Teacher's Wraparound Edition

GLENCOE LITERATURE

The Reader's Choice

Program Consultants

Beverly Ann Chin

Denny Wolfe

Jeffrey Copeland

Mary Ann Dudzinski

William Ray

Jacqueline Jones Royster

Jeffrey Wilhelm

American Literature

Glencoe McGraw-Hill

New York, New York   Columbus, Ohio   Woodland Hills, California   Peoria, Illinois

Acknowledgments

Grateful acknowledgment is given authors, publishers, photographers, museums, and agents for permission to reprint the following copyrighted material. Every effort has been made to determine copyright owners. In case of any omissions, the Publisher will be pleased to make suitable acknowledgments in future editions.

Acknowledgments continued on page R132.

The Standardized Test Practice pages in this book were written by The Princeton Review, the nation's leader in test preparation. Through its association with McGraw-Hill, The Princeton Review offers the best way to help students excel on standardized assessments.

The Princeton Review is not affiliated with Princeton University or Educational Testing Service.

Glencoe/McGraw-Hill

A Division of The McGraw·Hill Companies

Copyright © 2000 by The McGraw-Hill Companies, Inc. All rights reserved. Except as permitted under the United States Copyright Act of 1976, no part of this publication may be reproduced or distributed in any form or means, or stored in a database or retrieval system, without the prior written permission of the publisher.

Printed in the United States of America

Send all inquiries to:
Glencoe/McGraw-Hill
8787 Orion Place
Columbus, OH 43240

ISBN 0-02-635423-3
(Student Edition)

ISBN 0-02-635424-1
(Teacher's Wraparound Edition)

3 4 5 6 7 8 9 10 071/043 04 03 02 01 00

Book Overview

Table of Contents T8

To the Teacher

Student Edition

Reference Section

Senior Program Consultants

Beverly Ann Chin is Professor of English, Co-Director of the English Teaching Program, former Director of the Montana Writing Project, and former Director of Composition at the University of Montana in Missoula. In 1995–1996, Dr. Chin served as President of the National Council of Teachers of English. She currently serves as a Member of the Board of Directors of the National Board for Professional Teaching Standards. Dr. Chin is a nationally recognized leader in English language arts standards, curriculum, and assessment. Formerly a high school English teacher and adult education reading teacher, Dr. Chin has taught in English language arts education at several universities and has received awards for her teaching and service.

Denny Wolfe, a former high school English teacher and department chair, is Professor of English Education, Director of the Tidewater Virginia Writing Project, and Director of the Center for Urban Education at Old Dominion University in Norfolk, Virginia. For the National Council of Teachers of English, he has served as Chairperson of the Standing Committee on Teacher Preparation, President of the International Assembly, member of the Executive Committee of the Council on English Education, and editor of the SLATE Newsletter. Author of more than seventy-five articles and books on teaching English, Dr. Wolfe is a frequent consultant to schools and colleges on the teaching of English language arts.

Program Consultants

Jeffrey S. Copeland is Professor and Head of the Department of English Language and Literature at the University of Northern Iowa, where he teaches children's and young adult literature courses and a variety of courses in English education. A former public school teacher, he has published many articles in the professional journals in the language arts. The twelve books he has written or edited include *Speaking of Poets: Interviews with Poets Who Write for Children and Young Adults* and *Young Adult Literature: A Contemporary Reader.*

Mary Ann Dudzinski is a former high school English teacher and recipient of the Ross Perot Award for Teaching Excellence. She also has served as a member of the core faculty for the National Endowment for the Humanities Summer Institute for Teachers of Secondary School English and History at the University of North Texas. After fifteen years of classroom experience in grades 9–12, she currently is a language arts consultant.

William Ray has taught English in the Boston Public Schools; at Lowell University; University of Wroclaw, Poland; and, for the last fourteen years, at Lincoln-Sudbury Regional High School in Sudbury, Massachusetts. He specializes in world literature. He has worked on a variety of educational texts, as editor, consultant, and contributing writer.

Jacqueline Jones Royster is Associate Professor of English at The Ohio State University. She is also on the faculty of the Bread Loaf School of English at Middlebury College in Middlebury, Vermont. In addition to the teaching of writing, Dr. Royster's professional interests include the rhetorical history of African American women and the social and cultural implications of literate practices.

Jeffrey Wilhelm, a former English and reading teacher, is currently an assistant professor at the University of Maine where he teaches courses in middle and secondary level literacy. Author of several books and articles on the teaching of reading and the use of technology, he also works with local schools as part of the fledgling Adolescent Literacy Project and is the director of two annual summer institutes: the Maine Writing Project and Technology as a Learning Tool.

Teacher Reviewers

Rahn Anderson
Arapahoe High School
Littleton Public Schools
Littleton, Colorado

Linda Antonowich
West Chester Area School District
West Chester, Pennsylvania

Mike Bancroft
Rock Bridge High School
Columbia, Missouri

Luella Barber
Hays High School
Hays, Kansas

Lori Beard
Cypress Creek High School
Houston, Texas

Hugh Beattie
Bergenfield Public School District
Bergenfield, New Jersey

Patricia Blatt
Centerville High School
Centerville, Ohio

Edward Blotzer III
Wilkinsburg High School
Pittsburgh, Pennsylvania

Ruby Bowker
Mt. View High School
Mt. View, Wyoming

Darolyn Brown
Osborn High School
Detroit, Michigan

Rob Bruno
Atholton High School
Columbia, Maryland

Mary Beth Crotty
Bridgetown Junior High
Cincinnati, Ohio

Susan Dawson
Sam Barlow High School
Portland, Oregon

Thomas A. Della Salla
Schenectady City School District
Schenectady, New York

Sandra Denton
East High School
Columbus, Ohio

Charles Eisele
St. John Vianney High School
St. Louis, Missouri

Mel Farberman
Benjamin Cardozo High School
Bayside, New York

Caroline Ferdinandsen
San Joaquin Memorial High School
Fresno, California

Tye Ferdinandsen
San Joaquin Memorial High School
Fresno, California

Randle Frink
East Rowan High School
Salisbury, North Carolina

Pamela Fuller
Capital High School
Charleston, West Virginia

Tara Gallagher
River Hill High School
Columbia, Maryland

June Gatewood
Rio Americano
Sacramento, California

Ellen Geisler
Mentor High School
Mentor, Ohio

Leslie Gershon
Annapolis Senior High
Mitchellville, Maryland

Kim Hartman
Franklin Heights High School
Columbus, Ohio

Charlotte Heidel
Gaylord High School
Gaylord, Michigan

Keith Henricksen
Sutton Public Schools
Sutton, Nebraska

Patricia Herigan
Central Dauphin High School
Harrisburg, Pennsylvania

Azalie Hightower
Paul Junior High School
Washington, D.C.

Bobbi Ciriza Houtchens
San Bernardino High School
San Bernardino, California

Cheri Jefferson
Atholton High School
Columbia, Maryland

Marsha Jones
Seymour High School
Seymour, Indiana

Cheryl Keast
Glendale High School
Glendale, California

Glenda Kissell
Littleton High School
Littleton, Colorado

Jan Klein
Cypress Lake High School
Fort Myers, Florida

Beth Koehler
Nathan Hale High School
West Allis, Wisconsin

Sister Mary Kay Lampert
Central Catholic High School
Portland, Oregon

Elaine Loughlin
Palo Duro High
Amarillo, Texas

Tom Mann
Franklin Heights High School
Columbus, Ohio

Carolyn Sue Mash
Westerville North High School
Westerville, Ohio

Eileen Mattingly
McDonough High School
Pomfret, Maryland

Wanda McConnell
Statesville High School
Statesville, North Carolina

Victoria McCormick
John Jay High School
San Antonio, Texas

Sandra Sue McPherson
McKeesport Area High School
McKeesport, Pennsylvania

Jill Miller
Odessa High School
Odessa, Texas

Karmen Miller
Cypress Falls High School
Houston, Texas

Catherine Morse
Shelby High School
Shelby, Ohio

Tom Omli
Rogers High School
Puyallup, Washington

John O'Toole
Solon High School
Solon, Ohio

Helen Pappas
Bridgewater-Raritan High School
Bridgewater, New Jersey

Jill Railsback
Seymour High School
Seymour, Indiana

Doug Reed
Franklin Heights High School
Columbus, Ohio

Mary Jane Reed
Solon High School
Solon, Ohio

Dorlea Rikard
Bradshaw High School
Florence, Alabama

Diane Ritzdorf
Arapahoe High School
Littleton, Colorado

Leonor Rodriguez
Breckenridge High School
San Antonio, Texas

Susanne Rubenstein
Wachusett Regional High School
Holden, Massachusetts

Steve Slagle
San Gabriel High School
San Gabriel, California

Tammy Smiley
Littleton High School
Littleton, Colorado

Carol Smith
Moses Lake School District
Moses Lake, Washington

Helen Spaith
Franklin Heights High School
Columbus, Ohio

Marsha Spampinato
High School of Enterprise, Business,
and Technology
Smithtown, New York

Nora Stephens
Huntsville High School
Huntsville, Alabama

David Stocking
Wachusett Regional High School
Holden, Massachusetts

Mark Tavernier
Norfolk Public Schools
Norfolk, Virginia

Martin Tierney
Bishop Dwenger High School
Fort Wayne, Indiana

Elysa Toler-Robinson
Detroit Public Schools
Detroit, Michigan

Megan Trow
Sprague High School
Salem, Oregon

Joseph Velten Jr.
Archbishop Wood High School
Warminster, Pennsylvania

Margaret Wildermann
McDonough High School
Pomfret, Maryland

Kathy Young
Walnut Ridge High School
Columbus, Ohio

Mary Young
Greenville High School
Greenville, Illinois

Contents

Guide to Active Reading

UNIT § ONE

From the Earliest Days 36

Theme 1 Beginnings and Change 45

indicates world literature

CONTENTS

UNIT ✌ TWO

CONTENTS

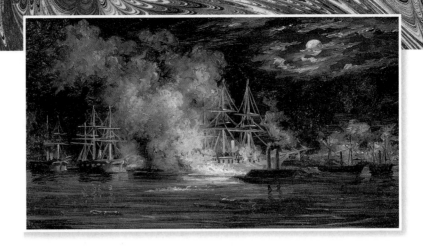

UNIT ❧ THREE

The Civil War and Its Aftermath

Theme 4 The Union Is Tested

CONTENTS

Theme 5 — Two New American Voices 397

CONTENTS

UNIT ❧ FOUR

Regionalism and Realism . . .448

Theme 6   The Energy of the Everyday 459

CONTENTS

CONTENTS

UNIT ❧ FIVE

Beginnings of the Modern Age .586

Theme 7 New Directions 597

CONTENTS

CONTENTS

UNIT ✤ SIX

CONTENTS

Theme 10   Acting on an Idea 907

UNIT ❧ SEVEN

CONTENTS

CONTENTS

Reference Section

Selections by Genre

Poetry

Features

COMPARING *selections*

Literature FOCUS

Active Reading Strategies

✎ Writing Workshop

Interdisciplinary Connection

Skills

Grammar Link

Listening, Speaking, and Viewing

Reading & Thinking Skills

Technology Skills

Vocabulary Skills

Writing Skills

Book Overview

THE LITERATURE UNITS

The literature that makes up the heart of the Student Edition is organized chronologically into seven units covering the major periods in American literature, from pre-Columbian times through the twentieth century. Each unit includes a variety of genres such as poetry, drama, short stories, and nonfiction. Each unit begins with a lively and engaging Unit Introduction that acquaints students with the history and culture of the period.

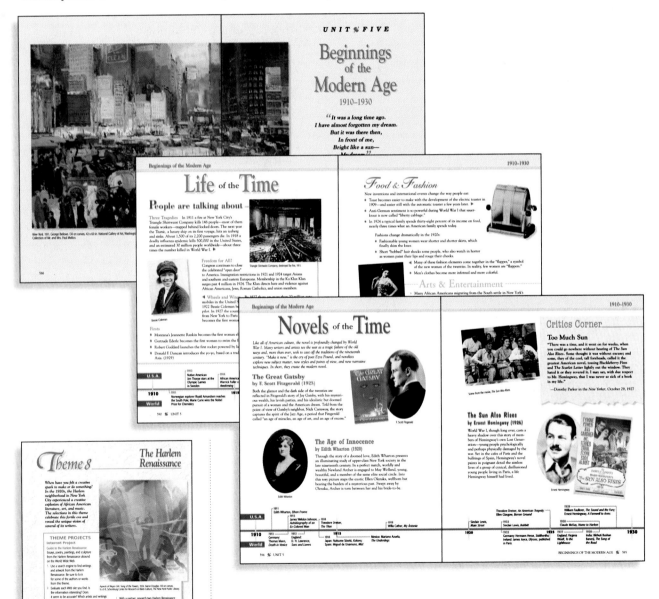

Within each unit, selections are organized into one or more sections, each based on a universal theme.

STUDENT EDITION

REFERENCE SECTION

This comprehensive set of handbooks provides a valuable resource for students. References throughout the textbook direct students to specific handbook pages for additional information and support.

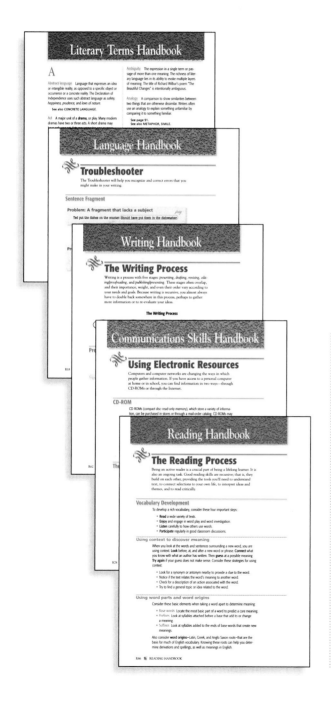

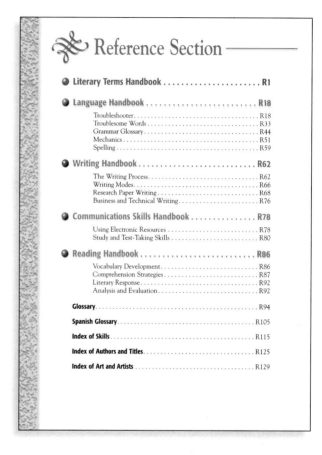

Literary Terms Handbook provides a glossary of all the literary terms taught with the selections in the book.

Language Handbook supplies ready reference and instructional support for grammar, usage, mechanics, and spelling.

Writing Handbook includes an overview of the writing process and the major writing modes as well as support for research paper writing.

Communications Skills Handbook addresses the use of electronic resources as well as study and test-taking skills.

Reading Handbook provides instructional support and models for a comprehensive set of reading strategies and skills.

Selection Plan

Each selection in the program is presented in a three-part format:
(1) Before You Read, (2) the selection pages and (3) Responding to Literature.

BEFORE YOU READ

This section prepares students for reading by helping them draw upon their personal experience, build background knowledge, and set a purpose for reading.

Meet the Author motivates students to read the selection by presenting high-interest author information and quotations in an inviting format.

Focus Activity creates a bridge into the selection by connecting the students' own experience to an important theme or aspect of the selection. Activities include quickwrites, journal entries, making graphic organizers, and group or whole class discussions.

 —Before You Read—

The Jilting of Granny Weatherall

Meet Katherine Anne Porter

"Ask what time it is in [Porter's] stories and you are certain to get the answer: the hour is fateful. It is not necessary to see the hands of the clock in her work. It is a time of racing urgency, and it is already too late."

—Eudora Welty

Over her long career, Katherine Anne Porter traveled far from the rural Texas landscape of her childhood. As a young woman she worked on newspapers in Chicago and Denver. She then spent most of her thirties living in Mexico and Europe, meeting other writers and gathering memories for some of her most famous stories.

Porter described herself as "a late starter," publishing her first collection of short stories, *Flowering Judas*, when she was forty. Several collections of short fiction and one novel, *Ship of Fools*, followed. At age seventy-six, Porter received a Pulitzer Prize and the National Book Award for *The Collected Stories of Katherine Anne Porter*.

Porter tried to tell each story "as clearly and purely and simply as I can." Many of her stories, like "The Jilting of Granny Weatherall," are set in the South and feature women who have profound self-realizations at crucial moments in their lives.

Katherine Anne Porter was born in 1890 and died in 1980.

FOCUS ACTIVITY

Life events occur in chronological order, but our conscious memories of them often unfold differently.

CHART IT! Chart five things you did yesterday in the order that you did them. Then chart five important events in your life in the order that they come to mind.

Yesterday's Events	Important Life Events

SETTING A PURPOSE Read to learn of one woman's memories and the order in which they unfold.

620 ❧ UNIT 5

BACKGROUND

The Time and Place
Porter sets her story in the American South in the early twentieth century. This was an era in which many southerners, including Porter's family, lived in extreme poverty. In addition, women of the time were often confined to the traditional roles of wife, mother, and homemaker.

Roman Catholicism figures prominently in Porter's story. Granny Weatherall's religious beliefs and her ideas of guilt and forgiveness are important elements in the story.

VOCABULARY PREVIEW

tactful (takt´ fəl) *adj.* able to speak or act without offending others; p. 622
dutiful (dōō´ ti fəl) *adj.* careful to fulfill obligations; p. 622
plague (plāg) *v.* to annoy; to pester; p. 623
vanity (van´ i tē) *n.* excessive pride, as in one's looks; p. 625

jilt (jilt) *v.* to drop or reject as a sweetheart; p. 625
piety (pī´ ə tē) *n.* religious devoutness; goodness; p. 627
dwindle (dwin´ dəl) *v.* to become gradually smaller; p. 628

Background presents nuggets of relevant background information to pique students' interest and enhance their understanding of the selection.

Vocabulary Preview introduces key vocabulary that students will encounter in reading the selection. (Generally, these are words that appear often on the SAT and in students' everyday and academic reading.)

SELECTION PAGES

The engaging design of the selection pages incorporates dynamic photography and fine art within a clean layout that promotes readability. A variety of carefully designed elements support and engage students as they read.

Viewing questions prompt students to connect the fine art and photographs to the selection.

The Seamstress, 1914.
Knud Larsen. Oil on canvas,
20 x 18⅛ in. Private collection.
Viewing the painting:
Why might the woman in the painting be like Cornelia at that age?

The White Bed Jacket, c. 1903. (Ida Cabot Perry. Pastel on tan paper, 25⅝ x 31⅝ in. Hirschl & Adler Galleries, Inc., New York.)

The Jilting of Granny Weatherall

Katherine Anne Porter ~

S he flicked her wrist neatly out of Doctor Harry's pudgy careful fingers and pulled the sheet up to her chin. The brat ought to be in knee-breeches. Doctoring around the country with spectacles on his nose. "Get along now, take your schoolbooks and go. There's nothing wrong with me."

Doctor Harry spread a warm paw like a cushion on her forehead where the forked green vein danced and made her eyelids twitch. "Now, now, be a good girl, and we'll have you up in no time."

"That's no way to speak to a woman nearly eighty years old just because she's down. I'd have you respect your elders, young man."

BEGINNINGS OF THE MODERN AGE 🙟 621

edges; it bored⁸ up into her head, and the agony was unbelievable. Yes, John, get the doctor now, no more talk, my time has come.

When this one was born it should be the last. The last. It should have been born first, for it was the one she had truly wanted. Everything came in good time. Nothing left out, left over. She was strong, in three days she would be as well as ever. Better. A woman needed milk in her to have her full health.

"Mother, do you hear me?"

"I've been telling you—"

"Mother, Father Connolly's here."

"I went to Holy Communion only last week. Tell him I'm not so sinful as all that."

"Father just wants to speak to you."

He could speak as much as he pleased. It was like him to drop in and inquire about her soul as if it were a teething baby, and then stay on for a cup of tea and a round of cards and gossip. He always had a funny story of some sort, usually about an Irishman who made his little mistakes and confessed them, and the point lay in some absurd thing he would blurt out in the confessional⁹ showing his struggles

8. Here, to *bore* means "to make a hole, as by drilling or pushing."

9. A *confessional* is a small booth in a Catholic church where a person confesses his or her sins to a priest and asks forgiveness from God through the priest.

626 🙟 UNIT 5

sake leave something to God." "Now, Ellen, you must believe what I tell you . . ."

So there was nothing, nothing to worry about any more, except sometimes in the night one of the children screamed in a nightmare, and they both hustled out shaking and hunting for the matches and calling, "There, wait a minute, here we are!" John, get the doctor now, Hapsy's time has come. But there was Hapsy standing by the bed in a white cap. "Cornelia, tell Hapsy to take off her cap. I can't see her plain."

Her eyes opened very wide and the room stood out like a picture she had seen somewhere. Dark colors with the shadows rising towards the ceiling in long angles. The tall black dresser gleamed with nothing on it but John's picture, enlarged from a little one, with John's eyes very black when they should have been blue. You never saw . . . . . , so how do you know how he looked? But the man insisted the copy was perfect, it was very rich and

10. *Assigns* are people to whom property is legally transferred.

Granny stepped up in the cart very lightly and reached for the reins, but a man sat beside her, and she knew him by his hands, driving the cart. She did not look in his face, for she knew without seeing, but looked instead down the road where the trees leaned over and bowed to each other and a thousand birds were singing a Mass. She felt like singing too, but she put her hand in the bosom of her dress and pulled out a rosary, and Father Connolly murmured Latin in a very solemn voice and tickled her feet.¹³ My God,

Did You Know?
A *rosary* is a string of beads used to help count specific prayers as they are recited.

11. *Frippery* is a showy, useless display.
12. A *nimbus* is a disk or ring of light; a halo.
13. The priest is administering the last rites, a Catholic ritual which includes saying prayers and applying oil to the dying person's feet.

Vocabulary
piety (pī′ a tē) *n.* religious devoutness; goodness

BEGINNINGS OF THE MODERN AGE 🙟 627

Footnotes support comprehension by explaining unfamiliar references or clarifying difficult passages in the text. Footnotes also supply pronunciations for many names of people and places and for words from other languages.

Vocabulary words are underscored at first use in the selection; a note at the bottom of the page provides the definition, pronunciation, and part of speech.

Did You Know? notes provide illustrated definitions to help students visualize unfamiliar settings or objects mentioned in the selection.

Selection Plan
(Continued)

RESPONDING TO LITERATURE

This section provides a variety of ways for students to respond to the literature through listening, speaking, and writing activities. It also provides students with an opportunity to make connections to the theme.

Personal Response questions and activities allow all students to express an immediate response to the selection. The goal here is exploration not closure.

Analyzing Literature questions help guide students to a thorough understanding of the selection. Recall questions focus students' attention on significant details of the selection, which they will use in answering the Interpret questions. Evaluate and Connect questions often include a Theme Connection.

Responding to Literature

Personal Response
What was your reaction to Granny Weatherall's train of thought?

——— ANALYZING LITERATURE ———

RECALL

1. At the beginning of the story, what attitudes does Granny have toward the doctor, toward Cornelia, and toward her own illness?
2. How does Granny describe her life since her husband John died? What examples does she give?
3. Who is Hapsy, and where does Granny see her?
4. Which event does Granny recall with particular anger and sadness? What "message" does she have for the person involved?
5. What does Granny ask of God in the next-to-last paragraph? What happens "for the second time"?

INTERPRET

6. What do Granny's attitudes early in the story reveal about her state of mind?
7. How might Granny have changed due to her experiences since her husband died? How does the name *Weatherall* fit Granny?
8. How does Granny's vision of Hapsy **foreshadow** the end of the story? (See Literary Terms Handbook, page R7.)
9. Think about Granny's "message" to the person who has hurt and saddened her. What does this message tell you about her feelings toward him? Explain.
10. Why do you think the jilting incident comes back to Granny so frequently as she faces death?

EVALUATE AND CONNECT

11. In your opinion, does Porter bring this story to an effective **climax** (see page R3)? Explain your answer using details from the story. Use a plot graph like the one on this page to help organize your ideas.
12. Which of Granny's memories did you find most touching? Why?
13. In your opinion, did Granny live a full life? Support your answer with details from the story.
14. Look back at the chart you created for the Focus Activity on page 620. Did you list your five important life events in chronological order? How is the order of your list similar to or different from Granny Weatherall's death-bed memories?
15. Would you like to have had Granny as a grandmother? Explain.

BEGINNINGS OF THE MODERN AGE ✿ 629

Literary ELEMENTS

Stream of Consciousness
Stream of consciousness is a technique that a writer uses to imitate the flow of thoughts, feelings, images, and memories of a character in a literary work. Stream of consciousness replaces traditional chronological order with a seemingly jumbled collection of impressions, forcing the reader to piece together the plot or theme. In "The Jilting of Granny Weatherall," Porter uses stream of consciousness to represent Granny's thoughts and memories.

1. Is stream of consciousness a good choice for telling the story "The Jilting of Granny Weatherall"? Explain.
2. What kinds of clues help the reader follow Granny's thoughts?
◉ See **Literary Terms Handbook**, p. R15.

Literary Elements teach traditional literary skills and provide students with the tools necessary to analyze and interpret literature.

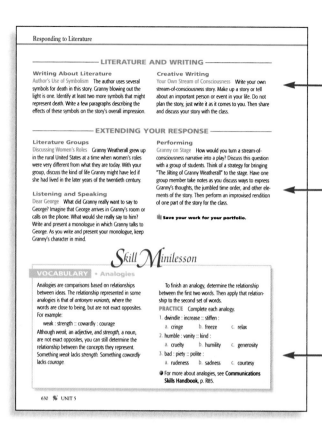

Responding to Literature

─────── LITERATURE AND WRITING ───────

Writing About Literature
Author's Use of Symbolism The author uses several symbols for death in this story. Granny blowing out the light is one. Identify at least two more symbols that might represent death. Write a few paragraphs describing the effects of these symbols on the story's overall impression.

Creative Writing
Your Own Stream of Consciousness Write your own stream-of-consciousness story. Make up a story or tell about an important person or event in your life. Do not plan the story, just write it as it comes to you. Then share and discuss your story with the class.

─────── EXTENDING YOUR RESPONSE ───────

Literature Groups
Discussing Women's Roles Granny Weatherall grew up in the rural United States at a time when women's roles were very different from what they are today. With your group, discuss the kind of life Granny might have led if she had lived in the later years of the twentieth century.

Performing
Granny on Stage How would you turn a stream-of-consciousness narrative into a play? Discuss this question with a group of students. Think of a strategy for bringing "The Jilting of Granny Weatherall" to the stage. Have one group member take notes as you discuss ways to express Granny's thoughts, the jumbled time order, and other elements of the story. Then perform an improvised rendition of one part of the story for the class.

Listening and Speaking
Dear George What did Granny really want to say to George? Imagine that George arrives in Granny's room or calls on the phone. What would she really say to him? Write and present a monologue in which Granny talks to George. As you write and present your monologue, keep Granny's character in mind.

📖 **Save your work for your portfolio.**

Skill Minilesson

VOCABULARY • Analogies

Analogies are comparisons based on relationships between ideas. The relationship represented in some analogies is that of *antonym variants*, where the words are close to being, but are not exact opposites. For example:

weak : strength :: cowardly : courage

Although *weak*, an adjective, and *strength*, a noun, are not exact opposites, you can still determine the relationship between the concepts they represent. Something *weak* lacks *strength*. Something *cowardly* lacks *courage*.

To finish an analogy, determine the relationship between the first two words. Then apply that relationship to the second set of words.

PRACTICE Complete each analogy.
1. dwindle : increase :: stiffen :
   a. cringe   b. freeze   c. relax
2. humble : vanity :: kind :
   a. cruelty   b. humility   c. generosity
3. bad : piety :: polite :
   a. rudeness   b. sadness   c. courtesy

● For more about analogies, see **Communications Skills Handbook**, p. R85.

630 📖 UNIT 5

Literature and Writing provides options that all students can use to respond in writing to a selection. One option is always a Writing About Literature prompt; the other option is either a Creative Writing prompt or a Personal Writing prompt.

Extending Your Response includes diverse activities that appeal to different types of learners. This section always includes Literature Groups as well as other activities chosen from the following menu: Interdisciplinary Activity, Learning for Life, Internet Connection, Listening and Speaking, Performing, and Reading Further.

Vocabulary minilessons teach or reinforce important vocabulary skills. Many focus on the type of analogies used in the SAT.

Single-Page Responding to Literature provides a more abbreviated set of response options for some selections. Students will encounter Literary Elements and/or two other options from the Literature and Writing and Extending Your Response menus above.

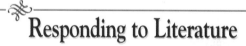

Responding to Literature

Personal Response
Which lines from the poem did you find most powerful or surprising? Copy these lines into your journal.

─────── ANALYZING LITERATURE ───────

RECALL AND INTERPRET
1. What has the snowfall done to the specific places and things mentioned in lines 1–14? What general atmosphere has the snowfall created? Use specific words from those lines to support your answer.
2. What does the speaker remember in lines 17–20? How would you characterize the tone of his remembrance in this stanza?
3. What answer does the speaker give Mabel when she asks where the snow comes from? What does his response tell you about his beliefs?
4. As the speaker again looks out at the snow, he is reminded of an event in the family's life. What is that event? How do you know?
5. What has the family experienced since the event described in lines 27–28? How is this experience similar to the snowfall?

EVALUATE AND CONNECT
6. How did the last stanza affect your understanding of the poem?
7. What might the speaker say to a family who had recently lost a child?
8. Does the **tone** change through this poem (see Literary Terms Handbook, page R16)? Use specific words and images to support your answer.
9. Think about your own writing experiences, including journals. How can writing about personal loss help people work through their sorrow?
10. Do you think this poem would comfort someone who had suffered a loss but did not share Lowell's religious beliefs? Why or why not?

Literary ELEMENTS

Theme
The **theme** of a work of literature is the main idea, or point, that it conveys to the reader. In some works, the theme is stated directly. In other works, events, dialogue, or imagery suggest the theme indirectly. Short stories, drama, and poetry often contain a suggested theme. One must read carefully to infer the theme from the details in the work.

1. State the theme of "The First Snow-Fall" in your own words.
2. Is the theme of the poem stated or implied? How do you know?
3. List details that point to or support the theme of this poem.
● See **Literary Terms Handbook**, p. R16.

─────── EXTENDING YOUR RESPONSE ───────

Personal Writing
Weather and Emotion Consider your response to the Focus Activity on page 230. Think of an intense feeling you have had. What kind of weather do you associate with that feeling? Connect the weather to the feeling or experience in a poem or short narrative. For help, you might use Lowell's poem as a model. Share your work with classmates.

Interdisciplinary Activity
Art: Expressive Images Images created by artists catch the eye and then the heart. Those created by poets capture the mind's eye and then the heart. Use paint, clay, a computer program, or other medium to create a work of art that expresses a particular emotion. Share your work with the class.

📖 **Save your work for your portfolio.**

A NEW NATION 📖 233

Features

A variety of special features enhance students' learning through attention to active reading, language arts skills, and connections to other literature, to other disciplines, and to technology.

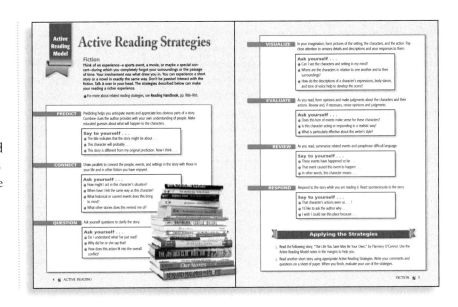

Guide to Active Reading models for students the kind of thinking and questioning that skillful readers do when reading fiction, poetry, and nonfiction. It also provides students with the opportunity to apply active reading strategies as they read sample fiction, poetry, and nonfiction selections.

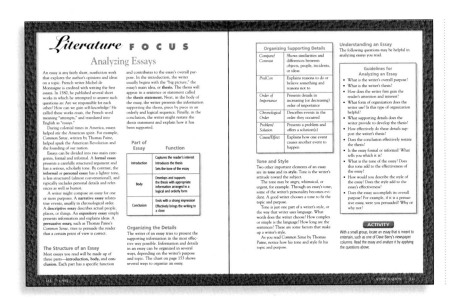

Literature Focus introduces students to the elements and characteristics of genres, literary movements, and literary forms, and provides historical information about major developments affecting American literature.

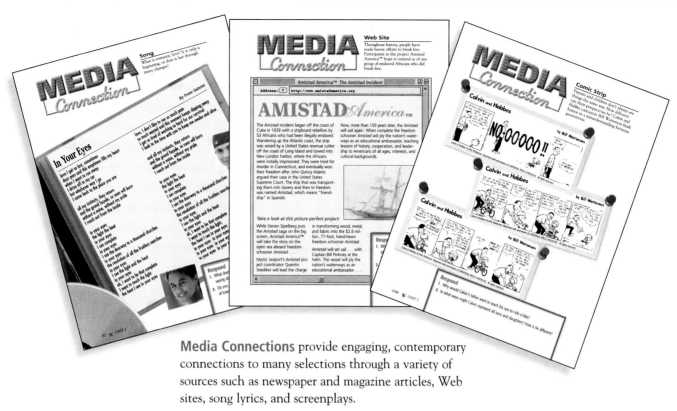

Media Connections provide engaging, contemporary connections to many selections through a variety of sources such as newspaper and magazine articles, Web sites, song lyrics, and screenplays.

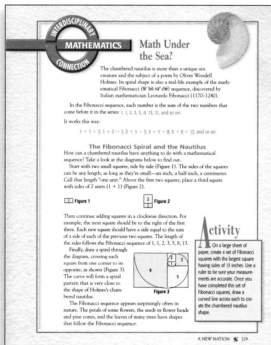

Interdisciplinary Connections connect selections to grade-level curricular goals in disciplines such as mathematics, science, history, and art.

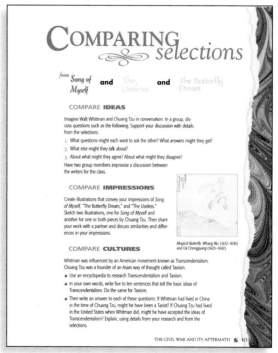

Comparing Selections Once or twice in each theme, a Comparing Selections page presents options for comparing an American selection with a selection from another country. Students will have the opportunity to explore themes that cross cultures through writing, discussion, and other engaging activities.

Features

(Continued)

Skills Features offer students opportunities to develop key language arts skills in the context of the literature they are reading. Features include

- ❧ *Vocabulary Skills*

- ❧ *Listening, Speaking, and Viewing*

- ❧ *Reading & Thinking Skills*

- ❧ *Writing Skills*

- ❧ *Grammar Link*

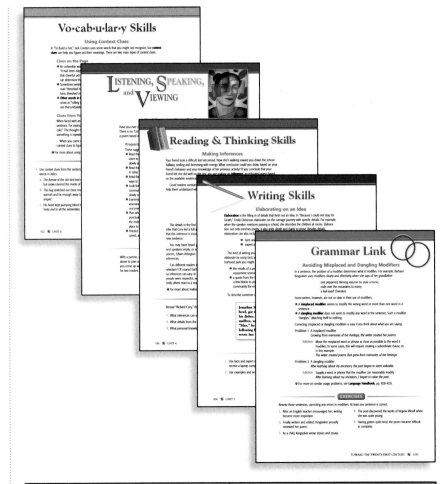

Technology Skills features enrich students' experience of literature through specific applications such as word processing, multimedia, databases, E-mail, and the Internet. For example, students will learn how to find writing resources on the Web and to use multimedia software to connect American history and American literature.

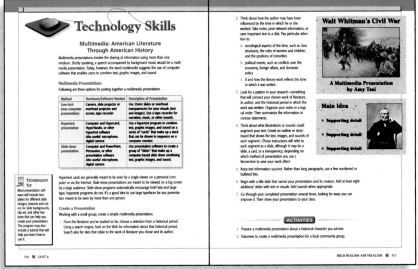

Nectar in a Sieve
BY KAMALA MARKANDAYA

Night
BY ELIE WIESEL

One Day in the Life of Ivan Denisovich
BY ALEKSANDR SOLZHENITSYN

Picture Bride
BY YOSHIKO UCHIDA

Pride and Prejudice
BY JANE AUSTEN

The Red Badge of Courage
BY STEPHEN CRANE

The Scarlet Letter
BY NATHANIEL HAWTHORNE

A Separate Peace
BY JOHN KNOWLES

The Strange Case of Dr. Jekyll and Mr. Hyde
BY ROBERT LOUIS STEVENSON

A Tale of Two Cities
BY CHARLES DICKENS

The Tempest
BY WILLIAM SHAKESPEARE

To Kill a Mockingbird
BY HARPER LEE

Wuthering Heights
BY EMILY BRONTË

The Yearling
BY MARJORIE KINNAN RAWLINGS

Study Guides

A separate Study Guide for each title in the Glencoe Literature Library provides teaching notes and reproducible activity pages for students.

For the Teacher
- Synopsis
- Media links
- Teaching options
- Answer key

For the Student
- Background information
- Active reading guides
- Response activities
- Test

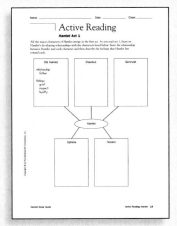

Active Reading pages include graphic organizers for students to complete as they read.

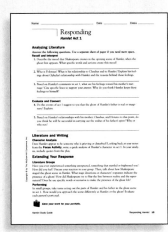

Responding pages include options for personal response, analyzing literature, and extending responses through writing and other activities.

Print Resources

Glencoe Literature has all the print resources you need to meet the needs of today's diverse classroom—and to save you valuable time.

Reading Resources
- Active Reading Guide
- inTime
- Literature Groups Sourcebook
- Media Connections Activities
- Reading Workbook

Language Arts Integration
- Critical Thinking Skills
- Grammar and Composition Handbook
- Grammar and Language Workbook
- Interdisciplinary Activities
- Language Arts Guide to the Internet and Other Electronic Resources
- Listening and Speaking Activities
- Research and Report Writing
- Selection Vocabulary Practice
- Spelling Power
- Style and Documentation Guide for Writers
- Viewing and Representing Activities
- Vocabulary Power
- Writing and Proofreading Practice

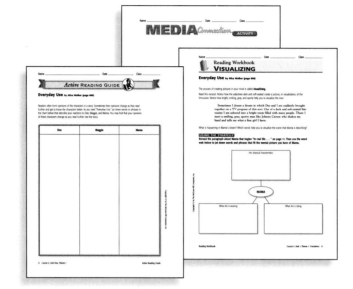

Grammar and Composition Handbook

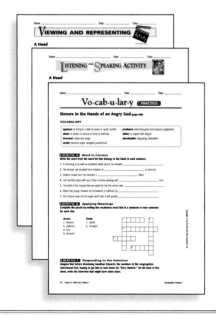

Teacher Management
- Block Scheduling Guide
- Unit Planning Guide

Meeting Individual Needs
- English Language Learners Sourcebook
- Inclusion Strategies Sourcebook

Spanish Resources
- Spanish Summaries
- Spanish Translations
- Active Reading Guide in Spanish
- Selection Quick Checks in Spanish

GLENCOE'S ASSESSMENT ADVANTAGE

Assessment Resources

- ❧ **Selection and Theme Assessment**
- ❧ **Selection Quick Checks**
- ❧ **Performance Assessment**
- ❧ **Writing Assessment and Portfolio Management**

THE PRINCETON REVIEW

The Princeton Review, the nation's leading test preparation firm, has developed the following assessment resource for *Glencoe Literature:*

- • **College Entrance Exams Preparation and Practice Workbook**

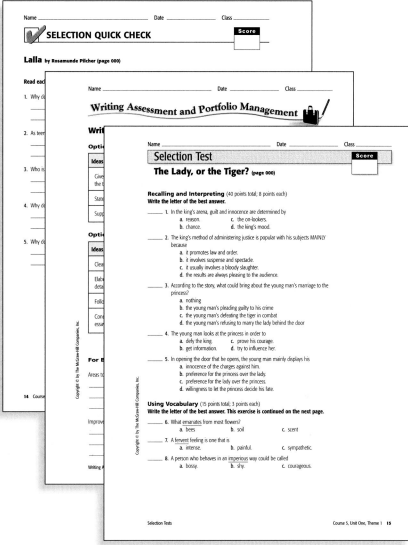

Name _____ Date _____ Class _____

✓ SELECTION QUICK CHECK

Score ▢

Lalla by Rosamunde Pilcher (page 000)

Read eac...

1. Why d...

2. As teen...

3. Who is...

4. Why d...

5. Why d...

Name _____ Date _____ Class _____

Writing Assessment and Portfolio Management 👜

Writ...

Optic...

Ideas...
Give... the t...
State...
Supp...

Optic...

Ideas...
Clea...
Elabo... deta...
Follo...
Conc... essa...

For E...

Areas t...

Improve...

Writing A...

Copyright © by The McGraw-Hill Companies, Inc.

14 Course...

Name _____ Date _____ Class _____

Selection Test

Score ▢

The Lady, or the Tiger? (page 000)

Recalling and Interpreting (40 points total; 8 points each)
Write the letter of the best answer.

____ 1. In the king's arena, guilt and innocence are determined by
   a. reason.   c. the on-lookers.
   b. chance.   d. the king's mood.

____ 2. The king's method of administering justice is popular with his subjects MAINLY because
   a. it promotes law and order.
   b. it involves suspense and spectacle.
   c. it usually involves a bloody slaughter.
   d. the results are always pleasing to the audience.

____ 3. According to the story, what could bring about the young man's marriage to the princess?
   a. nothing
   b. the young man's pleading guilty to his crime
   c. the young man's defeating the tiger in combat
   d. the young man's refusing to marry the lady behind the door

____ 4. The young man looks at the princess in order to
   a. defy the king.   c. prove his courage.
   b. get information.   d. try to influence her.

____ 5. In opening the door that he opens, the young man mainly displays his
   a. innocence of the charges against him.
   b. preference for the princess over the lady.
   c. preference for the lady over the princess.
   d. willingness to let the princess decide his fate.

Using Vocabulary (15 points total; 3 points each)
Write the letter of the best answer. This exercise is continued on the next page.

____ 6. What emanates from most flowers?
   a. bees   b. soil   c. scent

____ 7. A fervent feeling is one that is
   a. intense.   b. painful.   c. sympathetic.

____ 8. A person who behaves in an imperious way could be called
   a. bossy.   b. shy.   c. courageous.

Selection Tests   Course 5, Unit One, Theme 1 **15**

Copyright © by The McGraw-Hill Companies, Inc.

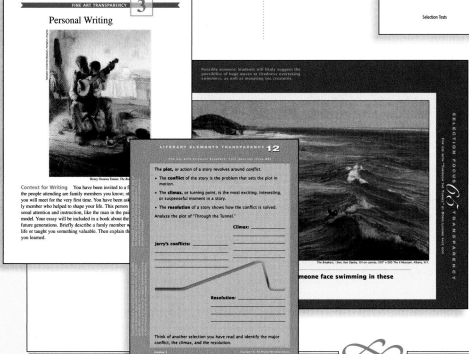

FINE ART TRANSPARENCY 3

Personal Writing

Henry Ossawa Tanner, *The Ba...*

Context for Writing You have been invited to a f... the people attending are family members you know; ot... you will meet for the very first time. You have been ask... ly member who helped to shape your life. This person... sonal attention and instruction, like the man in the pai... model. Your essay will be included in a book about the... future generations. Briefly describe a family member w... life or taught you something valuable. Then explain th... you learned.

Possible answers: Students will likely suggest the possibility of huge waves or tiredness overtaking swimmers, as well as menacing sea creatures.

LITERARY ELEMENTS TRANSPARENCY 12

The **plot**, or action of a story revolves around *conflict*.

- The **conflict** of the story is the problem that sets the plot in motion.
- The **climax**, or turning point, is the most exciting, interesting, or suspenseful moment in a story.
- The **resolution** of a story shows how the conflict is solved.

Analyze the plot of "Through the Tunnel."

Climax: _____

Jerry's conflicts: _____

Resolution: _____

Think of another selection you have read and identify the major conflict, the climax, and the resolution.

The Breakers, 19xx, Ken Danby. Oil on canvas, 00" x 000 The X Museum, Albany, N.Y.

...meone face swimming in these

Transparencies

Choose from a number of overhead transparencies to engage students and to reinforce and extend understanding.

- ❧ **Selection Focus Transparencies**
- ❧ **Literary Elements Transparencies**
- ❧ **Grammar and Language Transparencies**
- ❧ **Writing and Proofreading Transparencies**
- ❧ **Fine Art Transparencies**

Technology Resources

With *Glencoe Literature*, you can draw upon a wealth of audio, video, software, and Internet resources to help engage students' interest and enhance their experience of literature.

VIDEO RESOURCES

❧ **Literature Launchers** Short video segments that are motivating and engaging; available on videodisc or VHS tape

❧ **MindJogger Videoquizzes** One video quiz per unit, available on videodisc or VHS tape

❧ **Video Library** Collection of documentary and performance videos available on VHS tape

AUDIO RESOURCES

❧ **Audio Library** Literature selections available on audiotape or CD

❧ **Spanish Audio Library** Readings of many selections in Spanish available on audiotape or CD

Glencoe Literature Web Site lit.glencoe.com

On-line resources for you as well as for students and parents

Features include
❧ appropriate Web site links
❧ games and activities for lessons in the Student Edition
❧ state literary sites
❧ teacher-to-teacher exchange
❧ professional articles
❧ and much more!

Literature Classics CD-ROM

Literature Classics
Author   High School CD-ROM

Main Menu   Help

Selections by Title

A B C D E F G H I J K L M N O P Q R S T U V W X Y Z

Title	Author	Year	Genre
Macbeth	William Hazlitt (1778-1830)	1817	Essay
from *Macbeth*, from *On the Knocking at the Gate*	Thomas De Quincey (1785-1859)	c. 1823	Essay
Madame Celestin's Divorce	Kate Chopin (1851-1904)	1894	Short Story
Madame, Withouten Many Words	Sir Thomas Wyatt (c. 1503-1542)	c. 1503-1542	Poetry
Maese Perez, the Organist	Gustavo Adolfo Becquer (1836-1870)	c. 1836-1870	Short Story
The Magna Carta	Anonymous	1215	Historical Document
from *Magnalia Christi, Americana*	Cotton Mather (1663-1728)	1702	Biography

Internet
Help

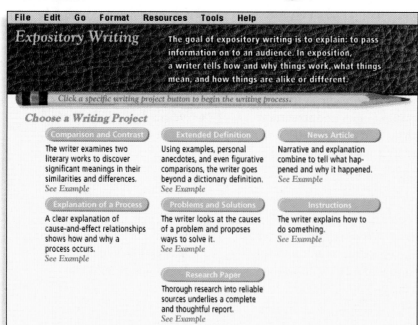

Writer's Assistant

File   Edit   Go   Format   Resources   Tools   Help

Expository Writing
The goal of expository writing is to explain: to pass information on to an audience. In exposition, a writer tells how and why things work, what things mean, and how things are alike or different.

Click a specific writing project button to begin the writing process.

Choose a Writing Project

Comparison and Contrast
The writer examines two literary works to discover significant meanings in their similarities and differences.
See Example

Extended Definition
Using examples, personal anecdotes, and even figurative comparisons, the writer goes beyond a dictionary definition.
See Example

News Article
Narrative and explanation combine to tell what happened and why it happened.
See Example

Explanation of a Process
A clear explanation of cause-and-effect relationships shows how and why a process occurs.
See Example

Problems and Solutions
The writer looks at the causes of a problem and proposes ways to solve it.
See Example

Instructions
The writer explains how to do something.
See Example

Research Paper
Thorough research into reliable sources underlies a complete and thoughtful report.
See Example

SOFTWARE

❧ **Literature Classics CD-ROM** More than 900 additional literature selections accessible by author, title, genre, theme, or date

❧ **Writer's Assistant** Easy-to-use, hands-on tools and templates to help students in all modes of writing

❧ **Presentation Plus** Dynamic multimedia PowerPoint® presentation tool

❧ **Testmaker** Editable electronic database of Selection and Theme Tests, with additional test items to customize your assessment to your needs

❧ **Vocabulary Puzzlemaker** Make vocabulary study fun with word searches based on selection vocabulary.

❧ **Language Arts Passkey™** Self-tutorial reading assistance for students

❧ **Electronic Teacher's Classroom Resources** All ancillary print resources available on CD-ROM

❧ **Interactive Grammar and Language Workbook**

Scope and Sequence Overview

Strand	Overview	Key Items for the Strand Student Edition
Literary Concepts and Techniques	Students develop knowledge of literary history and genres, analyze literary elements for their contribution to meaning in texts, and develop appreciation for aspects of writers' craft.	❧ Literary Elements ❧ Analyzing Literature ❧ Literature Focus ❧ Literary Terms Handbook
Reading and Thinking	Students develop proficiency with a full range of strategies and skills for comprehending a variety of texts and for thinking critically, creatively, and analytically.	❧ Active Reading Strategies ❧ Active Reading Models ❧ Reading and Thinking Skills ❧ Reading Handbook
Writing	Students write in a variety of forms for various purposes and audiences, using a recursive writing process as appropriate. Students write to learn and to make personal connections to literature.	❧ Writing Workshops ❧ Writing Skills features ❧ Focus Activities ❧ Literature and Writing ❧ Extending Your Response ❧ Theme Projects ❧ Writing Handbook
Vocabulary and Spelling	Students build vocabulary through wide reading, attention to context clues and structural analysis, and use of dictionaries and other reference tools.	❧ Vocabulary Preview ❧ Vocabulary Minilessons ❧ Vocabulary Skills features
Grammar and Language	Students develop mastery of the conventions of grammar, usage, mechanics, and style, and apply these conventions in their own writing.	❧ Grammar Link features ❧ Grammar Hints (in Writing Workshops) ❧ Language Handbook

The charts on these and the following two pages provide an overview of the program scope and sequence for *Glencoe Literature*. For a detailed scope and sequence of skills for each Theme, see the Theme Skills Scope and Sequence chart that immediately follows each Theme Opener. See also the Index of Skills (pages R115–R124) for a comprehensive listing of all skills and concepts taught in this level of *Glencoe Literature*.

Key Items for the Strand **Teacher's Wraparound Edition**	Key Items for the Strand **Program Resources**
❧ Literary Elements sidenotes ❧ Author's Craft sidenotes ❧ Thematic Focus ❧ Connecting to Other Selections	❧ Literary Elements Transparencies ❧ Literature Classics CD-ROM ❧ Literature Groups Sourcebook
❧ Active Reading sidenotes ❧ Critical Thinking sidenotes ❧ Reading Minilessons ❧ Less Proficient Readers ❧ English Language Learners	❧ Active Reading Guide ❧ Reading Workbook ❧ Critical Thinking Skills ❧ Inclusion Strategies Sourcebook ❧ English Language Learners Sourcebook ❧ Language Arts Passkey
❧ Writing Minilessons ❧ Meeting Individual Needs ❧ Reading Journals	❧ Writing and Proofreading Activities ❧ Writing and Proofreading Transparencies ❧ Grammar and Composition Handbook ❧ Writer's Assistant CD-ROM ❧ Style and Documentation Sourcebook for Writers
❧ Vocabulary Skills sidenotes ❧ English Language Learners	❧ Selection Vocabulary Practice ❧ Vocabulary Power ❧ Spelling Power ❧ Vocabulary Puzzlemaker
❧ Grammar and Language Minilessons ❧ Language Notes	❧ Grammar and Language Transparencies ❧ Grammar and Language Workbook ❧ Interactive Grammar and Language Workbook ❧ Grammar and Composition Handbook

Continued on T56–T57

Scope and Sequence Overview

(*Continued*)

Strand	Overview	Key Items for the Strand Student Edition
Listening, Speaking, and Viewing	Students develop proficiency with skills of oral communication and visual literacy and apply them in a variety of contexts.	• Extending Your Response • Theme Projects • Focus Activities • Literature Groups • Image captions (for Viewing)
Life Skills	Within the context of literature study, students develop skills of problem solving, decision making, and collaboration. They also perform a variety of real-world reading and writing tasks.	• Learning for Life Activities (Extending Your Response) • Theme Projects
Research and Study Skills	Students use reading and writing for inquiry and research and develop a variety of study and test-taking skills.	• Extending Your Response • Reading Handbook • Communications Skills Handbook • Theme Projects • Standardized Test Practice
Media and Technology	Students enhance their study of literature through the use of the Internet and other computer and media technologies.	• Internet Connections (Extending Your Response) • Theme Projects • Technology Skills
Interdisciplinary Studies	Students make frequent conceptual and thematic connections between literature and other fields of study.	• Interdisciplinary Connections • Interdisciplinary Activities (Extending Your Response) • Theme Projects

Key Items for the Strand **Teacher's Wraparound Edition**	Key Items for the Strand **Program Resources**
❧ Viewing the Painting sidenotes ❧ Listening and Speaking Minilessons	❧ Fine Art Transparencies ❧ Listening and Speaking Activities ❧ Viewing and Representing Activities ❧ Audio Library ❧ Video Library ❧ Literature Launchers
❧ Life Skills Connections ❧ Critical Thinking sidenotes ❧ Real-World Connections	❧ Critical Thinking Skills ❧ Unit Planning Guide (Life Skills Connections)
❧ Test-Taking Tips ❧ Multiple Learning Styles	❧ Research and Report Writing Guide ❧ Style and Documentation Sourcebook for Writers ❧ College Entrance Exams Preparation and Practice Workbook
❧ Technology Options ❧ Internet Connections ❧ Technology Tips	❧ Media Connections Activities ❧ Guide to Using the Internet and Other Electronic Resources ❧ Web Site (lit.glencoe.com) ❧ Writer's Assistant CD-ROM
❧ Interdisciplinary Connections ❧ Cultural Notes ❧ Historical Notes	❧ Interdisciplinary Activities ❧ Unit Planning Guide (Interdisciplinary Connections)

Program Philosophy

What are the goals of *Glencoe Literature*?

by Denny Wolfe

The impetus for *Glencoe Literature: The Reader's Choice* was the need for contemporary anthologies that would appeal to today's media-savvy students. A rich mix of classic and modern selections unites new and old voices chosen to represent our diverse communities. Each book's pages reflect a youthful energy, with color, images, media connections, interdisciplinary links, and quotations to enhance the featured literary works. The collection of poems and plays, stories and songs, letters and essays, myths and folklore enables teachers and students to explore together the literary legacies of many voices and many lands.

Glencoe Literature is particularly committed to supporting classroom teachers as they work
- to develop students' abilities as readers, writers, listeners, speakers, viewers, and critical and creative thinkers
- to guide students in developing interpretive skills that transcend specific literary voices, cultures, or times toward an understanding of the larger human experience
- to help students become life-long learners and responsible citizens for democracy in the twenty-first century

Through its varied and active instructional strategies, *Glencoe Literature* invites students to experience the entertaining and restorative powers of literature. Within this context students have frequent opportunities to
- engage in responsive reading, interpretation, and literary analysis through encounters with texts arranged by both theme and genre
- explore writing as a purposeful and flexible means of expression, reflection, and critical and creative thought
- use current and emerging technologies as tools for learning and extending the language arts
- participate in an approach to literacy development that integrates all the language arts
- experience multiple forms of assessment that are responsive to local, state, and national standards of achievement

Glencoe Literature prepares students for their literary encounters through prereading activities rooted in the experiences that students bring to texts. During and after the reading of a work, students respond personally to it; they share their responses with others; and they learn to probe ever more deeply into elements of the literary craft. This sequence enables students and teachers to create interpretive communities in their classrooms, to realize the highest standards of literary inquiry, and to participate vigorously in the cultural conversation of the twenty-first century.

Seymour Papert, one of the foremost authorities on computers and learning, writes that "the computer is the world's greatest construction kit." He concurs that literacy is intimately involved in technology and its critical use. Critical use, he tells us, can only occur if students find and design knowledge with technology. This kind of work is what Papert calls "hard fun," and it leads to powerful and exciting forms of learning. We have provided the context and support for this kind of learning in the text you hold in your hands. Buckle your seatbelts and get ready for some "hard fun" of your own.

How can we help students become media literate?

by Jeffrey Wilhelm

Media literacy is closely related to technology literacy, but it casts a wider net by considering how different technologies organize and represent information in different ways and with different effects. When my own students tell me that they "know" something because they read it on a Web site or saw it on MTV, I become very concerned that they have a critical understanding and standards for how knowledge is produced and represented. In response to these and similar needs, the National Communication Association created national standards for media literacy in 1996, and various states are now embedding similar standards into their curriculum and testing guidelines.

Because of the importance of media literacy, *Glencoe Literature* deals with media use and representation in a variety of ways. Students are asked to use and critique various media, often vis-à-vis literary texts so that they can compare the strengths and weaknesses of representing knowledge through different textual forms. Students are also asked to create media responses to literature they have read, and sometimes to create stories, arguments or presentations of their own using different media possibilities. Always, we have in mind to expand the notion of what it means to be literate to include an understanding of the nature of mass media, the techniques used by them, and the ability to both produce and critique meanings using various media. 🍃

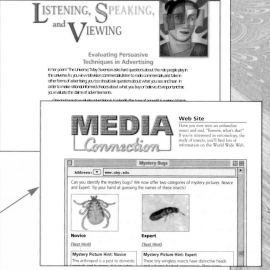

Internet Connections **engage students in online research and in building databases of shared knowledge in the classroom.**

Media Connections **and Listening, Speaking, and Viewing features help students become critical readers and viewers of media.**

Integrated Language Arts

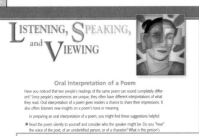

LISTENING, SPEAKING, and VIEWING

Oral Interpretation of a Poem

Have you noticed that two people's readings of the same poem can sound completely different? Since people's experiences are unique, they often have different interpretations of what they read. Oral interpretation of a poem gives readers a chance to share their impressions. It also offers listeners new insights on a poem's tone or meaning.

In preparing an oral interpretation of a poem, you might find these suggestions helpful:

● Read the poem silently to yourself and consider who the speaker might be. Do you "hear" the voice of the poet, of an unidentified person, or of a character? What is this person's

EXTENDING YOUR RESPONSE

Literature Groups
Do You Agree? The narrator contradicts himself at the end of the story, saying first, "And here I have lamely related to you the uneventful chronicle of two foolish children in a flat who most unwisely sacrificed for each other the greatest treasures of their house." Then he says, "Let it be said that of all who give gifts these two were the wisest. Of all who give and receive gifts, such as they, are wisest." With your group, discuss which of these statements is closer to your views about Della and Jim. Do you think there might be truth in both statements? Share your opinions with the rest of your classmates.

Reading Further
If you'd like to read more by O. Henry, you might enjoy these works:
Short Stories: "A Retrieved Reformation," which can be found in the collection *41 Stories*, shows how love can reform a criminal.
"The Cop and the Anthem" and "The Last Leaf," from the collection *The Best Short Stories of O. Henry*, both feature beloved, simple characters and twisting plots.
Viewing: *The Gift of Love* is a film adaptation of "The Gift of the Magi."

Skill features **help students develop key listening and speaking abilities, and** *Literature Groups* **activities provide opportunities for small group discussions with each selection.**

Skill Minilesson

VOCABULARY • The Latin Root *pos*

Latin roots form the basis of many English words. The root is usually combined with a prefix, a suffix, or both. The meaning of the English word is usually related to the meaning of the root it contains. For example, the words *disposition* (line 16) and *supposed* (line 27), from *Song of Myself*, contain the Latin root *pos*, meaning "to put" or "to place." *Disposition* can be interpreted as "the way a person's temperament or mood is arranged or placed"; *suppose* can mean "to place under belief."

PRACTICE Define each word below, using a dictionary if necessary. Then discuss with a partner how the meaning of the Latin root *pos* contributes to the meaning of each word.
1. deposit
2. oppose
3. transpose
4. position
5. expose

Skill Minilessons **provide frequent opportunities for students to develop reading and vocabulary skills in the context of their literature study.**

How can we integrate the language arts through our teaching of literature?

by Beverly Ann Chin

Integrating the English language arts into our teaching of literature is an effective way to help students improve their communication and thinking skills. Today, the English language arts include speaking, listening, reading, writing, viewing, and visually representing. We can use each of the language arts to engage our students in the study and appreciation of literature.

Listening and Speaking We integrate listening and speaking skills whenever students participate in class discussions and literature groups. Students orally share their understandings of literature, and they listen to other people's ideas and opinions. We teach speaking and listening skills when our students work in cooperative learning groups and collaborate on literature projects. Speaking and listening skills are basic components in creative drama activities, such as role playing, readers theater, improvisation, and choral reading. As students interpret literature through creative drama and oral interpretation, they discover how language and nonverbal communication affect the audience's understanding of the story. Whether students are responding to literature through a small group conversation, listening to someone read a selection aloud, or participating in a dramatic performance, they are using and improving their speaking and listening abilities.

Reading When we teach literature, we help our students develop important reading strategies. For example, before students read a literature selection, we invite students to draw upon their prior knowledge and experiences to help them make connections with the literature. During the reading process, we encourage students to make inferences about the characters' motivations and to use context clues to determine the meaning of unfamiliar vocabulary. After reading the selection, students discuss their responses and extend their comprehension. By encouraging students to respond to and reflect on literature, we help students develop their critical and creative reading abilities.

VISUALIZE In your imagination, form pictures of the setting, the characters, and the action. Pay close attention to sensory details and descriptions and your responses to them.

> **Ask yourself . . .**
> - Can I see the characters and setting in my mind?
> - Where are the characters in relation to one another and to their surroundings?
> - How do the descriptions of a character's expressions, body stance, and tone of voice help to develop the scene?

EVALUATE As you read, form opinions and make judgments about the characters and their actions. Review and, if necessary, revise opinions and judgments.

> **Ask yourself . . .**
> - Does this turn of events make sense for these characters?
> - Is this character acting or responding in a realistic way?
> - What is particularly effective about this writer's style?

REVIEW As you read, summarize related events and paraphrase difficult language.

> **Say to yourself . . .**
> - These events have happened so far . . .
> - That event caused this event to happen . . .
> - In other words, this character means . . .

RESPOND Respond to the story *while* you are reading it. React spontaneously to the story.

> **Say to yourself . . .**
> - That character's actions were so . . . !
> - I'd like to ask the author why . . .
> - I wish I could see this place because . . .

Applying the Strategies

1. Read the following story, "The Life You Save May Be Your Own," by Flannery O'Connor. Use the Active Reading Model notes in the margins to help you.

2. Read another short story using appropriate Active Reading Strategies. Write your comments and questions on a sheet of paper. When you finish, evaluate your use of the strategies.

 FICTION 5

Visualize

Emphasize that visualizing gives a sense of immediacy and helps readers connect to what is happening. It can help clear up misunderstandings or confusions about the text. Choose a scene from the story, and have students imagine the setting and the action that occurs.

Evaluate

Explain to students that judgments and opinions should always be a part of their reading strategies. Whether or not they write an evaluation or discuss it with others, their evaluation should be supported by evidence from the literature.

Review

Students who need help in summarizing may be encouraged to note, as they read, key words or phrases that help them keep track of each event or scene. Lengthy descriptions are unnecessary; a few phrases alone should help them recall what happens.

Respond

Remind students that their responses can take a variety of forms. A response may be an emotional reaction to a character or event, a reply to an idea in the text, or a question. Every response is acceptable, but students may want to analyze their reactions in order to understand why they feel or think as they do.

Objectives

- To read and analyze a work of fiction about first impressions
- To identify and assess the use of description in a story
- To write an evaluation of the title of a story

Skills

Reading/Thinking: Inferring; Comparing and Contrasting; Drawing Conclusions
Writing: Character Descriptions; Story
Vocabulary: Analogies
Grammar/Language: Double Negatives
Listening/Speaking: Interview
Life Skills: Lifelong Learning
Collaboration: Literature Groups; Play Proposal

Motivating

→OPTIONS

Selection Focus Transparency 1: Have students examine and discuss the photograph.

Focus Activity: As an extension of the Focus Activity, have students describe the things they look for when they are deciding whether or not to trust someone they are meeting for the first time. Encourage students to consider the judgments they make about people's speech, as well as their appearance and behavior.

Before You Read

The Life You Save May Be Your Own

Meet Flannery O'Connor

Award-winning author Flannery O'Connor often delighted in telling friends and interviewers that the highlight of her life occurred when, as a five-year-old, she taught a chicken to walk backwards. It was on such odd yet mundane experiences that O'Connor was later to base her work. "The first and most obvious characteristic of fiction," she said, "is that it deals with reality through what can be seen, heard, smelt, tasted, and touched."

Mary Flannery O'Connor grew up in Georgia. After graduating from college in 1945, she attended the prestigious Iowa Writers' Workshop at the University of Iowa. In 1952 O'Connor was stricken with a near fatal attack of lupus, the disease from which her father had died, and was forced to move back to her mother's farm. Her writing reflects the vivid details of these rural surroundings and describes seemingly simple yet extremely complex characters. Her themes are often the harsh and unsettling realities of hard luck, hypocrisy, and failed expectations.

O'Connor died at the age of thirty-nine, but her great talent had earned her recognition as a major literary voice of the American South. A review appearing in *Time* magazine hailed O'Connor as "highly unladylike [with] a brutal irony, a slam-bang humor, and a style of writing as balefully direct as a death sentence."

"Fiction is . . . the most modest and the most human of the arts."
—*O'Connor*

Flannery O'Connor was born in 1925 and died in 1964.

FOCUS ACTIVITY

What do you look for when you meet someone for the first time? Are your first impressions usually correct?

JOURNAL Briefly describe an experience you have had as you sized up a new acquaintance and then got to know the person better.

SETTING A PURPOSE Read to discover the first impressions two characters have about each other and whether those impressions prove to be correct.

BACKGROUND

The Time and Place

Widespread unemployment during the Depression of the 1930s brought hard times to many. Unemployed men, and occasionally women, often became wanderers, referred to as "tramps" or "hoboes." They went from city to city and house to house, particularly in rural areas, seeking odd jobs in return for food, clothes, or shelter. When World War II began, many regularly employed workers joined the armed forces. As a result, the previously unemployed and men wounded and sent home from the war frequently filled in at temporary jobs.

VOCABULARY PREVIEW

gaunt (gônt) *adj.* thin, bony, and hollow-eyed, as from hunger or illness; p. 8
list (list) *v.* to tilt or lean to one side; p. 8
ravenous (rav′ ə nəs) *adj.* extremely hungry; p. 11
stately (stāt′ lē) *adj.* noble; dignified; majestic; p. 12
morose (mə rōs′) *adj.* bad-tempered, gloomy, and withdrawn; p. 14
rue (rōō) *v.* to regret; to be sorry for; p. 16

RESOURCE MANAGER

Lesson Planning Resource
The *Unit One Planning Guide* (pp. vi–5) provides additional lesson notes and reduced versions of all print resources.

📁 **Other Print Resources**
- Active Reading Guide, p. 1
- Vocabulary Practice, p. 1
- Reading Workbook, pp. 1–2
- Grammar and Language Workbook, p. 203

- Grammar and Composition Handbook, Lesson 8.6
- Quick Checks, p. 1
- Selection and Theme Assessment, pp. 1–2
- Performance Assessment, p. 1
- Spanish Summaries, p. 1
- Inclusion Strategies
- English Language Learners Sourcebook

 Transparencies
- Selection Focus 1
- Literary Elements 1
- Grammar and Language 1

Technology
🎧 Audio Library
🎧 Spanish Audio Library
💻 Glencoe Literature Web Site
💾 Testmaker

"No'm, I don't," Mr. Shiftlet said.

"One that can't talk," she continued, "can't sass you back or use foul language. That's the kind for you to have. Right there," and she pointed to Lucynell sitting cross-legged in her chair, holding both feet in her hands.

"That's right," he admitted. "She wouldn't give me any trouble."

"Saturday," the old woman said, "you and her and me can drive into town and get married."

Mr. Shiftlet eased his position on the steps.

"I can't get married right now," he said. "Everything you want to do takes money and I ain't got any."

"What you need with money?" she asked.

"It takes money," he said. "Some people'll do anything anyhow these days, but the way I think, I wouldn't marry no woman that I couldn't take on a trip like she was somebody. I mean take her to a hotel and treat her. I wouldn't marry the Duchesser Windsor,[5] he said firmly, "unless I could take her to a hotel and give her something good to eat.

"I was raised thataway and there ain't a thing I can do about it. My old mother taught me how to do."

"Lucynell don't even know what a hotel is," the old woman muttered. "Listen here, Mr. Shiftlet," she said, sliding forward in her chair, "you'd be getting a permanent house and a deep well and the most innocent girl in the world. You don't need no money. Lemme tell you something: there ain't any place in the world for a poor disabled friendless drifting man."

The ugly words settled in Mr. Shiftlet's head like a group of buzzards in the top of a tree. He didn't answer at once. He rolled himself a cigarette and lit it and then he said in an even voice, "Lady, a man is divided into two parts, body and spirit."

The old woman clamped her gums together.

"A body and a spirit," he repeated. "The body, lady, is like a house: it don't go anywhere; but the spirit, lady, is like a automobile: always on the move, always . . ."

"Listen, Mr. Shiftlet," she said, "my well never goes dry and my house is always warm in the winter and there's no mortgage on a thing about this place. You can go to the courthouse and see for yourself. And yonder under that shed is a fine automobile." She laid the bait carefully. "You can have it painted by Saturday. I'll pay for the paint."

In the darkness, Mr. Shiftlet's smile stretched like a weary snake waking up by a fire. After a second he recalled himself and said, "I'm only saying a man's spirit means more to him than anything else. I would have to take my wife off for the weekend without no regards at all for cost. I got to follow where my spirit say to go."

---

5. Shiftlet is referring to the American woman for whom Britain's King Edward VIII gave up the throne in 1936. The new king gave them the titles Duke and Duchess of *Windsor*.

EVALUATE

Does Mr. Shiftlet's reason for needing money seem reasonable? Why or why not?

QUESTION

Why, do you think, does Mr. Shiftlet smile in the darkness?

FICTION ❧ 13

N   Critical Thinking

INFERRING Ask students how Mr. Shiftlet and Mrs. Crater are similar in their intentions. *(Each has a plan to foist off on the other. Mr. Shiftlet wants money and the car; Mrs. Crater wants an on-the-premises caretaker. Both use persuasive techniques to try to get what they want.)*

O   Active Reading

EVALUATE Help students recognize that Mr. Shiftlet's strongest personality trait is getting people to give him what he wants. He is always one step ahead of Mrs. Crater, and he is able to make even the most outrageous demands—in this case, for money—seem not only reasonable, but virtuous.

P   Active Reading

QUESTION Ask students what plan Mr. Shiftlet is pleased about. *(Students should understand that Mr. Shiftlet smiles at this point because he knows he has won his battle with Mrs. Crater. In the darkness she cannot see his smile. By agreeing to marry Lucynell, he will have money and a car for himself.)* You may want to call students' attention to the simile of a snake waking up by a fire, an apt comment on Mr. Shiftlet's slyness.

LIFE SKILLS CONNECTION

Lifelong Learning O'Connor's story teaches a lesson about trusting people. Mrs. Crater is fooled by Mr. Shiftlet; she trusts her first impressions, and her own desires blind her to his true intentions.

Activity Ask students to analyze a time when they made a faulty judgment about someone. Have them write a brief report about the reasons they made the judgment, and the problem with it. Students should address:

- their own and the other person's motivations.
- the behaviors of the person who misled them.
- the lesson they learned.
- the strategies that might have prevented their mistake.

After students have completed their reports, ask them to share them with a partner. **L2** **COLLAB. LEARN.**

14 ACTIVE READING

Active Reading

REVIEW Point out that Mr. Shiftlet had to seem unwilling to marry at first in order to obtain everything he wanted. *(When Mr. Shiftlet agrees to marry Lucynell on the following Saturday, Mrs. Crater promises him a picnic lunch, $17.50 in cash for a weekend wedding trip, and the use of her car.)*

Active Reading

CONNECT For this question students have to adopt Mr. Shiftlet's ideas and personality in order to imagine what he is thinking. They have to imagine themselves in his shoes. *(Mr. Shiftlet would most likely be thinking, "Oh well, it's worth it for the car." or "Now what am I going to do with Lucynell?")*

Teaching Options

The Life You Save May Be Your Own

Active Reading Model

REVIEW
What deal does Mrs. Crater offer to Mr. Shiftlet?

CONNECT
What would you be thinking here if you were Mr. Shiftlet?

"I'll give you fifteen dollars for a weekend trip," the old woman said in a crabbed voice. "That's the best I can do."

"That wouldn't hardly pay for more than the gas and the hotel," he said. "It wouldn't feed her."

"Seventeen-fifty," the old woman said. "That's all I got so it isn't any use you trying to milk me. You can take a lunch."

Mr. Shiftlet was deeply hurt by the word "milk." He didn't doubt that she had more money sewed up in her mattress but he had already told her he was not interested in her money. "I'll make that do," he said and rose and walked off without treating[6] with her further.

On Saturday the three of them drove into town in the car that the paint had barely dried on and Mr. Shiftlet and Lucynell were married in the Ordinary's[7] office while the old woman witnessed. As they came out of the courthouse, Mr. Shiftlet began twisting his neck in his collar. He looked morose and bitter as if he had been insulted while someone held him. "That didn't satisfy me none," he said. "That was just something a woman in an office did, nothing but paper work and blood tests. What do they know about my blood? If they was to take my heart and cut it out," he said, "they wouldn't know a thing about me. It didn't satisfy me at all."

"It satisfied the law," the old woman said sharply.

"The law," Mr. Shiftlet said and spit. "It's the law that don't satisfy me."

He had painted the car dark green with a yellow band around it just under the windows. The three of them climbed in the front seat and the old woman said, "Don't Lucynell look pretty? Looks like a baby doll." Lucynell was dressed up in a white dress that her mother had uprooted from a trunk and there was a Panama hat on her head with a bunch of red wooden cherries on the brim. Every now and then her placid[8] expression was changed by a sly isolated little thought like a shoot of green in the desert. "You got a prize!" the old woman said.

Mr. Shiftlet didn't even look at her.

They drove back to the house to let the old woman off and pick up the lunch. When they were ready to leave, she stood staring in the window of the car, with her fingers clenched around the glass. Tears began to seep sideways out of her eyes and run along the dirty creases in her face. "I ain't ever been parted with her for two days before," she said.

Mr. Shiftlet started the motor.

"And I wouldn't let no man have her but you because I seen you would do right. Good-bye, Sugarbaby," she said, clutching at the sleeve of the

---

6. Here, *treating* means "negotiating or discussing terms."
7. An *Ordinary* is a local judge who, in many states, is called the "justice of the peace."
8. *Placid* means "calm" or "peaceful."

Vocabulary
morose (mə rōs′) *adj.* bad-tempered, gloomy, and withdrawn

MULTIPLE LEARNING STYLES
MEETING INDIVIDUAL NEEDS

Interpersonal Interpersonal learners often have strong insights into the feelings and motivations of others. Invite them to explore Lucynell's character.

Activity Ask students to look for any clues to young Lucynell's character, needs, and desires. Then have them meet in small groups to share their insights. Each group can decide how to present their insights to the class. They may, for example, develop a series of abstract sketches, present a panel discussion, or retell the story from Lucynell's or an omniscient narrator's point of view. Encourage students to use their imaginations. **L3 COLLAB. LEARN.**

white dress. Lucynell looked straight at her and didn't seem to see her there at all. Mr. Shiftlet eased the car forward so that she had to move her hands.

The early afternoon was clear and open and surrounded by pale blue sky. Although the car would go only thirty miles an hour, Mr. Shiftlet imagined a terrific climb and dip and swerve that went entirely to his head so that he forgot his morning bitterness. He had always wanted an automobile but he had never been able to afford one before. He drove very fast because he wanted to make Mobile[9] by nightfall.

Occasionally he stopped his thoughts long enough to look at Lucynell in the seat beside him. She had eaten the lunch as soon as they were out of the yard and now she was pulling the cherries off the hat one by one and throwing them out the window. He became depressed in spite of the car. He had driven about a hundred miles when he decided that she must be hungry again and at the next small town they came to, he stopped in front of an aluminum-painted eating place called The Hot Spot and took her in and ordered her a plate of ham and grits. The ride had made her sleepy and as soon as she got up on the stool, she rested her head on the counter and shut her eyes. There was no one in The Hot Spot but Mr. Shiftlet and the boy behind the counter, a pale youth with a greasy rag hung over his shoulder. Before he could dish up the food, she was snoring gently.

---

9. *Mobile* (mō′ bēl) is a port city in southwestern Alabama.

Blue Diner with Figures, 1981. Ralph Goings. Oil on canvas, 48 x 62½ in. O.K. Harris Works of Art, New York.

Viewing the painting: How does this scene compare with your vision of the lunch counter where Mr. Shiftlet takes Lucynell? Explain.

VISUALIZE Picture Lucynell's appearance and actions on her wedding day. What might her actions suggest about her feelings?

VISUALIZE Before students attempt to visualize Lucynell in this situation, you may want them to skim the two full paragraphs on the page.

(Lucynell's actions suggest that she doesn't know what happened at the courthouse and doesn't understand why she is traveling with Mr. Shiftlet. However, the fact that she falls asleep at the lunch counter also suggests that she is unafraid and unconcerned about the outcome.)

VIEWING THE PAINTING

Ralph Goings (1928–) was one of the first participants in the Photorealist school of painters. He usually paints from photographs of a subject. Goings has said, "I use the impersonal, mechanical image of the photograph to paint a facsimile of reality. . . . However, the photograph is not the subject of my work but rather a source of information, information that must be translated into paint information. The painted image is more important than the reality or the photo image."

Viewing Response *Students will probably agree that the scene in the painting is much like The Hot Spot where Mr. Shiftlet takes Lucynell. However, the story takes place during the Great Depression, and The Hot Spot was likely more run-down and offered less than the diner in the painting.*

FICTION ✿ 15

Writing *Minilesson*

Character Descriptions Explain that many writers invent interesting characters by deliberately creating a contrast between their words and their actions. O'Connor does this with Mr. Shiftlet. Have students discuss O'Connor's technique, using descriptive passages from the story as examples.

Activity Ask students to create similar characters and write two- or three-paragraph vignettes about them. The characters don't necessarily have to be scoundrels; however, there should be clear differences between their words and actions. You may want to review the basics of written dialogue. **L2**

Additional Resources

Writer's Choice, Lesson 4.1

Active Reading

QUESTION If students have distrusted Mr. Shiftlet for some time, they may not be surprised that he decides to abandon Lucynell in the diner. He leaves her in relatively safe surroundings where she might eventually get some help. *(Mr. Shiftlet probably lies because he doesn't want to arouse suspicion about his relationship with Lucynell and wants to make a clean getaway.)*

Critical Thinking

DRAWING CONCLUSIONS Ask students what purpose the final scene with the young hitchhiker serves. *(Through Mr. Shiftlet's conversation with the boy, the author shows that his abandonment of Lucynell was hardly different from his abandonment of his own mother years before. Furthermore, Mr. Shiftlet's attempt to dissuade the boy from running away provides an ironic commentary on his own actions.)*

Active Reading Model

QUESTION
Why does Mr. Shiftlet lie to the boy behind the counter?

"Give it to her when she wakes up," Mr. Shiftlet said. "I'll pay for it now."

The boy bent over her and stared at the long pink-gold hair and the half-shut sleeping eyes. Then he looked up and stared at Mr. Shiftlet. "She looks like an angel of Gawd," he murmured.

"Hitchhiker," Mr. Shiftlet explained. "I can't wait. I got to make Tuscaloosa."[10]

The boy bent over again and very carefully touched his finger to a strand of the golden hair and Mr. Shiftlet left.

He was more depressed than ever as he drove on by himself. The late afternoon had grown hot and sultry and the country had flattened out. Deep in the sky a storm was preparing very slowly and without thunder as if it meant to drain every drop of air from the earth before it broke. There were times when Mr. Shiftlet preferred not to be alone. He felt too that a man with a car had a responsibility to others and he kept his eye out for a hitchhiker. Occasionally he saw a sign that warned: "Drive carefully. The life you save may be your own."

The narrow road dropped off on either side into dry fields and here and there a shack or a filling station stood in a clearing. The sun began to set directly in front of the automobile. It was a reddening ball that through his windshield was slightly flat on the bottom and top. He saw a boy in overalls and a gray hat standing on the edge of the road and he slowed the car down and stopped in front of him. The boy didn't have his hand raised to thumb the ride, he was only standing there, but he had a small cardboard suitcase and his hat was set on his head in a way to indicate that he had left somewhere for good. "Son," Mr. Shiftlet said, "I see you want a ride."

The boy didn't say he did or he didn't but he opened the door of the car and got in, and Mr. Shiftlet started driving again. The child held the suitcase on his lap and folded his arms on top of it. He turned his head and looked out the window away from Mr. Shiftlet. Mr. Shiftlet felt oppressed.[11] "Son," he said after a minute, "I got the best old mother in the world so I reckon you only got the second best."

The boy gave him a quick dark glance and then turned his face back out the window.

"It's nothing so sweet," Mr. Shiftlet continued, "as a boy's mother. She taught him his first prayers at her knee, she give him love when no other would, she told him what was right and what wasn't, and she seen that he done the right thing. Son," he said, "I never rued a day in my life like the one I rued when I left that old mother of mine."

The boy shifted in his seat but he didn't look at Mr. Shiftlet. He unfolded his arms and put one hand on the door handle.

---

10. *Tuscaloosa,* in west central Alabama, is nearly 200 miles north of Mobile.
11. Here, *oppressed* means "distressed" or "burdened."

Vocabulary
rue (rōō) *v.* to regret; to be sorry for

Teaching Options

INTERDISCIPLINARY CONNECTION

Sociology Students may wonder why Mr. Shiftlet would abandon a helpless, disabled young woman in unfamiliar surroundings without apparent remorse. Sociologists who have observed this phenomenon call it *anomie,* a social instability caused by a breakdown of standards and values. Note that Mr. Shiftlet is not a criminal; he doesn't physically harm Lucynell or leave her to die at the side of the road. O'Connor even describes him as depressed over his actions. Still, his behavior is deplorable.

Activity Interested students may enjoy researching this phenomenon. Have students report on anomie in American literature, in social settings, or in combat situations such as the Vietnam War. **L3**

I'll Take the High Road, 1944. Emil J. Kosa Jr. Oil on Masonite, 24 x 30 in. Private collection. Permission courtesy of Mrs. Emil J. Kosa, Jr.

Viewing the painting: What are the key images in this painting? How do they affect your response to Mr. Shiftlet's action?

"My mother was an angel of Gawd," Mr. Shiftlet said in a very strained voice. "He took her from heaven and giver to me and I left her." His eyes were instantly clouded over with a mist of tears. The car was barely moving.

The boy turned angrily in the seat. "You go to the devil!" he cried. "My old woman is a flea bag and yours is a stinking pole cat!" and with that he flung the door open and jumped out with his suitcase into the ditch.

Mr. Shiftlet was so shocked that for about a hundred feet he drove along slowly with the door still open. A cloud, the exact color of the boy's hat and shaped like a turnip, had descended over the sun, and another, worse looking, crouched behind the car. Mr. Shiftlet felt that the rottenness of the world was about to engulf him. He raised his arm and let it fall again to his breast. "Oh Lord!" he prayed. "Break forth and wash the slime from this earth!"

The turnip continued slowly to descend. After a few minutes there was a guffawing peal of thunder from behind and fantastic raindrops, like tin-can tops, crashed over the rear of Mr. Shiftlet's car. Very quickly he stepped on the gas and with his stump sticking out the window he raced the galloping shower into Mobile.

EVALUATE

Is Mr. Shiftlet's treatment of the young hitchhiker true to his character?

RESPOND

What is your opinion of Mr. Shiftlet at the end of the story?

V **Active Reading**

EVALUATE Have students summarize Mr. Shiftlet's actions from the beginning of the story before they make their evaluations. *(Mr. Shiftlet's treatment of the hitchhiker is true to his character. He continually seems unable to behave in a manner consistent with what he says he believes.)*

W **Active Reading**

RESPOND Challenge students to make a list of specific adjectives that describe Mr. Shiftlet. Then have them use their list to write a sentence or two stating their opinions about him.

☑ASSESSMENT OPTIONS

📁 *Quick Checks,* p. 1

Listening and Speaking *Minilesson*

Interview Students may gain a better understanding of characters by taking on their persona and exploring the characters' points of view.

Activity Have groups of five or six students create scenarios in which they play the roles of the characters in the story. For example, a police officer might interview Mr. Shiftlet about his abandonment of Lucynell, or Mrs. Crater might explain Lucynell's disappearance to a visiting relative. Group members should take turns performing impromptu conversations and those who are not participating in the conversations should critique the performances. **L2 COLLAB. LEARN.**

Responding to the Selection

Personal Response

Students may say that O'Connor prepares the reader for Lucynell's abandonment.

Active Reading Response

Students should explain how their strategies aided their understanding and enjoyment of the story.

ANALYZING LITERATURE

1. He presents himself as honest, down on his luck, and having an interest in fixing up the farm.

2. He repairs the garden house, patches the steps, builds a new hog pen, restores a fence, and teaches Lucynell to say "bird."

3. Lucynell is speech impaired and is likely mentally handicapped. Her disabilities make her vulnerable.

4. Mr. Shiftlet and Mrs. Crater first agree that he will work for food and will sleep in the car and then that he will marry Lucynell, take her on a trip, and return to live at the farm.

5. Lucynell is left at a diner; Mrs. Crater is left at home without Lucynell and her car; Mr. Shiftlet drives the car toward Mobile, Alabama.

6. Apparently tramps were common. Mrs. Crater doesn't realize the great interest Mr. Shiftlet has in her possessions; likewise, she is not aware that his behaviors don't always mirror his words.

7. Mr. Shiftlet wants whatever he can get out of Mrs. Carter, which students should infer from his interest in the farm.

8. Possible answer: Mrs. Crater thinks he is a good match; he is single, seems virtuous, and is handy.

9. Mr. Shiftlet makes the initial agreement because he needs food, a place to stay, and time. He agrees to marry Lucynell because it is an opportunity to get what he wants. Even if he intended to honor the second agreement, it is clear he is unable to do so.

10. Students could argue that Shiftlet saved himself from a life with Lucynell or that Mrs. Crater and Lucynell were saved from a lifetime of Shiftlet's irresponsible behaviors.

11. If the story were set in a modern city, the biggest difference might include the degree of violence present.

12. Students may say they judge new acquaintances by the way they look

---

Responding to Literature

Personal Response

Were you surprised by the outcome of the story? Explain.

Active Reading Response

Which one of the Active Reading Strategies described on pages 4–5 did you use most often? What did this strategy add to your appreciation of the story?

——— ANALYZING LITERATURE ———

RECALL

1. How does Mr. Shiftlet present himself to Mrs. Crater?
2. What does Mr. Shiftlet accomplish during his week on the Crater farm?
3. What is Lucynell's disability, and how does it affect her?
4. What two agreements do Mr. Shiftlet and Mrs. Crater make?
5. What happens to each of the characters at the end of the story?

INTERPRET

6. Why does Mrs. Crater assume that Mr. Shiftlet is no one to fear? What clues to his true character does she fail to notice?
7. What does Mr. Shiftlet want from Mrs. Crater? How do you know?
8. Why does Mrs. Crater think that Mr. Shiftlet is a good match for her daughter? Support your answer with examples from the story.
9. What factors might motivate Mr. Shiftlet to make each agreement? Do you think he intended to honor the second one? Why or why not?
10. Whose life, if anyone's, do you think may have been saved at the end of the story? Explain your choice.

EVALUATE AND CONNECT

11. How might this story be different if it were set in a modern-day city instead of on a country farm in the 1940s? Explain your answer.
12. How is your response to the Focus Activity on page 6 like Mrs. Crater's initial response to Shiftlet? How is it different?
13. The planting of clues about what may happen later in a story is **foreshadowing**. Which parts of the story foreshadow the end?
14. **Situational irony** occurs when the outcome of a situation is different from the expectations of a character or of a reader. Explain the situational irony in this story.
15. A hypocrite is someone who claims to have certain beliefs, but whose actions prove otherwise. Do you think Mr. Shiftlet is a hypocrite? Why or why not? Is Mrs. Crater a hypocrite? Explain.

Literary ELEMENTS

Description

A **description** is a detailed portrayal of a person, place, or thing. When authors write descriptions, they include vivid and precise adjectives, nouns, and verbs. Authors may use details to describe tangible things, such as the appearance of a character, place, or object. Or they may use details to describe intangible things, such as a character's personality traits. Authors often use **sensory details** to help readers understand what characters see, hear, touch, smell, or taste.

1. Identify details in the story that describe the Crater farm.
2. Which character in this story do you think is described most vividly? Cite details from the story to support your choice.

● See **Literary Terms Handbook**, p. R4.

---

and speak, as did Mrs. Crater; she was dead wrong. Responses are probably similar.

13. Whenever Mr. Shiftlet responds to Mrs. Crater, his thoughts and plans are different from what he says. Readers understand his duplicity because the narrator looks into Mr. Shiftlet's mind. The two main agreements foreshadow the end.

14. Making the two women the losers and the tramp the winner is situational irony.

15. Mr. Shiftlet matches most people's definitions of a hypocrite; his actions belie his words. Mrs. Crater is hypocritical in the way she baits Mr. Shiftlet to marry Lucynell.

LITERARY ELEMENTS

1. The author describes the farm as run-down but essentially intact. She has Mrs. Crater mention, for example, its sturdiness, its lack of encumbrance, its deep well, and its comfort in bad weather.
2. Mr. Shiftlet is probably described most vividly. He is shown as someone who agrees to Mrs. Crater's plan to get what he wants, but whose complexities prevent him from being honorable.

Additional Resources

 Literary Elements Transparency 1

LITERATURE AND WRITING

Writing About Literature

Evaluating the Title Why might O'Connor have chosen the slogan from a highway safety sign as the title of her story? Write a brief evaluation of the title's effectiveness. Explain why it is effective, or suggest an alternate title and provide support for your suggestion.

Creative Writing

Lucynell's Story What might happen to Lucynell after she wakes up? Will she be able to communicate her problem? Will she get home? Is it likely that anyone will befriend her? Write a one- or two-page sequel to the story, showing Lucynell's fate.

EXTENDING YOUR RESPONSE

Literature Groups

O'Connor's Characters Flannery O'Connor was known for having a flair for the absurd and for depicting characters who felt alone or isolated. With your group, discuss the appearance, thoughts, dialogue, manners, and actions of the characters in "The Life You Save May Be Your Own." In what ways are the characters loners? What exaggerated qualities do they have? How do these qualities affect the story? Share your conclusions with the class.

Learning for Life

Police Report Write up a police report on Shiftlet's theft and his abandonment of Lucynell. State the crime and note all the facts of the case, including descriptions of Shiftlet and the stolen car. Summarize his background, and record witnesses' statements.

Interdisciplinary Activity

Theater: Play Proposal Imagine that you are to stage a production of "The Life You Save May Be Your Own." With a partner, write a proposal stating your plans for sets, props, and costumes. If you wish, create a portfolio of detailed illustrations of how the scenes from the story should look.

 **Save your work for your portfolio.**

Skill Minilesson

VOCABULARY • Analogies

An **analogy** is a type of comparison that is based on the relationships between things or ideas. Some analogies are based on what may be called "degree of intensity."

> happy : ecstatic :: angry : furious

One who is extremely *happy* is *ecstatic,* just as one who is extremely *angry* is *furious.* In both cases, the second word conveys something similar to, but more intense than, the first.

● For more on analogies, see **Communications Skills Handbook,** pp. R83–R84.

PRACTICE Choose the word pair that best completes each analogy.

1. slender : gaunt ::
   a. true : accurate
   b. courageous : fearful
   c. good : excellent
   d. moral : ethical
   e. expensive : impractical

2. hungry : ravenous ::
   a. cold : frigid
   b. tall : heavy
   c. lucky : fortunate
   d. sad : lonely
   e. wise : educated

Writing About Literature

Students' evaluations should
- suggest why O'Connor chose the story's title.
- evaluate the title's effectiveness.
- suggest an alternate title if the title is deemed ineffective and provide support for the suggestion.

Creative Writing

Students' sequels should
- provide a satisfying plot.
- be consistent with the plot and characters in the story.
- tell what happens to Lucynell after she wakes up.

EXTENDING YOUR RESPONSE

Literature Groups Assign one student in each group to document the discussion and note the points that individuals make. Be sure that the content of the discussion focuses on the characters and the ways in which their qualities affect what happens in the story. **COLLAB. LEARN.**

Learning for Life For this activity students must look at the story from the point of view of a police investigator. Be sure students use in their reports typical police-report jargon.

Interdisciplinary Activity Students may begin by listing the principal scenes in the story and essential details given by O'Connor that describe each scene. Partners' proposals should include written plans and illustrations. **COLLAB. LEARN.**

Skill Minilesson

VOCABULARY • Analogies

1. c
2. a

Additional Resources
📁 *Vocabulary Practice,* p. 1

☑ ASSESSMENT OPTIONS

📁 ***Quick Checks,*** p. 1

📁 ***Selection and Theme Assessment,*** pp. 1–2

📁 ***Performance Assessment,*** p. 1

💾 ***Testmaker***

Active Reading Strategies

Objective

- To understand and apply strategies for reading and comprehending poetry

Teach the Strategies

Invite students to brainstorm a list of poetic elements, such as alliteration, imagery, metaphor, descriptive language, and rhythm. Guide a discussion of each element, and encourage students to provide examples. Ask how these techniques help them enjoy poetry.

Listen

Point out that readers often prefer to read a poem through completely before rereading for specific devices that contribute to how it sounds. On the first reading, students may simply identify enjoyable passages and get a sense of the overall sound and feeling of the poem.

Imagine

Suggest that while students read a poem, they pause occasionally to visualize the images. They should

- think about the associations that specific images create for them.
- consider how the images make them respond to a character, place, or thing.
- think about the mood created by the images.

Teaching Options

Active Reading Model

Active Reading Strategies

Poetry

"Poetry has always seemed the most natural way of saying what I feel," poet Elizabeth Bishop once said. How can poetry help us say what we feel? It can capture intense experiences or creative perceptions of the world with musical language. If prose is like talking, poetry is like singing. Also, poems can express deep thoughts or paint vivid images in just a few lines, or they can present extended comparisons and descriptive passages about a single idea. To get the most from a poem, try the following strategies.

● For more about related reading strategies, see **Reading Handbook**, pp. R86–R93.

LISTEN Read a poem aloud, concentrating on the way it sounds. As you read, pay attention to punctuation marks and the form of **stanzas**, or groups of lines. These items are signals for natural pauses.

Ask yourself . . .

- What type of rhythm do I hear in this poem? Is it rapid or slow?
- What rhyme scheme or pattern, if any, does each stanza have?
- Can I detect alliteration (the repetition of consonant sounds at the beginnings of words)?
- Do I hear assonance (the repetition of vowel sounds)?
- Does the poem have consonance (the repetition of consonant sounds within words or at the ends of words)?
- Is there onomatopoeia (the use of a word or phrase that imitates the sound it names)?
- How do these devices affect the musical quality of the poem?

IMAGINE Re-create in your mind the sights, sounds, smells, tastes, and feel of objects mentioned in the poem.

Ask yourself . . .

- Which specific details appeal to my senses?
- What comparisons does the poet make?
- What human attributes, if any, do the inanimate objects have?
- What types of visual images does the poet include?
- What figures of speech help me "see" objects in the poem?

THE LANGSTON HUGHES READER

T. S. ELIOT   SELECTED POEMS

HOMECOMING   JULIA ALVAREZ

SANDBURG THE PEOPLE, YES

FROST   The Road Not Taken

Collected Poems Edna St. Vincent Millay

ACROSS SPOON RIVER

Reading Journal

Nonverbal Responses

Point out that all responses in a reading journal need not be written in prose. Poetry, especially, often invites graphic responses. Students should respond in a form that is most comfortable for them. Spatial learners, for example, may find that visual representations of ideas are most effective in conveying information and aiding their reading comprehension.

Activity As students read the poem that follows, encourage them to incorporate graphic notes in their journals. These may include sketches of figures of speech or personal responses to images or ideas, diagrams of rhythms or patterns within the poem, or charts or diagrams showing the flow of ideas or images.

| **CLARIFY** | Work to unlock the meaning of each line or sentence. |

Ask yourself . . .
- What does this image (or line or phrase) mean? Why might the poet have chosen to include it?
- How does this image relate to other thoughts and ideas in the poem?

| **INTERPRET** | Reread the poem several times, focusing on its meaning. |

Ask yourself . . .
- What clues about the poem's message does the title provide?
- What words or phrases do the rhyme and rhythm help to emphasize?
- How do the images and symbols work together to support this message, or theme?
- How would I state the theme of this poem?

| **RESPOND** | Think about how the poem affects you. React spontaneously. Consider the ideas about your own life that come to mind as you read the poem. |

Say to yourself . . .
- This poem reminds me of . . .
- This poem makes me feel . . .
- I'd like to read or write a poem about . . .
- This image is so . . .

Applying the Strategies

Read the next selection, Elizabeth Bishop's poem "The Fish." Use the Active Reading Model notes in the margins to help you. Continue to use the strategies as you read other poems.

Clarify

Explain to students that understanding the details in a poem can help them make sense of it as a whole. For example, they may look for clues that reveal the poet's or narrator's attitude toward the subject. In the poem that follows, looking for adjectives that describe the fish would give students an idea of Elizabeth Bishop's feelings about it. The same technique, with different variables, would help them clarify the details in any poem.

Interpret

Remind students that interpreting something is like translating it. If parts of a poem seem difficult or cryptic, suggest they try putting those lines into their own words, checking a dictionary for definitions if needed. Remind them, too, that sometimes a single word can help them interpret an entire passage. Understanding one passage might help them interpret an entire poem. Encourage students to look for the speaker's tone and to consider what clues it gives to the poem's meaning.

Respond

As students read a poem, suggest they
- write words and phrases that come to mind as they read.
- identify the themes or messages of the poem and evaluate whether they agree or disagree with them.
- respond both to the entire poem and to specific lines, stanzas, images, metaphors, and other elements of the poem.

Before You Read

The Fish

Meet
Elizabeth Bishop

The poet Elizabeth Bishop once told her writing class at Harvard University, "Use the dictionary. It's better than the critics." Bishop's wit and devotion to careful, precise language came through in her own writing, which earned her nearly every major poetry prize in the United States.

For Bishop, writing poetry was an act of "self-forgetfulness," in which she focused on shaping and sharing her impressions of the physical world rather than on giving the details of her personal life. Her childhood in Worcester, Massachusetts, was difficult. When she was very young, her father died and her mother was permanently hospitalized, so Bishop was raised by her grandparents in Canada. After graduating from Vassar College in 1934, Bishop traveled frequently and lived in many places, including Florida, New York, and Europe. For sixteen years, she made her home in Brazil, writing, editing, and translating. She kept in touch with people she met in her travels through thousands of letters, some of which were collected and published in her book *One Art*.

Over her fifty-year writing career, Bishop published five slim volumes of poetry with a total of just 101 poems. However, she also wrote nonfiction, including several travel books. Besides writing, Bishop taught writing at Harvard for seven years and served as a poetry consultant to the Library of Congress.

❝I never intended to 'be' a poet, as I think people set out to do today. . . . [It is] far more important to just keep writing poetry than to think of yourself as a poet whose job is to write poetry all the time.❞

—Bishop

Elizabeth Bishop was born in 1911 and died in 1979.

FOCUS ACTIVITY

Imagine yourself fishing from a small boat. What might the fish you catch look like?

LIST IT! Make a list of words and phrases to describe the fish you "caught." Choose words that suggest your reaction to the fish.

SETTING A PURPOSE Read to discover one speaker's impressions of a fish she catches.

BACKGROUND

Literary Influences

Bishop was a college student when she met the poet Marianne Moore, who was to become her mentor and lifelong friend.

A lover of animals and the physical world, Bishop wrote careful descriptions of scenes she witnessed or experienced outdoors. The following passage from a letter Bishop wrote to Moore may have developed into her poem "The Fish."

> The other day I caught a parrot fish, almost by accident. They are ravishing fish—all iridescent, with a silver edge to each scale, and a real bull-like mouth just like turquoise; the eye is very big and wild, and the eyeball is turquoise too—they are very humorous-looking fish. A man on the dock immediately scraped off three scales, then threw him back; he was sure it wouldn't hurt him. I'm enclosing one [scale], if I can find it.

Objectives

- To read and analyze a narrative poem
- To identify and understand similes
- To write a short description using figurative language

Skills

Reading/Thinking: Drawing Conclusions; Monitoring Comprehension
Writing: Description
Collaboration: Literature Groups

Motivating
→OPTIONS

Selection Focus Transparency 2: Have students view the photograph and comment on the appearance of the fish.

Focus Activity: As an extension of the Focus Activity, ask volunteers to describe fishing experiences they have had, have read about, or have imagined. Encourage all students to respond by suggesting words to describe any of the experiences.

RESOURCE MANAGER

Lesson Planning Resource
The *Unit One Planning Guide* (pp. 6–10) provides additional lesson notes and reduced versions of all print resources.

📁 **Other Print Resources**
- Active Reading Guide, p. 2
- Reading Workbook, pp. 3–4
- Quick Checks, p. 2
- Selection and Theme Assessment, pp. 3–4

- Performance Assessment, p. 2
- Spanish Summaries, p. 2
- Inclusion Strategies
- English Language Learners Sourcebook

📖 **Transparencies**
- Selection Focus 2
- Literary Elements 2

Technology
- 🎧 Audio Library
- 🎧 Spanish Audio Library
- 💻 Glencoe Literature Web Site
- 💾 Testmaker

The Fish

Elizabeth Bishop

I caught a tremendous fish
and held him beside the boat
half out of water, with my hook
fast in a corner of his mouth.
5 He didn't fight.
He hadn't fought at all.
He hung a grunting weight,
battered and venerable°
and homely. Here and there
10 his brown skin hung in strips
like ancient wall-paper,
and its pattern of darker brown
was like wall-paper:
shapes like full-blown roses
15 stained and lost through age.
He was speckled with barnacles,
fine rosettes of lime,
and infested
with tiny white sea-lice,
20 and underneath two or three
rags of green weed hung down.
While his gills were breathing in
the terrible oxygen
—the frightening gills,
25 fresh and crisp with blood,
that can cut so badly—
I thought of the coarse white flesh
packed in like feathers,
the big bones and the little bones,
30 the dramatic reds and blacks
of his shiny entrails,°
and the pink swim-bladder°
like a big peony.
I looked into his eyes
35 which were far larger than mine

---

8 *Venerable* means "deserving respect because of age."
31 *Entrails* are internal organs.
32 A *swim-bladder*, or air bladder, is an air sac that enables some fish to maintain buoyancy and equilibrium.

LISTEN

Notice the rhythm of the sentence structure. Is it conversational, or does it have a regular, metrical rhythm?

IMAGINE

Picture the fish as the speaker describes it. What emotional effect does this description have on you?

Active Reading Model

Reading the Selection

A Active Reading

LISTEN Before students respond, ask a volunteer to read aloud lines 1–15. *(Students should recognize that the rhythm of the poem is conversational. It sounds as if the poet were describing her experience as she lived it, moment by moment.)*

Additional Resources
- *Active Reading Guide*, p. 2
- *Audio Library*
- *Spanish Audio Library*

B Active Reading

IMAGINE Ask students to point out specific images that resonate for them. Discuss how Bishop's images appeal to different senses. *(While some students may find the description of the fish repugnant, most will agree that its realism has overtones of admiration and sympathy. Images that appeal to the senses include "frightening gills . . . that can cut" [touch]; "dramatic reds and blacks of his shiny entrails" [sight]; "pink swim bladder like a big peony" [sight])* Ask students which details reveal the speaker's admiration for the fish. Which reveal her sympathy for its plight?

Teaching Options

MEETING INDIVIDUAL NEEDS — MULTIPLE LEARNING STYLES

Spatial Explain that Bishop's poem develops a detailed description of a fish. Spatial learners may benefit from visualizing Bishop's description.

Activity Have students create an illustration of the fish. Before beginning, instruct them to read the poem carefully, noting the details of Bishop's description. Encourage students to work in whatever medium in which they feel most comfortable. Students may choose to focus their illustrations on a particular image in the poem, or a specific aspect of the fish, such as the broken lines hanging from its mouth. Have students share their illustrations with the class. **L2**

C Active Reading

INTERPRET Encourage students to consider the signficance of the five times he got away. *(Students may conclude that the fish is too old or too weak to fight. Perhaps he is sick or injured from the old injuries; he may be tired of fighting.)*

D Active Reading

CLARIFY Explain that students may interpret the victory differently. *(Some may say the speaker celebrates the victory of catching such a prize fish—one that got away five times before. Others may say both the fish and the poet are victorious—the fish swims away free; the speaker chooses freedom—for him, a moral victory.)*

E Active Reading

RESPOND Encourage students to give reasons for their responses. *(Some may be surprised that the speaker releases the fish.)*

F Critical Thinking

DRAWING CONCLUSIONS In literature, real time is often compressed or extended. Ask students to estimate how much time elapses between the catching and the freeing of the fish. *(It is probably no more than a minute. It would take only seconds for the poet to note what the fish looks like, admire it, and decide to spare its life. In the poem the speaker's description makes the time seem longer.)*

✔ ASSESSMENT OPTIONS

📁 *Quick Checks*, p. 2

Teaching Options

Active Reading Model

but shallower, and yellowed,
the irises backed and packed
with tarnished tinfoil
seen through the lenses
40   of old scratched isinglass.°
They shifted a little, but not
to return my stare.
—It was more like the tipping
of an object toward the light.
45   I admired his sullen face,
the mechanism of his jaw,
and then I saw
that from his lower lip
—if you could call it a lip—
50   grim, wet, and weapon-like,
hung five old pieces of fish-line,
or four and a wire leader
with the swivel still attached,
with all their five big hooks
55   grown firmly in his mouth.
A green line, frayed at the end
where he broke it, two heavier lines,
and a fine black thread
still crimped from the strain and snap
60   when it broke and he got away.
Like medals with their ribbons
frayed and wavering,
a five-haired beard of wisdom
trailing from his aching jaw.
65   I stared and stared
and victory filled up
the little rented boat,
from the pool of bilge°
where oil had spread a rainbow
70   around the rusted engine
to the bailer rusted orange,
the sun-cracked thwarts,°
the oarlocks on their strings,
the gunnels°—until everything
75   was rainbow, rainbow, rainbow!
And I let the fish go.

INTERPRET
Why hasn't the fish fought for his survival this time?

CLARIFY
Whose victory fills up the boat?

RESPOND
What effect does the ending have on you?

Trout Leap, 1993. Paul Riley. Monoprint. Private collection.

---

40 *Isinglass* (ī′ zin glas′) was used in windows before glass panes became common.
68 *Bilge* (bilj) is stagnant water in the bottom of a boat.
72 *Thwarts* (thwôrts) are seats going across a small boat.
74 *Gunnels* (gun′ alz) are the upper edges of the sides of a boat.

Reading Minilesson

Monitoring Comprehension The vividly descriptive language of poetry can be difficult for students to understand. Clarifying and paraphrasing small sections at a time help students interpret the broader meaning.

Activity Give pairs of students copies of the poem. Have them follow these directions.

- Bracket small sections of text, ending with a complete thought or a complete sentence.
- Reread each section, restating in your own words what the passage is about.
- Use context to determine unfamiliar word meanings and to discuss figures of speech.
- Mark passages that remain unclear for further class discussion.

- Read the entire poem again to grasp its meaning as a whole. **L2**

Additional Resources
📁 *Reading Workbook,* pp. 3–4

Responding to Literature

Personal Response

Would you have thrown the fish back, as the speaker does? Why?

Active Reading Response

Which Active Reading Strategy was most helpful to you as you read the poem? Explain.

——— ANALYZING LITERATURE ———

RECALL AND INTERPRET

1. What details about the fish are provided in lines 1–21? How would you characterize the fish based on these details? Cite words and phrases from the poem to support your conclusion.
2. What thoughts does the speaker have while the fish's gills are breathing in "the terrible oxygen"? What do these thoughts suggest about her perception of the fish?
3. To what does the speaker compare the fish-lines hanging from the fish's mouth? What does this comparison tell you about how the speaker sees the fish? What might the fish symbolize?
4. In line 66, what does the speaker say fills the boat? What does everything become, according to line 75? What, in your opinion, motivates the speaker to let the fish go?

EVALUATE AND CONNECT

5. Have you ever experienced a sense of wonder or awe when confronted with some aspect of nature? What happened?
6. Do you think this poem is mostly about the fish or the speaker? Why?
7. How do the **sensory details** (see page R14) Bishop uses compare with the words you listed for the Focus Activity on page 22? Explain.
8. How is Bishop's description of the fish like that of a scientist or a naturalist? How is her description different? Which approach interests you more, and why?

——— EXTENDING YOUR RESPONSE ———

Literature Groups

Discuss the Question   One critic wrote that Bishop focused less on an event than on what she "saw and felt and shared with others." In your group, discuss the ways "The Fish" supports or contradicts this statement. Then present your conclusions to the class.

Creative Writing

Describing the Ordinary   Write ten or fifteen lines in which you describe an ordinary object, using **figurative language** (see page R6) as Bishop does in "The Fish."

📕 **Save your work for your portfolio.**

POETRY 🐟 25

Literary ELEMENTS

Simile

A **simile** states a comparison of two things by using a word or phrase that clearly indicates the comparison, such as *like* or *as*. Writers use similes to make an experience more vivid for the reader or to explain something unfamiliar by comparing it to something familiar. In this poem, Bishop uses similes to help the reader visualize the fish and to communicate her feelings about it.

1. To what does Bishop compare the fish's brown skin in line 11? What does this comparison reveal about Bishop's attitude toward the fish?
2. To what does the speaker compare the fish's white flesh? Why might she make this comparison?

● See **Literary Terms Handbook,** p. R14.

✔ ASSESSMENT OPTIONS

📁 *Quick Checks,* p. 2
📁 *Selection and Theme Assessment,* pp. 3–4
📁 *Performance Assessment,* p. 2
💾 *Testmaker*

LITERARY ELEMENTS

1. She compares the fish's skin to "ancient wall-paper." It suggests that the poet admires the fish for being so old.
2. The poet compares the fish's white flesh to feathers. They have a similar pattern, and the comparison gives the fish's flesh a sort of beauty.

Additional Resources

✎ *Literary Elements Transparency 2*

Responding to the Selection

Personal Response

Students may say that they would throw the fish back. Students should give reasons for their responses.

Active Reading Response

Many may say imagining the scene from the poet's words was the most helpful; it helped them shape their responses to the entire poem.

ANALYZING LITERATURE

1. The fish's weight and size are described, followed by his appearance. Students may characterize the fish as old and battered. They may cite his tattered skin, "like ancient wall-paper," and the barnacles, "fine rosettes of lime," and the weeds attached to his body like rags.
2. As the speaker holds the fish, she thinks about its internal organs, suggesting that she is in awe of its physiology.
3. She compares the fish lines to "medals with their ribbons frayed and wavering" and to "a five-haired beard of wisdom." The fish is venerable, brave, and distinguished, and symbolizes bravery and experience.
4. She says that victory fills the boat. Everything becomes a rainbow. The speaker's wonder and respect for the fish motivates her to let it go.
5. Students should give personal examples. They may say the memory of such sights lasts after the experience ends.
6. The poem seems mostly about the speaker. Her reactions to the fish's battle scars are strong; she refuses to be the agent of its death.
7. Students' details may be less precise and complex than are the details in this poem.
8. Bishop's description is like that of a scientist or a naturalist in its attention to detail. It is different because it is personal and subjective. Students should tell which description they prefer and explain why.

Active Reading Strategies

Objective

- To understand and apply strategies for reading and comprehending nonfiction

Teach the Strategies

Ask students to discuss the differences between nonfiction and fiction. Encourage students to review some of the strategies they use when reading fiction and explain how they might be used with nonfiction.

Predict

Ask students how they can predict
- the subject of a piece of nonfiction.
- the author's attitude or opinion.
- the author's purpose.

Connect

Stress that readers can connect to a piece of nonfiction by drawing on personal experiences and prior knowledge.

Question

Encourage students to ask questions
- to monitor their understanding of ideas, relationships, and purpose.
- to challenge the author's conclusions, facts, or reasons.
- to think beyond the text and apply ideas to other situations.

Teaching Options

Active Reading Model

Active Reading Strategies

Nonfiction

How can you get the most out of the essays, biographies, articles, and other types of nonfiction that you read? Active readers use many of the same strategies they use when reading fiction. However, as an active reader you'll need to adjust the strategies to the particular type of nonfiction you are reading.

● For more about related reading strategies, see **Reading Handbook,** pp. R86–R93.

PREDICT Make educated guesses about what you are reading. Preview the topic and the type of nonfiction. You can do this by making inferences from the title and skimming the text. Then try to figure out the author's main idea by looking for a thesis statement in the introductory paragraph. Also, think about the facts, reasons, and details the author may use to support the main idea.

Ask yourself . . .
● What will this selection be about?
● What main idea will the writer have about the topic?
● What evidence might the writer use to back up his or her ideas?

CONNECT Consider what you already know about the topic. Compare people and events with those in your own life. Reflect on any experiences you have had that relate to the topic. Read with the purpose of getting information or a new point of view on the topic.

Ask yourself . . .
● What have I heard or read about this topic?
● Whom or what does this selection remind me of?
● When have I been in a situation like the one described here?

QUESTION As you read, pause occasionally to question anything you do not understand. Reread any section that seems unclear to you. Read on to find answers to your questions. Discuss lingering questions with other readers.

Ask yourself . . .
● What is the writer's point here?
● Why is the writer giving me these facts?
● What does this point have to do with the writer's main idea?

Reading Journal

Writing While Reading

Encourage students to experiment with the Active Reading Strategies for nonfiction as they read Morrison's essay.

Activity Before reading the essay, direct students to divide several blank notebook pages in half vertically. As they read, have students use the left column to record responses to questions and directives in the Active Reading Strategy notes. Have them use the corresponding section of the right column to record personal thoughts, feelings, and questions about Morrison's essay as well as to comment on the active reading process. Use these two-column notes as a basis for classroom discussion.

VISUALIZE

Note details the writer provides, and use them to form mental images. Think about the physical appearance of people, places, and objects. In your mind, picture events, the steps in a process, or the way something works.

> **Ask yourself . . .**
> - What does this person or scene look like?
> - What happens after this step, and what came just before?
> - How does this part fit in with the rest of the selection?

EVALUATE

Make judgments about the material. Don't accept a statement if it isn't supported with plenty of evidence.

> **Ask yourself . . .**
> - Is this a fact or an opinion? Do I agree with it?
> - Do these facts and examples really support the author's point?
> - Are the author's cause-and-effect relationships logical and realistic?

REVIEW

As you read, pause occasionally to check your understanding of the material.

> **Say to yourself . . .**
> - The thesis statement is . . .
> - The evidence that supports the thesis is . . .
> - The steps in this process are . . .
> - This effect was caused by . . .
> - The author's purpose for writing is . . .

RESPOND

As you read, think about your reactions to the facts and ideas you are reading. Note the spontaneous thoughts and feelings that you have about what the author is saying.

> **Say to yourself . . .**
> - I'd like to ask the writer why . . .
> - I'd like to know more about . . .

Applying the Strategies

The next selection is an essay, "Thoughts on the African-American Novel," by Toni Morrison. As you read it, use the Active Reading Model notes in the margins. Then practice the strategies as you read another work of nonfiction.

Visualize

Point out that visualizing often works well in conjunction with the connecting strategy. By connecting to other experiences or knowledge of a subject, it is easier to visualize what the author describes.

Evaluate

Point out that readers can evaluate many aspects of a piece of writing. They may, for example, evaluate the logic and factual presentation, the imagery and figures of speech, the writing style and organization, and the author's purpose and bias.

Review

Explain that pausing periodically to review material will help students clarify their thinking and better understand the text. Reviewing will also help readers remember what the writer has said. Students may find it helpful to review while reading, immediately after finishing, and again a day or several days later.

Respond

Emphasize that any response to a piece of literature is valid if it reflects the reader's own experiences and attitudes. Readers should not be concerned that their reactions may be different from someone else's.

Objectives

- To read and analyze a work of non-fiction
- To understand the characteristics of an informal essay
- To write two passages of dialogue

Skills

Reading/Thinking: Varying Reading Rate
Writing: Journal Entry
Vocabulary: Etymology
Grammar/Language: Sentence Structure
Collaboration: Literature Groups

Motivating

→OPTIONS

Selection Focus Transparency 3: Have students examine the time line and then comment on the achievements of African Americans in literature.

Focus Activity: As an extension of the Focus Activity, ask students to describe the kinds of novels that they like best, giving reasons for their choices and naming some of their favorites. Encourage dialogue between students with similar interests.

 # —Before You Read—

Thoughts on the African-American Novel

Meet Toni Morrison

"Black people had some choices. They could say life is limited for you, make the best of it. . . . Or they said all things are possible and don't let anybody tell you that you can't do something. I came from a family that said the latter."

—*Morrison*

Highly acclaimed as a novelist, essayist, and literary critic, Toni Morrison won the Nobel Prize for Literature in 1993. Upon receiving it, Morrison responded, "I am outrageously happy. But what is most wonderful for me, personally, is to know that the prize at last has been awarded to an African American. Winning as an American is very special—but winning as a black American is a knockout."

Born Chloe Anthony Wofford, Morrison grew up in northern Ohio, a setting that figures prominently in many of her novels. She graduated from Howard University and received an M.A. degree from Cornell University. Throughout her career, Morrison has also held prestigious teaching positions at various colleges and universities.

When she was thirty-eight, she published *The Bluest Eye*, her first of seven novels. Her novel *Beloved* won the 1988 Pulitzer Prize for Fiction.

Morrison has always emphasized both her African American heritage and her experiences as a woman as influences that have shaped her storytelling talents. When asked whether she considered herself a black writer or a female writer, Morrison responded, "I've just insisted—insisted!—upon being called a black woman novelist."

Toni Morrison was born in 1931.

FOCUS ACTIVITY

In your opinion, why do people read novels?

FREEWRITE Spend a few minutes freewriting to explore this question.

SETTING A PURPOSE Read to explore one writer's ideas about why a society needs novels.

BACKGROUND

Literary Influences
The music, legends, and oral traditions of her African heritage influence Morrison's poetic and precise language. Much like some jazz music defies traditional structure, many of Morrison's own novels float back and forth through time.

VOCABULARY PREVIEW

aristocracy (ar´ is tok´ rə sē) *n.* people with high social status due to birth or title; p. 30
didactic (dī dak´ tik) *adj.* intended to instruct, especially with regard to morals; p. 30
exclusively (iks´ klōō´ siv lē) *adv.* without the inclusion or involvement of any others; p. 30
enlighten (en līt´ ən) *v.* to give knowledge or wisdom to; p. 31
meandering (mē an´ dər ing) *adj.* following a winding course; p. 33
unorthodox (un ôr´ thə doks´) *adj.* not customary or traditional; unusual; p. 33
paradigm (par´ ə dīm´) *n.* an example that acts as a model; a pattern; p. 33

 # RESOURCE MANAGER

Lesson Planning Resource
The *Unit One Planning Guide* (pp. 11–16) provides additional lesson notes and reduced versions of all print resources.

📁 **Other Print Resources**
- Active Reading Guide, p. 3
- Vocabulary Practice, p. 2
- Reading Workbook, pp. 5–6
- Grammar and Language Workbook, p. 111

- Grammar and Composition Handbook, Lesson 4.9
- Quick Checks, p. 3
- Selection and Theme Assessment, pp. 5–6
- Performance Assessment, p. 3
- Spanish Summaries, p. 3
- Inclusion Strategies
- English Language Learners Sourcebook

 Transparencies
- Selection Focus 3
- Literary Elements 3
- Grammar and Language 2

Technology
🎧 Audio Library
🎧 Spanish Audio Library
💻 Glencoe Literature Web Site
📖 Testmaker

Thoughts on the African-American Novel

Toni Morrison

Slow Down Freight Train, 1946–1947. Rose Piper. Oil on canvas, 29½ x 23⅛ in. Ackland Art Museum, University of North Carolina at Chapel Hill. Ackland Fund.

Reading the Selection

SUMMARY

In this essay Toni Morrison describes the origin of the novel as a genre, arguing that it evolved because the middle class had no art form and needed one in order to understand their culture and place in society. African Americans, she says, need novels for the same reasons, to define and explain their place in American society. Morrison says her goal is to write novels that respond to that need and that use the "characteristics of Black art."

📁 *Spanish Summaries*, p. 3

A Active Reading

PREDICT Ask students why Morrison uses the word *thoughts* in her title. What expectations does this title create? What does it tell the reader about the selection? *(Thoughts implies a level of informality. Rather than an exhaustive study of the African American novel, the reader might expect a less-structured, briefer rumination.)*

Additional Resources
📁 *Active Reading Guide*, p. 3
🎧 *Audio Library*
🎧 *Spanish Audio Library*

Teaching Options

MEETING INDIVIDUAL NEEDS INCLUSION STRATEGIES

Less-Proficient Readers Some students may need help developing strategies for determining Morrison's main ideas and identifying supporting details. Explain that Morrison's essay has a thesis and develops an argument.

Activity As students read, have them make a rough outline to identify each paragraph's main point and supporting details. They may write a topic sentence for each paragraph and then jot down supporting details. Then have students review their outlines and revise as necessary. Ask students to write a thesis statement which reflects Morrison's overall argument. **L1**

Additional Resources
📁 *Inclusion Strategies*

Teaching Options

Active Reading Model

The label "novel" is useful in technical terms because I write prose that is longer than a short story. My sense of the novel is that it has always functioned for the class or the group that wrote it. The history of the novel as a form began when there was a new class, a middle class, to read it; it was an art form that they needed. The lower classes didn't need novels at that time because they had an art form already: they had songs, and dances, and ceremony, and gossip, and celebrations. The aristocracy didn't need it because they had the art that they had patronized,[1] they had their own pictures painted, their own houses built, and they made sure their art separated them from the rest of the world. But when the industrial revolution[2] began, there emerged a new class of people who were neither peasants nor aristocrats. In large measure they had no art form to tell them how to behave in this new situation. So they produced an art form: we call it the novel of manners, an art form designed to tell people something they didn't know. That is, how to behave in this new world, how to distinguish between the good guys and the bad guys. How to get married. What a good living was. What would happen if you strayed from the fold. So that early works such as *Pamela*, by Samuel Richardson, and the Jane Austen material provided social rules and explained behavior, identified outlaws, identified the people, habits, and customs that one should approve of. They were didactic in that sense. That, I think, is probably why the novel was not missed among the so-called peasant cultures. They didn't need it, because they were clear about what their responsibilities were and who and where was evil, and where was good.

But when the peasant class, or lower class, or what have you, confronts the middle class, the city, or the upper classes, they are thrown a little bit into disarray. For a long time, the art form that was healing for Black people was music. That music is no longer *exclusively* ours, we don't have exclusive rights to it. Other people sing it and play it; it is the mode[3] of contemporary music everywhere. So another form has to take that place, and it seems to me that the novel is needed by African Americans now in a way that it was not needed before—and it is following along the lines of the function of novels everywhere. We don't live in places where we can hear those stories anymore; parents don't sit around and tell their children those classical, mythological archetypal stories[4] that we heard years ago. But new information has got to get out, and there are

---

1. Here, *patronize* (pā′ trə nīz′) means "to give financial support or encouragement to."
2. The *industrial revolution* helped develop a middle class of workers who began to gain some control over where, for whom, and for what wages they would work.
3. Here, *mode* means "a manner of expression." The type of music once considered an art form belonging to African Americans is now the preferred form of contemporary music for many modern listeners.
4. *Archetypal* (är′ kə tī′ pəl) *stories* come from ideas inherited through the ages by members of a race.

Vocabulary

aristocracy (ar′ is tok′ rə sē) *n.* people with high social status due to birth or title
didactic (dī dak′ tik) *adj.* intended to instruct, especially with regard to morals
exclusively (iks′ klōō′ siv lē) *adv.* without the inclusion or involvement of any others

---

Reading *Minilesson*

Church Picnic, 1988. Faith Ringgold. Painted canvas, pieced, dyed, printed fabrics, 74½ x 75½ in. Collection, High Museum at Georgia-Pacific Center, Atlanta, GA.

Viewing the quilt: In "Thoughts on the African-American Novel," Morrison says "one should be able to hear" a novel. What do you "hear" when you look at this quilt?

VIEWING THE QUILT

Faith Ringgold is an American artist and author, famous for her innovative story quilts about African American lives. One of her most notable stories, "Tar Beach," was named Caldecott Honor Book in 1992. The story quilt that accompanies her award winning picture book is one of her most beautiful creations.

Viewing Response *Students may note that the title of this quilt and the interactive social scene portrayed suggest laughter, music, and multiple vibrant conversations.*

several ways to do it. One is in the novel. I regard it as a way to accomplish certain very strong functions—one being the one I just described.

It should be beautiful, and powerful, but it should also *work*. It should have something in it that enlightens; something in it that opens the door and points the way. Something in it that suggests what the conflicts are, what the problems are. But it need not solve those problems because it is not a case study, it is not a recipe. There are things that I try to incorporate into my fiction that are directly and deliberately related to what I regard as the major characteristics of Black art, wherever it is. One of which is the ability to be both print and oral literature: to combine those two aspects so that the stories can be read in silence, of course, but one should be able to hear them as well. It should try deliberately to make you stand up and make you feel something profoundly in the same way that a Black preacher requires his congregation to speak, to join him in the sermon, to behave in a certain way, to stand up and to weep and to cry and to accede or to change and to modify—to expand on the sermon that is being delivered. In the same way that a musician's music is enhanced when there is a response from the audience. Now in a book, which closes, after all— it's of some importance to me to try to make that connection—to try to make that happen also. And, having at my disposal only the letters of the alphabet and some punctuation, I have to provide the places and spaces so that the reader can participate. Because it is the affective and participatory relationship[5] between the artist or the speaker and the audience that is of primary importance, as it is in these other art forms that I have described.

---

5. An *affective and participatory relationship* influences one's emotions and encourages one to take an active part in the relationship.

Vocabulary
enlighten (en līt′ ən) *v.* to give knowledge or wisdom to

Howardena Pindell (1943–) teaches art at the State University of New York at Stony Brook. She is a political activist and world traveler and has lived in both India and Japan. Often, her art is autobiographical and includes references to her travels and experiences, to racism and discrimination, and to other subjects that affect her.

Viewing Response *The art includes many images that echo the history and culture of African Americans, such as the white slave ship in the bottom left, the pictures of African Americans, and various symbols of African American culture. The art can be appreciated by most people, but it speaks most clearly to African Americans, who share the cultural background and sensitivity. This specific targeting of her audience is what Morrison is aiming for in her own work. She wants to write novels that evoke the shared memories of her African American readers and help them appreciate who they are and how they fit into the world.*

Autobiography: Water/Ancestors/Middle Passage/Family Ghosts, 1988. Howardena Pindell. Acrylic, tempera, cattle markers, oil stick, paper, polymer-photo transfer, and vinyl tape on sewn canvas, 299.7 x 180.3 cm. Wadsworth Atheneum, Hartford, CT. The Ella Galup Sumner and Mary Catlin Sumner Collection Fund. Courtesy the artist.

Viewing the art: How does your response to this image help you understand Morrison's point about the relationship between an artist and the audience?

32 ACTIVE READING

Teaching Options

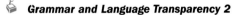

Grammar and Language *Minilesson*

Sentence Structure Point out that Morrison uses phrases and clauses that are meant to stand as sentences. For example, on page 31, Morrison writes, "One of which is the ability to be both print and oral literature: to combine those two aspects so that the stories can be read in silence, of course, but one should be able to hear them as well." This combination of clauses is a sentence fragment and serves to give the writing an informal, conversational tone that makes the serious, academic subject more approachable.

Activity Work with students to analyze the sentence structure of the first paragraph on this page. Then invite them to revise the fragments to form complete sentences. L2

Additional Resources

Grammar and Language Transparency 2

Grammar and Language Workbook, p. 111

Grammar and Composition Handbook, Lesson 4.9

Writer's Choice, Lesson 13.9

Toni Morrison ❧

To make the story appear oral, <u>meandering</u>, effortless, spoken—to have the reader *feel* the narrator without *identifying* that narrator, or hearing him or her knock about, and to have the reader work *with* the author in the construction of the book—is what's important. What is left out is as important as what is there. To describe sexual scenes in such a way that they are not clinical, not even explicit—so that the reader brings his own sexuality to the scene and thereby participates in it in a very personal way. And owns it. To construct the dialogue so that it is heard. So that there are no adverbs attached to them: "loudly," "softly," "he said menacingly." The menace should be in the sentence. To use, even formally, a chorus. The real presence of a chorus. Meaning the community or the reader at large, commenting on the action as it goes ahead.

In the books that I have written, the chorus has changed but there has always been a choral note, whether it is the "I" narrator of *Bluest Eye*, or the town functioning as a character in *Sula*, or the neighborhood and the community that responds in the two parts of town in *Solomon*. Or, as extreme as I've gotten, all of nature thinking and feeling and watching and responding to the action going on in *Tar Baby*, so that they are in the story: the trees hurt, fish are afraid, clouds report, and the bees are alarmed. Those are the ways in which I try to incorporate, into that traditional genre the novel, <u>unorthodox</u> novelistic characteristics—so that it is, in my view, Black, because it uses the characteristics of Black art. I am not suggesting that some of these devices have not been used before and elsewhere—only the reason why I do. I employ them as well as I can. And those are just some; I wish there were ways in which such things could be talked about in the criticism. My general disappointment in some of the criticism that my work has received has nothing to do with approval. It has something to do with the vocabulary used in order to describe these things. I don't like to find my books condemned as bad or praised as good, when that condemnation or that praise is based on criteria from other <u>paradigms</u>. I would much prefer that they were dismissed or embraced based on the success of their accomplishment within the culture out of which I write.

I don't regard Black literature as simply books written *by* Black people, or simply as literature written *about* Black people, or simply as literature that uses a certain mode of language in which you just sort of drop g's. There is something very special and very identifiable about it and it is my struggle to *find* that elusive but identifiable style in the books. My joy is when I think that I have approached it; my misery is when I think I can't get there.

REVIEW

What are some of the devices the author uses to inject aspects of black culture into her writing?

RESPOND

How does Morrison make you feel about writing?

Vocabulary

meandering (mē an′ dər ing) *adj.* following a winding course
unorthodox (un ôr′ thə doks′) *adj.* not customary or traditional; unusual
paradigm (par′ ə dīm′) *n.* an example that acts as a model; a pattern

---

*inter*NET CONNECTION

African American Artists Students who are interested in Pindell's art may enjoy using the Internet to research her works as well as those of other African American artists. Simply keying in the name *Howardena Pindell* will give them access to information on Pindell with links to information on other painters, printmakers, muralists, and mosaic artists.

Responding to the Selection

Personal Response

Students may mention her unorthodox sentence structure or her effort to create a dialogue with her readers.

Active Reading Response

Students should be able to explain how they used the strategy and how it helped them gain insight into the literature.

ANALYZING LITERATURE

1. Morrison asserts that the rise of the middle class caused the birth of the novel.

2. The novel of manners taught middle-class people how to behave in the industrial world, how to distinguish between good and bad, how to get married, what a good living was, and the effects of "straying from the fold."

3. Morrison states that the original African American art form was music, but when other cultures adopted it, African Americans had to search for a different art that spoke more specifically to them.

4. An African American novel should be beautiful, powerful, and enlightening; and it should engage the reader and elicit a response.

5. She is disappointed when critics do not judge her novels within an African American paradigm.

6. The novel dealt with matters that concerned the rising middle class, matters that had nothing to do with the lifestyle that the upper classes enjoyed.

7. The lower classes had to work very hard just to survive. They knew what their responsibilities were by what happened when they didn't live up to them: when they refused to work, they starved.

8. Early African Americans were able to express their emotions and ease the stress of their lives by singing.

9. Morrison says that a novel calls for a response from the reader in much the same way as a preacher calls for an active, vocal response from the congregation.

10. Morrison says that she constantly searches for ways to make her work "Black." When she feels that she hasn't achieved this goal, she is unhappy.

11. Students will probably find that their ideas about the novel do not go as far as those of Morrison.

12. Books can help readers distinguish between good and evil by presenting examples that readers can identify with and that correspond to the people and events in their lives.

13. Students may say that the writer's job is to present the reader with a view of life. Since problems aren't always resolved in real life, there is no reason why they should have to be resolved in a novel.

14. Students should state specific qualities they seek and explain why those are important in their writing.

15. Many students will say the essay makes them curious about Morrison's novels.

Responding to Literature

Personal Response

Which of Morrison's ideas about novels did you find most surprising?

Active Reading Response

Which one of the Active Reading Strategies on pages 26–27 best helped you understand Morrison's essay? Why?

ANALYZING LITERATURE

RECALL

1. According to Morrison, what event and what class of people caused the birth of the novel as a literary form?
2. In Morrison's view, what lessons did the novel of manners teach?
3. What reasons does Morrison give for explaining how African American culture developed a need for the novel?
4. What specific qualities does Morrison say an African American novel should contain?
5. What does Morrison find disappointing in criticism of her work?

INTERPRET

6. If the upper classes "made sure their art separated them from the rest of the world," why might the novel have been of little use to them?
7. What factors may have caused the lower classes to understand their responsibilities and to distinguish between good and evil?
8. Why might music have been a "healing" form of art to African Americans of an earlier time?
9. Explain Morrison's comparison between a novel and an African American preacher.
10. What do you think Morrison means by the final comment in her essay: "my misery is when I think I can't get there"?

EVALUATE AND CONNECT

11. Look at your response to the Focus Activity on page 28. How does your response compare with Morrison's ideas about the novel?
12. In your opinion, have novels the power to help readers distinguish between "the good guys and the bad guys"? Explain.
13. Morrison says that a novel should present problems but needn't solve them. Do you agree or disagree? Why?
14. Morrison strives for an African American **style** (see page R15) in her writing. What qualities do you strive to include in your work?
15. Does this essay make you want to read Morrison's novels? Explain.

Literary ELEMENTS

Informal Essay

An **essay** is a type of nonfiction that presents opinions and ideas on a specific topic. Essays may be formal or informal. An **informal essay** has a lighter tone and a more fluid structure than a **formal essay,** which features a carefully structured progression of opinions and supporting information. A formal essay may sound like a dignified speech, but an informal essay often sounds like a conversation. "Thoughts on the African-American Novel" is an informal essay.

1. An informal essay may contain sentence fragments and informal language. Find examples of each of these features in Morrison's essay.
2. How do these examples contribute to the overall **tone** of the essay?
3. An informal essay might include humor. Find one or more examples in Morrison's essay and explain what the humor adds to your reading of the piece.

● See **Literary Terms Handbook,** p. R5.

LITERARY ELEMENTS

1. Examples are on page 31, lines 9–17 and page 33, lines 1–12.
2. They make the tone more conversational and informal.
3. One source of humor occurs on page 31 where Morrison refers to having only the letters of the alphabet and some punctuation at her disposal for writing.

Additional Resources

✍ *Literary Elements Transparency 3*

LITERATURE AND WRITING

Writing About Literature

Dialogue Several critics have praised Morrison for her use of realistic dialogue in novels. Reread her comments about dialogue on page 33. Write a passage of dialogue that you think Morrison would not like. Then write a passage of dialogue that you believe she would like. Explain the differences between the two passages.

Personal Writing

Exploring New Insights If you've ever been to a concert, you may agree with Morrison that "a musician's music is enhanced when there is a response from the audience." Write a journal entry about a time when you had a strong response to something you read. Describe your response and explain how your reaction contributed to the experience of reading that piece.

EXTENDING YOUR RESPONSE

Literature Groups

Critic's Corner Toni Morrison's work is often the subject of critical reviews. With your group, begin a critical discussion about her essay. Which ideas did you particularly like or agree with? What did you dislike or disagree with? Why? Be sure to support your opinions with facts, examples, and sound reasoning. Summarize the group's views, and share them with the class.

Learning for Life

New Lessons for Novels The "novel of manners" emerged to tell people how to behave in the world after the Industrial Revolution. With a partner, brainstorm a list of lessons that novels should teach young readers today. Be prepared to explain the reasoning behind each choice when you share your list with the class.

Interdisciplinary Activity

Music: A Healing Source Research the roots of African American music, including spirituals, blues, and jazz. Select one African American musician and prepare a brief report about the person's contribution to African American culture.

 Save your work for your portfolio.

 Skill Minilesson

• Etymology

The **etymology** of a word is its history—a sort of family tree that helps explain the meanings carried by the word in a variety of times and by many writers. The word *novel,* for example, once meant "new." While it has that meaning today, it also refers to a literary genre, *the novel,* which is not new to modern readers.

PRACTICE Use the following words to complete the sentences.

unorthodox	enlighten	aristocracy
paradigm	meandering	didactic

1. In Greek, *krátos* means "strength" and *áristos* is "best." People who fit this description were the _____ .

2. The Büyük Menderes River winds through Turkey. Its name is related to a Greek word we use to describe anything or anyone that wanders: _____ .

3. The Greek word *orthós* means "correct," and *dóxa* means "opinion." Ideas not generally accepted as correct may be called _____ .

4. *Didaskein,* in Greek, means "to teach." Something that is designed to provide instruction is _____ .

NONFICTION 35

LITERATURE AND WRITING

Writing About Literature

Students' first dialogues should
• contain a great number of adverbs to describe a tone of voice or an attitude.
• sound rigid and unrealistic.

Students' second dialogues should
• indicate tone by the words that speakers use.
• sound conversational, inviting, and perhaps confrontational.

Personal Writing

Students' journal entries should
• describe a time when they felt a strong response to something they read.
• describe the response.
• explain how their response enhanced their enjoyment of reading.

EXTENDING YOUR RESPONSE

Literature Groups Remind students to appoint a note-taker to record the group's ideas to present to the class. Emphasize that reasons must be given for each opinion. **COLLAB. LEARN.**

Learning for Life Students' new "lessons" should emphasize the rewards as well as the difficulties of living in today's world. **COLLAB. LEARN.**

Interdisciplinary Activity Point out that students can find a great deal of information on the Internet by keying in the words *African American music.*

 Skill Minilesson

VOCABULARY • Etymology

1. aristocracy
2. meandering
3. unorthodox
4. didactic

Additional Resources

📁 *Vocabulary Practice,* p. 2

✔ ASSESSMENT OPTIONS

📁 *Quick Checks,* p. 3

📁 *Selection and Theme Assessment,* pp. 5–6

📁 *Performance Assessment,* p. 3

💾 *Testmaker*

UNIT INTRODUCTION

Theme 1:
BEGINNINGS AND CHANGE

SELECTIONS

SKILL FEATURES

WRITING WORKSHOP

UNIT WRAP-UP

- **Personal Response, Analyzing Literature, Evaluate and Set Goals** (p. 114)
- **Build Your Portfolio** (p. 114)
- **Reading on Your Own** (p. 115)

  The Autobiography of Benjamin Franklin by Benjamin Franklin

  The Account: Álvar Núñez Cabeza de Vaca's Relación translated by Martin A. Favata and José B. Fernández

  The Works of Anne Bradstreet edited by Jeannine Hensley

  The First Americans by Josepha Sherman

- **Standardized Test Practice** (pp. 116–117)

KEYS TO LITERARY CONNECTIONS

 Comparing Selections

In each theme of **Glencoe Literature,** the **Comparing Selections** feature gives students an opportunity to compare two selections they have just read. Each Comparing Selections page provides a variety of options to address diverse aspects of the reading and literature curriculum. For example, in Comparing Selections on page 98, students have the opportunity to compare the story of captivity in time of war in Mary Rowlandson's "A Narrative of the Captivity and Restoration of Mrs. Mary Rowlandson" and Pin Yathay's account of civil war in Cambodia. Through this comparison, students can gain insight into their own culture and into the ways it both resembles and differs from other cultures.

 World Literature

Glencoe Literature contains a variety of literature that represents cultures from around the world. World Literature selections are highlighted with this symbol: 🌐

KEYS TO TEACHING OPTIONS

🧊 **Block Scheduling**

Activities that are particularly suited to use within a block scheduling framework are identified throughout this unit by the following designation: 🧊. For detailed suggestions on block scheduling, see the **Block Scheduling Guide** for this grade level.

Key to Ability Levels

The Teaching Options throughout this unit have been coded for students of various abilities.

L1 BASIC activities for all students

L2 AVERAGE activities for average to above-average students

L3 CHALLENGING activities for above-average students

Reading Skills in this unit

Variety of Texts

In addition to numerous stories by Native American and early American authors, this unit also includes the following text types:

- mythology
- nonfiction
- poetry
- newspaper article
- song lyrics

Comprehension Skills

The following instructional support for comprehension skills appears in this unit of the Student Edition:

- Active Reading Strategies and Models (pp. 3–35)
- Recognizing Bias (p. 67)

See also the **Reading Minilessons** throughout the unit in this Teacher's Wraparound Edition.

Reading Resources

Comprehension Skills Resources

Active Reading Guides

The Active Reading Guide provides graphic organizers and study guide questions to support students' reading of each selection. (**Active Reading Guide**, pp. 4–12)

Reading Workbook

The Reading Workbook (pp. 7–18) includes additional instruction and reinforcement of reading strategies and skills.

Audio Library

Available both on tape and on CD, the Audio Library provides valuable comprehension support.

Resources for Reading Widely

Glencoe Literature Library

Each title in the Glencoe Literature Library includes a full-length novel or play plus related readings. A separate Study Guide is available for each title.

Literature Classics CD-ROM

The 900 selections on this CD-ROM can be searched by author, theme, or genre.

A coproduction of Glencoe and Time Inc., *inTime* includes a wealth of high-interest nonfiction related to the selections and themes in Unit One.

Assessment in this unit

Assessment Options in the Student Edition

Glencoe Literature offers a number of diverse ways to evaluate student understanding and skill proficiency. In the Student Edition, use the following:

- **Responding to Literature**
  Following each selection, students are asked to recall facts, interpret ideas, and evaluate concepts as they answer a variety of questions and complete activities to extend their understanding.
- **Unit Wrap-Up (pp. 114–115)**
  Here students respond to the selections on personal and analytical levels. They also assume ownership of their learning by setting and evaluating goals and by selecting work for their portfolios.

See also the many **Assessment Resources** listed on the facing page.

Standardized Test Practice

The Princeton Review has developed the Standardized Test Practice pages found at the end of this unit (pp. 116–117). These pages contain practice test questions that help students remain familiar with standardized test formats and content. For additional practice, you may want to use the following resource:

- **College Entrance Exam Preparation and Practice Workbook**

Writing Skills in this unit

Writing Skills

The Student Edition of Unit One offers strong instructional support for writing skills:

In **Extending Your Response**, which follows each selection:
- Writing About Literature
- Personal/Creative Writing

In **Writing Skills** Lessons:
- Using Specific, Vivid Words (p. 83)

See also the **Writing Minilessons** throughout the unit in this Teacher's Wraparound Edition.

Writing Workshops

Theme One in Unit One concludes with a **Writing Workshop** that guides students through the writing process.
- Narrative Writing: Historical Narrative (pp. 110–113)

Writing Resources

Writer's Assistant CD-ROM
Each Writing Workshop is supplemented by an interactive writing guide on the Writer's Assistant CD-ROM. This easy-to-use writing guide provides prompts, templates, and other tools that lead students through the writing process.

Writing and Proofreading Practice
Blackline masters present in-depth instruction and practice on a specific step in the writing process and proofreading. (pp. 1–15)

Writing and Proofreading Transparencies
Transparencies (1–8, 25–26) provide graphic organizers and proofreading exercises for whole class instruction.

Research and Report Writing Guide
This resource provides extensive tips and activities to guide students in their writing projects in the literature classroom as well as in classes across the curriculum.

Style and Documentation Sourcebook for Writers
This sourcebook is a combination reference and workbook, giving students the most up-to-date information and guidance regarding traditional as well as technological research strategies and documentation.

Grammar and Composition Handbook
The Grammar and Composition Handbook provides instruction that supplements activities in the student textbook.

Assessment Resources

Selection Quick Checks
For each selection, a Quick Check of three to five short-answer questions measures students' literal comprehension.

Selection and Theme Assessment
The Selection and Theme Assessment instrument tests students' abilities to recall, interpret, and evaluate what they've read. The tests consist of multiple-choice, short-answer, and essay questions.

Performance Assessment
Alternative assessment instruments and rubrics for Unit One are found in the Performance Assessment ancillary.

Writing Assessment and Portfolio Management
These notes and strategies, student models, and assessment tools assist with the task of measuring students' progress as writers and as monitors of their own writing.

Testmaker
Teachers can customize selection, theme, and Unit One tests by accessing the Testmaker database.

MindJogger Videoquizzes
Using a popular game show format, MindJogger Videoquizzes enable teachers to evaluate students' understanding of Unit One in a quick and fun manner.

Unit Objectives

- To enjoy reading a variety of literature focusing on beginnings and change
- To understand and appreciate how different ideas about life, religion, and morality shaped early literature
- To apply strategies for reading literature from the earliest days in North America

VIEWING THE ART

This deerskin mantle, or robe, was worn by Powhatan (?–1618), an Indian chief who united Native American tribes in Virginia to form the Powhatan Confederacy. Powhatan was the father of Pocahontas.

Responding to the Art Discussion questions:

- Ask students to discuss what the figures and circles might represent. *(Answers might include the following: The overall design suggests the chief's view of his world; the human figure is flanked by animals, which might be symbols of wealth and power; the circles might represent the areas under his control.)*

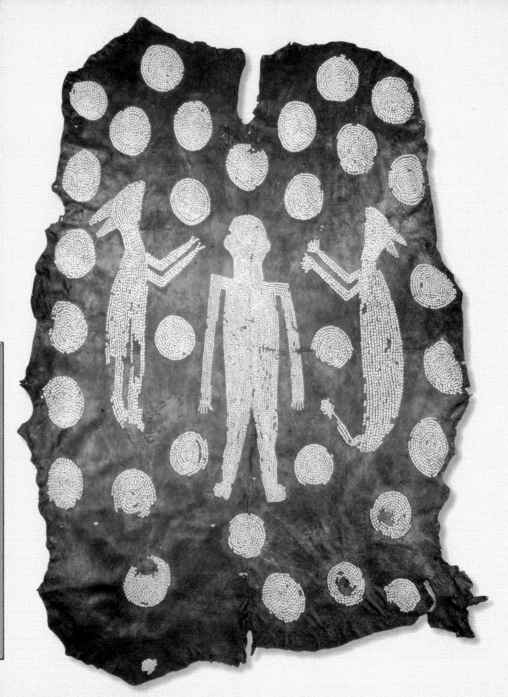

Powhatan's Mantle. Late 16th–early 17th century, Native North American, Virginia. Deerskin with shell patterns. The Ashmolean Museum, Oxford, UK.

36

STERLING SENIOR HIGH SCHOOL • HOUSTON, TEXAS

I have students with learning disabilities, which must be taken into consideration. Acting out the literature brings it alive for students. They use the library for research on the historical period to learn what the people of the times were thinking. Then each student takes a small piece from the text and paraphrases the passage for the class. Many of the students wear period costumes when they give their presentations. Even though this is not a requirement, the students like to wear the costumes.

HERMAN BURNS

UNIT ❦ ONE

From the Earliest Days
Prehistory to 1750

> *"Come with me now through time and mind,*
> *for the past beckons to be known.*
> *And the future,*
> *crouched like a panther on the bough of a tree,*
> *waits to see if we . . .*
> *if we*
> *have truly*
> *grown*
> *while it growls*
> *impatiently."*
>
> *—White Deer of Autumn*

Theme 1
Beginnings and Change
pages 45–113

Have students read the quotation. Then pose these questions for discussion:

- In what ways do you think the past has shaped who we, as Americans, are today?
- Do you think we have "truly grown," or become better, as a people over the time that the United States has existed?
- In what ways do you think the future is like a panther crouched on a tree branch?

Theme 1: Beginnings and Change

The literature in Theme 1 introduces students to writings from Native Americans, early European explorers, and settlers who came to North America to begin new lives. The selections explore the various new ideas and new ways of doing things that shaped our national character.

GLENCOE
TECHNOLOGY
LITERATURE CLASSICS
CD-ROM

Search for other selections about America's earliest days.

RESOURCE MANAGER

See the *Unit One Planning Guide* (pp. 18–19) for additional teaching notes, strategies, and resources for introducing the From the Earliest Days unit.

Introducing the Time Period

Ask students to share what they know about North America's first people. You may want to begin the discussion by asking these questions: Where did the first people in North America come from? Who were the first Europeans to visit North America? Who were the first Europeans to establish permanent settlements in North America? Why did they come? Students may have other interesting reactions to North America's early people. Ask them to describe what they think it would have been like to have crossed the land bridge with people from Asia. The ocean with Henry Hudson? The lands along the coast with the Puritans?

Historical Note

Although the people of North America celebrate Columbus Day on October 12, Columbus never landed on the North American continent. Between 1492 and 1504 Columbus completed four voyages to the Americas, sailing to the Caribbean islands on his first two trips, along the coast of South America on his third voyage (1498–1500), and along the coast of Central America on his fourth voyage (1502–1504).

From the Earliest Days

Setting the Scene

According to a story generations of Delaware Indians have passed down, Indians fishing off the Atlantic coast in the fall of 1609 saw "something remarkably large floating on the water." Some thought it was "an uncommonly large fish or animal, while others were of [the] opinion it must be a very big house floating on the sea." As the object approached the shore, the curious observers concluded that it was "positively a house full of human beings, of quite a different color from that of the Indians, and dressed quite differently from them."

The unusual looking visitors came ashore on the land that would one day be the state of New York. They held a brief, pleasant meeting with Indian leaders, explaining that they would return the following year. Then they sailed away. These visitors, probably Dutch sailors under the command of Henry Hudson, were among the first Europeans to visit the land that is now the United States. The Delaware, like other Native Americans throughout North America, would have many more encounters with white visitors, though not all would be so friendly.

The Landing of Henry Hudson, c. 1838. Robert W. Weir. Oil on canvas, 68 x 108 in. David David Gallery, Philadelphia.

North America				
c. 35,000 B.C. People begin moving across land bridge from Asia to North America		**1492** Christopher Columbus lands in America		**1565** Spain founds St. Augustine, Florida, the first permanent European settlement in what is now the United States
	Leif Eriksson visits North America			

40,000 B.C.	**1000**	**1275** **1500**	**1517**	**1546** **1575**
		Venetian traveler Marco Polo visits China	In Germany, Martin Luther ignites the Protestant Reformation	The Songhay defeat the Mali in West Africa

World

---

interNET CONNECTION

Early Fashions Students can take a look at the fashions of the day in Jamestown by visiting the Jamestown Web site. The site includes descriptions of the clothing in both England and the colonies during the colonial period, interesting facts about clothing of the period, and illustrations of the typical clothing of the time.

Extra Credit Projects

- Students can research any of America's early peoples—Asians who crossed the land bridge, Native American groups who spread across the continent, early European explorers, or early European settlers. Have them present the information they find as an oral report. **L2**
- Students may be fascinated by the everyday lives of people who lived before 1750. Encourage students to find the answers to the following questions: What was a typical meal like? What was an average home like? How often did people bathe? What did families and children do for fun? What kinds of jobs did most people have? What kinds of work did women do? **L2**

History of the Time

Native Americans

The Delaware Indians who greeted Hudson's sailors descended from migrants to America who probably arrived roughly 35,000 years earlier. Archeological evidence indicates that the first Americans came from Asia. They traveled across a land bridge that once linked Alaska and Russia across the Bering Strait. As groups of people migrated south and east throughout the Americas, they developed into hundreds of thriving societies. Though diverse, these Native Americans shared basic outlooks that in many ways differed dramatically from those of Europeans. Some central traditions of Native Americans were:

- The land is sacred—a living entity that benefits all life and that must be treated with great respect. No one can own the land.

- Lives are organized around cycles of nature, not around concepts of past, future, and progress.

- Traditions pass verbally from generation to generation through folktales, fables, and sacred stories.

- Speechmaking and storytelling are important parts of life.

Age of Exploration

Between 1000 and 1492, the year Christopher Columbus sailed across the Atlantic, a cultural revival known as the Renaissance increased Europeans' curiosity about the world. Trade with Arabs taught Europeans about the great wealth of Asia, as well as about improved techniques for building and navigating ships. These changes stimulated a period of European expansion in the 1400s that is often called the Age of Exploration. Led at first by the Portuguese and the Spanish, Europeans brought all parts of the world into meaningful contact with one another for the first time in history.

English Settlements

The first successful English settlement in North America began when a group of 105 colonists landed in Jamestown, Virginia, in 1607. Within seven months, all but thirty-two were dead. Still, the colony survived and began to prosper by the mid-1600s. About 550 miles north of Virginia, in Plymouth, Massachusetts, English immigrants started another colony in 1620. Many of the original settlers were Pilgrims, members of a reform movement known as Puritanism.

The English colonies also attracted many Dutch, German, and Scots-Irish immigrants. In addition, many Africans were captured and taken to America by force. By 1750, enslaved Africans accounted for about one-fifth of the population in the English colonies. By the late 1700s, the English colonies in North America were already a home for diverse cultures.

Historical Note

Like the Europeans who came thousands of years later, the first Americans were probably immigrants. Scientists believe that they walked across a land bridge from Siberia and subsequently spread throughout the Americas.

In the United States, evidence of some of these first Americans is found in an archaeological site in New Mexico. Called the Clovis people, they inhabited this area during a great ice age when glaciers extended as far south as Ohio. Today's Native Americans, who probably descended from the Clovis people, adjusted to different climates and conditions and became a diverse population. Starting in the 1600s when people from Europe and Africa became part of the mix, the people of the Americas became one of the most diverse populations on Earth.

Biography

The following videotape program is available from Glencoe. Be sure to preview the video for appropriateness for your class:

- "Pocahontas—Her True Story"

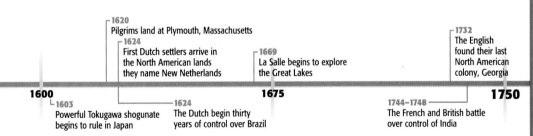

1600

└ **1603**
Powerful Tokugawa shogunate begins to rule in Japan

┌ **1620**
Pilgrims land at Plymouth, Massachusetts

┌ **1624**
First Dutch settlers arrive in the North American lands they name New Netherlands

1624
The Dutch begin thirty years of control over Brazil

┌ **1669**
La Salle begins to explore the Great Lakes

1675

┌ **1732**
The English found their last North American colony, Georgia

1744–1748
The French and British battle over control of India

1750

Native American Cultures Encourage students to learn more about contemporary Native American culture by visiting the *Native American Indian Plenty Stuff* Web site. The site connects to more than 300 Web pages in the United States and Canada, including maps, stories, astronomical information, recipes for Native American foods, pages showing Native American art, and bibliographies of books about Native Americans.

Cultural Note

Finding enough laborers to do the work in the new American colonies was a challenge. Even before the Southern and Chesapeake colonies began solving their labor problems by using enslaved Africans, colonists imported indentured servants by paying their way to America. In return, indentured servants contracted to work without pay as long as the person paying their passage also provided food, clothing, and shelter for a specified term—usually four years. Indentured servants were usually young men between the ages of 15 and 25. For a number of years, starting in 1630, more than half of the immigrants to the American colonies came as indentured servants.

FYI

Native Americans and the Horse Before the Spaniards brought horses to the Americas, Native Americans of the Great Plains used dogs and travois to carry things from place to place. A travois consisted of two long poles with a platform or netting between them. One end of each pole was fastened to a dog's shoulders, and the other end trailed behind on the ground. In a letter from 1541, Francisco de Coronado wrote that he had seen dogs carry the Native American houses, and that they had the sticks of their houses dragging along.

Life of the Time

People are talking about

Slavery Wanting laborers to work their land, colonists, particularly in Virginia, begin buying enslaved Africans. By 1700, ships crowded with enslaved men and women arrive regularly. Some colonists disapprove. In 1688, Quakers in Germantown, Pennsylvania, issue the first antislavery protest. Slave revolts become a constant fear among slaveholders. ▶

◀ **Religion** In the Massachusetts Bay Colony, Puritans exile Roger Williams in 1636 for his religious beliefs. He founds Rhode Island, which tolerates religious diversity. In 1660, Mary Dyer is publicly hanged on the Boston Common for her Quaker beliefs. Most Native Americans and enslaved Africans continue to practice their own beliefs.

New Fauna and Flora Everywhere in America, Europeans come upon exotic animals and vegetation unlike anything they have ever imagined—the opossum, for example.

"An animal which has a head like a sucking pig . . . hair like a badger . . . the tail like a rat, the paws like a monkey, which has a purse beneath its belly, where it produces its young and nourishes them." —*Le Moyne d'Iberville, 1699* ▶

Firsts

- Spanish explorers bring horses to the Americas. (1500s)
- John Rolfe harvests first tobacco crop in Virginia. (1612)
- Mail service in the colonies begins temporarily between Boston and New York. (1673)
- The first theater in the colonies opens in Williamsburg, Virginia. (1716)

Virginian Opossum, 1827–1836. John James Audubon. Color lithograph. Private collection.

North America			
	1619 Twenty enslaved Africans brought to Virginia	**1636** Roger Williams founds Rhode Island	**1640** The English colonies include about 26,000 Europeans and 600 Africans
40,000 B.C. **1600**	**1621** Potatoes first planted in Germany	**1630** **1632** Italian scientist Galileo publishes *Two Chief Systems of the World*	**1644** China's Ming Dynasty collapses **1653** Taj Mahal completed in India **1660** **1664–1665** Plague kills nearly 70,000 in London
World			

MEETING INDIVIDUAL NEEDS — MULTIPLE LEARNING STYLES

Logical and Mathematical The population of the English colonies in North America grew steadily during the seventeenth century. Refer students to the time line on pages 40 and 41, and point out the population figures for 1640 and 1700.

Activity Have students conduct population research using sources such as the *Historical Statistical Abstract of the United States*. Using the data they find, students can construct line, circle, or bar graphs showing how the population grew and changed during the first hundred years of colonial life.

As an alternative, students may construct graphs for regions such as the New England Colonies, the Middle Colonies, or the Southern Colonies. **L2**

Food & Fashion

- Native foods—corn, squash, beans, fish—are abundant, but cattle and pigs are brought from Europe. Some settlers adopt the Native American habit of chewing the resin of some trees.

- Puritans favor plain, dark clothing, though women still have to wear layers of petticoats and underskirts. Other colonists dress more lavishly, especially wealthy southern planter families. One Englishman writes from Virginia in 1759:

  "I assure you . . . the common Planter's Daughters here go every Day in finer Cloath than I have seen content you for a Summer's Sunday. . . . I'm nothing amongst the Lace and Lac'd fellows . . . here."

Arts & Entertainment

Native American cultures create objects both useful and beautiful—decorated clothing, baskets, pottery, and blankets. ▶

◀ Among European settlers, especially in the South, girls learn to sew and embroider. Samplers displaying a variety of stitches hang in many homes.

Amusements

- Native American recreations include sleight-of-hand games, dice games, and athletic games such as lacrosse and hoop-and-spear, in which a hoop rolling along the ground is speared with a wooden pole.
- Early colonists make their own entertainment. Many play musical instruments. Southern plantation owners give grand dance parties.
- Puritans outlaw dice, cards, and nine-pin bowling; some colonists invent a new game—ten-pin bowling.

Timeline

1692 Witchcraft trials begin in Salem, Massachusetts

1700 English colonies include about 220,000 Europeans and 27,000 Africans

1730s and 1740s Religious revivals, known as the Great Awakening, spread through colonies

1670s Ice cream becomes a popular treat in Paris

1669 Dutch painter Rembrandt dies

1687 English scientist Isaac Newton publishes his *Principia Mathematica*

1690

1720 German composer Johann Sebastian Bach completes his *Brandenburg Concertos*

1750

FROM THE EARLIEST DAYS 🦃 41

MEETING INDIVIDUAL NEEDS — MULTIPLE LEARNING STYLES

Interpersonal Remind students that community life was important to the colonists because their very survival depended on their neighbors. Recreational activities help bind people together. Local fairs were a popular activity.

Activity Have students work together in small groups to plan booths for a colonial fair. One group might plan a booth that displays typical colonial clothing. Another booth might feature colonial foods. A third might have contests based on colonial children's games or focus on colonial crafts. A speaker from the local historical society might explain life among Native Americans in your location during this time. **L2 COLLAB. LEARN.**

Literature of the Time

Literature of the Time

Cultural Note

For a colonial family, books were often a luxury item. The average home probably had fewer than two or three books. Share with students this inventory of the estate of John Smith, a Providence miller who died in 1682. He had only the Bible in his home.

- **In the upper room of the dwelling:** two bedsteads with beds and bedding.
- **In the lower room of the dwelling:** one bedstead with bed and bedding; one small piece of homemade cloth; a frying pan; two guns; a chamber pot; two pewter platters; two basins and three porringers (single-handled metal bowls); two spinning wheels and cards; an old Bible; four old chairs; several wooden dishes; four old spoons; two pounds of tallow candles; the corn mill and equipment . . .

Ask students what things might have been necessary in order for the colonists to have books.

(paper, printing presses, people with enough time to write books, sources of information, skilled printers, a reliable distribution system)

PEOPLE ARE READING . . .

Fliers and Pamphlets   In England, people are enticed by fliers that promote the delights of a "new life" across the sea but that often overlook the hardships and hazards that come with it.

> "Poor people (both Men and Women) of all kinds, can here get three times the Wages for their Labour they can in *England* or *Wales.* . . . Here are no Beggars to be seen." —Gabriel Thomas, *Historical and Geographical Account of Pensilvania* (1698) ▶

◀ **Religious Books**   After its publication in 1611, the English translation of the Bible ordered by King James I of England becomes the most widely read book in English. To enable more people to read the Bible, in 1647, Massachusetts Bay Colony passes the first colonial law requiring communities to support public schools. Another colonial best-seller is the hymnbook known as the *Bay Psalm Book*.

Newspapers   English settlers hungry for news get their first colonial newspaper in 1704, the *Boston News-Letter*. In 1734 officers arrest John Peter Zenger for allowing his *New York Weekly Journal* to criticize the governor. After ten months in prison, Zenger wins acquittal from a jury—an important victory for freedom of the press.

People Are Writing

Journals and Diaries   Puritans often keep diaries and include comments on their religious experiences. This allows people to reflect upon and examine their own spiritual development. Sarah Kemble Knight records her Boston-to-New York trip by horseback in 1704. The idea of a female traveling so far alone shocks many, including one woman who insists that she has never seen "a woman on the road so dreadful late in all the days of my versal [whole] life."

Letters   Educated colonists stay in touch with Europe and with one another through letters. Southern gentlemen and ladies who live far apart correspond often to share details of their daily lives.

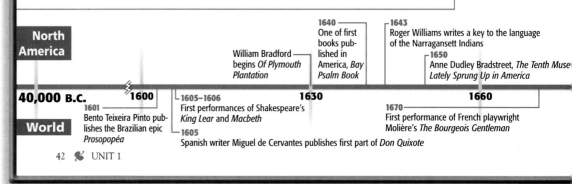

North America

40,000 B.C.	**1600**

- 1640 — One of first books published in America, *Bay Psalm Book*
- 1643 — Roger Williams writes a key to the language of the Narragansett Indians
- William Bradford begins *Of Plymouth Plantation*
- 1650 — Anne Dudley Bradstreet, *The Tenth Muse Lately Sprung Up in America*

World

- 1601 — Bento Teixeira Pinto publishes the Brazilian epic *Prosopopéa*
- 1605–1606 — First performances of Shakespeare's *King Lear* and *Macbeth*
- 1605 — Spanish writer Miguel de Cervantes publishes first part of *Don Quixote*
- 1630
- 1660
- 1670 — First performance of French playwright Molière's *The Bourgeois Gentleman*

42 UNIT 1

REAL-WORLD CONNECTION

The Issue That Won't Go Away
When the British governor of New York dismissed Chief Justice Lewis Morris, the *New York Weekly Journal* criticized the governor severely. John Peter Zenger, the paper's publisher, refused to reveal the critic's name to the British governor. With no one else to charge, the British arrested Zenger for criminal libel. Zenger was ultimately acquitted by a jury, but the issue of how much journalists must reveal in court is still controversial. Since 1984 at least a dozen reporters have been jailed for refusing to reveal sources, and since 1975 more than 20 have been fined for contempt. How do students feel about this issue?

Activity   Ask students to research the rights and responsibilities of reporters in today's world and write a short essay about the issues. **L2**

Literary Trends: Plain Style

"[John Billington was] found guilty of willful murder, by plain and notorious evidence. And was for the same accordingly executed. This, as it was the first execution among them [the Pilgrims], so was it a matter of great sadness unto them. . . . His fact was that he waylaid a young man, one John Newcomen, about a former quarrel and shot him with a gun, whereof he died." —*William Bradford*

The Puritans strive for simplicity in writing, just as they do in clothing, food, architecture, household furnishings, and religious practices. For example, Pilgrim leader William Bradford records the dramatic story of the settlement in "a plain style, with singular regard unto the simple truth in all things." Plain style focuses on communicating ideas as clearly as possible. This marks a change from ornate style, the complicated and decorative style used by writers in Europe at that time. Colonial writers such as Bradford think of writing as a practical tool for spiritual self-examination and religious instruction, not as an opportunity to demonstrate cleverness.

FOCUS ON . . .

The Power of Nature

The environment of North America astonishes newcomers to the continent. Some, like William Bradford, view it as a frightening place, a "hideous and desolate wilderness, full of wild beasts and wild men." However, others see in America an enormous garden, a vast, untouched earthly paradise:

"But the territorie and soil of the Chesepeans [Native Americans living on Chesapeake Bay] (being distant fifteene miles from the shoare) was for pleasantnes of seate, for temperature of climate, for fertilitie of soyle and for the commodity of the sea, besides multitude of beares (being an excellent good victuall [food]) with great woods of sassafras, and wallnut trees, . . . not to be excelled by any other whatsoever." —*Ralph Lane, 1585*

This view of a land filled with earthly blessings and of unlimited possibilities helps shape an emerging American spirit and literature.

Hooker and Company Journeying Through the Wilderness from Plymouth to Hartford, in 1636, 1846. Frederic Edwin Church. Oil on canvas, 40¼ x 60⅝ in. Wadsworth Atheneum, Hartford, CT.

A&E HOME VIDEO. ® *The following videotape program is available from Glencoe:*
- "Lives and Letters: Colonial America"

Timeline:

- **1679** Japanese poet Bashō writes poetry that breaks with the traditional haiku form
- **1682** *A Narrative of the Captivity and Restoration of Mrs. Mary Rowlandson* is published
- **1690**
- **1704** First English colonial newspaper, *Boston News-Letter*
- **1720**
- **1726** Irish-born writer Jonathan Swift publishes *Gulliver's Travels*
- **1735** The Zenger trial in New York helps establish free press
- **1741** Jonathan Edwards delivers sermon "Sinners in the Hands of an Angry God"
- **1750**

FROM THE EARLIEST DAYS 🐚 43

MEETING INDIVIDUAL NEEDS — GIFTED AND TALENTED ACTIVITY

"Colonial" Public Radio Students who are familiar with National Public Radio may have listened to the travel programs that take listeners along as broadcasters interview people from many different places. Ask gifted and talented students to imagine that they are colonial broadcasters who will interview people who have left Britain to start a new life in the colonies.

Activity Have students prepare five-minute radio scripts about one aspect of colonial life. Explain that they will need to research to find accurate information. Their audience will be people of the time who live in Great Britain. Once student scripts have been prepared, have groups of students perform a script for a five-minute program segment, either live or on tape. **L3 COLLAB. LEARN.**

Language of the Time

How People Speak

More Than One English Language In the early 1600s, each region of England has its own distinctive dialect. For example, Shakespeare uses rhymes based on the pronunciations common to his native town of Stratford-upon-Avon. English colonists carry their regional speech patterns with them to North America. Traces of these regional differences continue to distinguish American dialects today.

- Because most Virginia settlers come from western England while most settlers in Massachusetts come from eastern England, they speak differently. Certain distinguishing features of the two dialects will carry into modern speech—not pronouncing the r after vowels in New England, for instance.

- Scots-Irish people settle mostly in the middle colonies. Here, the r is still pronounced in words such as *lord* and *here*.

- The following language features of the 1600s and 1700s fade in England but persist in America:
  - "flat" a in *fast*, *path* (rather than "broad" a of *father*)
  - first vowel sound in *either* pronounced *ee* – *gotten* instead of *got*
  - *mad* for "angry" – *fall* for "autumn"

Thee, Thou, Thy *Thee, thou,* and *thy* are old-fashioned words for "you" and "your" that some people use to address children, close friends, and God. Quakers and Puritans use them to address everyone.

How People Write

Spelling More and more people are reading and writing in sixteenth-century England, and they cry out for spelling rules. The spelling system that settlers bring with them is similar to modern spelling. Exceptions include occasional final *e*: *kinde*; *ll* and *sse* at the end of words: *gratefull*, *kindnesse*; and *ick* for *ic*: *logick*, *magick*.

New Words and Expressions

From Other Languages In America, English speakers encounter new languages and new items that need names. Below are some of the useful words from Native American and African languages that enter English in colonial times.

Native American Languages		African Languages	
Original Word	**English Word**	**Original Word**	**English Word**
xocolatl (Aztec)	chocolate	mbanza (Kimbundu)	banjo
arathkone (Algonquian)	raccoon	banäna (Mande)	banana

44 ❧ UNIT 1

The following pictures illustrate a hornbook alphabet:

A	In *Adam's* Fall We Sinned all.
B	Thy Life to Mend This *Book* Attend.
C	The *Cat* doth play And after flay.
D	A *Dog* will bite A Thief at night.
E	An *Eagles* flight Is out of sight.
F	The *Idle Fool* Is whipt at School.

MEETING INDIVIDUAL NEEDS — ENGLISH LANGUAGE LEARNERS

Living Language Explain that American English is difficult for non-native speakers, partly because it has borrowed freely from many languages.

Activity Organize the class into groups, each containing at least one English language learner. Give groups a list of common words. Ask students to list as many synonyms for these common words as they can in as many languages as they can. Then have students share their lists with the class. How many words are similar? How many words from other languages are familiar to native English speakers?

Additional Resources
📁 *English Language Learners Sourcebook*

Theme 1 Beginnings and Change

How do you feel at the beginning of the school year? Excited? Nervous? How about other beginnings, such as the first days in a new neighborhood or the beginning of a friendship? After all these beginnings, things eventually change. How well do you adapt to change? Many of the writers in this theme tell of beginnings, from the beginnings of the world to the start of a life in a new land. And many of them faced great change, such as a change of government, a change in plans, or a change in their way of life.

THEME PROJECTS

Interdisciplinary Activity

Art   Choose two selections from this theme that tell of different kinds of beginnings. Create an illustration for each one.

1. Think about a critical moment in the selection that involves a beginning. What people or objects were present at that moment? What colors best describe that beginning?

2. Make a drawing or painting to represent each beginning. Include details that show how the two beginnings are alike and different.

3. Show your work to the class. Invite classmates to identify the beginnings you have illustrated and discuss their similarities and differences.

Performing

Theater   With a small group, choose a selection from this theme that shows a person or a group facing an important change. Rewrite the selection as a play, turning as much narrative as you can into dialogue and adding simple stage directions. Edit and revise your script. Assign roles to members of your group and put on an informal presentation of the play.

Sunrise–A Gift No Gem Could Equal, 1970. Charles F. Lovato. Oil on Masonite, 30½ x 21⅞ in. The Philbrook Museum of Art, Tulsa, OK.

LITERATURE & HUMANITIES

 Play "Ay Como Flecha" from Glencoe's **American Music: Cultural Traditions.** Volume 1, Track 3.

Theme 1

Teaching Strategies

The following suggestions may help your students plan and carry out their theme projects.

Interdisciplinary Activity

- Encourage students to identify a scene that can be represented well visually, such as the one from "The Sky Tree" illustrated on page 50.
- Have students identify their artistic strengths. Would it be better to draw? Paint? Make a collage?
- Before they begin, have students write a brief summary of what they want to show.
- Students should identify the comparison they want to make before they begin.

Performing

- Provide students with samples of plays for guidance.
- Explain that a play has a few central characters, a plot structure, and a theme(s) that is revealed through dialogue.

Additional Resources

- 📁 *Interdisciplinary Activities,* pp. 2–3
- 📁 *Viewing and Representing Activities,* pp. 7–8
- 📁 *Listening and Speaking Activities,* pp. 1–2
- 📁 *Critical Thinking Skills,* pp. 2–4
- 📁 *Selection and Theme Assessment,* pp. 215–216
- 📁 *Performance Assessment,* p. 125

GLENCOE TECHNOLOGY

LITERATURE CLASSICS CD-ROM

Search for other selections related to the theme of Beginnings and Change.

SELECTIONS	Literary Elements	Reading and Thinking	Writing	Vocabulary and Spelling	
How the World Was Made / **The Sky Tree** — ANONYMOUS	*TWE: Anthropomorphism,* p. 51	*TWE: Drawing Conclusions,* p. 49; *Inferring,* p. 51	SE: Origin Myth, p. 52		
from **The Iroquois Constitution** — DEKANAWIDA	SE: Repetition, p. 58 / *TWE: Author's Purpose,* p. 57	*TWE: Synthesizing,* p. 56; *Drawing Conclusions,* p. 56	SE: Analysis, p. 58		
from **La Relación** — ÁLVAR NÚÑEZ CABEZA DE VACA	SE: Narrator, p. 66 / *TWE: Setting,* p. 63; *Character,* p. 63	SE: Recognizing Bias, p. 67 / *TWE: Inferring,* p. 63; *Judging Credibility of a Source,* p. 64; *Distinguishing Fact from Opinion,* p. 65; *Sequencing Events,* p. 65	SE: Evaluation, p. 66		
from **Of Plymouth Plantation** — WILLIAM BRADFORD	SE: Diction, p. 73 / *TWE: Allusion,* p. 71; *Point of View,* p. 71	*TWE: Using Graphic Aids,* p. 71; *Evaluating,* p. 72	SE: Journal Entry, p. 73		
Upon the Burning of Our House July 10th, 1666 / **To My Dear and Loving Husband** — ANNE BRADSTREET	SE: Extended Metaphor, p. 81 / *TWE: Rhyme Scheme: Couplets,* p. 78; *Paradox,* p. 79	*TWE: Predicting,* p. 77; *Comparing and Contrasting,* p. 82	SE: Poem, p. 81		
from **A Narrative of the Captivity and Restoration of Mrs. Mary Rowlandson** — MARY ROWLANDSON	SE: Analogy, p. 91 / *TWE: Allusion,* p. 89; *Figures of Speech: Metaphor and Simile,* p. 90	*TWE: Judging Credibility of a Source,* p. 86; *Paraphrasing,* p. 87; *Sequencing,* p. 89	SE: Dialogue, p. 91	*TWE: Context Clues,* p. 88	
from **Stay Alive, My Son** — PIN YATHAY	SE: Rhetorical Question, p. 97 / *TWE: Climax,* p. 95	*TWE: Problem Solving,* p. 96	SE: Reflection Paragraphs, p. 97		
from **SINNERS IN THE HANDS OF AN ANGRY GOD** — JONATHAN EDWARDS	SE: Imagery, p. 105 / *TWE: Repetition,* p. 103; *Figurative Language: Symbol,* p. 104	*TWE: Main Idea and Supporting Details,* p. 102; *Establishing Criteria,* p. 103; *Analyzing Arguments,* p. 103	SE: Guidelines, p. 105 / *TWE: Rewrite Sentence Fragments,* p. 106		
Offer of Help — CANASSATEGO	SE: Tone, p. 109		SE: Letter, p. 109		

Key: Student material is in roman. Teacher material is in italic.   💻 Technology   **Collaboration**

Grammar and Language	Listening, Speaking, and Viewing	Life Skills	Study, Research, and Technology
TWE: *Recognizing Nouns, p. 48*	*TWE:* *The Oral Tradition, p. 50*		**SE:** Ecology, p. 53 **SE:** Interdisciplinary Activity, p. 58
			TWE: 🖳 *Internet Connection, p. 55*
TWE: *Relative Pronouns, p. 64*	**SE:** `COLLAB. LEARN.` Literature Groups, p. 66		
TWE: *Transitive and Intransitive Verbs, p. 70*			**SE:** Performing, p. 73 **SE:** Video Camera, p. 74
TWE: *Adjectives, p. 78; Adverbs, p. 83*	**SE:** `COLLAB. LEARN.` Literature Groups, p. 81; Designing a Quilt, p. 81; Performing an Oral Reading, p. 81		*TWE:* 🖳 *Internet Connection, p. 82*
TWE: *Interjections, p. 86*	**SE:** `COLLAB. LEARN.` Literature Groups, p. 91		
TWE: *Personal Pronouns, p. 94*	**SE:** `COLLAB. LEARN.` Literature Groups, p. 97 **SE:** Conducting an Interview, p. 99	*TWE:* *Decision Making, p. 95*	
SE: Sentence Fragments, p. 106	**SE:** `COLLAB. LEARN.` Creating a Visual Presentation, p. 105		*TWE:* 🖳 *Internet Connection, p. 104*
	SE: `COLLAB. LEARN.` Literature Groups, p. 109		*TWE:* 🖳 *Internet Connection, p. 108*

SELECTIONS	Print Resources		
How the World Was Made / **The Sky Tree** ANONYMOUS	Unit One Planning Guide, pp. 26–31 *Active Reading Guide, p. 4 Vocabulary Practice, p. 3	Grammar and Composition Handbook, Lesson 1.1 Grammar and Language Workbook, p. 47 Reading Workbook, pp. 7–8	*Quick Checks, p. 4 Selection and Theme Assessment, pp. 7–8 Performance Assessment, p. 4 Spanish Summaries, p. 4 Spanish Translations
from **The Iroquois Constitution** DEKANAWIDA	Unit One Planning Guide, pp. 32–37 *Active Reading Guide, p. 5 Vocabulary Practice, p. 4	Reading Workbook, pp. 9–10	*Quick Checks, p. 5 Selection and Theme Assessment, pp. 9–10 Performance Assessment, p. 5 Spanish Summaries, p. 5 Spanish Translations
from **La Relación** ÁLVAR NÚÑEZ CABEZA DE VACA	Unit One Planning Guide, pp. 38–43 *Active Reading Guide, p. 6 Vocabulary Practice, p. 5	Grammar and Composition Handbook, Lesson 1.2 Grammar and Language Workbook, p. 53 Reading Workbook, pp. 11–12	*Quick Checks, p. 6 Selection and Theme Assessment, pp. 11–12 Performance Assessment, p. 6 Spanish Summaries, p. 6
from **Of Plymouth Plantation** WILLIAM BRADFORD	Unit One Planning Guide, pp. 44–51 *Active Reading Guide, p. 7 Vocabulary Practice, p. 6	Grammar and Composition Handbook, Lesson 1.3 Grammar and Language Workbook, p. 55 Reading Workbook, p. 13	*Quick Checks, p. 7 Selection and Theme Assessment, pp. 13–14 Performance Assessment, p. 7 Spanish Summaries, p. 7
Upon the Burning of Our House July 10th, 1666 / **To My Dear and Loving Husband** ANNE BRADSTREET	Unit One Planning Guide, pp. 52–57 *Active Reading Guide, p. 8	Grammar and Composition Handbook, Lesson 1.4 Grammar and Language Workbook, p. 61 Reading Workbook, p. 14	*Quick Checks, p. 8 Selection and Theme Assessment, pp. 15–16 Performance Assessment, p. 8 Spanish Summaries, p. 8
from *A Narrative of the Captivity and Restoration of Mrs. Mary Rowlandson* MARY ROWLANDSON	Unit One Planning Guide, pp. 58–65 *Active Reading Guide, p. 9 Vocabulary Practice, p. 7	Grammar and Composition Handbook, Lesson 1.8 Grammar and Language Workbook, p. 69 Reading Workbook, pp. 15–16	*Quick Checks, p. 9 Selection and Theme Assessment, pp. 17–18 Performance Assessment, p. 9 Spanish Summaries, p. 9
from **Stay Alive, My Son** PIN YATHAY	Unit One Planning Guide, pp. 66–71 *Active Reading Guide, p. 10 Vocabulary Practice, p. 8	Grammar and Composition Handbook, Lesson 1.2 Grammar and Language Workbook, p. 51 Reading Workbook, pp. 15–16	*Quick Checks, p. 10 Selection and Theme Assessment, pp. 19–20 Performance Assessment, p. 10 Spanish Summaries, p. 10
from **SINNERS IN THE HANDS OF AN ANGRY GOD** JONATHAN EDWARDS	Unit One Planning Guide, pp. 72–79 *Active Reading Guide, p. 11 Vocabulary Practice, p. 9	Reading Workbook, pp. 17–18	*Quick Checks, p. 11 Selection and Theme Assessment, p. 21 Performance Assessment, p. 11 Spanish Summaries, p. 11
Offer of Help CANASSATEGO	Unit One Planning Guide, pp. 80–84 *Active Reading Guide, p. 12 Vocabulary Practice, p. 10	Reading Workbook, pp. 17–18	*Quick Checks, p. 12 Selection and Theme Assessment, p. 22 Performance Assessment, p. 12 Spanish Summaries, p. 12 Spanish Translations

*Also available in Spanish

Transparencies	Technology Resources
Selection Focus Transparency 4 Grammar and Language Transparency 3 Fine Art Transparency 2	Audio Library Spanish Audio Library Testmaker Web Site: *lit.glencoe.com*
Selection Focus Transparency 5 Literary Elements Transparency 4	Literature Launchers Audio Library Spanish Audio Library Testmaker Web Site: *lit.glencoe.com*
Selection Focus Transparency 6 Grammar and Language Transparency 4 Literary Elements Transparency 5	Audio Library Spanish Audio Library Testmaker Web Site: *lit.glencoe.com*
Selection Focus Transparency 7 Grammar and Language Transparency 5 Literary Elements Transparency 6	Literature Launchers Audio Library Spanish Audio Library Testmaker Web Site: *lit.glencoe.com*
Selection Focus Transparency 8 Grammar and Language Transparency 6 Literary Elements Transparency 7	Audio Library Testmaker Web Site: *lit.glencoe.com*
Selection Focus Transparency 9 Grammar and Language Transparency 8 Literary Elements Transparency 8	Audio Library Spanish Audio Library Testmaker Web Site: *lit.glencoe.com*
Selection Focus Transparency 10 Grammar and Language Transparency 9 Literary Elements Transparency 9 Fine Art Transparency 13	Audio Library Spanish Audio Library Testmaker Web Site: *lit.glencoe.com*
Selection Focus Transparency 11 Literary Elements Transparency 10	Audio Library Spanish Audio Library Testmaker Web Site: *lit.glencoe.com*
Selection Focus Transparency 12 Literary Elements Transparency 11	Audio Library Spanish Audio Library Testmaker Web Site: *lit.glencoe.com*

🗀 *Theme* RESOURCES

- Listening and Speaking Activities (pp. 1–2)
- Viewing and Representing Activities (pp. 7–8)
- Critical Thinking Skills (pp. 2–4)
- Media Connections Activities (pp. 1–2)
- Interdisciplinary Activities (pp. 2–3)

See also these additional planning resources:
- English Language Learners Sourcebook
- Inclusion Strategies Sourcebook
- Literature Groups Sourcebook

Use Glencoe's **Presentation Plus!** This multimedia teaching tool lets you present dynamic lessons that will engage your students. Using Microsoft Powerpoint,® you can customize the presentations to create your own personalized lessons.

Native American Mythology

Objective

- To recognize oral tradition as a form of literature

Teaching Strategies

Explain that the term *Native American* can be applied to dozens of distinct early American cultures. Remind students that *Native American* also includes such Mesoamerican cultures as the Zapotec, Aztec, Maya, and Olmec.

Cultural Sensitivity

Be aware that the term *mythology* as applied to Native American oral tradition may be offensive to some. Many Native Americans consider most of what other Americans call *mythology* to be an integral part of their spiritual beliefs.

Teaching Options

Literature **F O C U S**

Native American Mythology

Centuries before the first Europeans arrived on the shores of North America, Native Americans had established hundreds of thriving nations, each with a unique culture and heritage. Each nation had its own tradition of **oral literature**—stories that were passed down from one generation to the next as they were told and retold in the privacy of households and in tribal ceremonies.

An important part of the oral tradition of each culture was its myths. A **myth** is an anonymous, traditional story that relies on the supernatural to explain a natural phenomenon, an aspect of human behavior, or a mystery of the universe. Myths try to explain why the world is the way it is. They provide imaginative ways to help people feel at home in the world and make sense of it. **Creation myths** tell how the world and human life came to exist. Some myths, called **origin myths,** explain how natural phenomena such as the stars, moon, and mountains came to be or why a society has certain beliefs and customs. Often, the qualities of creation myths and origin myths appear in one story. A Taos Pueblo story explains:

"When Earth was still young and giants still roamed the land, a great sickness came upon them. All of them died except for a small boy. One day while he was playing, a snake bit him. The boy cried and cried. The blood came out, and finally he died. With his tears our lakes became. With his blood the red clay became. With his body our mountains became, and that was how Earth became."

Many Native American myths emphasize a strong spiritual bond between the Creator, humanity, and the entire natural world. They emphasize that it is the duty of humanity to maintain a balance within their natural world.

In many cultures, each family group, or clan, believed it descended from a particular animal or other natural object, called the **totem.** Members of the bear clan, for example, honored the bear. The bear in turn served as the group's guardian spirit, helping and protecting its members. The bear clan was responsible for preserving the myths of the bear.

Another common feature of Native American mythology is the **trickster.** These animal characters have two sides to their personalities. Tricksters are rebels who defy authority and sometimes create trouble and chaos. However, they are also curious, clever, and creative figures who can unexpectedly reveal wisdom. In many myths, the trickster is a coyote, a raven, or a mink. In one Native American myth, the coyote brings death into the world when he realizes the earth will become too crowded if people live forever.

Myths and rituals continue to play a central role in traditional Native American cultures. They are used to give people a sense of order and identity, to heal the sick, to ensure a plentiful supply of food, to initiate young people into adulthood, and to teach moral lessons.

MEETING INDIVIDUAL NEEDS **ENGLISH LANGUAGE LEARNERS**

Mythology Before they read, make sure that English language learners understand the subtitle. Who are Native Americans? What does *mythology* mean? Ask a volunteer to identify the parts of the word: *myth + ology*. Then ask which other words have the suffix. What does this suffix seem to mean?

Activity After students have read the Literature Focus, ask English language learners to share myths from their cultures with the class. Perhaps they know an entertaining trickster story. Students can write down these myths, or they can plan an oral storytelling.

Additional Resources
📁 *English Language Learners Sourcebook*

Before You Read
How the World Was Made and The Sky Tree

The Oral Tradition

Both of these stories come from an **oral tradition.** Storytellers passed along such tales by word of mouth. No one really knows where the stories originated. Native Americans have written down these stories only in the past hundred years. Long before that, however, the storytellers helped groups understand and record their daily lives and their history.

Native American storytellers often tell tales of nature. The two pieces you are about to read are **origin myths.** They tell how the world or some part of it came to be.

These two stories have been passed down for many hundreds of years. They come from different cultures, yet both stories show a great reverence for the natural world. "How the World

Was Made" comes from the Cherokee people, who lived in the forests of the Great Smoky Mountains. "The Sky Tree" comes from the Huron people of the Great Lakes region.

FOCUS ACTIVITY

In what ways does nature, or the natural world, affect your life? For example, are you more cheerful on a sunny day?

SHARE IDEAS In a group, share experiences of the natural world and your reactions to them—anything from the sense of awe at seeing a mountain to the frustration of being caught in a downpour.

SETTING A PURPOSE Read to learn the attitudes these tales reflect about nature and the place of humans in the natural world.

BACKGROUND

Recording the Oral Tradition

The Cherokee passed down the myth "How the World Was Made" from generation to generation. Then, around 1890, James Mooney, an anthropologist for the Smithsonian Institution in Washington, D.C., listened to the tale and wrote it down. He first published the story in 1891.

The Huron myth "The Sky Tree" is retold by Joseph Bruchac, a member of the Abenaki Native American group in northern New York State. Bruchac published this myth in 1991.

VOCABULARY PREVIEW

vault (vôlt) *n.* an arched structure forming a roof or ceiling; p. 48
alight (ə līt′) *v.* to descend and come to rest; p. 48

conjurer (kon′ jər ər) *n.* one who performs magic; sorcerer; p. 49

Objectives

- To read two Native American myths about the origin of the world
- To write a comparison of two Native American myths

Skills

Reading/Thinking: Drawing Conclusions; Inferring
Writing: Origin Myth
Grammar/Language: Recognizing Nouns
Listening/Speaking: The Oral Tradition

Motivating OPTIONS

Selection Focus Transparency 4: Have students view the transparency and then answer the question provided.

Focus Activity: As an extension of the Focus Activity, have students describe their favorite outdoor place and why they like it.

RESOURCE MANAGER

Lesson Planning Resource
The *Unit One Planning Guide* (pp. 26–31) provides additional lesson notes and reduced versions of all print resources.

📁 **Other Print Resources**
- Active Reading Guide, p. 4
- Vocabulary Practice, p. 3
- Reading Workbook, pp. 7–8
- Grammar and Language Workbook, p. 47

- Grammar and Composition Handbook, Lesson 1.1
- Quick Checks, p. 4
- Selection and Theme Assessment, pp. 7–8
- Performance Assessment, p. 4
- Spanish Summaries, p. 4
- Spanish Translations
- Inclusion Strategies
- English Language Learners Sourcebook

Transparencies
- Selection Focus 4
- Fine Art 2
- Grammar and Language 3

Technology
🎧 Audio Library
🎧 Spanish Audio Library
💻 Glencoe Literature Web Site
💾 Testmaker

SUMMARY

In "How the World Was Made," the world is created when the animals in Galunlati, a place in the sky, need more room. Water-beetle offers to find out what is below the water. The beetle stirs up mud to form land, which the animals settle on. Man and woman are created, and they grow quickly to dominate the land.

In "The Sky Tree," people live in Sky Land, above a water-covered Earth. The Sky Tree is felled, creating a giant hole through which it falls. The chief's wife jumps after it. Turtle sees and calls on the water animals to dive down the hole, gather mud, and place it on his back, creating an island. The tree then takes root in the new Earth.

📁 *Spanish Summaries,* p. 4

A **Active Reading**

PREDICT Read the first four sentences in the second paragraph aloud, and have students predict what will happen next.

Additional Resources

📁 *Active Reading Guide,* p. 4

🎧 *Audio Library*

🎧 *Spanish Audio Library*

Teaching Options

How the World

(Cherokee—Great Smoky Mountains)

Retold by James Mooney 〜

THE EARTH IS A GREAT ISLAND FLOATING IN A SEA OF WATER,

and suspended at each of the four cardinal points[1] by a cord hanging down from the sky vault, which is of solid rock. When the world grows old and worn out, the people will die and the cords will break and let the earth sink down into the ocean, and all will be water again. The Indians are afraid of this.

A When all was water, the animals were above in Gălûñ´lătĭ (go lun(g) lot´ i), beyond the arch; but it was very much crowded, and they were wanting more room. They wondered what was below the water, and at last Dâyuni´sĭ (dô yun ē´ si), "Beaver's Grandchild," the little Water-beetle, offered to go and see if it could learn. It darted in every direction over the surface of the water, but could find no firm place to rest. Then it dived to the bottom and came up with some soft mud, which began to grow and spread on every side until it became the island which we call the earth. It was afterward fastened to the sky with four cords, but no one remembers who did this.

At first the earth was flat and very soft and wet. The animals were anxious to get down, and sent out different birds to see if it was yet dry, but they found no place to alight and came back again to Gălûñ´lătĭ. At last it seemed to be time, and they sent out the Buzzard and told him to go and make ready for them. This was the Great Buzzard, the father of all the buzzards we see now. He flew all over the earth, low down near the ground, and it was still soft. When he reached the Cherokee country, he was very tired, and his wings began to flap and strike the ground, and wherever they struck the earth there was a valley, and where they turned up again there was a mountain. When the animals above saw this, they were afraid that the whole world would be mountains, so they called him back, but the Cherokee country remains full of mountains to this day.

When the earth was dry and the animals came down, it was still dark, so they got the sun and set it in a track to go every day across the island from east to west, just overhead. It was too hot this way, and Tsiska´gĭlĭ´ (chēs kä´ gi li´), the Red Crawfish, had his shell scorched a bright red, so that his meat was

---

1. The *four cardinal points* are the four main directions on a compass (north, south, east, and west).

Vocabulary
vault (vôlt) *n.* an arched structure forming a roof or ceiling
alight (ə līt´) *v.* to descend and come to rest

48 🦌 UNIT 1

Grammar and Language *Minilesson*

Recognizing Nouns Point out that nouns name persons, places, things, or ideas. Nouns may be subjects of sentences, objects of prepositions, direct or indirect objects, objects of infinitives, or predicate nominatives. Write the following on the board: "When they were through, Aataentsic settled down gently on the new Earth and the pieces of the great tree fell beside

her . . ." Discuss which words in the sentence are nouns.

Activity Write the following sentence on the board: "When the animals above saw this, they were afraid that the whole world would be mountains, so they called him back, but the Cherokee country remains full of mountains to this day." Have students identify which words are nouns. **L2**

Additional Resources

🖋 *Grammar and Language Transparency 3*

📗 *Grammar and Language Workbook,* p. 47

📗 *Grammar and Composition Handbook,* Lesson 1.1

📗 *Writer's Choice,* Lesson 10.1

Was Made

QUESTION Why did the Cherokee people explain the existence and creation of natural phenomena, such as mountains and animal characteristics, in this way? What purpose do these explanations serve? *(They tried to explain nature in terms they understood. These explanations reflect the Cherokee religious values.)*

Language Note

Discuss with students the meaning of *hair* in this context. Use the context clue "you [trees] shall lose your hair every winter" to help students pinpoint the meaning. Explain that the myth refers to the various trees' foliage as hair.

FYI

Forever Green The cedar, pine, spruce, holly, and laurel are not the only trees that do not "lose their hair" in Cherokee country. Three other trees that are "always green" are the juniper, the fir, and the cypress.

spoiled; and the Cherokee do not eat it. The conjurers put the sun another hand-breadth[2] higher in the air, but it was still too hot. They raised it another time, and another, until it was seven handbreadths high and just under the sky arch. Then it was right, and they left it so. This is why the conjurers call the highest place Gûlkwâ′gine Di′gălûñ′lătiyûñ′ (gul kwô′ gē nä̆   dē′ gol un(g) lot ē yun(g′)), "the seventh height," because it is seven handbreadths above the earth. Every day the sun goes along under this arch, and returns at night on the upper side to the starting place.

There is another world under this, and it is like ours in everything—animals, plants, and people—save that the seasons are different. The streams that come down from the mountains are the trails by which we reach this underworld, and the springs at their heads are the doorways by which we enter it, but to do this one must fast and go to water and have one of the underground people for a guide. We know that the seasons in the underworld are different from ours, because the water in the springs is always warmer in winter and cooler in summer than the outer air.

When the animals and plants were first made—we do not know by whom—they were told to watch and keep awake for seven nights, just as young men now fast and keep awake when they pray to their medicine.[3] They tried to do this, and nearly all were awake through the first night, but the next night several dropped off to sleep, and the third night others were asleep, and then others, until, on the seventh night, of all the animals only the owl, the panther, and one or two more were still awake. To these were given the power to see and to go about in the dark, and to make prey of the birds and animals which must sleep at night. Of the trees only the cedar, the pine, the spruce, the holly, and the laurel were awake to the end, and to them it was given to be always green and to be greatest for medicine, but to the others it was said: "Because you have not endured to the end you shall lose your hair every winter."

Men came after the animals and plants. At first there were only a brother and sister until he struck her with a fish and told her to multiply, and so it was. In seven days a child was born to her, and thereafter every seven days another, and they increased very fast until there was danger that the world could not keep them. Then it was made that a woman should have only one child in a year, and it has been so ever since.

---

2. A *hand-breadth* is a unit of measurement based on the width of a hand. It varies from 2½ to 4 inches.

3. Many Native American cultures believe that each plant, animal, and human has its own natural spirit that gives it power. *Medicine*, in this instance, refers to this spirit.

Vocabulary
conjurer (kon′ jər ər) *n.* one who performs magic; sorcerer

Reading *Minilesson*

Drawing Conclusions Remind students that creation myths are a culture's attempt to make sense of the world. The myth's details reflect how the culture interprets the world. Thus the crawfish has his meat "spoiled" in "How the World Was Made" to reflect the Cherokee aversion to eating crawfish.

Activity Have students select details from "How the World Was Made" and draw conclusions about what these details suggest about Cherokee culture. *(For example, students may say that the legend about the animals shows that the Cherokee were careful observers of nocturnal animals.)* **L2**

Additional Resources
📁 *Reading Workbook,* pp. 7–8

Sky Woman, 1936. Ernest Smith. Oil on canvas, 24¼ x 18⅛ in. Rochester Museum & Science Center, Rochester, NY.

50

The Sky Tree

(Huron—Eastern Woodland)

Retold by Joseph Bruchac

IN THE BEGINNING, EARTH WAS COVERED with water. In Sky Land, there were people living as they do now on Earth. In the middle of that land was the great Sky Tree. All of the food which the people in that Sky Land ate came from the great tree. The old chief of that land lived with his wife, whose name was Aataentsic, meaning "Ancient Woman," in their longhouse near the great tree. It came to be that the old chief became sick and nothing could cure him. He grew weaker and weaker until it seemed he would die. Then a dream came to him and he called Aataentsic to him.

"I have dreamed," he said, "and in my dream I saw how I can be healed. I must be given the fruit which grows at the very top of Sky Tree. You must cut it down and bring that fruit to me."

Aataentsic took her husband's stone ax and went to the great tree. As soon as she struck it, it split in half and toppled over. As it fell a hole opened in Sky Land and the tree fell through the hole. Aataentsic returned to the place where the old chief waited.

"My husband," she said, "when I cut the tree it split in half and then fell through a great hole. Without the tree, there can be no life. I must follow it."

Then, leaving her husband she went back to the hole in Sky Land and threw herself after the great tree.

As Aataentsic fell, Turtle looked up and saw her. Immediately Turtle called together all the water animals and told them what she had seen.

"What should be done?" Turtle said.

Beaver answered her. "You are the one who saw this happen. Tell us what to do."

"All of you must dive down," Turtle said. "Bring up soil from the bottom, and place it on my back."

Immediately all of the water animals began to dive down and bring up soil. Beaver, Mink, Muskrat, and Otter each brought up pawfuls of wet soil and placed the soil on the Turtle's back until they had made an island of great size. When they were through, Aataentsic settled down gently on the new Earth and the pieces of the great tree fell beside her and took root.

Did You Know?
A *longhouse* was a bark-covered communal home that could have space for as many as ten families as well as rooms for meetings and religious ceremonies.

E Critical Thinking

INFERRING Ask students to describe the relationship Turtle has with the other animals. From these descriptions, what can be inferred about her character? What position is Turtle likely to hold? *(Turtle must hold an esteemed position. She seems wise, understanding, and respectful. An experienced leader, she asks for the other animals' suggestions. She is counted on to solve the problem.)*

F Literary Elements

ANTHROPOMORPHISM Have students reread this last section of the myth. Ask students to list the animals' human attributes and write them on the board. Explain that these are examples of anthropomorphism. *(Turtle calls the animals together; Turtle recalls and tells what she has seen; Turtle and Beaver speak; Turtle recognizes that there is a problem; Beaver recognizes that Turtle is a leader; Turtle solves the problem; all of the other animals understand and complete the task.)*

Thematic Focus

Beginnings and Change Creation myths are closely tied to Native American religious beliefs and their respect for nature and the natural world. Have students discuss other creation accounts they have heard. How do creation myths demonstrate attitudes and beliefs?

✔ ASSESSMENT OPTIONS

📁 *Quick Checks,* p. 4

MEETING INDIVIDUAL NEEDS — MULTIPLE LEARNING STYLES

Bodily-Kinesthetic Students who think through somatic sensations often learn best when they approach a text in a nonlinguistic fashion. Performing, including pantomime, can be an effective learning tool for these and other students.

Activity Assemble students in small groups; then ask them to perform the events of "The Sky Tree," a relatively simple origin myth, in pantomine. Ask students to pretend that this pantomime will be performed at an important Native American cultural ceremony. Emphasize that the purpose of this pantomime is to present a basic outline of the myth to the audience.

L1 COLLAB. LEARN.

FINE ART — TRANSPARENCY 2

You may want to use **Fine Art Transparency 2** to discuss ancient time.

Personal Response

The most memorable passages will differ from student to student.

ANALYZING LITERATURE

1. Water-beetle dived into the water and brought up soft mud that grew into the earth. The Cherokee have respect even for the smallest of creatures.

2. The sun is too hot, so the conjurers move it seven hand-breadths above the earth. The conjurers are those able to perform feats of magic.

3. The myths explain the birth of mountains, the course of the sun across the sky, why trees lose their leaves, and why women bear only one child in a year.

4. The Cherokee believe all living things are equally important and interdependent. For example, they believe that the animals have/had a major role in the creation of Earth.

5. These phrases enhance the myth by making it more reverent, more mysterious; the unexplained phenomena elicit a certain respect from the reader.

6. The Sky Tree provided food for the inhabitants of Sky Land.

7. She cut down the Sky Tree because her husband believed the fruit at the top of the tree would cure his illness. This tells us that she would go to great lengths to obey her husband and make him well. In doing so, she risked the lives of all the Sky Land inhabitants, who depended on the tree.

8. Water animals brought up mud from underwater, put it on Turtle's back, and made an island. Aataentsic settled on Earth, and the pieces of the great tree fell beside her and took root. The imagery used to describe Earth includes "wet soil," "an island of great size," and "pieces of the great tree."

9. No, because his wife would not have cut down the Sky Tree, the hole would not have formed, and the water animals would not have created Earth. Because of the myth's positive tone, students may think the chief's dream came true.

10. Considering that Turtle was wise and that Earth was constructed on her back, she must occupy an important, respected position in Huron lore. Inclusion in a work of art would suggest the turtle's significance in the Huron's story of creation.

Responding to Literature

Personal Response

What passages from the myths are the most memorable to you? Why?

——— ANALYZING LITERATURE ———

How The World Was Made

RECALL AND INTERPRET

1. What is Water-beetle's role in the creation of Earth? What does this tell you about Cherokee reverence for all creatures?

2. What do the "conjurers" do? Who do you think the "conjurers" are? Explain.

3. Name three natural phenomena explained in this myth. Why might people create stories about how such things came to be?

EVALUATE AND CONNECT

4. For the Cherokee people, are humans more important than plants and animals, or are humans equal to them? Give examples from the myth to support your view.

5. At some points, the narrator says "No one remembers" or "We do not know." How do you think these phrases enhance the myth? Explain.

The Sky Tree

RECALL AND INTERPRET

6. Why was the Sky Tree important to the inhabitants of Sky Land?

7. Why does the old woman try to cut down the Sky Tree? What does this tell you?

8. According to the myth, how was the Earth formed? What **imagery** (see page R8) is used to describe Earth in the myth?

EVALUATE AND CONNECT

9. Theme Connections   Would this great beginning have occurred without the old chief's dream? Do you think his dream comes true?

10. Consider Turtle's role in this myth. If you saw a turtle in a Huron work of art, what might be its meaning within the work?

——— EXTENDING YOUR RESPONSE ———

Writing About Literature

Comparison of the Myths   Both selections tell how life on Earth came to be. Write a paragraph that compares and contrasts one of the following aspects of the myths: what life was like before Earth was created; how the sky and Earth are described; significant roles played by plants, animals, or humans.

Creative Writing

Your Own Myth   Using these two myths as a model, write an origin myth of your own about some element of nature. Tell what the world was like before this element existed. Tell how it came to be and how it made the world different. For ideas, think about the reactions to nature you shared in the Focus Activity on page 47.

📖 **Save your work for your portfolio.**

✔ ASSESSMENT OPTIONS

📁 **Quick Checks,** p. 4

📁 **Selection and Theme Assessment,** pp. 7–8

📁 **Performance Assessment,** p. 4

💾 **Testmaker**

ECOLOGY CONNECTION

Living in Harmony with Nature

The story of the Sky Tree reflects Native American understanding of and appreciation for the interdependence of all parts of nature. **Ecology** is the study of the relationship among plants, animals, and people and their environments.

In nature, a community of living things and its environment is called an **ecosystem.** A pond, for example, is an ecosystem. The microscopic life-forms, plants, insects, fish, birds, and animals that live in or near the pond or that visit the pond are all part of that ecosystem.

The living things in an ecosystem all pass through cycles of birth, reproduction, consumption, and death. Under normal circumstances, these cycles maintain a balance, but external influences can throw the cycles out of balance.

The North American prairie, for example, once consisted of millions of acres of grassland; it was the home of free-grazing bison and antelope. Natural predators such as wolves controlled the bison and antelope populations. Native Americans also helped by killing what they needed for food, clothing, and shelter.

As the United States expanded, bison, in particular, were killed by the tens of thousands. As settlers fenced the prairie for cattle and sheep, the remaining bison were forced into smaller areas. Starvation and disease devastated the bison herds.

Meanwhile, herds of cattle and sheep grazed countless acres of prairie grasses down to the bare ground. In other areas, farmers plowed up the prairie in order to plant crops. Without the deep-rooted grasses to anchor it, wind and rain eroded the rich topsoil. The once-fertile prairie was transformed into the "Dust Bowl" when a drought in the early 1930s attacked the already struggling ecosystem. Thousands of families lost their farms after watching their soil—and their life's work—blow away.

Decades later, ecologists are still learning how to maintain an ecological balance on the prairie. The North American prairie will never be what it once was. Perhaps through careful use, however, the plants, animals, and people that depend on one another for survival can find a balance.

Activity

 List the ways in which humans have affected the ecosystem of the North American prairie. Then work with a small group to do the following.

- Discuss what people might have done to maintain rather than destroy the prairie ecosystem.
- Find out how farmers and ranchers are maintaining the balance of the prairie's ecosystem today.

Teaching Options

ECOLOGY CONNECTION

Objective
- To investigate the balance among plants, animals, and humans

Teaching Strategies
Before they read, have students name some ways that the Cherokee and Huron respect nature. Then have students read this selection silently and discuss how the delicate balance of nature has been disrupted in the United States.

Activity
- Responses may include crop rotation and the planting of cover crops, rotating grazing pastures, planting shelterbelts, and terracing.
- Students' research should reveal that some farmers and ranchers are adopting no-till farming methods and that government policies no longer encourage fence-row-to-fence-row planting. As smaller family farms are bought up by larger corporate farming operations, however, many of the conservation methods used by individual farmers and ranchers are being discontinued.

MEETING INDIVIDUAL NEEDS — MULTIPLE LEARNING STYLES

Spatial Spatial learners may enjoy preparing maps for the class to use in discussing conservation in the Great Plains.

Activity Organize the class into groups of three or four students. Have each group prepare a map to give the class a visual representation of information about the Great Plains. Possible titles may include the following:

- Buffalo Grazing Lands—1850 and Today
- Acres in Federal Land Conservation Programs
- Native American Lands—1850 and Today
- Acres Devoted to Grazing in the Great Plains
- Acres Devoted to Growing Crops in the Great Plains **L2 COLLAB. LEARN.**

Objectives

- To read and analyze a constitution that charts a new beginning
- To identify repetition in The Iroquois Constitution
- To write an analysis of Iroquois values as revealed in their laws and procedures

Skills

Reading/Thinking: Synthesizing; Drawing Conclusions

Motivating

 →OPTIONS

Literature Launchers:
"Laying Down the Laws"

Videodisc Side A, Segment 2

Also available in VHS.

Selection Focus Transparency 5: Have students view the transparency and then answer the question provided.

Focus Activity: As an extension of the Focus Activity, have several students list on the board what the word *constitution* means to them. How do constitutions help nations? What may be some drawbacks to a constitution?

Meet Dekanawida

"The Word that I bring is that all peoples shall love one another and live together in peace."
—*Dekanawida*

Dekanawida (dək uhn′ ä wē′ dä), whose name means "Two River Currents Flowing Together," joined together not two, but five warring Iroquois tribes. Traditional accounts of his life vary. Some identify the great leader as a Huron, and others say he was born an Onondaga and later was adopted by the Mohawks. There is no doubt, however, that Dekanawida believed he was predestined to unite the Iroquois nation.

Dekanawida began to fulfill his destiny when he was a teenager. "It is my business to stop the shedding of blood among human beings," he said. Hiawatha, a Mohawk, forged a strong friendship with Dekanawida, and together the two men established an alliance among the Seneca, Cayuga, Oneida, Onondaga, and Mohawk nations. Because Dekanawida was not a gifted speaker, the eloquent Hiawatha presented their plan to the tribes. Once the Iroquois Confederacy was established and his task was completed, Dekanawida mysteriously vanished.

Dekanawida was born around 1550 and vanished around 1600.

FOCUS ACTIVITY

Read the following quotation, imagining that you are listening to Hiawatha speak these words:

"We must unite ourselves into one common band of brothers. We must have but one voice. . . . We must have one fire, one pipe, and one war. This will give us strength."

—*Hiawatha*

QUICKWRITE In your journal, describe your reaction to Hiawatha's call to unite.

SETTING A PURPOSE Read to learn Dekanawida's ideas about unity.

BACKGROUND

The Time and Place

In the 1400s, the Mohawk, Oneida, Onondaga, Cayuga, and Seneca tribes of the Iroquois nation occupied what is now New York State. These tribes continually fought with one another, which made them vulnerable to attack by other warring tribes. Then, around 1570, Dekanawida led them to form the Iroquois Confederacy, also known as the League of Five Nations. Two centuries after its formation, the confederacy came to an end as the remaining members withdrew to Canada or reluctantly settled on U.S. reservation lands.

VOCABULARY PREVIEW

disposition (dis′ pə zish′ ən) *n.* one's general way of thinking or feeling; p. 55

convene (kən vēn′) *v.* to come together; assemble; p. 56

posterity (pos ter′ ə tē) *n.* generations of the future; all of one's descendants; p. 56

progenitor (prō jen′ ə tər) *n.* direct ancestor; originator of an ancestral line; p. 57

mentor (men′ tər) *n.* wise and trusted adviser; p. 57

temper (tem′ pər) *v.* to modify or moderate; soften; p. 57

deliberation (di lib′ ə rā′ shən) *n.* careful consideration; p. 57

RESOURCE MANAGER

Lesson Planning Resource
The *Unit One Planning Guide* (pp. 32–37) provides additional lesson notes and reduced versions of all print resources.

Other Print Resources
- Active Reading Guide, p. 5
- Vocabulary Practice, p. 4
- Reading Workbook, pp. 9–10
- Quick Checks, p. 5

- Selection and Theme Assessment, pp. 9–10
- Performance Assessment, p. 5
- Spanish Summaries, p. 5
- Spanish Translations
- English Language Learners Sourcebook

 Transparencies
- Selection Focus 5
- Literary Elements 4

Technology
 Literature Launchers
Audio Library
Spanish Audio Library
 Glencoe Literature Web Site
 Testmaker

from

The Iroquois Constitution

Dekanawida

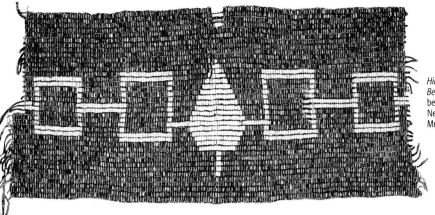

Hiawatha Wampum Belt. Iroquois. Woven beads, 21½ x 10½ in. New York State Museum, Albany.

The Tree of the Great Peace

I am Dekanawida and with the Five Nations' Confederate Lords I plant the Tree of the Great Peace. I plant it in your territory, Adodarho, and the Onondaga Nation, in the territory of you who are Firekeepers.

I name the tree the Tree of the Great Long Leaves. Under the shade of this Tree of the Great Peace we spread the soft white feathery down of the globe thistle[1] as seats for you, Adodarho, and your cousin Lords.

We place you upon those seats, spread soft with the feathery down of the globe thistle, there beneath the shade of the spreading branches of the Tree of Peace. There shall you sit and watch the Council Fire of the Confederacy of the Five Nations, and all the affairs of the Five Nations shall be transacted at this place.

Roots have spread out from the Tree of the Great Peace, one to the north, one to the east, one to the south, and one to the west. The name of these roots is the Great White Roots and their nature is Peace and Strength.

If any man or any nation outside the Five Nations shall obey the laws of the Great Peace and make known their <u>disposition</u> to the Lords of the Confederacy, they may trace the Roots to the Tree and if their minds are clean and they are obedient and promise to obey the wishes of the Confederate Council, they shall be welcomed to take shelter beneath the Tree of the Long Leaves.

---

1. *Globe thistle* is a plant that has prickly leaves and blue flowers. Like a dandelion, the flower becomes a mass of white, silky fuzz, or down, when it goes to seed.

Vocabulary
disposition (dis′ pə zish′ ən) *n.* one's general way of thinking or feeling

FROM THE EARLIEST DAYS 🐾 55

The Chief Firekeeper

At the time of the writing of The Iroquois Constitution, Adodarho was chief of the Onondaga nation. As the Chief Firekeeper, he was called on to decide whether a council should meet when the Confederate Council was not officially in session.

B Critical Thinking

SYNTHESIZING In "The Laws of the Council," Dekanawida discusses the possibility of changes to the law in the future. How is this provision similar to one in the U.S. Constitution? What do we call additions or changes to the U.S. Constitution? Might this constitution have influenced the writing of the U.S. Constitution?

Model: In this section Dekanawida must be talking about changes to the law. I know he uses symbolism, so the beams symbolize the constitution, which is the framework of the law, like the framework that holds up a building. "Added to the Rafters" refers to adding to the constitution. Additions to the U.S. Constitution are called amendments. I think the authors of both constitutions had foresight in realizing that future conditions might warrant new laws. Dekanawida's constitution was written around 1570. It may have influenced the U.S. Constitution, written much later in 1787.

Teaching Options

---

from The Iroquois Constitution

We place at the top of the Tree of the Long Leaves an Eagle who is able to see afar. If he sees in the distance any evil approaching or any danger threatening, he will at once warn the people of the Confederacy.

The Care of the Fire

The Smoke of the Confederate Council Fire shall ever ascend and pierce the sky so that other nations who may be allies may see the Council Fire of the Great Peace.

You, Adodarho, and your thirteen cousin Lords shall faithfully keep the space about the Council Fire clean and you shall allow neither dust nor dirt to accumulate. I lay a Long Wing before you as a broom. As a weapon against a crawling creature I lay a staff with you so that you may thrust it away from the Council Fire.

The Laws of the Council — B

Whenever the Confederate Lords shall assemble for the purpose of holding a council, the Onondaga Lords shall open it by expressing their gratitude to their cousin Lords and greeting them, and they shall make an address and offer thanks to the earth where men dwell, to the streams of water, the pools, the springs and the lakes, to the maize[2] and the fruits, to the medicinal herbs and trees, to the forest trees for their usefulness, to the animals that serve as food and give their pelts for clothing, to the great winds and the lesser winds, to the Thunderers, to the Sun, the mighty warrior, to the moon, to the messengers of the Creator who reveal his wishes and to the Great Creator who dwells in the heavens above, who gives all the things useful to

---

2. *Maize* is corn.

---

men, and who is the source and the ruler of health and life.

All the business of the Five Nations' Confederate Council shall be conducted by the two combined bodies of Confederate Lords. First the question shall be passed upon by the Mohawk and Seneca Lords; then it shall be discussed and passed by the Oneida and Cayuga Lords. Their decisions shall then be referred to the Onondaga Lords (Firekeepers) for final judgment.

When the Council of the Five Nation Lords shall <u>convene</u>, they shall appoint a speaker for the day. He shall be a Lord of either the Mohawk, Onondaga, or Seneca Nation.

No individual or foreign nation interested in a case, question, or proposition shall have any voice in the Confederate Council except to answer a question put to him or them by the speaker for the Lords.

If the conditions which shall arise at any future time call for an addition to or change of this law, the case shall be carefully considered, and if a new beam seems necessary or beneficial, the proposed change shall be voted upon and, if adopted, it shall be called, "Added to the Rafters."[3]

The Clans

Among the Five Nations and their <u>posterity</u> there shall be the following original clans: Great Name Bearer, Ancient Name Bearer,

---

3. The Iroquois leaders thought of their confederacy of five nations as a longhouse, a communal Iroquois dwelling with an east door, a west door, and a central fire. The terms *beam* and *Added to the Rafters* continue this comparison.

Vocabulary
convene (kən vēn′) *v.* to come together; assemble
posterity (pos ter′ ə tē) *n.* generations of the future; all of one's descendants

---

Reading *Minilesson*

Drawing Conclusions Students can draw conclusions about Iroquois society by looking at the values expressed in The Iroquois Constitution.

Activity Have students reread the first paragraph under "The Laws of the Council" and the last paragraph under "The Festivals." Write the following headings on the board: *Relationship with Other Nations, Relationship with Nature,* and *Relationship with the Creator.* Have students list evidence from the reading under each heading and identify any insights about Iroquois society that they can draw from the evidence. **L2**

Additional Resources
📂 *Reading Workbook,* pp. 9–10

Relationships		
Other Nations	**Nature**	**The Creator**
greet politely	thank the earth for streams, etc.	offer thanks
complete union of nations		

Reading & Thinking Skills

Recognizing Bias

Cabeza de Vaca's account of his travels was written for the king of Spain. The explorer hoped to give the king useful information about his discoveries and experiences. His report, how-ever, is not totally objective; it contains bias. **Bias** is "a mental inclination toward some opinion or position." A writer might have many reasons to be biased. Cabeza de Vaca, for example, probably wanted to present the best possible picture of himself as a loyal, courageous, and long-suffering servant of the Spanish king.

Good readers always look for an author's bias. To detect possible author bias, try these methods:

- Identify emotionally charged words. For example, Cabeza de Vaca uses words such as "picture of death," "misery," and "pity" to describe himself and his crew.
- Consider whether the author has a special interest in the issue. Cabeza de Vaca, for example, depended upon the generosity and support of the king for his livelihood. As a result, he wanted the king to think highly of him.
- Analyze the writer's reasoning. Does the writer give reliable evidence for certain claims? Consider Cabeza de Vaca's description of the Indians as "crude and untu-tored" in spite of the fact that they had homes, food, and a comfortable life.
- Look for oversimplification or exaggeration. Cabeza de Vaca describes the Indians as "giants."

Many pieces of writing, especially nonfiction, contain bias. Recognizing bias reminds you that there are differing viewpoints on many issues. Knowing that, you can decide to read fur-ther on an issue to gain a broader perspective.

- For more about related modes of reasoning, see **Reading Handbook,** pp. R86–R93.

EXERCISE

Identifying Bias   Identify any of the following state-ments that you think are biased. Write the word clues that led you to make that decision, and the strategy that helped you recognize the bias.

1. I, Cabeza de Vaca, am willing to perform without question any service for my king.

2. Because the Spaniards were the first Europeans to visit the island, the place and its people rightfully belonged to Spain.

3. Arrogant and careless of his crew's suffering, the cap-tain insisted on setting sail despite the heavy waves and approaching storm.

4. Cabeza de Vaca was the greatest and bravest explorer to visit the Americas.

5. When Lope de Oviedo saw that livestock lived on the island, he knew it was a land occupied by Christians.

Reading & Thinking Skills

Objective

- To identify bias in nonfiction writing

Teaching Strategies

Point out that a writer may exhibit bias in more than one way. Use the following example:

Cabeza de Vaca describes the Indians as "crude and untutored." This is an example of faulty reasoning and what other type of thought? *(Students may say oversimplification.)*

Exercise

1. Biased: The writer uses emotion-ally charged words, oversimplifies, and exaggerates. *without question*

2. Biased: The writer oversimplifies and may have a special interest in the issue; the reasoning is faulty. *Because, rightfully belonged*

3. Biased: The writer uses emotion-ally charged words and faulty reasoning. *Arrogant, careless, insisted, despite*

4. Biased: The writer exaggerates and may have a special interest. *greatest, bravest*

5. Biased: The writer uses faulty reasoning and oversimplifies. *knew*

Additional Resources
📁 *Reading Workbook*

Teaching Options

INCLUSION STRATEGIES

Less-Proficient Readers Review the various types of bias listed, and have students suggest additional examples for each. Point out that newspaper and magazine articles often contain bias. Have students find examples of bias in the media and share these with the class. Discuss the articles together, focusing on the bias in each.

Activity Have students choose a short passage from *La Relación* to rewrite as a bias-free newspaper article. As they draft their articles, have them check the list for any bias in their own writing. Then have students critique each other's writing. **L1**

Additional Resources
📁 *Inclusion Strategies*

Objectives

- To read and analyze an account of the Pilgrims' arrival in America
- To analyze Bradford's diction
- To write about the arrival of the Pilgrims from the Native American perspective

Skills

Reading/Thinking: Using Graphic Aids; Evaluating
Writing: Journal Entry
Grammar/Language: Transitive and Intransitive Verbs

Motivating
→ OPTIONS

Literature Launchers:
"Pilgrim Life"

Videodisc Side A, Segment 1

Also available in VHS.

Selection Focus Transparency 7: Have students view the transparency and then answer the question provided.

Focus Activity: As an extension of the Focus Activity, have students write in their journals about something that they are proud to have endured. Students may wish to keep their journal writing private.

Before You Read
from *Of Plymouth Plantation*

Meet William Bradford

> "All great and honorable actions are accompanied with great difficulties, and must be both enterprised and overcome with answerable courage."
> —*Bradford*

Violent storms tossed the creaking ship and blew it far off course. It was 1620 and the passengers aboard the *Mayflower* were traveling to the Americas. Among the passengers was thirty-year-old William Bradford.

Bradford was orphaned while still an infant and was raised by relatives. As a youth, he studied the Bible, and at about the age of seventeen he became a Separatist. Separatists were Puritans who wanted to break from the Church of England. Bradford and other Separatists decided to establish their own colony in the Americas.

Aboard the *Mayflower* Bradford helped write the Mayflower Compact (the colony's rules of government). In 1621 this group, known today as the Pilgrims, elected Bradford their leader. Although nearly half the colonists died of scurvy, fever, or starvation that first brutal winter, the colony grew into a thriving community under Bradford's leadership.

William Bradford was born in 1590 and died in 1657.

FOCUS ACTIVITY

Think of someone you have read about who has endured very harsh weather or other hardships. What were the main difficulties they faced?

MAP IT! What qualities do you think would help a person endure great hardship? List your ideas in a word web like the one shown.

Facing hardship

SETTING A PURPOSE Read to learn how the Pilgrims faced their hardships.

BACKGROUND

The Time and Place
Ocean travel in seventeenth-century England was hazardous. Ships were made of wood and were easily damaged if they hit shoals (sandbars or shallow spots in the water). Sometimes strong waves caused ships to "seele," or lurch suddenly from side to side. In fierce winds, sails were lowered by heavy ropes called "halyards," and ships would have to "hull" or drift at sea. Storms and wind shifts sometimes made it necessary for the *Mayflower* to change directions ("tack about") and to head for (or "stand for") a different course. Destined for Virginia, the *Mayflower* eventually landed on the coast of what is now Massachusetts.

VOCABULARY PREVIEW

resolve (ri zolv′) *v.* to decide; determine; p. 70
providence (prov′ ə dəns) *n.* divine care or guidance; foresight; p. 70
succor (suk′ ər) *n.* assistance in time of need; relief; p. 71

procure (prə kyo͞or′) *v.* to obtain by care or effort; p. 72
commodity (kə mod′ə tē) *n.* a product or economic good; p. 72
feigned (fānd) *adj.* fictitious; not genuine; p. 72

RESOURCE MANAGER

Lesson Planning Resource
The ***Unit One Planning Guide*** (pp. 44–51) provides additional lesson notes and reduced versions of all print resources.

 Other Print Resources
- Active Reading Guide, p. 7
- Vocabulary Practice, p. 6
- Reading Workbook, p. 13
- Grammar and Language Workbook, p. 55

- Grammar and Composition Handbook, Lesson 1.3
- Quick Checks, p. 7
- Selection and Theme Assessment, pp. 13–14
- Performance Assessment, p. 7
- Spanish Summaries, p. 7
- Inclusion Strategies
- English Language Learners Sourcebook

 Transparencies
- Selection Focus 7
- Literary Elements 6
- Grammar and Language 5

Technology
 Literature Launchers
 Audio Library
 Spanish Audio Library
 Glencoe Literature Web Site
Testmaker

The Landing of the Pilgrims at Plymouth, Mass. Dec. 22nd 1620, 1876. Currier & Ives.
Color lithograph. Museum of the City of New York.

from

Of Plymouth Plantation

William Bradford

SUMMARY

In 1620 the Puritans (Pilgrims) sail in treacherous seas from Holland to Virginia. A storm blows the *Mayflower* off course, and the ship lands in present-day Massachusetts. A few months after their arrival, nearly half of the 100 Pilgrims have died of disease. Native Americans befriend the Pilgrims and return the tools they had previously stolen. Squanto becomes an inter-preter, guide, and teacher to the Pilgrims, who learn to provide for themselves and celebrate the First Thanksgiving after the harvest.

📁 *Spanish Summaries,* p. 7

A Active Reading

CONNECT Have students study the lithograph of the Pilgrims landing at Plymouth and imagine how these people feel. *(No one looks especially happy; some are ill and need to be carried; they don't seem warmly dressed, so they will probably not have an easy time of it. They must be apprehensive.)*

Additional Resources

📁 *Active Reading Guide,* p. 7
🎧 *Audio Library*
🎧 *Spanish Audio Library*

Teaching Options

CONNECTING TO OTHER SELECTIONS

The chart at the right shows three ways to connect this excerpt from *Of Plymouth Plantation* to selections in this book.

For specific teaching strategies, see the **Unit One Planning Guide,** pp. 47–48.

Connection	Title
Life Skills: Supporting and Contributing	→ "Kitchens," p. 1073
Thematic: Overcoming Odds	→ "Frederick Douglass," p. 1146
Literary: Diction	→ "Weaver," p. 1153

B Author's Craft

DICTION Remind students that choice of words is called *diction*. It contributes greatly to Bradford's writing style and voice. How would students describe his style on the basis of his choice of words in this paragraph? *(Bradford writes in the plain language that characterizes the Puritans' sparse, ordinary lifestyle. His tone is direct, with little figurative language.)*

C Active Reading

QUESTION Despite the Pilgrims' suffering and hardships, they did not give up. What do students see as an important force in the Pilgrims' remaining determined despite their suffering? *(Students may focus on the Pilgrims' faith and belief in God that sustained them through hard times.)*

Historical Note

The Puritans held to a strict work ethic. They believed the devil finds work for idle hands. In England the calendar year included about 240 working days, but the Puritans worked at least 300 days a year, taking holidays only on the Sabbath, election day, Harvard commencement day, and public thanksgiving days. The Pilgrim calendar did not include Christmas as a holiday because it was viewed as a pagan remnant.

Teaching Options

---

from Chapter 9
Of Their Voyage, and How They Passed the Sea; and of Their Safe Arrival at Cape Cod

IN SUNDRY[1] OF THESE STORMS the winds were so fierce and the seas so high, as they could not bear a knot of sail, but were forced to hull for divers[2] days together. And in one of them, as they thus lay at hull in a mighty storm, a lusty[3] young man called John Howland, coming upon some occasion above the gratings was, with a seele of the ship, thrown into sea; but it pleased God that he caught hold of the topsail halyards which hung overboard and ran out at length. Yet he held his hold (though he was sundry fathoms under water) till he was hauled up by the same rope to the brim of the water, and then with a boat hook and other means got into the ship again and his life saved. And though he was something ill with it, yet he lived many years after and became a profitable member both in church and commonwealth. In all this voyage there died but one of the passengers, which was William Butten, a youth, servant to Samuel Fuller, when they drew near the coast.

But to omit other things (that I may be brief) after long beating at sea they fell with that land which is called **Cape Cod**; the which being made and certainly known to be it, they were not a little joyful. After some deliberation had amongst themselves and with the master of the ship, they tacked about and <u>resolved</u> to stand for the southward (the wind and weather being fair) to find some place about Hudson's River for their habitation. But after they had sailed that course about half the day, they fell amongst dangerous shoals and roaring breakers, and they were so far entangled therewith as they conceived themselves in great danger; and the wind shrinking upon them withal,[4] they resolved to bear up again for the Cape and thought themselves happy to get out of those dangers before night overtook them, as by God's good <u>providence</u> they did. And the next day they got into the Cape Harbor where they rid[5] in safety. . . .

Being thus arrived in a good harbor, and brought safe to land, they fell upon their knees and blessed the God of Heaven who had brought them over the vast and furious ocean, and delivered them from all the perils and miseries thereof, again to set their feet on the firm and stable earth, their proper element. And no marvel if they were thus joyful, seeing wise Seneca[6] was so affected with sailing a few miles on the coast of his own Italy, as he affirmed, that he had rather remain twenty years on his way by land than pass by sea to any place in a short time, so tedious and dreadful was the same unto him.

But here I cannot but stay and make a pause, and stand half amazed at this poor people's present condition; and so I think will the

Did You Know?
Cape Cod is a point of land on the east coast of Massachusetts.

---

1. *Sundry* refers to an indefinite number.
2. *Divers* means "several."
3. *Lusty* here means "strong."

4. *Also* is another word for *withal.*
5. *Rid* means "rode."
6. *Seneca* was a Roman philosopher and writer.

Vocabulary
resolve (ri zolv′) *v.* to decide; determine
providence (prov′ ə dəns) *n.* divine care or guidance; foresight

70 ❧ UNIT 1

Grammar and Language *Minilesson*

Transitive and Intransitive Verbs
Point out that transitive verbs take a direct object (Mary *gave* the gift) and that intransitive verbs have no object (John *lived* in Maine).

Activity Write the following sentences from Bradford's account on the board, and have students determine whether the verbs are transitive or intransitive.

1. He <u>lived</u> for many years after. *(intransitive)*
2. He <u>told</u> them also of another Indian. *(transitive)*
3. They <u>began</u> now to gather in the small harvest they had. *(intransitive)*

Then ask students to write four sentences of their own, two with transitive verbs and two with intransitive verbs. **L2**

Additional Resources

📖 *Grammar and Language Transparency 5*

📕 *Grammar and Language Workbook,* p. 55

📕 *Grammar and Composition Handbook,* Lesson 1.3

📕 *Writer's Choice,* Lesson 10.3

70

reader, too, when he well considers the same. Being thus passed the vast ocean, and a sea of troubles before in their preparation (as may be remembered by that which went before), they had now no friends to welcome them nor inns to entertain or refresh their weatherbeaten bodies; no houses or much less towns to repair to, to seek for succor. It is recorded in Scripture[7] as a mercy to the Apostle and his shipwrecked company, that the barbarians showed them no small kindness in refreshing them, but these savage barbarians, when they met with them (as after will appear) were readier to fill their sides full of arrows than otherwise. And for the season it was winter, and they that know the winters of that country know them to be sharp and violent, and subject to cruel and fierce storms, dangerous to travel to known places, much more to search an unknown coast.

from Chapter 11
The Starving Time

But that which was most sad and lamentable was, that in two or three months' time half of their company died, especially in January and February, being the depth of winter, and wanting houses and other comforts; being infected with the scurvy[8] and other diseases which this long voyage and their inaccommodate condition had brought upon them. So as there died some times two or three of a day in the foresaid time, that of 100 and odd persons, scarce fifty remained. And of these, in the time of most distress, there was but six or seven sound persons who to their great commendations, be it spoken, spared no pains

---

7. The reference here to *Scripture,* or the Bible, is Acts of the Apostles 28, which tells of the kindness shown to St. Paul and his companions by the natives of Malta after they were shipwrecked on that island.
8. A severe lack of vitamin C causes a disease called *scurvy.*

night nor day, but with abundance of toil and hazard of their own health, fetched them wood, made them fires, dressed them meat, made their beds, washed their loathsome clothes, clothed and unclothed them. In a word, did all the homely[9] and necessary offices for them which dainty and queasy stomachs cannot endure to hear named; and all this willingly and cheerfully, without any grudging in the least, showing herein their true love unto their friends and brethren; a rare example and worthy to be remembered. Two of these seven were Mr. William Brewster, their reverend Elder, and Myles Standish, their Captain and military commander, unto whom myself and many others were much beholden in our low and sick condition. And yet the Lord so upheld these persons as in this general calamity they were not at all infected either with sickness or lameness. . . .

Indian Relations

All this while the Indians came skulking about them, and would sometimes show themselves aloof off, but when any approached near them, they would run away; and once they [the Indians] stole away their [the colonists'] tools where they had been at work and were gone to dinner. But about the 16th of March, a certain Indian came boldly amongst them and spoke to them in broken English, which they could well understand but marveled at it. At length they understood by discourse with him, that he was not of these parts, but belonged to the eastern parts where some English ships came to fish, with whom he was acquainted and could name sundry of them by their names, amongst whom he had got his language. He became profitable to them in acquainting them with many things

---

9. *Homely* here means "domestic."

Vocabulary
succor (suk′ ər) *n.* assistance in time of need; relief

D **Literary Elements**

ALLUSION In this section, Bradford is referring, or alluding, to scripture from the Bible. Have students read the first 10 verses of Acts, Chapter 28, and find similarities between the Apostle Paul's experience on the island of Malta and the situation of William Bradford. Why would Bradford allude to this passage? *(Possibly Bradford felt like Paul; Bradford and the Apostle encountered "barbarians" who, at first, were intimidating but who turned out to be hospitable. In both cases, the so-called barbarians cared for the newcomers by building them fires, feeding them, and keeping them warm in the cold weather.)*

E **Literary Elements**

POINT OF VIEW Throughout the selection, Bradford writes as if he were not present during these experiences. What might be his reason for using the third person plural "they" instead of writing this as a first-person narrative? *(Possibly he wants to focus on the group as a whole rather than have his writing be viewed as a personal narrative. He wants to emphasize the Puritan ethic of community above self.)*

Reading *Minilesson*

Using Graphic Aids Maps and time lines can help students gain perspective on the difficulties of the Pilgrims' travels. After students have read the selection, have them create a time line of its events.

Activity Tell students that William Bradford grew up in Yorkshire, England, and then moved with other Separatists to the nearby town of Scrooby. Fearing persecution, the group then crossed the North Sea to Holland. After 12 years there, the group sailed to the New World, landing at Cape Cod. Hand out a map that shows the U.S., the Atlantic Ocean, England, and Holland, and have students trace Bradford's travels. **L2**

Additional Resources
📁 *Reading Workbook* p. 13

F **Critical Thinking**

EVALUATING After they have read the six terms of peace agreed to by Massasoit and the Pilgrims, have students evaluate the benefits of this new friendship to both the Pilgrims and the Native Americans.

Model: As a Native American, I have everything to lose but may want to help the Pilgrims in their time of need. If I follow this peace agreement, I will gain friends and be doing the right thing. As a Pilgrim, I have nothing to lose but my life. I could gain food, a home, and a future. The Native Americans can show me how to live here. Therefore, I think the Pilgrims have the most to gain from this agreement.

Thematic Focus

Beginnings and Change If students had lived during the seventeenth century and been given the opportunity to come to this new land, would they have come? Discuss the reasons given.

✔ ASSESSMENT OPTIONS

📁 *Quick Checks*, p. 7

Teaching Options

---

concerning the state of the country in the east parts where he lived, which was afterwards profitable unto them; as also of the people here, of their names, number and strength, of their situation and distance from this place, and who was chief amongst them. His name was Samoset. He told them also of another Indian whose name was Squanto, a native of this place, who had been in England and could speak better English than himself.

Being, after some time of entertainment and gifts dismissed, a while after he came again, and five more with him, and they brought again all the tools that were stolen away before, and made way for the coming of their great Sachem, called Massasoit. Who, about four or five days after, came with the chief of his friends and other attendance, with the aforesaid Squanto. With whom, after friendly entertainment and some gifts given him, they made a peace with him (which hath now continued this 24 years) in these terms:

F **1.** That neither he nor any of his should injure or do hurt to any of their people.

2. That if any of his did hurt to any of theirs, he should send the offender, that they might punish him.

3. That if anything were taken away from any of theirs, he should cause it to be restored; and they should do the like to his.

4. If any did unjustly war against him, they would aid him; if any did war against them, he should aid them.

5. He should send to his neighbors confederates to certify them of this, that they might not wrong them, but might be likewise comprised in the conditions of peace.

6. That when their men came to them, they should leave their bows and arrows behind them.

After these things he returned to his place called Sowams, some 40 miles from this place, but Squanto continued with them and was their interpreter and was a special instrument sent of God for their good beyond their expectation. He directed them how to set their corn, where to take fish, and to <u>procure</u> other <u>commodities</u>, and was also their pilot to bring them to unknown places for their profit, and never left them till he died.

from Chapter 12
First Thanksgiving

They began now to gather in the small harvest they had, and to fit up their houses and dwellings against winter, being all well recovered in health and strength and had all things in good plenty. For as some were thus employed in affairs abroad, others were exercised in fishing, about cod and bass and other fish, of which they took good store, of which every family had their portion. All the summer there was no want; and now began to come in store of fowl, as winter approached, of which this place did abound when they came first (but afterward decreased by degrees). And besides waterfowl there was great store of wild turkeys, of which they took many, besides venison, etc. Besides they had about a peck of meal a week to a person, or now since harvest, Indian corn to that proportion. Which made many afterwards write so largely of their plenty here to their friends in England, which were not <u>feigned</u> but true reports.

Vocabulary
procure (prə kyōōr´) *v.* to obtain by care or effort
commodity (kə mod´ə tē) *n.* a product or economic good; an article of trade
feigned (fānd) *adj.* fictitious; not genuine

ENGLISH LANGUAGE LEARNERS
MEETING INDIVIDUAL NEEDS

Interpretation English language learners may have difficulty interpreting Bradford's writing. Explain that he uses archaic English expressions that can also be difficult for native English speakers to understand.

Activity Pair each English language learner with a fluent English speaker. Each pair should read through the selection, focusing on sections of Bradford's writing that they have difficulty interpreting. Pairs should write down in their own words what they think Bradford is saying. Then have the entire class share their interpretations.

Additional Resources
📁 *English Language Learners Sourcebook*

Responding to Literature

Personal Response

What was your reaction to Bradford's experiences?

——— ANALYZING LITERATURE ———

RECALL AND INTERPRET

1. Theme Connections   What hardships did the Pilgrims face aboard the *Mayflower* and in Plymouth? Do you think the Pilgrims were skilled at adapting to unexpected changes? Explain.
2. Explain how the Pilgrims survived during "the Starving Time." What do Bradford's comments reveal about the Pilgrims?
3. What did Samoset and Squanto accomplish? Explain the effects of their actions on the Pilgrims. Give examples to support your response.
4. Compare the time of plenty in "the First Thanksgiving" to the Pilgrims' situation in "the Starving Time." What do you think might have happened to the Pilgrims without Squanto's help?

EVALUATE AND CONNECT

5. Think about your response to the Focus Activity on page 68. In your opinion, were the Pilgrims' qualities of endurance similar to those you listed? Use evidence from the selection to support your views.
6. Which episode from Bradford's account did you find the most interesting? Why?
7. In what ways might Bradford's narrative have meaning for people today? Explain your response.
8. Do you think that the celebration of Thanksgiving today has a strong connection to the experiences of the Pilgrims on the First Thanksgiving? Explain.

Literary ELEMENTS

Diction

Diction is the choice of words used by a writer. Bradford's diction reflects the language that was used in the seventeenth century. Many of the words and expressions he chose are rarely used in present-day writing. Also, compared with most writers today, Bradford uses long, complicated sentences.

1. Explain what you think the following sentence means: ". . . after long beating at sea they *fell with* that land. . . ."
2. Choose one of Bradford's long, complicated sentences with archaic words and reword it in language used today.

 See **Literary Terms Handbook**, p. R5.

——— EXTENDING YOUR RESPONSE ———

Creative Writing

Another Viewpoint   Imagine that you are one of the Native Americans who first encountered William Bradford and the other Pilgrims. What might be your impression of their arrival? How might you react to the newcomers' clothing and language? Record your observations and descriptions as a journal entry.

Performing

You Are There   Choose an event from Bradford's narrative and retell it to the class in the form of a dramatic monologue. Speak as if you were Bradford, but use modern language. If you would like, you may present your monologue to the class as a poem or rap.

 Save your work for your portfolio.

Personal Response

Students' responses to Bradford's experiences should display an understanding of the Pilgrims' hardships.

ANALYZING LITERATURE

1. Aboard ship they experienced harsh weather. On land they encountered a barren landscape, the lack of building materials, the onset of winter, and death. However, those who survived adapted to their new surroundings, supported by their faith in God and help from Native Americans.
2. Only six or seven people were well enough to care for the sick and dying. Bradford's comments reveal that the Pilgrims believed that they would be sustained if they cared for one another.
3. They helped unite two vastly different groups of people. They taught the Pilgrims how to survive in a new land, how to feed themselves, and how to build shelters.
4. During "the Starving Time" the Pilgrims were alone in an unfamiliar, strange land. By the time of "the First Thanksgiving," however, the Pilgrims had received help from Native Americans in growing food, had built shelters, and had made a peace agreement with the Native Americans. Without Squanto's help, all or most of the remaining Pilgrims might have died.
5. Students' lists of qualities for endurance should be similar to those exhibited by the Pilgrims.
6. Students may mention the help the Puritans received from the Native Americans, the first Thanksgiving, or other episodes.
7. Bradford's account has historical, inspirational, and religious significance.
8. It relates to today's celebration in that at Thanksgiving some people express gratitude for the privileges of a free country and a time to share with others.

✔ ASSESSMENT OPTIONS

🗀 *Quick Checks,* p. 7
🗀 *Selection and Theme Assessment,* pp. 13–14
🗀 *Performance Assessment,* p. 7
💾 *Testmaker*

LITERARY ELEMENTS

1. After being at sea for a long time, they finally came to land.
2. Responses should demonstrate reason and logic.

Additional Resources

  Literary Elements Transparency 6

Objectives

- To use a camcorder and other video equipment to create a video
- To adapt a literary work to a visual medium

Teaching Strategies

As a motivational introduction to this feature, show students a short film adaptation of a literary work. Point out how the visual and audio elements work together in the film to help convey the work's meaning.

Remind students to read the operating instructions to become familiar with the camera's operation. As they practice with the camera, the features of the camera can help generate creative ideas and help students avoid mistakes during filming. Remind students to read all safety rules and tips before they begin operating any equipment.

Point out that filmmakers generally use a logical progression in the sequence of shots. Moving from a *long shot* to a *medium shot* to a *close-up* and the reverse are effective techniques. Note that long shots allow the audience to see the entire set. Medium shots can highlight important physical elements of a scene. Close-ups help the audience recognize who is speaking and see facial expressions that show emotion.

Technology Skills

Using a Video Camera

Video cameras, or camcorders, are often used to record major life events—births, graduations, weddings, and holiday celebrations. A video camera also allows you the chance to respond to your reading in a way that stretches your imagination as you help create a work of art.

Choosing the Literature

Think over the literature selections you've read in class this year. Work with a group to choose a selection that provides material for an impressive video. Use the literature as a basis for the video, but don't feel you have to follow the writer's work exactly.

Using a Video Camera

TRY THIS TECHNIQUE	COMMENTS
Use a tripod	If you've ever gotten seasick watching a video of a family picnic, then you know the importance of a steady camera.
Lean against something	When a tripod is unavailable, try balancing yourself against something steady, like a wall or a piece of heavy furniture.
Experiment with the camera before you start filming	The time to push buttons is before you have actors on the set. Simulate filming conditions before shooting begins. The great thing about videotape is that you can try something over and over again on the same tape until you get it right.
Keep each scene short	Long, drawn-out scenes can be boring. Actors should stop at least every five minutes so you can move the camera to other angles, change to close-ups, or otherwise vary the shot.
Keep actors' faces visible	Unless the scene calls for the back of someone's head, keep the actors turned toward the camera.
Make sure your viewfinder image makes sense	When you zoom in or move the camera close to the actors, make sure the audience can see who is talking. Don't worry about keeping all the actors visible all the time.
Use cut-aways or cut-ins	When you just turn the camera off at the end of filming a scene, the next scene pops up in the video as if by magic. To avoid this, try panning to an inanimate object before turning the camera off, or focus on an inanimate object before filming the next action.
Don't "overzoom"	Constant zooming in and out disorients the viewer.
Experiment with composition	Practice various angles to achieve different effects. If you stand on a chair and shoot a scene from above, viewers feel they are listening in. If the camera is tilted away from horizontal, viewers will feel uneasy. Also, try to vary the position of the main subject within the frame.

 TECHNOLOGY TIP

The closer the camera gets to a specific actor, the closer the relationship he or she develops with the audience. Such camera work can help point out the main character.

Manuals and Specialized Vocabulary
Point out that manuals and operating instructions accompany audio/video (A/V) equipment. These manuals vary in clarity and may have been written in another language and then translated into English.

Activity Have students read the operating instructions for equipment they will use. Instruct them to take notes about any specialized vocabulary that may be unfamiliar. Then have each film team

meet and discuss terms or instructions that need explanation or clarification. Tell the groups to move ahead with their planning when they are sure that every member adequately comprehends his or her function as part of the filmmaking crew. **L2**

Making the Movie

Step 1: Planning

The most important (and longest) stage is planning. Time spent getting ready reduces the need for retakes and makes editing easier. Planning is best handled by several groups:

- **Script**   A script-writing team needs good writers, students who can envision each scene and the finished product, and a leader who can motivate others to stay on task and meet deadlines.
- **Storyboard**   This series of sketches translates the script into images and sounds. Each crucial shot has a sketch with the accompanying audio written beside it. The storyboarders work to maintain a consistent flow from scene to scene.
- **Equipment**   The equipment team locates, acquires, uses, maintains, and returns all necessary equipment. The group prepares for every need, from batteries and extension cords to extra recording tape and props. The group also develops a contingency plan in case something breaks. Each equipment team member should learn how to operate each piece of equipment.

Step 2: Rehearsal and Videotaping

The filming phase is often enjoyable, but it can have its pitfalls. Filming requires that all elements focused upon in the planning stage come together smoothly.

- **Actors**   All actors must memorize their lines from the script. They must also know the storyboard well enough to move through each scene. Actors need to rehearse until they can work smoothly with one another and with the crew.
- **Crew**   The crew includes a camera operator, several people to set up and monitor lighting and sound, and an equipment manager. You may also require people to work on makeup, costumes, and props.
- **Direction**   The direction team oversees all aspects of filming—the performance of the actors, the positioning of the camera, the length of scenes. It's best to have only one person as director. That person should make decisions based on input from several assistants.

Step 3: Editing and Final Production

The final product is created in the editing stage. Unnecessary takes are removed, and titles, credits, and music are added. Because editing equipment varies, the editing team should book training time with an A/V professional during the planning stage.

ACTIVITIES

1. Show your completed video to another class and get their response.

2. Produce a video illustrating literature concepts for younger viewers.

3. Volunteer to film activities at a local community center or a facility for the elderly.

Activities

After students have read the Using a Video Camera section, discuss the directions with the class to be certain that everyone understands how to complete the project. Answer any questions students have about the assignment or the equipment. You might ask an A/V professional to visit the class, assist with technical questions, and monitor hands-on experimentation with the equipment. *Students' films should:*

- demonstrate the group's ability to work together effectively as a unit and include a list of credits identifying the function or contribution of each member to the overall production.
- reflect thorough planning and the use of imagination in adapting a written work to the sound film medium.
- demonstrate adequate mastery of the available technology.
- include a series of scenes that flow continuously and, in combination, constitute a unified work.

TechnoTalk

Ready on the Set   Clear communication among cast and crew is essential to film production. Have students familiarize themselves with basic movie terms. Terms they might learn and discuss before filming include *places*, *marks*, *scene*, *take*, *lights*, *camera*, *action*, *prompt*, and *cut*. Suggest that they create a glossary of film terms for group members.

MEETING INDIVIDUAL NEEDS — MULTIPLE LEARNING STYLES

Spatial   Students with acute spatial abilities may respond well to tasks that involve synthesizing the diverse elements within a scene. Other group members can benefit from their ability and use their suggestions as springboards to generate other creative ideas.

Activity   Have students review the text of the literary work and create drawings that illustrate how they visualize the physical setting within which the action takes place. Tell the group to discuss these drawings, add new ideas as appropriate, and use the illustrations to design the movie set(s). Remind them of the practical limitations that cost and availability of materials place on independent filmmakers. Note that imagination frequently can overcome such obstacles. **L2**

Objectives

- To read and analyze two lyric poems
- To understand the use of extended metaphor
- To write a poetry review

Skills

Reading/Thinking: Predicting
Writing: Poem
Grammar/Language: Adjectives
Collaboration: Literature Groups; Designing a Quilt; Performing an Oral Reading

Reading Further

Be sure to review this title for appropriateness for your class before recommending it to students.

Cavanaugh, Jack. *Puritans: An American Family Portrait.* Colorado Springs: Chariot Victor Books, 1994. This historical fiction highlights the Morgan family's struggle against persecution in England and the family's efforts to come to America.

 # Before You Read

Upon the Burning of Our House and
To My Dear and Loving Husband

Meet Anne Bradstreet

"[Anne Bradstreet wrote] . . . the first good poems in America, while rearing eight children, lying frequently sick, keeping house at the edge of the wilderness, [and] managed a poet's range and extension within confines as severe as any American poet has confronted."

—*Adrienne Rich*

Anne Bradstreet wrote poems whenever she could—while caring for teething infants or mending clothes by the fire at night. She is remarkable not only because she was essentially the first American poet, but also because she composed her poems during a time when writing was considered an unsuitable occupation for a woman.

Bradstreet grew up in England, where she was educated by her father, Thomas Dudley. When she was eighteen, she traveled to the Massachusetts Bay Colony with her husband Simon and her parents to join the Puritan community there. Without her knowledge, her brother-in-law collected her poems and had them published in England under the title of *The Tenth Muse Lately Sprung Up in America.* Her best works explore her love for her husband, her sadness at the death of her parents and other family members, and her struggle to accept as God's will the losses she suffered.

Anne Bradstreet was born in 1612 and died in 1672.

FOCUS ACTIVITY

Think about something you own that you treasure. How would you feel if you lost that cherished object?

JOURNAL In your journal, write a short paragraph describing the object and your possible reaction to its loss.

SETTING A PURPOSE Read to find out the speaker's reactions to losing something she cherishes and her comments about someone she treasures.

BACKGROUND

The Time and Place

In seventeenth-century New England, poetry was acceptable reading for Puritans only if it was religious. However, as a Puritan, Anne Bradstreet viewed all events within the context of God's divine plan. She found similarities between the domestic details of daily life and the spiritual details of her religious life. Unlike traditional verse of her day, Bradstreet's poems speak of everyday occurrences and personal emotions. With directness and sincerity, Anne Bradstreet recorded both her earthly concerns and the Puritan faith that sustained her.

Literary Technique

Like many early poets, Bradstreet used **inversion**; that is, she changed the usual order of words. For example, in her poem "Upon the Burning of Our House" she wrote, "For sorrow near I did not look" instead of "I did not look nearby for sorrow." These inversions are designed to maintain the rhyme scheme and the rhythm of the poem.

RESOURCE MANAGER

Lesson Planning Resource
The *Unit One Planning Guide* (pp. 52–57) provides additional lesson notes and reduced versions of all print resources.

📁 **Other Print Resources**
- Active Reading Guide, p. 8
- Reading Workbook, p. 14
- Grammar and Language Workbook, p. 61
- Grammar and Composition Handbook, Lesson 1.4

- Quick Checks, p. 8
- Selection and Theme Assessment, pp. 15–16
- Performance Assessment, p. 8
- Spanish Summaries, p. 8
- Inclusion Strategies
- English Language Learners Sourcebook

 Transparencies
- Selection Focus 8
- Literary Elements 7
- Grammar and Language 6

Technology
🎧 Audio Library
💻 Glencoe Literature Web Site
📖 Testmaker

Upon the Burning of Our House

July 10th, 1666

Anne Bradstreet

77

More About Anne Bradstreet

A few years after her death, the second edition of *The Tenth Muse Lately Sprung Up in America* was published. This collection, as well as the first, was well received by critics, and it sold well. However, as time passed, praise for her work turned to scorn. Despite these attacks, more recent critical attention has acknowledged her talents and contributions to American literature.

Reading *Minilesson*

Predicting One way to engage students in a text is to have them predict the content before they read. Predicting helps students identify their expectations for what they will read before they begin. As they read, students can compare their expectations to the text, enhancing their comprehension and involvement with the content.

Activity Explain that "Upon the Burning of Our House" tells how a woman reacts when she loses her possessions. Ask students to write a paragraph predicting her possible reactions. After reading, students can compare their ideas to those in the poem. **L2**

Additional Resources
📁 *Reading Workbook,* p. 14

Reading the Selection

A **Active Reading**

VISUALIZE Ask students to use Bradstreet's details to form mental pictures of this tragic scene. Have students describe the scenes they visualize.

Model: It is dark, and I can see a two-story frame house with fire shooting from the rooftop. I picture a terrified young mother, who forces herself to run out of the house, carrying her children. Throughout this scene she is praying for God's help. Afterward, she is standing with her husband and children looking at the smoke and ashes that were their former belongings.

Additional Resources

📁 *Active Reading Guide,* p. 8

🎧 *Audio Library*

🎧 *Spanish Audio Library*

B **Literary Elements**

RHYME SCHEME: Couplets Ask students what rhyme scheme, or pattern, is evident in this poem. Have students provide examples from the poem. *(The poem is made up of couplets—two consecutive lines of poetry that are usually rhymed—with an aabbcc rhyme scheme.)*

In silent night when rest I took
For sorrow near I did not look
I wakened was with thund'ring noise
And piteous shrieks of dreadful voice.
5 That fearful sound of "Fire!" and "Fire!"
Let no man know is my desire.
I, starting up, the light did spy,
And to my God my heart did cry
To strengthen me in my distress
10 And not to leave me succorless.°
Then, coming out, beheld a space
The flame consume my dwelling place.
And when I could no longer look,
A I blest His name that gave and took,°
15 That laid my goods now in the dust.
Yea, so it was, and so 'twas just.
It was His own, it was not mine,
Far be it that I should repine;°
He might of all justly bereft°
20 But yet sufficient for us left.
When by the ruins oft I past
My sorrowing eyes aside did cast,
And here and there the places spy
Where oft I sat and long did lie:
25 Here stood that trunk, and there that chest,
There lay that store I counted best.
My pleasant things in ashes lie,
And them behold no more shall I.

Under thy roof no guest shall sit,
30 Nor at thy table eat a bit.
No pleasant tale shall e'er be told,
B Nor things recounted done of old.
No candle e'er shall shine in thee,
Nor bridegroom's voice e'er heard shall be.
35 In silence ever shall thou lie,
Adieu, Adieu,° all's vanity.°
Then straight I 'gin my heart to chide,°
And did thy wealth on earth abide?
Didst fix thy hope on mold'ring dust?
40 The arm of flesh didst make thy trust?
Raise up thy thoughts above the sky
That dunghill mists away may fly.
Thou hast an house on high erect,
Framed by that mighty Architect,
45 With glory richly furnished,
Stands permanent though this be fled.
It's purchased and paid for too
By Him who hath enough to do.
A price so vast as is unknown
50 Yet by His gift is made thine own;
There's wealth enough, I need no more,
Farewell, my pelf,° farewell my store.
The world no longer let me love,
My hope and treasure lies above.

---

10 *Succorless* means "without assistance" or "helpless."
14 This is a biblical reference to Job 1:21, ". . . the Lord gave, and the Lord hath taken away; blessed be the name of the Lord."
18 *Repine* means "to express unhappiness" or "to complain."
19 *Bereft* means "deprived of the possession or use of something."

36 *Adieu* (ə doo′) is French for "good-bye." *All's vanity* is a biblical reference to Ecclesiastes 1:2 and 12:8, "Vanity of vanities: all is vanity."
37 To *chide* is to find fault with or to blame.
52 *Pelf* is a term for money or wealth, often used disapprovingly.

Teaching Options

Grammar and Language *Minilesson*

Adjectives Point out to students that an adjective is a word that modifies a noun or pronoun by limiting or expanding its meaning. In the first lines of her poem, Bradstreet includes a number of adjectives: "silent" night, "thund'ring" noise, "piteous" shrieks, "dreadful" voice, and "fearful" sound.

Activity Ask students to rewrite the first six lines of the poem, replacing each of Bradford's adjectives with a synonym of their choosing. Then ask volunteers to read their rewrites aloud and ask how the tone of the poem is changed. **L2**

Additional Resources

🖺 *Grammar and Language Transparency 6*

📕 *Grammar and Language Workbook,* p. 61

📕 *Grammar and Composition Handbook,* Lesson 1.4

📗 *Writer's Choice,* Lesson 10.4

To My Dear and Loving Husband

Anne Bradstreet

If ever two were one, then surely we.
If ever man were loved by wife, then thee;
If ever wife was happy in a man,
Compare with me, ye women, if you can.
5   I prize thy love more than whole mines of gold
Or all the riches that the East doth hold.
My love is such that rivers cannot quench,
Nor ought° but love from thee, give recompense.°
Thy love is such I can no way repay,
10   The heavens reward thee manifold,° I pray.
Then while we live, in love let's so persevere

C — That when we live no more, we may live ever.

---

8 *Ought* means "anything." *Recompense* is "something given in return for something else" or "compensation."
10 Here, *manifold* means "in many different ways."

MEETING INDIVIDUAL NEEDS — ENGLISH LANGUAGE LEARNERS

Responding to the Selection

Personal Response

The most memorable lines for students will differ. Students may point to those that are most lyrical and descriptive.

ANALYZING LITERATURE

1. At first, she feels helpless and distressed, crying out to God for strength. For example, she says "And to my God my heart did cry."

2. Although the speaker does not directly address how she felt about her possessions before the fire, the reader can infer that they were important to her because "her sorrowing eyes" look over the ashes and mourn for all the "pleasant things." Later she realizes that her possessions really belong to God. She wants to dispel the idea that wealth "belongs" to anyone.

3. Bradstreet believes that her real hope and treasure awaits her in heaven after she dies.

4. Students may say they would not be so philosophical about a similar loss.

5. Students may say that today people are less likely to accept tragedy as a part of God's will; they are more likely to view the tragedy as hopeless rather than as a spiritual test as Bradstreet does. Others may say that such faith exists in our day too.

6. She prizes her husband's love more than gold; she uses this comparison to show the great value of this love.

7. His love for her is compensation. She hopes the heavens will reward him greatly. Students may find the ideas in these lines consistent with the ideas in the first four.

8. It sounds as if they will die yet live forever. It refers to her religious belief that when she and her husband die, they will live together in heaven.

9. If written today, the poem might be less formal and possibly less traditionally religious. Modern lyric poetry about love rarely includes strong allusions to faith and usually is not so direct in its declaration of love.

10. Students may mention figures from movies, television, or popular fiction, or people they know personally.

Responding to Literature

Personal Response

What lines from the poems do you find the most memorable? Share your ideas with the class.

———————— ANALYZING LITERATURE ————————

Upon the Burning of Our House

RECALL AND INTERPRET

1. At first, how does the speaker feel about the loss of her house in the fire? What different emotions does the speaker express? Point out specific lines to support your answer.

2. How did the speaker view her possessions before the fire, and how did she later change her views? Explain what she wanted to dispel.

3. In your opinion, what does the last sentence of the poem mean?

EVALUATE AND CONNECT

4. How is Bradstreet's reaction to losing the things she values similar to or different from your response to the Focus Activity on page 76?

5. How do people today accept or deal emotionally with losing their homes in a natural disaster? Do you think modern reactions are similar to or different from Bradstreet's reaction? Explain your response.

To My Dear and Loving Husband

RECALL AND INTERPRET

6. What does the speaker prize "more than whole mines of gold"? Why do you think she compares the way she feels to mines of gold?

7. What does the speaker say would compensate her for loving her husband, and how does she hope he will be rewarded for his love? In your opinion, how do the ideas in these lines relate to the ideas in the first four lines?

8. What is the seeming contradiction in the last line? What do you think this contradiction means?

EVALUATE AND CONNECT

9. If this poem were written today, how might the style and content be different? Explain your answer.

10. Describe a couple you know from real life, a movie, or a book who, in your opinion, feel for each other the way the speaker and her husband do.

Literary ELEMENTS

Extended Metaphor

A **metaphor** is a figure of speech that compares two things by saying that one thing is another. For example, in the sentence "the desert became a sweltering oven," the desert is said to be an oven—a fitting comparison because they are both hot. Occasionally, a writer will use an **extended metaphor,** developing a metaphor beyond a single line. This is what Bradstreet does,

beginning with line 43 of "Upon the Burning of Our House." Reread lines 43–50.

1. In your own words, summarize what you think the speaker is describing in the extended metaphor.
2. How do you think this extended metaphor relates to the speaker's description in lines 21–30?

● See **Literary Terms Handbook,** p. R6.

Writing About Literature

Students' reviews should

- give appropriate examples from the poem to support their opinions, which may range from admiration of Bradstreet's faith to astonishment of her calm acceptance of tragedy.
- explain clearly why they like or dislike the poem or agree or disagree with the speaker's views, offering reasoned judgments.

Creative Writing

Students' poems should

- relate to the subject they wrote about in the Focus Activity.
- express their feelings of loss in a lyrical fashion.
- use rhyme, repetition, or paradox.

LITERATURE AND WRITING

Writing About Literature

Poetry Review   Write a review of either "Upon the Burning of Our House" or "To My Dear and Loving Husband." Discuss what you liked or disliked about either of the two poems or whether you agreed with the speaker's views. You might also want to explain the effect of such devices as rhyme, rhythm, and metaphor. Use lines from the poems to support your opinions.

Creative Writing

Upon the Loss of . . .   Using the paragraph you wrote for the Focus Activity on page 76, write your own poem about what it feels like to lose something that is important to you. If you wish, you might try using **rhyme, repetition** (see page R13), or **paradox** (see page R11) as Bradstreet does in her poems.

EXTENDING YOUR RESPONSE

Literature Groups

Confusing Couplets   Both "To My Dear and Loving Husband" and "Upon the Burning of Our House" are written in **couplets,** or pairs of lines whose final syllables rhyme. To maintain the rhyme scheme, Bradstreet occasionally inverted word order or used unusual words, such as *succorless.* With your group, identify couplets that you find difficult to understand, and interpret their meaning. Then collaborate in rewording the sentences to make the meanings more clear.

Interdisciplinary Activity

Family and Consumer Sciences: Quilting Bee   With a partner, design squares for a quilt that Anne Bradstreet might have made. Use images from "To My Dear and Loving Husband" and "Upon the Burning of Our House" to illustrate your squares. Design individual squares and

then tape or glue them together and present your finished paper quilt to the class. If you have access to a computer graphics program, you could use it to design some or all of your squares. Print each square in color and assemble your quilt.

Performing

Oral Interpretation   With a small group of classmates, plan and perform an oral reading of "Upon the Burning of Our House." Decide which parts of the poem will be read by one person or several people. Agree on appropriate words to emphasize, gestures to make, and when to vary the tone and volume of speakers voices. Explain to the class how your reading helps to reveal the meaning of the poem.

✊ **Save your work for your portfolio.**

✔ ASSESSMENT OPTIONS

📁 ***Quick Checks,*** p. 8

📁 ***Selection and Theme Assessment,*** pp. 15–16

📁 ***Performance Assessment,*** p. 8

💾 ***Testmaker***

LITERARY ELEMENTS

1. She is describing a heavenly home, built by God for her. She explains that it has been purchased and paid for (alluding to Jesus' death on the cross).
2. In lines 21–30, she is describing her temporary possessions that she will "behold no more." In lines 43–50 she says that greater riches await her in heaven; it "stands permanent though this be fled."

Additional Resources

🖎 *Literary Elements Transparency 7*

MEDIA
Connection

Objective
- To understand and apply strategies for reading song lyrics

Literature LINK

To My Dear and Loving Husband
These song lyrics connect with "To My Dear and Loving Husband" on page 79. Discuss with students how these lyrics, like Bradstreet's lyrical work, express love in a very personal way. As in Bradstreet's poem, Peter Gabriel says that love makes him complete.

Respond
1. Love makes the speaker complete. Until the speaker comes back to this love, he or she feels lost. The love in the beloved's eyes strips away all pretense, and the speaker realizes that everything can be found with his or her beloved.
2. Some may identify with the image of driving off in a car but, at the same time, constantly seeking to be near the loved one; others may say love is much more than the need for physical proximity that is expressed in the lyric.

Additional Resources
📁 *Media Connections*, p. 2

Teaching Options

interNET CONNECTION

Peter Gabriel Students can find out more about Peter Gabriel and his work by going to the official Peter Gabriel Web site to learn about his dance, film, and environmental activities.

MEDIA
Connection

Song
What is romantic love? Is it only a beginning, or does it last through many changes?

By Peter Gabriel

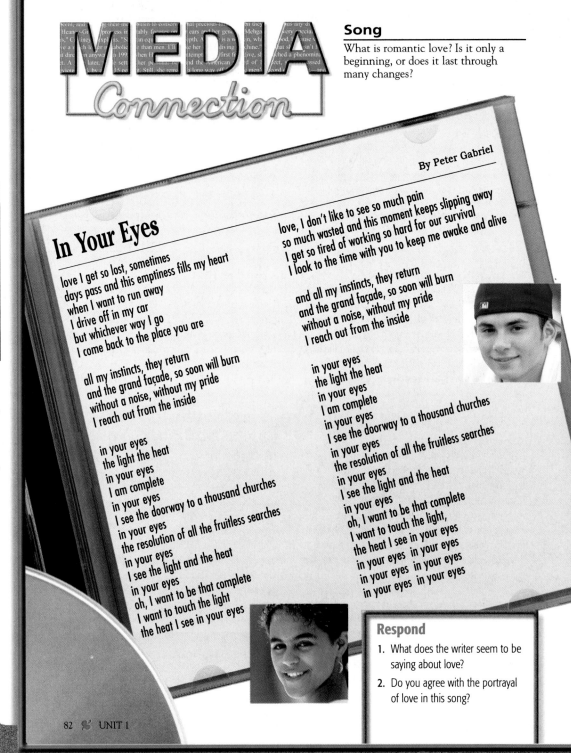

In Your Eyes

love I get so lost, sometimes
days pass and this emptiness fills my heart
when I want to run away
I drive off in my car
but whichever way I go
I come back to the place you are

all my instincts, they return
and the grand façade, so soon will burn
without a noise, without my pride
I reach out from the inside

in your eyes
the light the heat
in your eyes
I am complete
in your eyes
I see the doorway to a thousand churches
in your eyes
the resolution of all the fruitless searches
in your eyes
I see the light and the heat
in your eyes
oh, I want to be that complete
I want to touch the light
the heat I see in your eyes

love, I don't like to see so much pain
so much wasted and this moment keeps slipping away
I get so tired of working so hard for our survival
I look to the time with you to keep me awake and alive

and all my instincts, they return
and the grand façade, so soon will burn
without a noise, without my pride
I reach out from the inside

in your eyes
the light the heat
in your eyes
I am complete
in your eyes
I see the doorway to a thousand churches
in your eyes
the resolution of all the fruitless searches
in your eyes
I see the light and the heat
in your eyes
oh, I want to be that complete
I want to touch the light,
the heat I see in your eyes
in your eyes in your eyes
in your eyes in your eyes
in your eyes in your eyes

Respond
1. What does the writer seem to be saying about love?
2. Do you agree with the portrayal of love in this song?

82 UNIT 1

Reading Minilesson

Comparing and Contrasting "To My Dear and Loving Husband" and "In Your Eyes" are lyric poems of romantic love, the most common theme of poetry over the years. Ask students what differences and similarities they note between the two lyrics. Is the form or tone similar? How would they characterize the speaker in each piece? You may want to list on the board character traits for each speaker.

Activity Have each of your students bring in another love lyric—an old poem or a recent song—to read aloud. When all the poems and lyrics have been read, hold a discussion about common elements in love lyrics. **L2**

Additional Resources
📁 *Reading Workbook*

Writing Skills

Using Specific, Vivid Words

Consider these words from Anne Bradstreet's poem "Upon the Burning of Our House."

> **"I wakened was with thund'ring noise
> And piteous shrieks of dreadful voice."**

Notice the powerful way Bradstreet conveys her image of a *thund'ring noise, piteous shrieks,* and a *dreadful voice.*

Writers use various strategies to make scenes come alive. First, they choose specific rather than general words. For instance, how might the example be different if Bradstreet had used the word *calls* instead of *shrieks?* A call is a loud yell. A shriek is also a loud yell, but it is more specifically one that is frantic and high-pitched.

In selecting a specific word, writers consider the word's **connotation.** A word's connotation is made up of the feelings and values that readers associate with that word. In the example above, Bradstreet uses the term *dreadful.* She might have chosen words such as *horrible* or *terrifying.* The word *dreadful,* however, conveys an ominous feeling, fear of something that is about to happen. This connotation is different from the connotations of the other words.

Good writers also strive to use vivid, original words rather than overused ones. In the example, Bradstreet uses the word *thund'ring* to describe the noise she heard. *Great* and *loud* have similar meanings, but are more commonly used and no longer convey the vividness of the sound. For help in finding more precise, vivid, and fresh words, check a thesaurus.

EXERCISE

Replacing Overused Words   Rewrite the following sentences. Replace inexact or overused words with more specific, vivid ones. Use a thesaurus for help.

1. The moon shone over the lonely town.

2. The visitors were quite surprised by the tall buildings in our city.

3. Fed by a strong wind, the noisy fire burned one home after another.

4. The angry crowd moved closer and closer to the speaker.

5. Slowly, the tired stranger came out of the ugly old house.

Writing Skills

Objective
- To analyze an author's use of specific, vivid words

Teaching Strategies

It may be useful for students to reread "Upon the Burning of Our House" and look for additional examples of Bradstreet's use of specific, vivid words. Stress that, especially with lyrical works, the connotations of words are important because they express specific feelings and values.

Exercise
Sample answers:
1. A dim moon brooded over the desolate town.
2. Tourists marveled at the skyscrapers towering above our teeming streets.
3. Driven by the gale, voracious fires feasted on home after home.
4. An irate mob menaced the unpopular lecturer.
5. Wearily, the stranger shuffled from the ramshackle bungalow into the open air.

Additional Resources
📗 *Writer's Choice,* Lesson 3.1

Teaching Options

Grammar and Language *Minilesson*

Adverbs Point out that an adverb modifies a verb, adjective, or another adverb.

Activity Have students identify the adverbs in these sentences:
1. We entered a <u>richly</u> furnished living room.
2. She stands <u>solidly</u> behind her opinions.
3. The violinist played the music <u>slowly</u>.

L2

Additional Resources
📄 *Grammar and Language Transparency 7*

📗 *Grammar and Language Workbook,* p. 63

📗 *Grammar and Composition Handbook,* Lesson 1.5

📗 *Writer's Choice,* Lesson 10.5

Before Reading

Objectives

- To read and analyze a personal narrative about captivity
- To identify and understand analogies
- To write an imaginative dialogue

Skills

Reading/Thinking: Judging Credibility of a Source; Paraphrasing; Sequencing
Vocabulary: Context Clues
Grammar/Language: Interjections
Collaboration: Literature Groups

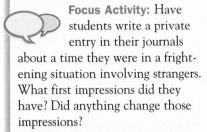

Motivating

→ OPTIONS

Selection Focus Transparency 9: Have students view the transparency and then discuss the question provided.

Focus Activity: Have students write a private entry in their journals about a time they were in a frightening situation involving strangers. What first impressions did they have? Did anything change those impressions?

Before You Read

from *The Captivity of Mrs. Mary Rowlandson*

Meet Mary Rowlandson

"I can remember the time, when I used to sleep quietly without workings in my thoughts, whole nights together, but now it is other ways with me."

Mary White Rowlandson wrote these words after being held prisoner for eleven weeks and five days. She had experienced the terror of war and kidnapping.

Born in England, Mary White moved to Lancaster, Massachusetts. Around 1656 she married Joseph Rowlandson, a minister in Lancaster.

When Lancaster was attacked at dawn on February 10, 1676, Rowlandson, her six-year-old daughter, and her two older children were among those captured by a party of Wampanoag warriors.

Looking back on her captivity, she wrote, "I have been in the midst of those roaring lions, and savage bears, that feared neither God, nor man, nor the devil." Yet her captors were neither "lions" nor "bears." Instead they were starving people displaced from their own land, and they wanted ransom money to buy food and other supplies. Indeed, they never hurt Rowlandson.

Eventually, Rowlandson's husband paid twenty pounds for her ransom, and Rowlandson was released. This narrative recounts parts of her ordeal.

Mary Rowlandson was born in approximately 1636 and died in 1710 or 1711.

FOCUS ACTIVITY

How do you feel when you find yourself in a group of strangers? What does the word *stranger* mean to you? What is the literal meaning of *stranger*?

SHARE IDEAS Talk with classmates about situations in which people who live near each other remain strangers. Share your ideas about the negative effects of such situations and how you might relieve them.

SETTING A PURPOSE Read this narrative to notice Mary Rowlandson's attitude toward Native Americans and to see whether it changes.

BACKGROUND

As a child, the Wampanoag chief Metacomet had watched his father, Massasoit, help the Pilgrims who arrived on the *Mayflower.* By 1665, there were about 25,000 Puritans in Massachusetts Bay Colony. With each passing year, more arrived; with each passing year, the Native Americans had less and less land, and some even had to work for the English to earn a living. Foreseeing the destruction of his own way of life and that of all the native people, Metacomet began forming alliances with other tribes against the settlers. In 1675, after three Wampanoag were executed by the Puritans, a swift, desperate war broke out.

VOCABULARY PREVIEW

doleful (dōl′ fəl) *adj.* full of grief or sorrow; sad; p. 85
desolation (des′ ə lā′ shən) *n.* devastation; misery; sadness; p. 85
daunt (dônt) *v.* to overcome with fear; intimidate; p. 86
compassion (kəm pash′ ən) *n.* deep awareness of another's suffering with a desire to help; p. 86

discern (di surn′) *v.* to recognize as different and distinct; distinguish; p. 88
lament (lə ment′) *v.* to express deep sorrow or grief; p. 89
savory (sā′ vər ē) *adj.* agreeable to the taste or smell; appetizing; p. 89

RESOURCE MANAGER

Lesson Planning Resource
The *Unit One Planning Guide* (pp. 58–65) provides additional lesson notes and reduced versions of all print resources.

📁 **Other Print Resources**
- Active Reading Guide, p. 9
- Vocabulary Practice, p. 7
- Reading Workbook, pp. 15–16
- Grammar and Language Workbook, p. 69

- Grammar and Composition Handbook, Lesson 1.8
- Quick Checks, p. 9
- Selection and Theme Assessment, pp. 17–18
- Performance Assessment, p. 9
- Spanish Summaries, p. 9
- Inclusion Strategies
- English Language Learners Sourcebook

Transparencies
- Selection Focus 9
- Literary Elements 8
- Grammar and Language 8

Technology
- Audio Library
- Spanish Audio Library
- Glencoe Literature Web Site
- Testmaker

I desired them that they would carry me to Albany upon one of those horses, and sell me for powder; for so they had sometimes discoursed.[9] I was utterly hopeless of getting home on foot the way that I came. I could hardly bear to think of the many weary steps I had taken to come to this place.

. . . My son being now about a mile from me, I asked liberty to go and see him; they bade me go, and away I went; but quickly lost myself, travelling over hills and through swamps, and could not find the way to him. And I cannot but admire at the wonderful power and goodness of God to me, in that though I was gone from home, and met with all sorts of Indians, and those I had no knowledge of, and there being no Christian soul near me; yet not one of them offered the least imaginable miscarriage to me. I turned homeward again, and met with my master; he showed me the way to my son: when I came to him I found him not well; and withal he had a boil on his side, which much troubled him; we bemoaned one another a while, as the Lord helped us, and then I returned again. When I was returned, I found myself as unsatisfied as I was before. I went up and down moaning and lamenting; and my spirit was ready to sink with the thoughts of my poor children; my son was ill, and I could not but think of his mournful looks; and no Christian friend was near him to do any office of love for him, either for soul or body. And my poor girl, I knew not where she was, nor whether she was sick or well, or alive or dead. I repaired under these thoughts to my Bible (my great comforter in that time) and that scripture came to my hand, *Cast thy burden upon the Lord, and he shall sustain thee.* Psal. lv. 22.

But I was fain[10] to go and look after something to satisfy my hunger; and going among the wigwams, I went into one, and there found a squaw who showed herself very kind to me, and gave me a piece of bear. I put it into my pocket, and came home; but could not find an opportunity to broil it, for fear they would get it from me, and there it lay all that day and night in my stinking pocket. In the morning I went again to the same squaw, who had a kettle of ground nuts boiling; I asked her to let me boil my piece of bear in her kettle, which she did, and gave me some ground nuts to eat with it, and I cannot but think how pleasant it was to me. I have seen bear baked very handsomely amongst the English, and some liked it, but the thoughts that it was bear made me tremble: but now that was savory to me that one would think was enough to turn the stomach of a brute creature.

One bitter cold day I could find no room to sit down before the fire; I went out, and could not tell what to do, but I went into another wigwam where they were also sitting round the fire; but the squaw laid a skin for me, and bid me sit down; and gave me some ground nuts, and bade me come again; and told me they would buy me if they were able; and yet these were strangers to me that I never knew before.

. . . *The fourteenth remove.*—Now must we pack up and be gone from this thicket, bending

---

9. *Discoursed* means "discussed."

10. In this instance, *fain* means "obliged."

Vocabulary
lament (lə ment´) *v.* to express deep sorrow or grief
savory (sā´vər ē) *adj.* agreeable to the taste or smell; appetizing

F Critical Thinking

SEQUENCING Point out to students that the sentence "I pray God he may remember these things, now he is returned in safety" on page 88 is written in the present tense, unlike the rest of the account, which is in the past tense. Rowlandson composed this sentence, and probably the entire account, after her release. Textual clues such as the tense of verbs can be critical to understanding the sequence of events.

G Literary Elements

ALLUSION The Puritans viewed writing, as well as all activities, as part of God's work. It was essential for their writing to contain references to God and to biblical passages, as Rowlandson's allusion to Psalm 22 demonstrates. What other allusions to the Bible does Rowlandson make in this narrative? *(She alludes to Job and Psalm 46 at the beginning of her account and to Moses and Psalm 55 at the conclusion of her account.)*

H Active Reading

CONNECT Some of the foods Rowlandson mentions (such as bear, bear's grease, deer, horseflesh, and an unborn fawn) would be an exotic diet for many cultures today. Have students name some foods that they consider unusual or exotic. *(Students may suggest ostrich, octopus, emu, alligator, rattlesnake, snails, or pig's feet.)*

MEETING INDIVIDUAL NEEDS

GIFTED AND TALENTED ACTIVITY

Write a Screenplay This excerpt from Rowlandson's account contains several dramatic moments that could make good scenes for a movie. Gifted and talented students may enjoy rewriting Rowlandson's narrative as a screenplay.

Activity Ask students to use the section titled "The second remove" to develop a brief script for a screenplay, adding dialogue and additional information as needed. When the screenplays are finished, have the students give a staged reading, using classmates as readers. **L3**

FIGURES OF SPEECH: Metaphor and Simile Have students identify instances in which Rowlandson uses metaphor and simile. Review with students the definitions for *metaphor* (an implied comparison of two seemingly unlike things) and *simile* (a direct comparison, which uses *like* or *as* to compare two seemingly unlike things). *(Simile: she compares cake crumbs to flint: "like little flints." Metaphor: she calls her captors roaring lions and savage bears: "I have been in the midst of those roaring lions and savage bears.")*

Thematic Focus

Beginnings and Change Have students discuss how this ordeal must have changed Rowlandson. In what ways would her life be different after her release? How would students have reacted to these changes?

☑ ASSESSMENT OPTIONS

📁 *Quick Checks,* p. 9

---

from **The Captivity of Mrs. Mary Rowlandson**

our course towards the bay-towns. I having nothing to eat by the way this day, but a few crumbs of cake, that an Indian gave my girl the same day we were taken. She gave it me, and I put it into my pocket; there it lay till it was so moldy (for want of good baking) that one could not tell what it was made of; it fell all to crumbs, and grew so dry and hard, that it was like little flints;[11] and this refreshed me many times when I was ready to faint. It was in my thoughts when I put it into my mouth; that if ever I returned, I would tell the world what a blessing the Lord gave to such mean food. As we went along, they killed a deer, with a young one in her; they gave me a piece of the fawn, and it was so young and tender, that one might eat the bones as well as the flesh, and yet I thought it very good. When night came on we sat down; it rained, but they quickly got up a bark wigwam, where I lay dry that night. I looked out in the morning, and many of them had lain in the rain all night. I saw by their reeking.[12] Thus the Lord dealt mercifully

> . . . O the wonderful power of God that I have seen, and the experiences that I have had!

with me many times; and I fared better than many of them.

. . . O the wonderful power of God that I have seen, and the experiences that I have had! I have been in the midst of those roaring lions and savage bears, that feared neither God nor man, nor the devil, by night and day, alone and in company, sleeping all sorts together; and yet not one of them ever offered the least abuse or unchastity to me in word or action. Though some are ready to say I speak it for my own credit; but I speak it in the presence of God, and to His glory.

. . . If trouble from smaller matters begins to arise in me, I have something at hand to check myself with, and say when I am troubled, it was but the other day, that if I had had the world, I would have given it for my freedom. . . . I have learned to look beyond present and smaller troubles, and to be quieted under them, as *Moses* said, *Exod.* xiv. 13, *Stand still, and see the salvation of the Lord.*

FINIS[13]

---

11. *Flints* refers to pieces of flint, a very hard type of quartz.
12. *Reeking* here means "steaming"; that is, water was evaporating from their hair and clothing.

---

13. *Finis* means "The End."

Teaching Options

MEETING INDIVIDUAL NEEDS — INCLUSION STRATEGIES

Less-Proficient Readers Some readers may have difficulty with unfamiliar words. Have students make a table like the one at the right, in which to define challenging words through context before consulting a dictionary.

Activity Copy the chart on the board as a model. Have students list difficult words as they read and try to define them through context. Then have students find dictionary definitions and write them in the third column. **L1**

Word	Meaning in Context	Definition

Additional Resources
📁 *Inclusion Strategies*

LISTENING, SPEAKING, and VIEWING

Conducting an Interview

In *Stay Alive, My Son,* Pin Yathay tells a horrifying story of war and the loss of a loved one. Stories like Pin Yathay's expose us to a variety of experiences and valuable lessons.

Another way to gather information about people's experiences is through an interview. In an interview, one person questions another person to obtain specific information. The interviewer then shares his or her findings—perhaps in a news article, a television broadcast, or a book.

In any career, however, you might conduct an interview. An employer might interview a potential employee, or a software developer might interview potential customers. For any interview, remember these guidelines.

Before the Interview
- Focus on the purpose of the interview. What do you want to learn?
- Find out as much as you can about the person and the topic.
- Plan a logical list of questions that ask *who, what, when, where, why,* and *how.*

During the Interview
- Be courteous.
- Do not argue or disagree. Focus on the ideas of the person being interviewed.
- Keep your questions brief and to the point.
- Listen carefully so you can ask appropriate and thoughtful follow-up questions.
- Take notes or, better yet, record the interview. (Be sure to ask permission.)

After the Interview
- Write a detailed account of the interview as soon as possible.
- If necessary, contact the person you interviewed or other sources to verify facts.
- Organize the material. Eliminate any information that is unrelated to your topic.
- Write an introduction for your interview that provides background and sets the scene.

ACTIVITIES

1. Interview a person who was a teenager a few decades ago. Focus on how that person's life as a teenager was similar to and different than yours. Discuss what you learn with your classmates.

2. Find a person who is an "expert" on football, TV trivia, gardening, or just about anything. Conduct a brief interview with that person to learn about his or her expertise. Report your findings to the class.

LISTENING, SPEAKING, and VIEWING

Objective
- To understand and apply interviewing strategies

Teaching Strategies

After students read and discuss the lesson, point out that the interviewer's main responsibility is to get the facts. One tactic for getting the facts is to avoid leading questions, which presuppose answers. For example, an interviewer might ask, "How did you react when you first felt the earthquake?" Not, "How scared were you when you first felt the earthquake?"

Activities

1. Students may say that their grandparents or great-grandparents talk of life without television, the importance of radio as a means of communication, and popular music and dances of their generations. Students may also have heard firsthand accounts of the events of World War II or the Vietnam War and the effect of the Vietnam War's protest movements on that era's teenagers.

2. Students' reports will depend on the interviewee's area of expertise. An athlete, for example, may discuss strategies, equipment, or famous figures of a particular sport.

Teaching Options

MEETING INDIVIDUAL NEEDS — ENGLISH LANGUAGE LEARNERS

Body Language Body language is the message conveyed through body movement, position, and gestures. Appropriate body language varies culturally. Discuss how body language affects communication during interviews.

Activity Have the class brainstorm to identify nonverbal cues that affect communication. Ask: How close should you stand when interviewing someone?

Should you make eye contact or avoid it? Should nearness or eye contact be based on sex? On age? As the class adds questions, write them on the board. Then have students answer the questions and identify differences.

Additional Resources
- *English Language Learners Sourcebook*

Objectives

- To read and analyze a sermon about the need for change
- To identify and analyze the use of imagery
- To write guidelines for the use of emotional appeals in persuasion

Skills

Reading/Thinking: Analyzing Arguments; Main Idea and Supporting Details; Establishing Criteria

Collaboration: Creating a Visual Presentation

Motivating
→ OPTIONS

Selection Focus Transparency 11: Have students view the transparency and then discuss the question provided.

Focus Activity: As an extension of the Focus Activity, have students suggest situations they have encountered that involved persuasion through appeals to emotion.

Before You Read

from Sinners in the Hands of an Angry God

Meet Jonathan Edwards

"I think it is a reasonable thing to fright persons away from hell. . . . Is it not a reasonable thing to fright a person out of a house on fire?"

—Edwards

The son and grandson of Puritan ministers, Jonathan Edwards was ordained a minister at the age of twenty-three. He soon became known for his "preaching of terror," which grew out of his belief that God was all powerful and human beings had no free will. Edwards preached that God had predestined people to go to heaven or hell. By 1750 some members of his congregation in Northampton, a village in the Massachusetts Bay Colony, were no longer comfortable with his extreme teachings and dismissed Edwards. He moved his family to a frontier village and worked as a missionary with Native Americans. During this time he wrote important theological works, including *Freedom of Will*.

Jonathan Edwards was born in 1703 and died in 1758.

FOCUS ACTIVITY

Think about a time you tried to change someone's mind. Did you use a gentle approach, scare tactics, or something in between?

QUICKWRITE In your journal, write about a time when you tried to persuade someone to accept your point of view. How did you do it? How successful were you?

SETTING A PURPOSE Read to discover how Edwards tries to persuade others.

BACKGROUND

The Time and Place

In 1740 the well-known British evangelist George Whitefield joined with Jonathan Edwards to spark a religious revival that swept New England. The Great Awakening, as it was called, was a backlash against what many believed was a church that had grown far too lenient. Edwards preached a return to strict Calvinism, religious teachings popular in the 1720s that had begun to fade. Calvinist ideas are reflected in his most famous sermon, "Sinners in the Hands of an Angry God."

Calvinism stressed predestination, the belief that only a select few chosen by God would be saved. No individual could earn grace by doing good deeds, so everyone was equally powerless to control their own fates.

VOCABULARY PREVIEW

wrath (rath) *n.* extreme anger; vengeful punishment; p. 102

appease (ə pēz′) *v.* to bring to a state of peace or quiet; soothe; p. 102

abate (ə bāt′) *v.* to lessen or reduce in force or intensity; p. 102

incensed (in senst′) *adj.* made very angry; p. 102

prudence (prōōd′ əns) *n.* exercise of good and cautious judgment; p. 102

abhor (ab hôr′) *v.* to regard with disgust; p. 103

abominable (ə bom′ə nə bəl) *adj.* disgusting; detestable; p. 103

RESOURCE MANAGER

Lesson Planning Resource
The *Unit One Planning Guide* (pp. 72–79) provides additional lesson notes and reduced versions of all print resources.

Other Print Resources
- Active Reading Guide, p. 11
- Vocabulary Practice, p. 9
- Reading Workbook, pp. 17–18
- Quick Checks, p. 11
- Selection and Theme Assessment, p. 21

- Performance Assessment, p. 11
- Spanish Summaries, p. 11
- Inclusion Strategies
- English Language Learners Sourcebook

Transparencies
- Selection Focus 11
- Literary Elements 10

Technology

- Audio Library
- Spanish Audio Library
- Glencoe Literature Web Site
- Testmaker

Responding to Literature

Personal Response

Imagine that you are in the congregation, listening to Edwards's sermon. How might you respond?

Literary ELEMENTS

——— ANALYZING LITERATURE ———

RECALL AND INTERPRET

1. In the first paragraph, what generalization does Edwards make about all people? Why do you think Edwards makes this statement?
2. A **metaphor** is a comparison made without using the words *like* or *as*. What metaphors does Edwards use to explain God's mercy? How do these metaphors reflect Edwards's view of the relationship between God and humanity?
3. What does the minister say to command the attention of those who think they will not fall victim to God's wrath?
4. Near the end of the sermon, what does Edwards say Christ has done? What might have been the minister's purpose in closing with this image?

EVALUATE AND CONNECT

5. **Repetition** is the frequent use of a word or phrase for emphasis. Evaluate the effect of repeating *you* throughout the sermon.
6. Edwards used fear to rekindle his congregation's interest. Compare his style with that of a more recent religious leader, such as Martin Luther King Jr. How are their appeals and goals similar and different?
7. Edwards wanted his sermon to frighten people into a "change of heart." In what other ways might a person have reacted to the sermon? Explain.
8. Reread what you wrote for the Focus Activity on page 100. Have your thoughts on persuasion changed at all since reading the sermon? Explain.

Imagery

Imagery is the collection of mental pictures, or images, in a literary work. Visual imagery is most common but a writer can also use other **sensory details** that appeal to the reader's sense of sound, taste, smell, or touch.

Edwards's sermon is filled with images meant to frighten listeners into seeking God and avoiding hell.

1. What frightening images occur in the first two paragraphs? To what senses do they appeal?
2. What sensory details does Edwards include in the fourth paragraph? What effect does the imagery have on the reader?
3. List five additional images in the sermon, each of which appeals to a different sense.

● See **Literary Terms Handbook,** p. R8.

——— EXTENDING YOUR RESPONSE ———

Personal Writing

Emotional Appeals   Edwards preached with a "fiery rhetoric," a speaking style intended to elicit a highly emotional response. In your opinion, when can emotional appeals be effective? In what situations are they inappropriate? Write a brief set of guidelines for the appropriate use of emotional appeals.

Interdisciplinary Activity

Art: Illustrating Images   Choose a passage from Edwards's sermon that contains vivid imagery, such as his comparison of sinners to "the most hateful and venomous serpent." Sketch the passage, or use a computer graphics program to illustrate the scene. Then, with other students, organize your images to create a visual presentation of the sermon.

 Save your work for your portfolio.

Responding to the Selection

Personal Response

Some students may find the vivid descriptions of hell and humanity's predicament convincing and therefore frightening; others may be put off by these images and so may dismiss them.

ANALYZING LITERATURE

1. He states that all people deserve God's wrath; he makes this statement to get the attention of the entire audience and because he believes the New Testament says this.
2. He uses several metaphors: the grace of God holds the sinner suspended over hell; grace stays the arrow from piercing the sinner's heart and keeps the flames of hell from consuming the thread that keeps the sinner, as abhorrent as a spider, from hell. The metaphors show how hopeless the sinner is without an all-powerful God.
3. He explains that none who do not repent will escape the sinners' punishment of hell.
4. He says that Christ has opened the door of mercy for them; this metaphor invites sinners to repent and change their ways.
5. The repetition emphasizes that Edwards speaks to each person in that audience specifically.
6. Many modern-day sermons invoke Christian values of compassion and mercy—the loving God as opposed to the avenger God. The goal, like the Puritans', is to change people's attitudes and behavior.
7. Some listeners may have been offended, rather than persuaded. Some may have found it difficult to relate to a God who regarded them as little better than spiders.
8. Some students may think that scare tactics are legitimate if the result is repentance; those who advocate gentler persuasion may see his frightening images as an example of how not to persuade someone.

✔ ASSESSMENT OPTIONS

📁 **Quick Checks,** p. 11
📁 **Selection and Theme Assessment,** p. 21
📁 **Performance Assessment,** p. 11
💾 **Testmaker**

LITERARY ELEMENTS

1. Images of a fiery pit and lake of brimstone appeal to sight and touch.
2. The weight of sin will make the sinner fall. The images frighten or intimidate.
3. Five images are the bow and arrow of God's wrath, souls born again, the sinner held over hell like a spider, a sinner who is like a venomous serpent, hell as a great furnace.

Additional Resources

🖌 **Literary Elements Transparency 10**

Grammar Link

Grammar Link

Grammar Link

Objective

• To recognize and correct sentence fragments

Teaching Strategies

Point out that writers often use sentence fragments for specific effects, but incomplete sentences are not correct in formal writing.

Exercises

1. *One solution:* Jonathan Edwards was born in 1703. He was a Puritan minister and one of the foremost early American writers. "Sinners in the Hands of an Angry God," written in 1741, may be his best-known sermon. In this sermon, he preaches about the dangers of sin. Edwards's theme, however, is not God's anger, but God's grace.
2. *Students' revisions should*
   • contain no sentence fragments.
   • reflect a variety of correction strategies.
   • maintain the style and meaning of their original work.

Additional Resources

Writer's Choice, Lesson 13.9

Avoiding Sentence Fragments

A fragment is something that is incomplete. It might be a fragment of a conversation, a fragment of a song, or a fragment of a sentence. A **sentence fragment** is a word or group of words that makes up only part of a sentence.

Problem 1 Some sentence fragments lack a subject, a verb, or both.
Succeeded his grandfather as a minister in Northampton, Massachusetts. [lacks a subject]
Many people in Edwards's church that Sunday. [lacks a verb]

   Solution Add the missing subject and/or verb.
   Edwards succeeded his grandfather as a minister in Northampton, Massachusetts.
   Many people sat in Edwards's church that Sunday.

Problem 2 Some sentence fragments are subordinate clauses that have been mistaken for a complete sentence. A subordinate clause has a subject and verb, but it does not express a complete thought and cannot stand alone as a sentence.
Because some Northampton Puritans disagreed with Edwards.

   Solution A Join the subordinate clause to a main clause.
   Because some Northampton Puritans disagreed with Edwards, he moved to the village of Stockbridge.

   Solution B Remove the subordinating conjunction at the beginning of the clause.
   Some Northampton Puritans disagreed with Edwards.

Writers sometimes deliberately use sentence fragments. Edwards uses the phrase "But alas!" in "Sinners in the Hands of an Angry God." It is an exclamation and its meaning is clear. Later, he uses the fragment "To see so many others feasting, while you are pining and perishing!" Here the meaning is less clear but can be understood within the context of the selection. Although you will find similar examples in other writing, beware of using fragments in your own writing because readers can often become confused.

● For more about sentence fragments, see **Language Handbook,** pp. R18–R19.

⟨ EXERCISES ⟩

1. **Proofreading** Use the strategies above to correct the sentence fragments in this paragraph.

   Jonathan Edwards was a Puritan minister and one of the foremost early American writers. Who was born in 1703. "Sinners in the Hands of an Angry God" may be his best known sermon. Written in 1741. In this sermon, preaches about the dangers of sin. Edwards's theme, however, is not the anger of God. But God's grace.

2. Revise a piece of your own writing using these strategies to eliminate sentence fragments.

Teaching Options

Writing *Minilesson*

Rewriting Fragments Have students identify and write down the sentence fragments Edwards uses on page 104. Discuss why Edwards used each fragment and whether or not its use is effective.

Activity Using their list of fragments, have students rewrite the paragraph or passage in which each sentence fragment occurs. Remind students that Edwards's sermon was meant to be delivered orally. Select a paragraph from each version and have a volunteer read the paragraphs aloud. Which version makes a more effective speech? Which is more effective for a formal, written presentation? **L2**

Additional Resources

  Writer's Choice, Lesson 13.9

Before You Read

Offer of Help

Meet Canassatego

"We are a powerful Confederacy; and by your observing the same methods our wise forefathers have taken, you will acquire such strength and power. Therefore whatever befalls you, never fall out with one another."

—Canassatego

Canassatego was a leader of the Onondaga people and a powerful *tadadaho,* or orator. A British colonial official, after hearing him speak, described Canassatego as "a tall, well-made man," with "a very full chest and brawny limbs. . . . He was about sixty years of age, very active, strong, and had a surprising liveliness in his speech."

The Onondaga were, in fact, allies of the British. Between 1689 and 1763, France and England battled over land in North America. To strengthen their forces, each nation developed alliances with Native American groups.

One powerful alliance forged by the British was with the Six Nations of the Iroquois—the Onondaga, Mohawk, Seneca, Oneida, Cayuga, and Tuscarora peoples. (The Tuscarora had joined the Iroquois in 1722.)

As leader of the Onondaga, Canassatego served as a representative of the united Iroquois at several meetings with British colonists. At one meeting in 1744, Canassatego urged the British colonies to unite, like the Iroquois, to form a strong, centralized government.

The unity of the colonies, based on the model of Canassatego's united Iroquois, ultimately came into being shortly before the American Revolution; inspired by Canassatego's original advice, "Never fall out with one another," the American patriots' rallying cry became, "United we stand, divided we fall."

Canassatego was born around 1690 and died in 1750.

FOCUS ACTIVITY

In your opinion, what skills should young people learn in school in order to prepare themselves most effectively for "real life"?

LIST IDEAS In your journal, create a list entitled "The Top Ten Skills a Person Needs for a Successful, Fulfilling Life."

SETTING A PURPOSE Read to see what one man valued as the best skills for his people.

BACKGROUND

The Time and Place

European settlers rarely respected the cultural traditions and territorial rights of Native Americans. A statement by Boston church leader Cotton Mather (1663–1728) illustrates the attitudes of many settlers: "We, God's chosen people, must conquer the earth. . . ." Ironically, such feelings of superiority occasionally led settlers to make gestures of "generosity." For example, representatives from Virginia gave an "offer of help" to Canassatego. They invited him to send a group of young Native Americans to Virginia to attend college, free of charge. The message you are about to read is Canassatego's response to this offer.

VOCABULARY PREVIEW

esteem (es tēm') *v.* to regard favorably; value highly; p. 108

proposal (prə pō'zəl) *n.* something put forward for consideration as a plan of action; p. 108

conception (kən sep'shən) *n.* mental image or idea; thought or notion; p. 108

Objectives

- To read and analyze a letter that refuses an offer of change
- To identify and analyze tone in writing
- To write a response letter

Skills

Collaboration: Literature Groups

Motivating →OPTIONS

Selection Focus Transparency 12: Have students view the transparency and then discuss the question provided.

Focus Activity: As an extension of the Focus Activity, have students work in pairs, discussing possible ways one culture can help another to strengthen education. What is an acceptable offer of help from one culture to another?

RESOURCE MANAGER

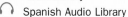

Lesson Planning Resource
The *Unit One Planning Guide* (pp. 80–84) provides additional lesson notes and reduced versions of all print resources.

📁 **Other Print Resources**
- Active Reading Guide, p. 12
- Vocabulary Practice, p. 10
- Reading Workbook, pp. 17–18
- Quick Checks, p. 12
- Selection and Theme Assessment, p. 22

- Performance Assessment, p. 12
- Spanish Summaries, p. 12
- Spanish Translations
- Inclusion Strategies
- English Language Learners Sourcebook

📖 **Transparencies**
- Selection Focus 12
- Literary Elements 11

Technology
- 🎧 Audio Library
- 🎧 Spanish Audio Library
- 💻 Glencoe Literature Web Site
- 📱 Testmaker

Reading the Selection

Offer of Help

Canassatego

SUMMARY

In his response to the colonists' proposal to educate a group of Onondaga young men, Canassatego acknowledges the colonists' good intentions and compliments them. Because they are so wise, he says, they will understand that different cultures value different types of learning. He ends by stating that his people would be glad to take 12 of the colonists' sons to educate them and make them into men.

📁 *Spanish Summaries*, p. 12

A **Active Reading**

RESPOND Ask students to describe their reactions to Canassatego as a person based on his message.

(Some students may say they like him —that he sounds like a humorous, wise person. Others may say he seems rather arrogant.)

Additional Resources

📁 *Active Reading Guide*, p. 12
🎧 *Audio Library*
🎧 *Spanish Audio Library*

We know you highly <u>esteem</u> the kind of learning taught in these colleges, and the maintenance of our young men, while with you, would be very expensive to you. We are convinced, therefore, that you mean to do us good by your <u>proposal</u>; and we thank you heartily. But you who are so wise must know that different nations have different <u>conceptions</u> of things; and you will not therefore take it amiss,[1] if our ideas of this kind of education happens not to be the same with yours. We have had some experience of it. Several of our young people were formerly brought up in the colleges of the northern provinces; they were instructed in all your sciences; but, when they came back to us, they were bad runners, ignorant of every means of living in the woods, unable to bear either cold or hunger, knew neither how to build a cabin, take a deer, or kill an enemy, spoke our language imperfectly, were therefore neither fit for hunters, warriors, nor counsellors, they were totally good for nothing. We are however not the less obliged for your kind offer, tho' we decline accepting it; and to show our grateful sense of it, if the gentlemen of Virginia shall send us a dozen of their sons, we will take great care of their education, instruct them in all we know, and make men of them.

---

1. To *take amiss* is "to take offense at."

Vocabulary
esteem (es tēm′) *v.* to regard favorably; value highly
proposal (prə pō′zəl) *n.* something put forward for consideration as a plan of action
conception (kən sep′shən) *n.* mental image or idea; thought or notion

Teaching Options

Educating Native Americans Students may be interested to learn that special schools for educating Native American children were established in many places. Have students use a search engine to find out more about these schools. Search for keywords such as *Indian schools*, *Native American schools*, or *Native American education*.

Responding to Literature

Personal Response

What questions would you like to ask Canassatego? Why?

ANALYZING LITERATURE

RECALL AND INTERPRET

1. Canassatego begins by thanking the colonists for their offer. What reasons does he give for saying that he knows they mean well? How might this beginning affect the colonists?
2. According to Canassatego, what skills did Iroquois men need? Why might these skills have been particularly important to them? Explain.
3. What does Canassatego say about the Native Americans who had gone to college in the northern provinces? How do you think the colonists might have responded to his comments? Why?
4. What counteroffer does Canassatego make? What reason does he give for making this offer? What might be his real reason? Explain.

EVALUATE AND CONNECT

5. In your own words, state what Canassatego wants the men from Virginia to understand. Do you think he makes his point effectively?
6. Theme Connections   In your opinion, why are the colonists interested in changing Canassatego's people? Explain.
7. Canassatego states, "Different nations have different conceptions of things." In your own life, would you say that different groups have different ideas about things? Support your response with details.
8. Being a diplomat requires tact and sensitivity, especially when dealing with people of different cultural backgrounds. Based on "Offer of Help," do you think Canassatego had effective skills as a diplomat? Explain.

Literary ELEMENTS

Tone

Tone is the attitude that a writer expresses toward his or her subject matter. When we speak, we choose a tone of voice to give clues to such underlying attitudes as humor, formality, anger, or sadness. Similarly, when we write, we carefully choose our words and structure our sentences in order to set the tone.

1. How would you describe the tone of Canassatego's speech? Cite examples of words or sentences that you feel indicate the tone.
2. In your opinion, why did Canassatego choose this particular tone?

● See **Literary Terms Handbook,** p. R16.

EXTENDING YOUR RESPONSE

Literature Groups

An Effective Education   In your group, discuss this question: *What practical skills should schools teach in order to prepare students for "real life"?* Refer to the list you created for the Focus Activity on page 107, adding any new ideas that you may have gained by reading Canassatego's thoughts. Present and explain the group's ideas to the class.

Creative Writing

R.S.V.P.   Write a letter that the representatives from Virginia might have written to respond to Canassatego. Choose your words carefully to express your reaction clearly. Be sure that your letter conveys respect for Canassatego and appreciation for his offer.

 Save your work for your portfolio.

LITERARY ELEMENTS

1. On the surface, his tone is very deferential and respectful. Examples include ". . . we thank you heartily," "But you who are so wise . . ." ". . . and you will not therefore take it amiss . . ." His final "and make men of them," however, implies sarcasm.
2. Students may say that the tone forces the audience to see his point without being overtly offensive.

Additional Resources

✍ *Literary Elements Transparency 11*

Responding to the Selection

Personal Response

Students should explain why the answers to their questions would be important for them to know.

ANALYZING LITERATURE

1. He says the colonists themselves value this kind of learning, and he realizes that this learning is expensive. The colonists may believe that Canassatego appreciates their offer.
2. Running, living in the woods, withstanding the heat and the cold, knowing how to build a cabin, killing a deer or an enemy, and speaking their native language were essential skills.
3. He said that they were "totally good for nothing." The colonists who understood the irony of his speech were probably offended; those who missed it probably believed Canassatego too ignorant to understand the value of education.
4. He offers to teach 12 of the colonists' sons to be men. Although his offer is couched in polite terms, it is sarcastic, indicating that the colonists' offer is insulting.
5. He wants them to understand that each culture has skills appropriate to that culture. Some students may say that his point is made subtly but effectively.
6. The colonists assume that Canassatego's people are "uncivilized" and need education in the things that the colonists value. The colonists do not understand or value Native American customs or education.
7. Students may say that different political parties, different religious values, and different cultural traditions—related to food, clothing, and music—all show that different groups have different ideas.
8. Those who say yes may believe that he makes a strong case without overtly offending the colonists; those who say no may indicate that although he is not overtly offensive, his tone is subtly biting and sarcastic.

Writing Workshop

Objectives

- To write a historical narrative in the first person
- To plan a historical narrative
- To draft, revise, edit, and present a historical narrative
- To reflect on and assess one's historical narrative

GLENCOE TECHNOLOGY

WRITER'S ASSISTANT
CD-ROM

Students can use Glencoe's templates and guidelines software for narrative writing to aid them in working through the steps in the writing process in this lesson.

Teaching Strategies

PREWRITING

Explore ideas Have students suggest further questions and situations to consider before writing and list these on the board for reference.

Choose an audience Students should consider appropriate language, level of difficulty, and details when they are choosing their audience.

Consider your purpose Before writing, have students identify their purpose and how to achieve it.

Teaching Options

·: Writing Workshop :·

Narrative Writing: Historical Narrative

Does reading about the past make you wonder what it would have been like to have lived during another time in history? If so, writing about a historical period is the next best thing to being there. **In this workshop, you will write a historical narrative in the first person.** In other words, you will use your imagination to enter into the time and place of one of the selections from this unit, then you'll write about the past from the point of view of someone who was there.

● As you write your narrative, refer to the **Writing Handbook,** pp. R62–R77.

The Writing Process

PREWRITING

PREWRITING TIP
If you find it difficult to imagine living in a different time period, think first about the similarities between people who lived then and people who live now. Then take it from there.

Explore ideas
Obviously, you weren't alive hundreds of years ago, so the personal experiences you describe in your narrative will be fictional. However, the sites and situations you write about should be real. To help you choose which literary setting to "visit," try some of these strategies.

● As you scan the selections, jot down "What if" questions, such as, "What if a group of colonists bumped into Mary Rowlandson and her captors?"
● Complete some sentence starters, such as, "When Aataentsic threw herself after the big tree, I went _____ ."
● Quiz yourself about your own strengths and limitations by asking such questions as, "How would I have survived the first winter at Plymouth?"

Choose an audience
To some extent, the content and style of your narrative will depend on your audience. For example, if you write for children, you might want to include a great deal of dialogue and action to keep them interested. If you write for your peers, you might have your narrator be a teenager.

Consider your purpose
No matter who your audience is, the main purpose of your narrative will probably be to help readers understand what it would have been like to live during a particular time in history.

MEETING INDIVIDUAL NEEDS · ENGLISH LANGUAGE LEARNERS

Cultural Connection Prepare for writing by asking students about their pasts. What stories about earlier times have they heard in their families? What historical stories are in their cultures?

Activity English language learners may write their historical narratives in their native language, using other native language speakers as their audience. Students can then focus on the narrative, using the steps in the writing process explained in this workshop. Have students read their narratives aloud to the class and then retell the story in English.

Additional Resources
📁 *English Language Learners Sourcebook*

Make a plan

The first step in developing a plan for your historical narrative is to decide on the time and place—the **setting**—of your narrative. Then, think about the other main elements of a story. You might want to jot down your thoughts on a chart like the one below:

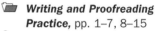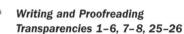

STUDENT MODEL

Setting	Where and when does the action occur? What does the place look like? What details will bring the setting to life?	The settlement of Plymouth, on the Atlantic coast, in 1620. I'll try to get pictures and a map of the reconstruction.
Point of view	Who's telling your story? Since this is a first-person narrative, the narrator of your tale will use words like *I* and *me*. However, that narrator doesn't have to be you. He or she can be a fictional character or a historical figure.	When I visited the modern reconstruction of Plymouth Plantation, I wondered about the people who used to live there. I think the narrator will be one of the colonists—a fictional one.
Characters	Who are they? Are they real people or fictional characters? How can you make them come alive in your narrative?	The other characters will be Captain Standish and the settlers that were really there. I'll re-read *Of Plymouth Plantation* and look in other sources to find out more about what they were like.
Plot	What is the problem or conflict? What relationship does your plot have to the actual historical events?	Problem = survival during the first winter. Captain Standish, one of the few healthy men, is struggling to keep the others alive. The climax will come when some of the sick people get well enough to bury the ones who didn't make it.

Note any factual information you will need to fill out background details. Is the information easily available from the library or other sources? If not, you may want to rethink your plans.

Make a plan Have students make a chart similar to the one described on this page. Then have them answer the questions in the model. They may find it helpful to refer to the notes they took when they were exploring ideas. Remind students that in this section they will just be jotting down notes to themselves that they will use later to draft their narratives. As students make their plans, they should review a selection with a similar setting from this theme to help them develop their own narratives. Encourage them to use self-stick notes to mark relevant passages.

Additional Resources

📁 ***Writing and Proofreading Practice,*** pp. 1–7, 8–15

✍ ***Writing and Proofreading Transparencies 1–6, 7–8, 25–26***

📕 ***Writer's Choice,*** Lessons 4.1–4.4

Special Needs Students with emotional difficulties are often better able to express their thoughts through the visual arts than verbally. Brainstorm with the students to find ways they can represent their historical narrative visually before writing it down.

Activity Point out that a visual representation can be anything from an illustration to a sculpture. Encourage students first to explore their narratives on paper, considering audience and purpose. Remind them to take notes as they plan. Then allow them to express their narratives visually before proceeding to write. **L1**

Additional Resources
📁 ***Inclusion Strategies***

Write your draft Remind students that drafting is the stage for ideas, not perfection. They should concentrate on the details their sensory images bring to them, not on whether or not these are important to the narrative or grammatically precise. Students can refine their work and take out unnecessary or unwanted details later in the writing process.

Set the scene Remind students that setting the scene involves engaging all of the senses of the reader—not just the sense of sight. Sounds and smells, especially, evoke a sense of place.

Be your own critic Allow students to wait for a few hours or a few days before revising their narratives. This will help students come to their work with a fresh approach, which often leads to new ideas and clarity.

Ask another critic Also, encourage students to provide positive suggestions when reviewing each other's work by focusing on the Questions for Revising.

Teaching Options

~: Writing Workshop :~

DRAFTING

DRAFTING TIP
To help imagine yourself in the role of the narrator, keep asking yourself such questions as, "What is the narrator feeling now?"

Write your draft
Before you start writing, you might want to close your eyes for a few minutes and imagine yourself in the role of your narrator. Notice what you see, hear, smell, and feel. Then open your eyes and start writing about all those things. Don't concern yourself with what is important and what's not. You'll have time to filter and refine your details later.

Set the scene
In order for your historical narrative to take readers somewhere they've never been before, you have to create a strong sense of time and place. Bring your readers into the narrative by using distinctive details and specific, vivid words that appeal to the readers' sense of smell, touch, or hearing as well as their sense of sight.

STUDENT MODEL

Wherever I looked, I saw gray—the murky gray sky, the restless gray sea, the bare and shivering gray trees. The smoke from the houses was gray, and it scratched at my throat painfully. It was as if a gray blanket of illness lay over everything and was seeping through our skin.

REVISING

REVISING TIP
Be selective. Ask yourself whether each detail really adds to the flow and impact of the narrative. If it doesn't, throw it out.

 TECHNOLOGY TIP
When revising on the computer, don't delete anything. Instead, cut unwanted sentences and paste them at the end of the file. Later, review this material for ideas or details to add.

Be your own critic
Do not review your narrative right away. Wait a few hours or a few days, then approach the story as if you were reading it for the first time. Put a check mark beside passages that are unclear, unnecessary, flat, or underdeveloped. When you're done reading, go back and try to improve those passages.

Ask another critic
Ask another student to review your narrative. Using the **Questions for Revising** as a guide, he or she should write questions and comments in the margins of your story. When you get your narrative back, consider which suggestions you want to follow.

QUESTIONS FOR REVISING

☑ Is the sense of time and place clear? How could it be strengthened?

☑ Where could details be added to make events or characters more vivid? Which details should be left out?

☑ How can the central conflict be strengthened?

☑ Which lines of dialogue sound realistic and which do not? How could the unrealistic ones be improved?

☑ Do the characters' thoughts and motivations seem real?

☑ Is the opening attention-getting? Is the ending satisfying?

STUDENT MODEL

I wondered where the deadly illness had come from. Had it come from the ship? Was it waiting
crowded, reeking
this new
for us on shore? (we had come so far to find)

112 🐚 UNIT 1

Writing Minilesson

Sensory Details Discuss the importance of vivid and precise sensory details in writing. In a historical narrative, words and expressions about time, place, and character are essential to an understanding of the history. The reader should be able to feel, taste, hear, smell, and see the images. Have students read the following two sentences and choose the clearer, more vivid description of the scene.

1. The harsh, bitter wind snapped at our backs as we trudged through the mounds of snow that first year at Plymouth.

2. It was cold, and there was a lot of snow during our first year at Plymouth.

Activity Have students work with a partner to look for vague or unclear descriptions in their narratives. Ask students to

discuss these passages and help each other develop more descriptive details. Then have them rewrite, using more sensory details. **L2**

Additional Resources

Writer's Choice, Lesson 3.2

EDITING/PROOFREADING

When you think your narrative reads smoothly, proofread it. Go over the story carefully several times, referring to the **Proofreading Checklist** on the inside back cover of this book to make sure you check for the most common types of errors.

Grammar Hint

Be sure each verb agrees with its subject, even when other words come between the subject and verb.

*The strong **arms** of Captain Standish gently **raise** the shivering woman's head so that she can sip the hot soup.*

● For more on subject-verb agreement, see **Language Handbook**, p. R21.

STUDENT MODEL

The days of last week ~~was~~ *were* bitter cold. This week, any warmth, even during our mid-day chores, ~~are~~ *is* hard to find.

PUBLISHING/PRESENTING

How will your narrative reach its proper audience? If you've written for children, you may want to turn your story into an illustrated mini-book for a grade-school library. If you've written for your peers, think about collaborating with them. You could form a historical fiction collection by binding your narrative with others that take place in the same setting.

PRESENTING TIP
Did you come across any maps of your story's setting? Consider making a copy to illustrate your narrative.

Reflecting

Think over your writing experience in this workshop. In your journal, comment on how writing about another time and place affected your process. Is your historical narrative something you would like to include in your portfolio? Why or why not?

Set goals for your next piece of writing. Consider what you hope to accomplish and what you plan to do differently.

Save your work for your portfolio.

Have students use the Proofreading Checklist on the inside back cover of their textbooks. Then have students work in pairs, reading their narratives aloud to one another. Reading their work aloud several times allows students to hear errors that they may overlook when reading silently.

PUBLISHING/PRESENTING

Allow students time to prepare and share their narratives with the appropriate audiences. If they are going to read aloud or present their narrative dramatically, they will need extra time for preparation.

Reflecting

Portfolio Encourage students to ask themselves these questions as they decide whether or not to include this work in their portfolios.

Does my historical narrative
- clearly express time and place to my audience?
- make the readers feel as if they are there?
- represent careful planning and revision on my part?

Suggest that if students answer yes to two or more of these questions, they should include their narratives in their portfolios.

✔ ASSESSMENT OPTIONS

📁 ***Writing Assessment and Portfolio Management***
- Writing Assessment, pp. 1–13, 14–16
- Portfolio Management, pp. 51–58

Unit Wrap-Up

Objectives

- To respond personally to the selections, discussions, and activities in this unit
- To write a comparison of the attitudes expressed in three selections
- To complete a self-evaluation, set a goal, and devise a plan for achieving that goal

PERSONAL RESPONSE

1. Students may rank the accounts of Mary Rowlandson and Cabeza de Vaca highly because they are high-interest tales that make the time and place seem real.
2. *Possible responses:*
   - Oral literature relies on tone of voice, pacing, and repetition. Written literature requires more formal structures.
   - Using several genres provides a fuller picture of a time and place.
   - History books give facts and figures. Literature offers first-hand information about what people thought and felt.
   - Reading Canassatego's letter showed me that I had misconceptions about the Native Americans.

ANALYZING LITERATURE

Students' writing should
- include an introductory paragraph that identifies the three selections and contains a thesis statement.
- provide details to support the conclusions.

EVALUATE AND SET GOALS

Evaluate

Have students list all contributions they made during this unit, such as positive peer review. Remind students to evaluate their unit work as a whole, not the strengths or weaknesses of one or two tasks.

Set Goals

Have students use a word web to visually represent their goal setting.

114 UNIT 1

Unit Wrap-Up

PERSONAL RESPONSE

1. Rank the selections in this unit from most to least interesting. Give a reason for each ranking.
2. What did your work in this unit teach you about:
   - differences and similarities between oral and written literature?
   - literary genres, such as myth, poetry, or narrative?
   - how to use literature to learn about history?
   - how to gain insight into different cultures from their literature?

ANALYZING LITERATURE

Comparing Attitudes   Compare and contrast the attitudes that Native Americans and Europeans displayed toward one another in the years covered by this unit. Use Cabeza de Vaca's *La Relación,* Canassatego's "Offer of Help," and Rowlandson's narrative of her captivity for evidence. Write a few paragraphs to explain your conclusions. Use specific facts and statements from the selections to support your ideas.

EVALUATE AND SET GOALS

Evaluate

1. Make a list of three things you contributed to the class as you studied this unit. Check the best one.
2. What aspect of this unit was the most challenging for you?
   - How did you approach the challenge?
   - What was the result?
3. If you had another week to work on this unit, what would you hope to learn; what skills would you hope to strengthen?
4. How would you assess your work in this unit using the following scale? Give at least two reasons for your assessment.
   4 = outstanding   **3** = good   **2** = fair   **1** = weak

Set Goals

1. Set a goal for your work in the next unit. Try to focus on improving a skill area, such as speaking or critical thinking.
2. Discuss your goal with your teacher.
3. Plan specific steps to achieve the goal.
4. Plan two or more points at which to stop and judge your work.
5. Think of a method to evaluate finished work.

BUILD YOUR PORTFOLIO

Select   From the writing you did in this unit, choose two pieces to put into your portfolio. Use the following questions as guides when choosing:
- Which taught you the most?
- Which are you likely to share?
- Which was the most difficult to complete?

Reflect   Include some explanatory notes with the portfolio pieces you chose. Use these questions to guide you:
- What are the piece's strengths and weaknesses?
- What did working on the piece teach you about writing (or about other skills the piece displays)?
- How would you revise the piece today to make it stronger?

114 UNIT 1

GLENCOE TECHNOLOGY

MINDJOGGER VIDEOQUIZZES
VIDEODISC

Use *MindJogger* to review the Unit One content.

Unit One
Side A

 Also available in VHS.

✔ ASSESSMENT OPTIONS

📁 ***Writing Assessment and Portfolio Management***
- Writing Assessment, pp. 1–13
- Portfolio Management, pp. 51–58

Reading on Your Own

If you have enjoyed the literature in this unit, you might also be interested in the following books.

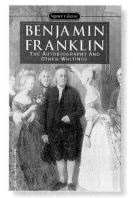

The Autobiography of Benjamin Franklin

by Benjamin Franklin While Franklin did not live to complete this autobiography, the great American leader tells of his life from an impoverished childhood in Boston to his successful careers as a printer, inventor, and writer.

The Account: Álvar Núñez Cabeza de Vaca's *Relación*

translated by Martin A. Favata and José B. Fernández This dramatic narrative, published in Spain in 1542, chronicles one of the first Spanish explorations of America. The story of the extreme hardships of the expedition is intertwined with vivid descriptions of the lush landscape and the cultures of native peoples.

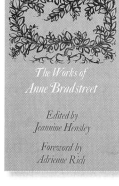

The Works of Anne Bradstreet

edited by Jeannine Hensley This book provides an opportunity to read more of the works of this skilled poet.

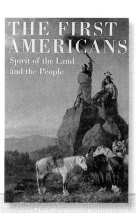

The First Americans

by Josepha Sherman An excellent, intelligent, and richly illustrated overview of Native American cultures, this book includes information about customs, beliefs, living conditions, and contacts with white settlers.

Reading on Your Own

Glencoe Literature Library

The Autobiography of Benjamin Franklin by Benjamin Franklin is available in the *Glencoe Literature Library*. For a complete listing, see p. T48 in this book.

The *Study Guides for Glencoe Literature* provide instructional support and student activities for works in the *Glencoe Literature Library*.

MEETING INDIVIDUAL NEEDS — INCLUSION STRATEGIES

You may wish to recommend *The First Americans* by Josepha Sherman to your less-proficient readers. The illustrations make this book particularly appropriate for these students. **L1**

The other books listed are rated for average readers (**L2**) or for students who need more challenging reading material (**L3**):

- *The Account: Álvar Núñez Cabeza de Vaca's Relación* translated by Martin A. Favata and José B. Fernández **L2**
- *The Autobiography of Benjamin Franklin* by Benjamin Franklin **L2**
- *The Works of Anne Bradstreet* edited by Jeannine Hensley **L3**

Additional Resources

 Inclusion Strategies

Standardized Test Practice

Answers and Analyses

1. **D** Since this sentence is composed of two independent clauses, a conjunction is needed to connect them. Choices C and D both have the conjunction *and*; Choice C, however, uses an awkward "ing" construction. The best choice is therefore D.

2. **E** In this sentence, the verbs *to explore* and *to ascend* must be in parallel form.

3. **B** Whenever possible, avoid the passive voice. Choices A, C, and D are all in passive voice. Choice E implies that the hurricane swayed, not the statue.

4. **D** To maintain parallel structure in the sentence, "has failed" is required. (Though the program *has excelled . . . it has failed*)

 TEST-TAKING TIP

Point out that on any multiple-choice question, there are two ways to find the "best" answer. Sometimes students know the right answer and find it in the choices. If this is not possible, they can start eliminating the choices that they are sure are wrong, and then choose from the remaining options.

Directions: The following sentences test correctness and effectiveness of expression. In choosing answers, follow the requirements of standard written English; that is, pay attention to grammar, choice of words, sentence construction, and punctuation.

In each of the following sentences, part of the sentence or the entire sentence is underlined. Beneath each sentence you will find five ways of phrasing the underlined part. Choice A repeats the original; the other four are different.

Choose the answer that best expresses the meaning of the original sentence. If you think the original is better than any of the alternatives, choose it; otherwise choose one of the others. Your choice should produce the most effective sentence—clear and precise, without awkwardness or ambiguity. Write the corresponding letter on your paper.

---

1. Many times reporters are privy to more information than they include in a piece, <u>this restraint helps create an especially compelling story</u>.

    (A) this restraint helps create an especially compelling story
    (B) with this restraint helping create an especially compelling story
    (C) and an especially compelling story being the creation of their restraint
    (D) and this restraint helps create an especially compelling story
    (E) an especially compelling story created from this restraint.

2. Climbing without supplemental oxygen at high altitudes is hard on the body, but it enables some climbers to explore remote areas <u>and they can ascend</u> without stopping.

    (A) and they can ascend
    (B) as well as ascending
    (C) so they can ascend
    (D) and an ascension
    (E) and to ascend

3. With all its high-powered winds, <u>the Statue of Liberty was caused to sway no more than five inches by the hurricane</u>.

    (A) the Statue of Liberty was caused to sway no more than five inches by the hurricane.
    (B) the hurricane caused the Statue of Liberty to sway no more than five inches
    (C) no more than five inches was how far the Statue of Liberty was swayed by the hurricane
    (D) the Statue of Liberty's movement was kept to no more than five inches by the hurricane
    (E) the hurricane swayed no more than five inches to the Statue of Liberty

4. The lecturer argued that though the program has excelled at training future scholars, <u>the failure is in its not educating</u> vocational students in the value of scholarly interests.

    (A) the failure is in its not educating
    (B) the failure it has is in its not educating
    (C) it failed not to educate
    (D) it has failed to educate
    (E) failing in its education of

SAT II Practice
Subject Test: Writing
Error Identification
Timed (4 minutes)

Directions: The following sentences test your knowledge of grammar, usage, diction (choice of words), and idiom.

Some sentences are correct.
No sentence contains more than one error.

You will find that the error, if there is one, is underlined and lettered. Elements of the sentence that are not underlined will not be changed. In choosing answers, follow the requirements of standard written English.

If there is an error, select the <u>one underlined part</u> that must be changed to make the sentence correct. Write the corresponding letter on your paper.

If there is no error, select answer E.

1. Only after the curtains had <u>rose</u> ten feet
<u>A</u>
<u>was</u> the crowd able <u>to see</u> the <u>layout</u> of the
<u>B</u>   <u>C</u>   <u>D</u>
stage. <u>No error</u>
         <u>E</u>

2. The new minor-league players <u>attracted a</u>
                               <u>A</u>
crowd of fans, <u>for</u> it had <u>never been seen</u>
               <u>B</u> <u>C</u>   <u>D</u>
in public before. <u>No error</u>
                   <u>E</u>

3. The building of a float for homecoming

<u>was first proposed</u> in the spring,
<u>A</u>
<u>but not until</u> school opened in the fall did
<u>B</u>
<u>such a project</u> become <u>a reality</u>. <u>No error</u>
<u>C</u>   <u>D</u>   <u>E</u>

4. If one is interested <u>in learning</u> <u>even more</u>
                        <u>A</u>   <u>B</u>   <u>C</u>
about aeronautics, <u>you should</u> take a flying
                    <u>D</u>
lesson. <u>No error</u>
          <u>E</u>

5. Meteorologists have discovered that public

concern is heightened <u>considerably</u>
                        <u>A</u>
whenever television stations <u>forecasted</u>
                             <u>B</u>   <u>C</u>
weather advisories early <u>in the day</u>.
                          <u>D</u>

<u>No error</u>
<u>E</u>

6. An organized team sport allows students

<u>to undertake</u> challenges that <u>encourages</u>
<u>A</u>   <u>B</u>
each of <u>them</u> to be <u>both</u> competitive
         <u>C</u>   <u>D</u>
and cooperative. <u>No error</u>
                   <u>E</u>

 STOP

Answers and Analyses

1. **A** The correct form of the verb is *had risen.*
2. **C** Students should look back to see that the subject *players* is plural. Therefore it needs a plural pronoun.
3. **E** There is no error in this sentence.
4. **D** The sentence begins by using the pronoun *one.* It should continue by saying *one should* . . .
5. **C** The sentence begins in the present tense (concern *is* heightened) and should continue in the present tense (*forecast*).
6. **B** The subject of the verb *to encourage* is *challenges.* This verb should agree with the plural subject and be written *encourage.*

 **TEST-TAKING TIP**

If you have students who are extremely anxious about the test they must take, try to help them put it in perspective. Let them know that standardized tests are not good indicators of how "smart" a student is. Help them see the many other factors that go into the college admissions process.

MORE PRACTICE

For additional practice with the SAT II: Writing Test, assign pp. 22–27 from the *College Entrance Exams Preparation and Practice Workbook.*

Unit Two — At a Glance
A New Nation

Theme 2: BREAKING FREE

KEYS TO LITERARY CONNECTIONS

 Comparing Selections

In each theme of **Glencoe Literature**, the **Comparing Selections** feature gives students an opportunity to compare two selections they have just read. Each Comparing Selections page provides a variety of options to address diverse aspects of the reading and literature curriculum.

World Literature

Glencoe Literature contains a variety of literature that represents cultures from around the world. World Literature selections are highlighted with this symbol:

Theme 3: GAINING INSIGHT

→ **UNIT WRAP-UP**

KEYS TO TEACHING OPTIONS

Block Scheduling

Activities that are particularly suited to use within a block scheduling framework are identified throughout this unit by the following designation: For detailed suggestions on block scheduling, see the **Block Scheduling Guide** for this grade level.

Key to Ability Levels

The Teaching Options throughout this unit have been coded for students of various abilities.

L1 BASIC activities for all students

L2 AVERAGE activities for average to above-average students

L3 CHALLENGING activities for above-average students

Reading Skills in this unit

Variety of Texts

In addition to many selections by early American writers, this unit also includes the following text types:

- autobiography
- nonfiction
- speech
- essay
- narrative
- historical document
- poetry
- letter
- rhetoric
- historic project
- script
- review

Comprehension Skills

The following instructional support for comprehension skills appears in this unit of the Student Edition:

- Active Reading Strategies and Model (pp. 3–35)
- Scanning (p. 284)

See also the **Reading Minilessons** throughout the unit in this Teacher's Wraparound Edition.

Reading Resources

Comprehension Skills Resources

Active Reading Guides

The Active Reading Guide provides graphic organizers and study guide questions to support students' reading of each selection. (**Active Reading Guide**, pp. 13–35)

Reading Workbook

The Reading Workbook (pp. 19–40) includes additional instruction and reinforcement of reading strategies and skills.

Audio Library

Available both on tape and on CD, the Audio Library provides valuable comprehension support.

Resources for Reading Widely

Glencoe Literature Library

Each title in the Glencoe Literature Library includes a full-length novel or play plus related readings. A separate Study Guide is available for each title.

Literature Classics CD-ROM

The 900 selections on this CD-ROM can be searched by author, theme, or genre.

 A coproduction of Glencoe and Time Inc., *inTime* includes a wealth of high-interest nonfiction related to the selections and themes in Unit Two.

✔ Assessment in this unit

Assessment Options in the Student Edition

Glencoe Literature offers a number of diverse ways to evaluate student understanding and skill proficiency. In the Student Edition, use the following:

- **Responding to Literature**
  Following each selection, students are asked to recall facts, interpret ideas, and evaluate concepts as they answer a variety of questions and complete activities to extend their understanding.
- **Unit Wrap-Up (pp. 312–313)**
  Here students respond to the selections on personal and analytical levels. They also assume ownership of their learning by setting and evaluating goals and by selecting work for their portfolios.

See also the many **Assessment Resources** listed on the facing page.

THE PRINCETON REVIEW

Standardized Test Practice

The Princeton Review has developed the Standardized Test Practice pages found at the end of this unit (pp. 314–315). These pages contain practice test questions that help students remain familiar with standardized test formats and content. For additional practice, you may want to use the following resources:

- **College Entrance Exam Preparation and Practice Workbook**

Writing Skills in this unit

Writing Skills

The Student Edition of Unit Two offers strong instructional support for writing skills:

In **Extending Your Response**, which follows each selection:
- Writing About Literature
- Personal/Creative Writing

In **Writing Skills** Lessons:
- Effective Conclusions (p. 181)

See also the **Writing Minilessons** throughout the unit in this Teacher's Wraparound Edition.

Writing Workshops

Both themes in Unit Two conclude with a **Writing Workshop** that guides students through the writing process.
- Personal Writing: Reflective Essay (pp. 196–200)
- Descriptive Writing: Travel Article (pp. 308–311)

Writing Resources

Writer's Assistant CD-ROM
Each Writing Workshop is supplemented by an interactive writing guide on the Writer's Assistant CD-ROM. This easy-to-use writing guide provides prompts, templates, and other tools that lead students through the writing process.

Writing and Proofreading Practice
Blackline masters present in-depth instruction and practice on a specific step in the writing process and proofreading. (pp. 16–29)

Writing and Proofreading Transparencies
Transparencies (9–12, 27–30) provide graphic organizers and proofreading exercises for whole class instruction.

Research and Report Writing Guide
This resource provides extensive tips and activities to guide students in their writing projects in the literature classroom as well as in classes across the curriculum.

Style and Documentation Sourcebook for Writers
This sourcebook is a combination reference and workbook, giving students the most up-to-date information and guidance regarding traditional as well as technological research strategies and documentation.

Grammar and Composition Handbook
The Grammar and Composition Handbook provides instruction that supplements activities in the student textbook.

Assessment Resources

Selection Quick Checks
For each selection, a Quick Check of three to five short-answer questions measures students' literal comprehension.

Selection and Theme Assessment
The Selection and Theme Assessment instrument tests students' abilities to recall, interpret, and evaluate what they've read. The tests consist of multiple-choice, short-answer, and essay questions.

Performance Assessment
Alternative assessment instruments and rubrics for Unit Two are found in the Performance Assessment ancillary.

Writing Assessment and Portfolio Management
These notes and strategies, student models, and assessment tools assist with the task of measuring students' progress as writers and as monitors of their own writing.

Testmaker
Teachers can customize selection, theme, and Unit Two tests by accessing the Testmaker database.

MindJogger Videoquizzes
Using a popular game show format, MindJogger Videoquizzes enable teachers to evaluate students' understanding of Unit Two in a quick and fun manner.

ᴬ New Nation

Unit Objectives

- To enjoy reading a variety of literary forms, including poetry, essays, autobiographies, and personal letters
- To analyze techniques used to inform and persuade in nonfiction works
- To apply strategies for reading nonfiction and poetry

Ⅴ IEWING THE PAINTING

American engraver and painter Asher B. Durand (1796–1886) became a leading figure of the Hudson River School's group of painters inspired by the unspoiled beauty of America. In *Kindred Spirits*, Durand portrays fellow painter Thomas Cole and poet William Cullen Bryant admiring a waterfall on the Hudson River in New York.

Responding to the Art Discussion questions:

- Why do you think the figures are so small and placed so far back in the painting? (*Durand wanted to emphasize the vastness of the landscape rather than the people.*)
- Why is the painting called *Kindred Spirits*? (*Artists of the time believed that contemplating nature connected them with the eternal. Thus the poet and painter shared this connection.*)
- How does the artist make the scene more dramatic? (*His techniques include the use of vertical and diagonal lines and high contrast.*)

Kindred Spirits, 1849. Asher Brown Durand. Oil on canvas, 46 x 36 in. The New York Public Library, New York.

118

TEACHER *to* TEACHER

R. N. SNIDER HIGH SCHOOL • FT. WAYNE, INDIANA

I take a social studies approach with this unit. I give students the historical background. We discuss the thoughts of the Age of Reason in England as well as in America. What is logical thinking and what does it have to do with literature? Students are interested in how literature comes out of the events of society. I use Jefferson's Declaration of Independence to explain "reason" as it was understood in the philosophy of the eighteenth century and to discuss the politics and logic of the period. I also show the video *1776* so that students can see the struggle over the ideas that went into writing this document.

JOHN HOUSER

UNIT ✤ TWO

A New Nation

1750–1850

*"Liberty, when it begins
to take root, is a plant
of rapid growth."*

—*George Washington*

Theme 2

Breaking Free
Pages 129–200

Theme 3

Gaining Insight
Pages 201–311

RESOURCE MANAGER

See the *Unit Two Planning Guide*
(pp. vi–1) for additional teaching notes,
strategies, and resources for introducing
Unit Two.

Introducing the Unit

Have students read the quotation.
Then pose these questions for
discussion:
• What do you think are the "roots"
  of liberty?
• What conditions are needed for
  freedom to grow?
• Has liberty in the United States
  grown quickly since the American
  Revolution? Why or why not?

Theme 2: Breaking Free

The literature in Theme 2 highlights
the determination and doubts of
early Americans in their quest to
break free. Additional world literature
shows that breaking free is a universal quest that can be as large as a
battle between two nations or as
small as a decision one person
must face.

Theme 3: Gaining Insight

The richly imagined, authentically
American literature in Theme 3 displays the maturation of America's
literary tastes and talent.

GLENCOE
TECHNOLOGY

LITERATURE CLASSICS
CD-ROM

Search for related pieces of literature by theme, author, or title.

Setting the Scene

Introducing the Time Period

Write the following quote from Thomas Paine on the board: "The Revolutionary War contributed more to enlighten the world, and diffuse a spirit of freedom and liberality among mankind, than any other human event . . . that ever preceded it." Explain to students that the selections in Unit 2 will focus on the attempts of people to break free from old traditions and do things their own way. Invite students to share anything they may know about this important period of U.S. history. Begin a discussion by posing such questions as: Why did the British colonies in America seek independence? Who are the key figures in this period of American history? How did the young nation grow and change during this time? How was life in America different in 1850 than it was in 1750?

Historical Note

Even at the time of the Revolution, many colonists did not consider themselves "Americans." They considered themselves British (which, in fact, they were). Moreover, they felt a stronger allegiance to the specific colony in which they made their home than to the colonies as a group.

Setting the Scene

On December 16, 1773, three British ships filled with chests of dried tea leaves lay in Boston harbor. A group of colonists, furious at the faraway king for taxing and restricting the sale of tea, refused to let the ships unload their cargo. That night about two hundred colonists decided to take more direct action. Disguised as Mohawk Indians, with red paint on their faces and blankets tied around their waists, the men marched to the waterfront. They used the ship's cranes to hoist 342 chests of tea out of the ship's hold and toss the chests into the harbor. The Boston Tea Party, as it came to be known, infuriated the British king and became a symbol of colonial resistance. Less than two years later, shots fired in Lexington, Massachusetts—what American author Ralph Waldo Emerson called "the shot heard 'round the world"—signaled the start of the American Revolution.

U.S.A.

- 1754 French and Indian War begins (French and British fight over control of North America)
- 1775 Revolutionary War begins
- 1765 Parliament imposes Stamp Act on colonies
- 1776 Declaration of Independence is signed
- 1783 United States wins its independence
- 1791 Bill of Rights is ratified

1750   **1770**   **1790**

World

- 1787 Sierra Leone is founded as a settlement for freed slaves
- 1789 The French Revolution begins
- 1791 Toussaint l'Ouverture leads African slaves in Haiti in a revolt against French rulers

120 🐚 UNIT 2

 interNET CONNECTION

Look into History Have students conduct research to learn about historical sites from the American Revolution that have been preserved or restored. Students might begin their searches using the following keywords: *American Revolution, historical parks,* and *American historical sites.*

Extra Credit Projects

- Have student groups create a time line of the period of American history covered by this unit, 1750–1850. The bottom of the time line should identify key American historical developments, and the top, key American literary events. Time line entries should add to those in this text. **L2** COLLAB. LEARN.

- Have students create biographical maps of one of the authors in the unit. Maps should show the locations of major events in the author's life, and indicate the key events that occurred at each place, such as writing a work, witnessing historical events, or meeting with influential figures. **L2**

History of the Time

"We hold these truths to be self-evident . . ."
—Thomas Jefferson

The Revolution

The American colonists were angry. They had hoped America would be a land of freedom and opportunity and had labored hard, endured severe weather, and risked disease and starvation in order to build towns and farms. They had fought alongside British soldiers to defeat France in the French and Indian War. However, that war had put Britain in debt, and to raise money, the British government looked to the colonies.

The British Parliament passed a series of unpopular laws, forcing the colonists to house British soldiers and taxing everyday items such as newspapers, almanacs, and legal documents. Some colonial political leaders refused to comply, and Britain "dissolved" their power. Then, in 1770, British troops fired on a disorderly mob in Boston. The event came to be known as the Boston Massacre.

After Parliament had levied new taxes on imports such as paint and tea, further violence broke out. In December 1773, the colonists dumped 342 chests of tea from British ships into Boston Harbor. King George III was furious and responded by passing the Intolerable Acts of 1774, a series of laws meant to punish the colonies for their disobedience.

The Acts so outraged the colonists that even the moderate George Washington declared, "the crisis is arrived when we must assert our rights." When the British troops fired at the colonial militia, on April 19, 1775, the colonists responded with force. The war had begun.

Independence

American leaders justified their revolt against British authority in the remarkable Declaration of Independence, approved by the Second Continental Congress on July 4, 1776. The United States went on to wage a war in which the ragtag colonial volunteers ultimately managed to defeat the splendidly outfitted and trained British soldiers.

Winning a war, however, does not create a nation. In 1781 the Second Continental Congress met to establish a government for the new nation. At first, they created a set of laws called the Articles of Confederation, which provided for a weak central government. Realizing the need for a more powerful national government, leaders of all the states met in Philadelphia in 1787. There they crafted the Constitution of the United States. Two years later, in 1789, George Washington was inaugurated as the first president of the United States.

The area and population of the new nation grew rapidly because of the acquisition of the Louisiana Territory and an influx of immigrants. This growth, as well as technological advances and other developments, helped create a flourishing and unique nation.

Timeline

- **1803** United States negotiates Louisiana Purchase
- **1808–1826** Most Latin American countries succeed in gaining independence
- **1810**
- **1812** War of 1812 against Britain begins
- **1815** Napoleon I is defeated at Waterloo and later exiled
- **1830**
- **1836** Texas declares independence from Mexico
- **1842** China opens five ports to trade with Western nations
- **1848** Mexican American War ends, adding territory to United States
- **1850**

Historical Note

Few delegates wanted to sever ties with Great Britain when the Second Continental Congress met in May 1775. In fact, John Dickinson of Pennsylvania wrote the Olive Branch Petition, which affirmed the colonists' loyalty to King George III and pleaded with him to remedy their complaints. Congress approved the petition in July 1775, but the king chose to ignore it. He declared all the colonies to be in rebellion on August 23, and closed American ports to overseas trade several months later. As a result, delegates became convinced that a peaceful settlement with the mother country was not possible.

Financing the War

Although the Continental Congress was supposed to pay for the Revolutionary War, it didn't have the power to tax the people. At the end of 1775, Congress issued paper currency called Continental dollars. It issued so many bills, however, that they lost most of their value. Congress was forced to rely on money from the states as well as on loans and gifts of cash from abroad, including France, the Netherlands, and Spain.

At the MOVIES

Be sure to review this movie before deciding whether to show it to your class.

• The movie **1776** is based on the hit broadway musical by Peter Stone and Sherman Edwards. Directed by Peter Hunt, the movie shows the events leading up to the Declaration of Independence.

Life of the Time

People are talking about

Life of the Time

◀ **The First "People's President"**   Americans inaugurate Andrew Jackson as their seventh president in 1829. Lacking the upper-class background and manners of previous presidents, Jackson is popular among the common people. Thousands attend Jackson's inauguration. As the new president arrives at the White House on horseback, a great crowd follows him.
"Thronging the East Room, the crowd fell on the refreshments, breaking china and smashing furniture."

—*William V. Shannon*

"We, the People"   Democracy is a hot topic in political circles, though its practice does not apply to all Americans. In 1848, Elizabeth Cady Stanton and Lucretia Mott hold the first women's rights convention at Seneca Falls, New York. They present a statement modeled on the Declaration of Independence. They call their resolutions the "Declaration of Sentiments" and profess "that all men and women are created equal."

Travel   Roads are still primitive. As late as 1842, visiting British novelist Charles Dickens reports riding on a road that was ". . . at the best but a track through the wild forest, and among the swamps, bogs, and morasses of the withered bush." Americans develop trails, turnpikes, canals, bridges, steamboats, and railroads. ▶

Firsts

- America's first streetlights are used in Philadelphia. (1757)
- Chocolate is first manufactured in the United States. (1765)
- Elizabeth Blackwell is the first American woman to receive a medical degree. (1849)

U.S.A.							
1752 Franklin experiments with electricity using kite and key	**1769** Dartmouth College is founded		**1772** Charles Wilson Peale, portrait of George Washington	**1780** American Academy of Arts and Sciences is established in Boston		**1789** Thanksgiving is first celebrated as national holiday	**1794** Eli Whitney patents cotton gin

1750		**1770**			**1790**

1700s Introduction of power-driven machinery heralds the Industrial Revolution in England

1782 King Rama I of Siam (now Thailand) makes Bangkok his capital

1786 Wolfgang Amadeus Mozart's comic opera *Le nozze de Figaro* premieres in Vienna

World

Since before the country's inception, Americans had been talking about heading west. Many dreamed of a country that covered all of North America. By the 1840s the United States controlled half the continent, and the term *manifest destiny* came into widespread use. Manifest destiny was the belief stated by New York newspaper editor John O'Sullivan, that the United States was destined to "possess the whole of the continent which Providence has given us." A combination of nationalism and expansionism, the belief in manifest destiny reflected the spirit of a growing country.

Historical Note

A transportation revolution radically changed American life during this period. Roads were improved. Steamboats began to ply America's rivers—its natural highways—in increasing numbers. The invention of the steam locomotive led to the creation of an extensive and impressive rail network. An equally impressive network of canals was also built. The net result was an infrastructure capable of supporting a growing nation and economy, as well as better communication among its citizens.

🖥 **Active Reading**

READING THE TIME LINE Ask students to research the time line entry for the United States in 1780. Have them explain why the academy was established. *(The American Academy of Arts and Sciences was founded to advance research and promote the study of both national and international problems.)*

MEETING INDIVIDUAL NEEDS — ENGLISH LANGUAGE LEARNERS

Cultural Contributions The story of America from 1750 to 1850 is largely the story of the contributions of other cultures. Although the United States was developing a unique culture and character, the contributions of other peoples and their ideas were fundamental.

Activity Have English language learners focus on the contributions their native cultures made to the United States during this time period. Students should conduct research to learn about individuals, groups, or ideas that influenced the United States. Have them share what they learn with the class.

Additional Resources
📁 *English Language Learners Sourcebook*

Food & Fashion

Most Americans are wearing comfortable, sturdy woolen clothing they make by hand.

- Most pioneer women wear smock-like dresses and petticoats over their skirts. Woolen or cotton bonnets protect their faces. ▶
- Frontiersmen wear loose-fitting, thigh-length hunting shirts—made from deerskin or homemade cloth—without buttons and belted or tied at the waist. Deerskin trousers are also worn. ▶

◀ Wealthy Americans are influenced by styles from England and France.

Diets vary, as do clothes.

- On the frontier and farms, a meal usually consists of corn grown in the family's fields and meat provided by the family's cattle, hogs, sheep, and chickens or from wild game.
- On southern plantations, wealthy owners may begin their dinner at three o'clock and continue into the evening. Most of what they eat is produced on their own property. Their meal may start with a rich soup, followed by a choice of mutton, ham, beef, turkey, duck, greens, vegetables, potatoes, beets, and hominy, and end with pudding, tarts, and ice cream.

Portrait of the Children of William Rankin Sr., 1838. Oliver Tarbell Eddy. Oil on canvas, 71 x 60 in. Collection of The Newark Museum, Newark, NJ.

Arts & Entertainment

- American artists such as John Singleton Copley, Charles Wilson Peale, and Gilbert Charles Stuart paint portraits of notable Americans.
- In 1787 Royall Tyler's *The Contrast* is the first American comedy performed by professional actors. The play compares the English and American people.
- In 1815 the Handel and Haydn Society of Boston is founded to perform choral music, and the Philharmonic Society of New York is established in 1842.
- Something close to modern baseball evolves in the 1840s when the British game "rounders" is modified by the use of a hard ball and the tagging of runners.
- In rural areas, at corn-gathering time, as many as forty or fifty people may gather to dance, hold contests, eat, and tell jokes.

Paul Revere, 1768. John Singleton Copley. Oil on canvas, 35 x 28½ in. Museum of Fine Arts, Boston. Gift of Joseph W. Revere, William B. Revere, and Edward H. R. Revere.

Timeline

- 1800 Library of Congress founded
- 1803 Ludwig van Beethoven completes his longest, grandest symphony, the *Third Symphony,* "Eroica"
- **1810**
- 1814 Francis Scott Key, "Star Spangled Banner"
- 1825 First successful steam railroad is built in England
- 1825 Erie Canal opens
- 1826 First overland route to California opens
- **1830**
- 1839 First successful photographic process, French physicist Louis Jacques Daguerre
- 1840 Samuel Morse patents telegraph
- 1849 Harriet Tubman escapes from slavery and joins the Underground Railroad
- **1850**

INTERDISCIPLINARY CONNECTION

Science Benjamin Franklin's most famous scientific experiment involved a kite, a key, and a thunderstorm. Invite students to find out more about Franklin's experiments.

Activity Ask students to research one of Franklin's scientific experiments. Then have them present their findings in an oral report. These questions may help students focus their thoughts: What was Franklin's experiment? What did he learn from it? What was he attempting to prove? What risks did he undergo to conduct this experiment? What lasting contributions to society resulted from this experiment? **L2**

Literature of the Time

Cultural Note

American abolitionist, writer, and editor Lydia Maria Child (1802–1880) founded the country's first children's magazine, *Juvenile Miscellany*, in 1826. She wrote several important abolitionist works, including *An Appeal in Favor of That Class of Americans Called Africans* (1833), and was editor of the *National Anti-Slavery Standard* from 1841 to 1843. Child also wrote about Native Americans. Additionally, she authored the famous poem "Boy's Thanksgiving," which begins "Over the river and through the woods . . ."

Pop Culture

Today there are approximately 1,800 daily newspapers in the United States, as well as 9,700 weekly and semiweekly newspapers. Total circulation of daily newspapers is about 60 million copies. Encourage students from other cultures to talk about their countries' newspapers. Students may be surprised to learn that newspapers in other countries are much smaller than U.S. newspapers and, in some cases, are severely limited by government controls in what they can publish.

Literature of the Time

PEOPLE ARE READING . . .

Magazines   Sarah Josepha Hale, American writer and editor, becomes well-known for being a forceful editor at *Ladies' Magazine* in Boston from 1828 to 1837 and at the *Godey's Lady's Book* in Philadelphia from 1837 to 1877. In addition to other works, in 1830 she writes *Poems for Our Children*, which contains the popular rhyme "Mary Had a Little Lamb."

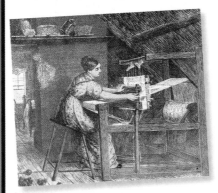

Newspapers   As of 1765, America has more than thirty newspapers, and by 1830 it has about a thousand. In 1833 Benjamin H. Day develops the "penny paper," which he says is designed "to lay before the public, at a price within the means of every one, all the news of the day."

◀ *The Frugal Housewife*
This bestseller by Lydia Maria Child is published in 1829. It is full of tips for cooking, housekeeping, and home remedies.

People Are Writing

About America   Americans and Europeans, ordinary and famous (including Charles Dickens), jot down their impressions of this new country. Some are published, such as Crévecoeur's *Letters of an American Farmer*, which describes the American as "a new man, who acts upon new principles."

About Politics   Americans like to express themselves on the issues of the day. Broadsides—sheets of papers containing various kinds of writing—are tacked up everywhere. The writing, though not sophisticated, is earnest and has popular appeal.

U.S.A.				
	1773 Phillis Wheatley, *Poems on Various Subjects, Religious and Moral*	**1783** Noah Webster, *American Spelling Book*, the first attempt to standardize spelling of American English		**1796** Amelia Simmons, *American Cookery*
1750		**1770**		**1790**
China: Wu Ching-tzu, *The Scholars*			**1792** England: Mary Wollstonecraft, *A Vindication of the Rights of Woman*	
World				

REAL-WORLD CONNECTION

Political Propaganda   As the text points out, people in the new nation enjoyed expressing themselves on the issues of the day in *broadsides,* sheets of paper that were posted in places for everyone to see. You may want to explain that the Internet is a good modern parallel, providing ample sites for posting personal opinions.

Activity   Have students use an Internet search engine to find examples of current political opinions and propaganda. Discuss how these postings may differ or resemble what early Americans would have written in their broadsides. **L2**

Literary Trends: From Reason to Romanticism

Nathaniel
Hawthorne

In the new century, as democracy is spreading, so is the importance of the common person. Romanticism, which focuses on individualism and the concerns of the heart, rather than the mind, emerges as a movement. Personal experience, emotions, intuition, the splendors of nature, and love of one's country find their way into poetry and prose. The new literature, still being shaped by European writing, begins to feature Americans dealing with American problems.

For the most part, as in the writings of Ralph Waldo Emerson, Romanticism is in tune with the optimism of the growing nation. However, the movement also has a dark side, expressed by such writers as Edgar Allan Poe and Nathaniel Hawthorne. Emerson finds Hawthorne's tales gloomy, while Hawthorne thinks Emerson is "a mystic, stretching his hand out of cloudland, in vain search for something real." Optimism and pessimism, individualism and nationalism, a love of nature and a fascination with the supernatural—all are part of the American consciousness.

Edgar Allan Poe

FOCUS ON . . .

Ralph Waldo
Emerson

The Transcendentalists

Transcendentalists such as Emerson believe that basic truths can be reached only by "going beyond," or transcending, reason and reflecting on the world of the spirit. Real knowledge, they argue, comes from a person's deep and free intuition and is available to everyone. They believe that the individual can transform the world—and that is what they aim to do, not only through their writings but through antislavery activity and other social action.

Timeline 1798–1850

- **1798** England: Samuel Taylor Coleridge and William Wordsworth, *Lyrical Ballads*
- **1810**
- **1812–1815** Germany: *Grimm's Fairy Tales*
- **1817** William Cullen Bryant, "Thanatopsis"
- **1828** Noah Webster, *American Dictionary of the English Language*
- **1830**
- **1833** Russia: Aleksandr Pushkin, *Eugene Onegin*
- **1841** Ralph Waldo Emerson, "Self-Reliance" and *Essays*
- **1847** England: Charlotte Brontë (under pseudonym Currer Bell), *Jane Eyre*
- **1849** Frances Parkman, *The Oregon Trail*
- Nathaniel Hawthorne, *The Scarlet Letter*
- **1850**

Novels of the Time

Novels of the Time

Cultural Note

Cooper's work is well known and remains popular, although many leading American literary figures have criticized it. Mark Twain, for one, panned it. He titled one essay "Fenimore Cooper's Literary Offenses." Twain wrote, "In one place in *Deerslayer* [one of the novels in *The Leather-Stocking Tales*], and in the restricted space of two-thirds of a page, Cooper has scored 114 offenses against literary art out of a possible 115. It breaks the record." Later, Twain writes that "Cooper [hasn't] any more invention than a horse; and I don't mean a high-class horse, either; I mean a clothes-horse . . . I feel sure, deep down in my heart, that Cooper wrote about the poorest English that exists in our language!"

Dana's Sea Journey

Richard Dana went to sea in an effort to improve his failing health. He worked aboard the *Pilgrim* on a difficult voyage around Cape Horn. Upon his return, he became a lawyer, working on behalf of mistreated sailors, with whom he empathized.

Stirred by the spirit of a young nation and its untarnished beauty, American writers during the second half of the eighteenth century hope to produce a truly American literature. At the same time, however, they remain strongly influenced by established European traditions. The first novels written by Americans use British models to explore American themes. Charles Brockden Brown's 1798 novel, Wieland, for example, follows the Gothic style—characterized by the grotesque and mysterious. By the 1820s, however, the first truly American novels emerge. By then, Romanticism is beginning to take hold in Europe—a movement stressing individualism, freedom from old forms, and a love of nature. American writers embrace the movement and make it their own.

The Last of the Mohicans
by James Fenimore Cooper (1826)

Cooper's popular five-part series *The Leather-Stocking Tales*, about a nature guide called Natty Bumppo, contains the first novels to depict realistic American frontier scenes and characters. *The Last of the Mohicans*, the second installment in the series, is set during the French and Indian War and portrays a group of Native Americans whose way of life is fast disappearing. The novel presents a thrilling chase, punctuated by captures, escapes, unexpected attacks, and heroic rescues. The novel contrasts two ways of life: the Native American's freedom and reverence of nature, and the settlers' drive to build farms and towns.

Two Years Before the Mast
by Richard Henry Dana (1840)

Dana's novel is based on his own experience on the crew of a ship for two years. Americans were fascinated by the day-to-day duties of a Yankee captain and crew. Dana's vivid descriptions of the captain's cruelty toward the crew lead to public outcry and legal action against such treatment aboard ship. The novel's factual details influence Herman Melville, whose novel *Moby-Dick* becomes the standard for all sea adventures.

U.S.A.				
			1789 — William Hill Brown, *The Power of Sympathy*	1792–1815 — H. H. Brackenridge, *Modern Chivalry*
1750	1759–1767 England: Laurence Sterne, *Tristram Shandy*	**1770**	1787— Germany: Johann Wolfgang von Goethe, *The Sorrows of Young Werther*	**1790**
World				

MEETING INDIVIDUAL NEEDS — GIFTED AND TALENTED ACTIVITY

Reading a Novel Challenge outstanding students by asking them to read one of the novels mentioned on these pages in its entirety. All of *The Leather-Stocking Tales* are enjoyable and action-packed. *Two Years Before the Mast* is filled with action as well. *The Scarlet Letter* is more difficult, in both language and subject matter.

Activity Ask students to prepare for the class a 15-minute lesson that connects the themes and concerns of the novel with other selections in this unit. Their focus should not be to give a book report, but rather to make connections between the novel they read and the larger literary and historical issues in the unit. **L3**

the others knew not where we were, so we put toward the shore, got into a creek, landed near an old fence, with the rails of which we made a fire, the night being cold, in October, and there we remained till daylight. Then one of the company knew the place to be Cooper's Creek, a little above Philadelphia, which we saw as soon as we got out of the creek, and arrived there about eight or nine o'clock on the Sunday morning and landed at Market Street wharf.

I have been the more particular in this description of my journey, and shall be so of my first entry into that city, that you may in your mind compare such unlikely beginnings with the figure I have since made there. I was in my working dress, my best clothes coming round by sea. I was dirty, from my being so long in the boat. My pockets were stuffed out with shirts and stockings, and I knew no one nor where to look for lodging. Fatigued with walking, rowing, and the want of sleep, I was very hungry; and my whole stock of cash consisted in a single dollar, and about a shilling[4] in copper coin, which I gave to the boatmen for my passage. At first they refused it, on account of my having rowed; but I insisted on their taking it. Man is sometimes more generous when he has little money than when he has plenty; perhaps to prevent his being thought to have but little.

I walked toward the top of the street, gazing about till near Market Street, when I met a boy with bread. I had often made a meal of dry bread, and inquiring where he had bought it, I went immediately to the baker's he directed me to. I asked for biscuits, meaning such as we had at Boston; that sort, it seems, was not made at Philadelphia. I then asked for a threepenny loaf and was told they had none. Not knowing the different prices nor the names of the different sorts of bread, I told him to give me threepenny worth of any sort. He gave me accordingly three great puffy rolls. I was surprised at the quantity, but took it, and having no room in my pockets, walked off with a roll under each arm and eating the other. Thus I went up Market Street as far as Fourth Street, passing by the door of Mr. Read, my future wife's father; when she, standing at the door, saw me, and thought I made, as I certainly did, a most awkward, ridiculous appearance. Then I turned and went down Chestnut Street and part of Walnut Street, eating my roll all the way; and coming round found myself again at Market Street wharf, near the boat I came in, to which I went for a draught[5] of the river water; and being filled with one of my rolls, gave the other two to a woman and her child that came down the river in the boat with us and were waiting to go further.

Thus refreshed I walked again up the street, which by this time had many clean-dressed people in it, who were all walking the same way. I joined them, and thereby was led into the great meeting-house of the Quakers,[6] near the market. I sat down among them, and after looking round a while and hearing nothing said,[7] being very drowsy through labor and want of rest the preceding night, I fell fast asleep and continued so till the meeting broke up, when some one was kind enough to rouse me. This, therefore, was the first house I was in, or slept in, in Philadelphia.

---

5. Here, *draught* means "a gulp" or "a swallow."
6. *Quakers* are members of the Society of Friends, a Christian religious group founded in the seventeenth century.
7. Quaker religious meetings often include long periods of silence.

---

4. A *shilling* is a British coin equal to one-twentieth of a pound.

C Active Reading

VISUALIZE Encourage students to picture in their minds what Franklin looked like during his journey. Ask students what images stand out in their minds. To help them visualize, use a map to point out the length of the route from Burlington to Philadelphia.

Model: Franklin's description of the way he looked when he arrived in Philadelphia shows how exhausting the experience must have been. Even though he was tired and had little money, Franklin was fascinated by his new surroundings.

A&E HOME VIDEO. ® *The following videotape program is available from Glencoe. Be sure to preview the video for appropriateness for your class:*

- **Biography: Benjamin Franklin—Citizen of the World**

D Critical Thinking

DRAWING CONCLUSIONS What do Franklin's actions reveal about the kind of person he is? *(Franklin shows he is proud when he insists on paying his fare. He shows his generosity when he shares the rolls. His comments about the meetinghouse show his sense of humor.)*

Sequence of Events English language learners may find Franklin's vocabulary and sentence structure challenging. Point out that Franklin tells the events in sequential order.

Activity Suggest that students mark the events on time lines, or write individual events on index cards and put the cards in the correct order from beginning to end. You may want to have the students work in small groups. **COLLAB. LEARN.**

Additional Resources
📁 *English Language Learners Sourcebook*

Literary Elements

E **Literary Elements**

APHORISM An aphorism is a short, memorable statement that expresses some truth or observation about life. Are any of these aphorisms familiar to students? These aphorisms were written more than 200 years ago. If they are familiar, what does their familiarity reveal about them? *(These aphorisms stand the test of time because they were written using memorable language and still apply to situations today.)*

F **Literary Elements**

FIGURES OF SPEECH: *Metaphor*
Franklin illustrates his points with colorful metaphors. Have students explain the metaphors in the aphorisms. *(In the third aphorism, for example, the wheel of the cart is a metaphor for a person who makes a lot of noise and prevents things from running smoothly.)*

Teaching Options

---

from POOR RICHARD'S ALMANACK

E

Benjamin Franklin

Who judges best of a man, his enemies or himself?

If you would keep your secret from an enemy,
    tell it not to a friend.

F The worst wheel of the cart makes the most noise.

He that cannot obey, cannot command.

No gains without pains.

'Tis easier to prevent bad habits than to break them.

A rolling stone gathers no moss.

Today is yesterday's pupil.

Most fools think they are only ignorant.[1]

An empty bag cannot stand upright.

_____

1. *Ignorant* means "uneducated" or "uninformed."

REAL-WORLD CONNECTION

Adjusting to Change Have students put themselves in Benjamin Franklin's shoes by talking about a time when they had to adjust to a new situation, such as a new neighborhood or community, a new job, or a different school. Ask students: What obstacles did you face? How were your experiences similar to Franklin's? How did your experiences help you break free? What advice would you give to others in the same situation?

Activity After the class discussion, have students write short autobiographical essays in which they try to duplicate Franklin's writing style. **L2**

Experience keeps a dear[2] school, yet fools will learn
in no other.

What signifies[3] your patience, if you can't find it
when you want it.

He that lies down with dogs, shall rise up with fleas.

Well done is better than well said.

What you would seem to be, be really.

Honesty is the best policy.

Dost thou love life? Then do not squander time;
for that's the stuff life is made of.

 Keep thy shop, and thy shop will keep thee.

Beware of little expenses,
a small leak will sink a great ship.

A penny saved is a penny earned.

Don't count your chickens before they are hatched.

Buy what thou hast no need of;
and e'er long thou shalt sell thy necessaries.

Not to oversee workmen, is to leave them your purse open.

Fish and visitors smell in three days.

Quarrels never could last long,
if on one side only lay the wrong.

Love thy neighbor; yet don't pull down your hedge.

---

2. Here, *dear* means "expensive."
3. *Signifies* means "has importance or meaning."

G Critical Thinking

INFERRING Many of the aphorisms do not have explicit meanings. Rather, their meanings must be inferred. Encourage students to make inferences.

Model: In the eighteenth aphorism, Franklin probably is not referring to keeping an actual shop, because his aphorisms apply to life in general. A shop could refer to a business, a family, or even a community. If you take care of each of these, they will also take care of you.

H Author's Craft

LITERARY HISTORY The great masters of aphorisms—Pascal and La Rochefoucauld—wrote before Franklin's lifetime. Franklin's *Poor Richard's Almanack* sayings are thought to be reworked English and French aphorisms.

Thematic Focus

Breaking Free Encourage students to look at how Benjamin Franklin portrays himself in the autobiography. Do his thoughts and observations in the aphorisms show that he has broken free from his humble beginnings in Philadelphia? In what ways? How might the aphorisms reveal what Franklin has learned from his experiences?

☑ ASSESSMENT OPTIONS

📁 *Quick Checks,* p. 13

MEETING INDIVIDUAL NEEDS — MULTIPLE LEARNING STYLES

Interpersonal Some students may understand the aphorisms better if they have an opportunity to discuss them with others.

Activity Organize students into small groups. Ask each student to choose an aphorism that ties into something that has happened in his or her life. Students can read their chosen aphorisms aloud, restate the aphorisms in their own words, and tell how the aphorism was demonstrated in their lives. Encourage students to ask group members to explain aphorisms they do not understand. This activity may help students see how Franklin's truths apply to modern-day situations as well as to life more than 200 years ago. **L2**
COLLAB. LEARN.

Personal Response

Students may answer that they would be excited and somewhat scared if they were in Franklin's position.

ANALYZING LITERATURE

1. Franklin meets Dr. Brown. Franklin portrays Brown as mischievous and a quack. The portrayal of Brown reveals Franklin's sense of humor. The encounter with an old woman shows Franklin's appreciation of the many kindnesses he was shown.

2. Because Franklin did part of the rowing, the boatmen do not expect him to pay. Franklin's sense of pride compels him to pay his way.

3. Franklin falls asleep. His play on the word "house" shows Franklin's wit. His attitude toward the experience could also reveal cynicism.

4. As part of their answers, students should give specific examples of situations from both the past and present that call for self-reliance.

5. An enemy will not find out a secret if the secret is not told to a friend. In other words, if you want to keep something a secret, don't tell it to anyone—not even a friend.

6. A small leak can sink a great ship. This may mean that many small expenses can add up, until all the small expenses are as much as or more than one large expense.

7. Franklin asserts that one should love his or her neighbor, but maintaining some boundaries is desirable.

8. Students should provide reasons for whatever aphorism they select.

Responding to Literature

Personal Response

Do you think you would have felt as young Franklin did arriving in a new city, with little money, no place to live, and no job? Explain.

ANALYZING LITERATURE

from
The Autobiography of Benjamin Franklin

RECALL AND INTERPRET

1. Whom does Franklin meet before he takes the boat to Philadelphia? What do you learn about him from these encounters?

2. Why do the boatmen at first refuse to accept money from Franklin? Why do you think he offers to pay?

3. What does Franklin do during the Quakers' meeting? What do you think the last sentence of this selection reveals about Franklin?

EVALUATE AND CONNECT

4. How important is self-reliance in the world today? Do you think people are more or less self-reliant today than they were in Franklin's time? Explain.

from
POOR RICHARD'S ALMANACK

RECALL AND INTERPRET

5. According to Franklin, how can a secret be kept from an enemy? Describe in your own words the advice given in the second saying.

6. What does Franklin say will sink a great ship? What do you think he means by this?

7. In the final aphorism, what does Franklin say about "thy neighbor"? What might he mean by "don't pull down your hedge"?

EVALUATE AND CONNECT

8. In your opinion, which aphorism gives the best advice? Explain.

Literary ELEMENTS

Aphorisms

Aphorisms are short, memorable statements that convey a general truth or an observation about life. The aphorisms that Franklin wrote in *Poor Richard's Almanack* reflect his clever use of language. For example, when Franklin says, "An empty bag cannot stand upright," he presents a humorous **metaphor** for a spineless person who can't stand up for his or her beliefs.

1. Choose one aphorism. Explain how Franklin's word choices help make it easy to remember.

2. Using language of today and references to contemporary life, reword one of Franklin's aphorisms.

● See **Literary Terms Handbook,** p. R1.

LITERARY ELEMENTS

1. One example: In the aphorism, "What you would seem to be, be really," Franklin repeats the word *be*. The repetition makes the aphorism seem like poetry. The poetic sound of the aphorism makes it easy to remember.

2. One possible response: "Live up to the image you present to the public."

Additional Resources

Literary Elements Transparency 12

— LITERATURE AND WRITING —

Writing About Literature
Personality Profile   What do you know about Franklin from the two selections that you have read? What personal characteristics does Franklin reveal? Use the personal details and experiences that Franklin presents to create a personality profile of Franklin as a young man. Use vivid language and quotes from the selections to enliven Franklin's profile.

Creative Writing
Advice by Aphorism   The colonists found advice in the aphorisms of the *Almanack*, while today we read advice columns in the newspaper. Select a letter written to a newspaper advice columnist and compose an aphorism that sums up your advice to the letter writer. Refer to your response to the Focus Activity on page 130 and review the elements that made your favorite saying effective. Then use those elements to help you write your own aphorism.

— EXTENDING YOUR RESPONSE —

Literature Groups
Getting the Point   The meanings of some of Franklin's aphorisms, such as "Honesty is the best policy," are clear and straightforward. With others, however, the meaning must be inferred, or figured out. Take turns in your group choosing the aphorisms you find most thought-provoking, or perhaps hardest to understand, and discuss their meanings with your group.

Listening and Speaking
On My Own   Ask one or more family members or older friends to recall a time in their life when they went out on their own, had to make a new start, or, like Franklin, arrived in a city as a stranger. Invite them to discuss the thoughts and feelings they had at the time. Take notes or tape record their memories and then share the oral histories with your classmates.

Internet Connection
Franklin on the Web   You can find the entire text of Benjamin Franklin's *Autobiography* on-line, made available by Project Gutenberg. For further information about Franklin, including a visit to the Benjamin Franklin National Memorial, type "Benjamin Franklin" into a search engine and surf the Web sites listed.

 Save your work for your portfolio.

VOCABULARY • The Latin Root *gen*

The word *ingenious* contains the Latin root *gen*, which means "to give birth to" or "to produce." To *generate* is to bring into existence.

Recognizing the root *gen* in an unfamiliar word can help you get a sense of the word's meaning.

PRACTICE   Use your knowledge of the root *gen* and these clues to match each word to its meaning.

Clues: *con-* means "with"; *de-* means "away from"; *pro-* means "forth"; *primo-* means "first"; *-alogy* means "the study of"

1. congenital
2. degenerate
3. progeny
4. primogenitor
5. genealogy

a. offspring
b. oldest ancestor
c. acquired at birth
d. recorded history of one's ancestry
e. to fall away from a former condition

LITERATURE AND WRITING

Writing About Literature
Students' profiles should
- give specific details about Franklin's personality.
- include evidence from the selections, such as quotations and incidents from Franklin's life.

Creative Writing
Students' aphorisms should
- offer sensible advice based on the letters they chose.
- include elements that students mentioned in the Focus Activity.

EXTENDING YOUR RESPONSE

Literature Groups Have each student choose a difficult aphorism, devise questions about it, and write possible meanings before the group meets. **COLLAB. LEARN.**

Listening and Speaking Before students interview family members or friends, work with them to devise a list of interview tips, such as avoiding yes or no questions or leading questions that cause the person being interviewed to give the "expected" answer.

VOCABULARY • The Latin Root *gen*

1. c   2. e   3. a
4. b   5. d

Additional Resources
Vocabulary Practice, p. 11

✔ ASSESSMENT OPTIONS

- 📁 *Quick Checks,* p. 13
- 📁 *Selection and Theme Assessment,* pp. 23–24
- 📁 *Performance Assessment,* p. 13
- 💾 *Testmaker*

*inter*NET CONNECTION

Benjamin Franklin Have students research Franklin's contributions to American letters.

Objectives

- To read an expository selection about *dichos*, sayings that make a point
- To identify elements of exposition in nonfiction
- To write a brief essay about proverbs in the English language

Skills

Reading/Thinking: Paraphrasing; Evaluating

Grammar/Language: Linking Verbs in Predicates

Motivating

→ **OPTIONS**

Selection Focus Transparency 14: Have students view the transparency and then answer the question provided.

Focus Activity: As an extension of the Focus Activity, have students compile a dictionary of sayings and determine what each saying means. Do students agree on the meanings of the sayings?

 # Before You Read

Dichos

Meet Américo Paredes

"The proverb presents conventional wisdom in a neat package . . ."

—*Paredes*

To many people it might not sound like work at all: visiting restaurants and other public gathering places and listening to people tell jokes. Yet, some of Américo Paredes's most serious writings are his analyses of such informal humor. Paredes is a folklorist—a scholar who collects and records the oral traditions, including the sayings, beliefs, tales, and practices of a particular people. His focus is the folklore of Mexican Americans. Having grown up in a Mexican American family that has called the Rio Grande region of Texas home since the 1700s, Paredes brings an insider's insight to his work. He was a professor at the University of Texas at Austin for more than forty years, teaching anthropology and English. Paredes is also a prolific poet, has published a novel, and has been a professional singer, guitarist, and composer, performing throughout the Texas-Mexico border region. His essay "Dichos" appeared in the book *Mexican-American Authors* in 1972.

". . . For I was born beside your waters, And since very young I knew That my soul had hidden currents, That my soul resembled you, . . ."

—*Paredes*

Américo Paredes was born in 1915 in Brownsville, Texas, and died in 1999.

FOCUS ACTIVITY

Think of an occasion when you made what you would classify as a perfect comment—or when you later thought of what would have been a perfect comment.

DISCUSS In a small group, share your "perfect" sayings and describe the situations in which they occurred. Discuss possible improvements on the sayings.

SETTING A PURPOSE Read to learn what *dichos* are and how they are helpful to speakers and writers.

BACKGROUND

Literary Influences

A rich oral tradition has always been an important part of Mexican American culture. This culture includes people who have lived in Texas, New Mexico, and California since Europeans first came to North America. It also embraces the urban lifestyles of the Mexican American neighborhoods of most major cities in the United States. Paredes sheds light on this varied culture with his collection of sayings in common usage among Mexican Americans.

VOCABULARY PREVIEW

distinctive (dis ting′ tiv) *adj.* different in quality or kind; separate; p. 139

absolute (ab′ sə loot′) *adj.* complete; certain; final; p. 140

sluggard (slug′ ərd) *n.* one who is usually lazy or idle; p. 141

conspire (kən spīr′) *v.* to join or act together, especially to carry out some secret or evil deed or for a hidden or illegal purpose; p. 141

RESOURCE MANAGER

Lesson Planning Resource

The *Unit Two Planning Guide* (pp. 14–19) provides additional lesson notes and reduced versions of all print resources.

📁 **Other Print Resources**
- Active Reading Guide, p. 14
- Vocabulary Practice, p. 12
- Reading Workbook, p. 19
- Grammar and Language Workbook, p. 57

- Grammar and Composition Handbook, Lesson 1.3
- Quick Checks, p. 14
- Selection and Theme Assessment, pp. 23–24
- Performance Assessment, p. 13
- Spanish Summaries, p. 14
- Spanish Translations
- Inclusion Strategies
- English Language Learners Sourcebook

 **Transparencies**
- Selection Focus 14
- Literary Elements 13
- Grammar and Language 11

Technology
🎧 Audio Library
🎧 Spanish Audio Library
🖥 Glencoe Literature Web Site
💾 Testmaker

LISTENING, SPEAKING, and VIEWING

Analyzing Advertising Slogans

As Américo Paredes explains, people remember *dichos* because the sayings use just the right words. Advertising slogans are somewhat similar to *dichos* in that they are meant to be memorable—to stay in our minds and influence our buying decisions. Like *dichos* they might have two balanced parts or use contrasting words within a statement. Other times, they use alliteration (repeated first sounds of words) or assonance (repeated vowel sounds). Some might compare one thing to another. Following are some advertising slogans that use these techniques:

Balanced parts: "The quality of platinum. The strength of steel."
Balanced parts with contrast: "Tough on stains. Easy on your hands."
Alliteration or assonance: "Discover the difference."
"Care for what you wear."
Comparison: "Like the tools your grandfather cherished."

When you see or hear such slogans, certain images usually come to mind. These mental images connect you with the slogan's message and help you to remember it. Also, because of a slogan's rhythm, rhyme, or perhaps its association with a catchy tune or melody, you often "hear" a slogan over and over in your mind, which in turn helps you remember it. Viewing slogans on billboards or on television fixes the words visually in your mind, and when you see or hear the slogan again, you are more easily persuaded because you are familiar with the message. Being aware of advertising techniques can help you understand how slogans persuade you to buy a product or service.

ACTIVITY

As you watch a television program or listen to the radio, jot down any ads you hear that use the techniques mentioned. Analyze the words and/or the visuals of the ads to determine what makes the ads effective. Then use similar techniques to create and present an advertising slogan for a product you use every day. Use visuals and/or music to help you present your slogan in a memorable and persuasive way.

LISTENING, SPEAKING, and VIEWING

Objective
- To analyze advertising techniques to understand the persuasive power of slogans

Teaching Strategies

Have students apply the strategies outlined in this lesson to actual advertising. They can list slogans they already know from radio, television, and print ads and identify the techniques used in the advertisements. Then students can answer these questions: What do the slogans imply about the products? Do the implications in the slogans match the reality of the products? Why or why not? How can slogans make the products seem more attractive than they really are?

Activity

Students' slogans should
- use the techniques of balanced parts, balanced parts with contrast, alliteration, assonance, and/or comparison.
- tell something about the product.
- convey that the product is a "must-have" item.
- incorporate appropriate visuals and/or music to increase the appeal of the product.

Teaching Options

MEETING INDIVIDUAL NEEDS — ENGLISH LANGUAGE LEARNERS

The Language of Advertising
English language learners may have trouble understanding an ad's colloquial language. Sentence fragments in advertisements may cause further confusion. Help students understand the meanings of the slogans on this page.

Activity Cut out several ads from newspapers and magazines. Have pairs of students work together to paraphrase the slogans. Explain that slogans may lose their meanings when translated. Ask English language learners to translate some advertising slogans from their native languages.

Additional Resources
📁 *English Language Learners Sourcebook*

Objectives

- To read and analyze a speech about breaking free
- To determine a writer's purpose
- To write a news report

Skills

Reading/Thinking: Evaluating; Synthesizing
Writing: News Report
Collaboration: Performing

Motivating

→OPTIONS

Literature Launchers: "What Makes a Good Speech?"

Videodisc Side A, Segment 3

Also available in VHS.

Selection Focus Transparency 15: Have students view the transparency and then answer the question provided.

Focus Activity: As an extension of the Focus Activity, have students share their journal entries in small groups to discuss what a day might be like without all their freedoms.

Before You Read

Speech to the Second Virginia Convention

Meet Patrick Henry

"Give me liberty, or give me death."

—Henry

On March 23, 1775, Patrick Henry stood before fellow delegates at the Second Virginia Convention and thundered his famous challenge. Thomas Marshall, a delegate to the convention, recalled that the speech was "one of the most bold, vehement, and animated pieces of eloquence that had ever been delivered."

As a young lawyer, Henry developed his gift for public speaking. That talent served him well when he became a member of the Virginia House of Burgesses at the age of twenty-nine.

Supporting the colonists' right to make their own laws, Henry defiantly exclaimed, "If this be treason, make the most of it." For the next decade, he continued to argue boldly for colonial rights.

A man of action as well as a compelling speaker, Henry played a prominent role in the Revolution that soon followed his famous speech. In 1776, as the battles of the Revolution raged around them, the citizens of Virginia elected Henry to be the first governor of the commonwealth under its new constitution. He served three terms as governor.

Patrick Henry was born in 1736 and died in 1799.

FOCUS ACTIVITY

What does the phrase "Give me liberty, or give me death" mean to you?

LIST IDEAS In your journal, explore some of the liberties you enjoy. Would you risk your life to preserve any one of these freedoms? Why or why not?

SETTING A PURPOSE Read to find out what Patrick Henry says about liberty.

BACKGROUND

The Time and Place

The speech you are about to read was delivered in 1775 to the Second Virginia Convention meeting in Richmond, Virginia.

Colonists' Protests

The Seven Years War with France in the mid-eighteenth century strained Britain's treasury. Consequently, the British Parliament passed a series of taxes on its colonies designed to replenish Britain's treasury. American colonists protested these taxes, and thousands of British troops were sent to Boston to keep the peace.

VOCABULARY PREVIEW

arduous (är′jōō əs) *adj.* requiring great exertion or endurance; difficult; p. 148
insidious (in sid′ē əs) *adj.* slyly treacherous and deceitful; deceptive; p. 148
subjugation (sub′jə gā′shən) *n.* act of bringing under control; domination; p. 148
remonstrate (ri mon′strāt) *v.* to object; to protest; p. 148
spurn (spurn) *v.* to reject with disdain; p. 149

RESOURCE MANAGER

Lesson Planning Resource
The *Unit Two Planning Guide* (pp. 20–25) provides additional lesson notes and reduced versions of all print resources.

Other Print Resources
- Active Reading Guide, p. 15
- Vocabulary Practice, p. 13
- Reading Workbook, p. 20
- Quick Checks, p. 15

- Selection and Theme Assessment, pp. 25–26
- Performance Assessment, p. 14
- Spanish Summaries, p. 15
- Spanish Translations
- Inclusion Strategies
- English Language Learners Sourcebook

 Transparencies
- Selection Focus 15
- Literary Elements 14

Technology

 Literature Launchers
 Audio Library
 Spanish Audio Library
 Glencoe Literature Web Site
Testmaker

COMPARING selections

from The Crisis, No. 1 **and** *from* **THE HISTORIES**

COMPARE **SITUATIONS**

Both Paine and Herodotus describe nations at war. On a separate piece of paper, write a few paragraphs answering the following questions:

1. How is the war between the Persians and the Greeks similar to the war between the British and the colonists?
2. In what ways are the two wars different? You might use encyclopedias or other reference books to learn more about ancient Greece and Persia.
3. In your opinion, what could the British and the colonists have learned from reading Herodotus's account of the Persian Wars?

COMPARE **IDEAS OF BRAVERY**

Both Herodotus and Paine give their views on true bravery against an invading enemy. With a small group, discuss the following:

1. Which statements from each selection show the writer's idea of bravery?
2. What idea does Herodotus have of true bravery? What idea does Paine have?
3. Compare and contrast the ideas of bravery expressed by Herodotus and Paine.

COMPARE **SOLDIERS**

More than two thousand years separate the battle at Thermopylae from the battle at Trenton. Despite this time gap, many aspects of soldiering remained unchanged.

- With a small group of classmates, research the Persian, Greek, British, or the Patriot (colonial) soldiers. Learn about their weapons, battle preparations, and fighting tactics.
- On a piece of poster board, make a large drawing representing a soldier from the group you selected. Label the various parts of the uniform and fighting gear. Add margin notes to provide additional details about the soldier.
- Display your poster with those of classmates. Then discuss your work with the class. Make a class chart of the similarities and differences among the soldiers.

COMPARING selections

Objective

- To compare two nonfiction works about fighting for a cause

COMPARE **SITUATIONS**

1. Both are wars for independence.
2. They take place in different eras, the armies use different strategies and weapons, and the combatants have different reasons for fighting.
3. The colonists could have learned that true bravery is not solely dependent on strength. The British could have learned not to underestimate the colonists.

COMPARE **IDEAS OF BRAVERY**

1. Students should identify specific statements from each selection.
2. Herodotus believes that bravery means fighting for a cause, even if it means being killed in the process. Paine believes that bravery means showing "your faith by your works," acting on principles, and trusting God to look after you.
3. Both believe in fighting for a just cause, but their ideas about bravery differ greatly.

COMPARE **SOLDIERS**

Students' posters should

- show evidence of careful planning.
- include details related to soldiers, battle preparations, weapons, fighting tactics, and feelings about war.
- be visually appealing and clearly labeled.

Teaching Options

PORTFOLIO OPTIONS

Select and Reflect Have students reflect on their investigations of soldiers by asking themselves these questions:

- Is my investigation balanced, including information about the personal characteristics of the soldiers?
- Does my poster reflect the information that I found?
- Did my poster contribute to the class discussion about soldiers?

Students should place their reflections in their portfolios. At a later time, they might consider using their research materials to write portfolio showcase pieces. **L2**

Additional Resources
📁 *Writing Assessment and Portfolio Management,* pp. 51–58

Before Reading

Objectives

- To read and analyze a historic document on independence
- To identify words with strong connotations
- To write an analysis on the elements of a persuasive essay

Skills

Reading/Thinking: Identifying Bias; Evaluating
Vocabulary: Usage
Grammar/Language: Objects of Prepositions
Collaboration: Literature Groups

Motivating
→OPTIONS

Literature Launchers: "Liberty's Eloquent Author"

Videodisc Side A, Segment 4

Also available in VHS.

Selection Focus Transparency 18: Have students view the transparency and then answer the question provided.

Focus Activity: As an extension of the Focus Activity, have pairs of students compare and contrast their webs.

Before You Read
Declaration of Independence

Meet Thomas Jefferson

"... to place before mankind the common sense of the subject, in terms so plain and firm as to command their assent, and to justify ourselves in the independent stand we are compelled to take."
—Jefferson

With his purpose defined, Thomas Jefferson crafted what many believe is the most powerful argument for freedom ever written. When the Continental Congress debated breaking away from Britain in 1776, the members turned to Jefferson to put their ideas about liberty and freedom into writing. Jefferson did indeed express those ideas in the writing of the Declaration of Independence.

This skilled writer was also a man of many other talents and interests. James Parton, a Jefferson biographer, describes him as "a gentleman of thirty-two who could calculate an eclipse, tie an artery, plan an edifice, try a case, break a horse, dance a minuet, and play the violin."

Jefferson was a native Virginian. He graduated from the College of William and Mary, studied law, and became a member of the Virginia House of Burgesses. He served as governor of Virginia, minister to France, secretary of state, vice-president, and president of the United States.

Jefferson died on July 4, 1826, the fiftieth anniversary of the signing of the Declaration of Independence.

Thomas Jefferson was born in 1743 and died in 1826.

FOCUS ACTIVITY

Just how much freedom should an individual or a country have? What, if anything, should limit freedom?

WORD WEB Create a word web with the word "freedom" at the center. Then complete the word web with your ideas on personal and national freedom.

Right to vote

Freedom

SETTING A PURPOSE Read to learn more about Jefferson's views of freedom.

168 ❧ UNIT 2

BACKGROUND

The Time and Place

In 1776 the Second Continental Congress created a committee to draft a statement declaring independence from Britain. Jefferson did most of the writing.

The Idea of Natural Law

Some of Jefferson's ideas about independence were not new. He studied John Locke's theory of "natural law." According to Locke, people are "by nature free, equal and independent . . ." Following his lead, Jefferson stressed that the American Revolution was a struggle for the basic rights of all.

VOCABULARY PREVIEW

usurpation (u′ sər pā′ shən) *n.* act of seizing power without legal right or authority; p. 169

endeavor (en dev′ ər) *v.* to make an effort to; to try; p. 171

tenure (ten′ yər) *n.* conditions or terms under which something is held; p. 171

acquiesce (ak′ wē es′) *v.* to consent or agree silently, without objections; to comply passively; p. 172

rectitude (rek′ tə tōōd′) *n.* uprightness of moral character; honesty; p. 172

RESOURCE MANAGER

Lesson Planning Resource
The *Unit Two Planning Guide* (pp. 40–47) provides additional lesson notes and reduced versions of all print resources.

📁 **Other Print Resources**
- Active Reading Guide, p. 18
- Vocabulary Practice, p. 16
- Reading Workbook, pp. 23–24
- Grammar and Language Workbook, p. 85

- Grammar and Composition Handbook, Lesson 1.6
- Quick Checks, p. 18
- Selection and Theme Assessment, pp. 31–32
- Performance Assessment, p. 17
- Spanish Summaries, p. 18
- Inclusion Strategies
- English Language Learners Sourcebook

🖨 **Transparencies**
- Selection Focus 18
- Literary Elements 17
- Grammar and Language 13

Technology
 Literature Launchers
🎧 Audio Library
🎧 Spanish Audio Library
💻 Glencoe Literature Web Site
📼 Testmaker

Declaration of Independence

In Congress, July 4, 1776

Thomas Jefferson ~

WHEN, IN THE COURSE OF HUMAN EVENTS, it becomes necessary for one people to dissolve the political bands which have connected them with another, and to assume, among the powers of the earth, the separate and equal station to which the laws of nature and nature's God entitle them, a decent respect to the opinions of mankind requires that they should declare the causes which impel them to the separation.

We hold these truths to be self-evident: that all men are created equal, that they are endowed by their Creator with certain unalienable rights;[1] that among these are life, liberty, and the pursuit of happiness; that to secure these rights, governments are instituted among men, deriving their just powers from the consent of the governed; that whenever any form of government becomes destructive of these ends, it is the right of the people to alter or to abolish it, and to institute new government, laying its foundation on such principles, and organizing its powers in such form, as to them shall seem most likely to effect their safety and happiness. Prudence,[2] indeed, will dictate that governments long established should not be changed for light and transient causes; and accordingly all experience hath shown that mankind are more disposed to suffer, while evils are sufferable, than to right themselves by abolishing the forms to which they are accustomed. But when a long train of abuses and usurpations, pursuing invariably the same object, evinces[3] a design to reduce

---

1. *Unalienable rights* cannot be taken away.
2. The exercise of good judgment is called *prudence*.
3. *Evinces* means "makes clear or evident."

Vocabulary
usurpation (uˊ sər pāˊ shən) *n.* act of seizing power without legal right or authority

---

SUMMARY

The Declaration of Independence explains precisely why the colonists believe they deserve their freedom and lays the groundwork for establishing the basic freedoms that are the foundation of our democracy.

📁 *Spanish Summaries,* p. 18

A Active Reading

PREDICT Explain to students that the first sentence of the Declaration of Independence acts as a kind of thesis statement. Have students read the statement carefully. Then ask them to predict what information Jefferson will convey. *(Answers might include that the Declaration will show why it is necessary for the colonists to dissolve political ties, why the laws of God and nature entitle them to independence, and why they are taking action.)*

Additional Resources

📁 *Active Reading Guide,* p. 18
🎧 *Audio Library*
🎧 *Spanish Audio Library*

Teaching Options

CONNECTING TO OTHER SELECTIONS

The chart at the right shows three ways to connect the Declaration of Independence to selections in this book.

For specific teaching strategies, see the **Unit Two Planning Guide,** pages 43–44.

Connection	Title
Life Skills: Leading and Organizing	→ "Se me enchina el cuerpo al oír tu cuento," p. 1097
Thematic: The Fight for Freedom	→ "Go Down, Moses," p. 338
Literary: Diction	→ "The Portrait," p. 851

Declaration of Independence

them under absolute despotism,[4] it is their right, it is their duty, to throw off such government, and to provide new guards for their future security.

Such has been the patient sufferance of these colonies; and such is now the necessity which constrains[5] them to alter their former systems of government. The history of the present King of Great Britain is a history of repeated injuries and usurpations, all having in direct object the establishment of an absolute

tyranny[6] over these states. To prove this, let facts be submitted to a candid world.

He has refused his assent[7] to laws, the most wholesome and necessary for the public good.

He has forbidden his governors to pass laws of immediate and pressing importance, unless suspended in their operation till his assent should be obtained; and when so suspended, he has utterly neglected to attend to them.

He has refused to pass other laws for the accommodation of large districts of people,

---

4. *Despotism* is government by a ruler who has absolute authority.
5. *Constrains* means "forces."

6. The arbitrary or oppressive exercise of power is *tyranny.*
7. *Assent* is agreement.

Declaration of Independence, 1824. John Trumbull. Oil on canvas, 21⅛ x 31⅛ in. Yale University Art Gallery, New Haven, CT.

Viewing the painting: Do you think the artist accurately captured the spirit of the moment? Explain why or why not.

170 ❧ UNIT 2

unless those people would relinquish the right of representation in the legislature, a right inestimable to them, and formidable to tyrants only.

He has called together legislative bodies at places unusual, uncomfortable, and distant from the depository of their public records, for the sole purpose of fatiguing them into compliance with his measures.

He has dissolved representative houses repeatedly, for opposing, with manly firmness, his invasions on the rights of the people.

He has refused, for a long time after such dissolutions, to cause others to be elected; whereby the legislative powers, incapable of annihilation, have returned to the people at large for their exercise; the state remaining, in the meantime, exposed to all the dangers of invasion from without and convulsions within.

B He has endeavored to prevent the population of these states; for that purpose obstructing the laws for naturalization[8] of foreigners, refusing to pass others to encourage their migrations hither, and raising the conditions of new appropriations of lands.

He has obstructed the administration of justice, by refusing his assent to laws for establishing judiciary powers.

He has made judges dependent on his will alone for the tenure of their offices, and the amount of payment of their salaries.

He has erected a multitude of new offices, and sent hither swarms of officers to harass our people and eat out their substance.

He has kept among us, in times of peace, standing armies, without the consent of our legislatures.

He has affected to render the military independent of, and superior to, the civil power.

He has combined with others to subject us to a jurisdiction foreign to our constitution and unacknowledged by our laws, giving his assent to their acts of pretended legislation:

For quartering[9] large bodies of armed troops among us;

For protecting them, by a mock trial, from punishment for any murders which they should commit on the inhabitants of these states;

For cutting off our trade with all parts of the world;

For imposing taxes on us without our consent;

For depriving us, in many cases, of the benefits of trial by jury;

For transporting us beyond seas, to be tried for pretended offenses;

For abolishing the free system of English laws in a neighboring province,[10] establishing therein **C** an arbitrary government, and enlarging its boundaries, so as to render it at once an example and fit instrument for introducing the same absolute rule into these colonies;

For taking away our charters, abolishing our most valuable laws, and altering fundamentally the forms of our governments;

For suspending our own legislatures, and declaring themselves invested with power to legislate for us in all cases whatsoever.

He has abdicated government here, by declaring us out of his protection and waging war against us.

He has plundered our seas, ravaged our coasts, burned our towns, and destroyed the lives of our people.

He is at this time transporting large armies of foreign mercenaries[11] to complete the works

---

8. *Naturalization* is the process by which foreigners become citizens of another country.
9. Here, *quartering* means "providing with living accommodations; lodging."
10. The *neighboring province* is Quebec, Canada.
11. Soldiers who serve in a foreign army for pay are *mercenaries*.

Vocabulary
endeavor (en dev′ ər) *v.* to make an effort to; to try
tenure (ten′ yər) *n.* conditions or terms under which something is held

A NEW NATION 171

Grammar and Language *Minilesson*

Objects of Prepositions Explain to students that in the phrase "For transporting us beyond the seas," transporting is a gerund, a verb form that ends in *-ing* and is used in the same way a noun is used. *Transporting* is the object of the preposition *for*.

Activity Ask students to identify other gerunds being used as the objects of prepositions in the selection. Remind students that they should <u>not</u> simply look for words that end in *-ing*. These words are usually verbs that are not gerunds. **L2**

Additional Resources
- *Grammar and Language Transparency 13*
- *Grammar and Language Workbook,* p. 85
- *Grammar and Composition Handbook,* Lesson 1.6
- *Writer's Choice,* Lesson 10.6

Language Note

Students usually use *excited* as an adjective. In the second paragraph, *excited* is a verb meaning "stirred up" or "roused."

Active Reading

RESPOND Ask students to imagine that they are members of the British Parliament and have just received the Declaration of Independence from the colonies. How would they react? Would they think that Jefferson had made a good case for freedom for the colonies? Why or why not?

Model: I'm not sure that the British Parliament would find Jefferson's Declaration of Independence as persuasive as the colonists would. No matter how well he argued his points, the Parliament would probably resist.

Thematic Focus

Breaking Free Discuss with students what the Declaration of Independence says about breaking free. Be sure that students understand that Jefferson respects tradition and advocates breaking free only as a last resort.

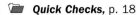

☑ **ASSESSMENT OPTIONS**

📁 *Quick Checks,* p. 18

Teaching Options

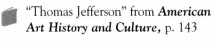

LITERATURE & HUMANITIES

📖 "Thomas Jefferson" from *American Art History and Culture,* p. 143

Declaration of Independence

of death, desolation, and tyranny already begun with circumstances of cruelty and perfidy[12] scarcely paralleled in the most barbarous ages, and totally unworthy the head of a civilized nation.

He has constrained our fellow-citizens, taken captive on the high seas, to bear arms against their country, to become the executioners of their friends and brethren, or to fall themselves by their hands.

He has excited domestic insurrections among us, and has endeavored to bring on the inhabitants of our frontiers, the merciless Indian savages, whose known rule of warfare is an undistinguished destruction of all ages, sexes, and conditions.

In every stage of these oppressions we have petitioned for redress[13] in the most humble terms; our repeated petitions have been answered only by repeated injury. A prince whose character is thus marked by every act which may define a tyrant is unfit to be ruler of a free people.

Nor have we been wanting in our attentions to our British brethren. We have warned them, from time to time, of attempts by their legislature to extend an unwarrantable jurisdiction over us. We have reminded them of the circumstances of our emigration and settlement here. We have appealed to their native justice and magnanimity;[14] and we have conjured[15] them, by the ties of our common kindred, to disavow these usurpations, which would inevitably interrupt our connections and correspondence. They, too, have been deaf to the voice of justice and consanguinity.[16] We must, therefore, <u>acquiesce</u> in the necessity which denounces[17] our separation, and hold them, as we hold the rest of mankind, enemies in war, in peace, friends.

We, therefore, the representatives of the United States of America, in General Congress assembled, appealing to the Supreme Judge of the world for the <u>rectitude</u> of our intentions, do, in the name and by the authority of the good people of these colonies, solemnly publish and declare that these United Colonies are, and of right ought to be, free and independent states; that they are absolved from all allegiance to the British crown, and that all political connection between them and the state of Great Britain is, and ought to be, totally dissolved; and that, as free and independent states, they have full power to levy war, conclude peace, contract alliances, establish commerce, and do all other acts and things which independent states may of right do. And for the support of this declaration, with a firm reliance on the protection of Divine Providence, we mutually pledge to each other our lives, our fortunes, and our sacred honor.

---

12. *Perfidy* means "a deliberate betrayal of trust."
13. A compensation for a wrong done is a *redress.*
14. *Magnanimity* means "nobility of mind and heart."
15. Here, *conjured* means "solemnly appealed to."

16. *Consanguinity* is a relationship based on having ancestors in common; a blood relationship.
17. Here, *denounces* means "announces" or "proclaims."

Vocabulary

acquiesce (ak′ wē es′) *v.* to consent or agree silently, without objections; to comply passively
rectitude (rek′ tə tōōd′) *n.* uprightness of moral character; honesty

---

MEETING INDIVIDUAL NEEDS — ENGLISH LANGUAGE LEARNERS

Negative Prefixes On the board, list these words from the selection: *<u>in</u>estimable, <u>un</u>usual, <u>un</u>comfortable.* Explain that each word contains a negative prefix which makes the meaning the opposite of the root word.

Activity As students read, have them list words with negative prefixes. Ask students to explain how the negative prefixes change the meanings of words. Encourage students to make a prefix bank for reference.

Additional Resources

📁 *English Language Learners Sourcebook*

Responding to Literature

Personal Response

How has your reading of the Declaration of Independence affected your ideas about freedom?

ANALYZING LITERATURE

RECALL AND INTERPRET

1. What is the purpose of the document? To which "opinions of mankind" might Jefferson be referring?
2. According to Jefferson, which human rights are unalienable? How do you interpret the phrase "pursuit of happiness"?
3. What accusations does Jefferson make against the British king? In a statement, summarize the complaints against the king.
4. How have the colonists met with "these oppressions"? Why might the King have ignored the colonists' petitions for redress?
5. What do the signers pledge in the final paragraph? What does the pledge in the final paragraph reveal about the signers' commitment?

EVALUATE AND CONNECT

6. In listing the grievances, Jefferson uses the technique of **repetition** (see page R13), beginning each item with the phrase *He has.* How does this technique help make the document clear?
7. Identify and explain what you consider to be Jefferson's strongest argument for freedom.
8. Think back to the ideas you expressed for the Focus Activity on page 168. Do you think the basic ideas expressed in the Declaration of Independence reflect your beliefs? Use details from the document to support your opinion.

Literary ELEMENTS

Connotation
Beyond their literal meaning, words carry with them suggestions or associations of feeling. Such suggestions or associations are called the word's **connotations.** In the Declaration of Independence, Jefferson uses words having strongly negative connotations: He speaks of the king's "abuses," "usurpations," and "despotism."

Identify words having negative connotations in the following passage: "He has plundered our seas, ravaged our Coasts, burned our towns, and destroyed the lives of our people." Explain the connotation of each.

● See **Literary Terms Handbook,** p. R4.

EXTENDING YOUR RESPONSE

Writing About Literature
Effective Presentation of Ideas   Jefferson's presentation of the rights of all people proved so effective that the Declaration of Independence is universally admired. Identify at least three elements in the Declaration that, in your opinion, give it strength. Explain how each contributes to the power of the whole.

Literature Groups
Freedom for All   "When in the course of human events it becomes necessary for one people to dissolve the political bands which have connected them with another . . ." With your group, discuss what conditions or situations in today's world might justify such a declaration of independence.

📖 **Save your work for your portfolio.**

Responding to the Selection

Personal Response

Students should link their ideas about freedom to specific passages in the Declaration of Independence.

ANALYZING LITERATURE

1. The document explains why the colonists desire to be free. Jefferson refers to people in general—all people deserve these rights and should think they are reasonable.
2. Among the unalienable rights are life, liberty, and the pursuit of happiness. Students may say that the "pursuit of happiness" means that people can do what they want if it is legal and does not hurt others.
3. The king has refused the colonists a voice in running their country and has made laws without their consent.
4. The document says that the colonists have asked to be compensated. When polite requests did not work, the colonists threatened more severe action. The king may have ignored the requests because he did not believe the colonists would carry out their threats.
5. The signers pledge that the colonies are independent and claim the rights of an independent nation. The signers believe God will help them in their undertaking.
6. The repetition provides an orderly list and helps give the impression that Jefferson has clearly thought out exactly what the king's offenses are.
7. Students should provide clear reasons for their choices.
8. Students should provide support for their answers.

✔ ASSESSMENT OPTIONS

📁 *Quick Checks,* p. 18
📁 *Selection and Theme Assessment,* pp. 31–32
📁 *Performance Assessment,* p. 17
💾 *Testmaker*

LITERARY ELEMENTS

Plundered and *ravaged* have particularly strong negative connotations. Plunder literally means "pillage or sack" and the use here connotes thievery. *Ravage* means "to commit destructive actions." It connotes violence, even rape. Students might also identify *burned* and *destroyed* as having negative connotations in this passage. Used here, they connote violent, senseless destruction.

Additional Resources
🖌 *Literary Elements Transparency 17*

Technology Skills

Objectives

- To understand the guidelines for effective communication via E-mail
- To write business letters stating a personal opinion using E-mail

Teaching Strategies

Discuss with students the advantages of sending messages via E-mail. E-mail messages arrive at their destination in a matter of seconds and at no additional cost. The same message can be sent to large numbers of people.

Discuss the layout and special features of the E-mail system. Students should first familiarize themselves with the system. Note that an E-mail address must be complete and accurate.

Adapting to Available E-mail Systems

Point out that the E-mail systems in different on-line services may vary. For example, one service may allow the sender to write and receive E-mail at the same location while another service may not.

E-mail: Business Writing

E-mail has made exercising your right of free speech easier than ever. Many newspapers, magazines, television shows, and radio broadcasts list their E-mail addresses so you can voice your opinion with a few minutes at the keyboard and the click of a mouse button. But if you decide to comment via E-mail, you'll need to remember several points about business writing.

The E-mail Business Letter

Server space on office computers is valuable. Mail that is too memory-intensive has been known to bring more than one network crashing down. Consequently, a business letter via E-mail should not be as lengthy or as elaborate as those destined for the post office. Look at the sample below:

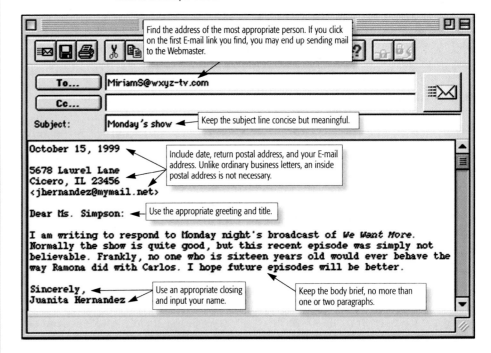

As with any letter, business E-mails should be checked for grammar and spelling *before* they are sent. Though most E-mail programs offer an "unsend" feature, you shouldn't make a habit of relying upon it too heavily.

Teaching Options

E-mail Spelling and Grammar Checking
Some E-mail systems provide spelling and grammar checking options. Students may choose to use these features, but remind them that they should personally check the spelling of proper names, titles, and other pertinent information.

MEETING INDIVIDUAL NEEDS — MULTIPLE LEARNING STYLES

Linguistic Students with acute linguistic abilities may respond well to activities that involve adapting written communications to electronic specifications and creating original correspondence. Others can benefit from their abilities as well.

Activity Before the class begins the E-mail activity, ask linguistically talented students to write the kind of detailed letter that a correspondent might send to a newspaper or television station through the post office. Then ask them to edit that letter to meet the limitations imposed by E-mail constraints. If possible, have them use the kind of computer editing feature that permits revisions to appear alongside the original copy. Ask them to share their completed work with the class. **L3**

TIPS FOR EFFECTIVE BUSINESS E-MAIL COMMUNICATIONS
• **Be certain.** If you respond immediately to something you view or read, you may react with emotion, which can get in the way of what you want to express. If you're writing an E-mail to voice an extreme response, you might want to wait a day or two before clicking Send.
• **Be cordial.** Even if you are writing to express displeasure, don't neglect common courtesy. You don't need to be overly gracious in your letter, but don't flame the reader.
• **Be brief.** Dispense with any unnecessary formalities, and say what you want to say.
• **Be clear.** Because we know what we mean, sometimes we mistakenly think others will, too. Ask a friend to read through your E-mail before you send it if you think there might be confusing elements.
• **Avoid E-mail acronyms and emoticons.** Acronyms (such as BTW for By the Way) and emoticons (like smiley faces) are useful for saving valuable server space, but save them for your friendly letters.
• **Remember your audience.** Adapt your correspondence to the needs of the person to whom you are writing. A business E-mail should be formal, but not stilted.
• **Include your addresses.** Make sure you include your E-mail address as well as your postal address.

E-mail is an excellent way of sharing your opinions quickly and easily, but you might consider following up your electronic correspondence with a letter mailed through the post office. E-mail is often viewed as remote, whereas traditional forms of business communication add a personal touch.

ACTIVITIES

1. Surf the Web to find sites of major newspapers and television programs. Search within the site to locate the E-mail address of a public relations official or customer service representative. (Note: the E-mail address at the bottom of the Web site is usually that of the Webmaster. Only comments about the site itself should be sent to her or him.) Practice writing E-mail letters that provide feedback to the newspaper or television show. Ask an older friend or relative to critique your letters and offer suggestions on how they might be improved.

2. Working with a partner, role-play a consumer and a television executive engaged in an E-mail correspondence. Some possible situations include: a letter of praise, a comment or suggestion, a criticism, a request for information.

REAL-WORLD CONNECTION

Before You Read

To His Excellency, General Washington

Objectives

- To read and analyze a poem celebrating our nation's freedoms
- To examine the use of heroic couplets in a poem
- To write a poem

Skills

Reading/Thinking: Visualizing; Drawing Conclusions
Writing: Poem

More About Phillis Wheatley

Wheatley, a devout Christian, began writing religious verse at about the age of thirteen. Her first published poem was an elegy on the death of George Whitehead, a well-known evangelical preacher. The sensation resulting from this poem led to the publication of Wheatley's only volume of poetry. Reverend Whitehead had been a close friend of an English countess, who was so impressed with Wheatley's elegy that she invited her to London and assisted her in publishing her poetry in England.

Meet Phillis Wheatley

"We whose Names are underwritten, do assure the World, that the Poems . . . were (as we verily believe) written by Phillis, a young Negro Girl, who . . . [is] under the Disadvantage of serving as a Slave. . . ."

In 1773 most readers would have doubted that an enslaved woman had written a book of poetry. The above statement was taken from the introduction to Phillis Wheatley's book of poetry, *Poems on Various Subjects, Religious and Moral*, published when Wheatley was only nineteen or twenty years old. Signed by eighteen of "the most respectable characters in Boston," including John Hancock and the royal governor, the letter was testimony to the authenticity of the poems. Wheatley was the first African American to publish a book of poetry.

Wheatley was kidnapped from her home in the Senegal/Gambia region on the west coast of Africa and brought to New England on the slave ship *Phillis* when she was just seven or eight. In 1761 John Wheatley, a wealthy Bostonian, purchased her to be a personal attendant for his wife, Susanna. Recognizing the child's intelligence, the Wheatley family took great interest in educating her.

Given the family name Wheatley and the first name Phillis (the name of the ship she arrived on), the young woman gained free use of the home library and was supported and encouraged in her studies and writing. She quickly mastered English and Latin. She studied the Bible and read many of the ancient Greek and Latin classics.

In May of 1773, the Wheatleys sent Phillis to London. A doctor had recommended a sea voyage for Phillis's health, and the Wheatley's son Nathaniel was bound for London on business. It was there that Wheatley was finally able to publish her only volume of poetry, *Poems on Various Subjects, Religious and Moral*. On her return from England, the family freed her from enslavement. The poet remained in the Wheatley household until the death of John Wheatley in 1778.

In April of that same year, Phillis Wheatley married John Peters, a freed African American. Poverty and the death of two infants marked their difficult marriage. In 1784 Wheatley wrote her last poem, her husband died in debtor's prison, and on December 5, she died of malnutrition. A brief announcement in Boston's *Independent Chronicle* read, "Last Lord's Day, died Mrs. Phillis Peters (formerly Phillis Wheatley), aged thirty-one, known to the world by her celebrated miscellaneous poems."

"You were . . . a sickly little Black girl, snatched from your home and country and made a slave; a woman who still struggled to sing the song that was your gift . . . It is not so much what you sang, as that you kept alive, in so many of our ancestors, the notion of song."

—Alice Walker

Phillis Wheatley was born around 1753 and died in 1784.

Reading Further

If you would like to read more by Phillis Wheatley, you might read:

The Collected Works of Phillis Wheatley, edited by John C. Shields.

RESOURCE MANAGER

Lesson Planning Resource
The *Unit Two Planning Guide* (pp. 48–52) provides additional lesson notes and reduced versions of all print resources.

Other Print Resources
- Active Reading Guide, p. 19
- Reading Workbook
- Quick Checks, p. 19
- Selection and Theme Assessment, pp. 33–34

- Performance Assessment, p. 18
- Spanish Summaries, p. 19
- Inclusion Strategies
- English Language Learners Sourcebook

Transparencies
- Selection Focus 19
- Literary Elements 18

Technology
- Audio Library
- Glencoe Literature Web Site
- Testmaker

FOCUS ACTIVITY

What would you write in a letter to the President or another leader? Would you ask the leader to support new laws? Would you propose solutions to problems?

FREEWRITE List messages you might send to the President or to another leader. Consider local or national problems that need to be solved. Think about accomplishments you might thank the leader for.

SETTING A PURPOSE Read to learn Phillis Wheatley's message to George Washington.

BACKGROUND

The Time and Place
When General George Washington traveled to Boston in 1775 to assume leadership of the Continental Army and to rid the city of occupying British soldiers, Phillis Wheatley wrote to him. Her letter and poem to the General were sent to his headquarters in nearby Cambridge. Washington responded by expressing his appreciation for the poem and invited her to visit him. The two met at his Cambridge headquarters.

Liberty vs. Slavery
The "Columbia" Wheatley speaks of in her poem is America, personified as a goddess of liberty. Wheatley herself, however, had not yet attained her own freedom in the New England colonies. Critics have ridiculed Wheatley for glorifying our nation's freedom yet never speaking out against slavery. Others, however, see Wheatley as a woman who was painfully aware of the need to ingratiate herself with her supporters and patrons.

Literary Influences
Wheatley's poetry is written in the neoclassical style, characterized by formal elegance, simplicity, dignity, order, and proportion. The content of her poetry reflects her strong Christian values.

George Washington. Artist unknown, after Charles Willson Peale. Oil on canvas. Chateau de Versailles, France.

A NEW NATION 🐚 177

Reading Further

Be sure to review these titles for appropriateness for your class before recommending them to students.

Mason, Julian (editor). *The Poems of Phillis Wheatley.* Chapel Hill, North Carolina: University of North Carolina Press, 1989.

Shields, John (editor). *The Collected Works of Phillis Wheatley.* New York: Oxford University Press, 1989.

VIEWING THE PAINTING

Ask students to identify qualities of Washington that are evident in the painting.

Viewing Response *From Washington's dress and the cannon upon which he is leaning, the viewer can infer that he was an important military figure. His pose is relaxed and authoritative.*

Reading *Minilesson*

Visualizing Wheatley uses striking visual images to describe the United States in its quest for freedom. Visualizing what students "see" as they read or hear the poem will help them better understand Wheatley's view of the United States.

[Activity] As students read, they can sketch what they visualize as Wheatley's picture of America. Ask students to examine their drawings. What feelings or emotions do the drawings convey? Do students think Wheatley's images produce the effect she desires? Why or why not? **L2**

Additional Resources
📁 *Reading Workbook*

A Active Reading

PREDICT Ask students to read the "letter" that precedes the poem and then pause. Based on this letter, what can they predict about the poem's content and tone? *(Students might predict that the poem will praise Washington and his cause unequivocally; the tone will probably be formal.)*

Additional Resources
📁 *Active Reading Guide,* p. 19
🎧 **Audio Library**

Teaching Options

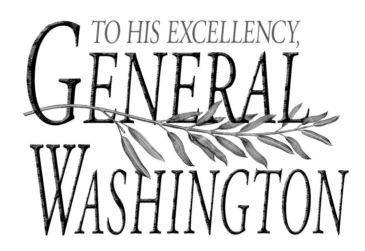

TO HIS EXCELLENCY, GENERAL WASHINGTON

Phillis Wheatley ∾

> *Sir.*
>
> *I Have taken the freedom to address your Excellency in the enclosed poem, and entreat your acceptance, though I am not insensible of its inaccuracies. Your being appointed by the Grand Continental Congress to be Generalissimo of the armies of North America, together with the fame of your virtues, excite sensations not easy to suppress. Your generosity, therefore, I presume, will pardon the attempt. Wishing your Excellency all possible success in the great cause you are so generously engaged in. I am,*
>
> > *Your Excellency's most obedient humble servant,*
> > *Phillis Wheatley.*

Providence, Oct. 26, 1775.
His Excellency Gen. Washington.

> Celestial choir! enthron'd in realms of light,
>   Columbia's scenes of glorious toils I write.
> While freedom's cause her anxious breast alarms,
> She flashes dreadful in refulgent° arms.
> 5 See mother earth her offspring's fate bemoan,
> And nations gaze at scenes before unknown!
> See the bright beams of heaven's revolving light
> Involved in sorrows and the veil of night!

---

4 *Refulgent* means "radiant."

178 🦋 UNIT 2

The goddess comes, she moves divinely fair,
10 Olive and laurel binds her golden hair:
B Wherever shines this native of the skies,
Unnumber'd charms and recent graces rise.

Muse!° bow propitious° while my pen relates
C How pour her armies through a thousand gates,
15 As when Eolus° heaven's fair face deforms,
Enwrapp'd in tempest and a night of storms;
Astonish'd ocean feels the wild uproar,
The refluent° surges beat the sounding shore;
Or thick as leaves in Autumn's golden reign,
20 Such, and so many, moves the warrior's train.
In bright array they seek the work of war,
D Where high unfurl'd the ensign° waves in air.
Shall I to Washington their praise recite?
Enough thou know'st them in the fields of fight.
25 Thee, first in peace and honours,—we demand
The grace and glory of thy martial band.
Fam'd for thy valour, for thy virtues more,
Hear every tongue thy guardian aid implore!
One century scarce perform'd its destined round,
30 When Gallic° powers Columbia's fury found;
And so may you, whoever dares disgrace
The land of freedom's heaven-defended race!
Fix'd are the eyes of nations on the scales,
For in their hopes Columbia's arm prevails.
35 Anon° Britannia° droops the pensive head,
While round increase the rising hills of dead.
Ah! cruel blindness to Columbia's state!
Lament thy thirst of boundless power too late.
Proceed, great chief, with virtue on thy side,
40 Thy ev'ry action let the goddess guide.
A crown, a mansion, and a throne that shine,
With gold unfading, WASHINGTON! be thine.

---

13 The poet asks for aid from a *Muse*. In Greek mythology, the Muses
(goddesses) preside over arts and sciences. Here, *propitious* means "favorably."
15 In Greek mythology, *Eolus* is the god of the winds.
18 *Refluent* means "back-flowing."
22 The *ensign* here is a flag.
30 *Gallic* means "French." Washington had fought the French during the French
and Indian War (1754–1763).
35 *Anon* means "soon." *Britannia* is Great Britain, personified as a goddess.

MEETING INDIVIDUAL NEEDS — ENGLISH LANGUAGE LEARNERS

Responding to the Selection

Personal Response

Some students may say that Wheatley believes in liberty and the colonists' cause; others may say Wheatley gives Washington more credit than he is due.

ANALYZING LITERATURE

1. Wheatley wants General Washington to know that the country has confidence in him. She views Washington as a man of great virtue.
2. She asks the celestial choir to look at the noble struggle for freedom; the war being fought in America is unlike any other.
3. Columbia is graceful, divine, and draped with symbols of peace. Wheatley views America in a similar light and sees America as refined, not aggressive.
4. She compares the army to winds, waves, and leaves. Students may say that she chooses forces of nature because the army's power is beyond human measurements.
5. The lines are addressed to Britain. They warn rather than admire.
6. For most students, the letter will show Wheatley's motivation and make the poem's intent clearer.
7. Students may cite images, allusions, or difficult words.
8. Students should cite specific details from different portrayals of George Washington.
9. Today's readers might view Wheatley's opinions as overly fervent. Some might find it ironic that an ex-slave was praising her country's virtues. Modern readers might find the poem's images and allusions difficult.
10. Students should clearly explain their reactions.

Responding to Literature

Personal Response

What is your impression of Wheatley from reading this letter and poem?

——— ANALYZING LITERATURE ———

RECALL AND INTERPRET

1. In your own words, restate the message in Wheatley's letter to General Washington. What seems to have been her opinion of Washington?
2. In lines 1–8, describe what the speaker asks the Celestial Choir to see.
3. What image of Columbia is described in lines 9–12? What does the **imagery** convey about the speaker's view of America?
4. In lines 13–22, to what three things does the speaker compare the colonial army? In your opinion, why did she choose these images?
5. To whom are lines 29–38 addressed? How does this section of the poem differ from the rest?

EVALUATE AND CONNECT

6. Did reading the letter help you understand the poem? Why or why not?
7. Which lines from the poem did you have the most trouble understanding? Why do you think they were especially troublesome?
8. How does Wheatley's portrait of Washington compare with other interpretations of him, based on your reading and on television or film portrayals?
9. How might most readers today view Wheatley's poem if it appeared in a newspaper or magazine? Give examples.
10. **Theme Connections** What is your reaction to Wheatley's attitude toward the colonial cause of freedom? Explain your response.

Literary ELEMENTS

The Heroic Couplet
A **couplet** is two consecutive lines of poetry that rhyme. A **heroic couplet** has a specific rhythm, or meter, called **iambic pentameter.** In this meter, each line consists of five units, or feet, and each foot consists of two syllables, an unstressed one followed by a stressed one. This form of couplet became known as "heroic" because it was commonly used in epics that told of heroes and heroic deeds.

1. Read aloud three heroic couplets from the poem. In your opinion, does the heroic couplet form add to or detract from the meaning and tone of the poem? Explain your position.
2. Why do you think Wheatley might have chosen to write this poem in heroic couplets?

● See **Literary Terms Handbook,** p. R7.

——— EXTENDING YOUR RESPONSE ———

Creative Writing

Letter to a Leader Review your freewrite from the Focus Activity on page 177. Choose one message you would like to send to the President or any other leader. Then write a short poem that captures the essence of your message. Write your poem in couplets; if you want a greater challenge, try writing it in heroic couplets. Read your work to the class.

Interdisciplinary Activity

Art: Create an Image Choose one of the images from Wheatley's poem to illustrate. Then, in a drawing or a painting, create your own visual image to convey the image in the poem. If possible, you might use a computer to create your image. Display your art for the class.

📖 **Save your work for your portfolio.**

LITERARY ELEMENTS

1. Students may note that the regularity of the couplets creates a rational, dignified tone.
2. Students may say that Wheatley sees General Washington and his cause as being heroic, so she chooses a form that is used to record heroic deeds.

Additional Resources

✑ *Literary Elements Transparency 18*

✔ ASSESSMENT OPTIONS

📁 *Quick Checks,* p. 19
📁 *Selection and Theme Assessment,* pp. 33–34
📁 *Performance Assessment,* p. 18
💾 *Testmaker*

MEDIA Connection

Web Site

Throughout history, people have made heroic efforts to break free. Participants in the project Amistad America™ hope to remind us of one group of enslaved Africans who did break free.

Amistad America™ The Amistad Incident

Address: http://www.amistadamerica.org

AMISTAD America™

The *Amistad* incident began off the coast of Cuba in 1839 with a shipboard rebellion by 53 Africans who had been illegally enslaved. Wandering up the Atlantic coast, the ship was seized by a United States revenue cutter off the coast of Long Island and towed into New London harbor, where the Africans were initially imprisoned. They were tried for murder in Connecticut, and eventually won their freedom after John Quincy Adams argued their case in the United States Supreme Court. The ship that was transporting them into slavery and then to freedom was named *Amistad,* which means "friendship" in Spanish.

Now, more than 150 years later, the *Amistad* will sail again. When complete the freedom schooner *Amistad* will ply the nation's waterways as an educational ambassador, teaching lessons of history, cooperation, and leadership to Americans of all ages, interests, and cultural backgrounds.

Take a look at this picture perfect project:

While Steven Spielberg puts the *Amistad* saga on the big screen, Amistad America™ will take the story on the open sea aboard freedom schooner *Amistad.* . . .

Mystic Seaport's *Amistad* project coordinator Quentin Snediker will lead the charge in transforming wood, metal, and fabric into the $2.8 million, 77-foot, hand-hewn freedom schooner *Amistad.*

Amistad will set sail . . . with Captain Bill Pinkney at the helm. The vessel will ply the nation's waterways as an educational ambassador. . . .

Respond

1. What do you think motivates people to participate in a project like Amistad America™?
2. Do you think the project will be successful? Explain your answer.

MEDIA Connection

Objective

- To understand and apply strategies for reading a Web page

Literature — LINK

Letter to Her Daughter from the New and Unfinished White House This Web page relates the role of John Quincy Adams, Abigail Adams's son, in the *Amistad* case. Students can analyze how the mother's personality traits were mirrored in her son.

From The Life of Olaudah Equiano By learning firsthand of the horrors of the slave trade, students will understand the pressing need for projects like Amistad America.

Respond

1. Students may say that people do projects like these because they want a better understanding of the past. The projects try to teach the present generation not to repeat past mistakes.
2. Students may say that the project will be a success because it is well organized and well funded.

Additional Resources
📁 *Media Connections,* p. 4

Teaching Options

Reading *Minilesson*

Activating Prior Knowledge If students consider what they already know about both the Internet and the *Amistad,* they will be able to judge the accuracy of the content of the Web sites more effectively.

Activity Before students read the Web sites, ask them to list what they already know about the *Amistad.* Ask them what else they would like to know about the incident. As they read, they can look for the answers to their questions. You may also ask them to predict what they will find at each of the different areas of the Web site. **L2**

Additional Resources
📁 *Reading Workbook*

The *Amistad* Suggest that students find other Web sites about the *Amistad.* They can enter *Amistad* as a keyword.

Objectives

- To read and analyze a slave narrative on the loss of freedom
- To analyze the methods a slave narrative uses to expose the horrors of slavery
- To write a press release

Skills

Reading/Thinking: Making Critical Judgments; Drawing Conclusions; Synthesizing

Grammar/Language: Compound Subjects

Life Skills: Planning and Designing

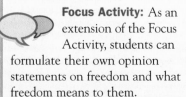

Motivating

→OPTIONS

Selection Focus Transparency 21: Have students view the transparency and then answer the question provided.

Focus Activity: As an extension of the Focus Activity, students can formulate their own opinion statements on freedom and what freedom means to them.

Before You Read

from *The Life of Olaudah Equiano*

Meet Olaudah Equiano

"*. . . I might say my sufferings were great; but when I compare my lot with that of most of my countrymen, I regard myself as a particular favorite of heaven. . . .*"

—Equiano

Olaudah Equiano (ō lau′ dä   e kwē ä′ nō), the son of a chieftain of the Igbo group, was born in 1745 in the African village of Essaka (now northeastern Nigeria). When he was only eleven years old, he was kidnapped by slave traders and shipped to the island of Barbados in the Caribbean Sea.

In Barbados, Equiano traded the "cheerfulness and affability . . . the leading characteristics of our nation" for the "shrieks of the women and the groans of the dying [that made] a scene of horror almost inconceivable."

Equiano had been in Barbados for nearly a year when an officer of the British Royal Navy bought him and renamed him Gustavus Vassa. By the age of twelve Equiano learned to read and write. At age twenty-one he was finally able to buy his freedom. He settled in England and devoted himself to the antislavery movement. His autobiography, *The Interesting Narrative of the Life of Olaudah Equiano, or Gustavus Vassa, the African*, was first published in 1789. It would forever change the European and American view of slavery.

Olaudah Equiano was born in 1745 and died in 1797.

FOCUS ACTIVITY

"No man has received from nature the right to give orders to others. Freedom is a gift from heaven, and every individual of the same species has the right to enjoy it as soon as he is in enjoyment of his reason."

—*Denis Diderot*

SHARE IT! Discuss with a classmate this statement by French philosopher Diderot. Try to summarize the statement in just a few words. Consider how you might feel if someone took away your freedom.

SETTING A PURPOSE Read to discover Equiano's attitude toward his loss of freedom.

BACKGROUND

The Time and Place

From the 1500s to the 1800s, about twelve million Africans suffered unspeakable horrors on the forced journey from their homes to enslavement in the Western Hemisphere. The longest and most arduous portion of the journey, known as the Middle Passage, was a two-month voyage from West Africa to the West Indies. Almost two million Africans died from malnutrition, disease, suffocation, beatings, and despair.

VOCABULARY PREVIEW

countenance (koun′ tə nens) *n.* face; facial features; p. 190

apprehension (ap′ ri hen′ shən) *n.* fear of what may happen in the future; anxiety; p. 191

copious (kō′ pē əs) *adj.* large in quantity; plentiful; p. 192

gratify (grat′ ə fī′) *v.* to satisfy or indulge; p. 193

clamor (klam′ ər) *n.* confused, insistent shouting; p. 194

scruple (skrōō′ pəl) *n.* moral principle that restrains action; p. 194

RESOURCE MANAGER

Lesson Planning Resource
The *Unit Two Planning Guide* (pp. 59–66) provides additional lesson notes and reduced versions of all print resources.

Other Print Resources
- Active Reading Guide, p. 21
- Vocabulary Practice, p. 18
- Reading Workbook, pp. 25–26
- Grammar and Language Workbook, p. 75

- Grammar and Composition Handbook, Lesson 2.3
- Quick Checks, p. 21
- Selection and Theme Assessment, pp. 37–38
- Performance Assessment, p. 20
- Spanish Summaries, p. 21
- Spanish Translations
- Inclusion Strategies
- English Language Learners Sourcebook

Transparencies
- Selection Focus 21
- Literary Elements 20
- Grammar and Language 15

Technology
- Audio Library
- Spanish Audio Library
- Glencoe Literature Web Site
- Testmaker

Responding to Literature

Personal Response

What images or details from this narrative linger in your mind?

ANALYZING LITERATURE

RECALL AND INTERPRET

1. What does Equiano fear will happen to him when he is taken aboard the ship? Why might he be so afraid?
2. How does Equiano react to the fatal flogging of a white crew member? Why do you think the incident has such a strong impact on Equiano?
3. Although terrified, Equiano also displays great curiosity. Relate an incident that reveals his curiosity. What does it reveal about his character?
4. In the last paragraph, what does Equiano describe as perhaps the greatest tragedy of slavery? What do you think he means when he says it "adds fresh horrors even to the wretchedness of slavery"?

EVALUATE AND CONNECT

5. Theme Connections   In this part of his story, does Equiano give any indication that he might soon break free of his enslavement? Explain.
6. Describe the **tone** (see page R16) of this work. At what point does the tone shift? Evaluate the effectiveness of this change in tone.
7. Think back to your discussion for the Focus Activity on page 188. How would you describe Equiano's attitude toward his loss of freedom? How might you react to such an extreme loss of freedom?
8. What insights have you gained from reading this work? For example, has it affected your attitudes about personal freedom, human nature, or our nation's history of enslavement of Africans?

EXTENDING YOUR RESPONSE

Internet Connection

First-Hand Accounts   Log on to the Library of Congress's on-line African American History and Culture page. There you can find photographs of original texts, letters, and posters related to the topic of slavery. You can also find art by and about enslaved African Americans. Download and print a story or photograph you find interesting and share it with your class.

Writing About Literature

Two Thumbs Up   Imagine that you have just produced a feature film based on the life of Olaudah Equiano. Write a press release that summarizes the story and encourages viewers to attend a screening of the film.

 Save your work for your portfolio.

Personal Response

Students should articulate what made certain images stand out.

ANALYZING LITERATURE

1. He fears that the white men will eat him. His fears probably result from his never having seen a white person before. He is also young and has been taken by force.
2. He becomes even more terrified of the white men on the ship. Their flogging and discarding one of their own shows their inhumanity.
3. Equiano observes the sailors to see how they use instruments. He remains curious and eager to learn, despite the conditions.
4. Equiano feels that the greatest tragedy is the separation of families. He probably means that slavery is made even more horrible without family support.
5. Students may say that Equiano uses strong images and powerful words to display his will to be free and become educated. His words challenge slavery directly.
6. The tone for most of the piece is objective. In the last paragraph, the tone directly challenges those who trade and hold slaves.
7. Equiano is desperate and anxious at his loss of freedom. Students may say they would be scared, unhappy, or angry.
8. Responses should correspond to the major issues of the selection.

Writing ✎ Workshop

Objectives

- To create a personal response to literature for a particular audience
- To plan a reflective essay that explores ideas and connects personal thoughts to the literature
- To draft, revise, edit, and present a reflective essay
- To assess the reflective essay

Teaching Strategies

PREWRITING

Explore ideas Ask students to identify which selection made the most powerful impression. Then group students who chose the same selection to explore the impressions in more detail.

Teaching Options

⌁: Writing ✎ Workshop :⌁

Personal Writing: Reflective Essay

What does "breaking free" mean to you? What are your thoughts about oppression and independence? Your mind is deep, and when you take the trouble to explore it, you can find surprising wisdom. The selections you have read so far express ideas about oppression, freedom, and crucial choices. One way to explore such ideas is to write a reflective essay, a piece of writing that examines in-depth your own thoughts on a particular subject. **In this workshop, you will write a reflective essay.** You will examine, develop, and write about your own insights on one of the ideas in this theme.

● As you write your reflective essay, refer to **Writing Handbook,** pp. R62–R77.

The Writing Process

PREWRITING

PREWRITING TIP
To start your exploration, ask a friend to interview you about freedom, oppression, or choices in this theme and in today's world. Jot down your answers to the interview questions.

Explore ideas
Many selections in this theme are more than two hundred years old, yet they speak to people today. Look back through the theme for selections or passages that have special meaning for you. Ask yourself questions like these:

● How do these selections make me feel? Proud? Angry? Hopeful? Confused? Sad? Curious? Why do I feel this way?
● With which of Benjamin Franklin's proverbs do I agree or disagree? Why?
● What are Patrick Henry's ideas about freedom? What are my ideas about freedom?
● What parts of Thomas Paine's *The Crisis, No. 1* do I still remember from my first reading? Why?
● What aspects of Abigail Adams's personality do I like or dislike?
● What current events or issues came to mind when I read the Declaration of Independence?
● If Phillis Wheatley saw the world today, what would she think?
● How can I understand or relate to Olaudah Equiano's experience?
● Of the selections I have read, which ones might apply to my life or to the lives of people I know? How do they apply?

MEETING INDIVIDUAL NEEDS — ENGLISH LANGUAGE LEARNERS

Developing a Topic Make sure English language learners understand that in a reflective essay they will reflect, or comment, on what they feel and think about a topic.

Activity To simplify the assignment, break it down into a series of carefully sequenced questions that students can work through one at a time.

- What selection will you write about?
- What did you most like about it?
- What two or three elements about it were most important for you?
- What did the selection mean to your life?

Additional Resources
📁 *English Language Learners Sourcebook*

Theme 3 — Gaining Insight

Think of a time when you had a flash of understanding and saw the deeper, hidden meaning of something. Maybe you suddenly saw the logic behind a geometry proof, or discovered the perfect new ingredient to add to your chili recipe. In either case you would have gained an insight, an understanding that goes deeper than the surface of things. In this theme you will read selections that reflect the writers' insights—about themselves, about nature, and about humankind.

THEME PROJECTS

Internet Connection

Design a Web Site   With a partner, design a Web site for one of the authors in this theme.

1. Together, choose an author and plan what to include about his or her life, works, and thoughts.

2. Search the Internet to find other sites related to the author and add "links" to those sites on your own Web site.

3. Design your Web site to be visually appealing and to reflect the nature of the author's insights.

4. If possible, design an actual Web site. Otherwise, create your site on paper as it would look on a monitor screen. Share your Web site with the class.

Interdisciplinary Project

Art: Collage Gallery   Choose three speakers or authors from this theme and create a collage for each one that conveys that person's ideas.

1. Use paper, newspaper and magazine clippings, fabric, photographs, objects from nature, and any other media you can think of to express your view of the subject. However, do not use your subject's name in the collage.

2. Display your collages for the class. Ask classmates to try to name the person each collage represents and to give reasons for their guesses.

Shield of Memory, Robin Holder. Stencil monotype, 19¾ x 30 in. Collection of the artist.

Theme 3

Teaching Strategies

The following suggestions may help your students plan and carry out their theme projects.

Internet Connection

- Share sample Web site pages with students and discuss their features, including "links."
- Encourage students to research their author in encyclopedias, on-line, in biographies and critical studies, and in the Before You Read pages of this book.
- Encourage students to create visual appeal through graphics/illustrations, photos.

Interdisciplinary Project

- Collages do not have to represent the person but rather the person's ideas. Students do not need to re-create a physical likeness.
- Encourage students to first identify a few key elements that they believe best convey the ideas of each subject and then to think about how to represent these ideas visually.
- Students may use words or brief quotations in their collages.

Additional Resources

- *Interdisciplinary Activities,* pp. 6–7
- *Viewing and Representing Activities,* pp. 11–12
- *Listening and Speaking Activities,* pp. 5–6
- *Critical Thinking Skills,* pp. 8–10
- *Selection and Theme Assessment,* pp. 219–220
- *Performance Assessment,* p. 127

LITERATURE & HUMANITIES

Play "Come Life, Shaker Life," and "'Tis a Gift to Be Simple," from Glencoe's *American Music: Cultural Traditions,* Volume 1, Track 14.

GLENCOE TECHNOLOGY

LITERATURE CLASSICS CD-ROM

Search for other short stories by theme, author, or title.

SELECTIONS	Literary Elements	Reading and Thinking	Writing	Vocabulary and Spelling	
The Devil and Tom Walker WASHINGTON IRVING	SE: Tall Tale, p. 214 *TWE: Motif, p. 204; Figures of Speech: Simile, p. 205; Character: Context Clues, p. 206; Tall Tale, p. 207; Tone: Satire, p. 209; Theme: Universal Truths, p. 210; Symbol, p. 213*	*TWE: Visualizing, p. 205; Drawing Conclusions, p. 206; Inferring, p. 211*	SE: Song Lyrics, p. 215 *TWE: Writing About Action, p. 212; Character Sketch, p. 215*	SE: Analogies, p. 215; Using Roots to Understand New Words, p. 217	
To a Waterfowl Thanatopsis WILLIAM CULLEN BRYANT	*TWE: Figures of Speech: Oxymoron, p. 220*	*TWE: Synthesizing, p. 219;* COLLAB. LEARN. Paraphrasing, p. 219; *Inferring, p. 221; Elaborating, p. 221*	SE: Comparison, p. 223		
Old Ironsides THE CHAMBERED NAUTILUS OLIVER WENDELL HOLMES	SE: Verbal Irony, p. 228 *TWE: Tone, p. 225; Figures of Speech: Metaphor, p. 226*	*TWE: Setting a Purpose for Reading, p. 225; Drawing Conclusions, p. 227*			
The First Snow-Fall JAMES RUSSELL LOWELL	SE: Theme, p. 233 *TWE: Imagery, p. 231; Figurative Language, p. 232*	*TWE: Inferring, p. 232*	SE: Poem or Narrative, p. 233 *TWE: Descriptive Paragraph, p. 234*		
The Tide Rises, the Tide Falls HENRY WADSWORTH LONGFELLOW	SE: Rhythm, p. 237 *TWE: Figure of Speech: Personification, p. 236*	*TWE: Using Sensory Details, p. 236*	SE: Interview Questions and Answers, p. 237		
Concord Hymn *from* Self-Reliance *from* Nature RALPH WALDO EMERSON	SE: Metonymy, p. 241; Figurative Language, p. 248 *TWE: Figurative Language: Apostrophe, p. 240*	*TWE: Elaborating, p. 243; Comparing and Contrasting, p. 245; Logical Reasoning, p. 246*	SE: Modern Song, p. 241; Journal Entry, pp. 244, 249	SE: The Prefix com-, p. 249	
from WALDEN *from* CIVIL DISOBEDIENCE HENRY DAVID THOREAU	SE: Argument, p. 262 *TWE: Tone, p. 253; Figures of Speech: Metaphor, p. 254; Motif, p. 254; Figures of Speech: Analogy, p. 255; Allusion, p. 261*	*TWE: Problems and Solutions, p. 251; Inferring, pp. 255, 261; Elaborating, p. 259; Making Assumptions, p. 260; Main Points and Supporting Details, p. 261*	SE: Arrest Report, p. 263	SE: Analogies, p. 263	
The Minister's Black Veil NATHANIEL HAWTHORNE	SE: Short Story, p. 276 *TWE: Foreshadowing, p. 269; Tone: Ambiguity, p. 270; Motif, p. 271; Character, p. 271; Imagery, p. 272*	*TWE: Previewing, p. 267; Inferring, pp. 270, 272*	SE: Dialogue, p. 277 *TWE: Character Sketch, p. 273*	SE: Etymology, p. 277 *TWE: Root Words, p. 268*	
The Three-Piece Suit ALI DEB	SE: Rising Action, p. 282 *TWE: Tone: Irony, p. 280*	*TWE: Identifying Fallacies in Reasoning, p. 281* SE: Scanning, p. 284	SE: Wardrobe Description, p. 282		
To HELEN THE RAVEN THE PIT AND THE PENDULUM EDGAR ALLAN POE	SE: Suspense, p. 305 *TWE: Meter, p. 288; Alliteration and Assonance, p. 288;* Rhyme, p. 289; *Figurative Language: Imagery, p. 293; Plot: Suspense, p. 296; Hyperbole, p. 301; Plot: Deus ex Machina, p. 304*	*TWE: Classifying, p. 287; Evaluating, pp. 296, 301, 303; Identifying Audience, p. 307*	SE: Character Description, p. 291; Advice Letter, p. 291; Poem, p. 306; Analyzing Description, p. 306 *TWE: Analyzing Description, p. 299*	SE: Pronunciation, p. 306	

Key: Student material is in roman. Teacher material is in italic. 🖥 Technology COLLAB. LEARN. Collaboration

Grammar and Language	Listening, Speaking, and Viewing	Life Skills	Study, Research, and Technology
TWE: Appositives & Appositive Phrases, p. 204; **COLLAB. LEARN.** *Absolute Phrases*, p. 208	SE: **COLLAB. LEARN.** Literature Groups, p. 215; Monologue, p. 215 *TWE: Oral Presentation*, p. 211	SE: Learning for Life: The Cost of Borrowing, p. 215	*TWE: History*, p. 207
TWE: Present Participles as Adjectives, p. 220			SE: 🖥 Internet Connection, p. 223
TWE: Past Participles as Adjectives, p. 226			
SE: Making Pronouns and Their Antecedents Agree, p. 234 *TWE: Gerunds*, p. 231			
	SE: **COLLAB. LEARN.** Performing Rhythms, p. 237		
TWE: Gerund Phrases, p. 239; *Infinitives*, p. 242	SE: **COLLAB. LEARN.** Literature Groups, pp. 241, 244, 249; **COLLAB. LEARN.** Performing a Press Conference, p. 249		SE: 🖥 **COLLAB. LEARN.** Internet Connection, p. 249 *TWE: Research Culture*, p. 247
TWE: Infinitive Phrases, p. 252; *Split Infinitives*, p. 258	SE: **COLLAB. LEARN.** Literature Groups, pp. 256, 263; Lecture, p. 256; Speech, p. 263; **COLLAB. LEARN.** Performing a Play, p. 263		*TWE: Disobedience and Change*, p. 260
TWE: Dangling Participles, p. 268	SE: **COLLAB. LEARN.** Literature Groups, p. 277; Sermon, p. 277; Dramatic Scene, p. 277		*TWE: Religion and Architecture*, p. 271
TWE: Object of an Infinitive, p. 280	SE: **COLLAB. LEARN.** Literature Groups, p. 282		
TWE: Combining Main Clauses, p. 290; *Identifying Main Clauses*, p. 293	SE: **COLLAB. LEARN.** Literature Groups, p. 306	SE: Learning for Life: A Marketing Plan, p. 306 *TWE: Logical Reasoning*, p. 296	SE: 🖥 Internet Connection, p. 306 *TWE: The Spanish Inquisition*, p. 295

SELECTIONS	Print Resources		
The Devil and Tom Walker WASHINGTON IRVING	Unit Two Planning Guide, pp. 74–81 * Active Reading Guide, p. 22 Vocabulary Practice, p. 19	Grammar and Composition Handbook, Lessons 3.2, 3.4 Grammar and Language Workbook, pp. 87, 89 Reading Workbook, pp. 27–28	* Quick Checks, p. 22 Selection and Theme Assessment, pp. 39–40 Performance Assessment, p. 21 Spanish Summaries, p. 22 Spanish Translations
To a Waterfowl Thanatopsis WILLIAM CULLEN BRYANT	Unit Two Planning Guide, pp. 82–87 * Active Reading Guide, p. 23	Grammar and Composition Handbook, Lesson 3.3 Grammar and Language Workbook, p. 93 Reading Workbook	* Quick Checks, p. 23 Selection and Theme Assessment, pp. 41–42 Performance Assessment, p. 22 Spanish Summaries, p. 23
Old Ironsides THE CHAMBERED NAUTILUS OLIVER WENDELL HOLMES	Unit Two Planning Guide, pp. 88–93 * Active Reading Guide, p. 24	Grammar and Composition Handbook, Lesson 3.3 Grammar and Language Workbook, p. 93 Reading Workbook	* Quick Checks, p. 24 Selection and Theme Assessment, pp. 43–44 Performance Assessment, p. 23 Spanish Summaries, p. 24
The First Snow-Fall JAMES RUSSELL LOWELL	Unit Two Planning Guide, pp. 94–99 * Active Reading Guide, p. 25	Grammar and Composition Handbook, Lesson 3.3 Grammar and Language Workbook, p. 89 Reading Workbook	* Quick Checks, p. 25 Selection and Theme Assessment, p. 45 Performance Assessment, p. 24 Spanish Summaries, p. 25 Spanish Translations
The Tide Rises, the Tide Falls HENRY WADSWORTH LONGFELLOW	Unit Two Planning Guide, pp. 100–104 * Active Reading Guide, p. 26	Reading Workbook	* Quick Checks, p. 26 Selection and Theme Assessment, p. 46 Performance Assessment, p. 25 Spanish Summaries, p. 26 Spanish Translations
Concord Hymn from Self-Reliance from Nature RALPH WALDO EMERSON	Unit Two Planning Guide, pp. 105–111 * Active Reading Guide, pp. 27–29 Vocabulary Practice, p. 20	Grammar and Composition Handbook, Lesson 3.3 Grammar and Language Workbook, pp. 89, 91 Reading Workbook, pp. 29–30	* Quick Checks, pp. 27–29 Selection and Theme Assessment, pp. 47–48 Performance Assessment, p. 26 Spanish Summaries, p. 27
from CIVIL DISOBEDIENCE from WALDEN HENRY DAVID THOREAU	Unit Two Planning Guide, pp. 112–120 * Active Reading Guide, pp. 30–31 Vocabulary Practice, p. 21	Grammar and Composition Handbook, Lesson 3.3 Grammar and Language Workbook, p. 91 Reading Workbook, pp. 31–34	* Quick Checks, pp. 30–31 Selection and Theme Assessment, pp. 49–50 Performance Assessment, p. 27 Spanish Summaries, p. 28 Spanish Translations
The Minister's Black Veil NATHANIEL HAWTHORNE	Unit Two Planning Guide, pp. 121–128 * Active Reading Guide, p. 32 Vocabulary Practice, p. 22	Grammar and Composition Handbook, Lesson 3.3 Grammar and Language Workbook, p. 207 Reading Workbook, pp. 35–36	* Quick Checks, p. 32 Selection and Theme Assessment, pp. 51–52 Performance Assessment, p. 28 Spanish Summaries, p. 29
The Three-Piece Suit ALI DEB	Unit Two Planning Guide, pp. 129–134 * Active Reading Guide, p. 33 Vocabulary Practice, p. 23	Grammar and Composition Handbook, Lesson 3.3 Grammar and Language Workbook, p. 91 Reading Workbook, pp. 35–36	*Quick Checks, p. 33 Selection and Theme Assessment, pp. 53–54 Performance Assessment, p. 29 Spanish Summaries, p. 30 Spanish Translations
To Helen THE RAVEN THE PIT AND THE PENDULUM EDGAR ALLAN POE	Unit Two Planning Guide, pp. 135–143 * Active Reading Guide, pp. 34–35 Vocabulary Practice, p. 24	Grammar and Composition Handbook, Lessons 4.1, 12.4 Grammar and Language Workbook, p. 97 Reading Workbook, pp. 37–40	* Quick Checks, pp. 34–35 Selection and Theme Assessment, pp. 55–56 Performance Assessment, p. 30 Spanish Summaries, p. 31 Spanish Translations

*Also available in Spanish

Transparencies	Technology Resources
Selection Focus Transparency 22 Grammar and Language Transparencies 16, 17 Literary Elements Transparency 21	Audio Library Spanish Audio Library Testmaker Web Site: *lit.glencoe.com*
Selection Focus Transparency 23 Grammar and Language Transparency 18	Audio Library Testmaker Web Site: *lit.glencoe.com*
Selection Focus Transparency 24 Grammar and Language Transparency 19 Literary Elements Transparency 22	Audio Library Testmaker Web Site: *lit.glencoe.com*
Selection Focus Transparency 25 Grammar and Language Transparency 20 Literary Elements Transparency 23	Audio Library Spanish Audio Library Testmaker Web Site: *lit.glencoe.com*
Selection Focus Transparency 26 Literary Elements Transparency 24	Audio Library Spanish Audio Library Testmaker Web Site: *lit.glencoe.com*
Selection Focus Transparency 27 Grammar and Language Transparencies 21, 22 Literary Elements Transparencies 25, 26	Audio Library Testmaker Web Site: *lit.glencoe.com*
Selection Focus Transparency 28 Grammar and Language Transparencies 23, 24 Literary Elements Transparency 27 Fine Art Transparency 16	Literature Launchers Audio Library Spanish Audio Library Testmaker Web Site: *lit.glencoe.com*
Selection Focus Transparency 29 Grammar and Language Transparency 25 Literary Elements Transparency 28 Fine Art Transparency 11	Audio Library Spanish Audio Library Testmaker Web Site: *lit.glencoe.com*
Selection Focus Transparency 30 Grammar and Language Transparency 26 Literary Elements Transparency 29 Fine Art Transparency 24	Audio Library Spanish Audio Library Testmaker Web Site: *lit.glencoe.com*
Selection Focus Transparency 31 Grammar and Language Transparencies 27, 28 Literary Elements Transparency 30	Literature Launchers Audio Library Spanish Audio Library Testmaker Web Site: *lit.glencoe.com*

Theme RESOURCES

- Listening and Speaking Activities (pp. 5–6)
- Viewing and Representing Activities (pp. 11–12)
- Critical Thinking Skills (pp. 8–10)
- Media Connections Activities (pp. 5–6)
- Interdisciplinary Activities (pp. 6–7)

See also these additional planning resources:
- English Language Learners Sourcebook
- Inclusion Strategies Sourcebook
- Literature Groups Sourcebook

Use Glencoe's **Presentation Plus!** This multimedia teaching tool lets you present dynamic lessons that will engage your students. Using Microsoft Powerpoint,® you can customize the presentations to create your own personalized lessons.

Objectives

- To read and analyze a short story about the consequences of a man's pact with the devil
- To identify the elements of a tall tale
- To write an effective character sketch

Skills

Reading/Thinking: Visualizing; Drawing Conclusions; Inferring
Writing: Writing About Action; Song Lyrics
Vocabulary: Analogies
Grammar/Language: Appositives and Appositive Phrases; Absolute Phrases
Listening/Speaking: Oral Presentation
Collaboration: Literature Groups

Motivating
→ OPTIONS

Selection Focus Transparency 22: Have students view the transparency and then answer the question provided.

Focus Activity: As an extension of the Focus Activity, have students talk about the long-term effects of their decisions.

Before You Read
The Devil and Tom Walker

Meet Washington Irving

The youngest of eleven children, Washington Irving trained to be a lawyer, but his real love was writing.

Irving's first book, *A History of New York*, was a humorous, tongue-in-cheek combination of history, folklore, and opinion. Published under the pseudonym Diedrich Knickerbocker when Irving was twenty-six, it extended his reputation worldwide and established him as the first American writer to achieve international fame. A few years later Irving traveled to Europe, where he stayed for almost two decades.

While in London, he published *The Sketch Book of Geoffrey Crayon, Gent.* An immediate success, this book contained two of Irving's most famous stories, "The Legend of Sleepy Hollow" and "Rip Van Winkle."

In his sixties, Irving returned to New York to stay. When asked which of his works was his favorite, he said:

"I scarcely look with full satisfaction on any. . . . I often wish that I could have twenty years more, to take them down from the shelf one by one, and write them over."

Washington Irving was born in 1783 and died in 1859.

FOCUS ACTIVITY

Have you ever made a decision or commitment that you later regretted?

JOURNAL Write for a few minutes in your journal about the results of your decision and how you might have acted differently.

SETTING A PURPOSE Read to find out the results of the main character's decision.

BACKGROUND

The Time and Place

"The Devil and Tom Walker" takes place in New England in the 1720s—when Puritanism was fading and the urge to acquire wealth was growing.

Literary Influences

Both Irving and his readers would have been familiar with two references that appear in this tale. The first reference is to Captain William Kidd (c. 1645–1701), a real pirate who became the subject of many legends. The second is to Faust, who makes a deal with the devil. A version of this story had been published by Johann Wolfgang von Goethe.

VOCABULARY PREVIEW

prevalent (prev′ ə lent) *adj.* widespread; p. 204
discord (dis′ kôrd) *n.* lack of agreement or harmony; conflict; p. 204
impregnable (im preg′ nə bəl) *adj.* incapable of being taken by force; able to resist attack; p. 205
melancholy (mel′ ən kol′ ē) *adj.* depressing; dismal; gloomy; p. 205

surmise (sər mīz′) *v.* to infer from little evidence; to guess; p. 207
obliterate (ə blit′ ə rāt) *v.* to remove all traces of; to erase; p. 207
speculate (spek′ yə lāt′) *v.* to engage in risky business ventures, hoping to make quick profits; p. 210
parsimony (pär′ sə mō nē) *n.* excessive frugality; stinginess, p. 211

RESOURCE MANAGER

Lesson Planning Resource
The *Unit Two Planning Guide* (pp. 74–81) provides additional lesson notes and reduced versions of all print resources.

📁 **Other Print Resources**
- Active Reading Guide, p. 22
- Vocabulary Practice, p. 19
- Reading Workbook, pp. 27–28
- Grammar and Language Workbook, pp. 89, 87

- Grammar and Composition Handbook, Lessons 3.2, 3.4
- Quick Checks, p. 22
- Selection and Theme Assessment, pp. 39–40
- Performance Assessment, p. 21
- Spanish Summaries, p. 22
- Spanish Translations
- Inclusion Strategies
- English Language Learners Sourcebook

 **Transparencies**
- Selection Focus 22
- Literary Elements 21
- Grammar and Language 16, 17

Technology
🎧 Audio Library
🎧 Spanish Audio Library
💻 Glencoe Literature Web Site
💾 Testmaker

The Devil and Tom Walker, 1856. John Quidor. Oil on canvas, 27 x 34 in.
The Cleveland Museum of Art, Cleveland, OH.

The Devil and Tom Walker

Washington Irving ∿

A FEW MILES FROM BOSTON, in Massachusetts, there is a deep inlet,
winding several miles into the interior of the country from Charles Bay,
and terminating in a thickly wooded swamp or morass. On one side of this
inlet is a beautiful dark grove; on the opposite side the land rises abruptly
from the water's edge into a high ridge, on which grow a few scattered oaks
of great age and immense size.

A NEW NATION ❧ 203

SUMMARY

One day the devil offers Tom Walker a
pirate's treasure. When Tom's greedy
wife urges him to accept, he refuses
out of spite, so she tries to make her
own bargain with the devil, but disappears. Tom then accepts the devil's
offer and becomes a rich moneylender.
Hoping to cheat the devil, he adopts
the pretense of religion. When a borrower asks Tom for an extension on a
loan, citing all the interest he has paid,
Tom replies, "The devil take me if I have
made a farthing." Tom's ever-present
Bible, buried beneath a mortgage, fails
to protect him. The devil whisks Tom
away, and his riches turn to cinders.

📁 **Spanish Summaries,** p. 22

A Active Reading

PREDICT Help students predict the
direction the story will take by focusing on the details in the title and the
first four paragraphs of the story.

Additional Resources
📁 **Active Reading Guide,** p. 22
🎧 **Audio Library**
🎧 **Spanish Audio Library**

Reading the Selection

Teaching Options

CONNECTING TO OTHER SELECTIONS

The chart at the right shows three ways
to connect "The Devil and Tom Walker"
to selections in this book.

For specific teaching strategies, see the
Unit Two Planning Guide, pp. 77–78.

Connection	Title
Life Skills: Making Decisions →	"Traveling Through the Dark," p. 1143
Critical Thinking: Causes & Effects →	"The Story of an Hour," p. 525
Literary: Characterization →	"A Worn Path," p. 833

Language Note

The word *facility* often refers to a place. It comes from *facilis,* the Latin word for easy. *Facility* here denotes an "easy means."

B **Literary Elements**

MOTIF Irving mentions Captain Kidd shortly before he introduces Tom and his wife. Ask students why he does this. *(Irving implies that both Kidd and the Walkers are dedicated to self-ishness and greed.)* Greed is a recurring motif in the story. It is evident in the wife's plan to meet the devil, in Tom's eventual acceptance of the devil's bargain, and in his sharp dealing as a moneylender.

The Devil and Tom Walker

Under one of these gigantic trees, according to old stories, there was a great amount of treasure buried by Kidd the pirate. The inlet allowed a facility to bring the money in a boat, secretly and at night, to the very foot of the hill; the elevation of the place permitted a good lookout to be kept that no one was at hand; while the remarkable trees formed good landmarks by which the place might easily be found again. The old stories add, moreover, that the devil presided at the hiding of the money, and took it under his guardianship; but this, it is well known, he always does with buried treasure, particularly when it has been ill gotten. Be that as it may, Kidd never returned to recover his wealth, being shortly after seized at Boston, sent out to England, and there hanged for a pirate.

About the year 1727, just at the time that earthquakes were <u>prevalent</u> in New England and shook many tall sinners down upon their knees, there lived near this place a meager, miserly fellow, of the name of Tom Walker. He had a wife as miserly as himself; they were so miserly that they even conspired to cheat each other. Whatever the woman could lay hands on she hid away; a hen could not cackle but she was on the alert to secure the new laid egg. Her husband was continually prying about to detect her secret hoards, and many and fierce were the conflicts that took place about what ought to have been common property. They lived in a forlorn-looking house that stood alone and had an air of starvation. A few straggling savin trees, emblems of sterility, grew near it; no

Did You Know?
Savin trees are a type of juniper. Dark green in summer, their scalelike leaves turn a dingy green in winter.

smoke ever curled from its chimney, no traveler stopped at its door. A miserable horse, whose ribs were as articulate as the bars of a gridiron, stalked about a field where a thin carpet of moss, scarcely covering the ragged beds of pudding stone,[1] tantalized and balked his hunger; and sometimes he would lean his head over the fence, look piteously at the passer-by, and seem to petition deliverance from this land of famine.

The house and its inmates had altogether a bad name. Tom's wife was a tall termagant,[2] fierce of temper, loud of tongue, and strong of arm. Her voice was often heard in wordy warfare with her husband, and his face sometimes showed signs that their conflicts were not confined to words. No one ventured, however, to interfere between them. The lonely wayfarer shrunk within himself at the horrid clamor and clapperclawing,[3] eyed the den of <u>discord</u> askance, and hurried on his way, rejoicing, if a bachelor, in his celibacy.

One day that Tom Walker had been to a distant part of the neighborhood, he took what he considered a short cut homeward, through the swamp. Like most short cuts it was an ill-chosen route. The swamp was thickly grown with great gloomy pines and hemlocks, some of them ninety feet high, which made it dark at noonday, and a retreat for all the owls of the neighborhood. It was full of pits and quagmires, partly covered with weeds and mosses, where the green surface often betrayed the traveler into a gulf of black, smothering mud; there were also dark and stagnant pools, the abodes of the

---

1. *Pudding stone* is a rock consisting of pebbles and gravel embedded in cement, like plums in a pudding.
2. A *termagant* is a quarrelsome, scolding woman.
3. *Clapperclawing* is scratching or clawing with the fingernails.

Vocabulary
prevalent (prev′ ə lent) *adj.* widespread
discord (dis′ kôrd) *n.* lack of agreement or harmony; conflict

Teaching Options

Grammar and Language *Minilesson*

Appositives and Appositive Phrases
An appositive is a noun or pronoun placed next to another noun or pronoun to identify or give additional information about it. An appositive phrase consists of an appositive plus any modifiers. Nonessential appositives are set off with commas. For example, in the sentence "We have two dogs, Pepper and Spot," the appositive phrase *Pepper and Spot* renames the

direct object, *dogs.* It could be eliminated from the sentence.

Activity Write a few examples on the board. Then have students write five sentences containing appositives and five containing appositive phrases. Have them exchange sentences with other students to check for correct punctuation. **L2**

Additional Resources

Grammar and Language Transparency 16

Grammar and Language Workbook, p. 89

Grammar and Composition Handbook, Lesson 3.2

Writer's Choice, Lesson 12.2

tadpole, the bullfrog, and the water snake, where the trunks of pines and hemlocks lay half drowned, half rotting, looking like alligators sleeping in the mire.

Tom had long been picking his way cautiously through this treacherous forest, stepping from tuft to tuft of rushes and roots, which afforded precarious footholds among deep sloughs, or pacing carefully, like a cat, along the prostrate[4] trunks of trees, startled now and then by the sudden screaming of the bittern or the quacking of a wild duck rising on the wing from some solitary pool. At length he arrived at a firm piece of ground, which ran out like a peninsula into the deep bosom of the swamp. It had been one of the strongholds of the Indians during their wars with the first colonists. Here they had thrown up a kind of fort, which they had looked upon as almost impregnable, and had used as a place of refuge for their squaws and children. Nothing remained of the old Indian fort but a few embankments, gradually sinking to the level of the surrounding earth, and already overgrown in part by oaks and other forest trees, the foliage of which formed a contrast to the dark pines and hemlocks of the swamp.

It was late in the dusk of evening when Tom Walker reached the old fort, and he paused there awhile to rest himself. Any one

Did You Know?
A *bittern* is a marsh-dwelling wading bird with mottled brownish plumage and a deep, booming cry.

but he would have felt unwilling to linger in this lonely, melancholy place, for the common people had a bad opinion of it, from the stories handed down from the time of the Indian wars, when it was asserted that the savages held incantations[5] here, and made sacrifices to the evil spirit.

Tom Walker, however, was not a man to be troubled with any fears of the kind. He reposed himself for some time on the trunk of a fallen hemlock, listening to the boding cry of the tree toad, and delving with his walking staff into a mound of black mold at his feet. As he turned up the soil unconsciously, his staff struck against something hard. He raked it out of the vegetable mold, and lo! a cloven[6] skull, with an Indian tomahawk buried deep in it, lay before him. The rust on the weapon showed the time that had elapsed since this death blow had been given. It was a dreary memento of the fierce struggle that had taken place in this last foothold of the Indian warriors.

"Humph!" said Tom Walker, as he gave it a kick to shake the dirt from it.

"Let that skull alone!" said a gruff voice. Tom lifted up his eyes, and beheld a great black man seated directly opposite him on the stump of a tree. He was exceedingly surprised, having neither heard nor seen any

Did You Know?
A male *tree toad*, or tree frog, calls to attract females. When certain types of these frogs call, their throat expands to look like a bubble.

---

4. *Prostrate* means "lying down."

5. *Incantations* are the recitations of verbal charms or spells to produce a magical effect.
6. *Cloven* means "split" or "divided."

Vocabulary
impregnable (im preg′ nə bəl) *adj.* incapable of being taken by force; able to resist attack
melancholy (mel′ ən kol′ ē) *adj.* depressing; dismal; gloomy

FIGURES OF SPEECH: *Simile* Remind students that a simile is a comparison that uses the word *like* or *as* to show a likeness between two seemingly unlike things. Point out Irving's use of a simile to compare the "trunks of pines and hemlocks" to "alligators sleeping in the mire." Have students discuss the appropriateness of this comparison. (*It is appropriate on both the physical and symbolic level: the texture of a tree trunk resembles the skin of an alligator, and an alligator is a reptile, suggesting the satanic snake of the Garden of Eden.*)

D **Active Reading**

QUESTION Ask students what Irving's purpose might have been in going into such detail about the Indian fort. (*The details foreshadow Tom's discovery of the skull. The tomahawk's association with "savages" and their "sacrifices to the evil spirit" connects the Indians with the devil. Tom's kick initiates the devil's sudden appearance.*)

Reading *Minilesson*

Visualizing The ability to visualize places and people is often indispensable to understanding a story, especially when students are faced with the extended descriptive openings used by many nineteenth century writers. Too often students skim description quickly or skip it altogether. As a result, they miss important clues to the mood and the events that follow.

Activity Have students reread the opening paragraph of "The Devil and Tom Walker," and make one or more rough sketches of the setting. Ask students what atmosphere Irving establishes. Remind students that at the time, many regarded nature as malevolent. **L2**

Additional Resources
📁 *Reading Workbook,* pp. 27–28

E Critical Thinking

DRAWING CONCLUSIONS Have students focus on the stranger's appearance, words, and actions before Tom asks his direct question about the stranger's identity. Ask students what details help them identify the stranger. *(His blackened face links him to the "fires and forges" of hell, and he has an evil "pair of great red eyes." Saying "I am likely to have a good stock of firewood [that is, souls to burn] for winter" is an allusion to his identity.)*

F Active Reading

VISUALIZE Tom learns that the tall trees, "fair and flourishing without," are actually "rotten at the core." Have students discuss the link between Crowninshield and these trees. *(Crowninshield, rich through piracy, was morally as rotten as the trees.)*

G Literary Elements

CHARACTER: *Context Clues* Discuss the common thread running through the devil's nicknames. *(Huntsman, miner, woodsman—they are all gatherers.)* What is it that the devil gathers? *(souls)*

Language Note

The nickname "Old Scratch" comes from *skratte,* an Old Norse word meaning "monster" or "devil."

---

one approach, and he was still more perplexed on observing, as well as the gathering gloom would permit, that the stranger was neither negro nor Indian. It is true he was dressed in a rude, half Indian garb,[7] and had a red belt or sash swathed round his body, but his face was neither black nor copper color, but swarthy and dingy, and begrimed with soot, as if he had been accustomed to toil among fires and forges. He had a shock of coarse black hair, that stood out from his head in all directions, and bore an ax on his shoulder.

He scowled for a moment at Tom with a pair of great red eyes.

"What are you doing on my grounds?" said the black man, with a hoarse, growling voice.

"Your grounds!" said Tom with a sneer, "no more your grounds than mine; they belong to Deacon Peabody."

"Deacon Peabody be d——d," said the stranger, "as I flatter myself he will be if he does not look more to his own sins and less to those of his neighbors. Look yonder, and see how Deacon Peabody is faring."

Tom looked in the direction that the stranger pointed, and beheld one of the great trees, fair and flourishing without, but rotten at the core, and saw that it had been nearly hewn through, so that the first high wind was likely to blow it down. On the bark of the tree was scored the name of Deacon Peabody, an eminent man who had waxed[8] wealthy by driving shrewd bargains with the Indians. He now looked around, and found most of the tall trees marked with the name of some great man of the colony, and all more or less scored by the ax. The one on which he had been seated, and which had evidently just been hewn down, bore the name of Crowninshield, and he recollected a mighty rich man of that

name, who made a vulgar display of wealth which it was whispered he had acquired by buccaneering.[9]

"He's just ready for burning!" said the black man, with a growl of triumph. "You see I am likely to have a good stock of firewood for winter."

"But what right have you," said Tom, "to cut down Deacon Peabody's timber?"

"The right of a prior claim," said the other. "This woodland belonged to me long before one of your white-faced race put foot upon the soil."

"And pray, who are you, if I may be so bold?" said Tom.

"Oh, I go by various names. I am the wild 'huntsman' in some countries, the 'black miner' in others. In this neighborhood I am known by the name of the 'black woodsman.' I am he to whom the red men consecrated this spot, and in honor of whom they now and then roasted a white man, by way of sweet-smelling sacrifice. Since the red men have been exterminated by you white savages, I amuse myself by presiding at the persecutions of Quakers and Anabaptists;[10] I am the great patron and prompter of slave dealers, and the grand master of the Salem witches."

"The upshot of all which is that, if I mistake not," said Tom sturdily, "you are he commonly called 'Old Scratch.'"[11]

"The same, at your service!" replied the black man, with a half civil nod.

Such was the opening of this interview, according to the old story, though it has almost too familiar an air to be credited. One would think that to meet with such a singular personage, in this wild, lonely place, would have shaken any man's nerves; but Tom was a hard-minded fellow, not easily

---

7. *Garb* means "clothing" or "attire."
8. Here, *waxed* means "grown" or "become."

9. *Buccaneering* is robbing ships at sea (piracy).
10. The *Quakers* and the *Anabaptists* were two religious groups in Massachusetts that were persecuted for their beliefs.
11. *Old Scratch* is a nickname for the devil.

Teaching Options

Understanding Cultural Symbols

The devil tells Tom he's called the "black woodsman," the "wild huntsman," and the "black miner," and Tom adds "Old Scratch" to the list. Invite students to discuss what names are used for such figures in their countries.

Activity Organize students into groups of mixed backgrounds and have them brainstorm as many names as they can for the figure that symbolizes evil, both in their own and in other cultures.

Additional Resources

📁 *English Language Learners Sourcebook*

daunted, and he had lived so long with a termagant wife that he did not even fear the devil.

It is said that after this commencement they had a long and earnest conversation together, as Tom returned homeward. The black man told him of great sums of money buried by Kidd the pirate under the oak trees on the high ridge, not far from the morass. All these were under his command, and protected by his power, so that none could find them but such as propitiated[12] his favor. These he offered to place within Tom Walker's reach, having conceived an especial kindness for him; but they were to be had only on certain conditions. What these conditions were may be easily surmised, though Tom never disclosed them publicly. They must have been very hard, for he required time to think of them, and he was not a man to stick at trifles when money was in view. When they had reached the edge of the swamp the stranger paused. "What proof have I that all you have been telling me is true?" said Tom. "There's my signature," said the black man, pressing his finger on Tom's forehead. So saying, he turned off among the thickets of the swamp, and seemed, as Tom said, to go down, down, down into the earth, until nothing but his head and shoulders could be seen, and so on, until he totally disappeared.

When Tom reached home he found the black print of a finger burned, as it were, into his forehead, which nothing could obliterate.

The first news his wife had to tell him was the sudden death of Absalom Crowninshield, the rich buccaneer. It was announced in the papers with the usual

flourish, that a great man had fallen in Israel.[13]

Tom recollected the tree which his black friend had just hewn down, and which was ready for burning. "Let the freebooter[14] roast," said Tom; "who cares!" He now felt convinced that all he had heard and seen was no illusion.

He was not prone to let his wife into his confidence, but as this was an uneasy secret he willingly shared it with her. All her avarice was awakened at the mention of hidden gold, and she urged her husband to comply with the black man's terms, and secure what would make them wealthy for life. However Tom might have felt disposed to sell himself to the devil, he was determined not to do so to oblige his wife, so he flatly refused, out of the mere spirit of contradiction. Many and bitter were the quarrels they had on the subject, but the more she talked the more resolute was Tom not to be damned to please her.

At length she determined to drive the bargain on her own account, and, if she succeeded, to keep all the gain to herself. Being of the same fearless temper as her husband, she set off for the old Indian fort towards the close of a summer's day. She was many hours absent. When she came back she was reserved and sullen in her replies. She spoke something of a black man whom she had met about twilight hewing at the root of a tall tree. He was sulky, however, and would not come to terms; she was to go again with a

---

13. Here, *Israel* is a biblical reference to 2 Samuel 3:38: "Know ye not that there is a prince and a great man fallen this day in Israel?" The Puritans referred to New England as "Israel," their Promised Land.
14. A *freebooter* is a pirate.

---

12. *Propitiated* means "won over" or "gained by pleasing acts."

Vocabulary
surmise (sər mīz′) *v.* to infer from little evidence; to guess
obliterate (ə blit′ ə rāt) *v.* to remove all traces of; to erase

---

Historical Note

During a period of months beginning in 1692, over a hundred people in Salem, Massachusetts were accused of witchcraft and imprisoned. In 1693 all were released by order of Governor William Phips. By then 19 had been hanged and one had been pressed to death, a process in which heavy objects, such as stones, are piled on someone's body until the victim suffocates.

H **Active Reading**

QUESTION Have students brainstorm the "certain conditions" that Tom might accept to get the hidden money. Students may pick up on the implications of the phrase a few paragraphs later when Irving writes, "the more resolute was Tom not to be damned to please her." Emphasize the need to raise questions as a way of engaging and interacting with a text.

I **Literary Elements**

TALL TALE Typically a tall tale contains exaggerations. Have students point out the exaggerations in the first column on this page. (*The disappearance of the stranger "down, down, down into the earth" and the permanent imprint of a finger burned into [Tom's] forehead.*)

INTERDISCIPLINARY CONNECTION

History Remind students that early in the story Irving mentions the pirate Kidd; later Crowninshield, a "mighty rich man," is reputed to have become rich through "buccaneering," another reference to piracy. Was Irving fascinated by tales he had heard, or were pirates a real and present danger in the late eighteenth century?

Activity Have students use both the library and the Internet to research the prevalence of piracy during the years 1790–1810. Ask students to answer the following questions: Who were famous pirates? What led them into piracy? Where did they sail? Some students may want to investigate whether piracy still occurs today and, if so, where. **L2**

Active Reading

EVALUATE Ask students if Tom's uneasiness is caused by a genuine concern about his wife's safety or concern for the loss of the silver articles. *(Since Irving links the disappearance of both Tom's wife and his household valuables, some students may argue that he is concerned that an unscrupulous thief took the valuables and did away with her. Others, remembering the Walkers' history of marital conflict, may think Tom worries more about the loss of property than the loss of his wife.)*

VIEWING THE PAINTING

Harold Rudolph (c. 1850–1884) began his career by painting portraits. After 1877, however, he increasingly turned his attention to landscapes, particularly those of Louisiana.

Viewing Response *Students may say that the mood is dark, somber, or eerie. The mood might be more upbeat if the scene had been depicted in daylight. The painting resembles Irving's description of the swamp, and Tom went there at dusk.*

propitiatory offering, but what it was she forbore to say.

The next evening she set off again for the swamp, with her apron heavily laden. Tom waited and waited for her, but in vain; midnight came, but she did not make her appearance; morning, noon, night returned, but still she did not come. Tom now grew uneasy for her safety, especially as he found she had carried off in her apron the silver teapot and spoons and every portable article of value. Another night elapsed, another morning came, but no wife. In a word, she was never heard of more.

What was her real fate nobody knows, in consequence of so many pretending to know. It is one of those facts which have become confounded by a variety of historians. Some asserted that she lost her way among the tangled mazes of the swamp, and sank into some pit or slough; others, more uncharitable, hinted that she had eloped with the household booty,[15] and made off to some other province; while others surmised that the tempter had decoyed her into a dismal quagmire, on the top of which her hat was found lying. In confirmation of this it was said a great black man, with an ax on his shoulder, was seen late that very evening coming out of the swamp, carrying a bundle tied in a check apron, with an air of surly triumph.

_____
15. *Booty* is stolen goods.

Swamp Sunset. Harold Rudolph (c. 1850–1884). Oil on canvas, 12 x 18 in. The Ogden Museum of Southern Art, University of New Orleans.

Viewing the painting: What mood does this painting evoke? How would the mood change if the scene had been depicted in broad daylight? How is the swamp scene in the painting similar to or different from the one where Tom Walker first met the Devil?

208 🐦 UNIT 2

Teaching Options

Grammar and Language *Minilesson*

Absolute Phrases Point out to students that an absolute phrase, also called a nominative absolute, consists of a noun or pronoun that is modified by a participle or a participial phrase. An absolute phrase has no grammatical relation to the rest of the sentence. For example, the sentence "His wife being ill-tempered, Tom was not saddened to lose her" contains a nominative absolute (underlined).

Activity Organize the class into small groups, and have each student write and then share a sentence with an absolute phrase. Then have a representative from each group write one sentence on the board to share with the class. Discuss any problem sentences, and have the class rewrite them as necessary. **L2**
COLLAB. LEARN.

Additional Resources

📜 *Grammar and Language Transparency 17*

📗 *Grammar and Language Workbook,* p. 87

📗 *Grammar and Composition Handbook,* Lesson 3.4

📗 *Writer's Choice,* Lesson 12.4

The most current and probable story, however, observes that Tom Walker grew so anxious about the fate of his wife and his property that he set out at length to seek them both at the Indian fort. During a long summer's afternoon he searched about the gloomy place, but no wife was to be seen. He called her name repeatedly, but she was nowhere to be heard. The bittern alone responded to his voice, as he flew screaming by, or the bullfrog croaked dolefully from a neighboring pool. At length, it is said, just in the brown hour of twilight, when the owls began to hoot and the bats to flit about, his attention was attracted by the clamor of carrion crows[16] hovering about a cypress tree. He looked up, and beheld a bundle tied in a check apron and hanging in the branches of the tree, with a great vulture perched hard by, as if keeping watch upon it. He leaped with joy, for he recognized his wife's apron and supposed it to contain the household valuables.

"Let us get hold of the property," said he consolingly to himself, "and we will endeavor to do without the woman."

As he scrambled up the tree the vulture spread its wide wings and sailed off, screaming, into the deep shadows of the forest. Tom seized the check apron, but, woeful sight! found nothing but a heart and liver tied up in it!

K Such, according to this most authentic old story, was all that was to be found of Tom's wife. She had probably attempted to deal with the black man as she had been accustomed to deal with her husband; but though a female scold is generally considered a match for the devil, yet in this instance she appears to have had the worst of it. She must have died game, however, for it is said Tom noticed many prints of cloven feet deeply stamped about the tree, and found handfuls of hair

16. *Carrion crows* are crows that feed on dead or decaying flesh.

that looked as if they had been plucked from the coarse black shock of the woodman. Tom knew his wife's prowess by experience. He shrugged his shoulders as he looked at the signs of a fierce clapperclawing. "Egad," said he to himself, "Old Scratch must have had a tough time of it!"

Tom consoled himself for the loss of his property with the loss of his wife, for he was a man of fortitude. He even felt something like gratitude towards the black woodman, who, he considered, had done him a kindness. He sought, therefore, to cultivate a further acquaintance with him, but for some time without success; the old blacklegs played shy, for whatever people may think, he is not always to be had for calling for; he knows how to play his cards when pretty sure of his game.

At length, it is said, when delay had whetted Tom's eagerness to the quick, and prepared him to agree to anything rather than not gain the promised treasure, he met the black man one evening in his usual woodman's dress, with his ax on his shoulder, sauntering along the swamp, and humming a tune. He affected to receive Tom's advances with great indifference, made brief replies, and went on humming his tune.

By degrees, however, Tom brought him to business, and they began to haggle about the terms on which the former was to have the pirate's treasure. There was one condition which need not be mentioned, being generally understood in all cases where the devils grants favors; but there were others about which, though of less importance, he was inflexibly obstinate. He insisted that the money found through his means should be employed in his service. He proposed, therefore, that Tom should employ it in the black traffic,—that is to say, that he should fit out a slave ship. This, however, Tom resolutely refused; he was bad enough, in all conscience, but the devil himself could not tempt him to turn slave trader.

K **Literary Elements**

TONE: *Satire* Explain that literature that uses wit and irony to ridicule human vice or folly is called satire. Some works are entirely satiric; others, like "The Devil and Tom Walker," contain satiric passages. Have students discuss which passages in this and the following paragraph appear satiric. *(Two satiric comments include "a female scold is generally considered a match for the devil" and "Tom consoled himself for the loss of his property with the loss of his wife." Both rely on humor growing out of the war between the sexes.)*

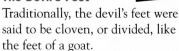

The Devil's Feet
Traditionally, the devil's feet were said to be cloven, or divided, like the feet of a goat.

MEETING INDIVIDUAL NEEDS **INCLUSION STRATEGIES**

Less-Proficient Readers In one long sentence in the second paragraph on page 208, the narrator relates three theories to explain the wife's disappearance.

Activity Working in pairs or small groups, students should look up unfamiliar words, then discuss the three theories in this sentence. After students have discussed each theory, have them create a three-column chart with: (1) the theory number, (2) the beginning and ending text words for each theory, and (3) what the words mean.

Additional Resources
📁 *Inclusion Strategies*

Finding Tom so squeamish on this point, he did not insist upon it, but proposed, instead, that he should turn usurer,[17] the devil being extremely anxious for the increase of usurers, looking upon them as his peculiar[18] people.

To this no objections were made, for it was just to Tom's taste.

"You shall open a broker's shop in Boston next month," said the black man.

"I'll do it tomorrow, if you wish," said Tom Walker.

"You shall lend money at two percent a month."

"Egad, I'll charge four!" replied Tom Walker.

"You shall extort[19] bonds, foreclose mortgages, drive the merchants to bankruptcy"—

"I'll drive them to the d—l!" cried Tom Walker.

"You are the usurer for my money!" said blacklegs with delight. "When will you want the rhino?"[20]

"This very night."

"Done!" said the devil.

"Done!" said Tom Walker. So they shook hands and struck a bargain.

A few days' time saw Tom Walker seated behind his desk in a countinghouse in Boston.

His reputation for a ready-moneyed man, who would lend money out for a good consideration, soon spread abroad. Everybody remembers the time of Governor Belcher,[21] when money was particularly scarce. It was a time of paper credit. The country had been deluged with government bills; the famous Land Bank[22] had been established; there had been a rage for speculating; the people had run mad with schemes for new settlements, for building cities in the wilderness; land jobbers[23] went about with maps of grants and townships and Eldorados,[24] lying nobody knew where, but which everybody was ready to purchase. In a word, the great speculating fever which breaks out every now and then in the country had raged to an alarming degree, and everybody was dreaming of making sudden fortunes from nothing. As usual the fever had subsided, the dream had gone off, and the imaginary fortunes with it; the patients were left in doleful plight, and the whole country resounded with the consequent cry of "hard times."

At this propitious time of public distress did Tom Walker set up as usurer in Boston. His door was soon thronged by customers. The needy and adventurous, the gambling speculator, the dreaming land jobber, the thriftless tradesman, the merchant with cracked credit,— in short, everyone driven to raise money by desperate means and desperate sacrifices hurried to Tom Walker.

Thus Tom was the universal friend of the needy, and acted like a "friend in need"; that is to say, he always exacted good pay and good security. In proportion to the distress of

---

17. A *usurer* is a person who lends money, especially at an excessive or unlawfully high rate of interest.
18. Here, *peculiar* means "special."
19. *Extort* means "to obtain by threats, force, or other types of oppression."
20. *Rhino* is a slang term for money.
21. Jonathan *Belcher* was governor of Massachusetts and New Hampshire from 1730 to 1741.
22. Boston merchants organized the *Land Bank* in 1739. Landowners could borrow money in the form of mortgages on their property and then repay the loans with cash or manufactured goods. When the bank was outlawed in 1741, many colonists lost money.
23. *Land jobbers* are people who buy and sell land for profit.
24. *Eldorados* are places of great wealth or opportunity. The term comes from the name El Dorado, a legendary region of South America sought by Spanish explorers for its gold and jewels.

Vocabulary
speculate (spek' yə lāt') v. to engage in risky business ventures, hoping to make quick profits

the applicant was the hardness of his terms. He accumulated bonds and mortgages, gradually squeezed his customers closer and closer, and sent them at length, dry as a sponge, from his door.

In this way he made money hand over hand, became a rich and mighty man, and exalted his cocked hat upon 'Change.[25] He built himself, as usual, a vast house, out of ostentation,[26] but left the greater part of it unfinished and unfurnished, out of parsimony. He even set up a carriage in the fullness of his vainglory,[27] though he nearly starved the horses which drew it; and as the ungreased wheels groaned and screeched on the axletrees you would have thought you heard the souls of the poor debtors he was squeezing.

As Tom waxed old, however, he grew thoughtful. Having secured the good things of this world, he began to feel anxious about those of the next. He thought with regret on the bargain he had made with his black friend, and set his wits to work to cheat him out of the conditions. He became, therefore, all of a sudden, a violent churchgoer. He prayed loudly and strenuously, as if heaven were to be taken by force of lungs. Indeed, one might always tell when he had sinned most during the week by the clamor of his Sunday devotion. The quiet Christians who had been modestly and steadfastly traveling Zionward,[28] were struck with self-reproach at seeing themselves so suddenly outstripped in their career by this new-made convert. Tom was as rigid in religious, as in money, matters; he was a stern supervisor and

censurer of his neighbors, and seemed to think every sin entered up to their account became a credit on his own side of the page. He even talked of the expediency of reviving the persecution of Quakers and Anabaptists. In a word, Tom's zeal became as notorious as his riches.

Still, in spite of all this strenuous attention to forms, Tom had a lurking dread that the devil, after all, would have his due. That he might not be taken unawares, therefore, it is said he always carried a small Bible in his coat pocket. He had also a great folio Bible on his countinghouse desk, and would frequently be found reading it when people called on business. On such occasions he would lay his green spectacles in the book, to mark the place, while he turned round to drive some usurious bargain.

Some say that Tom grew a little crack-brained in his old days, and that, fancying his end approaching, he had his horse new shod, saddled, and bridled, and buried with his feet uppermost, because he supposed that at the last day the world would be turned upside down, in which case he should find his horse standing ready for mounting, and he was determined at the worst to give his old friend a run for it. This, however, is probably a mere old wives' fable. If he really did take such a precaution it was totally superfluous; at least, so says the authentic old legend, which closes his story in the following manner.

One hot summer afternoon in the dog days,[29] just as a terrible, black thunder gust was coming up, Tom sat in his counting-house, in his white linen cap and India silk morning gown. He was on the point of foreclosing a mortgage, by which he would complete the ruin of an

---

25. The 'Change, or Exchange, was a financial center where merchants, bankers, and brokers met to do business.
26. *Ostentation* means "a display meant to impress others."
27. *Vainglory* is boastful, undeserved pride in one's accomplishments or qualities.
28. *Zionward* means "toward heaven."

29. *Dog days* are the hot, sultry days of summer.

Vocabulary
parsimony (pär′ sə mō nē) *n.* excessive frugality; stinginess

---

Language Note
Ask students to use a thesaurus to investigate *parsimony*, or its variant, *parsimonious*. This word leads to a rich source of synonyms that further describe Tom Walker: *scrimpy, stingy, mean, miserly*.

N **Critical Thinking**

INFERRING Ask students if they think Tom is a hypocrite. What details support their inference? *(Tom's public appearance masks his real self. Instead of being a "universal friend of the needy," he squeezes his customers dry; his "vast house" is actually "unfinished and unfurnished"; he owns a carriage but starves his horse; he attempts to compensate for his great sins with outward and zealous religious acts; he points out his neighbors' sins but never acknowledges his own.)*

O **Active Reading**

PREDICT Ask students to predict what Irving's "black thunder gust" might anticipate in this story. *(The coming "black thunder gust" suggests that Tom's life is about to change— and not for the better. Weather plays a similar role in other works, including Shakespeare's plays and in many horror movies.)*

Listening and Speaking *Minilesson*

Oral Presentation Ask each student to assume the identity of a Boston citizen who has an encounter with Tom Walker and who will now testify for or against him in court. For example: a borrower, the grocer, a churchgoer, or a stable boy.

Activity Establish guidelines for a one-minute student presentation.

Students should
- identify their characters by name.
- state their relationships to Tom.
- memorize comments or use note cards rather than read.
- use vocal tone and gestures to imply their attitudes toward Tom.

Have students deliver, in character, a one-minute statement to the class. **L2**

VIEWING THE PAINTING

Of the 35 extant paintings by John Quidor (1801–1881), 17 of them illustrate tales by Washington Irving.

Viewing Response *Students may say that the exaggerated representation of the characters and their actions reflects the fantastic nature of Irving's story.*

P Author's Craft

ALLITERATION The repetition of initial letters can give emphasis (as in the product name *Coca Cola*), can connect two concepts (as in "patience" and "piety"), and can create humor (as in tongue twisters). Here, Irving's alliteration creates ironic humor since losing one's patience is far different from losing one's religious devotion.

Cultural Note

In America the meaning of the expression *an old wives' fable* (or more commonly, *tale*) comes from a European tradition that held the wisdom of the elder woman of the community to be of little value, hence Irving's use of the adjective *mere*.

unlucky land speculator for whom he had professed the greatest friendship. The poor land jobber begged him to grant a few months' indulgence. Tom had grown testy and irritated, and refused another day.

"My family will be ruined and brought upon the parish," said the land jobber.

"Charity begins at home," replied Tom; "I must take care of myself in these hard times."

"You have made so much money out of me," said the speculator.

Tom lost his patience and his piety. "The devil take me," said he, "if I have made a farthing."[30]

Just then there were three loud knocks at the street door. He stepped out to see who was there. A black man was holding a black horse, which neighed and stamped with impatience.

"Tom, you're come for," said the black fellow gruffly. Tom shrank back, but too late. He

---

30. A *farthing* was a British coin worth one-fourth of a penny.

Tom Walker's Flight, c. 1856. John Quidor. Oil on canvas, 26¾ x 33¾ in. The Fine Arts Museums of San Francisco.
Viewing the painting: In what ways does this painting reflect the fantastic nature of the story?

Teaching Options

Writing Minilesson

Writing About Action In describing a dramatic action, writers should choose verbs that convey the event and have strong connotations. Ask students to pick out the verbs and verbals used to describe Tom's last earthly ride. *("whisked," "galloped," "dashing," "bobbing," "fluttering," and "striking fire")* Then have students suggest possible synonyms with

more neutral connotations and discuss why Irving might have rejected them.

Activity Have students choose a dramatic action, one that in real time would take less than a minute to occur. Then have each student write two different paragraphs describing the event in no more than three to five sentences each. One paragraph should be written using bland,

generic verbs *(talked, walked, threw)*. The second paragraph should feature more vivid terms *(babbled, strolled, hurled)*. Compare and discuss a few of these paragraphs as a class. **L2**

Additional Resources

📗 **Writer's Choice,** Lesson 3.1

212

had left his little Bible at the bottom of his coat pocket, and his big Bible on the desk buried under the mortgage he was about to foreclose; never was sinner taken more unawares. The black man whisked him like a child into the saddle, gave the horse a lash, and away he galloped, with Tom on his back, in the midst of the thunderstorm. The clerks stuck their pens behind their ears, and stared after him from the windows. Away went Tom Walker, dashing down the streets, his white cap bobbing up and down, his morning gown fluttering in the wind, and his steed striking fire out of the pavement at every bound. When the clerks turned to look for the black man he had disappeared.

Tom Walker never returned to foreclose the mortgage. A countryman, who lived on the border of the swamp, reported that in the height of the thunder gust he had heard a great clattering of hoofs and a howling along the road, and running to the window caught sight of a figure such as I have described, on a horse that galloped like mad across the fields, over the hills, and down into the black hemlock swamp towards the old Indian fort, and that shortly after, a thunderbolt falling in that direction seemed to set the whole forest in a blaze.

The good people of Boston shook their heads and shrugged their shoulders, but had been so much accustomed to witches and goblins, and tricks of the devil, in all kinds of shapes, from the first settlement of the colony, that they were not so much horror-struck as might have been expected. Trustees were appointed to take charge of Tom's effects. There was nothing, however, to administer upon. On searching his coffers,[31] all his bonds and mortgages were found reduced to cinders. In place of gold and silver his iron chest was filled with chips and shavings; two skeletons lay in his stable instead of his half starved horses; and the very next day his great house took fire and was burned to the ground.

Such was the end of Tom Walker and his ill-gotten wealth. Let all griping money brokers lay this story to heart. The truth of it is not to be doubted. The very hole under the oak trees, whence he dug Kidd's money, is to be seen to this day, and the neighboring swamp and old Indian fort are often haunted in stormy nights by a figure on horseback, in morning gown and white cap, which is doubtless the troubled spirit of the usurer. In fact, the story has resolved itself into a proverb, and is the origin of that popular saying, so prevalent throughout New England, of "the devil and Tom Walker."

---

31. *Coffers* are strongboxes used to hold money or other valuables.

Q Literary Elements

SYMBOL Ask students to discuss how the description of "big Bible . . . buried under the mortgage" is symbolic. *(God's word is "buried" under a potent symbol of Tom's greed.)*

Thematic Focus

Gaining Insight Have students consider which, if any, of the events in Tom's life helps him gain a deeper insight into himself or the implications of his bargain. If students point out his turn toward religion, ask them to support their assertion with specific details from the text. Discuss whether Tom's insights involve a complete understanding of the implications of his greed or if his understanding is superficial. Ask students to support their judgments.

☑ ASSESSMENT OPTIONS

📁 *Quick Checks,* p. 22

REAL-WORLD CONNECTION

The Price of a Soul Tom's desire to become a wealthy man leads him to sell his soul to the devil.

Activity Have students discuss the following questions: Do some people today figuratively sell their souls for gain? What are some of those gains? Fame? Power? Status? Do such people seem to be punished? If so, how?

Encourage students to discuss whether the television script for the Simpsons episode on page 216 indicates that people today take selling one's soul to the devil more or less seriously than the people in Irving's time did. **L2**

Responding to the Selection

Personal Response

Students should describe and explain their reactions.

ANALYZING LITERATURE

1. Each tries to cheat the other; the wife attacks Tom; there does not seem to be any love between them.
2. Not repelled, Tom asks for time to consider the devil's offer.
3. She disappears, and Tom later finds a heart and liver tied in her apron.
4. The devil persuades Tom to become a moneylender and supplies the money at a time when feverish speculation and get-rich-quick schemes are flourishing.
5. He is whisked away by the devil, and his wealth is reduced to cinders.
6. Both are greedy. Tom's wife encourages him to cultivate a friendship with the devil, which he does after she disappears.
7. Tom is so avaricious that he sacrifices his soul for wealth and status.
8. The narrator wants us to believe Tom's wife was killed by the devil. It is "the most current and probable" and "authentic" version.
9. The narrator implies that people overly fond of money are in the grip of the devil: Tom's wife disappears in search of it; ruined speculators are called "patients"; Tom himself "goes to the devil" because of it.
10. Material wealth is "perishable."
11. The purpose is twofold: to entertain with lively characters and far-fetched occurrences and to warn against putting worldly goods above spiritual matters. The message is entertaining.
12. The story satirizes marriage, the expectation that characters will be heroes, and the social institutions fostering uncontrolled growth and greed.
13. Students may say that Tom's only regret would be that he got "caught."
14. Students should note that the disclaimers establish a distance between the narrator and the tale.
15. Greed endangers the soul, and insincere religious zeal does not offer redemption. Explanations may vary.

Responding to Literature

Personal Response

How did you react to Tom and his wife? Share your responses.

——— ANALYZING LITERATURE ———

RECALL

1. What kind of people are Tom Walker and his wife? Describe what you know about them.
2. How does Tom react to the devil and his offer?
3. What happens to Tom's wife?
4. What business does Tom go into? What makes this possible, and what makes this a good time to go into such a business?
5. What finally happens to Tom Walker?

INTERPRET

6. How are Tom and his wife alike? In your opinion, does Tom's wife contribute to Tom's cooperation with the devil? Explain.
7. What does Tom's agreement with the devil tell you about Tom?
8. The narrator offers different versions of what might have happened to Tom's wife. What might the narrator want us to believe? Explain.
9. What can you infer about the narrator's attitude toward money and the people who care about it? What evidence supports your inference?
10. The narrator tells us what happens to Tom's possessions. What do you understand from this?

EVALUATE AND CONNECT

11. What do you think is the purpose of this story? How does this story differ from the histories, religious tracts, and political papers that most American writers of the time were producing?
12. **Satire** is a form of writing that uses humor, not as an end in itself, but as a weapon against someone or something—a person, a group, or a habit. In what ways is this story a satire? What is made fun of?
13. Think about your response to the Focus Activity on page 202. Compare the decision you regretted with Tom Walker's decision and its consequences.
14. The narrator often issues disclaimers by saying "people said" or "it is said." How did you respond to these disclaimers? How do you think other readers might respond? Explain.
15. Theme Connections   What are some of the insights that this story conveys? In your opinion what is the most powerful message? Explain.

Literary ELEMENTS

Tall Tale

"The Devil and Tom Walker" is a **tall tale**, a type of folklore associated with the American frontier. Tall tales are humorous stories that contain exaggerations and invention. Typically, their heroes are bold but foolish characters who may have superhuman abilities or who may act as if they do. Tall tales are not intended to be believable; their exaggerations are used for comic effect. When Irving writes that Tom "had lived so long with a termagant wife that he did not even fear the devil," he stretched the truth to gain a laugh.

1. When Tom's wife disappears, what does Tom do and say? What makes this comic instead of sad?
2. Tom's greed is exaggerated. How does Irving show this?
3. What other comic exaggerations can you find?

● See **Literary Terms Handbook**, p. R16.

LITERARY ELEMENTS

1. Tom says, "Let us get hold of the property, and we will endeavor to do without the woman." The phrasing makes this line more comic than sad.
2. In making the bargain, Tom doubles each of the devil's requirements.
3. Other exaggerations include the wife's treatment of Tom and Tom's excessive religious zeal.

Additional Resources

 Literary Elements Transparency 21

LITERATURE AND WRITING

Writing About Literature

Character Sketch Irving describes Tom Walker's appearance, his actions, his words, and the reactions of other characters to him. Write a brief character sketch of Tom using details from the story to support your description.

Creative Writing

Story in Song Many folk songs tell the story of events and characters from history and legends. Using the tune of a song that you like, write a few verses that tell what happened to Tom Walker.

EXTENDING YOUR RESPONSE

Literature Groups

Test of Time Do you think "The Devil and Tom Walker" has lasting appeal, or is it interesting mainly as a historical piece? Give your opinion, using evidence from the story to support your answer. Then, as a group, summarize the opinions expressed and report to the class.

Learning for Life

The Cost of Borrowing What kind of living would Tom Walker earn today as a moneylender? Work with a group to investigate how much interest would be charged on a loan of $1,000. Examine several sources, such as a cash advance from a credit card company, a long-term mortgage, and a loan from a commercial lender. Present your findings in a brief report.

Performing

The Devil to Pay Imagine that you are one of the minor characters from this story and you are giving an interview years later. In a monologue, tell what happened to the Walker family. Include your reactions, opinions, and any gossip of the time. Present your monologue to the class.

Reading Further

To read more by Washington Irving, look for these books:

Short Story: *The Legend of Sleepy Hollow: Found Among the Papers of the Late Diedrich Knickerbocker,* an illustrated edition of the story about a schoolmaster and a headless horseman.

Collection: *The Sketch Book,* contains short stories, travel sketches, and essays.

 **Save your work for your portfolio.**

 *Skill Minilesson*

Analogies are comparisons based on relationships between ideas. The word pairs in some analogies are antonym variants. For example,

   weak : strong :: dark : light

Weak is the opposite of *strong; dark* is the opposite of *light.*

   To finish an analogy, decide on the relationship represented by the first pair of words. Then apply that relationship to the second set of words.

● For more about analogies, see **Communications Skills Handbook,** pp. R83–R85.

PRACTICE Choose the word that best completes each analogy.

1. discord : harmony :: conflict :
   a. agreement   b. fight   c. tension

2. calm : nervous :: melancholy :
   a. gloomy   b. cheerful   c. sad

3. generosity : parsimony :: wealth :
   a. greed   b. riches   c. poverty

4. prevalent : uncommon :: often :
   a. frequent   b. common   c. seldom

LITERATURE AND WRITING

Writing About Literature

Students' character sketches should
• cover at least three character traits.
• support each trait with details from the story.
• use quotation marks to indicate material taken from the story.
• be between three and five paragraphs long.

Creative Writing

Students' song lyrics should
• be at least 12 lines long.
• be divided into stanzas of equal length.
• show evidence of a repeated rhyme scheme.

EXTENDING YOUR RESPONSE

Literature Groups Encourage students to assign one opinion to each group member so that everyone has a chance to participate. **COLLAB. LEARN.**

Learning for Life Advise students that a visual aid, such as a chart, would enable the class to grasp their findings more easily.

Performing Suggest that costume details—a hat, shoes, or overgarment—can help students convey their characters.

Skill Minilesson

VOCABULARY • Analogies
1. a   2. b
3. c   4. c

Additional Resources
📁 *Vocabulary Practice,* p. 19

✔ ASSESSMENT OPTIONS

📁 *Quick Checks,* p. 22

📁 *Selection and Theme Assessment,* pp. 39–40

📁 *Performance Assessment,* p. 21

💾 *Testmaker*

Objective

• To understand and apply strategies for reading a television script

The Devil and Tom Walker

Most students will see the link between the script and Irving's story "The Devil and Tom Walker." Each main character "sells his soul" for monetary gain, and then has to face the consequences of his decision. The major difference is that Tom loses his life as a result of his bargain with the devil while Bart is saved by his sister.

Respond

1. In his dream, Bart finds that by selling his soul, he will have no friends, he will be the butt of jokes, and he will never reach the "glowing Emerald City."

2. Some will think Lisa exhibits great love and concern; others will think she should have let Bart face the consequences of his decision.

Additional Resources

📁 *Media Connections,* p. 5

Teaching Options

MEDIA Connection

Television Script

In this *Simpsons* episode, Bart jokingly sells his "soul" ("Bart Simpson's Soul" written on a piece of paper) to his friend, Milhouse, for five dollars. Later, Bart has a dream about his soul.

Bart Sells His Soul

EXTERIOR: SPRINGFIELD CENTRAL PARK

[*As Bart approaches the park, he hears sounds of kids having fun. As he gets closer, he sees that each child is playing with his or her own soul (milky-white ghostly versions of themselves). He sees kids and their souls pushing each other on swings, riding bicycles built for two, and having chicken fights.*]

*   *   *

[*Martin and his soul, in matching sailor outfits, run down to the shore of a lake and stand by a bunch of rowboats. They hop into a rowboat, each grabbing an oar, and row off. Other kids and their souls follow and head off toward a glowing Emerald City on the other side of the lake. Milhouse runs by, hand-in-hand with his own soul and Bart's soul. The souls get on the bench and do all the rowing as Milhouse relaxes in the back of the boat. Bart tries to follow, but without a soul to grab the other oar, he can only row around and around in a circle.*]

BART
Wait! Wait for me!

[*Sherri, Terri, and their souls row by.*]

SHERRI, TERRI, & THEIR SOULS
Bart, it's time to end this dream / And don't forget the standard scream.

BACK TO REALITY
[*Bart sits upright in bed.*] [*Scream.*]

*   *   *

EXTERIOR: SPRINGFIELD STREET— MORNING
[*As Bart walks home, it starts to rain.*]

INTERIOR: BART'S ROOM—A LITTLE LATER

[*Bart walks into his room, kneels by his bed, and prays.*]

BART
Are you there, God? It's me, Bart Simpson. I know I never paid too much attention in church, but I could really use some of that good stuff now. . . . I'm afraid some weirdo's got my soul and I don't know what they're doing to it. I just want it back. Please. [*Starts to cry.*] I hope you can hear this . . .

[*The soul flutters down onto the bed, ragged and . . . crumpled. Bart looks up to see Lisa.*]

BART
Lisa? You bought this?

LISA
With the change in my piggy bank.

BART
There's no change in your piggy bank.

LISA
Not in any of the ones *you* know about.

BART
Oh, Lisa, thank you.

[*Bart is so happy he kisses her.*]

Respond

1. How does Bart's "joke" backfire on him?

2. Do you think Lisa does the right thing by helping Bart? Explain.

REAL-WORLD CONNECTION

Reading Scripts Encourage students to find scripts on the Internet using key-words such as *scripts* and the name of their favorite show. Explain that in one respect, a television sitcom (situation comedy) script and a short story are alike: both tell a story. But television stories don't rely on words alone. To help tell their stories, they use pictures. The pictures, both settings and characters' actions, are described in italicized stage directions. To understand the sequence of events and the dialogue, a reader must read the stage directions.

Activity Ask students to form small groups, assign parts, and enact a scene from a script they find on the Internet, including what occurs in the italicized stage directions. **L2** **COLLAB. LEARN.**

Vo·cab·u·lar·y Skills

Using Roots to Understand New Words

When you read, you are likely to come across unfamiliar words. There are several techniques that can help you understand these words. One good way to begin is to identify the word's **root**—the element that expresses the basic meaning of the word. Although English borrows words from many languages, a great number of root words trace their origins to Greek or Latin words. Knowing some common Greek and Latin roots can boost your understanding of what you read.

In "The Devil and Tom Walker," Washington Irving uses the word *recognize*. The word's root comes from the Latin *cogn,* meaning "to know." In the story, Tom Walker *recognizes* his wife's apron as he searches for her. In other words, he sees something he has previously *known.* The following words contain the same root as *recognize:*

cognitive   cognizant   cognition   incognito

Since a number of words may come from the same root, a knowledge of common roots can help you recognize the meaning of many words. Here are a few useful roots to know.

Root	Meaning	Example
facilis	easy	facilitate
cult	to care for	agriculture
vivi	live	vivacious
verb	word	verbal

Words change over time, of course, and you may not know what a word means even if you recognize its root. Still, looking at the root of an unfamiliar word is one good place to begin as you try to figure out that word's meaning.

EXERCISES

1. The words below appear in "The Devil and Tom Walker." The root of each word is listed above. Find the word in the story and define it as it is used there.

   a. facility (page 204)   c. reviving (page 211)

   b. cultivate (page 209)   d. proverb (page 213)

2. The root of each word below is underlined. For each word, write another word with the same root.

   a. de<u>termin</u>e   d. un<u>fin</u>ished

   b. <u>vers</u>atile   e. re<u>port</u>

   c. ob<u>ject</u>ion

Vo·cab·u·lar·y Skills

Objective
- To use word roots to help understand new words

Teaching Strategies

Show students how to look up the etymology of a word in a dictionary. Students may need to refer to a dictionary for help with Exercise 2. Remind students that words can be formed by using a root word and various prefixes and/or suffixes.

Exercises

1. *Acceptable definitions include:*
   a. facility: easy means
   b. cultivate: to promote, foster, or develop
   c. reviving: bringing back into existence
   d. proverb: short, pithy saying expressing popular wisdom
2. *Acceptable answers include:*
   a. terminate, terminal, interminable, terminology
   b. reverse, converse, version
   c. projectile, conjecture, rejection, subject
   d. finite, final, finale, finality
   e. transport, porter, report, portable

Additional Resources
📁 *Vocabulary Power: Weekly Lessons and Activities*

Teaching Options

MEETING INDIVIDUAL NEEDS — ENGLISH LANGUAGE LEARNERS

Understanding Root Words English language learners may need help finding word roots. Point students to the etymological information in dictionaries. As an example, share this etymological note for *launder:* from Middle English *launder;* from Old French *lavandier;* going back to Latin *lavanda,* things to be washed, from *lavare,* to wash.

Activity Have students compile a "root garden" of word roots using word webs. For example, students might place a Latin word at the center of a word web and surround it with common English words derived from the Latin.

Additional Resources
📁 *English Language Learners Sourcebook*

Objectives

- To read and analyze two Romantic poems about the insights to be gained from nature
- To write a thematic comparison

Skills

Reading/Thinking: Synthesizing; Paraphrasing; Inferring; Elaborating

Grammar/Language: Present Participles as Adjectives

Motivating

→ OPTIONS

Selection Focus Transparency 23: Have students view the transparency and then answer the question provided.

Focus Activity: As an extension of the Focus Activity, have students summarize, orally or in writing, the experience that led to a personal insight about nature.

Before You Read

To a Waterfowl and Thanatopsis

Meet William Cullen Bryant

❝ **The remarkable thing about 'Thanatopsis' was not that Bryant entertained the thoughts it contains . . . but that he expressed them in verses that were so beautiful and so different from anything ever written before in America.** ❞

—*Percy H. Boynton*

As a boy, William Cullen Bryant spent much time exploring the mysteries of the forests and hills in the isolated countryside of Cummington, Massachusetts. Encouraged by his father, who loved poetry, Bryant also enjoyed literary pursuits. While still in his teens, Bryant wrote "Thanatopsis," which his father sent to the *North American Review*, a major literary magazine. The editors found the poem so impressive that some doubted its true origins. "No one on this side of the Atlantic is capable of writing such verse," said one editor.

The doubts arose because until that point, no American poet of any importance had created poetry in the free-flowing, unrhymed form that Bryant used. Nor had any American poet before Bryant celebrated nature and expressed emotion following the trend of English Romantic poetry. The public loved the poem. Nevertheless, Bryant continued to revise it over the next ten years.

Bryant first worked as a lawyer, but at thirty-one, he gave up the profession and moved to New York City. There he became the editor of the *Evening Post* newspaper, a position he held for half a century. As an editor, Bryant became an outspoken advocate of freedom and human rights. He supported women's rights, the abolition of slavery, and freedom of speech. Bryant continued to express his ideas through poetry and speeches into his eighties.

William Cullen Bryant was born in 1794 and died in 1878.

FOCUS ACTIVITY

"Let nature be your teacher," advised the English Romantic poet William Wordsworth. What lessons have you learned from nature?

LIST IDEAS List some personal insights you have gained from natural events and scenes.

SETTING A PURPOSE Read to discover the insights that one poet gained from observing and contemplating nature.

BACKGROUND

Literary Influences

Romanticism began in Europe during the late eighteenth century and has affected art, music, and literature ever since. A reaction against earlier, rational schools of thought, Romanticism celebrated the individual and emotional, imaginative, and spiritual experiences. Bryant was influenced by the English Romantics, including William Wordsworth and Samuel Taylor Coleridge.

Blank Verse

The poem "Thanatopsis" is written in **blank verse** (see page R2), a poetic form not used by American poets before Bryant. Blank verse is unrhymed poetry that is written in a rhythmic pattern called **iambic pentameter.** In iambic pentameter, each line has five feet, or beats; each foot contains one unstressed syllable followed by a stressed syllable. Pauses do not always come at the ends of lines but wherever they make sense. Bryant introduced this poetic form into mainstream American poetry.

218 ❧ UNIT 2

RESOURCE MANAGER

Lesson Planning Resource
The *Unit Two Planning Guide* (pp. 82–87) provides additional lesson notes and reduced versions of all print resources.

📁 **Other Print Resources**
- Active Reading Guide, p. 23
- Reading Workbook
- Grammar and Language Workbook, p. 93

- Grammar and Composition Handbook, Lesson 3.3
- Quick Checks, p. 23
- Selection and Theme Assessment, pp. 41–42
- Performance Assessment, p. 22
- Spanish Summaries, p. 23
- Inclusion Strategies
- English Language Learners Sourcebook

🔖 **Transparencies**
- Selection Focus 23
- Grammar and Language 18

Technology
🎧 Audio Library
💻 Glencoe Literature Web Site
💾 Testmaker

Math Under the Sea?

The chambered nautilus is more than a unique sea creature and the subject of a poem by Oliver Wendell Holmes. Its spiral shape is also a real-life example of the mathematical Fibonacci (fē′ bō nä′ chē) sequence, discovered by Italian mathematician Leonardo Fibonacci (1170–1240).

In the Fibonacci sequence, each number is the sum of the two numbers that come before it in the series: 1, 1, 2, 3, 5, 8, 13, 21, and so on.

It works this way:

$1 + 1 = \underline{2}, 1 + 2 = \underline{3}, 2 + 3 = \underline{5}, 3 + 5 = \underline{8}, 5 + 8 = \underline{13}$, and so on

The Fibonacci Spiral and the Nautilus

How can a chambered nautilus have anything to do with a mathematical sequence? Take a look at the diagrams below to find out.

Start with two small squares, side by side (Figure 1). The sides of the squares can be any length, as long as they're small—an inch, a half-inch, a centimeter. Call that length "one unit." Above the first two squares, place a third square with sides of 2 units (1 + 1) (Figure 2).

☐☐ **Figure 1**

⊞ **Figure 2**

Then continue adding squares in a clockwise direction. For example, the next square should be to the right of the first three. Each new square should have a side equal to the sum of a side of each of the previous two squares. The length of the sides follows the Fibonacci sequence of 1, 1, 2, 3, 5, 8, 13.

Finally, draw a spiral through the diagram, crossing each square from one corner to its opposite, as shown (Figure 3). The curve will form a spiral pattern that is very close to the shape of Holmes's chambered nautilus.

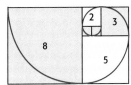

Figure 3

The Fibonacci sequence appears surprisingly often in nature. The petals of some flowers, the seeds in flower heads and pine cones, and the leaves of many trees have shapes that follow the Fibonacci sequence.

Activity

On a large sheet of paper, create a set of Fibonacci squares with the largest square having sides of 13 inches. Use a ruler to be sure your measurements are accurate. Once you have completed this set of Fibonacci squares, draw a curved line across each to create the chambered nautilus shape.

Objective

• To understand and calculate mathematical sequences

Teaching Strategies

Supply students with large sheets of paper and pens, or have students bring in newspapers and colored felt-tipped pens. Assign pairs of students to work on this connection activity, pairing a skilled math student with a less-proficient math student.

Activity

Check students' drawings for accuracy.

MEETING INDIVIDUAL NEEDS — MULTIPLE LEARNING STYLES

Spatial Students with highly developed spatial abilities may enjoy building a three-dimensional model of the nautilus.

Activity Suggest that students construct a model of the chambered nautilus using folded paper or wooden toothpicks and white glue or a material of their choosing. Remind students to use the information in the activity to make sure that their models are accurate. The full-grown nautilus has 36 chambers. Display the models in the classroom.

Objectives

- To read and analyze a poem about the emotion evoked by a snowfall
- To identify and examine the theme of a poem
- To write a poem or short narrative connecting weather to an emotional experience

Skills

Reading/Thinking: Inferring
Writing: Poem or Narrative
Grammar/Language: Gerunds

Motivating

→ OPTIONS

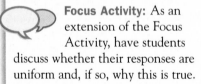

Selection Focus Transparency 25: Have students view the transparency and then answer the question provided.

Focus Activity: As an extension of the Focus Activity, have students discuss whether their responses are uniform and, if so, why this is true.

Before You Read

The First Snow-Fall

Meet James Russell Lowell

"[Reading] enables us to see with the keenest eyes, hear with the finest ears, and listen to the sweetest voices of all time."

—*Lowell*

Born in Cambridge, Massachusetts, James Russell Lowell had a happy childhood. At age fifteen, he entered Harvard College. Lowell wrote many letters to friends in those Harvard days, and from evidence in these letters has been described as "a scatterbrain, eagerly enthusiastic, devoted to his friends, . . . [opposed] to hard work." Still, he graduated from Harvard and then from Harvard Law School four years later. At twenty-five Lowell married Maria White, a poet and abolitionist. Maria White provided a stabilizing influence on Lowell's often unfocused life. In fact, he published his first book of poetry the year after they were engaged to be married.

Then, at the height of his literary fame, three of his four children died. These losses were followed by the death of Maria in 1853. For a time, it seemed that Lowell had buried with Maria his enthusiasm for poetry. He turned his energy toward interests other than writing. Lowell married Frances Dunlap in 1857 but continued to grieve over the death of Maria.

In 1855 he became a professor of modern languages at Harvard. He helped found the *Atlantic Monthly,* a literary magazine that is still published today, and he served as its first editor. By the 1860s, Lowell began writing extensively again. His poetry and essays during this period helped him regain his literary fame, yet Lowell took on new challenges.

In 1877, he served as ambassador to Spain, and then in 1880 he became ambassador to Great Britain. In 1885 Lowell returned home from England and lived until his death at Elmwood, the house of his birth.

James Russell Lowell was born in 1819 and died in 1891.

FOCUS ACTIVITY

Sometimes our moods seem to match the weather. What kind of weather do you associate with joy? with sorrow?

CHART IT! Make a chart that matches different moods to the weather you would associate with each. For example, what weather do you associate with anger?

SETTING A PURPOSE Read to see how a snowfall brings out a strong emotion in the speaker.

BACKGROUND

The Time and Place
The time is the mid-1800s. Lowell is at home with his daughter Mabel in Cambridge, Massachusetts.

Lowell's Tragedy
Lowell's experience of the death of a child was not uncommon in the 1800s. About one-third of the children who lived in urban areas died before they reached the age of twenty-one. Most were victims of diseases that are now controlled by vaccines and medication. Measles, diphtheria, and smallpox—all contagious—took the lives of many children. The death of women from childbirth, or from complications following birth, was also common.

RESOURCE MANAGER

Lesson Planning Resource
The *Unit Two Planning Guide* (pp. 94–99) provides additional lesson notes and reduced versions of all print resources.

📁 **Other Print Resources**
- Active Reading Guide, p. 25
- Reading Workbook
- Grammar and Language Workbook, p. 89
- Grammar and Composition Handbook, Lesson 3.3

- Quick Checks, p. 25
- Selection and Theme Assessment, p. 45
- Performance Assessment, p. 24
- Spanish Summaries, p. 25
- Spanish Translations
- Inclusion Strategies
- English Language Learners Sourcebook

 **Transparencies**
- Selection Focus 25
- Literary Elements 23
- Grammar and Language 20

Technology
🎧 Audio Library
🎧 Spanish Audio Library
💻 Glencoe Literature Web Site
💾 Testmaker

The First Snow-Fall

James Russell Lowell

The snow had begun in the gloaming,°
  And busily all the night
Had been heaping field and highway
  With a silence deep and white.

5 Every pine and fir and hemlock
  Wore ermine° too dear° for an earl,
And the poorest twig on the elm-tree
  Was ridged inch deep with pearl.

10 From sheds new-roofed with Carrara°
  Came Chanticleer's° muffled crow,
The stiff rails softened to swan's-down,
  And still fluttered down the snow.

I stood and watched by the window
  The noiseless work of the sky,
15 And the sudden flurries of snow-birds,
  Like brown leaves whirling by.

---

1 *Gloaming* means "twilight" or "dusk."
6 The fur of an *ermine*, a weasel of northern regions, turns white in winter. Here, *dear* means "expensive."

9 *Carrara* is a type of white marble from Italy.
10 A *chanticleer* is a rooster.

A Literary Elements

IMAGERY Have students find alternate words for *snow* in lines 1–12 and then discuss their effect. *(The words "ermine," "pearl," "Carrara," and "swan's-down" have positive connotations; they contrast with the speaker's feelings of sorrow.)*

Additional Resources
📁 *Active Reading Guide*, p. 25
🎧 *Audio Library*
🎧 *Spanish Audio Library*

B Active Reading

PREDICT Ask students to determine the link between stanzas 1–4 and stanza 5.

Model: In stanzas 1–4, the speaker describes the overnight fall of snow on the land, the trees, the shed, and the fence. In stanza 5, the speaker introduces the image of a snow-covered graveyard, then narrows to a specific headstone. Perhaps someone the speaker knows is buried there. If so, the reference to "babes in the wood" may imply that the buried person is a child—perhaps the speaker's child.

Teaching Options

Grammar and Language *Minilesson*

Gerunds A gerund, a verb form ending in *-ing* used as a noun, can be subjects of sentences, direct objects, indirect objects, objects of prepositions, predicate nominatives, or appositives.

Activity On the board, create a chart of the ways to use gerunds. Then ask students to find one verb ending in *-ing* from the poem and use that word as a gerund in each way listed. **L2**

Additional Resources
✍ *Grammar and Language Transparency 20*

📘 *Grammar and Language Workbook*, p. 89

📘 *Grammar and Composition Handbook*, Lesson 3.3

📘 *Writer's Choice*, Lesson 12.3

VIEWING THE PAINTING

John Henry Twachtman (1853–1902) studied in Cincinnati, Ohio, and in Europe. He was influenced by Impressionism.

Viewing Response *Students may refer to the images presented in lines 3–4, 5–8, 9, or 25–26.*

C Critical Thinking

INFERRING Have students discuss whether readers need to know about the deaths of Lowell's children to understand the "first great sorrow." *(Some may say readers would be puzzled; others, who saw the meaning of "headstone" and "mound," may disagree.)*

D Literary Elements

FIGURATIVE LANGUAGE Ask if the speaker's statement to Mabel could have a figurative meaning. *(The statement suggests that the speaker is talking about death resulting from God's will.)*

Thematic Focus

Gaining Insight Have students discuss whether the father's acceptance of what happened seems genuine.

☑ ASSESSMENT OPTIONS

📁 *Quick Checks,* p. 25

Teaching Options

The First Snow-Fall

I thought of a mound in sweet Auburn°
    Where a little headstone stood;
How the flakes were folding it gently,
20   As did robins the babes in the wood.

Up spoke our own little Mabel,
    Saying, "Father, who makes it snow?"
And I told of the good All-father
    Who cares for us here below.

25 Again I looked at the snow-fall,
    And thought of the leaden sky
That arched o'er our first great sorrow,
    When that mound was heaped so high.

I remembered the gradual patience
30   That fell from that cloud like snow,
Flake by flake, healing and hiding
    The scar that renewed our woe.

And again to the child I whispered,
    "The snow that husheth all,
35 Darling, the merciful Father
    Alone can make it fall!"

Then, with eyes that saw not, I
    kissed her;
And she, kissing back, could
    not know
That *my* kiss was given to her sister,
40   Folded close under deepening snow.

17 *Auburn* is Mt. Auburn Cemetery in Cambridge, Massachusetts.

Last Touch of Sun. John Henry Twachtman (1853–1902). Oil on canvas, 24¾ x 30 in. Private collection.
Viewing the painting: Which images from "The First Snow-Fall" are reflected in this painting?

MEETING INDIVIDUAL NEEDS ENGLISH LANGUAGE LEARNERS

Elegies Lowell's poem could be considered an elegy to a lost child. Elegies express a poet's sense of loss and sorrow over a death. Elegies may be unfamiliar to some English language learners.

Activity Explain the function of an elegy. Then ask English language learners to share ways that people in their native cultures respond to grief. What formal ways of expressing grief exist? What are the culture's beliefs about death? Ask students to explain how someone in their native culture might respond to the loss of a child. Then discuss with the class cultural variations in responses to death.

Additional Resources
📁 *English Language Learners Sourcebook*

Henry David Thoreau

one lot of grasshoppers in the winter,—we never need read of another. One is enough. If you are acquainted with the principle, what do you care for a <u>myriad</u> instances and applications? . . .

Time is but the stream I go a-fishing in. I drink at it; but while I drink I see the sandy bottom and detect how shallow it is. Its thin current slides away, but eternity remains. I would drink deeper; fish in the sky, whose bottom is pebbly with stars. I cannot count one. I know not the first letter of the alphabet. I have always been regretting that I was not as wise as the day I was born. The intellect is a cleaver; it discerns and rifts its way into the secret of things. I do not wish to be any more busy with my hands than is necessary. My head is hands and feet. I feel all my best faculties concentrated in it. My instinct tells me that my head is an organ for burrowing, as some creatures use their snout and fore-paws, and with it I would mine and burrow my way through these hills. I think that the richest vein is somewhere hereabouts; so by the divining rod[12] and thin rising vapors I judge; and here I will begin to mine.

from Conclusion

. . . I left the woods for as good a reason as I went there. Perhaps it seemed to me that I had several more lives to live, and could not spare any more time for that one. It is remarkable how easily and insensibly we fall into a particular route, and make a beaten track for ourselves. I had not lived there a week before my feet wore a path from my door to the pondside; and though it is five or six years since I trod it, it is still quite distinct. It is true, I fear that others may have fallen into it, and so helped to keep it open. The surface of the earth is soft and impressible by the feet of men; and so with the paths which the mind travels. How worn and dusty, then, must be the highways of the world, how deep the ruts of tradition and conformity! I did not wish to take a cabin passage,[13] but rather to go before the mast and on the deck of the world, for there I could best see the moonlight amid the mountains. I do not wish to go below now.

I learned this, at least, by my experiment; that if one advances confidently in the direction of his dreams, and endeavors to live the life which he has imagined, he will meet with a success unexpected in common hours. He will put some things behind, will pass an invisible boundary; new, universal, and more liberal laws will begin to establish themselves around and within him; or the old laws be expanded, and interpreted in his favor in a more liberal sense, and he will live with the license of a higher order of beings. In proportion as he simplifies his life, the laws of the universe will appear less complex, and solitude will not be solitude, nor poverty poverty, nor weakness weakness. If you have built castles in the air, your work need not be lost; that is where they should be. Now put the foundations under them. . . .

12. A *divining rod* is a forked stick believed to indicate the presence of underground minerals or water.

13. A person who took a *cabin passage* on a sailing ship would travel in a private compartment, sheltered from the weather.

Vocabulary
myriad (mir′ ē əd) *adj.* countless; innumerable

A NEW NATION 255

REAL-WORLD CONNECTION

The E-Mail Connection Thoreau comments that for his part, he could easily do without the post office. He had, he said, received only one or two letters "that were worth the postage." Today, approximately 147 million people worldwide receive electronic mail. Of those, about 87 million people have on-line service in the United States and Canada. Electronic mail messages can be received seconds after they are sent. Have students conduct an informal survey among their peers to determine how many of them receive electronic mail and what percentage of that mail they find valuable. As students share the results of their surveys, discuss the positive and negative effects of instantaneous communication. Does it makes our lives more or less complex? **L2**

F Literary Elements

FIGURES OF SPEECH: *Analogy* Unlike a metaphor with its single comparison, an analogy is an extended metaphor that notes several points of similarity. Ask students if Thoreau extends any of the three metaphors in this paragraph into an analogy. *(Yes, all three: "Time is but the stream I go a-fishing in"; "The intellect is a cleaver"; and "My head is hands and feet.")*

G Critical Thinking

INFERRING Ask students if these final two sentences mean Thoreau is planning a sea voyage.

Model: I don't think Thoreau is planning a sea voyage. The sentences seem figurative. I think they mean Thoreau is ready for a less isolated life. He seems afraid of settling for "tradition and conformity." He wants to experience more of the real world and the world of the mind.

Thematic Focus

Gaining Insight Thoreau was influenced by Emerson. As students read, have them examine how Thoreau's insights compare with those of Emerson, paying particular attention to Emerson's transcendentalist ideas.

✓ ASSESSMENT OPTIONS

📁 *Quick Checks,* p. 30

Responding to the Selection

Personal Response

Suggest that students identify specific ideas from Thoreau's writing with which they agree or disagree.

ANALYZING LITERATURE

1. He wanted to find out the essence of life; Walden offered the opportunity for a simple life, which helped him live intensely.

2. He disdains news and mail, thinking them unimportant. He values deeper, more essential knowledge.

3. He says he had other lives to live, suggesting he wanted to get many different experiences from life.

4. He learned both the practical and the philosophical essentials of life. His time was well spent because it taught him self-reliance and expanded his awareness.

5. Students' responses should reflect priorities in keeping with Thoreau's outlook.

6. Emphasize that students need not be limited to three effects.

7. He confirmed his belief that most lives are too complicated and need to be simplified. The experience helped him understand himself and the universe better.

8. Encourage students to provide specific examples of ways to live life more fully.

EXTENDING YOUR RESPONSE

Literature Groups Emphasize that students should establish their definition before they debate the statement. **COLLAB. LEARN.**

Listening and Speaking Challenge students to update Thoreau's content by having them extrapolate his probable views on TV, E-mail, video games, and other aspects of contemporary culture.

Responding to Literature

Personal Response
Which of Thoreau's ideas do you strongly agree or disagree with? Note them in your journal.

ANALYZING LITERATURE

RECALL AND INTERPRET

1. What did Thoreau hope to do at Walden? How might being there have helped him achieve his goal?
2. What are Thoreau's views of the news and the mail? Why do you think he held these views? What does his discussion tell you about what he values?
3. Why did Thoreau leave Walden? What might this suggest about him?
4. What did Thoreau learn at Walden? In your opinion, did he see his time there as well spent or wasted? Give reasons for your response.

EVALUATE AND CONNECT

5. Look back at the list of "What's Really Important" that you created in response to the Focus Activity on page 251. Which of those items do you think Thoreau might have considered unessential? Explain.
6. How do you think your life might change if you took Thoreau's advice to "Simplify, simplify"? To help answer this question, use a cause-and-effect diagram.
7. Theme Connections   In your opinion, what insights did Thoreau gain by his "experiment" in the woods?
8. Thoreau urges us to "live deep and suck out all the marrow of life." How could you apply this to your own life? Explain and give examples.

Cause: Take Thoreau's advice to "Simplify, simplify."

Effect: Effect: Effect:

EXTENDING YOUR RESPONSE

Literature Groups
No Ambition?   Ralph Waldo Emerson once said of Thoreau, "I cannot help counting it a fault in him that he had no ambition." In your group, discuss whether or not you agree with Emerson. First, define *ambition*. Debate the statement with your group and use evidence to support your opinions. Summarize the group's ideas for the class.

Listening and Speaking
Guest Speaker   Thoreau earned money and spread his ideas by giving lectures to local groups. Write and deliver a lecture that Thoreau might have given to high school students in which he explains his ideas about nature, materialism, and progress. Include examples from *Walden*.

📖 **Save your work for your portfolio.**

✔ ASSESSMENT OPTIONS

📁 *Quick Checks,* p. 30
📁 *Selection and Theme Assessment,* pp. 49–50
📁 *Performance Assessment,* p. 27
💾 *Testmaker*

from

CIVIL DISOBEDIENCE

Henry David Thoreau

SUMMARY

Although government exists to execute the will of the governed, too often its actions are contrary to that will. Government actions should be based in conscience, not expedience or law. Thoreau was once jailed for refusing to pay his poll tax. The experience confirmed Thoreau's belief that the State has power only over people's bodies, not their minds or souls. Thoreau describes his cellmate, the mores of jail life, and a "foreign" Concord at night. He leaves prison convinced that the best government is just and respectful even to citizens who "live aloof from it."

📁 *Spanish Summaries,* p. 28

Additional Resources

📁 *Active Reading Guide,* p. 31
🎧 *Audio Library*
🎧 *Spanish Audio Library*

Language Note

In modern usage the word *motto* (see Thoreau's first sentence) refers to a brief sentence that expresses a principle, goal, or ideal.

Teaching Options

CONNECTING TO OTHER SELECTIONS

The chart at the right shows three ways to connect the excerpt from *Civil Disobedience* to selections in this book.

For specific teaching strategies, see the **Unit Two Planning Guide,** pp. 116–117.

Connection	Title
Life Skills: Analyzing Arguments →	"Let Us Examine the Facts," p. 519
Thematic: The Courage of One's Convictions →	"Speech to the Second Virginia Convention," p. 147
Literary: Essay →	"Stride Toward Freedom," p. 892

Historical Note

The 21-month Mexican-American War began in 1846, ten years after the fall of the Alamo and one year after Texas entered the Union. As a result of the war, the United States acquired nearly all of the territory included in present-day Texas, Utah, New Mexico, Nevada, Arizona, California, and western Colorado.

A **Active Reading**

EVALUATE Ask students if they find Thoreau's criticism of majority rule and justice fair. *(Many will wonder why he connects the two; others will disagree since a basic tenet of democracy is the fairness of majority rule; some will also point to Thoreau's real concern: the rights of the minority.)*

I heartily accept the motto, "That government is best which governs least"; and I should like to see it acted up to more rapidly and systematically. Carried out, it finally amounts to this, which also I believe—"That government is best which governs not at all"; and when men are prepared for it, that will be the kind of government which they will have. Government is at best but an expedient; but most governments are usually, and all governments are sometimes, inexpedient. The objections which have been brought against a standing army, and they are many and weighty, and deserve to prevail, may also at last be brought against a standing government. The standing army is only an arm of the standing government. The government itself, which is only the mode which the people have chosen to execute their will, is equally liable to be abused and perverted before the people can act through it. Witness the present Mexican war, the work of comparatively a few individuals using the standing government as their tool; for, in the outset, the people would not have consented to this measure.

This American government—what is it but a tradition, though a recent one, endeavoring to transmit itself unimpaired to posterity,[1] but each instant losing some of its integrity? It has not the vitality and force of a single living man; for a single man can bend it to his will. It is a sort of wooden gun to the people themselves. But it is not the less necessary for this; for the people must have some complicated machinery or other, and hear its din, to satisfy that idea of government which they have. Governments show thus how successfully men can be imposed on, even impose on themselves, for their own advantage. It is excellent, we must all allow. Yet this government never of itself furthered any

enterprise, but by the alacrity with which it got out of its way. *It* does not keep the country free. *It* does not settle the West. *It* does not educate. The character inherent in the American people has done all that has been accomplished; and it would have done somewhat more, if the government had not sometimes got in its way. For government is an expedient by which men would fain[2] succeed in letting one another alone; and, as has been said, when it is most expedient, the governed are most let alone by it. Trade and commerce, if they were not made of india-rubber, would never manage to bounce over the obstacles which legislators are continually putting in their way; and, if one were to judge these men wholly by the effects of their actions and not partly by their intentions, they would deserve to be classed and punished with those mischievous persons who put obstructions on the railroads.

But, to speak practically and as a citizen, unlike those who call themselves no-government men, I ask for, not at once no government, but *at once* a better government. Let every man make known what kind of government would command his respect, and that will be one step toward obtaining it.

After all, the practical reason why, when the power is once in the hands of the people, a majority are permitted, and for a long period continue, to rule is not because they are most likely to be in the right, nor because this seems fairest to the minority, but because they are physically the strongest. But a government in which the majority rule in all cases cannot be based on justice, even as far as men understand it. Can there not be a government in which majorities do not virtually decide right and wrong, but conscience?—in which majorities

A

---

1. *Posterity* means "future generations."

2. *Fain* means "gladly" or "willingly."

Vocabulary
expedient (iks pē′ dē ənt) *n.* something employed to bring about a desired result; a means to an end
din (din) *n.* loud, continuous noise
alacrity (ə lak′ rə tē) *n.* speed; swiftness
inherent (in hēr′ ənt) *adj.* existing as a basic quality; belonging to by nature

258 ❧ UNIT 2

Teaching Options

Grammar and Language *Minilesson*

Split Infinitives Remind students that an infinitive is a verb form preceded by the word *to* and used as a noun, an adjective, or an adverb. Explain that although the split infinitive (inserting a modifier between the *to* and the verb) is becoming more accepted, in most instances, split infinitives are to be avoided in formal writing except when an awkward construction may result.

Activity Have students rewrite the following sentences to eliminate the split infinitives:
1. "To practically speak, . . . I ask for, not at once no government, but at once a better government." *(To speak practically)*
2. "It is not desirable to then cultivate a respect for the law . . ." *(then, to cultivate)* **L2**

Additional Resources

📖 *Grammar and Language Transparency 24*

📘 *Grammar and Language Workbook,* p. 91

📘 *Grammar and Composition Handbook,* Lesson 3.3

📘 *Writer's Choice,* Lesson 12.3

decide only those questions to which the rule of expediency is applicable? Must the citizen ever for a moment, or in the least degree, resign his conscience to the legislator? Why has every man a conscience, then? I think that we should be men first, and subjects afterward. It is not desirable to cultivate a respect for the law, so much as for the right. The only obligation which I have a right to assume is to do at any time what I think right. It is truly enough said that a corporation has no conscience; but a corporation of conscientious men is a corporation *with* a conscience. Law never made men a whit[3] more just; and, by means of their respect for it, even the well-disposed are daily made the agents of injustice. . . .

Some years ago, the State met me in behalf of the Church, and commanded me to pay a certain sum toward the support of a clergyman whose preaching my father attended, but never I myself. "Pay," it said, "or be locked up in the jail." I declined to pay. But, unfortunately, another man saw fit to pay it. I did not see why the schoolmaster should be taxed to support the priest, and not the priest the schoolmaster; for I was not the State's schoolmaster, but I supported myself by voluntary subscription. I did not see why the lyceum[4] should not present its tax-bill, and have the State to back its demand, as well as the Church. However, at the request of the selectmen,[5] I condescended to make some such statement as this in writing:—"Know all men by these presents, that I, Henry Thoreau, do not wish to be regarded as a member of any incorporated society which I have not joined." This I gave to the town clerk; and he has it. The State, having thus learned that I did not wish to be regarded as a member of that church, has never made a like demand on me since; though it said that it must adhere to its original presumption

> *The only obligation which I have a right to assume is to do at any time what I think right.*

that time. If I had known how to name them, I should then have signed off in detail from all the societies which I never signed on to; but I did not know where to find a complete list.

I have paid no poll-tax[6] for six years. I was put into a jail once on this account, for one night; and, as I stood considering the walls of solid stone, two or three feet thick, the door of wood and iron, a foot thick, and the iron grating which strained the light, I could not help being struck with the foolishness of that institution which treated me as if I were mere flesh and blood and bones, to be locked up. I wondered that it should have concluded at length that this was the best use it could put me to, and had never thought to avail itself of my services in some way. I saw that, if there was a wall of stone between me and my townsmen, there was a still more difficult one to climb or break through before they could get to be as free as I was. I did not for a moment feel confined, and the walls seemed a great waste of stone and mortar. I felt as if I alone of all my townsmen had paid my tax. They plainly did not know how to treat me, but behaved like persons who are underbred. In every threat and in every compliment there was a blunder; for they thought that my chief desire was to stand the other side of that stone wall. I could not but smile to see how industriously they locked the door on my meditations, which followed them out again without let[7] or hindrance, and *they* were really all that was dangerous. As they could not reach me, they had resolved to punish my body; just as boys, if they cannot come at some person against whom they have a spite, will abuse his dog. I saw that the State was half-witted, that it was timid as a lone woman with her silver spoons, and that it did not know its friends from its foes, and I lost all my remaining respect for it, and pitied it.

---

3. *Whit* means "a tiny amount" or "a bit."
4. A *lyceum* is an organization that sponsors educational programs, such as concerts and lectures.
5. *Selectmen* refers to a group of elected local officials.

6. A *poll-tax*, now illegal, was a tax on people (not property). Payment was often required in order to vote.
7. Here, *let* means "an obstruction" or "an obstacle."

Active Reading

REVIEW Ask students to summarize in no more than three sentences Thoreau's main points so far.

Model: Thoreau distrusts government and wants little of it. He believes in individualism and conscience, not the power of the majority. He is willing even to go to jail for the sake of principle.

Critical Thinking

MAKING ASSUMPTIONS Have students review what Thoreau has said. Then ask students to speculate on what Thoreau's reaction might be to such contemporary issues as welfare, mandatory "three-strikes-and-you're-out" jail sentences, and the Internet. *(He would certainly oppose welfare; he might find the jail sentences anti-individual and illogical; he might be intrigued by the individualism possible on the Internet but appalled by its potential for complicating people's lives with trivialities.)*

Thus the State never intentionally confronts a man's sense, intellectual or moral, but only his body, his senses. It is not armed with superior wit or honesty, but with superior physical strength. I was not born to be forced. I will breathe after my own fashion. Let us see who is the strongest. What force has a multitude? They only can force me who obey a higher law than I. They force me to become like themselves. I do not hear of *men* being *forced* to live this way or that by masses of men. What sort of life were that to live? When I meet a government which says to me, "Your money or your life," why should I be in haste to give it my money? It may be in a great strait, and not know what to do: I cannot help that. It must help itself; do as I do. It is not worth the while to snivel about it. I am not responsible for the successful working of the machinery of society. I am not the son of the engineer. I perceive that, when an acorn and a chestnut fall side by side, the one does not remain inert to make way for the other, but both obey their own laws, and spring and grow and flourish as best they can, till one, perchance, overshadows and destroys the other. If a plant cannot live according to its nature, it dies; and so a man.

The night in prison was novel and interesting enough. The prisoners in their shirt-sleeves were enjoying a chat and the evening air in the doorway, when I entered. But the jailer said, "Come, boys, it is time to lock up"; and so they dispersed, and I heard the sound of their steps returning into the hollow apartments. My roommate was introduced to me by the jailer as "a first-rate fellow and a clever man." When the door was locked, he showed me where to hang my hat, and how he managed matters there. The rooms were whitewashed once a month; and this one, at least, was the whitest, most simply furnished, and probably the neatest apartment in the town. He naturally wanted to know where I came from, and what brought me there; and, when I had told him, I asked him in my turn how he came there, presuming him to be an honest man, of course; and, as the world goes, I believe he was. "Why," said he, "they accuse me of burning a barn; but I never did it." As near as I could discover, he had probably gone to bed in a barn when drunk, and smoked his pipe there; and so a barn was burnt. He had the reputation of being a clever man, had been there some three months waiting for his trial to come on, and would have to wait as much longer; but he was quite domesticated and contented, since he got his board for nothing, and thought that he was well treated.

He occupied one window, and I the other; and I saw that if one stayed there long, his principal business would be to look out the window. I had soon read all the tracts[8] that were left there, and examined where former prisoners had broken out, and where a grate had been sawed off, and heard the history of the various occupants of that room; for I found that even here there was a history and a gossip which never circulated beyond the walls of the jail. Probably this is the only house in the town where verses are composed, which are afterward printed in a circular form, but not published. I was shown quite a long list of verses which were composed by some young men who had been detected in an attempt to escape, who avenged themselves by singing them.

I pumped my fellow-prisoner as dry as I could, for fear I should never see him again; but at length he showed me which was my bed, and left me to blow out the lamp.

It was like traveling into a far country, such as I had never expected to behold, to lie there for one night. It seemed to me that I never had heard the town clock strike before, nor the evening sounds of the village; for we slept with the windows open, which were inside the grating. It was to see my native village in the light of the Middle Ages, and our Concord[9] was turned into a Rhine[9] stream, and visions of knights and

---

8. *Tracts* are leaflets or pamphlets, especially those on religious or political topics.
9. *Concord* refers to the Concord River. The *Rhine* River flows through Germany and the Netherlands.

Teaching Options

LITERATURE & HUMANITIES

🎧 Play "Get Off the Track," from Glencoe's *American Music,* Volume 1, Track 18.

GIFTED AND TALENTED ACTIVITY
MEETING INDIVIDUAL NEEDS

Disobedience and Change Gifted students may enjoy investigating how effective civil disobedience has been as an agent for change. Remind students that in his 1999 State of the Union speech, President Clinton introduced Rosa Parks whose simple act of civil disobedience sparked the Civil Rights movement.

Activity Have students research to find figures whose civil disobedience inspired social changes. Students should prepare an oral report on that person for the class. Help students get started by suggesting research areas such as woman suffrage or the Vietnam War.

Henry David Thoreau

F castles passed before me. They were the voices of old burghers[10] that I heard in the streets. I was an involuntary spectator and auditor[11] of whatever was done and said in the kitchen of the adjacent village inn—a wholly new and rare experience to me. It was a closer view of my native town. I was fairly inside of it. I never had seen its institutions before. This is one of its peculiar institutions; for it is a shire town.[12] I began to comprehend what its inhabitants were about.

In the morning, our breakfasts were put through the hole in the door, in small oblong-square tin pans, made to fit, and holding a pint of chocolate, with brown bread, and an iron spoon. When they called for the vessels again, I was green enough to return what bread I had left; but my comrade seized it, and said that I should lay that up for lunch or dinner. Soon after he was let out to work at haying in a neighboring field, whither he went every day, and would not be back till noon; so he bade me good-day, saying that he doubted if he should see me again.

G When I came out of prison—for some one interfered, and paid that tax—I did not perceive that great changes had taken place on the common, such as he observed who went in a youth and emerged a tottering and gray-headed man; and yet a change had to my eyes come over the scene—the town, and State, and country—greater than any that mere time could effect. I saw yet more distinctly the State in which I lived. . . .

Is a democracy, such as we know it, the last improvement possible in government?

The authority of government, even such as I am willing to submit to—for I will cheerfully obey those who know and can do better than I, and in many things even those who neither know nor can do so well—is still an impure one: to be strictly just, it must have the sanction and consent of the governed. It can have no pure right over my person and property but what I concede to it. The progress from an absolute to a limited monarchy, from a limited monarchy to a democracy, is a progress toward a true respect for the individual. Even the Chinese philosopher[13] was wise enough to regard the individual as the basis of the empire. Is a democracy, such as we know it, the last improvement possible in government? Is it not possible to take a step further towards recognizing and organizing the rights of man? There will never be a really free and enlightened State until the State comes to recognize the individual as a higher and independent power, from which all its own power and authority are derived, and treats him accordingly. I please myself with imagining a State at least which can afford to be just to all men, and to treat the individual with respect as a neighbor; which even would not think it inconsistent with its own repose if a few were to live aloof from it, not meddling with it, nor embraced by it, who fulfilled all the duties of neighbors and fellow-men. A State which bore this kind of fruit, and suffered it to drop off as fast as it ripened, would prepare the way for a still more perfect and glorious State, which also I have imagined, but not yet anywhere seen.

---

10. *Burghers* is a term for inhabitants of a city.
11. Here, *auditor* means "someone who hears" or "a listener."
12. A *shire town*, or county town, is similar to a county seat.

13. The *Chinese philosopher* referred to is Confucius (c. 551–479 B.C.).

Vocabulary
sanction (sangk′ shən) *n.* approval or support

F ### Critical Thinking

INFERRING Ask students what they may infer about Thoreau from his statement about a "new and rare experience." *(Thoreau's vantage point in the prison provides him with a new point of view, giving him new insights into the lives of the townspeople. These new insights make him realize that he has held himself aloof from others in the past.)*

G ### Literary Elements

ALLUSION An allusion is an indirect reference. When Thoreau refers to the man who "went in a youth and emerged a tottering and gray-headed man," he is probably alluding to Rip van Winkle in Washington Irving's story. Ask students what he might mean by this allusion. *(Like Rip van Winkle, Thoreau feels he has woken up to a town that has changed while he has "slept" for what seems like years.)*

Thematic Focus

Gaining Insight Have students discuss the one idea they found most startling in this essay, and have them explain how that idea might manifest itself in today's world. What insights into today's world does reading Thoreau's essay provide?

✔ ASSESSMENT OPTIONS

📁 *Quick Checks*, p. 31

Reading *Minilesson*

Main Points and Supporting Details
Have students identify the main points and supporting details for the mottoes which express Thoreau's thesis.

Activity Write on the board:
- Does Thoreau support his thesis with facts or with opinions? Give examples.
- Do Thoreau's facts and examples really support his thesis?

- What do the arguments and actions in the essay reveal about Thoreau?

Have small groups each answer one of the questions and provide evidence. Then discuss each group's answer. **L2**
COLLAB. LEARN.

Additional Resources
📁 *Reading Workbook,* pp. 33–34

Personal Response

Students should cite reasons for their opinions and present examples to support their conclusions.

ANALYZING LITERATURE

1. The best government is one "which governs not at all."
2. Thoreau will follow his conscience.
3. A man paid the tax for Thoreau but Thoreau stated, in writing, why he had refused; he was never required to pay this tax again.
4. He was jailed for not paying his poll tax. He was at times amused, affronted, and intrigued.
5. The governed must "sanction and consent."
6. The problems are loss of integrity and the tyranny of the majority.
7. He means that people should follow their consciences before laws. The majority rules because they are physically stronger, not because they are right; laws do not necessarily equal justice.
8. By refusing to pay taxes, Thoreau asserts his right to act based on what is right for him.
9. Freedom is the knowledge that one has done what is right.
10. A government must have the consent of those it governs.
11. Answers could include knowing the issues and candidates; writing letters; working for justice, questioning laws; and examining majority decisions in light of individual conscience.
12. Students may mention the income tax, undeclared wars, broken treaties with Native Americans, or the internment of Japanese Americans during World War II.
13. It adds concrete detail to an abstract subject.
14. Thoreau is against too much governmental authority. Having recently won independence from a monarchy, Thoreau's audience may have been very receptive to individual liberties.
15. Students may suggest that the essay is essentially optimistic; it proposes a society where laws and government are hardly necessary because humankind has progressed to a degree where right and justice are the measures of all actions.

Responding to Literature

Personal Response

Did Thoreau persuade you to share his views of government? Why or why not?

ANALYZING LITERATURE

RECALL

1. What kind of government does Thoreau say is best?
2. What is the one thing Thoreau feels obligated to follow?
3. What action did Thoreau take after refusing to pay the tax to support a clergyman? What was the outcome of this action?
4. Why was he put in jail? How did he feel about being there? Explain.
5. In Thoreau's opinion, what is needed for a government to be just?

INTERPRET

6. According to Thoreau, what problems might arise from government?
7. What does Thoreau mean when he says "we should be men first, and subjects afterward"? Cite specific details from the essay to support your response.
8. How do Thoreau's actions reflect his thoughts about himself as part of society?
9. What does Thoreau conclude about freedom while he is in jail?
10. What does Thoreau suggest should be the relationship between government and the individual?

EVALUATE AND CONNECT

11. Based on the ideas in "Civil Disobedience," how might Thoreau suggest that people today become involved in their government?
12. Thoreau mentions the Mexican-American War as an example of a government acting against the people's will. What other examples of unpopular government actions can you think of? Explain.
13. An **anecdote** is a short account of an interesting event in a person's life. What does Thoreau's anecdote about his night in jail contribute to his essay?
14. In general, what is Thoreau trying to persuade readers to believe? Why might this essay have been persuasive in a country that was relatively newly independent?
15. Do you think this essay is optimistic or pessimistic? In what ways? Explain.

Literary
ELEMENTS

Argument

In "Civil Disobedience," Thoreau presents an **argument**, a piece of writing in which reason is used to influence someone else's ideas or actions. An argument is a form of persuasive writing. Some persuasive writing depends mainly on emotion for its power. An argument uses logic, reasons, and evidence. For instance, Thoreau writes that government does not further any enterprise. He supports this by giving examples: *It does not keep the country free. It does not settle the West. It does not educate.*

1. List the reasons that Thoreau presents for not paying a tax to support a clergyman.
2. Identify another of Thoreau's topics and give examples of the supporting logic, reasons, and evidence he uses.

● See **Literary Terms Handbook**, p. R2.

LITERARY ELEMENTS

1. He was not a church member; the State used its power to force payment; the tax was not reciprocal.
2. Premise: majority rules can't be just. Arguments: the majority makes the law; conscience is an attribute of individuals; conscience should determine justice.

Additional Resources

Literary Elements Transparency 27

LITERATURE AND WRITING

Writing About Literature

A Different Drummer? Look again at the first quote on page 250. Do you think Thoreau followed his own advice? In a few paragraphs explain whether Thoreau's actions or writings followed the idea he expressed in the quote. Use evidence from these selections to support your ideas.

Creative Writing

Report on the Prisoner When Thoreau refused to pay the poll tax, Samuel Staples, the local tax collector, constable, and jailer, had to arrest him. Write the arrest report that Staples might have submitted to his boss about taking Thoreau into custody and putting him in jail.

EXTENDING YOUR RESPONSE

Literature Groups

Debate Hold a debate on one of the issues that Thoreau writes about. In your group, form two teams—one to defend Thoreau's point of view, and the other to defend an opposing view. Each team should work together to provide evidence to support their arguments. Summarize the key points and arguments presented by each team, and share your summary with the class.

Performing

A One-Act Play Use the jail scene in "Civil Disobedience" as the basis for a one-act play or a short skit. Experiment with using minimal props to create the physical place and the atmosphere. Use some of the quotes Thoreau provides as starting points for dialogue. You may also want to have a narrator explain the historical setting or provide other information. Rehearse your play and present it to the class.

Listening and Speaking

"I Have a Dream" "Civil Disobedience" influenced many world leaders, including Dr. Martin Luther King Jr. Locate a copy of Dr. King's speech "I Have a Dream." Select a passage that you think relates to Thoreau's essay. Deliver that passage to the class and explain how Dr. King's speech shows the influence of "Civil Disobedience."

Reading Further

If you'd like to read more by and about Henry David Thoreau, look for these books:

Memoirs: *Journal 1837–1844: The Writings of Henry D. Thoreau,* a personal glimpse into the writer's life.

Walking, a celebration of the joys of "sauntering."

Biography: *The Cambridge Companion to Henry David Thoreau,* edited by Joel Myerson, essays about Thoreau.

📖 **Save your work for your portfolio.**

Skill Minilesson

VOCABULARY • **Analogies**

Analogies are comparisons based on relationships between ideas. Some analogies are based on a relationship of *definition.*

    teacher : instructs :: carpenter : builds

A *teacher* by definition *instructs;* a *carpenter builds.*

To finish an analogy, decide on the relationship of the first pair of words. Apply that relationship to the second set of words.

PRACTICE Choose the word that best completes each analogy.

1. hindrance : obstructs :: sanction :
   a. assists   b. shelters   c. approves

2. sentinels : guard :: chaperones :
   a. flourish   b. watch   c. founder

● For more about analogies, see **Communications Skills Handbook,** pp. R83–R85.

LITERATURE AND WRITING

Writing About Literature

Students' essays should
- have a thesis that takes a stance on whether or not Thoreau followed a "different drummer."
- link Thoreau's actions and writings to the thesis.
- use citations from the Thoreau selections as support.

Creative Writing

Suggest that students ask local police or security personnel about what information is required for such a report. 📇

EXTENDING YOUR RESPONSE

Literature Groups Suggest that students use books, periodicals, and the Internet to find contemporary examples to support their arguments. **COLLAB. LEARN.**

Performing Encourage groups using props and set pieces to rehearse enough to feel comfortable with them. 📇

Listening and Speaking

Students' speeches should
- begin with an assertion of Thoreau's influence on Dr. Martin Luther King Jr.
- convey the relevant passage with pauses and vocal inflection.
- establish the ideological links with appropriate quotations and references.

Skill Minilesson

VOCABULARY • Analogies
1. c   2. b

Additional Resources
📁 *Vocabulary Practice,* p. 21

ASSESSMENT OPTIONS

📁 ***Quick Checks,*** p. 31
📁 ***Selection and Theme Assessment,*** pp. 49–50
📁 ***Performance Assessment,*** p. 27
💾 ***Testmaker***

Before Reading

Objectives

- To read and analyze a short story about a minister whose black veil symbolizes the secret barriers people use to hide their impurities from others
- To understand the elements of a short story
- To write an analysis of Hawthorne's parable

Skills

Reading/Thinking: Previewing; Inferring
Writing: Character Sketch; Dialogue
Vocabulary: Root Words; Etymology
Grammar/Language: Dangling Participles
Listening/Speaking: Sermon
Collaboration: Literature Groups

More About Nathaniel Hawthorne

Hawthorne edited a magazine, the monthly *American Magazine of Useful and Entertaining Knowledge,* and worked on several children's books. In this same period, he worked at the Boston Custom House and tried a brief stay at Brook Farm, an experimental commune based on Transcendentalist philosophies. His experience at Brook Farm did not suit him, and he eventually distanced himself from Transcendentalism.

Before You Read

The Minister's Black Veil

Meet Nathaniel Hawthorne

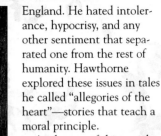

❝I don't want to be a doctor, and live by men's diseases; nor a minister to live by their sins; nor a lawyer to live by their quarrels. So I don't see there's anything left for me but to be an author.❞

—*Hawthorne*

Thus, some may say, Nathaniel Hawthorne became one of the United States' great writers by default.

Hawthorne was born in the port town of Salem, Massachusetts. When Hawthorne was only four, his father, a sea captain, died of yellow fever in South America. Raised by his eccentric, reclusive mother, young Hawthorne became an avid reader of poetry and exotic adventure stories.

At age seventeen Hawthorne began his four years at Bowdoin College in Maine. His friends there included a future president and a future poet: Franklin Pierce and Henry Wadsworth Longfellow.

After graduating from Bowdoin, Hawthorne sought seclusion in Salem, where he spent twelve years studying Puritan history and developing his writing skills. Out of those twelve years came two books, a novel called *Fanshawe* and a collection of short stories called *Twice-Told Tales. Fanshawe* was never popular—Hawthorne himself destroyed all the copies he could find—but reviewers praised *Twice-Told Tales*, and the book enjoyed a modest success with the public.

In his writing, Hawthorne explored issues of moral and social responsibility in Puritan New England. He hated intolerance, hypocrisy, and any other sentiment that separated one from the rest of humanity. Hawthorne explored these issues in tales he called "allegories of the heart"—stories that teach a moral principle.

At the age of thirty-eight, Hawthorne married Sophia Peabody and moved to the Old Manse, the house in Concord, Massachusetts, where writer Ralph Waldo Emerson had lived. However, unable to support his family as a writer, Hawthorne returned to Salem. There he served as Surveyor of the Port but lost the job when the political administration changed. Hawthorne then began writing *The Scarlet Letter.* This novel, published when Hawthorne was forty-six, was a sensation. He followed up the success with another novel, *The House of the Seven Gables.*

In 1853, when his friend Franklin Pierce became president of the United States, Hawthorne was awarded the position of U.S. consul to the city of Liverpool, England. He held that position for four years. Then he toured Italy and returned to England to write his last complete novel, *The Marble Faun.* By 1860, he returned to the United States— in ill health, struggling to continue writing, and despondent. Four years later, while traveling with Franklin Pierce, Hawthorne died in his sleep.

❝Mr. Hawthorne's distinctive trait is invention, creation, imagination.❞

—*Edgar Allan Poe*

Nathaniel Hawthorne was born in 1804 and died in 1864.

RESOURCE MANAGER

Lesson Planning Resource
The *Unit Two Planning Guide* (pp. 121–128) provides additional lesson notes and reduced versions of all print resources.

📁 **Other Print Resources**
- Active Reading Guide, p. 32
- Vocabulary Practice, p. 22
- Reading Workbook, pp. 35–36
- Grammar and Language Workbook, p. 207

- Grammar and Composition Handbook, Lesson 3.3
- Quick Checks, p. 32
- Selection and Theme Assessment, pp. 51–52
- Performance Assessment, p. 28
- Spanish Summaries, p. 29
- Inclusion Strategies
- English Language Learners Sourcebook

 Transparencies
- Selection Focus 29
- Fine Art 11
- Literary Elements 28
- Grammar and Language 25

Technology
🎧 Audio Library
🎧 Spanish Audio Library
💻 Glencoe Literature Web Site
💾 Testmaker

FOCUS ACTIVITY

How do you behave when you feel guilty about something?

CREATE A WEB Make a word web like the one below. Write the word *guilt* in the center oval. Take five minutes to complete the web with ways people might behave when they feel guilty.

SETTING A PURPOSE Read to notice how guilt affects the people in the story.

BACKGROUND

The Time and Place
Seventeenth-century Puritan New England, the setting of "The Minister's Black Veil," was steeped as much in superstition as in religion. Hawthorne's story balances on the line that separated the two.

The Puritans
Puritanism was a movement that began in the Church of England in the 1500s. Puritans wanted to "purify" the church of practices they said had no basis in the Bible. In the 1600s, Puritans came to New England and founded a community based on biblical laws. They believed that God was all-powerful and all-knowing. They also held that people were sinful by nature and deserved eternal punishment but that God had "elected" some to be saved. No one could be sure of salvation, but Puritans strove to lead

a moral life as a sign that they had been saved. This involved keeping a constant watch over oneself and others to fight the "natural" tendency to sin.

Parables
The subtitle of "The Minister's Black Veil" is "A Parable." A parable is a story that illustrates a moral lesson. In this way, parables resemble fables. Fables, however, usually have animal characters, whereas parables have human characters. Many famous parables appear in the Bible. The parable of the prodigal son, for example, teaches that one who turns away from evil should be forgiven. Hawthorne included the subtitle "A Parable" to alert his readers that he intended "The Minister's Black Veil" to convey a moral lesson.

VOCABULARY PREVIEW

perturbation (pur′ tər bā′ shən) *n.* agitation; anxiety; uneasiness; p. 268
venerable (ven′ ər ə bəl) *adj.* deserving respect because of age, character, or position; p. 268
iniquity (in ik′ wə tē) *n.* sin; p. 268
sagacious (sə gā′ shəs) *adj.* having or showing wisdom and keen perception; p. 269

irreproachable (ir′ i prō′ chə bəl) *adj.* free from blame; faultless; p. 274
zealous (zel′ əs) *adj.* filled with enthusiastic devotion; passionate; p. 274
torpor (tôr′ pər) *n.* a state of being unable to move or feel; p. 274

Reading Further
Be sure to view these titles for appropriateness for your class before recommending them to students.

Hawthorne, Nathaniel. *Young Goodman Brown and Other Short Stories.* New York: Dover, 1992. This is a collection of short stories by Hawthorne.

James, Henry. *Hawthorne.* Ithaca, New York: Cornell University Press, 1998. This reprint of James's biography provides insight into Hawthorne as both a writer and a man.

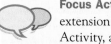

Selection Focus Transparency 29: Have students view the transparency and then answer the question provided.

Focus Activity: As an extension of the Focus Activity, ask students how a person's body language may convey guilt. How would different kinds of guilt affect body language?

The Minister's Black Veil

A Parable

Nathaniel Hawthorne

THE SEXTON STOOD IN THE PORCH of Milford meeting-house, pulling busily at the bell-rope. The old people of the village came stooping along the street. Children, with bright faces, tripped merrily beside their parents, or mimicked a graver gait, in the conscious dignity of their Sunday clothes. Spruce[1] bachelors looked sidelong at the pretty maidens, and fancied that the Sabbath sunshine made them prettier than on week days. When the throng had mostly streamed into the porch, the sexton[2] began to toll the bell, keeping his eye on the Reverend Mr. Hooper's door. The first glimpse of the clergyman's figure was the signal for the bell to cease its summons.

"But what has good Parson Hooper got upon his face?" cried the sexton in astonishment.

All within hearing immediately turned about, and beheld the semblance of Mr. Hooper, pacing slowly his meditative way towards the meeting-house. With one accord[3]

they started,[4] expressing more wonder than if some strange minister were coming to dust the cushions of Mr. Hooper's pulpit.[5]

"Are you sure it is our parson?" inquired Goodman[6] Gray of the sexton.

"Of a certainty it is good Mr. Hooper," replied the sexton. "He was to have exchanged pulpits with Parson Shute, of Westbury; but Parson Shute sent to excuse himself yesterday, being to preach a funeral sermon."

The cause of so much amazement may appear sufficiently slight. Mr. Hooper, a gentlemanly person, of about thirty, though still a bachelor, was dressed with due clerical neatness, as if a careful wife had starched his band, and brushed the weekly dust from his Sunday's garb. There was but one thing remarkable in his appearance. Swathed[7] about his forehead, and hanging down over his face, so low as to be

---

1. *Spruce* means "neat and trim in appearance" or "dapper."
2. A *sexton* is a church employee who cares for church property and who may also ring the bells and dig graves.
3. *With one accord* means "with complete agreement" or "with unity."

4. Here, *started* means "made a sudden involuntary movement, as from fear or surprise."
5. A *pulpit* is a raised structure from which a minister delivers a sermon or conducts a worship service.
6. *Goodman* is a title of polite address similar to "Mister."
7. *Swathed* means "wrapped."

266 UNIT 2

shaken by his breath, Mr. Hooper had on a black veil. On a nearer view it seemed to consist of two folds of crepe,[8] which entirely concealed his features, except the mouth and chin, but probably did not intercept his sight, further than to give a darkened aspect to all living and inanimate things. With this gloomy shade before him, good Mr. Hooper walked onward, at a slow and quiet pace, stooping somewhat, and looking on the ground, as is customary with abstracted[9] men, yet nodding kindly to those of his parishioners who still waited on the meeting-house steps. But so wonder-struck were they that his greeting hardly met with a return.

"I can't really feel as if good Mr. Hooper's face was behind that piece of crepe," said the sexton.

---

8. *Crepe* is a light, soft fabric with a crinkled surface.
9. Here, *abstracted* means "lost in thought" or "preoccupied."

"I don't like it," muttered an old woman, as she hobbled into the meeting-house. "He has changed himself into something awful, only by hiding his face."

"Our parson has gone mad!" cried Goodman Gray, following him across the threshold.

A rumor of some unaccountable phenomenon had preceded Mr. Hooper into the meeting-house, and set all the congregation astir. Few could refrain from twisting their heads towards the door; many stood upright, and turned directly about; while several little boys clambered upon the seats, and came down again with a terrible racket. There was a general bustle, a rustling of the women's gowns and shuffling of the men's feet, greatly at variance with that hushed repose which should attend the entrance of the minister. But Mr. Hooper appeared not to notice the

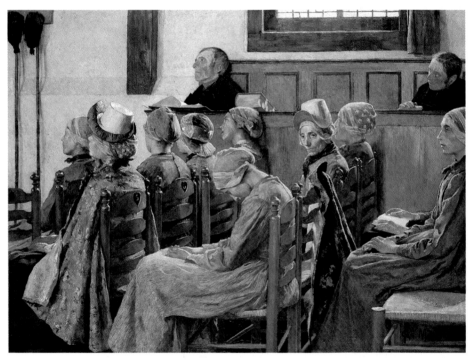

The Sermon, 1886. Julius Gari Melchers. Oil on canvas, 62⅝ x 86½ in. National Museum of American Art, Smithsonian Institution, Washington, D.C.

Viewing the painting: In what ways do the attitudes of the people in the painting reflect those of Mr. Hooper's congregation?

Pulpits A pulpit is generally a raised, hexagonal or octagonal stone or wooden platform with an enclosed, often carved, wooden front. The pulpit usually stands on a base and is accessible only by stairs.

VIEWING THE SKETCH

Viewing Response *The position of the minister is elevated. Students may see his position as a symbol for the high esteem with which he is initially viewed by his congregation.*

Vo•cab•u•lar•y Skills

Root Words The Latin root word *turba* denotes a whirling motion. Romans used it to describe the agitated crowds. In English it is the basis of such words as *disturb, imperturbable, turbid,* and *turbine.*

C Active Reading

PREDICT Ask students why Mr. Hooper may find his congregation a "fearful" sight. *(Because he fears their reaction when he confronts them.)*

Viewing the sketch: How might the pulpit's placement in this sketch reflect Mr. Hooper's position in Milford?

perturbation of his people. He entered with an almost noiseless step, bent his head mildly to the pews on each side, and bowed as he passed his oldest parishioner, a white-haired great-grandsire, who occupied an arm-chair in the center of the aisle. It was strange to observe how slowly this venerable man became conscious of something singular in the appearance of his pastor. He seemed not fully to partake of the prevailing wonder, till Mr. Hooper had ascended the stairs, and showed himself in the pulpit, face to face with his congregation, except for the black veil. That mysterious emblem was never once withdrawn. It shook with his measured breath, as he gave out the psalm; it threw its obscurity between him and the holy page, as he read the Scriptures; and while he prayed, the veil lay heavily on his uplifted countenance.[10] Did he

seek to hide it from the dread Being whom he was addressing?

Such was the effect of this simple piece of crepe, that more than one woman of delicate nerves was forced to leave the meeting-house. Yet perhaps the pale-faced congregation was almost as fearful a sight to the minister, as his black veil to them.

Mr. Hooper had the reputation of a good preacher, but not an energetic one: he strove to win his people heavenward by mild, persuasive influences, rather than to drive them thither by the thunders of the Word. The sermon which he now delivered was marked by the same characteristics of style and manner as the general series of his pulpit oratory. But there was something, either in the sentiment of the discourse itself, or in the imagination of the auditors,[11] which made it greatly the most powerful effort that they had ever heard from their pastor's lips. It was tinged, rather more darkly than usual, with the gentle gloom of Mr. Hooper's temperament. The subject had reference to secret sin, and those sad mysteries which we hide from our nearest and dearest, and would fain[12] conceal from our own consciousness, even forgetting that the Omniscient[13] can detect them. A subtle power was breathed into his words. Each member of the congregation, the most innocent girl, and the man of hardened breast, felt as if the preacher had crept upon them, behind his awful veil, and discovered their hoarded iniquity of deed or thought. Many spread their clasped hands on their bosoms. There was nothing terrible in what Mr. Hooper said, at least, no violence; and yet, with every tremor of his melancholy voice, the hearers quaked. An

C

---

10. *Countenance* means "face."

11. *Auditors* are "those who hear" or "listeners."
12. *Fain* means "gladly" or "willingly."
13. *The Omniscient* is "the all knowing," or God.

Vocabulary

perturbation (pur´ tər bā´ shən) *n.* agitation; anxiety; uneasiness
venerable (ven´ ər ə bəl) *adj.* deserving respect because of age, character, or position
iniquity (in ik´ wə tē) *n.* sin

Teaching Options

Grammar and Language *Minilesson*

Dangling Participles Point out to students that a participle is a verb form that can function as an adjective and that a participial phrase contains a participle plus any complements and modifiers. A participial phrase at the beginning of a sentence must modify the sentence's subject.

Activity Write the following sentences on the board:

Rising over the horizon, the Reverend Mr. Hooper saw the morning sun.

Veiling the minister's countenance, I saw a piece of somber black cloth.

Have students identify the participial phrase and the grammatical subject of the sentence. Then have students rewrite the sentences to eliminate the dangling participle. **L2**

Additional Resources

✍ *Grammar and Language Transparency 25*

📖 *Grammar and Language Workbook,* p. 207

📖 *Grammar and Composition Handbook,* Lesson 3.3

📖 *Writer's Choice,* Lesson 12.3

unsought pathos[14] came hand in hand with awe. So sensible were the audience of some unwonted[15] attribute in their minister, that they longed for a breath of wind to blow aside the veil, almost believing that a stranger's visage[16] would be discovered, though the form, gesture, and voice were those of Mr. Hooper.

At the close of the services, the people hurried out with indecorous confusion, eager to communicate their pent-up amazement, and conscious of lighter spirits the moment they lost sight of the black veil. Some gathered in little circles, huddled closely together, with their mouths all whispering in the center; some went homeward alone, wrapped in silent meditation; some talked loudly, and profaned the Sabbath day with ostentatious laughter. A few shook their sagacious heads, intimating that they could penetrate the mystery; while one or two affirmed that there was no mystery at all, but only that Mr. Hooper's eyes were so weakened by the midnight lamp, as to require a shade. After a brief interval, forth came good Mr. Hooper also, in the rear of his flock. Turning his veiled face from one group to another, he paid due reverence to the hoary heads,[17] saluted the middle aged with kind dignity as their friend and spiritual guide, greeted the young with mingled authority and love, and laid his hands on the little children's heads to bless them. Such was always his custom on the Sabbath day. Strange and bewildered looks repaid him for his courtesy. None, as on former occasions, aspired to the honor of walking by their pastor's side. Old Squire Saunders, doubtless by an accidental lapse of memory, neglected to invite Mr. Hooper to his table, where the good clergyman had been wont[18] to

bless the food, almost every Sunday since his settlement. He returned, therefore, to the parsonage, and, at the moment of closing the door, was observed to look back upon the people, all of whom had their eyes fixed upon the minister. A sad smile gleamed faintly from beneath the black veil, and flickered about his mouth, glimmering as he disappeared.

"How strange," said a lady, "that a simple black veil, such as any woman might wear on her bonnet should become such a terrible thing on Mr. Hooper's face!"

"Something must surely be amiss with Mr. Hooper's intellects," observed her husband, the physician of the village. "But the strangest part of the affair is the effect of this vagary,[19] even on a sober-minded man like myself. The black veil, though it covers only our pastor's face, throws its influence over his whole person, and makes him ghostlike from head to foot. Do you not feel it so?"

"Truly do I," replied the lady; "and I would not be alone with him for the world. I wonder he is not afraid to be alone with himself!"

"Men sometimes are so," said her husband.

The afternoon service was attended with similar circumstances. At its conclusion, the bell tolled for the funeral of a young lady. The relatives and friends were assembled in the house, and the more distant acquaintances stood about the door, speaking of the good qualities of the deceased, when their talk was interrupted by the appearance of Mr. Hooper, still covered with his black veil. It was now an appropriate emblem. The clergyman stepped into the room where the corpse was laid, and bent over the coffin, to take a last farewell of his deceased parishioner. As he stooped, the veil hung straight down from his forehead, so that, if her eyelids had not been closed forever,

---

14. *Pathos* is a feeling of pity, compassion, or sorrow.
15. *Unwonted* means "not customary" or "unusual."
16. *Visage* means "face."
17. *Hoary heads* are white-haired heads.
18. *Wont* means "accustomed."

19. A *vagary* is an odd or erratic action or idea.

Vocabulary
sagacious (sə gā′ shəs) *adj.* having or showing wisdom and keen perception

---

D **Literary Elements**

FORESHADOWING Ask students to consider what the events in this paragraph may foreshadow. *(They suggest a change in the parishioners' attitudes toward Hooper and his rueful realization of it.)*

E **Active Reading**

CONNECT Ask students if funeral customs have changed since the time of the story. *(Most will say yes, since bodies are rarely "laid out" in homes these days. Some will say that present-day funeral parlor visitations are similar.)*

Language Note

The word *profane* can have different meanings, depending on how it is used. Here, Hawthorne says that some members of the congregation "profaned the Sabbath day with ostentatious laughter." The meaning of the word can vary from "nonreligious," as in "sacred and profane music," to "blasphemous or contemptuous of God," or simply, "vulgar and coarse." It is a variant of the Latin word *profanus*, which means "outside the temple." Here, the most likely meaning is "not respectful" to the Sabbath.

MEETING INDIVIDUAL NEEDS
ENGLISH LANGUAGE LEARNERS

Funeral Customs Many countries and cultural groups deal with death in different ways. As a result, students from other cultures may find the actions of Mr. Hooper quite strange.

Activity Have students think about the role of religious leaders, friends, and families in their communities at the time of someone's death. Have

them share with the class the funeral customs of their cultures.

Additional Resources
📁 *English Language Learners Sourcebook*

F Critical Thinking

INFERRING Ask students if this allusion to the veil reveals what it symbolizes. *(No, but the allusion plus the words "dreadful hour" intimate that the veil masks something revealed only after death.)*

G Literary Elements

TONE: *Ambiguity* The ambiguity of this story has continually fascinated readers by allowing a number of possible meanings and enriching the reading experience. Have students discuss how this dialogue reinforces the ambiguity of the story's meaning. *(The dialogue suggests a supernatural element in the story. This reinforces the earlier reference to the shuddering corpse, and it anticipates the sensations of the bride as well as the minister's odd reaction in the next paragraph. What it means, however, is unclear.)*

H Active Reading

QUESTION Encourage students to discuss why Hawthorne juxtaposed the funeral and the wedding paragraphs. *(Both are ceremonies Hooper would conduct; they represent a beginning and an end; at each the minister seems to bring evil, not comfort or joy, thus increasing the mystery of the story.)*

the dead maiden might have seen his face. Could Mr. Hooper be fearful of her glance, that he so hastily caught back the black veil? A person who watched the interview between the dead and living, scrupled[20] not to affirm, that, at the instant when the clergyman's features were disclosed, the corpse had slightly shuddered, rustling the shroud[21] and muslin cap, though the countenance retained the composure of death. A superstitious old woman was the only witness of this prodigy.[22] From the coffin Mr. Hooper passed into the chamber of the mourners, and thence to the head of the staircase, to make the funeral prayer. It was a tender and heart-dissolving prayer, full of sorrow, yet so imbued with celestial hopes, that the music of a heavenly harp, swept by the fingers of the dead, seemed faintly to be heard among the saddest accents of the minister. The people trembled, though they but darkly understood him when he prayed that they, and himself, and all of mortal race, might be ready, as he trusted this young maiden had been, for the dreadful hour that should snatch the veil from their faces. The bearers went heavily forth, and the mourners followed, saddening all the street, with the dead before them, and Mr. Hooper in his black veil behind.

"Why do you look back?" said one in the procession to his partner.

"I had a fancy," replied she, "that the minister and the maiden's spirit were walking hand in hand."

"And so had I, at the same moment," said the other.

That night, the handsomest couple in Milford village were to be joined in wedlock. Though reckoned a melancholy man, Mr. Hooper had a placid cheerfulness for such occasions, which often excited a sympathetic

smile where livelier merriment would have been thrown away. There was no quality of his disposition which made him more beloved than this. The company at the wedding awaited his arrival with impatience, trusting that the strange awe, which had gathered over him throughout the day, would now be dispelled. But such was not the result. When Mr. Hooper came, the first thing that their eyes rested on was the same horrible black veil, which had added deeper gloom to the funeral, and could portend[23] nothing but evil to the wedding. Such was its immediate effect on the guests that a cloud seemed to have rolled duskily from beneath the black crepe, and dimmed the light of the candles. The bridal pair stood up before the minister. But the bride's cold fingers quivered in the tremulous hand[24] of the bridegroom, and her deathlike paleness caused a whisper that the maiden who had been buried a few hours before was come from her grave to be married. If ever another wedding were so dismal, it was that famous one where they tolled the wedding knell.[25] After performing the ceremony, Mr. Hooper raised a glass of wine to his lips, wishing happiness to the new-married couple in a strain of mild pleasantry that ought to have brightened the features of the guests, like a cheerful gleam from the hearth. At that instant, catching a glimpse of his figure in the looking-glass, the black veil involved his own spirit in the horror with which it overwhelmed all others. His frame shuddered, his lips grew white, he spilt the untasted wine upon the carpet, and rushed forth into the darkness. For the Earth, too, had on her Black Veil.

The next day, the whole village of Milford talked of little else than Parson Hooper's black veil. That, and the mystery concealed behind it, supplied a topic for discussion between acquaintances meeting in the street, and good

---

20. *Scrupled* means "hesitated."
21. A *shroud* is a cloth used to wrap a dead body for burial.
22. Here, *prodigy* means "an extraordinary event that causes amazement."

23. *Portend* means "to be a warning or an indication of."
24. A *tremulous hand* is one that is trembling or shaking.
25. Hawthorne is referring to his own short story "The Wedding Knell." A *knell* is the solemn sound of a bell ringing, as at a funeral.

Teaching Options

INCLUSION STRATEGIES
MEETING INDIVIDUAL NEEDS

Learning Disabled Hawthorne places the paragraphs about the funeral and the wedding one after the other so that the reader will compare and contrast what occurs at each event.

Activity To help students discern the similarities and differences, have them fill in the chart to the right. **L1**

	Funeral	Wedding
Behavior of Hooper		
Hooper's Effect on Event		
Reactions of Those Present		

Additional Resources
📁 *Inclusion Strategies*

women gossiping at their open windows. It was the first item of news that the tavern-keeper told to his guests. The children babbled of it on their way to school. One imitative little imp covered his face with an old black handkerchief, thereby so affrighting his playmates that the panic seized himself, and he well-nigh lost his wits by his own waggery.[26]

It was remarkable that of all the busybodies and impertinent people in the parish, not one ventured to put the plain question to Mr. Hooper, wherefore he did this thing. Hitherto, whenever there appeared the slightest call for such interference, he had never lacked advisers, nor shown himself averse to be guided by their judgment. If he erred at all, it was by so painful a degree of self-distrust, that even the mildest censure would lead him to consider an indifferent action as a crime. Yet, though so well acquainted with this amiable weakness, no individual among his parishioners chose to make the black veil a subject of friendly remonstrance. There was a feeling of dread, neither plainly confessed nor carefully concealed, which caused each to shift the responsibility upon another, till at length it was found expedient to send a deputation[27] of the church, in order to deal with Mr. Hooper about the mystery, before it should grow into a scandal. Never did an embassy so ill discharge its duties. The minister received them with friendly courtesy, but became silent, after they were seated, leaving to his visitors the whole burden of introducing their important business. The topic, it might be supposed, was obvious enough. There was the black veil swathed round Mr. Hooper's forehead, and concealing every feature above his placid mouth, on which, at times, they could perceive the glimmering of a melancholy smile. But that piece of crepe, to their imagination, seemed to hang down before his heart, the symbol of a fearful secret between him and

them. Were the veil but cast aside, they might speak freely of it, but not till then. Thus they sat a considerable time, speechless, confused, and shrinking uneasily from Mr. Hooper's eye, which they felt to be fixed upon them with an invisible glance. Finally, the deputies returned abashed[28] to their constituents, pronouncing the matter too weighty to be handled, except by a council of the churches, if, indeed, it might not require a general synod.[29]

But there was one person in the village unappalled by the awe with which the black veil had impressed all beside herself. When the deputies returned without an explanation, or even venturing to demand one, she, with the calm energy of her character, determined to chase away the strange cloud that appeared to be settling round Mr. Hooper, every moment more darkly than before. As his plighted wife,[30] it should be her privilege to know what the black veil concealed. At the minister's first visit, therefore, she entered upon the subject with a direct simplicity, which made the task easier both for him and her. After he had seated himself, she fixed her eyes steadfastly upon the veil, but could discern nothing of the dreadful gloom that had so overawed the multitude: it was but a double fold of crepe, hanging down from his forehead to his mouth, and slightly stirring with his breath.

"No," said she aloud, and smiling, "there is nothing terrible in this piece of crepe, except that it hides a face which I am always glad to look upon. Come, good sir, let the sun shine from behind the cloud. First lay aside your black veil: then tell me why you put it on."

Mr. Hooper's smile glimmered faintly.

"There is an hour to come," said he, "when all of us shall cast aside our veils. Take it not amiss, beloved friend, if I wear this piece of crepe till then."

---

26. *Waggery* is mischievous or joking behavior.
27. A *deputation* is a delegation.

28. *Abashed* means "ashamed" or "embarrassed."
29. A *synod* is a council of church officials or a governing body of all the churches.
30. *Plighted wife* means "intended wife" or "fiancée."

Language Note

Remind students that the archaic word *wherefore* means "why." Students may remember this from *Romeo and Juliet* or other Shakespearean plays.

I Literary Elements

MOTIF In literature a motif is a repeated or dominant theme, idea, or event. Ask students to decide whether *secret* is a motif in the story. *(Yes. The subject of the sermon is secret sin, and the word is repeated in various contexts.)* Suggest that students trace the use of the word throughout the story.

J Literary Elements

CHARACTER Have students discuss the change in the parishioners' attitudes toward Mr. Hooper before and after he puts on the veil. *(They once freely advised him and commented on his actions. Now they are "speechless, confused," and "abashed.")*

MEETING INDIVIDUAL NEEDS — GIFTED AND TALENTED ACTIVITY

Religion and Architecture Explain to students that the design used for a place of worship often reflects the philosophy and beliefs of the religious group that uses it.

Activity Ask gifted and talented students to select the place of worship of one group as the focus for research. Students may consider, for example, a Jewish synagogue, an Islamic mosque, one of several varieties of Christian churches, a Buddhist temple, or an outdoor ceremonial area of a Native American group. Ask students to conduct research and gather visual aids that show how the place of worship provides insights into the group's beliefs. Students should present their findings to the class in oral reports. **L3**

IMAGERY Hawthorne often describes Mr. Hooper's sad smile as glimmering. Ask students to discuss what this image of light may mean. *(To Christians light is associated with Christ and is an image of hope. Here it may connote the minister's hope that others will perceive why he is veiled.)*

L Active Reading

EVALUATE Ask students how Elizabeth has been characterized before this scene. What adjectives have been used to describe her? *(She is described as composed, good-humored, concerned, confident, and troubled.)*

M Critical Thinking

INFERRING Ask students to speculate on the reason behind Elizabeth's reaction. *(Students may conclude that she thinks he is mad or that he indeed has a secret sin.)*

Teaching Options

FINE ART
TRANSPARENCY 11

You may want to use *Fine Art Transparency 11* to discuss different ways an individual might view reality.

The Minister's Black Veil

"Your words are a mystery, too," returned the young lady. "Take away the veil from them, at least."

"Elizabeth, I will," said he, "so far as my vow may suffer me. Know, then, this veil is a type and a symbol, and I am bound to wear it ever, both in light and darkness, in solitude and before the gaze of multitudes, and as with strangers, so with my familiar friends. No mortal eye will see it withdrawn. This dismal shade must separate me from the world: even you, Elizabeth, can never come behind it!"

"What grievous affliction hath befallen you," she earnestly inquired, "that you should thus darken your eyes forever?"

"If it be a sign of mourning," replied Mr. Hooper, "I, perhaps, like most other mortals, have sorrows dark enough to be typified by a black veil."

"But what if the world will not believe that it is the type of an innocent sorrow?" urged Elizabeth. "Beloved and respected as you are, there may be whispers that you hide your face under the consciousness of secret sin. For the sake of your holy office, do away this scandal!"

The color rose into her cheeks as she intimated the nature of the rumors that were already abroad in the village. But Mr. Hooper's mildness did not forsake him. He even smiled again—that same sad smile, which always appeared like a faint glimmering of light, proceeding from the obscurity beneath the veil.

"If I hide my face for sorrow, there is cause enough," he merely replied; "and if I cover it for secret sin, what mortal might not do the same?"

And with this gentle, but unconquerable obstinacy did he resist all her entreaties.[31] At length Elizabeth sat silent. For a few moments she appeared lost in thought, considering, probably, what new methods might be tried to withdraw her lover from so dark a fantasy, which, if it had no other meaning, was perhaps a symptom of mental disease. Though of a firmer

---

31. *Entreaties* are pleas.

272 UNIT 2

---

character than his own, the tears rolled down her cheeks. But, in an instant, as it were, a new feeling took the place of sorrow: her eyes were fixed insensibly on the black veil, when, like a sudden twilight in the air, its terrors fell around her. She arose, and stood trembling before him.

"And do you feel it then, at last?" said he mournfully.

She made no reply, but covered her eyes with her hand, and turned to leave the room. He rushed forward and caught her arm.

"Have patience with me, Elizabeth!" cried he, passionately. "Do not desert me, though this veil must be between us here on earth. Be mine, and hereafter there shall be no veil over my face, no darkness between our souls! It is but a mortal veil—it is not for eternity! O! you know not how lonely I am, and how frightened, to be alone behind my black veil. Do not leave me in this miserable obscurity forever!"

"Lift the veil but once, and look me in the face," said she.

"Never! It cannot be!" replied Mr. Hooper.

"Then farewell!" said Elizabeth.

She withdrew her arm from his grasp, and slowly departed, pausing at the door, to give one long shuddering gaze, that seemed almost to penetrate the mystery of the black veil. But, even amid his grief, Mr. Hooper smiled to think that only a material emblem had separated him from happiness, though the horrors, which it shadowed forth, must be drawn darkly between the fondest of lovers.

From that time no attempts were made to remove Mr. Hooper's black veil, or, by a direct appeal, to discover the secret which it was supposed to hide. By persons who claimed a superiority to popular prejudice, it was reckoned merely an eccentric whim, such as often mingles with the sober actions of men otherwise rational, and tinges them all with its own semblance of insanity. But with the multitude, good Mr. Hooper was irreparably a bugbear.[32] He

---

32. A *bugbear* is a real or imaginary object of fear.

MULTIPLE LEARNING STYLES
MEETING INDIVIDUAL NEEDS

Bodily-Kinesthetic Many students prefer to hear rather than read dialogue. Certainly a well-acted scene clarifies and intensifies its emotional content for both the actors involved and the audience.

Activity Have students enact the scene between Hooper and Elizabeth. Before presenting it in class, the actors should
- analyze the characters and their motivations.
- analyze the text for clues to physical movements and the emotional dynamics of the scene.
- block the scene and rehearse it a few times.
- determine appropriate vocal inflections and gestures.
- use set or costume props as needed. **L2**

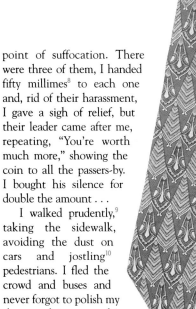

Ali Deb ~

point of suffocation. There were three of them, I handed fifty millimes[8] to each one and, rid of their harassment, I gave a sigh of relief, but their leader came after me, repeating, "You're worth much more," showing the coin to all the passers-by. I bought his silence for double the amount . . .

I walked prudently,[9] taking the sidewalk, avoiding the dust on cars and jostling[10] pedestrians. I fled the crowd and buses and never forgot to polish my shoes and iron my shirts carefully, often using the fire to dry them faster. The January cold suddenly came to mind and I anticipated the need to buy a coat and change my suit when winter had passed. Should I hold out my hand for a loan or draw directly from the company's cash box? Finally, I got on the train. I breathed in the fetid[11] breath of the passengers. I leaned on the armrest of a seat; a lady grumbled and said to her neighbor, "They're even contesting our second-class seats."

So I slipped into the first class where a seat and a supplementary fee of some consequence awaited me. I went into the local supermarket. It had been quite some time since I had taken care of my shopping. Upon seeing me, a neighbor literally shrieked for joy, shook my hand and then, raising his flat voice, asked me for a loan that I would have naturally refused him if I had not been wearing my suit.

I bought several items and held them in my arms against my chest. The salesgirl greeted me and unhooked a suitable basket. I had no other alternative but to deposit my purchases inside, and since the proper sort of people, my sort, buy without consideration for the price, I did not even bother to look at the cash register total. When I had returned home, my blood pressure was at its peak, my head was literally boiling, my tongue twisted and my chest heaving. I no longer saw where I walked or where I threw my jacket, vest, and trousers. I clenched my teeth and gritted them as I cursed the traps of this century and the folly of fools. I finally went back to being my old self and since that day no one has troubled me anymore.

---

8. The *millime* (mə lēm´) is a Tunisian unit of money of very low value.
9. To walk *prudently* is to do so cautiously, in a way that shows good judgment.
10. *Jostling* pedestrians are bumping, pushing, or shoving each other in a crowd.
11. *Fetid* (fet´ id) breath is offensive-smelling.

Responding to the Selection

Personal Response

Some students may have been surprised; others may think that the ending had adequate preparation.

ANALYZING LITERATURE

1. He stayed within his budget and has extra money. He feels awed and proud to be able to dress well now.
2. The friend implies that they demean the suit. The narrator purchases a new shirt and tie.
3. He instantly replaces his old shoes. He is "overcome by a delicious peace." He thinks his ensemble is now "perfection."
4. He dumps the suit and goes back to being his old self. He learns that how he dresses is not who he is.
5. The story is both serious and humorous because it deals with hypocrisy, but in an exaggerated manner.
6. It puts readers into his mind and makes evident his pride, extravagances, desperate economies, and increasing snobbery.
7. Some students would compliment their friend; others may admit to jealousy. Students may compare their actions to the friend's question about the shirt and tie.
8. Most students, like the narrator, feel good about being dressed well. A few may feel uncomfortable.

EXTENDING YOUR RESPONSE

Literature Groups Have students give equal consideration to both parts of the question before coming to a conclusion. **COLLAB. LEARN.**

Personal Writing

Students' paragraphs should
- have a clear topic sentence that controls the paragraph content.
- have concrete, vivid examples.
- have a concluding sentence that summarizes why the choices are appropriate to the writer.

Responding to Literature

Personal Response

Did the story's ending surprise you, or not? Explain.

——— ANALYZING LITERATURE ———

RECALL AND INTERPRET

1. What enables the narrator to buy the new suit? How does he feel about the suit? What conclusions can you draw from this about his usual financial status and way of dressing?
2. What comment does a friend in the café make about the narrator's clothing? What is the friend implying? What does this comment cause the narrator to do?
3. What does the narrator do when someone calls attention to his shoes? How does he feel when his friends compliment him? Why do you think he feels this way?
4. Theme Connections   What decision does the narrator make at the end of the story? What insights do you think he has gained into his own identity—about who he really is—from this experience?

EVALUATE AND CONNECT

5. Did you find this story humorous, serious, or both? Explain.
6. This story is told from the **first-person point of view** (see page R12). What does this point of view add to the story? Explain.
7. How do you feel when a friend wears something new and very appealing? Are you at all like any of the characters in the story? Support your response using details from the selection.
8. Review what you wrote for the Focus Activity on page 278. How do you act when you are dressed up or wearing new clothes? How does your response compare to the narrator's behavior?

Literary ELEMENTS

Rising Action

The **rising action** in a plot is the action that leads up to the climax of the story. In this part of the story, the complications and plot twists help develop the conflict. For example, in "The Three-Piece Suit" the rising action consists of a series of problems for the narrator. Each time he attempts to solve a problem, a new one arises.

1. What is the first problem that the narrator encounters? How does it set the stage for the next problem?
2. What additional problems does the narrator face? How does each one prepare the reader for what will follow?

● See **Literary Terms Handbook,** p. R13.

——— EXTENDING YOUR RESPONSE ———

Literature Groups

Discuss the Issue   Was the narrator responsible for his own problems in this story, or was he the victim of other people's reactions? Let each member of your group give an opinion on this question. Use evidence from the story to support your position. Summarize the group's responses and share the results with the class.

Personal Writing

The Real You   Imagine that you have just won a contest and your prize is the opportunity to choose a completely new wardrobe. Price is no object. In one paragraph, describe in detail the clothing you would choose. Tell what pieces really shout, "This is who I am!" and explain why.

💾 **Save your work for your portfolio.**

LITERARY ELEMENTS

1. When a friend notes his shabby shirt and tie, he instantly buys new ones. The reader anticipates that other articles of clothing, such as his shoes, might also need to be replaced.
2. The young girl, the weather, beggars, train passenger, and sales clerk episodes impel him into greater physical or economic danger.

Additional Resources

✍ *Literary Elements Transparency 29*

✔ ASSESSMENT OPTIONS

📁 *Quick Checks,* p. 33
📁 *Selection and Theme Assessment,* pp. 53–54
📁 *Performance Assessment,* p. 29
💾 *Testmaker*

COMPARING selections

The Minister's Black Veil **and** *The Three-Piece Suit*

COMPARE **SYMBOLS**

In both selections, an article of clothing becomes a symbol—an object that represents something else. Write a brief essay that answers the following questions about these symbols.

1. What is the symbol in each story and what might it represent? How are the symbols alike? How are they different?

2. In which story does the symbol more accurately represent the character who wears it? Explain.

3. With which symbol or character do you identify? Why?

COMPARE **MOTIVATION**

Which character has the greater motivation to change his appearance the way he does—Mr. Hooper or the narrator of "The Three-Piece Suit"? With a small group of classmates, discuss the reasons each character has for changing his appearance. Support your opinions with details from the stories. Discuss points such as these:

- What statement was each character trying to make with the change in appearance?

- What might be the effects of these statements?

- How important might these effects be to the characters and to others around them?

COMPARE **CULTURES**

With a partner, research modes of dress in seventeenth-century Puritan New England and in modern-day Tunisia or another Islamic nation. What importance does each culture place on attire? What symbolic meaning do various articles of clothing carry? On poster board, create a visual presentation of the clothing of each culture.

A NEW NATION 🦢 283

Objective

- To compare two short stories in which the characters' clothing gives insight into their identities.

COMPARE **SYMBOLS**

Students' answers should include

1. that both symbols are articles of clothing; the minister's veil has darker connotations.

2. that both symbols accurately represent the characters.

3. reasons to support their choices.

COMPARE **MOTIVATION**

Discussions may cover the following:

- The minister shows how secret sin separates people from each other and from God; the character in the three-piece suit is trying to show he is wealthy and, thus, important.

- The minister illustrates the separation; the character wearing the three-piece suit looks wealthy but misjudges the consequences.

- The minister's veil offers spiritual insights to himself and others; the man in the three-piece suit learns about his own values.

Additional Resources
📁 *Literature Groups Sourcebook*

COMPARE **CULTURES**

Students' visual presentations should
- identify important symbols.
- point out similarities and differences between the cultures.

Teaching Options

PORTFOLIO OPTIONS _____

Select and Reflect Have students reflect on the essays they wrote for the activity above by asking themselves these questions:

- Does my essay include sufficient citations from the story?
- Is my reasoning logical?
- Does my final paragraph conclude, or does it just end?

Students should place their reflections in their portfolios. Later they may consider using the comments to revise their essays as portfolio showcase pieces. **L2**

Additional Resources
📁 *Writing Assessment and Portfolio Management*, pp. 51–58

Objective

- To understand and apply the technique of scanning to find information

Teaching Strategies

After students read the explanation in their textbooks, have them think of keywords or phrases they can use to scan a story or nonfiction work read earlier. For example, if a reader wants to know what Thoreau says about government in "Civil Disobedience," he or she might scan for the following keywords: *government, state, authority,* or *democracy.*

Activities

1. *Some possible keywords:*
   a. attire, buy (bought), shop
   b. pay (paid), price loan
2. *Students' responses to this activity should*
   - result in a question that is neither too obvious nor too obscure.
   - limit the number of keywords to three.
   - contain keywords actually found in the article.

Additional Resources
📁 *Reading Workbook*

Teaching Options

Reading & Thinking Skills

Scanning

Let's say you have just read a fascinating news story. It might be about a discovery on Mars or under Egypt's desert sands. It might be about a student summer work program in national parks. You'd like to learn more.

You might begin by checking the listings in your library or by using a search engine on the Internet. You might find a vast amount of information but not have time to read it all. Once you have chosen an appropriate source, how can you quickly find the specific information you need?

Many readers use a technique called scanning. **Scanning** is one process of searching through writing for a particular fact or piece of information. When you scan, your eyes sweep across a page, looking for key words that may lead you to information you want. Whether you're looking through library listings, a textbook, or the want ads, scanning can make your information searches more efficient.

You can also use scanning to find specific information in material that you've already read. For example, when it's time to answer the questions following "The Three-Piece Suit" or another selection, scanning can help you locate relevant sections to review.

Use the following guidelines to make scanning work for you.

- Choose from two to four key words or phrases that relate to your topic and the information you want to locate. For example, to learn more about summer work programs in national parks, you might look for *work program* and *national parks.*
- Move your eyes quickly over the material. Stay focused. Look only for the key words you have chosen; don't try to read every word.
- Pay special attention to titles, headings and subheadings, and boldfaced words.
- When you find a key word, read the material around it.

● For more about related reading strategies, see **Reading Handbook,** pp. R86–R93.

ACTIVITIES

1. Scan "The Three-Piece Suit" to find answers to the following questions. List the key words you used in your search. Write your answers.

   a. In addition to the suit, what other articles of clothing did the narrator buy?

   b. What other financial burdens did the narrator accept in his effort to appear rich?

2. Read a brief magazine article and write a question about it. Then write three key words or phrases that will lead to the answer. Exchange articles and questions with a partner. Scan the article to answer your partner's question. Did you find the information quickly? Discuss what other approaches you might have taken to find the information.

MEETING INDIVIDUAL NEEDS — INCLUSION STRATEGIES

Less-Proficient Readers Ask students to bring in the automobile classified ads of the local newspaper. Invite them to shop for a used car based on the following criteria:

- It is no older than (have students set age).
- It costs no more than (have students set price).
- It is being sold by the owner, not by a used car lot.

Activity Ask students for keywords they would use in scanning for a suitable used car. Then have them scan the ads. **L1**

Additional Resources
📁 *Inclusion Strategies*

Edgar Allan Poe

50 Much I marveled this ungainly fowl to hear discourse so plainly,
Though its answer little meaning—little relevancy bore;
For we cannot help agreeing that no living human being
Ever yet was blessed with seeing bird above his chamber door—
Bird or beast upon the sculptured bust above his chamber door,
        With such name as "Nevermore."

55 But the Raven, sitting lonely on the placid° bust, spoke only
That one word, as if his soul in that one word he did outpour.
Nothing farther then he uttered—not a feather then he fluttered—
Till I scarcely more than muttered "Other friends have flown before—
On the morrow *he* will leave me, as my Hopes have flown before."
60   Then the bird said "Nevermore."

Startled at the stillness broken by reply so aptly spoken,
"Doubtless," said I, "what it utters is its only stock and store
Caught from some unhappy master whom unmerciful Disaster
Followed fast and followed faster till his songs one burden bore—
65 Till the dirges° of his Hope that melancholy burden bore
        Of 'Never—nevermore.' "

But the Raven still beguiling all my fancy into smiling,
Straight I wheeled a cushioned seat in front of bird, and bust and door;
Then, upon the velvet sinking, I betook myself to linking
70 Fancy unto fancy, thinking what this ominous bird of yore—
What this grim, ungainly, ghastly, gaunt, and ominous bird of yore
        Meant in croaking "Nevermore."

This I sat engaged in guessing, but no syllable expressing
To the fowl whose fiery eyes now burned into my bosom's core;
75 This and more I sat divining,° with my head at ease reclining
On the cushion's velvet lining that the lamplight gloated o'er,
But whose velvet violet lining with the lamplight gloating o'er,
        She shall press, ah, nevermore!

---

55 *Placid* means "calm," "peaceful," or "undisturbed."
65 *Dirges* are slow, mournful pieces of music, such as funeral hymns.
75 *Divining* means "knowing through insight or intuition" or "guessing."

G Literary Elements

RHYME Have students study Poe's rhymes in this stanza and note both his rhyme scheme and any internal rhymes; then examine earlier stanzas to see if these patterns are regular. *(Three rhymes, the first and third internal and the second at the end of line 4, occur in lines 4 and 5; the rhyme scheme is a consistently repeated abcbbb.)*

H Active Reading

CLARIFY Ask students to clarify the meaning and tone of the statement in this line. *(The speaker fears that the raven will leave him just as Lenore did; the tone is melancholy.)*

I Active Reading

INTERPRET Ask students what adjectives in these lines make the mood of the poem sinister. *(The bird's "fiery eyes" and the "gloating" lamplight make the mood sinister.)*

MULTIPLE LEARNING STYLES

Spatial Students with acute spatial abilities will easily visualize the scene descriptions in the first eight stanzas. Their classmates might benefit from this skill in conveying what is occurring in the poem.

Activity Ask students to depict the events of the first eight stanzas of the poem in a comic strip format.

Have them decide whether

- each stanza should become a separate scene or if stanzas can be combined.
- words from the poem or modern words that convey the same ideas and emotional intensity should be used.

Have artists post their comic strips. **L2**

THE RAVEN

> Then, methought, the air grew denser, perfumed from an unseen censer°
> 80 Swung by Seraphim° whose foot-falls tinkled on the tufted floor.
> "Wretch," I cried, "thy God hath lent thee—by these angels he hath sent thee
> Respite°—respite and nepenthe° from thy memories of Lenore;
> Quaff,° oh quaff this kind nepenthe and forget this lost Lenore!"
>   Quoth the Raven "Nevermore."
>
> 85 "Prophet!" said I, "thing of evil!—prophet still, if bird or devil!—
> Whether Tempter° sent, or whether tempest° tossed thee here ashore,
> Desolate yet all undaunted, on this desert land enchanted—
> On this home by Horror haunted—tell me truly, I implore—
> Is there—*is there* balm° in Gilead?°—tell me—tell me, I implore!"
> 90   Quoth the Raven "Nevermore."
>
> "Prophet!" said I, "thing of evil!—prophet still, if bird or devil!
> By that Heaven that bends above us—by that God we both adore—
> Tell this soul with sorrow laden if, within the distant Aidenn,°
> It shall clasp a sainted maiden whom the angels name Lenore—
> 95 Clasp a rare and radiant maiden whom the angels name Lenore."
>   Quoth the Raven "Nevermore."
>
> "Be that word our sign of parting, bird or fiend!" I shrieked, upstarting—
> "Get thee back into the tempest and the Night's Plutonian shore!
> Leave no black plume as a token of that lie thy soul hath spoken!
> 100 Leave my loneliness unbroken!—quit the bust above my door!
> Take thy beak from out my heart, and take thy form from off my door!"
>   Quoth the Raven "Nevermore."
>
>
> And the Raven, never flitting, still is sitting, *still* is sitting
> On the pallid° bust of Pallas just above my chamber door;
> 105 And his eyes have all the seeming of a demon's that is dreaming,
> And the lamp-light o'er him streaming throws his shadow on the floor;
> And my soul from out that shadow that lies floating on the floor
>   Shall be lifted—nevermore!

---

79 A *censer* is a container in which incense is burned. During a religious service, it may be swung from connecting chains.
80 *Seraphim* are angels of the highest rank.
82 A *respite* is a period of rest or relief, as from work or sorrow. The ancient Greeks believed the drug *nepenthe* (ni pen′ thē) would ease pain and grief by causing forgetfulness.
83 *Quaff* means "to drink heartily and deeply."
86 *Tempter* refers to the devil. A *tempest* is a violent storm.
89 *Balm* is something that heals or soothes, as an ointment. *Gilead* was a region in ancient Palestine. Here Poe uses a phrase from the Bible (Jeremiah 8:22): "Is there no balm in Gilead?" By this he means, "Is there no relief from my suffering?"
93 Aidenn means "Eden" or "Heaven."
104 *Pallid* means "lacking in color" or "pale."

290 🦢 UNIT 2

Grammar and Language *Minilesson*

Combining Main Clauses Point out that a main clause has a subject and a verb and expresses a complete thought. Main clauses may be combined to form compound sentences.

Activity Write the following sentences on the board:

The last line of every stanza contains a variation of the word *more*, and repetition is found in other places as well.

"The Raven" opens with sorrow; it ends with insanity.

Have students identify the main clauses in these sentences. Explain that main clauses combined to make a compound sentence must be separated by a semicolon or by a coordinating conjunction preceded by a comma. Then ask students to write two sentences about the poem using combined main clauses. **L2**

Additional Resources

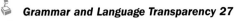 *Grammar and Language Transparency 27*

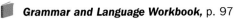 *Grammar and Language Workbook,* p. 97

 *Grammar and Composition Handbook,* Lesson 12.4

Writer's Choice, Lesson 13.1

Responding to Literature

Personal Response

In your opinion, what is the most haunting image from either of these poems?

ANALYZING LITERATURE

TO HELEN

RECALL AND INTERPRET

1. In the first stanza, to what does the speaker compare Helen's beauty? What might the speaker be saying about the way Helen's beauty makes him feel?
2. What does the **imagery** (see page R8) in lines 7–8 suggest to you about the speaker's feelings for Helen?
3. In lines 11–12, where is Helen when the speaker sees her? What does that detail and his description of her in the following lines suggest about his relationship with her?

EVALUATE AND CONNECT

4. The speaker in this poem describes his response to a beautiful woman. What, in your mind, is perfect beauty? Explain.

THE RAVEN

RECALL AND INTERPRET

5. Why is the speaker reading at the beginning of the poem? How would you describe his emotional state in the first six stanzas?
6. How does the speaker's mood change after the raven enters his room? What conclusion does the speaker express in lines 81–83 about the raven's presence?
7. Summarize the speaker's questions to the raven in lines 85–95. How does he react to the raven's response? Describe the speaker's emotional response by the end of the poem.

EVALUATE AND CONNECT

8. Reread the poem, paying particular attention to the repetition of sounds Poe uses. How does this repetition influence the effect of the poem?

EXTENDING YOUR RESPONSE

Writing About Literature

Character Description   Based on the statements and actions of the speaker in "The Raven," write a description of his character. Be sure to mention events that seem to have had a strong influence on his mental and emotional state. Comment on whether you think the raven's visit helped or harmed the speaker's condition.

Creative Writing

My Advice to You   Imagine that the speaker in "To Helen" has written to you for advice on how to pursue a relationship with his love. Write a letter of advice in reply. Be sure to consider what you know about Helen, the speaker's feelings for her, and the nature of their relationship.

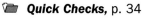 **Save your work for your portfolio.**

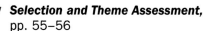

ASSESSMENT OPTIONS

📁 **Quick Checks,** p. 34

📁 **Selection and Theme Assessment,** pp. 55–56

📁 **Performance Assessment,** p. 30

💾 **Testmaker**

Reading the Selection

SUMMARY

After being sentenced to death by the Spanish inquisitors, a prisoner wakens and explores his dark cell. He faints and barely avoids falling into a deep pit. Awakening yet again, he finds that he is strapped to a wooden table with a great sharp pendulum swinging above him. As the blade descends, he rubs food onto his bonds so that rats will gnaw his bindings. Freed, he realizes that the heated metal walls are slowly closing in. Just before he is forced into the pit, French soldiers enter the city, and he is saved.

📁 **Spanish Summaries,** p. 31

🅰 Active Reading

VISUALIZE Have students read silently the second paragraph. Then ask students to visualize the scene by imagining how a filmmaker might set the mood for the story using the details in Poe's account.

Additional Resources
📁 **Active Reading Guide,** p. 35
🎧 **Audio Library**
🎧 **Spanish Audio Library**

Teaching Options

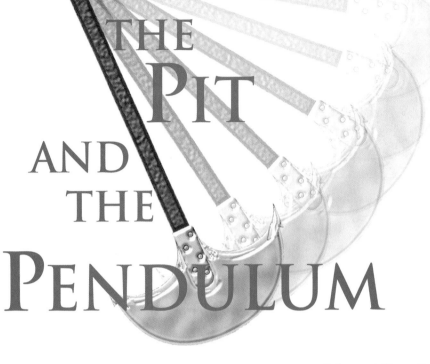

THE PIT AND THE PENDULUM

Edgar Allan Poe ～

I WAS SICK—sick unto death with that long agony; and when they at length unbound me, and I was permitted to sit, I felt that my senses were leaving me. The sentence—the dread sentence of death—was the last of distinct accentuation which reached my ears.

After that, the sound of the inquisitorial voices seemed merged in one dreamy indeterminate hum. It conveyed to my soul the idea of *revolution*—perhaps from its association in fancy with the burr of a millwheel. This only for a brief period; for presently I heard no more. Yet, for a while, I saw; but with how terrible an exaggeration! I saw the lips of the black-robed judges. They appeared to me white—whiter than the sheet upon which I trace these words—and thin even to grotesqueness;[1] thin with the intensity of their expression of firmness—of immovable resolution—of stern contempt of human torture. I saw that the decrees of what to me was Fate, were still issuing from those lips. I saw them writhe with a deadly locution.[2] I saw them fashion the syllables of my name; and I shuddered because no sound succeeded. I saw, too, for a few moments of delirious horror, the soft and nearly imperceptible waving of the sable draperies which enwrapped the walls of the apartment. And then my vision fell upon the seven tall candles upon the table. At first they wore the aspect of charity, and seemed white slender angels who would save me; but then, all

---

1. *Grotesqueness* is the state of being distorted or unnatural in shape or appearance.

2. *Locution* is a form or style of verbal expression.

CONNECTING TO OTHER SELECTIONS

The chart at the right shows three ways to connect "The Pit and the Pendulum" to selections in this book.

For specific teaching strategies, see the **Unit Two Planning Guide,** pp. 139–140.

Connection	Title
Life Skills: Problem Solving	→ from *Black Boy,* p. 822
Thematic: Matters of Life and Death	→ *The Crucible,* p. 913
Literary: Setting	→ "The First Snow-Fall," p. 231

at once, there came a most deadly nausea over my spirit, and I felt every fiber in my frame thrill as if I had touched the wire of a galvanic battery,[3] while the angel forms became meaningless specters,[4] with heads of flame, and I saw that from them there would be no help. And then there stole into my fancy, like a rich musical note, the thought of what sweet rest there must be in the grave. The thought came gently and stealthily, and it seemed long before it attained full appreciation; but just as my spirit came at length properly to feel and entertain it, the figures of the judges vanished, as if magically, from before me; the tall candles sank into nothingness; their flames went out utterly; the blackness of darkness superdvened; all sensations appeared swallowed up in a mad rushing descent as of the soul into Hades.[5] Then silence, and stillness, and night were the universe.

I had swooned; but still will not say that all of consciousness was lost. What of it there remained I will not attempt to define, or even to describe; yet all was not lost. In the deepest slumber—no! In delirium—no! In a swoon—no! In death—no! even in the grave all *is not* lost. Else there is no immortality[6] for man. Arousing from the most profound[7] of slumbers, we break the gossamer web of *some* dream. Yet in a second afterward, (so frail may that web have been) we remember not that we have dreamed. In the return to life from the swoon there are two stages; first, that of the sense of mental or spiritual; secondly, that of the sense of physical, existence. It seems probable that if, upon reaching the second stage, we could recall the impressions of the first, we should find these impressions eloquent in memories of the gulf beyond. And that gulf is—what? How at least shall we distinguish its shadows from

3. In a *galvanic battery*, direct electric current is produced by means of chemical action.
4. *Specters* are ghosts or ghostly visions.
5. In Greek myth, *Hades* is the underground place of the dead.
6. Here, *immortality* means "eternal life."
7. Here, *profound* means "complete" or "deep."

those of the tomb? But if the impressions of what I have termed the first stage, are not, at will, recalled, yet, after long interval, do they not come unbidden, while we marvel whence they come? He who has never swooned, is not he who finds strange palaces and wildly familiar faces in coals that glow; is not he who beholds floating in midair the sad visions that the many may not view; is not he who ponders over the perfume of some novel[8] flower—is not

8. A *novel* flower is new and unusual.

Seven Tall Candles. Barry Moser. Watercolor, 6½ x 3⅞ in. Private collection.

Viewing the painting: The narrator describes the candles first as "white slender angels," then as "specters, with heads of flame." How would you describe the candles in the painting?

FIGURATIVE LANGUAGE: *Imagery* Poe is noted for his sensory imagery. Ask students to identify the sensory images that dominate the paragraph and what their effect is. *(The senses are sound, sight, and, to a lesser extent, touch. They make the action more vivid and intense, and they begin the narrator's characterization.)*

VIEWING THE PAINTING

Barry Moser (1940–) is an award-winning illustrator. He has illustrated nearly 200 books, including many famous titles. He is also known for an idiosyncrasy: he often marks his projects with his face. "I've done two editions of *The Odyssey*, and in the first one I was Odysseus. It can be that straightforward, or it can be something as small as the face on a brooch on a woman's bodice," said Moser.

Viewing Response *Students may agree with either of the narrator's descriptions or invent one of their own based on these descriptions.*

Grammar and Language *Minilesson*

Identifying Main Clauses Point out to students that a main clause has a subject and a predicate and can stand alone.

Activity Point out the paragraph at the end of the first column on page 294. Only one of the sentences in the paragraph meets the definition of a main clause. Ask students to add the missing element to make "sentences" into main clauses (verbs). **L2**

Additional Resources

🖌 ***Grammar and Language Transparency 28***

📗 ***Grammar and Language Workbook,*** p. 97

📙 ***Grammar and Composition Handbook,*** Lesson 4.1

📗 ***Writer's Choice,*** Lesson 13.1

Active Reading

VISUALIZE Ask students to visualize what the speaker vaguely remembers happening. *(tall figures silently carrying him down to a flat, damp place)*

Language Note

Combined with various prefixes and suffixes, the Latin word *duc*, meaning "lead," forms the basis of a number of English words. A *duct* is a channel that conducts air or water. The root can also be a title: the Italian leader Benito Mussolini was called Il *Duce*; Queen Elizabeth's husband is the *Duke* of Edinburgh; a similarly titled Spaniard is a *duque*. Ask students to name other words using *duc* as a root. *(Possibilities include: abduct, adduce, conduct, educate, induct, introduce, produce, and reduce.)*

he whose brain grows bewildered with the meaning of some musical cadence which has never before arrested his attention.

Amid frequent and thoughtful endeavors to remember; amid earnest struggles to regather some token of the state of seeming nothingness into which my soul had lapsed, there have been moments when I have dreamed of success; there have been brief, very brief periods when I have conjured up remembrances which the lucid reason of a later epoch assures me could have had reference only to that condition of seeming unconsciousness. These shadows of memory tell, indistinctly, of tall figures that lifted and bore me in silence down—down—still down—till a hideous dizziness oppressed me at the mere idea of the interminableness[9] of the descent. They tell also of a vague horror at my heart, on account of that heart's unnatural stillness. Then comes a sense of sudden motionlessness throughout all things; as if those who bore me (a ghastly train!) had outrun, in their descent, the limits of the limitless, and paused from the wearisomeness of their toil. After this I call to mind flatness and dampness; and that all is *madness*—the madness of a memory which busies itself among forbidden things.

Very suddenly there came back to my soul motion and sound—the tumultuous motion of the heart, and, in my ears, the sound of its beating. Then a pause in which all is blank. Then again sound, and motion, and touch—a tingling sensation pervading my frame. Then the mere consciousness of existence, without thought—a condition which lasted long. Then, very suddenly, *thought*, and shuddering terror, and earnest endeavor to comprehend my true state. Then a strong desire to lapse into insensibility.[10] Then a rushing revival of soul and a successful

effort to move. And now a full memory of the trial, of the judges, of the sable draperies, of the sentence, of the sickness, of the swoon. Then entire forgetfulness of all that followed; of all that a later day and much earnestness of endeavor have enabled me vaguely to recall.

So far, I had not opened my eyes. I felt that I lay upon my back, unbound. I reached out my hand, and it fell heavily upon something damp and hard. There I suffered[11] it to remain for many minutes, while I strove to imagine where and *what* I could be. I longed, yet dared not to employ my vision. I dreaded the first glance at objects around me. It was not that I feared to look upon things horrible, but that I grew aghast lest there should be *nothing* to see. At length, with a wild desperation at heart, I quickly unclosed my eyes. My worst thoughts, then, were confirmed. The blackness of eternal night encompassed me. I struggled for breath. The intensity of the darkness seemed to oppress and stifle me. The atmosphere was intolerably close. I still lay quietly, and made effort to exercise my reason. I brought to mind the inquisitorial proceedings,[12] and attempted from that point to deduce my real condition. The sentence had passed; and it appeared to me that a very long interval of time had since elapsed. Yet not for a moment did I suppose myself actually dead. Such a supposition, notwithstanding what we read in fiction, is altogether inconsistent with real existence;—but where and in what state was I? The condemned to death, I knew, perished usually at the *autos-da-fé*,[13] and one of these had

---

9. *Interminableness* means "endlessness."
10. The narrator is describing his wish to return to unconsciousness *(insensibility)*.

11. Here, *suffered* means "allowed."
12. During the Inquisition, a person's refusal to confess was taken as evidence of guilt.
13. Often, the sentence was to be burned alive in public ceremonies called *autos-da-fé* (ô′ tōz də fā′). The phrase is Portuguese for "acts of faith," referring to the Inquisitors' faith that the condemned persons were guilty as charged.

Vocabulary
deduce (di dōos′) *v.* to draw a conclusion from something known or assumed

Teaching Options

MEETING INDIVIDUAL NEEDS — ENGLISH LANGUAGE LEARNERS

Diction Poe's diction, or word choice, is always quite precise. To create the kind and degree of terror the narrator experiences, Poe selects richly connotative words.

Activity Select a student reader to read the paragraph in the first column of page 297 beginning, "I saw clearly . . ." As students reread it

silently, have them look up unfamiliar words. When students understand the passage, have them point out words with negative connotations, such as *doom, tyranny, direst, agonies, hideous, torture.*

Additional Resources
📁 *English Language Learners Sourcebook*

Brücke, 1987. Christa Näher. Oil on canvas, 90 x 50 cm. Private collection.
Viewing the painting: How might you feel if you were isolated, as the narrator was, in a place like the one depicted in the painting? Explain.

been held on the very night of the day of my trial. Had I been remanded to my dungeon, to await the next sacrifice which would not take place for many months? This I at once saw could not be. Victims had been in immediate demand. Moreover, my dungeon, as well as all the condemned cells at Toledo,[14] had stone floors, and light was not altogether excluded.

A fearful idea now suddenly drove the blood in torrents upon my heart, and for a brief period, I once more relapsed into insensibility. Upon recovering, I at once started to my feet, trembling convulsively in every fiber. I thrust my arms wildly above and around me in all directions. I felt nothing; yet dreaded to move a step, lest I should be impeded by the walls of the *tomb*. Perspiration burst from every pore and stood in cold big beads on my forehead. The agony of suspense grew at length intolerable, and I cautiously moved forward, with my arms extended, and my eyes straining from their sockets, in the hope of catching some faint ray of light. I proceeded for many paces; but still all was blackness and vacancy. I breathed more freely. It seemed evident that mine was not, at least, the most hideous of fates.

And now, as I still continued to step cautiously onward, there came thronging upon my recollection a thousand vague rumors of the horrors of Toledo. Of the dungeons there

14. The Spanish city of *Toledo* was important during the Inquisition.

Vocabulary
impede (im pēd′) *v.* to slow or block progress or action; obstruct

D Active Reading

CONNECT AND EVALUATE Explain to students that in an era when electric lights are everywhere, it is hard for modern readers to conceive of total darkness. Ask students to think about any instances when they could see absolutely nothing. *(Students may mention dark, windowless rooms, tours of caves where the guide turns off the lights, and so on.)* Then ask students to identify the comparison that Poe makes to characterize the darkness and why it is appropriate to the narrator's state of mind. *(He compares the darkness to a tomb; given the character's preoccupation with death, the comparison is logical both emotionally and literally.)*

GIFTED AND TALENTED ACTIVITY

The Spanish Inquisition Poe's story describes the experience of being a prisoner during the Spanish Inquisition. Today, the Inquisition is synonymous with mercilessness and torture, but few students know much about it.

Activity Gifted and talented students may enjoy researching more about the Spanish Inquisition and the Roman Catholic Church of this period. Encourage students to investigate why the Inquisition began, what its goals were, and whether torture chambers like the one in this story really existed. Encourage each student to focus on a specific aspect of the Inquisition, and then report the findings to the class. **L3**

Literary Elements

E

PLOT: *Suspense* Ask students how Poe creates suspense in this passage. *(He portrays the confused state and heightened emotions of the narrator; he foreshadows horrific events to come.)*

Critical Thinking

F

EVALUATING Ask students to evaluate the prisoner's mental condition at this point. *(He is calm enough to use his intelligence to assess his surroundings.)*

Language Note

Both *apprehend* and *comprehend* denote "to perceive mentally," but their meanings are slightly different. When you comprehend, you take in the meaning and the implications of something. When you apprehend, you take in the meaning, but not the implications.

Teaching Options

---

had been strange things narrated—fables I had always deemed them—but yet strange, and too ghastly to repeat, save in a whisper. Was I left to perish of starvation in the subterranean[15] world of darkness; or what fate, perhaps even more fearful, awaited me? That the result would be death, and a death of more than customary bitterness, I knew too well the character of my judges to doubt. The mode and the hour were all that occupied or distracted me.

E My outstretched hands at length encountered some solid obstruction. It was a wall, seemingly of stone masonry—very smooth, slimy, and cold. I followed it up; stepping with all the careful distrust with which certain antique narratives had inspired me. This process, however, afforded me no means of ascertaining the dimensions of my dungeon; as I might make its circuit, and return to the point whence I set out, without being aware of the fact; so perfectly uniform seemed the wall. I therefore sought the knife which had been in my pocket, when led into the inquisitorial chamber; but it was gone; my clothes had been exchanged for a wrapper of coarse serge. I had thought of forcing the blade in some minute crevice of the masonry, so as to identify my point of departure. The difficulty, nevertheless, was but trivial; although, in the disorder of my fancy, it seemed at first insuperable.[16] I tore a part of the hem from the robe and placed the fragment at full length, and at right angles to the wall. In groping my way around the prison I could not fail to encounter this rag upon completing the circuit. So, at least I thought: but I had not counted upon the extent of the dungeon, or upon my own weakness. The ground was moist and slippery. I staggered onward for some time, when I stumbled and fell. My excessive fatigue

---

15. Most commonly, *subterranean* describes things that exist or occur below the earth's surface, but it can also mean "out of sight" or "secret."
16. Something that's *insuperable* cannot be overcome.

---

induced me to remain prostrate; and sleep soon overtook me as I lay.

Upon awakening, and stretching forth an arm, I found beside me a loaf and a pitcher with water. I was too much exhausted to reflect upon this circumstance, but ate and drank with avidity.[17] Shortly afterward, I resumed my tour around the prison, and with much toil, came at last upon the fragment of the serge. Up to the period when I fell I had counted fifty-two paces, and upon resuming my walk, I counted forty-eight more;—when I arrived at the rag. There were in all, then, a hundred paces; and admitting two paces to the yard, I presumed the dungeon to be fifty yards in circuit. I had met, however, with many angles in the wall, and thus I could form no guess at the shape of the vault; for vault I could not help supposing it to be.

I had little object—certainly no hope—in these researches; but a vague curiosity prompted me to continue them. Quitting the wall, I resolved to cross the area of the enclosure. At first I proceeded with extreme caution, for the floor, although seemingly of solid material, was treacherous with slime. At length, however, I took courage, and did not hesitate to step firmly; endeavoring to cross in as direct a line as possible. I had advanced some ten or twelve paces in this manner, when the remnant of the torn hem of my robe became entangled between my legs. I stepped on it, and fell violently on my face. **F**

In the confusion attending my fall, I did not immediately apprehend a somewhat startling circumstance, which yet, in a few seconds afterward, and while I still lay prostrate, arrested my attention. It was this—my chin rested upon the floor of the prison, but my lips and the upper portion of my head, although seemingly at a less elevation than the chin, touched nothing. At the same time my forehead seemed bathed in a clammy vapor, and the peculiar smell of decayed fungus arose to

---

17. *Avidity* is eagerness and enthusiasm.

LIFE SKILLS CONNECTION

Logical Reasoning To investigate his surroundings without being able to see them, the narrator must rely upon his other senses and his intelligence.

Activity Have students close their eyes and imagine that they, too, have been confined in a dark place. Ask students to use sensory details and memory to describe that place. Have the class try to guess

where the speaker is. Students may complete a chart such as the sensory wheel here. **L2**

See · Hear · Deduce — What I . . . — Taste · Touch · Smell

Writing Skills in this unit

Writing Skills

The Student Edition of Unit Three offers strong instructional support for writing skills:

In **Extending Your Response**, which follows each selection:
- Writing About Literature
- Personal/Creative Writing

In **Writing Skills** Lessons:
- Elaborating on an Idea (p. 434)

See also the **Writing Minilessons** throughout the unit in this Teacher's Wraparound Edition.

Writing Workshops

The themes in Unit Three conclude with a **Writing Workshop** that guides students through the writing process.
- Persuasive Writing: Essay (p. 392)
- Expository Writing: Analyzing a Poem (p. 440)

Writing Resources

Writer's Assistant CD-ROM
Each Writing Workshop is supplemented by an interactive writing guide on the Writer's Assistant CD-ROM. This easy-to-use writing guide provides prompts, templates, and other tools that lead students through the writing process.

Writing and Proofreading Practice
Blackline masters present in-depth instruction and practice on a specific step in the writing process and proofreading. (pp. 30–44)

Writing and Proofreading Transparencies
Transparencies (13–14, 31–34) provide graphic organizers and proofreading exercises for whole class instruction.

Research and Report Writing Guide
This resource provides extensive tips and activities to guide students in their writing projects in the literature classroom as well as in classes across the curriculum.

Style and Documentation Sourcebook for Writers
This sourcebook is a combination reference and work-book, giving students the most up-to-date information and guidance regarding traditional as well as technological research strategies and documentation.

Grammar and Composition Handbook
The Grammar and Composition Handbook provides instruc-tion that supplements activities in the student textbook.

Assessment Resources

Selection Quick Checks
For each selection, a Quick Check of three to five short-answer questions measures students' literal comprehension.

Selection and Theme Assessment
The Selection and Theme Assessment instrument tests students' abilities to recall, interpret, and evaluate what they've read. The tests consist of multiple-choice, short-answer, and essay questions.

Performance Assessment
Alternative assessment instruments and rubrics for Unit Three are found in the Performance Assessment ancillary.

Writing Assessment and Portfolio Management
These notes and strategies, student models, and assessment tools assist with the task of measuring students' progress as writers and as monitors of their own writing.

Testmaker
Teachers can customize selection, theme, and Unit Three tests by accessing the Testmaker database.

MindJogger Videoquizzes
Using a popular game show format, MindJogger Videoquizzes enable teachers to evaluate students' understanding of Unit Three in a quick and fun manner.

Unit Objectives

- To read and enjoy a variety of literature selections that bring to life the turmoil of the Civil War era
- To analyze the literary elements in various kinds of literature
- To apply strategies for reading various kinds of literature

VIEWING THE PAINTING

Xanthus R. Smith (1839–1929), whose father was the painter Russell Smith, was born in Philadelphia. He enlisted in the Union navy, was given special privileges as an artist, and received time off for painting.

Responding to the Art Discussion questions:

- What is happening in this picture? *(A Confederate ship is trying to set a Union ship on fire.)*
- What do the details of the painting suggest about the attack? *(The use of dark and light suggests an ominous tone. The moon indicates the attack took place at night, probably to surprise sleeping Union soldiers.)*

> *"Our National Sin has found us out. . . .*
> *We have sown the wind, only to reap the whirlwind."*
>
> —Frederick Douglass, 1861,
> speaking of slavery and the Civil War

C.S.S. Manassas Pushing a Fire Barge into the U.S.S. Hartford in New Orleans Harbor.
Xanthus R. Smith (1839–1929). Oil on paper, 5¼ x 9¼ in. Private collection.

316

TEACHER to TEACHER

STEARNS HIGH SCHOOL • MILLINOCKET, MAINE

I look for ways to help lower-ability students shine while keeping upper-level students challenged. Personally-based research works well for all students. To introduce the Civil War, we talk about the names of places involved in the war, such as battle sites. We then discuss those places that are in our part of the country, especially the places where students have lived or have visited. Students use the library and the Internet to research these towns. This personally-based research leads into historic research as we go through the unit.

LINDA NEAL

UNIT ❧ THREE

The
Civil War
and
Its Aftermath

1845–1880

Theme 4
The Union Is Tested
pages 327–396

Theme 5
Two New American Voices
pages 397–443

Have students read the quotation. Then pose these questions for discussion.
- What is the "National Sin" to which Frederick Douglass refers? *(slavery)*
- What is "the whirlwind"? *(the Civil War)*
- What sort of literature would you expect people caught in "the whirlwind" to produce? *(Persuasive, critical, provocative, or angry are possible choices.)*

Theme 4: The Union Is Tested

The selections in Theme 4 explore the tragedy of slavery that helped cause the Civil War and its wrenching impact on all Americans, Northerners and Southerners.

Theme 5: Two New American Voices

Students investigate the contributions of Walt Whitman and Emily Dickinson to American thought and literature through representative selections of their works.

GLENCOE
TECHNOLOGY
LITERATURE CLASSICS
CD-ROM

Search for other Civil War era works by theme, author, or title.

RESOURCE MANAGER

See the *Unit Three Planning Guide* (pp. vi–1) for additional teaching notes, strategies, and resources for introducing the Civil War unit.

Setting the Scene

Setting the Scene

Introducing the Time Period

Ask the students to share what they know about the Civil War. You may wish to pose these questions to begin the discussion: What issue divided the North from the South? Who was the president, and what was his position on that issue?

VIEWING THE PAINTING

Conrad Wise Chapman (1842–1910) was a Confederate soldier serving in the South Carolina coastal defenses. He saw little action at this post and spent much time in 1863 sketching the harbor. Chapman's paintings can be seen at the Museum of the Confederacy in Richmond.

Responding to the Art Discussion questions:
- What is the most noticeable object in this painting? (*the Confederate flag*)
- What does the condition of the flag suggest about the length of time that the Confederacy has held the fort? (*Its worn condition suggests a long siege.*)
- What is the sentry looking at? (*the Union blockade in the harbor*)

Mary Boykin Chesnut went to bed on April 11, 1861, but could not sleep. Like many others in Charleston, South Carolina, that night, she knew that federal troops under Major Robert Anderson were holed up in Fort Sumter on a rocky island in the city's harbor. South Carolina, which had seceded from the Union four months earlier, had issued these troops an ultimatum. "If Anderson will not surrender," Chesnut noted in her private journal, "tonight the bombardment begins." At 4:30 A.M. on April 12, she heard the sound she had dreaded: "the booming of the cannon." Racing to her rooftop, she witnessed the beginning of the thirty-four-hour shelling of Fort Sumter—the event that began the American Civil War.

Flag of Fort Sumter, October 20, 1863, 1864. Conrad Wise Chapman. Oil on board, 10 x 14 in. The Museum of the Confederacy, Richmond, VA.

U.S.A.	┌1846 War begins between the United States and Mexico	┌1848 First women's rights convention held in Seneca Falls, New York ┌1850 Compromise of 1850 strengthens the Fugitive Slave Act	1859 John Brown leads antislavery raid	┌1860 Abraham Lincoln elected president	┌1861 Confederate forces win First Battle of Bull Run
1845	└1847 In West Africa, formerly enslaved African Americans declare Liberia an independent nation	1850 Taiping Rebellion erupts in China **1855**	└1858 Benito Juárez becomes president of Mexico	└1861 Nationalists proclaim a united Italy; Russian serfs freed	
World					

interNET CONNECTION

Fort Sumter Students can take a walking tour of Fort Sumter by viewing the Charleston Public Library Web site. For additional information about the battle at Fort Sumter, students can connect to the Tulane University Library to read Professor Latner's *Crisis at Fort Sumter.*

Extra Credit Projects

- Students can review books of Currier and Ives prints to select those that show interesting aspects of nineteenth-century life. Have them present the prints, along with their comments and impressions, for class discussion. **L2**

- Students can investigate the Civil War era on the Internet. Have them use keywords such as *Smithsonian, American history,* and the *Library of Congress.* Have students list additional information and details for the time lines on pages 318–325. **L2**

History of the Time

The Path to War

Regional economic differences helped bring about the outbreak of the Civil War in 1861. In the South, enslaved African Americans provided the labor needed for an agricultural economy based on raising and selling cotton. In the North, free people, both white and black, worked for wages in the mines, factories, and trading companies of a growing industrial economy.

As the nation expanded westward, many Southerners wanted slavery to expand with it, but most Northerners did not. In November 1860, Abraham Lincoln, who opposed the expansion of slavery, won the presidential election. In response, South Carolina and other Southern states—together known as the Confederacy—began to secede from the United States. Lincoln vowed to preserve the Union. When Confederate cannons fired at Fort Sumter, the Civil War began.

The War

The long tradition of military service in the South gave the eleven states that seceded an edge during the first year of fighting. By the end of 1862, however, the North's naval blockades and larger armies began to bring it victories. Then, on January 1, 1863, events took a dramatic turn. Lincoln issued the Emancipation Proclamation, which declared that all enslaved people in the rebellious states were free. The North's fight to save the Union immediately became a war to end slavery. In the spring of 1865, after more than 600,000 deaths, the war ended in a victory for the North. The slave economy was destroyed.

The Aftermath

The eleven-year period after the Civil War, referred to as Reconstruction, was marked by economic growth. Northern industry had prospered during the Civil War and continued to expand. The South, devastated by the war, began to rebuild. In both regions, however, groups fought against long-existing oppression:

- African Americans, though no longer enslaved, still battled discrimination and racism. One victory was the ratification of the Fourteenth Amendment in 1868, which required states to provide "equal protection of the laws" to all persons.
- Women fought for equality and the right to vote. One leader, Susan B. Anthony, was arrested in 1872 for attempting to vote in a New York election.
- Sioux, Cheyenne, Arapaho, and other Native Americans continued the struggle to protect their land from the spread of white settlements.

The efforts of African Americans, women, and Native Americans to achieve justice would help shape American history after the Civil War.

Historical Note

Shortly after President Lincoln took office, he was faced with the crisis that began the Civil War. The newly declared Confederacy had refused to allow provisions to be delivered to Fort Sumter. Instead, General Beauregard demanded that the Union surrender the fort. Rather than acknowledge Southern autonomy, Lincoln ordered that provisions be sent to the men. General Beauregard opened fire on the fort, and on the second day, with Fort Sumter badly damaged from the attack, Union General Anderson surrendered. The South held Fort Sumter in full view of Union blockades throughout the war.

Biography

The following videotape program is available from Glencoe. Be sure to preview this video before showing it to your class.

- **Abraham Lincoln: Preserving the Union**

Active Reading

READING THE TIME LINE Have students identify entries on the time line that deal with inventions. *(sewing machine patent, improved machine gun, steel-making process, dynamite, electrical lightbulb)*

Timeline:

- Civil War ends; Lincoln is assassinated; Thirteenth Amendment bans slavery
- 1867 — United States buys Alaska from Russia
- 1870 — Hiram Revels becomes the first African American in the U.S. Senate
- 1876 — Sioux forces defeat General George Custer at the Battle of Little Bighorn
- **1865**
- 1868 — Meiji Restoration reforms Japan's government
- 1870 — Franco-Prussian War begins in Europe
- **1875**
- 1879 — Zulu War starts in South Africa
- **1880**

African American Soldiers One of the most famous African American Civil War regiments was the 54th Regiment of the Massachusetts Volunteer Infantry. Have students check the Internet for the story of one of its famous battles. Suggest they use keywords such as *Civil War* and *54th Regiment of the Massachusetts Volunteer Infantry.*

Life of the Time

Life of the Time

People are talking about

The Underground Railroad   Harriet Tubman escapes slavery and then secretly returns to the South nineteen times to help others escape. She becomes the most famous guide on the Underground Railroad—a secret network of hideouts for people fleeing slavery.

"I had reasoned this out in my mind: There was two things I had a right to, liberty and death. If I could not have one, I would have the other, for no man should take me alive." —*Harriet Tubman*

Harriet Tubman

Portrait of John Brown, c. 1859. Ole Peter Hansen Balling. Oil on canvas, 30 x 25 in. The National Portrait Gallery, Washington, DC.

◄ John Brown's Raid   Brown and his followers kill five proslavery men in Kansas in 1856. Three years later, he and about twenty followers seize weapons and ammunitions from a federal arsenal at Harpers Ferry, Virginia. Brown hopes his actions will ignite an uprising to free enslaved African Americans "on a larger scale." He is captured, tried, and executed.

Otis's Elevators   In 1852, Elisha Otis announces his invention of the first elevator with an automatic safety device to prevent it from falling if the cable breaks. Otis personally demonstrates his new elevator by having the cable cut after he has ascended. The device works. ►

Firsts

- The first transatlantic telegraph cable is laid. (1858)
- Christopher Sholes and associates produce the first practical typewriter. (1867)
- Alexander Graham Bell demonstrates the first telephone. (1876)

U.S.A.

1846 Elias Howe patents the sewing machine

1848 Discovery of gold ignites the California Gold Rush; Stephen Foster publishes "Oh! Susannah"

1850 Printmakers Currier and Ives begin working together

1863 James Whistler exhibits *Arrangement in Grey and Black No 1: The Artist's Mother*

1862 Richard J. Gatling demonstrates an improved machine gun

1845

1855

World

Potato blight causes the Great Famine in Ireland

British explorer David Livingstone names Victoria Falls in Africa

1856 British inventor Henry Bessemer develops an efficient steel making process

MEETING INDIVIDUAL NEEDS   MULTIPLE LEARNING STYLES

Musical Students with strong musical abilities may be interested in contributing musically to this unit on the Civil War period.

Activity Have students, alone, with a partner, or as a group, research the songs of Stephen Foster. Students could learn to play a few of the pieces and then plan a live performance for the class that includes narration. Before each piece is played, the narrator could identify any interesting information that students uncovered in their research. **L2** **COLLAB. LEARN.**

Food & Fashion

- Whiskey, long a staple drink in the United States, comes under increasing attack. Between 1846 and 1857, thirteen states pass laws prohibiting consumption of alcohol.

- Machine production transforms what people wear. Invention of the sewing machine makes possible production of inexpensive, ready-to-wear clothing.

- In the 1870s, a clothing maker in San Francisco begins making rugged pants out of blue denim reinforced with copper rivets. Levi's blue jeans will eventually become widely popular.

- Fashionable women wear skirts that are held out from their bodies with wire frameworks. ▶

Arts & Entertainment

◀ Winslow Homer draws and paints scenes of army camp life. His work often makes the cover of *Harper's Weekly* magazine. Critics will later praise Homer as one of the greatest American painters.

More than one thousand photographers record the Civil War. The best known is Mathew Brady, who will produce 3,500 photographs of the war. ▶

Home, Sweet Home, c. 1863. Winslow Homer. Oil on canvas, 21½ x 16½ in. The National Gallery of Art, Washington, DC.

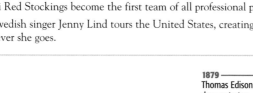

Amusements

- Baseball is a popular pastime. In 1869, the Cincinnati Red Stockings become the first team of all professional players.

- In 1850 Swedish singer Jenny Lind tours the United States, creating a sensation wherever she goes.

Pop Culture

Technological Gadgets The drive for new technology was just getting started as the nineteenth century dawned. At that time, stereoscopes were the latest gadgets; today we have CDs, remote controls, and videophones. Ask students how many consider themselves to be "gadget lovers." Find out what gadgets intrigue them and ask what gadget, existing or yet to be invented, would make their lives easier or more fun?

FYI

How Did Baseball Start? Baseball in the United States evolved from several bat-and-ball games, such as cricket, rounders, one-cat, and town ball, played in England. Each game required a batter to strike an object with a bat and then run between two or more points before being put out. The runner was put out if the object was caught or if touched by the object. In 1845, the first club, the New York Knickerbockers, was formed, and over the next decade, the Knickerbockers and other clubs adopted a series of rules that eventually led to modern baseball.

Timeline:

- **1865**
- **1867** Swedish industrialist Alfred Nobel receives a British patent on dynamite; diamond rush begins in South Africa
- **1869** The Suez Canal opens in Egypt
- **1871** Chicago Fire destroys much of the city, killing 250 people
- **1873** French painter Claude Monet completes *Impression: Sunrise*
- **1875** Thomas Eakins paints *The Gross Clinic*
- **1876** The first full production of German composer Richard Wagner's opera *The Ring of Nibelung* is staged
- **1879** Thomas Edison demonstrates the first practical electrical lightbulb
- **1880**

MEETING INDIVIDUAL NEEDS — MULTIPLE LEARNING STYLES

Spatial Spatial learners may like to demonstrate their visual abilities in their study of the Civil War period.

Activity Invite students to make a catalog of men's and women's clothing styles of the Civil War era. Students should first research to find the standards of the period and the cost of clothing at that time in history. Students can make copies of pictures of fashions that they find in their research and organize them into categories for their catalogs. Some students may prefer to create their own clothing designs based on the standards and styles of the time period. For each item in their catalog, students should provide a flattering description, color choices, sizes, and price. Have students display their catalogs for all to enjoy. **L2**

Literature of the Time

Literature of the Time

A Memorable Introduction When Abraham Lincoln met Harriet Beecher Stowe, he reportedly greeted her as the "little woman who made the book that made this great war." Stowe's story of Uncle Tom, an enslaved man who is murdered because he refuses to deny God and accept Simon Legree, his cruel overseer, as his master, gave momentum to the abolitionist movement.

® The following videotape program is available from Glencoe. Be sure to preview this video before showing it to your class.

- **Civil War Journal: Robert E. Lee***

 Also available in the Glencoe Literature Video Library.

Biography

The following videotape program is available from Glencoe. Be sure to preview this video before showing it to your class.

- **Frederick Douglass***

Also available in the Glencoe Literature Video Library.

PEOPLE ARE READING . . .

Antislavery Writings *The Liberator,* a newspaper founded by William Lloyd Garrison in 1831, is dedicated to the abolition of slavery. Harriet Beecher Stowe's anti-slavery novel, *Uncle Tom's Cabin,* appears first as a newspaper serial and then in book form in 1852. It sells 300,000 copies in its first year.

William Lloyd Garrison

William Gilmore Simms A proud native of South Carolina, Simms writes a popular series of romantic tales about his state's frontier past. He emerges as a defender of slavery and a critic of excessive federal government power.

Harper's Weekly Readers look forward to the political cartoons of Thomas Nast, a Union supporter. Nast popularizes the Democratic Party's donkey symbol and creates the Republican elephant. ▶

"A LIVE JACKASS KICKING A DEAD LION." And such a Lion! and such a Jackass!

People Are Writing

Letters and Diaries During the war many people record their daily lives in letters and diaries. In 1873 they begin using postcards to correspond.

Memoirs Soldiers and civilians publish their memoirs after the war. These accounts provide day-to-day details of the major campaigns of the war.

U.S.A.

Frederick Douglass publishes his autobiography

1847 Henry Wadsworth Longfellow, *Evangeline*

1854 Sara Josepha Hale, *Woman's Record* (encyclopedia)

Walt Whitman, *Leaves of Grass*

1863 Abraham Lincoln, "The Gettysburg Address"

World

1845

1850 England: Elizabeth Barrett Browning, *Sonnets from the Portuguese*

1855

1854 England: Alfred Tennyson, "The Charge of the Light Brigade"

1858 Kenya: Mwana Kupona binti Msham, "Poem of Mwana Kupona"

REAL-WORLD CONNECTION

Political Cartoons Ask students to bring to class current political cartoons from both local and national sources.

Activity In pairs or in groups, have students discuss each of their selections to interpret its message and to evaluate its effectiveness. What are the cartoons saying about current events?

Who would agree? Disagree? Are the cartoons too subtle? Too heavy-handed? **L2 COLLAB. LEARN.**

Literary Trends: From Romanticism to Realism

"The new age [after the Civil War] began with the putting away of the outworn dress of eighteenth-century romantic liberalism. In the hurrying new days there was no time for abstract theories. . . . [There] emerged eventually a spirit of realistic criticism, seeking to evaluate the worth of this new America, and discover if possible other philosophies to take the place of those which had gone down in the fierce battles of the Civil War." —*Vernon L. Parrington*

Before the Civil War, most fiction and poetry depicts people and situations that are highly imaginative, like Poe's and Irving's, or romanticized and idealized, like Hawthorne's. All of that changes. People who have entertained romantic notions of war are shocked into reality by war's brutality.

The Ambrose Bierce story in this unit, "An Occurrence at Owl Creek Bridge," represents the new wave in fiction: Realism. Writers such as Bierce portray real human experience with all of its imperfections and find truth in everyday people and experiences.

FOCUS ON . . .

Two Unique Geniuses
Walt Whitman and Emily Dickinson redefine American poetry, but it would be hard to find two more different people. Whitman, outgoing and outspoken, publishes nine editions of *Leaves of Grass,* creating both enemies and admirers. Dickinson, reserved and reclusive, publishes only seven poems in her lifetime. Both writers, however, are innovators who set the stage for twentieth-century poetry.

Mark Twain, "The Celebrated Jumping Frog of Calaveras County"

1868 Bret Harte, "The Luck of Roaring Camp"

1873 Henry Timrod, "The Cotton Boll"

Mary Baker Eddy, *Science and Health*

1879 George W. Cable, *Old Creole Days*

1865

England: Lewis Carroll, *Alice's Adventures in Wonderland*

1872 Argentina: José Hernández, *The Gaucho Martin Fierro*

1875

1879 Norway: Henrik Ibsen, *A Doll's House*

1880

THE CIVIL WAR AND ITS AFTERMATH 323

Novels of the Time

Introductory Note

An obsessed sea captain pursues a legendary whale; four young sisters face an uncertain future in sedate New England; a young soldier confronts the horrors of war. *Moby-Dick*, *Little Women*, and *The Red Badge of Courage* are worlds apart, socially and psychologically; yet together they suggest the evolution of the American novel. Melville's Ahab is a romantic figure, grappling madly but heroically with the forces of nature and questions of good and evil; Alcott's Meg, Jo, Beth, and Amy face the realities of growing up in a difficult time; and Crane's Henry Fleming is a hapless pawn, buffeted by forces and feelings he barely understands. As America became more industrialized and impersonal, novelists dramatized the changes, showing how difficult it was for ordinary people to assert their wills in the face of powerful political, social, and economic realities.

Cultural Note

Although the English novel flourished in the eighteenth century, few serious novels were written in the United States before 1800. James Fenimore Cooper's *The Leatherstocking Tales* established the genre in America, paving the way for classic works such as Nathaniel Hawthorne's *The Scarlet Letter* (1850) and Melville's *Moby-Dick* (1851).

Novels of the Time

Responding to the brutality of the Civil War, American novelists turn more and more toward realism. Writers of this time try to observe society closely and to show life as it really is. Many important books of this period analyze economic conditions of the day and conflicts between people from different social classes.

Moby-Dick: or, The Whale
by Herman Melville (1851)

Although Melville's previous novels of sea adventure are quite successful, this story of a whaling voyage is dismissed as absurd, wild, or mad by most readers of his time. In years to come, however, *Moby-Dick* becomes recognized as one of the greatest American novels, the first to struggle with such profound issues as the place of humanity in the universe. The tragic figure of Captain Ahab and his obsessive, doomed search for a great white whale dominate the story.

The Red Badge of Courage
by Stephen Crane (1895)

Although written thirty years after the Civil War ends, this short novel realistically depicts the psychological terror experienced by soldiers. It portrays young Henry Fleming's intense fear in his first battle and his response to that fear. Crane uses what is most likely the Battle of Chancellorsville as the model for the fighting portrayed in the book.

Herman Melville

U.S.A.		1850 — Nathaniel Hawthorne, *The Scarlet Letter*	1852 Harriet Beecher Stowe, *Uncle Tom's Cabin*	1853 William Wells Brown, *Clotelle*	1857 Herman Melville, *The Confidence-Man*	1860 Ann Sophia Stephens, *Malaeska: The Indian Wife of the White Hunter*
1845		1847 England: Emily Brontë, *Wuthering Heights*	1849 England: Charles Dickens, *David Copperfield*	**1855**	1857 France: Gustave Flaubert, *Madame Bovary*	1864 Germany: Wilhelm Raabe, *The Hunger-pastor*
World						

MEETING INDIVIDUAL NEEDS — MULTIPLE LEARNING STYLES

Interpersonal Students who learn best by working with others and through discussion can collaboratively explore important novels of the era.

Activity Have students gather as many as possible of the books listed on the time line on pages 322 and 323. Organize the class into small groups, and have students create brief synopses of the books. Students can use as a resource the supplementary information at the front and back of the novels, including any critic's remarks, book introductions, author information, summaries, and other notes on the inside and back covers. Invite students to present their synopses for class discussion. **L2 COLLAB. LEARN.**

FOCUS ACTIVITY

Do you agree with the saying "knowledge is power"? Does knowledge give you greater control over your life?

QUICKWRITE Spend three or four minutes writing to explore your response to this question. Include specific examples.

SETTING A PURPOSE Read to see what kind of power knowledge gives to one young man.

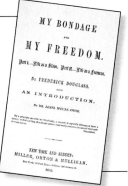

MY BONDAGE
AND
MY FREEDOM.

Part I.—Life as a Slave, Part II.—Life as a Freeman.

By FREDERICK DOUGLASS.

WITH
AN INTRODUCTION.

By DR. JAMES McCUNE SMITH.

NEW YORK AND AUBURN:
MILLER, ORTON & MULLIGAN.

BACKGROUND

The Time and Place
When Douglass first arrived in Baltimore in 1825, the city was already a busy seaport on Chesapeake Bay. Shipbuilding thrived, and the docks along the Patapsco River were crowded with goods headed for inland cities. Unlike other parts of Maryland, free blacks formed a majority of the black population in Baltimore. The seaport thus seemed a haven for African Americans living in the state.

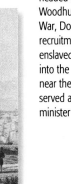

Baltimore, 1857.

Life as a Free Man
Once Douglass no longer had to worry about being captured and sent back to slavery, he funneled all of his energy into the promotion of justice. Not only did he speak against slavery, he championed the rights of African Americans and women. He participated in the first women's rights convention in Seneca Falls, New York, in 1848. He also became involved in politics. In 1872 he ran for vice-president on the Equal Rights Party ticket headed by feminist Victoria Woodhull. During the Civil War, Douglass supported the recruitment of free and enslaved African Americans into the Union Army, and near the end of his life, he served as United States minister to Haiti.

VOCABULARY PREVIEW

benevolent (bə nev′ə lent) *adj.* doing or desiring to do good; kind; p. 330

depravity (di prav′ə tē) *n.* the state of being morally bad or corrupt; p. 330

induce (in do͞os′) *v.* to lead by persuasion or influence; p. 330

upbraiding (up brā′ding) *adj.* criticizing or harshly scolding; p. 333

vanquish (vang′ kwish) *v.* to defeat; p. 333

avarice (av′ər is) *n.* excessive desire for wealth; greed; p. 333

censure (sen′ shər) *v.* to express disapproval of; to find fault with; to blame; p. 334

THE CIVIL WAR AND ITS AFTERMATH 🐚 329

from MY BONDAGE AND MY FREEDOM

Frederick Douglass

I LIVED IN THE FAMILY OF MASTER Hugh, at Baltimore, seven years, during which time—as the almanac[1] makers say of the weather—my condition was variable. The most interesting feature of my history here, was my learning to read and write, under somewhat marked disadvantages. In attaining this knowledge, I was compelled to resort to indirections by no means congenial to my nature, and which were really humiliating to me. My mistress—who, as the reader has already seen, had begun to teach me—was suddenly checked in her benevolent design, by the strong advice of her husband. In faithful compliance with this advice, the good lady had not only ceased to instruct me, herself, but had set her face as a flint against my learning to read by any means. It is due, however, to my mistress to say, that she did not adopt this course in all its stringency at the first. She either thought it unnecessary, or she lacked the depravity indispensable to shutting me up in mental darkness. It was, at least, necessary for her to have some training, and some hardening, in the exercise of the slaveholder's prerogative, to make her equal to forgetting my human nature and character, and to treating me as a thing destitute of a moral or an intellectual nature. Mrs. Auld—my mistress—was, as I have said, a most kind and tender-hearted woman; and, in the humanity of her heart, and the simplicity of her mind, she set out, when I first went to live with her, to treat me as she supposed one human being ought to treat another.

It is easy to see, that, in entering upon the duties of a slaveholder, some little experience is needed. Nature has done almost nothing to prepare men and women to be either slaves or slaveholders. Nothing but rigid training, long persisted in, can perfect the character of the one or the other. One cannot easily forget to love freedom; and it is as hard to cease to respect that natural love in our fellow creatures. On entering upon the career of a slave-holding mistress, Mrs. Auld was singularly deficient; nature, which fits nobody for such an office, had done less for her than any lady I had known. It was no easy matter to induce her to think and to feel that the curly-headed boy, who stood by her side, and even leaned on her lap; who was loved by little Tommy, and who loved little Tommy in turn; sustained to her only the relation of a chattel.[2] I was *more* than that, and she felt me to be more than that. I could talk and sing; I could laugh and weep; I could reason and remember; I could

---

1. An *almanac* is a reference book that is published yearly. It includes calendars with weather forecasts and astronomical information.

2. An article of movable, personal property, such as furniture or livestock, is *chattel*. Enslaved people were sometimes referred to as *chattel*.

Vocabulary
benevolent (bə nev′ ə lent) *adj.* doing or desiring to do good; kind
depravity (di prav′ ə tē) *n.* the state of being morally bad or corrupt
induce (in dōōs′) *v.* to lead by persuasion or influence

Grammar and Language *Minilesson*

Subordinate Clauses Explain that a subordinate clause has a subject and a predicate but cannot stand alone as a sentence. Subordinate clauses can be introduced by a subordinating conjunction or introduced by a relative pronoun.

Activity Have students write three sentences about the selection. Each sentence should contain a subordinate clause and a main clause. Have students underline the main clause in their sentences once and the subordinate clause twice. **L2**

Additional Resources
✏️ *Grammar and Language Transparency 29*
📕 *Grammar and Language Workbook,* p. 97
📕 *Grammar and Composition Handbook,* Lesson 4.2
📗 *Writer's Choice,* Lesson 13.2

Frederick Douglass Series No. 8, 1938–39. Jacob Lawrence. Casein tempera on gessoed hardboard, 17⅞ x 12 in. Hampton University Museum, Hampton, VA.

love and hate. I was human, and she, dear lady, knew and felt me to be so. How could she, then, treat me as a brute, without a mighty struggle with all the noble powers of her own soul. That struggle came, and the will and power of the husband was victorious. Her noble soul was overthrown; but, he that overthrew it did not, himself, escape the consequences. He, not less than the other parties, was injured in his domestic peace by the fall.

When I went into their family, it was the abode of happiness and contentment. The mistress of the house was a model of affection and tenderness. Her fervent piety and watchful uprightness made it impossible to see her without thinking and feeling—"*that woman is a Christian.*" There was no sorrow nor suffering for which she had not a tear, and there was no innocent joy for which she had not a smile. She had bread for the hungry, clothes for the naked, and comfort for every mourner that came within her reach. Slavery soon proved its ability to divest her of these excellent qualities, and her home of its early happiness. Conscience cannot stand much violence. Once thoroughly broken down, *who* is he that can repair the damage? It may be broken toward the slave, on Sunday, and toward the master on Monday. It cannot endure such shocks. It must stand entire, or it does not stand at all. If my condition waxed bad, that of the family waxed not better. The first step, in the wrong direction, was the violence done to nature and to conscience, in arresting the

benevolence that would have enlightened my young mind. In ceasing to instruct me, she must begin to justify herself *to* herself; and, once consenting to take sides in such a debate, she was riveted to her position. One needs very little knowledge of moral philosophy, to see *where* my mistress now landed. She finally became even more violent in her opposition to my learning to read, than was her husband himself. She was not satisfied with simply doing as *well* as her husband had commanded her, but seemed resolved to better his instruction. Nothing appeared to make my poor mistress—after her turning toward the downward path—more angry, than seeing me, seated in some nook or corner, quietly reading a book or

VIEWING THE PAINTING

Jacob Lawrence (1917–) is famous for his series of paintings about African American historical figures and topics. He studied art in New York City and taught there and at the University of Washington in Seattle, where he retired as professor emeritus in 1983.

B **Literary Elements**

AUTHOR'S PURPOSE Douglass's autobiography is more than the telling of his life story: It is a carefully constructed and compelling argument against the institution of slavery. Have students identify and discuss the argument Douglass makes against slavery in this passage. *(Douglass argues that a person's conscience "must stand entire, or it does not stand at all." When Mrs. Auld ceases to be kind and considerate to Douglass, she will soon cease to have these qualities toward other people. Thus Douglass argues that slavery damages the slaveholder as well as the slave.)*

Reading *Minilesson*

Verifying Predictions Predicting what will happen involves students in a selection by giving them a purpose for their reading. Verifying their predictions can build confidence in the study of literature.

Activity After students read the first paragraph of the selection, have them predict ways in which Douglass might learn to read after his mistress refuses

to teach him. Have students write down their ideas and then, as they read, confirm which of their ideas appear in the selection. **L2**

Additional Resources
📁 *Reading Workbook,* pp. 41–42

FYI

C Author's Craft

PERSUASION Douglass couches an argument against slavery in the form of a recollection from his boyhood. He recalls discussing the question of slavery with his white playmates and asserts that their condemnation of slavery sprang "from nature, unseared and unperverted" by a society that condoned it. His description of the way Mrs. Auld's good conscience was disrupted by being a slaveholder reinforces his argument that slavery goes against people's good nature.

D Author's Craft

TRANSITION The reference to the age at which Douglass learned to read and write provides a narrative flow and a transition to his ensuing state of mind.

Teaching Options

---

from MY BONDAGE *and* MY FREEDOM

a newspaper. I have had her rush at me, with the utmost fury, and snatch from my hand such newspaper or book, with something of the wrath and consternation which a traitor might be supposed to feel on being discovered in a plot by some dangerous spy.

Mrs. Auld was an apt woman, and the advice of her husband, and her own experience, soon demonstrated, to her entire satisfaction, that education and slavery are incompatible with each other. When this conviction was thoroughly established, I was most narrowly watched in all my movements. If I remained in a separate room from the family for any considerable length of time, I was sure to be suspected of having a book, and was at once called upon to give an account of myself. All this, however, was entirely *too late*. The first, and never to be retraced, step had been taken. In teaching me the alphabet, in the days of her simplicity and kindness, my mistress had given me the *"inch,"* and now, no ordinary precaution could prevent me from taking the *"ell."*[3]

Seized with a determination to learn to read, at any cost, I hit upon many expedients to accomplish the desired end. The plea which I mainly adopted, and the one by which I was most successful, was that of using my young white playmates, with whom I met in the street, as teachers. I used to carry, almost constantly, a copy of Webster's spelling book in my pocket; and, when sent of errands, or when play time was allowed me, I would step, with my young friends, aside, and take a lesson in spelling. I generally paid my *tuition fee* to the boys, with bread, which I also carried in my pocket. For a single biscuit, any of my hungry little comrades would give me a lesson more valuable to me than bread. Not every one, however, demanded this consideration, for there were those who took pleasure in

teaching me, whenever I had a chance to be taught by them. I am strongly tempted to give the names of two or three of those little boys, as a slight testimonial of the gratitude and affection I bear them, but prudence forbids; not that it would injure me, but it might, possibly, embarrass them; for it is almost an unpardonable offense to do any thing, directly or indirectly, to promote a slave's freedom, in a slave state. It is enough to say, of my warm-hearted little play fellows, that they lived on Philpot street, very near Durgin & Bailey's shipyard.

Although slavery was a delicate subject, and very cautiously talked about among grown up people in Maryland, I frequently talked about it—and that very freely—with the white boys. I would, sometimes, say to them, while seated on a curb stone or a cellar door, "I wish I could be free, as you will be when you get to be men." "You will be free, you know, as soon as you are twenty-one, and can go where you like, but I am a slave for life. Have I not as good a right to be free as you have?" Words like these, I observed, always troubled them; and I had no small satisfaction in wringing from the boys, occasionally, that fresh and bitter condemnation of slavery, that springs from nature, unseared and unperverted. Of all consciences, let me have those to deal with which have not been bewildered by the cares of life. I do not remember ever to have met with a *boy*, while I was in slavery, who defended the slave system; but I have often had boys to console me, with the hope that something would yet occur, by which I might be made free. Over and over again, they have told me, that "they believed *I* had as good a right to be free as *they* had"; and that "they did not believe God ever made any one to be a slave." The reader will easily see, that such little conversations with my play fellows, had no tendency to weaken my love of liberty, nor to render me contented with my condition as a slave. **C**

When I was about thirteen years old, and had succeeded in learning to read, every increase of knowledge, especially respecting **D**

---

3. An *ell* is an old English measure of length used mainly for cloth. It is equal to forty-five inches. Douglass is referring to the adage "Give him an inch and he'll take an ell."

Frederick Douglass ∾

the FREE STATES, added something to the almost intolerable burden of the thought— "I AM A SLAVE FOR LIFE." To my bondage I saw no end. It was a terrible reality, and I shall never be able to tell how sadly that thought chafed my young spirit. Fortunately, or unfortunately, about this time in my life, I had made enough money to buy what was then a very popular school book, viz:[4] the "Columbian Orator." I bought this addition to my library, of Mr. Knight, on Thames street, Fell's Point, Baltimore, and paid him fifty cents for it. I was first led to buy this book, by hearing some little boys say that they were going to learn some little pieces out of it for the Exhibition. This volume was, indeed, a rich treasure, and every opportunity afforded me, for a time, was spent in diligently perusing it. Among much other interesting matter, that which I had perused and reperused with unflagging satisfaction, was a short dialogue between a master and his slave. The slave is represented as having been recaptured, in a second attempt to run away; and the master opens the dialogue with an upbraiding speech, charging the slave with ingratitude, and demanding to know what he has to say in his own defense. Thus upbraided, and thus called upon to reply, the slave rejoins, that he knows how little anything that he can say will avail, seeing that he is completely in the hands of his owner; and with noble resolution, calmly says, "I submit to my fate." Touched by the slave's answer, the master insists upon his further speaking, and recapitulates the many acts of kindness which he has performed toward the slave, and tells him he is permitted to speak for himself. Thus invited to the debate, the quondam[5] slave made a spirited defense of himself, and thereafter the whole argument, for and against slavery, was brought out. The master was vanquished at every turn in the argument; and seeing himself to be thus vanquished, he generously and meekly emancipates the slave, with his best wishes for his prosperity. It is scarcely necessary to say, that a dialogue, with such an origin, and such an ending—read when the fact of my being a slave was a constant burden of grief— powerfully affected me; and I could not help feeling that the day might come, when the well-directed answers made by the slave to the master, in this instance, would find their counterpart in myself. . . .

I had now penetrated the secret of all slavery and oppression, and had ascertained their true foundation to be in the pride, the power and the avarice of man. The dialogue and the speeches were all redolent of the principles of liberty, and poured floods of light on the nature and character of slavery. . . . Nevertheless, the increase of knowledge was attended with bitter, as well as sweet results. The more I read, the more I was led to abhor and detest slavery, and my enslavers. "Slaveholders," thought I, "are only a band of successful robbers, who left their homes and went into Africa for the purpose of stealing and reducing my people to slavery." I loathed them as the meanest and the most wicked of men. As I read, behold! the very discontent so graphically predicted by Master Hugh, had already come upon me. I was no longer the light-hearted, gleesome boy, full of mirth and play, as when I landed first at Baltimore. Knowledge had come; light had penetrated the moral dungeon where I dwelt; and, behold! there lay the bloody whip, for my back, and here was the iron chain; and my good,

---

4. *Viz* is an abbreviation for the Latin word *videlicet,* meaning "namely" or "that is."

5. *Quondam* means "that once was" or "former."

Vocabulary
upbraiding (up brā′ ding) *adj.* criticizing or harshly scolding
vanquish (vang′ kwish) *v.* to defeat
avarice (av′ ər is) *n.* excessive desire for wealth; greed

THE CIVIL WAR AND ITS AFTERMATH 333

INFERRING Douglass is held in slavery, yet he manages to earn fifty cents—a relatively large sum at the time—to purchase a book. Challenge students with these questions about Douglass's purchase: How might a young enslaved person have managed to earn money? What does his choice about how he spends this money say about Douglass? *(Douglass might have earned the money by doing odd jobs, perhaps for neighbors. That he chooses to spend his money on a schoolbook indicates how much his education means to him.)*

F Literary Elements

AUTOBIOGRAPHY Douglass's reading and rereading of this dialogue proves to be a turning point in his life. Discuss with students both why and how the dialogue "powerfully affected" him. *(In the dialogue between an enslaved person and a master, the enslaved person prevails. Douglass is inspired and hopeful that perhaps someday he will be able to make a similar argument for his own life.)*

G Active Reading

QUESTION There is no climax in an autobiography, but this passage may seem like one to the reader. Douglass's struggle to learn to read and write has "bitter, as well as sweet results." What were each of these results? *(The "sweet" results are the triumph of literacy and Douglass's penetration of "the secret of all slavery." The bitter results include increased loathing of slavery and despair for his own state.)*

TEACHER to TEACHER

FELS HIGH SCHOOL • PHILADELPHIA, PENNSYLVANIA

More than 40 culture groups are represented in our school, so to help students relate to American literature, I use short stories of other cultures with related themes. I use stories students are familiar with as a bridge to go from what they know to what they're going to learn. Many of my students' families come from southeast Asia, so they make the connection between that part of the world being torn apart by war and the Civil War in this country. We live close to Gettysburg, so students have visited the Civil War battle site, and we include their experiences in the classroom discussion.

NOELLE KODROFF

Critical Thinking

SYNTHESIZING With "We were both victims to the same overshadowing evil . . . ," Douglass says slavery has harmed both himself and Mrs. Auld. Later he said, "No man can put a chain about the ankle of his fellow man without at last finding the other end fastened about his own neck." Ask students to create a para-phrased statement combining the ideas in both quotations. *(Students can suggest that both Douglass and Mrs. Auld are victims. The chain is a symbol of slavery. One end is attached to the slave; the other is attached to the slaveholder. Both are chained by, or victims of, slavery.)*

Thematic Focus

The Union Is Tested Point out that at the outbreak of the Civil War, about 4 million enslaved Africans lived in the United States (in a population of about 31 million). Emphasize that all of them had experiences similar to those of Douglass—some better, some much worse. The impact of these experiences helped drive the nation to civil war.

✔ ASSESSMENT OPTIONS

📁 *Quick Checks,* p. 36

Teaching Options

---

kind master, he was the author of my situation. The revelation haunted me, stung me, and made me gloomy and miserable. As I writhed under the sting and torment of this knowledge, I almost envied my fellow slaves their stupid contentment. This knowledge opened my eyes to the horrible pit, and revealed the teeth of the frightful dragon that was ready to pounce upon me, but it opened no way for my escape. I have often wished myself a beast, or a bird—any-thing, rather than a slave. I was wretched and gloomy, beyond my ability to describe. I was too thoughtful to be happy. It was this everlasting thinking which distressed and tormented me; and yet there was no getting rid of the subject of my thoughts. All nature was redolent of it. Once awakened by the silver trump[6] of knowl-edge, my spirit was roused to eternal wakeful-ness. Liberty! the inestimable birthright of every man, had, for me, converted every object into an asserter of this great right. It was heard in every sound, and beheld in every object. It was ever present, to torment me with a sense of my wretched condition. The more beautiful and charming were the smiles of nature, the more horrible and desolate was my condition. I saw nothing without seeing it, and I heard nothing without hearing it. I do not exaggerate, when I say, that it looked from every star, smiled in every calm, breathed in every wind, and moved in every storm.

I have no doubt that my state of mind had something to do with the change in the treat-ment adopted, by my once kind mistress toward me. I can easily believe, that my leaden, down-cast, and discontented look, was very offensive to her. Poor lady! She did not know my trouble, and I dared not tell her. Could I have freely

---

6. *Trump* is a trumpet.

---

made her acquainted with the real state of my mind, and given her the reasons therefor, it might have been well for both of us. Her abuse of me fell upon me like the blows of the false prophet upon his ass; she did not know that an *angel* stood in the way;[7] and—such is the rela-tion of master and slave—I could not tell her. Nature had made us *friends;* slavery made us *ene-mies.* My interests were in a direction opposite to hers, and we both had our private thoughts and plans. She aimed to keep me ignorant; and I resolved to know, although knowledge only increased my discontent. My feelings were not the result of any marked cruelty in the treat-ment I received; they sprung from the consider-ation of my being a slave at all. It was *slavery*—not its mere *incidents*—that I hated. I had been cheated. I saw through the attempt to keep me in ignorance; I saw that slaveholders would have gladly made me believe that they were merely acting under the authority of God, in making a slave of me, and in making slaves of others; and I treated them as robbers and deceivers. The feeding and clothing me well, could not atone for taking my liberty from me. The smiles of my mistress could not remove the deep sorrow that dwelt in my young bosom. Indeed, these, in time, came only to deepen my sorrow. She had changed; and the reader will see that I had changed, too. We were both vic-tims to the same overshadowing evil—*she,* as mistress, *I,* as slave. I will not censure her harshly; she cannot censure me, for she knows I speak but the truth, and have acted in my oppo-sition to slavery, just as she herself would have acted, in a reverse of circumstances.

---

7. Douglass is referring to a biblical tale (Numbers 22:21–35) in which an ass (donkey), despite being beaten by its master, Balaam, cannot obey and move on because its way is blocked by an angel whom Balaam cannot see.

Vocabulary
censure (sen′shər) *v.* to express disapproval of; to find fault with; to blame

---

Writing *Minilesson*

Critical Response Explain to students that Douglass sought to tell his life story and to argue against slavery. Elicit exam-ples from the selection that show each purpose and discuss how well each exam-ple conveys the intended information.

Activity Write this question on the board: How does Douglass use details from his life story to argue against slavery? Direct students to write a paragraph that uses a declarative form of the question as the topic sentence and to use specific examples from the text. **L2**

Additional Resources

📙 *Writer's Choice,* Lesson 5.1

Responding to Literature

Personal Response

How did this narrative affect your attitude toward your own personal freedom?

ANALYZING LITERATURE

RECALL AND INTERPRET

1. How does Mrs. Auld treat Douglass when he first arrives? How does Mrs. Auld's "inexperience" with slavery help Douglass?

2. How and why does Mrs. Auld's behavior toward Douglass change? In your opinion, who is hurt more by the change, Douglass or the Auld family? Support your answer with details from the selection.

3. Who finally agrees to teach Douglass to read and why? Compare these teachers' attitudes toward slavery with Mrs. Auld's attitudes.

4. To whom is Douglass referring and what do you think he means when he says, "Nature had made us *friends;* slavery made us *enemies*"?

EVALUATE AND CONNECT

5. Evaluate the effectiveness of Douglass's use of the **first-person point of view** in conveying his message. (See Literary Terms Handbook, page R12.)

6. How did knowledge help Douglass gain control over his life? Refer to your notes from the Focus Activity on page 329. Do you think that Douglass might agree with the ideas you expressed there? Explain.

7. Douglass blames the system of slavery more than he blames the Aulds for his situation. Do you agree or disagree? Explain, using a chart like the one on this page.

8. Douglass was physically held captive in slavery; yet, his mind and spirit were free. In what ways might a person held in captivity keep his or her mind free? Explain your response.

Literary ELEMENTS

Autobiography

An **autobiography** is the story a person writes about his or her own life. Douglass's autobiography recounts his experiences both during his enslavement and as a free man, but it has another purpose—to provide a persuasive argument against slavery.

1. What do you think is Douglass's main idea or purpose in this particular portion of his autobiography?

2. Do you think that Douglass presents himself as he really was, or might he be presenting a **biased**, or one-sided, view? Support your response.

● See **Literary Terms Handbook**, p. R2.

Blame for Douglass's situation	
the institution of slavery	the Aulds

EXTENDING YOUR RESPONSE

Creative Writing

Mrs. Auld's Journal   Take Mrs. Auld's point of view. Write three journal entries that show how you feel about teaching young Frederick to read. Write the first entry from a time soon after Douglass's arrival in your household; the second, from the day of the confrontation with your husband; the third, from one year later.

Performing

Role-Play   Picture Frederick Douglass meeting Mrs. Auld again later in life, when he is famous and free. In a group, discuss what they might talk about. Then write a dialogue between these two characters and have two group members act out the dialogue for the class.

📖 **Save your work for your portfolio.**

Responding to the Selection

Personal Response

Encourage students to appreciate their freedoms by comparing theirs with those of the young Douglass.

ANALYZING LITERATURE

1. She treats him kindly at first. She teaches him to read.

2. She stops teaching and treats him cruelly. Some may say that Mrs. Auld becomes a less humane person; others, that Douglass suffers by having his education obstructed.

3. Douglass's white playmates agree to teach him to read in exchange for biscuits and out of friendship. They, like Mrs. Auld, are uncomfortable with the idea of slavery. Unlike her, they speak out against it.

4. He refers to Mrs. Auld and himself. As human beings, Mrs. Auld and Douglass are by nature "friends." The institution of slavery has changed this.

5. The first-person point of view conveys the day-to-day realities of slavery and intensifies Douglass's authority.

6. Students may say that Douglass was inspired to oppose slavery.

7. Students who agree may say that the system of slavery forced the Aulds to mistreat Douglass. Those who disagree may say that the Aulds could have chosen not to be slaveholders.

8. Students may suggest captives could be free through reading or prayer.

✔ ASSESSMENT OPTIONS

📁 ***Quick Checks,*** p. 36

📁 ***Selection and Theme Assessment,*** pp. 57–58

📁 ***Performance Assessment,*** p. 31

💾 ***Testmaker***

LITERARY ELEMENTS

1. Slavery is an evil that victimizes the slave and the slaveholder.

2. Douglass reports nothing negative about himself, which might indicate bias.

Additional Resources

📖 ***Literary Elements Transparency 31***

Objectives

- To read and interpret lyrics from African American spirituals
- To define *refrain* and to analyze the refrains in three spirituals
- To investigate and write about the role and appeal of spirituals

Skills

Reading/Thinking: Responding; Analyzing; Inferring
Writing: Poem or Song
Grammar/Language: Simple and Compound Sentences
Listening/Speaking: Brief Talk Using Visual Aid
Collaboration: Literature Groups; Performing a Spiritual

Motivating
→ OPTIONS

Selection Focus Transparency 33: Have students review the transparency and then discuss the question provided.

Focus Activity: As an extension of the Focus Activity, direct partners to agree on a song they both find inspirational. Have them write the lyrics, relying on memory. Partners should then discuss why they found the song inspirational.

Before You Read

Three Spirituals

Who Wrote These Spirituals?

The spirituals featured here came out of the oral tradition of African Americans enslaved in the South before the outbreak of the Civil War. These "sorrow songs," as they were called, were created by anonymous artists and transmitted by word of mouth. As a result, several versions of a spiritual may exist.

African American spirituals combined the tunes and texts of Christian hymns with the rhythms, finger-snapping, clapping, and stamping of traditional African music. Many followed a call-and-response pattern in which a leader sang the verses and was answered by a group of singers.

Enslaved African Americans sang spirituals both in worship and while laboring in the field. Many of the songs have a dual meaning, expressing both religious faith and a hunger for freedom from slavery.

Some spirituals served as encoded messages through which enslaved field workers, forbidden to speak to each other, could communicate practical information about escape. Some typical "code" words included *Egypt*, referring to the South or the state of bondage, and the *Promised Land* or *Heaven*, referring to the North or freedom. The spiritual "Follow the Drinking Gourd," for example, tells people escaping enslavement how to follow the Underground Railroad, a secret network of free blacks and white sympathizers who accompanied and sheltered thousands on the dangerous journey north to freedom.

FOCUS ACTIVITY

Think of a song you find particularly inspiring, such as a patriotic song, a school fight song, or even a popular song from the radio.

DISCUSS Talk with a partner about what makes your song inspirational. Is it the music, the lyrics, an association with a particular time or place, or is it a combination of these elements?

SETTING A PURPOSE Read to enjoy songs that have inspired millions of people.

BACKGROUND

The Biblical Connection

Some enslaved African Americans likened their situation to that of the Jews in Egypt in biblical times. According to the Bible, the Jews were forced into slavery by a pharaoh, or ruler of Egypt. Moses, a leader of the Jews, asked the pharaoh to free his people. Moses explained that if his people were not freed, God would send ten plagues upon the Egyptians. The plagues indeed came and the pharaoh released the Jews. Moses led his people out of Egypt, but the pharaoh changed his mind and sent soldiers after them. The soldiers chased the Jews to the shores of the Red Sea. Then Moses called upon God to part the waters so his people could cross. The sea rolled back for the Jews to pass, but closed in on the Egyptian soldiers. Thus, when the Jews "reached the other shore," they were free people once again.

Gourd instrument made by enslaved African Americans.

336 UNIT 3

RESOURCE MANAGER

Lesson Planning Resource
The *Unit Three Planning Guide* (pp. 16–21) provides additional lesson notes and reduced versions of all print resources.

📁 Other Print Resources
- Active Reading Guide, p. 37
- Reading Workbook
- Grammar and Language Workbook, p. 99
- Grammar and Composition Handbook, Lesson 4.7

- Quick Checks, p. 37
- Selection and Theme Assessment, p. 59
- Performance Assessment, p. 32
- Spanish Summaries, p. 33
- Inclusion Strategies
- English Language Learners Sourcebook

🖥 Transparencies
- Selection Focus 33
- Literary Elements 32
- Grammar and Language 30

Technology
- 🎧 Audio Library
- 💻 Glencoe Literature Web Site
- 💾 Testmaker

Swing Low, Sweet Chariot A

Swing low, sweet chariot,
Coming for to carry me home,
Swing low, sweet chariot,
Coming for to carry me home.

5   I looked over Jordan° and what did I see,
Coming for to carry me home?
A band of angels coming after me,
Coming for to carry me home.

10   If you get there before I do,
Coming for to carry me home,
Tell all my friends I'm coming too;
Coming for to carry me home.

I'm sometimes up, I'm sometimes down,
Coming for to carry me home,
15   But still my soul feels heavenly bound;
Coming for to carry me home.

Swing low, sweet chariot,
Coming for to carry me home,
Swing low, sweet chariot,
20   Coming for to carry me home.

---

5 *Jordan* refers to the Jordan River. In the Book of Exodus in the
Bible, when the Jews were fleeing from slavery in Egypt, they
had to cross the Jordan to reach their Promised Land.

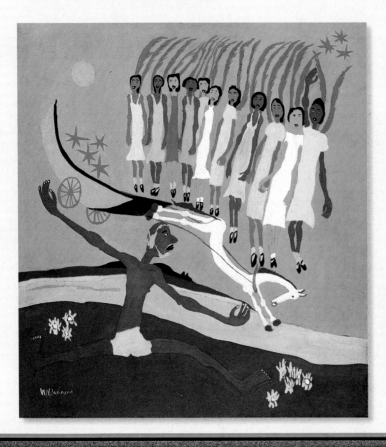

Swing Low, Sweet Chariot,
c. 1939. William H. Johnson. Oil
on board, 28½ x 26½ in. National
Museum of American Art,
Smithsonian Institution,
Washington, DC. Do you think
this painting effectively conveys
the mood of the song? Which
details seem to relate specifically
to lines in the song?

337

Reading the Selection

A Active Reading

EVALUATE Ask why this spiritual held special meaning for enslaved African Americans. Share the following model to illustrate the thinking process involved in evaluating.

Model: The Bible tells how the Jews were held captive in Egypt until Moses led them to freedom. I think Moses and the "children of Israel" are a metaphor for the enslaved African Americans.

VIEWING THE PAINTING

William H. Johnson was a Harlem Renaissance painter who enjoyed a prestigious art education in Paris. He borrowed from European expressionists in a bold attempt to portray the African American experience.

Viewing Response *The mood of the painting is hopeful and expectant, like the song. The painting shows the band of angels, the chariot, the Jordan, and a soul bound for heaven.*

Additional Resources
📁 *Active Reading Guide,* p. 37
🎧 *Audio Library*

Teaching Options

Reading *Minilesson*

Responding to Aesthetic Elements
Initiate a brief discussion with the question, "How are song lyrics the same as poems?"

Activity Have volunteers who have not heard these spirituals sung read them aloud as they would read poems. Then play recordings of the three spirituals. Return to the class discussion, and have students explain which form is more compelling and effective, and why. **L2**

Additional Resources
📁 *Reading Workbook*

B **Literary Elements**

REFRAIN Ask students to identify the refrain and explain how it sums up the meaning of the song. *(The refrain "Let my people go," simply and powerfully expresses the deepest desire of the enslaved African Americans.)*

A Direct Quotation

Moses says, "Let my people go" in the Bible in Exodus 5:1. The people of Israel were held in captivity by the Egyptians. Moses pleads with the pharaoh to release his people in this famous quotation.

C **Active Reading**

VISUALIZE Guide students in visualizing the physical conditions under which this spiritual was sung. Discuss how the spiritual might have comforted people living under these conditions.

D **Critical Thinking**

ANALYZING Douglass wrote of spirituals, "Every tone was a testimony against slavery, and a prayer to God for deliverance from chains." How does this spiritual support what he wrote? *(Its allusion to the freedom demanded by Moses echoes the singer's own desire for freedom. Moses makes it clear that his demand for freedom for his people comes directly from God.)*

Go Down, Moses

B
Go down, Moses,
'Way down in Egypt's land;
Tell ole Pharaoh
Let my people go.

C
5 When Israel was in Egypt's land,
Let my people go;
Oppressed so hard they could not stand,
Let my people go.

D
Thus saith the Lord, bold Moses said,
10 Let my people go;
Let them come out with Egypt's spoil,
Let my people go.

The Lord told Moses what to do,
Let my people go;
15 To lead the children of Israel thro',
Let my people go.

When they had reached the other shore,
Let my people go;
They sang a song of triumph o'er.
20 Let my people go.

Go down, Moses,
'Way down in Egypt's land;
Tell ole Pharaoh
Let my people go.

Harriet Tubman Series No. 11, 1939–40. Jacob Lawrence. Casein tempera on gessoed hardboard, 12 x 17⅞ in. Hampton University Museum, Hampton, VA.

338   UNIT 3

Teaching Options

Grammar and Language *Minilesson*

Simple and Compound Sentences

Explain that a **simple sentence** has one main clause and no subordinate clauses. It can, however, have a compound subject, a compound predicate, or both. A **compound sentence** has two or more main clauses.

Activity Have students write four original sentences conveying their thoughts on slavery using the following patterns:
1. simple sentence with a compound subject
2. simple sentence with a compound subject and a compound predicate
3. compound sentence
4. compound sentence with two main clauses **L2**

Additional Resources

📖 *Grammar and Language Transparency 30*

📕 *Grammar and Language Workbook,* p. 99

📗 *Grammar and Composition Handbook,* Lesson 4.7

📘 *Writer's Choice,* Lesson 13.3

338

Follow the Drinking Gourd

Harriet Tubman Series No. 10, 1939–40. Jacob Lawrence. Casein tempera on gessoed hardboard, 17⅞ x 12 in. Hampton University Museum, Hampton, VA.

E **F** When the sun comes back and the first
    quail calls,
    Follow the drinking gourd,°
For the old man is a-waiting for to carry
    you to freedom
If you follow the drinking gourd.

5   Follow the drinking gourd,
    Follow the drinking gourd,
For the old man is a-waiting for to carry
    you to freedom
If you follow the drinking gourd.

The river bank will make a very good
    road,
10   The dead trees show you the way,

Left foot,° peg foot° traveling on
    Follow the drinking gourd.

The river ends between two hills
    Follow the drinking gourd.
15   There's another river on the other side,
    Follow the drinking gourd.

Where the little river meets the great
    big river,°
    Follow the drinking gourd.
The old man is a-waiting for to carry
    you to freedom,
20   If you follow the drinking gourd.

G

---

2 The *drinking gourd* was the Big Dipper, which points directly to Polaris, the North Star, and the direction of freedom for African Americans escaping from enslavement.

11 One "conductor," or guide, on the Underground Railroad was a man named Peg Leg Joe. This one-legged sailor taught slaves this song and made marks—a *left foot* and a *peg foot*—for them to follow on their journey north.
13–17 The first river is the Tombigbee River in Alabama; the second is the Tennessee River; and the third is the Ohio River.

THE CIVIL WAR AND ITS AFTERMATH 🐿 339

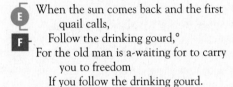

Personal Response

Have student pairs share their responses and see if certain phrases are commonly chosen. If these choices come mainly from the refrains, ask students what they can conclude from that.

ANALYZING LITERATURE

1. The chariot represents escape, either to the North or in death. The "band of angels" might be angels, literally, or Underground Railroad "conductors."

2. The speaker wants to go "home," to freedom or to heaven.

3. The speaker sometimes feels okay and sometimes depressed but always believes he or she will attain freedom, either by escaping slavery or by dying. The soul might feel "heavenly bound" because the speaker has faith.

4. Answers should be supported by facts from history and recent trends in civil rights.

5. Answers should include a comparison of lyrics and the feelings they generate.

6. The speaker asks Moses to demand freedom for the Jews. Its hidden message might be to look for a modern "Moses."

7. Moses is directed by God. Enslaved African Americans believed freedom was what God intended for them.

8. Students may say that the mood of the song is plaintive or demanding. The song is about a people who are unjustly oppressed, but who are supported by their faith in God.

9. Students should identify people who face discrimination or oppression.

10. The reward is "freedom." The drinking gourd represents the Big Dipper, which points North, and symbolizes the path to freedom.

11. Landmarks include a river bank, dead trees, two hills, another river, and the confluence of this river with a third river. These would guide someone traveling in unfamiliar territory.

12. The combination of powerful language and down-to-earth travel directions might have brought to life the help that could be provided by the Underground Railroad.

Responding to Literature

Personal Response

Which phrases or lines from these spirituals do you find most memorable? Share your reactions with a partner.

--- **ANALYZING LITERATURE** ---

Swing Low, Sweet Chariot

RECALL AND INTERPRET

1. To what vehicle does the speaker refer? What might this vehicle represent? Whom or what might the "band of angels" in line 7 represent?

2. Where does the speaker want to go? In your opinion, where or what is this place? Explain.

3. How does the speaker feel in lines 13–16? Why do you think the speaker's "soul feels heavenly bound"?

EVALUATE AND CONNECT

4. In what ways does this spiritual reflect the history of enslaved African Americans? Might the spiritual in any way point to their future? Explain.

5. Think about your discussion for the Focus Activity on page 336. Then explain how the song you picked compares with "Swing Low, Sweet Chariot" both in terms of its words and its effect on you.

Go Down, Moses

RECALL AND INTERPRET

6. In lines 1–8, what is the speaker asking Moses to do? What hidden message might these words have given to enslaved African Americans?

7. According to the song, who is telling Moses what to do? What might these lines say about the hopes and beliefs of many enslaved African Americans?

EVALUATE AND CONNECT

8. Describe the **mood**, or overall feeling or emotion, created by this song. Use specific examples from the song to support your response.

9. Who might have reason to sing this song or another like it today? Why?

Follow the Drinking Gourd

RECALL AND INTERPRET

10. According to the song, what reward would come to a person who followed the drinking gourd? What might the drinking gourd be a **symbol** for (see page R16)?

11. What other landmarks does the song mention? How might these landmarks have been helpful to people escaping enslavement?

EVALUATE AND CONNECT

12. Imagine that you are an enslaved person. Might this song have helped you to build up courage and trust in the Underground Railroad? Explain your answer.

ASSESSMENT OPTIONS

📁 *Quick Checks,* p. 37

📁 *Selection and Theme Assessment,* p. 59

📁 *Performance Assessment,* p. 32

💾 *Testmaker*

Responding to Literature

Personal Response

Which character in this passage did you identify with most strongly? Why?

ANALYZING LITERATURE

RECALL AND INTERPRET

1. Why does Eliza flee her home? What conclusions can you draw about Eliza from the manner in which she left?
2. Who first helps Eliza? What can you infer about his views on slavery? Use specific examples to support your response.
3. Identify the obstacles that Eliza faces on her journey. In your opinion, if she had known the danger she was about to face, would she have left her home? Explain.
4. According to the narrator, what could have happened to Reverend Rankin if he had confessed to helping Eliza? What does Rankin's silence and the behavior of Eliza's first helper suggest about the risks involved in helping fugitives escape?

EVALUATE AND CONNECT

5. Do you detect any **bias**—a mental inclination toward some opinion or position—in this story? Cite specific lines in this account that point to bias, or explain why you think there might be no bias.
6. In *Uncle Tom's Cabin,* Harriet Beecher Stowe gives a melodramatic, or highly emotional, account of Eliza's flight. Describe the **tone** Parker uses to tell the same story. (See Literary Terms Handbook, page R16.)
7. Refer to your list from the Focus Activity on page 349. Would you ever take risks comparable to those taken by Eliza? Explain.
8. In this account, several persons take risks to attain freedom for a stranger and her baby. What degree of risk might you take to protect a family member, a friend, or a stranger? Explain.

Literary ELEMENTS

Foreshadowing

Foreshadowing is a method of increasing suspense by presenting events or characters in such a way as to hint at what is going to happen. Writers often foreshadow what will occur in a story by giving hints or clues. Sometimes these clues are subtle. Sometimes they are ominous and are used to create an aura of **suspense**. For example, when the dogs refuse to follow Eliza onto the ice, you realize that they sense danger. This detail foreshadows Eliza's first fall through the ice, and prompts the reader to continue reading to learn the outcome of the story.

1. What other examples of foreshadowing can you find in the narrative about Eliza?
2. How does foreshadowing build suspense in the story?

● See **Literary Terms Handbook,** p. R7.

EXTENDING YOUR RESPONSE

Interdisciplinary Activity
American History: Routes to Freedom   With a partner, create a map that shows major routes on the Underground Railroad from the South to the North and into Canada. Indicate the place on the Ohio River where Eliza crossed. Share your work with the class.

Creative Writing
My Name Is Eliza   Write this story from Eliza's perspective. Tell about your harrowing river crossing and what kept you going. Explain why you risked your life and that of your baby.

 **Save your work for your portfolio.**

Responding to the Selection

Personal Response

Students should give reasons for their choices.

ANALYZING LITERATURE

1. She fled to prevent her baby from being sold. She is brave, desperate, and devoted to her child.
2. The man in the cabin is the first person to help Eliza. He probably opposes slavery.
3. Obstacles include the slave-chasers, the weather, the river, and the lack of both supplies and a plan. Students may say Eliza would have left anyway to save her baby. Others may say she had second thoughts during the journey and would not have left.
4. Consequences include a fine, jail, and loss of property. Their actions suggest great risks.
5. Despite the objective language and tone, using the points of view of Eliza and those who help her, creates antislavery bias.
6. The tone is suspenseful without being melodramatic.
7. Students' may explain motivation or their physical condition in their answers.
8. The degree of risk probably would vary with the circumstances.

EXTENDING YOUR RESPONSE

Interdisciplinary Activity Have students use encyclopedias and historical atlases to find Underground Railroad routes. **COLLAB. LEARN.**

Creative Writing

Students' stories should
• include Eliza's thoughts.
• be based on Parker's account.
• convey the event's trauma.

✔ ASSESSMENT OPTIONS

📁 ***Quick Checks,*** p. 39
📁 ***Selection and Theme Assessment,*** pp. 61–62
📁 ***Performance Assessment,*** p. 34
💾 ***Testmaker***

LITERARY ELEMENTS

1. Examples include the statement that Eliza leaves with no plan or supplies in midwinter, that the helpful man in the cabin cautions her not to go, and that she hesitates after first stepping onto the ice.
2. Foreshadowing suggests that certain events are likely to take place but that their outcome is unknown.

Additional Resources
⚑ ***Literary Elements Transparency 34***

Technology Skills

Objectives

- To understand the broad range of research resources available on the Internet
- To use Internet resources for assistance with grammar, usage, and mechanics errors
- To evaluate the usefulness of specific Web sites

Teaching Strategies

If you are not familiar with National Writing Centers Association resources, you may visit its Internet site and browse its links before students begin this activity. Use the information you discover to tailor instruction to the Internet experience and remedial needs of individual students.

Brainstorm with students to determine how adept they are at locating primary resource sites and using links to connect with sites containing related information and assistance.

Activities

Suggest students use the following tips to complete this activity:

- Organize questions under the categories *Grammar*, *Usage*, and *Mechanics*. This can save time moving between links.
- Copy the URL completely and correctly to easily access the site again.

Teaching Options

Internet: Writing Resources on the Web

Unless you have a photographic memory, you might find it difficult to recall the countless rules of grammar and mechanics. As you compose, you may ask yourself:

- Do I use commas or semicolons to separate items in a list?
- Is it really wrong to end a sentence with a preposition?
- When do I use a colon?
- How can I tell if this is a sentence fragment?
- Is this a run-on sentence?

The answers to these questions and more are available on the World Wide Web.

Find Your Problems

Look back at papers you have written that were marked and returned to you. Based on your teacher's comments, record the major grammar, usage, and mechanics items that gave you trouble. To supplement your list, or, in the unlikely event that you don't have a single item of your own to list, refer to the following items:

Do you get confused between the words in these pairs?		
accept / except	complement / compliment	it's / its
affect / effect	confident / confidante	lay / lie
allusion / illusion	counsel / council	personal / personnel
a lot / allot	desert / dessert	principal / principle
already / all ready	every day / everyday	stationary / stationery
altogether / all together	farther / further	their / there / they're
beside / besides	fewer / less	whose / who's
capital / capitol	immigrate / emigrate	your / you're
Can you explain the difference between each of the following pairs?		
• an adjective and an adverb		
• a relative pronoun and a demonstrative pronoun		
• a transitive verb and an intransitive verb		
• a compound sentence and a complex sentence		
• a direct object and an indirect object		
Do you always know when and how to use each kind of punctuation?				

period	comma	colon	semicolon	quotation marks
apostrophe	hyphen	dash	italics	parentheses

 INCLUSION STRATEGIES

MEETING INDIVIDUAL NEEDS

interNET CONNECTION

On-line Dictionaries Explain that students can locate Internet sites devoted to the definitions of computer and technical Internet terms. Have students use a search engine and enter keywords such as *computer terms*, *Internet language*, or *Webopaedia*.

Less-Proficient Readers The specialized vocabulary and unusual abbreviations associated with the Internet may challenge less-proficient readers. The following activity may aid their comprehension.

Activity Have students create notebooks in which they keep an alphabetical list of specialized vocabulary and abbreviations. Have partners work together to find and write a definition for each entry. Suggest that they also collaborate on a definition in their own words that can be entered alongside the formal definition. **L1**

Activities

After students complete the Writing Resources activity, divide the class into small, heterogeneous groups. Answer any questions students have about the assignment.

To ensure consistency in rating systems, brainstorm with students to reach consensus on criteria to be included in the evaluation. Determine requirements for each of the ratings in the evaluation system.

Students' reference handbooks should:
- list several diverse Web sites that offer assistance to writers.
- describe pertinent strengths and weaknesses of each site.
- accurately and consistently rate each site.

Students who volunteer to assist in the middle school may receive extra credit.

From the list you compiled, and including at least one item from each group in the boxed lists, write ten questions or problems about grammar, usage, and mechanics you'd like answered. You will then find the answers to your questions.

1. Use a search engine to locate the resources listed below. Write their URLs in your notebook for future reference. A good place to begin your search is at the National Writing Centers Association site: http://departments.colgate.edu/diw/NWCA.html.
   - an on-line writing lab (OWL)
   - a grammar hotline
   - Modern Language Association (MLA) guidelines for citing electronic sources
   - an on-line dictionary
   - an on-line thesaurus

2. On a sheet of paper, or on your word processor, write your ten questions, their answers, and the URLs of the Web sites where you found the information.

ACTIVITIES

1. With a partner or a small group, create a reference handbook of Web sites that offer assistance to writers. Describe the features of each site and rate it using a star system.
   - ★★★★ Super Site
   - ★★★ Good Site
   - ★★ Fair Site
   - ★ Don't Bother

2. Volunteer to help students in a nearby middle school use the Internet to improve their writing skills.

TechnoTalk

Internet Terms Point out that common Internet terms have become part of our technology language. A *search engine* is a program that searches the Internet for sites that match or may contain information related to the keyword(s) you have entered. A *URL* (Universal Resource Locator) is the Web address of a particular site. Each site usually contains *http://www* in its address. *HTTP* is short for hypertext transfer protocol, or the way in which the computer language is transferred correctly across the Web. *WWW* means World Wide Web.

INTERDISCIPLINARY CONNECTION

Economics Point out that the Internet began as a consortium of universities. Their goal was to advance research by sharing information and resources. Entrepreneurs quickly saw the potential for creating private companies to provide information services to individuals. In a few short years, businesses operating on the Internet have become a major force in the national economy.

Activity Students might enjoy researching Internet companies that have become highly attractive to investors in the stock market. Instruct them to use library and magazine resources to identify and report on one such company. Each report should include the year in which the company began operations, a summary of its services, and information on the current value of its stock, as well as projections by financial experts on its future. **L3**

Surfing the Net Remind students that they also can use a search engine and enter keywords *Modern Language Association guidelines*.

Objectives

- To read a firsthand account of events surrounding the start of the Civil War
- To read excerpts from a journal and to identify a journal's salient characteristics
- To write a one-act play based on a journal

Skills

Reading/Thinking: Inferring; Questioning; Distinguishing Fact and Opinion
Writing: One-Act Play
Grammar/Language: Sentence Fragments
Collaboration: Literature Groups

Motivating
→ OPTIONS

Selection Focus Transparency 36: Have students view the transparency and then discuss the question.

Focus Activity: As an extension of the Focus Activity, explore how students would feel about living through a landmark historical event.

FINE ART
TRANSPARENCY 7

You might want to use *Fine Art Transparency 7* to discuss the lives of families like Chesnut's in the mid-nineteenth century.

Before You Read

from Mary Chesnut's Civil War

Meet Mary Chesnut

"If the only true history concerns itself not so much with what statesmen and generals did at a given time as with what men and women were, then this diary is a masterpiece of history in the highest and fullest sense."

—Ben Ames Williams

Mary Boykin Chesnut's life was one of opposites. Before the Civil War, she experienced the kind of luxury that accompanied growing up on a large South Carolina plantation. After the war, she struggled to make ends meet. While she abhorred slavery, her family owned hundreds of enslaved people and her father was a proslavery senator and governor.

At seventeen she married James Chesnut Jr., a lawyer from a large, neighboring plantation. When James was elected to the Senate in 1858, the Chesnuts moved to Washington, where they entertained politicians who would become the leading figures of the Confederacy. When not charming friends with her sharp wit and keen intellect, Chesnut immersed herself in reading, enjoying English and French novels and history books above all.

When the war broke out, Chesnut remained loyal to the South despite her opposition to slavery. She visited hospitals, rejoiced with her friends at Confederate victories, and cried with them over Confederate defeats. Through it all, she lamented the cruelties and evils of war in detailed journals that recorded what people of the time believed, felt, and said. Hers is an insider's view of the real war as it ripped through the South.

Mary Chesnut was born in 1823 and died in 1886.

FOCUS ACTIVITY

Picture yourself and your friends at a time of crisis–perhaps during a flood, an ice storm, a hurricane, an earthquake, or a war.

JOURNAL Choose one of the crisis situations listed above. Visualize yourself in the middle of it. What part might you play? How might other people behave? What might you talk about? Write your ideas in your journal.

SETTING A PURPOSE Read to find out Mary Chesnut's thoughts and observations during a crisis.

BACKGROUND

The Time and Place

By early 1861, South Carolina had seceded from the Union and claimed ownership of all federal property within the state. Only Fort Sumter remained under federal control. Confederate authorities demanded the removal of U.S. troops from Fort Sumter. President Lincoln refused their request, and on April 12, 1861, Confederate forces opened fire on the fort.

VOCABULARY PREVIEW

allusion (ə lōō′ zhən) *n.* an indirect or casual reference; an incidental mention; p. 358
capitulate (kə pich′ ə lāt′) *v.* to surrender or yield; to give up; p. 358
audaciously (ô dā′ shəs lē) *adv.* boldly; arrogantly; p. 358

prostrate (pros′ strāt) *adj.* bowing or kneeling down in humility, adoration, or submission; p. 359
delusion (di lōō′ zhən) *n.* a false impression or belief; p. 359
pervade (pər vād′) *v.* to spread through every part; p. 360

RESOURCE MANAGER

Lesson Planning Resource
The ***Unit Three Planning Guide*** (pp. 34–41) provides additional lesson notes and reduced versions of all print resources.

📁 **Other Print Resources**
- Active Reading Guide, p. 40
- Vocabulary Practice, p. 27
- Reading Workbook, pp. 43–44
- Grammar and Language Workbook, p. 111

- Grammar and Composition Handbook, Lesson 4.9
- Quick Checks, p. 40
- Selection and Theme Assessment, pp. 63–64
- Performance Assessment, p. 35
- Spanish Summaries, p. 36
- Spanish Translations
- Inclusion Strategies
- English Language Learners Sourcebook

📖 **Transparencies**
- Selection Focus 36
- Fine Art 7
- Literary Elements 35
- Grammar and Language 33

Technology
🎧 Audio Library
🎧 Spanish Audio Library
💻 Glencoe Literature Web Site
💾 Testmaker

Before You Read

Shiloh

Meet Herman Melville

"A whale ship was my Yale College and my Harvard."
—*Melville*

Herman Melville was a writer ahead of his time—and he knew it. During his lifetime, Melville's readers and critics never appreciated his greatest and most serious works. Years later, however, a new generation of readers recognized Melville as one of America's finest writers—a writer who had spoken for them before their time.

Melville's youthful experiences probably contributed to the dark vision of humankind reflected in his writings. Though Melville was born into a prominent New York family, his father went bankrupt, suffered a nervous breakdown, and died when Melville was twelve. Melville had to discontinue much of his schooling to help support his family.

Melville's real adventures began when, at the age of twenty-one, he sailed on a whaling ship bound for the South Pacific. He abandoned ship in the Marquesas Islands and lived for a month with the supposedly cannibalistic Typee people, who, in fact, turned out to be gentle and gracious.

After numerous voyages, Melville returned to New York, where he wrote adventure novels inspired by his seagoing experiences. He quickly became one of the country's most celebrated writers. Melville then began to write his greatest work, *Moby-Dick* (1851), a complex story of the hunt for a fierce white whale.

Ironically, the same critics who had loved Melville's adventure tales panned his serious work; worse yet, the public ignored it. A few years later, Melville abandoned novel writing for poetry and, for financial reasons, took a job as a customs inspector. He composed "Shiloh" and the other poems contained in the book *Battle-Pieces and Aspects of the War* (1866) in response to the horrific sights he encountered visiting a cousin in the Union army.

Herman Melville was born in 1819 and died in 1891.

FOCUS ACTIVITY

Think about a time when you visited or saw pictures of a cemetery, a former battlefield, or a monument. What emotions did you experience?

QUICKWRITE Jot down some reactions you had when visiting or viewing a place that honors the dead.

SETTING A PURPOSE Read to discover one speaker's reactions to visiting a Civil War battlefield.

BACKGROUND

The Time and Place
The Battle of Shiloh, named after a church on the battlefield, was fought in Pittsburg Landing, Tennessee, on April 6 and 7, 1862. The Union Army suffered 13,000 casualties (dead, wounded, missing, or captured), and the smaller Confederate contingent had 10,700 casualties.

A Poetic Tribute
Melville subtitled this poem a **requiem.** In the Roman Catholic Church, a requiem is a mass, or ceremony, held for a deceased person in which people pray for the person's soul. Many composers, including Wolfgang Mozart and Giuseppe Verdi, have written compositions for requiem masses. Writers, too, have used the concept in poetic tributes to the dead.

THE CIVIL WAR AND ITS AFTERMATH 381

A Active Reading

INTERPRET What natural elements does Melville use? *(swallows, clouds, forest-field, rain, night, morning, eve)* What do they contribute to the poem's meaning? *(melancholy, peace)*

B Literary Elements

POEM: *Requiem* A **requiem** is a song, poem, or service that accompanies the laying to rest of the dead. Why might Melville have focused on the dead soldiers? *(He may have wanted to emphasize the true tragedy of war and not glorify a bloody battle.)*

C Literary Elements

ALLITERATION Have students review **alliteration.** Then ask them to identify several examples of alliteration in the poem. *(s sound in lines 1–2 and 18–19; f sound in lines 3–5; p sound in lines 6–7; l sound in line 10; f and c sounds in lines 14–15.)*

Additional Resources
📁 *Active Reading Guide,* p. 43
🎧 *Audio Library*

Shiloh

Herman Melville

Shiloh National Battlefield, Tennessee.

A Requiem
(April 1862)

Skimming lightly, wheeling° still,
    The swallows fly low
Over the field in clouded days,
    The forest-field of Shiloh—
5 Over the field where April rain
    Solaced° the parched° ones stretched
      in pain
Through the pause of night
That followed the Sunday fight
    Around the church of Shiloh—

10 The church so lone, the log-built one,
    That echoed to many a parting groan
      And natural prayer
    Of dying foemen° mingled there—
Foemen at morn, but friends at eve—
15   Fame or country least their care:
    (What like a bullet can undeceive!)
      But now they lie low,
    While over them the swallows skim,
      And all is hushed at Shiloh.

---

1 *Wheeling* means "moving in a circle."
6 *Solaced* means "comforted" or "soothed." *Parched* means "dried" or "thirsty."

13 *Foemen* are opponents, or enemies, in a war.

Writing Minilesson

Poetry and Pain Remind students that poetry often grows out of painful experiences which are transformed by time and the poet's skill into something beautiful.

Activity Ask students to recall a painful experience from their past, think about the emotional impact of the experience, and, in their journals, write a short poem or prose paragraph in which they try to transform or give meaning to the experience.

Additional Resources
📙 *Writer's Choice,* Lesson 1.1

Responding to Literature

Personal Response

Describe your emotions after you finished reading the poem. Were they similar to those you described for the Focus Activity on page 381?

—— ANALYZING LITERATURE ——

RECALL AND INTERPRET

1. Describe the movements of the swallows in lines 1–4. What does this sight suggest to you about the speaker's reaction to the battlefield?
2. What does the rain do for the wounded soldier? What might this suggest about the speaker's view of the natural world and human pain?
3. According to lines 13–16, what happens between Union and Confederate soldiers following the battle? What accounts for the change between them? What attitude toward war do you think the speaker expresses in this poem?
4. What might the speaker mean by "What like a bullet can undeceive!"?

EVALUATE AND CONNECT

5. List the pairs of words Melville uses to create **end rhyme** (see page R13) with *Shiloh*. What **mood** do these rhymes create?
6. Why do you think Melville focuses on the church at Shiloh? What might the church symbolize? Explain.
7. If you had been a family member or friend of a soldier killed at Shiloh, how might you have responded to this poem? Explain your answer.
8. Theme Connections   If those responsible for the Civil War had experienced the insight offered by Melville in "Shiloh," do you think the war would have been fought? Explain.

—— EXTENDING YOUR RESPONSE ——

Creative Writing

Capture the Feeling   Melville wrote "Shiloh" after visiting the scene of a bloody battle. Choose a place that is often crowded with people, such as a football stadium or a school auditorium. Then write either a paragraph or a poem describing the way it looks on the day after a major event. Try to convey your feelings about what happened and to capture echoes or memories of the event. Share your work with the class.

Listening and Speaking

The Sounds of Shiloh   How would you present the poem "Shiloh" on the radio? Would you emphasize the poem's **rhyme** and **alliteration?** Would you add sound effects? How and where would you vary the volume and pitch of your voice? Plan, practice, and audiotape a dramatic reading of "Shiloh" and then play the tape for the class.

📖 **Save your work for your portfolio.**

Responding to the Selection

Personal Response

Encourage students to appreciate the way a poem can evoke emotional responses in a reader.

—— ANALYZING LITERATURE ——

1. The swallows fly in low circles. The sight of the battlefield may have had a dizzying effect on the speaker.
2. The rain comforted him. The speaker feels the gentleness of nature can help alleviate human suffering.
3. They become friends in their dying because they are no longer enemies but human beings suffering the same pain. The poem focuses on the tragedy of a war that makes enemies out of those who should be allies.
4. Answers should point out that bullets erase all pretense or motivation. The reality of war is disillusioning.
5. Melville rhymes Shiloh with "fly low" and "lie low." The mood is somber.
6. It may symbolize death or peace. Students should give explanations.
7. Students may express gratitude that the poet is honoring the dead or dismay at the tragedy of the lost lives.
8. There can be many ways to justify either position. Answers should refer to the poem.

✔ ASSESSMENT OPTIONS

📁 ***Quick Checks,*** p. 43
📁 ***Selection and Theme Assessment,*** pp. 69–70
📁 ***Performance Assessment,*** p. 38
💾 ***Testmaker***

LITERARY ELEMENTS

1. Students may say the soft sound of the *f* enhances the somber and soft qualities of the poem.
2. Some may say the hard sound of the *p* reinforces the harsh image. To others it may echo falling rain.

Additional Resources

✍ ***Literary Elements Transparency 38***

Objectives

- To analyze a famous piece of Civil War literature
- To identify examples of parallelism and explain its value
- To write an analysis of the use of antithesis

Skills

Writing: Letter
Vocabulary: Analogies
Collaboration: Literature Groups

Motivating

→ OPTIONS

Literature Launchers:
"Heeding the Call of Duty: A Soldier's Letter"

Videodisc Side A, Segment 8

Also available in VHS.

Selection Focus Transparency 40: Have students view the transparency and then discuss the question provided.

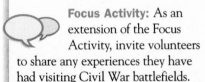

Focus Activity: As an extension of the Focus Activity, invite volunteers to share any experiences they have had visiting Civil War battlefields.

 # Before You Read

The Gettysburg Address

Meet Abraham Lincoln

❝With malice toward none, with charity for all . . . let us strive on to finish the work we are in, to bind up the nation's wounds, to care for him who shall have borne the battle, and for his widow and his orphan, to do all which may achieve and cherish a just and lasting peace among ourselves, and with all nations.❞

—*Lincoln*

One of the United States' greatest presidents, Abraham Lincoln led the country through the Civil War, helping to preserve the Union and to end slavery. Lincoln and the United States showed the world that democracy can be a durable form of government.

For many, Lincoln's journey from a Kentucky log cabin to the White House symbolizes American opportunity. Born in Hardin County, Kentucky, Lincoln grew up mainly on frontier farms in Indiana, where he received little formal education. He read every book he could find, and, following a move to New Salem, Illinois, studied the law. At twenty-five, Lincoln was elected to the Illinois state legislature, marking the beginning of an astounding political career that led to his election as president in 1860.

A man who had once described military glory as "that attractive rainbow that rises in showers of blood—that serpent's eye that charms to destroy" became a great war leader only because it was necessary to preserve the Union. Lincoln believed that a Confederate victory would most likely have resulted in at least two separate nations. That, he felt, would have marked the failure of democracy.

Abraham Lincoln was born in 1809 and died from an assassin's bullet in 1865.

FOCUS ACTIVITY

What do you know about President Abraham Lincoln? What kind of person was he? What were his accomplishments as president?

JOURNAL Write for a few minutes in your journal to explore your own impression of Lincoln.

SETTING A PURPOSE Read to find out Lincoln's thoughts when he visits the site of a major Civil War battle.

BACKGROUND

The Time and Place

On November 19, 1863, a solemn group of people gathered on the battlefield at Gettysburg, Pennsylvania, to dedicate a cemetery to the soldiers killed there. Edward Everett, a highly respected orator and politician, spoke before Lincoln—for two hours. Lincoln then spoke for just two minutes. Afterward, the press all but ignored Lincoln's speech. Even Lincoln regarded it as a "flat failure." Everett, however, said, "I should be glad if I could flatter myself that I came as near to the central idea of the occasion, in two hours as you did in two minutes."

VOCABULARY PREVIEW

score (skôr) *n.* a group of twenty items; p. 385
consecrate (kon′sə krāt′) *v.* to set apart as sacred; to make or declare holy; p. 385
hallow (hal′ō) *v.* to make or select as holy; to regard or honor as sacred; p. 385
perish (per′ish) *v.* to pass from existence; to disappear; p. 385

RESOURCE MANAGER

Lesson Planning Resource
The *Unit Three Planning Guide* (pp. 60–64) provides additional lesson notes and reduced versions of all print resources.

📁 **Other Print Resources**
- Active Reading Guide, p. 44
- Vocabulary Practice, p. 30
- Quick Checks, p. 44
- Selection and Theme Assessment, pp. 71–72

- Performance Assessment, p. 39
- Spanish Summaries, p. 40
- Inclusion Strategies
- English Language Learners Sourcebook

 Transparencies
- Selection Focus 40
- Literary Elements 39

Technology
 Literature Launchers
 Audio Library
 Spanish Audio Library
💻 Glencoe Literature Web Site
💾 Testmaker

Transparencies	Technology Resources
Selection Focus Transparency 42 Grammar and Language Transparencies 35–36 Fine Art Transparency 6	Literature Launchers Audio Library Testmaker Web Site: *lit.glencoe.com*
Selection Focus Transparency 43 Literary Elements Transparency 41	Audio Library Testmaker Web Site: *lit.glencoe.com*
Selection Focus Transparency 44	Audio Library Testmaker Web Site: *lit.glencoe.com*
Selection Focus Transparency 45 Grammar and Language Transparencies 37–38 Literary Elements Transparency 42 Fine Art Transparency 21	Literature Launchers Audio Library Testmaker Web Site: *lit.glencoe.com*

Theme RESOURCES

- Listening and Speaking Activities (pp. 9–10)
- Viewing and Representing Activities (pp. 15–16)
- Critical Thinking Skills (pp. 14–16)
- Media Connections Activities (pp. 9–10)
- Interdisciplinary Activities (pp. 10–11)

See also these additional planning resources:
- English Language Learners Sourcebook
- Inclusion Strategies Sourcebook
- Literature Groups Sourcebook

PRESENTATION Plus!

Use Glencoe's **Presentation Plus!** This multimedia teaching tool lets you present dynamic lessons that will engage your students. Using Microsoft Powerpoint,® you can customize the presentations to create your own personalized lessons.

Literature FOCUS

Poetry

Objectives

- To identify and understand the basic elements of a poem
- To learn how to analyze a poem

Teaching Strategies

Explain that recognizing the elements of a poem and their interactions are important tools for analyzing a poem.

Cultural Sensitivity

Be aware that imagery and its associations may differ from culture to culture. In many Latin American cultures, for example, purple—not black—is the color associated with mourning.

Speaker

Remind students that the poet creates a speaker in a poem much as a writer of fiction creates a character. A first-person speaker is not necessarily the author. It is, therefore, important to identify the speaker.

Rhythm

Read aloud a stanza of "The Raven," emphasizing Poe's use of rhythm.

Rhyme

Invite students to think about why readers, and particularly young readers, like poems that **rhyme**. (The sound of rhyming words can be a pleasurable experience for the ears.)

Teaching Options

Literature FOCUS

Poetry

Poetry is a type of literature that shares intense experiences or unique insights through the imaginative use of language. Poets rely on the **form** of their writing to convey meaning, using **lines** and **stanzas** rather than sentences and paragraphs as the basic units of composition. Understanding these and other basic elements of poetry will help you analyze the poems you read.

ELEMENTS OF POETRY   MODELS

Speaker

Every poem has a **speaker,** or voice, that talks to the reader. Like a narrator in prose, the speaker is not necessarily the author. The speaker can be a fictional person, an animal, or even a thing.

> The speaker in "The Raven" is a man who has just lost his beloved Lenore.

Rhythm

Rhythm is the pattern of sound created by the arrangement of stressed and unstressed syllables in a line. Rhythm can be regular or irregular. **Meter** is a regular pattern of stressed and unstressed syllables that sets the overall rhythm of certain poems. The basic unit of meter is the **foot,** which typically is made up of at least one stressed and one unstressed syllable. Stressed syllables are marked with (´) and unstressed syllables with (˘).

> For the ráre and rádiant máiden whóm the ángels náme Lenóre—
> *from "The Raven" by Edgar Allan Poe*

Rhyme

Rhyme is the repetition of similar sounds in words that appear close to each other in a poem.

- **Internal rhyme** occurs within a line of poetry.
- **End rhyme** occurs at the ends of lines.
- **Slant rhyme** refers to words that almost rhyme, but not quite.
- **Rhyme scheme,** the pattern of rhyme formed by end rhyme, is identified by assigning a different letter of the alphabet to each new rhyme.

> Judge Tenderly—of Me   internal rhyme
> *from "This is my letter to the World"*
> *by Emily Dickinson*

> How statue-like I see thee stand,   end rhyme
> The agate lamp within thy hand!
> *from "To Helen" by Edgar Allan Poe*

> Who took the Flag today   slant rhyme
> Can tell the definition
> So clear of Victory
> *from "Success is counted sweetest" by Emily Dickinson*

MEETING INDIVIDUAL NEEDS — ENGLISH LANGUAGE LEARNERS

Figurative Language Understanding the concept of figurative language can be difficult for English language learners. Tell students that they are using figurative language when they say "slow as molasses," "as cold as ice," or "as big as a house," as well as other clichés and idioms.

Activity Challenge students to record in a notebook all of the figurative language they use or hear in normal conversation for one week.

Additional Resources
📁 *English Language Learners Sourcebook*

Other Sound Devices

Sound devices contribute to the musical nature of a poem and help emphasize certain words.

- **Alliteration** is the repetition of sounds, most often consonant sounds, at the beginning of words.
- **Assonance** is the repetition of vowel sounds.
- **Consonance** is the repetition of consonant sounds within words or at the ends of words.
- **Onomatopoeia** is the use of a word or phrase that imitates or suggests the sound it describes.

> While I nodded, nearly napping — alliteration
>
> And the Raven, never flitting, still is sitting, *still* is sitting — assonance
>
> Some late visitor entreating entrance at my chamber door. — consonance
>
> tapping, rapping — onomatopoeia
> *from "The Raven"*

Imagery

Imagery is descriptive language that evokes an emotional response and appeals to the senses—sight, sound, touch, taste, or smell. Some images appeal to more than one sense at the same time.

> And the silken, sad, uncertain rustling of each purple curtain — (appeals to the senses of touch, sound, and sight)
> *from "The Raven"*

Figurative Language

Figurative language is language that is used for descriptive effect and is not meant to be read literally. Usually, figurative language expresses meaning beyond the literal level.

- A **simile** is a figure of speech that uses words such as *like* or *as* to compare seemingly unlike things.
- A **metaphor** compares or equates seemingly unlike things by stating that one thing *is* another. Metaphors do not use *like* or *as*.
- A **symbol** is a person, place, or object that has meaning in itself and also stands for something other than itself. Poets often use symbols to suggest something without actually stating it.
- **Personification** is a figure of speech in which an animal, an object, or an idea is given human characteristics.

> Helen, thy beauty is to me Like those Nicean barks of yore — simile
> *from "To Helen"*
>
> [the grass] is the handkerchief of the Lord, — metaphor
> *from Song of Myself by Walt Whitman*
>
> The agate lamp in "To Helen" is a classic symbol of immortality
>
> Quoth the Raven "Nevermore." — personification
> *from "The Raven"*

Other Sound Devices

Ask students to think of words that imitate the sound of what they describe. *(pop, hush, crackle, whoosh, crunch)*

Imagery and Figurative Language

To help students understand the effects of imagery, have them describe a favorite food, appealing to their listeners' sense of sight, sound, touch, taste, and smell. To help students understand figurative language, have them employ first a simile and then a metaphor to describe a prominent object in the classroom. Discuss how imagery and figurative language affect us as readers. *(Some students may answer that imagery and figurative language allow readers to have a clearer idea of the author's thoughts.)*

MEETING INDIVIDUAL NEEDS — MULTIPLE LEARNING STYLES

Musical Poets use rhythm to emphasize an idea, to create a mood, and to bring out the musical quality of language. To extend the study of rhythm, provide students with examples of iambic, trochaic, anapestic, dactylic, and spondaic lines of poetry. (See the Literary Terms Handbook.)

Activity Select students with musical ability to demonstrate the rhythm pattern, using drumsticks or pencils on a desktop. Then have other students read the lines aloud, emphasizing the rhythm. **L2**

MEDIA
Connection

Objective
- To read a newspaper article and understand how journalists present information

Literature ———— LINK

Whitman's Poetry This newspaper article connects to the poetry of Walt Whitman and particularly to his Civil War poems (pages 406–407). Ask students to think about how drafts of Whitman's poetry would be of interest to scholars. Explore these questions.
- What might the documents show?
- What differences might occur between Whitman's actual notebook and a copy of the poems reprinted here?

Respond
1. The notebooks can give insight into the author's work and life. Documents by a famous author are also attractive to collectors.
2. Students may want to know details about the theft and where the remaining notebooks are.

Additional Resources
📁 *Media Connections*, p. 9

Teaching Options

interNET CONNECTION

Walt Whitman For more about Walt Whitman's notebooks, students can see the *Library of Congress Learning Page* and look in the *American Memory Collection*.

MEDIA
Connection

Newspaper Article
Walt Whitman was truly a new American voice during the 1800s. He remained a significant figure throughout the 1900s, as shown by this story of thievery and an FBI investigation.

Stolen Whitman Papers Surface After 50 Years

by David Streitfeld and Elizabeth Kastor—Washington Post, February 18, 1995

Four long-lost notebooks by Walt Whitman, stolen from the Library of Congress a half-century ago, have been recovered, Sotheby's auction house said yesterday. Found by a man among his late father's papers, the notebooks will be returned to the library.

"This is definitely the most important literary material we could have hoped to recover of anything known in American literature," said David Wigdor, assistant chief of the library's manuscript division.

Six Whitman notebooks are still missing. The 10 stolen volumes were part of a total of 24 donated to the library in 1920 by Thomas B. Harned.

The man who brought the notebooks to Sotheby's in New York has chosen to remain anonymous. He told the auction house that his father had received the material as a gift about 30 years ago. The FBI, which investigated the case in the '40s, is once again pursuing it, according to the Library of Congress.

If the notebooks were not stolen material, they would have brought a presale estimate of $350,000 to $500,000, said Selby Kiffer, a vice president in Sotheby's books and manuscripts department.

The man who approached Sotheby's with the documents was "stunned" when he was told what he had, Kiffer said. "When he realized that he wouldn't be selling them he was stunned and I think slightly depressed, as I think anyone would be. On the other hand, he was incredibly cooperative. . . . He feels he has done his part, and his role is ended." No money is changing hands in the return of the papers.

The rediscovered notebooks include essays on perception and the human senses, names and addresses of friends, and drafts of Civil War poems. Whitman also kept notes about some of the wounded soldiers he tended in Washington [D.C.] in 1862. "bed 15—wants an orange . . . bed 59 wants some liquorice . . . 27 wants some figs and a book," he wrote. Next to some of these jottings were crosses, suggesting the nameless subjects had died.

Respond
1. Why, in your opinion, would the notebooks of a nineteenth-century poet be so valuable?
2. What more would you like to know about this story? Why?

Reading *Minilesson*

Previewing Previewing a text prepares students for what they are about to read. For a newspaper article, students should pay particular attention to headlines and dates for clues to the article's content.

Activity Show students sample headlines from the day's newspaper and have them predict what the articles that follow are likely to describe. **L2**

Additional Resources
📁 *Reading Workbook*

Before You Read

Whitman's Poetry

Meet Walt Whitman

As a young man, Walt Whitman loved to wander through the streets of Manhattan. As he walked, he recorded in a notebook his impressions of the city's sights, sounds, and intriguing cast of characters. Using these notes, Whitman created a revolutionary kind of poetry that celebrated the democratic spirit of his native land.

Whitman lived almost his entire life in Long Island, Manhattan, and Brooklyn, New York. A great believer in gathering a wide range of experiences, he worked as a schoolteacher, office boy, journalist, editor, printer, house builder, and nurse. He also traveled down the Mississippi River, soaking up the voices and sights of America.

In 1854, when Whitman was in his mid-thirties, he began to devote more of his energy to writing poetry. By this time he had moved back in with his parents in Brooklyn. "Walt," his mother later said, "had no business [during this period] but going out and coming in to eat, drink, write, and sleep." Little did she know that her son was at that time composing what would be one of the greatest books in American literature—*Leaves of Grass*.

In long, unmetered lines called free verse, Whitman celebrated the diversity, energy, and turbulence of nineteenth-century American life. No subject was too commonplace for his attention: not the mechanic or the prisoner, or the lowly blade of grass. Many people were shocked by the poems' unconventional style and by their content. One poet, John Greenleaf Whittier, was even said to have thrown his copy into the fire. Ralph Waldo Emerson, on the other hand, wrote to Whitman: "I greet you at the beginning of a great career."

Through the years, Whitman revised, rearranged, and added new poems to *Leaves of Grass*, publishing a total of nine editions. He imagined the work as one long poem that expressed his all-embracing view of the world. Despite the acclaim from Emerson and others, Whitman had to publish the first five editions of the work at his own expense and lived all his life close to poverty. Today, the 383 poems included in the final edition of *Leaves of Grass* (1892) are read and celebrated throughout the world for capturing the colorful speech and brash, optimistic spirit of a vital young nation.

❝You cannot really understand America without Walt Whitman, without *Leaves of Grass*.❞

—*Mary Smith Whitall Costelloe*

❝I think of art as something to serve the people—the mass: when it fails to do that it's false to its promises.❞

❝The United States themselves are essentially the greatest poem.❞

—*Whitman*

Walt Whitman was born in 1819 and died in 1892.

THE CIVIL WAR AND ITS AFTERMATH 401

Objectives

- To read and analyze poetry focusing on the theme of "new voices" in American literature
- To write a prose version of "A Sight in Camp in the Daybreak Gray and Dim"

Skills

Reading/Thinking: Paraphrasing
Writing: Interview Questions and Possible Answers; Short Story
Grammar/Language: Sentence Fragments; Run-on Sentences

More About Walt Whitman

Whitman published *Leaves of Grass* in July 1855 and began immediately to promote it. He sent copies of his book to famous writers such as Emerson and even undertook to write anonymous reviews of his own book. At one point, he went so far as to pass along Emerson's flattering review of *Leaves of Grass* to a newspaper, hoping to bring attention to his work.

FINE ART
TRANSPARENCY 6

You may want to use *Fine Art Transparency 6* to discuss ways to celebrate the spirit and energy of American workers.

RESOURCE MANAGER

Lesson Planning Resource
The *Unit Three Planning Guide* (pp. 76–82) provides additional lesson notes and reduced versions of all print resources.

📁 **Other Print Resources**
- Active Reading Guide, pp. 46–47
- Reading Workbook
- Grammar and Language Workbook, pp. 111, 113

- Grammar and Composition Handbook, Lessons 4.9, 4.10
- Quick Checks, pp. 46–47
- Selection and Theme Assessment, pp. 73–74
- Performance Assessment, p. 40
- Spanish Summaries, p. 42
- Inclusion Strategies
- English Language Learners Sourcebook

🖐 **Transparencies**
- Selection Focus 42
- Fine Art 6
- Grammar and Language 35, 36

Technology
- 💿 Literature Launchers
- 🎧 Audio Library
- 💻 Glencoe Literature Web Site
- 💾 Testmaker

Motivating
→OPTIONS

Reading Further

Be sure to review these titles for appropriateness for your class before recommending them to students.

Whitman, Walt. *Memoranda During the War.* Boston: Applewood Books, 1990. Whitman's experiences in the Civil War reveal his sympathy for those who participated. His reporting shows the deep emotional insights characteristic of a poet, but it is also detailed and accurate.

Greenspan, Ezra (editor). *The Cambridge Companion to Walt Whitman.* Cambridge: Cambridge University Press, 1995. Essays written by a team of scholars cover contemporary issues in Whitman's art and life.

Before You Read

FOCUS ACTIVITY

What kind of spirit do you see in the people you know? For example, do you think they feel mostly optimistic or pessimistic? Why?

THINK-PAIR-SHARE Think about these questions on your own for a few minutes. Then discuss your responses with a partner. Finally, share your responses with your classmates and briefly discuss whether people in the United States seem generally optimistic or pessimistic.

SETTING A PURPOSE Read to find out how Whitman views the spirit of his country and its citizens.

BACKGROUND

Whitman and the War
In 1862 Whitman's brother was wounded in the first battle of Fredericksburg, and Whitman traveled to the battlefront in Virginia to care for him. Deeply moved by the suffering he encountered and finding his brother's condition stable, Whitman went on to Washington, D.C., to work as a volunteer nurse in army hospitals. There he comforted and cared for both Union and Confederate soldiers, dressing their wounds, writing letters for them, and bringing them items they needed, such as apples, oranges, and books. Writing about this experience, Whitman noted, "I supply often to some of these dear suffering boys . . . that which doctors nor medicines nor skill nor any routine assistance can give."

The Time and Place
Following the Civil War, the United States experienced tremendous economic growth and social change. Railroad construction and a series of new technological advances, such as the telephone, the typewriter, and the automobile, led to a burst of industrial activity. Great social and political change accompanied this growth. For example, many people moved from farms to cities, the number of immigrants increased dramatically, and the country expanded westward. While some individuals profited greatly from these changes, many others suffered. Deplorable working and living conditions in the cities led to labor disputes and eventually to the

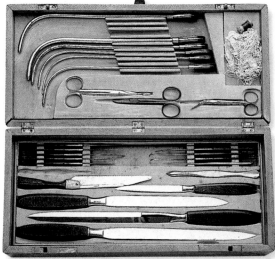

Civil War surgeon's kit

creation of labor unions and political organizations serving workers' needs.

In this growth and turmoil, Whitman saw common people coming alive and asserting their freedom as individuals. He imagined Americans breaking free from conventional ways of life and following their own visions. Recalling this time, Whitman said, "My Book and I—what a period we have presumed to span! those thirty years from 1850 to '80—and America in them!"

Reading *Minilesson*

Paraphrasing Paraphrasing is a particularly useful skill for students who may have difficulty with the line breaks and diction of poetry.

Activity Organize the class into two groups. Assign half the class "I Hear America Singing," and the other half "When I Heard the Learn'd Astronomer." Each student should write a paraphrase of the assigned poem and then exchange paraphrases with a partner in the other group. Partners should read each other's paraphrases, compare the paraphrase to the appropriate poem, and help their partners clarify any unclear language. Then have students revise their paraphrases as needed. **L2**

Additional Resources
📁 *Reading Workbook*

I Hear America Singing

Walt Whitman ∾

I hear America singing, the varied carols I hear,
Those of mechanics, each one singing his as it should be blithe° and strong,
The carpenter singing his as he measures his plank or beam,
The mason singing his as he makes ready for work, or leaves off work,
5   The boatman singing what belongs to him in his boat,
     the deckhand singing on the steamboat deck,
The shoemaker singing as he sits on his bench, the hatter singing as he stands,
The wood-cutter's song, the ploughboy's on his way in the morning,
     or at noon intermission or at sundown,
The delicious singing of the mother, or of the young wife at work,
     or of the girl sewing or washing,
Each singing what belongs to him or her and to none else,
10   The day what belongs to the day—at night the party of young fellows,
     robust, friendly,
Singing with open mouths their strong melodious songs.

_____
2 *Blithe* means "lighthearted" or "cheerful."

Cradling Wheat, 1938. Thomas Hart Benton. Tempera and oil on board, 31 x 38 in. ©T.H. Benton and R.P. Benton Testamentary Trusts/Licensed by VAGA, New York/The St. Louis Art Museum, St. Louis, MO. Look closely at the people in this painting. What words might Whitman have used to describe them in "I Hear America Singing"? Explain.

C Author's Craft

REPETITION Have students note the repetition of the phrase "When I" in "When I Heard the Learn'd Astronomer." Ask them why Whitman might have chosen to do this. *(Possible responses: The repetition emphasizes the tedium of the proofs, figures, charts, diagrams, and mathematical analyses and is a key part of the poem's rhythm.)*

D Active Reading

CONNECT Ask students to recall a time when they found themselves daydreaming because something they expected to be interesting was dull and tedious. How did Whitman's description compare with their experience? *(Students may mention learning rules for a complex game when they simply wanted to play it, or hearing a lecture on painters when they really wanted to paint.)* What do they think was happening to the poet when he "Look'd up in perfect silence at the stars"? *(He responded emotionally, appreciating their beauty and majesty.)*

Thematic Focus

Two New American Voices Have students discuss whether Whitman's poetry is different from the poetry in previous units. Then ask if Whitman's optimism is similar to or different from that of earlier poets.

ASSESSMENT OPTIONS

📁 *Quick Checks,* p. 46

Teaching Options

Twilight #4, 1997. Peter Sickles. Oil on canvas, 18 x 24 in. Private collection.

When I Heard the Learn'd Astronomer

Walt Whitman

C
When I heard the learn'd astronomer,
When the proofs, the figures, were ranged in columns before me,
When I was shown the charts and diagrams, to add, divide, and measure them,
When I sitting heard the astronomer where he lectured with much applause
in the lecture-room,
D
How soon unaccountable I became tired and sick,
Till rising and gliding out I wander'd off by myself,
In the mystical moist night-air, and from time to time,
Look'd up in perfect silence at the stars.

Responding to Literature

Personal Response

Which poem did you prefer? Why?

ANALYZING LITERATURE

I Hear America Singing

RECALL AND INTERPRET

1. What occupations does the speaker say represent America? What do these occupations tell you about Whitman's view of his country?
2. According to line 9, what does each laborer sing about? What do the laborers' "songs" suggest about the work they do?
3. What happens at night? Why do you think the poem ends the way it does?

EVALUATE AND CONNECT

4. What **catalog**, or list of images and details, is included in this poem? What effect does the catalog have on your reading of the poem?
5. Look back at your responses to the Focus Activity on page 402. Based on this poem, do you think Whitman would agree or disagree with your ideas? Explain.

When I Heard the Learn'd Astronomer

RECALL AND INTERPRET

6. What techniques does the astronomer use to present information? What does this suggest to you about the astronomer's approach to his subject?
7. What does the speaker do in lines 6–8? What conclusions can you draw about the speaker based on these actions?
8. How does the speaker's method for "studying" the stars differ from the astronomer's method? What does this difference imply about the speaker's values?

EVALUATE AND CONNECT

9. How does the use of **parallelism** (see page R11) reinforce the message of the poem?
10. What might be some advantages of viewing the stars as the astronomer does? as the speaker does? Which way of viewing do you prefer?

EXTENDING YOUR RESPONSE

Creative Writing

Interview What would you like to ask Whitman about the themes and distinctive features of "I Hear America Singing" and "When I Heard the Learn'd Astronomer"? With a partner, write questions for Whitman and answers from his point of view.

Interdisciplinary Activity

Astronomy: Your View In "When I Heard the Learn'd Astronomer," Whitman expresses one opinion about astronomy. Form your own opinion by researching the field. Report your findings to the class.

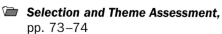
Save your work for your portfolio.

ASSESSMENT OPTIONS

📁 **Quick Checks,** p. 46

📁 **Selection and Theme Assessment,** pp. 73–74

📁 **Performance Assessment,** p. 40

💾 **Testmaker**

---

speaker's method has greater appeal for times of meditation and reflection.

EXTENDING YOUR RESPONSE

Creative Writing

Have students discuss the features of good interview questions and how questions that can be answered with a simple "yes" or "no" discourage conversation.

Interdisciplinary Activity Brainstorm with the class for keywords to use in their research on astronomy, either from an encyclopedia or from the Internet.

Personal Response

Expect students to offer specific evidence from the poems to support their preferences.

ANALYZING LITERATURE

1. The speaker mentions a mechanic, carpenter, mason, boatman, deckhand, shoemaker, hatter, wood-cutter, plough-boy, girl sewing or washing, young wife at work, and a mother. They reflect the belief that such labor makes the country strong and unique.
2. Each sings about his or her own work. These songs suggest that their work is satisfying.
3. At night young fellows rest and blend their voices. Students may say that the final image suggests that it takes all of the workers to make a strong America.
4. Whitman's catalog of occupations provides a montage of the sights and sounds of daily life in the United States in the mid-1800s. The catalog's listing of concrete details makes the poem more immediate and intense.
5. Whitman's view of the Americans' spirit is extremely optimistic.
6. The astronomer uses mathematics, charts, and diagrams in his lecture. His approach is analytical, scientific, and impersonal.
7. The speaker rises and glides out, wandering off. Students might conclude that he is bored with the astronomer because his own response to the stars is mystical and emotional, not logical.
8. The speaker's method is spontaneous, mysterious, and emotional; it implies that the speaker values artistic experience over scientific analysis.
9. Use of parallel structures reinforces Whitman's message by suggesting the tedious nature of the astronomer's lecture.
10. The astronomer's methods have obvious advantages in terms of scientific inquiry and application. The

A Active Reading

EVALUATE Point out to students that they will need to explore at least two major issues to understand Whitman's meaning—the identity of the three dead soldiers and the reason that he sees the third soldier's face as the "face of the Christ himself."

Model: The first dead soldier is an elderly man; the second is a youth; the third is neither young nor old. The speaker must mean that death in war can come at any age. The speaker uses a metaphor to describe the third soldier, comparing him to Christ, so I need to think about the ways this soldier is like Christ.

Additional Resources
📁 *Active Reading Guide,* p. 47
🎧 *Audio Library*

A Sight in Camp in the Daybreak Gray and Dim

Walt Whitman ⌁

A sight in camp in the daybreak gray and dim,
As from my tent I emerge so early sleepless,
As slow I walk in the cool fresh air the path near by the hospital tent,
Three forms I see on stretchers lying, brought out there untended lying,
5 Over each the blanket spread, ample brownish woolen blanket,
Gray and heavy blanket, folding, covering all.

Curious I halt and silent stand,
Then with light fingers I from the face of the nearest the first just lift the blanket;
A Who are you elderly man so gaunt and grim, with well-gray'd hair, and flesh all sunken
    about the eyes?
10 Who are you my dear comrade?

Then to the second I step—and who are you my child and darling?
Who are you sweet boy with cheeks yet blooming?

Then to the third—a face nor child nor old, very calm, as of beautiful yellow-white ivory;
Young man I think I know you—I think this face is the face of the Christ himself,
15 Dead and divine and brother of all, and here again he lies.

Civil War soldiers awaiting medical treatment, 1864.

Grammar and Language *Minilesson*

Run-on Sentences Point out to students that a run-on sentence is two or more complete sentences written as though they were one sentence. Students may correct run-ons by joining them with a semicolon or a comma and a coordinating conjunction, or by breaking the run-on into two sentences.

Activity Have students correct each of the following run-on sentences, using each of the three methods.

1. They took many books from the library none of them were returned overdue.
2. The student searched for information about Walt Whitman, the library had more than 20 of his books.
3. Each of the books seemed interesting and worthwhile none of them helped with the report. **L2**

Additional Resources
✍ *Grammar and Language Transparency 36*
📕 *Grammar and Language Workbook,* p. 113
📕 *Grammar and Composition Handbook,* Lesson 4.10
📘 *Writer's Choice,* Lesson 13.10

Beat! Beat! Drums!

Walt Whitman

The Wounded Drummer Boy, 1871.
Eastman Johnson. Oil on canvas,
40 x 36 in. The Brooklyn Museum,
New York.

Beat! beat! drums!—blow! bugles! blow!
Through the windows—through doors—burst like a ruthless force,
Into the solemn church, and scatter the congregation,
Into the school where the scholar is studying;
5 Leave not the bridegroom quiet—no happiness must he have now with his bride,
Nor the peaceful farmer any peace, ploughing his field or gathering his grain,
So fierce you whirr and pound you drums—so shrill you bugles blow.

Beat! beat! drums!—blow! bugles! blow!
Over the traffic of cities—over the rumble of wheels in the streets;
10 Are beds prepared for sleepers at night in the houses? no sleepers must sleep in those beds,
No bargainers' bargains by day—no brokers or speculators°—would they continue?
Would the talkers be talking? would the singer attempt to sing?
Would the lawyer rise in the court to state his case before the judge?
Then rattle quicker, heavier drums—you bugles wilder blow.

15 Beat! beat! drums!—blow! bugles! blow!
Make no parley°—stop for no expostulation,°
Mind not the timid—mind not the weeper or prayer,
Mind not the old man beseeching the young man,
Let not the child's voice be heard, nor the mother's entreaties,
20 Make even the trestles° to shake the dead where they lie awaiting the hearses,
So strong you thump O terrible drums—so loud you bugles blow.

---

11 *Speculators* are people who engage in risky business ventures hoping to make quick or large profits.
16 A *parley* is a conference between enemies to discuss terms of a truce or an agreement. *Expostulation* is the act of reasoning with a person to correct or dissuade him or her.
20 *Trestles* are structures in which a beam is supported by four diverging legs.

THE CIVIL WAR AND ITS AFTERMATH 🌾 407

B Active Reading

CONNECT How do you think the speaker in "Beat! Beat! Drums!" feels about this war? *(The speaker sees the war as a "ruthless force" that overpowers and invades every aspect of life.)*

C Literary Elements

ALLITERATION AND CONSONANCE
Point out Whitman's use of alliteration and consonance in the last stanza. Ask students how Whitman's use of repetition of the *m* sound (make, mind, man, and mother's) affected their response to the poem. Point out that the sound is also repeated in the words timid, thump, and drums. *(Students may note that the repetition of the m sounds sets up a kind of hum or moan, which is appropriate to the weeping, prayer, beseeching, and entreaties cataloged as responses to the death and destruction of war.)*

Thematic Focus

Two New American Voices Ask students to discuss why Whitman seems to condemn the Civil War itself, rather than the Union or Confederate sides. Why might this view represent a "new voice" about war?

✓ ASSESSMENT OPTIONS

📁 *Quick Checks,* p. 47

INTERDISCIPLINARY CONNECTION

Health Interested students may wish to investigate medical and general health practices common during the Civil War.

Activity Encourage students to check Web sites devoted to the Civil War, as well as to check reference tools in the media center or library. Students may present their information to the class using artwork, panel discussion, or a short script. **L2**

Personal Response

Urge students to explain the reasons why a particular word or image affected them as they read.

ANALYZING LITERATURE

1. The speaker sees three forms lying on stretchers. He focuses on the blanket; it covers the dead as a sign of respect, but it also hides the bodies. The repetition of the word *lying* with its multiple meanings suggests that hiding the bodies somehow makes death impersonal. The remaining stanzas belie the impersonality.

2. The first is an older man, gaunt, grim, gray-haired. The second is a rosy-cheeked boy. The speaker's questions imply his sorrow at the waste; the way he phrases them implies that the deaths *are* personal, even though he does not know the victims.

3. The speaker compares the third body with that of Christ. Like Christ, the soldier has died for the sins of others. In this case the sin is the country's sin: slavery. The speaker is profoundly moved by the deaths.

4. The three images show the scope of sacrifice and suffering in the war. The old soldier died before finishing his life's work; the young soldier before realizing his potential; and the third, like Christ, died in his prime.

5. Some may say they would avoid looking at the bodies to put death out of their minds, others that they would look to see if they knew the victims.

6. The drums and bugles in this poem symbolize how the war invades every aspect of life. Sound images are appropriate because it is very difficult to ignore loud sounds.

7. The instruments interrupt people sleeping, praying, ploughing, studying, talking, and singing. The variety suggests that war disrupts all aspects of life.

8. The instruments should ignore the attempts to avoid war, the timid, the religious, the destruction of families. The message is that war is oblivious

Responding to Literature

Personal Response

Which image or idea from these two poems stands out in your mind? Why?

--- **ANALYZING LITERATURE** ---

A Sight in Camp in the Daybreak Gray and Dim

RECALL AND INTERPRET

1. According to the first stanza, what does the speaker see at daybreak? What item does the speaker describe in lines 5–6? Why might the speaker have focused on this item?

2. Describe the first two soldiers. What do the speaker's questions imply about his feelings toward the soldiers?

3. To whom does the speaker compare the third soldier? What does this tell you about the speaker's emotional reaction to what he sees?

EVALUATE AND CONNECT

4. What does each soldier add to your understanding of the poem's message?

5. How do you think you might have reacted to the situation described in the poem?

Beat! Beat! Drums!

RECALL AND INTERPRET

6. What instruments are mentioned in this poem? What might they represent?

7. What kinds of activities do the instruments interrupt? What does the variety of activities suggest to you about the speaker's message?

8. According to the third stanza, what should the instruments ignore? What message does this stanza convey? Explain your answer.

EVALUATE AND CONNECT

9. To whom is the poem addressed? How does this add to its impact?

10. What attitude toward war does this poem express? Support your answer.

--- **EXTENDING YOUR RESPONSE** ---

Creative Writing

A Story Gray and Dim Write a short story based on "A Sight in Camp in the Daybreak Gray and Dim." Think of this brief event as the beginning of the story. Begin by writing an outline of your story. Then complete the story and present it to a group of classmates.

Interdisciplinary Activity

Music History: The Sounds of Drums and Bugles Research Civil War drums and bugles. What did they look like? What did they sound like? What roles did these instruments play on the battlefront? Report your findings to the class.

📖 **Save your work for your portfolio.**

to reason and emotion; the drums and bugles drown out all other voices.

9. Whitman addresses the instruments directly, perhaps because they have no humanity and cannot respond to reason or compassion. As symbols of war, they make intrusive noise and disrupt life. Ironically, personifying the instruments gives them volition, but not humanity.

10. The speaker's attitude is bitterly ironic; once it begins, war "bursts like a ruthless force" over all aspects of life, and mere humans seem powerless to stop it.

✔️ **ASSESSMENT OPTIONS**

📁 *Quick Checks,* p. 47

📁 *Selection and Theme Assessment,* pp. 73–74

📁 *Performance Assessment,* p. 40

💾 *Testmaker*

Before You Read

from *Song of Myself*

FOCUS ACTIVITY

Have you ever felt "connected" to nature or to all of humankind? What would it take for you to have such feelings?

DISCUSS As a class, have a brief discussion of what it might mean to feel "connected" to nature or to all of humankind and about what might make someone feel that way.

SETTING A PURPOSE Read to learn of the speaker's feelings of connection to the natural world and to all of humankind.

BACKGROUND

Literary Influences

When Whitman was young, he read Homer's classic epic poem the *Iliad* while "in a shelter'd hollow of rocks and sand, with the sea on each side." He felt that only the "presence of Nature" prevented him from being completely overwhelmed by the experience of reading this poem and other great works of world literature. Several years later Whitman would create his own epic poem—*Song of Myself.* As in the *Iliad,* this poem describes the journey of a hero. The hero in this poem, however, is the poet himself, not a fictional or historic character, and his journey is in part a spiritual one. As the poem progresses, the poet attempts to connect with the spirit of the reader, of the American landscape, of the American people, and, finally, of the universe itself.

    Song of Myself encourages each reader to share the poet's journey and to celebrate his or her own heroic spirit. In writing this work, Whitman tried to show that his fellow citizens were as heroic as the "god-like or lordly born characters" written of in ancient Greece.

Authors Among Ourselves

In the 1840s and 1850s, the most popular novelists among readers in the United States were the Scottish writer Sir Walter Scott and the English novelist Charles Dickens. Although Whitman admired these two authors, he deplored what he described as the "tinsel sentimentality" of much of European writing at that time. He asked in one of his essays, "Shall [Nathaniel] Hawthorne get a paltry *seventy-five dollars* for a two-volume work—shall real American genius shiver with neglect—while the public run after this foreign trash?" He urged his fellow citizens to cast aside the "unwholesome reading from abroad" and look for authors among "ourselves."

Eaton's Neck, Long Island, 1872. John Frederick Kensett. Oil on canvas, 18 x 36 in. The Metropolitan Museum of Art, New York.

RESOURCE MANAGER

Lesson Planning Resource
The *Unit Three Planning Guide* (pp. 83–89) provides additional lesson notes and reduced versions of all print resources.

📁 Other Print Resources
- Active Reading Guide, p. 48
- Reading Workbook
- Quick Checks, p. 48
- Selection and Theme Assessment, pp. 75–76

- Performance Assessment, p. 41
- Spanish Summaries, p. 43
- Spanish Translations
- Inclusion Strategies
- English Language Learners Sourcebook

📠 Transparencies
- Selection Focus 43
- Literary Elements 41

Technology
- 🎧 Audio Library
- 💻 Glencoe Literature Web Site
- 💾 Testmaker

Before Reading

Objectives

- To read the work of a "new voice" in American poetry
- To analyze free verse rhythms
- To write an analysis of details in a poem

Skills

Reading/Thinking: Summarizing
Writing: Poem
Vocabulary: The Latin Root *pos*
Life Skills: Making Decisions
Collaboration: Literature Groups; Choral Reading

Motivating
→OPTIONS

 Selection Focus Transparency 43: Have students view the transparency and discuss the question.

Focus Activity: As an extension of the Focus Activity, have students think about the stages of a journey that heroes make in movies. Most follow Joseph Campbell's pattern in *The Hero with a Thousand Faces*: a test, a call to action, and return home with new understanding.

LITERATURE & HUMANITIES

🎧 Play "Come Life, Shaker Life" and "Tis a Gift to Be Simple" from Glencoe's *American Music: Cultural Traditions* and compare the lyrics of each song with the words of Whitman's poem.

Reading the Selection

A **Active Reading**

RESPOND Why do you think the speaker connects the reader so closely with himself at the beginning of the poem? *(The speaker may want readers to accept him as a representative of humanity.)*

Model: The speaker uses the word *celebrate* in the very first line and then says that everything that belongs to him belongs to the reader. It seems that the speaker wants the reader to identify with and celebrate their common feelings. Then the speaker says that not only are the reader and the speaker connected, but all people are connected because they are all part of the natural world.

Additional Resources

📁 *Active Reading Guide*, p. 48
🎧 *Audio Library*

B **Literary Elements**

METAPHOR Remind students that a metaphor compares two unlike things. Draw students' attention to the image of grass as a metaphor for the speaker's thoughts about humanity and America.

Teaching Options

---

from

Song of Myself

Walt Whitman ∾

1

A
I celebrate myself, and sing myself,
And what I assume you shall assume,
For every atom belonging to me as good belongs to you.

B
I loafe and invite my soul,
5   I lean and loafe at my ease observing a spear of summer grass.

My tongue, every atom of my blood, form'd from this soil, this air,
Born here of parents born here from parents the same, and their parents the same,
I, now thirty-seven years old in perfect health begin,
Hoping to cease not till death.

10   Creeds and schools in abeyance,°
Retiring back a while suffic'd at what they are, but never forgotten,
I harbor for good or bad, I permit to speak at every hazard,
Nature without check with original energy.

 6

A child said *What is the grass?* fetching it to me with full hands;
15   How could I answer the child? I do not know what it is any more than he.

I guess it must be the flag of my disposition, out of hopeful green stuff woven.

Or I guess it is the handkerchief of the Lord,
A scented gift and remembrancer° designedly dropt,
Bearing the owner's name someway in the corners, that we may see and remark,
    and say *Whose?*

20   What do you think has become of the young and old men?
And what do you think has become of the women and children?

---

10 *In abeyance* means "suspended" or "in a state of being undetermined."
18 A *remembrancer* is a reminder.

CONNECTING TO OTHER SELECTIONS

COMPARING *selections*

This selection is paired with "The Butterfly Dream" and "The Useless," on page 419. A lesson for teaching a comparison of the two selections appears on page 421.

The chart at the right shows three ways to connect this excerpt from *Song of Myself* to selections in this book.

For specific teaching strategies, see the *Unit Three Planning Guide*, pp. 86–87.

Connection	Title
Critical Thinking: Comparing and Contrasting	→ "I, Too," p. 740
Thematic: Spirit of a People	→ "Chicago," p. 671
Literary: Alliteration	→ "My City," p. 720

Haymaking, 1864. Winslow Homer. Oil on canvas, 16 x 11 in. The Columbus Museum of Art, Columbus, OH.

Viewing the painting: In what ways does this painting capture the mood of the poem? Explain, using details from both the painting and the poem.

Reading *Minilesson*

Summarizing For long poems, such as *Song of Myself,* students may find it helpful to break the poem into parts, summarize each part, and reflect on what the poet says before proceeding.

Activity Organize the class into pairs or small groups. Assign each group a section of *Song of Myself.* Have students write a summary of the assigned section. Then have the groups share their summaries with the class. Students may find it necessary to make additions and corrections as they hear the summaries of other sections of the poem. When all the summaries have been discussed, put the poem back together by focusing on themes and tone in Whitman's poem. **L2**

Additional Resources
📁 *Reading Workbook*

INTERPRET Point out that in lines 28–46, Whitman catalogs many of the people he is and many of the places in which he is at home. Ask students what the catalogs suggest about Whitman's view of humanity. *(Whitman thinks that he speaks for all people, whatever their occupations or frames of reference.)* Invite students to discuss Whitman's basis for this connection.

Model: When the speaker says he is all those people with all those different jobs, it seems he is saying that what all these people have in common is more important than what makes them different. Whitman may be saying that all people are connected by their common humanity.

D Literary Elements

TONE Point out line 49: "And am not stuck up, and am in my place." Then ask students to identify the tone in the parenthetic lines 50–53. *(Some may say the lines convey a self-deprecating humor. Others may say these lines help locate humans in the chain of being; that is, they describe moths and fish eggs, the sun, the universe [the dark suns], and the "impalpable" [a universal spirit or God].)*

They are alive and well somewhere,
The smallest sprout shows there is really no death,
And if ever there was it led forward life, and does not wait at the end to arrest it,
25 And ceas'd the moment life appear'd.

All goes onward and outward, nothing collapses,
And to die is different from what any one supposed, and luckier.

I am of old and young, of the foolish as much as the wise,
Regardless of others, ever regardful of others,
30 Maternal as well as paternal, a child as well as a man,
Stuff'd with the stuff that is coarse and stuff'd with the stuff that is fine,
One of the Nation of many nations, the smallest the same and the largest the same,
A Southerner soon as a Northerner, a planter nonchalant° and hospitable down by the
    Oconee° I live,
A Yankee bound my own way ready for trade, my joints the limberest joints on earth and
    the sternest joints on earth,
35 A Kentuckian walking the vale of the Elkhorn in my deer-skin leggings, a Louisianian
    or Georgian,
A boatman over lakes or bays or along coasts, a Hoosier,° Badger,° Buckeye;°
At home on Kanadian snow-shoes or up in the bush, or with fishermen off Newfoundland,
At home in the fleet of ice-boats, sailing with the rest and tacking,
At home on the hills of Vermont or in the woods of Maine, or the Texan ranch,
40 Comrade of Californians, comrade of free North-Westerners, (loving their big proportions,)
Comrade of raftsmen and coalmen, comrade of all who shake hands and welcome
    to drink and meat,
A learner with the simplest, a teacher of the thoughtfullest,
A novice beginning yet experient of myriads of seasons,
Of every hue and caste am I, of every rank and religion,
45 A farmer, mechanic, artist, gentleman, sailor, quaker,
Prisoner, fancy-man, rowdy,° lawyer, physician, priest.

I resist any thing better than my own diversity,
Breathe the air but leave plenty after me,
And am not stuck up, and am in my place.

50 (The moth and the fish-eggs are in their place,
The bright suns I see and the dark suns I cannot see are in their place,

The palpable° is in its place and the impalpable is in its place.)

---

33 *Nonchalant* means "showing a lack of interest or enthusiasm." The *Oconee* is a river in Georgia.
36 *Hoosier, Badger,* and *Buckeye* are nicknames for natives or residents of Indiana, Wisconsin, and Ohio, respectively.
46 A *rowdy* is a rough, disorderly person.
52 *Palpable* means "able to be touched or felt."

ENGLISH LANGUAGE LEARNERS

MEETING INDIVIDUAL NEEDS

Geography Lesson English language learners may be overwhelmed by unfamiliar place names.

Activity Before students read section 16 of *Song of Myself*, discuss the locations identified in the poem. On a map of the United States, have students locate the places mentioned. Challenge students to find the Oconee and Elkhorn Rivers (in Georgia and Nebraska,

respectively). Discuss the meanings of the terms *Yankee, Hoosier, Badger,* and *Buckeye.* What might Whitman be saying about himself when he says he is "at home" everywhere?

Additional Resources
📁 *English Language Learners Sourcebook*

17

These are really the thoughts of all men in all ages and lands, they
    are not original with me,
If they are not yours as much as mine they are nothing, or next to nothing,
55 If they are not the riddle and the untying of the riddle they are nothing,
If they are not just as close as they are distant they are nothing.

This is the grass that grows wherever the land is and the water is,
This is the common air that bathes the globe.

46

I know I have the best of time and space, and was never measured and
    never will be measured.

60 I tramp a perpetual journey, (come listen all!)
My signs are a rain-proof coat, good shoes, and a staff cut from the woods,
No friend of mine takes his ease in my chair,
I have no chair, no church, no philosophy,
I lead no man to a dinner-table, library, exchange,
65 But each man and each woman of you I lead upon a knoll,°
My left hand hooking you round the waist,
My right hand pointing to landscapes of continents and the public road.

Not I, not any one else can travel that road for you,
You must travel it for yourself.

70 It is not far, it is within reach,
Perhaps you have been on it since you were born and did not know,
Perhaps it is everywhere on water and on land.

Shoulder your duds° dear son, and I will mine, and let us hasten forth,
Wonderful cities and free nations we shall fetch as we go.

75 If you tire, give me both burdens, and rest the chuff of your hand° on my hip,

And in due time you shall repay the same service to me,
For after we start we never lie by again.

This day before dawn I ascended a hill and look'd at the crowded heaven,
And I said to my spirit *When we become the enfolders of those orbs, and the pleasure and*
    knowledge of every thing in them, shall we be fill'd and satisfied then?
80 And my spirit said *No, we but level that lift to pass and continue beyond.*

---

65 A *knoll* is a small, rounded hill.
73 *Duds* are personal belongings.
75 *Chuff of your hand* refers to the fat part of the palm.

Historical Note

When Walt Whitman published his first edition of *Leaves of Grass* on or around July 4, 1855, he believed he was embarking on a personal literary journey of national significance. Setting out to define the American experience, Whitman consciously hoped to answer Ralph Waldo Emerson's 1844 essay, "The Poet." Emerson called for a truly original national poet who would sing of the new country in a new voice.

E Literary Elements

STYLE Remind students that style involves the choice and arrangement of words in a written work. Ask students how Whitman's choice of ordinary, everyday language in section 46 helps reinforce his theme. *(Whitman's words are simple and straightforward, appropriate for a conversation among friends and appropriate to his message about the connectedness of all people.)*

TEACHER to TEACHER

ALOHA HIGH SCHOOL • ALOHA, OREGON

I have students select and memorize 10 to 15 lines from one of Walt Whitman's poems. Students recite the lines in class and suggest interpretations. Students then tell what may have influenced the poet to write these lines.

After this introductory exercise, students write their own poems, building from a line of Whitman's. For example, students may begin "I hear . . ." after reading from the section on sound in *Song of Myself*. Finally, students read their poems to the class.

KEN MARTINEZ

VIEWING THE PAINTING

George Bellows (1882–1925) was a leading American artist during the early 1900s. He studied with Robert Henri in New York City. He is noted for his paintings of his family, the sea, and boxing matches.

Viewing Response *Students should recognize that the painting depicts robust, hard-working Americans, just as Whitman conveys the spirit of a powerful, young, and hard-working nation.*

You are also asking me questions and I hear you,
I answer that I cannot answer, you must find out for yourself.

Sit a while dear son,
Here are biscuits to eat and here is milk to drink,
85   But as soon as you sleep and renew yourself in sweet clothes, I kiss you with a good-by kiss
      and open the gate for your egress hence.°

Long enough have you dream'd contemptible dreams,
Now I wash the gum from your eyes,
You must habit yourself to the dazzle of the light and of every moment of your life.

Long have you timidly waded holding a plank by the shore,
90   Now I will you to be a bold swimmer,
To jump off in the midst of the sea, rise again, nod to me, shout, and laughingly dash with your hair.

---

85 *Egress hence* means "departure from this place."

The Sand Team, 1917. George Bellows. Oil on canvas, 30½ x 44¼ in. The Brooklyn Museum, New York.

Viewing the painting: In your opinion, what spirit of America does this painting convey? How is it similar to or different from Whitman's view of the American spirit?

Teaching Options

MEETING INDIVIDUAL NEEDS — MULTIPLE LEARNING STYLES

Interpersonal Whitman creates catalogs of visual images in section 16 of the poem. Have students work in groups to translate Whitman's word pictures into actual portraits displayed as a mural.

Activity Have each group of students use a long strip of paper to create a progression of portraits of all the people the speaker describes. Before beginning their portraits, students should plan how they will handle the subject and agree on a medium for their artwork, such as collage, tempera paint, or ink drawings. Have a spokesperson from each group present the completed mural to the class and explain the group's selection of materials and portraits. **L2 COLLAB. LEARN.**

51

The past and present wilt—I have fill'd them, emptied them,
And proceed to fill my next fold of the future.

Listener up there! what have you to confide to me?
95   Look in my face while I snuff the sidle of evening,°
(Talk honestly, no one else hears you, and I stay only a minute longer.)

Do I contradict myself?
Very well then I contradict myself,
(I am large, I contain multitudes.)

100 I concentrate toward them that are nigh,° I wait on the door-slab.

Who has done his day's work? who will soonest be through with his supper?
Who wishes to walk with me?

Will you speak before I am gone? will you prove already too late?

52

 The spotted hawk swoops by and accuses me, he complains of my gab and my loitering.

105 I too am not a bit tamed, I too am untranslatable,
I sound my barbaric yawp° over the roofs of the world.

The last scud° of day holds back for me,
It flings my likeness after the rest and true as any on the shadow'd wilds,
It coaxes me to the vapor and the dusk.

110 I depart as air, I shake my white locks at the runaway sun,
I effuse° my flesh in eddies, and drift it in lacy jags.

I bequeath myself to the dirt to grow from the grass I love,
If you want me again look for me under your boot-soles.

You will hardly know who I am or what I mean,
115 But I shall be good health to you nevertheless,
And filter and fibre your blood.

Failing to fetch me at first keep encouraged,
Missing me one place search another,
I stop somewhere waiting for you.

---

95 *Snuff the sidle of evening* means "to put out the last light of the day, which is moving sideways across the sky."
100 *Nigh* means "near."
106 A *yawp* is a loud, sharp cry.
107 *Scud* refers to wind-driven clouds or rain.
111 *Effuse* means "to pour out or forth."

THE CIVIL WAR AND ITS AFTERMATH ❦ 415

Personal Response

Some students may find the narrator irresponsible. Others may see his words as inspirational.

ANALYZING LITERATURE

1. In section 1, the speaker connects himself to the reader and to all people; he invites the reader to follow him on a mystical exploration of himself, of nature, and of life. Lines 10–13 inform readers that he is putting aside formal education for new and uncharted experiences and knowledge.
2. The speaker believes that in death we are reunited with nature and in this way continue to live.
3. The speaker's paradoxes include being both old and young, foolish and wise, careful and careless, male and female, coarse and cultured, and others.
4. The speaker enjoins the boy to put on traveler's clothing and follow him, to hand over his burdens if he tires, and do the same for the speaker later in life. He tells the boy to savor life and to find his own answers.
5. Sections 51 and 52 are the speaker's farewell to the reader. He explains that he will always be accessible through communion with nature. After a life of geographical and philosophical exploration, he addresses a Supreme Being for validation.
6. The speaker views himself as in harmony with nature and the rest of the world and would like others to follow his lead.
7. The speaker believes in the continuity of life in nature, in a cyclical pattern of life, death, and rebirth. Death is not an end.
8. The paradoxes suggest that the speaker embraces all aspects of himself, including the contradictions, and all of humankind, both virtuous and unholy. These exemplify the diversity of human life.
9. The deeper meaning of the speaker's advice is to learn about life first-hand. The best ways of learning are intuitive and mystical rather than empirical. One should savor life for all it offers. The human spirit is boundless.
10. The speaker sees no great division between body and spirit. One is the manifestation of the other. Humankind is simply one more creature in the natural world.

Responding to Literature

Personal Response

How did you react to the speaker in the poem? Explain your answer.

—— ANALYZING LITERATURE ——

RECALL

1. What is the main topic of section 1? What is the speaker saying in lines 10–13 about his past learning and his future?
2. What does the speaker say about death in lines 20–27?
3. A **paradox** is a statement that seems to contradict itself, but may actually be true. What paradoxes does Whitman list in section 16?
4. Summarize the speaker's advice to his "son" in lines 73–91.
5. Briefly state what the speaker is saying in sections 51 and 52.

INTERPRET

6. How does the speaker seem to view himself in relation to nature and to the rest of the world?
7. What do lines 20–27 suggest about the speaker's ideas of life and death?
8. What, in your opinion, do the paradoxes in section 16 reveal about the speaker's feelings toward humankind? What do these lines suggest about Whitman's attitude toward himself?
9. In your opinion, what is the deeper meaning of the advice the speaker gives? Explain your answer using details from the poem.
10. What do sections 51 and 52 suggest to you about the speaker's attitude toward the relationship between his physical body and his spirit? between humankind and nature?

EVALUATE AND CONNECT

11. How does Whitman's use of **catalogs** in this selection help get across his message? (See Literary Terms Handbook, page R3.)
12. Which of Whitman's ideas about nature, death, or people do you find most interesting? Explain, using details from the poem.
13. An **epic poem** recounts the adventures of a hero. In your opinion, is the speaker of *Song of Myself* a hero? Explain your answer with details from the poem.
14. Think back to the ideas you discussed for the Focus Activity on page 409. Then use a chart like the one shown to compare Whitman's ideas about being connected to nature and humankind with yours.
15. What would you like to say to the speaker after reading this poem?

Literary ELEMENTS

Free Verse

Whitman is famous for using **free verse**—a type of poetry that has no set **meter**, line length, stanza arrangement, or rhyme. Though free verse lacks a regular pattern of stressed and unstressed syllables, it does not lack rhythm. Whitman used free verse because it echoes the rising and falling cadences of everyday speech.

1. With a partner, read one of Whitman's poems aloud, paying close attention to its rhythm. Do you find the rhythm of the poem similar to everyday speech? Explain.
2. In what ways might *Song of Myself* have a different effect if it were written in a regular rhythm pattern?

● See **Literary Terms Handbook**, p. R7.

Connection to nature, humankind	
Whitman's ideas	**My ideas**

11. The catalogs provide emphasis and examples to support the tremendous scope of the poem.
12. Have students reflect upon what their choices say about their own attitudes toward nature, death, or people.
13. Students may say that anyone who accepts the risks Whitman does must be heroic; others that a real hero has other qualities, such as being responsible for a home, family, and job.
14. Answers should display an understanding of Whitman's view of the connectedness of people and nature.
15. Accept all responses that reflect an understanding of the poem and Whitman's message.

LITERARY ELEMENTS

1. Students will probably find the rhythms of Whitman's poetry close to natural speech patterns. This is due to the free verse form.
2. A more regular rhythm pattern might contradict the message of freedom and openness to all experience that is at the heart of this poem.

Additional Resources

🖋 *Literary Elements Transparency 41*

LITERATURE AND WRITING

Writing About Literature

Details, Details In *Song of Myself* and other poems, Whitman uses specific details to enrich his poetry. Choose one of Whitman's poems and list the details in that poem that you find most powerful. Then write a few paragraphs explaining the effect those details have on the poem. For example: Do they bring out the meaning more clearly? Do they make the images more memorable? Be specific in supporting your explanations.

Creative Writing

Celebrate! Write a short poem celebrating your America. Use free verse and other devices Whitman used to create rhythm in his work, such as **repetition** and **parallelism** (see pages R11 and R13). Begin the poem with one of the following lines:

   "I celebrate myself, and sing myself."
   "I hear America singing."

EXTENDING YOUR RESPONSE

Literature Groups

Nature, Death, and Spirit Debate whether or not Whitman succeeds in reaching today's reader. Consider, for example, whether his ideas about nature, death, the spirit of America, and the human spirit are still relevant, and whether his style remains fresh. Summarize the group's responses and share the results with the class.

Internet Connection

Where's Walt? Search the Internet for sites devoted to Whitman. Determine your favorite site and present a short review of it to your classmates. Include the address, the options at the site, and any interesting facts you discovered.

Performing

Sing "a Song" With a group of classmates, perform a choral reading of a section of *Song of Myself*. Decide beforehand who will read each line or stanza: an individual, a pair of students, or the entire group. Also decide when a line should be read loudly or softly, fast or slowly. Try to speak as naturally as possible.

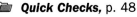 **Save your work for your portfolio.**

VOCABULARY • The Latin Root *pos*

Latin roots form the basis of many English words. The root is usually combined with a prefix, a suffix, or both. The meaning of the English word is usually related to the meaning of the root it contains. For example, the words *disposition* (line 16) and *supposed* (line 27), from *Song of Myself*, contain the Latin root *pos*, meaning "to put" or "to place." *Disposition* can be interpreted as "the way a person's temperament or mood is arranged or placed"; *suppose* can mean "to place under belief."

PRACTICE Define each word below, using a dictionary if necessary. Then discuss with a partner how the meaning of the Latin root *pos* contributes to the meaning of each word.

1. deposit
2. oppose
3. transpose
4. position
5. expose

LITERATURE AND WRITING

Writing About Literature

Students' explanations should
- demonstrate an understanding of Whitman's meaning.
- show how specific details contribute to this meaning.

Creative Writing

Students' poems should
- reflect an understanding of free verse.
- include examples of repetition and parallelism.

EXTENDING YOUR RESPONSE

Literature Groups Point out to students that they should explore both sides to this question before they determine their group's position.
COLLAB. LEARN.

Internet Connection Remind students to consider the reliability of their source of information. Help students determine possible bias.
COLLAB. LEARN.

Performing Help student groups choose what section each will perform to avoid duplication. Encourage students to spend time planning and rehearsing their choral readings. If possible, videotape the readings in the order presented in the poem.

VOCABULARY • The Latin Root *pos*

1. something placed for safekeeping
2. to place opposite or against something
3. to change in form or nature of expression
4. an act of placing or arranging
5. to deprive of shelter, protection, or care

ASSESSMENT OPTIONS

📁 *Quick Checks,* p. 48
📁 *Selection and Theme Assessment,* pp. 75–76
📁 *Performance Assessment,* p. 41
💾 *Testmaker*

Objectives

- To read and analyze literature written from a Taoist perspective
- To identify symbolism in Chuang Tzu's poetry

Skills

Reading/Thinking: Interpreting; Using Text Structures
Writing: Journal Writing
Collaboration: Literature Groups

Motivating
→ OPTIONS

Selection Focus Transparency 44: Have students view the transparency and then discuss the question provided.

Focus Activity: As an extension of the Focus Activity, ask students to think about a person for whom politics, fame, or fortune may have created new perspectives. Students may suggest rock and movie stars. Discuss the price these individuals pay for celebrity.

—Before You Read—

The Useless and The Butterfly Dream

Meet Chuang Tzu

"I know about letting the world alone, not interfering. I do not know about running things. Letting things alone so that men will not blow their nature out of shape! Not interfering, so that men will not be changed into something they are not!"

—*Chuang Tzu*

Chuang Tzu (zhwäng dzoo) was born more than two thousand years ago into a world of war and chaos. From the 900s to about 220 B.C., China was embroiled in civil war, as warlords fought for power and land. In search of peace and stability, Chuang Tzu and other philosophers tried to show China's rulers a better way to govern. Great thinkers sought to create a society in harmony with nature.

Little is known of Chuang Tzu's life. According to one Chinese historian, Chuang may have been born in the town of Meng, somewhere in the present-day province of Anhui or Henan. His given name was Chuang Chou. The title *Tzu*, meaning "Master," was added to honor his role as a founder of the way of thinking that became known as Taoism (dou′iz′ əm).

Philosophers Chuang Tzu, Lao Tzu, and Lieh Tzu are considered the founders of Taoism—a philosophy based on the principle that happiness and tranquility can be achieved by understanding one's own true nature and living in harmony with it.

"Tao" is the name given to the powerful, invisible reality believed by Taoists to be the source of everything in the universe. Followers believe that if they live by Taoist principles they will eventually become good and enlightened beings. Chuang Tzu believed that an individual gains freedom by living a life of purity and simplicity. In his writings, he described politics, fame, and fortune as threats to health, freedom, and integrity.

Chuang Tzu was born c. 369 B.C. and died c. 286 B.C.

FOCUS ACTIVITY

Think of a time when something made you look at your life from an entirely different perspective. Maybe the new view was spurred by a dream, an event, or advice.

CHART IT! Use a flow chart like the one on this page to describe the chain of events that led you to a new and unusual perspective on life.

SETTING A PURPOSE Read to discover the new perspectives Chuang Tzu offers.

| Event 1 | ⟹ | Event 2 | ⟹ | New perspective |

BACKGROUND

Ancient Words

The book that shares its author's name—*Chuang Tzu*—is considered a masterpiece of Chinese literature and philosophy. Only the first seven chapters, or "Inner Chapters," are attributed to Chuang Tzu. The other writings have been added or edited over the centuries and contain a wide variety of stories, essays, and legends that deal with Taoist philosophy. Many legends about the life of Chuang Tzu appear throughout the book, although historians do not consider them to be reliable.

RESOURCE MANAGER

Lesson Planning Resource
The *Unit Three Planning Guide* (pp. 90–94) provides additional lesson notes and reduced versions of all print resources.

📁 **Other Print Resources**
- Active Reading Guide, p. 49
- Reading Workbook, pp. 47–48
- Quick Checks, p. 49
- Selection and Theme Assessment, pp. 75–76

- Performance Assessment, p. 41
- Spanish Summaries, p. 44
- Inclusion Strategies
- English Language Learners Sourcebook

 Transparencies
- Selection Focus 44

Technology
- 🎧 Audio Library
- 🎧 Spanish Audio Library
- 💻 Glencoe Literature Web Site
- 💾 Testmaker

The Useless

Chuang Tzu

Translated by Martin Palmer

Hui Tzu said to Chuang Tzu:
"All your teaching is centered on what has no use."

Chuang replied:
"If you have no appreciation for what has no use
You cannot begin to talk about what can be used.
The earth, for example, is broad and vast
But of all this expanse a man uses only a few inches
Upon which he happens to be standing.
Now suppose you suddenly take away
All that he is not actually using
So that, all around his feet a gulf
Yawns, and he stands in the Void,
With nowhere solid except right under each foot:
How long will he be able to use what he is using?"

Hui Tzu said: "It would cease to serve any purpose."

Chuang Tzu concluded:
"This shows
The absolute necessity
Of what has 'no use.'"

Magical Butterfly. Wang Wu (1632–1690) and Da Chongguang (1623–1692). Ink and color on paper. Private collection.

The Butterfly Dream

Chuang Tzu

Translated by Martin Palmer

ONCE UPON A TIME, I, Chuang Tzu, dreamt that I was a butterfly, flitting around and enjoying myself. I had no idea I was Chuang Tzu. Then suddenly I woke up and was Chuang Tzu again. But I could not tell, had I been Chuang Tzu dreaming I was a butterfly, or a butterfly dreaming I was now Chuang Tzu?

Reading the Selection

A Active Reading

EVALUATE Some students may think that teaching should have a practical rather than a philosophical basis. Encourage students to articulate the basis for this point of view, as well as for that of Chuang Tzu.

Additional Resources
- *Active Reading Guide,* p. 49
- *Audio Library*

B Critical Thinking

INTERPRETING Point out the development of Chuang Tzu's argument about teaching. Share the model below to illustrate the thinking process.

Model: Chuang uses an analogy to explain the concept of what is useful. He says that if you take away everything that is not being used at the moment, what is being used right now also becomes useless. I think he means that everything you learn may not be useful at the time you learn it, but it is important to learn as much as you can because all knowledge is connected and important.

Teaching Options

Reading *Minilesson*

Using Text Structures Point out that Chuang Tzu's argument in "The Useless" contains four parts, each of which serves a different function.

Activity Have students read the poem and then create a visual representation of what each speaker in the poem does.

Students may, for example, use four boxes with the following labels:

> Hui Tzu presents a problem.

> Chuang Tzu provides a solution.

> Hui Tzu sees Chuang's logic.

> Chuang Tzu summarizes the solution.

Additional Resources
Reading Workbook, pp. 47–48

Responding to the Selection

Personal Response

Students may say that the poems make them think about what "useful" really means.

ANALYZING LITERATURE

1. Hui Tzu accuses Chuang Tzu of teaching him about things that have no use. The student believes that only knowledge that has a practical application is valuable.

2. Chuang replies that if Hui has no understanding of the useless, he will never understand the nature of true usefulness. He says if one understands only a small part of the world, only that part is useful, but the rest is important, too. Students will probably say the response is appropriate because it clearly illustrates Chuang's point.

3. Chuang concludes that "useless" knowledge is absolutely necessary for survival.

4. Students' answers might depend upon their attitudes toward practical applications versus philosophical ideas. Urge students to support their answers with examples.

5. The paradox is that "useless" knowledge is vital to someone's understanding of his or her place in the world. The use of a paradox challenges readers to see that the contradiction is only apparent, not necessarily real.

6. Chuang Tzu says that he once dreamed he was a butterfly. He may have wanted to relate the story of the dream in order to explore the paradox of the dreamer and the dream.

7. Chuang Tzu had forgotten that he was himself. He includes this information to demonstrate how completely he experienced the butterfly's life.

8. Waking from the dream, Chuang Tzu wonders whether he had dreamt of being a butterfly or if a butterfly was dreaming of being him. Chuang Tzu wonders about the nature of reality and perception.

Responding to Literature

Personal Response

What do "The Useless" and "The Butterfly Dream" leave you thinking about?

──── ANALYZING LITERATURE ────

The Useless

RECALL AND INTERPRET

1. What statement does Hui Tzu first make to Chuang Tzu? What do you think the statement means?
2. How does Chuang reply to Hui? What example does Chuang use to support his reply? Is the example, in your opinion, an appropriate response to Hui's statement? Explain.
3. What is Chuang's final conclusion? Restate this conclusion in your own words and explain what Chuang seems to be saying.

EVALUATE AND CONNECT

4. Did Chuang's argument convince you? Why or why not?
5. A **paradox** is a statement that seems to contradict itself but may actually be true. What effect does paradox have on your reading of the selection?

The Butterfly Dream

RECALL AND INTERPRET

6. What does Chuang Tzu say he once dreamt? Why do you think he would want to relate the story of such a dream?
7. During the dream, what does he have "no idea" of? Why might he have added this statement to the story of his dream?
8. What does Chuang Tzu wonder when he wakes from the dream? What does this tell you about his way of thinking?

EVALUATE AND CONNECT

9. What do you think the butterfly might symbolize? Do you think it is an effective **symbol** (see page R16)? Explain your answer with details from the selection.
10. What lesson, or **moral**, do you gain from this story? Explain your conclusion.

──── EXTENDING YOUR RESPONSE ────

Personal Writing

Your Own Dream   In your journal, write about an interesting and unique dream you have had. Tell what lesson you might learn from that dream. You might try to write your dream in the style of Chuang Tzu. Also look for symbols in your dream—like the butterfly in Chuang's dream.

Literature Groups

New Views   With your group, discuss the question: Do "The Butterfly Dream" and "The Useless" cause you to look at life in a different way? If so, how? Review your answers to the Focus Activity on page 418 to help you. Share your ideas with other groups.

📖 **Save your work for your portfolio.**

9. The butterfly may symbolize an alternative view of reality because Chuang Tzu cannot tell which view, his or the butterfly's, is more real.
10. Chuang says it is impossible to determine for certain whether we are real or characters in someone else's dream; therefore to define reality only as what we can perceive with our senses does not make sense.

LITERATURE AND WRITING

Personal Writing

Students' journal entries should
- describe their dreams in detail.
- explore possible symbolic interpretations of the dreams.

Literature Groups Students' discussion should reflect an understanding of the poems, and compare the literature to their own ideas about usefulness and reality.

COMPARING selections

COMPARING *selections*

from **Song of Myself**   **and**   The Useless   **and**   The Butterfly Dream

COMPARE **IDEAS**

Imagine Walt Whitman and Chuang Tzu in conversation. In a group, discuss questions such as the following. Support your discussion with details from the selections.

1. What questions might each want to ask the other? What answers might they get?

2. What else might they talk about?

3. About what might they agree? About what might they disagree?

Have two group members improvise a discussion between the writers for the class.

COMPARE **IMPRESSIONS**

Create illustrations that convey your impressions of *Song of Myself,* "The Butterfly Dream," and "The Useless." Sketch two illustrations, one for *Song of Myself* and another for one or both pieces by Chuang Tzu. Then share your work with a partner and discuss similarities and differences in your impressions.

Magical Butterfly. Wang Wu (1632–1690) and Da Chongguang (1623–1692).

COMPARE **CULTURES**

Whitman was influenced by an American movement known as Transcendentalism. Chuang Tzu was a founder of an Asian way of thought called Taoism.

- Use an encyclopedia to research Transcendentalism and Taoism.

- In your own words, write five to ten sentences that tell the basic ideas of Transcendentalism. Do the same for Taoism.

- Then write an answer to each of these questions: If Whitman had lived in China in the time of Chuang Tzu, might he have been a Taoist? If Chuang Tzu had lived in the United States when Whitman did, might he have accepted the ideas of Transcendentalism? Explain, using details from your research and from the selections.

Objectives

- To compare the poems of Chuang Tzu with *Song of Myself*
- To recognize distinctive and shared characteristics of cultures

COMPARE **IDEAS**

Similarities Both Whitman and Chuang Tzu explore the meaning of what they see in the world. **Differences** The speaker in *Song of Myself* believes knowledge comes from direct experience; Chuang Tzu looks inward for understanding.

COMPARE **IMPRESSIONS**

Students' illustrations should

- illustrate the students' impressions of Chuang Tzu and Whitman's work.
- portray the distinctive features in each poet's style.
- reflect students' interpretations.

COMPARE **CULTURES**

Students' answers should

- show that Transcendentalists believed that people can use intuition to gain truth. Taoists believe that the ideal life focuses on simple, meditative living in harmony with nature.
- explore how time periods might influence the writers.
- use information from their research effectively.

Additional Resources
📁 *Literature Groups Sourcebook*

Teaching Options

 PORTFOLIO OPTIONS _____

Select and Reflect Have students reflect on the analyses they wrote for the activity above by asking themselves these questions:
- Does my explanation include background information about both Taoism and Transcendentalism?
- How well does my analysis explain how cultural influences affect a writer and influence his work?

Students should attach their reflections to their explanations and place them in their portfolios. Later, they might use the comments in revisions. **L2**

Additional Resources
📁 *Writing Assessment and Portfolio Management,* pp. 51–58

Vo·cab·u·lar·y Skills

Objective

- To learn the meanings of prefixes, roots, and suffixes to identify meanings of unfamiliar words

Teaching Strategies

Invite students to add to the list of examples for each of the prefixes and suffixes listed. Be sure that students understand that a prefix can completely reverse the meaning of a word: *legal*, *illegal*. Then reinforce the idea of looking at the base or root word.

Exercise

1. a
2. c

Additional Resources

📁 *Vocabulary Power: Weekly Lessons and Activities*

Vo·cab·u·lar·y Skills

Understanding Prefixes and Suffixes

One way to determine the meaning of an unfamiliar word is to analyze its parts. If you recognize the root, or base of a word, you are well on your way to understanding the new word's meaning. By learning the meanings of **prefixes** (word parts attached to the beginning of a word) and **suffixes** (word parts attached to the end of a word) you can decipher new words. For example, here is how you might analyze the word *expostulation* from Walt Whitman's "Beat! Beat! Drums!"

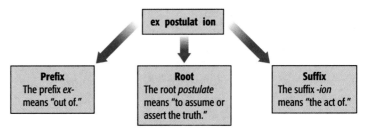

ex postulat ion		
Prefix	**Root**	**Suffix**
The prefix *ex-* means "out of."	The root *postulate* means "to assume or assert the truth."	The suffix *-ion* means "the act of."

The word *expostulation* means "the act of reasoning with someone to correct or dissuade"—that is, the act of trying to talk someone out of an idea. Although a word's parts usually add up to its meaning, it is a good idea to confirm your interpretation with a dictionary.

Here are some frequently used prefixes and suffixes and their meanings:

	Meaning	Examples
Prefixes		
il-, im-, in-, ir-	without, not	illegal, incomplete
trans-	across	translate, transport
Suffixes		
-able, -ible	capable of	laughable, visible
-ical	related to	symmetrical, geological

EXERCISE

Use prefixes and suffixes from the lists to help you complete the following sentences.

1. A transcontinental airline flight would fly
   a. across a continent.
   b. between more than two continents.
   c. from one continent to another.

2. A hierarchy can be a classification of people based on their status. So, in a hierarchical society, people would
   a. all have the same status.
   b. all be related to one another.
   c. be divided by their status.

Teaching Options

MEETING INDIVIDUAL NEEDS ENGLISH LANGUAGE LEARNERS

Analyzing Word Parts Explain to English language learners that comparing the prefixes and suffixes in their native languages to those in English may help them learn English prefixes and suffixes.

Activity Have English language learners chart prefixes and suffixes in their own languages and in English.

Meaning	(Own Language) prefixes, suffixes	English prefixes, suffixes
without, not		in-
capable of		-able

Additional Resources

📁 *English Language Learners Sourcebook*

Before You Read

Dickinson's Poetry

Meet Emily Dickinson

"Forgive me if I am frightened; I never see strangers and hardly know what I say," Emily Dickinson said to Thomas Wentworth Higginson the first time she met him in her home in Amherst, Massachusetts. Higginson was a well-known critic, with whom she had been corresponding for eight years but had never met. Indeed, Dickinson didn't see strangers often: she rarely went out into the world or received visitors.

Dickinson lived almost her entire life in her family's home, watching the life of Amherst from her second-story bedroom window and writing poetry. She composed approximately eighteen hundred poems, though only seven were published during her lifetime. After Dickinson died, her younger sister Lavinia discovered a number of Dickinson's poems in a dresser drawer and became the principal agent of their publication. Dickinson enjoyed a close relationship with Lavinia and with her older brother Austin, but felt distant from her mother and intimidated by her stern, but loving, father, who was one of Amherst's most distinguished citizens.

As she neared the end of her life, Dickinson hardly ever ventured downstairs, instead sending little notes to visitors who waited below. Dickinson's quiet exterior, however, disguised a passionate inner life. She was a poet far ahead of her time, a poet of keen awareness and startling originality. She created her own distinctive style, experimenting with grammar, capitalization, punctuation, rhyme, and meter—and heartily confusing the few critics of her day who actually saw her poems. Many years would pass before most readers came to fully understand the genius that spoke from her poems.

No matter how common or ordinary the occurrence, Dickinson could find meaning in it. A slant of light during the afternoon, a bird coming down a walk, a long shadow on the lawn; in just eight, twelve, or sixteen lines, she could turn the everyday into the miraculous, and the apparently meaningless into the deeply meaningful. After reading Dickinson's poems, critic Allen Tate rejected Dickinson's description of herself as "frightened" and the world's assessment of her life as quiet or barren. He said, "All pity for Miss Dickinson's 'starved life' is misdirected. Her life was one of the richest and deepest ever lived on this continent." So it is that the "facts" of Dickinson's outer life seem to tell one story, but the proof of Dickinson's inner life, her poetry, tells an entirely different story.

> "To live is so startling, it leaves but little room for other occupations."

> "I had no monarch in my life, and cannot rule myself; and when I try to organize, my little force explodes and leaves me bare and charred."

—*Dickinson*

Emily Dickinson was born in 1830 and died in 1886.

THE CIVIL WAR AND ITS AFTERMATH 423

Before Reading

Objectives

- To read and analyze Emily Dickinson's poetry as a "new American voice"
- To identify the different types of rhyme, such as slant rhyme, used by Dickinson
- To identify common themes in Dickinson's poems

Skills

Reading/Thinking: Paraphrasing; Drawing Conclusions; Inferring
Writing: Compare and Contrast; Remodeling
Grammar/Language: Noun Clauses; Using a Dash
Collaboration: Literature Groups; Performing

More About Emily Dickinson

Emily Dickinson came from a prosperous and intellectual family. Her family was one of the most distinguished in Amherst. Edward, her father, was treasurer of Amherst College and served in Congress. Emily herself had many advantages. She attended Amherst Academy and Mt. Holyoke Female Seminary, and thus was better educated than most people of her day.

LITERATURE & HUMANITIES

Display the painting *Christina's World* from Glencoe's **American Art, History, and Culture** to discuss ways in which the painting reflects themes expressed in "If you were coming in the Fall."

RESOURCE MANAGER

Lesson Planning Resource
The *Unit Three Planning Guide* (pp. 95–103) provides additional lesson notes and reduced versions of all print resources.

📁 **Other Print Resources**
- Active Reading Guide, pp. 50–53
- Reading Workbook
- Grammar and Language Workbook, p. 107
- Grammar and Composition Handbook, Lessons 4.5, 11.7

- Quick Checks, pp. 50–53
- Selection and Theme Assessment, pp. 77–78
- Performance Assessment, p. 42
- Spanish Summaries, p. 45
- Inclusion Strategies
- English Language Learners Sourcebook

Transparencies
- Selection Focus 45
- Fine Art 21
- Literary Elements 42

- Grammar and Language 37

Technology
- 💿 Literature Launchers
- 🎧 Audio Library
- 🖥 Glencoe Literature Web Site
- 💾 Testmaker

423

Reading Further

Be sure to review this title for appropriateness for your class before recommending it to students.

Lundin, Roger. *Emily Dickinson and the Art of Belief.* Grand Rapids, Michigan: Wm. B. Eerdmans Publishing Co., 1998. This readable biography focuses on Dickinson's religious views and her "inner debate" about Christianity.

Motivating
→ OPTIONS

Literature Launchers:
"The Belle of Amherst"

Videodisc Side A,
Segment 10

Also available in VHS.

Selection Focus Transparency 45: Have students view the transparency and then answer the question provided.

Focus Activity: As an extension of the Focus Activity, ask students to imagine a writer who is the opposite of the wandering Walt Whitman, one who hardly ever left home and came into contact with few people. How might these circumstances shape this poet's work?

Before You Read

———— **FOCUS ACTIVITY** ————

How important are your friends to you? What are your views of death? What is success? What is wisdom?

FREEWRITE Spend three or four minutes freewriting to explore your response to one of the questions above.

SETTING A PURPOSE Read to learn one poet's views of relationships, death, success, and other topics.

———— **BACKGROUND** ————

Dickinson's Dashes and Capitalization

Much of Dickinson's poetry features her characteristic use of dashes. The dashes serve as interrupters. They signal pauses, but more than that, they call attention to the words they enclose. They may break off a line or thought suddenly; they may call attention to a shift in meaning or action; they may interrupt the rhythm; or they may draw attention to the moment of silence they create in an oral reading of the poems. To understand these poems, you need to think about not only the words but also the dashes. Each one is carefully placed, and each one affects the reading of the poem.

Dickinson was also innovative in her use of capitalization. Like most poets of her day, she capitalized the first letter of each line of a poem and all proper nouns. Additionally, however, she capitalized many common nouns, thereby calling attention to them and emphasizing their importance.

Literary Influences

Books, Dickinson once said, were her "enthralling friends." She particularly enjoyed reading William Shakespeare, Ralph Waldo Emerson, and women writers of her day, including George Eliot, Charlotte and Emily Brontë, and Elizabeth Barrett Browning. Dickinson's interest in the complexity and turmoil of the human soul and in humankind's relationship to nature drew her to these writers. Dickinson also steeped herself in the Bible, particularly the Book of Revelation. Her poems refer to various religious concepts, such as heaven, hell, sin, and immortality.

Technically, Dickinson's poems owe much to the hymns she heard in childhood, whose rhythms she adapted to her poetry. Many of her poems consist of alternating six- and eight-syllable lines. This is the most popular form of rhythm in old Protestant hymns.

Dickinson Homestead, Amherst, Massachusetts.

CONNECTING TO OTHER SELECTIONS

The chart at the right shows three ways to connect "Because I could not stop for Death" to other selections in this book.

For specific teaching strategies, see the *Unit Three Planning Guide,* pp. 99–100.

Connection	Title
Critical Thinking: Evaluating	→ "If We Must Die," p. 734
Thematic: Matters of Life and Death	→ "Death of the Ball Turret Gunner," p. 857
Literary: Metaphor	→ "Birches," p. 698

If you were coming in the Fall

Emily Dickinson

If you were coming in the Fall,
I'd brush the Summer by
With half a smile, and half a spurn,
As Housewives do, a Fly.

5   If I could see you in a year,
I'd wind the months in balls—
And put them each in separate Drawers,
For fear the numbers fuse—

If only Centuries, delayed,
10 I'd count them on my Hand,
Subtracting, till my fingers dropped
Into Van Dieman's Land.°

If certain, when this life was out—
That yours and mine, should be
15 I'd toss it yonder, like a Rind,
And take Eternity—

But, now, uncertain of the length
Of this, that is between,
It goads me, like the Goblin Bee—
20 That will not state—its sting.

---

12 *Van Dieman's Land* is the former name for Tasmania, an island that is part of Australia.

Waiting, 1885. Clement Rollins Grant. Oil on canvas, 20 x 30 in. Private collection.

CONNECT Point out that Dickinson observes that people select soul-mates and close the door to others, but does not explain how the "soul selects" that "society." Ask students to jot down the qualities that they would look for in a soulmate, ranking these from most important to least important. Have volunteers share their lists with the class and discuss their similarities and differences. *(Students may choose empathy, listening skills, a sense of humor, good moral character, trustworthiness, intelligence, or other traits.)* Focus on the ranking of their choices. Are the same qualities at the top of most lists, or are there important differences?

D Critical Thinking

DRAWING CONCLUSIONS Based on their reading of these three poems, have students draw conclusions about Dickinson's personality. *(Students may conclude that the speaker in the poems is reflective, somewhat introverted, and capable of deep feelings. Some may say the poet places a high value on relationships.)*

Thematic Focus

Two New Voices Discuss with students how these two poems give voice to Dickinson's inner feelings.

ASSESSMENT OPTIONS

 Quick Checks, p. 50

Teaching Options

My life closed twice before its close

Emily Dickinson

My life closed twice before its close—
It yet remains to see
If Immortality unveil
A third event to me

So huge, so hopeless to conceive
As these that twice befell.
Parting is all we know of heaven,
And all we need of hell.

The Soul selects her own Society

C

Emily Dickinson **D**

The Soul selects her own Society—
Then—shuts the Door—
To her divine Majority—
Present no more—

5 Unmoved—she notes the Chariots—pausing—
At her low Gate—
Unmoved—an Emperor be kneeling
Upon her Mat—

I've known her—from an ample nation—
10 Choose One—
Then—close the Valves of her attention—
Like Stone—

MEETING INDIVIDUAL NEEDS — ENGLISH LANGUAGE LEARNERS

Concepts of Heaven and Hell
Cultures with different religious beliefs also have differing concepts of what happens when someone dies. How do the English language learners in your class view death?

Activity Have small groups from different cultural backgrounds explore Dickinson's concepts of heaven and hell. Discuss whether similar ideas and questions are common across cultures. Encourage English language learners to contribute their beliefs.

Additional Resources
 English Language Learners Sourcebook

Responding to Literature

Personal Response

What questions would you like to ask the speakers of these poems?

ANALYZING LITERATURE

If you were coming in the Fall

RECALL AND INTERPRET

1. What periods of time does the speaker suggest in each of the first four stanzas? What action does the speaker take in the first four stanzas? Why, in your opinion, do the periods of time change from stanza to stanza?

2. According to the fifth stanza, what is the speaker uncertain about? Why might she compare this uncertainty to a bee's sting?

EVALUATE AND CONNECT

3. Would you call this a love poem? Why or why not?

4. What might Dickinson be saying about the nature of waiting? Do you agree? Explain.

My life closed twice before its close

RECALL AND INTERPRET

5. What has already happened twice to the speaker? To what kind of event might the speaker be referring?

6. What does the speaker say about parting? How, in your opinion, do partings affect the speaker?

EVALUATE AND CONNECT

7. Have you ever seen a life close before its close? What form did that closing take?

8. Only one dash is used in this poem, and only one word is capitalized that isn't at the beginning of a line. What effect, in your opinion, do the dash and capitalized word have on the meaning of the poem? Explain your answer.

The Soul selects her own Society

RECALL AND INTERPRET

9. What does the soul select? From among how many does the soul choose just one? What does this suggest about the soul?

10. According to the second stanza, what things fail to "move" the soul? In your opinion, why are the examples of what the soul is "unmoved" by significant?

11. What words does the speaker use to refer to the soul? From these words, what can you infer about the speaker's relationship to the soul?

EVALUATE AND CONNECT

12. What image do you see in your mind's eye when you imagine the soul closing "the Valves of her attention"? How does the use of this **metaphor** affect your understanding of the poem? (See Literary Terms Handbook, page R9.)

THE CIVIL WAR AND ITS AFTERMATH 427

Personal Response

Students' questions may extend the poems' meanings: who is the person for whom the speaker waits in "If you were coming in the Fall," or how did the speaker's life close twice?

ANALYZING LITERATURE

1. The speaker suggests months, years, centuries, and eternity. In stanza 1 she brushes aside Summer, in stanza 2 she puts the months away, in stanza 3 she counts and subtracts, and in stanza 4 she tosses her life away. The increasing lengths of time emphasize the depth of her feelings.

2. The speaker is uncertain about when or if the person she waits for will return, so the uncertainty buzzes around in her mind like a bee.

3. Some may say it is a love poem because it speaks of the pain and uncertainty of separation; the speaker says she would give up life for an eternity with the "you" in the poem. Others may say that what the speaker longs for is the love experience itself.

4. Students may say that Dickinson views waiting as something that can be survived, however long, providing an end moment is given.

5. The speaker experienced a darkness similar to death when she twice lost someone she loved. This might refer to the actual death of a person close to her or the loss of a friendship.

6. The speaker likens partings to death. The pain of parting makes her wonder if immortality will be equally devastating. The speaker muses that all we really know about heaven is that it represents parting and that knowing what parting is like is also everything we need to know of hell.

7. Students may mention people who are injured or those who have had devastating emotional experiences. Discuss what can assist a life to reopen after such a closing.

8. The dash suggests that the reader should pause and reflect. The capitalization of "Immortality" connects the concept of eternal life with God. The speaker speculates, however, on what heaven might be if it also represents eternal parting—the "third event."

9. The soul selects its friend from among many. The soul is extremely particular about its company and has one soulmate forever.

ASSESSMENT OPTIONS

- 📁 ***Quick Checks,*** p. 50
- 📁 ***Selection and Theme Assessment,*** pp. 77–78
- 📁 ***Performance Assessment,*** p. 42
- 💾 ***Testmaker***

10. The soul fails to be moved by either the noise of the crowd at her gate or by an important person kneeling at her doorstep. The soul chooses its company based upon its own private criteria.

11. The speaker refers to the soul as "her" and "she," suggesting that the speaker refers to her own soul and relationships.

12. Students may say that the valves, coupled with the reference to stone, suggest closing off a stream behind a dam. The metaphor is apt; valves completely stop the flow of water, just as the soul's choice might prevent feelings being given to others.

Reading the Selection

A Active Reading

CONNECT Explain that new ideas are often considered madness until they are proven. Challenge students to think of examples of "much madness" being "divinest Sense." *(Students may mention historical ideas such as the idea that the earth is round. Other students may say that the democratic government was once thought to be madness because the masses were too uneducated to make good decisions.)*

B Author's Craft

PARADOX A paradox is a statement that seems to contradict itself but nevertheless suggests an important truth. Emily Dickinson often uses paradoxes in her poetry, for example, "Much Madness is divinest Sense—." Ask students to explain the truth contained in this apparent contradiction. *(Students may say that unusual thinking and actions, which on the surface might be construed as "madness," often reflect a higher order of "sense" than is commonly recognized.)*

Additional Resources
📁 *Active Reading Guide,* p. 51
🎧 *Audio Library*

A Day Dream, 1877. Eastman Johnson. Oil on paperboard, 24 x 12 in. Fine Arts Museums of San Francisco. Gift of Mr. and Mrs. John D. Rockefeller III.

Much Madness is divinest Sense

Emily Dickinson ∿

Much Madness is divinest Sense—
To a discerning Eye—
Much Sense—the starkest Madness—
'Tis the Majority
In this, as All, prevail—
Assent—and you are sane—
Demur°—you're straightway dangerous—
And handled with a Chain—

---

7 *Demur* means "to hesitate" or "to protest."

Teaching Options

INCLUSION STRATEGIES

Special Needs Students with deep emotional sensitivity may identify strongly with the poem "Much Madness is divinest Sense."

Activity Allow students time to write about situations in their lives when they acted or thought differently from the majority, and felt or were considered unlike family or peers around them.

Journal entries will be shared only if the student chooses to share. **L2**

Additional Resources
📁 *Inclusion Strategies*

Responding to Literature

Personal Response

Which images from these poems did you find the most surprising and memorable? Why?

─── ANALYZING LITERATURE ───

I heard a Fly buzz when I died

RECALL AND INTERPRET

1. According to the first stanza, what is the atmosphere in the room like? What effect does the buzzing fly seem to have on the speaker?
2. In lines 5 and 6, what are the "eyes" and "breaths" doing? What do the "eyes" and "breaths" await? Explain your answer.
3. According to stanzas three and four, what does the fly come between? What happens next? In your opinion, what point about dying does the speaker make in this poem?

EVALUATE AND CONNECT

4. How does Dickinson's account of someone dying compare with other representations you have read or seen?

The Bustle in a House

RECALL AND INTERPRET

5. What words does the speaker use that suggest everyday household chores? In your opinion, is the poem really referring to everyday household chores? Explain.
6. According to the second stanza, when will we again "use" the love we put aside on the morning after death? What does this suggest about Dickinson's religious faith?

EVALUATE AND CONNECT

7. In your opinion, is bustle helpful or burdensome in times of grief? Explain.
8. An **analogy** is a comparison between two things to show their similarities. What analogy does the speaker make in this poem? In your opinion, is this an effective comparison?

Because I could not stop for Death

RECALL AND INTERPRET

9. According to the first stanza, why does "Death" stop? How is "Death" portrayed?
10. What places and things does the speaker pass while taking the ride with "Death"? What might these places and things represent?
11. What revelation does the speaker make in the last stanza? Why? What can you infer from this about the speaker's attitude toward death?

EVALUATE AND CONNECT

12. If you wrote a poem with this title, what places and things would the speaker pass in your poem? How would the speaker be dressed? Where would the speaker end up?

THE CIVIL WAR AND ITS AFTERMATH 🐞 433

✔ ASSESSMENT OPTIONS

- 📁 **Quick Checks,** p. 52
- 📁 **Selection and Theme Assessment,** pp. 77–78
- 📁 **Performance Assessment,** p. 42
- 💾 **Testmaker**

---

ripe grain = maturity, setting sun = death. The last image in stanza 5 is a house in the ground—perhaps a tomb.

11. In the final stanza, the speaker reveals that she has been dead for centuries, but it seems only a day in the face of eternity. Against eternity, a lifetime is very short.

12. Encourage students to use concrete images for their last ride, as Dickinson has done in the poem.

Personal Response

Students may mention the fly buzzing, "Sweeping up the Heart," or the horses' heads that were "toward Eternity."

ANALYZING LITERATURE

1. The atmosphere in the room is solemn. Loved ones encircle the speaker's deathbed. The fly distracts the speaker from the heaviness of this moment, from dying; the fly is annoying and makes the speaker lose concentration.

2. The "eyes" and "breaths" refer to those standing watch. They await the appearance of the King—the savior, or death personified.

3. The fly interposes its buzzing self between the dying person and "the light," between life and death. At that moment the speaker dies. Dickinson seems to say that even at the moment of death, life in the shape of this fly—trivial, annoying, ugly—reasserts itself.

4. Dickinson's portrayal of dying is unsentimental. Unlike many dramatic deathbed scenes, the tone is matter-of-fact. The fly is rather original.

5. The terms *bustle*, *sweeping*, and *putting away* all suggest household chores. Dickinson compares the chores to the emotional tasks necessary when a loved one dies.

6. According to the second stanza, we will not use the love we put aside until we meet the person who has died in the afterworld, suggesting that Dickinson believed in life after death.

7. Student may say that the bustle can be helpful for getting through sorrowful times.

8. Dickinson compares the cleaning of a house with the cleaning of a heart required after the death of a loved one.

9. Death stops for the speaker because her time on Earth is over. Death is portrayed as a kindly gentleman, a coach driver.

10. While taking the ride with death, the speaker passes the schoolyard, fields of grain, the setting sun, and a house. These places represent the phases of life: school = youth,

Writing Skills

Objective

- To develop a writing idea by providing specific supporting details appropriate for the purpose of the piece

Teaching Strategies

Explain that expert opinions provide elaboration and strengthen the writer's position. Tell students that newspaper reporters often consult experts when developing stories. Ask students to bring in samples of elaboration from a current newspaper.

Activities

1. *Student elaborations should*
   - employ relevant facts.
   - cite expert opinion.
   - include persuasive reasons.
2. *Students' revisions should*
   - include elaboration strategies.
   - use elaboration to strengthen their arguments.

Additional Resources

Writer's Choice, Lesson 3.2

Writing Skills

Elaborating on an Idea

Elaboration is the filling in of details that flesh out an idea. In "Because I could not stop for Death," Emily Dickinson elaborates on the carriage journey with specific details. For example, when the speaker mentions passing a school, she describes the children at recess. Elaboration not only enriches poetry, it also adds depth and clarity to prose. Besides details, elaboration can also include the following:

- facts and statistics
- expert opinions
- anecdotes
- quotations
- reasons
- examples

The kind of writing you do determines how you will elaborate. To prove a point, you might elaborate by using facts and quotations. For example, in a letter to protest the loss of a neighborhood park you might include

- the results of a poll showing that 150 preschool children use the playground equipment several times a week.
- a quote from the former mayor: "The citizens of Midville need travel no more than a few blocks to picnic or play ball in one of the many small parks that make our community the envy of its neighbors."

To describe someone or something, you might use an anecdote.

> Jonathan Marks finished the last bit of oatmeal in his bowl, got to his feet, and ambled to the sink to wash his dishes. He walked to the door, checked the empty mailbox, and brought in the morning newspaper. "Max," he said to the old mixed-breed hound devotedly following him, "wait until I reread this letter my niece wrote last week. Then we'll go for our morning walk."

ACTIVITIES

1. Use facts and expert opinions to elaborate for your parents on the reasons you should receive a laptop computer (or any other gift).

2. Use examples and an anecdote to describe one friend to another.

Grammar and Language *Minilesson*

Using a Dash Dashes indicate an abrupt break or change in thought or add emphasis within a sentence.

Activity Have students write sentences using dashes either for emphasis or to indicate an abrupt change or break.

L2

Additional Resources

- *Grammar and Language Transparency 38*
- *Grammar and Language Workbook,* p. 267
- *Grammar and Composition Handbook,* Lesson 11.7
- *Writer's Choice,* Lesson 21.7

There's a certain Slant of light

Emily Dickinson ∾

There's a certain Slant of light,
Winter Afternoons—
That oppresses, like the Heft°
Of Cathedral Tunes—

5 Heavenly Hurt, it gives us—
We can find no scar,
But internal difference,
Where the Meanings, are—

None may teach it—Any—
10 'Tis the Seal° Despair—
An imperial affliction
Sent us of the Air—

When it comes, the Landscape listens—
Shadows—hold their breath—
15 When it goes, 'tis like the Distance
On the look of Death—

---

3 Here, *heft* means "heaviness."
10 Here, *seal* means "emblem."

CONNECT Point out to students that Emily Dickinson's letter to the world is very brief and seemingly simple. It contains only eight short lines. Give students a few minutes to write their own letters to the world, in which they explain in about 40 words how they would like to be remembered. Then ask how many students listed personality or character traits, how many listed accomplishments, and how many listed relationships. Then ask students which, if any of these things, apply to the speaker in "This is my letter to the World."

(Students should note that the speaker mentions none of these directly; however, the eight lines suggest that she is referring to her body of poetry. She says that people should judge her tenderly because she was engaged in relaying nature's messages.)

Thematic Focus

Two New Voices Ask students to discuss which elements of Dickinson's poetry might inspire her readers to judge her tenderly. Which of these elements might be characteristic of new voices in American literature during the mid-1800s?

✔ **ASSESSMENT OPTIONS**

📁 *Quick Checks,* p. 53

This is my letter to the World

Emily Dickinson ∾

At the Window, 1870. Karl Harald Alfred Broge. Oil on canvas, 21 x 17¼ in. Private collection.

This is my letter to the World
That never wrote to Me—
The simple News that Nature told—
With tender Majesty

Her Message is committed°
To Hands I cannot see—
For love of Her—Sweet—countrymen—
Judge tenderly—of Me

———————————————
5 *Committed* means "entrusted."

Teaching Options

MEETING INDIVIDUAL NEEDS — **ENGLISH LANGUAGE LEARNERS**

Nature's Message Students from other cultures often have a different awareness of and appreciation for nature. English language learners may enjoy sharing their views with the rest of the class.

Activity Divide the class into groups with native speakers and English language learners. Ask each group to brainstorm images of nature from the land they are most familiar with. Students may know legends or stories connected with particular places. Provide time in class for a discussion of the beauties of nature.

Additional Resources
📁 *English Language Learners Sourcebook*

Responding to Literature

Personal Response

What reactions did you have while reading these poems?

ANALYZING LITERATURE

There's a certain Slant of light

RECALL AND INTERPRET

1. When does the speaker observe the "certain Slant of light"? What effect does the light have on the speaker?
2. In the third stanza, what words or phrases does the speaker use to name the slant of light? What can you infer about the speaker's feelings toward the light?
3. What happens when the light comes, and what happens when it goes? What might the light **symbolize,** or represent?

EVALUATE AND CONNECT

4. Have you ever experienced the kind of winter afternoon light the speaker describes? What might be different about the light or a person's mood on a winter afternoon than at other times of year or day?
5. What feelings does Dickinson evoke as she describes that "certain Slant of light"? Does she bring out these feelings effectively? Use details from the poem to explain your answer.
6. **Personification** is the giving of human qualities or characteristics to an object, an idea, or an animal. Identify two or more examples of personification in this poem. Explain how they affect the poem's meaning.

This is my letter to the World

RECALL AND INTERPRET

7. To whom is the speaker's letter addressed? To what do you think the speaker is referring with the words "my letter"?
8. What "News" does the letter contain? What, in your opinion, is the speaker's relationship to nature?
9. What plea does the speaker make in the second stanza? Why do you think the speaker makes this plea?

EVALUATE AND CONNECT

10. Do you think this poem would make a suitable introduction to a collection of Dickinson's work? Explain your answer.
11. What new impressions of Dickinson did this poem give you?
12. If you could send a letter to the world, what would it say?

Responding to the Selection

Personal Response

Students may say that "There's a certain Slant of light" is sad or depressing, and that "This is my letter to the World" made them think about qualities that give life significance.

ANALYZING LITERATURE

1. The speaker observes this "certain Slant of light" in the late afternoon on a winter's day. She finds it oppressive.
2. In the third stanza the speaker names the light "the Seal Despair" and calls it "An imperial affliction." One can infer from this choice of words that the speaker thinks of the light as a kind of cosmic malaise, inexplicable desperation caused by nature.
3. When the light comes, the speaker feels overcome by the weight of her mood. When it leaves, she feels relief. The light may symbolize a mood in which the awareness of death becomes oppressive.
4. A winter afternoon is often gloomy and dark, possibly contributing to depression that might otherwise be dispelled by sunshine.
5. Dickinson elicits feelings of oppressive weight and inexplicable depression. She accomplishes this through precise word choice: "oppresses," "Heft," "Hurt," "Despair."
6. The "Landscape" and "Shadows" are personified in this poem. Like the speaker, both are affected by the "Slant of light," and are seen as the speaker sees them.
7. The letter is addressed to the public. By "letter" Dickinson is probably referring to her poetry.
8. The "News" is the information Dickinson has culled from careful observation, experience, and communion with nature.
9. The speaker asks "the World" to be gentle in judging her. She has communicated nature's message as well as she can. It is now committed

---

ASSESSMENT OPTIONS

- 📁 **Quick Checks,** p. 53
- 📁 **Selection and Theme Assessment,** pp. 77–78
- 📁 **Performance Assessment,** p. 42
- 💾 **Testmaker**

to the public—"Hands I cannot see." Dickinson, like all artists, seeks an appreciative audience.

10. Students are likely to concur that this poem would make a good introduction to a collection of Dickinson's poetry because it is an explanation and a plea for understanding from the author to her readers.

11. The poem gives the impression of a writer who, despite reclusiveness, wants others to read her poems and who cares about how others may judge her work.

12. Ask students if they would change anything in the letters they wrote, after studying and thinking about Dickinson's poems.

LITERATURE AND WRITING

Writing About Literature

Students' paragraphs should
- state Dickinson's primary themes, such as nature, success, or death as the focus for their writing.
- support this focus statement with evidence from the poems.
- compare Dickinson's themes with issues and ideas that are important to them.

Creative Writing

Students' presentations should
- demonstrate an understanding of Dickinson's treatment of a topic, such as cleaning a house in preparation for a funeral.
- use a form other than poetry to express this topic.

EXTENDING YOUR RESPONSE

Literature Groups After groups have shared their interpretations with the class, discuss how difficult literature becomes more accessible through collaborative readings. **COLLAB. LEARN.**

Internet Connection Help students determine the credibility of various Web sites by examining which seem to be the work of scholars and which the work of enthusiasts.

Performing Encourage students to practice their charade several times before performing it for the other group. **COLLAB. LEARN.**

Literary ELEMENTS

Slant Rhyme

Slant rhyme, also called imperfect rhyme or eye rhyme, refers to the words at the ends of lines of poetry that almost–but don't quite–rhyme. Dickinson makes constant use of slant rhyme in her poems. For example, in "I heard a Fly buzz when I died," the words *room* and *storm,* which appear at the ends of lines 2 and 4, almost rhyme. Similarly, the words *be* and *fly,* at the ends of lines 10 and 12, are slant rhymes. In this case, the words do not almost rhyme; instead, they end with letters that sometimes rhyme or may look as if they rhyme.

1. Identify one other use of slant rhyme in "I heard a Fly buzz when I died."
2. Identify the two examples of slant rhyme in "The Bustle in a House."
3. Identify two other uses of slant rhyme in other poems by Dickinson. Give at least one reason why Dickinson may have chosen to use slant rhyme in each case.

● See **Literary Terms Handbook,** p. R13.

LITERATURE AND WRITING

Writing About Literature

Identify Themes Based on the poems you have read, what would you identify as the **themes,** or central messages, of Dickinson's poetry? Begin by jotting down notes about the theme of each poem in this lesson. Then write two or three paragraphs in which you identify Dickinson's primary themes and give examples of how she states them. Finally, compare Dickinson's themes with the ideas you expressed in the Focus Activity on page 424.

Creative Writing

Remodeling Job Take one of the topics expressed in Dickinson's poems, such as "Death" picking up a rider and taking the rider to the cemetery, and present the topic in a different form. For example, you might choose to create a cartoon, comic strip, diary entry, monologue, script, or itinerary. Title your work with a relevant quote from Dickinson's poetry.

EXTENDING YOUR RESPONSE

Literature Groups

Finding the Meaning With your group, go back over two or three poems and identify words, phrases, and lines that you found difficult to understand. Discuss these passages with one another and offer ideas on how to interpret them. Build an interpretation of each poem based on everyone's combined input. Be ready to share your interpretations with the class.

Internet Connection

Visit Emily Dickinson On-line The life of this very private poet has become very public on the Internet. Conduct a search to find Web sites devoted to Dickinson's life and poetry. Visit one site and present a short review of it to your classmates. Include the address, the options at the site, and aspects of the site that make visiting it a worthwhile or time-wasting experience.

Performing

Play Charades Working as a group, choose an image or scene from one of the poems to act out for another group. See how quickly others can identify the poem. When you are done, watch the charades of other groups and identify the poems they correspond to.

■ Save your work for your portfolio.

LITERARY ELEMENTS

1. firm/Room.
2. Death/Earth, away/Eternity.
3. In "Because I could not stop for Death," slant rhymes include away/Civility, chill/Tulle, Day/Eternity. Dickinson's style includes frequent rhymes. Rather than use an imprecise word for the sake of rhyme, Dickinson chose slant rhyme.

Additional Resources

🖑 *Literary Elements Transparency 42*

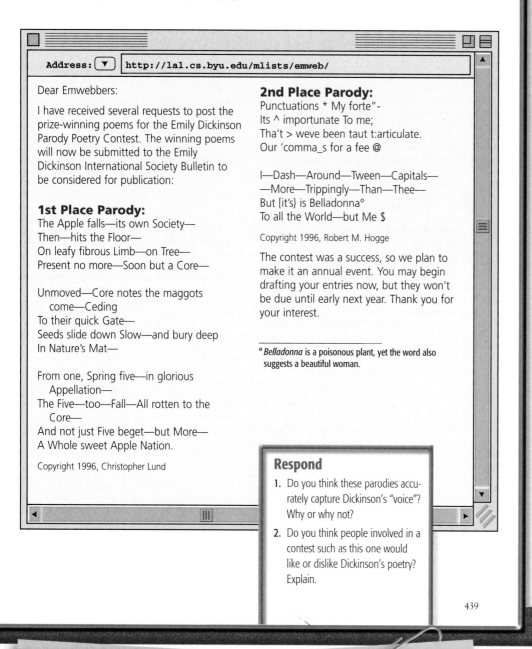

MEDIA Connection

Web Page

Imitation, people say, is the highest form of flattery. Does that statement include humorous imitation, or **parody?** The poems below placed first and second in an on-line Emily Dickinson Parody Poetry Contest.

Address: ▼ http://lal.cs.byu.edu/mlists/emweb/

Dear Emwebbers:

I have received several requests to post the prize-winning poems for the Emily Dickinson Parody Poetry Contest. The winning poems will now be submitted to the Emily Dickinson International Society Bulletin to be considered for publication:

1st Place Parody:
The Apple falls—its own Society—
Then—hits the Floor—
On leafy fibrous Limb—on Tree—
Present no more—Soon but a Core—

Unmoved—Core notes the maggots
　　come—Ceding
To their quick Gate—
Seeds slide down Slow—and bury deep
In Nature's Mat—

From one, Spring five—in glorious
　　Appellation—
The Five—too—Fall—All rotten to the
　　Core—
And not just Five beget—but More—
A Whole sweet Apple Nation.

Copyright 1996, Christopher Lund

2nd Place Parody:
Punctuations * My forte"-
Its ^ importunate To me;
Tha't > weve been taut t:articulate.
Our 'comma_s for a fee @

I—Dash—Around—Tween—Capitals—
—More—Trippingly—Than—Thee—
But [it's} is Belladonna°
To all the World—but Me $

Copyright 1996, Robert M. Hogge

The contest was a success, so we plan to make it an annual event. You may begin drafting your entries now, but they won't be due until early next year. Thank you for your interest.

° *Belladonna* is a poisonous plant, yet the word also suggests a beautiful woman.

Respond

1. Do you think these parodies accurately capture Dickinson's "voice"? Why or why not?

2. Do you think people involved in a contest such as this one would like or dislike Dickinson's poetry? Explain.

439

Writing Workshop

Objectives

- To create a personal response to a poem
- To plan an analytical essay on the meaning in a poem
- To draft, revise, edit, and present an expository essay

GLENCOE
TECHNOLOGY

WRITER'S ASSISTANT CD-ROM

Students can use Glencoe's templates and guidelines software for expository writing to aid them in working through the steps in the writing process in this lesson.

Teaching Strategies

PREWRITING

Explore Ideas Have students share ideas about their poem with a partner; then remind them that if their analysis reveals things about the poem which they no longer wish to write about, they may choose another poem.

Choose an audience Suggest that students aim their analysis for students a grade or two younger and that they keep their style simple.

Teaching Options

∾: Writing ✶ Workshop :∾

Expository Writing: Analyzing a Poem

Using relatively few words, poets can communicate vast meanings and evoke deep emotions. How do they do it? They use rhythm, sound, form, figurative language, and numerous other methods to get the most out of their words. As a reader, you try to understand the poem, and one of the best ways to understand a poem is to write an analysis of it. **In this workshop, you will analyze a poem by identifying its meaning and then writing an essay that explains how various techniques help create that meaning.** You may choose a poem from this theme or any other poem that appeals to you.

● As you write your analysis, refer to the **Writing Handbook**, pp. R62–R77.

The Writing Process

PREWRITING

> **PREWRITING TIP**
>
> Keep a dictionary beside you as you read the poem. You will need to understand the meaning of each word.

Explore ideas

Choose a poem from this unit or any poem that has made a strong impression on you. For example, you might want to write about a poem that gave you a surprising view of death, as in Dickinson's "I heard a Fly buzz when I died." Or you might choose a poem that expresses your own feelings about nature, as in Whitman's *Song of Myself.* Then use the following steps to help you get inside the poem.

● Read the poem once all the way through, noting how it makes you feel and any new insights it provides.
● Read the poem again, highlighting sections you might not understand.
● Read it a third and fourth time, jotting down questions, thoughts, feelings—anything you think of.
● Discuss the poem with a partner. Remember, though, that you don't have to agree on everything.

Choose an audience

You can write your poetry analysis for other high school students. Perhaps your class can even put together a literary magazine with articles on favorite poems.

Consider your purpose

No matter who your audience is, you must explain your interpretation of the poem and show how the poet conveys that meaning. To do this, you will have to identify the techniques the poet uses and give examples from the poem.

MEETING INDIVIDUAL NEEDS ENGLISH LANGUAGE LEARNERS

Vocabulary Development Poetic language is often more dense than that of prose. A single misunderstood word can impede comprehension. English language learners should pay particular attention to a poem's vocabulary.

Activity Before students read, have them scan the poems for unfamiliar words. Suggest that they try to determine the words' meanings from context and then consult a dictionary to verify the definition. If they are still confused, tell students to ask a peer or you for help. Finally, have students make lists of these words and their definitions to use as references.

Additional Resources
📁 *English Language Learners Sourcebook*

Make a plan

In the introduction to your essay, state your interpretation of the poem's meaning. You will also want to summarize the techniques that the poet uses to convey the meaning. Then, in the body of your essay, you will devote a separate paragraph to each technique. The chart below will help you plan the content of your essay.

STUDENT MODEL

Meaning	Does the poem focus on an idea? Does it focus on a feeling? What message is the poet trying to convey?	"I heard a Fly buzz" focuses on the moment of death. It makes me imagine what it must be like to die.
Form	Do the poem's form and content seem related? Has the poet done anything unusual with punctuation or capitalization? If so, how does that help communicate the poet's message?	The poem's form does not really relate to its content. Certain words are capitalized, though, and that's probably important.
Meter	Does the poem have regular meter, or is it written in free verse? Why might the poet have chosen one pattern instead of another?	The poem is in free verse, but it has a distinct rhythm. The poet uses dashes to break up the rhythm and hold our attention.
Language	What images does the poet create? To what senses do the images appeal? Does the poet use figurative language, such as metaphors or similes? Does the poem contain any symbols? Do the imagery and figurative language help you see new connections between ideas? How do the imagery and figurative language help bring out the poem's meaning?	Room's stillness is compared to the stillness between a storm's heaves. Other figurative language: Eyes had wrung dry, breaths gathering, failing windows.
Speaker	Is there a definite speaker? If so, does the speaker's identity affect the poem's meaning?	The speaker is someone who has just died. The poet is imagining what it must be like to die.

Remember you don't need to discuss all the techniques mentioned in the chart. Focus on the ones that contribute to the meaning of the poem you are writing about and discuss them in order of importance.

Consider your purpose To demonstrate how the poet conveys meaning, students will need to identify the techniques the poet employs. Review the definitions of common poetic techniques and remind students to identify them in their essays.

Make a plan Have students make a chart similar to the one described. Have them answer the questions about meaning, form, meter, language, and speaker. Remind students that at this point they are only jotting down notes.

Once they have answered the questions, students should reread their poems to find specific examples to support their ideas. If they can find no supporting evidence, students should reconsider what they have generalized about the poems.

Additional Resources

📁 *Writing and Proofreading Practice*, pp. 1–7, 38–44

✍ *Writing and Proofreading Transparencies 1–6, 33–34*

📓 *Writer's Choice,* Lessons 2.2, 2.7

Writing *Minilesson*

Oral Prewriting Students who are gifted talkers may find that their most effective prewriting strategy is to explain the plan for their essay aloud to a partner.

Activity Put students in pairs and have the partners answer the model questions in conversation before they put their ideas on paper. Encourage the listening partner to ask probing questions of the writing partner. Remind students that it is especially important to ask where in the text the writer finds evidence for his or her assumptions about the poem. **L2**

Additional Resources

📓 *Writer's Choice,* Lesson 2.2

442 🐾 UNIT 3

DRAFTING

Draft openings Discuss various ways to get a reader's attention in an essay. Ask students to think about effective openings.

Write your draft Have students free-write for about 20 minutes, keeping their audience in mind before they think about formal structure.

REVISING

Evaluate your work Remind students to use the Questions for Revising as they reread their drafts. If they answer "no" to every question, the best solution may be to choose another poem and re-start the writing process.

Talk it over Encourage students to ask their writing partners for specific help with the parts of the essay that seem most problematic. Often a reluctant respondent comes to life when asked specific questions.

TECHNOLOGY TIP

The cut-and-paste feature of word processing programs allows students to rearrange whole sections of their essays for greater impact. Encourage students to reconsider the order of their supporting paragraphs.

Teaching Options

~ *Writing Workshop* ~

DRAFTING

DRAFTING TIP
Keep your plan in mind, but don't be afraid to change it if you discover new ideas about the poem as you draft.

Draft openings
When drafting, you can experiment with different openings until you find the best way to get your readers' attention. One approach is to begin your essay with a provocative question.

Write your draft
Elaborate on each point you make by giving examples from the poem. For more help with elaboration, refer to Writing Skills page 434.

STUDENT MODEL

FIRST OPENING	SECOND OPENING
In the poem "I heard a Fly buzz when I died," Emily Dickinson sets out to describe the moment of death. This essay will examine three techniques Dickinson uses to convey her vision of death.	The moment of death— what is it like? In the poem "I heard a Fly buzz when I died," Emily Dickinson thinks about death and imagines what the experience must be like. This essay will discuss her use of three techniques in an unromantic portrayal of death.

REVISING

REVISING TIP
Make sure the lines you cite from the poem are stated correctly.

TECHNOLOGY TIP
Use the cut-and-paste function on your computer to be sure your sentences and paragraphs are concise. Cut out all words, phrases, and sentences that are redundant or unnecessary.

Evaluate your work
Let your draft sit for at least a few hours before you begin revising it. Then look for places where you could have expressed your ideas more clearly. Using the **Questions for Revising** as a guide, make revisions to your draft.

Talk it over
Read your essay aloud to a partner. Take notes on your partner's comments and questions, and consider his or her responses as you revise.

STUDENT MODEL

By focusing
~~Because Dickinson looks at~~ on the
moment of death, the poem makes
    what that moment might be like
me think about ~~death.~~

QUESTIONS FOR REVISING

- ☑ Does the opening generate interest?
- ☑ Is your thesis, or central idea, clearly stated in the opening paragraph?
- ☑ Do the points you make support your thesis?
- ☑ Is there evidence from the poem to support each point?
- ☑ Does the concluding paragraph sum up your major points?

MEETING INDIVIDUAL NEEDS — GIFTED AND TALENTED ACTIVITY

A Creative Writing Magazine Constructing a class magazine to showcase students' creative writing efforts can be an excellent way to teach collaboration skills. It also allows students to evaluate, edit, compose, and format a magazine.

Activity Assign an editor, designer, and technical expert as the magazine's staff. Encourage the staff to plan the magazine's focus, prepare editorial guidelines, and accept submissions that include original poetry, short stories, criticism, and expository articles. Include original illustrations as appropriate and available. Suggest that students solicit manuscripts and artwork from fellow students. Set a publication date for the magazine. **L3** **COLLAB. LEARN.**

~ Writing ~ Workshop ~

EDITING/PROOFREADING

When you are satisfied with the content and flow of your essay, proofread it carefully for errors in grammar, usage, mechanics, and spelling.

PROOFREADING TIP
Use the **Proofreading Checklist** on the inside back cover of this book to help catch mistakes.

Grammar Hint

Nonessential appositives should be preceded and followed by commas.

To see if an appositive is nonessential, ask yourself, "Does the sentence still make sense without the appositive?"

Giselle Gonzales, last year's winner of the poetry contest, will present the award.

● For more on using commas, see **Language Handbook**, p. R53.

The appositive phrase, *last year's winner of the poetry contest,* is not essential to the meaning of the sentence and therefore is set off by commas.

STUDENT MODEL

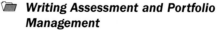

PUBLISHING/PRESENTING

If you are planning to put together a class literary magazine, agree on ways to make the essays look similar. For example, you might decide to use the same lettering and the same size headings. If you are presenting your essay to teachers or classmates, make the copy as attractive as you can. Remember to check it one final time for mistakes.

PRESENTING TIP
Giving your essay an intriguing title will help focus your readers' attention on what you want to say.

Reflecting

Think about the writing experience you have just had. In your journal, reflect on other ways you might use the analyzing skills you developed while writing this essay. What would you do differently in your next analysis of a literary work?

Save your work for your portfolio.

EDITING/PROOFREADING

Discuss with students the reasons for careful proofreading. What happens when mechanical errors persist in the final copy of an essay? Encourage students to think about how mechanical errors distract the reader from the message and interfere with meaning. Students should also consider how careless proofreading can diminish credibility. All the reader has to go on is what is on the page.

PUBLISHING/PRESENTING

A literary magazine needs an introduction to orient readers to the publication's content. Suggest that students use Emily Dickinson's "This is my letter to the World" as a model for the opening page of their magazine. How would they like their readers to judge these essays?

Reflecting

Portfolio Encourage students to ask themselves this question as they review their writing.

Does my essay
- reflect a candid appraisal of my strengths and weaknesses as a writer?
- represent some of my best work?
- include ideas I would like to pursue further?

Suggest that if students answer "yes" to more than one of these questions, they consider including their essays in their portfolios.

✔ ASSESSMENT OPTIONS

📁 **Writing Assessment and Portfolio Management**
- Writing Assessment, pp. 1–13, 26–28
- Portfolio Management, pp. 51–58

Unit Wrap-Up

Objective

- To review the literature, discussions, and activities in this unit

PERSONAL RESPONSE

1. Students may choose materials that elicit an emotional response, such as "Mary Chesnut's Civil War" or "I Hear America Singing."
2. Students may choose the Whitman selections that teach about the emotions associated with the Civil War.
3. Students may say that literature often reflects the historical setting, events, and developments of an era.
4. Be sure students provide specific examples to show how poems may have changed their feelings about poetry.

ANALYZING LITERATURE

Students' writing should
- have an introductory paragraph that identifies the two pieces of literature and the two topics being compared.
- include details from both pieces to support their conclusions.

EVALUATE AND SET GOALS

Evaluate

Have students list the assignments they completed throughout the unit and evaluate their own performance for each one of these.

Set Goals

Ask students to identify their goals as well as the steps they intend to take toward achieving them. Suggest that students make a time line with milestones clearly indicated. Discuss students' plans in individual conferences.

Unit Wrap-Up

PERSONAL RESPONSE

1. Which selection in Unit 3 made the strongest impression on you? What created this impression—the events of a story, the language and imagery of a poem, the facts you learned, or some other element?
2. Which selection or selections taught you the most about our nation's history?
3. What new ideas do you have about understanding history through different kinds of literature?
4. How did the poems in Unit 3 affect your feelings and ideas about poetry?

ANALYZING LITERATURE

Compare and Contrast   A number of the selections in Unit 3 focus on the topics of slavery and the Civil War. Choose one of those topics and then select two pieces of literature from Unit 3 on that topic. (Count Whitman's two Civil War poems as one selection.) Explain the ways the two pieces are alike and different. For example, do they provide similar or different viewpoints? Do they convey impressions and lessons that are similar or different? Which piece taught you more about the topic you chose?

EVALUATE AND SET GOALS

Evaluate

1. What was the most significant thing you contributed to the class as you studied this unit?
2. Which aspect of this unit was the most interesting to you?
   - What made it so interesting?
   - In what ways could you pursue this interest further?
3. How would you assess your work in this unit using the following scale? Give at least two reasons for your assessment.
   4 = outstanding   **3** = good   **2** = fair   **1** = weak
4. If you had another week to work on this unit, what would you hope to learn? What would you hope to make or create? What skills would you hope to strengthen?

Set Goals

1. Set a goal for your work in the next unit. Try to focus on improving a skill such as writing or listening.
2. Discuss your goal with your teacher.
3. Plan specific steps to achieve the goal.
4. Plan checkpoints at which you can judge your work.
5. Think of a method to evaluate your finished work.

BUILD YOUR PORTFOLIO

Select   From the writing you have done for this unit, choose two pieces to put in your portfolio. Use the following questions as guides when choosing:
- Which taught you the most?
- Which are you likely to share?
- Which was the most fun to do?
- Which was the most difficult to complete?

Reflect   Include some explanatory notes with the portfolio pieces you have chosen. Use these questions to guide you:
- What are the piece's strengths and weaknesses?
- What did working on the piece teach you about writing (or about other skills the piece displays)?
- How would you revise the piece today to make it stronger?

✔ ASSESSMENT OPTIONS

📁 ***Writing Assessment and Portfolio Management***
- Writing Assessment, pp. 1–13
- Portfolio Management, pp. 51–58

GLENCOE
TECHNOLOGY

 **MINDJOGGER VIDEOQUIZZES**
VIDEODISC
Use *MindJogger* to review the Unit Three content.

Unit 3
Side A

 Also available in VHS.

Reading on Your Own

If you have enjoyed the literature in this unit, you might also be interested in the following books.

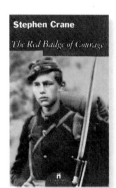

The Red Badge of Courage
by Stephen Crane A Civil War soldier's grand notions of glory abandon him as he faces the slaughter of battle. Crane had no experience of warfare when he wrote this novel, yet he successfully depicts the experiences, the terror, and the bravery of an ordinary soldier.

America Goes to War: The Civil War and Its Meaning in American Culture
by Bruce Catton Catton offers many interesting and useful facts and insights into the Civil War. The author also relates the Civil War to more current events in American and world history.

The Negro's Civil War: How American Blacks Felt and Acted During the War for the Union
by James M. McPherson This book reads like a well-written diary with the addition of historical explanations. Numerous quotations reveal the ideas and feelings of African American Union soldiers in their own words. Photographs, songs, tables, and charts offer a variety of additional source materials.

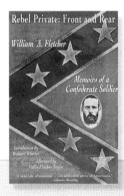

Rebel Private: Front and Rear
by William A. Fletcher In this memoir, a former Confederate soldier tells of the harsh realities of the Civil War. Fletcher describes many important battles, including the Battle of Gettysburg. The book provides an interesting perspective—that of an ordinary citizen and Confederate soldier.

THE CIVIL WAR AND ITS AFTERMATH 🐾 445

Reading on Your Own

Glencoe Literature Library

The Red Badge of Courage by Stephen Crane is available in the *Glencoe Literature Library*. For a complete listing, see p. T48 in this book.

The *Study Guides for Glencoe Literature* provide instructional support and student activities for works in the *Glencoe Literature Library*.

At the MOVIES

Be sure to preview the following video for appropriateness for your class:

• *An Occurrence at Owl Creek Bridge**

* Also available in the Glencoe Literature *Video Library*

MEETING INDIVIDUAL NEEDS INCLUSION STRATEGIES

While *The Red Badge of Courage* by Stephen Crane might be difficult for your less-proficient readers, they might increase their understanding of the novel by making a story map as they read.

• *America Goes to War: The Civil War and Its Meaning in American Culture* by Bruce Catton **L2**

• *The Negro's Civil War* by James M. McPherson **L2**

• *Rebel Private: Front and Rear* by William A. Fletcher **L2**

Additional Resources
📁 *Inclusion Strategies*

Standardized Test Practice

Answers and Analyses

1. **D** This sentence contains a problem of diction. The appropriate word is an *indefinite* period, not an *indecisive* period.

2. **B** The word *cautious* describes the manner in which mountain bikes are ridden. Since it modifies a verb, it should be the adverb *cautiously*.

3. **B** The two verbs in the sentence must be in parallel form. (People *are* sometimes employed . . . and so *have* no sense . . .)

4. **E** There is no error in this sentence.

5. **C** The *university* is doing the fund-raising. The *university* is singular and requires the possessive adjective *its* rather than *their*.

6. **C** The word *contributions* is plural, and therefore requires the plural form *have been recorded*.

Tell students that, when taking the actual SAT, it is best to fill in the answer oval for each question as they answer it. If students need to skip a question, they should be very careful to skip it on the answer sheet also. They should check periodically to be sure that they are on the same question in the test booklet and on the answer sheet.

Standardized Test Practice

> **Directions:** The following sentences test your knowledge of grammar, usage, diction (choice of words), and idiom.
>
> Some sentences are correct.
> No sentence contains more than one error.
>
> You will find that the error, if there is one, is underlined and lettered. Elements of the sentence that are not underlined will not be changed. In choosing answers, follow the requirements of standard written English.
>
> If there is an error, select the <u>one underlined part</u> that must be changed to make the sentence correct. Write the corresponding letter on your paper.
>
> If there is no error, select answer E.

1. <u>Despite</u> the community's urgent appeal,
     A
   the city government <u>decided</u> to build a
            B
   new highway <u>through</u> the park and close
           C
   the park for an <u>indecisive</u> period. <u>No error</u>
            D   E

2. <u>No matter</u> how <u>cautious</u> mountain bikes
     A   B
   are ridden, they <u>are</u> capable <u>of damaging</u>
           C   D
   the land over which they travel. <u>No error</u>
            E

3. People are sometimes employed <u>to complete</u>
            A
   a small part of one process in one section
   of one company, and so <u>having</u> no sense
           B
   <u>of</u> the process <u>in its entirety</u>. <u>No error</u>
    C   D   E

4. The doctor <u>omitted from</u> his article any
          A
   mention of subjects who <u>had experienced</u>
            B
   adverse reactions <u>to</u> the medication
           C
   prescribed for <u>them</u>. <u>No error</u>
         D   E

5. An administrator at the state university
   announced that an <u>extraordinarily high</u>
        A   B
   percentage of <u>their</u> fund-raising results
           C
   directly <u>from</u> money donated to it by
        D
   generous alumni. <u>No error</u>
          E

6. Many scholars have <u>written about</u> the
          A
   Renaissance, but <u>never before</u> <u>has</u> the
           B   C
   contributions of the painters been
   <u>so completely</u> recorded. <u>No error</u>
      D   E

Directions: The following sentences test correctness and effectiveness of expression. In choosing answers, follow the requirements of standard written English; that is, pay attention to grammar, choice of words, sentence construction, and punctuation.

In each of the following sentences, part of the sentence or the entire sentence is underlined. Beneath each sentence you will find five ways of phrasing the underlined part. Choice A repeats the original; the other four are different.

Choose the answer that best expresses the meaning of the original sentence and write the corresponding letter on your paper. If you think the original is better than any of the alternatives, choose it; otherwise choose one of the others. Your choice should produce the most effective sentence—clear and precise, without awkwardness or ambiguity.

1. Jean Louis David's art depicts classical <u>figures and they were</u> both historically and stylistically accurate for the neo-classical period.

   (A) figures and they were
   (B) figures that were
   (C) figures, being that they were
   (D) figures, and making them
   (E) figures, they

2. <u>The community center, once about to close due to lack of funds, is</u> now a busy, fun place to visit.

   (A) The community center, once about to close due to lack of funds, is
   (B) The community center was once about to close due to lack of funds, it is
   (C) The community center that once having been about to close due to lack of funds is
   (D) The community center, because it was once about to close due to lack of funds, is
   (E) The community center was once about to close due to lack of funds, and it is

3. For many a talented writer, <u>being free to create is more important</u> than being highly paid.

   (A) being free to create is more important
   (B) having freedom to create is more important
   (C) there is more importance in the freedom to create
   (D) freedom to create has more importance
   (E) to have the freedom to create is more important

4. In most offices, employees keep copies of all documents, <u>a focus on detail that is important</u>.

   (A) a focus on detail that is important
   (B) inasmuch as they show a focus on detail, it is important
   (C) this makes it important in showing their focus on detail
   (D) an idea that is important in showing their focus on detail
   (E) which is important and it shows a focus on detail

 STOP

SAT II Practice
Subject Test: Writing
Sentence Correction
Timed (3 minutes)

Answers and Analyses

1. **B** Choice E makes a run-on sentence; choices C and D are awkward. Choice A requires a comma after *figures*. Choice B is, therefore, the correct choice.

2. **A** Choice B requires a conjunction (or a semicolon) to connect the two independent clauses. Choice C is an incomplete sentence. Choices D and E illogically connect (with *because* and *and*) the two clauses; if any conjunction is used, it should have the sense of contrasting the two clauses (by using a conjunction such as *but*).

3. **A** To maintain parallel structure in this sentence, the first part of the comparison must match the second part (*being free . . . is more important than being highly paid*).

4. **A** In choices B, C, and E, the referent of the pronoun *it* is unclear. Choice D is awkward. Therefore the best choice is A.

 TEST-TAKING TIP

Advise students to carefully read the directions for each section of the test if they have not practiced on actual released tests. If they have taken many practice tests, they should simply skim the directions to prepare their minds for the task at hand.

MORE PRACTICE

For additional practice with the SAT II Writing Test, assign pp. 28–33 from the *College Entrance Exams Preparation and Practice Workbook.*

UNIT INTRODUCTION

Theme 6:
THE ENERGY OF THE EVERYDAY

SELECTIONS

SKILL FEATURES

WRITING WORKSHOP

UNIT WRAP-UP

- **Personal Response, Analyzing Literature, Evaluate and Set Goals** (p. 582)
- **Build Your Portfolio** (p. 582)
- **Reading on Your Own** (p. 583)

  My Ántonia by Willa Cather

  Manners and Customs by Jim Barmeier

  Edith Wharton Abroad: Selected Travel Writings, 1888–1920 edited by Sarah Bird Wright

  Ellis Island: Land of Hope by Joan Lowery Nixon

KEYS TO LITERARY CONNECTIONS

 Comparing Selections

In this theme of **Glencoe Literature,** the **Comparing Selections** feature gives students an opportunity to compare two selections they have just read. The Comparing Selections page provides a variety of options to address diverse aspects of the reading and literature curriculum. For example, in Comparing Selections on page 493, students compare people who are labeled as outcasts because of their professions in Bret Harte's "The Outcasts of Poker Flat" with a woman who is outcast because she lives "a secret and mysterious life" in Bessie Head's "Chief Sekoto Holds Court." Through this comparison, students can gain insight into their own culture and into the ways in which it both resembles and differs from other cultures.

 World Literature

Glencoe Literature contains a variety of literature that represents cultures from around the world. World literature selections are highlighted with this symbol: 🌐.

KEYS TO TEACHING OPTIONS

🧊 **Block Scheduling**

Activities that are particularly suited to use within a block scheduling framework are identified throughout this unit by the following designation: 🧊. For detailed suggestions on block scheduling, see the **Block Scheduling Guide** for this grade level.

Key to Ability Levels

The Teaching Options throughout this unit have been coded for students of various abilities.

L1 BASIC activities for all students

L2 AVERAGE activities for average to above-average students

L3 CHALLENGING activities for above-average students

Reading Skills in this unit

Variety of Texts

In addition to many stories by American authors, this unit also includes the following text types:
- short story
- nonfiction
- poetry
- photography/science book
- Web site

Comprehension Skills

The following instructional support for comprehension skills appears in this unit of the Student Edition:
- Active Reading Strategies and Models (pp. 3–35)
- Making Inferences (p. 556)

See also the **Reading Minilessons** throughout the unit in this Teacher's Wraparound Edition.

Reading Resources

Comprehension Skills Resources

 Active Reading Guides

The Active Reading Guide provides graphic organizers and study guide questions to support students' reading of each selection. (**Active Reading Guide**, pp. 54–65)

Reading Workbook

The Reading Workbook (pp. 49–58) includes additional instruction and reinforcement of reading strategies and skills.

 Audio Library

Available both on tape and on CD, the Audio Library provides valuable comprehension support.

Resources for Reading Widely

Glencoe Literature Library

Each title in the Glencoe Literature Library includes a full-length novel or play plus related readings. A separate Study Guide is available for each title.

Literature Classics CD-ROM

The 900 selections on this CD-ROM can be searched by author, theme, or genre.

A coproduction of Glencoe and Time Inc., *inTime* includes a wealth of high-interest nonfiction related to the selections and themes in Unit Four.

✔ Assessment in this unit

Assessment Options in the Student Edition

Glencoe Literature offers a number of diverse ways to evaluate student understanding and skill proficiency. In the Student Edition, use the following:

- **Responding to Literature**

  Following each selection, students are asked to recall facts, interpret ideas, and evaluate concepts as they answer a variety of questions and complete activities to extend their understanding.

- **Unit Wrap-Up (pp. 582–583)**

  Here students respond to the selections on personal and analytical levels. They also assume ownership of their learning by setting and evaluating goals and by selecting work for their portfolios.

See also the many **Assessment Resources** listed on the facing page.

Standardized Test Practice

The Princeton Review has developed the Standardized Test Practice pages found at the end of this unit (pp. 584–585). These pages contain practice test questions that help students remain familiar with standardized test formats and content. For additional practice, you may want to use the following resource:

- **College Entrance Exam Preparation and Practice Workbook**

Writing Skills in this unit

Writing Skills

The Student Edition of Unit Four offers strong instructional support for writing skills:

In **Extending Your Response**, which follows each selection:
- Writing About Literature
- Personal/Creative Writing

In **Writing Skills** Lessons:
- Using Transitions Effectively (p. 522)

See also the **Writing Minilessons** throughout the unit in this Teacher's Wraparound Edition.

Writing Workshops

Theme Six in Unit Four concludes with a **Writing Workshop** that guides students through the writing process.
- Business Writing: Problem-Solution Proposal (pp. 578–581)

Writing Resources

Writer's Assistant CD-ROM

Each Writing Workshop is supplemented by an interactive writing guide on the Writer's Assistant CD-ROM. This easy-to-use writing guide provides prompts, templates, and other tools that lead students through the writing process.

Writing and Proofreading Practice

Blackline masters present in-depth instruction and practice on a specific step in the writing process and proofreading. (pp. 1–6, 45–52)

Writing and Proofreading Transparencies

Transparencies (1–7, 35–36) provide graphic organizers and proofreading exercises for whole class instruction.

Research and Report Writing Guide

This resource provides extensive tips and activities to guide students in their writing projects in the literature classroom as well as in classes across the curriculum.

Style and Documentation Sourcebook for Writers

This sourcebook is a combination reference and work-book, giving students the most up-to-date information and guidance regarding traditional as well as technological research strategies and documentation.

Grammar and Composition Handbook

The Grammar and Composition Handbook provides instruction that supplements activities in the student textbook.

Assessment Resources

Selection Quick Checks

For each selection, a Quick Check of three to five short-answer questions measures students' literal comprehension.

Selection and Theme Assessment

The Selection and Theme Assessment instrument tests students' abilities to recall, interpret, and evaluate what they've read. The tests consist of multiple-choice, short-answer, and essay questions.

Performance Assessment

Alternative assessment instruments and rubrics for Unit Four are found in the Performance Assessment ancillary.

Writing Assessment and Portfolio Management

These notes and strategies, student models and assessment tools assist with the task of measuring students' progress as writers and as monitors of their own writing.

Testmaker

Teachers can customize selection, theme, and Unit Four tests by accessing the Testmaker database.

MindJogger Videoquizzes

Using a popular game show format, MindJogger Videoquizzes enable teachers to evaluate students' understanding of Unit Four in a quick and fun manner.

UNIT ☙ FOUR
Regionalism and Realism

Unit Objectives

- To enjoy reading short stories, expository speeches, and poems
- To identify elements of and apply strategies for short stories, expository speeches, and poems

Vɪᴇᴡɪɴɢ THE PAINTING

Winslow Homer (1836–1910) began his career as a pictorial reporter and magazine illustrator. After spending time in France, where he was exposed to the Impressionist movement, Homer concentrated his efforts on painting. Homer lived in Prout's Neck, Maine, where he painted small watercolors of the countryside and daily life. Homer is also well-known for his brilliant seascapes.

Responding to the Art Discussion questions:

- Would you describe the painting style as realistic? (*While the painting does not precisely depict the faces of the people, its treatment of the boat, sea, and sky are realistic.*)
- Does nature seem to be a benevolent or threatening force? (*It is benevolent. The people aboard the boat are relying on nature to get them someplace, and nature is obliging.*)

Breezing Up (A Fair Wind), 1873–1876. Winslow Homer. Oil on canvas, 24⅛ x 38⅛ in. National Gallery of Art, Washington, DC. Gift of the W. L. and May T. Mellon Foundation.

448

TEACHER to TEACHER

Lɪᴛᴛʟᴇ Wᴏᴜɴᴅ • Kʏʟᴇ, Sᴏᴜᴛʜ Dᴀᴋᴏᴛᴀ

As I discuss regionalism and realism with the class, I explain that many writers in this unit went out and lived, and then wrote about their experiences which contribute to the power of their work. I encourage students to immerse themselves in a "nature experience," and then write a short fiction piece drawing on their experiences. I also create other immersion experiences. For example, to prepare my students for reading Native American selections, I immerse them in Native American culture by having a South Dakota spiritual leader come in and talk to the students about the importance of the buffalo for the Plains Indian tribes. We discuss the relationship between the Plains Indians and the natural world and enact Lakota ceremonies relating to the buffalo. Then students write pieces of fiction drawing on their experiences.

Rᴏʙᴇʀᴛ Cᴏᴏᴋ

UNIT ❧ FOUR

Regionalism and Realism

1865–1910

❝The history of every country begins in the heart of a man or a woman.❞

—Willa Cather

Theme 6
The Energy of the Everyday
pages 459–581

Introducing the Unit

Have students read the quotation. Then pose these questions for discussion:

- In what ways do individual people affect changes in the history of a nation?
- Do you think individual perceptions of events and movements shape recorded history?
- How does literature both shape and reflect the time in which it is written?

Theme 6: The Energy of the Everyday

The short stories, expository speech, and poems in Theme 6 focus on the experiences of everyday people living in different regions.

GLENCOE
TECHNOLOGY

LITERATURE CLASSICS
CD-ROM

Search for other short stories, speeches, and poems by theme, author, or title.

RESOURCE MANAGER

See the *Unit Four Planning Guide* (p. 1) for additional teaching notes, strategies, and resources for introducing the Regionalism and Realism unit.

Setting the Scene

Setting the Scene

Introducing the Time Period

Invite students to share what they know about the aftermath of the Civil War. You may wish to pose these questions to begin the discussion: How were the lives of the newly-freed African Americans affected by the end of the war? What problems did both the North and the South face after the war? What changes in business and industry occurred during the era?

Historical Note

The steam engine made possible all kinds of machinery, but it was the locomotive that spurred the public's desire to see the country from east to west. Invented in England in 1804, the locomotive revolutionized the transportation industry. The first full-sized locomotive running a regular schedule in the United States was the *Stourbridge Lion*.

VIEWING THE PAINTING

English painter Thomas Hill (1829–1908) settled in California in 1861. He painted *The Last Spike* during his years in San Francisco. Today the canvas hangs in the California State Railroad Museum in Sacramento.

Viewing Response Discussion question:

• What conclusion can you draw about the crowd shown in the painting? (*People from all over the country came to see the driving of the last spike because they considered it a historic occasion.*)

On May 10, 1869, at Promontory Point, Utah, Grenville M. Dodge, chief engineer of the Union Pacific Railway, witnessed "the driving of the last spike." This famous spike marked the completion of the long, arduous work of connecting two railway lines across North America. Workers had extended the Central Pacific line eastward from California and the Union Pacific line westward from Iowa. Dodge recorded what he saw:

"The two trains pulled up facing each other, each crowded with workmen. . . . The officers and invited guests formed on each side of the track. . . . a number of spikes were driven in the two adjoining rails, each one of the prominent persons present taking a hand, but very few hitting the spikes, to the great amusement of the crowd. . . . thus the two roads were wedded into one great trunk line from the Atlantic to the Pacific."

The Last Spike, 1877–1881 (detail). Thomas Hill. Oil on canvas, 96½ x 240½ in. California State Railroad Museum, Sacramento.

U.S.A.

1869 Elizabeth Cady Stanton and Susan B. Anthony organize the National Woman Suffrage Association

1870 John D. Rockefeller forms the Standard Oil Company

1877 Pursued by the U.S. Army, Chief Joseph and the Nez Percé surrender in Montana

1886 Labor leaders organize the American Federation of Labor; the Statue of Liberty is dedicated in New York

1865   **1875**   **1885**

World

1870 General Tomás Guardia begins his twelve-year dictatorship in Costa Rica

1871 German regions unite to form the German Empire

The Indian National Congress is formed to give the people of India more power in that British-ruled nation

450   UNIT 4

Extra Credit Projects

• Between 1865 and 1910, bison, wolves, and grizzly bears were hunted nearly to extinction. During the same period, Yellowstone National Park was established, and the Sierra Club was founded. Have students investigate environmental events of the period. **L2**

• In 1893 Frederick Jackson Turner delivered a speech explaining the importance of the frontier in the development of the American character. His thesis has been called "the single most influential piece of writing in the history of American history." Ask students to explore Turner's thesis and evaluate the validity of his conclusions. **L3**

History of the Time

An Age of Growth

The railroads—their mighty engines hauling raw materials, hopeful migrants, and wealthy business owners across the country—symbolized the United States in the late 1800s. Like the nation itself, the railroads were powerful, noisy money-makers and always on the move.

Part of this movement was from rural to urban areas. The rapid growth of cities and industry undermined Thomas Jefferson's vision of a nation of small towns and family farms. Between 1870 and 1910, the nation's largest city, New York, tripled in size. In Chicago, the city that poet Carl Sandburg labeled "the nation's freight handler," the population multiplied an astounding seven times. Each major industry created a handful of incredibly wealthy men. Among the richest were Andrew Carnegie in steel, John D. Rockefeller in oil, J. P. Morgan in finance, and Cornelius Vanderbilt in railroads.

Reconstruction in the South

From 1865 to 1877 the South went through a period known as Reconstruction. As the former Confederate states reentered the Union, the U.S. Congress supported the establishment of new state governments. These governments were led by African Americans,

Northerners who came to the South, and "scalawags," Southern whites who cooperated with the new governments. There was significant resistance, however, to these new governments and the policies of Reconstruction, and by 1877 the Democratic Party—then the party of conservative white Southerners—had regained control of state governments in the South.

The shifting of economic power and Reconstruction were two of the many developments occurring in the nation.

- The last great land rush took place when the government opened Cherokee territory in Oklahoma for settlement by non-Indians. At noon on April 22, 1889, fifty thousand frantic settlers rode wagons, ran, pushed, and stumbled to claim plots of land.

- Immigrants poured into the country—more than 15 million between 1885 and 1910, mostly from southern or eastern Europe. In 1882 the Chinese Exclusion Act prohibited Chinese workers from immigrating to the United States.

- Laborers, including many children, suffered low wages, long hours, and hazardous conditions. Despite sometimes violent opposition from factory owners, workers formed unions and used strikes to demand fair treatment on the job.

- A burst of inventiveness led to dazzling changes in the daily lives of Americans. Cameras, lightbulbs, telephones, typewriters, automobiles, phonographs, bicycles, moving pictures, skyscrapers, airplanes—new or improved products came in a flurry.

History of the Time

Historical Note

One of the chief galvanizing forces for newly-freed African Americans in the South was the church. Thousands of new African American churches sprang up, and by 1870 there was an African American church in nearly every southern town. From this base evolved the numerous fraternal, benevolent, and mutual-aid societies that characterized the early Reconstruction era.

FYI

Native Americans So widespread was the westward movement of the post-Civil War era that the lifestyle of Native Americans was compromised. Yet many frontiersmen and soldiers openly sympathized with their adversaries even as they stole their land and livelihood. Among them was General George Custer, who commented: "If I were an Indian, I often think I would greatly prefer to cast my lot among those of my people [who] adhered to the free open plains, rather than submit to the confined limits of a reservation, there to be the recipient of the blessed benefits of civilization."

1890 Congress creates Yosemite National Park in California

1893 New Zealand adopts woman suffrage

1894 War begins between China and Japan

1895

1896 The Supreme Court upholds laws supporting racial segregation; the Klondike gold rush begins in Canada and Alaska

1899 The South African (Boer) War between British and Dutch settlers begins

1901 Theodore Roosevelt becomes president after the assassination of William McKinley

1905 Strikes and mass protests bring reform in Russia

1906 An earthquake kills 500 people in San Francisco

1910

REGIONALISM AND REALISM 🐾 451

Inventions The national Invention Hall of Fame Index of Inventions contains information on many inventions patented during the post-Civil War years. Have students explore inventions from the period and create labeled schematic diagrams using information they find on the Internet.

Life of the Time

Life of the Time

FYI

Steam Power Visitors to the Centennial Exposition of 1876 in Philadelphia were amazed by the giant Corliss steam engine displayed in Machinery Hall. When President Ulysses S. Grant pulled the levers that started the engine, the floor trembled and the hall reverberated with sound. This single engine powered thirteen acres of machinery in the great hall.

Biography

The following videotape program is available from Glencoe. Be sure to preview the following video for appropriateness for your class:

• **Biography: Sitting Bull—Chief of the Lakota Nation**

interNET CONNECTION

Historic Expositions Students may enjoy "visiting" the Philadelphia Centennial Exposition and the Chicago Columbian Exposition on the Internet. These and several other historic expositions are featured on the Internet. Have students enter keywords and phrases such as *exposition* and *world exposition*.

People are talking about

A Continuing Struggle Although African Americans have gained freedom and citizenship, they still must struggle for equality and opportunity. The U.S. Freedmen's Bureau provides food and medical assistance and builds hospitals and more than 1,000 schools. However, President Andrew Johnson returns abandoned lands to pardoned Southerners, thus forcing many freed African Americans into oppressive sharecropping arrangements.

◀ **Grand Expositions** At the 1876 Centennial Exposition in Philadelphia, people are amazed by typewriters, telephones, and a gigantic steam engine. In 1893 a highlight for many of the 21 million visitors to the World's Columbian Exposition in Chicago is the gigantic Ferris wheel. Each car on the 264-foot-high Ferris wheel holds up to sixty people.

Going Places In addition to moving around the country on railroads, people travel about cities on trolleys. The first subways in the country open in Boston in 1897 and in New York in 1904. Then, in 1908, Henry Ford presents his Model T automobile, the car that will enable Americans to take to the road.

A Welcome for Immigrants Beginning in 1886, the Statue of Liberty, a gift from France, welcomes immigrants to New York Harbor. In 1892 a receiving facility for immigrants opens on New York's Ellis Island that will be an entry point for about 17 million immigrants over the next fifty years. ▶

Firsts

• Scientists create the first plastics—celluloid (1869) and Bakelite in (1909).

• Orville and Wilbur Wright make the first airplane flight (1903).

Immigrants at Ellis Island, 1905.

U.S.A.

- 1866 More than eighty African Americans are killed in Memphis and New Orleans race riots
- 1871 P. T. Barnum's circus, the "Greatest Show on Earth," opens in Brooklyn
- 1879 F. W. Woolworth opens his first five-and-ten-cent store
- 1880 George Eastman patents roll film for cameras
- 1883 Buffalo Bill Cody opens his first Wild West show

1865 — **1875** — **1885**

World

- 1869 Russian chemist Dmitry Mendeleyev devises the periodic table of the elements
- 1876 China's first railway opens
- 1883 On an island between Java and Sumatra, the volcano Krakatoa explodes, killing 36,000

Critics Corner

Huckleberry Finn Barred Out

The Concord, Mass. Public Library committee has decided to exclude Mark Twain's latest book from the library. One member of the committee says that, while he does not wish to call it immoral, he thinks [it] contains but little humor, and that of a very coarse type. He regards it as the veriest trash. The librarian and the other members of the committee entertain similar views, characterizing it as rough, coarse and inelegant, dealing with a series of experiences not elevating, the whole book being more suited to the slums than to intelligent, respectable people.

—*The Boston Transcript, March 17, 1885*

"All modern American literature comes from one book by Mark Twain called *Huckleberry Finn.*"

—*Ernest Hemingway*

The Adventures of Huckleberry Finn
by Mark Twain (1885)

Huckleberry Finn first appears as a character in Mark Twain's popular book *The Adventures of Tom Sawyer,* about a boy growing up in Missouri. *The Adventures of Huckleberry Finn* tells of the travels of the runaway orphan Huck, and of Jim, who is escaping enslavement. Huck's reflections on various aspects of life in the prewar South are delivered in a slangy, colloquial voice that will be influential for later writers. The story moves between funny episodes of satire or slapstick and touching portrayals of the relationship between Huck and Jim.

Mark Twain

Timeline

- **1888** Edward Bellamy, *Looking Backward, 2000–1887*
- **1888** Nicaragua: Rubén Darío, *Azul*
- **1890** Bengal: Rabindranath Tagore, *Mānāsi*
- **1892** Germany: Gerhart Hauptmann, *The Weavers*
- **1895**
- **1899** Charles Waddell Chesnutt, *The Conjure Woman*
- **1900** L. Frank Baum, *The Wonderful Wizard of Oz;* Theodore Dreiser, *Sister Carrie*
- **1901** Frank Norris, *The Octopus*
- **1902** England: Beatrix Potter, *The Tale of Peter Rabbit*
- **1904–07** China: Liu E, *The Travels of Lao Ts'an*
- **1905**
- **1906** Upton Sinclair, *The Jungle*
- **1907** Basutoland (Lesotho): Thomas Mofolo, *The Traveller of the East*
- **1910**

Historical Note

Samuel Langhorne Clemens (1835–1910), whose pseudonym was Mark Twain, grew up in the Mississippi River town of Hannibal, Missouri, during the age of the steamboat. The Mississippi provides the setting for many of his novels, including *The Adventures of Huckleberry Finn* (1885), *The Adventures of Tom Sawyer* (1876), and *Life on the Mississippi* (1883). His pen name derives from the riverboat term that means the water is two fathoms deep. Clemens also traveled beyond the Mississippi, and his novels and short stories are set in many times and places. Examples include *Roughing It* (1872), which autobiographically describes Clemens's prospecting attempts in the West, and *The Prince and the Pauper* (1882), a novel set in England in the sixteenth century.

At the MOVIES

Please be sure to review this movie for appropriateness before showing it to the students.

- *Huckleberry Finn* is available from Live Home Video Inc. (1981) 72 minutes.

INTERDISCIPLINARY CONNECTION

Civics Point out that the response to *Huckleberry Finn* described in the Critics Corner above was not unique. This novel has been the subject of censorship attempts since its publication. Point out to students that debates of this nature are part of being a member of a democratic society.

Activity Invite students to investigate the censorship of *Huckleberry Finn.* Students should determine the reasons behind the efforts to censor this novel. Have the reasons changed since the novel was first published? How successful have these efforts been? Do the censorship arguments have any validity? After students investigate the subject, have them present their findings in a panel discussion. **L2 COLLAB. LEARN.**

Language of the Time

Language of the Time

How People Speak

◄ **On the Phone** By 1887 there are more than 150,000 telephones in the United States. The need for something to say when one picks up a ringing phone makes the word "Hello" popular. Compared with letters, phone conversations tend to be brisk and informal.

Recorded Voices Thomas Edison's phonograph, patented in 1877, preserves the sound of voices for the first time. Florence Nightingale's voice is among those preserved on a recording kept at London's Science Museum. ►

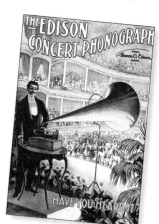

How People Write

On Postcards Postcards become a craze after their introduction in the United States in 1873 as a promotional device. As the telephone does with the spoken language, postcards encourage a clipped, conversational style of writing.

As They Speak Regional writers try to capture the flavor of local dialects, including the increasing use of Americanisms. In 1886 one of the nation's leading literary figures, William Dean Howells, writes, "I would have them [our novelists] use 'Americanisms' whenever these serve their turn; and when their characters speak, I should like to hear them speak true American, with all the varying Tennesseean, Philadelphian, Bostonian, and New York accents."

New Words and Expressions

Phone Language New telephone-related expressions are heard:

Give me a ring.	exchange	long distance
I'll give you a buzz.	trunk line	phone book
Number, please.	central	telephone booth
operator	telephone number	yellow pages
switchboard	party line	

The Melting Pot The title of a 1908 play by British writer Israel Zangwill, the term *melting pot* becomes part of American English, meaning "a location in which a blending of peoples and cultures takes place." Immigrants contribute numerous words to the language, including *delicatessen, kindergarten, kosher, spaghetti,* and *tutti-frutti.*

Historical Note

The telephone was publicly introduced at the 1876 Centennial Exposition in Philadelphia. At first, telephones were rented to subscribers, and the cost of stringing telephone lines was absorbed in subscribers' use charges. In its early years of use only doctors and successful businesspeople could afford regular telephone service, but as telephones became more common, prices decreased. Eventually, instead of hanging telephone lines in tree branches, companies began erecting telephone poles to carry multiple lines. Soon many cities and towns were connected and "hello girls," or operators, put the calls through.

MEETING INDIVIDUAL NEEDS — ENGLISH LANGUAGE LEARNERS

Dialects Explain that one effect of the telephone, which was later enhanced by radio, television, computer, and other communications technology, has been to reduce the dialectical differences between regions of the country; everyone is beginning to talk more and more alike.

Activity Have a group of students that includes both English language learners and language proficient speakers investigate regional difference in American English to find out how these dialects developed and spread. Ask them to provide examples of words that are pronounced differently in different regions. Then invite English language learners to share with the class their knowledge of dialect within their native cultures. **COLLAB. LEARN.**

Frog of Calaveras County

Mark Twain

The Country Store, 1872. Winslow Homer. Oil on wood, 11⅞ x 18⅛ in. Hirshhorn Museum and Sculpture Garden, Smithsonian Institution, Washington, D.C. Gift of Joseph H. Hirshhorn, 1966.

Viewing the painting: What do the attitudes of the men in this painting suggest to you about the ways stories such as the one about Jim Smiley might have spread in the mid-1800s?

B Simon Wheeler backed me into a corner and blockaded me there with his chair, and then sat me down and reeled off the monotonous narrative which follows this paragraph. He never smiled, he never frowned, he never changed his voice from the gentle-flowing key to which he tuned the initial sentence, he never betrayed the slightest suspicion of enthusiasm; but all through the interminable

Vocabulary
interminable (in tur′ mi nə bəl) *adj.* seemingly endless

B **Literary Elements**
CHARACTERIZATION Students should notice a sharp contrast between the language of the narrator and the language of Wheeler. Ask students to find examples of words or phrases used by the narrator that seem formal. Then ask them what this formal language might suggest about the narrator. *(Some examples include "hereunto append the result," "infernal reminiscence," and "reeled off the monotonous narrator." The language suggests that the narrator has some education.)*

FYI

Frame Story Explain to students that a frame story is a story that "frames" or surrounds another story. The story Wheeler tells is framed by the narrator's story.

VIEWING THE PAINTING
Winslow Homer (1836–1910) was an American naturalist painter. He began his career as a magazine illustrator and went on to paint vivid and realistic scenes from the Civil War. During the 1870s, when this painting was produced, Homer painted mostly rural scenes.

Viewing Response *Students may suggest that stories spread by word of mouth as men sat around the fire.*

Reading *Minilesson*

Classifying Explain to students that good writers create well-rounded characters by describing their appearance, actions, and personalities. Ask students to read paragraphs two and three of this story, looking for descriptions of Simon Wheeler. Have them decide if each description provides information about Wheeler's appearance, his actions, or his personality.

Activity As they read, have students fill in a chart, putting each description in the appropriate column. Ask volunteers to share their descriptions. **L2**

Actions	Appearance	Personality

Additional Resources
📁 *Reading Workbook,* p. 49

Author's Craft

TONE Explain to students that Twain's tone helps make the story humorous. Although the tale of Smiley might seem absurd to most people, Wheeler relates it in a serious manner, as if he believes it is a true story. This juxtaposition between tone and content adds a comic element to the story.

Critical Thinking

DRAWING CONCLUSIONS Ask students what they can conclude about Smiley's character and his attitude toward gambling based on the story about Parson Walker's wife. *(They may conclude that he lacks empathy, is highly inconsiderate, and is so obsessed with gambling that he will place a bet at even the most inappropriate of times.)*

---

narrative there ran a vein of impressive earnestness and sincerity, which showed me plainly that, so far from his imagining that there was any thing ridiculous or funny about his story, he regarded it as a really important matter, and admired its two heroes as men of transcendent[5] genius in finesse.[6]

To me, the spectacle of a man drifting serenely along through such a queer yarn without ever smiling, was exquisitely absurd. As I said before, I asked him to tell me what he knew of Rev. Leonidas W. Smiley, and he replied as follows. I let him go on in his own way, and never interrupted him once:

There was a feller here once by the name of *Jim Smiley*, in the winter of '49—or may be it was the spring of '50—I don't recollect exactly, somehow, though what makes me think it was one or the other is because I remember the big flume wasn't finished when he first came to the camp; but any way, he was the curiosest man about always betting on any thing that turned up you ever see, if he could get any body to bet on the other side; and if he couldn't he'd change sides. Any way that suited the other man would suit him—any way just so's he got a bet, *he* was satisfied. But still he was lucky, uncommon lucky; he most always come out winner. He was always ready and laying for a chance; there couldn't be no solitry thing mentioned but that feller'd offer to bet on it, and take any side you please, as I was just telling you. If there was a horse race, you'd find him flush,[7] or you'd find

Did You Know?
A *flume* is a trough or chute, often inclined, that carries water.

him busted at the end of it; if there was a dog-fight, he'd bet on it; if there was a cat-fight, he'd bet on it; if there was a chicken-fight, he'd bet on it; why, if there was two birds setting on a fence, he would bet you which one would fly first; or if there was a camp-meeting,[8] he would be there reg'lar, to bet on Parson Walker, which he judged to be the best exhorter[9] about here, and so he was, too, and a good man. If he even seen a straddle-bug[10] start to go anywheres, he would bet you how long it would take him to get wherever he was going to, and if you took him up, he would foller that straddle-bug to Mexico but what he would find out where he was bound for and how long he was on the road. Lots of the boys here has seen that Smiley, and can tell you about him. Why, it never made no difference to *him*—he would bet on *any* thing—the dangdest feller. Parson Walker's wife laid very sick once, for a good while, and it seemed as if they warn't going to save her; but one morning he come in, and Smiley asked how she was, and he said she was considerable better—thank the Lord for his inf'nit mercy—and coming on so smart that, with the blessing of Prov'dence,[11] she'd get well yet; and Smiley, before he thought, says, "Well, I'll risk two-and-a-half[12] that she don't, any way."

Thish-yer[13] Smiley had a mare—the boys called her the fifteen-minute nag, but that was only in fun, you know, because, of course, she was faster than that—and he used to win money on that horse, for all she was so slow and always had the asthma, or the distemper, or the consumption,[14] or something of that kind. They

---

5. *Transcendent* means "surpassing others" or "superior."
6. *Finesse* is the smooth or artful handling of a situation.
7. Here, *flush* means "having a large amount of money" or "rich."

8. A *camp-meeting* is an outdoor religious gathering, sometimes held in a tent.
9. An *exhorter* is someone who urges by giving strong advice or warnings; here, a preacher.
10. A *straddle-bug* is a long-legged beetle.
11. *Prov'dence* (Providence) is God.
12. *Risk two-and-a-half* means "risk, or bet, $2.50."
13. *Thish-yer* is dialect for "this here."
14. *Consumption* is another name for tuberculosis.

Teaching Options

MEETING INDIVIDUAL NEEDS — ENGLISH LANGUAGE LEARNERS

Contractions Some of the contractions in this selection may present a problem for English language learners. Write the following on the board: *I don't see, you've been,* and *you'd think.* Explain that the underlined words are contractions; that is, they are two words joined by an apostrophe. Point out that *don't* is a contraction of *do* and *not*; *you've* is a contraction of *you* and *have*; *you'd* is a contraction of *you* and *would*. Invite students to find other contractions.

Activity Work with students as a group to find and define contractions in the story. Discuss Twain's use of contractions to show informal speech.

Additional Resources
📁 *English Language Learners Sourcebook*

Mark Twain

used to give her two or three hundred yards start, and then pass her under way; but always at the fag-end[15] of the race she'd get excited and desperate-like, and come cavorting[16] and straddling up, and scattering her legs around limber, sometimes in the air, and sometimes out to one side amongst the fences, and kicking up m-o-r-e dust, and raising m-o-r-e racket with her coughing and sneezing and blowing her nose—and always fetch up at the stand[17] just about a neck ahead, as near as you could cipher it down.[18]

And he had a little small bull pup, that to look at him you'd think he wan't worth

Did You Know?
The *fo'castle*, or forecastle (fōk′ səl), of a steamboat is a raised deck at the front of the boat.

a cent, but to set around and look ornery, and lay for a chance to steal something. But as soon as money was up on him, he was a different dog; his under-jaw'd begin to stick out like the fo'castle of a steamboat, and his teeth would uncover, and shine savage like the furnaces. And a dog might tackle him, and bully-rag[19] him, and bite him, and throw him over his shoulder two or three times, and Andrew Jackson—which was the name of the pup—Andrew Jackson would never let on but what *he* was satisfied, and hadn't expected nothing else—and the bets being doubled and doubled on the other side all the time, till the money was all up; and then all of a sudden he would grab that other dog jest by the j'int of his hind leg and freeze to it—not chaw, you understand, but only jest grip and hang on till they throwed up the

15. The *fag-end* is the last part.
16. *Cavorting* means "running and jumping around playfully."
17. *Fetch up at the stand* means "arrive at the grandstand," which was placed at the finish line.
18. *Cipher it down* means "calculate it."
19. *Bully-rag* means "to intimidate" or "to abuse."

sponge,[20] if it was a year. Smiley always come out winner on that pup, till he harnessed[21] a dog once that didn't have no hind legs, because they'd been sawed off by a circular saw, and when the thing had gone along far enough, and the money was all up, and he come to make a snatch for his pet holt,[22] he saw in a minute how he'd been imposed on, and how the other dog had him in the door,[23] so to speak, and he 'peared surprised, and then he looked sorter discouraged-like, and didn't try no more to win the fight, and so he got shucked out[24] bad. He give Smiley a look, as much as to say his heart was broke, and it was *his* fault, for putting up a dog that hadn't no hind legs for him to take holt of, which was his main dependence in a fight, and then he limped off a piece and laid down and died. It was a good pup, was that Andrew Jackson, and would have made a name for hisself if he'd lived, for the stuff was in him, and he had genius—I know it, because he hadn't had no opportunities to speak of, and it don't stand to reason that a dog could make such a fight as he could under them circumstances, if he hadn't no talent. It always makes me feel sorry when I think of that last fight of his'n, and the way it turned out.

Well, thish-yer Smiley had rat-tarriers,[25] and chicken cocks,[26] and tom-cats, and all them kind of things, till you couldn't rest, and you couldn't fetch nothing for him to bet on but he'd match you. He ketched a frog one day, and took him home, and said he cal'klated[27] to edercate him; and so he never done nothing

20. *Throwed up the sponge* means "gave up the contest."
21. Here, *harnessed* means "set up a fight with."
22. A *pet holt* is a favorite hold.
23. *Had him in the door* means "had him at a disadvantage or in a tight place."
24. *Shucked out* means "beaten" or "defeated."
25. *Rat-tarriers* are dogs (terriers) once used for catching rats.
26. *Chicken cocks* are adult male chickens (roosters) that are trained to fight.
27. *Cal'klated* is dialect for calculated, meaning "planned."

REGIONALISM AND REALISM 465

E **Author's Craft**

SIMILE Point out that Twain makes absurd comparisons to add humor to the story. Using similes, he says that the underjaw of Smiley's dog sticks out "like the fo'castle of a steamboat," and that his teeth "shine savage like the furnaces."

F **Active Reading**

EVALUATE Ask students if they think this story rings true. Ask them why they think Wheeler told it. *(Students may think that this story is a "tall tale," told simply to amuse or entertain the stranger.)*

G **Critical Thinking**

DRAWING CONCLUSIONS Encourage students to draw conclusions about Smiley's character based on the stories about his animals. Have them consider their feelings toward Smiley at this point in the story by describing what they like and dislike about his character.

Model: Based on what I've read so far, I think Smiley is a pretty self-centered, cruel person. I know he abused his horse and his dog. He only keeps animals around so that he can train them and bet on them. He doesn't seem to care about anyone but himself. He also appears to be quite foolish: the idea of educating a frog is absurd.

INCLUSION STRATEGIES

Less-Proficient Readers Write the following words on the board: *Thish-yer; wan't; j'int.* Tell less-proficient readers that Twain used *colloquialisms* to add color and realism to his stories. Explain that Twain altered the spelling of words to suggest the way they were pronounced. Ask students to read aloud the words on the board to uncover their meanings. *(this here; wasn't; joint)*

Activity Ask students to read the description of Smiley's frog. As they read, have students look for examples of Smiley's everyday speech. Have them write these examples in their journals, read them aloud, and then guess their meanings. **L1**

Additional Resources

📁 *Inclusion Strategies*

REGIONALISM AND REALISM 465

Point out that the cartoon-like appearance of Pierre's frog suits the humorous, "tall tale" atmosphere of this story.

Viewing Response *Most students will say that the frog is sitting rather than jumping, since all four of its feet are on the ground. Some students will say that the frog's position could indicate that it is preparing to jump.*

FYI

Frogtown, USA Every year on the third weekend in May, Calaveras County holds its annual Frog Jump Championship. In 1998 first prize in this unusual competition was $5,000.

Yellow Frog. Christian Pierre (b. 1962). Oil on canvas, 18 x 25 in. Private collection.

Viewing the painting: Do you think the frog depicted in this painting is a "jumping frog" like Dan'l Webster? Why or why not?

Teaching Options

MIAMI JACKSON SENIOR HIGH SCHOOL • MIAMI, FLORIDA

I use Twain's story as a school-to-work lesson. We begin with a class discussion on the Civil War and westward expansion. We discuss why people went west, the opportunities they sought, and the realities they encountered. We talk about Twain's life, including his experiences in the West, and then I show the movie *Mark Twain's America*. I call on my acting background to read the story to the class, so that students hear the dialect and catch the humor. We talk about the story and how Smiley made a career of gambling. I encourage students to think about imaginative ways to make money that, unlike gambling, are legitimate.

JOHN KNIGHT

for three months but set in his back yard and learn[28] that frog to jump. And you bet you he *did* learn him, too. He'd give him a little punch behind, and the next minute you'd see that frog whirling in the air like a doughnut—see him turn one summerset, or may be a couple, if he got a good start, and come down flat-footed and all right, like a cat. He got him up so in the matter of catching flies, and kept him in practice so constant, that he'd nail a fly every time as far as he could see him. Smiley said all a frog wanted was education, and he could do most any thing—and I believe him. Why, I've seen him set Dan'l Webster[29] down here on this floor—Dan'l Webster was the name of the frog—and sing out, "Flies, Dan'l, flies!" and quicker'n you could wink, he'd spring straight up, and snake a fly off'n the counter there, and flop down on the floor again as solid as a gob of mud, and fall to scratching the side of his head with his hind foot as indifferent as if he hadn't no idea he'd been doin' any more'n any frog might do. You never see a frog so modest and straightfor'ard as he was, for all he was so gifted. And when it come to fair and square jumping on a dead level, he could get over more ground at one straddle[30] than any animal of his breed you ever see. Jumping on a dead level was his strong suit, you understand; and when it come to that, Smiley would ante up[31] money on him as long as he had a red.[32] Smiley was monstrous proud of his frog, and well he might be, for fellers that had traveled and been everywheres, all said he laid over any frog that ever *they* see.

Well, Smiley kept the beast in a little lattice box, and he used to fetch him down town sometimes and lay for a bet. One day a feller—

---

28. Here, *learn* means "teach."
29. *Dan'l Webster* refers to Daniel Webster (1782–1852), a famous orator who served as a U.S. senator and a U.S. secretary of state.
30. Here, *straddle* means "to jump."
31. *Ante up* means "to put into the pool" or "to bet."
32. *A red* refers to a red cent, meaning "any money at all."

a stranger in the camp, he was—come across him with his box, and says:

"What might it be that you've got in the box?"

And Smiley says, sorter indifferent like, "It might be a parrot, or it might be a canary, may be, but it an't—it's only just a frog."

And the feller took it, and looked at it careful, and turned it round this way and that, and says, "H'm—so 'tis. Well, what's *he* good for?"

"Well," Smiley says, easy and careless, "He's good enough for *one* thing, I should judge—he can outjump any frog in Calaveras county."

The feller took the box again, and took another long, particular look, and give it back to Smiley, and says, very deliberate, "Well, I don't see no p'ints[33] about that frog that's any better'n any other frog."

"May be you don't," Smiley says, "May be you understand frogs, and may be you don't understand 'em; may be you've had experience, and may be you an't only a amature, as it were. Anyways, I've got *my* opinion, and I'll risk forty dollars that he can outjump any frog in Calaveras county."

And the feller studied a minute, and then says, kinder sad like, "Well, I'm only a stranger here, and I an't got no frog; but if I had a frog, I'd bet you."

And then Smiley says, "That's all right—that's all right—if you'll hold my box a minute, I'll go and get you a frog." And so the feller took the box, and put up his forty dollars along with Smiley's, and set down to wait.

So he set there a good while thinking and thinking to hisself, and then he got the frog out and prized his mouth open and took a teaspoon and filled him full of quail shot[34]— filled him pretty near up to his chin—and set him on the floor. Smiley he went to the

---

33. *P'ints* is dialect for points, meaning "qualities" or "characteristics."
34. *Quail shot* is ammunition made up of small lead pellets.

H **Literary Elements**

PERSONIFICATION Explain that Twain endows the frog with the human qualities of modesty and straightforwardness. This technique, called personification, adds humor to the story.

I **Active Reading**

PREDICT Based on what they already know about Smiley, have students predict whether the stranger or Smiley will win the bet. *(Some students may be surprised that, given his betting history, Smiley loses the wager; others may say that the story prepares the reader for Smiley's loss.)*

J **Literary Elements**

CHARACTER The fact that the stranger thinks of his plan while waiting for Smiley indicates that his decision to fill the frog with quail shot was premeditated. Ask students if they think Smiley would have done the same thing in the stranger's situation. *(Smiley has not cheated to win bets in the past, so students may say that he would not have acted as the stranger did.)*

MULTIPLE LEARNING STYLES

Musical Students with strong musical abilities may enhance their understanding of a literary text by setting events in the text to music. Have students rewrite parts of the story as a song. Lively tales such as this one, which were shared among residents of frontier camps, will make humorous and upbeat songs.

Activity Ask students to write the lyrics to a song about "Gamblin' Jim Smiley." They may find an appropriate tune to which they can set their lyrics, or they can compose an original song. Remind them that whatever they choose or compose should be as light in tone as their lyrics. Ask volunteers to perform their songs for the class. **L3**

Critical Thinking

EVALUATING Have students evaluate the story about the jumping frog by asking them if they agree with the narrator's poor opinion of the story of Smiley. Ask them if they found the story amusing or interminable. *(Some students may have enjoyed Wheeler's story about Smiley; others may agree with the narrator that it is simply ridiculous.)*

Active Reading

INTERPRET Tell students that Twain once wrote, "The humorous story may be spun out to great length and may wander around as much as it pleases, and arrive nowhere in particular." Ask students whether this story fits Twain's description. *(The story fits this description: Wheeler's tale has no real purpose, he recounts a number of incidents in no particular order, and he only stops because the narrator refuses to hear any more.)*

Thematic Focus

The Energy of the Everyday Point out that Twain uses humor, colloquial language, and colorful descriptions to transform this story about everyday people into a lively tale. Ask students what techniques in Twain's story they found most effective.

☑ ASSESSMENT OPTIONS

📁 *Quick Checks,* p. 54

Teaching Options

---

swamp and slopped around in the mud for a long time, and finally he ketched a frog, and fetched him in, and give him to this feller, and says:

"Now, if you're ready, set him alongside of Dan'l, with his fore-paws just even with Dan'l, and I'll give the word." Then he says, "One—two—three—jump!" and him and the feller touched up the frogs from behind, and the new frog hopped off, but Dan'l give a heave, and hysted up his shoulders—so—like a Frenchman, but it wan't no use—he couldn't budge; he was planted as solid as an anvil, and he couldn't no more stir than if he was an-chored out. Smiley was a good deal surprised, and he was dis-gusted too, but he didn't have no idea what the matter was, of course.

The feller took the money and started away; and when he was going out at the door, he sorter jerked his thumb over his shoulders—this way—at Dan'l, and says again, very deliberate, "Well, *I* don't see no p'ints about that frog that's any better'n any other frog."

Smiley he stood scratching his head and looking down at Dan'l a long time, and at last he says, "I do wonder what in the nation that frog throw'd off for—I wonder if there an't something the matter with him—he 'pears to look mighty baggy, somehow." And he ketched

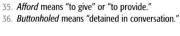

"Well, thish-yer Smiley had a yaller one-eyed cow that didn't have no tail . . ."

Dan'l by the nap of the neck, and lifted him up and says, "Why, blame my cats, if he don't weigh five pound!" and turned him upside down, and he belched out a double handful of shot. And then he see how it was, and he was the maddest man—he set the frog down and took out after that feller, but he never ketched him. And—

[Here Simon Wheeler heard his name called from the front yard, and got up to see what was wanted.] And turning to me as he moved away, he said: "Just set where you are, stranger, and rest easy—I an't going to be gone a second."

But, by your leave, I did not think that a continuation of the history of the enterprising vagabond *Jim* Smiley would be likely to afford[35] me much information concerning the Rev. *Leonidas W.* Smiley, and so I started away.

At the door I met the sociable Wheeler returning, and he buttonholed[36] me and recommenced:

"Well, thish-yer Smiley had a yaller one-eyed cow that didn't have no tail, only jest a short stump like a bannanner, and——"

"Oh! hang Smiley and his afflicted cow!" I muttered, good-naturedly, and bidding the old gentleman good-day, I departed.

---

35. *Afford* means "to give" or "to provide."
36. *Buttonholed* means "detained in conversation."

Vocabulary
enterprising (en' tər prī' zing) *adj.* showing energy and initiative, especially in beginning new projects
vagabond (vag' ə bond') *n.* someone who wanders from place to place, having no visible means of support

---

REAL-WORLD CONNECTION

Frogs Twain's story describes Dan'l Webster, a rather amazing jumping frog. After students read the Media Connection on page 471, ask them if Twain's description is plausible. Why or why not? Based on Twain's description, what kind of frog is Dan'l Webster?

Activity Have students look through science or nature books to find out more about frogs. Ask them to research such details as what frogs eat, where they live, and how long they live. Suggest that they try to find information about one of the types of frogs mentioned in the Media Connection. Have students share their findings with the class. **L2**

Responding to Literature

Personal Response

What questions would you like to ask Simon Wheeler?

— ANALYZING LITERATURE —

RECALL

1. How does the narrator come to meet Simon Wheeler and to hear his story? How does the narrator describe Wheeler's storytelling style?
2. For what reason does Wheeler call Smiley "the curiosest man"? What evidence does Wheeler use to support his statement?
3. Summarize the methods that Smiley's mare and bull pup use to win. What eventually becomes of Smiley's dog?
4. What amazing things can Smiley's frog do? What personality traits does Wheeler attribute to the frog?
5. Summarize what happens after Smiley meets the stranger.

INTERPRET

6. What can you infer about the narrator's attitude toward Wheeler? Support your answer using details from the story.
7. What conclusions can you draw about Smiley's character, based on the tale Wheeler tells? Use details from the story to support your ideas.
8. Why do you think Wheeler tells about the mare and bull pup first, before focusing on the frog?
9. What aspects of Wheeler's description of Smiley's frog do you find particularly absurd?
10. What event or events determine the outcome of the encounter with the stranger? Explain your answer.

EVALUATE AND CONNECT

11. Refer to your response to the Focus Activity on page 461. Compare the exaggerations you listed with your favorite exaggerations from this story. Which ones are funnier? Why?
12. How do Wheeler's personality and manner of speaking add to the story's humor? Use specific examples to support your ideas.
13. Would you have stayed to hear Wheeler's story about Smiley's "yaller one-eyed cow that didn't have no tail"? Why or why not?
14. Think of a performer who uses exaggeration for comic effect. How does this person's use of exaggeration compare with Wheeler's?
15. In this selection, one story serves as a **frame** for another story. Why might Mark Twain have chosen this structure? What role does the narrator play? (See Literary Terms Handbook, page R7.)

Literary ELEMENTS

Colloquial Language
Colloquial language refers to the informal speech that people use in everyday conversation. Often, the vocabulary and expressions people use, as well as their manner of speaking, are specific to a particular geographical region. To represent colloquial language accurately, writers often break the standard rules of punctuation, spelling, and grammar. In "The Celebrated Jumping Frog of Calaveras County," Twain uses colloquial language to evoke the region and the people he is writing about, as in this example: "He *ketched* a frog one day, and took him home, and said he *cal'klated* to *edercate* him . . ."

1. Identify at least two other examples of colloquial language in the story. Explain which rules of grammar, spelling, or punctuation are ignored in the characters' speech.
2. Why might colloquial language be inappropriate in a formal essay or an article that explains how to do something?

● See **Literary Terms Handbook,** p. R3.

Personal Response

Students may ask if Smiley existed. Others may ask Wheeler about Smiley's "yaller one-eyed cow."

ANALYZING LITERATURE

1. The narrator's friend tells him to call on Wheeler to ask after Leonidas W. Smiley. He says Wheeler is monotonous but earnest.
2. Smiley bets on anything and any side. He even bets on whether the parson's wife will live or die.
3. The mare falls behind and then scrambles to the end. The pup bites its opponent's hind leg. The dog dies of a broken heart.
4. It can out-jump any frog, turn somersaults and land on its feet, and catch flies out of the air. Wheeler says the frog is modest and straightforward.
5. Smiley bets the stranger that his frog will out-jump any frog. When Smiley leaves to find a competitor, the stranger fills Smiley's frog with quail shot, making him too heavy to jump. Smiley loses the bet.
6. He thinks Wheeler is boring (Wheeler almost bores him to death) and ignorant (he thinks Wheeler does not realize that the story is absurd).
7. Smiley is obsessed with gambling, heartless (he bets on a sick woman), and naïve (he leaves the stranger alone with his frog).
8. Wheeler wants to establish Smiley's obsession with gambling first and then build up to the story.
9. Students may find it absurd to call a frog modest and straightforward.
10. The stranger cheats by filling Smiley's frog with quail shot so that he is too heavy to jump.
11. Students may compare their exaggerations to such exaggerations as the mare "always had the asthma, or the distemper, or the consumption," or the dog died of a broken heart.

LITERARY ELEMENTS

1. Some students might note that *curiosest* is an incorrect superlative form of *curious; summerset* is *somersault* spelled and pronounced incorrectly; and *ketched* is an incorrect past tense of *catch.*
2. Colloquial language is not always Standard English; therefore, it may be difficult for people in other regions to understand it.

Additional Resources

 Literary Elements Transparency 43

12. Wheeler's monotone and sincerity, and the tale's implausibility, make his story funnier.
13. Students' answers will depend on their response to the jumping frog story.
14. Comedians exaggerate on purpose; Wheeler does not.
15. Twain contrasts Wheeler's colorful regional language with the narrator's dry Standard English. The frame structure permits Twain to comment on Wheeler and his story. The narrator's departure also provides a logical conclusion.

LITERATURE AND WRITING

Writing About Literature
Students' analyses should
- describe the setting using details from the text.
- give logical reasons why Twain might have chosen this setting.
- explain how another setting would change the story.

Creative Writing
Students' stories should
- accurately present Wheeler's speech patterns, using Twain's dialogue as a guide.
- present humorous exaggerations.

EXTENDING YOUR RESPONSE

Literature Groups Remind students to support their conclusions with textual evidence. **COLLAB. LEARN.**

Performing Tell students to refer frequently to the story when composing answers. **COLLAB. LEARN.**

Learning for Life Before students begin this exercise, ask them to name their favorite advertisements and explain why they are effective. Encourage students to borrow these ideas in creating their advertisements.

LITERATURE AND WRITING

Writing About Literature
Analyze the Effect of Setting In three paragraphs, describe the **setting** in which Simon Wheeler tells his story, and explore the following questions: Why might Twain have selected this setting? How might the story have been different if the narrator had met Wheeler in a city? Support your opinions with details from the selection.

Creative Writing
Smiley's Yaller Cow Tell your version of the story of Smiley's "yaller one-eyed cow," using Simon Wheeler as the narrator. In your story, bend the standard rules of grammar, punctuation, and spelling in order to accurately represent Wheeler's manner of speaking. Try to include as many humorous exaggerations as you can.

EXTENDING YOUR RESPONSE

Literature Groups
Believe It or Not A **tall tale** is narrated in a sober manner in order to convince the listener that the story is true, no matter how fantastic the events or characters may be. In your group, compare and contrast Smiley's three tales—the mare, the dog, and the frog—and discuss which story was the most convincing. Use specific details from the selection to support your ideas. Share your conclusions with the class.

Performing
An Interview with Simon Wheeler Work with another student to write an interview with Simon Wheeler. Compose answers that you think would be consistent with his character. Present your interview to the class, with one student playing the role of interviewer and the other the role of Wheeler.

Learning for Life
An Advertisement Create a newspaper advertisement for a performance by Jim Smiley's amazing frog. For ideas, look at real newspaper advertisements for plays, circuses, and other live performances. Use language and graphics to capture readers' attention and to persuade them that they won't want to miss this performance by a truly amazing amphibian.

💾 **Save your work for your portfolio.**

Skill Minilesson

VOCABULARY • The Latin Root *ject*

The word *conjecture* comes from the Latin prefix *con-*, meaning "together," and the root *ject*, meaning "to throw." When you *conjecture*, you don't have enough evidence to draw a logical conclusion, so you throw thoughts together; you guess.

Since the prefix *e-* means "out," an ejected player is one who is thrown out of a game. A rejected suitor or fish or idea is thrown back.

PRACTICE Use your knowledge of the root *ject* and familiar prefixes to answer the following questions.

1. Does a person with *dejected* spirits feel hopeful, sad, or outraged?
2. What might a person giving a speech do to *inject* some humor?
3. Which is used as a *projectile*—a cannonball, a life raft, or a rocking chair?
4. In the following sentence, which word is an *interjection?* "No, I did not tell him what I thought; but—oh!—how I wanted to!"

Skill Minilesson

VOCABULARY • The Latin Root *ject*

1. sad
2. say something funny
3. a cannonball
4. oh!

Additional Resources
📁 *Vocabulary Practice,* p. 31

✔️ ASSESSMENT OPTIONS

📁 *Quick Checks,* p. 54
📁 *Selection and Theme Assessment,* pp. 79–80
📁 *Performance Assessment,* p. 43
💾 *Testmaker*

Photography/ Science Book

The frogs many of us know from everyday life are green and they jump. The red-eyed tree frog (below), however, usually just strolls around the rain forest. Read to learn more frog facts.

Frogs

from *Frogs*, by David Badger, photographs by John Netherton

"Well, I don't see no p'ints about that frog that's any better'n any other frog."

That sentiment, voiced by a compulsive gambler in Mark Twain's acclaimed short story, "The Celebrated Jumping Frog of Calaveras County," first appeared in a New York literary journal in 1865. Of course, that was before color photography was invented—and before nature photographers like John Netherton began to distill the beauty of the natural world through their artistic images.

Frog-jumping contests such as the annual event in Calaveras County, California, have conditioned many people to think of frogs primarily as "leapers," but these adroit animals move by other means as well. Toads, for example, hop. Arboreal tree frogs climb. Flying frogs glide (or freefall) with webbed feet serving as makeshift parachutes. Senegal running frogs walk or run. Walking frogs stride slowly. Burrowing toads shuffle and dig. Northern cricket frogs skitter. And all manner of aquatic and terrestrial species swim.

Still, it is the leapers and the climbers, endowed with long hind legs, that amaze observers. When a leopard frog launches itself into the air, or a jittery bullfrog jumps into the water, the powerful extensor muscles in its rear legs perform a remarkable feat [allowing it to leap incredibly long distances].

The size of a frog sometimes fools observers into assuming that the bigger the frog, the longer the leap. Yet the goliath frog of Africa, which exceeds 15 inches (375 mm) from snout to rump, is actually a rather poor jumper, and entrants in the Calaveras County frog-jumping contest have proved embarrassing duds.

Well-hyped bullfrogs can excite audiences with their proven ability to leap nine times the length of their body, but smaller frogs can jump even farther relative to their size. The leopard frog, for example, can leap fifteen times its body length, and the southern cricket frog can jump an astonishing thirty-six times its body length.

Respond

1. Which fact about frogs surprised you the most? Explain.
2. Why do you think frogs have developed so many ways of getting around?

Objective

• To read and understand a science book

Literature — LINK

The Celebrated Jumping Frog of Calaveras County The author uses a quote from Twain's story to introduce the article because his scientific description of different kinds of frogs reveals that there are "p'ints" that distinguish one frog from another. Note that science also plays a role in Twain's story. The stranger uses scientific knowledge to win the bet: he knew that making Smiley's frog heavier would hinder the frog's ability to jump.

Respond

1. Students may be surprised to learn that some frogs climb trees.
2. Frogs may have developed several ways of getting around to adjust to their environments.

Additional Resources
📁 *Media Connections,* p. 11

Teaching Options

Reading *Minilesson*

Author's Purpose Point out to students that writers have different purposes for writing, listing on the board what those purposes might be. Direct students to identify that "Frogs" is nonfiction while Twain's story is fiction, and ask them to think about how the purposes for each type of writing might be different.

Activity Have students work in pairs to write a brief statement describing the purpose of Badger's article, "Frogs." Ask them to state what specific information about frogs Badger conveys. Have students compare the language Badger uses to convey the information in his article to the language Twain uses in his story. **L2** **COLLAB. LEARN.**

Additional Resources
📁 *Reading Workbook*

Frogs Have students learn more about the frog-jumping competition in Calaveras County by searching with keywords *frogtown* or *Calaveras Frog Contest*.

Objective

- To understand the elements of a short story

Teaching Strategies

As students read the lesson, use the following strategies to discuss the elements. You may want to refer to other stories from this theme to further explain these elements.

Setting

Explain to students that the setting consists of a physical place and the values and beliefs in that place. Ask students to name some of the beliefs and values of the people in their town, and explore how these values and beliefs are an integral part of the town's setting.

Characters

Point out that nature is the antagonist in "To Build a Fire"; the biting cold temperature in the Yukon prevents the man from lighting a fire.

Point of View

Explain that the point of view of a story influences the information a reader obtains. In a first-person point of view, for example, the narrator's thoughts and feelings dominate the story.

Teaching Options

Literature **F O C U S**
Short Story

A **short story** is a brief piece of fiction, usually focusing on a single major event and on a few characters. In a review of Nathaniel Hawthorne's *Twice-Told Tales*, Edgar Allan Poe wrote that the short story belonged "to the loftiest region of art." Learning the language of literary analysis can help you understand and discuss how short stories are created and what makes them effective.

SHORT STORY ELEMENTS

MODEL: "The Celebrated Jumping Frog of Calaveras County"

Setting

Setting is the time and location of a story's events; it may also include the ideas, beliefs, and values of the characters or of the particular society.

> Since the story is a tale within a tale, it has two settings. It opens in the mining community of Angel's Camp, California, some years after a particular frog-jumping contest.

Characters

Characters are the actors in a story. Most characters are people, but they can also be animals, elements of nature, or other forces.

- The **protagonist** is the main character.
- The **antagonist** is the person or thing that opposes the main character. Not all stories have antagonists.

> The **protagonist** of the inner story is Jim Smiley, and the **antagonist** is the stranger who bets against Smiley's frog.

Point of View

Point of view is the perspective from which the narrator tells a story.

- In **first-person** point of view, the narrator is a character in the story and uses "I" or "me" in telling it.
- In **third-person** point of view, the narrator is not a character, but describes the action and the characters from outside the story. In **third-person omniscient** point of view, the narrator is all-knowing. In **third-person limited**, the narrator describes only what one character could know.

> The narrator describes his visit with Simon Wheeler from a **first-person point of view.**

MEETING INDIVIDUAL NEEDS — ENGLISH LANGUAGE LEARNERS

Learning the Short Story Elements
Have English language learners choose a story from their own cultures or a movie they have seen recently. Ask students to identify the elements in the story or movie that correspond to the elements on these pages. Encourage fluent speakers to help English language learners with the elements.

Activity After English language learners have described the elements, ask them to write each element on a separate note card with a brief definition and an example from the story they discussed.

Additional Resources
📁 *English Language Learners Sourcebook*

Responding to Literature

Personal Response

Did the ending of the story surprise you? Why or why not?

ANALYZING LITERATURE

RECALL

1. What has the secret committee of Poker Flat decided to do? Why? How is this decision carried out?
2. Summarize what happens on the outcasts' first day together.
3. What happens on the second day in camp?
4. What happens to Mother Shipton? Why? What actions does Mr. Oakhurst take in the last part of the story?
5. When the people from Poker Flat arrive at the camp, what do they find?

INTERPRET

6. What is the narrator's **tone**, or attitude, toward Poker Flat's secret committee and its "improper persons"? What words convey that tone?
7. What can you infer about Mr. Oakhurst's character, based on the way he treats Tom and Piney?
8. What do you learn about the characters, based on the way each one behaves on the second day in camp?
9. What do you think the narrator means when he says that Oakhurst is "at once the strongest and yet the weakest of the outcasts"?
10. In your opinion, what message, or lesson, does this story convey? Support your ideas, using details from the selection.

EVALUATE AND CONNECT

11. Which story character or characters do you admire the most? the least? Give reasons for your answers.
12. How does the author use **foreshadowing** (see page R7) to help prepare the reader for future events? Give specific examples.
13. Do you think the secret committee of Poker Flat is justified in acting as it does? Why or why not?
14. Recall the ideas you discussed in response to the Focus Activity on page 475. Which story characters resemble the stereotypical characters you've seen in films or television series about the Old West? Explain.
15. Do you believe that people are sometimes capable of acting in a completely unselfish way—even sacrificing themselves for the good of others? Explain.

Literary ELEMENTS

Character

A **character** is a person in a literary work. Some characters are **flat**—that is, they reveal or represent a single personality trait. Stereotypes, or stock characters, such as the noble hero or the innocent young lover, are usually flat characters. A **round character**, on the other hand, shows varied and sometimes contradictory traits—just as real people do. A **static character** remains mostly the same throughout a story; a **dynamic character** grows and changes. In "The Outcasts of Poker Flat," Harte creates both flat and round characters; some characters are static, while others are dynamic.

1. What flat characters does Harte create in this story? What personality trait does each character reveal or represent?
2. Who are the round characters in this story? What varied and contradictory traits does each one exhibit?
3. Who are the static characters? Who are the dynamic characters? Explain your choices.

⬤ See **Literary Terms Handbook,** p. R3.

---

12. The ominous tone of the first paragraph foreshadows future events. The party is not equipped for delay, foreshadowing their difficulties.
13. Students may note the hypocrisy of the committee's actions; they oust Oakhurst though many of them also gambled.
14. Students may say that the Duchess is the call girl, Oakhurst the hero, Uncle Billy the cheating drunk, and Piney Woods the ingenue.
15. Some students may find it possible to be completely unselfish; others may think that this is unrealistic.

Responding to the Selection

Personal Response

Some students may have been surprised by Oakhurst's actions and the deaths of several characters, expecting instead a happy ending.

ANALYZING LITERATURE

1. The committee banishes all "improper persons" because the town has suffered losses. The outcasts are marched to the outskirts of town and told not to return.
2. They head toward Sandy Bar, but stop when the Duchess declares she can go no farther. They make camp and are joined by Tom Simson and his fiancée, who are coming from Sandy Bar. Tom points out an old cabin, where the women sleep the first night.
3. Uncle Billy has stolen the animals; the outcasts are snowed in; they fix up the cabin and get through the day by entertaining each other.
4. Mother Shipton dies of starvation, having saved her food for Piney. Oakhurst kisses the Duchess, leaves, and shoots himself.
5. They find Piney and the Duchess dead in the cabin and Oakhurst dead under a tree.
6. His tone is bitter: he emphasizes their hypocrisy by their "spasm of virtuous reaction," unfamiliarity with "Sabbath influences," and "lawless and ungovernable" action.
7. He is honorable because he tries to stop them from delaying their trip and endangering their lives.
8. Oakhurst is protective; he doesn't tell Simson and Piney about Uncle Billy. Tom is naive and generous; he offers the cabin to the outcasts. Piney is naive and good-natured.
9. He is strong because he assumes leadership and because he remains calm and rational. He is weak because he kills himself.
10. One message is that hard times bring out the best in people. (Mother Shipton sacrifices herself, Oakhurst behaves selflessly, and the Duchess finds peace.)
11. Students may admire Oakhurst but be disappointed that he kills himself.

LITERATURE AND WRITING

Writing About Literature

Students' analyses should
- describe Harte's re-creation of the language, customs, geography, and habits of the people and region.
- include specific examples.
- explain how local color affected their understanding.

Creative Writing

Students' happy endings should
- reflect a thorough knowledge of the story.
- mention several of the story's characters.
- provide a reasonable resolution.

Skill Minilesson

VOCABULARY • Etymology

1. Perhaps from an English dialect *gulch* to gulp; from the Middle English *gulchen*
2. From the Middle English, from the Latin *billicosus*, from *bellicus,* of war, from *bellum* war
3. From the Spanish, from *castaña* meaning chestnut, from the Latin *castanea*, from the Greek *kastanea*
4. From the Middle English, from the Latin *pastoralis,* from *pastor* herdsman
5. From the Tamil (Indian), *paraiyan* drummer
6. From the French, *impropriété,* or Latin, *improprietat*
7. From Latin, *malevolent*—from *male,* badly, and *velle,* to wish
8. From the Latin, *aequanimitas* or French *aequo animo,* with even mind
9. From Latin, *jocularis*
10. From Greek, *hypotithenai*

Additional Resources
📁 *Vocabulary Practice,* p. 32

LITERATURE AND WRITING

Writing About Literature
Analyzing Local Color   When writers evoke a particular region by recreating the language, customs, and geography of the area, they use a technique called **local color** (see page R9). In a few paragraphs, analyze how Harte uses local color in "The Outcasts of Poker Flat." Explain how local color adds to your understanding of the story.

Creative Writing
Happily Ever After   Write a happy ending for this story—if not for all the characters, at least for the ones you like the best. Share and compare your new ending with those created by your classmates.

EXTENDING YOUR RESPONSE

Literature Groups
Frontier Justice   In your group, discuss the type of "justice" that is meted out to the characters in this story. Consider questions like these: What gives the secret committee of Poker Flat the authority to force the outcasts to leave town? Shouldn't the outcasts be given a chance to defend themselves? Should the members of the secret committee be held responsible for what happens to the outcasts? Why or why not? Use specific details from the selection to support your opinions. Share your opinions with the class.

Learning for Life
Incident Report   Imagine that Poker Flat has a sheriff's office and you work for it. Tom Simson, looking half-frozen and utterly exhausted, stumbles into your office on a December afternoon in 1850. Write an incident report based on the information Tom gives you.

Listening and Speaking
Discussing a Film   View the 1952 film *The Outcasts of Poker Flat,* directed by Joseph M. Newman and starring Anne Baxter. Note similarities and differences between the film and Harte's original story. Then hold a roundtable discussion in which you compare the story and the film. Which did you prefer? Why?

📖 **Save your work for your portfolio.**

Skill Minilesson

VOCABULARY • Etymology

A word's etymology is its history or an explanation of its origin. Often a word can be traced back through several languages, as is the case with the word *querulous.*

> *querulous:* Middle English *querulose,* from Old French *querelos,* from Late Latin *querulosus,* from Latin *querulus,* from *queri,* meaning "to complain."

Dictionaries usually list etymologies in brackets.

PRACTICE   Use a dictionary to find the etymology of each of the following words from "The Outcasts of Poker Flat."

1. gulch
2. bellicose
3. castanet
4. pastoral
5. pariah
6. impropriety
7. malevolent
8. equanimity
9. jocular
10. hypothesis

✓ ASSESSMENT OPTIONS

📁 *Quick Checks,* p. 55
📁 *Selection and Theme Assessment,* pp. 81–82
📁 *Performance Assessment,* p. 44
💾 *Testmaker*

Before You Read

Chief Sekoto Holds Court

Meet Bessie Head

"I write best if I can hear the thunder behind my ears."

—Head

One of Africa's best-known writers, Bessie Head began her life in a South African mental hospital. Because of racist attitudes in South Africa, Head's Scottish mother was judged insane and committed to an asylum when she became pregnant by a black man. Taken from her mother at birth, Head was brought up in a foster home until she was thirteen; then she was sent to a mission school.

After training to be a teacher and teaching a few years, Head launched a new career as a journalist. She had difficulty achieving recognition for her work, however, because of prejudice and discrimination toward her gender and racial heritage. The white minority that ruled South Africa at that time practiced apartheid, an official policy of racial segregation and discrimination against nonwhites. This policy made it difficult for people like Head to advance in their careers.

In 1964 Head abandoned journalism and moved to Botswana. There, in a small rural village, she wrote the novels that brought her international acclaim: *When Rain Clouds Gather* (1969), *Maru* (1971), and *A Question of Power* (1973). In these works, Head drew upon her own experiences to explore the themes of racial and sexual discrimination and poverty. While Head's writings often tell of brutality, they also express faith in the power of love and the belief that justice ultimately triumphs.

Bessie Head was born in 1937 and died in 1986.

FOCUS ACTIVITY

How might you respond if your friends and neighbors unjustly accused you of committing a horrible crime? To whom might you turn for help?

FREEWRITE Spend three minutes exploring your response to these questions.

SETTING A PURPOSE Read to find out what happens when a woman is accused of committing a terrible crime.

BACKGROUND

The Time and Place

This story takes place in Botswana, a small nation in southern Africa, some time between the 1960s and the early 1980s. During that period, ninety-four percent of the population lived in small rural villages ruled by tribal chiefs. In addition to their village duties, these chiefs also served as regional law enforcement officers, judges, and representatives at tribal conferences. A House of Chiefs, representing the eight major tribes of the Botswanan people, advised the national government on various tribal matters.

VOCABULARY PREVIEW

concede (kən sēd′) *v.* to acknowledge as true; to admit; p. 489
dally (dal′ ē) *v.* to linger; to delay; to waste time; p. 489
ashen (ash′ ən) *adj.* pale; p. 490

grievously (grē′ vəs lē) *adv.* very seriously; gravely; p. 490
derangement (di rānj′ ment) *n.* disturbance of normal functioning; disorder; p. 491

Objectives

- To read and analyze a short story about justice
- To identify and describe the climax and resolution of a short story

Skills

Reading/Thinking: Inferring; Identifying Assumptions; Distinguishing Fact and Opinion
Writing: Journal Entry
Grammar/Language: Verb Tense
Collaboration: Literature Groups

Motivating OPTIONS

Selection Focus Transparency 48: Have students examine and discuss the map of Botswana.

Focus Activity: As an extension of the Focus Activity, have students compare their responses with those of a partner.

RESOURCE MANAGER

Lesson Planning Resource
The *Unit Four Planning Guide* (pp. 22–27) provides additional lesson notes and reduced versions of all print resources.

Other Print Resources
- Active Reading Guide, p. 56
- Vocabulary Practice, p. 33
- Reading Workbook, pp. 51–52
- Grammar and Language Workbook, p. 137

- Grammar and Composition Handbook, Lesson 5.4
- Quick Checks, p. 56
- Selection and Theme Assessment, pp. 83–84
- Performance Assessment, p. 45
- Spanish Summaries, p. 48
- Spanish Translations
- English Language Learners Sourcebook

Transparencies
- Selection Focus 48
- Literary Elements 45
- Grammar and Language 41

Technology
- 🎧 Audio Library
- 🎧 Spanish Audio Library
- 💻 Glencoe Literature Web Site
- 💾 Testmaker

Beaded Panel (detail). c. 1980, Zulu people, Inanda area, South Africa. Glass beads.

Chief Sekoto Holds Court

Bessie Head

Woman Walking, 1990. Tilly Willis. Oil on canvas. Private collection.

SUMMARY

Chief Sekoto, a judge who values reason and optimism, is faced with an angry mob of villagers who have unreasonably accused a woman of murder. He reacts in his usual logical manner. He examines the evidence and finds the woman innocent. Chief Sekoto fines the villagers one beast per household, scolds them for their narrow-mindedness, and offers the woman a room in his home.

 **Spanish Summaries,** p. 48

A Active Reading

CONNECT Explain to students that this story concerns a case brought to a tribal court in Botswana. Ask students what they know about the justice system in the United States. What are its principles? What rights does the defendant have? Encourage students to look for similarities and differences between the U.S. and Botswanan systems as they read.

Additional Resources
- **Active Reading Guide,** p. 56
- **Audio Library**
- **Spanish Audio Library**

Teaching Options

COMPARING selections

This selection is paired with "The Outcasts of Poker Flat" on page 476. A lesson for teaching a comparison of the two selections appears on page 493.

Even those who did not like chiefs had to concede that Paramount Chief Sekoto was a very charming man. His charm lay not so much in his outer appearance as in his very cheerful outlook on life. In fact, so fond was he of the sunny side of life that he was inclined to regard any gloomy, pessimistic person as insane and make every effort to avoid his company. It was his belief that a witty answer turneth away wrath and that the oil of reason should always be poured on troubled waters.[1]

Every weekday morning, Chief Sekoto listened to cases brought before his court, while the afternoons were spent at leisure unless there were people who had made appointments to interview him. This particular Monday morning a lively and rowdy case was in session when, out of the corner of his eye, Chief Sekoto saw his brother Matenge drive up and park his car opposite the open clearing where court was held. Nothing upset Chief Sekoto more than a visit from his brother, whom he had long classified as belonging to the insane part of mankind. He determined to dally over the proceedings for as long as possible in the hope that his brother would become bored and leave. Therefore he turned his full attention on the case at hand.

The case had been brought in from one of the outlying villages, called Bodibeng, and the cause of its rowdiness was that the whole village of Bodibeng had turned up to witness the trial. A certain old woman of the village, named Mma-Baloi, was charged with allegedly[2] practising witchcraft, and so certain were the villagers of her guilt that they frequently forgot themselves and burst out into loud chatter and had to be brought to order by the president of the court with threats of fines.

---

1. The Chief's first belief is a variation of Proverbs 15:1, which says, "A soft answer turneth away wrath." The second belief refers to the fact that oil floats on, rather than mixing with, water; thus, metaphorically, the *oil of reason* would have a calming effect on the *troubled waters* of a dispute.
2. Here, *allegedly* (ə lej' id lē) means "presumedly" or "supposedly."

Vocabulary
concede (kən sēd') *v.* to acknowledge as true; to admit
dally (dal' ē) *v.* to linger; to delay; to waste time

B Active Reading
QUESTION Ask students what they learned about Chief Sekoto from this passage. *(He is cheerful, and he is impatient with anyone who does not share his cheerful outlook. He values wit and reason.)*

C Author's Craft
JUXTAPOSITION Although the description of the setting and events of this story might make readers think that it takes place in the distant past, Head uses juxtaposition to remind readers that this is a modern story. Explain that Head juxtaposes her description of Sekoto and the village to her description of Matenge driving up in a car, emphasizing that although the events may sound like something from a different era, they are not.

D Critical Thinking
INFERRING Ask students what can be inferred about Sekoto's brother, given Sekoto's classification of him as belonging to "the insane part of mankind." *(Sekoto regards all gloomy and pessimistic people as insane, so it is likely that he feels his brother is gloomy and pessimistic.)*

Reading *Minilesson*

Identifying Assumptions Explain to students that everyone makes assumptions about others based on their appearance, how they speak, or how they interact. These assumptions are often wrong, especially when they are based solely on appearances. When making assumptions, people may be stereotyping, or making inaccurate generalizations about others.

Activity In a class discussion, ask these questions: What assumptions did the villagers make about Mma-Baloi? On what basis? In your opinion, are these assumptions true or false? **L2**

Additional Resources
📁 *Reading Workbook,* pp. 51–52

E Active Reading

EVALUATE Have students describe the evidence the villagers use to conclude that Mma-Baloi is a witch. Then ask them to evaluate this evidence.

Model: The "evidence" the villagers use is that Mma-Baloi keeps to herself, her only guests are strangers, several children have died in the village, and a woman died in her hut. The villagers blame Mma-Baloi to alleviate their own sense of guilt and grief over the loss of their children. The fact that a woman died in her hut is not proof of her guilt. The villagers' logic is severely flawed; they have no proof that Mma-Baloi had anything to do with these deaths.

F Author's Craft

FIGURATIVE LANGUAGE Instead of simply saying that Chief Sekoto's gesture was meant to deflate their confidence, the author provides a more powerful image by saying that it was meant to "puncture a hole in" their confidence.

G Critical Thinking

DISTINGUISHING FACT AND OPINION Ask students why they think Chief Sekoto would ask to see the issuer of the death certificates. How does this request help Sekoto to distinguish between fact and opinion?
(The issuer is more qualified to determine the cause of death; with his medical training, he offers facts, while the villagers offer only opinions.)

Teaching Options

E Evidence was that Mma-Baloi had always lived a secret and mysterious life apart from the other villagers. She was also in the habit of receiving strangers from far-off places into her home who would not state what dealings they had with Mma-Baloi. Now, over a certain period, a number of the children of the village had died sudden deaths, and each time a mother stood up to describe these sudden deaths, the crowd roared in fury because the deaths of the children and the evil practices of Mma-Baloi were one and the same thing in their minds. The accused, Mma-Baloi, sat a little apart from the villagers in a quaking, <u>ashen</u>, crumpled heap and each time the villagers roared, she seemed about to sink into the earth. Noting this, Chief Sekoto's kindly heart was struck with pity.

Further evidence was that about a week ago a strange young woman had turned up in the village of Bodibeng and made straight for the hut of Mma-Baloi, where she had died a sudden death. This had made Mma-Baloi run screaming from her hut, and it was only the intervention[3] of the police that had saved Mma-Baloi from being torn to pieces by the villagers.

Chief Sekoto was silent for some time. The insanity of mankind never ceased to amaze him. At last he turned to the accused and said gently, "Well, mother, what do you have to say in defense of yourself?"

"Sir, I am no witch," said the quavering old voice. "Even though I am called the mother of the witches, I am no witch. Long ago I was taught by the people who live in the bush how to cure ailments with herbs and that is my business."

---

3. Here, *intervention* means "the act of coming between opposing parties."

She pointed a shaking finger at a bag placed near her.

"I would like to see the contents of the bag," Chief Sekoto said with a great show of interest. The bag was brought to him and its contents tipped out on the ground. They were a various assortment of dried leaves, roots, and berries. He examined them leisurely, picking up a few items for closer inspection. This very deliberate gesture was meant to puncture a hole in the confidence of the crowd, who annoyed him. While he fiddled about he was aware of how silent and intent they had become, following his every movement with their eyes. Thus holding the stage, he turned to the old woman and said: **F**

"Proceed with your defense, mother."

"About the deaths of the children of which I am accused, I know nothing, sir," she said. "About the young woman who died in my home last Saturday, I am also innocent. This young woman came to me on recommendation, being <u>grievously</u> ill. We were discussing the ailment when she fell dead at my feet. Never has such a thing occurred before, and this caused me to lose my mind and run out of the house."

"That is quite understandable, mother," Chief Sekoto said sympathetically. "Even I should have been grieved if some stranger was struck with death in my home."

He swept the crowd with a stern glance. **G** "Who issues the certificates of death in Bodibeng?" he asked.

There was a short, bewildered silence. Then a car and a messenger had to be found to fetch the doctor of the Bodibeng hospital. There was a delay of two hours as the doctor was engaged in an operation. Throughout this long wait the court remained in session. At one stage Chief Sekoto received an impatient

---

Vocabulary
ashen (ash′ ən) *adj.* pale
grievously (grē′ vəs lē) *adv.* very seriously; gravely

Grammar and Language *Minilesson*

Verb Tense Write the following sentence on the board: "About a week ago, a strange young woman <u>had turned up</u> in the village of Bodibeng and <u>made</u> straight for the hut of Mma-Baloi." Explain to students that *had turned up* is the past perfect tense of the verb phrase "to turn up." The past perfect tense indicates that one past action or condition began and ended

before another past action started. Tell students that the past perfect tense is formed with *had* and the past participle of a verb, as in the following examples: *had bought, had found, had shopped.*

Activity Have students look on pages 489 and 490 for examples of the past perfect tense. Ask them to explain why the verb is in the past perfect tense. **L2**

Additional Resources

Grammar and Language Transparency 41

Grammar and Language Workbook, p. 137

Grammar and Composition Handbook, Lesson 5.4

Writer's Choice, Lesson 15.3, 15.4

note: "Dear Brother," it said. "Please spare a few moments to discuss an urgent matter."

Chief Sekoto replied: "Is it life or death? I am at the moment faced with the life or death of an old woman. I cannot move."

It was near noon when the doctor arrived. His evidence was brief and to the point. Yes, it was true, he said. There had been a surprising number of child deaths in the village of Bodibeng, and death in each case had been due to pneumonia; and yes, he said, he had performed a postmortem[4] on the body of a young woman last Saturday afternoon. The young woman had died of a septic womb. . . .[5] He would say that the septic condition of the womb had been of three months' duration.

All that was left now was for Chief Sekoto to pass judgement on the case. This he did sternly, drawing himself up to his full height.

"People of Bodibeng," he said. "It seems to me you are all suffering from derangement of the brain."

He paused long enough to allow the villagers to look at each other uneasily.

"Your children die of pneumonia," he thundered, "and to shield yourselves from blame you accuse a poor old woman of having bewitched them into death. Not only that.

---

4. A *postmortem,* or autopsy, is the examination of a corpse that a physician performs to discover the cause of death.
5. In this case, the doctor's discovery of a *septic womb* indicated the absorption of certain poisonous bacteria into the bloodstream from an infection in the womb.

You falsely accuse her of a most serious crime which carries the death sentence. How long have you planned the death of a poor old woman, deranged people of Bodibeng? How long have you caused her to live in utter misery, suspicion, and fear? I say: Can dogs bark forever? Oh no, people of Bodibeng, today you will make payment for the legs of the old mother who has fled before your barking. I say: The fault is all with you, and because of this I fine each household of Bodibeng one beast. From the money that arises out of the sale of these beasts, each household is to purchase warm clothing for the children so that they may no longer die of pneumonia."

He turned and looked at the old woman, changing his expression to one of kindness.

"As for you, mother," he said. "I cannot allow you to go and live once more among the people of Bodibeng. It is only hatred that the people of Bodibeng feel for you, and this has driven them out of their minds. As hatred never dies, who knows what evil they will not plot against you. I have a large house, and you are welcome to the protection it offers. Besides, I suffer from an ailment for which I am always given penicillin injections at the hospital. Now I am tired of the penicillin injections and perhaps your good herbs may serve to cure me of my troubles."

He stood up, signifying the end of the case. The people of Bodibeng fled in confusion from the courtyard, but the old woman sat for a long time on the ground, silent tears of gratitude dripping down into her lap.

Vocabulary
derangement (di rānj′ ment) *n.* disturbance of normal functioning; disorder

---

H **Active Reading**

QUESTION Ask students how the doctor's testimony affects the villagers' claim. *(It disproves it; the doctor shows that Mma-Baloi was not responsible for the children's or the woman's death.)*

I **Active Reading**

EVALUATE Discuss the way Chief Sekoto punishes the villagers. Ask students if they agree with his punishment. *(Most students will agree that the villagers deserve to be punished for having unfairly accused Mma-Baloi and that the punishment produced more good than bad.)*

Thematic Focus

The Energy of the Everyday Ask students to discuss this story's theme about an ordinary person who must face an extraordinary challenge. Mma-Baloi must prove herself innocent despite having been accused by people to whom logic and reasoning is inconsequential.

✓ **ASSESSMENT OPTIONS**

📁 *Quick Checks,* p. 56

MEETING INDIVIDUAL NEEDS ENGLISH LANGUAGE LEARNERS

Law and Order In this story, Mma-Baloi must defend herself against the villagers' charges that she is a witch and a murderer. Explain to students that if she had been accused of this crime in the United States, she would have been represented by a lawyer, and she might not have been required to speak in her own defense.

Activity Have English language learners share information about the criminal justice systems in other countries. Invite native English speakers to join the discussion, adding ways in which the systems and laws compare to those in the United States.

Additional Resources
📁 *English Language Learners Sourcebook*

Personal Response

Many students will be pleased with the Chief's verdict. They may also be saddened by the pain the villagers caused Mma-Baloi.

ANALYZING LITERATURE

1. He is warm, cheerful, and reasonable. The narrator likes him; he or she says that he is a "very charming man."
2. Mma-Baloi is charged with murder because she is a loner who receives strange visitors, because many children have died in the village, and because a woman died in her hut. The judge doubts the villagers' sanity because their argument is illogical.
3. She says that she is not a witch, that she treats people with herbs, and that she is not responsible for the woman's death. Chief Sekoto asks to see her medicine and calls in the doctor who performed the autopsy. This suggests that Chief Sekoto is a reasonable man.
4. He says that the children died of pneumonia and the woman died of a septic womb. His evidence is based on proven medical knowledge.
5. He rules that Mma-Baloi is not guilty and fines each village household one beast, which may make the villagers think twice before rashly accusing anyone in the future.
6. Some students may feel that they, too, would be terrified if unjustly accused.
7. The story teaches that it is wrong to judge people merely because they are different. It also teaches that it is necessary to have evidence before accusing someone of a crime.
8. Students may discuss cases they have read about in newspapers or seen on television.

Responding to Literature

Personal Response

What was your reaction to the end of the story?

—— ANALYZING LITERATURE ——

RECALL AND INTERPRET

1. Describe Chief Sekoto's personality. What can you infer about the narrator's attitude toward him? Support your ideas by using details from the story.
2. What charge is brought against Mma-Baloi? What evidence do her accusers use to support this charge? Why do you think Chief Sekoto doubts the sanity of the woman's accusers?
3. Summarize what Mma-Baloi says in her own defense. How does Chief Sekoto respond to the woman's testimony? What do his words and actions seem to suggest about his character?
4. What evidence does the doctor present? Compare this evidence with that presented by the villagers and by Mma-Baloi.
5. Summarize Chief Sekoto's verdict in this case. What punishment does he impose? What effect might this punishment have on the villagers?

EVALUATE AND CONNECT

6. Refer to your response in the Focus Activity on page 487. Compare your imagined response with Mma-Baloi's actual response to being accused of a horrible crime.
7. In your opinion, what lesson, or **moral,** does this story teach? Explain your answer.
8. Have you ever witnessed or heard a story about a person being accused of wrongdoing based on flimsy evidence? Explain the situation and its outcome.

Climax and Resolution
Most stories contain a central conflict, or struggle between two opposing forces. In the story you have just read, the central conflict involves the decision that Chief Sekoto must make regarding Mma-Baloi's guilt or innocence. The point at which the central conflict reaches its highest emotional pitch is called the **climax.** The **resolution** is the point in the story when the outcome of the central conflict is revealed.

1. Identify the climax of "Chief Sekoto Holds Court." What gives this event such emotional impact?
2. Describe the resolution of the central conflict.
3. How might the ending of the story differ if Chief Sekoto had reached a different verdict? Explain.

● See **Literary Terms Handbook,** pp. R3 and R13.

—— EXTENDING YOUR RESPONSE ——

Literature Groups

Judge the Judge   In your group, discuss and evaluate Chief Sekoto's ruling in the case of *The People of Bodibeng* v. *Mma-Baloi.* Do you agree or disagree with his ruling? Do you think the fine he imposes is fair? Support your opinions with facts and reasons. Share your conclusions with the class.

Personal Writing

Mob Mentality?   How did you respond to the way Mma-Baloi was treated by the villagers? Why, do you think, didn't a single villager speak out in her defense? Record your responses to these questions in your journal.

📖 **Save your work for your portfolio.**

LITERARY ELEMENTS

1. The moment of Chief Sekoto's verdict is the climax; it is emotional because Mma-Baloi's life hangs in the balance.
2. The conflict is resolved by the excitement of Chief Sekoto's ruling.
3. If he had convicted her of the crime, the ending would have been surprising because all evidence pointed to her innocence.

Additional Resources

✍ *Literary Elements Transparency 45*

✔ ASSESSMENT OPTIONS

📁 *Quick Checks,* p. 56
📁 *Selection and Theme Assessment,* pp. 83–84
📁 *Performance Assessment,* p. 45
💾 *Testmaker*

COMPARING *selections*

The OUTCASTS of Poker Flat and Chief Sekoto Holds Court

COMPARE **CONFLICTS AND RESOLUTIONS**

Each selection contains a central conflict involving one or more characters labeled as outcasts. On a separate sheet of paper, write a few paragraphs answering the following questions:

1. In each story, who are the outcasts? What reasons do others have for labeling these characters as outcasts?

2. What punishment does each group intend for its outcasts? In each story, compare the intended punishment with what actually happens to the outcasts.

3. Evaluate the resolution of the central conflict in each story. Do you think the characters deserve their fates? Why or why not?

COMPARE **CULTURES**

Each story demonstrates the power of the accepted rules or customs of a particular culture or subculture, such as its ideas of justice. In a small group, discuss how the following cultural factors affected the characters in each story. Have one member record your group's ideas and opinions.

- accepted ideas about law and justice
- accepted rules of social behavior
- time and place in which events occur

COMPARE **PROTAGONISTS**

In "The Outcasts of Poker Flat," John Oakhurst is the **protagonist,** or central character; Chief Sekoto is the protagonist in "Chief Sekoto Holds Court." Think about the major traits of each character. Then create a diagram like the one at the right to compare and contrast the two protagonists. Identify traits they share as well as traits that set them apart from each other. Share your diagram with a small group of classmates.

Traits of John Oakhurst | Traits of both | Traits of Chief Sekoto

COMPARING *selections*

Objective
- To compare two short stories about outcasts

COMPARE **CONFLICTS AND RESOLUTIONS**

1. In "The Outcasts of Poker Flat," Mr. Oakhurst, Uncle Billy, the Duchess, and Mother Shipton are the outcasts because of their professions. In "Chief Sekoto Holds Court," Mma-Baloi is the outcast because she keeps to herself.

2. In Harte's story the outcasts are banned from the town; all except Uncle Billy die as the result. In "Chief Sekoto Holds Court," Mma-Baloi is to be executed, but she actually lives.

3. The outcasts in Harte's story did not deserve to die simply because the townspeople did not like them; Mma-Baloi deserved to live because she was innocent.

COMPARE **CULTURES**
Students' discussions should
- cite ways in which the cultural factors affected characters.
- demonstrate an understanding that each culture has different accepted rules or customs.

COMPARE **PROTAGONISTS**
Students' diagrams should
- include shared traits in the center.
- include traits that set the characters apart in the outer circles.

Teaching Options

PORTFOLIO OPTIONS

Select and Reflect Have students evaluate their comparisons of the conflicts and resolutions in these stories by asking themselves the following questions:
- Do my paragraphs answer each of the questions asked?
- Have I included appropriate transitions to connect the ideas in my paragraphs?

Ask students to write answers to these questions and use them to revise their paragraphs for inclusion in their portfolios. **L2**

Additional Resources
📁 *Writing Assessment and Portfolio Management,* pp. 51–58

LISTENING, SPEAKING, and VIEWING

Objective

- To acquire the tools to become an effective storyteller

Teaching Strategies

Suggest that students choose stories with which they are already familiar so that they do not have to worry about memorizing unfamiliar plot details for their performance. Encourage students to select a story that interests them so that they convey enthusiasm when they perform it. You may also suggest that they choose one of their own stories from their portfolios.

Activities

1. *Students' analyses should*
   - rate each of the elements—voice, gestures, and interest—on a scale of one to ten.
   - include descriptions of specific elements of the performance.
2. *Students could*
   - share their audiences' responses and suggestions with the class in order to develop a plan for improvement.

Teaching Options

LISTENING, SPEAKING, and VIEWING

Storytelling

Through stories, people pass traditions, customs, and values from generation to generation. In "Chief Sekoto Holds Court," for example, listeners learn that they should not condemn an innocent person just because she is different from them.

Good storytellers don't just tell a story; they perform it, with dramatic pauses, lively gestures, and sound effects. You can use these techniques to become an effective storyteller yourself.

Before Your Performance

- Read your story several times to remember the key events in the order they appear. Don't try to memorize the words; you might panic if you forget exactly what comes next. However, don't bore your listeners by simply reading the story aloud.
- Experiment with gestures, facial expressions, and posture to show excitement, confusion, and other emotions. Practice in front of a mirror, varying your voice to help listeners distinguish among the characters in the story.
- Consider playing background music to set the mood for your story. Alternatively, add sound effects using your voice, hands, simple instruments, or other tools.
- Ask a friend to watch and listen for ways you can tell your story more effectively, or videotape your performance and critique it.

During Your Performance

- Begin by telling your audience where and when the story takes place, but don't give away the plot. You might pose a question such as, "Do you ever wonder what your cat is thinking? The boy in this story was even more curious than his cat."
- Relax and enjoy yourself. If you're tense, your audience will sense it. If you forget an important detail, add it later, saying something like, "Oops! There's something else you need to know."

ACTIVITIES

1. Watch a storyteller in a taped performance or in person. Notice how he or she uses a variety of voices, gestures, and expressions to create interesting characters and an intriguing plot. Present a brief analysis of the performance to the class.

2. Choose a myth, folktale, or other story to tell. Practice it; then tell the story to an appropriate audience. Young children will let you know if you need to add more drama or perhaps shorten your presentation for your next performance.

494   UNIT 4

 ENGLISH LANGUAGE LEARNERS

Stories from Home To help English language learners with this lesson, encourage them to choose stories from their cultures—either ones that have been passed down through oral tradition or ones they have read.

Activity Have students choose a story to retell. Pair them with fluent English speakers and have them practice telling their stories. Tell them to focus at first on becoming comfortable telling the story aloud in English. As students master the stories, have them focus on other details: gestures, intonation, and facial expressions. **COLLAB. LEARN.**

Additional Resources

📁 *English Language Learners Sourcebook*

Web Site

Some people, in their everyday lives, face powerful natural forces such as bitterly cold weather. For anyone in such a frigid setting, this Web site could be quite important.

Feeling Chilly? Check Out These Hypothermia Tips

Address: http://www.alaska-movie.com

Hypothermia occurs when a person gets too cold. It is very dangerous and can even kill. People can get hypothermia gradually (which is called exposure) through cool temperatures, sweating, wet clothes, or clothes that aren't warm enough. They can also get acute hypothermia if they fall into cold water or are outside without shelter during a blizzard or other extremely cold weather.

Gradual hypothermia is especially dangerous because it can occur even when the temperature is mild, and because people often don't realize it is even happening.

The Warning Signs of Hypothermia

These are some of the symptoms of hypothermia. A person who is suffering from exposure (or extreme low temperatures) may demonstrate some or all of these symptoms:

1. Shivering, which means the body is trying to warm itself.

2. Increased heart rate and faster breathing.

3. Cold and [pallid] hands and feet, which means that the body is diverting blood from the person's extremities to try to keep the internal organs warm.

4. Irritable, irrational, and/or confused behavior.

5. Blue-colored lips or skin (an indication the hypothermia is getting severe).

6. Eventual unconsciousness.

How to Help People with Hypothermia

Mild cases of hypothermia are easier to treat than severe ones. For [people] with a mild case, you can encourage them to stay active, which will help them to warm up. Try to get them to a warm, dry shelter, and make sure that their clothes are dry and their heads are covered. If possible, it is good to apply warm objects (like a hot water bottle). They should drink something warm, but not if it has caffeine or alcohol in it.

[When] suffering from extreme acute hypothermia, [people] may become drowsy or nearly unconscious. It is important to get them to a hospital as soon as possible. In the meantime, [locate] a warm dry place, and handle them very gently (jostling them around or rubbing their skin can actually cause them to have a heart attack!).

Make sure they are gently warmed, but not by placing anything hot on them, because that can cause a heart attack as well.

Respond

1. What are the different types of hypothermia and how do they differ?

2. Describe some things you should do or not do to help someone suffering from hypothermia.

Teaching Options

Objective

• To understand and apply strategies for reading a Web site

Literature LINK

To Build a Fire Point out that this article provides tips for recognizing and treating the severe effects of cold on the human body. The main character in "To Build a Fire" (page 498) must battle alone to save himself from these same terrible effects.

Respond

1. Hypothermia builds over time and can occur when temperatures are mild; its causes include cool temperatures, sweating, and insufficiently warm clothing. People can experience acute hypothermia when they are outside during severe weather or after falling into cold water.

2. To treat mild hypothermia, apply hot water bottles, find warm shelter, cover the person's head, and give the person warm drinks without alcohol or caffeine. For acute hypothermia, handle the person gently and get him or her to a hospital as soon as possible.

Additional Resources
📁 *Media Connections,* p. 12

Hypothermia Have students choose a search engine to look for additional information about hypothermia. Suggest that they use the keyword *hypothermia*.

496 UNIT 4

Objectives

- To read and analyze a short story about a man who battles the elements threatening his survival
- To identify and analyze the setting in a story
- To write an explanation of a literary technique

Skills

Reading/Thinking: Sequencing; Making Critical Judgments; Drawing Conclusions; Evaluating
Writing: Letter
Vocabulary: Analogies
Grammar/Language: Compatibility of Verb Tenses
Life Skills: Planning
Collaboration: Literature Groups

More About Jack London

London had a difficult life, experiencing financial hardships as a child, and illness as an adult. When he was 13, he worked as many as 18 hours a day jarring pickles. At 15, he became known as the "Prince of the Oyster Pirates" for illegally raiding commercial oyster beds. After only one semester of college, he was forced to leave for financial reasons. He went to the Yukon but left empty-handed after he became ill.

London credited his hardships for enhancing his art. He believed that he developed his storytelling skills during his time as a hobo, when he was forced to beg for food.

Before You Read

To Build a Fire

Meet Jack London

"It was in the Klondike I found myself. There nobody talks. Everybody thinks. You get your true perspective. I got mine."

—London

In 1897 Jack London left college and went to the Yukon to join the Klondike gold rush. He never found gold, but he did find something that proved more precious to him: a wealth of raw material for the stories that eventually made him famous.

Born in San Francisco to an unstable mother and a father who refused to claim him, London was raised mainly by a family friend and a stepsister. From the age of eleven, the boy worked to earn money for his family. London loved the sea, so he hung around the harbor, doing odd jobs and learning to be an expert sailor. While still in his teens, he signed on to a schooner sailing to Siberia. From that adventure came his first published story.

At eighteen, London set off to ride the rails, living the life of a hobo as he traveled across the country on freight trains. This journey became a turning point in his life as he saw up close the raw, painful lives of men who did not seem to belong. London vowed to educate himself so he could survive by his mental powers rather than his physical strength.

After completing high school in one year, London attended college for a semester before rushing off to the Klondike. He failed to strike it rich, so he came home and turned to writing for his livelihood. In 1903 London published *The Call of the Wild*, the novel that firmly established his reputation. In time, he became the country's best-paid author—a stunning reversal of fortune for the once-impoverished writer.

Throughout his life, London worked under pressure to support not only himself but also family members and friends. He set himself the task of writing at least a thousand publishable words every day, and he rarely deviated from that schedule. But despite publishing more than fifty books and becoming the country's first millionaire author, London habitually spent more than he earned, and he often wrote stories in order to pay urgent debts.

In the last years of his life, London bought a ranch in northern California and began to build his dream house on it. In 1913, shortly before he was to move into the house, it burned down. The fire devastated London both emotionally and financially. He continued to live on the ranch but never rebuilt the house. Three years later, plagued by health problems and financial difficulties, London died. He was forty years old.

"The proper function of [a person] is to live, not to exist. I shall not waste my days in trying to prolong them. I shall use my time."

—London

Jack London was born in 1876 and died in 1916.

RESOURCE MANAGER

Lesson Planning Resource
The *Unit Four Planning Guide* (pp. 28–35) provides additional lesson notes and reduced versions of all print resources.

Other Print Resources
- Active Reading Guide, p. 57
- Vocabulary Practice, p. 34
- Reading Workbook, pp. 53–54
- Grammar and Language Workbook, p. 143

- Grammar and Composition Handbook, Lesson 5.6
- Quick Checks, p. 57
- Selection and Theme Assessment, pp. 85–86
- Performance Assessment, p. 46
- Spanish Summaries, p. 49
- Spanish Translations
- Inclusion Strategies
- English Language Learners Sourcebook

 **Transparencies**
- Selection Focus 49
- Literary Elements 46
- Grammar and Language 42

Technology

- Audio Library
- Spanish Audio Library
- Glencoe Literature Web Site
- Testmaker

trail was plainly visible, but a dozen inches of snow covered the marks of the last runners. In a month no man had come up or down that silent creek. The man held steadily on. He was not much given to thinking, and just then particularly he had nothing to think about save that he would eat lunch at the forks and that at six o'clock he would be in camp with the boys. There was nobody to talk to; and, had there been, speech would have been impossible because of the ice muzzle on his mouth. So he continued monotonously to chew tobacco and to increase the length of his amber beard.

Once in a while the thought reiterated[12] itself that it was very cold and that he had never experienced such cold. As he walked along he rubbed his cheekbones and nose with the back of his mittened hand. He did this automatically, now and again changing hands. But rub as he would, the instant he stopped his cheekbones went numb, and the following instant the end of his nose went numb. He was sure to frost his cheeks; he knew that, and experienced a pang of regret that he had not devised a nose strap of the sort Bud wore in cold snaps. Such a strap passed across the cheeks, as well, and saved them. But it didn't matter much, after all. What were frosted cheeks? A bit painful, that was all; they were never serious.

Empty as the man's mind was of thoughts, he was keenly observant, and he noticed the changes in the creek, the curves and bends and timber jams, and always he sharply noted where he placed his feet. Once, coming around the bend, he shied[13] abruptly, like a startled horse, curved away from the place where he had been walking, and retreated several paces back along the trail. The creek he knew was frozen clear to the bottom—no creek could contain water in

12. *Reiterated* means "repeated."
13. *Shied* means "moved suddenly, as in fear."

that arctic winter—but he knew also that there were springs that bubbled out from the hillsides and ran along under the snow and on top the ice of the creek. He knew that the coldest snaps never froze these springs, and he knew likewise their danger. They were traps. They hid pools of water under the snow that might be three inches deep, or three feet. Sometimes a skin of ice half an inch thick covered them, and in turn was covered by the snow. Sometimes they were alternate layers of water and ice skin, so that when one broke through he kept on breaking through for a while, sometimes wetting himself to the waist.

That was why he had shied in such panic. He had felt the give under his feet and heard the crackle of a snow-hidden ice skin. And to get his feet wet in such a temperature meant trouble and danger. At the very least it meant delay, for he would be forced to stop and build a fire, and under its protection to bare his feet while he dried his socks and moccasins. He stood and studied the creek bed and its banks, and decided that the flow of water came from the right. He reflected awhile, rubbing his nose and cheeks, then skirted to the left, stepping gingerly and testing the footing for each step. Once clear of the danger, he took a fresh chew of tobacco and swung along at his four-mile gait.

In the course of the next two hours he came upon similar traps. Usually the snow above the hidden pools had a sunken, candied appearance that advertised the danger. Once again, however, he had a close call; and once, suspecting danger, he compelled the dog to go on in front. The dog did not want to go. It hung back until the man shoved it forward, and then it went quickly across the white, unbroken surface. Suddenly it broke through, floundered to one side, and got away to firmer footing. It had wet its forefeet and legs, and almost immediately the water that clung to it turned to ice. It made

Vocabulary
compel (kəm pel′) *v.* to force

I Literary Elements
CHARACTER Explain to students that the man has a crucial character flaw. He is unable to look beyond the present to see the possible terrible consequences of not having prepared for his journey. His lack of imagination is his flaw.

J Author's Craft
FORESHADOWING Discuss how London prepares the reader for later events by saying that it would mean "trouble and danger" if the man were to get his feet wet. When the man later falls into the spring, the reader is instantly aware of the gravity of the act.

FYI
Deadly Water Water conducts (draws) heat away from the body 25 times faster than air does. This is why experts emphasize the importance of keeping dry in extremely cold environments.

K Active Reading
INTERPRET As they read, students can make connections between the man's actions and his character. Ask students what the man's actions toward his dog suggest about his character. *(His actions suggest that he is selfish and mean.)*

INTERDISCIPLINARY CONNECTION

Science The man in this story suffers from hypothermia, a condition caused by heat loss. The body loses heat through radiation, conduction, convection, and evaporation.

Activity Divide the class into four groups. Have each group research one of the forms of heat loss, giving an example of how the body loses heat in each form. Ask each group to present an explanation of the process to the class. Suggest that they use visual aids such as charts or diagrams to enhance their presentations. Remind students that heat loss is biologically necessary. Encourage students to discuss both the harmful and beneficial effects of heat loss in their presentations.
L2 COLLAB. LEARN.

Active Reading

L

QUESTION Discuss how the dog's instinct protects it from the elements in this instance. *(The dog knows to bite at the ice to prevent frostbite.)* Ask students what the man's action reveals about him. *(By taking off his mittens, he reveals that he lacks instinct.)*

Literary Elements

M

SYMBOL Explore with students the symbolism in the disappearance of the man's shadow. *(Nature is so powerful here that the man becomes inconsequential: nature literally makes the man's shadow disappear.)*

Literary Elements

N

CHARACTER Point out that only when he senses real danger does the man begin to realize his mistake in ignoring the old-timer from Sulphur Creek.

Literary Elements

O

FORESHADOWING Ask students what is suggested when the narrator qualifies the sentence "the cold of space was outwitted" with the modifier "for the moment." *(This suggests that nature has only temporarily been overcome.)*

TO BUILD A FIRE

L

quick efforts to lick the ice off its legs, then dropped down in the snow and began to bite out the ice that had formed between the toes. This was a matter of instinct. To permit the ice to remain would mean sore feet. It did not know this. It merely obeyed the mysterious prompting that arose from the deep crypts[14] of its being. But the man knew, having achieved a judgment on the subject, and he removed the mitten from his right hand and helped tear out the ice particles. He did not expose his fingers more than a minute, and was astonished at the swift numbness that smote[15] them. It certainly was cold. He pulled on the mitten hastily, and beat the hand savagely across his chest.

M

At twelve o'clock the day was at its brightest. Yet the sun was too far south on its winter journey to clear the horizon. The bulge of the earth intervened between it and Henderson Creek, where the man walked under a clear sky at noon and cast no shadow. At half-past twelve, to the minute, he arrived at the forks of the creek. He was pleased at the speed he had made. If he kept it up, he would certainly be with the boys by six. He unbuttoned his jacket and shirt and drew forth his lunch. The action consumed no more than a quarter of a minute, yet in that brief moment the numbness laid hold of the exposed fingers. He did not put the mitten on, but, instead, struck the fingers a dozen sharp smashes against his leg. Then he sat down on a snow-covered log to eat. The sting that followed upon the striking of his fingers against his leg ceased so quickly that he was startled. He had had no chance to take a bite of biscuit. He struck the fingers repeatedly and returned them to the mitten, baring the other hand for the purpose of eating. He tried to take a mouthful, but the ice muzzle prevented. He had forgotten to build a

fire and thaw out. He chuckled at his foolishness, and as he chuckled he noted the numbness creeping into his exposed fingers. Also, he noted that the stinging which had first come to his toes when he sat down was already passing away. He wondered whether the toes were warm or numb. He moved them inside the moccasins and decided that they were numb.

He pulled the mitten on hurriedly and stood up. He was a bit frightened. He stamped up and down until the sting returned into the feet. It certainly was cold, was his thought. That man from Sulphur Creek had spoken the truth when telling how cold it sometimes got in the country. And he had laughed at him at the time! That showed one must not be too sure of things. There was no mistake about it, it *was* cold. He strode up and down, stamping his feet and threshing his arms, until reassured by the returning warmth. Then he got out matches and proceeded to make a fire. From the undergrowth, where high water of the previous spring had lodged a supply of seasoned twigs, he got his firewood. Working carefully from a small beginning, he soon had a roaring fire, over which he thawed the ice from his face and in the protection of which he ate his biscuits. For the moment the cold of space was outwitted. The dog took satisfaction in the fire, stretching out close enough for warmth and far enough away to escape being singed.

N

O

When the man had finished, he filled his pipe and took his comfortable time over a smoke. Then he pulled on his mittens, settled the earflaps of his cap firmly about his ears, and took the creek trail up the left fork. The dog was disappointed and yearned back toward the fire. This man did not know cold. Possibly all the generations of his ancestry had been ignorant of cold, of real cold, of cold one hundred and seven degrees below freezing point. But the dog knew; all its ancestry knew, and it had

---

14. Here, *crypts* means "hidden recesses."
15. *Smote* (past tense of *smite*) means "afflicted" or "attacked."

Vocabulary
intervene (in´ tər vēn´) *v.* to come or lie between

MEETING INDIVIDUAL NEEDS

GIFTED AND TALENTED ACTIVITY

Naturalism Challenge gifted and talented students to analyze this story in a larger literary context. Explain that London was a naturalist. The Naturalism movement began in France during the nineteenth century and became popular in the United States before the beginning of the twentieth century.

Activity Ask students to write an essay connecting this story to the

literary trends of the time. Have students read about the ideas and philosophies of the naturalists in references such as the *Oxford Companion to American Literature* or *Benét's Reader's Encyclopedia*. Have students write about Naturalism in this story, paying particular attention to the role nature plays in the man's life and death. **L3**

inherited the knowledge. And it knew that it was not good to walk abroad in such fearful cold. It was the time to lie snug in a hole in the snow and wait for a curtain of cloud to be drawn across the face of outer space whence this cold came. On the other hand, there was no keen intimacy between the dog and the man. The one was the toil slave of the other, and the only caresses it had ever received were the caresses of the whiplash and of harsh and menacing throat sounds that threatened the whiplash. So the dog made no effort to communicate its apprehension to the man. It was not concerned in the welfare of the man; it was for its own sake that it yearned back toward the fire. But the man whistled, and spoke to it with the sound of whiplashes, and the dog swung in at the man's heels and followed after.

The man took a chew of tobacco and proceeded to start a new amber beard. Also, his moist breath quickly powdered with white his mustache, eyebrows, and lashes. There did not seem to be so many springs on the left fork of the Henderson, and for half an hour the man saw no signs of any. And then it happened. At a place where there were no signs, where the soft, unbroken snow seemed to advertise solidity beneath, the man broke through. It was not deep. He wet himself to the knees before he floundered out to the firm crust.

He was angry, and cursed his luck aloud. He had hoped to get into camp with the boys at six o'clock, and this would delay him an hour, for he would have to build a fire and dry out his foot gear. This was imperative[16] at that low temperature—he knew that much; and he turned aside to the bank, which he climbed. On top, tangled in the underbrush about the trunks of several small spruce trees, was a high-water deposit of dry firewood—sticks and twigs, principally, but also larger portions of seasoned branches and fine, dry, last-year's grasses. He threw down several large pieces on

16. *Imperative* means "absolutely necessary."

top of the snow. This served for a foundation and prevented the young flame from drowning itself in the snow it otherwise would melt. The flame he got by touching a match to a small shred of birch bark that he took from his pocket. This burned even more readily than paper. Placing it on the foundation, he fed the young flame with wisps of dry grass and with the tiniest dry twigs.

He worked slowly and carefully, keenly aware of his danger. Gradually, as the flame grew stronger, he increased the size of the twigs with which he fed it. He squatted in the snow, pulling the twigs out from their entanglement in the brush and feeding directly to the flame. He knew there must be no failure. When it is seventy-five below zero, a man must not fail in his first attempt to build a fire—that is, if his feet are wet. If his feet are dry, and he fails, he can run along the trail for half a mile and restore his circulation. But the circulation of wet and freezing feet cannot be restored by running when it is seventy-five below. No matter how fast he runs, the wet feet will freeze the harder.

All this the man knew. The old-timer on Sulphur Creek had told him about it the previous fall, and now he was appreciating the advice. Already all sensation had gone out of his feet. To build the fire he had been forced to remove his mittens, and the fingers had quickly gone numb. His pace of four miles an hour had kept his heart pumping blood to the surface of his body and to all the extremities. But the instant he stopped, the action of the pump eased down. The cold of space smote the unprotected tip of the planet, and he, being on that unprotected tip, received

P Critical Thinking

MAKING CRITICAL JUDGMENTS
Ask students to compare the dog's instinct to the man's intellect. Have them explore which form of knowledge seems better suited to this situation and why.

Model: The dog uses its instinct to protect itself from the cold. It knows, for example, the danger of walking in such cold weather, and that it should take cover. London implies that, lacking the protection of instinct, the man must imagine the consequences of such extreme temperatures. Lacking both instinct and imagination, the man will probably suffer terribly.

Q Author's Craft

SUSPENSE Discuss how London adds suspense in this paragraph by delaying when he provides information. Instead of simply stating that the man broke through the ice, he begins with the ominous phrase, "And then it happened." Ask students to continue reading to find another instance in which London uses this device to build suspense. *(He delays information on page 504, paragraph 3, when the tree extinguishes the fire.)*

R Critical Thinking

DRAWING CONCLUSIONS Encourage students to draw conclusions about the man from his comment here about the old-timer from Sulphur Creek. *(Students may conclude that he lives only in the moment, which is another example of his lack of imagination. Others may conclude that he is arrogant.)*

S Literary Elements

SIMILE Remind students that a simile is a comparison using the words *like* or *as*. Ask students to identify the two similes in this paragraph. *(London compares the man's socks to "sheaths of iron" and his moccasin strings to "rods of steel." These similes emphasize the difficulties the man faces in trying to remove his socks and shoes.)*

FYI

Men Only? Men were not the only ones who went north in search of adventure. In 1898 a pregnant woman, Martha Louise Black, hiked over the Chilkoot Pass and sailed down the Yukon River in a homemade boat after her first husband abandoned her on the way to the Klondike. Among Black's feats in the Yukon were running a saw-mill and supervising 16 men on a mining claim. Black later became Canada's second female member of Parliament.

Teaching Options

---

the full force of the blow. The blood of his body recoiled before it. The blood was alive, like the dog, and like the dog it wanted to hide away and cover itself up from the fearful cold. So long as he walked four miles an hour, he pumped that blood, willy-nilly,[17] to the surface; but now it ebbed[18] away and sank down into the recesses of his body. The extremities were the first to feel its absence. His wet feet froze the faster, and his exposed fingers numbed the faster, though they had not yet begun to freeze. Nose and cheeks were already freezing, while the skin of all his body chilled as it lost its blood.

But he was safe. Toes and nose and cheeks would be only touched by the frost, for the fire was beginning to burn with strength. He was feeding it with twigs the size of his finger. In another minute he would be able to feed it with branches the size of his wrist, and then he could remove his wet foot gear, and, while it dried, he could keep his naked feet warm by the fire, rubbing them at first, of course, with snow. The fire was a success. He was safe. He remembered the advice of the old-timer on Sulphur Creek, and smiled. The old-timer had been very serious in laying down the law that no man must travel alone in the Klondike after fifty below. Well, here he was; he had had the accident; he was alone; and he had saved himself. Those old-timers were rather womanish, some of them, he thought. All a man had to do was to keep his head, and he was all right. Any man who was a man could travel alone. But it was surprising, the rapidity with which his cheeks and nose

All a man had to do was to keep his head, and he was all right.

17. *Willy-nilly* means "without choice."
18. *Ebbed* means "flowed back" or "receded."

Vocabulary
conflagration (kon′ flə grā′ shən) *n.* a large, destructive fire

---

were freezing. And he had not thought his fingers could go lifeless in so short a time. Lifeless they were, for he could scarcely make them move together to grip a twig, and they seemed remote from his body and from him. When he touched a twig, he had to look and see whether or not he had hold of it. The wires were pretty well down between him and his finger-ends.

All of which counted for little. There was the fire, snapping and crackling and promising life with every dancing flame. He started to untie his moccasins. They were coated with ice; the thick German socks were like sheaths of iron halfway to the knees; and the moccasin strings were like rods of steel all twisted and knotted as by some conflagration. For a moment he tugged with his numb fingers, then, realizing the folly of it, he drew his sheath-knife.

But before he could cut the strings, it happened. It was his own fault or, rather, his mistake. He should not have built the fire under the spruce tree. He should have built it in the open. But it had been easier to pull twigs from the brush and drop them directly on the fire. Now the tree under which he had done this carried a weight of snow on its boughs. No wind had blown for weeks, and each bough was fully freighted. Each time he had pulled a twig he had communicated a slight agitation to the tree—an imperceptible agitation, so far as he was concerned, but an agitation sufficient to bring about the disaster. High up in the tree one bough capsized its load of snow. This fell on the boughs beneath, capsizing them. This process continued, spreading out and involving the whole tree. It grew like an avalanche, and it descended without warning upon the man and

---

MEETING INDIVIDUAL NEEDS

MULTIPLE LEARNING STYLES

Linguistic Have students imitate one of London's techniques in their own writing. Tell students that many writers use suspense to keep readers "at the edge of their seats." One technique for building suspense is to delay or slow down time at a crucial point in a story. Remind students that London uses delaying techniques before he describes the man stepping into the spring and the tree extinguishing the fire.

Activity Have students write two paragraphs describing an event. Ask them to use the line, "And then it happened," in their paragraphs. Students should build suspense by providing extra details prior to telling the reader what happened. Invite volunteers to share their anecdotes. **L2**

the fire, and the fire was blotted out! Where it had burned was a mantle of fresh and disordered snow.

The man was shocked. It was as though he had just heard his own sentence of death. For a moment he sat and stared at the spot where the fire had been. Then he grew very calm. Perhaps the old-timer on Sulphur Creek was right. If he had only had a trail mate he would have been in no danger now. The trail mate could have built the fire. Well, it was up to him to build the fire over again, and this second time there must be no failure. Even if he succeeded, he would most likely lose some toes. His feet must be badly frozen by now, and there would be some time before the second fire was ready.

Such were his thoughts, but he did not sit and think them. He was busy all the time they were passing through his mind. He made a new foundation for a fire, this time in the open, where no treacherous tree could blot it out. Next, he gathered dry grasses and tiny twigs from the high-water flotsam.[19] He could not bring his fingers together to pull them out, but he was able to gather them by the handful. In this way he got many rotten twigs and bits of green moss that were undesirable, but it was the best he could do. He worked methodically, even collecting an armful of the larger branches to be used later when the fire gathered strength. And all the while the dog sat and watched him, a certain yearning wistfulness[20] in its eyes, for it looked upon him as the fire provider, and the fire was slow in coming.

When all was ready, the man reached in his pocket for a second piece of birch bark. He knew the bark was there, and, though he

could not feel it with his fingers, he could hear its crisp rustling as he fumbled for it. Try as he would, he could not clutch hold of it. And all the time, in his consciousness, was the knowledge that each instant his feet were freezing. This thought tended to put him in a panic, but he fought against it and kept calm. He pulled on his mittens with his teeth, and threshed his arms back and forth, beating his hands with all his might against his sides. He did this sitting down, and he stood up to do it; and all the while the dog sat in the snow, its wolf brush of a tail curled around warmly over its forefeet, its sharp wolf ears pricked forward intently as it watched the man. And the man, as he beat and threshed with his arms and hands, felt a great surge of envy as he regarded the creature that was warm and secure in its natural covering.

After a time he was aware of the first faraway signals of sensation in his beaten fingers. The faint tingling grew stronger till it evolved into a stinging ache that was excruciating, but which the man hailed with satisfaction. He stripped the mitten from his right hand and fetched forth the birch bark. The

---

19. *Flotsam* (flot' səm) is floating debris, here left behind by a river or stream in the spring when the water rises with the runoff from melting snow and ice.
20. *Wistfulness* means "thoughtful sadness."

T Active Reading

QUESTION Ask students why the man feels as though he has just heard his own death sentence. *(He needs a fire to thaw out his wet and frozen feet; without one, he probably will die of hypothermia.)*

U Literary Elements

CLIMAX The story's climax begins in this paragraph where the conflict reaches its highest point. Ask students to identify the climax. *(The man's struggle to light the fire signifies the climax because the conflict in this story is the struggle between the man and nature. If the man does not triumph in this struggle, he will die.)*

V Active Reading

QUESTION Ask students why the man might have been glad to feel the stinging in his fingers. *(It indicated his fingers were still alive.)*

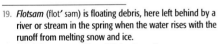

The Klondike Suggest that students use the keywords *Yukon, Klondike,* and *gold rush* to find more information about life in the Yukon during the gold rush. Remind students that they may want to use combinations of keywords when researching this topic on the Internet: typing only *gold rush* may also yield a great deal of information about the California gold rush. Have students share their findings with the class.

Teaching Options

TO BUILD A FIRE

exposed fingers were quickly going numb again. Next he brought out his bunch of sulphur matches. But the tremendous cold had already driven the life out of his fingers. In his effort to separate one match from the others, the whole bunch fell in the snow. He tried to pick it out of the snow, but failed. The dead fingers could neither touch nor clutch. He was very careful. He drove the thought of his freezing feet, and nose, and cheeks, out of his mind, devoting his whole soul to the matches. He watched, using the sense of vision in place of that of touch, and when he saw his fingers on each side of the bunch, he closed them— that is, he willed to close them, for the wires were down, and the fingers did not obey. He pulled the mitten on the right hand, and beat it fiercely against his knee. Then, with both mittened hands, he scooped the bunch of matches, along with much snow, into his lap. Yet he was no better off.

After some manipulation he managed to get the bunch between the heels of his mittened hands. In this fashion he carried it to his mouth. The ice crackled and snapped when by a violent effort he opened his mouth. He drew the lower jaw in, curled the upper lip out of the way, and scraped the bunch with his upper teeth in order to separate a match. He succeeded in getting one, which he dropped on his lap. He was no better off. He could not pick it up. Then he devised a way. He picked it up in his teeth and scratched it on his leg. Twenty times he scratched before he succeeded in lighting it. As it flamed he held it with his teeth to the birch bark. But the burning brimstone[21] went up his nostrils and into his lungs, causing him to cough spasmodically.[22] The match fell into the snow and went out.

The old-timer on Sulphur Creek was right, he thought in the moment of controlled despair that ensued;[23] after fifty below, a man should travel with a partner. He beat his hands, but failed in exciting any sensation. Suddenly he bared both hands, removing his mittens with his teeth. He caught the whole bunch between the heels of his hands. His arm muscles not being frozen enabled him to press the hand heels tightly against the matches. Then he scratched the bunch along his leg. It flared into flame, seventy sulphur matches at once! There was no wind to blow them out. He kept his head to one side to escape the strangling fumes, and held the blazing bunch to the birch bark. As he so held it, he became aware of sensation in his hand. His flesh was burning. He could smell it. Deep down below the surface he could feel it. The sensation developed into pain that grew acute. And still he endured it, holding the flame of the matches clumsily to the bark that would not light readily because his own burning hands were in the way, absorbing most of the flame.

At last, when he could endure no more, he jerked his hands apart. The blazing matches fell sizzling into the snow, but the birch bark was alight. He began laying dry grasses and the tiniest twigs on the flame. He could not pick and choose, for he had to lift the fuel between the heels of his hands. Small pieces of rotten wood and green moss clung to the twigs, and he bit them off as well as he could with his teeth. He cherished the flame carefully and awkwardly. It meant life, and it must not perish. The withdrawal of blood from the surface of his body now made him begin to shiver, and he grew more awkward. A large piece of green moss fell squarely on the little fire. He tried to poke it out with his fingers, but his shivering frame made him poke too far, and he disrupted the nucleus of

---

21. *Brimstone* is sulfur.
22. *Spasmodically* means "in a sudden, violent manner" or "convulsively."

23. *Ensued* means "happened afterward" or "followed."

Vocabulary
acute (ə kūt′) *adj.* intense; severe

MEETING INDIVIDUAL NEEDS — MULTIPLE LEARNING STYLES

Spatial Students who learn through visual stimuli may benefit from visualizing the setting, events, and characters in a story. Art, for example, can help engage spatial learners and enhance their reading comprehension.

Activity Have students look through art or photography books that contain landscapes or portraits to find a painting or photograph they would use to illustrate this selection. The picture should either remind them of an aspect of the selection or reflect the tone or mood of the story. Have students show their choices to the class, and explain why they would make good illustrations for the selection. **L1**

the little fire, the burning grasses and tiny twigs separating and scattering. He tried to poke them together again, but in spite of the tenseness of the effort, his shivering got away with him, and the twigs were hopelessly scattered. Each twig gushed a puff of smoke and went out. The fire provider had failed. As he looked apathetically about him, his eyes chanced on the dog, sitting across the ruins of the fire from him, in the snow, making restless, hunching movements, slightly lifting one forefoot and then the other, shifting its weight back and forth on them with wistful eagerness.

The sight of the dog put a wild idea into his head. He remembered the tale of the man, caught in a blizzard, who killed a steer and crawled inside the carcass, and so was saved. He would kill the dog and bury his hands in the warm body until the numbness went out of them. Then he could build another fire. He spoke to the dog, calling it to him; but in his voice was a strange note of fear that frightened the animal, who had never known the man to speak in such way before. Something was the matter, and its suspicious nature sensed danger—it knew not what danger, but somewhere, somehow, in its brain arose an apprehension of the man. It flattened its ears down at the sound of the man's voice, and its restless, hunching movements and the liftings and shiftings of its forefeet became more pronounced; but it would not come to the man. He got on his hands and knees and crawled toward the dog. This unusual posture again excited suspicion, and the animal sidled mincingly[24] away.

The man sat up in the snow for a moment and struggled for calmness. Then he pulled on his mittens, by means of his teeth, and got upon his feet. He glanced down at first in order to assure himself that he was really standing up, for the absence of sensation in his feet left him unrelated to the earth. His erect position in itself started to drive the webs of suspicion from the dog's mind; and when he spoke peremptorily,[25] with the sound of whiplashes in his voice, the dog rendered its customary allegiance and came to him. As it came within reaching distance, the man lost his control. His arms flashed out to the dog, and he experienced genuine surprise when he discovered that his hands could not clutch, that there was neither bend nor feeling in the fingers. He had forgotten for the moment that they were frozen and that they were freezing more and more. All this happened quickly, and before the animal could get away, he encircled its body with his arms. He sat down in the snow, and in this fashion held the dog, while it snarled and whined and struggled.

Viewing the photograph: As you look at this photograph, jot down the first five words that come to mind. Which of these words best describes the tone of "To Build a Fire"? Explain.

---

24. *Sidled mincingly* means "moved sideways in a careful manner."

25. *Peremptorily* (pe remp′ tə rə lē) means "authoritatively" or "dictatorially."

Vocabulary
apathetically (ap′ ə the′ ti klē) *adv.* in a manner showing little interest or concern

Point out to students that the artist depicts the Yukon during a different time of year than when this story is set.

Viewing Response *Some students will think this painting depicts a much calmer, less menacing view of the Yukon's landscape than the one described in London's story.*

Z Literary Elements

THEME The dog's instinct saves it from the man. Discuss with students the story's recurring theme of instinct versus intellect.

AA Literary Elements

CONFLICT Explore with students the different kinds of conflict in the story, including internal and external conflict. *(In addition to the man's struggle with an outside force [nature], he must face an internal struggle to stay calm despite his increasingly desperate circumstances.)*

LIFE SKILLS CONNECTION

Planning One of the main reasons the man in the story does not survive his journey is that he is ill prepared. Explain to students that taking time to prepare makes many aspects of life easier.

Activity Divide the class into pairs, and have each partner share one major goal for the future, such as finding a job, traveling, or attending college. Have the partners take turns explaining what they have done to prepare for this goal and their future plans for accomplishing it. Ask students to write a list of at least five things they can do to prepare for their goals. Encourage students to keep their lists as a checklist for the future. **L1 COLLAB. LEARN.**

BB Critical Thinking

EVALUATING Ask students to evaluate the man's plan to kill the dog. Then ask them to determine what this plan suggests about his state of mind. *(The plan is cruel and desperate. It may seem like a logical plan, but it is impossible for him to execute because he cannot possibly kill a dog if he has so little control over his hands that he cannot light a fire. The plan suggests that the man is so desperate at this stage that he is willing to try anything to survive.)*

CC Literary Elements

CONFLICT The man struggles to avoid thinking about his imminent death. He is battling an internal conflict to stay focused under extremely tense circumstances.

DD Literary Elements

CHARACTER Even with death near, the man refuses to think the worst, revealing his lack of imagination and his arrogance. Although some may view his determination as admirable, it proves a weak contestant against the wild, indifferent forces of nature and illustrates his misplaced pride in his own power to survive against the indifferent power of nature. Had the man recognized the strength and power of nature earlier in his journey, he would never have been faced with such a terrible situation.

Teaching Options

But it was all he could do, hold its body encircled in his arms and sit there. He realized that he could not kill the dog. There was no way to do it. With his helpless hands he could neither draw nor hold his sheath knife nor throttle the animal. He released it, and it plunged wildly away, with tail between its legs, and still snarling. It halted forty feet away and surveyed him cautiously, with ears sharply pricked forward. The man looked down at his hands in order to locate them, and found them hanging on the ends of his arms. It struck him as curious that one should have to use his eyes in order to find out where his hands were. He began threshing his arms back and forth, beating the mittened hands against his sides. He did this for five minutes, violently, and his heart pumped enough blood up to the surface to put a stop to his shivering. But no sensation was aroused in the hands. He had an impression that they hung like weights on the ends of his arms, but when he tried to run the impression down, he could not find it.

A certain fear of death, dull and oppressive, came to him. This fear quickly became poignant[26] as he realized that it was no longer a mere matter of freezing his fingers and toes, or of losing his hands and feet, but that it was a matter of life and death with the chances against him. This threw him into a panic, and he turned and ran up the creek bed along the old, dim trail. The dog joined in behind and kept up with him. He ran blindly, without intention, in fear such as he had never known in his life. Slowly, as he ploughed and floundered through the snow, he began to see things again—the banks of the creek, the old timber jams, the leafless aspens, and the sky. The running made him feel better. He did not shiver. Maybe, if he ran on, his feet would thaw out; and, anyway, if he ran far enough, he would reach camp and the boys. Without doubt he would lose some fingers and

---

26. *Poignant* (poin′ yənt) means "sharply felt" or "intensely distressing."

toes and some of his face; but the boys would take care of him, and save the rest of him when he got there. And at the same time there was another thought in his mind that said he would never get to the camp and the boys; that it was too many miles away, that the freezing had too great a start on him, and that he would soon be stiff and dead. This thought he kept in the background and refused to consider. Sometimes it pushed itself forward and demanded to be heard, but he thrust it back and strove to think of other things.

It struck him as curious that he could run at all on feet so frozen that he could not feel them when they struck the earth and took the weight of his body. He seemed to himself to skim along above the surface, and to have no connection with the earth. Somewhere he had once seen a winged Mercury, and he wondered if Mercury felt as he felt when skimming over the earth.

Did You Know?
In Roman mythology, *Mercury* is the messenger of the gods. He is portrayed wearing a winged hat and winged sandals.

His theory of running until he reached camp and the boys had one flaw in it: he lacked the endurance. Several times he stumbled, and finally he tottered, crumpled up, and fell. When he tried to rise, he failed. He must sit and rest, he decided, and next time he would merely walk and keep on going. As he sat and regained his breath, he noted that he was feeling quite warm and comfortable. He was not shivering, and it even seemed that a warm glow had come to his chest and trunk. And yet, when he touched his nose or cheeks, there was no sensation. Running would not thaw them out. Nor would it thaw out his hands and feet. Then the thought came to him that the frozen portions of his

---

MULTIPLE LEARNING STYLES

MEETING INDIVIDUAL NEEDS

Intrapersonal Some students respond well to activities that are reflective or that require them to work alone. One way to draw on this strength is to ask students to write about their reactions to a story.

Activity Have students write in their journals about the man and his journey. Ask them to consider their reactions to the man and his death. How were their reactions influenced by their feelings toward the man? For example, if they did not like the man, how did this influence their reaction to his death? Would they have felt more sympathy if they had liked him better? Why or why not? **L2**

Jack London ~

body must be extending. He tried to keep this thought down, to forget it, to think of something else; he was aware of the panicky feeling that it caused, and he was afraid of the panic. But the thought asserted itself, and persisted, until it produced a vision of his body totally frozen. This was too much, and he made another wild run along the trail. Once he slowed down to a walk, but the thought of the freezing extending itself made him run again.

And all the time the dog ran with him, at his heels. When he fell down a second time, it curled its tail over its forefeet and sat in front of him, facing him, curiously eager and intent. The warmth and security of the animal angered him, and he cursed it till it flattened down its ears appeasingly. This time the shivering came more quickly upon the man. He was losing in his battle with the frost. It was creeping into his body from all sides. The thought of it drove him on, but he ran no more than a hundred feet, when he staggered and pitched headlong. It was his last panic. When he had recovered his breath and control, he sat up and entertained in his mind the conception of meeting death with dignity. However, the conception did not come to him in such terms. His idea of it was that he had been making a fool of himself, running around like a chicken with its head cut off—such was the simile that occurred to him. Well, he was bound to freeze anyway, and he might as well take it decently. With this new-found peace of mind came the first glimmerings of drowsiness. A good idea, he thought, to sleep off to death. It was like taking an anaesthetic.[27] Freezing was not so bad as people thought. There were lots worse ways to die.

27. An *anaesthetic* is something that produces a loss of sensation.

He pictured the boys finding his body next day. Suddenly he found himself with them, coming along the trail and looking for himself. And, still with them, he came around a turn in the trail and found himself lying in the snow. He did not belong with himself any more, for even then he was out of himself, standing with the boys and looking at himself in the snow. It certainly was cold, was his thought. When he got back to the States he could tell the folks what real cold was. He drifted on from this to a vision of the old-timer on Sulphur Creek. He could see him quite clearly, warm and comfortable, and smoking a pipe.

"You were right, old hoss; you were right," the man mumbled to the old-timer on Sulphur Creek.

Then the man drowsed off into what seemed to him the most comfortable and satisfying sleep he had ever known. The dog sat facing him and waiting. The brief day drew to a close in a long, slow twilight. There were no signs of a fire to be made, and, besides, never in the dog's experience had it known a man to sit like that in the snow and make no fire. As the twilight drew on, its eager yearning for the fire mastered it, and with a great lifting and shifting of its forefeet, it whined softly, then flattened its ears down in anticipation of being chidden[28] by the man. But the man remained silent. Later, the dog whined loudly. And still later it crept close to the man and caught the scent of death. This made the animal bristle and back away. A little longer it delayed, howling under the stars that leaped and danced and shone brightly in the cold sky. Then it turned and trotted up the trail in the direction of the camp it knew, where were the other food providers and fire providers.

28. *Chidden* (past participle of *chide*) means "scolded."

Active Reading

QUESTION Ask students why they think the dog continues to run alongside the man? *(The dog continues to run alongside the man because the man is the fire provider.)*

Literary Elements

PLOT: *Falling Action* With death nearby, the man suddenly feels a sense of warmth and calm. This scene presents the falling action of the plot; London shares the man's sense of warmth to indicate that the end is near. The image of the stars leaping, dancing, and shining brightly in the sky at the end of the story suggests nature's indifference to the plight of the man.

Thematic Focus

The Energy of the Everyday
The man in this story must struggle against the elements to survive. His story, although too common during this time in the history of the Klondike Gold Rush, is rendered extraordinary by London's use of vivid details in relating the man's internal and external struggles for survival.

✔ ASSESSMENT OPTIONS

📁 ***Quick Checks,*** p. 57

REAL-WORLD CONNECTION

Hypothermia Today scientists know more about hypothermia and its treatment than they did when this story took place.

Activity Have students work in groups to read the warning signs of hypothermia in Media Connection on page 495. Ask them to determine if the man in the story exhibited any of these warning signs. Have students give an example of each sign. **L2** COLLAB. LEARN.

® *The following videotape program is available from Glencoe. Be sure to preview the video for appropriateness for your class.*

- **To Build a Fire***

  **Also available in the Glencoe Literature Video Library.*

Responding to the Selection

Personal Response

Students may mention the image of the man burning his flesh as he attempts to build the fire, or images of the wild and imposing setting.

ANALYZING LITERATURE

1. He is going to Henderson Creek to meet his friends at camp. He is unconcerned about his journey, feeling no danger.

2. The dog is fearful of the man (because the man whips it), and it wants to stop and hide (because it knows the temperature is too low for travel).

3. The man steps in a spring and gets his feet wet. He tries to light a fire, but it is extinguished by a tree. His hands are so cold that he cannot light another fire.

4. He thrashes his arms back and forth, beating them against his chest. He does this violently and then begins to run wildly because he is panicked.

5. The man dies; the dog survives and heads toward the camp.

6. He is unimaginative, arrogant, does not prepare well, and lacks an understanding of danger.

7. Its nervous behavior and its desire to find shelter foreshadow the man's hypothermia and death.

8. The man must struggle against an external force, nature. Internal forces he struggles against are his own fear and desperation.

9. Some may think he does not truly know his fate until he passes out in the snow; others may think he knows when his fire is extinguished.

10. One lesson is that one must listen to experts and be prepared; another is that one must be able to imagine consequences.

11. The mood becomes more ominous and desperate as the story progresses, which is a reflection of the man's advancing desperation.

12. Charts may include the following effects: *Physical:* frostbite, frozen, numb; *Mental:* desperation, frenzy, fear, avoidance, acceptance.

13. Some sensory images include the burning flesh, the warmth of the fire, and the man's frozen beard. These images help the reader "feel" the man's experiences by appealing to various senses.

Responding to Literature

Personal Response

Which images from the story are the most vivid and memorable?

ANALYZING LITERATURE

RECALL

1. Where is the man going? What is his attitude toward his journey and the conditions he faces?
2. Describe how the man's dog behaves. What reasons does the narrator give for this behavior?
3. What mishap occurs shortly after the man eats lunch and resumes his journey? Summarize his attempts to recover from this mishap.
4. Describe what the man does after releasing the dog. How do his feelings of panic affect his behavior?
5. What happens to the man and the dog at the end of the story?

INTERPRET

6. What can you infer about the man's personality and character, based on the information in the first five paragraphs?
7. What events does the dog's behavior **foreshadow** (see page R7)?
8. What external and internal forces must the man struggle against?
9. At what point do you think the man knows his fate? Explain.
10. What lesson or lessons might be learned from reading this story? Support your ideas by using details from the selection.

EVALUATE AND CONNECT

11. Explain how the **mood,** or atmosphere, changes as the story develops. How are the events of the story reflected in the change of mood?
12. Complete a chart like the one you made for the Focus Activity on page 497 for the man in this story. Compare your chart with this new one and explain any differences.
13. Find at least three examples of **sensory details** (see page R14) in the selection and evaluate how well each one helps you see, hear, feel, smell, or taste what is being described.
14. Is the dog merely a **foil,** a character used to contrast with another character, or is it an important character in its own right? Explain.
15. Think of a time when you faced a dangerous or potentially dangerous situation alone. How did you handle it? Would you do anything differently in a similar situation today? Explain.

Literary ELEMENTS

Setting

The **setting** is the time and place in which the events of a literary work occur. "To Build a Fire" is set in a specific historical time and place. The setting of London's story is well defined and essential; without the setting, this particular story could not have been written. The setting establishes the story's central **conflict,** or struggle between opposing forces, and is vital to the development of the plot, or sequence of events that make up the story's action. The setting also allows London to develop the character of the man through his interactions with the physical environment.

1. In what historical time and place is this story set? What details and references in the story help establish the setting?
2. How does the setting of the story establish the central conflict? How does it influence the resolution, or final outcome, of this conflict?
3. How does London reveal the man's character through his interactions with the physical environment? Give specific examples.

● See **Literary Terms Handbook,** p. R14.

14. Some may think the dog is a character in its own right because it expresses emotions such as fear. Others may think it is a foil used to contrast the man's display of arrogance and ignorance.

15. Suggest that students mention only those situations they do not mind sharing with the class.

LITERARY ELEMENTS

1. It is set in the Klondike during the Gold Rush at the beginning of the twentieth century. The narrator mentions several places to set the scene in the Yukon.
2. The harsh natural elements provide the conflict—the man must build a fire or die of hypothermia, but the extreme cold prevents him from building the fire.
3. He lacks respect for the bitter cold. He builds the fire too close to the tree.

Additional Resources

Literary Elements Transparency 46

— LITERATURE AND WRITING —

Writing About Literature

Explain a Literary Technique   London names specific places in the story but does not give names to any of the characters. In a paragraph, explain why you think the places are named but the people are not. How does London's choice help you better understand the story's **theme**, or message? Support your ideas with evidence.

Creative Writing

I'm So Sorry to Inform You   Imagine that you are one of the main character's camp mates and that you are writing to the man's family to inform them of his death. Write a tactful letter in which you gently break the news without dwelling on all the gory details. Focus on the fact that the man died while pursuing an adventurous dream.

— EXTENDING YOUR RESPONSE —

Literature Groups

Consider the Possibilities   In your opinion, how might the man have altered his fate? What decisions might he have made if he had not been a person "without imagination"? In your group, brainstorm different actions the man might have taken at each turn of events in the story. Share your ideas with the class.

Interdisciplinary Activity

Biology: The Effects of Extreme Cold   Investigate how different parts of the human body are affected by severe cold. Find out what actually happens when a person freezes to death. Use diagrams, charts, or other visual aids to present your findings to the class.

Learning for Life

News Story   Imagine that you are a journalist covering the Klondike gold rush in 1897. Write a news story in which you report the death of the man in this selection. In your story's lead, or opening paragraph, be sure to cover the five Ws: *who, what, where, when,* and *why.* Give additional details in the body of your news story.

Reading Further

You might enjoy reading these novels by Jack London: *The Call of the Wild, White Fang,* and *The Sea Wolf* are based on London's adventures in the Yukon and at sea.

 Save your work for your portfolio.

Analogies are comparisons based on relationships between words and ideas. Sometimes the relationship between the words in a pair is that of *synonym variants.* Such words have similar meanings, but they are not exact synonyms. The words in each pair may or may not be the same part of speech.

   surprised : astonishment :: joyful : happiness

Someone who is *surprised* is astonished; he or she exhibits *astonishment.* Someone who is *joyful* is happy; he or she exhibits *happiness.*

● For more about analogies, see **Communications Skills Handbook,** p. R83.

PRACTICE   Choose the pair that best completes each analogy.

1. funny : humor ::
   a. angry : gloom
   b. cold : ice
   c. strong : muscles
   d. brave : courage
   e. dishonest : integrity

2. acute : severity ::
   a. strong : weakness
   b. lively : energy
   c. friendly : hostility
   d. careful : accident
   e. white : blizzard

LITERATURE AND WRITING

Writing About Literature

Students' explanations should
• reflect an understanding that the man is insignificant compared to the great forces of nature.
• use specific details from the story as evidence.

Creative Writing

Students' letters should
• include specific details from the story.
• present the information in a tactful manner while helping to console the family.

EXTENDING YOUR RESPONSE

Literature Groups   Suggest that students pay particular attention to the man's decision to travel alone and his treatment of the dog. **COLLAB. LEARN.**

Interdisciplinary Activity   Tell students that the Internet may be a valuable research tool in finding this information.

Learning for Life   Remind students that as journalists, they have a responsibility to ensure that their stories are both interesting and accurate.

1. d
2. b

Additional Resources
   Vocabulary Practice, p. 34

ASSESSMENT OPTIONS

   Quick Checks, p. 57
   Selection and Theme Assessment, pp. 85–86
   Performance Assessment, p. 46
   Testmaker

Vo·cab·u·lar·y Skills

Objective

• To learn how to use context clues to determine a word's meaning

Teaching Strategies

Tell students that learning to recognize context clues will save them time as they read; they will no longer have to reach for a dictionary every time they encounter a new word. Remind students that synonyms are different words that have the same meaning.

Exercises

1. *Some acceptable definitions:*
   a. mark or track
   b. burned
   c. the limbs of the body (arms, hands, legs, and feet)
2. *Some acceptable replacements:*
   a. systematically or with method or order
   b. far away
   c. told off or scolded

Make sure that students have replaced the italicized words with words that are the same part of speech.

Additional Resources

📁 *Vocabulary Power: Weekly Lessons and Activities*

Teaching Options

Vo·cab·u·lar·y Skills

Using Context Clues

In "To Build a Fire," Jack London uses some words that you might not recognize, but **context clues** can help you figure out their meanings. There are two main types of context clues.

Clues on the Page

● An unfamiliar word may be used as a **synonym** for another term. Jack London writes, "It had been days since he had seen the sun; . . . a few more days must pass before that cheerful *orb* . . . would just peep above the skyline." By reading carefully, you can determine that *orb,* in this context, is another word for *sun.*

● Sometimes writers **define** unusual words. For instance, London says the nearly frozen man "*threshed* his arms back and forth, beating his hands with all his might." So here, *threshed* means "beat."

● **Other words in the sentence** may also provide clues, as when London describes snow as "rolling in gentle *undulations.*" The words *rolling* and *gentle* can help you see that *undulation* means "a rising and falling in waves."

Clues from Your Own Knowledge

When faced with an unfamiliar word, think of other words that would make sense in the sentence. For example, London writes, ". . . the thought *reiterated* itself that it was very cold." The thought must have "presented" itself. You know the prefix *re-* means that something is repeated, so *reiterate* means "to present again" or "to repeat something."

When you come upon an unfamiliar word in your reading, don't skip over it. Use context clues to figure out what it means.

● For more about using context clues, see **Reading Handbook,** pp. R86–R93.

EXERCISES

1. Use context clues from the sentences to define the words in italics.

   a. The *furrow* of the old sled-trail was plainly visible, but snow covered the marks of the last runners.

   b. The dog stretched out close enough to the fire for warmth and far enough away to escape being *singed.*

   c. His heart kept pumping blood to the surface of his body and to all the *extremities.*

2. For each sentence, think of a word or phrase that would make sense in place of the italicized word. Then use a dictionary to find out whether your word or phrase is similar in meaning to the italicized word.

   a. He worked *methodically,* even collecting an armful of the larger branches to be used later.

   b. He could barely move his fingers together, and they seemed *remote* from his body and from him.

   c. The dog flattened its ears in anticipation of being *chidden* by the man.

MEETING INDIVIDUAL NEEDS   ENGLISH LANGUAGE LEARNERS

Building Vocabulary Help English language learners look for context clues. Explain the part of speech of each italicized word. Then work through the second exercise together.

Activity Explain that in the first sentence, *methodically* is an adverb; it describes the way the man worked. Ask students to think of another adverb to replace it. In the second sentence, the adjective *remote* describes a noun, "his *fingers.*" In the third sentence, *chidden* is a form of the verb *to chide.* They will need a past participle in this sentence.

Additional Resources

📁 *English Language Learners Sourcebook*

Before You Read

I Will Fight No More Forever

Meet Chief Joseph

"Whenever the white man treats the Indian as they treat each other, then they shall have no more wars."

—Chief Joseph

Joseph—whose given name was Hinmaton Yalaktit (hin mə tō′ yä läkh′ tet) or "Thunder Rolling Down the Mountain"—was born in the Wallowa Valley in what is now northeastern Oregon. When his father died in 1871, Joseph was elected to succeed him as a chief of the Nez Percé (nez purs).

Although this tribe had maintained peace with the whites for seventy years, Chief Joseph inherited a volatile situation. Eight years earlier, following a gold rush into Nez Percé territory, the U.S. government had reclaimed nearly all the land it had ceded to the tribe in an 1855 treaty. Chief Joseph successfully resisted efforts to remove his band from the Wallowa Valley until 1877, when the government threatened removal by force.

To avoid bloodshed, Chief Joseph decided to cooperate, but as he led his band toward a reservation, some of his men killed a group of white settlers. To protect his people from retaliation by the U.S. Army, he led them on a long, grueling march for the Canadian border. Within forty miles of their destination, however, they were forced to surrender.

Chief Joseph's people were then removed to what is now Oklahoma, where many became sick and died. In 1885 the tribe was returned to the Pacific Northwest, but about half, including Chief Joseph, were taken to a non–Nez Percé reservation in Washington. There Chief Joseph died, according to his doctor, "of a broken heart."

"I have asked some of the great white chiefs where they get their authority to say to the Indian that he shall stay in one place, while he sees white men going where they please. They can not tell me."

—Chief Joseph

Chief Joseph was born around 1840 and died in 1904.

FOCUS ACTIVITY

Have you ever been forced to defend yourself, either physically or verbally?

JOURNAL Write about a time when you had to defend yourself. How did you handle the situation?

SETTING A PURPOSE Read to understand a man's defense of his decisions.

BACKGROUND

The Long Trek to Canada

Chief Joseph tried to take his people to Canada because he felt he had no choice. For more than three months, from June 17 to September 30, 1877, he led some two hundred warriors and their families on a journey that covered more than a thousand miles. The warriors fought off pursuing federal troops again and again, despite being outnumbered at least ten to one. Because of his constant attention to the needs of the women, children, and aged among his people, because of his humane treatment of prisoners, and because of his honorable behavior in victory and defeat, Chief Joseph won many admirers and supporters among Native Americans and whites.

REGIONALISM AND REALISM 513

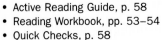

SUMMARY

In the midst of a desperate flight to Canada, Chief Joseph sees that the tribe's leaders are dead and the women and children are freezing and starving. After years of fighting the white people to protect the Nez Percé land and way of life, he realizes that his tribe is too devastated to fight any longer.

 Spanish Summaries, p. 50

 Active Reading

RESPOND Chief Joseph's speech is written in a series of sentences with similar grammatical structures. Ask students what response these sentences evoke. *(Students may say that naming many of the people who have died and repeating the words "is dead" helps them understand the enormity of his loss.)*

Additional Resources

 Active Reading Guide, p. 58

🎧 **Audio Library**

🎧 **Spanish Audio Library**

Chief Joseph Rides to Surrender, 1979. Howard Terpning. Oil on canvas. ©1979 Howard Terpning. ©1979 The Greenwich Workshop® Inc. Courtesy of The Greenwich Workshop Inc., Shelton, CT.

I Will Fight No More Forever

Chief Joseph ∿

"Tell General Howard[1] I know his heart. What he told me before, I have in my heart. I am tired of fighting. Our chiefs are killed. Looking Glass[2] is dead. Too Hul Hul Suit[3] is dead. The old men are all dead. It is the young men who say yes and no. He who led on the young men is dead.[4] It is cold and we have no blankets. The little children are freezing to death. My people, some of them, have run away to the hills and have no blankets, no food; no one knows where they are—perhaps freezing to death. I want to have time to look for my children and see how many I can find. Maybe I shall find them among the dead. Hear me, my chiefs. I am tired; my heart is sick and sad. From where the sun now stands I will fight no more forever."

1. *General* (Oliver Otis) *Howard* (1830–1909) had been a Union general in the Civil War. He sent troops to fight the Nez Percé in the Battle of White Bird Canyon.
2. *Looking Glass* was a respected leader of the Nez Percé. He took part in the 1877 retreat.
3. *Too Hul Hul Suit,* or Tu Ku Lxu C'uut (tœ kœl´ hu sœt´), leader of the White Bird tribe, was a member of the negotiating team that met with General Howard. He favored fighting for the Nez Percé land rather than moving to a reservation.
4. *[He who led . . . dead.]* refers to Chief Joseph's younger brother, Ollikut (ōl okh´ ut).

514 🦃 UNIT 4

interNET CONNECTION

The Nez Percé Students may enjoy learning more about the Nez Percé. Have them use a search engine to research this Native American group, using keywords *Nez Percé, Native Americans,* or *Chief Joseph.*

Responding to Literature

Personal Response

If you could speak to Chief Joseph, what would you say to him?

─── ANALYZING LITERATURE ───

RECALL AND INTERPRET

1. What has happened to the chiefs and the old men of the tribe? Who is left to carry on the fight? In your opinion, how might these developments have affected Chief Joseph's decision?

2. What other reasons does Chief Joseph give for his decision? What can you infer about his values and his character, based on these reasons?

3. What words does Chief Joseph use to describe his heart? How do the feelings he describes help you better understand the decision he has made?

4. In your words, restate the last sentence of Chief Joseph's speech.

EVALUATE AND CONNECT

5. What words and phrases does Chief Joseph repeat? What is the effect of this **repetition?** (See Literary Terms Handbook, page R13.)

6. In this short speech, Chief Joseph explains a decision that will have an enormous impact on the lives of his people. Do you think a longer, more detailed speech would have been more effective or more convincing? Why or why not?

7. Chief Joseph was a brave, proud warrior. In your opinion, what inner qualities did he summon in order to accept defeat with dignity? Explain.

8. Read the journal entry you made for the Focus Activity on page 513. After reading Chief Joseph's speech, can you imagine a different solution to the situation you wrote about? Explain.

Literary ELEMENTS

Tone

Tone is the writer's attitude toward the subject of a work. The tone of a piece of writing conveys one or more emotions. In "I Will Fight No More Forever," the tone conveys feelings of weariness, resignation, sadness, and dignity. Writers create the tone of a work primarily through word choice, but sentence structure and length can also be important. For example, Chief Joseph's use of brief sentences and simple, direct language emphasizes the overwhelming sense of loss.

1. What words and phrases help create a tone that is weary, resigned, and sad, yet dignified?

2. Find examples of simple, direct language and brief sentences. How do they affect the tone of the speech?

● See **Literary Terms Handbook,** p. R16.

─── EXTENDING YOUR RESPONSE ───

Personal Writing

In Defense   In "I Will Fight No More Forever," Chief Joseph eloquently defends his decision to surrender. Using the selection as a model, write a speech defending your response to the situation you described for the Focus Activity on page 513.

Internet Connection

Wounded Knee   In 1890 federal troops killed more than 150 unarmed Sioux men, women, and children at Wounded Knee, South Dakota. Use the Internet to research the massacre. In a presentation to the class, compare this situation with that of Chief Joseph and his people.

 Save your work for your portfolio.

REGIONALISM AND REALISM ❦ 515

LITERARY ELEMENTS

1. Phrases may include: "I am tired of fighting," "I am tired; my heart is sick and sad," and "From where the sun now stands I will fight no more forever."

2. "The old men are all dead" is one example of a brief sentence that adds to the sad, resigned tone of the speech.

Additional Resources

✍ *Literary Elements Transparency 47*

Responding to the Selection

Personal Response

Students may want to express their sympathy for his loss, ask him if he later regretted his decision, or ask what General Howard told him.

ANALYZING LITERATURE

1. The chiefs and the old men have all died. The young men must carry on the fight. Chief Joseph may believe that it is up to a new generation to decide what to do next.

2. He wants to look for the children, and he is tired and full of sorrow. His desire to save the remainder of his people reveals that he is a kind and honorable person.

3. His heart is "sick" and "sad." The feelings he describes make his decision to cease fighting more understandable.

4. From this moment on, I will never fight again.

5. He repeats the words, "is dead" and "freezing to death," which reinforces his sorrow and feelings of helplessness over the deaths of many of his people.

6. Many students will feel that his speech is very effective in expressing his feelings. The shortness of the speech implies that he is too tired to say more.

7. Students may mention such qualities as courage, faith, and honor.

8. Students may say that they realized that walking away from confrontation can be honorable.

EXTENDING YOUR RESPONSE

Personal Writing

Students' speeches should
● persuasively defend a position.
● use Chief Joseph's speech as a model.

Internet Connection Suggest that students begin their search with the keywords *Wounded Knee 1890.*

Technology Skills

Objectives

- To use available technology to create a multimedia presentation
- To make a connection between a historical period and the literature of that time

Teaching Strategies

As a motivational introduction to this feature, show students a multimedia presentation of the kind they will be encouraged to create. It need not be elaborate. You may choose to show only highly relevant segments of the model, but it would be helpful to demonstrate how a variety of media—visual (written text and illustrations) and audio (narrative, music, and sound effects)—can work together to create an exciting learning experience. In addition, an initial presentation could serve as an introduction to the kinds of hardware and software your groups will use for their presentations.

Adapting to Available Technology

As the chart on this page shows, the kinds of media used to create a multimedia experience can vary from the relatively low-tech equipment likely to be available in almost any school to sophisticated, state-of-the-art computer software. Help students adapt to the equipment to which they have access and know (or can learn) how to use.

Teaching Options

Technology Skills

Multimedia: American Literature Through American History

Multimedia presentations involve the sharing of information using more than one medium. Strictly speaking, a speech accompanied by background music would be a multimedia presentation. Today, however, the word *multimedia* suggests the use of computer software that enables users to combine text, graphic images, and sound.

Multimedia Presentations

Following are three options for putting together a multimedia presentation.

Method	Hardware/Software Needed	Description of Presentation
Low-tech (non-computer presentation)	Camera, slide projector or overhead projector and screen, tape recorder	Use 35mm slides or overhead transparencies for your visuals (text and images). Use a tape recorder for narration, music, or other sounds.
Hypertext presentation	Computer and Hypercard, HyperStudio, or other hypertext software *Also useful:* microphone, digital camera	Use a hypertext program to combine text, graphic images, and sound on a series of "cards" that make up a stack that can be shown in sequence on a computer monitor.
Slide-show presentation	Computer and PowerPoint, Persuasion, or other presentation software *Also useful:* microphone, digital camera	Use presentation software to create a group of "slides" that make up a computer-based slide show combining text, graphic images, and sound.

Hypertext cards are generally meant to be seen by a single viewer on a personal computer or via the Internet. Slide-show presentations are meant to be viewed on a big screen by a large audience. Slide-show programs automatically encourage brief text and large type; hypertext programs do not. It's a good idea to use large typefaces for any presentation meant to be seen by more than one person.

Create a Presentation

Working with a small group, create a simple multimedia presentation.

1. From the literature you've studied so far, choose a selection from a historical period. Using a search engine, look on the Web for information about that historical period. Search also for sites that relate to the work of literature you chose and its author.

> ### TECHNOLOGY TIP
> Most presentation software will include templates for different slide designs, textures and colors for slide backgrounds, clip art, and other features that can help you create your presentation. The program may also include a tutorial that will help you learn how to use it.

---

interNET CONNECTION

Slide-Show Demonstrations If time is a factor in creating a multimedia presentation, try finding an example on the Web to show students. The PBS Online site usually has presentations similar to electronic slide shows. They can be accessed from the site or, in some cases, downloaded to your hard drive.

MEETING INDIVIDUAL NEEDS — INCLUSION STRATEGIES

Special Needs If you have students with low vision, try to ensure that they have full and equal opportunity to participate. Low-vision students also may be able to contribute knowledge or skills involving audio equipment.

Activity Consult privately with low-vision students. Ask them to help you identify ways to enhance features of a multimedia presentation for an audience that includes individuals who are visually challenged. You also might ask if they have experience using the audio equipment available to the class. If so, they might offer clarification about its effective use and innovative ideas for adapting it to the presentation. Students may share this information with the class. **L2**

2. Think about how the author may have been influenced by the time in which he or she worked. Take notes, print relevant information, or save important text to a disk. Pay particular attention to:

   a. sociological aspects of the time, such as class structures, the roles of women and children, and the positions of minorities

   b. political events, such as conflicts over the economy, foreign affairs, and domestic policy

   c. if and how the literary work reflects the time in which it was written

3. Look for a pattern in your research—something that will connect your chosen work of literature, its author, and the historical period in which the work was written. Organize your notes in a logical order. Then summarize the information in concise statements.

4. Think about what illustrations or sounds could augment your text. Create an outline or storyboard that shows the text, images, and sounds of each segment. (These instructions will refer to each segment as a slide, although it may be a slide, a card, or a transparency, depending on which method of presentation you use.) Remember to save your work often!

5. Keep text information succinct. Rather than long paragraphs, use a few numbered or bulleted lists.

6. Begin with a title slide that names your presentation and its creators. Add at least eight additional slides with text or visuals. Add sounds when appropriate.

7. Go through your completed presentation several times, looking for ways you can improve it. Then show your presentation to your class.

ACTIVITIES

1. Prepare a multimedia presentation about a historical character you admire.

2. Volunteer to create a multimedia presentation for a local community group.

Walt Whitman's Civil War

A Multimedia Presentation by Amy Tsai

Main Idea

- **Supporting detail**

- **Supporting detail**

- **Supporting detail**

Activities

After students have read the Create a Presentation section, discuss the directions with the class to be sure that everyone understands how to complete the project and to answer any questions students have about the assignment or the technology.

Students' presentations should:
- demonstrate the group's ability to cooperate in the preparation and execution of a multimedia presentation.
- demonstrate an ability to use the available technology.
- imaginatively combine text, images, and sounds (subject to any restrictions in available technology).
- contain at least nine slides, including a title slide with the names of the student authors.

TechnoTalk

Old Terms for New Concepts The multimedia software programs mentioned on the chart on page 516 refer to a single screen as a "card" or a "slide." Use the chart descriptions to demonstrate to students how a new technology often adopts the vocabulary methods. As an additional example, point out that typesetters today, although their work is done electronically, still use many terms that were familiar to Ben Franklin, who worked as a printer when type (individual letters cast in lead) was set by hand. Examples of these terms include *font, type, character,* and *leading.* Discuss the advantages of using a familiar term for a new concept.

REAL-WORLD CONNECTION

Presentations Suggest to students that the ability to make effective presentations with electronic media is an important skill in the working world. Discuss how people might use such technology in a work environment. (Some examples include electronic resumes, sales presentations, business proposals, and advertisements.)

Activity Have students look for examples of such presentations on the Web. Suggest that they use a search engine and enter keywords such as *multimedia presentation* or *slide show*. Ask them to share any examples they find with the class. Invite the students to critique the presentations. **L2**

Objectives

- To read and analyze a speech by a chief of the Cherokee explaining his reaction to a peace treaty
- To recognize and evaluate the elements of an expository speech

Skills

Reading/Thinking: Analyzing Arguments; Identifying Supporting Details
Writing: Poem, Song, or Essay About Loss
Collaboration: Literature Groups

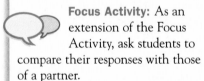

Motivating
→OPTIONS

Selection Focus Transparency 51: Have students discuss the original Cherokee homeland and create a map showing areas to which they were removed.

Focus Activity: As an extension of the Focus Activity, ask students to compare their responses with those of a partner.

Before You Read

Let Us Examine the Facts

Meet the Cherokee of Corn Tassel's Era

❝Remember that the whites are near us. . . . [U]nless you can speak their language, read and write as they do, they will be able to cheat you and trample on your rights.❞

—*Cherokee elder*

Until the middle of the 1700s, the Cherokee were a powerful nation of more than 20,000 people who occupied 40,000 square miles of land in the central and southeastern regions of what became the United States. They lived in villages and made their living by hunting, farming, fishing, and trading. Their prosperity diminished during the 1760s and 1770s, when white settlers began to move into Cherokee territory and claim ownership of the land.

During the American Revolution, some Cherokee sided with the British, who supplied them with food and other goods. Unwilling to distinguish between neutral and hostile Cherokee, revolutionary militias destroyed nearly forty Cherokee towns. In 1777 they forced the Cherokee to sign a binding "peace" treaty. Like many Native American peoples, the Cherokee soon learned that white officials designed such treaties primarily to deprive them of their lands.

In the selection you are about to read, Corn Tassel, a head chief of the Cherokee, responds to a peace treaty proposed by U.S. officials. Though suspicious of the treaty, the Cherokee signed it on November 28, 1785. Three years later Corn Tassel was killed by a young white man in retribution for a crime the chief did not commit.

The date of Corn Tassel's birth is unknown; he died in 1788.

FOCUS ACTIVITY

Imagine that someone comes to your home and demands that you and your family agree to move out so that he or she can move in. How would you react? What would you say and do?

FREEWRITE Spend three minutes writing a response to these questions.

SETTING A PURPOSE Find out how a head chief of the Cherokee responds to the demands of a treaty.

BACKGROUND

Did You Know?
In 1821 a Cherokee named Sequoyah presented to tribal elders the alphabet he had invented to represent the sounds and syllables in the Cherokee language. The elders immediately adopted this alphabet. Because the Cherokee had no written language before 1821, this selection, dated 1785, probably does not contain Corn Tassel's actual words. The ideas communicated in the selection, however, do most likely reflect those that Corn Tassel expressed.

VOCABULARY PREVIEW

exorbitant (ig zôr′ bə tənt) *adj.* exceeding what is reasonable; excessive; p. 519
pretension (pri ten′ shən) *n.* a claim; an assertion; p. 519
vigilance (vij′ ə ləns) *n.* the state of being alert or watchful; p. 520
mishap (mis′ hap′) *n.* an unfortunate accident or mistake; a misfortune; p. 520

propriety (prə prī′ ə tē) *n.* the quality of being proper; appropriateness; p. 520
doctrine (dok′ trin) *n.* a principle that is taught and advocated; a tenet; p. 520
sustenance (sus′ tə nəns) *n.* that which sustains life, especially food; p. 520

RESOURCE MANAGER

Lesson Planning Resource
The *Unit Four Planning Guide* (pp. 41–46) provides additional lesson notes and reduced versions of all print resources.

📁 **Other Print Resources**
- Active Reading Guide, p. 59
- Vocabulary Practice, p. 35
- Reading Workbook, pp. 53–54
- Quick Checks, p. 59
- Selection and Theme Assessment, p. 88

- Performance Assessment, p. 48
- Spanish Summaries, p. 51
- Inclusion Strategies

Transparencies
- Selection Focus 51
- Fine Art 23
- Literary Elements 48

Technology
🎧 Audio Library
🎧 Spanish Audio Library
💻 Glencoe Literature Web Site
💾 Testmaker

Let Us Examine the Facts

Corn Tassel ∽

Our People Lived Here, c. 1967. Paul Pahsetopah (Four Hills or Humps on the Buffalo). Watercolor on board, 24½ x 31¹⁵⁄₁₆ in. The Philbrook Museum of Art, Tulsa, OK.

It is a little surprising that when we entered into treaties with our brothers, the whites, their whole cry is *more land!* Indeed, formerly it seemed to be a matter of formality with them to demand what they knew we durst[1] not refuse. But on the principles of fairness, of which we have received assurances during the conducting of the present treaty, and in the name of free will and equality, I must reject your demand. Suppose, in considering the nature of your claim (and in justice to my nation I shall and will do it freely), I were to ask one of you, my brother warriors, under what kind of authority, by what law, or on what pretense he makes this exorbitant demand of nearly all the lands we hold between your settlements and our towns, as the cement and consideration of our peace.

Would he tell me that it is by right of conquest? No! If he did, I should retort on him that *we* had last marched over his territory; even up to this very place which he has *fortified* so far within his former limits; nay, that some of our young warriors (whom we have not yet had an opportunity to recall or give

notice to, of the general treaty) are still in the woods, and continue to keep his people in fear, and that it was but till lately that these identical walls were your strongholds, out of which you durst scarcely advance.

If, therefore, a bare march, or reconnoitering[2] a country is sufficient reason to ground a claim to it, we shall insist upon transposing the demand, and your relinquishing your settlements on the western waters and removing one hundred miles back towards the east, whither some of our warriors advanced against you in the course of last year's campaign.

Let us examine the facts of your present eruption into our country, and we shall discover your pretensions on that ground. What

---

1. *Durst* means "dared."

2. *Reconnoitering* (rē kə noi′ tər ing) is inspecting or surveying an area in order to obtain information.

Vocabulary

exorbitant (ig zôr′ bə tənt) *adj.* exceeding what is reasonable; excessive
pretension (pri ten′ shən) *n.* a claim; an assertion

SUMMARY

Corn Tassel presents his reasons for refusing to sign a peace treaty proposed by U.S. officials. He argues that white people have no claim to his nation's land because they never conquered it. He claims that white people have tried to force their values on his people but have not proven these values worthy of adoption. He describes how his people have been hurt by the hunting and killing of animals on Cherokee land.

📁 *Spanish Summaries,* p. 51

A **Active Reading**

REVIEW Remind students that this selection was written in response to a peace treaty proposed by U.S. officials. Ask students what the first paragraph of the selection reveals about the terms of the treaty. *(The U.S. government asks for all of the lands between U.S. settlements and Cherokee towns.)*

Additional Resources
📁 *Active Reading Guide,* p. 59
🎧 *Audio Library*
🎧 *Spanish Audio Library*

Teaching Options

FINE ART
TRANSPARENCY 23

You may want to have students use *Fine Art Transparency 23* to discuss necessities of Cherokee life destroyed by the U.S. government.

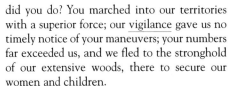

B Author's Craft

ARGUMENT Explain that Corn Tassel downplays the military skills of the United States by saying that his people were outnumbered and only a few "defenseless" individuals were killed. Ask students to identify Corn Tassel's purpose in pointing out the "essential point" that the United States missed in the attempted conquest. *(His purpose is to mock the United States for missing the opportunity to fortify more land.)*

C Critical Thinking

ANALYZING ARGUMENTS Ask students what Corn Tassel says white people should do instead of forcing his people to adopt the white way of life. What implication does he make about white people's way of life? *(He says they should show his people the "good effect" of this way of life, implying that he has little respect for it.)*

Thematic Focus

The Energy of the Everyday Corn Tassel rejects this treaty in an effort to allow his people to return to their normal lives. He shows how the lives of the white people differ from those of the Cherokee, but explains that with understanding, the two nations can coexist.

 ASSESSMENT OPTIONS

📁 *Quick Checks*, p. 59

Teaching Options

 **LITERATURE & HUMANITIES**

Art Talk: "Indian Drawing Lesson," Transparency 20

Have students examine the collage in small groups. What is the dominant image? What images are less dominant? How are the themes of unity and disunity expressed?

---

did you do? You marched into our territories with a superior force; our <u>vigilance</u> gave us no timely notice of your maneuvers; your numbers far exceeded us, and we fled to the stronghold of our extensive woods, there to secure our women and children.

B Thus, you marched into our towns; they were left to your mercy; you killed a few scattered and defenseless individuals, spread fire and desolation wherever you pleased, and returned again to your own habitations. If you meant this, indeed, as a conquest you omitted the most essential point; you should have fortified the junction of the Holstin and Tennessee rivers, and have thereby conquered all the waters above you. But, as all are fair advantages during the existence of a state of war, it is now too late for us to suffer for your <u>mishap</u> of generalship!

Again, were we to inquire by what law or authority you set up a claim, I answer, *none!* Your laws extend not into our country, nor ever did. You talk of the law of nature and the law of nations, and they are both against you.

C Indeed, much has been advanced on the want of what you term civilization among the Indians; and many proposals have been made to us to adopt your laws, your religion, your manners, and your customs. But, we confess that we do not yet see the <u>propriety</u>, or practicability of such a reformation, and should be better pleased with beholding the good effect of these <u>doctrines</u> in your own practices than with hearing you talk about them, or reading your papers to us upon such subjects.

You say: Why do not the Indians till the ground and live as we do? May we not, with equal propriety, ask, Why the white people do not hunt and live as we do? You profess[3] to think it no injustice to warn us not to kill our deer and other game from the mere love of waste; but it is very criminal in our young men if they chance to kill a cow or a hog for their <u>sustenance</u> when they happen to be in your lands. We wish, however, to be at peace with you, and to do as we would be done by. We do not quarrel with you for killing an occasional buffalo, bear or deer on our lands when you need one to eat; but you go much farther; your people hunt to gain a livelihood by it; they kill all our game; our young men resent the injury, and it is followed by bloodshed and war.

This is not a mere affected[4] injury; it is a grievance which we equitably[5] complain of, and it demands a permanent redress.[6]

The great God of Nature has placed us in different situations. It is true that he has endowed you with many superior advantages; but he has not created us to be your slaves. *We are a separate people!* He has given each their lands, under distinct considerations and circumstances; he has stocked yours with cows, ours with buffalo; yours with hog, ours with bear; yours with sheep, ours with deer. He has, indeed, given you an advantage in this, that your cattle are tame and domestic while ours are wild and demand not only a larger space for range, but art[7] to hunt and kill them; they are, nevertheless, as much our property as other animals are yours, and ought not to be taken away without our consent, or for something equivalent.

---

3. *Profess* means "claim."
4. *Affected* means "assumed for show to make an impression."
5. *Equitably* means "fairly" or "justly."
6. *Redress* means "compensation."
7. Here, *art* means "skill."

Vocabulary

vigilance (vij′ ə lans) *n.* the state of being alert or watchful
mishap (mis′ hap′) *n.* an unfortunate accident or mistake; a misfortune
propriety (prə prī′ ə tē) *n.* the quality of being proper; appropriateness
doctrine (dok′ trin) *n.* a principle that is taught and advocated; a tenet
sustenance (sus′ tə nəns) *n.* that which sustains life, especially food

520 ❦ UNIT 4

Reading *Minilesson*

Identifying Supporting Details In an effective expository speech or essay, the thesis is supported with details. Looking for supporting details will improve students' reading comprehension.

Activity Explain that Corn Tassel rejects the demands of the white people, giving two main reasons: 1) white people do not have a legal right to take the land, and 2) white people's laws do not apply to Corn Tassel's people. Write these reasons on the board, and have students find two details that support each reason. **L2**

Additional Resources

📁 *Reading Workbook*, pp. 53–54

Responding to Literature

Personal Response

Were you convinced by Corn Tassel's arguments? Explain why or why not.

——— ANALYZING LITERATURE ———

RECALL AND INTERPRET

1. How much land are the white officials demanding from the Cherokee? What are they promising in return?
2. According to Corn Tassel, what is the basis of the white officials' claim to Cherokee lands? What is Corn Tassel's opinion of that claim? Use details from the selection to support your answer.
3. What specific grievance do the Cherokee have against the white people? In your opinion, how does this grievance reflect the cultural clash between the two groups?
4. Summarize the ideas that Corn Tassel expresses in the last paragraph. What can you infer about his view of the rights held by the Cherokee and the white people?

EVALUATE AND CONNECT

5. Compare your response to the Focus Activity on page 518 with Corn Tassel's response to the proposed peace treaty.
6. Describe Corn Tassel's **tone,** or attitude toward his subject. Do you think his tone suits the subject? Why or why not?
7. If you could interview Corn Tassel, what questions would you ask him? What advice might you give to him?
8. Theme Connections   Corn Tassel points out how the everyday lives of the Cherokee and the white people differ. Do you think one group of people ever has the right to force another group to change or give up its way of life? Explain.

Literary ELEMENTS

Argument

Argument is the use of reason to influence ideas or actions. In "Let Us Examine the Facts," Corn Tassel argues that the white officials are wrong to think that Cherokee lands belong to them. To support his argument, he presents facts and reasons, such as the failure of the whites to occupy the Cherokee towns that they entered and destroyed.

1. What facts and reasons does Corn Tassel give to support his statement that both "the law of nature and the law of nations" are against the claim of the white officials?
2. Would you have been influenced by Corn Tassel's argument? Explain, using details from the selection as support.

⬤ See **Literary Terms Handbook,** p. R2.

——————— EXTENDING YOUR RESPONSE ———————

Literature Groups
Mediating Conflict   People involved in conflict sometimes call in a mediator to help them work toward a compromise. Imagine that Corn Tassel has asked your group to mediate the conflict between the Cherokee and the white officials. As a group, use specific details from Corn Tassel's speech and suggest compromises to resolve the problems. Share your ideas with the class.

Creative Writing
The Pain of Loss   Corn Tassel, like many Native American leaders of the 1700s and 1800s, had learned from experience that "peace" treaties often led to the loss of tribal lands. In a poem, a song, or an essay, try to capture how Corn Tassel might have felt about that loss.

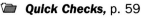 **Save your work for your portfolio.**

REGIONALISM AND REALISM 521

Responding to the Selection

Personal Response

Many students will feel that Corn Tassel gives convincing evidence to support his argument.

ANALYZING LITERATURE

1. They are demanding "nearly all the lands" in exchange for peace.
2. Their basis is that they won it by conquest. Corn Tassel thinks there was no conquest.
3. The white people hunt on Cherokee land but do not allow the Cherokee to hunt on the white land. The white people are territorial, believing they own the land and all the animals on it, and they hunt for profit. The Cherokee hunt for survival, and they believe that they should be able to hunt where they wish.
4. Corn Tassel believes that the whites and the Cherokee should live separately and respect each other's right to have a different lifestyle. He thinks that white people have more rights than his people.
5. Many students will say that they would not be willing to sign the treaty either.
6. Corn Tassel's tone is logical and defensive. Most students will think it suits his purpose.
7. Some students may want to ask him what he would say if he wanted to appeal to emotion instead of reason.
8. Many students may think that no group has this right. Encourage students to support their answers.

✔ ASSESSMENT OPTIONS

📁 **Quick Checks,** p. 59
📁 **Selection and Theme Assessment,** p. 88
📁 **Performance Assessment,** p. 48
💾 **Testmaker**

LITERARY ELEMENTS

1. They didn't secure the junction at the Holstin and Tennessee Rivers, so they didn't conquer all rivers above them.
2. The whites have discriminated against the Cherokee. They have a double standard. They hunt anywhere while the Cherokee are restricted to their own land. The Cherokee are a separate nation; they should not have to live by white laws.

Additional Resources

📖 **Literary Elements Transparency 48**

REGIONALISM AND REALISM 🐿 521

Objective

- To use transitions effectively

Teaching Strategies

After students have read the explanation on this page, write the following sentences on the board and have students fill in an appropriate transition.

1. I got wet _____ I got caught in the rain.
2. I often buy sweets. _____, this morning I bought a chocolate bar.
3. I often travel in the summer; _____, this year I stayed at home.

(Possible answers: 1. because;
2. For instance; 3. however.)

Exercises

1. *First* (indicates order), *for example* (alerts reader to an example), *because* (shows causality), *Second* (indicates order), *but* (shows contrast), *Most importantly* (shows priority).
2. Ensure that students have underlined all transitions and have used each one appropriately.

Additional Resources

Writer's Choice, Lessons 5.1, 5.4

Teaching Options

Writing Skills

Using Transitions Effectively

When you read a story or an article, do you ever think, "This is too choppy and hard to understand"? The selection might be missing transitions, words and phrases that help show the relationships between ideas in a piece of writing. Transitions lead readers smoothly from sentence to sentence and from paragraph to paragraph.

Contrast

One group of transitional words and phrases, including *but, yet, on the other hand, however,* and *nevertheless,* indicates that two ideas contradict or contrast with each other. Notice how transitions are used to show contradictions between ideas in these sentences from "Let Us Examine the Facts."

- *It is true that he has endowed you with many superior advantages; but he has not created us to be your slaves.*
- *Your cattle are tame . . . while ours are wild . . . ; they are, nevertheless, as much our property as other animals are yours.*

Other Transitions

Transitional words such as *because* or *as a result* also indicate relationships, showing that one event caused another. Phrases such as *for instance* and *that is* alert readers to expect an example. Transitions also indicate time *(first, next, now),* position *(above, in the middle, outside),* and importance *(especially, above all, in fact).*

EXERCISES

1. Copy the following summary of "Let Us Examine the Facts," underlining the transitional words and phrases you find. Indicate the relationship each transition shows.

> Corn Tassel, the author, explained why his people would continue to resist white domination. First, the whites had no legal claim to his people's land. The whites could not, for example, claim the land just because they marched over it. Second, the whites wanted the Indians to adopt their religion, but the whites did not themselves live according to the values they professed to hold dear. Most importantly, the whites and the Indians were separate peoples.

2. Write a paragraph responding to "Let Us Examine the Facts" or to another selection, using transitions to make your ideas flow more smoothly. Underline the transitions that you include.

Grammar and Language *Minilesson*

Future Perfect Tense The future perfect tense is formed with *will have* or *shall have* and the past participle of a verb, as in *will have gone.*

Activity Have students write sample sentences changing a verb tense from the future to the future perfect and adding to each sentence as necessary. **L2**

Additional Resources

Grammar and Language Transparency 43

Grammar and Language Workbook, p. 137

Grammar and Composition Handbook, Lesson 5.4

Writer's Choice, Lesson 15.4

Before You Read

The Story of an Hour

Meet Kate Chopin

Kate Chopin (shō′ pan) was the first female writer in the United States to portray frankly the passions and discontents of women confined to traditional roles as wives and mothers. For this she was roundly condemned in her time and is widely praised today.

She was born Katherine O'Flaherty in St. Louis to an Irish-born merchant and a mother of French descent. When Kate was five, her father died in a railroad accident. She left school, and for the next two years, she studied at home with her mother, grandmother, and great-grandmother, who became her tutor. Growing up in a household of strong, independent women did much to shape Kate as a person and a writer.

At age twenty, Kate married Oscar Chopin, a cotton broker, and moved with him to New Orleans. The cosmopolitan city suited her, and she was unhappy when business problems forced them to move to Oscar's rural hometown of Cloutierville, Louisiana. At first the small town held little attraction for Kate, but the area would later inspire many of her stories.

When her husband died in 1882, Chopin was left with children to raise and support. She ran her husband's businesses for a year. Then she moved her household back to St. Louis to be near her family there. When her mother died a year later, Chopin was overwhelmed with grief. At her doctor's advice, she turned to writing and published her first work in 1889.

Chopin earned praise for stories that captured the local color of Louisiana, but drew criticism for those that questioned the role of women in contemporary society. Her novel *The Awakening*, published in 1899, was acknowledged for its technique and harshly criticized for its content. Possibly as a result of that criticism, the publication of Chopin's last story collection, which included "The Story of an Hour," was canceled.

❝When the theme of a story occurs to her, she writes it out immediately, often at one sitting, then, after a little, copies it out carefully, seldom making corrections. She never retouches after that.❞

—*William Schuyler*

❝There are stories that seem to write themselves, and others which positively refuse to be written—which no amount of coaxing can bring to anything.❞

❝Story-writing—at least with me—is the spontaneous expression of impressions gathered from goodness knows where.❞

❝The artist must possess the courageous soul that dares and defies.❞

—*Chopin*

Kate Chopin was born in 1851 and died in 1904.

REGIONALISM AND REALISM 🐦 523

Objectives

- To read and analyze a short story about one woman's reaction to the news of her husband's death
- To identify and analyze the elements of plot in a short story
- To evaluate the title of a short story

Skills

Reading/Thinking: Building Background Knowledge; Analyzing Arguments; Inferring
Grammar/Language: Past Progressive Verb Form

More About Kate Chopin

Kate Chopin's great-grandmother, Madame Victoria Verdon Charleville, gave Chopin French and piano lessons. She cultivated Chopin's love of music and her unconventional attitude toward life. In keeping with her unconventionality, many of Chopin's stories contain themes that were considered controversial at the time. "The Story of an Hour" was published in *Vogue* magazine, which provided Chopin with an audience when book publishing houses were unwilling to do so. Chopin composed many of her short stories in one sitting, rarely editing them later. She wrote in her living room, surrounded by her young children. To have time for her favorite pastimes, such as attending concerts, Chopin wrote only one or two days per week.

RESOURCE MANAGER

Lesson Planning Resource
The *Unit Four Planning Guide* (pp. 47–52) provides additional lesson notes and reduced versions of all print resources.

📁 **Other Print Resources**
- Active Reading Guide, p. 60
- Vocabulary Practice, p. 36
- Reading Workbook, pp. 55–56
- Grammar and Language Workbook, p. 141

- Grammar and Composition Handbook, Lesson 5.5
- Quick Checks, p. 60
- Selection and Theme Assessment, pp. 89–90
- Performance Assessment, p. 49
- Spanish Summaries, p. 52
- Inclusion Strategies
- English Language Learners Sourcebook

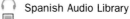 **Transparencies**
- Selection Focus 52
- Fine Art 27
- Literary Elements 49
- Grammar and Language 44

Technology
🎧 Audio Library
🎧 Spanish Audio Library
💻 Glencoe Literature Web Site
💾 Testmaker

Motivating
→OPTIONS

Selection Focus Transparency 52: Have students examine and discuss the painting "At The Window" by William Merritt Chase.

Focus Activity: Ask students to write several adjectives that describe their emotions during this time.

Reading Further

Be sure to review this title for appropriateness for your class before recommending it to students.

The Complete Works of Kate Chopin, edited by Per Seyersted. Baton Rouge: Louisiana State University Press, 1969, is a two-volume collection of Chopin's writing.

FINE ART
TRANSPARENCY 27

You may want to use **Fine Art Transparency 27** to discuss reactions to unexpected news.

At the MOVIES

Be sure to preview the following video for appropriateness for your class.

• *Kate Chopin: Five Stories of an Hour* is available in the *Glencoe Literature Video Library*.

FOCUS ACTIVITY

Have you ever experienced a feeling of great relief—a moment when you suddenly felt very free and unburdened?

QUICKWRITE Take five minutes to write about a time when you felt as though the weight of the world had just been lifted from your shoulders. What caused you to feel this way? How long did the feeling last?

SETTING A PURPOSE Read to discover how quickly one woman's emotions change.

BACKGROUND

The Time and Place

The 1890s were a period of social tension. Organizations were pushing hard for woman suffrage. Women were also meeting for social, intellectual, and philanthropic purposes. Some women began attending college and entering professions previously open only to men.

Women marching for the right to vote, early 1900s.

At the same time, however, many women, especially in the South, were being raised with a special sense of "a woman's place" in the home. Although their roles as wives and mothers were glorified, women had few legal rights. For example, when Chopin's husband died, she had to petition the court to be appointed the legal guardian of her own children.

Chopin was critical of cultural expectations for women. In much of her fiction, she criticized the institution of marriage and wrote about women who struggled against social convention to be individuals.

Literary Influences

Perhaps the strongest influence on Chopin's writing style was the French writer Guy de Maupassant. Here she talks about his ability to craft a story:

"I read his stories and marveled at them. Here was life, not fiction. . . . Here was a man who had escaped from tradition and authority, who had entered into himself and looked out upon life through his own being and with his own eyes; and who, in a direct and simple way, told us what he saw."

VOCABULARY PREVIEW

repression (ri presh′ ən) *n.* the state of being held back or kept under control; p. 526
elusive (i lōō′ siv) *adj.* difficult to explain or grasp; p. 526
tumultuously (tōō mul′ chōō əs lē) *adv.* in an agitated manner; violently; p. 526
exalted (ig zôl′ təd) *adj.* elevated; p. 527
perception (pər sep′ shən) *n.* an awareness; an insight; p. 527

persistence (pər sis′ təns) *n.* stubborn or determined continuance; p. 527
impose (im pōz′) *v.* to inflict, as by authority; to dictate; p. 527
illumination (i lōō′ mə nā′ shən) *n.* intellectual enlightenment; p. 527

LITERATURE & HUMANITIES

 "Mr. and Mrs. Isaac Newton Phelps" from **American Art and Culture**

Have students examine the picture in small groups. How does the painting express Mrs. Mallard's attitudes toward herself and her husband?

THE STORY OF AN HOUR

Kate Chopin

The Lady Anne, 1899. Edwin Austin Abbey. Oil on canvas, 48 x 24 in. The Butler Institute of American Art, Youngstown, OH.

525

SUMMARY

Mrs. Mallard is at first devastated to hear of her husband's sudden death in a train accident. However, as she realizes the freedom that his death will allow her, she grows so ecstatic that when her husband suddenly appears at the door, unharmed and unaware of the accident, she dies of a heart attack. Doctors declare her death the result of a "joy that kills," but the real cause of her death is her great unhappiness at her husband's return.

📁 *Spanish Summaries*, p. 52

A **Active Reading**

PREDICT Before reading the story, have students examine the title page. Based on its content, ask students what they can predict about this story. *(Based on the title, students may predict that the story takes place in only one hour, possibly recounting a dramatic event. The art may prompt students to suggest that the story will concern a woman who lived at the turn of the century.)*

Additional Resources
📁 *Active Reading Guide*, p. 60
🎧 *Audio Library*
🎧 *Spanish Audio Library*

Teaching Options

Reading *Minilesson*

Building Background Knowledge
Mrs. Mallard's thoughts and actions may confuse students who do not understand the story's context.

Activity Ask students to share thoughts they might have about marriages in the late nineteenth century. Then have them read the information on page 524 about the setting of this story. Organize the students in groups and ask them to reach

some conclusions about marriages in the 1890s. Tell students to consider what it must have been like to live without any legal rights. When students have finished reading, ask them to share how their pre-reading and discussion affected their understanding of the selection.
L2 **COLLAB. LEARN.**

B Active Reading

INTERPRET Richards and Mrs. Mallard's sister cautiously tell Mrs. Mallard of her husband's death. Ask students what this reveals about their perception of Mrs. Mallard's relationship with her husband. *(It shows that they think Mrs. Mallard loves her husband and that she will be extremely upset to hear that he is dead.)*

C Literary Elements

SETTING Point out that these descriptions of the setting also describe Mrs. Mallard's reaction to her husband's death. She thinks that her old, dark life will be replaced by a new, bright one.

D Literary Elements

CONFLICT The woman fights her response, which presents an internal conflict. She is, however, "powerless" and cannot avoid her reaction because the thought of her impending freedom is too appealing.

E Active Reading

RESPOND Ask students what their response was to Mrs. Mallard's reaction. Did they find it heartless or were they sympathetic?

Model: At first, I felt that she was heartless in her reaction to her husband's death. But as I read on, I realized that although she did love her husband, her marriage to him did not give her any freedom. Considering this fact, I think her reaction may be understandable.

B Knowing that Mrs. Mallard was afflicted with a heart trouble, great care was taken to break to her as gently as possible the news of her husband's death. It was her sister Josephine who told her, in broken sentences; veiled[1] hints that revealed in half concealing. Her husband's friend Richards was there, too, near her. It was he who had been in the newspaper office when intelligence of the railroad disaster was received, with Brently Mallard's name leading the list of "killed." He had only taken the time to assure himself of its truth by a second telegram, and had hastened to forestall[2] any less careful, less tender friend in bearing the sad message.

She did not hear the story as many women have heard the same, with a paralyzed inability to accept its significance. She wept at once, with sudden, wild abandonment, in her sister's arms. When the storm of grief had spent[3] itself she went to her room alone. She would have no one follow her.

There stood, facing the open window, a comfortable, roomy armchair. Into this she sank, pressed down by a physical exhaustion that haunted her body and seemed to reach into her soul.

C She could see in the open square before her house the tops of trees that were all aquiver with the new spring life. The delicious breath of rain was in the air. In the street below a peddler was crying his wares. The notes of a distant song which some one was singing reached her faintly, and countless sparrows were twittering in the eaves.

There were patches of blue sky showing here and there through the clouds that had met and piled one above the other in the west facing her window.

She sat with her head thrown back upon the cushion of the chair, quite motionless, except when a sob came up into her throat and shook her, as a child who has cried itself to sleep continues to sob in its dreams.

She was young, with a fair, calm face, whose lines bespoke repression and even a certain strength. But now there was a dull stare in her eyes, whose gaze was fixed away off yonder on one of those patches of blue sky. It was not a glance of reflection, but rather indicated a suspension of intelligent thought.

There was something coming to her and she was waiting for it, fearfully. What was it? She did not know; it was too subtle and elusive to name. But she felt it, creeping out of the sky, reaching toward her through the sounds, the scents, the color that filled the air.

D Now her bosom rose and fell tumultuously. She was beginning to recognize this thing that was approaching to possess her, and she was striving to beat it back with her will— as powerless as her two white slender hands would have been.

E When she abandoned herself a little whispered word escaped her slightly parted lips. She said it over and over under her breath: "free, free, free!" The vacant stare and the look of terror that had followed it went from her eyes. They stayed keen and bright. Her pulses beat fast, and the coursing[4] blood warmed and relaxed every inch of her body.

She did not stop to ask if it were or were not a monstrous joy that held her. A clear and

---

1. *Veiled* means "disguised" or "obscure."
2. *Forestall* means "to hinder or prevent by action taken in advance."
3. Here, *spent* means "exhausted."
4. *Coursing* means "swiftly moving."

Vocabulary
repression (ri presh′ ən) *n.* the state of being held back or kept under control
elusive (i lōō′ siv) *adj.* difficult to explain or grasp
tumultuously (tōō mul′ chōō əs lē) *adv.* in an agitated manner; violently

526 🐚 UNIT 4

Teaching Options

Grammar and Language *Minilesson*

Past Progressive Verb Form Point out that each tense has a progressive form that expresses continuing action. The past progressive form, which expresses a continuing action in the past, consists of the past tense of the verb *be* and the present participle of the main verb. Remind students that the present participle of a verb is formed by adding *-ing* to the base form: *walking, running, speaking.*

Activity Have students write three sentences using past progressive forms of the verbs *to walk, to run,* and *to speak.* Then have students find five examples of the past progressive tense in the story. Ask volunteers to share their examples with the class. *(Possible examples: was crying, was singing, were twittering, was beginning, was striving.)*

Additional Resources

🖳 *Grammar and Language Transparency 44*

📙 *Grammar and Language Workbook,* p. 141

📙 *Grammar and Composition Handbook,* Lesson 5.5

📙 *Writer's Choice,* Lesson 15.5

Kate Chopin

exalted perception enabled her to dismiss the suggestion as trivial.

She knew that she would weep again when she saw the kind, tender hands folded in death; the face that had never looked save[5] with love upon her, fixed and gray and dead. But she saw beyond that bitter moment a long procession of years to come that would belong to her absolutely. And she opened and spread her arms out to them in welcome.

There would be no one to live for her during those coming years; she would live for herself. There would be no powerful will bending hers in that blind persistence with which men and women believe they have a right to impose a private will upon a fellow-creature. A kind intention or a cruel intention made the act seem no less a crime as she looked upon it in that brief moment of illumination.

And yet she had loved him—sometimes. Often she had not. What did it matter! What could love, the unsolved mystery, count for in face of this possession of self-assertion which she suddenly recognized as the strongest impulse of her being!

"Free! Body and soul free!" she kept whispering.

Josephine was kneeling before the closed door with her lips to the keyhole, imploring for admission. "Louise, open the door! I beg; open the door—you will make yourself ill.

---

5. Here, *save* means "except."

What are you doing, Louise? For heaven's sake open the door."

"Go away. I am not making myself ill." No; she was drinking in a very elixir of life[6] through that open window.

Her fancy was running riot along those days ahead of her. Spring days, and summer days, and all sorts of days that would be her own. She breathed a quick prayer that life might be long. It was only yesterday she had thought with a shudder that life might be long.

She arose at length and opened the door to her sister's importunities.[7] There was a feverish triumph in her eyes, and she carried herself unwittingly like a goddess of Victory. She clasped her sister's waist, and together they descended the stairs. Richards stood waiting for them at the bottom.

Some one was opening the front door with a latchkey. It was Brently Mallard who entered, a little travel-stained, composedly carrying his grip-sack[8] and umbrella. He had been far from the scene of accident, and did not even know there had been one. He stood amazed at Josephine's piercing cry; at Richards' quick motion to screen him from the view of his wife.

But Richards was too late.

When the doctors came they said she had died of heart disease—of joy that kills.

---

6. An *elixir* (i lik′ sər) *of life* is a substance thought to prolong life indefinitely.
7. *Importunities* are persistent requests or demands.
8. A *grip-sack* is a small traveling bag.

Vocabulary

exalted (ig zôl′ təd) *adj.* elevated
perception (pər sep′ shən) *n.* an awareness; an insight
persistence (pər sis′ təns) *n.* stubborn or determined continuance
impose (im pōz′) *v.* to inflict, as by authority; to dictate
illumination (i lōō′ mə nā′ shən) *n.* intellectual enlightenment

REGIONALISM AND REALISM ❧ 527

F Critical Thinking

ANALYZING ARGUMENTS Discuss the argument Mrs. Mallard makes to justify her happiness. *(She says that there is no distinction between a kind and a cruel intention if the intention is to control somebody. Despite his kindness, her husband could not make her happy because the institution of marriage is so limiting.)*

G Active Reading

QUESTION Ask students why Mrs. Mallard might never before have recognized self-assertion as "the strongest impulse of her being." *(She may not have allowed herself to realize an impulse about which she could do nothing.)*

H Critical Thinking

INFERRING Have students infer what they can about Mrs. Mallard's life from this paragraph. *(One can infer that her life was miserable because she shuddered at the thought that her life might be long.)*

Thematic Focus

The Energy of the Everyday After her husband's supposed death, Mrs. Mallard believes that her life has improved irrevocably. She feels hope instead of grief. When her husband returns and she realizes that her life will return to normal, she grieves for her personal loss and dies.

 ASSESSMENT OPTIONS

📁 *Quick Checks,* p. 60

MEETING INDIVIDUAL NEEDS — ENGLISH LANGUAGE LEARNERS

Love and Marriage Some English language learners may have views about marriage that differ from those held by native-born students.

Activity Ask English language learners to describe marriage in their cultures. At what age do most men and women marry? Are divorces permitted? Are marriages arranged? Ask students to describe the roles men and women play in a marriage, and encourage students to discuss the roles of husbands and wives in the United States. Then connect students' discussions to the story by asking them about their thoughts on Mrs. Mallard's reaction.

Additional Resources

📁 *English Language Learners Sourcebook*

Personal Response

Many students will be shocked by the ending, but they will probably understand Mrs. Mallard's reaction.

ANALYZING LITERATURE

1. She is shocked and grieved, which indicates that she loves her husband.
2. She realizes that she will be free without her husband. She is saddened by losing him, but is thrilled that she will not be responsible to anyone. She probably fears her reaction because it is socially unacceptable.
3. She has a "feverish triumph in her eyes" and carries herself "like a goddess of Victory." The description implies that she is happy, self-confident, and hopeful about her future.
4. She dies from the shock of her husband's return, which means the loss of her freedom, not from a "joy that kills."
5. Many students will think that she is a free spirit who has been trapped by the conventions of marriage.
6. The dramatic irony reinforces how misunderstood Mrs. Mallard was, and how good she was at hiding her feelings. No one understands her unhappiness, so they assume her death is the result of joy.
7. Most students will note that their emotions were not as exaggerated as hers.
8. Many students will feel that Mrs. Mallard would have had other options, such as divorce or separation, and that she would not have needed to await her husband's death to find freedom.

Responding to Literature

Personal Response

What emotions did you experience as you read this story? How did the ending affect you?

ANALYZING LITERATURE

RECALL AND INTERPRET

1. How does Mrs. Mallard first react to the news her sister tells her? What does her reaction seem to indicate about her feelings toward her husband?
2. Summarize what happens while Mrs. Mallard is in her room. How do her feelings change? Why, do you think, does she fear this change at first but later welcomes it?
3. What words does the narrator use to describe Mrs. Mallard's appearance and behavior as she leaves her room? Based on this description, what might you infer about her attitude and outlook?
4. What happens to Mrs. Mallard at the end of the story? Do you agree with the explanation the doctors give? Why or why not?

EVALUATE AND CONNECT

5. What is your opinion of Mrs. Mallard's character? Support your evaluation by using details from the story.
6. **Dramatic irony** occurs when the reader knows something that characters in a literary work do not. How does the dramatic irony in the last paragraph add to your understanding and appreciation of the story?
7. Review your response to the Focus Activity on page 524. Compare and contrast Mrs. Mallard's experience with your own.
8. This story takes place more than a century ago, at a time when most American women lived very restricted lives. Do you think this story would be believable if it were set in the present? Why or why not?

EXTENDING YOUR RESPONSE

Writing About Literature

Evaluate the Title   The original title of "The Story of an Hour" was "The Dream of an Hour." Why might the title have been changed? How are the titles similar? different? Which title do you think is more appropriate? Why? Write a paragraph or two in which you answer these questions.

Interdisciplinary Activity

History: Women's Roles   Reread the Time and Place section on page 524. Then research the social, political, and legal issues that concerned Kate Chopin and other women of her time. Share your findings with the class.

 Save your work for your portfolio.

528   UNIT 4

Literary ELEMENTS

Plot

The **plot** is the sequence of events in a story. The events of a story develop its central **conflict,** or struggle between opposing forces. When a character struggles against an outside force, the conflict is external; when a character experiences a struggle inside his or her own mind, the conflict is internal. The conflict builds until the story reaches its **climax**—the point of greatest emotional intensity. The story concludes with the **resolution,** or final outcome of the conflict.

1. What is the central conflict of "The Story of an Hour"? Is this conflict external, internal, or both? Explain.
2. Identify the climax. Do you think this story might have two climaxes?
3. How does the resolution of the story help you better understand its **theme,** or message?

● See **Literary Terms Handbook,** p. R12.

LITERARY ELEMENTS

1. The conflict is internal and external. Mrs. Mallard fights her own desire for freedom and the conventions of society.
2. One climax occurs when Mrs. Mallard realizes how wonderful her life will be without her husband. The other climax is when Mr. Mallard comes home.
3. The resolution shows that Mrs. Mallard's life is defined by her marriage.

Additional Resources

✍ *Literary Elements Transparency 49*

✔ ASSESSMENT OPTIONS

📁 *Quick Checks,* p. 60
📁 *Selection and Theme Assessment,* pp. 89–90
📁 *Performance Assessment,* p. 49
💾 *Testmaker*

I received one morning a letter, written in pale ink on glassy, blue-lined note-paper, and bearing the postmark of a little Nebraska village. This communication, worn and rubbed, looking as if it has been carried for some days in a coat pocket that was none too clean, was from my uncle Howard, and informed me that his wife had been left a small <u>legacy</u> by a bachelor relative, and that it would be necessary for her to go to Boston to attend to the settling of the estate. He requested me to meet her at the station and render[1] her whatever services might be necessary. On examining the date indicated as that of her arrival, I found it to be no later than tomorrow. He had characteristically delayed writing until, had I been away from home for a day, I must have missed my aunt altogether.

The name of my Aunt Georgiana opened before me a gulf of recollection so wide and deep that, as the letter dropped from my hand, I felt suddenly a stranger to all the present conditions of my existence, wholly ill at ease and out of place amid the familiar surroundings of my study. I became, in short, the gangling farmer-boy my aunt had known, scourged[2] with chilblains[3] and bashfulness, my hands cracked and sore from the corn husking. I sat again before her parlour organ, fumbling the scales with my stiff, red fingers, while she, beside me, made canvas mittens for the huskers.

The next morning, after preparing my landlady for a visitor, I set out for the station. When the train arrived I had some difficulty in finding my aunt. She was the last of the passengers to alight, and it was not until I got her into the carriage that she seemed really to recognize me. She had come all the way in a day coach; her linen duster[4] had become black with soot and her black bonnet grey with dust during the journey. When we arrived at my boarding-house the landlady put her to bed at once and I did not see her again until the next morning.

Whatever shock Mrs. Springer experienced at my aunt's appearance, she considerately concealed. As for myself, I saw my aunt's battered figure with that feeling of awe and respect with which we behold explorers who have left their ears and fingers north of Franz-Joseph-Land,[5] or their health somewhere along the Upper Congo.[6] My Aunt Georgiana had been a music teacher at the Boston Conservatory, somewhere back in the latter sixties. One summer, while visiting in the little village among the Green Mountains[7] where her ancestors had dwelt for generations, she had <u>kindled</u> the callow[8] fancy of my uncle, Howard Carpenter, then an idle, shiftless boy of twenty-one. When she returned to her duties in Boston, Howard followed her, and the upshot of this infatuation was that she eloped with him, eluding the <u>reproaches</u> of her family and the criticism of her friends by going

---

4. A *duster* is a long, lightweight coat worn to protect one's clothing from dust.
5. *Franz-Joseph-Land* is a group of islands in the Arctic Ocean.
6. The *Congo* River in central Africa is also called the Zaire River.
7. The *Green Mountains* extend from western Massachusetts through Vermont and into Canada.
8. *Callow* means "inexperienced" or "immature."

---

1. *Render* means "to make available" or "to provide."
2. *Scourged* means "afflicted."
3. *Chilblains* are red, swollen sores on the skin caused by exposure to the cold.

Vocabulary
legacy (leg′ ə sē) *n.* an inheritance
kindle (kind′ əl) *v.* to stir up; to excite
reproach (ri prōch′) *n.* an expression of disapproval; a reprimand

REGIONALISM AND REALISM 🎵 533

Childe Hassam (1859–1935) was born in Dorchester, Massachusetts. He attended art school in Boston and then in Paris, where he learned the techniques of Impressionism. He often depicted rural and city scenes with brilliant light and color.

Viewing Response *Students may say that Georgiana may have been excited to see such a bustling, vibrant city or that she may have been overwhelmed and intimidated by a city much more advanced than Red Cloud.*

FYI

Music and Math The mathematician Pythagoras, author of the famous Pythagorean Theorem, defined musical intervals in mathematical terms. The system used for today's musical notes is based on the work of Pythagoras. For an example of musical notes, tell students to look at page 533 of the selection.

Boston Commons, 1901. Childe Hassam. Oil on canvas, 16 x 20 in. David David Gallery, Philadelphia.

Viewing the painting: Look closely at the painting. Suppose Aunt Georgiana saw this scene as soon as she arrived in Boston. How might she have reacted? Explain.

Teaching Options

MEETING INDIVIDUAL NEEDS

ENGLISH LANGUAGE LEARNERS

Home Away from Home Students who have recently moved to the United States may connect to Georgiana. When she leaves Boston, she no longer has the opportunity to hear performances of the music she loves.

Activity Ask students to write a list of words that describe the one aspect of everyday life in their cultures that they miss most. Tell them that their lists should include words that will describe the aspect for another person. Have students share their lists with a partner and discuss how the sights, sounds, or smells of their examples bring back memories of home.

Additional Resources
📁 *English Language Learners Sourcebook*

with him to the Nebraska frontier. Carpenter, who, of course, had no money, took up a homestead in Red Willow County, fifty miles from the railroad. There they had measured off their land themselves, driving across the prairie in a wagon, to the wheel of which they had tied a red cotton handkerchief, and counting its revolutions. They built a dug-out in the red hillside, one of those cave dwellings whose inmates so often reverted to primitive conditions. Their water they got from the lagoons where the buffalo drank, and their slender stock of provisions was always at the mercy of bands of roving Indians. For thirty years my aunt had not been farther than fifty miles from the homestead.

Did You Know?
Early settlers on the prairie often lived in a *dug-out,* a home dug into the side of a hill or ravine, until they were able to build an above-ground home.

I owed to this woman most of the good that ever came my way in my boyhood, and had a reverential[9] affection for her. During the years when I was riding herd for my uncle, my aunt, after cooking the three meals—the first of which was ready at six o'clock in the morning—and putting the six children to bed, would often stand until midnight at her ironing-board, with me at the kitchen table beside her, hearing me recite Latin declensions and conjugations,[10] gently shaking me when my drowsy head sank down over a page of irregular verbs. It was to her, at her ironing or mending, that I read my first Shakspere, and her old text-book on mythology was the first that ever came into my empty hands. She taught me my scales and exercises on the little parlor organ which her husband had bought her after fifteen years, during which she had not so much as seen a musical instrument. She would sit beside me by the hour, darning and counting, while I struggled with the "Joyous Farmer."[11] She seldom talked to me about music, and I understood why. Once when I had been doggedly beating out some easy passages from an old score of *Euryanthe*[12] I had found among her music books, she came up to me and, putting her hands over my eyes, gently drew my head back upon her shoulder, saying tremulously,[13] "Don't love it so well, Clark, or it may be taken from you."

When my aunt appeared on the morning after her arrival in Boston, she was still in a semi-somnambulant[14] state. She seemed not to realize that she was in the city where she had spent her youth, the place longed for hungrily half a lifetime. She had been so wretchedly train-sick throughout the journey that she had no recollection of anything but her discomfort, and, to all intents and purposes, there were but a few hours of nightmare between the farm in Red Willow County and my study on Newbury Street. I had planned a little pleasure for her that afternoon, to repay her for some of the glorious moments she had given me when we used to milk together in the straw-thatched cowshed and she, because I was more than usually tired, or because her husband had spoken

---

11. *Joyous Farmer* is one of a series of compositions for children by Robert Shumann (1810–1856).
12. *Euryanthe* (ā ûr i än tā) is an opera by the German composer Carl Maria von Weber (1786–1826).
13. *Tremulously* means "in a trembling or shaking manner."
14. *Semi-somnambulant* (sem' ē   som nam' byə lənt) means "bewildered or dazed, as if sleepwalking."

---

9. *Reverential* means "with a feeling of deep respect and awe."
10. *Declensions* are different forms of nouns, pronouns, and adjectives. *Conjugations* are different forms of verbs. Students often memorize these forms when learning a new language.

Vocabulary
doggedly (dô′ gid lē) *adv.* in a stubbornly persistent manner; obstinately

WORD CHOICE Discuss with students the words Cather chooses to describe Aunt Georgiana (an inmate who reverted to primitive conditions) and her home in Nebraska (a cave dwelling). These words imply that Georgiana took a step backward when she moved from civilized Boston to become a prisoner in primitive Nebraska.

F **Critical Thinking**

INTERPRETING Ask students why they think Aunt Georgiana warns Clark not to love music so well and why she seldom discusses the subject with him.

Model: I know that Aunt Georgiana misses music; she feels that it has been taken from her. She may not have talked to her nephew about music very often because she didn't want music to be taken from him, too. On the other hand, Georgiana may have become depressed talking about something that was no longer part of her life.

INCLUSION STRATEGIES

Learning Disabled Students with learning disabilities respond to approaches that appeal to a variety of senses, engage prior knowledge, and spark their curiosity about a text.

Activity Ask students to describe what they know about life on a farm. Then read to students the passage on this page that begins, "There they had measured off their land . . ." Ask students to describe Georgiana's life in Nebraska. Show them a videotaped concert or a photograph of people attending the symphony. Ask students to imagine how Georgiana might react if she attended such a concert after living on a farm for 30 years. **L1**

Additional Resources
Inclusion Strategies

G Literary Elements

THEME Note the contrast between Aunt Georgiana's everyday life before her marriage—attending concerts in Paris and teaching in Boston—and her everyday life in Nebraska—fixing breakfast before 6 A.M. and ironing until midnight.

H Active Reading

QUESTION Ask students why Aunt Georgiana seems more concerned with life in Nebraska than with life in Boston. *(She has lived in Nebraska for so long that her concerns are there. She may also feel more comfortable concerning herself with something she knows.)*

I Literary Elements

METAPHOR Discuss the contrast between the colorful scene at the opera and the black and grim house with the black pond where Aunt Georgiana lives. The dark colors serve as a metaphor for her "dark" life in Nebraska and are juxtaposed with the colorful life she would have had in Boston.

J Literary Elements

PLOT Point out that Aunt Georgiana's awakening from her semi-somnambulant state serves as the rising action in this story. As the musicians enter the music hall, Aunt Georgiana begins to awaken.

Teaching Options

A Wagner Matinée

sharply to me, would tell me of the splendid performance of the *Huguenots*[15] she had seen in Paris, in her youth.

At two o'clock the Symphony Orchestra was to give a Wagner program, and I intended to take my aunt; though, as I conversed with her, I grew doubtful about her enjoyment of it. I suggested our visiting the Conservatory and the Common[16] before lunch, but she seemed altogether too timid to wish to venture out. She questioned me absently about various changes in the city, but she was chiefly concerned that she had forgotten to leave instructions about feeding half-skimmed milk to a certain weakling calf, "old Maggie's calf, you know, Clark," she explained, evidently having forgotten how long I had been away. She was further troubled because she had neglected to tell her daughter about the freshly-opened kit of mackerel in the cellar, which would spoil if it were not used directly.

I asked her whether she had ever heard any of the Wagnerian operas, and found that she had not, though she was perfectly familiar with their respective situations, and had once possessed the piano score of *The Flying Dutchman*. I began to think it would be best to get her back to Red Willow County without waking her, and regretted having suggested the concert.

From the time we entered the concert hall, however, she was a trifle less passive and inert, and for the first time seemed to perceive her surroundings. I had felt some trepidation lest she might become aware of her queer, country clothes, or might experience some painful embarrassment at stepping suddenly into the world to which she had been dead for a quarter of a century. But, again, I found how superficially

I had judged her. She sat looking about her with eyes as impersonal, almost as stony, as those with which the granite Rameses[17] in a museum watches the froth and fret that ebbs and flows[18] about his pedestal. I have seen this same aloofness in old miners who drift into the Brown hotel at Denver, their pockets full of bullion,[19] their linen soiled, their haggard faces unshaven; standing in the thronged corridors as solitary as though they were still in a frozen camp on the Yukon.[20]

The matinée audience was made up chiefly of women. One lost the contour of faces and figures, indeed any effect of line whatever, and there was only the color of bodices past counting, the shimmer of fabrics soft and firm, silky and sheer; red, mauve, pink, blue, lilac, purple, écru,[21] rose, yellow, cream, and white, all the colors that an impressionist[22] finds in a sunlit landscape, with here and there the dead shadow of a frock coat. My Aunt Georgiana regarded them as though they had been so many daubs of tube-paint on a palette.

When the musicians came out and took their places, she gave a little stir of anticipation, and looked with quickening interest down over the rail at that invariable grouping, perhaps the first wholly familiar thing that had greeted her eye since she had left old Maggie and her weakling calf. I could feel how all those details sank into her soul, for I had not forgotten how they had sunk into mine when I came fresh from

---

15. *Huguenots* (hū′ gə nots′) is a French opera by the German composer Giacomo Meyerbeer (1791–1864).
16. *Common* refers to Boston Common, a public park.

17. *Rameses* (ram′ ə sēz) is the name shared by several kings of ancient Egypt.
18. *[froth and fret . . . flows]* This phrase refers to the general busy activity that would come and go past a museum statue.
19. Here, *bullion* (bool′ yən) is gold.
20. *Yukon* refers to the Yukon River, a major route to the Klondike gold fields in Canada.
21. *Écru* (ā′ krōō) is beige.
22. An *impressionist* is a member of a movement in French painting that emphasized the play of light and color.

Vocabulary
inert (i nurt′) *adj.* inactive; sluggish
trepidation (trep′ ə dā′ shən) *n.* nervous anticipation; anxiety

LIFE SKILLS CONNECTION

Decision Making Tell students they will have to make many important decisions in their lives—decisions that will change their lives and the lives of others.

Activity Have students form groups to discuss Aunt Georgiana's decision to marry Howard Carpenter. Ask them to answer the following questions: Do you think that Georgiana made her decision based on reason or emotion? What does Clark imply about Georgiana's decision?

Do you agree with him? What were the consequences of her decision? What did she lose? What did she gain? If she could go back in time, do you think she would have married him again? Why or why not? What would you advise someone in Aunt Georgiana's position to do? Have students share a summary of their discussions with the class. **L2 COLLAB. LEARN.**

ploughing forever and forever between green aisles of corn, where, as in a treadmill, one might walk from daybreak to dusk without perceiving a shadow of change. The clean profiles of the musicians, the gloss of their linen, the dull black of their coats, the beloved shapes of the instruments, the patches of yellow light on the smooth, varnished bellies of the 'cellos and the bass viols in the rear, the restless, wind-tossed forest of fiddle necks and bows—I recalled how, in the first orchestra I ever heard, those long bow-strokes seemed to draw the heart out of me, as a conjurer's stick reels out yards of paper ribbon from a hat.

Did You Know?
The *cello* (short for violoncello) and the *bass viol* (also called the double bass) are stringed instruments played with a bow. Cellos are usually located on one side of an orchestra, with bass viols on the same side in the back.

The first number was the *Tannhauser* overture. When the horns drew out the first strain of the Pilgrim's chorus, Aunt Georgiana clutched my coat sleeve. Then it was I first realized that for her this broke a silence of thirty years. I saw again the tall, naked house on the prairie, black and grim as a wooden fortress; the black pond where I had learned to swim, its margin pitted with sun-dried cattle tracks; the rain gullied clay banks about the naked house, the four dwarf ash seedlings where the dish-cloths were always hung to dry before the kitchen door. The world there was the flat world of the ancients;[23] to the east, a cornfield that stretched to daybreak; to the west, a corral that reached to sunset; between, the conquests of peace, dearer-bought than those of war.

The overture closed, my aunt released my coat sleeve, but she said nothing. She sat staring dully at the orchestra. What, I wondered, did she get from it? She had been a good pianist in her day, I knew, and her musical education had been broader than that of most music teachers of a quarter of a century ago. She had often told me of Mozart's operas and Meyerbeer's, and I could remember hearing her sing, years ago, certain melodies of Verdi.[24] When I had fallen ill with a fever in her house she used to sit by my cot in the evening—when the cool, night wind blew in through the faded mosquito netting tacked over the window and I lay watching a certain bright star that burned red above the cornfield—and sing "Home to our mountains, O, let us return!" in a way fit to break the heart of a Vermont boy near dead of homesickness already.

I watched her closely through the prelude to *Tristan and Isolde*, trying vainly to conjecture what that seething <u>turmoil</u> of strings and winds might mean to her, but she sat mutely staring at the violin bows that drove <u>obliquely</u> downward, like the pelting streaks of rain in a summer shower. Had this music any message for her? Had she enough left to at all comprehend this power which had kindled the world since she had left it? I was in a fever of curiosity, but Aunt Georgiana sat silent upon her peak in Darien.[25]

---

24. Wolfgang Amadeus *Mozart* (woolf′ gang′   ä′ mə dā′ əs mōt′ särt), 1756–1791, was an Austrian composer. Giuseppe *Verdi* (jōō zep′ pe   ver′ dē), 1813–1901, was an Italian composer of opera.

25. The phrase *"peak in Darien"* (dãr′ ē en′) alludes to the poem "On First Looking into Chapman's Homer" by John Keats. The poem describes Spanish explorers on a mountain in Darien, now Panama, who stand silently and in awe, as the first Europeans to view the Pacific Ocean.

Vocabulary
turmoil (tur′ moil) *n.* a state of confused agitation; commotion
obliquely (ə blēk′ lē) *adv.* in a slanting or sloping direction

FYI

The Power of Music
The ancient Greeks believed that certain musical scales had the power to affect mood, to impel people to act, and in some cases, even to make people lose consciousness. Scientists today still believe that some forms of music can calm us during times of stress, helps us fight fatigue, and make us more productive.

K Active Reading

CONNECT Ask students if they have attended a symphony or seen a concert on television. Ask those students who have seen a classical music concert to comment on Cather's description of the musicians. Are there any other sights or sounds these students would add to this description? Ask students who have not seen such a concert to state which images from this description are the most vivid or interesting.

L Author's Craft

WORD CHOICE Point out that Cather implies throughout the story that the prairie house in Nebraska is a kind of prison for Aunt Georgiana. Here, she compares the house to a fortress.

M Literary Elements

NARRATOR Discuss with students that Clark understands that music can make a person homesick because he, too, felt homesick when his aunt sang to him in Nebraska.

INCLUSION STRATEGIES

Less-Proficient Readers Less-proficient readers will benefit from working in groups to learn the vocabulary words identified at the bottom of the pages of the selection.

Activity Have students form small groups and write each of the vocabulary words on one side of a note card and the definition on the other. Then ask students to take turns quizzing each other on the words, providing clues when necessary. After students have defined each word, have them repeat the exercise, this time using each of the words in an original sentence. **L1**

COLLAB. LEARN.

Additional Resources
📁 *Inclusion Strategies*

Rehearsal of the Pasdeloup Orchestra at the Cirque d'Hiver, 1879-1880. John Singer Sargent. Oil on canvas, 21¾ x 18¼ in. Museum of Fine Arts Boston. Charles Henry Hayden Fund.

Viewing the painting: How does this painting help you sense the "deluge of sound poured on and on"?

turned to my aunt. Her eyes were closed, but the tears were glistening on her cheeks, and I think, in a moment more, they were in my eyes as well. It never really died, then—the soul which can suffer so excruciatingly and so interminably; it withers to the outward eye only; like that strange moss which can lie on a dusty shelf half a century and yet, if placed in water, grows green again. She wept so throughout the development and elaboration of the melody.

During the intermission before the second half, I questioned my aunt and found that the "Prize Song" was not new to her. Some years before there had drifted to the farm in Red Willow County a young German, a tramp cowpuncher,[26] who had sung in the chorus at Bayreuth[27] when he was a boy, along with the other peasant boys and girls. Of a Sunday morning he used to sit on his gingham-sheeted bed in the hands' bedroom which opened off the kitchen, cleaning the leather of his boots and saddle, singing the "Prize

N She preserved this utter immobility throughout the number from *The Flying Dutchman,* though her fingers worked mechanically upon her black dress, as if, of themselves, they were recalling the piano score they had once played. Poor hands! They had been stretched and twisted into mere tentacles to hold and lift and knead with; on one of them a thin, worn band that had once been a wedding ring. As I pressed and gently quieted one of those groping hands, I remembered with quivering eyelids their services for me in other days.

Soon after the tenor began the "Prize Song," I heard a quick drawn breath and

---

26. *Cowpuncher* means "cowboy."
27. *Bayreuth* (bī roit′) is a German city famous for its annual Wagnerian music festival.

Song," while my aunt went about her work in the kitchen. She had hovered over him until she had <u>prevailed</u> upon him to join the country church, though his sole fitness for this step, in so far as I could gather, lay in his boyish face and his possession of this divine melody. Shortly afterward, he had gone to town on the Fourth of July, been drunk for several days, lost his money at a faro[28] table, ridden a saddled Texas steer on a bet, and disappeared with a fractured collar-bone. All this my aunt told me huskily, wanderingly, as though she were talking in the weak lapses of illness.

"Well, we have come to better things than the old *Trovatore*[29] at any rate, Aunt Georgie?" I queried, with a well meant effort at jocularity.[30]

Her lip quivered and she hastily put her handkerchief up to her mouth. From behind it she murmured, "And you have been hearing this ever since you left me, Clark?" Her question was the gentlest and saddest of reproaches.

The second half of the program consisted of four numbers from the *Ring*, and closed with Siegfried's funeral march. My aunt wept quietly, but almost continuously, as a shallow vessel overflows in a rain-storm. From time to time her dim eyes looked up at the lights, burning softly under their dull glass globes.

The <u>deluge</u> of sound poured on and on; I never knew what she found in the shining current of it; I never knew how far it bore her, or past what happy islands. From the trembling of her face I could well believe that before the last number she had been carried out where the myriad[31] graves are, into the grey, nameless burying grounds of the sea; or into some world of death vaster yet, where, from the beginning of the world, hope has lain down with hope and dream with dream and, renouncing,[32] slept.

The concert was over; the people filed out of the hall chattering and laughing, glad to relax and find the living level again, but my kinswoman made no effort to rise. The harpist slipped the green felt cover over his instrument; the flute-players shook the water from their mouthpieces; the men of the orchestra went out one by one, leaving the stage to the chairs and music stands, empty as a winter cornfield.

I spoke to my aunt. She burst into tears and sobbed pleadingly. "I don't want to go, Clark, I don't want to go!"

I understood. For her, just outside the concert hall, lay the black pond with the cattle-tracked bluffs; the tall, unpainted house, with weather-curled boards, naked as a tower; the crook-backed ash seedlings where the dish-cloths hung to dry; the gaunt,[33] moulting turkeys picking up refuse about the kitchen door.

---

28. *Faro* (fār' ō) is a gambling game played with a deck of cards.
29. *Trovatore* (tro və tōr' e) refers to *Il Trovatore,* an opera by Giuseppe Verdi.
30. *Jocularity* means "joking" or "humor."

31. *Myriad* means "countless" or "innumerable."
32. *Renouncing* means "giving up."
33. *Gaunt* means "extremely thin."

Vocabulary
prevail (pri vāl') *v.* to use persuasion successfully
deluge (del' ūj) *n.* anything that overwhelms or rushes like a flood

REGIONALISM AND REALISM 539

Literary Elements

CHARACTERIZATION This anecdote tells the reader a great deal about Aunt Georgiana's personality. Her love for music is so great that she befriends a young boy based solely on his musical ability.

Active Reading

QUESTION Ask students why the "Prize Song" in particular might cause Aunt Georgiana to cry. *(The song is one that she had heard in Nebraska; it probably reminds her that she must return to that life in Nebraska.)*

Thematic Focus

The Energy of the Everyday In this story, that which is an everyday event to some—attending a concert—becomes an extraordinary event to a woman who has been deprived of such an experience for many years.

✔ASSESSMENT OPTIONS

📁 *Quick Checks,* p. 61

REAL-WORLD CONNECTION

Listening to Music Tell students that music plays an even greater role in people's lives today than it did 100 years ago. People now have access to music on the radio, in their cars, while shopping, at the movies, and in their homes.

Activity Have students describe times when they enjoy listening to music. How does music affect their moods? What emotions do they associate with music? **L1**

*inter*NET CONNECTION

Wagner Richard Wagner was only 16 when he composed his first music. Suggest that students use the keywords *Wagner* and *Romanticism* to find out more about this remarkable musician.

Responding to the Selection

Personal Response

Many students will feel sorry for Aunt Georgiana, and they may think she made a mistake when she married Howard Carpenter and moved to Nebraska.

ANALYZING LITERATURE

1. He feels like the shy farm boy he was when he last saw her.
2. She gave up music to work on the farm.
3. She read to him and taught him Latin, Shakespeare, and music.
4. She seems tired and distant. She reacts to the music by moving her hands.
5. She cries because she does not want to go home. The narrator knows that she must return to a harsh and unfulfilling farm life.
6. The narrator was deeply affected by Aunt Georgiana's kindness to him and has a reverential affection for her. He also realizes that she had longed to return to Boston for half a lifetime and that this trip might be significant for her.
7. She gave up teaching and the culture of Boston and Paris.
8. They reveal empathy and kindness but also that he feels life in Boston is preferable to life in Nebraska.
9. Aunt Georgiana had wanted to attend such a concert for so long that when she finally does, she is overwhelmed. Her tears indicate her passion for music.
10. The concert hall symbolizes the life of her youth and missed opportunities.
11. The elaborate, colorful concert hall provides a contrast to the flat, unvarying prairie where Aunt Georgiana lives, reinforcing the theme of regret for things lost.
12. Students may say that they have more opportunities to visit a previous home than Georgiana does.
13. Students may find it difficult and isolating.
14. Students may mention such emotions as grief, joy, empathy, or horror.
15. Students unfamiliar with opera or classical music may think the references detract from their understanding. Others may appreciate more deeply Georgiana's enjoyment and sense of loss.

Responding to Literature

Personal Response

What went through your mind as you read about Aunt Georgiana's reaction to the concert?

——— ANALYZING LITERATURE ———

RECALL

1. How does the narrator react to the letter from his uncle?
2. What changes occurred in Aunt Georgiana's life after she married?
3. The narrator says that he owed to his aunt "most of the good that ever came my way in my boyhood." What is he grateful for?
4. Why does the narrator grow doubtful that his aunt will enjoy the concert? How does she react to it?
5. How does Aunt Georgiana behave after the concert ends? How does the narrator explain this behavior?

INTERPRET

6. Why, do you think, does the narrator react so strongly to his uncle's letter?
7. What, in your opinion, did Aunt Georgiana give up in getting married and moving to Nebraska? Explain, using details from the story.
8. What do the narrator's thoughts and observations about his aunt reveal about his own character and personality?
9. Why do you think the concert affects Aunt Georgiana so deeply?
10. At the end of the story, what does the concert hall seem to symbolize for Aunt Georgiana?

EVALUATE AND CONNECT

11. How do Cather's descriptions of the Boston concert hall and the Nebraska prairie help you better understand the **theme,** or central message, of this story? Explain.
12. Look back at your response to the Focus Activity on page 531. How does your real or imagined experience with moving compare with Aunt Georgiana's experience?
13. How has this story affected your impressions of frontier life? Organize your response in a spider diagram like the one shown.
14. Describe a time when you experienced a deep, emotional response to a work of art, such as a painting, a poem, or a piece of music.
15. In what ways do the musical references contribute to or detract from your understanding of the story?

Literary ELEMENTS

Point of View

Point of view refers to the relationship of the narrator, or storyteller, to the story. The first-person pronouns *I, my,* and *me* in the opening paragraph of "A Wagner Matinée" reveal that this story is told from the **first-person point of view.** Everything that the reader learns is filtered through the eyes, ears, and thoughts of the narrator, a character named Clark.

1. How does the narrator help the reader understand Aunt Georgiana and her life? Use details from the story to support your answer.
2. How might the story be different if it had been told from Georgiana's point of view instead of Clark's? Give specific examples.

● See **Literary Terms Handbook,** p. R12.

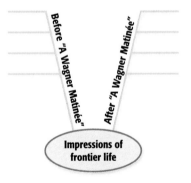

Before "A Wagner Matinée"   After "A Wagner Matinée"

Impressions of frontier life

LITERARY ELEMENTS

1. He provides details about her life before marriage and her life in Nebraska, which he witnessed firsthand.
2. Some students may say that Georgiana would have described her feelings during the journey, when reuniting with her nephew, and at the concert. Others may say that she might admit that her marriage was a mistake and that she longed to return to Boston.

Additional Resources

 Literary Elements Transparency 50

———— LITERATURE AND WRITING ————

Writing About Literature

Analyze Comparisons Willa Cather compares Georgiana to an explorer, to a statue, and to moss; she compares aisles of corn to a treadmill, bowstrokes to the action of a conjurer's stick, and music to a water current. Choose a comparison and write a paragraph explaining how it contributes to the story's meaning.

Creative Writing

The Beat Goes On Put yourself in Georgiana's place. Imagine that you have recently returned to your Nebraska home. Write a thank-you letter to Clark, updating him on your life since your return. Share with him your impressions of your visit to Boston and your trip home. Also include your thoughts about being back on the farm.

———— EXTENDING YOUR RESPONSE ————

Literature Groups

Time for a Rest? In your group, discuss these questions: What might happen if Georgiana decided to stay in Boston for an extended vacation? Would she feel at home there? Why or why not? How might she spend her time? Who would do her work back home in Nebraska? Would she find it difficult to finally return home? Be sure to support your opinions with specific details from the story. Then summarize your group's opinions for the class.

Interdisciplinary Connection

Music: Appreciating Wagner Locate a recording of one of Richard Wagner's operas and research the story behind it. Play some of the recording for the class, explaining the story.

Learning for Life

Mapping a Route Aunt Georgiana traveled by train from Nebraska to Boston. Research and create a map that shows the route the train would have traveled (in about 1900), the terrain through which it would have passed, and major geographical landmarks along the way.

Reading Further

You might enjoy these novels by Willa Cather:
My Ántonia and *O Pioneers!* explore the life of the early pioneers in Nebraska.

 Save your work for your portfolio.

Skill Minilesson

VOCABULARY • **Analogies**

Analogies are comparisons based on relationships between words and ideas. The relationship in some analogies is that of an action and its significance.

> kiss : affection :: scowl : anger

A *kiss* is a sign of *affection;* a *scowl* is a sign of *anger.*

To finish an analogy, decide what relationship is represented by the first pair of words. Then apply that relationship to the second pair.

● For more on analogies, see **Communications Skills Handbook,** p. R83.

PRACTICE Choose the word that best completes each analogy.

1. reproaches : disapproval :: compliments :
      a. criticism   b. approval   c. affection
2. sweat : trepidation :: wink :
      a. anxiety   b. blink   c. mischief
3. riot : turmoil :: truce :
      a. peace   b. noise   c. conflict

Writing About Literature

Students' paragraphs should
- include one comparison and explain the two things being compared.
- explain how the comparison adds to an understanding of the story.

Creative Writing

Students' letters should
- be in the format of an informal letter.
- include impressions of Boston based on descriptions in the text.
- present the information in an appropriate style and tone.

EXTENDING YOUR RESPONSE

Literature Groups Remind students that divorce was considered socially unacceptable at this time and that married women had few legal rights. **COLLAB. LEARN.**

Interdisciplinary Connection You may want to have several students prepare a brief presentation about the history of opera to enhance students' appreciation. **COLLAB. LEARN.**

Learning for Life Have students work in small groups to complete this activity. Encourage them to color their maps and present them on large sheets of poster board. **COLLAB. LEARN.**

Skill Minilesson

VOCABULARY • **Analogies**

1. b   2. c   3. a

Additional Resources
📁 *Vocabulary Practice,* p. 37

 **ASSESSMENT OPTIONS**

📁 *Quick Checks,* p. 61
📁 *Selection and Theme Assessment,* pp. 91–92
📁 *Performance Assessment,* p. 50
💾 *Testmaker*

Objectives

- To read and analyze two poems about the African American experience in late nineteenth-century America
- To identify and analyze the elements of a sonnet

Skills

Reading/Thinking: Enhancing Comprehension
Grammar/Language: Present Perfect Tense

Motivating

→ OPTIONS

Selection Focus Transparency 54: Have students view the transparency and then answer the question provided.

Focus Activity: As an extension of the Focus Activity, have students draw or describe the face they wear when they feel most comfortable—with friends, with family members, or alone at home. How does this face compare to the others they drew?

Before You Read

Douglass and *We Wear the Mask*

Meet Paul Laurence Dunbar

"I know why the caged bird sings!"

—*Dunbar*

These words, perhaps better than any, describe the complex plight of Paul Laurence Dunbar. To get a hearing for his poetry he often felt he had to "sing" within the constraints of taste and prejudice that dominated his times.

One of the first African American writers to attain national recognition, Dunbar was the son of formerly enslaved people from Kentucky. Their stories of pre-Emancipation days would provide a sea of material for his work.

Dunbar was the only African American student at his Dayton, Ohio, high school. There he excelled at his studies, edited the school paper, and became class president. Despite his success in school, however, the adult world was reluctant to give Dunbar a chance to prove himself. When he could not find a job in a newspaper or a legal office because of his color, he took a four-dollar-a-week elevator operator job. Between calls for the elevator, he wrote.

Dunbar took out a loan to publish his first volume of poetry, *Oak and Ivy*. His second volume, *Majors and Minors*, came out in 1895. When the influential writer and critic William Dean Howells favorably reviewed it, Dunbar found himself famous. Much to Dunbar's growing despair, however, the poems that got a hearing were not those written with serious artistic intent, but those written in black dialect that he called "jingles in a broken tongue."

Paul Laurence Dunbar was born in 1872 and died in 1906.

FOCUS ACTIVITY

Do you sometimes feel that you have to "wear" more than one face? Are you one person at home, another at school, and yet another when you are out with friends?

SKETCH IT! Draw pictures showing different faces you might "wear" in different situations.

SETTING A PURPOSE Read "We Wear the Mask" to understand why some people show different faces at different times.

BACKGROUND

The Poet's Twin Masks

Who was Paul Laurence Dunbar? Was he a "city person" who in just one generation had lost touch with the reality of his parents' lives in slavery? Or was he a poet who understood his primarily white audience well enough to give them the poetry they wanted?

Dunbar wrote two kinds of poetry. Although he was known and loved for his sentimental verse, written in dialect, about an idyllic, pastoral, pre–Civil War plantation life, he has sometimes been criticized for this work and for failing to confront the issues of racial stereotypes and discrimination. However, Dunbar also produced poems in Standard English that meditate on love, nature, or death; express pride in African Americans; or lament thwarted efforts to live and create freely.

RESOURCE MANAGER

Lesson Planning Resource
The *Unit Four Planning Guide* (pp. 61–65) provides additional lesson notes and reduced versions of all print resources.

Other Print Resources
- Active Reading Guide, p. 62
- Reading Workbook
- Grammar and Language Workbook, p. 137

- Grammar and Composition Handbook, Lesson 5.4
- Quick Checks, p. 62
- Selection and Theme Assessment, pp. 93–94
- Performance Assessment, p. 51
- Spanish Summaries, p. 54
- Spanish Translations
- Inclusion Strategies

 Transparencies
- Selection Focus 54
- Literary Elements 51
- Grammar and Language 45

Technology
- Audio Library
- Glencoe Literature Web Site
- Testmaker

Responding to Literature

Personal Response

Do you know anyone whose outlook resembles that of Lucinda Matlock or Fiddler Jones? Explain.

ANALYZING LITERATURE

Lucinda Matlock

RECALL AND INTERPRET

1. Describe how Lucinda Matlock spent her life. What were her joys? her sorrows?
2. What can you infer about Lucinda's character and outlook on life, based on the information she gives in lines 1–17? Support your answer, using details from the poem.
3. What is Lucinda talking about in lines 18–22? What do you think she means when she says, "It takes life to love Life"?
4. Describe Lucinda's **tone,** or attitude toward her subject, in lines 1–17. How does her tone change in lines 18–22? What might you infer from this change?

EVALUATE AND CONNECT

5. Find several examples of **alliteration** and describe the effect created by the repetition of initial consonant sounds.
6. Theme Connections   What advice might Lucinda give about facing the ups and downs of everyday life?
7. What simple pleasures in life do you most enjoy? Explain why.

Fiddler Jones

RECALL AND INTERPRET

8. What does Fiddler Jones say you must do if people find out that you can fiddle? What does this statement suggest about his outlook on life?
9. In lines 5–14, Fiddler describes different ways of perceiving the same things. Summarize these descriptions. What point do you think he is trying to make?
10. What reasons does Fiddler give for neglecting his farm? How does he seem to feel about his work habits?
11. What did Fiddler Jones have at the end of his life? Why might he have had no regrets?

EVALUATE AND CONNECT

12. What does Fiddler's philosophy of life seem to be? What do you think of his philosophy?
13. Theme Connections   Do you think Fiddler's life exemplifies "the energy of the everyday"? Give reasons for your answer.
14. Apply the statement in lines 1–2 to your own life. What "vibration" is at the center of your heart and your life? How does this force define who you are?

11. He had "forty acres," "a broken fiddle," "a broken laugh," and "a thousand memories." He had no regrets because he enjoyed life.
12. His philosophy is to be positive and enjoy life. Some students will agree; others will think it is equally important to work hard in school or at a career.
13. Most students will think that it does—he expends all his energy enjoying his everyday life.
14. Students may mention such "vibrations" as athletics or art.

Responding to the Selection

Personal Response

Students should mention people who have positive attitudes toward life.

ANALYZING LITERATURE

1. She spent her life caring for her family. Her joys were her family and nature. Her sorrow was losing eight children.
2. Readers can infer that she had a positive outlook, worked hard, and cared for others. For example, she lived with her husband "enjoying, working, raising the twelve children."
3. Lucinda is talking about people with negative attitudes. Students may say that only through experiencing both the good and the bad can a person truly love life.
4. Lucinda's tone in lines 1–17 is happy and satisfied. In lines 18–22, her tone is serious and reprimanding, implying that she disapproves of complainers.
5. Examples of alliteration include "moonlight," "middle" (line 4); "discontent," "drooping," "degenerate," "daughters" (lines 19–20); "life," "love," "Life" (line 22). This alliteration provides rhythm and pattern.
6. Lucinda might say that people must accept both the good and the bad and that they should celebrate life's small pleasures.
7. Students may mention such pleasures as talking with friends or taking walks.
8. He says "fiddle you must," which suggests that he has a positive outlook and that he believes in being accommodating and friendly.
9. He says some people see "a harvest of clover"; others see "a meadow to walk through." Cooney Potter sees drought where Fiddler Jones sees Red-Head Sammy dancing. His point is that people's attitudes affect their perceptions.
10. He neglects his farm because people stop him to play his fiddle at a dance or a picnic. He seems to think that his work habits are fine.

LITERATURE AND WRITING

Writing About Literature

Students' paragraphs should

- refer to elements of the poems as a basis for their comparisons such as the characters' love of life, their impatience with those who complain, and their ability to rise above hardships, and contrasts, such as Lucinda's dedication to hard work and Fiddler Jones's easily distracted and somewhat disconnected attitude toward it.
- conclude whether these characters would agree about what constitutes a good life and provide valid reasons for their conclusions. Students might say, for example, that although many aspects of their personalities differed, they both took enjoyment from their lot in life.
- organize their comparisons and contrasts logically.

Personal Writing

Students' statements should

- express complete thoughts about their philosophies of life.
- express their true feelings, but not list aphorisms.
- reflect students' outlooks, whether optimistic or pessimistic.

EXTENDING YOUR RESPONSE

Literature Groups As students devise answers to their questions, remind them to consider each character's philosophy of life. **COLLAB. LEARN.**

Performing Encourage students to read their monologues to partners before the performance. Ask partners to offer suggestions for improving performances. **COLLAB. LEARN.**

Interdisciplinary Activity Tell students who prefer not to sketch that they may find a photograph or painting of a person who resembles the character. Ask these students to give reasons for their choices.

Literary ELEMENTS

Dramatic Monologue

A **dramatic monologue** is a form of dramatic poetry in which a single speaker addresses a silent audience. "Lucinda Matlock" and "Fiddler Jones" appear among a group of interrelated dramatic monologues in *Spoon River Anthology*. The speakers, who lived and died in Spoon River, all have something to say about their lives, and they want their audience—the living—to heed the lessons they have learned.

1. What did you learn about the meaning of life by reading "Lucinda Matlock" and "Fiddler Jones"?
2. Paraphrase one of the dramatic monologues you have just read. Do you think this work would be as effective in prose as it is in poetry? Explain your response.

● See **Literary Terms Handbook,** p. R5.

LITERATURE AND WRITING

Writing About Literature

Comparing Characters   Write several paragraphs in which you compare and contrast Lucinda Matlock and Fiddler Jones. What is similar about their outlooks and philosophies of life? What is different? How did they spend their lives? What was most important to each character? Do you think they would agree about what constitutes a good life? Why or why not?

Personal Writing

The Meaning of Life   Review the ideas you listed in response to the Focus Activity on page 546. What ideas would you add or change, now that you have read two poems about the meaning of life? After revising your list of ideas, write a statement that expresses your own philosophy of life.

EXTENDING YOUR RESPONSE

Literature Groups

What's the Scoop?   Lucinda Matlock and Fiddler Jones apparently led very active, full lives. Readers learn about the characters in a general way, but the details are missing. As a group, devise a list of questions that you would like to ask these characters. After you write the questions, discuss possible answers. Share your questions and answers with the class.

Performing

Dramatic Monologue   Prepare a dramatic reading of "Lucinda Matlock" or "Fiddler Jones." As you practice your monologue, try to vary the volume, pitch, and tone of your voice to communicate the speaker's message more effectively. You may want to use facial expressions and hand or body gestures to dramatize your presentation. Perform your monologue for your classmates.

Interdisciplinary Activity

Art: Character Sketch   After reading the two poems, can you imagine what each speaker might have looked like? Make a sketch of either Lucinda Matlock or Fiddler Jones. You might show the character engaged in an activity described in the poem. Share your sketch with the class.

Reading Further

You might enjoy another depiction of small-town America in the early twentieth century:

Our Town, by Thorton Wilder, is a play that affirms the simple values of life in a New Hampshire village.

📖 **Save your work for your portfolio.**

LITERARY ELEMENTS

1. Students may have learned that life is precious and that they must savor every moment. They may also have learned that having a positive attitude towards life will improve the quality of their lives.
2. Answers will depend on students' appreciation for elements that distinguish poetry from prose.

Additional Resources

✍ *Literary Elements Transparency 52*

✔ ASSESSMENT OPTIONS

📁 *Quick Checks,* p. 63

📁 *Selection and Theme Assessment,* pp. 95–96

📁 *Performance Assessment,* p. 52

💾 *Testmaker*

Moonlit Shipwreck at Sea, 1901. Thomas Moran. Oil on canvas, 76.2 x 102.2 cm. Private collection.

The Open Boat

Stephen Crane ∾

A tale intended to be after the fact. Being the experience of four men from the sunk steamer Commodore . . .

559

SUMMARY

Four men—a cook, an oiler, a captain, and a correspondent—must travel toward land in a dinghy after their ship sinks. After several unsuccessful attempts to make it ashore in the boat, the men finally get as close to shore as they can and swim the rest of the way. A swimmer at the shore sees them and saves the cook, the correspondent, and the captain from the ocean. Only the oiler dies. As the correspondent sits on the shore, he mourns the oiler, for whom the long and difficult journey was in vain.

🗀 *Spanish Summaries,* p. 57

A Active Reading

PREDICT Have a volunteer read the text beneath the title. Ask the class what this information tells them about the story. *("The Open Boat" is a survival story, and at least one of the four men, the author, must have either lived to tell it or else kept a record of it.)*

Additional Resources
🗀 *Active Reading Guide,* p. 65
🎧 *Audio Library*

Teaching Options

Reading *Minilesson*

Visualizing Spatial Relationships
Visualizing aids understanding and requires careful attention to details, which, in turn, enhances reading comprehension.

Activity Ask students to read part 1 of the story. Have four students demonstrate the amount of room in the dinghy by measuring a space of approximately 10 by 5 feet and seating themselves in the positions in which the men are seated. Then have them visualize the boat in relation to the ocean. Tell students that they should continue to visualize as they read the story. **L2**
COLLAB. LEARN.

Additional Resources
🗀 *Reading Workbook,* pp. 57–58

B Active Reading

QUESTION Ask students what this paragraph suggests about the focus of the men's attention. Why might these characters not know the color of the sky? *(The characters' attention is focused on the sea and their battle to survive. They do not know the color of the sky because they dare not look away from their enemy, the sea.)*

C Active Reading

EVALUATE Ask students if they think this is an effective description of the boat. *(Many students will feel that Crane's description is effective because he compares the size of the boat to the size of something his readers know—a bathtub.)*

D Literary Elements

FIGURATIVE LANGUAGE: *Simile* Point out that Crane provides the reader with a comparison to explain what it feels like inside the boat. He compares riding in the boat to a wild ride on a bucking bronco.

The Open Boat

I

B None of them knew the color of the sky. Their eyes glanced level, and were fastened upon the waves that swept toward them. These waves were of the hue of slate, save for the tops, which were of foaming white, and all of the men knew the colors of the sea. The horizon narrowed and widened, and dipped and rose, and at all times its edge was jagged with waves that seemed thrust up in points like rocks.

C Many a man ought to have a bathtub larger than the boat which here rode upon the sea. These waves were most wrongfully and barbarously abrupt and tall, and each froth-top was a problem in small boat navigation.

The cook squatted in the bottom and looked with both eyes at the six inches of gunwale[1] which separated him from the ocean. His sleeves were rolled over his fat forearms, and the two flaps of his unbuttoned vest dangled as he bent to bail out the boat. Often he said: "Gawd! That was a narrow clip." As he remarked it he invariably gazed eastward over the broken sea.

The oiler,[2] steering with one of the two oars in the boat, sometimes raised himself suddenly to keep clear of water that swirled in over the stern.[3] It was a thin little oar and it seemed often ready to snap.

The correspondent, pulling at the other oar, watched the waves and wondered why he was there.

The injured captain, lying in the bow, was at this time buried in that profound dejection and indifference which comes, temporarily at least, to even the bravest and most enduring when, willy nilly,[4] the firm fails, the army loses, the ship

goes down. The mind of the master of a vessel is rooted deep in the timbers of her, though he command for a day or a decade, and this captain had on him the stern impression of a scene in the grays of dawn of seven turned faces, and later a stump of a top-mast with a white ball on it that slashed to and fro at the waves, went low and lower, and down. Thereafter there was something strange in his voice. Although steady, it was deep with mourning, and of a quality beyond oration[5] or tears.

"Keep'er a little more south, Billie," said he.

"'A little more south,' sir," said the oiler in the stern.

D A seat in this boat was not unlike a seat upon a bucking bronco, and, by the same token, a bronco is not much smaller. The craft pranced and reared, and plunged like an animal. As each wave came, and she rose for it, she seemed like a horse making at a fence outrageously high. The manner of her scramble over these walls of water is a mystic thing, and, moreover, at the top of them were ordinarily these problems in white water, the foam racing down from the summit of each wave, requiring a new leap, and a leap from the air. Then, after scornfully bumping a crest, she would slide, and race, and splash down a long incline and arrive bobbing and nodding in front of the next menace.

A singular disadvantage of the sea lies in the fact that after successfully surmounting one wave you discover that there is another behind it just as important and just as nervously anxious to do something effective in the way of swamping boats. In a ten-foot dinghy one can get an idea of the resources of the sea in the line of waves that is not probable to the average experience, which is never

---

1. A *gunwale* is the upper edge of the side of a boat.
2. The *oiler* is the person responsible for oiling machinery in the engine room on a ship.
3. The *stern* is the rear part of a boat or ship.
4. *Willy nilly* means "whether one wishes it or not."

5. An *oration* is a formal speech.

Vocabulary
profound (prə found′) *adj.* coming from the depth of one's being; intensely felt

---

Grammar and Language *Minilesson*

Emphatic Forms of Verbs Explain to students that a verb in the emphatic form receives additional emphasis. The emphatic forms of verbs consist of *do, does,* or *did* plus the base form of the verb: *He does fear that you are right.*

Activity Have students rewrite the following sentences about "The Open Boat" using the emphatic form of the underlined

verb. Ensure that students do not change the verb's tense. **L2** **COLLAB. LEARN.**
1. The ship <u>sank</u>. *(did sink)*
2. The captain <u>lay</u> in the bow. *(did lie)*
3. The cook believed that houses of refuge <u>carry</u> crews. *(do carry)*
4. The captain <u>chuckled</u>. *(did chuckle)*
5. The men <u>fear</u> drowning. *(do fear)*

Additional Resources

Grammar and Language Transparency 48

Grammar and Language Workbook, p. 141

Grammar and Composition Handbook, Lesson 5.5

Writer's Choice, Lesson 15.5

at sea in a dinghy. As each slaty[6] wall of water approached, it shut all else from the view of the men in the boat, and it was not difficult to imagine that this particular wave was the final outburst of the ocean, the last effort of the grim water. There was a terrible grace in the move of the waves, and they came in silence, save for the snarling of the crests.

In the wan[7] light, the faces of the men must have been gray. Their eyes must have glinted in strange ways as they gazed steadily astern. Viewed from a balcony, the whole thing would doubtlessly have been weirdly picturesque. But the men in the boat had no time to see it, and if they had had leisure there were other things to occupy their minds. The sun swung steadily up the sky, and they knew it was broad day because the color of the sea changed from slate to emerald green, streaked with amber lights, and the foam was like tumbling snow. The process of the breaking day was unknown to them. They were aware only of this effect upon the color of the waves that rolled toward them.

In disjointed sentences the cook and the correspondent argued as to the difference between a lifesaving station and a house of refuge. The cook had said: "There's a house of refuge just north of the Mosquito Inlet Light, and as soon as they see us, they'll come off in their boat and pick us up."

"As soon as who see us?" said the correspondent.

"The crew," said the cook.

"Houses of refuge don't have crews," said the correspondent. "As I understand them, they are only places where clothes and grub are stored for the benefit of shipwrecked people. They don't carry crews."

"Oh, yes, they do," said the cook.

"No, they don't," said the correspondent.

"Well, we're not there yet, anyhow," said the oiler, in the stern.

---

6. *Slaty* means "having the bluish-gray color of slate."
7. *Wan* means "pale."

"Well," said the cook, "perhaps it's not a house of refuge that I'm thinking of as being near Mosquito Inlet Light. Perhaps it's a life-saving station."

"We're not there yet," said the oiler, in the stern.

II

As the boat bounced from the top of each wave, the wind tore through the hair of the hatless men, and as the craft plopped her stern down again the spray slashed past them. The crest of each of these waves was a hill, from the top of which the men surveyed, for a moment, a broad tumultuous[8] expanse, shining and wind-riven. It was probably splendid. It was probably glorious, this play of the free sea, wild with lights of emerald and white and amber.

"Bully good thing it's an onshore wind,"[9] said the cook. "If not, where would be we? Wouldn't have a show."

"That's right," said the correspondent.

The busy oiler nodded his assent.

Then the captain, in the bow, chuckled in a way that expressed humor, contempt, tragedy, all in one. "Do you think we've got much of a show, now, boys?" said he.

Whereupon the three were silent, save for a trifle of hemming and hawing. To express any particular optimism at this time they felt to be childish and stupid, but they all doubtless possessed this sense of the situation in their mind. A young man thinks doggedly[10] at such times. On the other hand, the ethics of their condition was decidedly against any open suggestion of hopelessness. So they were silent.

"Oh, well," said the captain, soothing his children, "we'll get ashore all right."

But there was that in his tone which made them think, so the oiler quoth: "Yes! If this wind holds!"

---

8. *Tumultuous* means "agitated" or "turbulent."
9. An *onshore wind* is one that blows toward the shore.
10. *Doggedly* means "in a stubbornly persistent manner."

561

E Literary Elements

IMAGERY Point out the adjectives used to describe the waves' movement, such as "terrible grace." Explain that throughout the story, the ocean is described in terms of its beauty and its power.

F Literary Elements

NARRATOR The narrator often provides only those details that the men would notice. For instance, the use of the words *must have* reinforces the men's lack of time or energy to consider their positions; they expend all their energy fighting to survive.

G Critical Thinking

INFERRING Ask students why the cook and the correspondent fight over such a minor detail. *(They may be fighting to distract themselves from their thoughts about dying. Maybe the men are taking out on each other their fear of and anger about their situation.)*

MEETING INDIVIDUAL NEEDS ENGLISH LANGUAGE LEARNERS

Building Vocabulary Help English language learners determine the meaning of unfamiliar words from context clues.

Activity Have students work with a fluent English speaker to use context clues to determine the meaning of the words *bronco* (page 560), *gulls* (page 562), *diabolical* (page 564), and *billows* (page 566). In the first column,

have students write the word and then complete the rest of the chart, using a dictionary to check their work.

Word	Clues	Meaning

Additional Resources

📁 *English Language Learners Sourcebook*

The Open Boat

The cook was bailing. "Yes! If we don't catch hell in the surf."

Canton flannel gulls[11] flew near and far. Sometimes they sat down on the sea, near patches of brown seaweed that rolled over the waves with a movement like carpets on a line in a gale. The birds sat comfortably in groups, and they were envied by some in the dinghy, for the wrath of the sea was no more to them than it was to a covey of prairie chickens a thousand miles inland. Often they came very close and stared at the men with black bead-like eyes. At these times they were uncanny and sinister[12] in their unblinking scrutiny, and the men hooted angrily at them, telling them to be gone. One came, and evidently decided to alight on the top of the captain's head. The bird flew parallel to the boat and did not circle, but made short sidelong jumps in the air in chicken-fashion. His black eyes were wistfully fixed upon the captain's head. "Ugly brute," said the oiler to the bird. "You look as if you were made with a jackknife." The cook and the correspondent swore darkly at the creature. The captain naturally wished to knock it away with the end of the heavy painter,[13] but he did not dare do it, because anything resembling an emphatic gesture would have capsized this freighted boat, and so with his open hand, the captain gently and carefully waved the gull away. After it had been discouraged from the pursuit the captain breathed easier on account of his hair, and others breathed easier because the bird struck their minds at this time as being somehow gruesome and ominous.

In the meantime the oiler and the correspondent rowed. And also they rowed.

They sat together in the same seat, and each rowed an oar. Then the oiler took both oars; then the correspondent took both oars; then the oiler; then the correspondent. They rowed and they rowed. The very ticklish part of the business was when the time came for the reclining one in the stern to take his turn at the oars. By the very last star of truth, it is easier to steal eggs from under a hen than it was to change seats in the dinghy. First the man in the stern slid his hand along the thwart[14] and moved with care, as if he were of Sèvres.[15] Then the man in the rowing seat slid his hand along the other thwart. It was all done with the most extraordinary care. As the two sidled past each other, the whole party kept watchful eyes on the coming wave, and the captain cried: "Look out now! Steady there!"

The brown mats of seaweed that appeared from time to time were like islands, bits of earth. They were traveling, apparently, neither one way nor the other. They were, to all intents, stationary. They informed the men in the boat that it was making progress slowly toward the land.

The captain, rearing cautiously in the bow, after the dinghy soared on a great swell, said that he had seen the lighthouse at Mosquito Inlet. Presently the cook remarked that he had seen it. The correspondent was at the oars, then, and for some reason he too wished to look at the lighthouse, but his back was toward the far shore and the waves were important, and for some time he could not seize an opportunity to turn his head. But at last there came

---

11. *Canton flannel gulls* are gulls whose feathers resemble Canton flannel, a strong cotton fabric that is soft on one side and ribbed on the other.
12. *Sinister* means "evil" or "ominous."
13. A *painter* is a rope attached to the front of a boat, used for tying up to a dock.

14. A *thwart* is a seat going across a boat, on which a rower or passenger sits.
15. *Sèvres* (sev′rə) refers to fine porcelain made in Sèvres, France.

Vocabulary
uncanny (un ka′nē) *adj.* strangely unsettling; eerie
emphatic (em fa′tik) *adj.* forceful

a wave more gentle than the others, and when at the crest of it he swiftly scoured the western horizon.

"See it?" said the captain.

"No," said the correspondent, slowly, "I didn't see anything."

"Look again," said the captain. He pointed. "It's exactly in that direction."

At the top of another wave, the correspondent did as he was bid, and this time his eyes chanced on a small still thing on the edge of the swaying horizon. It was precisely like the point of a pin. It took an anxious eye to find a lighthouse so tiny.

"Think we'll make it, Captain?"

"If this wind holds and the boat don't swamp, we can't do much else," said the captain.

The little boat, lifted by each towering sea, and splashed viciously by the crests, made progress that in the absence of seaweed was not apparent to those in her. She seemed just a wee thing wallowing, miraculously, top up, at the mercy of five oceans. Occasionally, a great spread of water, like white flames, swarmed into her.

"Bail her, cook," said the captain, serenely.

"All right, Captain," said the cheerful cook.

III

It would be difficult to describe the subtle brotherhood of men that was here established on the seas. No one said that it was so. No one mentioned it. But it dwelt in the boat, and each man felt it warm him. They were a captain, an oiler, a cook, and a correspondent, and

The Derelict, 1975. Donald McAdoo. Watercolor, 14 x 21 in. Collection Mr. & Mrs. Robert A. Kopp Jr.

Viewing the painting: What struggle might have occurred involving the boat in this painting? How does the struggle you imagine compare with the struggles faced by the men in "The Open Boat"?

they were friends, friends in a more curiously iron-bound degree than may be common. The hurt captain, lying against the water jar in the bow, spoke always in a low voice and calmly, but he could never command a more ready and swiftly obedient crew than the motley three of the dinghy. It was more than a mere recognition of what was best for the common safety.

There was surely in it a quality that was personal and heartfelt. And after this devotion to the commander of the boat there was this comradeship that the correspondent, for instance, who had been taught to be cynical of men, knew even at the time was the best experience of his life. But no one said that it was so. No one mentioned it.

"I wish we had a sail," remarked the captain. "We might try my overcoat on the end of an oar and give you two boys a chance to rest." So the cook and the correspondent held the mast and spread wide the overcoat. The oiler steered, and the little boat made good way with her new rig. Sometimes the oiler had to scull[16] sharply to keep a sea from breaking into the boat, but otherwise sailing was a success.

Meanwhile the lighthouse had been growing slowly larger. It had now almost assumed color, and appeared like a little gray shadow on the sky. The man at the oars could not be prevented from turning his head rather often to try for a glimpse of this little gray shadow.

---

16. *Scull* means "to propel a boat forward by moving a single oar from side to side over the stern of a boat."

563

L Literary Elements

CHARACTERIZATION The captain sees the lighthouse when the others still cannot because he knows the ocean better than they do. Despite his injuries, he is the leader in the dinghy because of his knowledge.

M Literary Elements

PLOT: *Rising Action* Explain that the men are always looking for reasons to believe that they will survive. Their will to survive drives the plot's action.

N Critical Thinking

INFERRING Ask what the captain's response to the correspondent suggests about the role fate will play in their survival. *(It suggests that fate will determine their outcome.)*

Historical Note

As Stephen Crane was writing "The Open Boat," he met with Edward Murphy, the real captain of the *Commodore*. Crane read Murphy "The Open Boat" and said to him, "Listen, Ed, I want to have this *right*, from your point of view. How does it sound so far?" "You've got it, Steve," Murphy is said to have replied.

O Active Reading

CONNECT Ask if students have ever been in a situation that forced them to become close to people they would not otherwise have known.

GIFTED AND TALENTED ACTIVITY

Comparing Two Media Challenge gifted and talented students to participate in the following research project.

Activity Have students locate in the library a copy of "Stephen Crane's Own Story," Crane's article about the sinking of the *Commodore*, which first appeared in the *New York Press* on January 7, 1897. Which of the events

Crane describes in the article do not appear in the story? How does the article compare in tone and style to the story? How does the information in the article add to students' understanding of the story? Have students present their findings in an essay or oral report. **L3**

QUESTION Ask students what two details Crane provides to show that the men are not prepared for this dangerous situation. What is ironic about the second detail? *(Crane says that they had not had any sleep for two days and two nights and that no one had eaten well before the ship sank. The second detail is ironic because one would not expect someone to remember to eat well when a boat is sinking.)*

Q **Critical Thinking**

ANALYZING Point out that the narrator goes into great detail about the men's physical exhaustion. Ask them to compare this description with the captain's warning. What might this foreshadow about the ending of the story? *(The captain warns them that they will need all of their strength if they have to swim ashore, but the narrator has already said that they have little strength. This may suggest that the men will not survive.)*

R **Author's Craft**

IMAGERY Point out that writers often appeal to more than one sense when they describe a setting. Here, Crane appeals to both sight and sound in his description of the sea and the shore.

Teaching Options

The Open Boat

At last, from the top of each wave the men in the tossing boat could see land. Even as the lighthouse was an upright shadow on the sky, this land seemed but a long black shadow on the sea. It certainly was thinner than paper. "We must be about opposite New Smyrna,"[17] said the cook, who had coasted this shore often in schooners. "Captain, by the way, I believe they abandoned that lifesaving station there about a year ago."

"Did they?" said the captain.

The wind slowly died away. The cook and the correspondent were not now obliged to slave in order to hold high the oar. But the waves continued their old impetuous swooping at the dinghy, and the little craft, no longer under way, struggled woundily over them. The oiler or the correspondent took the oars again.

Shipwrecks are *apropos*[18] of nothing. If men could only train for them and have them occur when the men had reached pink condition, there would be less drowning at sea. Of the four in the dinghy none had slept any time worth mentioning for two days and two nights previous to embarking in the dinghy, and in the excitement of clambering about the deck of a foundering[19] ship they had also forgotten to eat heartily.

For these reasons, and for others, neither the oiler nor the correspondent was fond of rowing at this time. The correspondent wondered ingenuously how in the name of all that was sane could there be people who thought it amusing to row a boat. It was not an amusement; it was a diabolical punishment, and even a genius of mental aberrations could never conclude that it was anything but a

horror to the muscles and a crime against the back. He mentioned to the boat in general how the amusement of rowing struck him, and the weary-faced oiler smiled in full sympathy. Previously to the foundering, by the way, the oiler had worked doublewatch in the engine-room of the ship.

"Take her easy, now, boys," said the captain. "Don't spend yourselves. If we have to run a surf you'll need all your strength, because we'll sure have to swim for it. Take your time."

Slowly the land arose from the sea. From a black line it became a line of black and a line of white—trees and sand. Finally, the captain said that he could make out a house on the shore. "That's the house of refuge, sure," said the cook. "They'll see us before long, and come out after us."

The distant lighthouse reared high. "The keeper ought to be able to make us out now, if he's looking through a glass," said the captain. "He'll notify the lifesaving people."

"None of those other boats could have got ashore to give word of the wreck," said the oiler, in a low voice. "Else the lifeboat would be out hunting us."

Slowly and beautifully the land loomed out of the sea. The wind came again. It had veered from the northeast to the southeast. Finally, a new sound struck the ears of the men in the boat. It was the low thunder of the surf on the shore. "We'll never be able to make the lighthouse now," said the captain. "Swing her head a little more north, Billie."

"'A little more north,' sir," said the oiler.

Whereupon the little boat turned her nose once more down the wind, and all but the oarsman watched the shore grow. Under the influence of this expansion doubt and direful apprehension was leaving the minds of the men. The management of the boat was still most absorbing, but it could not prevent a

---

17. *New Smyrna* refers to the town of New Smyrna Beach, on the east coast of Florida.
18. *Apropos* means "relevant" or "pertinent."
19. *Foundering* means "sinking."

Vocabulary
ingenuously (in jen′ ū as lē) *adv.* honestly; frankly; candidly

Writing *Minilesson*

Using Descriptive Language Explain that good writers use precise words in their writing. Write the following sentence on the board: "The men in the boat were tired." Have students compare it to Crane's description: "Of the four in the dinghy none had slept any time worth mentioning for two days and two nights." Students should note Crane's use of specific details.

Activity Have students rewrite the following sentences to add precise details.
1. The boy was ill, so he missed the event.
2. The weather was bad when the women arrived.
3. The girl played rugby. **L2**

Additional Resources
Writer's Choice, Lesson 3.2

quiet cheerfulness. In an hour, perhaps, they would be ashore.

Their backbones had become thoroughly used to balancing in the boat and they now rode this wild colt of a dinghy like circus men. The correspondent thought that he had been drenched to the skin, but happening to feel in the top pocket of his coat, he found therein eight cigars. Four of them were soaked with sea-water; four were perfectly scatheless. After a search, somebody produced three dry matches, and thereupon the four waifs[20] rode impudently in their little boat, and with an assurance of an impending rescue shining in their eyes, puffed at the big cigars and judged well and ill of all men. Everybody took a drink of water.

IV

"Cook," remarked the captain, "there don't seem to be any signs of life about your house of refuge."

"No," replied the cook. "Funny they don't see us!"

A broad stretch of lowly coast lay before the eyes of the men. It was of dunes topped with dark vegetation. The roar of the surf was plain, and sometimes they could see the white lip of a wave as it spun up the beach. A tiny house was blocked out black upon the sky. Southward, the slim lighthouse lifted its little gray length.

Tide, wind, and waves were swinging the dinghy northward. "Funny they don't see us," said the men.

The surf's roar was here dulled, but its tone was, nevertheless, thunderous and mighty. As the boat swam over the great rollers, the men sat listening to this roar. "We'll swamp sure," said everybody.

It is fair to say here that there was not a lifesaving station within twenty miles in either

direction, but the men did not know this fact and in consequence they made dark and opprobrious[21] remarks concerning the eyesight of the nation's lifesavers. Four scowling men sat in the dinghy and surpassed records in the invention of epithets.[22]

"Funny they don't see us."

The light-heartedness of a former time had completely faded. To their sharpened minds it was easy to conjure pictures of all kinds of incompetency and blindness and, indeed, cowardice. There was the shore of the populous land, and it was bitter and bitter to them that from it came no sign.

"Well," said the captain, ultimately, "I suppose we'll have to make a try for ourselves. If we stay out here too long, we'll none of us have strength left to swim after the boat swamps."

And so the oiler, who was at the oars, turned the boat straight for the shore. There was a sudden tightening of muscles. There was some thinking.

"If we don't all get ashore—" said the captain. "If we don't all get ashore, I suppose you fellows know where to send news of my finish?"

They then briefly exchanged some addresses and admonitions.[23] As for the reflections of the men, there was a great deal of rage in them. Perchance they might be formulated thus: "If I am going to be drowned—if I am going to be drowned—if I am going to be drowned, why, in the name of the seven mad gods who rule the sea,[24] was I allowed to come thus far and contemplate sand and trees? Was I brought here merely to have my nose dragged away as I was about to nibble the sacred cheese of life? It is

21. *Opprobrious* (ə prō′ brē əs) means "derogatory."
22. *Epithets* are descriptive, sometimes abusive, words or phrases used with or in place of a name.
23. *Admonitions* are warnings or advice.
24. [*seven . . . the sea*] This description probably refers to the seven major seas, each at the mercy of a deity.

20. *Waifs* are persons having no apparent home.

Vocabulary
impudently (im′ pyə dənt lē) *adv.* in an offensively bold manner; arrogantly

565

Literary Elements

W Literary Elements

CONFLICT Point out that the man threatens fate, or nature, by shaking his fists to the clouds. Ask students how nature "responds" to this threat in the next paragraph. *(The waves become so "formidable," or powerful, that the men are forced back to sea.)* Explain that nature has, at least temporarily, won the fight.

X Literary Elements

FORESHADOWING One of the men jokingly suggests that the lifesavers believe they are fishing. This joke foreshadows the reaction of the man on the shore, who does indeed believe that the men are fishermen.

VIEWING THE PAINTING

Albert Pinkham Ryder (1847–1917) was a mystic and a romantic. He was an imaginative, solitary American painter who is noted for his highly personal seascapes.

Viewing Response *The mood of the painting is serious and somewhat foreboding. The dark sea and the solitary boater suggest the same view of man against nature that Crane develops in his story.*

Teaching Options

preposterous. If this old ninny-woman, Fate,[25] cannot do better than this, she should be deprived of the management of men's fortunes. She is an old hen who knows not her intention. If she has decided to drown me, why did she not do it in the beginning and save me all this trouble. The whole affair is absurd. . . . But, no, she cannot mean to drown me. She dare not drown me. She cannot drown me. Not after all this work." Afterward the man might have had an impulse to shake his fist at the clouds. "Just you drown me, now, and then hear what I call you!"

The billows that came at this time were more formidable. They seemed always just about to break and roll over the little boat in a turmoil of foam. There was a preparatory and long growl in the speech of them. No mind unused to the sea would have concluded that the dinghy could ascend these sheer heights in time. The shore was still afar. The oiler was a wily[26] surfman. "Boys," he said, swiftly, "she won't live three minutes more and we're too far out to swim. Shall I take her to sea again, Captain?"

"Yes! Go ahead!" said the captain.

This oiler, by a series of quick miracles, and fast and steady oarsmanship, turned the boat

Moonlight, c. 1885. Albert Pinkham Ryder. Oil on canvas, 16 x 17¾ in. National Museum of American Art, Smithsonian Institution, Washington, DC.

Viewing the painting: In your opinion, what is the mood of this painting? How does this mood help convey the experience of the men during their night at sea?

in the middle of the surf and took her safely to sea again.

There was a considerable silence as the boat bumped over the furrowed sea to deeper water. Then somebody in gloom spoke. "Well, anyhow, they must have seen us from the shore by now."

The gulls went in slanting flight up the wind toward the gray desolate east. A squall,[27] marked by dingy clouds, and clouds brick-red, like smoke from a burning building, appeared from the southeast.

"What do you think of those lifesaving people? Ain't they peaches?"

"Funny they haven't seen us."

"Maybe they think we're out here for sport? Maybe they think we're fishin'. Maybe they think we're damned fools."

It was a long afternoon. A changed tide tried to force them southward, but wind and wave said northward. Far ahead, where coastline, sea, and sky formed their mighty angle, there were little dots which seemed to indicate a city on the shore.

"St. Augustine?"

The captain shook his head. "Too near Mosquito Inlet."

And the oiler rowed, and then the correspondent rowed. Then the oiler rowed. It was a weary business. The human back can become the seat of more aches and pains than

---

25. *Fate* implies a supernatural power guiding one to an inevitable end. In classical mythology, the three Fates were portrayed as old women.
26. *Wily* means "cunning" or "sly."

---

27. A *squall* is a short, sudden, strong windstorm, often accompanied by rain or snow.

Vocabulary
preposterous (pri pos′ tər əs) *adj.* absurd; ridiculous

MEETING INDIVIDUAL NEEDS **MULTIPLE LEARNING STYLES**

Logical and Mathematical Students strong in logical and mathematical thinking may enjoy finding analogies.

Activity Model reading an analogy: "Bird is to sky as <u>fish</u> is to lake." Explain that analogies pair words with similiar relationships. Have students complete the following analogies.

1. ingenuously : deceptively :: *(b)*
   a. honestly : frankly
   b. graciously : impolitely
   c. candid : genuinely
2. preposterous : absurd :: *(a)*
   a. genuine : authentic
   b. pious : disrespectful
   c. deep : shallow
3. arrogant : impudently :: *(c)*
   a. foolish : absurd
   b. impious : respectfully
   c. honest : truthfully **L3**

are registered in books for the composite anatomy of a regiment. It is a limited area, but it can become the theater of innumerable muscular conflicts, tangles, wrenches, knots, and other comforts.

Y "Did you ever like to row, Billie?" asked the correspondent.

"No," said the oiler. "Hang it."

When one exchanged the rowing-seat for a place in the bottom of the boat, he suffered a bodily depression that caused him to be careless of everything save an obligation to wiggle one finger. There was cold seawater swashing to and fro in the boat, and he lay in it. His head, pillowed on a thwart, was within an inch of the swirl of a wave crest, and sometimes a particularly obstreperous[28] sea came inboard and drenched him once more. But these matters did not annoy him. It is almost certain that if the boat had capsized he would have tumbled comfortably out upon the ocean as if he felt sure that it was a great soft mattress.

Z "Look! There's a man on the shore!"

"Where?"

"There! See 'im? See 'im?"

"Yes, sure! He's walking along."

"Now he's stopped. Look! He's facing us!"

"He's waving at us!"

AA "So he is! By thunder!"

"Ah, now, we're all right! Now we're all right! There'll be a boat out here for us in half an hour."

"He's going on. He's running. He's going up to that house there."

The remote beach seemed lower than the sea, and it required a searching glance to discern the little black figure. The captain saw a floating stick and they rowed to it. A bath-towel was by some weird chance in the boat, and, tying this on the stick, the captain waved it. The oarsman did not dare turn his head, so he was obliged to ask questions.

---

28. *Obstreperous* (əb strep′ ər əs) means "unruly."

"What's he doing now?"

"He's standing still again. He's looking, I think. . . . There he goes again. Toward the house. . . . Now he's stopped again."

"Is he waving at us?"

"No, not now! he was, though."

"Look! There comes another man!"

"He's running."

"Look at him go, would you."

"Why, he's on a bicycle. Now he's met the other man. They're both waving at us. Look!"

"There comes something up the beach."

"What the devil is that thing?"

"Why, it looks like a boat."

"Why, certainly it's a boat."

"No, it's on wheels."

"Yes, so it is. Well, that must be the lifeboat. They drag them along shore on a wagon."

"That's the lifeboat, sure."

"No, by——, it's—it's an omnibus."[29]

"I tell you it's a lifeboat."

BB "It is not! It's an omnibus. I can see it plain. See? One of those big hotel omnibuses."

"By thunder, you're right. It's an omnibus, sure as fate. What do you suppose they are doing with an omnibus? Maybe they are going around collecting the lifecrew, hey?"

"That's it, likely. Look! There's a fellow waving a little black flag. He's standing on the steps of the omnibus. There come those other two fellows. Now they're all talking together. Look at the fellow with the flag. Maybe he ain't waving it!"

"That ain't a flag, is it? That's his coat. Why, certainly, that's his coat."

"So it is. It's his coat. He's taken it off and is waving it around his head. But would you look at him swing it!"

"Oh, say, there isn't any lifesaving station there. That's just a winter resort hotel omnibus that has brought over some of the boarders to see us drown."

---

29. An *omnibus*, or bus, would have been pulled by horses during this time period.

Y **Author's Craft**

HUMOR Crane uses touches of humor to lighten the tone of this story. The correspondent, for example, refers frequently to his disbelief that people row as a hobby.

Z **Literary Elements**

PLOT When the men see the man ashore, they have renewed belief that they will be rescued. This belief builds the dramatic tension and leads to rising action.

AA **Author's Craft**

DIALOGUE Point out Crane's use of dialogue to relate the events that happen next. This technique is particularly effective because the reader realizes what is occurring at the same time the men do. Thus, the reader is able to feel their sense of disbelief when the man waves his flag at them. Their increasing sense of disbelief and fear builds dramatic tension and suspense, as the reader awaits the plot's outcome.

BB **Literary Elements**

IRONY Ask students to discuss how the situation here is an example of situational irony. *(The men expect that the people on shore will call for help, but instead they simply wave and smile.)* The people on shore are tragically unaware of the men's desperate situation. Explain that this incident expresses the naturalists' belief that people are incapable of overcoming the forces of nature.

MEETING INDIVIDUAL NEEDS **MULTIPLE LEARNING STYLES**

Spatial Students with acute spatial abilities may enjoy drawing a picture of the scene in which the people on shore smile and wave at the four men in the dinghy. Explain that despite the seriousness of the situation, there is an element of humor in the scene.

Activity Have students draw a sketch of this scene. Remind them to reread

the scene, using the men's dialogue as a guide for depicting their facial expressions and gestures. Ask volunteers to share their sketches with the class. **L2**

Active Reading

QUESTION Point out that Crane does not always indicate which of the four men is speaking. Ask students to consider why he might do this. *(He may want to indicate that all of the men experienced similar periods of surprise, shock, and anger. He may also wish to emphasize their feelings of confusion, exhaustion, and disorientation.)*

Literary Elements

PLOT After a brief period of hope, the men must return to their former, monotonous duty—rowing.

Literary Elements

METAPHOR In this metaphor, which compares man's quest for survival to nibbling "the sacred cheese of life," humans are compared to mice. Naturalists believe that people are as small and insignificant as mice when compared to the powerful forces of nature.

The Open Boat

"What's that idiot with the coat mean? What's he signaling, anyhow?"

"It looks as if he were trying to tell us to go north. There must be a lifesaving station up there."

"No! He thinks we're fishing. Just giving us a merry hand. See? Ah, there, Willie."

"Well, I wish I could make something out of those signals. What do you suppose he means?"

"He don't mean anything. He's just playing."

"Well, if he'd just signal us to try the surf again, or to go to sea and wait, or go north, or go south, or go to hell—there would be some reason in it. But look at him. He just stands there and keeps his coat revolving like a wheel. The ass!"

"There come more people."

"Now there's quite a mob. Look! Isn't that a boat?"

"Where? Oh, I see where you mean. No, that's no boat."

"That fellow is still waving his coat."

"He must think we like to see him do that. Why don't he quit it. It don't mean anything."

"I don't know. I think he is trying to make us go north. It must be that there's a lifesaving station there somewhere."

"Say, he ain't tired yet. Look at 'im wave."

"Wonder how long he can keep that up. He's been revolving his coat ever since he caught sight of us. He's an idiot. Why aren't they getting men to bring a boat out. A fishing boat—one of those big yawls[30]—could come out here all right. Why don't he do something?"

"Oh, it's all right, now."

"They'll have a boat out here for us in less than no time, now that they've seen us."

A faint yellow tone came into the sky over the low land. The shadows on the sea slowly deepened. The wind bore coldness with it, and the men began to shiver.

"Holy smoke!" said one, allowing his voice to express his impious mood, "if we keep on monkeying out here! If we've got to flounder out here all night!"

"Oh, we'll never have to stay here all night! Don't you worry. They've seen us now, and it won't be long before they'll come chasing out after us."

The shore grew dusky. The man waving a coat blended gradually into this gloom, and it swallowed in the same manner the omnibus and the group of people. The spray, when it dashed uproariously over the side, made the voyagers shrink and swear like men who were being branded.

"I'd like to catch the chump who waved the coat. I feel like soaking him one, just for luck."

"Why? What did he do?"

"Oh, nothing, but then he seemed so damned cheerful."

In the meantime the oiler rowed, and then the correspondent rowed, and then the oiler rowed. Gray-faced and bowed forward, they mechanically, turn by turn, plied the leaden oars. The form of the lighthouse had vanished from the southern horizon, but finally a pale star appeared, just lifting from the sea. The streaked saffron[31] in the west passed before the all-merging darkness, and the sea to the east was black. The land had vanished, and was expressed only by the low and drear thunder of the surf.

"If I am going to be drowned—if I am going to be drowned—if I am going to be drowned, why, in the name of the seven mad gods who rule the sea, was I allowed to come thus far and contemplate sand and trees? Was I brought here merely to have my nose dragged away as I was about to nibble the sacred cheese of life?"

---

30. A *yawl* is a sailboat with two masts, the large mast near the front of the boat and the smaller one near the back.

31. Here, *saffron* means "yellow-orange in color."

Vocabulary
impious (im′ pē əs) *adj.* lacking in reverence; disrespectful

---

MULTIPLE LEARNING STYLES

Musical Students with musical abilities respond well to activities that incorporate music. Tell students that people have always told stories; in England and Scotland, people sometimes told stories as ballads, which they often sang. Ballads use dialogue to present action, recounting tales of love, adventure, courageous feats and sudden disasters. You may give students examples of ballads such as "Sir Patrick Spens" and "The Wreck of the Edmund Fitzgerald."

Activity Have students compose their own ballads about the adventures of these four men. Students may either set their ballads to a favorite tune or compose their own. Ask volunteers to share their ballads with the class. **L3**

The patient captain, drooped over the water jar, was sometimes obliged to speak to the oarsman.

"Keep her head up! Keep her head up!"

"'Keep her head up,' sir." The voices were weary and low.

This was surely a quiet evening. All save the oarsman lay heavily and listlessly in the boat's bottom. As for him, his eyes were just capable of noting the tall black waves that swept forward in a most sinister silence, save for an occasional subdued growl of a crest.

The cook's head was on a thwart, and he looked without interest at the water under his nose. He was deep in other scenes. Finally he spoke. "Billie," he murmured, dreamfully, "what kind of pie do you like best?"

V

"Pie," said the oiler and the correspondent, agitatedly. "Don't talk about those things, blast you!"

"Well," said the cook, "I was just thinking about ham sandwiches, and—"

A night on the sea in an open boat is a long night. As darkness settled finally, the shine of the light, lifting from the sea in the south, changed to full gold. On the northern horizon a new light appeared, a small bluish gleam on the edge of the waters. These two lights were the furniture of the world. Otherwise there was nothing but waves.

Two men huddled in the stern, and distances were so magnificent in the dinghy that the rower was enabled to keep his feet partly warmed by thrusting them under his companions. Their legs indeed extended far under the rowing seat until they touched the feet of the captain forward. Sometimes, despite the efforts of the tired oarsman, a wave came piling into the boat, an icy wave of the night, and the chilling water soaked them anew. They would twist their bodies for a moment and groan, and sleep the dead sleep once more, while the water in the boat gurgled about them as the craft rocked.

The plan of the oiler and the correspondent was for one to row until he lost the ability, and then arouse the other from his sea-water couch in the bottom of the boat.

The oiler plied the oars until his head drooped forward, and the overpowering sleep blinded him. And he rowed yet afterward. Then he touched a man in the bottom of the boat, and called his name. "Will you spell me for a little while?" he said, meekly.

"Sure, Billie," said the correspondent, awakening and dragging himself to a sitting position. They exchanged places carefully, and the oiler, cuddling down in the seawater at the cook's side, seemed to go to sleep instantly.

The particular violence of the sea had ceased. The waves came without snarling. The obligation of the man at the oars was to keep the boat headed so that the tilt of the rollers would not capsize her, and to preserve her from filling when the crests rushed past. The black waves were silent and hard to be seen in the darkness. Often one was almost upon the boat before the oarsman was aware.

In a low voice the correspondent addressed the captain. He was not sure that the captain was awake, although this iron man seemed to be always awake. "Captain, shall I keep her making for that light north, sir?"

The same steady voice answered him. "Yes. Keep it about two points off the port bow."[32]

The cook had tied a life belt around himself in order to get even the warmth which this clumsy cork contrivance could donate, and he seemed almost stove-like when a rower, whose teeth invariably chattered wildly as soon as he ceased his labor, dropped down to sleep.

The correspondent, as he rowed, looked down at the two men sleeping under foot. The cook's arm was around the oiler's shoulders, and, with their fragmentary clothing and haggard faces, they were the babes of the

---

32. The *bow* is the forward part of a boat or ship. The *port bow*, then, would be the left side of the forward part.

Active Reading

QUESTION Ask students why the cook might think about food at such a time. *(The cook can temporarily escape his feelings of fear and hunger by thinking about food, which he obviously loves.)*

Literary Elements

SETTING This description of the golden lights on the ocean creates a beautiful scene. This tranquil setting provides a sharp contrast to the anxiety and discomfort experienced by the men in the boat.

Literary Elements

PLOT The men's ability to sleep under such terrible conditions indicates their great exhaustion.

Literary Elements

CHARACTER Point out that the oiler's will to survive is greater than his fatigue. The oiler's determination makes his death in the final stages of the journey even more tragic.

ENGLISH LANGUAGE LEARNERS

Summarizing and Predicting English language learners may find the action in part 4 difficult because of the dialogue.

Activity Pair English language learners with fluent English speakers and have them answer the following questions about part 4: What do the men see on the shore? What happens? Why are the men not rescued? How do the men react to what happens?

Suggest that partners take turns reading part 4, stopping to discuss any confusing passages. Will the men be rescued? Ask students to read further to verify their predictions. **COLLAB. LEARN.**

Additional Resources
📁 *English Language Learners Sourcebook*

Literary Elements

SETTING The sad voice of the wind reflects the men's own sadness. Point out that the men's mood is often reflected in the setting. At this point in the story, as the men begin to lose hope, the setting becomes still and calm.

Critical Thinking

DRAWING CONCLUSIONS Challenge students to draw conclusions by having them answer the following questions: What is this "thing" the correspondent sees? What details does he give that support your response? (*It is a shark—he describes its dark fin, its speed and power, and the horror a picnicker would have upon seeing it.*) Then ask students to consider why he might have had a different reaction to the shark had he been a picnicker. (*Students may note that in his current situation, he has many fears and that he has become used to danger. If he were a picnicker, he would not expect to encounter such a dangerous creature.*)

Literary Elements

NATURALISM Although the man feels it would be "unnatural" to die at such a time, he begins to realize that "nature does not regard him as important." After battling nature for so long, he is finally aware of its power and indifference.

Teaching Options

---

sea, a grotesque rendering of the old babes in the wood.

Later he must have grown stupid at his work, for suddenly there was a growling of water, and a crest came with a roar and a swash into the boat, and it was a wonder that it did not set the cook afloat in his life belt. The cook continued to sleep, but the oiler sat up, blinking his eyes and shaking with the new cold.

"Oh, I'm awful sorry, Billie," said the correspondent, contritely.

"That's all right, old boy," said the oiler, and lay down again and was asleep.

Presently it seemed that even the captain dozed, and the correspondent thought that he was the one man afloat on all the oceans. The wind had a voice as it came over the waves, and it was sadder than the end.

There was a long, loud swishing astern of the boat, and a gleaming trail of phosphorescence, like blue flame, was furrowed on the black waters. It might have been made by a monstrous knife.

Then there came a stillness, while the correspondent breathed with the open mouth and looked at the sea.

Suddenly there was another swish and another long flash of bluish light, and this time it was alongside the boat, and might almost have been reached with an oar. The correspondent saw an enormous fin speed like a shadow through the water, hurling the crystalline spray and leaving the long glowing trail.

The correspondent looked over his shoulder at the captain. His face was hidden, and he seemed to be asleep. He looked at the babes of the sea. They certainly were asleep. So, being bereft[33] of sympathy, he leaned a little way to one side and swore softly into the sea.

But the thing did not then leave the vicinity of the boat. Ahead or astern, on one side or the other, at intervals long or short, fled the long sparkling streak, and there was to be

---

33. *Bereft* means "lacking something needed."

---

heard the whiroo of the dark fin. The speed and power of the thing was greatly to be admired. It cut the water like a gigantic and keen projectile.

The presence of this biding thing did not affect the man with the same horror that it would if he had been a picnicker. He simply looked at the sea dully and swore in an undertone.

Nevertheless, it is true that he did not wish to be alone with the thing. He wished one of his companions to awaken by chance and keep him company with it. But the captain hung motionless over the water jar and the oiler and the cook in the bottom of the boat were plunged in slumber.

VI

"If I am going to be drowned—if I am going to be drowned—if I am going to be drowned, why, in the name of the seven mad gods who rule the sea, was I allowed to come thus far and contemplate sand and trees?"

During this dismal night, it may be remarked that a man would conclude that it was really the intention of the seven mad gods to drown him, despite the abominable injustice of it. For it was certainly an abominable injustice to drown a man who had worked so hard, so hard. The man felt it would be a crime most unnatural. Other people had drowned at sea since galleys[34] swarmed with painted sails, but still—

When it occurs to a man that nature does not regard him as important, and that she feels she would not maim the universe by disposing of him, he at first wishes to throw bricks at the temple, and he hates deeply the fact that there are no bricks and no temples. Any visible expression of nature would surely be pelleted with his jeers.

Then, if there be no tangible thing to hoot he feels, perhaps, the desire to confront a personification and indulge in pleas, bowed

---

34. A *galley* is a medieval ship propelled by sails and a row (or rows) of oars on either side.

INCLUSION STRATEGIES

Learning Disabled Students with learning disabilities may have difficulty with passages that do not contain much action. Part 6, for example, focuses on the correspondent's feelings.

Activity Before students read part 6, ask them if they have ever felt a connection to a character in a book, movie, or television show. What did they have in common with this character? Explain that in part 6, the correspondent will be reminded of a character he read about in school. As they read part 6, have students write down what the correspondent and the character have in common. Meet with students to discuss their responses. **L1**

Additional Resources
📁 *Inclusion Strategies*

to one knee, and with hands supplicant, saying: "Yes, but I love myself."

A high cold star on a winter's night is the word he feels that she says to him. Thereafter he knows the pathos[35] of his situation.

The men in the dinghy had not discussed these matters, but each had, no doubt, reflected upon them in silence and according to his mind. There was seldom any expression upon their faces save the general one of complete weariness. Speech was devoted to the business of the boat.

To chime the notes of his emotion, a verse mysteriously entered the correspondent's head. He had even forgotten that he had forgotten this verse, but it suddenly was in his mind.

A soldier of the Legion[36] lay dying in Algiers,[37]
There was lack of woman's nursing, there was dearth of woman's tears;
But a comrade stood beside him, and he took that comrade's hand,
And he said: "I never more shall see my own, my native land."[38]

In his childhood, the correspondent had been made acquainted with the fact that a soldier of the Legion lay dying in Algiers, but he had never regarded it as important. Myriads of his schoolfellows had informed him of the soldier's plight, but the dinning[39] had naturally ended by making him perfectly indifferent. He had never considered it his affair that a soldier of the Legion lay dying in Algiers, nor had it appeared to him as a matter for sorrow. It was less to him than the breaking of a pencil's point.

Now, however, it quaintly came to him as a human, living thing. It was no longer merely a picture of a few throes[40] in the breast of a poet, meanwhile drinking tea and warming his feet at the grate; it was an actuality—stern, mournful, and fine.

The correspondent plainly saw the soldier. He lay on the sand with his feet out straight and still. While his pale left hand was upon his chest in an attempt to thwart the going of his life, the blood came between his fingers. In the far Algerian distance, a city of low square forms was set against a sky that was faint with the last sunset hues. The correspondent, plying the oars and dreaming of the slow and slower movements of the lips of the soldier, was moved by a profound and perfectly impersonal comprehension. He was sorry for the soldier of the Legion who lay dying in Algiers.

The thing which had followed the boat and waited had evidently grown bored at the delay. There was no longer to be heard the slash of the cut water, and there was no longer the flame of the long trail. The light in the north still glimmered, but it was apparently no nearer to the boat. Sometimes the boom of the surf rang in the correspondent's ears, and he turned the craft seaward then and rowed harder. Southward, some one had evidently built a watch fire on the beach. It was too low and too far to be seen, but it made a shimmering, roseate reflection upon the bluff back of it, and this could be discerned from the boat. The wind came stronger, and sometimes a wave suddenly raged out like a mountain cat and there was to be seen the sheen and sparkle of a broken crest.

The captain, in the bow, moved on his water jar and sat erect. "Pretty long night," he observed to the correspondent. He looked at the shore. "Those lifesaving people take their time."

"Did you see that shark playing around?"

---

35. *Pathos* means "deep sadness."
36. *Legion* refers to the French Foreign Legion, an army composed mainly of foreign volunteers.
37. *Algiers* (al jērz′) is the capital of Algeria, a country in northern Africa that was once ruled by France.
38. This verse compresses the first stanza of "Bingen on the Rhine" by English poet Caroline E. S. Norton (1808–1877).
39. *Dinning* means "insistent repetition."
40. *Throes* are pains.

571

MM **Literary Elements**

SYMBOL Point out that the star, which is "high" and "cold," symbolizes the aloofness and indifference of nature. Ask students to recall other aspects of nature that Crane uses to symbolize aloofness and indifference. (*Students may mention the gulls and the waves.*)

FYI

Misquoting You may want to point out that Crane has misquoted Norton's poem, cutting about 20 words from it. Critics have argued over whether Crane omitted the lines on purpose or whether he simply forgot them. He may have omitted them to show that the poem meant so little to the correspondent in his youth that he has only a vague recollection of it.

NN **Critical Thinking**

MAKING CRITICAL JUDGMENTS Ask students why this poem may mean more to the correspondent now than it did in his youth. (*The correspondent is now able to empathize with the soldier—he, too, fears that he will never again see his home, and he, too, relies on his "comrades" for support and companionship.*)

MULTIPLE LEARNING STYLES

Linguistic Students with strong linguistic skills excel at activities that ask them to respond to material through writing.

Activity Have students write a letter to a movie director, convincing him or her to make a movie based on "The Open Boat." Tell students that they must assume the director has not read the story, so their letters should include a brief summary of the plot. Remind them that people in the movie industry receive hundreds of script ideas, so their letters should include an introduction that will capture the director's attention. Students may describe one particularly exciting scene or give a brief synopsis of their ideas for the movie. They may also want to suggest actors who could play the roles of the captain, the cook, the oiler, and the correspondent. **L2**

00 Critical Thinking

INFERRING Remind students that the captain has injured his arm and cannot row. Why, then, might the correspondent have wished he had known the captain was awake? *(The correspondent probably just wanted to be comforted—the four men now have such good rapport with each other that they can comfort each other even though they are all equally incapable of doing anything about their condition.)*

PP Literary Elements

PLOT Explain that as the day breaks and the shore once again comes into view, the men have another chance for survival. This indicates the beginning of the rising action.

VIEWING THE PAINTING

This painting depicts an impressionist view of the moon and portrays the unfocused effect of light filtering through the night sky.

Viewing Response *This scene might have made the men think about the isolated quality of their circumstances and about their inability to clearly see their future.*

The Open Boat

"Yes, I saw him. He was a big fellow, all right."

"Wish I had known you were awake."

Later the correspondent spoke into the bottom of the boat.

"Billie!" There was a slow and gradual disentanglement. "Billie, will you spell me?"

"Sure," said the oiler.

As soon as the correspondent touched the cold comfortable seawater in the bottom of the boat, and had huddled close to the cook's life belt he was deep in sleep, despite the fact that his teeth played all the popular airs. This sleep was so good to him that it was but a moment before he heard a voice call his name in a tone that demonstrated the last stages of exhaustion. "Will you spell me?"

"Sure, Billie."

The light in the north had mysteriously vanished, but the correspondent took his course from the wide-awake captain.

Later in the night they took the boat farther out to sea, and the captain directed the cook to take one oar at the stern and keep the boat facing the seas. He was to call out if he should hear the thunder of the surf. This plan enabled the oiler and the correspondent to get respite together. "We'll give those boys a chance to get into shape again," said the captain. They curled down and, after a few preliminary chatterings and trembles, slept once more the dead sleep. Neither knew they had bequeathed to the

Veiled Moon, 1995. Jane Wilson. Oil on linen, 18 x 18 in. Fischbach Gallery, New York.

Viewing the painting: Imagine the men on the boat viewing this scene. What might the scene make them think about? Explain.

cook the company of another shark, or perhaps the same shark.

As the boat caroused on the waves, spray occasionally bumped over the side and gave them a fresh soaking, but this had no power to break their repose. The ominous slash of the wind and the water affected them as it would have affected mummies.

"Boys," said the cook, with the notes of every reluctance in his voice, "she's drifted in pretty close. I guess one of you had better take her to sea again." The correspondent, aroused, heard the crash of the toppled crests.

As he was rowing, the captain gave him some whiskey and water, and this steadied the chills out of him. "If I ever get ashore and anybody shows me even a photograph of an oar—"

At last there was a short conversation.

"Billie . . . Billie, will you spell me?"

"Sure," said the oiler.

VII

When the correspondent again opened his eyes, the sea and the sky were each of the gray hue of the dawning. Later, carmine and gold was painted upon the waters. The morning appeared finally, in its splendor, with a sky of pure blue, and the sunlight flamed on the tips of the waves.

On the distant dunes were set many little black cottages, and a tall white windmill reared above them. No man, nor dog, nor bicycle

PP

INTERDISCIPLINARY CONNECTION

Art Impressionist artists, like naturalists, wanted to convey their impressions of nature. They painted with tiny brush strokes, breaking light into its many colors, as the human eye does when it looks at natural scenes.

Activity Have students find out more about the impressionists. Suggest that they present their findings in the form of a pamphlet, a brochure, or a brief oral presentation. Some questions for study

include: Where and when did the impressionists paint? Which artists were impressionists? Where did the name "Impressionist" come from? Have students research two Impressionist painters and make photocopies of these paintings to include in their reports. **L3**

Theme 8:
THE HARLEM RENAISSANCE → **UNIT WRAP-UP**

SELECTIONS

My City (p. 718)

Media Connection: Magazine Article—A Place To Be Free (p. 722)

from Dust Tracks on a Road (p. 723)

If We Must Die (p. 733)

The Tropics in New York (p. 733)

Media Connection: Radio Transcript Artist Jacob Lawrence (p. 737)

I, Too (p. 738)

The Negro Speaks of Rivers (p. 738)

from Songs for Signare (p. 744)

Sonnet to a Negro in Harlem (p. 748)

Storm Ending (p. 752)

November Cotton Flower (p. 752)

A black man talks of reaping (p. 756)

Any Human to Another (p. 756)

SKILL FEATURES

Writing Skills (p. 732)

Interdisciplinary Connection (p. 751)

WRITING WORKSHOP

Creative Writing: Poem (pp. 762–765)

- **Personal Response, Analyzing Literature, Evaluate and Set Goals** (p. 766)
- **Build Your Portfolio** (p. 766)
- **Reading on Your Own** (p. 767)

  Their Eyes Were Watching God by Zora Neale Hurston

  The Great Gatsby by F. Scott Fitzgerald

  Having Our Say: The Delaney Sisters' First 100 Years by Sarah and A. Elizabeth Delaney

  Collected Poems by Edna St. Vincent Millay; Norma Millay, editor

- **Standardized Test Practice** (pp. 768–769)

KEYS TO TEACHING OPTIONS

Block Scheduling

Activities that are particularly suited to use within a block scheduling framework are identified throughout this unit by the following designation: 🔳. For detailed suggestions on block scheduling, see the **Block Scheduling Guide** for this grade level.

Key to Ability Levels

The Teaching Options throughout this unit have been coded for students of various abilities.

L1 BASIC activities for all students

L2 AVERAGE activities for average to above-average students

L3 CHALLENGING activities for above-average students

Reading Skills in this unit

Variety of Texts

This unit includes the following text types, which reflect the different literary perspectives of early twentieth century American writers.

- poetry
- short story
- lyric poetry
- autobiography
- newspaper article
- magazine article
- radio transcript

Comprehension Skills

The following instructional support for comprehension skills appears in this unit of the Student Edition:

- Active Reading Strategies and Model (pp. 4–35)
- Identifying the Author's Purpose (p. 611)

See also the **Reading Minilessons** throughout the unit in this Teacher's Wraparound Edition.

Reading Resources

Comprehension Skills Resources

📁 **Active Reading Guides**

The Active Reading Guide provides graphic organizers and study guide questions to support students' reading of each selection. (**Active Reading Guide**, pp. 66–91)

📁 **Reading Workbook**

The Reading Workbook (pp. 59–70) includes additional instruction and reinforcement of reading strategies and skills.

🎧 **Audio Library**

Available both on tape and on CD, the Audio Library provides valuable comprehension support.

Resources for Reading Widely

 Glencoe Literature Library

Each title in the Glencoe Literature Library includes a full-length novel or play plus related readings. A separate Study Guide is available for each title.

💿 **Literature Classics CD-ROM**

The 900 selections on this CD-ROM can be searched by author, theme, or genre.

 *in*TIME

A coproduction of Glencoe and Time Inc., *inTime* includes a wealth of high-interest nonfiction related to the selections and themes in Unit Five.

✓ Assessment in this unit

Assessment Options in the Student Edition

Glencoe Literature offers a number of diverse ways to evaluate student understanding and skill proficiency. In the Student Edition, use the following:

- **Responding to Literature**

  Following each selection, students are asked to recall facts, interpret ideas, and evaluate concepts as they answer a variety of questions and complete activities to extend their understanding.

- **Unit Wrap-Up (pp. 766–767)**

  Here students respond to the selections on personal and analytical levels. They also assume ownership of their learning by setting and evaluating goals and by selecting work for their portfolios.

See also the many **Assessment Resources** listed on the facing page.

Standardized Test Practice

The Princeton Review has developed the Standardized Test Practice pages found at the end of this unit (pp. 768–769). These pages contain practice test questions that help students remain familiar with standardized test formats and content. For practice, you may want to use the following resource:

- **College Entrance Exam Preparation and Practice Workbook**

Writing Skills in this unit

Writing Skills

The Student Edition of Unit Five offers strong instructional support for writing skills:

In **Extending Your Response**, which follows each selection:
- Writing About Literature
- Personal/Creative Writing

In **Writing Skills** Lessons:
- Creating Unified Paragraphs (p. 732)

See also the **Writing Minilessons** throughout the unit in this Teacher's Wraparound Edition.

Writing Workshops

Both themes in Unit Five conclude with a **Writing Workshop** that guides students through the writing process, focusing on the narrative mode of writing.
- Persuasive Writing: Editorial (pp. 712–716)
- Creative Writing: Poem (pp. 762–765)

Writing Resources

Writer's Assistant CD-ROM
Each Writing Workshop is supplemented by an interactive writing guide on the Writer's Assistant CD-ROM. This easy-to-use writing guide provides prompts, templates, and other tools that lead students through the writing process.

Writing and Proofreading Practice
Blackline masters present in-depth instruction and practice on a specific step in the writing process and proofreading. (pp. 53–66)

Writing and Proofreading Transparencies
Transparencies (15–16, 37–40) provide graphic organizers and proofreading exercises for whole class instruction.

Research and Report Writing Guide
This resource provides extensive tips and activities to guide students in their writing projects in the literature classroom as well as in classes across the curriculum.

Style and Documentation Sourcebook for Writers
This sourcebook is a combination reference and workbook, giving students the most up-to-date information and guidance regarding traditional as well as technological research strategies and documentation.

Grammar and Composition Handbook
The Grammar and Composition Handbook provides instruction that supplements activities in the student textbook.

Assessment Resources

Selection Quick Checks
For each selection, a Quick Check of three to five short-answer questions measures students' literal comprehension.

Selection and Theme Assessment
The Selection and Theme Assessment instrument tests students' abilities to recall, interpret, and evaluate what they've read. The tests consist of multiple-choice, short-answer, and essay questions.

Performance Assessment
Alternative assessment instruments and rubrics for Unit Five are found in the Performance Assessment ancillary.

Writing Assessment and Portfolio Management
These notes and strategies, student models, and assessment tools assist with the task of measuring students' progress as writers and as monitors of their own writing.

Testmaker
Teachers can customize selection, theme, and Unit Five tests by accessing the Testmaker database.

MindJogger Videoquizzes
Using a popular game show format, MindJogger Videoquizzes enable teachers to evaluate students' understanding of Unit Five in a quick and fun manner.

Unit Objectives

- To enjoy reading the poetry and prose of the period
- To analyze the literary elements in poetry and prose
- To apply strategies for reading poems and prose

VIEWING THE PAINTING

George Bellows (1882–1925) attended Ohio State University and then moved to New York City to study art. He is known for his broad and slashing brushstrokes and for his urban scenes, landscapes, seascapes, and portraits.

Responding to the Art Discussion questions:

- What words does the painting bring to mind? *(busy, chaotic, crowded, loud, alive, overwhelming, energetic)*
- Why does Bellows place the wagon in such a dominant position? *(The wagon suggests the energy of construction in the city, an idea reinforced by the wall of buildings.)*
- To what extent are people an important element? *(The people are dwarfed by the buildings in this bustling city and lose their individuality.)*

New York, 1911. George Bellows. Oil on canvas, 42 x 60 in. National Gallery of Art, Washington, DC. Collection of Mr. and Mrs. Paul Mellon.

586

TEACHER *to* TEACHER

NEWCOMER HIGH SCHOOL • SAN FRANCISCO, CALIFORNIA

Before we begin the unit, I have students brainstorm what they know about the twentieth century. We use the board for mapping. In the center of the board, I write a word that students connect to the twentieth century, such as *technology*. From that word, other words and thoughts come to mind, and I write these on the board. This process reveals what students already know about the century, from its history to its culture. As we study the literature, we break into groups and read to each other. Each group picks a selection, or part of a selection, and reports to the whole class. This can also be done as a panel, where one group presents questions to another.

Then students create a video—written, produced, and acted by them—that demonstrates their knowledge of the literature. The video can take a variety of forms—it might be a quiz show, a scripted panel discussion, or a scene from a selection.

NIMFA RODEHEAVER

UNIT FIVE

Beginnings
of the
Modern Age
1910–1930

"It was a long time ago.
I have almost forgotten my dream.
But it was there then,
In front of me,
Bright like a sun—
My dream."

—Langston Hughes, from "As I Grew Older"

Theme 7
New Directions
pages 597–716

Theme 8
The Harlem Renaissance
pages 717–765

Introducing the Unit

Have students read the quotation. Then pose these questions for discussion:
- Why do people turn to literature to express their dreams?
- Why is it important to read about others' dreams?
- How do people's dreams change as they grow older?

Theme 7: New Directions

The poems and short stories in Theme 7 demonstrate the new directions taken by writers and by society during the early years of the twentieth century, a period of rapid industrialization, advances in technology, urbanization, and social change. The selections in this theme reflect the new ways of viewing the world which developed during this dynamic time.

Theme 8: The Harlem Renaissance

In the 1920s, the art and literature of the African American community experienced a rush of new vitality and creativity. The selections in this theme highlight some of the best creations of this renaissance.

GLENCOE
TECHNOLOGY
LITERATURE CLASSICS
CD-ROM

Search for other selections related to the themes of New Directions and the Harlem Renaissance.

RESOURCE MANAGER

See the *Unit Five Planning Guide* (p. 1) for additional teaching notes, strategies, and resources for introducing the Beginnings of the Modern Age unit.

Setting the Scene

Setting the Scene

Introducing the Time Period

Ask students what events come to mind as they think about the United States during the period between 1910 and 1930. You may wish to pose these questions to begin the discussion: What was the most important international event of this period? What is the decade of the 1920s often called and why? What economic event signaled the end of this era? What population shifts took place during this period? What cultural changes took place?

Historical Note

The election of Woodrow Wilson was something of a surprise. He ran against two formidable opponents, former President Theodore Roosevelt and incumbent President William Howard Taft. Roosevelt and Taft divided the electorate, and Wilson was elected president with only a minority of the votes. Wilson's presidency marked a transition in American history. In 1910 there were 500,000 cars in America. By 1920 there were more than 8 million. Modern roads began snaking across America. Electricity spread into more and more homes. Skyscrapers were built. Industry expanded at an enormous rate. The speed and flurry of modern life was ushered in during this pivotal era.

A&E HOME VIDEO.® *The following videotape program is available from Glencoe. Be sure to preview the following video for appropriateness for your class.*

• **Biography: Henry Ford**

On March 3, 1913, a lanky, long-faced, scholarly man—Woodrow Wilson—arrived in Washington, D.C. Though he would be sworn in as President of the United States the following day, he arrived almost unnoticed. That same day, crowds flocked to a controversial march by women demanding the right to vote. As the women marched, supporters cheered and opponents yelled insults and jeered.

The next day, no competition drew attention from Wilson. A huge crowd of 50,000 people or more gathered to applaud his stirring inaugural address and his promise of a "New Freedom" for ordinary people. Women's right to vote, however, was not on his ambitious agenda, nor was the devastating world war that was to come. But these issues would come, and Wilson and the nation would face them.

U.S.A.

The National Urban League is formed to assist African Americans moving into cities

German submarines sink a British ship, the *Lusitania,* killing 1,198 people, including 128 Americans

1917 The United States declares war on Germany

1910

1915

1911 Japan takes over Korea

Mexican President Porfirio Diaz is ousted; Manchu dynasty is overthrown in China

1914 The Panama Canal opens

1915–16 Approximately one million Armenians die as Turkish troops force them from their land

1917 In Russia, a revolution overthrows the government of the Czar

World

Extra Credit Projects

• Ask students to review costume books, illustrations, and portraits of the time, selecting pictures of what the fashionable man and woman wore in 1910. Have them present their pictures to the class and discuss how the clothing reflects the spirit of the times. **L2**

• Have students investigate immigration and migration patterns between 1910 and 1930 by consulting reference books and the Internet. They should focus on both the number of immigrants from foreign countries and the migration of U.S. citizens from rural to urban areas. Have students present their findings and the implications raised by these findings to the class. **L2**

History of the Time

History of the Time

The New Freedom

"There is one great basic fact which underlies all the questions that are discussed on political platforms at the present moment," declared Woodrow Wilson in 1913. "That singular fact is that nothing is done in this country as it was done twenty years ago." New technology—the automobile, the radio, the movies, the telephone, and the airplane—opened up the world and bound the expansive nation together.

Wilson's election reflected a number of popular demands. Many people wanted the government to limit the power of huge business interests. Congress passed laws to protect the rights of consumers and lowered tariffs, or taxes, on imports into the United States. Imported products could better compete with the products of large U.S. corporations, reducing the profits of these corporations. In addition, state governments ratified constitutional amendments that granted women the right to vote.

At the same time, more Americans left rural areas for cities. By 1920, for the first time in the nation's history, city inhabitants outnumbered rural dwellers. Many African Americans left the rural South with hopes of greater freedom in northern cities.

War!

In August 1914, Europe burst into war. Great Britain, France, Japan, Belgium, Serbia, Russia, and Italy formed an alliance against Germany, Austria-Hungary, Turkey, and Bulgaria. In the Atlantic Ocean, German submarines torpedoed ships carrying supplies to Great Britain. As American passengers died on these ships, anti-German sentiment grew in the United States. In 1917, with Wilson declaring that "the world must be made safe for democracy," the United States formally entered the war against Germany.

In this war, tanks, artillery, machine guns, planes, and poison gas caused death and destruction on a scale previously unmatched. Finally, on November 11, 1918, the exhausted, bloodied opponents stopped fighting after Germany and its allies surrendered. About 115,000 Americans died in the war, but Europe lost a generation—nearly 10 million people.

The Roaring Twenties

Repulsed by the senseless slaughter of the war, Americans attempted to withdraw from the rest of the world. Politicians rejected Wilson's pleas to join the new League of Nations and approved severe immigration restrictions.

Many Americans expressed a desperate yet creative hysteria in new jazz rhythms, outrageous fashions, and wacky fads, and in obsessions with money, motorcars, and youth. On October 29, 1929, however, the excitement ended. The stock market crashed and countless investors lost all their savings. An extraordinary era had come to an end.

Timeline

┌ The Nineteenth Amendment gives women the right to vote; prohibition on the sale of alcohol begins

┌ 1921
Congress passes the first law sharply limiting European immigration

┌ 1924
Congress declares all Native Americans to be citizens of the United States

1929
The stock market crashes, marking the beginning of the Great Depression

1920 — **1925** — **1930**

└ The League of Nations meets for first time, in Geneva, Switzerland; Mohandas Gandhi starts a nonviolent movement against British rule in India

└ 1926
Economic turmoil leads to a general strike in Great Britain

└ 1928
Fifteen countries sign the Kellogg-Briand Pact, renouncing war

BEGINNINGS OF THE MODERN AGE 589

Historical Note

After World War I, Democratic President Wilson became a passionate advocate for the League of Nations, an organization whose purpose was to arbitrate international disputes. Because Republican senators refused to approve U.S. membership in the League, Wilson set out on a whirlwind speaking tour to gather support. After delivering a speech in Pueblo, Colorado, Wilson collapsed and was unable to finish his tour. During the last 15 months of his presidency, his poor health prevented him from fighting for the League. As a consequence, the Senate refused to sign the Treaty of Versailles, which would have committed the United States to the League of Nations.

Women Get the Vote

In 1920 the U.S. Congress adopted the Nineteenth Amendment, which granted women the right to vote. For Carrie Chapman Catt, a feminist leader, the amendment was the culmination of 25 years of work. Catt was so committed to this goal that before her marriage to George Catt in 1890, she demanded a prenuptial agreement guaranteeing that during four months each year she could devote herself to working for woman suffrage.

---

interNET CONNECTION

Influenza Although the carnage of World War I resulted in the deaths of more than 8,500,000 soldiers and the wounding of about 21,000,000, the influenza epidemic of 1918–1919 killed far more people than died in World War I. Have students search the Internet for statistical information about this worldwide scourge using such keywords as *influenza epidemic* or *Spanish influenza.*

At the MOVIES

Be sure to review this movie before deciding whether to show it to your class.

• *All Quiet on the Western Front,* an antiwar story about a German soldier, won an Oscar in 1930 for best picture.

Life of the Time

Life of the Time

People are talking about

Three Tragedies In 1911 a fire at New York City's Triangle Shirtwaist Company kills 146 people—most of them female workers—trapped behind locked doors. The next year the *Titanic*, a luxury ship on its first voyage, hits an iceberg and sinks. About 1,500 of its 2,200 passengers die. In 1918 a deadly influenza epidemic kills 500,000 in the United States, and an estimated 30 million people worldwide—about three times the number killed in World War I. ▶

Triangle Shirtwaist Company, destroyed by fire, 1911.

Freedom for All?
Congress continues to close the celebrated "open door" to America. Immigration restrictions in 1921 and 1924 target Asians and southern and eastern Europeans. Membership in the Ku Klux Klan surges past 4 million in 1924. The Klan directs hate and violence against African Americans, Jews, Roman Catholics, and union members.

Bessie Coleman

◀ **Wheels and Wings** By 1927 there are more than 20 million automobiles in the United States. In the air, stunt flyers become popular. In 1921 Bessie Coleman becomes the first licensed female African American pilot. In 1927 the country goes wild when Charles Lindbergh flies solo from New York to Paris in 33½ hours. Five years later, Amelia Earhart becomes the first woman to fly solo across the Atlantic Ocean.

Firsts

- Montana's Jeannette Rankin becomes the first woman elected to Congress. (1916)
- Gertrude Ederle becomes the first woman to swim the English Channel. (1926)
- Robert Goddard launches the first rocket powered by liquid fuel. (1926)
- Donald F. Duncan introduces the yo-yo, based on a traditional toy from East Asia. (1929)

Time Line

U.S.A.		1912 — Native American Jim Thorpe stars at the Olympic Games in Sweden	1914 — African American sculptor Meta Vaux Warrick Fuller completes *Ethiopia Awakening*		1918 — The United States goes on daylight saving time for the first time
1910	1911 — Norwegian explorer Roald Amundsen reaches the South Pole; Marie Curie wins the Nobel Prize for Chemistry		**1915**	1916 — German-born physicist Albert Einstein announces his general theory of relativity	1918 — A worldwide influenza epidemic kills an estimated 30 million people
World					

Cultural Note

In 1950 sportswriters and broadcasters named Jim (James Francis) Thorpe (1888–1953) America's best athlete of the century's first 50 years. Thorpe, born in Oklahoma of Fox and Sauk heritage, won the gold medal for the decathlon and pentathlon in the 1912 Olympic Games. From 1913 to 1919, he was an outfielder for National League baseball teams in New York, Boston, and Cincinnati. He starred as a professional football player from 1919 to 1926.

FYI

Car Culture Although in 1921 the United States still did not have numbered highways, more and more Americans were driving. By 1925 nearly 20 million cars traveled U.S. roads. Before World War I, almost no one borrowed money to pay for a car. By 1925, 75 percent of all cars were purchased on the installment plan.

📖 Active Reading

READING THE TIME LINE Ask students to speculate about the significance of the 1918 time line entry about influenza. *(Thirty million deaths is an enormous number. The fact that so many people died from influenza, an illness that is now easily treatable, demonstrates how modern medicine has advanced since 1918.)*

At the MOVIES

Be sure to review this movie before deciding whether to show it to your class.

- *Jim Thorpe—All American* Burt Lancaster plays the lead role in this 1951 black-and-white film about the sports great.

MEETING INDIVIDUAL NEEDS — MULTIPLE LEARNING STYLES

Mathematical In the language of mathematicians, the formula expressing Albert Einstein's theory of relativity is considered elegant; it is characterized by simplicity and precision. Many people recognize $E = mc^2$, but few understand its meaning or its implications.

Activity Have a small group of students who are interested in math or science investigate Einstein's theory of relativity and present an explanation to the class. They will want to produce graphics to help clarify the explanation. In addition to explaining the theory, ask them to discuss its past and present significance and its practical applications. **L3 COLLAB. LEARN.**

Food & Fashion

New inventions and international events change the way people eat:

- Toast becomes easier to make with the development of the electric toaster in 1909—and easier still with the automatic toaster a few years later. ▶

- Anti-German sentiment is so powerful during World War I that sauerkraut is now called "liberty cabbage."

- In 1924 a typical family spends thirty-eight percent of its income on food, nearly three times what an American family spends today.

Fashions change dramatically in the 1920s:

- Fashionable young women wear shorter and shorter skirts, which finally skim the knee.

- Short "bobbed" hair shocks some people, who also watch in horror as women paint their lips and rouge their cheeks.

- ◀ Many of these fashion elements come together in the "flapper," a symbol of the new woman of the twenties. In reality, few women are "flappers."

- Men's clothes become more informal and more colorful.

Arts & Entertainment

- Many African Americans migrating from the South settle in New York's Harlem. By the mid-1920s, African American writers, artists, and musicians usher in the Harlem Renaissance.

- The rhythms of jazz come north from the African American clubs of New Orleans, spread by masters such as Louis Armstrong, Jelly Roll Morton, Duke Ellington, and Bessie Smith. The music gives the Jazz Age its name and influences composers such as George Gershwin and Aaron Copland.

Amusements

- "The Sultan of Swat," Babe Ruth, hits sixty home runs in 1927, setting a record that will last thirty-four years.

- Movies become the most popular form of entertainment. In 1930 weekly admissions totals reach ninety million.

Timeline:

1920
- The population of the United States reaches 106 million
- An earthquake in northwest China kills nearly 200,000 people

1924
- Duke Ellington and the Washingtonians make their first recording

1925
- Chamonix, France, hosts the first Winter Olympics; anthropologists find the fossils of an ancient hominid, *Australopithecus,* in southern Africa

1927
- *The Jazz Singer* is the first talking motion picture

1928
- Walt Disney's Mickey Mouse makes his first appearance in *Steamboat Willie*

1930
- The world population approaches 2 billion

BEGINNINGS OF THE MODERN AGE 591

Pop Culture

Mind Your Manners Emily Post (1872–1960) first tried her hand at writing fiction, publishing books such as *The Flight of the Moth*. Real success, however, came with the publication of *Etiquette*, which was originally titled *Etiquette in Society, in Business, in Politics, and at Home*. It was later rechristened *Etiquette: The Blue Book of Social Usage*. The book was hugely successful, with more than 90 printings. The work established Post as the final authority on socially acceptable behavior. She became a nationally syndicated columnist and radio program host. *Etiquette* was followed by *How to Behave Though a Debutante, The Personality of a House, Children Are People,* and *Motor Manners*.

Cultural Note

In 1925 Harold Ross founded the *New Yorker*, a sophisticated, liberal weekly magazine that initially focused on New York City's social and cultural life. Over time it has become renowned for its short fiction, essays, foreign reportage, profiles, and cartoons.

Literature of the Time

PEOPLE ARE READING . . .

War Propaganda When the United States goes to war in 1917, the government's Committee on Public Information blankets the country with 75 million leaflets, pamphlets, and posters aimed at recruiting soldiers and explaining President Wilson's war aims to the people. ▶

About Manners The loosening of conventions after World War I leaves people confused about proper behavior. Their search for guidance makes Emily Post's 1922 book, *Etiquette*, a best-seller. Post remains America's chief arbiter of manners for more than three decades.

Magazines, Magazines, Magazines New magazines reflect the changing times. In the *American Mercury*, H. L. Mencken expresses the critical, mocking spirit of the day. *Time* summarizes the news, and *Reader's Digest* condenses magazine articles. "Confession" magazines and gossipy movie magazines sell well.

People Are Writing

Parodies Americans react to political and social events with clever slogans and humorous parodies in verse and song. Even the sacrifices of war (such as sending supplies to the armed forces through the Y.M.C.A.) are parodied in rhyme:

> "My Tuesdays are meatless,
> My Wednesdays are wheatless,
> I'm getting more eatless each day.
> My coffee is sweetless,
> My bed it is sheetless.
> All sent to the Y.M.C.A."

Petitions Supporters of woman suffrage produce a petition 18,000 feet long with nearly 500,000 names. However, during World War I, the government jails petitioners demanding repeal of repressive laws designed to prevent antiwar protests. ▶

U.S.A.	Jane Addams, *Twenty Years at Hull-House*	**1914** Gertrude Stein, *Tender Buttons*
	1912 Edna St. Vincent Millay, "Renascence"	Edgar Lee Masters, *Spoon River Anthology*
		1917 William Carlos Williams, "All Que Quiere"

1910   **1915**

World	**1912** Switzerland: Carl Jung, *Psychology of the Unconscious*	**1913** England: George Bernard Shaw, *Pygmalion*
	India: Muhammad Iqbāl, *The Secrets of the Self;* Japan: Akutagawa Ryūnosuke, *Rashōmon*	**1918** China: Lu Hsün, "A Madman's Diary"

MEETING INDIVIDUAL NEEDS — MULTIPLE LEARNING STYLES

Spatial For many devotees, the heart of the *New Yorker* is its cartoons. Over its nearly 75 years of continuous publication, it has featured the visual humor of Charles Addams, George Price, Helen Hokinson, James Thurber (also a writer), Roz Chast, and many others.

Activity Have students interested in drawing or social history explore one of the cartoonists from the magazine's early years at the *New Yorker's* Cartoon Bank Web site. In a class presentation, students should comment on the artist's technique and discuss what sense of the 1920s emerges from the cartoons and their subject matter. **L2**

Literary Trends: Modernism

"World War I . . . destroyed faith in progress, but it did more than that—it made clear to perceptive thinkers . . . that violence prowled underneath man's apparent harmony and rationality."

—William E. Leuchtenburg, *The Perils of Prosperity*

With their belief in human reason shaken by war, artists strive for new ways to portray the world. Painter Pablo Picasso, instead of reproducing what one sees from a single perspective, shows multiple perspectives in one painting. Composer Arnold Schoenberg abandons the traditional eight-note scale and creates music using a twelve-tone scale.

Writers also abandon conventions. Many create characters who, like real people, think in a continuous flow of ideas that seem to go in several directions at once. T. S. Eliot, William Faulkner, and Irish writer James Joyce make this stream-of-consciousness style famous. Another writer, E. E. Cummings, writes poetry without punctuation, capitalization, or even straight lines of text. These and other Modernists, with their emphasis on the new and untried, throw open the doors of possibility to all who follow.

E. E. Cummings

Portrait of Gertrude Stein, 1906. Pablo Picasso. Oil on canvas, 100 x 81.3 cm. The Metropolitan Museum of Art, New York.

FOCUS ON . . .

The Harlem Renaissance

African Americans who throng to New York's Harlem turn it into a vigorous, fertile cultural center. As W. E. B. Du Bois and others urge the expression of racial pride, writers focus on their own lives, culture, and identity. The fresh, new subjects and skillful writing attracts publishers and readers to the works of many writers, including Langston Hughes, Jean Toomer, Countee Cullen, and later, Zora Neale Hurston. However, with the economic depression of the 1930s, the Harlem Renaissance fades.

Harlem Renaissance novelist and literary editor Jessie Fauset

1923 —
Jean Toomer, "Song of the Son"; Claude McKay, *Harlem Shadows*

1922 —
T. S. Eliot, *The Waste Land*

1924 —
Robert Frost wins the first of his four Pulitzer Prizes for Poetry

1926 —
Langston Hughes, *The Weary Blues*

1927 —
Carl Sandburg, *The American Songbag*

1928 —
Margaret Mead, *Coming of Age in Samoa*

1920

1922 —
England: Katherine Mansfield, *The Garden Party*

1924 —
Chile: Pablo Neruda, *Twenty Love Poems and a Song of Despair*

1925

Germany: Adolf Hitler, *Mein Kampf*

1926 —
England: A. A. Milne, *Winnie-the-Pooh*

1930

BEGINNINGS OF THE MODERN AGE 593

Novels of the Time

Introductory Note

Call students' attention to the phrase "explore new subject matter, new styles and points of view, and new narrative techniques." As a class, discuss these elements as they apply to nineteenth-century novels that students have read. Have students give examples from their reading. Then invite students to talk about the differences between nineteenth- and twentieth-century novels. Encourage students to tell about modern novels they've read and to summarize the differences. What exactly are modern novelists doing that's different with regard to subject matter, style, point of view, and narrative technique?

Cultural Note

A theme common to novelists of this period was high society and how to succeed within it, but these writers brought surprisingly different outlooks to the theme. In *The Great Gatsby*, Fitzgerald paints an intriguing if lurid picture of wealth and social climbing. In contrast, Wharton, in novels like *The Age of Innocence* and *Old New York*, often plants her novels in the nineteenth century and describes the suffocating effects of society, social climbing, and even wealth. Hemingway gives a different emphasis to society by turning his back on it. His characters, as in *The Sun Also Rises*, are outcasts, not members of high society.

At the MOVIES

Be sure to review this movie before deciding whether to show it to your class.

• *The Great Gatsby* This 1974 film of F. Scott Fitzgerald's novel is directed by Jack Clayton and stars Robert Redford, Mia Farrow, Sam Waterston, Karen Black, and Bruce Dern.

Novels of the Time

Like all of American culture, the novel is profoundly changed by World War I. Many writers and artists see the war as a tragic failure of the old ways and, more than ever, seek to cast off the traditions of the nineteenth century. "Make it new," is the cry of poet Ezra Pound, and novelists explore new subject matter, new styles and points of view, and new narrative techniques. In short, they create the modern novel.

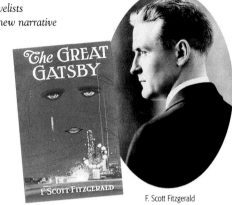

F. Scott Fitzgerald

The Great Gatsby
by F. Scott Fitzgerald (1925)

Both the glamor and the dark side of the twenties are reflected in Fitzgerald's story of Jay Gatsby, with his mysterious wealth, his lavish parties, and his idealistic but doomed pursuit of a woman and the American dream. Told from the point of view of Gatsby's neighbor, Nick Carraway, the story captures the spirit of the Jazz Age, a period that Fitzgerald called "an age of miracles, an age of art, and an age of excess."

Edith Wharton

The Age of Innocence
by Edith Wharton (1920)

Through the story of a doomed love, Edith Wharton presents an illuminating study of upper-class New York society in the late nineteenth century. In a perfect match, worldly and wealthy Newland Archer is engaged to May Welland, young, beautiful, and a member of the same elite social circle. Into this rosy picture steps the exotic Ellen Olenska, wellborn but bearing the burden of a mysterious past. Swept away by Olenska, Archer is torn between her and his bride-to-be.

U.S.A.				
	1911 Edith Wharton, *Ethan Frome*			
		1912 James Weldon Johnson, *Autobiography of an Ex-Colored Man*	1914 Theodore Dreiser, *The Titan*	1918 Willa Cather, *My Ántonia*
1910	1912 Germany: Thomas Mann, *Death in Venice*	1913 England: D. H. Lawrence, *Sons and Lovers*	**1915** 1914 Japan: Natsume Sōseki, *Kokoro;* Spain: Miguel de Unamuno, *Mist*	Mexico: Mariano Azuela, *The Underdogs*
World				

MEETING INDIVIDUAL NEEDS — MULTIPLE LEARNING STYLES

Linguistic Students with linguistic abilities are often excellent oral interpreters of literature. Their empathy with the style and the characters and their enthusiasm for literature can be infectious.

Activity Ask students to choose two or three novels from the period. Have them practice reading only the first paragraph or two of each novel and then read those paragraphs aloud to the class. This demonstration will provide a good opportunity to compare the styles and tones of the different novelists and to examine their techniques for getting a novel started. Invite the class to vote on the most intriguing beginning. **L1**

Scene from the movie, *The Sun Also Rises.*

Critics Corner

Too Much Sun

"There was a time, and it went on for weeks, when you could go nowhere without hearing of *The Sun Also Rises.* Some thought it was without excuse; and some, they of the cool, tall foreheads, called it the greatest American novel, tossing *Huckleberry Finn* and *The Scarlet Letter* lightly out the window. They hated it or they revered it. I may say, with due respect to Mr. Hemingway, that I was never so sick of a book in my life."

—Dorothy Parker in the *New Yorker,* October 29, 1927

The Sun Also Rises
by Ernest Hemingway (1926)

World War I, though long over, casts a heavy shadow over this story of members of Hemingway's own Lost Generation—young people psychologically and perhaps physically damaged by the war. Set in the cafes of Paris and the bullrings of Spain, Hemingway's novel paints in poignant detail the aimless lives of a group of cynical, disillusioned young people living in Paris, a life Hemingway himself had lived.

Ernest Hemingway

Sinclair Lewis,
Main Street

1920

1922
Sinclair Lewis, *Babbitt*

1922
Germany: Hermann Hesse, *Siddhartha;*
Ireland: James Joyce, *Ulysses,* published
in Paris

Theodore Dreiser, *An American Tragedy;*
Ellen Glasgow, *Barren Ground*

1925

1927
England: Virginia
Woolf, *To the
Lighthouse*

1929
William Faulkner, *The Sound and the Fury;*
Ernest Hemingway, *A Farewell to Arms*

1928
Claude McKay, *Home to Harlem*

1928
India: Bibhuti Bushan
Banerji, *The Song of
the Road*

1930

BEGINNINGS OF THE MODERN AGE   595

GIFTED AND TALENTED ACTIVITY

Film Adaptations *The Great Gatsby,* *The Age of Innocence,* and *The Sun Also Rises* were successful novels that were made into major motion pictures. After reviewing these movies for appropriateness for your students, have students view these films to get a taste of the novels of the period.

Activity Invite gifted and talented students to work in pairs or small groups to locate and view one of the films and also to read the novel. Then have them consider these questions: How faithfully does the film present the novel? Does it accurately portray the time in which it was written? Do the actors seem well chosen? Are there problems in the adaptation? Finally, have them give the film a thumbs up or thumbs down.

L3 **COLLAB. LEARN.**

Language of the Time

Language of the Time

How People Speak

Radio Talk Individuals and families spend hours in front of the radio, which delivers not only news and entertainment but a uniform English that begins to influence the way people talk.

Marvelous! The Roaring Twenties generation goes to extremes in speech as in everything else. Things are not merely good, they are "divine," "keen," "super," or "marvelous!" People take delight in clever, slangy expressions, such as the following terms of approval:

- the cat's meow
- the bee's knees
- the tiger's spots

Wordplay

Jazz What is the origin of *jazz*, the word that names a decade? Some believe it came from the name of an African American musician, Jasbo, or Jas, Brown. Others trace it to West Africa. The Tshilubia word *jaja* means "to cause one to dance," and the Temne word *yas* means "lively or energetic." No one knows for certain.

Jazz Horns, 1930s or early 1940s. Adolf Arthur Dehn. Watercolor on paper, 15⅛ x 22⅝ in. Private collection.

Crosswords On December 21, 1913, the first crossword puzzle—called a word-cross—appears in the *New York World* newspaper. In the 1920s, a book of crosswords is published, setting off a national craze.

New Words and Expressions

"We could almost write the history of civilization merely from linguistic evidence." —*Albert C. Baugh* and *Thomas Cable*

From World War I		From the Automobile	
parachute	camouflage	sedan	filling station, service
bomber	shell shock	sports car	station, gas station
tank (weapon)	bail out	convertible	backseat driver
blimp	flame thrower	blowout	parking lot
dog tag	slacker	retread	hitchhike
gas mask		jalopy	

Historical Note

The first known American radio broadcast occurred in 1906. In 1910 engineer Lee De Forest installed a transmitter in New York's Metropolitan Opera House and broadcast a performance by famed tenor Enrico Caruso. In 1920 radio station KDKA in Pittsburgh became the first commercial radio station in the country when it broadcast the returns of the Harding-Cox presidential election. Beginning in 1921, the sale of radios sky-rocketed, and radios became a status symbol in American homes.

FYI

Valentino During the 1920s, modern young women, called flappers, often referred to the men they dated as *sheiks*, presumably because of Rudolf Valentino, who starred in a movie titled *The Sheik*. Valentino (1895–1926) was born in Italy and came to the United States in 1913. He worked as a gardener, a polisher of brass on the fronts of houses, and a member of a dance team until he got his big break in the movies in 1921. He became famous immediately, and Hollywood's first screen idol was created. Fewer than six years later, Valentino died of a perforated ulcer.

interNET CONNECTION

Radio Have students search for the history of radio from 1895 to 1995 using keywords such as *broadcasting history, AM stations,* and *FM stations*.

MEETING INDIVIDUAL NEEDS — ENGLISH LANGUAGE LEARNERS

Slang Tell English language learners that slang terms identify people in many professions. During World War I, American soldiers were called dough-boys. During World War II, soldiers were sometimes referred to as GIs, from the general issue uniforms they wore.

Activity Ask students to identify slang expressions for professions in their countries of origin. What are soldiers in their countries called? What names are given to politicians, journalists, mechanics, and computer specialists? Have students compare these terms to English terms.

Additional Resources
📁 *English Language Learners Sourcebook*

anyone lived in a pretty how town

E. E. Cummings

A Summer Evening on the Lake in Alexandra Park. Helen Bradley (1900–1979). Oil on canvas board, 24 x 30 in. Private collection.

anyone lived in a pretty how town
(with up so floating many bells down)
spring summer autumn winter
he sang his didn't he danced his did.

5   Women and men(both little and small)
cared for anyone not at all
they sowed their isn't they reaped their same
sun moon stars rain

children guessed(but only a few
10 and down they forgot as up they grew
autumn winter spring summer)
that noone loved him more by more

when by now and tree by leaf
she laughed his joy she cried his grief
15 bird by snow and stir by still
anyone's any was all to her

someones married their everyones
laughed their cryings and did their dance
(sleep wake hope and then)they
20 said their nevers they slept their dream

stars rain sun moon
(and only the snow can begin to explain
how children are apt to forget to remember
with up so floating many bells down)

25 one day anyone died i guess
(and noone stooped to kiss his face)
busy folk buried them side by side
little by little and was by was

all by all and deep by deep
30 and more by more they dream their sleep
noone and anyone earth by april
wish by spirit and if by yes.

Women and men(both dong and ding)
summer autumn winter spring
35 reaped their sowing and went their came
sun moon stars rain

Reading the Selection

A Active Reading

INTEPRET Have students discuss why Cummings repeats, with a variation, the four seasons in lines 3, 11, and 34. Ask, too, if it relates to the other repeated line: "sun moon stars rain." What do these lines contribute to the theme of the poem? *(Both sets of repeated lines focus on the changelessness of the universe. The seasons repeat themselves in an endless cycle. The sun, moon, stars, and rain are constant elements of life. The suggestion is that life goes on without change through generations.)*

Additional Resources
📁 *Active Reading Guide,* p. 74
🎧 *Audio Library*

B Literary Elements

RHYTHM Discuss the rhythm of the poem with students. You might wish to divide the stanzas among pairs of students. Ask them to mark the stressed and unstressed syllables and then to share their results in class. Is the rhythm of the poem regular or irregular? *(Irregular)*

✔ ASSESSMENT OPTIONS
📁 *Quick Checks,* p. 74

Teaching Options

 MULTIPLE LEARNING STYLES

Spatial Cummings's poem describes everyday life in a typical town. Each stanza presents an image of a different representative event in the life of the town and its people.

Activity Divide the class into nine groups, one for each stanza. Have each group illustrate a stanza. Explain that they should capture the stanza's central image (for example, sowing and reaping, marriage, or death). Encourage students to be creative with their choice of media, but explain that all illustrations must be no larger than a page in a book. When all illustrations are complete, have the class design a volume containing the fully illustrated poem. **L2** **COLLAB. LEARN.**

Personal Response

Students may be puzzled and/or fascinated by Cummings's use of lowercase letters, lack of punctuation, unexpected diction, and repetition of word groups.

ANALYZING LITERATURE

1. The main character is anyone; his wife is noone. Their names suggest both anonymity and universality.
2. Men and women (other people) do not care for anyone; they spend their lives in negative ("their isn't") or conforming ("their same") activities. Such words imply the speaker's disdain for them.
3. The children guess that noone loves anyone. As they grow, they forget it. This suggests that children are more in touch with true emotion than are adults.
4. Anyone dies and noone shortly follows him. The townspeople seem indifferent to their deaths. Cummings may suggest that only in personal relationships do people find satisfaction and love and that isolation, alienation, conformity, and indifference are the norms.
5. Like the refrain in traditional ballads, Cummings repeats, with variation, two phrases signifying the changelessness of life: "spring summer autumn winter" and "sun moon stars rain."
6. Cummings might envision the "pretty how town" situated in a valley ("down") above ("up") which the sound of "many bells" floats. The bells echo the children's growth ("up they grew"). Together, the impression is of a pristine and lovely setting.
7. Students may reply that Cummings's description of average citizens is still accurate.
8. Some students will respond that the lack of such conventions creates a barrier to their understanding; others may see that they force readers into a special attentiveness and result in increased appreciation.

Responding to Literature

Personal Response

What reactions did you have as you read this poem? Explain.

ANALYZING LITERATURE

RECALL AND INTERPRET

1. What is the name of the main character of the poem and what is the name of his wife? What do their names suggest to you?
2. According to the speaker, what do "women and men" do? What seems to be the speaker's attitude toward these people? How can you tell?
3. What does the speaker say about what children know? What happens to them? What might Cummings be trying to convey about the difference between children and adults?
4. What happens to the two main characters at the end of the poem? How do the townspeople seem to react to this event? What lesson about life do you think Cummings is trying to communicate with this poem?

EVALUATE AND CONNECT

5. What two series of words are repeated in the poem? What might the poet have meant to emphasize through the use of **repetition** (see page R13)?
6. The words in lines 2 and 24 don't seem to make much sense. How do these words contribute to your impression of the town?
7. How does the poem's depiction of the "average person" compare with your response to the Focus Activity on page 642? Based on your comparison, would you say the poem also describes people of today?
8. In this poem, Cummings uses unconventional word order and few capital letters and punctuation marks. In your opinion, how do these techniques contribute to the impact and meaning of the poem?

Literary ELEMENTS

Rhythm
In poetry, **rhythm** is the arrangement of stressed and unstressed syllables. Rhythm can convey meaning by emphasizing certain words and phrases. It can also add a musical quality to a poem and help set the tone. Regular rhythm has a predictable pattern, while irregular rhythm has no definite pattern. Although "anyone lived in a pretty how town" has irregular rhythm, the particular arrangement of stressed and unstressed syllables plays an important role in the poem.

Women and men (both little and small)
cared for anyone not at all

1. Which lines seem to have the same or nearly the same rhythm? Which have rhythm that is quite different?
2. What do you think the differences in rhythm emphasize?
- See **Literary Terms Handbook,** p. R13.

EXTENDING YOUR RESPONSE

Writing About Literature
What Does It Really Mean? In choosing words, poets consider both the **denotation** (literal meaning) and **connotation** (suggested meaning). In a few paragraphs, describe how the difference between the denotation and the connotation of the words *little, small, same,* and *never* might affect the reading of the poem.

Internet Connection
E. E. Cummings on the Web Look for Web sites devoted to Cummings. Print out or copy down two more of his poems. Compare your reactions to these poems with those you had to "anyone lived in a pretty how town." Share your thoughts with a partner.

📓 **Save your work for your portfolio.**

LITERARY ELEMENTS

1. The lines vary in length from four to 12 syllables. All the first lines and all the second lines are rhythmically similar. Lines 8, 21, and 36 consist of four stressed syllables.
2. Two of these three lines end a stanza. Line 21 begins stanza 6 and is the only first stanza line with a rhythm different from other first lines. This line signals the emotional turn of the poem.

Additional Resources
📖 **Literary Elements Transparency 60**

✔ ASSESSMENT OPTIONS

📁 *Quick Checks,* p. 74
📁 *Selection and Theme Assessment,* p. 111
📁 *Performance Assessment,* p. 62
💾 *Testmaker*

Anecdote

Marianne Moore's fellow poet Alfred Kreymborg once decided to take her in a new direction—to a baseball game. Here's what happened, as Kreymborg described it in his autobiography.

from *The Oxford Book of American Literary Anecdotes*

edited by Donald Hall

Never having found her at a loss on any topic whatsoever, I wanted to give myself the pleasure of at least once hearing her stumped about something. Certain that only an experience completely strange to her would be the thing, I invited her to a game at the Polo Grounds [baseball stadium where the New York Giants played].

Well, I got her safely to her seat and sat down beside her. Without so much as a glance toward the players at practice grabbing grounders and chasing fungos [practice fly balls], she went on giving me her impression of the respective technical achievements of [poets] Mr. Pound and Mr. Aldington without missing a turn in the rhythm of her speech, until I, a little impatient, touched her arm and, indicating a man in the pitcher's box winding up with the movement Matty's [Hall of Fame pitcher Christy Mathewson] so famous for, interrupted: "But Marianne, wait a moment, the game's about to begin. Don't you want to watch the first ball?" "Yes indeed," she said, stopped, blushed and leaned forward. The old blond boy [Mathewson] delivered a tantalizing fadeaway [pitch] which hovered in the air and then, just as it reached the batter, Shorty Slagle, shot from his shoulders to his knees and across the plate. "Strike!" bawled Umpire Emslie. "Excellent," said Marianne.

Delighted, I quickly turned to her with: "Do you happen to know the gentleman who threw that strike?"

"I've never seen him before," she admitted, "but I take it it must be Mr. Mathewson."

I could only gasp, "Why?"

"I've read his instructive book on the art of pitching—"

"Strike two!" interrupted Bob Emslie.

"And it's a pleasure," she continued, "to note how unerringly his execution supports his theories."

Respond

1. Does Kreymborg really take Marianne Moore in a new direction? Explain.

2. If you were in Kreymborg's position, would you be so surprised? Why or why not?

Objective

- To read and understand an anecdote

Literature LINK

Poetry This anecdote connects to Marianne Moore's "Poetry" on page 648. In lines 10–11 of "Poetry," Moore asserts that "we do not admire what/we cannot understand . . ." She then provides examples, one of which is "the baseball fan." She may have read Mathewson's book in order to fill in this gap in her own understanding.

Respond

1. No. Kreymborg assumes that Moore will have no knowledge of baseball, but she startles him by having read Mathewson's book on pitching.

2. Students will probably say that they, too, would be surprised if a friend of theirs, who seemed so uninterested in sports, showed such a surprising technical knowledge of the game.

Additional Resources
📁 *Media Connections*, p. 14

Teaching Options

Reading *Minilesson*

Author's Purpose Remind students that authors write to persuade, to inform, to entertain, to analyze, or to express ideas. Point out that looking at an author's choice of subject matter, word choice, and sentence structure can help a reader identify the author's purpose.

Activity Ask students to determine the author's purpose in this anecdote. *(to*

entertain, to provide information about poet Marianne Moore) Then ask students to point out clues that helped them determine the author's purpose. *(subject matter: funny story word choice: formal language at a ball game, "gasp")* What clues were helpful in identifying purpose?
L2 COLLAB. LEARN.

*inter*NET CONNECTION

Writers and Sports Have students search the Internet to learn more about writers interested in sports. Suggest they use keywords such as *literary anecdotes* and *literature and sports*.

Objectives

- To read a poem about the purpose of poetry
- To identify enjambment and to understand its effect on the meaning of a poem
- To paraphrase a poem for a younger audience

Skills

Reading/Thinking: Summarizing
Listening/Speaking: Oral Reading

Motivating

→ **OPTIONS**

Selection Focus Transparency 67: Have students look at and read the cartoon. Then discuss the question.

Focus Activity: As an extension of the Focus Activity, have students share with the class one or two items from their list.

Before You Read

Poetry

Meet Marianne Moore

"We [writers] must not be too sensitive about not being liked or not being printed. . . . The thing is to see the vision and not deny it; to care and admit that we do."

—Moore

Marianne Moore followed her own advice: she cared more about writing poetry than about achieving fame. She wasn't discouraged when she was called a "poet's poet" (meaning that only other poets appreciated her "difficult" poetry) or when her *Selected Poems* sold only 864 copies in seven years.

This original and whimsical writer was born in Missouri, grew up in Pennsylvania, and attended Bryn Mawr College where she began writing poetry. At the age of thirty-one, Moore moved with her mother to New York City, a place that offered her "accessibility to experience." There she worked in a school and a library, edited an influential literary magazine called *The Dial,* and mingled with other avant-garde writers and painters. In her spare time, she wrote many books of poetry, one of which won a Pulitzer Prize.

Moore believed that poets should write with what she called "unbearable accuracy." She revised her own poems again and again, never really considering any to be truly finished. While her use of obscure words and complex stanza patterns gave Moore a reputation for being difficult, she was greatly admired by fellow poets, including T. S. Eliot and William Carlos Williams. The poet John Ashbery once said of her, "I am tempted to call her our greatest modern poet."

Marianne Moore was born in 1887 and died in 1972.

FOCUS ACTIVITY

Do you think you understand what poetry is?

THINK-PAIR-SHARE Spend three minutes jotting down a list of things you know about poetry. Then share your list with a partner.

SETTING A PURPOSE Read to learn one writer's ideas of what poetry is.

——— BACKGROUND ———

Scientific Influences

At Bryn Mawr College, Moore majored in biology and histology, the study of plant and animal tissue structure. She even considered pursuing a career in medicine. Moore's interest in science never left her, as is apparent in both the subject matter and the precision of her verse. Moore wrote extensively of the natural world, and in a 1961 interview she discussed the importance of her scientific training to her poetry: "Precision, economy of statement, logic employed to ends that are disinterested, drawing and identifying, liberate—at least have some bearing on—the imagination."

RESOURCE MANAGER

Lesson Planning Resource
The *Unit Five Planning Guide* (pp. 59–63) provides additional lesson notes and reduced versions of all print resources.

📁 **Other Print Resources**
- Active Reading Guide, p. 75
- Reading Workbook
- Quick Checks, p. 75
- Selection and Theme Assessment, p. 112

- Performance Assessment, p. 63
- Spanish Summaries, p. 67
- Inclusion Strategies
- English Language Learners Sourcebook

 Transparencies
- Selection Focus 67
- Literary Elements 61

Technology
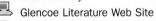
- Audio Library
- Glencoe Literature Web Site
- Testmaker

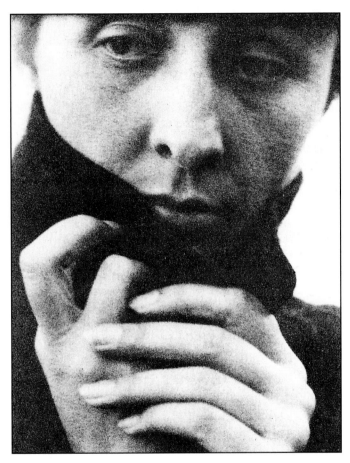

A *Poetry*

Marianne Moore ∿

Georgia O'Keeffe, 1918. Alfred Stieglitz. Photograph. Metropolitan Museum of Art, New York.

A Active Reading

CONNECT Explain that Moore's poem describes some of the difficulties of poetry. Before they read, ask students to write down three things that they find difficult about reading poetry. Encourage students to think about how Moore's poem addresses these difficulties as they read.

Additional Resources
📁 *Active Reading Guide,* p. 75
🎧 *Audio Library*

VIEWING THE PHOTOGRAPH

Art critic Robert Hughes characterized Alfred Stieglitz (1864–1946) as "courageous, obdurately persistent, impatient with fools, and sometimes an arrogant prig." Nonetheless, it was Stieglitz who forced Americans to recognize photography as a legitimate art form. Six years before he married artist Georgia O'Keeffe (1887–1986), Stieglitz took this evocative photograph of her.

Viewing Response What is the main focus of this photograph? *(Many students will say that the focus is on the hands because they are made to stand out against the dark background.)*

Teaching Options

Reading *Minilesson*

Summarizing Moore's poem describes what good poetry is and what it is not. Although she presents her ideas in the poem, she has a thesis and supporting ideas much like those found in an essay.

Activity Ask students to summarize Moore's poem by identifying Moore's main point(s), supporting ideas, and examples. Explain that students' summaries should be organized as a brief essay, rather than a line-by-line paraphrase. Students may outline their summaries before writing. Have students compare their summaries with a partner. Do students agree on Moore's main ideas? **L2 COLLAB. LEARN.**

Additional Resources
📁 *Reading Workbook*

647

Poetry

I, too, dislike it: there are things that are important beyond all this fiddle.°
  Reading it, however, with a perfect contempt for it, one discovers in
  it after all, a place for the genuine.
    Hands that can grasp, eyes
5   that can dilate,° hair that can rise
      if it must, these things are important not because a

B high-sounding interpretation can be put upon them but because they are
  useful. When they become so derivative° as to become unintelligible,
  the same thing may be said for all of us, that we
10   do not admire what
    we cannot understand: the bat
     holding on upside down or in quest of something to

eat, elephants pushing, a wild horse taking a roll, a tireless wolf under
  a tree, the immovable critic twitching his skin like a horse that feels a flea, the base-
15 ball fan, the statistician—
    nor is it valid
     to discriminate against 'business documents and

C school-books'; all these phenomena are important. One must make a distinction
  however: when dragged into prominence by half poets, the result is not poetry,
20 nor till the poets among us can be
    'literalists° of
    the imagination'—above
     insolence° and triviality and can present

for inspection, 'imaginary gardens with real toads in them', shall we have
25 it. In the meantime, if you demand on the one hand,
  the raw material of poetry in
    all its rawness and
    that which is on the other hand
     genuine, you are interested in poetry.

---

1 Here, *fiddle* means "nonsense" or "aimless, trifling, or experimental activity."
5 *Dilate* means "to become larger or wider."
8 Here, *derivative* (di riv′ ə tiv) may mean "unoriginal" or "based on someone else's experience."
21 Here, *literalists* are people who stick to observable facts.
23 *Insolence* is arrogance.

Responding to Literature

Personal Response

Were you convinced by the writer's argument? Why or why not?

——— ANALYZING LITERATURE ———

RECALL AND INTERPRET

1. What attitudes about poetry does the speaker express in lines 1–3?

2. What things does the speaker present in lines 4–5? Why are they important? What can you infer about the speaker's attitude toward poetry?

3. How does the speaker say people react to poems that "become so derivative as to become unintelligible"? According to the speaker, what kinds of "phenomena" make good subjects for poetry? What point do you think Moore is trying to make in lines 8–18?

4. According to lines 18–25, what accounts for the difference between the work of "half poets" and that of poets? How do you think presenting "'imaginary gardens with real toads in them'" results in poetry? Explain.

5. According to lines 25–29, what two demands indicate that a person is interested in poetry? In your opinion, what characteristics does the speaker believe a good poem should have?

EVALUATE AND CONNECT

6. Moore begins the poem by stating a provocative opinion. Do you think this is an effective way to begin the poem? Explain.

7. Look back at your response to the Focus Activity on page 646. How do the ideas presented in this poem help you understand what poetry is?

8. What subjects might the speaker suggest for poems written today?

Literary ELEMENTS

Enjambment

Enjambment is a verse technique in which the sense and grammatical structure of one line carries over to the next line without a punctuated pause. Enjambed lines contrast with end-stopped lines, in which both meaning and grammatical structure come to an end or a definitive pause. In "Poetry," enjambment serves to emphasize certain words or to expand their meanings by relating them to different contexts. This technique also serves to express the flow of the speaker's thought.

1. Identify three examples of enjambment in "Poetry."

2. In each example, what word or words might Moore be trying to emphasize or expand?

● See **Literary Terms Handbook,** p. R5.

——— EXTENDING YOUR RESPONSE ———

Writing About Literature

In Support of Poetry   Make poetry fans out of an audience of fourth or fifth graders. In your own words, rewrite Moore's ideas about poetry as stated in the poem. Be sure to write for your younger audience. Then make your presentation to a fourth- or fifth-grade class.

Listening and Speaking

Reading "Poetry"   Moore's **rhythm, rhyme,** and **enjambment** create challenges for reading aloud. (See Literary Terms Handbook, pages R13 and R5.) With a partner, prepare an oral reading of "Poetry." Present your reading to the class, alternating stanzas with your partner.

📖 **Save your work for your portfolio.**

Personal Response

Make certain that students explain their understanding of Moore's words *genuine* and *useful* as a defense for poetry.

ANALYZING LITERATURE

1. The speaker says that, like many readers, she dislikes poetry but acknowledges that it sometimes contains what is genuine.

2. The speaker mentions grasping hands, dilating eyes, and rising hair. These are important because they are "useful." The speaker values the concrete and the real, not "high-sounding interpretation."

3. People don't admire what they cannot understand. Good subjects can be anything from bats to schoolbooks, if they are imbued with the quality of genuineness.

4. True poets are "'literalists of the imagination'" while "half-poets" are mired in "insolence and triviality." A real poet can describe an "imaginary garden" in so genuine a way that even a toad becomes real and therefore important.

5. People who demand and respond to real subjects and genuineness, or honesty, are interested in poetry. The speaker believes a good poem should not be derivative but should deal honestly with subjects readers will understand.

6. Students will probably agree that it is effective. Its provocativeness catches the reader's attention.

7. Students may find that Moore has sharpened their judgment of what poetry should be about.

8. Moore strongly suggests that any subject, if presented with honesty, can be a proper subject for a poem.

✔ ASSESSMENT OPTIONS

📁 *Quick Checks,* p. 75

📁 *Selection and Theme Assessment,* p. 112

📁 *Performance Assessment,* p. 63

💾 *Testmaker*

LITERARY ELEMENTS

1. Enjambment occurs in the majority of lines. It is especially effective in lines 6–8, 17–18, and 20–22.

2. After lines 6–7, Moore surprises the reader with the unexpected word *useful;* after line 17, another unexpected word *school-books;* after line 20, Moore emphasizes the phrase *literalists of/the imagination.*

Additional Resources

 Literary Elements Transparency 61

Before Reading

Objectives

- To read a short story about a young man trying to regain the woman he loves
- To identify the methods of characterization used by an author
- To write an analysis of a story's point of view

Skills

Reading/Thinking: Drawing Conclusions; Sequencing; Making Critical Judgments; Identifying Assumptions; Inferring

Writing: Dramatizing a Scene; Journal Entry

Vocabulary: Word Meaning and Pronunciation; Connotations; Using Prior Knowledge

Grammar/Language: Subject-Verb Agreement

Listening/Speaking: Formal Discussion; Monologue; Jazz Soundtrack

Life Skills: Problem Solving

Collaboration: Literature Groups

More About F. Scott Fitzgerald

In 1937 Fitzgerald decided to give up writing serious literature and try to earn a living writing screenplays in Hollywood. However, he soon became discouraged when his scripts were continually revised and changed. In 1939, a year before his death, he returned to writing novels. *The Last Tycoon* was unfinished at his death but was revised and completed by Edmund Wilson and published in 1941.

Before You Read

The Bridal Party

Meet F. Scott Fitzgerald

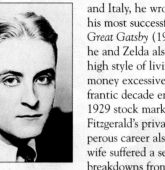

F. Scott Fitzgerald once wrote that "all the stories that came into my head had a touch of disaster in them. . . . I was pretty sure living wasn't the reckless, careless business these people thought." Many of Fitzgerald's stories and novels describe the lifestyle of young, wealthy Americans in the 1920s. Fitzgerald shared this lifestyle, and the heroes in his fiction often have values and conflicts that are very similar to his own.

Fitzgerald was born in 1896 in St. Paul, Minnesota, into a family of little wealth but great social ambition. A failure at business, Fitzgerald's father was often criticized by his wife. She had high expectations for their children and sent them to the best schools so that they could mingle with the upper classes.

As a student, Fitzgerald had difficulty disciplining himself. He spent his time at Princeton University writing for the newspaper and participating in the drama club, trying to achieve social status through school clubs. After failing several courses, he left college in his junior year to enlist in the army. While stationed in the South, he fell in love with Zelda Sayre.

Following his stint in the army, Fitzgerald settled in New York City and struggled to earn a living. His financial worries ended with the publication of *This Side of Paradise* when he was twenty-four. This novel about his life at Princeton was an overnight success, making it possible for Fitzgerald to marry Zelda.

In the 1920s, Fitzgerald wrote short stories and novels and mingled with the rich in the United States and in Europe. While in France and Italy, he wrote and revised his most successful novel, *The Great Gatsby* (1925). However, he and Zelda also maintained a high style of living and spent money excessively. When the frantic decade ended with the 1929 stock market crash, Fitzgerald's private life and prosperous career also crashed. His wife suffered a series of nervous breakdowns from which she never recovered, and his high-paying magazine jobs dwindled with the onset of the Great Depression.

Though Fitzgerald struggled in the 1930s with alcoholism and with his marriage, he continued to write stories, novels, and essays; "The Bridal Party" was written during this period. He also spent some time in Hollywood as a screenwriter in an attempt to pay his debts. Fitzgerald then began work on a fifth novel, *The Last Tycoon*, but died of a heart attack at age forty-four before he completed it.

"Draw your chair up close to the edge of the precipice and I'll tell you a story."

"Show me a hero and I will write you a tragedy."

"Mostly, we authors repeat ourselves. . . . We have two or three great and moving experiences in our lives . . . and we tell our two or three stories—each time in a new disguise."

—Fitzgerald

F. Scott Fitzgerald was born in 1896 and died in 1940.

RESOURCE MANAGER

Lesson Planning Resource
The *Unit Five Planning Guide* (pp. 64–71) provides additional lesson notes and reduced versions of all print resources.

📁 **Other Print Resources**
- Active Reading Guide, p. 76
- Vocabulary Practice, p. 40
- Reading Workbook, pp. 63–64
- Grammar and Language Workbook, p. 155

- Grammar and Composition Handbook, Lesson 6.2
- Quick Checks, p. 76
- Selection and Theme Assessment, pp. 113–114
- Performance Assessment, p. 64
- Spanish Summaries, p. 68
- Inclusion Strategies
- English Language Learners Sourcebook

🖼 **Transparencies**
- Selection Focus 68
- Literary Elements 62
- Grammar and Language 51

Technology
- 💿 Literature Launchers
- 🎧 Audio Library
- 🎧 Spanish Audio Library
- 💻 Glencoe Literature Web Site
- 💾 Testmaker

FOCUS ACTIVITY

Have you ever found yourself in a situation in which wanting to fit in with a group was an issue?

FREEWRITE Take a few minutes to freewrite about a time in your life when you especially wanted to fit in with a certain group. Why was it so important to fit in? How did you handle the situation?

SETTING A PURPOSE Read to see how the narrator hopes to "fit in."

BACKGROUND

The Time and Place

The Jazz Age The 1920s have been called the Jazz Age for the relatively new musical form that was popular during the era. Jazz's vibrant and rebellious rhythms mirrored the spirit of a decade in which young people were rebelling against the social rules of the previous generation.

Economic prosperity fed the decade's party atmosphere. Business was booming, and some people made huge profits on their investments. Giddy from the sudden wealth, people partied and spent money recklessly.

The Stock Market Crash In the 1920s, manufacturing experienced a great rise in productivity, but other sectors of the economy, most notably agriculture and energy, were sagging. Mergers between numerous small companies meant that by the end of the decade a relatively small number of corporations were earning nearly half of the nation's income. Stock prices rose sharply as many investors bought stocks, hoping to make quick profits before the boom ended. In August 1929, production dropped drastically, and two months later, panic began as many investors began selling off their stocks. Banks and

Paris, around 1930.

investment companies tried to intervene, but the situation proved irreversible; on October 29, 1929–"Black Tuesday"–the stock market collapsed completely. Stocks became worthless, and the Great Depression, the worst period of economic hardship in U.S. history, dragged on through most of the next decade.

VOCABULARY PREVIEW

imminent (im′ ə nənt) *adj.* about to take place; p. 652

reciprocate (ri sip′ rə kāt′) *v.* to give, feel, or show in return; p. 652

exhilarated (ig zil′ ə rā təd) *adj.* cheerful, lively, or excited; filled with vigor; p. 656

exploit (iks ploit′) *v.* to use or develop for profit, often in a selfish, unjust, or unfair way; p. 657

impetuously (im pech′ ōō əs lē) *adv.* impulsively; suddenly; rashly; p. 658

tentative (ten′ tə tiv) *adj.* not fully worked out; somewhat undecided; p. 658

Motivating
→OPTIONS

 Literature Launchers: "F. Scott, Zelda and the Roaring Twenties"

Videodisc Side B, Segment 13

Also available in VHS.

 Selection Focus Transparency 68: Discuss what clothing today reflects about people. Then discuss the poster.

Focus Activity: As an extension of the Focus Activity, have students write a brief evaluation of their experience. Based on what they know now, ask students if fitting in is really so important.

Reading Further

Be sure to review these titles for appropriateness for your class before recommending them to students.

Fitzgerald, F. Scott. *The Great Gatsby.* New York: Simon & Schuster, 1996. Fitzgerald's most famous novel chronicles life in the Jazz Age.

Fitzgerald, F. Scott. *The Short Stories of F. Scott Fitzgerald: A New Collection.* Penny Kaganoff (editor). New York: Simon & Schuster, 1995.

CONNECTING TO OTHER SELECTIONS

The chart at the right shows three ways to connect "The Bridal Party" to selections in this book.

For specific teaching strategies, see the *Unit Five Planning Guide,* pp. 67–68.

Connection	Title
Life Skills: Decision Making →	"To Build a Fire," p. 498
Thematic: Turning Point →	"The Second Tree from the Corner," p. 783
Literary: Irony →	"The Three-Piece Suit," p. 279

THE BRIDAL PARTY

SUMMARY

Michael had hoped to marry Caroline, but felt his poverty and her family's disdain caused them to breakup. While living in Paris, where Caroline is visiting, he receives a note announcing her imminent marriage. Later, he runs into Caroline and her wealthy fiancé, Hamilton, and is invited to several pre-nuptial parties. Michael is convinced that Caroline still loves him. After learning that he has inherited $250,000, he decides to fight for her. He leaves Hamilton's bachelor party to talk to Caroline. Soon after, Hamilton arrives and announces that he has lost all his money. Caroline says it doesn't matter. At the wedding reception, Michael realizes he is "cured" of his love.

📁 *Spanish Summaries,* p. 68

A **Active Reading**

PREDICT After they read the title and first page, have students predict what might happen: What will become of Michael and Caroline?

Additional Resources

📁 *Active Reading Guide,* p. 76

🎧 *Audio Library*

🎧 *Spanish Audio Library*

≈ I ≈

There was the usual insincere little note saying: "I wanted you to be the first to know." It was a double shock to Michael, announcing, as it did, both the engagement and the <u>imminent</u> marriage; which, moreover, was to be held, not in New York, decently and far away, but here in Paris under his very nose, if that could be said to extend over the Protestant Episcopal Church of the Holy Trinity, Avenue George-Cinq.[1] The date was two weeks off, early in June.

At first Michael was afraid and his stomach felt hollow. When he left the hotel that morning, the *femme de chambre*,[2] who was in love with his fine, sharp profile and his pleasant buoyancy, scented the hard abstraction that had settled over him. He walked in a daze to his bank, he bought a detective story at Smith's on the Rue de Rivoli,[3] he sympathetically stared for a while at a faded panorama of the battlefields in a tourist-office window and cursed a Greek tout who followed him with a half-displayed packet of innocuous[4] post cards warranted to be very dirty indeed.

But the fear stayed with him, and after a while he recognized it as the fear that now he would never be happy. He had met Caroline Dandy when she was seventeen, possessed her young heart all through her first season in New York, and then lost her, slowly, tragically, uselessly, because he had no money and could make no money; because, with all the energy and good will in the world, he could not find himself; because, loving him still, Caroline had lost faith and begun to see him as something pathetic, futile and shabby, outside the great, shining stream of life toward which she was inevitably drawn.

Since his only support was that she loved him, he leaned weakly on that; the support broke, but still he held on to it and was carried out to sea and washed up on the French coast with its broken pieces still in his hands. He carried them around with him in the form of photographs and packets of correspondence and a liking for a maudlin[5] popular song called "Among My Souvenirs." He kept clear of other girls, as if Caroline would somehow know it and <u>reciprocate</u> with a faithful heart. Her note informed him that he had lost her forever.

It was a fine morning. In front of the shops in the Rue de Castiglione,[6] proprietors and

---

1. *George-Cinq* (zhōrzh sănk)
2. The *femme de chambre* (fem də shäm′ br) is the hotel's housekeeper.
3. *Rue de Rivoli* (rōō də rē vo lē′); *Rue de* is French for "street of."
4. The *tout* (tōō), an aggressive peddler, offers pornographic pictures disguised as ordinary, innocent, or *innocuous,* post cards.

5. *Maudlin* means "overly sentimental."
6. *Castiglione* (käs′ tēl yō′ nä)

Vocabulary
imminent (im′ ə nənt) *adj.* about to take place
reciprocate (ri sip′ rə kāt′) *v.* to give, feel, or show in return

---

Grammar and Language *Minilesson*

Subject-Verb Agreement Remind students to pay particular attention to subject-verb agreement when prepositional phrases intervene between the subject and the verb of a sentence. The verb must agree with the subject, not with the object of the preposition.

Activity Write these sentences on the board and have students pick the correct verbs.

1. Members of the bridal party (is/are) excited. *(are)*
2. The music of the piano and other instruments (was/were) energetic. *(was)*
3. The dance floor in the center of the room (appear/appears) too crowded. *(appears)*
4. People at the back of the room (cheer/cheers) when Caroline and Hamilton arrive. *(cheer)* **L2**

Additional Resources

📖 *Grammar and Language Transparency 51*

📖 *Grammar and Language Workbook,* p. 155

📖 *Grammar and Composition Handbook,* Lesson 6.2

📖 *Writer's Choice,* Lesson 16.1

B Critical Thinking

DRAWING CONCLUSIONS Ask students if they can deduce the kind of job Michael has. *(The references to Guaranty Trust, Morgan, and National City suggest that he works in a bank.)*

F. Scott Fitzgerald ∾

patrons were on the sidewalk gazing upward, for the Graf Zeppelin,[7] shining and glorious, symbol of escape and destruction—of escape, if necessary, through destruction—glided in the Paris sky. He heard a woman say in French that it would not her astonish if that commenced to let fall the bombs. Then he heard another voice, full of husky laughter, and the void in his stomach froze. Jerking about, he was face to face with Caroline Dandy and her fiancé.

"Why, Michael! Why, we were wondering where you were. I asked at the Guaranty Trust, and Morgan and Company, and finally sent a note to the National City——"

Why didn't they back away? Why didn't they back right up, walking backward down the Rue de Castiglione, across the Rue de Rivoli, through the Tuileries Gardens,[8] still walking backward as fast as they could till they grew vague and faded out across the river?

"This is Hamilton Rutherford, my fiancé."

"We've met before."

"At Pat's, wasn't it?"

"And last spring in the Ritz Bar."

"Michael, where have you been keeping yourself?"

"Around here." This agony. Previews of Hamilton Rutherford flashed before his eyes—a quick series of pictures, sentences. He remembered hearing that he had bought a seat in 1920 for a hundred and twenty-five thousand of borrowed money, and just before the break[9] sold it for more than half a million. Not handsome like Michael, but vitally attractive, confident, authoritative, just the right height over Caroline there—Michael had always been too short for Caroline when they danced.

Rutherford was saying: "No, I'd like it very much if you'd come to the bachelor dinner. I'm taking the Ritz Bar from nine o'clock on. Then right after the wedding there'll be a reception and breakfast at the Hotel George-Cinq."

"And, Michael, George Packman is giving a party day after tomorrow at Chez[10] Victor, and I want you to be sure and come. And also to tea Friday at Jebby West's; she'd want to have you if she knew where you were. What's your hotel, so we can send you an invitation? You see, the reason we decided to have it over here is because mother has been sick in a nursing home here and the whole clan is in Paris. Then Hamilton's mother's being here too——"

The entire clan; they had always hated him, except her mother; always discouraged his courtship. What a little counter he was in this game of families and money! Under his hat his brow sweated with the humiliation of the fact

---

7. The *Graf Zeppelin,* a German airship, carried passengers in the 1930s. During World War I, such airships served as bombers.

8. The *Tuileries* (twhēl′ rē) *Gardens* are located in Paris, France, and are noteworthy in that their design has changed little since they were created in 1664.

9. A *seat,* or membership, in a stock exchange is expensive because only a limited number of memberships exist. The *break* is the October 1929 stock market crash.

10. *Chez* (shā) is French for "at." It is often used in the names of restaurants, and here, means "at the house of."

C Literary Elements

CHARACTERIZATION Point out that the writer develops Michael's character in two ways. He tells readers directly about Michael, as when he says on page 652 that "Michael was afraid and his stomach felt hollow." He also gives indirect information about Michael, as in this paragraph. Ask students what this look into Michael's thoughts tells them about his personality. *(He is sensitive and very much in love. It is painful for him to see Caroline with Hamilton, and he doesn't understand why she is so insensitive as to bring Hamilton to him.)*

Language Note

In many board games, a counter, or round disk of metal or plastic, is used for keeping score. The word reduces Michael to an inanimate object in the "game" of love. Its use implies that Michael doesn't count for much.

Reading *Minilesson*

Sequencing A relatively long story such as "The Bridal Party" includes many events. Although they occur in chronological order, students may lose track of them and how they affect each other and the relationships among characters.

Activity Encourage students to track the main events of the story as they read by constructing a sequence-of-events chart like the one shown. Students may work individually and then meet in small groups to compare their charts. **L1**

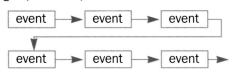

Additional Resources

📁 *Reading Workbook,* pp. 63–64

Viewing the sketch: How do the people in the sketch seem similar to or different from the characters in "The Bridal Party"?

that for all his misery he was worth just exactly so many invitations. Frantically he began to mumble something about going away.

D Then it happened—Caroline saw deep into him, and Michael knew that she saw. She saw through to his profound[11] woundedness, and something quivered inside her, died out along the curve of her mouth and in her eyes. He had moved her. All the unforgettable impulses of first love had surged up once more; their hearts had in some way touched across two feet of Paris sunlight. She took her fiancé's arm suddenly, as if to steady herself with the feel of it.

They parted. Michael walked quickly for a minute; then he stopped, pretending to look in a window, and saw them farther up the street, walking fast into the Place Vendôme,[12] people with much to do.

11. *Profound* means "deep" or "complete."
12. *Place Vendôme* (pläs   vän dōm')

He had things to do also—he had to get his laundry.

"Nothing will ever be the same again," he said to himself. "She will never be happy in her marriage and I will never be happy at all any more."

The two vivid years of his love for Caroline moved back around him like years in Einstein's physics. Intolerable memories arose—of rides in the Long Island moonlight; of a happy time at Lake Placid with her cheeks so cold there, but warm just underneath the surface; of a despairing afternoon in a little café on Forty-eighth Street in the last sad months when their marriage had come to seem impossible.

"Come in," he said aloud.

The concierge with a telegram; brusque because Mr. Curly's clothes were a little shabby. Mr. Curly gave few tips; Mr. Curly was obviously a *petit client*.[13]

Michael read the telegram.

"An answer?" the concierge asked.

"No," said Michael, and then, on an impulse: "Look."

"Too bad—too bad," said the concierge. **E** "Your grandfather is dead."

"Not too bad," said Michael. "It means that I come into a quarter of a million dollars."

Too late by a single month; after the first flush of the news his misery was deeper than ever. Lying awake in bed that night, he listened endlessly to the long caravan of a circus moving through the street from one Paris fair to another.

13. A *concierge* (kōn syerzh') assists hotel guests by taking messages, making reservations, and so on. A *brusque* person is blunt and rude. The French phrase *petit client* (pe' tē klē' ən) means "small (unimportant) customer."

F. Scott Fitzgerald

When the last van had rumbled out of hearing and the corners of the furniture were pastel blue with the dawn, he was still thinking of the look in Caroline's eyes that morning—the look that seemed to say: "Oh, why couldn't you have done something about it? Why couldn't you have been stronger, made me marry you? Don't you see how sad I am?"

Michael's fists clenched.

"Well, I won't give up till the last moment," he whispered. "I've had all the bad luck so far, and maybe it's turned at last. One takes what one can get, up to the limit of one's strength, and if I can't have her, at least she'll go into this marriage with some of me in her heart."

◆ II ◆

Accordingly he went to the party at Chez Victor two days later, upstairs and into the little salon[14] off the bar where the party was to assemble for cocktails. He was early; the only other occupant was a tall lean man of fifty. They spoke.

"You waiting for George Packman's party?"

"Yes. My name's Michael Curly."

"My name's——"

Michael failed to catch the name. They ordered a drink, and Michael supposed that the bride and groom were having a gay time.

"Too much so," the other agreed, frowning. "I don't see how they stand it. We all crossed on the boat together; five days of that crazy life and then two weeks of Paris. You"—he hesitated, smiling faintly—"you'll excuse me for saying that your generation drinks too much."

"Not Caroline."

"No, not Caroline. She seems to take only a cocktail and a glass of champagne, and then she's had enough, thank God. But Hamilton drinks too much and all this crowd of young people drink too much. Do you live in Paris?"

"For the moment," said Michael.

"I don't like Paris. My wife—that is to say, my ex-wife, Hamilton's mother—lives in Paris."

"You're Hamilton Rutherford's father?"

"I have that honor. And I'm not denying that I'm proud of what he's done; it was just a general comment."

"Of course."

Michael glanced up nervously as four people came in. He felt suddenly that his dinner coat was old and shiny; he had ordered a new one that morning. The people who had come in were rich and at home in their richness with one another—a dark, lovely girl with a hysterical little laugh whom he had met before; two confident men whose jokes referred invariably to last night's scandal and tonight's potentialities, as if they had important rôles in a play that extended indefinitely into the past and the future. When Caroline arrived, Michael had scarcely a moment of her, but it was enough to note that, like all the others, she was strained and tired. She was pale beneath her rouge; there were shadows under her eyes. With a mixture of relief and wounded vanity,[15] he found himself placed far from her and at another table; he needed a moment to adjust himself to his surroundings. This was not like the immature set in which he and Caroline had moved; the men were more than thirty and had an air of sharing the best of this world's good. Next to him was Jebby West, whom he knew; and, on the other side, a jovial man who immediately began to talk to Michael about a stunt for the bachelor dinner: They were going to hire a French girl to appear with an actual baby in her arms, crying: "Hamilton, you can't desert me now!" The idea seemed stale and unamusing to Michael, but its originator shook with anticipatory laughter.

Farther up the table there was talk of the market—another drop today, the most appreciable[16] since the crash; people were kidding Rutherford about it: "Too bad, old man. You better not get married, after all."

---

14. The French word *salon* means "drawing room."

15. *Vanity* is excessive pride.

16. *Appreciable* means "enough to be noticed."

BEGINNINGS OF THE MODERN AGE ❧ 655

Historical Note

Remind students that in 1919 Congress passed the Volstead Act, a law that effectively prohibited the sale of liquor. During Prohibition, however, many Americans continued to drink alcohol. They made their own alcoholic beverages and drank illegally in speakeasies. Doctors also prescribed alcohol for medicinal purposes. After years of being ignored and subverted in the United States and derided in Europe, the Volstead Act was repealed in 1933.

F Literary Elements

CHARACTERIZATION Have students discuss what Michael's conversation and thoughts reveal about his character. *(His defense of Caroline to Mr. Rutherford and his assessment of her looks reveal his love; his nervousness at his shiny dinner jacket reinforces his sense of inferiority to the rich.)*

FYI

Dinner Apparel During the more formal 1920s, wealthy people dressed for dinner. Men changed from three-piece suits to tuxedos; women typically wore long dresses and, often, wispy feather hats and elbow-length gloves.

Writing *Minilesson*

Dramatizing a Scene If students were going to present the arrival of Caroline and Hamilton at the Chez Victor as a television play, the arrival might be somewhat longer than in the story.

Activity Have small groups of students write a one- or two-minute scene that includes Caroline and Hamilton's arrival, their greeting of guests, and Caroline's brief moment with Michael. They should include stage directions and dialogue to cover the three discrete segments of the scene. After rehearsing they should enact it in class and have the audience comment on how effective their scene was.
L3 **COLLAB. LEARN.**

Additional Resources

▌ *Writer's Choice,* Lesson 3.1

655

Michael asked the man on his left, "Has he lost a lot?"

"Nobody knows. He's heavily involved, but he's one of the smartest young men in Wall Street. Anyhow, nobody ever tells you the truth."

It was a champagne dinner from the start, and toward the end it reached a pleasant level of conviviality,[17] but Michael saw that all these people were too weary to be exhilarated by any ordinary stimulant; for weeks they had drunk cocktails before meals like Americans, wines and brandies like Frenchmen, beer like Germans, whisky-and-soda like the English, and as they were no longer in the twenties, this preposterous *mélange*,[18] that was like some gigantic cocktail in a nightmare, served only to make them temporarily less conscious of the mistakes of the night before. Which is to say that it was not really a gay party; what gayety existed was displayed in the few who drank nothing at all.

But Michael was not tired, and the champagne stimulated him and made his misery less acute. He had been away from New York for more than eight months and most of the dance music was unfamiliar to him, but at the first bars of the "Painted Doll," to which he and Caroline had moved through so much happiness and despair the previous summer, he crossed to Caroline's table and asked her to dance.

She was lovely in a dress of thin ethereal[19] blue, and the proximity of her crackly yellow hair, of her cool and tender gray eyes, turned his body clumsy and rigid; he stumbled with their first step on the floor. For a moment it seemed that there was nothing to say; he wanted to tell her about his inheritance, but the idea seemed abrupt, unprepared for.

"Michael, it's so nice to be dancing with you again."

He smiled grimly.

"I'm so happy you came," she continued. "I was afraid maybe you'd be silly and stay away. Now we can be just good friends and natural together. Michael, I want you and Hamilton to like each other."

The engagement was making her stupid; he had never heard her make such a series of obvious remarks before.

"I could kill him without a qualm,"[20] he said pleasantly, "but he looks like a good man. He's fine. What I want to know is, what happens to people like me who aren't able to forget?"

As he said this he could not prevent his mouth from dropping suddenly, and glancing up, Caroline saw, and her heart quivered violently, as it had the other morning.

"Do you mind so much, Michael?"

"Yes."

For a second as he said this, in a voice that seemed to have come up from his shoes, they were not dancing; they were simply clinging together. Then she leaned away from him and twisted her mouth into a lovely smile.

"I didn't know what to do at first, Michael. I told Hamilton about you—that I'd cared for you an awful lot—but it didn't worry him, and he was right. Because I'm over you now—yes, I am. And you'll wake up some sunny morning and be over me just like that."

He shook his head stubbornly.

"Oh, yes. We weren't for each other. I'm pretty flighty, and I need somebody like Hamilton to decide things. It was that more than the question of—of——"

"Of money." Again he was on the point of telling her what had happened, but again something told him it was not the time.

---

17. *Conviviality* is merriment and the enjoyment of good company.
18. *Mélange* (mä′ länzh) means "mixture."
19. An *ethereal* (i thēr′ ē əl) blue would be very light and delicate.

20. *Qualm* means "doubt," "misgiving," or "twinge of conscience."

Vocabulary
exhilarated (ig zil′ ə rā təd) *adj.* cheerful, lively, or excited; filled with vigor

"Then how do you account for what happened when we met the other day," he demanded helplessly—"what happened just now? When we just pour toward each other like we used to—as if we were one person, as if the same blood was flowing through both of us?"

"Oh, don't," she begged him. "You mustn't talk like that; everything's decided now. I love Hamilton with all my heart. It's just that I remember certain things in the past and I feel sorry for you—for us—for the way we were."

Over her shoulder, Michael saw a man come toward them to cut in. In a panic he danced her away, but inevitably the man came on.

"I've got to see you alone, if only for a minute," Michael said quickly. "When can I?"

"I'll be at Jebby West's tea tomorrow," she whispered as a hand fell politely upon Michael's shoulder.

But he did not talk to her at Jebby West's tea. Rutherford stood next to her, and each brought the other into all conversations. They left early. The next morning the wedding cards arrived in the first mail.

Then Michael, grown desperate with pacing up and down his room, determined on a bold stroke; he wrote to Hamilton Rutherford, asking him for a rendezvous[21] the following afternoon. In a short telephone communication Rutherford agreed, but for a day later than Michael had asked. And the wedding was only six days away.

They were to meet in the bar of the Hotel Jena. Michael knew what he would say: "See here, Rutherford, do you realize the responsibility you're taking in going through with this marriage? Do you realize the harvest of trouble and regret you're sowing in persuading a girl into something contrary to the instincts of her

heart?" He would explain that the barrier between Caroline and himself had been an artificial one and was now removed, and demand that the matter be put up to Caroline frankly before it was too late.

Rutherford would be angry, conceivably there would be a scene, but Michael felt that he was fighting for his life now.

He found Rutherford in conversation with an older man, whom Michael had met at several of the wedding parties.

"I saw what happened to most of my friends," Rutherford was saying, "and I decided it wasn't going to happen to me. It isn't so difficult; if you take a girl with common sense, and tell her what's what, and do your stuff damn well, and play decently square with her, it's a marriage. If you stand for any nonsense at the beginning, it's one of these arrangements—within five years the man gets out, or else the girl gobbles him up and you have the usual mess."

"Right!" agreed his companion enthusiastically. "Hamilton, boy, you're right."

Michael's blood boiled slowly.

"Doesn't it strike you," he inquired coldly, "that your attitude went out of fashion about a hundred years ago?"

"No, it didn't," said Rutherford pleasantly, but impatiently. "I'm as modern as anybody. I'd get married in an aeroplane next Saturday if it'd please my girl."

"I don't mean that way of being modern. You can't take a sensitive woman——"

"Sensitive? Women aren't so darn sensitive. It's fellows like you who are sensitive; it's fellows like you they <u>exploit</u>—all your devotion and kindness and all that. They read a couple of books and see a few pictures because they haven't got anything else to do, and then they say they're finer in grain than you are, and to prove it they take the bit in their teeth and

---

21. A *rendezvous* is an appointment to meet at a certain place or time.

Vocabulary

exploit (iks ploit′) *v.* to use or develop for profit, often in a selfish, unjust, or unfair way

---

THE BRIDAL PARTY

tear off for a fare-you-well—just about as sensitive as a fire horse."

"Caroline happens to be sensitive," said Michael in a clipped voice.

At this point the other man got up to go; when the dispute about the check had been settled and they were alone, Rutherford leaned back to Michael as if a question had been asked him.

"Caroline's more than sensitive," he said. "She's got sense."

His combative eyes, meeting Michael's, flickered with a gray light. "This all sounds pretty crude to you, Mr. Curly, but it seems to me that the average man nowadays just asks to be made a monkey of by some woman who doesn't even get any fun out of reducing him to that level. There are darn few men who possess their wives any more, but I am going to be one of them."

To Michael it seemed time to bring the talk back to the actual situation: "Do you realize the responsibility you're taking?"

"I certainly do," interrupted Rutherford. "I'm not afraid of responsibility. I'll make the decisions—fairly, I hope, but anyhow they'll be final."

"What if you didn't start right?" said Michael impetuously. "What if your marriage isn't founded on mutual love?"

"I think I see what you mean," Rutherford said, still pleasant. "And since you've brought it up, let me say that if you and Caroline had married, it wouldn't have lasted three years. Do you know what your affair was founded on? On sorrow. You got sorry for each other. Sorrow's a lot of fun for most women and for some men, but it seems to me that a marriage ought to be based on hope." He looked at his watch and stood up.

"I've got to meet Caroline. Remember, you're coming to the bachelor dinner day after tomorrow."

Michael felt the moment slipping away. "Then Caroline's personal feelings don't count with you?" he demanded fiercely.

"Caroline's tired and upset. But she has what she wants, and that's the main thing."

"Are you referring to yourself?" demanded **M** Michael incredulously.[22]

"Yes."

"May I ask how long she's wanted you?"

"About two years." Before Michael could answer, he was gone.

During the next two days Michael floated in an abyss of helplessness. The idea haunted him that he had left something undone that would sever this knot drawn tighter under his eyes. He phoned Caroline, but she insisted that it was physically impossible for her to see him until the day before the wedding, for which day she granted him a tentative rendezvous. Then he went to the bachelor dinner, partly in fear of an evening alone at his hotel, partly from a feeling that by his presence at that function he was somehow nearer to Caroline, keeping her in sight.

The Ritz Bar had been prepared for the occasion by French and American banners and by a great canvas covering one wall, against which the guests were invited to concentrate their proclivities[23] in breaking glasses.

At the first cocktail, taken at the bar, there were many slight spillings from many trembling hands, but later, with the champagne, there was a rising tide of laughter and occasional bursts of song.

---

22. *Incredulously* means "with unwillingness or inability to believe."
23. At this bachelor party, the guests' tendencies, or *proclivities,* are to drink toasts repeatedly to the groom and then smash their drinking glasses.

Vocabulary
impetuously (im pech′ o͞o əs lē) *adv.* impulsively; suddenly; rashly
tentative (ten′ tə tiv) *adj.* not fully worked out; somewhat undecided

Rooftop Café, 1925. Everett Shinn. Pastel on blue paper laid down on board, 11¼ x 15¼ in. Berry Hill Galleries Inc., New York.

Viewing the painting: In what ways does the mood of the painting reflect the mood of the parties described in "The Bridal Party"?

VIEWING THE PAINTING

Everett Shinn (1876–1953) was a painter, illustrator, designer, playwright, and film director. A member of a group of painters called The Eight, his early paintings are realistic urban scenes.

Viewing Response *Like the party at Chez Victor, the soft pastels of Shinn's painting create a mood of wealth, elegance, and gaiety.*

N **Author's Craft**

MOTIF Point out to students that Fitzgerald again refers to the stock market. This motif is clearly going to be important to the plot.

O **Active Reading**

PREDICT Ask students to speculate on the significance of this second woman. How will her appearance affect the characters? *(Most students will conclude that there has been another woman in Hamilton's life. Students might predict that if she is involved with Hamilton, Caroline may return to Michael.)*

Michael was surprised to find what a difference his new dinner coat, his new silk hat, his new, proud linen made in his estimate of himself; he felt less resentment toward all these people for being so rich and assured. For the first time since he had left college he felt rich and assured himself; he felt that he was part of all this, and even entered into the scheme of Johnson, the practical joker, for the appearance of the woman betrayed, now waiting tranquilly in the room across the hall.

"We don't want to go too heavy," Johnson said, "because I imagine Ham's had a pretty anxious day already. Did you see Fullman Oil's sixteen points off this morning?"

N

"Will that matter to him?" Michael asked, trying to keep the interest out of his voice.

"Naturally. He's in heavily; he's always in everything heavily. So far he's had luck; anyhow, up to a month ago."

The glasses were filled and emptied faster now, and men were shouting at one another across the narrow table. Against the bar a group of ushers was being photographed, and the flash light surged through the room in a stifling cloud.

"Now's the time," Johnson said. "You're to stand by the door, remember, and we're both to try and keep her from coming in—just till we get everybody's attention."

He went on out into the corridor, and Michael waited obediently by the door. **O** Several minutes passed. Then Johnson reappeared with a curious expression on his face.

"There's something funny about this."

"Isn't the girl there?"

"She's there all right, but there's another woman there, too; and it's nobody we engaged either. She wants to see Hamilton Rutherford, and she looks as if she had something on her mind."

BEGINNINGS OF THE MODERN AGE 🌿 659

GIFTED AND TALENTED ACTIVITY

Marriage Rituals Ask students to consider certain rituals associated with American marriages, such as the choosing of rings, showers for the bride, bachelor parties for the groom, the throwing of rice at the newly married couple, and honeymoons. Ask them what other rituals they can think of.

Activity Have students research the history and purpose of these and other marriage rituals. Ask them to consider
• when the ritual began.
• what the ritual originally signified.
• what the ritual presently means.
• why some rituals have disappeared.

Have students share their findings with the class in a panel discussion. **L3**

P **Literary Elements**

CHARACTERIZATION Ask students to describe what they learn about Hamilton from these lines. *(Although he is shocked and then angered by the news of Marjorie Collins's appearance, he is a man who recovers quickly and can take charge in an emergency. He seems to think quickly on his feet because he evidently knows immediately what he'll do.)*

Q **Active Reading**

QUESTION Ask students what the phrase "house of cards" means and why Michael thinks it is about to fall. *(Literally a structure made with playing cards, a house of cards is, figuratively, something so flimsy that it can easily be destroyed. Michael hopes that Marjorie Collins's appearance will force Hamilton and Caroline to break up.)*

R **Literary Elements**

FORESHADOWING Ask students what events these telegrams may foreshadow. *(Given the references to Hamilton's investments, the telegrams may foreshadow important news about them.)*

THE BRIDAL PARTY

They went out into the hall. Planted firmly in a chair near the door sat an American girl a little the worse for liquor, but with a determined expression on her face. She looked up at them with a jerk of her head.

"Well, j'tell him?" she demanded. "The name is Marjorie Collins, and he'll know it. I've come a long way, and I want to see him now and quick, or there's going to be more trouble than you ever saw." She rose unsteadily to her feet.

"You go in and tell Ham," whispered Johnson to Michael. "Maybe he'd better get out. I'll keep her here."

P Back at the table, Michael leaned close to Rutherford's ear and, with a certain grimness, whispered:

"A girl outside named Marjorie Collins says she wants to see you. She looks as if she wanted to make trouble."

Hamilton Rutherford blinked and his mouth fell ajar; then slowly the lips came together in a straight line and he said in a crisp voice:

"Please keep her there. And send the head barman to me right away."

Michael spoke to the barman, and then, without returning to the table, asked quietly for his coat and hat. Out in the hall again, he passed Johnson and the girl without speaking and went out into the Rue Cambon.[24] Calling a cab, he gave the address of Caroline's hotel.

Q His place was beside her now. Not to bring bad news, but simply to be with her when her house of cards came falling around her head.

Rutherford had implied that he was soft—well, he was hard enough not to give up the girl he loved without taking advantage of every chance within the pale[25] of honor. Should she turn away from Rutherford, she would find him there.

She was in; she was surprised when he called, but she was still dressed and would be

down immediately. Presently she appeared in a dinner gown, holding two blue telegrams in her hand. They sat down in armchairs in the deserted lobby.

"But, Michael, is the dinner over?"

"I wanted to see you, so I came away."

"I'm glad." Her voice was friendly, but matter-of-fact. "Because I'd just phoned your **R** hotel that I had fittings and rehearsals all day tomorrow. Now we can have our talk after all."

"You're tired," he guessed. "Perhaps I shouldn't have come."

"No. I was waiting up for Hamilton. Telegrams that may be important. He said he might go on somewhere, and that may mean any hour, so I'm glad I have someone to talk to."

Michael winced at the impersonality in the last phrase.

"Don't you care when he gets home?"

"Naturally," she said, laughing, "but I haven't got much say about it, have I?"

"Why not?"

"I couldn't start by telling him what he could and couldn't do."

"Why not?"

"He wouldn't stand for it."

"He seems to want merely a housekeeper," said Michael ironically.

"Tell me about your plans, Michael," she asked quickly.

"My plans? I can't see any future after the day after tomorrow. The only real plan I ever had was to love you."

Their eyes brushed past each other's, and the look he knew so well was staring out at him from hers. Words flowed quickly from his heart:

"Let me tell you just once more how well I've loved you, never wavering for a moment, never thinking of another girl. And now when I think of all the years ahead without you, without any hope, I don't want to live, Caroline darling. I used to dream about our home, our children, about holding you in my

---

24. *Cambon* (käm′ bon)
25. A *pale* is a boundary, an enclosure, or a limit.

Teaching Options

interNET CONNECTION

High Finance Students interested in the stock market might wish to discover what information is available on the Web. Have them use such keywords as *finance, stock market, investing,* or *funds.*

INTERDISCIPLINARY CONNECTION

History The Roaring Twenties came to an abrupt end when the stock market crashed on Black Monday, October 29, 1929. Ever since, economists and historians have offered various explanations for this crash.

Activity Have interested students research and report on the causes of the crash of 1929 and the safeguards government put in place to prevent a

second occurrence. Consider having each student research a specific aspect of the crash and its effects. **L3**

arms and touching your face and hands and hair that used to belong to me, and now I just can't wake up."

Caroline was crying softly. "Poor Michael—poor Michael." Her hand reached out and her fingers brushed the lapel of his dinner coat. "I was so sorry for you the other night. You looked so thin, and as if you needed a new suit and somebody to take care of you." She sniffled and looked more closely at his coat. "Why, you've got a new suit! And a new silk hat! Why, Michael, how swell!" She laughed, suddenly cheerful through her tears. "You must have come into money, Michael; I never saw you so well turned out."

For a moment, at her reaction, he hated his new clothes.

"I have come into money," he said. "My grandfather left me about a quarter of a million dollars."

"Why, Michael," she cried, "how perfectly swell! I can't tell you how glad I am. I've always thought you were the sort of person who ought to have money."

"Yes, just too late to make a difference."

The revolving door from the street groaned around and Hamilton Rutherford came into the lobby. His face was flushed, his eyes were restless and impatient.

"Hello, darling; hello, Mr. Curly." He bent and kissed Caroline. "I broke away for a minute to find out if I had any telegrams. I see you've got them there." Taking them from her, he remarked to Curly, "That was an odd business there in the bar, wasn't it? Especially as I understand some of you had a joke fixed up in the same line." He opened one of the telegrams, closed it and turned to Caroline with the divided expression of a man carrying two things in his head at once.

"A girl I haven't seen for two years turned up," he said. "It seemed to be some clumsy form of blackmail, for I haven't and never have had any sort of obligation toward her whatever."

"What happened?"

"The head barman had a Sûreté Générale[26] man there in ten minutes and it was settled in the hall. The French blackmail laws make ours look like a sweet wish, and I gather they threw a scare into her that she'll remember. But it seems wiser to tell you."

"Are you implying that I mentioned the matter?" said Michael stiffly.

"No," Rutherford said slowly. "No, you were just going to be on hand. And since you're here, I'll tell you some news that will interest you even more."

He handed Michael one telegram and opened the other.

"This is in code," Michael said.

"So is this. But I've got to know all the words pretty well this last week. The two of them together mean that I'm due to start life all over."

Michael saw Caroline's face grow a shade paler, but she sat quiet as a mouse.

"It was a mistake and I stuck to it too long," continued Rutherford. "So you see I don't have all the luck, Mr. Curly. By the way, they tell me you've come into money."

"Yes," said Michael.

"There we are, then." Rutherford turned to Caroline. "You understand, darling, that I'm not joking or exaggerating. I've lost almost every cent I had and I'm starting life over."

Two pairs of eyes were regarding her—Rutherford's noncommittal[27] and unrequiring, Michael's hungry, tragic, pleading. In a minute she had raised herself from the chair and with a little cry thrown herself into Hamilton Rutherford's arms.

"Oh, darling," she cried, "what does it matter! It's better; I like it better, honestly I do! I want to start that way; I want to! Oh, please don't worry or be sad even for a minute!"

---

26. In Paris, *Sûreté Générale* (sœr′ tā   zhen ā′ räl′) is the police department's criminal investigation unit.

27. *Noncommittal* means "unwilling to pledge oneself to a particular opinion, view, or course of action."

Critical Thinking

INFERRING Have students consider why Michael might hate his new clothes. *(Michael's reaction is linked to Caroline's statement that he had looked "as if [he] needed . . . somebody to take care of [him]." He may fear that his sudden prosperity will diminish her concern.)*

Active Reading

RESPOND Hamilton has made two important announcements before Michael and Caroline. Invite students to give their opinion of Hamilton and his actions. *(Most students will admire Hamilton for his courage and honesty. They should give reasons for their responses.)*

Literary Elements

PLOT: *Climax* Ask students whether Caroline's action could be the climax of the plot. *(Yes. By choosing Hamilton instead of Michael, Caroline resolves the plot issue of who gets the girl.)*

REAL-WORLD CONNECTION

Honesty Hamilton faces two crises: a woman who wants to blackmail him and his disaster on the stock market. He freely acknowledges both situations to Caroline. He evidently believes that honesty is the best policy. Invite students to consider if this is always the case.

Activity Have students find magazine, newspaper, or Internet articles that either exemplify or debunk the adage "Honesty is the best policy." The articles can focus on personal relations, business dealings, even international relations. Ask students to summarize their articles in three to five sentences. Then have a class discussion. Ask students: What is the connection between honesty and honor? Are there degrees of honesty? Are there circumstances in which complete honesty can be harmful? **L2**

The Wedding. Walter Richard Sickert (1860–1942). Oil on canvas. Private collection.

Viewing the painting: What adjectives would you use to describe the bride in the painting? Could the adjectives you chose also apply to Caroline? Why or why not?

662   UNIT 5

"All right, baby," said Rutherford. His hand stroked her hair gently for a moment; then he took his arm from around her.

"I promised to join the party for an hour," he said. "So I'll say good night, and I want you to go to bed soon and get a good sleep. Good night, Mr. Curly. I'm sorry to have let you in for all these financial matters."

But Michael had already picked up his hat and cane. "I'll go along with you," he said.

~III~

It was such a fine morning. Michael's cutaway[28] hadn't been delivered, so he felt rather uncomfortable passing before the cameras and moving-picture machines in front of the little church on the Avenue George-Cinq.

It was such a clean, new church that it seemed unforgivable not to be dressed properly, and Michael, white and shaky after a sleepless night, decided to stand in the rear. From there he looked at the back of Hamilton Rutherford, and the lacy, filmy back of Caroline, and the fat back of George Packman, which looked unsteady, as if it wanted to lean against the bride and groom.

The ceremony went on for a long time under the gay flags and pennons[29] overhead, under the thick beams of June sunlight slanting down through the tall windows upon the well-dressed people.

As the procession, headed by the bride and groom, started down the aisle, Michael realized with alarm he was just where everyone would dispense with their parade stiffness, become informal and speak to him.

So it turned out. Rutherford and Caroline spoke first to him; Rutherford grim with the strain of being married, and Caroline lovelier than he had ever seen her, floating all softly down through the friends and relatives of her youth, down through the past and forward to the future by the sunlit door.

Michael managed to murmur, "Beautiful, simply beautiful," and then other people passed and spoke to him—old Mrs. Dandy, straight from her sickbed and looking remarkably well, or carrying it off like the very fine old lady she was; and Rutherford's father and mother, ten years divorced, but walking side by side and looking made for each other and proud. Then all Caroline's sisters and their husbands and her little nephews in Eton suits,[30] and then a long parade, all speaking to Michael because he was still standing paralyzed just at that point where the procession broke.

He wondered what would happen now. Cards had been issued for a reception at the George-Cinq; an expensive enough place, heaven knew. Would Rutherford try to go through with that on top of those disastrous telegrams? Evidently, for the procession outside was streaming up there through the June morning, three by three and four by four. On the corner the long dresses of girls, five abreast, fluttered many-colored in the wind. Girls had become gossamer again, perambulatory flora;[31] such lovely fluttering dresses in the bright noon wind.

Michael needed a drink; he couldn't face that reception line without a drink. Diving into a side doorway of the hotel, he asked for the bar, whither a *chasseur*[32] led him through half a kilometer of new American-looking passages.

But—how did it happen?—the bar was full. There were ten—fifteen men and two—four girls, all from the wedding, all needing a drink. There were cocktails and champagne in the bar; Rutherford's cocktails and champagne, as

---

28. A *cutaway,* also called a morning coat, is a man's long, formal coat with tails sloping back from the waistline.
29. *Pennons* are long, triangular flags.
30. *Eton* is a prestigious boys' school near London; the *suits* are of the style—black, with short pants and waist-length jackets—worn by Eton students.
31. *Gossamer* is light, filmy, delicate, and cobweb-like. *Perambulatory flora* are walking plants or flowers.
32. A *chasseur* (shä sœr′) runs errands and attends to guests' needs.

Critical Thinking

INFERRING Ask students how they would describe Michael's state of mind at this point. (*Michael seems numb to every stimulus.*)

Active Reading

RESPOND Fitzgerald emphasizes what Michael has heard before but rejected: that Caroline has been after Hamilton for two years. Students might discuss whether this second verification changes their attitude toward Michael or Caroline.

Vo•cab•u•lar•y Skills

Connotations The word *poignant* comes from a French verb that means "to prick." Thus, its connotation is not sentimental, but sharp and hurtful.

---

it turned out, for he had engaged the whole bar and the ballroom and the two great reception rooms and all the stairways leading up and down, and windows looking out over the whole square block of Paris. By and by Michael went and joined the long, slow drift of the receiving line. Through a flowery mist of "Such a lovely wedding," "My dear, you were simply lovely," "You're a lucky man, Rutherford" he passed down the line. When Michael came to Caroline, she took a single step forward and kissed him on the lips, but he felt no contact in the kiss; it was unreal and he floated on away from it. Old Mrs. Dandy, who had always liked him, held his hand for a minute and thanked him for the flowers he had sent when he heard she was ill.

"I'm so sorry not to have written; you know, we old ladies are grateful for——" The flowers, the fact that she had not written, the wedding—Michael saw that they all had the same relative importance to her now; she had married off five other children and seen two of the marriages go to pieces, and this scene, so poignant,[33] so confusing to Michael, appeared to her simply a familiar charade in which she had played her part before.

A buffet luncheon with champagne was already being served at small tables and there was an orchestra playing in the empty ballroom. Michael sat down with Jebby West; he was still a little embarrassed at not wearing a morning coat, but he perceived now that he was not alone in the omission and felt better. "Wasn't Caroline divine?" Jebby West said. "So entirely self-possessed. I asked her this morning if she wasn't a little nervous at stepping off like this. And she said, 'Why should I be? I've been after him for two years, and now I'm just happy, that's all.'"

"It must be true," said Michael gloomily.

"What?"

"What you just said."

He had been stabbed, but, rather to his distress, he did not feel the wound.

He asked Jebby to dance. Out on the floor, Rutherford's father and mother were dancing together.

"It makes me a little sad, that," she said. "Those two hadn't met for years; both of them were married again and she divorced again. She went to the station to meet him when he came over for Caroline's wedding, and invited him to stay at her house in the Avenue du Bois[34] with a whole lot of other people, perfectly proper, but he was afraid his wife would hear about it and not like it, so he went to a hotel. Don't you think that's sort of sad?"

An hour or so later Michael realized suddenly that it was afternoon. In one corner of the ballroom an arrangement of screens like a moving-picture stage had been set up and photographers were taking official pictures of the bridal party. The bridal party, still as death and pale as wax under the bright lights, appeared, to the dancers circling the modulated semidarkness of the ballroom, like those jovial or sinister[35] groups that one comes upon in The Old Mill at an amusement park.

After the bridal party had been photographed, there was a group of the ushers; then the bridesmaids, the families, the children. Later, Caroline, active and excited, having long since abandoned the repose implicit[36] in her flowing dress and great bouquet, came and plucked Michael off the floor.

"Now we'll have them take one of just old friends." Her voice implied that this was best, most intimate of all. "Come here, Jebby, George—not you, Hamilton; this is just my friends—Sally——"

A little after that, what remained of formality disappeared and the hours flowed easily down

---

34. *du Bois* (dōō bwä)

35. A *jovial* group is lively and full of fun; a *sinister* one threatens harm or evil.

36. *Repose* means "peacefulness." Something *implicit* is suggested but not directly expressed.

---

33. *Poignant* (poin′ yənt) means "calling up sad emotions."

664 ❧ UNIT 5

Teaching Options

Listening and Speaking *Minilesson*

Formal Discussion A formal group discussion about literature is constructed around several participants who agree in advance to discuss specific questions. They prepare by rereading the literature, thinking about the questions, and supporting their opinions with quotations, examples, and other evidence from the source. The group should select a leader who will monitor the discussion, keep participants focused on the question under consideration, and see to it that all questions are discussed in the time allowed. The questions can address one or more of the elements of fiction.

Activity Have students work in groups of five or six and plan a formal group discussion of this story. They should first choose the questions they will discuss. Then, in a 10- or 15-minute discussion, students should examine those questions before the rest of the class. **L2** **COLLAB. LEARN.**

CHICAGO

Carl Sandburg

A **Active Reading**

CONNECT Explain to students that this poem is about the city of Chicago. Before they read, ask students what they already know about the city. What images come to mind when they think of Chicago? You might suggest that they create a word web with "Chicago" at the center, and add words and phrases that they associate with the city around it. Encourage students to compare their impressions of Chicago with Sandburg's as they read.

Additional Resources
📁 *Active Reading Guide,* p. 77
🎧 *Audio Library*

VIEWING THE PHOTOGRAPH

Ask students the following questions:
• **What is the mood of the picture?** *(It is a mood of frenzied activity and confusion.)*
• **What impression of Chicago does this photograph convey?** *(It conveys the impression of a busy, dynamic, crowded city.)*

Teaching Options

Reading Minilesson

Classifying Poets often imply their attitude toward their subject through their choice of words and images. In "Chicago" Sandburg uses a series of epithets and images to convey his attitude toward the city of Chicago.

[Activity] Have small groups use the chart to identify the characteristics of Chicago that Sandburg describes and then evaluate whether or not Sandburg admires them. **L2** **COLLAB. LEARN.**

Characteristic	Does Sandburg admire?

Additional Resources
📁 *Reading Workbook*

671

Supported by nine railroads and several of Chicago's leading meat packers, Union Stock Yards opened on Christmas Day, 1865. Not until August 1971 did all meat-processing activities cease at that location. Today, extensive stockyards are located in Nebraska, South Dakota, and Minnesota.

B Active Reading

CLARIFY Ask students to discuss the phrase "Flinging magnetic curses" in line 11. *(Students should conclude that Sandburg uses the word* magnetic *in its sense of attracting or charming others. Some students may point out that magnets can both attract and repel. Sandburg suggests that Chicago's qualities may do both.)*

Thematic Focus

New Directions Ask students how Sandburg's poem reflects the changes in American society and American cities in the early twentieth century. In what ways does the poem celebrate urbanization and industrialization? In what ways does it criticize these developments?

✓ ASSESSMENT OPTIONS

📁 *Quick Checks,* p. 77

Teaching Options

CHICAGO

Hog Butcher for the World,
Tool Maker, Stacker of Wheat,
Player with Railroads and the Nation's Freight Handler;
Stormy, husky, brawling,
5   City of the Big Shoulders:
They tell me you are wicked and I believe them, for I have seen your painted
    women under the gas lamps luring the farm boys.
And they tell me you are crooked and I answer: Yes, it is true I have seen the
    gunman kill and go free to kill again.
And they tell me you are brutal and my reply is: On the faces of women and
    children I have seen the marks of wanton° hunger.
And having answered so I turn once more to those who sneer at this my city,
    and I give them back the sneer and say to them:
10   Come and show me another city with lifted head singing so proud to be alive
    and coarse and strong and cunning.
B Flinging magnetic curses amid the toil of piling job on job, here is a tall bold
    slugger set vivid against the little soft cities;
Fierce as a dog with tongue lapping for action, cunning as a savage pitted
    against the wilderness,
        Bareheaded,
        Shoveling,
15   Wrecking,
        Planning,
        Building, breaking, rebuilding,
Under the smoke, dust all over his mouth, laughing with white teeth,
Under the terrible burden of destiny laughing as a young man laughs,
20   Laughing even as an ignorant fighter laughs who has never lost a battle,
Bragging and laughing that under his wrist is the pulse, and under his ribs the
    heart of the people,
        Laughing!
Laughing the stormy, husky, brawling laughter of Youth, half-naked, sweat-
    ing, proud to be Hog Butcher, Tool Maker, Stacker of Wheat, Player
    with railroads and Freight Handler to the Nation.

_____

8 *Wanton* means "resulting from extreme cruelty or neglect."

ENGLISH LANGUAGE LEARNERS

Epithets Point out to English language learners that the poem begins with a series of epithets, short descriptive phrases that characterize a person or place. Sandburg uses them to emphasize traits that he thinks are special to Chicago. Ask volunteers to paraphrase or explain and discuss the epithets.

Activity Ask English language learners to create epithets about cities or other places where they have lived. Invite students to share them with the class, and explain why they believe these phrases capture some special quality of these places. **COLLAB. LEARN.**

Additional Resources
📁 *English Language Learners Sourcebook*

Responding to Literature

Personal Response

What are your impressions of the Chicago the speaker describes?

Literary ELEMENTS

Apostrophe

Apostrophe is a figure of speech in which a writer directly addresses an inanimate object, an idea, or an absent person. For example, in "Chicago," the speaker says to the city, "they tell me you are crooked and I answer . . ." Poets often use apostrophe to achieve either a formal tone or a sense of emotional immediacy.

1. Would you say the speaker in "Chicago" addresses the city directly in the first five lines? Explain.
2. In which lines does the speaker address the city as "you"? In your opinion, what effect does this use of apostrophe create?
3. What effects do you think Sandburg's overall use of apostrophe in the poem creates?

● See **Literary Terms Handbook,** p. R1.

─── ANALYZING LITERATURE ───

RECALL AND INTERPRET

1. What names does the speaker give Chicago in lines 1–5? What do these names reveal about the city?
2. In lines 6–8, what three negative adjectives describe the city? What problems in the city do these adjectives indicate? What overall impressions do these problems give of Chicago? Explain.
3. Name some of the positive adjectives the speaker uses to describe Chicago. What do these words reveal about the city's inhabitants and the speaker's attitude toward them?
4. To what does Sandburg compare Chicago in lines 10–23? What final impression do these comparisons give of the city?

EVALUATE AND CONNECT

5. How does Sandburg's **diction,** or choice of words, help create a vivid image of the city? Provide examples from the poem.
6. Notice two **similes,** or comparisons using the word *like* or *as,* that Sandburg uses in lines 19–20. In your opinion, how effective are these similes in expressing the **theme** (see page R16) of the poem?
7. How does Sandburg's portrayal of early twentieth-century Chicago compare with a big city of today? Consider similarities as well as differences.
8. Review what you wrote for the Focus Activity on page 670. How does your defense compare with Sandburg's defense of Chicago? Would any of Sandburg's methods have helped you in your defense? Explain.

─── EXTENDING YOUR RESPONSE ───

Creative Writing

Defending Your Community   With a partner, write a poem or a brief essay defending your own city, town, or neighborhood. Use Sandburg's poem as a model. What special characteristics does your community have? What might some people say to criticize it? How will you defend it against those criticisms? Share your poem or essay with the class.

Literature Groups

Proud or Defensive?   Is the speaker in "Chicago" proud of the city or defensive about its poor public image? What do you think? Debate this question in your group, and provide examples from the poem to support your opinion. Share your group's ideas with the class.

 Save your work for your portfolio.

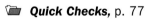

✔ ASSESSMENT OPTIONS

📁 *Quick Checks,* p. 77
📁 *Selection and Theme Assessment,* p. 115
📁 *Performance Assessment,* p. 65
💾 *Testmaker*

LITERARY ELEMENTS

1. Yes, Sandburg's series of descriptive epithets are used as forms of direct address.
2. He addresses the city as "you" in lines 6–8. The use of personification creates emotional intimacy and immediacy.
3. The apostrophe creates a paradoxical effect: it entices the reader to share the speaker's feelings while also distancing the reader with its artificiality.

Additional Resources

 Literary Elements Transparency 63

Personal Response

Some will be repelled by the negative images; others will find them compelling.

─── ANALYZING LITERATURE ───

1. The speaker calls the city the "Hog Butcher for the World, Tool Maker, Stacker of Wheat, Player with Railroads, and the Nation's Freight Handler." The names reveal that the city is a commercial and industrial center.
2. The adjectives "wicked," "crooked," and "brutal" refer to prostitution, crime, and poverty. They suggest a city beset with urban problems.
3. The positive adjectives—"proud to be alive," "coarse and strong and cunning," "tall bold," "Bareheaded, Shoveling, Wrecking, Planning, Building, breaking, rebuilding"—suggest the speaker's admiration.
4. Sandburg compares the city to a laughing youth, which suggests the city's newness and indomitability.
5. Sandburg uses concrete images and strong connotative words such as "painted women" not "prostitutes"; "wanton hunger" instead of mere "hunger"; "magnetic curses" and "slugger" to suggest strength. These are vivid, strong words that help the reader sense the vitality of the city.
6. The similes "laughing as a young man laughs" and "as an ignorant fighter laughs" provide an effective comparison that helps readers appreciate the youth, strength, and brashness of the city.
7. Students might point out that the energy and brutality of life in many cities remains much the same, but most cities are now built around service industries rather than manufacturing. Workers are more likely to sit in front of computers than to roll up their sleeves and shovel coal.
8. Students' defenses may be based on logic and reasoned arguments, whereas Sandburg uses powerful images and forceful assertions.

Objectives

- To read poems written by Chinese immigrants
- To identify literal language and understand its power
- To write a short poem about a disappointing moment

Skills

Reading/Thinking: Inferring
Writing: Editorial
Collaboration: Literature Groups

Motivating
→OPTIONS

Selection Focus Transparency 70: Before viewing the cartoon, ask students their views on immigration.

Focus Activity: As an extension of the Focus Activity, have students think about how they overcame their disappointment. Did it last long? How do they feel about it now?

Before You Read

from Songs of Gold Mountain

> **"Right after we were wed, Husband,**
> **you set out on a journey.**
> **How was I to tell you how I felt?**
> **Wandering around a foreign country,**
> **when will you ever come home?"**
>
> —*Anonymous*

"Gold Mountain Poems" were written by numerous anonymous poets—Chinese immigrants to the United States who were detained at an immigration center in San Francisco.

In the mid-nineteenth century, Chinese people began immigrating to the United States in large numbers. Many left China to escape intense fighting between the British and the Chinese and between peasant farmers and the ruling class. Others left China hoping to improve their economic prospects by working in this country.

The first wave of Chinese immigrants consisted mostly of adventurous young men who dreamed of striking it rich in the mines of "Gold Mountain," as the United States was called. Circulars distributed by labor brokers fueled such dreams: "Americans are very rich people. They want the China man to come and make him very welcome. There you will have great pay, large houses, and food and clothing of the finest description."

Many of the young men who came to California were married and planned to remain just long enough to make their fortune. In reality, however, about half of this group never returned to China. When mining profits began to dwindle, many went to work on the Central Pacific Railroad and on farms in California.

FOCUS ACTIVITY

Think about a time when you experienced great disappointment. How did you feel? What did you do?

QUICKWRITE Spend three or four minutes exploring your response to these questions.

SETTING A PURPOSE Read to learn about the feelings of disappointment experienced by many Chinese immigrants as described by anonymous poets.

BACKGROUND

The Time and Place
In 1849, the first year of the great gold rush, 325 Chinese immigrants arrived in California to prospect for gold. In 1852 more than 20,000 arrived. Americans welcomed these newcomers at first, but they soon began crying "California for Americans," resulting in a special miner's tax for foreigners. In 1882 the Chinese Exclusion Act was passed, which prohibited the immigration of

Chinese railroad workers, 1877.

Chinese laborers and eventually of all Chinese. The law remained in effect until 1943. Because of it, Chinese arriving after 1882 were detained for anywhere from several weeks to more than a year in a place called the "Wooden Barracks" on San Francisco Bay. On the walls of this place, they wrote short, powerful poems expressing their reactions to being detained.

RESOURCE MANAGER

Lesson Planning Resource
The *Unit Five Planning Guide* (pp. 77–81) provides additional lesson notes and reduced versions of all print resources.

📁 **Other Print Resources**
- Active Reading Guide, p. 78
- Reading Workbook
- Quick Checks, p. 78
- Selection and Theme Assessment, p. 116

- Performance Assessment, p. 66
- Spanish Summaries, p. 70
- Inclusion Strategies
- English Language Learners Sourcebook

 Transparencies
- Selection Focus 70
- Literary Elements 64

Technology
🎧 Audio Library
🖥 Glencoe Literature Web Site
💾 Testmaker

FOCUS ACTIVITY

How would you react if you suffered a serious injury to your leg or hand?

DISCUSS With a small group of classmates, briefly discuss how you would react to a life-changing injury. Explore how you might feel and how your outlook on the future might change.

SETTING A PURPOSE Read to discover how the narrator and other characters cope with their injuries and wounds.

BACKGROUND

Literary Influences

Hemingway recalled that when he was a young reporter on the *Kansas City Star,* the newspaper's style sheet instructed reporters to "avoid the use of adjectives, especially such extravagant ones as *splendid, gorgeous, grand, magnificent,* etc." Short sentences, brief opening paragraphs, and "vigorous English" were also required. Hemingway later called these "the best rules I ever learned for the business of writing." He learned much from Gertrude Stein's efforts to write with concise, spare prose that created repetitive sentence rhythms. Hemingway also noted that Stephen Crane, another American writer who had been trained as a journalist and served as a war correspondent, greatly influenced his prose style.

Kansas City Star newsroom, c. 1918.

VOCABULARY PREVIEW

lurch (lurch) *v.* to move suddenly and unevenly; p. 680
withered (with′ ərd) *adj.* shriveled; p. 680
detached (di tacht′) *adj.* not involved emotionally; indifferent; p. 681

jostle (jos′ əl) *v.* to bump, push, or shove while moving, as in a crowd; p. 681
resign (ri zīn′) *v.* to make oneself accept; p. 683

In Another Country

SUMMARY

During World War I, the narrator, a wounded American officer, and three Italian officers meet daily for physical therapy at an Italian hospital. The narrator works at a machine that mechanically bends his knee. One day, when the narrator says he hopes to marry, the Italian major exclaims, "A man must not marry" because "he should not place himself in a position to lose" his wife. Later the major explains that his wife has just died. Thereafter, the major stares out the window as he works on his rehabilitation.

📁 *Spanish Summaries,* p. 71

A Active Reading

VISUALIZE As students read the first two paragraphs, urge them to pause to visualize the scene. Ask them to describe the setting. Why does the author spend so much time developing the setting? *(It establishes mood and creates a sense of reality.)*

Additional Resources
📁 *Active Reading Guide,* p. 79
🎧 *Audio Library*
🎧 *Spanish Audio Library*

In the fall the war[1] was always there, but we did not go to it any more. It was cold in the fall in Milan[2] and the dark came very early. Then the electric lights came on, and it was pleasant along the streets looking in the windows. There was much game[3] hanging outside the shops, and the snow powdered in the fur of the foxes and the wind blew their tails. The deer hung stiff and heavy and empty, and small birds blew in the wind and the wind turned their feathers. It was a cold fall and the wind came down from the mountains.

We were all at the hospital every afternoon, and there were different ways of walking across the town through the dusk to the hospital. Two of the ways were alongside canals, but they were long. Always, though, you crossed a bridge across a canal to enter the hospital. There was a choice of three bridges. On one of them a woman sold roasted chestnuts. It was warm, standing in front of her charcoal fire, and the chestnuts were warm afterward in your pocket. The hospital was very old and very beautiful, and you entered through a gate and walked across a courtyard and out a gate on the other side. There were usually funerals starting from the courtyard. Beyond the old hospital were the new brick pavilions, and there we met every afternoon and were all very polite and interested in what was the matter, and sat in the machines that were to make so much difference.

The doctor came up to the machine where I was sitting and said: "What did you like best to do before the war? Did you practice a sport?"

I said: "Yes, football."

"Good," he said. "You will be able to play football again better than ever."

My knee did not bend and the leg dropped straight from the knee to the ankle without a calf, and the machine was to bend the knee and make it move as in riding a tricycle. But it did not bend yet, and instead the machine lurched when it came to the bending part. The doctor said: "That will all pass. You are a fortunate young man. You will play football again like a champion."

In the next machine was a major who had a little hand like a baby's. He winked at me when the doctor examined his hand, which was between two leather straps that bounced up and down and flapped the stiff fingers, and said: "And will I too play football, captain-doctor?" He had been a very great fencer, and before the war the greatest fencer in Italy.

The doctor went to his office in the back room and brought a photograph which showed a hand that had been withered almost as small as the major's, before it had taken a machine course, and after was a little larger. The major held the photograph with his good hand and looked at it very carefully. "A wound?" he asked.

"An industrial accident," the doctor said.

"Very interesting, very interesting," the major said, and handed it back to the doctor.

"You have confidence?"

"No," said the major.

There were three boys who came each day who were about the same age I was. They were all three from Milan, and one of them was to be a lawyer, and one was to be a painter, and

---

1. The *war* is World War I (1914–1918). The United States, Italy, and other countries fought Germany and its allies.
2. *Milan* is a city in northern Italy.
3. Here, *game* refers to wild animals and birds that have been hunted and killed for food.

Vocabulary
lurch (lurch) *v.* to move suddenly and unevenly
withered (with′ ərd) *adj.* shriveled

Teaching Options

Reading *Minilesson*

Identifying Author's Purpose Students may be confused by this story since it seems to have little plot and virtually no conflict. Further, the sequence of incidents seems unrelated, and it appears to end, rather than conclude. The theme may appear obscure. Suggest to students that Hemingway's prose style reflects some of the beliefs of the imagist poets.

Activity Have students identify a place in the story where Hemingway uses each of the following imagist principles: the juxtaposition of images; emotion and theme conveyed through images; and brief, clear, concrete language. Have each student find three examples of imagist principles and write a brief paragraph, analyzing what Hemingway's use of the principles might suggest about his purpose for writing in the story. **L2**

Additional Resources
📁 *Reading Workbook,* pp. 65–66

Grammar Link

Using Commas in a Series

In Hemingway's writing, as in your own, you will often find a sentence with three or more elements in a series. These three elements might be words, phrases, or clauses. Use commas after each element in a series, including the element that precedes the conjunction.

Problem 1 Missing commas in a series of words
Hemingway writes of physical emotional and spiritual loss.

   Solution   Use commas after the words in a series, including the word that comes before the conjunction.
Hemingway writes of physical, emotional, and spiritual loss.

Problem 2 Missing commas in a series of phrases
They were maimed in battle numbed by pain and defeated by loss.

   Solution   Use commas after the phrases in a series, including the phrase that comes before the conjunction.
They were maimed in battle, numbed by pain, and defeated by loss.

Problem 3 Missing commas in a series of clauses
One boy wanted to be a lawyer one wanted to be a painter and the third had intended to be a soldier.

   Solution   Use commas after the clauses in a series, including the clause that comes before the conjunction.
One boy wanted to be a lawyer, one wanted to be a painter, and the third had intended to be a soldier.

● For more about using commas in a series, see **Language Handbook,** p. R32.

EXERCISE

Rewrite each of the incorrect sentences, applying the solutions shown above. (One of the sentences is correct.)

1. In our band Larry plays guitar, Yolanda plays keyboards and Tom plays percussion.

2. He wants ice cream milk and cake.

3. They took a plane to Boston, a train to New York, and a bus to Baltimore.

4. Linda saw the balloon floating in the sky riding the air currents higher and higher, and disappearing into a cloud.

5. I cleaned my room swept the kitchen floor and took out the trash.

6. Hemingway has a concise, simple and unadorned style.

Grammar Link

Objective

- To use commas correctly in a series

Teaching Strategies

Emphasize that a series consists of three or more elements. If the sentence contains only two elements, no separating comma is needed.

Exercise

1. In our band Larry plays guitar, Yolanda plays keyboards*[,]* and Tom plays percussion.
2. He wants ice cream*[,]* milk*[,]* and cake.
3. Correct
4. Linda saw the balloon floating in the sky*[,]* riding the air currents higher and higher, and disappearing into a cloud.
5. I cleaned my room*[,]* swept the kitchen floor*[,]* and took out the trash.
6. Hemingway has a concise, simple*[,]* and unadorned style.

Additional Resources

▮ *Grammar and Language Workbook,* p. 251

▮ *Grammar and Composition Handbook,* Lesson 11.6

▮ *Writer's Choice,* Lesson 21.6

Teaching Options

Writing *Minilesson*

Writing Directions In the second paragraph of "In Another Country," Hemingway gives partial directions to the hospital and the pavilions where the men work at their rehabilitation. Point out that he uses the canals, bridges, and even the woman selling chestnuts as landmarks to identify the route.

Activity As a class, have students choose a central point or a well-known landmark in their town. Then ask each student to write detailed directions for getting from that point to his or her home. Tell students not to include maps or other graphics in their directions. Ask selected students to read their directions in class. **L2**

Additional Resources

▮ *Writer's Choice,* Lessons 3.1, 3.2

Objectives

- To use available technology to create a spreadsheet
- To use spreadsheet software to create a productivity chart

Teaching Strategies

To help motivate students, point out two major benefits of spreadsheets. First, they take advantage of a computer's ability to compute (or calculate) at phenomenal speed. Second, using spread-sheet formulas avoids the careless mistakes humans sometimes make when tired or rushed.

Tell students that a computer does exactly what it is told. Spreadsheet commands are designed to tell the computer precisely what to do.

Stress the importance of entering correct and complete information in each cell. Inserting wrong information may generate incorrect or incomplete answers. Incomplete information does not permit the computer to identify the cell in which the information is to be stored or recognize the procedure it should carry out.

Adapting to Available Spreadsheet Software

Explain that although the principles are the same, spreadsheet software may vary in commands, details of use, and sophistication of application.

Teaching Options

Spreadsheet: Determining Productivity

Spreadsheet software can help you manage your time better by allowing you to see, in graphic form, how you actually spend your days. Start by listing everything you do on a typical school day. Group the activities into categories such as sleeping, school, homework, time spent with family, and so on. Then record how much time you spend on each group of activities during an average twenty-four-hour day. Round each figure to the nearest half hour, and record the times in decimals (for example, 3.5 hours). Make sure your hours add up to 24.

> **TECHNOLOGY TIP**
>
> Spreadsheet programs differ slightly, so if you have trouble at any time in this activity, browse through the program's Help menu or consult with your teacher or lab instructor.

Reviewing Spreadsheet Tools

Take a few minutes to review the major functions of spreadsheets.

TERM	FUNCTION
Worksheet	A worksheet is the "page" where you insert and manipulate data.
Cells	Each worksheet is divided into cells, the basic units for storing data.
Cell address	The intersection of a column and a row forms a cell. The cell at column D and row 4, for example, is called D4.
Chart	Various types of graphs (bar graph, line graph, and so on) are referred to as charts in spreadsheet programs. The data on a spreadsheet can be made into a chart.
Formulas	Formulas mathematically combine the data in cells to produce a new value. For example, a formula may tell the program to add up all the figures in a column or a row.

Estimating Your Productivity

Have your list of activities handy as you open your spreadsheet. Most spreadsheet software opens to a blank worksheet. You will see columns, rows, and empty cells. You will also see pull-down menus, one or more toolbars, a formula bar, and a cell-content space. When

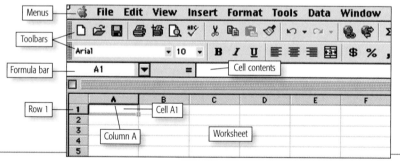

MEETING INDIVIDUAL NEEDS — MULTIPLE LEARNING STYLES

Logical and Mathematical Students with acute logical and mathematical abilities may respond well to creating an application of spreadsheet software.

Activity Before they begin the spreadsheet activity, organize students in groups. Include one or more students who have demonstrated logical and mathematical aptitude in each group.

Have members discuss the directions, asking questions and seeking clarification concerning theory and specific numbered directions. Encourage hands-on activities in which individual members experiment with using commands, entering data in appropriate locations, moving about among cells, and applying the formulas. **L2**

45   'What did he say? Did he say anything?'

      'But little.'

           'Anything? Mary, confess
     He said he'd come to ditch° the meadow for me.'

     'Warren!'

50   'But did he? I just want to know.'

     'Of course he did. What would you have him say?
     Surely you wouldn't grudge the poor old man
     Some humble way to save his self-respect.
     He added, if you really care to know,
55   He meant to clear the upper pasture, too.
     That sounds like something you have heard before?
     Warren, I wish you could have heard the way
     He jumbled everything. I stopped to look
     Two or three times—he made me feel so queer°—
60   To see if he was talking in his sleep.
     He ran on° Harold Wilson—you remember—
     The boy you had in haying four years since.
     He's finished school, and teaching in his college.
     Silas declares you'll have to get him back.
65   He says they two will make a team for work:
     Between them they will lay this farm as smooth!
     The way he mixed that in with other things.
     He thinks young Wilson a likely lad, though daft°
     On education—you know how they fought
70   All through July under the blazing sun,
     Silas up on the cart to build the load,
     Harold along beside to pitch it on.'

     'Yes, I took care to keep well out of earshot.'

     'Well, those days trouble Silas like a dream.
75   You wouldn't think they would. How some things linger!°

---

48 Here, *ditch* means "to dig long, narrow channels." These channels, or ditches, are often used for drainage or irrigation.
59 *Queer* means "odd" or "strange."
61 *Ran on* means "talked continuously about."
68 *Daft* means "foolish."
75 *Linger* means "to continue to exist" or "to endure."

E Critical Thinking

LOGICAL REASONING Ask students with what emotion Mary exclaims, "Warren!" *(Possible answers: surprise, anger, reproof, warning, or disappointment.)*

Language Note

In line 55, Frost alludes to *clearing*. The word could have several applications: clearing land of trees, shrubs or weeds; of previously planted crops; or, more likely in this case, of the rocks common to New England soil.

F Critical Thinking

DRAWING CONCLUSIONS Ask students to examine Mary's comments and speculate on what is happening to Silas.

Model: Mary is describing mental confusion. Based on what I've heard and read, Silas might be suffering from something like senile dementia or maybe even Alzheimer's disease. Silas speaks in non sequiturs, jumbles everything, and has lost track of real time. He thinks Harold is still a college student available for summer farm work. According to Mary, his conversation is very confused.

LIFE SKILLS CONNECTION

Teaching and Mentoring Silas wants another opportunity to teach Harold Wilson to build a load of hay. Often in life, people have the chance to pass along some skill they have developed: throwing a curve, breaking an egg with one hand, setting up a personal Web site, or playing a simple tune on the guitar.

Activity Invite students to think about a skill they have that they'd like to pass on to someone else. The skill might be really important, or not very important at all. Have students write their names and skills on 3″ x 5″ index cards and post them in the classroom. Then have students choose skills and participate in mentoring each other in the acquisition of the new skills. **L2**

G Active Reading

CONNECT Ask students if they agree with Mary's statement in lines 79–80. *(Most students will agree that they, too, have had this experience.)*

H Critical Thinking

EVALUATING Ask students what they think of Silas's "one accomplishment." *(Most students will find the accomplishment not very important and think that it's sad that this is all he has to feel proud of and to teach.)*

I Active Reading

RESPOND Ask students to discuss whether Mary's comment in lines 101–105 makes them more or less sympathetic toward Silas. *(Most students will be more sympathetic to Silas. He seems to be a man who has nothing and only one skill, and yet he cares a great deal about others. He seems hard to dislike.)*

G
Harold's young college boy's assurance piqued° him.
After so many years he still keeps finding
Good arguments he sees he might have used.
I sympathise.° I know just how it feels
80 To think of the right thing to say too late.
Harold's associated in his mind with Latin.
He asked me what I thought of Harold's saying
He studied Latin like the violin
Because he liked it—that an argument!
85 He said he couldn't make the boy believe
He could find water with a hazel prong°—
Which showed how much good school had ever done him.
He wanted to go over that. But most of all
He thinks if he could have another chance
90 To teach him how to build a load of hay—'

H
'I know, that's Silas' one accomplishment.
He bundles every forkful in its place,
And tags and numbers it for future reference,
So he can find and easily dislodge° it
95 In the unloading. Silas does that well.
He takes it out in bunches like big birds' nests.
You never see him standing on the hay
He's trying to lift, straining to lift himself.'

I
'He thinks if he could teach him that, he'd be
100 Some good perhaps to someone in the world.
He hates to see a boy the fool of books.
Poor Silas, so concerned for other folk,
And nothing to look backward to with pride,
And nothing to look forward to with hope,
105 So now and never any different.'

J
Part of a moon was falling down the west,
Dragging the whole sky with it to the hills.
Its light poured softly in her lap. She saw it
And spread her apron to it. She put out her hand
110 Among the harp-like morning-glory° strings,

---

76 *Piqued* means "aroused a feeling of anger or resentment in."
79 *Sympathise* means "to share in or to agree with the feelings or ideas of another."
86 A *hazel prong* is a stick believed to indicate the presence of underground water.
94 *Dislodge* means "to move or to force from a position."
110 A *morning glory* is a vine that produces trumpet-shaped flowers. Gardeners often position a lattice or strings for a vine to grow along.

Teaching Options

MEETING INDIVIDUAL NEEDS — GIFTED AND TALENTED ACTIVITY

Analyze a Poem Frost wrote a number of other dramatic poems, including "The Mountain," "A Hundred Collars," "Home Burial," "Blueberries," "A Servant to Servants," "The Code," "The Generations of Men," "The Housekeeper," and "The Fear."

Activity Have students work individually to read one of the poems listed above or another dramatic poem by Frost and then write an analysis of it. Encourage students to compare and contrast the poem they select with "The Death of the Hired Hand." You might have a few students read the poems they selected to the class and present their analyses. **L3**

Taut° with the dew from garden bed to eaves,
As if she played unheard some tenderness
That wrought° on him beside her in the night.
'Warren,' she said, 'he has come home to die:
115   You needn't be afraid he'll leave you this time.'

'Home,' he mocked gently.

                         'Yes, what else but home?
It all depends on what you mean by home.
Of course he's nothing to us, any more
120   Than was the hound that came a stranger to us
Out of the woods, worn out upon the trail.'

'Home is the place where, when you have to go there,
They have to take you in.'

                       'I should have called it
125   Something you somehow haven't to deserve.'

Warren leaned out and took a step or two,
Picked up a little stick, and brought it back
And broke it in his hand and tossed it by.
'Silas has better claim on us you think
130   Than on his brother? Thirteen little miles
As the road winds would bring him to his door.
Silas has walked that far no doubt to-day.
Why didn't he go there? His brother's rich,
A somebody—director in the bank.'

135   'He never told us that.'

               'We know it though.'

'I think his brother ought to help, of course.
I'll see to that if there is need. He ought of right
To take him in, and might be willing to—
140   He may be better than appearances.
But have some pity on Silas. Do you think
If he had any pride in claiming kin
Or anything he looked for from his brother,
He'd keep so still about him all this time?'

---

111 *Taut* means "stretched tight."
113 *Wrought* means "worked."

J **Literary Elements**

DRAMATIC POETRY Explain that description can be part of dramatic poetry just as dialogue can. Ask students to discuss what this passage reveals about Mary. How does this description reinforce the character that is revealed through dialogue.
(Mary is very sensitive and sympathetic to the world around her; she opens her apron to catch the moonlight and puts her hands on the "morning-glory strings." The description reinforces the character we see arguing forcefully to take Silas in.)

K **Author's Craft**

METAPHOR Ask students to identify the metaphor in these lines. *(Silas is compared to a hound.)* How does this metaphor affect the way you might look at Silas? *(It makes him appear tired and sad, like a homeless hound.)*

L **Active Reading**

CLARIFY Ask students the difference between Mary's view of a person's home and Warren's.

Model: Mary has a very compassionate view. She says home is "Something you somehow haven't to deserve," but she implies that home is a harbor, a safe place that a person can count on no matter what. I think Warren is more cynical about Silas; he argues that home is a place that has to take you in because the people in the home are responsible even if the person in need—Silas—isn't.

MULTIPLE LEARNING STYLES

Musical Students who are especially skilled in music will find it interesting to analyze the poem in terms of music. Other students will also benefit by learning to recognize how music can mirror and enhance the emotions and events in a dramatic piece of work.

Activity Have students work individually or in small groups to identify and locate music to accompany "The Death of the Hired Man." Encourage them to think about mood, tone, the characters' thoughts and feelings, and the plot. Then have them present their selections to the class, identifying which lines from the poem will be accompanied by each piece and explaining why the piece was chosen and how it corresponds to events in the poem. **L2** **COLLAB. LEARN.**

Author's Craft

DICTION Frost's choice of words for Mary characterizes her as a woman who speaks in plain, often one-syllable words. In line 150, the ungrammatical "He don't" achieves two purposes: First, it develops Mary's character, showing that she is a country woman who speaks nonstandard English, probably because she has not had much education. Secondly, it sustains the iambic rhythm of the poem.

Language Note

The word *lounge* refers to a sofa, often with a headrest and sometimes with no back. Consequently, it can be used as a bed.

Thematic Focus

New Directions Have students look back at all of Frost's poems in this cluster and review the new directions taken by the characters. Ask students which of the new directions taken by the characters troubles them most. Which appeals to them most? For which are they most sympathetic?

☑ ASSESSMENT OPTIONS

📂 **Quick Checks,** p. 83

---

145   'I wonder what's between them.'

                                 'I can tell you.
     Silas is what he is—we wouldn't mind him—
     But just the kind that kinsfolk can't abide.°
     He never did a thing so very bad.
150   He don't know why he isn't quite as good
     As anybody. Worthless though he is,
     He won't be made ashamed to please his brother.'

     'I can't think Si ever hurt anyone.'

     'No, but he hurt my heart the way he lay
155   And rolled his old head on that sharp-edged chair-back.
     He wouldn't let me put him on the lounge.
     You must go in and see what you can do.
     I made the bed up for him there to-night.
     You'll be surprised at him—how much he's broken.
160   His working days are done; I'm sure of it.'

     'I'd not be in a hurry to say that.'

     'I haven't been. Go, look, see for yourself.
     But, Warren, please remember how it is:
     He's come to help you ditch the meadow.
165   He has a plan. You mustn't laugh at him.
     He may not speak of it, and then he may.
     I'll sit and see if that small sailing cloud
     Will hit or miss the moon.'

                         It hit the moon.
170   Then there were three there, making a dim row,
     The moon, the little silver cloud, and she.

     Warren returned—too soon, it seemed to her,
     Slipped to her side, caught up her hand and waited.

     'Warren?' she questioned.

175   'Dead,' was all he answered.

---

148 *Abide* means "to put up with" or "to tolerate."

Teaching Options

MEETING INDIVIDUAL NEEDS — MULTIPLE LEARNING STYLES

Spatial Students with strong spatial abilities may respond more readily to this poem if they transform the verbal descriptions into a visual image.

Activity Ask students to imagine that they are set designers hired to create the set for a play or a movie based on "The Death of the Hired Man." Have them create sketches depicting the porch and stairs where Warren and Mary sit and discuss Silas, the view from the porch, and any interior spaces of the house that are mentioned. Additional sketches might depict the changing night sky. Students should display and be ready to explain their interpretations. **L2**

The Tropics in New York

Claude McKay

Fruit Stand Vendor, 1994. Hyacinth Manning. Acrylic on canvas, 28 x 22 in. Private collection. How does this painting help you visualize the tropics McKay describes?

Bananas ripe and green, and ginger-root,
    Cocoa in pods and alligator pears,
And tangerines and mangoes and grape fruit,
    Fit for the highest prize at parish fairs,

5 Set in the window, bringing memories
    Of fruit-trees laden by low-singing rills,
And dewy dawns, and mystical blue skies
    In benediction° over nun-like hills.

10 My eyes grew dim, and I could no more gaze;
    A wave of longing through my body swept,
And, hungry for the old, familiar ways,
    I turned aside and bowed my head and wept.

_____
8 A *benediction* is a blessing.

C Author's Craft

SOUND DEVICES Ask students to identify the use of sound devices in the first stanza. *(Examples of alliteration: ripe, root; pods, pears. Assonance: highest, prize. Rhyme: root, fruit; pears, fairs.)* How does the use of sound devices in this poem compare to the use of sound devices in "If We Must Die"? *("The Tropics in New York" depends much more heavily on sound devices. "If We Must Die" has a pattern of rhymed lines and occasional alliteration, but sound devices are used only sparingly.)*

D Critical Thinking

EVALUATING Ask students which of the two poems evokes a stronger response as they read. Why? *(Many students will suggest that "If We Must Die" provokes stronger reactions; its images are searing and concern bravery in the face of imminent death. "The Tropics in New York" does convey a feeling of sorrow, but many students will find this poem more sad than militant.)*

Thematic Focus

The Harlem Renaissance McKay wrote that he wanted to look for ways to counter the "ignoble cruelty" of racism. What message about racism can be learned from either or both of these poems? Do you think these poems expose the ignoble cruelty of racism?

ASSESSMENT OPTIONS

   Quick Checks, p. 86

 ENGLISH LANGUAGE LEARNERS

Paraphrasing a Poem In order to conform to a set pattern of rhyme and rhythm, and to construct a powerful argument, Claude McKay uses sentence structures and vocabulary that may confuse English language learners.

  Activity Have students work in pairs to paraphrase the poem. Suggest that they first break the poem into sentences and look at one sentence at a time. They can break up long sentences into several small ones and look up or talk through the meanings of words they don't know. Once they have broken down the poem into manageable pieces, ask pairs to paraphrase the poems.

Additional Resources
  English Language Learners Sourcebook

 FINE ART
TRANSPARENCY 19

You may want to use **Fine Art Transparency 19** to discuss memories of past homes.

Personal Response

Students will most likely say that images from "If We Must Die" make them feel angry, whereas those from "The Tropics in New York" make them feel nostalgic or sad.

ANALYZING LITERATURE

1. The speaker names dogs (hunter) and hogs (hunted). The speaker identifies with the hogs, in that he feels hunted and penned in.
2. He wants them to fight back. Even though he acknowledges that they are outnumbered, he believes that it is important for them to show courage and stand up for themselves.
3. McKay creates a mood of defiance and inspiration. Most students will say the technique is very effective.
4. The poem may have heralded the beginning of the Harlem Renaissance because it encouraged African Americans to "fight back." Expressing their outrage was one way to do that. The new sense of pride it gave African Americans also inspired other artists.
5. The speaker sees beautiful fruit in the window. The sight brings back memories of the speaker's homeland.
6. He cries at the thought of home. His reaction may be caused by the contrast between the beauty that was home and the ugliness now. He may also simply be homesick.
7. Students may cite the descriptions of the fruit, the sounds of the birds, and the rhythm conveyed by the lines of the poem.
8. Students should clearly link the poem to their own experiences.

Responding to Literature

Personal Response

Which image from the poems stands out in your mind? What effect does this image have on you?

ANALYZING LITERATURE

If We Must Die

RECALL AND INTERPRET

1. What two animals does the speaker name? Which is the hunter and which is the hunted? With whom does the speaker identify? Explain.
2. How does the speaker want his kinsmen to behave? Why is this important to him?

EVALUATE AND CONNECT

3. How do the reactions advocated by the speaker compare with those of the person or people you wrote about for the Focus Activity on page 733?
4. Theme Connections   Some critics believe "If We Must Die" marks the start of the Harlem Renaissance. Why might this poem have led to such a creative outpouring?

The Tropics in New York

RECALL AND INTERPRET

5. What does the speaker see in the window? What memories does the sight bring?
6. How does the speaker react physically when he recalls his memories? Why might he have this reaction?

EVALUATE AND CONNECT

7. Which **sensory details** (see page R14) in the poem help you picture the tropics best? Explain.
8. What feelings about times or places in your past does this poem express for you?

Literary ELEMENTS

Shakespearean Sonnet

A **Shakespearean,** or **English,** sonnet is a type of sonnet developed in England and made famous by William Shakespeare. It is organized into three **quatrains** (groups of four lines) followed by a rhymed **couplet** (a pair of lines). The lines have the rhyme scheme *abab cdcd efef gg.* A main thought is presented in the three quatrains, and the couplet contains the conclusion.

1. Which of the McKay poems is a Shakespearean sonnet? How do you know?
2. Explain the main idea presented in the three quatrains of the Shakespearean sonnet McKay wrote. Then describe the conclusion.

● See **Literary Terms Handbook,** p. R15.

LITERARY ELEMENTS

1. "If We Must Die" has the correct number of lines and rhyme scheme.
2. The first quatrain says that African Americans should not die like hogs; the second says that standing up in defiance will make their tormentors admire them; the third, that they should deal one death blow. The poem ends with a call to the fight.

Additional Resources

 Literary Elements Transparency 70

✔ ASSESSMENT OPTIONS

📁 *Quick Checks,* p. 86

📁 *Selection and Theme Assessment,* pp. 127–128

📁 *Performance Assessment,* p. 72

💾 *Testmaker*

MEDIA Connection

Radio Transcript

People's lives are often influenced by their communities and the events that take place there. Artists, such as the one featured below, help give expression to that influence.

Artist Jacob Lawrence

National Public Radio, from *Morning Edition*, June 9, 1998

BOB EDWARDS, host
As part of the Harlem Renaissance, Jacob Lawrence was among those who helped move the black experience into the mainstream of America's artistic consciousness after World War I. Many of the writers and musicians went on to gain worldwide recognition—Zora Neale Hurston, Langston Hughes, Duke Ellington.

Behind those famous figures was a vibrant community of visual artists whose participation in the Harlem Renaissance often is overlooked. Jacob Lawrence is the last living member of the group and his work is part of a touring exhibition dedicated to it.

WILLIAM DRUMMOND, reporter
One particular series of paintings stands out. [Jacob Lawrence's] scenes from the life of Toussaint l'Ouverture . . . consist of forty-one panels depicting the life of the Haitian general who came to be a symbol of black pride in 1930s America because of his successful rebellion against French rule a century earlier.

The paintings were the subject of Lawrence's first exhibition in 1938 at the Harlem YMCA. By then, Jacob Lawrence was just 20 years old and the Harlem Renaissance was coming to an end.

When the movement began Lawrence was just a toddler, but he grew up taking in all that was going on around him.

LAWRENCE
I knew many of the older people. Some, like Langston Hughes, I met. Claude McKay I knew well. He befriended me. I'm sure it had a great deal of influence on me and my work.

DRUMMOND
Lawrence's paintings tell stories, says Patricia Hills, who teaches art history at Boston University and has written frequently about Lawrence. That's why she calls him a pictorial Gryot.

PATRICIA HILLS
"Gryot," as you know, is a French word, it comes from West Africa. It means "a storyteller." You know, the person in the community who knows the history and tells the story. That's one of the reasons he's [Lawrence] done a lot of works in series, because the series allows him to tell the kind of story that he wants to tell. He's really interested in people. He's interested in his own community.

Respond

1. Are storytellers important in today's society? Explain why or why not.

2. Based on this interview, what, in your opinion, is Jacob Lawrence's significance to the Harlem Renaissance?

MEDIA Connection

Objective

- To read and understand a radio program transcript

If We Must Die and The Tropics of New York Claude McKay inspired many of the artists and writers of the Harlem Renaissance, among them Jacob Lawrence. Lawrence was just two years old when McKay wrote "If We Must Die" in 1919, but Lawrence grew up surrounded by the artistic excitement of the Renaissance during the 1920s.

Respond

1. Many students will say storytellers help people stay in touch with their roots and stimulate the imagination.

2. Lawrence broadened the Harlem Renaissance into the visual arts. He extended the influence of this period and helped to "move the black experience into the mainstream of America's artistic consciousness."

Additional Resources
📁 *Media Connections*, p. 16

Teaching Options

Reading *Minilesson*

Sequence of Events The way the radio transcript seems to jump randomly from one person's comments to the next may confuse students.

Activity Have students draw five large boxes in a row on a sheet of paper and place an arrow leading from each box to the next box on the right. In the first box, have students write the name of the host, and summarize his or her comments. Then, following the arrow to the right, have students repeat the process for each speaker. Point out that radio transcripts often lack transitional phrases found in prose selections. **L1**

Additional Resources
📁 *Reading Workbook*

Before Reading

Objectives

- To read and analyze two poems about African American identity
- To examine the effect of repetition in a poem
- To write a paragraph that compares and contrasts the themes of two poems

Skills

Reading/Thinking: Drawing Conclusions
Writing: Poem, Song Lyrics, or Essay
Collaboration: Literature Groups; Choral Reading
Listening/Speaking: Choral Reading

More About Langston Hughes

Students may be surprised to know that Hughes wrote several books on jazz as well as a series of children's books. Dismayed by the lack of information available to children about music and about famous African Americans, Hughes wrote several biographies for children.

"The Negro Speaks of Rivers" was Hughes's first published poem. In 1921 it appeared in *Crisis,* a newspaper and literary magazine featuring the works of African Americans.

Before You Read

I, Too and *The Negro Speaks of Rivers*

Meet Langston Hughes

When Langston Hughes was nineteen, his father offered to send him to college in Europe so Hughes could escape from the racism and segregation that affected every part of American life. Hughes refused, however, explaining, "More than Paris, or the Shakespeare country, or Berlin, or the Alps, I wanted to see Harlem, the greatest Negro city in the world." Hughes spent the rest of his life celebrating Harlem and African American life.

Despite having a wealthy father, Hughes knew what it meant to live in poverty. By the age of twelve he had already lived in six different cities because his divorced mother was always moving around looking for work. He also lived for a time with his grandmother, who told him stories about heroic ancestors who had fought slavery and racism. She helped instill in Hughes a lasting sense of pride in his heritage and culture.

Hughes began writing poetry in high school. He attended Columbia University for a year but found the school to be too large and impersonal. Instead he went to live in his beloved Harlem, where he had a hard time finding a job. Finally he took a job as a merchant sailor, traveling to Africa and Europe. When he returned to the United States he continued writing poetry and eventually earned a college degree from Lincoln University. In 1926 his first book, *The Weary Blues,* was published.

Throughout his life Hughes was a "poet of the people" who spent much time traveling across the country to read his poetry. He integrated the rhythms of blues and jazz music in his writings and used the language of the people he encountered. Hughes saw beauty in the wisdom, humor, and strength of the people he portrayed.

Although best known as a poet, Hughes also wrote fiction, drama, popular songs, and satirical sketches about an uneducated but perceptive character named Simple. In addition, he worked on anthologies and translations and helped the careers of many younger writers.

"It is the duty of the younger Negro artist . . . to change through the force of his art that old whispering 'I want to be white' to 'why should I want to be white? I am a Negro—and beautiful!'"

"I didn't know the upper-class Negroes well enough to write much about them. I knew only the people I had grown up with, and they weren't people whose shoes were always shined, who had been to Harvard, or who had heard of Bach. But they seemed to me good people, too."

—*Hughes*

"Hughes . . . was unashamedly black at a time when blackness was démodé [not fashionable], and he didn't go much beyond one of his earliest themes, black *is* beautiful."

—*Lindsay Patterson*

Langston Hughes was born in 1902 and died in 1967.

RESOURCE MANAGER

Lesson Planning Resource
The *Unit Five Planning Guide* (pp. 128–132) provides additional lesson notes and reduced versions of all print resources.

Other Print Resources
- Active Reading Guide, p. 87
- Reading Workbook
- Quick Checks, p. 87
- Selection and Theme Assessment, pp. 129–130

- Performance Assessment, p. 73
- Spanish Summaries, p. 77
- Inclusion Strategies
- English Language Learners Sourcebook

 Transparencies
- Selection Focus 77
- Literary Elements 71

Technology
 Audio Library
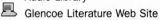 Glencoe Literature Web Site
Testmaker

Literary ELEMENTS

Stanza

A **stanza** is a group of lines that form a unit in a poem. The stanzas in a poem are separated by white space and are similar in structure, often having the same number of lines, **meter**, and **rhyme scheme** (see pages R9 and R13). A stanza usually focuses on a single idea, much like a paragraph does, and each new stanza typically has a new focus.

1. Look at "A black man talks of reaping." How many stanzas does it have? How many lines are in each stanza? What idea is presented in each stanza?

2. Cullen's "Any Human to Another" uses a freer type of stanza form than that used in Bontemps's "A black man talks of reaping." In what ways do the stanzas in Cullen's poem reflect the definition given above? How do they differ?

3. What effect does each poet create through his choice of stanza form?

● See **Literary Terms Handbook**, p. R15.

LITERATURE AND WRITING

Writing About Literature

Extended Metaphor   The poem "A black man talks of reaping" includes an **extended metaphor**, a metaphor that is developed over more than one line. The metaphor is implied instead of stated directly. What comparison is the poet making in this poem? Write two or three paragraphs stating what the metaphor is and how it is extended through the poem.

Creative Writing

Responding Through Poetry   Both poets wrote their poems in response to events and attitudes of the time. Think of an event or an issue that troubles you today. Write a poem responding to the topic. Include your personal thoughts and hopes, but also consider whether you plan to speak for just yourself or for a group of people. If you wish, share your finished poem with your class.

EXTENDING YOUR RESPONSE

Literature Groups

What's in a Name?   Bontemps has been called "the conscience of his era." Judging from "A black man talks of reaping," does the name fit Bontemps? Based on "Any Human to Another," do you think Cullen should share this title? Discuss these questions with your group. Then present the results of your discussion to the class.

Learning for Life

Interview Questions   Suppose that you are a reporter and you have the opportunity to interview Bontemps or Cullen about their poems. Choose the author you'd most like to interview, and prepare a list of questions. If possible, research the answers to your questions. Then share your findings with the class.

Interdisciplinary Activity

Music: Companion Piece   People have always used music to help tell their stories. Research one type of music, such as blues or folk music, and select a song that would be a good companion piece to one of the poems.

Reading Further

If you enjoyed these poems, you might try this collection:
The Lost Zoo, by Countee Cullen, a book for children that contains Cullen's poems with illustrations by Brian Pinkney.

 Save your work for your portfolio.

BEGINNINGS OF THE MODERN AGE ❧ 761

LITERATURE AND WRITING

Writing About Literature

Students' paragraphs should
• directly state the two items or ideas implied by the extended metaphor.
• include specific examples from the poem that support the ideas.

Creative Writing

Students' poems should
• focus on contemporary issues.
• include personal thoughts and hopes.

EXTENDING YOUR RESPONSE

Literature Groups   Before the discussions begin, encourage students to write a response to the questions and to include reasons and supporting evidence for their view. **COLLAB. LEARN.**

Learning for Life   After students prepare their interviews, have them practice doing them "live" with partners and then present the interviews before the class.

Interdisciplinary Activity
Encourage students to set the poems to music and perform dramatic readings. Their tone, volume, and gestures should correspond to musical pieces.

✔ ASSESSMENT OPTIONS

📁 *Quick Checks,* p. 91

📁 *Selection and Theme Assessment,* pp. 135–136

📁 *Performance Assessment,* p. 76

💾 *Testmaker*

Writing Workshop

Objectives
- To write a poem about a place
- To plan, draft, revise, edit a poem
- To reflect on and assess the poem

GLENCOE
TECHNOLOGY

**WRITER'S ASSISTANT
CD-ROM**

Students can use Glencoe's templates and guidelines software for creative writing to aid them in working through the steps in the writing process in this lesson.

Teaching Strategies

PREWRITING

Explore ideas Encourage students to meet in small groups to discuss possible topics. Students may talk to family who often have good insight into experiences of the past.

Explore your responses Have students copy their poems so that they can write on and around the text and then organize their thoughts on the chart.

Teaching Options

~: Writing Workshop :~

Creative Writing: Poem

Many of the poems you have read in this theme involve places or ideas that inspire deep affection or desire. Langston Hughes's expression of cultural hope and pride is evident in "The Negro Speaks of Rivers," as is Claude McKay's intense longing for the "dewy dawns, and mystical blue skies" of his native Jamaica in his poem "The Tropics in New York." What places or ideas inspire you? **In this workshop, you will write a poem about a place or idea that has influenced or affected you.**

● As you write your poem, refer to the **Writing Handbook,** pp. R62–R77.

The Writing Process

PREWRITING

PREWRITING TIP
You will be presenting your poem to others, so be sure to write about only those feelings, places, and ideas you are willing to share.

Explore ideas
Here are some suggestions for helping you find a subject for your poem.

● Skim the poems in Theme 8. Do any of the places or ideas in these poems remind you of something you want to write about?

● Think of a place or idea that intrigues you. Could you write about a childhood getaway place, an idea or feeling inspired by a trip, or a holiday with family or friends?

Explore your responses
Sometimes the ideas and feelings expressed in a poem are so similar to yours that you respond to the poem immediately. That poem might then inspire you to write on a similar topic or in a similar style. Choose a poem from this theme that especially appealed to you. In a chart like the one begun here, write the idea or place described in the poem and the poet's response to it. Then record connections the poem has to your life.

STUDENT MODEL

Poem	"My City"
Idea or Place	Manhattan
Poet's Response	Poet loves the sights, sounds, smells, and crowds
My Response	Reminds me of when I visit my uncle in Chicago. The bustling people downtown always interest me.

MEETING INDIVIDUAL NEEDS
ENGLISH LANGUAGE LEARNERS

Speaking Before Writing Have English language learners talk about experiences that have affected them to help them develop their ideas.

Activity In small groups, have native and nonnative English speakers discuss the experiences they wish to write about in their poems. Experiences can be places they have visited, or ideas they have had or read about. Give students

these questions to guide them: What is inspiration? What people or events have inspired you? How will you describe your inspiration in a poem? Encourage students to help each other determine ways in which to express their ideas.

Additional Resources
📁 *English Language Learners Sourcebook*

Reading on Your Own

If you have enjoyed the literature in this unit, you might also be interested in the following books.

Their Eyes Were Watching God
by Zora Neale Hurston In Hurston's famous novel of the 1930s, Janie Crawford, a strong and self-reliant African American woman, makes a journey back to her roots in search of her own identity.

The Great Gatsby
by F. Scott Fitzgerald The "roaring 1920s" come to life in this famous story of Jay Gatsby, a self-made man, and the woman he has loved for years.

Having Our Say:
The Delaney Sisters' First 100 Years
by Sarah and A. Elizabeth Delaney Two feisty women who lived to be more than a century old tell their life stories. They describe the social history of the twentieth century as they witnessed and enjoyed it.

Collected Poems
by Edna St. Vincent Millay; Norma Millay, editor The definitive collection of Millay's poetry, this volume was compiled by Millay's sister after the poet's death. Published in 1957, the collection continues to appeal to today's readers. One reviewer of this book refers to the "grace and depth" and "stunning beauty" of Millay's poetry.

BEGINNINGS OF THE MODERN AGE 767

Reading on Your Own

Reading on Your Own

At the MOVIES

Be sure to review this movie before deciding whether to show it to your class.

• The 1974 movie version of *The Great Gatsby* offers stellar performances by Robert Redford as Gatsby, Mia Farrow as Daisy, and Sam Waterston as Nick. The screenplay, written by Francis Ford Coppola, was adapted from the novel.

MEETING INDIVIDUAL NEEDS — INCLUSION STRATEGIES

You may wish to recommend *Having Our Say* by the Delaney sisters to your less-proficient readers. The subject matter and writing style are accessible for these students. **L1**

The books listed at the right are rated for average readers (**L2**) or for students who need more challenging reading material (**L3**):

• *Their Eyes Were Watching God* by Zora Neale Hurston **L2**
• *The Great Gatsby* by F. Scott Fitzgerald **L2**
• *Collected Poems* by Edna St. Vincent Millay **L3**

Additional Resources
📁 *Inclusion Strategies*

ACT Practice
Reading
Timed (7 minutes)

TEST-TAKING TIP

Unlike the SAT, the ACT does not arrange questions in order from easiest to hardest. Students who want to answer easy questions first have to find them for themselves on the ACT. Suggest that they make two passes through the test. They can find the easy questions first, then on the second pass try to answer any difficult questions they can.

TEST-TAKING TIP

Once a student has found the answer to a question in the text, he or she should look at the possible answer choices and eliminate the worst choices first. The correct answer is a paraphrase of the information in the passage, but it may not be immediately apparent. Therefore it is safest for a student to first eliminate the choices that are most obviously wrong, and then work toward the best answer.

The passage below is followed by seven questions based on its content. Select the best answer and write the corresponding letter on your paper.

NATURAL SCIENCE: This passage is adapted from Stephen Hawking's *The Illustrated Brief History of Time* (©1988 and 1996 by Stephen Hawking).

Our present ideas about the motion of bodies date back to Galileo and Newton. Before them people believed Aristotle, who said that the natural state of a body was to be
5 at rest and that it moved only if driven by a force or impulse. It followed that a heavy body should fall faster than a light one, because it would have a greater pull toward the earth.

The Aristotelian tradition also held that
10 one could work out all the laws that govern the universe by pure thought: it was not necessary to check by observation. So no one until Galileo bothered to see whether bodies of different weight did in fact fall at different
15 speeds. It is said that Galileo demonstrated that Aristotle's belief was false by dropping weights from the leaning tower of Pisa. The story is almost certainly untrue, but Galileo did do something equivalent: he rolled balls
20 of different weights down a smooth slope. The situation is similar to that of heavy bodies falling vertically, but it is easier to observe because the speeds are lesser. Galileo's measurements indicated that each body
25 increased its speed at the same rate, no matter what its weight. For example, if a ball is released on a slope that drops by one meter for every ten meters of length, the ball will travel down the slope at a speed of about one
30 meter per second after one second, two meters per second after two seconds, and so on, however heavy the ball. Of course a lead weight would fall faster than a feather, but that is only because a feather is slowed by air
35 resistance. If one drops two bodies that don't have much air resistance, such as two different lead weights, they fall at the same rate. On the moon, where there is no air to slow things down, the astronaut David R. Scott
40 performed the feather and lead weight experiment and found that indeed they did hit the ground at the same time.

Galileo's measurements were used by Newton as the basis of his laws of motion. In
45 Galileo's experiments, as a body rolled down the slope it was always acted on by the same force (its weight), and the effect was to make it constantly increase its speed. This showed that the real effect of a force is always to change the
50 speed of a body, rather than just to set it moving, as was previously thought. It also meant that whenever a body is not acted on by any force, it will keep on moving in a straight line at the same speed. This idea was first stated
55 explicitly in Newton's *Principia Mathematica*, published in 1687, and is known as Newton's first law. What happens to a body when a force does act on it is given by Newton's second law. This states that the body will accelerate, or
60 change its speed, at a rate that is proportional to the force. (For example, the acceleration is twice as great if the force is twice as great.) The acceleration is also smaller the greater the mass (or quantity of matter) of the body. (The
65 same force acting on a body of twice the mass will produce half the acceleration.) A familiar example is provided by a car: the more powerful the engine, the greater the acceleration, but the heavier the car, the smaller the accelera-
70 tion for the same engine. In addition to his laws of motion, Newton discovered a law to describe the force of gravity, which states that every body attracts every other body with a force that is proportional to the mass of each
75 body. Thus the force between two bodies would be twice as strong if one of the bodies (say, body A) had its mass doubled. This is what you might expect because one could think of the new body A as being made of two
80 bodies with the original mass. Each would attract body B with the original force. Thus the total force between A and B would be twice the original force. And if, say, one of the bodies had twice the mass, and the other had

85 three times the mass, then the force would be six times as strong. One can now see why all bodies fall at the same rate: a body of twice the weight will have twice the force of gravity pulling it down, but it will also have twice the 90 mass. According to Newton's second law, these two effects will exactly cancel each other, so the acceleration will be the same in all cases.

1. According to the passage, Galileo rolled balls of different weight down a smooth slope in order to:

A. show that a body in motion will continue moving.
B. measure the distance the balls traveled.
C. compare the speed of the balls.
D. demonstrate the force of gravity.

2. As it is used in line 55, the word *explicitly* most nearly means:

F. definitively.
G. scientifically.
H. radically.
J. vaguely.

3. According to the passage, Galileo determined that whenever a body is not acted on by another force, the body will:

A. stop moving.
B. decelerate and move at a slower speed.
C. accelerate to move at a faster speed.
D. continue to move at the current speed.

4. According to the passage, all of the following are involved in Newton's second law EXCEPT:

F. proportional rate.
G. force.
H. air resistance.
J. acceleration.

5. The passage suggests that one feature of the moon is that the moon:

A. has no gravity.
B. is a terrible place to perform experiments.
C. has a large amount of air resistance.
D. has no atmosphere to create air resistance.

6. One of the main observations made in the second paragraph (lines 9–42) is that:

F. the natural state of a body is at rest.
G. no one can tell if bodies of different weight fall at different times.
H. Galileo dropped weights from the leaning tower of Pisa to prove Aristotle's theory.
J. according to Aristotle, it was not necessary to prove the laws that govern the universe by observation.

7. How does the example of a car (lines 66–70) function in the passage?

A. It distinguishes between heavy cars and lighter cars.
B. It provides an example of Newton's second law in everyday terms.
C. It makes the point that cars with bigger engines accelerate faster.
D. It revises the theory that a heavy car will move more quickly.

7. **B** On lines 66–67 the purpose of the car example is stated in these terms: *A familiar example is provided by a car.* Since this immediately follows a discussion of Newton's second law, we can infer that the car example is intended to explain Newton's second law.

Answers and Analyses

1. **C** Students should reread the relevant lines in the passage and look for evidence to support their answer. Galileo's experiment with the balls can be found on lines 18–26. There it states that *Galileo's measurements indicated that each body increased its speed at the same rate.*

2. **F** In the lines prior to 55, the passage states that Galileo's experiments showed that a body will continue to move in a straight line if not acted upon. This idea, however, was first stated as such by Newton. The word that comes closest to conveying this idea is F.

3. **D** Again, students should reread the relevant lines of the passage. Lines 51–54 state *that whenever a body is not acted on by any force, it will keep on moving in a straight line at the same speed.* Choice D is a restatement of these lines.

4. **H** On lines 57–61, which describe Newton's second law, all of the choices except air resistance are mentioned. Remind students to work carefully when they see the word EXCEPT in a question.

5. **D** The discussion of the moon takes place on lines 38–42. There it states *On the moon, where there is no air to slow things down . . .*

6. **J** Students should watch out for careless errors on this question. Choice F comes from paragraph 1, not from paragraph 2. Choice G is incorrect because the passage states that Galileo *rolled balls of different weights down a smooth slope.* Choice H cannot be right, since the passage states that Galileo did not in fact drop weights from the tower of Pisa. On lines 11–12, it states that, according to Aristotle, *it was not necessary to check by observation.* Therefore the best choice is J.

MORE PRACTICE

For additional practice with the ACT, assign pp. 40–61 from the *College Entrance Exams Preparation and Practice Workbook.*

Unit Six At a Glance
Midcentury Voices

UNIT INTRODUCTION

Theme 9:
PERSONAL DISCOVERIES

- **U.S.A./World Time Lines** (pp. 772–779)
- **Setting the Scene** (p. 772)
- **History of the Time** (p. 773)
- **Life of the Time** (pp. 774–775)
- **Literature of the Time** (pp. 776–777)
- **Novels of the Time** (pp. 778–779)

  The Grapes of Wrath by John Steinbeck

  The Member of the Wedding by Carson McCullers

  Invisible Man by Ralph Ellison
- **Language of the Time** (p. 780)

SELECTIONS

The Second Tree from the Corner (p. 782)

Media Connection: Television Transcript—The Mystery of Happiness (p. 790)

Ode to My Socks (p. 791)

Breakfast (p. 796)

A Rose for Emily and **Address upon Receiving the Novel Prize for Literature** (p. 802)

Father's Bedroom (p. 816)

from **Black Boy** (p. 820)

Media Connection: Newspaper Article—100-Mile Run to Agony and Ecstasy (p. 830)

A Worn Path (p. 831)

The Explorer (p. 842)

February (p. 846)

The Portrait (p. 850)

The Death of the Ball Turret Gunner (p. 856)

The Beautiful Changes (p. 860)

The Rockpile (p. 863)

The Magic Barrel (p. 874)

from **Stride Toward Freedom** (p. 890)

Choice: A Tribute to Dr. Martin Luther King Jr. (p. 896)

KEYS TO LITERARY CONNECTIONS

Comparing Selections

In each theme of **Glencoe Literature,** the **Comparing Selections** feature gives students an opportunity to compare two selections they have just read. Each Comparing Selections page provides a variety of options to address diverse aspects of the reading and literature curriculum.

World Literature

Glencoe Literature contains a variety of literature that represents cultures from around the world. World Literature selections are highlighted with this symbol:

SKILL FEATURES

Vocabulary Skills (p. 815)

Writing Skills (p. 819)

Grammar Link (p. 849)

Interdisciplinary Connection (p. 855)

Reading & Thinking Skills (p. 859)

WRITING WORKSHOP

Narrative Writing: College Application (pp. 902–906)

Theme 10:
ACTING ON AN IDEA

UNIT WRAP-UP

SELECTIONS

Media Connection: Radio Transcript—Blacklisted Woman Vindicated by Federal Court Ruling (p. 910)

The Crucible (p. 911)

Nineteen Thirty-Seven (p. 998)

- **Personal Response, Analyzing Literature, Evaluate and Set Goals** (p. 1014)

- **Build Your Portfolio** (p. 1014)

- **Reading on Your Own** (p. 1015)

  A Separate Peace by John Knowles

  I Have a Dream: Writings and Speeches That Changed the World by Martin Luther King Jr., edited by James Melvin Washington

  Death of a Salesman by Arthur Miller

  The Glass Menagerie by Tennessee Williams

-

SKILL FEATURES

Literature Focus: Drama (pp. 908–909)

Listening, Speaking, & Viewing (p. 1009)

WRITING WORKSHOP

Narrative Writing: Dramatic Scene (pp. 1010–1013)

Reading Skills in this unit

Variety of Texts

In addition to short stories by authors from the United States, this unit also includes the following text types:

- poetry
- speech
- autobiography
- essay
- play
- television transcript
- newspaper article
- radio interview

Comprehension Skills

The following instructional support for comprehension skills appears in this unit of the Student Edition:

- Active Reading Strategies and Model (pp. 3–35)
- Summarizing (p. 859)

See also the **Reading Minilessons** throughout the unit in this Teacher's Wraparound Edition.

Reading Resources

Comprehension Skills Resources

📁 **Active Reading Guides**

The Active Reading Guide provides graphic organizers and study guide questions to support students' reading of each selection. (**Active Reading Guide**, pp. 92–112)

📁 **Reading Workbook**

The Reading Workbook (pp. 71–82) includes additional instruction and reinforcement of reading strategies and skills.

🎧 **Audio Library**

Available both on tape and on CD, the Audio Library provides valuable comprehension support.

Resources for Reading Widely

📖 **Glencoe Literature Library**

Each title in the Glencoe Literature Library includes a full-length novel or play plus related readings. A separate Study Guide is available for each title.

💿 **Literature Classics CD-ROM**

The 900 selections on this CD-ROM can be searched by author, theme, or genre.

 *in*TIME

A coproduction of Glencoe and Time Inc., *inTime* includes a wealth of high-interest nonfiction related to the selections and themes in Unit Six.

✓ Assessment in this unit

THE PRINCETON REVIEW

Assessment Options in the Student Edition

Glencoe Literature offers a number of diverse ways to evaluate student understanding and skill proficiency. In the Student Edition, use the following:

- **Responding to Literature**
  Following each selection, students are asked to recall facts, interpret ideas, and evaluate concepts as they answer a variety of questions and complete activities to extend their understanding.
- **Unit Wrap-Up (pp. 1014–1015)**
  Here students respond to the selections on personal and analytical levels. They also assume ownership of their learning by setting and evaluating goals and by selecting work for their portfolios.

See also the many **Assessment Resources** listed on the facing page.

Standardized Test Practice

The Princeton Review has developed the Standardized Test Practice pages found at the end of this unit (pp. 1016–1017). These pages contain practice test questions that help students remain familiar with standardized test formats and content. For additional practice, you may want to use the following resource:

- College Entrance Exam Preparation and Practice Workbook

History of the Time

Depression and New Deal

After the crash, the economic depression—a term chosen by President Herbert Hoover as less frightening than *panic* or *crisis*—steadily worsened. From 1929 to 1932, approximately 9,000 banks closed, 100,000 businesses failed, and 12 million people lost their jobs—and the numbers were still climbing. The unemployed filled city streets, breadlines, and soup kitchens.

Franklin Delano Roosevelt

With the economy crumbling, voters rejected Hoover's bid for a second term in 1932 and elected Franklin Delano Roosevelt, who promised "a new deal for the American people." Roosevelt's "alphabet agencies" poured out of the federal government, in hopes of pulling the nation out of its economic crisis. These included programs such as the Works Progress Administration (WPA) and the Civilian Conservation Corps (CCC), formed to provide emergency financial aid and temporary jobs. Besides easing the suffering caused by the depression, these agencies returned hope to people and established a larger role for the federal government in promoting prosperity.

World War II

As the depression of the 1930s worsened, some countries turned to menacing dictators for leadership: Benito Mussolini in Italy, Adolf Hitler in Germany, and a military government in Japan. Soon Japanese troops invaded China, and Hitler's army stormed through Europe. Then, on December 7, 1941, Japanese bombers attacked an American naval base at Pearl Harbor, Hawaii. America immediately went to war, joining the Allies, which included Great Britain and the Soviet Union.

Four years and some 45 to 50 million deaths later, peace returned to the world. Germany surrendered in May 1945. Japan surrendered four months later, after the United States dropped atomic bombs on the Japanese cities of Hiroshima and Nagasaki.

Progress and Anxiety

The years after World War II brought changes to the United States. Many Americans began to challenge racial discrimination at home. The devastation in Europe allowed American industries to dominate world markets and the wartime economic boom continued throughout the 1950s.

However, the United States and the Soviet Union became tense rivals in a worldwide struggle for power—a conflict that became known as the cold war. The two world powers never went to war against each other, but they continued developing and stockpiling nuclear weapons. An anxious world now lived under a new cloud—the mushroom cloud of the atomic age.

Historical Note

The "baby boom" started in 1946—the year after World War II ended—as American soldiers returning from the war married, settled down, and had families. This era of high birth rates continued until 1964. The effect on the U.S. population was dramatic. In 1940, there were about 132 million Americans. By 1950, that number had grown to about 150 million. By 1960, the population had grown to about 180 million people—an increase of nearly 40 percent over the pre-war figure.

FYI

The Greatest Event in History? Some historians call World War II the most significant single occurrence in history. A total of 59 countries participated in the truly global conflict that cost about 56 million lives, resulted in more than $1 trillion in destruction, and had inestimable effects on countless individuals.

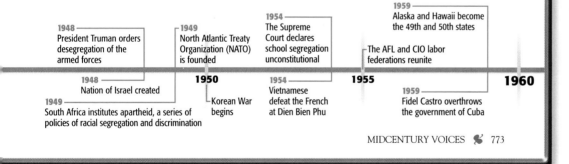

1948 — President Truman orders desegregation of the armed forces

1949 — North Atlantic Treaty Organization (NATO) is founded

1954 — The Supreme Court declares school segregation unconstitutional

1959 — Alaska and Hawaii become the 49th and 50th states

The AFL and CIO labor federations reunite

1948 — Nation of Israel created

1950

1954 — Vietnamese defeat the French at Dien Bien Phu

1955

1959 — Fidel Castro overthrows the government of Cuba

1960

1949 — South Africa institutes apartheid, a series of policies of racial segregation and discrimination

Korean War begins

The Cold War Students interested in the cold war will find a site at Kansas State University dedicated to the topic. Numerous links will lead them to fascinating information. Students interested in the military preparations for the potential real war that lurked throughout this period can find intriguing information at one of the U.S. military Web sites.

Midcentury Voices

Cultural Note

Television became a staple of American life during this period. Regular broadcasting began in 1941, but it wasn't until after World War II, in 1946, that the "television boom" began. In 1945 there were perhaps 10,000 television sets in the United States receiving local, black-and-white broadcasts. By 1950, the figure was 6 million sets receiving national broadcasts. Just 10 years later there were a stunning 60 million television sets in the country—a tenfold increase in a decade. Television stars and newscasters played a major role in setting the tone of the life of the time.

FYI

Highways to America

Today the more than 40,000 miles of interstate highways in the United States are a familiar fact of American life. But during the 1930s, 1940s, and most of the 1950s, few miles of "freeway" existed. It wasn't until 1956 that President Eisenhower signed the acts into law that created the interstate system. Its official name—the National System of Interstate and Defense Highways—reflects its birth from the fears generated by World War II and the cold war; it was conceived largely as a system for moving military vehicles and for evacuating civilians.

Midcentury Voices

Life of the Time

People are talking about

Broadcasts By 1940 about eighty percent of American households include radios. Listeners get to know President Roosevelt through his "fireside chats." In 1938 radio listeners fill the streets in panic, fearing that Martians are invading the earth, as Orson Welles broadcasts a very believable performance of H. G. Wells's *War of the Worlds*. After World War II, more and more families have a new form of entertainment in their living rooms—television. ▶

◀ The Road to Suburbia

America was the only nation "that ever went to the poorhouse in an automobile," notes humorist Will Rogers during the depression. The love of cars, combined with government subsidies for roads and new housing, leads to a post-war construction boom. Homes, malls, and motels engulf cities. Suddenly much of America becomes suburban.

Thurgood Marshall (center), 1954.

Brown v. Board of Education Civil Rights activists, led by lawyer Thurgood Marshall, win a dramatic victory in 1954. The Supreme Court rules that "Separate educational facilities are inherently unequal," and, in a follow-up ruling, that schools should desegregate "with all deliberate speed." While more than 500 school districts obey quietly and quickly, more than seventy-five percent of southern schools are still segregated in 1965.

Firsts

- Frances Perkins becomes Secretary of Labor—the first female cabinet member. (1933)
- Chuck Yeager flies the first airplane that breaks the sound barrier. (1947)
- Disneyland, the first theme park, opens. (1955)

U.S.A.			1936 — African American Jesse Owens wins four gold medals in Berlin Olympics	1944 — Aaron Copland's *Appalachian Spring* ballet opens, danced by Martha Graham and company
	1931 — The "Star Spangled Banner" becomes national anthem		1937 — Amelia Earhart disappears while attempting to fly across the Atlantic Ocean	
1930		**1935**	**1940**	**1945**
World	1931 — The first trans-African railroad is completed	1934 — In Germany, Wernher von Braun launches experimental rockets	1938 — Geologists discover significant reserves of oil in Saudi Arabia; In Hungary, Ladislao and George Biró patent a ballpoint pen	

MEETING INDIVIDUAL NEEDS — MULTIPLE LEARNING STYLES

Musical Students with strong musical talents, abilities, or interests can achieve a better understanding of the life of the time through exploring the popular music of the 1930s, 1940s, and 1950s.

Activity Have students work as a group to conduct research about the music of the 1930s, 1940s, and 1950s. Have them investigate the kinds of music popular at the time and the composers, song writers, and performers who made names for themselves. Ask students to obtain representative recordings of the music from the different decades to play for the class. They should provide background on the music, including its history, its significance to the period, and its influence on later music. **L2 COLLAB. LEARN.**

Food & Fashion

Jean Harlow

- Some women dye their hair during the 1930s, attempting to copy the look of "platinum blonde bombshell" Jean Harlow and other movie stars. ▶
- Young "hepcats" show off their zoot suits in the 1940s, featuring thigh-length jackets with padded shoulders and baggy pants with narrow cuffs.
- With silk stockings unavailable and factory jobs common, wartime women turn to wearing slacks. ▶
- The drive for greater convenience continues to shape eating habits. Stores begin selling sliced bread in 1930 and TV dinners in 1953.
- Meat consumption increases to its highest level since 1909. Many more people can afford meat thanks to the wartime economic boom.

Women railroad mechanics, 1942.

Arts & Entertainment

- In the 1950s, television cuts into the appeal of movies, and theater attendance drops by half between 1948 and 1955.
- ◀ America's varied voices are heard through its music—swing tunes by Duke Ellington, bebop jazz by Charlie Parker, nightclub crooning by Frank Sinatra, country ballads by Hank Williams, and rock and roll by Chuck Berry and Elvis Presley.
- Artists stirred by the drama of real life and funded by a handful of New Deal programs use a documentary approach that influences every medium. Government-sponsored photographs, with their stark, vivid images of the depression, visually define the period for most Americans.

Duke Ellington (at piano) and his orchestra.

Amusements

- In 1947 Jackie Robinson becomes the major leagues' first African American player in the twentieth century.
- Critics condemn the acrobatic jitterbug of the 1930s as too wild for polite dancers. By 1943 it is so popular that *Life* magazine proclaims it "the true national folk dance."

Time line:

- **1947** Levittown, the first mass-produced housing development, is started on Long Island, NY
- **1946** In Italy, women gain the right to vote
- Ralph Bunche becomes the first African American to win the Nobel Peace Prize
- **1951** The U.S. Census Bureau begins using UNIVAC, the first commercially available computer
- **1950**
- **1953** Mountain climbers Edmund Hillary, New Zealand, and Tenzing Norgay, Nepal, conquer Mt. Everest in Nepal
- **1955**
- **1959** Frank Lloyd Wright's spiral building for the Guggenheim Museum opens in New York City
- **1959** Sirimavo Bandaranaike of Ceylon (Sri Lanka) becomes world's first woman prime minister
- **1960**

MULTIPLE LEARNING STYLES

Logical and Mathematical To help students who learn logically acquire basic information about American life during the period covered by this unit, encourage them to study the time lines and create individual charts that will help them organize the information.

Activity Have students make a chart similar to the one shown and write notes in the appropriate places. **L2**

Time Period	History of the Time	Life of the Time	Literature of the Time
1930s			
1940s			
1950s			

Literature of the Time

African American

Magazines Magazines by, for, and about African Americans made their national debuts during the 1940s, largely because of the efforts of one man. John Johnson began publishing *Negro Digest* in 1942. Within a year, it had a circulation of more than 50,000—an impressive figure that disproved the white establishment's belief that such a magazine would be a failure. In 1945 Johnson launched another magazine, *Ebony*, targeted at black veterans of World War II. A third Johnson magazine, *Jet*, became, like *Ebony*, a premier African American magazine.

Midcentury Voices

Literature of the Time

PEOPLE ARE READING . . .

Paperbacks Poverty in the 1930s and war shortages in the 1940s encourage publishers to shift toward smaller, less expensive soft-covered books. The public loves them, and the inexpensive paperback revolutionizes American reading habits. One paperpack, Dr. Benjamin Spock's *Baby and Child Care*, outsells every other book in American history—except the Bible.

◀ **New Magazines** New uses of technology stimulate new magazines. The powerful photographic images of the depression spur the founding of two magazines devoted to real-life photographs—*Life* (1936) and *Look* (1937). The advent of TV is followed in 1953 by the publication of *TV Guide*, which quickly becomes the most successful new periodical of the 1950s.

1940s paperback

The Lonely Crowd This 1950 book by David Riesman and others helps define the era. Americans absorbed into large corporations, Riesman claims, find their independence and creativity squashed by their need for approval and hopes for advancement. Suffocating conformity and personal loneliness become themes in fictional works such as Sloan Wilson's *The Man in the Gray Flannel Suit*, Saul Bellow's *The Adventures of Augie March*, and J. D. Salinger's *Catcher in the Rye*.

People Are Writing

About America Under the New Deal, the government hires writers to describe the sites and history of America in books, pamphlets, brochures, and other documentary literature. Among these writers are Conrad Aiken, Saul Bellow, and Ralph Ellison.

Letters Even though wartime security censors check and edit personal letters, soldiers share their experiences with friends and family. Letters provide a vital link between the battlefront and the homefront.

U.S.A.					
Katherine Anne Porter, *Flowering Judas*	1934 Ruth Benedict, *Patterns of Culture*	1936 Dale Carnegie, *How to Win Friends and Influence People*	1938 Thornton Wilder, *Our Town*	1941 Eudora Welty, *A Curtain of Green*	1944 Tennessee Williams, *The Glass Menagerie*; Gunnar Myrdal, *An American Dilemma*

1930		**1935**		**1940**	1943	**1945**
World	Madagascar: Jean-Joseph Rabéarivelo, *Translation of the Night*		1939 Martinique: Aimé Césaire, *Return to My Native Land*		Germany: Bertolt Brecht, *The Good Woman of Setzuan*	France: Jean-Paul Sartre, *No Exit*

REAL-WORLD CONNECTION

Magazines Evolve Point out that magazines changed drastically in content, design, and readership during the mid-twentieth century.

Activity Have students research magazines published in the 1930s, 1940s, and 1950s. They should try to obtain copies of magazines of this period on microfiche or microfilm. Then have students compare and contrast the look and feel of these publications with those published today.

Students should compare the design of the publications, their content, and their readership. How are the publications similar? How are they different? What conclusions can students draw about life in America from these similarities and differences? **L2**

Literary Trends: Reflection and Protest

"In St. Louis, an Inquiring Reporter stopped a young mother and asked about her personal expectations for the postwar. 'Oh, things are going along just wonderfully,' she bubbled. 'Harry has a grand job, there's the new baby—'

Then she frowned. 'Do you think it's really all going to last?'

A zest in today, wondrous hopes for tomorrow—but always, in the America of V-J [Victory over Japan], there were shadows. A nation accustomed to the categorical yes and no, to war or peace and prosperity or depression, found itself in the nagging realm of maybe." —*Eric Goldman*

Some writers answer the "maybe" by setting off on personal journeys of discovery. For example, poet Robert Lowell revisits "My Father's Bedroom," and James Baldwin journeys back to his Harlem childhood in the short story "The Rockpile."

FOCUS ON . . .

Protest Writers

Many writers of the time respond to the uncertainty of their world by portraying human stories energized by social commitment. John Steinbeck and Arthur Miller demonstrate how writers can use their work as a weapon in the war for social justice. Steinbeck, stirred by the plight of migrant farm families, crafts one of the great novels of social protest, *The Grapes of Wrath*. In his play *The Crucible*, Arthur Miller uses the seventeenth-century Salem, Massachusetts, witch trials to protest the 1950s anticommunist hysteria. Both works arouse strong reactions, demonstrating how literature affects, as well as reflects, the world around it.

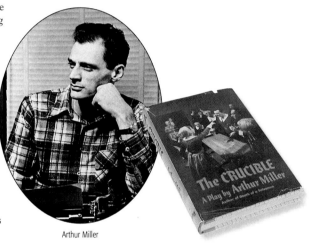

Arthur Miller

Cultural Note

World War II had a profound influence on all aspects of American life, including the literature of the time. Popular novels based on the war included *The Naked and the Dead* (1948) by Norman Mailer and *The Caine Mutiny* (1951) by Herman Wouk. More popular still were individual soldiers' remembrances of the war, which filled magazines and bookshelves in the post-war years.

Pop Culture

The Beat Movement Many protest writers of the 1950s were beatniks, or members of the so-called beat generation. These were young people who came of age early in the post-war period. Disillusioned by World War II and the cold war that followed, they protested against American society. The leading beat writer was Jack Kerouac. His autobiographical novel, *On the Road* (1957), told the tale of a cross-country trip.

1947
W. H. Auden, *The Age of Anxiety;* James Michener, *Tales of the South Pacific*

1949
Arthur Miller, *Death of a Salesman;* Gwendolyn Brooks, *Annie Allen*

1951
Marianne Moore, *Collected Poems;* Langston Hughes, *Montage of a Dream Deferred*

1959
Lorraine Hansberry, *A Raisin in the Sun*

1947
Netherlands: Anne Frank, *The Diary of a Young Girl*

1950

Chile: Pablo Neruda, *General Song;* Mexico: Octavio Paz, *The Labyrinth of Solitude*

1955

1956
Soviet Union: Yevgeny Yevtushenko, *Zima Junction*

1960

MIDCENTURY VOICES ❦ 777

MEETING INDIVIDUAL NEEDS — MULTIPLE LEARNING STYLES

Intrapersonal Students who acquire knowledge and insight through reflection will empathize with the reflective nature of literature about personal discoveries.

Activity Have students reread the quote in Literary Trends at the top of this page. Emphasize the phrase, "the nagging realm of maybe." Students should use the phrase as the basis for journal entries. In their entries, they should attempt to define or explain what the "realm of maybe" is and why it would be "nagging." Remind them to use examples from their own lives to explore its effects and to suggest solutions to it. **L2**

Novels of the Time

The literature of the period from 1930 through 1960 is as varied as the times that produce it. Some writers react directly to conditions in the world in which they find themselves, while others explore private experiences and feelings.

The Grapes of Wrath
by John Steinbeck (1939)

Set during the Great Depression, this gripping novel tells the story of the Joads, an Oklahoma farm family driven by poverty to seek out the natural paradise of California. Through the struggles of their journey and the disillusionment that awaits them, they learn how poor, exploited people can unite as a community to survive. The novel arouses widespread sympathy for the plight of migrant farm workers. In 1940 Steinbeck wins a Pulitzer Prize for *The Grapes of Wrath,* and the story is made into a memorable movie starring Henry Fonda.

John Steinbeck

The Member of the Wedding
by Carson McCullers (1946)

Carson McCullers

In this sensitive, beautifully written novel, as in much of her other work, Carson McCullers reveals the inner lives of isolated, lonely people. Frankie is a motherless twelve-year-old girl who, yearning for a connection, imagines that she will join her brother and his bride on their honeymoon trip. In the meantime, she finds refuge in her kitchen, talking with John Henry, her sickly six-year-old cousin, and Berenice, the wise and maternal cook. McCullers adapts the novel into a successful stage play in 1950 that is made into a film in 1952.

U.S.A.	1931 Pearl Buck, *The Good Earth*	1932 William Faulkner, *Light in August*	1934 F. Scott Fitzgerald, *Tender Is the Night*	1936 John Dos Passos, *The Big Money* 1937 Zora Neale Hurston, *Their Eyes Were Watching God*	Richard Wright, *Native Son;* Carson McCullers, *The Heart Is a Lonely Hunter;* Thomas Wolfe, *You Can't Go Home Again*	Jessamyn West, *Friendly Persuasion*
1930		**1932**	**1935**		**1940**	**1945**
World		England: Aldous Huxley, *Brave New World*	1937–40 Iceland: Halldór Laxness, *World Light*	1939 Ireland: James Joyce, *Finnegans Wake*	1942 France: Albert Camus, *The Stranger* China: Lao She, *Rickshaw Boy*	

Introductory Note

Have students define the word *diversity* and briefly discuss why *diverse* is one of the best adjectives to apply to American life and to the American population. Remind students that literature is a reflection of a culture, so it makes sense that American literature is also diverse. Narrow the discussion to one form of American literature—the novel—and elicit from the class examples of novels they have read to emphasize the diversity of the American novel. After they have read Novels of the Time, ask them how the three novels highlighted here exemplify that diversity.

Historical Note

John Steinbeck's works provide a window to the history of his time. *The Grapes of Wrath* remains the quintessential expression of the hardships wrought by the Great Depression of the 1930s. During the 1940s, Steinbeck served as a war correspondent, capturing the triumph and tragedy of World War II in nonfiction works and a novel. His post-war novel, *Cannery Row,* and its sequel, *Sweet Thursday,* recount the lives of ordinary Americans during the 1940s and 1950s. The nonfiction *Travels With Charley* is Steinbeck's account of his reflections of a road trip across the United States at the end of this period.

MEETING INDIVIDUAL NEEDS — MULTIPLE LEARNING STYLES

Interpersonal Students who learn best through working with others will benefit by collaborating on the preparation of a biographical time line of an important novelist of the era.

Activity Have students form groups to research the landmark biographical events in the life of a novelist of this era. Students should present what they learn in the form of a time line. Their time lines should include such entries as birth and death dates, geographical moves, travels, meetings and relationships with other significant literary figures, publications of major works, and major awards. Encourage students to enhance their time lines with illustrations and quotations. **L2 COLLAB. LEARN.**

Critics Corner

The Visible Ellison

"*Invisible Man* is not a great Negro novel; it is a work of art any contemporary writer could point to with pride."

—Harvey Curtis Wester, *Saturday Review*, April 12, 1952

"Ellison has an abundance of that primary talent without which neither craft nor intelligence can save a novelist; he is richly, wildly inventive; his scenes rise and dip with tension; his people bleed; his language stings. No other writer has captured so much of the confusion and agony, the hidden gloom and surface gaiety of Negro life."

—Irving Howe, *Nation*, May 10, 1952

Ralph Ellison

Invisible Man
by Ralph Ellison (1952)

Ralph Ellison spends seven years writing his only novel, which shocks and impresses readers when it first appears and goes on to win great acclaim and the 1953 National Book Award for fiction. Ellison looks at America through the eyes of a nameless young African American man. Full of idealism when he first leaves the South for the streets of Harlem, he journeys through a variety of strange and disillusioning experiences. Along the way, he realizes that he has been made invisible—that is, rejected and robbed of his identity—by racism and by an impersonal modern society.

invisible man

a novel by **Ralph Ellison**

A MODERN LIBRARY BOOK

Historical Note

Ralph Waldo Ellison, a literary spokesperson of twentieth-century America, shares part of his name with an American literary voice—Ralph Waldo Emerson—of the previous century. However, Ellison was not as prolific as Emerson. His reputation rests on *Invisible Man*, his only novel. Ellison did, however, publish numerous short stories and essays. He spent most of his career as a teacher at several colleges and universities. During the 1970s, he was the Albert Schweitzer Professor of the Humanities at New York University.

At the MOVIES

Be sure to preview the following video for appropriateness for your class.

- *Lives and Letters: Mid-Century America*.

1952
Ernest Hemingway, *The Old Man and the Sea*

1946
Robert Penn Warren, *All the King's Men*

1953
James Baldwin, *Go Tell It on the Mountain*

1957
Jack Kerouac, *On the Road*

1948
Japan: Kawabata Yasunari, *Snow Country*

1950

1957
Soviet Union: Boris Pasternak, *Doctor Zhivago*

Uruguay: Juan Carlos Onetti, *A Brief Life*

1955

1958
Nigeria: Chinua Achebe, *Things Fall Apart*

1960

GIFTED AND TALENTED ACTIVITY

Literary Critics Students are familiar with literary critics but may know little about who they are, what they do, or why they are an important part of the American literary landscape.

Activity Have students, individually or in small groups, investigate the role of the literary critic. They might begin by looking for answers to these questions: Who were the leading critics of the mid-twentieth century? What is the function and usefulness of literary criticism? How does literary criticism influence the work of writers and what the American public reads? Students who are especially motivated may also want to investigate one of the trends or schools of criticism, such as Deconstructionism and New Criticism, that developed during this period. **L3**

Midcentury Voices

Language of the Time

How People Speak

Cab Calloway

Jive Talk   Jive talk, the jargon of "cool" jazz musicians of the 1930s, works its way into American speech. Cab Calloway, a bandleader of the swing era, declares himself the heppest of hepcats and talks jive talk to his audiences, with the help of his "Hepster's Dictionary." During the decade, *hep* turns into *hip*. In the 1940s, jazz expressions move increasingly into general use, especially among the young, who take to describing good things as *cool, crazy, far out, real gone, out of sight, wild,* and *weird.*

American English Goes to War   Young Americans take their casual, slangy speech to war, creating expressions that enter the speech of the time. "Sighted sub. Sank same," radios a naval aviator. The most famous response of the war comes from General Anthony McAuliffe. When an opposing German general suggests that McAuliffe surrender, he replies simply, "Nuts!" The German general has no idea what McAuliffe means.

How People Write

Office Memos   Large corporations need a way to communicate with their employees, and the office memo is born. Memos are efficient, but they are also impersonal, reducing the human feeling in office life still further.

Braille   Louis Braille invented his raised-dot system of writing for the blind in 1824, when he was only sixteen years old. A universal braille code for English is adopted in 1932 and improved in 1957.

Office files in braille, 1955.

New Words and Expressions

Baseball, War, and Fashion   The years from 1930 to 1960 produce a multitude of new experiences that, in turn, produce a multitude of new words and expressions. Here are some examples:

Baseball	World War II	Korean War	Fashion
farm system	bazooka	brainwashing	bikini
send to the showers	GI	chopper	Bermuda shorts
All-Star Game	gung ho	germ warfare	button-down shirt
Little League	radar	honcho	Capri pants
have a strike against you	roger!		loafers
	walkie-talkie		

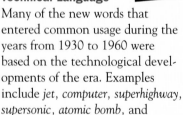

Theme 9 — Personal Discoveries

What are you like? What do you want out of life? Many of the characters and speakers in this theme make startling personal discoveries—about love, beauty, hope, family, and other crucial issues. Others teach lessons to help readers or listeners reach such personal discoveries.

THEME PROJECTS

Performing

Lessons to Be Learned With a partner, role-play a five- to ten-minute dialogue between two characters or speakers from the selections in this theme.

1. Choose two characters or speakers who might have an interesting dialogue. Perhaps their discoveries are similar, opposite, or just seem interesting when compared.

2. Plan your dialogue. Make sure the two people explain their own discoveries or lessons; they should really listen and speak to each other—agreeing, disagreeing, comparing, and contrasting.

3. Present your dialogue to the class, allowing classmates to critique the content.

Interdisciplinary Project

Art: A Cast of Characters With a small group, create a mural that includes characters or speakers from the selections and illustrates one discovery each has made.

1. Discuss the personal discoveries of the main character or speaker of each selection. How can you illustrate these discoveries?

2. Draw or paint your mural on a large sheet of paper. Divide the tasks among group members. Then, on the mural, write a small caption for each subject's personal discovery.

3. Display your mural on the classroom wall.

Study in Gray, 1933. Lucy Drake Marlow. Oil on Masonite, 28 x 23 in. The Lucy Drake Marlow Art Collection Trust.

GLENCOE TECHNOLOGY

LITERATURE CLASSICS CD-ROM

Search for other selections related to the theme of Personal Discoveries.

Theme 9

Teaching Strategies

The following suggestions may help your students plan and carry out their theme projects.

Performing

- Make sure that students understand that their dialogues can be between characters from different selections.
- Students can script their dialogues completely or perform the dialogues extemporaneously.
- Remind students that their dialogues should be in keeping with the nature and speech of the characters they are portraying; students should stay in character.

Interdisciplinary Project

- Have students write each caption in the first person, from the character's point of view, and in language appropriate to the character.
- Encourage students to include images that symbolize the characters' personal discoveries.
- Students may want to arrange their characters so that those who made similar personal discoveries are next to each other, and perhaps include labels on the mural to define certain types of personal discoveries.

Additional Resources

- *Interdisciplinary Activities,* pp. 18–19
- *Viewing and Representing Activities,* pp. 23–24
- *Listening and Speaking Activities,* pp. 17–18
- *Critical Thinking Skills,* pp. 26–27
- *Selection and Theme Assessment,* p. 231
- *Performance Assessment,* p. 133

SELECTIONS	Literary Elements	Reading and Thinking	Writing	Vocabulary and Spelling	
The Second Tree from the Corner E. B. WHITE	SE: Internal Conflict, p. 788 TWE: Internal Conflict, pp. 784, 786; Rising Action, p. 786	TWE: Drawing Conclusions, p. 784; Inferring, p. 785; Focusing on a Question, p. 787; Evaluating Sources, p. 790	SE: Journal Entry, p. 789 Character Exposition, p. 789	SE: Parts of Speech, p. 789	
Ode to My Socks PABLO NERUDA	SE: Metaphor, p. 794 TWE: Imagery, p. 793; Metaphor, p. 793	TWE: Establishing Criteria, p. 793	SE: Poem, p. 794		
Breakfast JOHN STEINBECK	SE: Implied Theme, p. 801 TWE: Implied Theme, p. 799	TWE: Identifying Spatial Relationships, p. 798; Inferring, p. 799	SE: Description, p. 801		
A Rose for Emily Address upon Receiving the Nobel Prize for Literature WILLIAM FAULKNER	SE: Flashback, p. 813 TWE: Flashback, pp. 805, 806, 810; Setting, p. 806; Foreshadowing, pp. 807, 810; Characterization, pp. 807, 809; Symbolism, pp. 810, 811	TWE: Using Text Structures, p. 803; Drawing Conclusions, pp. 806, 807, 808; Paraphrasing, p. 812	SE: Diary Entry, p. 814; Descriptive Paragraphs, p. 814 TWE: Using Adjectival Lists, p. 810	SE: Denotation and Connotation, p. 814 Defining Compound Words, p. 815	
Father's Bedroom ROBERT LOWELL	SE: Confessional Poetry, p. 818 TWE: Confessional Poetry, p. 817		SE: Description of a Place, p. 818; Organizing Details, p. 819		
from Black Boy RICHARD WRIGHT	SE: Flash-forward, p. 828 TWE: Characterization, pp. 823, 826; Conflict, p. 825; Flash-forward, p. 826	TWE: Inferring, p. 825; Comparing and Contrasting, p. 827	SE: Letters, p. 829; Author's Use of Dialogue, p. 829	SE: Latin Roots: vit and viv, p. 829	
A Worn Path EUDORA WELTY	SE: Characterization, p. 840 TWE: Characterization, pp. 834, 838; Extended Metaphor, pp. 834, 835; Symbolism, pp. 835, 836; Character, p. 836	TWE: Identifying Author's Purpose, p. 830; Inferring, p. 836; Comparing and Contrasting, p. 838	SE: Comparison, p. 841; Short Story, p. 841	SE: Analogies, p. 841	
The Explorer GWENDOLYN BROOKS	SE: Alliteration, p. 845 TWE: Theme, p. 844		SE: Poem, p. 845		

Key: Student material is in roman. Teacher material is in italic. 💻 Technology **COLLAB. LEARN.** Collaboration

Grammar and Language	Listening, Speaking, and Viewing	Life Skills	Study, Research, and Technology
TWE: Pronoun Antecedents, p. 785	SE: COLLAB. LEARN. Literature Groups, p. 789	SE: Follow-up Report, p. 789	*TWE:* 🖥 *Internet Connection*, p. 790
	SE: COLLAB. LEARN. Literature Groups, p. 794		
TWE: Using Good *and* Well, p. 800			SE: History, p. 801 *TWE:* 🖥 *Internet Connection*, p. 797
TWE: Degrees of Comparison, p. 806	SE: COLLAB. LEARN. Literature Groups, p. 814		SE: 🖥 Internet Connection, p. 814 *TWE: Old Family Homes*, p. 809; COLLAB. LEARN. *The Critics' View*, p. 811
TWE: Using Bad and Badly, p. 819	SE: COLLAB. LEARN. Literature Groups, p. 818		
TWE: Using Who *and* Whom, p. 824	SE: COLLAB. LEARN. Literature Groups, p. 829; Interview, p. 829		SE: History, p. 829 *TWE:* COLLAB. LEARN. *Sharecropping*, p. 826
TWE: Incorrect Verb Tense, p. 838	SE: COLLAB. LEARN. Literature Groups, p. 841; Story Reading, p. 841 *TWE: Mini Readers Theater*, p. 839		SE: Geography, p. 841 *TWE:* 🖥 *Internet Connection*, p. 830; *Marathon Races*, p. 836
	SE: COLLAB. LEARN. Literature Groups, p. 845		

SELECTIONS	Literary Elements	Reading and Thinking	Writing	Vocabulary and Spelling	
February RALPH ELLISON	SE: Personal Essay, p. 848 TWE: Personal Essay, p. 847		SE: Descriptive Paragraphs, p. 848 TWE: **COLLAB. LEARN.** A Personal Essay, pp. 847, 849		
The Portrait TOMÁS RIVERA	SE: Idiom, p. 854 TWE: Rising Action, p. 852; Climax, p. 852; Idiom, p. 853	TWE: Making Critical Judgments, p. 853	SE: Journal Entry, p. 854		
The Death of the Ball Turret Gunner RANDALL JARRELL	SE: Author's Note, p. 858 TWE: Author's Note, p. 857	SE: Summarizing, p. 859	SE: Expository Paragraphs, p. 858 TWE: Tone, p. 857		
The Beautiful Changes RICHARD WILBUR	SE: Sensory Details, p. 862	TWE: Comparing and Contrasting, p. 861	SE: Identifying Sound Devices, p. 862		
The Rockpile JAMES BALDWIN	SE: Foil, p. 872 TWE: Symbolism, pp. 868, 869; Foreshadowing, p. 868; Characterization, pp. 868, 869; Foil, pp. 870, 871	TWE: Previewing, p. 865; Inferring, p. 866; Drawing Conclusions, p. 870; Paraphrasing, p. 871	SE: Conflict Analysis, p. 873; Journal Entry, p. 873 TWE: **COLLAB. LEARN.** Advice Letter, p. 873	SE: Analogies, p. 873 TWE: Etymology, p. 867	
The Magic Barrel BERNARD MALAMUD	SE: Dialect, p. 888 TWE: Characterization, pp. 876, 882; Dialect, pp. 877, 879; Point of View, p. 880; Conflict, p. 884; Foreshadowing, p. 885; Simile, p. 885; Motivation, p. 886	TWE: Interpreting, p. 876; Comparing and Contrasting, pp. 876, 879, 883, 886, 887; Making Critical Judgments, p. 877; Inferring, p. 878; Drawing Conclusions, p. 881	SE: Supporting Viewpoint, p. 889; Short Story, p. 889 TWE: Extended Definition: Love, p. 882; Evaluating Elements, p. 884	SE: The Latin Roots ami-, anim-, and ama (amo), p. 889 TWE: Word Families, p. 881; Word Meaning, p. 882	
from Stride Toward Freedom MARTIN LUTHER KING JR.	SE: Structure, p. 895 TWE: Structure, p. 894	TWE: Analyzing Arguments, p. 892; Logical Reasoning, p. 893; Paraphrasing, p. 894			
Choice: A Tribute to Dr. Martin Luther King Jr. ALICE WALKER	SE: Anecdote, p. 901 TWE: Anecdote, p. 899; Theme, p. 899	TWE: Activating Prior Knowledge, p. 898; Inferring, p. 900	SE: Journal Entry, p. 901		

Key: Student material is in roman. Teacher material is in italic. ⌨ Technology **COLLAB. LEARN.** Collaboration

Grammar and Language	Listening, Speaking, and Viewing	Life Skills	Study, Research, and Technology
	SE: **COLLAB. LEARN.** Literature Groups, p. 848		
	SE: **COLLAB. LEARN.** Literature Groups, p. 854		TWE: 🖥 Internet Connection, p. 851
	SE: **COLLAB. LEARN.** Literature Groups, p. 858		
	SE: Dramatic Reading, p. 862		
TWE: Double Negatives, p. 870	SE: **COLLAB. LEARN.** Literature Groups, p. 873; **COLLAB. LEARN.** Performing, p. 873	TWE: Problem Solving, p. 867	SE: 🖥 Internet Connection, p. 873
TWE: Subject Complements, p. 878	SE: **COLLAB. LEARN.** Literature Groups, p. 889; Reading Dialogue, p. 889	SE: Brochure, p. 889 TWE: Decision Making, p. 880	TWE: Geography, p. 881; New York's Jewish Community, p. 886
TWE: Compound and Compound-Complex Sentences, p. 894	SE: **COLLAB. LEARN.** Literature Groups, p. 895	SE: Interview, p. 895	
TWE: Past Perfect Tense, p. 900	SE: **COLLAB. LEARN.** Literature Groups, p. 901		TWE: 🖥 Internet Connection, p. 898

SELECTIONS	📁 Print Resources		
The Second Tree from the Corner E. B. WHITE	Unit Six Planning Guide, pp. 8–15 * Active Reading Guide, p. 92 Vocabulary Practice, p. 44	Grammar and Composition Handbook, Lesson 7.6 Grammar and Language Workbook, p. 187 Reading Workbook, pp. 71–72	* Quick Checks, p. 92 Selection and Theme Assessment, pp. 137–138 Performance Assessment, p. 77 Spanish Summaries, p. 82 Spanish Translations
Ode to My Socks PABLO NERUDA	Unit Six Planning Guide, pp. 16–20 * Active Reading Guide, p. 93	Reading Workbook	* Quick Checks, p. 93 Selection and Theme Assessment, pp. 137–138 Performance Assessment, p. 77 Spanish Summaries, p. 83 Spanish Translations
Breakfast JOHN STEINBECK	Unit Six Planning Guide, pp. 21–26 * Active Reading Guide, p. 94 Vocabulary Practice, p. 45	Grammar and Composition Handbook, Lesson 8.5 Grammar and Language Workbook, p. 201 Reading Workbook, pp. 73–74	* Quick Checks, p. 94 Selection and Theme Assessment, pp. 139–140 Performance Assessment, p. 78 Spanish Summaries, p. 84
A Rose for Emily Address upon Receiving the Nobel Prize for Literature WILLIAM FAULKNER	Unit Six Planning Guide, pp. 27–34 * Active Reading Guide, p. 95 Vocabulary Practice, p. 46	Grammar and Composition Handbook, Lesson 8.1 Grammar and Language Workbook, p. 195 Reading Workbook, pp. 75–76	* Quick Checks, p. 95 Selection and Theme Assessment, pp. 141–142 Performance Assessment, p. 79 Spanish Summaries, p. 85
Father's Bedroom ROBERT LOWELL	Unit Six Planning Guide, pp. 35–39 * Active Reading Guide, p. 96	Grammar and Composition Handbook, Lesson 8.5 Grammar and Language Workbook, p. 201 Reading Workbook	* Quick Checks, p. 96 Selection and Theme Assessment, pp. 143–144 Performance Assessment, p. 80 Spanish Summaries, p. 86
from **Black Boy** RICHARD WRIGHT	Unit Six Planning Guide, pp. 40–47 * Active Reading Guide, p. 97 Vocabulary Practice, p. 47	Grammar and Composition Handbook, Lesson 7.5 Grammar and Language Workbook, p. 181 Reading Workbook, pp. 77–78	* Quick Checks, p. 97 Selection and Theme Assessment, pp. 145–146 Performance Assessment, p. 81 Spanish Summaries, p. 87
A Worn Path EUDORA WELTY	Unit Six Planning Guide, pp. 48–55 * Active Reading Guide, p. 98 Vocabulary Practice, p. 48	Grammar and Composition Handbook, Lesson 5.6 Grammar and Language Workbook, pp. 135–143 Reading Workbook, pp. 77–78	* Quick Checks, p. 98 Selection and Theme Assessment, pp. 147–148 Performance Assessment, p. 82 Spanish Summaries, p. 88 Spanish Translations
The Explorer GWENDOLYN BROOKS	Unit Six Planning Guide, pp. 56–60 * Active Reading Guide, p. 99	Reading Workbook	* Quick Checks, p. 99 Selection and Theme Assessment, p. 149 Performance Assessment, p. 83 Spanish Summaries, p. 89

*Also available in Spanish

Transparencies	**Technology Resources**
Selection Focus Transparency 82 Grammar and Language Transparency 58 Literary Elements Transparency 75 Fine Art Transparency 30	Audio Library Spanish Audio Library Testmaker Web Site: *lit.glencoe.com*
Selection Focus Transparency 83 Literary Elements Transparency 76	Audio Library Spanish Audio Library Testmaker Web Site: *lit.glencoe.com*
Selection Focus Transparency 84 Grammar and Language Transparency 59 Literary Elements Transparency 77	Literature Launchers Audio Library Spanish Audio Library Testmaker Web Site: *lit.glencoe.com*
Selection Focus Transparency 85 Grammar and Language Transparency 60 Literary Elements Transparency 78	Audio Library Spanish Audio Library Testmaker Web Site: *lit.glencoe.com*
Selection Focus Transparency 86 Grammar and Language Transparency 61 Literary Elements Transparency 79 Fine Art Transparency 12	Audio Library Testmaker Web Site: *lit.glencoe.com*
Selection Focus Transparency 87 Grammar and Language Transparency 62 Literary Elements Transparency 80	Audio Library Spanish Audio Library Testmaker Web Site: *lit.glencoe.com*
Selection Focus Transparency 88 Grammar and Language Transparency 63 Literary Elements Transparency 81	Literature Launchers Audio Library Spanish Audio Library Testmaker Web Site: *lit.glencoe.com*
Selection Focus Transparency 89 Literary Elements Transparency 82	Audio Library Testmaker Web Site: *lit.glencoe.com*

SELECTIONS	📁 Print Resources		
February RALPH ELLISON	Unit Six Planning Guide, pp. 61–65 * Active Reading Guide, p. 100 Vocabulary Practice, p. 49	Reading Workbook	* Quick Checks, p. 100 Selection and Theme Assessment, p. 150 Performance Assessment, p. 84 Spanish Summaries, p. 90
The Portrait TOMÁS RIVERA	Unit Six Planning Guide, pp. 66–70 * Active Reading Guide, p. 101	Reading Workbook, pp. 79–80	* Quick Checks, p. 101 Selection and Theme Assessment, pp. 151–152 Performance Assessment, p. 85 Spanish Summaries, p. 91
The Death of the Ball Turret Gunner RANDALL JARRELL	Unit Six Planning Guide, pp. 71–75 * Active Reading Guide, p. 102	Reading Workbook	* Quick Checks, p. 102 Selection and Theme Assessment, p. 153 Performance Assessment, p. 86 Spanish Summaries, p. 92
The Beautiful Changes RICHARD WILBUR	Unit Six Planning Guide, pp. 76–80 * Active Reading Guide, p. 103	Reading Workbook	* Quick Checks, p. 103 Selection and Theme Assessment, p. 154 Performance Assessment, p. 87 Spanish Summaries, p. 93
The Rockpile JAMES BALDWIN	Unit Six Planning Guide, pp. 81–88 * Active Reading Guide, p. 104 Vocabulary Practice, p. 50	Grammar and Composition Handbook, Lesson 8.6 Grammar and Language Workbook, p. 203 Reading Workbook, pp. 79–80	* Quick Checks, p. 104 Selection and Theme Assessment, pp. 155–156 Performance Assessment, p. 88 Spanish Summaries, p. 94
The Magic Barrel BERNARD MALAMUD	Unit Six Planning Guide, pp. 89–96 * Active Reading Guide, p. 105 Vocabulary Practice, p. 51	Grammar and Composition Handbook, Lesson 2.5 Grammar and Language Workbook, p. 81 Reading Workbook, pp. 79–80	* Quick Checks, p. 105 Selection and Theme Assessment, pp. 157–158 Performance Assessment, p. 89 Spanish Summaries, p. 95
from Stride Toward Freedom MARTIN LUTHER KING JR.	Unit Six Planning Guide, pp. 97–102 * Active Reading Guide, p. 106 Vocabulary Practice, p. 52	Grammar and Composition Handbook, Lesson 4.8 Grammar and Language Workbook, p. 101 Reading Workbook, pp. 79–80	* Quick Checks, p. 106 Selection and Theme Assessment, pp. 159–160 Performance Assessment, p. 90 Spanish Summaries, p. 96
Choice: A Tribute to Dr. Martin Luther King Jr. ALICE WALKER	Unit Six Planning Guide, pp. 103–108 * Active Reading Guide, p. 107 Vocabulary Practice, p. 53	Grammar and Composition Handbook, Lesson 5.4 Grammar and Language Workbook, p. 137 Reading Workbook, pp. 79–80	* Quick Checks, p. 107 Selection and Theme Assessment, pp. 161–162 Performance Assessment, p. 91 Spanish Summaries, p. 97

*Also available in Spanish

Transparencies	Technology Resources
Selection Focus Transparency 90 Literary Elements Transparency 83	Audio Library Spanish Audio Library Testmaker Web Site: *lit.glencoe.com*
Selection Focus Transparency 91 Literary Elements Transparency 84 Fine Art Transparency 3	Audio Library Spanish Audio Library Testmaker Web Site: *lit.glencoe.com*
Selection Focus Transparency 92 Literary Elements Transparency 85	Audio Library Testmaker Web Site: *lit.glencoe.com*
Selection Focus Transparency 93 Literary Elements Transparency 86	Audio Library Testmaker Web Site: *lit.glencoe.com*
Selection Focus Transparency 94 Grammar and Language Transparency 64 Literary Elements Transparency 87	Audio Library Testmaker Web Site: *lit.glencoe.com*
Selection Focus Transparency 95 Grammar and Language Transparency 65 Literary Elements Transparency 88	Audio Library Spanish Audio Library Testmaker Web Site: *lit.glencoe.com*
Selection Focus Transparency 96 Grammar and Language Transparency 66 Literary Elements Transparency 89	Audio Library Spanish Audio Library Testmaker Web Site: *lit.glencoe.com*
Selection Focus Transparency 97 Grammar and Language Transparency 67 Literary Elements Transparency 90	Audio Library Spanish Audio Library Testmaker Web Site: *lit.glencoe.com*

Theme RESOURCES

- Listening and Speaking Activities (pp. 17–18)
- Viewing and Representing Activities (pp. 23–24)
- Critical Thinking Skills (pp. 25–27)
- Media Connections Activities (pp. 17–18)
- Interdisciplinary Activities (pp. 18–19)

See also these additional planning resources:
- English Language Learners Sourcebook
- Inclusion Strategies Sourcebook
- Literature Groups Sourcebook

Use Glencoe's *Presentation Plus!* This multi-media teaching tool lets you present dynamic lessons that will engage your students. Using Microsoft Powerpoint,® you can customize the presentations to create your own personalized lessons.

Objectives

- To read and analyze a short story about a man who makes a personal discovery
- To define external and internal conflict and to analyze the internal conflict of a character
- To write an analysis of how visual imagery contributes to characterization

Skills

Reading/Thinking: Drawing Conclusions; Inferring; Focusing on a Question
Writing: Journal Entry
Vocabulary: Parts of Speech
Grammar/Language: Pronoun Antecedents
Life Skills: Follow-Up Report
Collaboration: Literature Groups

Motivating
→OPTIONS

Selection Focus Transparency 82: Have students view the transparency and then answer the question provided.

Focus Activity: As an extension of the Focus Activity, invite students to compare their lists and determine if everyone wants the same kinds of things.

Before You Read
The Second Tree from the Corner

Meet E. B. White

"I arise in the morning torn between a desire to improve (or save) the world and a desire to enjoy (or savor) the world. This makes it hard to plan the day."
—*White*

Although the beloved children's classics *Charlotte's Web* and *Stuart Little* remain two of Elwyn Brooks (E. B.) White's best-known works, he is also highly acclaimed for his essays and short stories. In fact, it was while working for the *New Yorker* magazine in his late twenties that White first captivated the American public through his essays, sketches, and editing style. There he worked with other legendary writers such as James Thurber and Robert Benchley to create a sophisticated and clever "New York" voice for the newly established magazine.

White was born and raised in rural Mount Vernon, New York. In 1938, at age thirty-nine, after many years in New York City, he decided to leave the city and return to a simpler rural life, this time in Maine. There he continued writing essays and penned his famed children's stories, which were originally intended to entertain a visiting niece.

White was awarded the Presidential Medal of Freedom in 1963, the Laura Ingalls Wilder Award from the American Library Association in 1970, and, in 1973, he was elected to the American Academy of Arts and Letters.

E. B. White was born in 1899 and died in 1985.

FOCUS ACTIVITY

Imagine that someone asks you, "What do you want out of life?" How would you answer?

QUICKWRITE Jot down some answers to this question. Include tangible things, such as a college education or a car, as well as intangible things, such as wisdom or happiness.

SETTING A PURPOSE Read to see how two characters respond to the question "What do you want out of life?"

BACKGROUND

The Time and Place

This story takes place in Manhattan, a part of New York City, probably in the late 1940s. One clue to the story's time frame comes from a reference to Ethel Merman, a popular Broadway singer and actress of the time. Other references to famous New York institutions and places appear in the story as well. The narrator mentions the *Times,* which is the *New York Times* newspaper, the "Park," which is Central Park, and the "East Seventies," a section of Manhattan known for its wealthy residents.

VOCABULARY PREVIEW

amorphous (ə môr′ fəs) *adj.* without definite form; p. 784
retractable (ri trak′ tə bəl) *adj.* capable of being drawn back or in; p. 784
hemorrhage (hem′ ər ij) *n.* a severe discharge of blood; p. 785
inquisitor (in kwiz′ ə tər) *n.* one who asks questions; p. 786
intimation (in′ tə mā′ shən) *n.* a hint; a suggestion; p. 787
invigorated (in vig′ ə rā′ tid) *adj.* filled with strength and energy; p. 787

782 ❧ UNIT 6

RESOURCE MANAGER

Lesson Planning Resource
The *Unit Six Planning Guide* (pp. 8–15) provides additional lesson notes and reduced versions of all print resources.

📂 **Other Print Resources**
- Active Reading Guide, p. 92
- Vocabulary Practice, p. 44
- Reading Workbook, pp. 71–72
- Grammar and Language Workbook, p. 187

- Grammar and Composition Handbook, Lesson 7.6
- Quick Checks, p. 92
- Selection and Theme Assessment, pp. 137–138
- Performance Assessment, p. 77
- Spanish Summaries, p. 82
- Spanish Translations
- Inclusion Strategies
- English Language Learners Sourcebook

📖 **Transparencies**
- Selection Focus 82
- Fine Art 30
- Literary Elements 75
- Grammar and Language 58

Technology
🎧 Audio Library
🎧 Spanish Audio Library
💻 Glencoe Literature Web Site
💾 Testmaker

The Second Tree from the Corner

E. B. White

Washington Square Park. Anthony Springer (1928–1995). Oil on canvas. Private Collection. Permission courtesy of Mrs. Sylvia Springer.

SUMMARY

Mr. Trexler is plagued by "bizarre thoughts," depression, mysterious physical symptoms, and anxiety. The author describes Trexler's visits to a psychiatrist and implies that Trexler's problem is fear. The story ends soon after a visit, during which the doctor asks Trexler pointedly, "What do you want?" This question leads to Trexler's epiphany: he realizes that "all men" want something "deep, formless, enduring, and impossible of fulfillment"; something he can't explain but recognizes when he sees the second tree from the corner "saturated" with the evening light.

📁 *Spanish Summaries,* p. 82

A **Active Reading**

PREDICT Trexler's internal conflict is implied from the very beginning. Challenge students to predict what this conflict is, based on the opening paragraphs. *(Trexler wrestles with bizarre thoughts, though what these are remains unknown.)*

Additional Resources
📁 *Active Reading Guide,* p. 92
🎧 *Audio Library*
🎧 *Spanish Audio Library*

Teaching Options

CONNECTING TO OTHER SELECTIONS

COMPARING *selections*

This selection is paired with "Ode to My Socks" on page 792. A lesson for teaching a comparison of the two selections appears on page 795.

The chart at the right shows three ways to connect "The Second Tree from the Corner" to selections in this book.

For specific teaching strategies, see the *Unit Six Planning Guide,* pp. 11–12.

Connection	Title
Critical Thinking: Comparing and Contrasting →	"Because I could not stop for Death," p. 432
Thematic: Turning points →	"The Bridal Party," p. 652
Literary: Conflict →	"Chief Sekoto Holds Court," p. 488

B Author's Craft

TONE Discuss the tone of these lines with students and ensure that they appreciate how the author integrates humor into the story. Ask students how this humor affects the tone of the story and whether it adds to or detracts from the plot. *(The use of humor here and elsewhere engages the reader, lightens up an otherwise dreary and oppressive situation, and makes the story more enjoyable.)*

C Literary Elements

INTERNAL CONFLICT Ask students to identify and discuss the internal conflicts that Trexler is struggling with in this passage. *(He is struggling with choosing a bizarre thought to share with the doctor. He is worrying about how the doctor will interpret his thoughts. He is worrying about the time he is taking to decide what to do.)*

"Ever have any bizarre thoughts?" asked the doctor.

Mr. Trexler failed to catch the word. "What kind?" he said.

"Bizarre," repeated the doctor, his voice steady. He watched his patient for any slight change of expression, any wince. It seemed to Trexler that the doctor was not only watching him closely but was creeping slowly toward him, like a lizard toward a bug. Trexler shoved his chair back an inch and gathered himself for a reply. He was about to say "Yes" when he realized that if he said yes the next question would be unanswerable. Bizarre thoughts, bizarre thoughts? Ever have any bizarre thoughts? What kind of thoughts *except* bizarre had he had since the age of two?

Trexler felt the time passing, the necessity for an answer. These psychiatrists were busy men, overloaded, not to be kept waiting. The next patient was probably already perched out there in the waiting room, lonely, worried, shifting around on the sofa, his mind stuffed with bizarre thoughts and <u>amorphous</u> fears. Poor fellow, thought Trexler. Out there all alone in that misshapen antechamber,[1] staring at the filing cabinet and wondering whether to tell the doctor about that day on the Madison Avenue bus.

Let's see, bizarre thoughts. Trexler dodged back along the dreadful corridor of the years to see what he could find. He felt the doctor's eyes upon him and knew that time was running out. Don't be so conscientious, he said to himself. If a bizarre thought is indicated here, just reach into the bag and pick anything at all. A man as well supplied with bizarre thoughts as you are should have no difficulty producing one for the record. Trexler

darted into the bag, hung for a moment before one of his thoughts, as a hummingbird pauses in the delphinium. No, he said, not that one. He darted to another (the one about the rhesus monkey), paused, considered. No, he said, not that.

Trexler knew he must hurry. He had already used up pretty nearly four seconds since the question had been put. But it was an impossible situation—just one more lousy, impossible situation such as he was always getting himself into. When, he asked himself, are you going to quit maneuvering yourself into a pocket? He made one more effort. This time he stopped at the asylum, only the bars were lucite[2]— fluted, <u>retractable</u>. Not here, he said. Not this one.

He looked straight at the doctor. "No," he said quietly. "I never have any bizarre thoughts."

The doctor sucked in on his pipe, blew a plume of smoke toward the rows of medical books. Trexler's gaze followed the smoke. He managed to make out one of the titles, *The Genito-Urinary System*. A bright wave of fear swept cleanly over him and he winced under

Did You Know?
Delphinium (del fin′ ē əm), also called larkspur, is a tall, flowering plant. The flowers are usually blue or purple.

Did You Know?
Fluted means "having decorative, usually rounded grooves."

---

1. An *antechamber*, or waiting room, is a smaller room serving as an entrance to a larger or main room.

2. *Lucite* is the trademark name of a transparent plastic.

Vocabulary
amorphous (ə môr′ fəs) *adj.* without definite form
retractable (ri trak′ tə bəl) *adj.* capable of being drawn back or in

---

Teaching Options

Reading *Minilesson*

Drawing Conclusions Most short stories require readers to draw conclusions early in the story based on the exposition. By focusing on this essential reading task, students can ensure that they understand what they are reading on a literal level and so create the foundation for a deeper understanding of a story.

Activity Have students reread the first four paragraphs of this story. Based on

their reading, have them list everything about the setting and characters that they know. For each fact, they should jot a note explaining how they came to that conclusion. Have students share their lists with the class and point out the conclusions they drew in order to develop their lists. **L2**

Additional Resources
📁 ***Reading Workbook,*** pp. 71–72

the first pain of kidney stones.[3] He remembered when he was a child, the first time he ever entered a doctor's office, sneaking a look at the titles of the books—and the flush of fear, the shirt wet under the arms, the book on t.b.,[4] the sudden knowledge that he was in the advanced stages of consumption,[5] the quick vision of the hemorrhage. Trexler sighed wearily. Forty years, he thought, and I still get thrown by the title of a medical book. Forty years and I still can't stay on life's little bucky horse. No wonder I'm sitting here in this dreary joint at the end of this woebegone[6] afternoon, lying about my bizarre thoughts to a doctor who looks, come to think of it, rather tired.

The session dragged on. After about twenty minutes, the doctor rose and knocked his pipe out. Trexler got up, knocked the ashes out of his brain, and waited. The doctor smiled warmly and stuck out his hand. "There's nothing the matter with you—you're just scared. Want to know how I know you're scared?"

"How?" asked Trexler.

"Look at the chair you've been sitting in! See how it has moved back away from my desk? You kept inching away from me while I asked you questions. That means you're scared."

"Does it?" said Trexler, faking a grin. "Yeah, I suppose it does."

They finished shaking hands. Trexler turned and walked out uncertainly along the passage, then into the waiting room and out

past the next patient, a ruddy pin-striped man who was seated on the sofa twirling his hat nervously and staring straight ahead at the files. Poor, frightened guy, thought Trexler, he's probably read in the *Times* that one American male out of every two is going to die of heart disease by twelve o'clock next Thursday. It says that in the paper almost every morning. And he's also probably thinking about that day on the Madison Avenue bus.

A week later, Trexler was back in the patient's chair. And for several weeks thereafter he continued to visit the doctor, always toward the end of the afternoon, when the vapors hung thick above the pool of the mind and darkened the whole region of the East Seventies.[7] He felt no better as time went on, and he found it impossible to work. He discovered that the visits were becoming routine and that although the routine was one to which he certainly did not look forward, at least he could accept it with cool resignation, as once, years ago, he had accepted a long spell with a dentist who had settled down to a steady fooling with a couple of dead teeth. The visits, moreover, were now assuming a pattern recognizable to the patient.

Each session would begin with a resumé of symptoms—the dizziness in the streets, the constricting pain in the back of the neck, the apprehensions, the tightness of the scalp, the inability to concentrate, the despondency[8] and the melancholy times, the feeling of pressure and tension, the anger at not being able to work, the anxiety over work not done, the gas on the stomach. Dullest set of neurotic

---

3. *Kidney stones* are small, hard calcium deposits that sometimes form in the kidneys and cause pain.
4. Tuberculosis, a disease that often affects the lungs, is sometimes referred to as *t.b.*
5. *Consumption* is another name for tuberculosis.
6. *Woebegone* means "sorrowful" or "filled with grief"; it can also suggest "dreary and miserable."

7. Most of the streets that run east to west in Manhattan are identified by numbers rather than names. *East Seventies* refers to the section of streets from 70–79 that are on the east side of Manhattan.
8. *Despondency* means "hopelessness" or "depression."

Vocabulary
hemorrhage (hem′ ər ij) *n.* a severe discharge of blood

Active Reading

RESPOND Ask students how they feel about Mr. Trexler at this point in the story and why. *(Most students will feel sympathetic toward Mr. Trexler. He is presented in a sympathetic light as a troubled man trying to figure out how to get over his illnesses.)*

Active Reading

RESPOND Ask students how they feel about the psychiatrist at this point in the story. Ask how their reactions to him compare to their reactions to Mr. Trexler. *(The psychiatrist is presented as a stock character, flat and level, as opposed to the depth and complexity of Trexler.)*

Critical Thinking

INFERRING Mr. Trexler makes a quick analysis of his fellow patient. Why might Trexler think he knows what's happening in the other man's life and mind? *(Trexler is projecting his own experiences and thoughts onto the other man.)*

Grammar and Language *Minilesson*

Pronoun Antecedents A pronoun refers to a noun or another pronoun that usually comes before it in a text. The word to which a pronoun refers is called its antecedent or referent. In the sentence, "I gave Mary the apple she wanted," *she* is a pronoun that refers to *Mary*.

Activity Ask students to find 10 pronouns in the story. For each, have them identify its antecedent and tell whether

the antecedent is a noun or another pronoun. If it is a pronoun, they should identify its antecedent, and continue the process until they identify the original noun. You may do the activity orally or have students copy the sentences in which pronouns and their antecedents appear. Then have them circle each pronoun and draw a line to its antecedent. **L2**

Additional Resources

Grammar and Language Transparency 58

Grammar and Language Workbook, p. 187

Grammar and Composition Handbook, Lesson 7.6

Writer's Choice, Lesson 17.6

TAXI! TAXI! The United States had its first motor-driven taxicab in about 1898, but it wasn't powered by a gasoline engine. It was electric. Almost a decade later, taxicabs with gasoline engines and taximeters came to New York City. Today, so many taxis use New York City streets that a group of concerned New Yorkers hopes to have them and other automobiles banned from parts of the city's Central Park.

Teaching Options

---

symptoms in the world, Trexler would think, as he obediently trudged back over them for the doctor's benefit.

As he became familiar with the pattern Trexler found that he increasingly tended to identify himself with the doctor, transferring himself into the doctor's seat—probably (he thought) some rather slick form of escapism. At any rate, it was nothing new for Trexler to identify himself with other people. Whenever he got into a cab, he instantly became the driver, saw everything from the hackman's angle (and the reaching over with the right hand, the nudging of the flag, the pushing it down, all the way down along the side of the meter), saw everything—traffic, fare, everything—through the eyes of Anthony Rocco, or Isidore Freedman, or Matthew Scott. In a barbershop, Trexler was the barber, his fingers curled around the comb, his hand on the tonic. Perfectly natural, then, that Trexler should soon be occupying the doctor's chair, asking the questions, waiting for the answers. He got quite interested in the doctor, in this way. He liked him, and he found him a not too difficult patient.

It was on the fifth visit, about halfway through, that the doctor turned to Trexler and said, suddenly, "What do you want?" He gave the word "want" special emphasis.

"I d'know," replied Trexler uneasily. "I guess nobody knows the answer to that one."

"Sure they do," replied the doctor.

"Do *you* know what *you* want?" asked Trexler narrowly.

"Certainly," said the doctor. Trexler noticed that at this point the doctor's chair slid slightly backward, away from him. Trexler stifled a small, internal smile. Scared as a rabbit, he said to himself. Look at him scoot!

"What *do* you want?" continued Trexler, pressing his advantage, pressing it hard.

The doctor glided back another inch away from his inquisitor. "I want a wing on the small house I own in Westport.[9] I want more money, and more leisure to do the things I want to do."

Trexler was just about to say, "And what are those things you want to do, Doctor?" when he caught himself. Better not go too far, he mused. Better not lose possession of the ball. And besides, he thought, what the hell goes on here, anyway—me paying fifteen bucks a throw for these séances[10] and then doing the work myself, asking the questions, weighing the answers. So he wants a new wing! There's a fine piece of theatrical gauze for you! A new wing.

Trexler settled down again and resumed the role of patient for the rest of the visit. It ended on a kindly, friendly note. The doctor reassured him that his fears were the cause of his sickness, and that his fears were unsubstantial. They shook hands, smiling.

Trexler walked dizzily through the empty waiting room and the doctor followed along to let him out. It was late; the secretary had shut up shop and gone home. Another day over the dam. "Goodbye," said Trexler. He stepped into the street, turned west toward Madison, and thought of the doctor all alone there, after hours, in that desolate hole—a man who worked longer hours than his secretary. Poor, scared, over-worked guy, thought Trexler. And that new wing!

It was an evening of clearing weather, the Park showing green and desirable in the distance, the last daylight applying a high

---

9. *Westport* is a residential community and summer resort on the coast of Connecticut.
10. A *séance* is a meeting in which people attempt to communicate with the spirits of the dead. Here, Trexler is questioning the scientific validity of his psychiatric sessions.

Vocabulary
inquisitor (in kwiz′ ə tər) *n.* one who asks questions

MEETING INDIVIDUAL NEEDS — ENGLISH LANGUAGE LEARNERS

Difficult Words To comprehend the story's meaning, readers must fully understand some relatively difficult words, such as *apprehensions, melancholy, inexpressible,* and *unattainable.* English language learners can benefit from consulting outside resources for words not defined in footnotes.

Activity Pair English language learners and have students complete a chart for each unfamiliar word using English dictionaries. **COLLAB. LEARN.**

Word	Definition	Word's Importance to the Story

Additional Resources
 English Language Learners Sourcebook

Did You Know?
Brownstone is the name of a reddish-brown sandstone as well as a type of house made with it.

lacquer to the brick and brownstone walls and giving the street scene a luminous and intoxicating splendor. Trexler meditated, as he walked, on what he wanted. "What do you want?" he heard again. Trexler knew what he wanted, and what, in general, all men wanted; and he was glad in a way, that it was both inexpressible and unattainable, and that it wasn't a wing. He was satisfied to remember that it was deep, formless, enduring, and impossible of fulfillment, and that it made men sick, and that when you sauntered along Third Avenue and looked through the doorways into the dim saloons, you could sometimes pick out from the unregenerate ranks the ones who had not forgotten, gazing steadily into the bottoms of the glasses on the long chance that they could get another little peek at it. Trexler found himself renewed by the remembrance that what he wanted was at once great and microscopic, and that although it borrowed from the nature of large deeds and of youthful love and of old songs and early intimations, it was not any one of these things, and that it had not been isolated or pinned down, and that a man who attempted to define it in the privacy of a doctor's office would fall flat on his face.

Trexler felt invigorated. Suddenly his sickness seemed health, his dizziness stability. A small tree, rising between him and the light, stood there saturated with the evening, each gilt-edged leaf perfectly drunk with excellence and delicacy. Trexler's spine registered an ever so slight tremor as it picked up this natural disturbance in the lovely scene. "I want the second tree from the corner, just as it stands," he said, answering an imaginary question from an imaginary physician. And he felt a slow pride in realizing that what he wanted none could bestow, and that what he had none could take away. He felt content to be sick, unembarrassed at being afraid; and in the jungle of his fear he glimpsed (as he had so often glimpsed them before) the flashy tail feathers of the bird courage.

Then he thought once again of the doctor, and of his being left there all alone, tired, frightened. (The poor, scared guy, thought Trexler.) Trexler began humming "Moonshine Lullaby," his spirit reacting instantly to the hypodermic of Merman's[11] healthy voice. He crossed Madison, boarded a downtown bus, and rode all the way to Fifty-second Street before he had a thought that could rightly have been called bizarre.

---

11. Ethel *Merman* (1909–1984) was an American actress and singer known for her powerful voice.

Vocabulary
intimation (in' tə mā' shən) *n.* a hint; a suggestion
invigorated (in vig' ə rā' tid) *adj.* filled with strength and energy

FOCUSING ON A QUESTION Point out that the key to understanding the story is finding an answer to the question: what does Trexler want?

Model: It is difficult to say exactly what Trexler wants. He describes it as "inexpressible." But he provides some important clues about it: it is "what all men wanted," "deep, formless, enduring," and "at once great and microscopic." It's made up of many things yet not any one of them. I think that he might be referring to a sense of peace or happiness, since everyone wants that but it may be different for each person.

FINE ART
TRANSPARENCY 30

You may want to use *Fine Art Transparency 30* to discuss the use of sensory details in description.

Thematic Focus

Personal Discoveries Ask students whether Trexler's personal discovery seems valid. Remind students that his discovery, although undefined has the power to resolve Trexler's internal conflict.

✓ ASSESSMENT OPTIONS

📁 *Quick Checks,* p. 92

MEETING INDIVIDUAL NEEDS
GIFTED AND TALENTED ACTIVITY

Expressing the Inexpressible
Trexler discovers that what he wants is "inexpressible," yet he finds a symbol that expresses it perfectly. Advanced students can get more from this selection by exploring what Trexler and "all men" want in greater detail.

Activity Direct them to the first column of this page and have them list the words used to describe what "all men wanted" (*unattainable, deep, formless, enduring,* and so on). Once they have created their lists, have them attempt to define what is described. They may present their definition in written form or as an appropriate visual symbol that makes the tree symbolism more concrete. **L3**

Responding to the Selection

Personal Response

Students may say that they would like to ask about Trexler's bizarre thoughts or the incident on the Madison Avenue bus, since Trexler alludes to it twice in the story without explaining it.

ANALYZING LITERATURE

1. "Ever have any bizarre thoughts?" "No, I never have any bizarre thoughts."
2. He is scared.
3. A fellow patient and the psychiatrist; Trexler thinks that both of them are scared.
4. He sees the world through their eyes.
5. He challenges the doctor with the same question. Trexler thinks about what "all men want" and what characteristics this thing has.
6. He is confused, fearful, and unsure of how to express his thoughts.
7. Trexler is in fact scared, but probably not of what the doctor thinks he is.
8. Students may say that Trexler is compassionate and identifies with others; he longs to share his struggles. Students may say his observations seem reasonable.
9. Students may say that Trexler is extremely empathetic.
10. He wants fulfillment, happiness, and a sense of his place in the universe; he seeks inner peace.
11. Students may say it was realistic. It is certainly something that people seek to attain.
12. Students may agree that it is an effective symbol. Trees are traditional symbols for life, the universe, and life processes.
13. Students should distinguish between the types of answers that the doctor and Trexler give.
14. Most students will find Trexler to be a sympathetic character.
15. Trexler discovers that in his "sickness," his undefinable aspirations and desires are more meaningful than the limited, but "healthy" wants of the doctor.

Responding to Literature

Personal Response

What questions would you like to ask Mr. Trexler? Explain.

ANALYZING LITERATURE

RECALL

1. What question does the doctor ask Mr. Trexler at the beginning of the story? What is Trexler's answer?
2. What, according to the doctor, is wrong with Trexler?
3. What two people does Trexler pity? What thoughts does he have about them?
4. Describe the ways that Trexler identifies with the cab driver, the barber, and the doctor.
5. How does Trexler respond to the question "What do you want?" What does the question make him think about after his visit to the doctor?

INTERPRET

6. In your opinion, what does Trexler's reaction to the doctor's first question reveal about his state of mind?
7. Do you agree with the doctor's early diagnosis of Trexler? Explain.
8. Why do you think Trexler pities others? Do you think his observations are accurate? Why or why not?
9. What does Trexler's tendency to identify with others suggest to you about his personality?
10. In your opinion, what does Trexler want?

EVALUATE AND CONNECT

11. Was Trexler's reaction to his discovery of what he wants in life realistic? Why or why not?
12. Do you think the "second tree from the corner" is an effective **symbol** for what Trexler wants from life? (See Literary Terms Handbook, page R16.)
13. Refer to your response to the Focus Activity on page 782. Are your answers more similar to Trexler's answer or to the doctor's? Explain.
14. In your opinion, is Trexler a sympathetic character or not? Use a chart like the one on this page to help organize your thoughts.
15. Theme Connections   What personal discovery does Trexler make? Describe a personal discovery you've made about yourself. What lesson did you learn? How did you learn that lesson?

Literary ELEMENTS

Internal Conflict

At the center of each story there is usually a struggle, or **conflict**, between two opposing forces. The conflict might be **external**—between the main character and another person or an outside force—or it may be **internal**—between two opposing thoughts or desires within the mind of the main character.

1. Is the main struggle in this story an internal or external conflict? Describe that struggle, using details from the selection as evidence.
2. Does this story have a secondary conflict? If so, is it internal or external? Support your answer with details from the text.
- See **Literary Terms Handbook**, p. R3.

Trexler	
Positive traits	Negative traits
1.	1.

LITERARY ELEMENTS

1. It is an internal conflict. Trexler's internal conflict is expressed through bizarre thoughts, melancholy, anxiety, and a variety of physical symptoms.
2. Trexler engages in a kind of secondary external conflict with the doctor, whom Trexler challenges with the doctor's own question.

Additional Resources

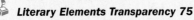 *Literary Elements Transparency 75*

LITERATURE AND WRITING

Writing About Literature
"Like a Lizard Toward a Bug"   E. B. White uses many visual images to describe Trexler's feelings. For example, Trexler thinks the doctor "was creeping slowly toward him, like a lizard toward a bug." In a paragraph, explain how this image and two others fit Trexler's character.

Creative Writing
Trexler's Bizarre Thoughts   Select one of Trexler's incomplete references to a bizarre thought, such as "the Madison Avenue bus," "the rhesus monkey," or "the asylum." Write a journal entry for Trexler describing one of these thoughts more fully. Share your entry with the class.

EXTENDING YOUR RESPONSE

Literature Groups
What, Exactly, Does He Want?   With your group, look at the description on page 787 of Trexler's discovery and its effect on his outlook. Discuss what message the author intends to convey with this scene. Consider what events take place and the author's general attitude toward the characters. Share your group's views with the class.

Interdisciplinary Activity
Art: The Second Tree from the Corner   Visualize Trexler's view of the second tree from the corner. Why was it such a dramatic sight? Based on the details in the story, create a painting, a drawing, a collage, or other visual representation of what Trexler might have seen. Include a glimpse of a bird or other symbols you think might be appropriate.

Learning for Life
A Follow-Up Report   Following a session with a patient or client, psychiatrists and psychologists often write a report. Write a report that the psychiatrist might have written to summarize his observations and analysis of Trexler. The report should be based on details from the story.

Reading Further
If you would like to read more by E. B. White, you might enjoy these books:

Collections: *The Second Tree from the Corner* and *The Essays of E. B. White* showcase a variety of White's talents.

Children's Books: *Stuart Little, Charlotte's Web,* and *The Trumpet of the Swan,* are stories based on the ageless themes of friendship and love.

 Save your work for your portfolio.

VOCABULARY • Parts of Speech

When a word is changed from one part of speech to another—such as from a noun to an adjective—the central part of the word's meaning remains the same. For example, if you know that the noun *despondency* means "hopelessness" or "depression," you can figure out that the adjective *despondent* means "hopeless" or "depressed."

PRACTICE   Use your knowledge of the vocabulary words in "The Second Tree from the Corner" to figure out the meanings of the words below. For each, write a definition of the word and use the word in a sentence.

1. inquisitive (adj.)   3. intimate (v.)
2. invigorate (v.)   4. retract (v.)

LITERATURE AND WRITING

Writing About Literature
Students' paragraphs should
- analyze the image mentioned and two other images. The image mentioned, for example, is appropriate because Trexler views himself as small and vulnerable.
- explain how two more images are consistent with Trexler's character.

Creative Writing
Students' journal entries should
- be written from Trexler's point of view.
- expand on one of Trexler's bizarre thoughts.
- maintain a tone and content that are consistent with Trexler's thoughts.

EXTENDING YOUR RESPONSE

Literature Groups Focus students' attention on the adjectives that Trexler uses. Remind them to consider the tree as a symbol.  COLLAB. LEARN.

Interdisciplinary Activity Remind students that they should use the symbolic aspect of the tree in their representations.

Learning for Life Emphasize that the reports should be written from the psychiatrist's point of view.

VOCABULARY • Parts of Speech

1. Curious and questioning; the sentence should use the word as an adjective.
2. To enliven or strengthen; the sentence should use the word as a verb.
3. To imply or suggest; the sentence should use the word as a verb.
4. To rescind or take away; the sentence should use the word as a verb.

Additional Resources
📁 *Vocabulary Practice,* p. 44

✓ ASSESSMENT OPTIONS

📁 *Quick Checks,* p. 92
📁 *Selection and Theme Assessment,* pp. 137–138
📁 *Performance Assessment,* p. 77
💾 *Testmaker*

MEDIA Connection

Objective

- To read and understand an excerpt from a television transcript

Literature LINK

The Second Tree from the Corner This television transcript connects to "The Second Tree from the Corner," page 783. The main idea of both the story and this script is what people want in life. The script suggests that happiness is the most important thing, although how that can be attained is left unanswered. The idea that happiness is a mystery may also be the root of Trexler's internal conflict over what he wants.

Respond

1. Students may agree with Myers's conclusion that "close, supportive, connected relationships make for happiness."
2. Students should describe their experiences. They may mention a good deed that was especially rewarding, close friendships, community or environmental activities.

Additional Resources
📁 *Media Connections,* p. 17

Teaching Options

interNET CONNECTION

Happiness Suggest that students look up the keywords *happiness, self-realization,* and *personal satisfaction.*

MEDIA Connection

Television Transcript

What is happiness? What do you need in order to attain it? Is happiness something you can discover within yourself? See if your views change after reading the excerpt that follows.

The Mystery of Happiness

ABC Special Report, hosted by John Stossel, September 4, 1997

JOHN STOSSEL
If you had just one wish for your children, that they have wealth, high intelligence, a successful job or career, or an overall happy life, wouldn't you pick happiness? Actually, I know most of you would, because we just took an ABC News poll of 1,500 adults. A happy life outpolled all the other choices combined. . . .

What makes for a happy life—more possessions? And how would we know what makes for a happy life?

Psychologist David Myers, who spent six years examining hundreds of studies on happiness for [his] book, says once you get past poverty, money doesn't help, no matter how much stuff you buy.

DAVID MYERS
The stockpiles of CDs, the closets full of clothes, the big-screen stereo TV systems . . .

JOHN STOSSEL
Doesn't do it.

DAVID MYERS
Clearly it doesn't do it. People having achieved that level of wealth have now adapted to it, and it takes new increments—a faster computer, a bigger TV screen or whatever—to rejuice the joy that the initial purchase gained for them. . . . And that's why today, with double the incomes and double what money buys for us, we're no happier than we were 40 years ago. . . . Close, supportive, connected relationships make for happiness, and we have fewer of those relationships today in the United States. Three times as many of us today live alone as lived alone a half century ago.

LEO WINGATE, guest
You don't have to search for happiness, you just have to know it, recognize it when you find it, when you see it. And it might be in the strangest places sometimes.

Respond

1. After reading this excerpt, do you agree with Myers's conclusion of what makes people happy? Why or why not?
2. Describe a time when you found happiness in an unexpected place.

Reading Minilesson

Evaluating Sources In their reading and in their lives, students are presented with a dizzying array of choices that advocates claim will lead to happiness. The ability to evaluate the sources of these claims is crucial to making informed and healthy choices.

Activity Have students reread this excerpt from a television transcript to identify the sources of information cited. In small groups, have students evaluate each source for its credibility, reliability, and authority. Then discuss the groups' evaluations as a class. **L2** **COLLAB. LEARN.**

Additional Resources
📁 *Reading Workbook*

Before You Read

Ode to My Socks

Meet Pablo Neruda

"I have always wanted the hands of the people to be seen in poetry. I have always preferred a poetry where the fingerprints show. A poetry of loam where water can sing. A poetry of bread, where everyone may eat."

—*Neruda*

Pablo Neruda (pä' blō   nä rōō' dä) was born in a small town in rural Chile. His father, a railway worker, and his mother, a teacher, named him Neftalí Ricardo Reyes Basoalto. His mother died of tuberculosis shortly after his birth, and two years later his father remarried.

Reyes began writing poetry at the age of ten. He published his first book of poems when he was just nineteen, under the pen name Pablo Neruda, a name most likely inspired by his appreciation of the works of Czech poet Jan Neruda. In 1924 his second book, *Twenty Love Poems and a Song of Despair*, became an instant success, and Neruda was well on his way to becoming a world-renowned poet. Not long after the publication of his first two books, Neruda went to Asia as Chile's honorary consul. It was the first position in a consular career that would take him to Spain, France, and Mexico.

Despite such high-ranking diplomatic positions and worldwide acclaim for his poetry, Neruda never lost the eloquent, yearning voice of his rural past. In 1945 Chile awarded him the National Literature Prize. In 1949, while living in France, he completed his major work, *Canto General*, a book of 340 poems, which took Neruda fourteen years to complete. In 1971 he received the Nobel Prize for Literature "for a poetry that with the action of an elemental force brings alive a continent's destiny and dreams."

Pablo Neruda was born in 1904 and died in 1973.

FOCUS ACTIVITY

What was the best gift that you ever received?

CHART IT! Use an idea tree like the one below to come up with reasons why the gift pleased you.

SETTING A PURPOSE Read to learn one speaker's reaction to a special gift.

BACKGROUND

Literary Influences

Neruda felt that writers of the Americas, due to the relative youth of their countries, had great opportunities to explore creative possibilities and find fresh, new voices. As an example, he cited the often "unorthodox" poetic vision of Walt Whitman. Of Whitman he said, "He was not only intensely conscious, but he was open-eyed! He had tremendous eyes to see everything–he taught us to see things. He was our poet."

The Ode

Neruda calls this poem an **ode**–a type of lyric poem in which strong personal emotion is expressed directly and spontaneously. Traditionally odes have rhyming lines and are dignified in subject, feeling, and style. One famous ode glorifies a nightingale. Neruda's ode departs somewhat from the traditional style.

Objectives

- To read and analyze a poem in which the speaker makes an important personal discovery through a commonplace experience
- To identify metaphors in a poem and explain how they contribute to the poem's message
- To write a poem modeled on the selection

Skills

Reading/Thinking: Establishing Criteria
Collaboration: Literature Groups

Motivating → OPTIONS

Selection Focus Transparency 83: Have students view the transparency and then answer the question provided.

Focus Activity: As an extension of the Focus Activity, challenge students to explain how they can choose gifts to create feelings of happiness in others.

RESOURCE MANAGER

Lesson Planning Resource
The *Unit Six Planning Guide* (pp. 16–20) provides additional lesson notes and reduced versions of all print resources.

📁 **Other Print Resources**
- Active Reading Guide, p. 93
- Reading Workbook
- Quick Checks, p. 93
- Selection and Theme Assessment, pp. 137–138

- Performance Assessment, p. 77
- Spanish Summaries, p. 83
- Spanish Translations
- Inclusion Strategies
- English Language Learners Sourcebook

📑 **Transparencies**
- Selection Focus 83
- Literary Elements 76

Technology
🎧 Audio Library
🎧 Spanish Audio Library
💻 Glencoe Literature Web Site
💾 Testmaker

Reading the Selection

A Active Reading

CONNECT Challenge students to think of a favorite or especially meaningful small gift they have received. Ask volunteers to share the examples with the class. Are there similarities among the gifts?

Additional Resources

📁 *Active Reading Guide*, p. 93
🎧 *Audio Library*
🎧 *Spanish Audio Library*

B Active Reading

REVIEW Ask students who Maru Mori is. What do they know about this person? *(Maru Mori is the gift-giver; she is a woman and sheepherder.)*

FYI

A Poet Translator The translator of this poem, Robert Bly, won the National Book Award for *The Light Around the Body*, a book of poetry.

Teaching Options

COMPARING selections

This selection is paired with "The Second Tree from the Corner" on page 783. A lesson for teaching a comparison of the two selections appears on page 795.

WORLD LITERATURE

Ode to My Socks A

Pablo Neruda

Translated by Robert Bly

The Magician, 1992. Maria Angelica Ruiz-Tagle. Oil on canvas, 130 x 97 cm. Private collection.

FOCUS ACTIVITY

What memories of people, places, or events are extremely vivid in your mind?

JOURNAL Write a journal entry describing one of these memories. Include a brief explanation of why you think the memory remains strong.

SETTING A PURPOSE Read to experience one person's vivid memory of an early morning.

BACKGROUND

The Time and Place
This story takes place in northern California in the 1930s. Steinbeck originally published this piece in a short-story collection called *The Long Valley* in 1938. He later adapted it and included it as part of a chapter in *The Grapes of Wrath*. The main character in "Breakfast" is not identified. In *The Grapes of Wrath*, however, the main character is Tom Joad, a young man who has traveled with his family from Oklahoma to California in search of work and opportunity.

Literary Influences
The odd jobs that Steinbeck held during the early 1920s gave him a firsthand look at the desperate working and living conditions forced upon most farm laborers. These observations helped Steinbeck develop the themes and plots of many of his major works. Steinbeck also was inspired by the terrain of his northern California background. He wrote about the working person's quest for dignity and deliverance, and the stark challenges presented by external forces, such as nature, society, and fate.

From the movie *The Grapes of Wrath*.

VOCABULARY PREVIEW

scuffle (skuf′ əl) *v.* to move with a quick, shuffling gait; p. 798
dissipate (dis′ ə pāt′) *v.* to cause to scatter and gradually vanish; to break up and drive off; p. 798
avert (ə vurt′) *v.* to turn away or aside; p. 800

Motivating
→OPTIONS

 Literature Launchers: "John Steinbeck's World"

Videodisc Side B, Segment 18

Also available in VHS.

 Selection Focus Transparency 84: Have students view the transparency and then answer the question provided.

Focus Activity: As an extension of the Focus Activity, challenge students to identify details of their memories that draw upon each of their five senses.

Reading Further

Be sure to review these titles for appropriateness for your class before recommending them to students.

Novels: Steinbeck, John. *The Grapes of Wrath*. New York: Knopf, 1993.

Steinbeck, John. *The Red Pony*. New York: Viking Penguin, 1992.

Biography: Benson, Jackson J. *The True Adventures of John Steinbeck, Writer*. New York: Viking Penguin, 1990.

Migrant Workers Students can learn more about migrant workers by searching for the keywords *migrant workers* on the Internet.

SUMMARY

"Breakfast" is a remembrance of an early morning encounter in northern California during the Great Depression. The narrator comes across a family of migrant workers. A young mother is fixing breakfast. With her are a baby, an older man, and a younger man. The older man generously invites the narrator to breakfast, and the campers tell of their good luck in finding work. The younger man kindly offers to help the narrator find a job. The narrator remembers the encounter as one "of great beauty" that gives him a "rush of warmth."

📁 *Spanish Summaries,* p. 84

A Active Reading

PREDICT Based on the first paragraph, the use of the word *curious,* and the story's title, what can students predict about the story?

(The tone will be pleasant, and the story will be a memory about a breakfast. The use of the word curious implies something special or unusual.)

Additional Resources
📁 *Active Reading Guide,* p. 94
🎧 *Audio Library*
🎧 *Spanish Audio Library*

Teaching Options

Breakfast

John Steinbeck

This thing fills me with pleasure. I don't know why, I can see it in the smallest detail. I find myself recalling it again and again, each time bringing more detail out of a sunken memory, remembering brings the curious warm pleasure.

It was very early in the morning. The eastern mountains were black-blue, but behind them the light stood up faintly colored at the mountain rims with a washed red, growing colder, grayer and darker as it went up and overhead until, at a place near the west, it merged with pure night.

And it was cold, not painfully so, but cold enough so that I rubbed my hands and shoved them deep into my pockets, and I hunched my shoulders up and scuffled my feet on the ground. Down in the valley where I was, the earth was that lavender gray of dawn. I walked along a country road and ahead of me I saw a tent that was only a little lighter gray than the ground. Beside the tent there was a flash of orange fire seeping out of the cracks of an old rusty iron stove. Gray smoke spurted up out of the stubby stovepipe, spurted up a long way before it spread out and dissipated.

I saw a young woman beside the stove, really a girl. She was dressed in a faded cotton skirt and waist.[1] As I came close I saw that she

───────────

1. Here, a *waist* is a blouse.

Vocabulary
scuffle (skuf′ əl) *v.* to move with a quick, shuffling gait
dissipate (dis′ ə pāt′) *v.* to cause to scatter and gradually vanish; to break up and drive off

Reading *Minilesson*

Identifying Spatial Relationships
Steinbeck's memorable characters are matched by his memorable descriptions of the settings. To appreciate Steinbeck's work, students need to focus on both the characters and the settings. By isolating each of these literary elements, students can form more complete pictures of Steinbeck's works.

Activity Call students' attention to the second and third paragraphs, and point out how they establish the setting of the story. Have students identify the words and phrases that describe the scene ("the eastern mountains," "down in the valley where I was," "a country road," and so on). Ask students to use this information to sketch rough maps that depict the setting of "Breakfast." **L2**

Additional Resources
📁 *Reading Workbook,* pp. 73–74

IMPLIED THEME Point out that the implied theme of a work is developed through details and descriptions. Here, Steinbeck paints an appealing picture of the campsite as a place of warmth and goodness. Ask students to identify the ways he accomplishes this. *(The presence of a mother nursing a baby indicates warmth and love. Her "practiced" movements, as she cooks and nurses her baby, demonstrate the nature of her caregiving. The aroma of the breakfast is the "warmest, pleasantest" one the narrator knows. As he approaches, the scene is illuminated quickly by the dawn. When he arrives, the warmth strikes him and makes him shiver.)*

Cultural Note

The campsite is, in fact, the family's home. During the Great Depression, countless Americans were what we would today call homeless. They lived in tents near wherever they could find work, staying as long as the work lasted, and then moving on.

C **Critical Thinking**

INFERRING Why are the two men's faces and hair wet? *(They have just washed up in the tent at the beginning of the day.)*

---

carried a baby in a crooked arm and the baby was nursing, its head under her waist out of the cold. The mother moved about, poking the fire, shifting the rusty lids of the stove to make a greater draft, opening the oven door; and all the time the baby was nursing, but that didn't interfere with the mother's work, nor with the light quick gracefulness of her movements. There was something very precise and practiced in her movements. The orange fire flicked out of the cracks in the stove and threw dancing reflections on the tent.

I was close now and I could smell frying bacon and baking bread, the warmest, pleasantest odors I know. From the east the light grew swiftly. I came near to the stove and stretched my hands out to it and shivered all over when the warmth struck me. Then the tent flap jerked up and a young man came out

and an older man followed him. They were dressed in new blue dungarees[2] and in new dungaree coats with the brass buttons shining. They were sharp-faced men, and they looked much alike.

The younger had a dark stubble beard and the older had a gray stubble beard. Their heads and faces were wet, their hair dripped with water, and water stood out on their stiff beards and their cheeks shone with water. Together they stood looking quietly at the lightening east; they yawned together and looked at the light on the hill rims. They turned and saw me.

"Morning," said the older man. His face was neither friendly nor unfriendly.

"Morning, sir," I said.

---

2. *Dungarees* are blue denim pants.

Tracking Dialogue English language learners sometimes encounter difficulty when reading dialogue. If the speaker isn't directly identified, students may not be sure which character is speaking.

Activity Pair English language learners with fluent English speakers. Direct each pair of students to identify all of the instances in "Breakfast" in

which sentences in quotation marks are not directly attributed to a character. For each, students should identify who speaks the line or lines and explain how they identified the character. **COLLAB. LEARN.**

Additional Resources

📁 *English Language Learners Sourcebook*

REVIEW Ask students what "some of the reasons" are for the narrator's pleasant experience. What is "the great beauty"?

Model: I think one reason it was so pleasant for him is that the family treated him so kindly. Another reason may be the family's demeanor: although they were poor, they seemed happy. This might have inspired the narrator, who seems poor himself. A third reason could be that the nice events of the story take place during a time of hardship—the Great Depression—making them more special. I think the "great beauty" is just a combination of these things—all of which are beautiful.

Thematic Focus

Personal Discoveries Ask students to identify and discuss the "personal discovery" the narrator makes. Is he explicit in identifying this discovery? Could he be explicit if he wanted to? Does he need to be? Students should explain their answers.

☑ ASSESSMENT OPTIONS

📁 *Quick Checks,* p. 94

Breakfast

"Morning," said the young man.

The water was slowly drying on their faces. They came to the stove and warmed their hands at it.

The girl kept to her work, her face averted and her eyes on what she was doing. Her hair was tied back out of her eyes with a string and it hung down her back and swayed as she worked. She set tin cups on a big packing box, set tin plates and knives and forks out too. Then she scooped fried bacon out of the deep grease and laid it on a big tin platter, and the bacon cricked[3] and rustled as it grew crisp. She opened the rusty oven door and took out a square pan full of high big biscuits.

When the smell of that hot bread came out, both of the men inhaled deeply.

The elder man turned to me, "Had your breakfast?"

"No."

"Well, sit down with us, then."

That was the signal. We went to the packing case and squatted on the ground about it. The young man asked, "Picking cotton?"

"No."

"We had twelve days' work so far," the young man said.

The girl spoke from the stove. "They even got new clothes."

The two men looked down at their new dungarees and they both smiled a little.

The girl set out the platter of bacon, the brown high biscuits, a bowl of bacon gravy and a pot of coffee, and then she squatted down by the box too. The baby was still nursing, its head

---

3. Here, *cricked* means "turned or twisted."

up under her waist out of the cold. I could hear the sucking noises it made.

We filled our plates, poured bacon gravy over our biscuits and sugared our coffee. The older man filled his mouth full and he chewed and chewed and swallowed. Then he said, "God Almighty, it's good," and he filled his mouth again.

The young man said, "We been eating good for twelve days."

We all ate quickly, frantically, and refilled our plates and ate quickly again until we were full and warm. The hot bitter coffee scalded our throats. We threw the last little bit with the grounds in it on the earth and refilled our cups.

There was color in the light now, a reddish gleam that made the air seem colder. The two men faced the east and their faces were lighted by the dawn, and I looked up for a moment and saw the image of the mountain and the light coming over it reflected in the older man's eyes.

Then the two men threw the grounds from their cups on the earth and they stood up together. "Got to get going," the older man said.

The younger turned to me. "'Fyou want to pick cotton, we could maybe get you on."

"No. I got to go along. Thanks for breakfast."

The older man waved his hand in a negative. "O.K. Glad to have you." They walked away together. The air was blazing with light at the eastern skyline. And I walked away down the country road.

That's all. I know, of course, some of the reasons why it was pleasant. But there was some element of great beauty there that makes the rush of warmth when I think of it. **D**

※

Vocabulary

avert (ə vurt′) *v.* to turn away or aside

Teaching Options

Grammar and Language *Minilesson*

***Using* Good *and* Well** The words *good* and *well* pose a common usage challenge. Write the following sentence from "Breakfast" on the board: "We been eating good for twelve days." Focus attention on the second error: the misuse of the word *good.* Guide students to identify *good* as an adjective and *well* as an adverb.

Activity Then have students identify the correct word in each sentence:
1. The child behaved (good, <u>well</u>).
2. The coffee smelled (<u>good</u>, well).
3. The new job paid (good, <u>well</u>). **L2**

Additional Resources

📖 *Grammar and Language Transparency 59*

📙 *Grammar and Language Workbook,* p. 201

📙 *Grammar and Composition Handbook,* Lesson 8.5

📘 *Writer's Choice,* Lesson 18.5

doing more running *away* from than running *toward* something. I stopped. The streets seemed dangerous. The buildings were massive and dark. The moon shone and the trees loomed frighteningly. No, I could not go on. I would go back. But I had walked so far and had turned too many corners and had not kept track of the direction. Which way led back to the orphan home? I did not know. I was lost.

I stood in the middle of the sidewalk and cried. A "white" policeman came to me and I wondered if he was going to beat me. He asked me what was the matter and I told him that I was trying to find my mother. His "white" face created a new fear in me. I was remembering the tale of the "white" man who had beaten the "black" boy. A crowd gathered and I was urged to tell where I lived. Curiously, I was too full of fear to cry now. I wanted to tell the "white" face that I had run off from an orphan home and that Miss Simon ran it, but I was afraid. Finally I was taken to the police station where I was fed. I felt better. I sat in a big chair where I was surrounded by "white" policemen, but they seemed to ignore me. Through the window I could see that night had completely fallen and that lights now gleamed in the streets. I grew sleepy and dozed. My shoulder was shaken gently and I opened my eyes and looked into a "white" face of another policeman who was sitting beside me. He asked me questions in a quiet, confidential tone, and quite before I knew it he was not "white" any more. I told him that I had run away from an orphan home and that Miss Simon ran it.

It was but a matter of minutes before I was walking alongside a policeman, heading toward the home. The policeman led me to the front gate and I saw Miss Simon waiting for me on the steps. She identified me and I was left in her charge. I begged her not to beat me, but she yanked me upstairs into an empty room and lashed me thoroughly. Sobbing, I slunk off to bed, resolved to run away again. But I was watched closely after that.

My mother was informed upon her next visit that I had tried to run away and she was terribly upset.

"Why did you do it?" she asked.

"I don't want to stay here," I told her.

"But you must," she said. "How can I work if I'm to worry about you? You must remember that you have no father. I'm doing all I can."

"I don't want to stay here," I repeated.

"Then, if I take you to your father . . ."

"I don't want to stay with him either," I said.

"But I want you to ask him for enough money for us to go to my sister's in Arkansas," she said.

Again I was faced with choices I did not like, but I finally agreed. After all, my hate for my father was not so great and urgent as my hate for the orphan home. My mother held to her idea and one night a week or so later I found myself standing in a room in a frame house. My father and a strange woman were sitting before a bright fire that blazed in a grate. My mother and I were standing about six feet away, as though we were afraid to approach them any closer.

"It's not for me," my mother was saying. "It's for your children that I'm asking you for money."

"I ain't got nothing," my father said, laughing.

"Come here, boy," the strange woman called to me.

I looked at her and did not move.

"Give him a nickel," the woman said. "He's cute."

"Come here, Richard," my father said, stretching out his hand.

I backed away, shaking my head, keeping my eyes on the fire.

"He is a cute child," the strange woman said.

"You ought to be ashamed," my mother said to the strange woman. "You're starving my children."

MIDCENTURY VOICES ❦ 825

Active Reading

QUESTION Ask students why they think Wright puts the word *white* in quotation marks. *(He may be emphasizing the split between white people and black people that is such a fundamental part of his life.)*

Critical Thinking

INFERRING Wright says that the policeman was "not 'white' any more." Ask students what he means by this, why the change occurs, and what it says about the author. *(Wright begins to see the policeman as a person and not just a member of a race. This change is brought about by the policeman's kindness and attention. For Wright, it may represent a revelation that a person's character is not dependent on his skin color.)*

Literary Elements

CONFLICT This paragraph identifies many of the conflicts that Wright faces. Challenge students to identify them and classify them as internal or external. *(Wright is faced with dilemmas [internal]: he is given these choices by his mother [external]; he hates his father and the "strange woman" [external]; he hates Miss Simon and the orphan home [external].)*

MULTIPLE LEARNING STYLES

Linguistic Students with strong linguistic talents, abilities, or interests can achieve a deeper and more personal understanding of the selection by identifying the words that they associate with each character in the selection.

Activity Have students create a list of all the characters in the selection, including minor characters. For each character, students should brainstorm and write down words and phrases that Wright used to describe the character or that they associate with the character. When they have finished, challenge students to identify the connotations of the words and phrases for each character. **L2**

Author's Craft

CHARACTERIZATION This passage gives indirect clues to the father's character. Point out that he has repeatedly claimed that he is unable to help Wright's mother support the children. Ask students how they account for his claim that he wants the child to stay with him and will give him "plenty to eat." *(Wright's father has probably been lying about his inability to provide child support. He may not really want Richard; he may be seeking to undermine or punish the mother.)*

Literary Elements

FLASH-FORWARD Wright quickly takes the reader a quarter of a century ahead in time. Have students describe what has happened to Wright's father and to Wright during this time. *(His father has become a sharecropper, and Wright's mind and consciousness have been so "greatly and violently altered" that he and his father inhabit different realities.)*

---

from **Black Boy**

"Now, don't you-all fight," my father said, laughing.

"I'll take that poker and hit you!" I blurted at my father.

He looked at my mother and laughed louder.

"You told him to say that," he said.

"Don't say such things, Richard," my mother said.

"You ought to be dead," I said to the strange woman.

The woman laughed and threw her arms about my father's neck. I grew ashamed and wanted to leave.

"How can you starve your children?" my mother asked.

"Let Richard stay with me," my father said.

"Do you want to stay with your father, Richard?" my mother asked.

"No," I said.

"You'll get plenty to eat," he said.

"I'm hungry now," I told him. "But I won't stay with you."

"Aw, give the boy a nickel," the woman said.

My father ran his hand into his pocket and pulled out a nickel.

"Here, Richard," he said.

"Don't take it," my mother said.

"Don't teach him to be a fool," my father said. "Here, Richard, take it."

I looked at my mother, at the strange woman, at my father, then into the fire. I wanted to take the nickel, but I did not want to take it from my father.

"You ought to be ashamed," my mother said, weeping. "Giving your son a nickel when he's hungry. If there's a God, He'll pay you back."

"That's all I got," my father said, laughing again and returning the nickel to his pocket.

We left. I had the feeling that I had had to do with something unclean. Many times in the years after that the image of my father and the strange woman, their faces lit by the dancing flames, would surge up in my imagination so vivid and strong that I felt I could reach out and touch it; I would stare at it, feeling that it possessed some vital meaning which always eluded me.

A quarter of a century was to elapse between the time when I saw my father sitting with the strange woman and the time when I was to see him again, standing alone upon the red clay of a Mississippi plantation, a sharecropper, clad in ragged overalls, holding a muddy hoe in his gnarled, veined hands—a quarter of a century during which my mind and consciousness had become so greatly and violently altered that when I tried to talk to him I realized that, though ties of blood made us kin, though I could see a shadow of my face in his face, though there was an echo of my voice in his voice, we were forever strangers, speaking a different language, living on vastly distant planes of reality. That day a quarter of a century later when I visited him on the plantation—he was standing against the sky, smiling toothlessly, his hair whitened, his body bent, his eyes glazed with dim recollection, his fearsome aspect of twenty-five years ago gone forever from him—I was overwhelmed to realize that he could never understand me or the scalding experiences that had swept me beyond his life and into an area of living that he could never know. I stood before him, poised, my mind aching as it embraced the simple nakedness of his life, feeling how completely his soul was imprisoned by the slow flow of the seasons, by wind and rain and sun, how fastened were his memories to a crude and raw past, how chained were his actions and emotions to the direct, animalistic impulses of his withering body . . .

From the white landowners above him there had not been handed to him a chance to learn

Vocabulary

vivid (viv′ id) *adj.* lifelike; realistic; distinct

vital (vīt′ əl) *adj.* of critical importance; essential

poised (poizd) *adj.* having a calm, controlled, and dignified manner; composed

---

REAL-WORLD CONNECTION

Sharecropping Sharecropping—in which farmers who live on and work the land receive a share of the crop in compensation—still exists in many parts of the world. Sharecropping often results in a kind of semi-slavery because the sharecroppers are often indebted to the owners and so are unable to leave. In the United States, sharecropping has virtually ended as farms have become mechanized. But in a few isolated pockets, it still exists.

Activity Have groups conduct research to learn about sharecropping in the United States or another country today. Have them investigate the economic and social impact of this system on the sharecroppers and on the owners. **L2** **COLLAB. LEARN.**

Negro Cabin, Sedalia, North Carolina (No. 1), 1930. Loïs Mailou Jones. Watercolor on paper, 14⅛ x 19⅛ in. Collection of the artist.

Viewing the painting: In what ways does the scene depicted in the painting capture the difficult life of Wright's father and of sharecroppers in general?

VIEWING THE PAINTING

Loïs Mailou Jones (1905–1998) was an American painter whose body of work reflects a variety of styles and influences. She established the art department at the Palmer Memorial Institute, an African American school.

Viewing Response *The cabin is small and ramshackle, and the residents probably have few possessions, mostly utilitarian. Wright's father, like most sharecroppers, was extremely poor.*

K **Critical Thinking**

COMPARING AND CONTRASTING What does Wright find that he has in common with his father? What differences does he identify? *(Wright has recognized that they share some facial and vocal characteristics, but they have little else in common. The city prevented the father from seeing joy or despair. In contrast, the city has enabled Wright to have a fuller understanding of life.)*

Thematic Focus

Personal Discoveries Challenge students to identify at least three important discoveries that Wright has made. Discuss how these discoveries change as Wright matures.

☑ **ASSESSMENT OPTIONS**

🗀 *Quick Checks,* p. 97

the meaning of loyalty, of sentiment, of tradition. Joy was as unknown to him as was despair. As a creature of the earth, he endured, hearty, whole, seemingly indestructible, with no regrets and no hope. He asked easy, drawling questions about me, his other son, his wife, and he laughed, amused, when I informed him of their destinies. I forgave him and pitied him as my eyes looked past him to the unpainted wooden shack. From far beyond the horizons that bound this bleak plantation there had come to me through my living the knowledge that my father was a black peasant who had gone to the city seeking life, but who had failed in the city; a black peasant whose life had been hopelessly snarled in the city, and who had at last fled the city—that same city which had lifted me in its burning arms and borne me toward <u>alien</u> and undreamed-of shores of knowing.

Vocabulary
alien (ā′ lē ən) *adj.* strange; unfamiliar; foreign

Personal Response

Most students will respond sympathetically to Wright's experiences and appreciate his success in overcoming obstacles.

ANALYZING LITERATURE

1. They go to court to obtain child support from Wright's father. The judge accepts the father's explanation that he's doing all he can.

2. They go to the orphan home because their mother is too poor to provide for them and must work. His main feelings include hunger, fear, nervousness, and distrust.

3. Wright runs away to escape the miserable life at the orphan home; his encounter with Miss Simon over the blotter precipitates his attempted escape. He becomes lost, cries, and is taken to the police station. The policemen feed him and return him to the orphan home.

4. She offers to take him out of the orphan home if he asks his father for money. Wright doesn't like the deal, but he hates the orphan home even more.

5. He becomes a poor sharecropper.

6. Wright begins to hate his father, who refuses to help support his family and laughs easily about it.

7. The home is different because he is surrounded by strangers and fears the woman managing it. It is the same because he is hungry and unhappy there. His unhappiness increases because he feels abandoned and is mistreated.

8. Wright is at first keenly aware that the policemen are white. When one policeman is kind to him, he views the policeman as a person and not just a member of a race.

9. Wright is strong-willed, capable of great anger, and has a strong sense of right and wrong.

10. Wright has learned of loyalty, sentiment, tradition, joy, and despair. He values the full range of human experience, unlike his father, who appears to Wright as "a creature of the earth."

11. Every major development is moving. Students should give reasons for their choices.

12. Many students will relate a personal discovery that has to do with empathy for the disadvantaged.

Responding to Literature

Personal Response

What was your reaction to the events of Wright's life? Explain.

──── ANALYZING LITERATURE ────

RECALL

1. Why do Wright, his mother, and his brother go to court? What happens there?

2. Why do Wright and his brother go to the orphan home? What are the three main feelings Wright experiences while there?

3. Why does Wright run away? What happens during this incident?

4. What deal does Wright's mother make with him as she takes him out of the orphan home? How does Wright feel about the deal?

5. What ultimately happens to Wright's father?

INTERPRET

6. How do you think the events in court affect Wright's relationship with his father? Explain.

7. For Wright, how is the orphan home different from his old home? How is it similar? Why might his unhappiness increase there?

8. What do you learn about Wright's attitudes and perceptions about race from the runaway incident?

9. What do you learn about Wright's character from his interactions with his father just after he leaves the orphan home?

10. What does the visit with his elderly father reveal about Wright and what he values in life? Explain, using details from the selection.

EVALUATE AND CONNECT

11. Which **anecdote** from the selection did you find most moving? Why? (See Literary Terms Handbook, page R1.)

12. Theme Connections   What is the most important personal discovery you gained from reading this selection? Explain.

13. How did knowing that this selection is an **autobiography** (see page R2) affect your reaction to it? Would you have reacted differently if it were fiction? Explain.

14. How would you describe this selection's **tone,** or the author's attitude? How effective is this tone in expressing the author's main points?

15. Based on this selection, do you think you would like to read the rest of Richard Wright's autobiography? Why or why not?

Literary ELEMENTS

Flash-forward

Writers have different ways of ordering events in a story. Most often they describe events in chronological order, or the order in which events naturally occur. Sometimes, however, writers interrupt this flow of events. A skip back to the past is called a **flashback.** A leap forward into the future is called a **flash-forward.** A writer might signal a flash-forward with a new paragraph or with a description of a new setting, so readers know exactly how the time frame has shifted. In other instances, writers shift the setting back and forth in time without giving any signal.

1. Where is the flash-forward in this selection?

2. How does Wright signal that he is skipping ahead from the main narrative?

3. What effect does this flash-forward create in Wright's narrative? In your opinion, does it strengthen or weaken the narrative? Explain.

● See **Literary Terms Handbook,** p. R6.

---

13. The events have a greater impact because they are true. Reactions to fiction may be less personal.

14. The tone seems to be matter of fact with a bitter undercurrent. It is effective.

15. Students may find the excerpt intriguing and may express interest in reading the rest of the autobiography.

LITERARY ELEMENTS

1. The flash-forward begins in column two on page 826.

2. He signals with the phrase, "A quarter of a century was to elapse . . ."

3. The flash-forward breaks the narrative; it gives a view of the mature Wright. Some may want more of what happened next; others may say the flash-forward helps them understand the meaning better.

Additional Resources

 Literary Elements Transparency 80

LITERATURE AND WRITING

Writing About Literature
Author's Use of Dialogue   Find four examples of **dialogue** (see page R4) in the selection. Note the setting in which each occurs, the people who are talking, what they talk about, and any other details that you find significant. Then write several paragraphs explaining what each example reveals about the characters.

Creative Writing
Letters from the Heart   Imagine that you are Wright living in the orphan home. Write a letter to your mother describing the conditions, your feelings about being there, and your hopes for how things will change. Then imagine that you are Wright's mother, and write a reply. Use the selection as a guide for details and characterization.

EXTENDING YOUR RESPONSE

Literature Groups
What Is Hunger?   What does hunger feel like to you? Look back at your freewriting for the Focus Activity on page 821, and share your responses with your group. Then look in the selection for Wright's descriptions of hunger. How do his descriptions compare with those your group came up with? What "kills" his hunger? What else might he hunger for? Share your ideas with the class.

Interdisciplinary Activity
History: Life in the South   Find out what life was like for African Americans in the South around 1915. Look for interesting statistics as you research voting laws, Jim Crow laws, business ownership, farming, schools, or any other

topic of interest to you. Then, in an oral report, explain how what you have learned is related to Wright's story.

Listening and Speaking
Interview Richard Wright   What questions would you like to ask Richard Wright after reading this excerpt from his autobiography? With a partner, create a list of questions. Then discuss how Wright might answer each one. Finally, plan and perform your interview with Richard Wright for a group of classmates. After the interview, discuss its content with the class.

 Save your work for your portfolio.

 Skill Minilesson

VOCABULARY • Latin Roots: *vit* and *viv*

Latin roots form the basis of many English words. The root is usually combined with a prefix, a suffix, or both. The meaning of the English word is usually related to the meaning of the root it contains. For example, the Latin roots *vit* and *viv* mean "life" or "to live." Notice how these roots affect the meanings of two vocabulary words:

*vit*al–essential; necessary to continued existence or life

*viv*id–lifelike; realistic

PRACTICE   Write a definition that includes the meaning of the root *vit* or *viv* for each word below. Then write each word in an original sentence.

1. **vit**ality
2. re**viv**e
3. **viv**acious
4. **vit**a
5. con**viv**ial

LITERATURE AND WRITING

Writing About Literature
Students' explanations should
- identify four examples of dialogue.
- identify the setting, speakers, subject matter, and other significant details of each dialogue.
- analyze how each example contributes to the characterization of the people speaking the dialogue.

Creative Writing
Students' letters should
- consist of one written from Wright's point of view and one written from the point of view of Wright's mother.
- be in keeping with the setting of the selection and with the characters.

 Skill Minilesson

VOCABULARY • Latin Roots: *vit* and *viv*

Definitions may vary somewhat. Sample sentences are provided.
1. the power to live or grow; Although his life was short, Wright lived it with vitality.
2. to bring back to life; Does this excerpt revive your interest in Wright's writing?
3. showing a love of life; Are you sullen and withdrawn, or vivacious?
4. a summary of key events in an individual's professional or educational life; You may need to prepare a vita in order to find a job.
5. festively sharing life; People become convivial around the holidays.

Additional Resources
📁 *Vocabulary Practice,* p. 47

✔ **ASSESSMENT OPTIONS**

📁 *Quick Checks,* p. 97
📁 *Selection and Theme Assessment,* pp. 145–146
📁 *Performance Assessment,* p. 81
💾 *Testmaker*

Objective

• To read and respond to a newspaper article

Respond

1. Students who find the race appealing might cite the personal challenge and potential triumph. Other students might find the race pointless and cite other ways to challenge themselves.

2. People often push their physical limits to determine what these limits truly are and to discover how they respond to difficult situations. They often discover that they are stronger than they realized and can survive hardships.

Additional Resources

📁 *Media Connections,* pp. 17–18

Newspaper Article

Most professional athletes are relatively young, but amateurs of all ages can amaze people with their physical endurance. In California, the Angeles Crest 100-Mile Endurance Run attracts athletes who push their limits to the max.

100-Mile Run to Agony and Ecstasy

by Sonia Nazario, *Los Angeles Times,* September 30, 1996

Runner John Canby of La Canada Flintridge had been plodding on his feet most of the previous 29 hours when finally, at 11 A.M., he walked across the finish line, bowlegged, stepping as if walking on broken glass. His first request to friends: Could they pull the car closer to him, please, so he could escape without having to take another step? Some of the endurance runners [in this race] concede that this equivalent of four back-to-back marathons may seem a bit nutty to outsiders.

Frank Pitts, 65, began to ponder this point around midnight Saturday, as he ran up and down mountains in the wilderness darkness. Below, he could see the twinkling city lights.

"I thought: 'I could be in a nice soft bed,'" he said, quickly adding, "Then I thought: 'I'm out here having fun and all those people aren't.'" Pitts acknowledges some disadvantages to such a race, his eleventh:

Sometimes, in the dead of night, running, he hallucinates. During one race, he was convinced that he had to take a train between two first aid stops along the route. "Your legs feel like they've been beaten by baseball bats. You can't imagine taking another step. Yet you have to keep moving. And somehow you do," Pitts said. The retired Los Angeles County machinist, who began endurance running when he was 52, trained six to eight hours a day for the event.

Pitts, who had to drop out at the 74th mile but has finished the race six times before, plans to try again next year.

No matter one's age or fitness, the rocky trail is grueling, with eight major peaks, a total climb of 21,610 feet, and then 26,700 feet of quad-busting descent. Of the 140 who started the race Saturday, 18 finished in less than 24 hours. One Tarahumara Indian lost eight

pounds in the first 75 miles. [The Tarahumara of Mexico are noted for their ability to run long distances.]

And there are real dangers: rattlesnakes at night, and in the 1992 race, a mountain lion.

Respond

1. Does this endurance run sound appealing to you? Why or why not?

2. Why, in your opinion, do people push their physical limits? What might they discover about themselves by doing so?

Reading *Minilesson*

Identifying Author's Purpose Explain to students the two basic types of newspaper articles: news articles and feature articles. News articles convey information and report current news events objectively. Feature articles entertain, are often not about current news events, and may have a subjective tone and content.

Activity Have students identify the article on this page as a news article or as a

feature article. Then have students read a newspaper and classify the articles that they read. Students should be able to explain why they classified each article as they did. **L2**

Additional Resources

📁 *Reading Workbook*

Before You Read

A Worn Path

Meet Eudora Welty

Eudora Welty admits to having lived a sheltered life. She grew up in Jackson, Mississippi, and has lived in her family's house there almost her entire life. Welty has maintained, though, that "a sheltered life can be a daring life as well. For all serious daring starts from within."

Welty's parents filled their house with books and loved to read on their own and to their children. Once she learned to read herself, Welty read everything she could get her hands on. Her mother, however, put one restriction on her reading. She told the town librarian that Eudora could read anything in the library except the then-popular novel *Elsie Dinsmore*. When Eudora asked why, her mother explained that the main character fainted and fell off her piano stool after being made to practice for a long time. Her mother told Eudora that she was too impressionable: "You'd read that and the very first thing you'd do, you'd fall off the piano stool." Thereafter, Welty could never hear the word *impressionable* without calling up the image of falling off a piano stool.

Welty's love of reading and her lively imagination inspired her decision to become a writer. Her first full-time job was as a publicity writer for the Works Progress Administration (WPA). This government agency, founded during the Great Depression, gave people work on public projects, such as constructing roads and buildings, clearing trails in parks, and painting murals. For her job, Welty traveled around Mississippi and wrote articles about WPA projects in the state. Welty later said that, through her travels, she gained her first glimpses of the very different ways that people live. Her musings and imaginings about the people she saw, talked to, and photographed inspired her writing throughout her life.

Welty had her first short story published when she was twenty-seven. Five years later, she published *A Curtain of Green*, a collection of short stories in which "A Worn Path" first appeared. In her thirties, she published her first novels, *The Robber Bridegroom* (1942) and *Delta Wedding*. Welty went on to write award-winning fiction for many years, until severe arthritis forced her to give up writing at age eighty-five.

"Through travel I first became aware of the outside world; it was through travel that I found my own introspective way into becoming part of it."

"Writing a story is one way of discovering *sequence* in experience, of stumbling upon cause and effect in the happenings of a writer's own life. This has been the case with me. Connections slowly emerge."

"Writing fiction has developed in me an abiding respect for the unknown in a human lifetime."

—*Welty*

Eudora Welty was born in 1909.

Before Reading

Objectives

- To read and analyze a short story about an old woman's journey
- To distinguish between direct and indirect characterization
- To compare and contrast two characters

Skills

Reading/Thinking: Inferring; Comparing and Contrasting
Writing: Comparison; Short Story
Vocabulary: Analogies
Grammar/Language: Incorrect Verb Tense
Listening/Speaking: Mini Readers Theater; Reading Aloud
Collaboration: Literature Groups

More About Eudora Welty

Eudora Welty has lived virtually all her life in Mississippi, and her writing demonstrates a deep and enduring love of the South. Despite the limitations of her experience and subject matter, Welty's writing is truly universal. It has been accurately observed that "she sees in each life a piece of all life." She began writing while very young and had several pieces published in children's magazines before she was a teen. Welty won the Pulitzer Prize in 1972 for *The Optimist's Daughter*.

RESOURCE MANAGER

Lesson Planning Resource
The *Unit Six Planning Guide* (pp. 48–55) provides additional lesson notes and reduced versions of all print resources.

Other Print Resources
- Active Reading Guide, p. 98
- Vocabulary Practice, p. 48
- Reading Workbook, pp. 77–78
- Grammar and Language Workbook, pp. 135–143

- Grammar and Composition Handbook, Lesson 5.6
- Quick Checks, p. 98
- Selection and Theme Assessment, pp. 147–148
- Performance Assessment, p. 82
- Spanish Summaries, p. 88
- Spanish Translations
- Inclusion Strategies
- English Language Learners Sourcebook

Transparencies
- Selection Focus 88
- Literary Elements 81
- Grammar and Language 63

Technology
- Literature Launchers
- Audio Library
- Spanish Audio Library
- Glencoe Literature Web Site
- Testmaker

Motivating
→ OPTIONS

Literature Launchers:
"Eudora Welty: Listening and Writing"

Videodisc Side B, Segment 17

Also available in VHS.

Selection Focus Transparency 88: Have students view the transparency and then answer the question provided.

Focus Activity: As an extension of the Focus Activity, have students compare the traits they admire in each elderly person and look for common elements. You may wish to have students compare their lists.

Reading Further

Be sure to review these titles for appropriateness for your class before recommending them to students.

Welty, Eudora. *The Optimist's Daughter.* New York: Random House, 1990.

Welty, Eudora. *The Collected Stories of Eudora Welty.* New York: Harcourt, 1982.

— FOCUS ACTIVITY —

Think about elderly people you respect and admire–people you know personally or people you know about.

LIST IDEAS Make a list of five to ten admirable elderly people, and write down what it is you admire about them.

SETTING A PURPOSE Read to discover the qualities of one elderly woman.

— BACKGROUND —

The Time and Place

"A Worn Path" is set near the city of Natchez (nach′ iz), Mississippi, probably sometime around 1930. The *Natchez Trace* mentioned in the story was an old trail that led from the Native American villages along the banks of the lower Mississippi River northeastward six hundred miles to settlements along the Cumberland River, in what is now

Tennessee. Travelers who boated down the Mississippi had to walk or ride the Natchez Trace to return to locations upstream. In the 1700s, two towns grew up at the ends of the trail–Nashville and Natchez.

Around the turn of the nineteenth century, the Natchez Trace was one of the most well-traveled trails in the United States. However, it fell into disuse around 1820. New, powerful steamships that could travel against the Mississippi's strong current allowed river travelers to make their way upstream by boat, making the overland trail unnecessary. The Natchez Trace fell into disrepair. Some sections were farmed; others became parts of local roads.

Literary Influences

Eudora Welty has written that her story ideas come, in large part, from "what I see and hear and learn and feel and remember of my living world." In an interview, she explained an experience that inspired "A Worn Path":

"I was with a painter friend who was doing a landscape, and I just came along for company. I was reading under a tree, and just looking up saw this small, distant figure come out of the woods and move across the whole breadth of my vision and disappear into the woods on the other side. . . . I knew she was going somewhere. I knew that she was bent on an errand, even at that distance."

— VOCABULARY PREVIEW —

grave (grāv) *adj.* dignified and gloomy; somber; p. 833
quivering (kwiv′ ər ing) *n.* a shaking with a slight, rapid vibration; a trembling; p. 834
thicket (thik′ it) *n.* an area of dense growth, as of shrubs or bushes; p. 834
limber (lim′ bər) *adj.* able to bend or move easily; nimble; p. 834

vigorously (vig′ ər əs lē) *adv.* with power, energy, and strength; p. 835
ceremonial (ser′ ə mō′ nē əl) *adj.* formal; p. 838
solemn (sol′ əm) *adj.* serious; grave; p. 838
comprehension (kom pri hen′ shən) *n.* the act of grasping mentally; understanding; p. 839

832 🐾 UNIT 6

CONNECTING TO OTHER SELECTIONS

The chart at the right shows three ways to connect "A Worn Path" to selections in this book.

For specific teaching strategies, see the **Unit Six Planning Guide,** pp. 51–52.

Connection	Title
Life Skills: Supporting and Contributing	→ "In Another Country," p. 680
Thematic: The Power of Love	→ "The Soul selects her own Society," p. 426
Literary: Characterization	→ "The Devil and Tom Walker," p. 203

A Worn Path

Eudora Welty ~

Day's End, Jackson, 1930s. Eudora Welty. Photograph. Mississippi Department of Archives and History, Jackson, MS. Eudora Welty Collection.

IT WAS DECEMBER—a bright frozen day in the early morning. Far out in the country there was an old Negro woman with her head tied in a red rag, coming along a path through the pinewoods. Her name was Phoenix Jackson. She was very old and small and she walked slowly in the dark pine shadows, moving a little from side to side in her steps, with the balanced heaviness and lightness of a pendulum in a grandfather clock. She carried a thin, small cane made from an umbrella, and with this she kept tapping the frozen earth in front of her. This made a <u>grave</u> and persistent noise in the still air, that seemed meditative like the chirping of a solitary little bird.

She wore a dark striped dress reaching down to her shoe tops, and an equally long apron of bleached sugar sacks, with a full pocket: all neat and tidy, but every time she took a step she might have fallen over her shoelaces, which dragged from her unlaced shoes. She looked straight ahead. Her eyes were blue with age. Her skin had a pattern all its own of numberless branching wrinkles and as though a whole little tree stood in the middle of her forehead, but a golden color ran underneath, and the two knobs of her cheeks were illumined by a yellow burning under the dark. Under the red rag her hair came down on her neck in the frailest of ringlets, still black, and with an odor like copper.

Vocabulary
grave (grāv) *adj.* dignified and gloomy; somber

SUMMARY

"A Worn Path" tells of an elderly African American woman's journey from her home in the woods to the city of Natchez, Mississippi. Phoenix Jackson makes the difficult walk whenever she needs more medicine for her grandson, her only companion, who was injured from accidentally swallowing lye. The walk is a metaphor of her life's journey, filled with hardships and joy.

📁 *Spanish Summaries,* p. 88

Additional Resources
📁 *Active Reading Guide,* p. 98
🎧 *Audio Library*
🎧 *Spanish Audio Library*

Ⓐ Active Reading

PREDICT Explain that the phoenix is a mythological bird that lives for hundreds of years and then sets itself on fire, dies, and is reborn from the ashes. Have students predict what the character might be like, based on her name. *(Phoenix may be someone who has lived long and who rises to meet new challenges.)*

Teaching Options

TEACHER to TEACHER

ALBERTVILLE HIGH SCHOOL • ALBERTVILLE, ALABAMA

To introduce "A Worn Path," I ask a question all students can answer: What is the setting for *Batman* movies? With Gotham City as our starting point, we discuss gothic elements in literature. Then we prepare a chart that compares European gothic, American gothic, and Southern gothic. As we read "A Worn Path" orally, students watch for darkness, journeys, secret places, and entrapment. This southern gothic story is rich in symbolism and characterization, which spurs discussions about topics ranging from students' fascination with the macabre to thoughts about racism.

JOANN ELLIS

B Literary Elements

B Literary Elements

CHARACTERIZATION Ask students what they can infer about Phoenix's character from this paragraph. *(That she talks to herself suggests that she spends a lot of time alone. Her diction and grammar reveal her as a rural southerner with little education. Her threatening words directed to the animals may indicate nervousness with animals and yet a determination to proceed no matter what.)*

C Literary Elements

EXTENDED METAPHOR Point out that this story may be read as an extended metaphor that compares Phoenix's journey with all people's journeys through life. She refers to her day's journey, which, like life's journey for the elderly, is getting short.

VIEWING THE PHOTOGRAPH

Welty, a skilled photographer and writer, worked for the WPA from 1933 to 1936 during the Great Depression. She crisscrossed Mississippi taking photographs of the poor.

Viewing Response *The path in the photograph is old, sunken, and tree-lined, like part of the path that Phoenix travels.*

Teaching Options

Now and then there was a <u>quivering</u> in the <u>thicket</u>. Old Phoenix said, "Out of my way, all you foxes, owls, beetles, jack rabbits, coons and wild animals! . . . Keep out from under these feet, little bob-whites. . . .[1] Keep the big wild hogs out of my path. Don't let none of those come running my direction. I got a long way." Under her small black-freckled hand her cane, <u>limber</u> as a buggy whip, would switch at the brush as if to rouse up any hiding things.

On she went. The woods were deep and still. The sun made the pine needles almost too bright to look at, up where the wind rocked. The cones

---

1. *Bob-whites,* also called quails or partridges, are birds with mottled brown plumage and white markings.

Road Between High Banks, Hinds County, 1940s. Eudora Welty. Photograph. Mississippi Department of Archives and History, Jackson, MS. Eudora Welty Collection.

Viewing the photograph: In what ways is the path in the photograph similar to or different from the path in the story?

Vocabulary
quivering (kwiv' ər ing) *n.* a shaking with a slight, rapid vibration; a trembling
thicket (thik' it) *n.* an area of dense growth, as of shrubs or bushes
limber (lim' bər) *adj.* able to bend or move easily; nimble

834   UNIT 6

---

dropped as light as feathers. Down in the hollow[2] was the mourning dove—it was not too late for him.

The path ran up a hill. "Seem like there is chains about my feet, time I get this far," she said, in the voice of argument old people keep to use with themselves. "Something always take a hold of me on this hill—pleads I should stay."

After she got to the top she turned and gave a full, severe look behind her where she had come. "Up through pines," she said at length. "Now down through oaks."

Her eyes opened their widest, and she started down gently. But before she got to the bottom of the hill a bush caught her dress.

Her fingers were busy and intent, but her skirts were full and long, so that before she could pull them free in one place they were caught in another. It was not possible to allow the dress to tear. "I in the thorny bush," she said. "Thorns, you doing your appointed[3] work. Never want to let folks pass, no sir. Old eyes thought you was a pretty little *green* bush."

Finally, trembling all over, she stood free, and after a moment dared to stoop for her cane.

"Sun so high!" she cried, leaning back and looking, while the thick tears went over her eyes. "The time getting all gone here."

At the foot of this hill was a place where a log was laid across the creek.

"Now comes the trial," said Phoenix.

Putting her right foot out, she mounted the log and shut her eyes. Lifting her skirt, leveling her cane fiercely before her, like a festival figure

---

2. *A hollow* is a small valley.
3. *Appointed* means "assigned" or "designated."

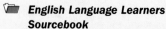

MEETING INDIVIDUAL NEEDS — ENGLISH LANGUAGE LEARNERS

Understanding Dialect English language learners may need help to appreciate Eudora Welty's use of southern dialect and colloquial speech.

Activity Pair English language learners with fluent English speakers. Direct each pair to a create a chart like the one shown. In the first column, students should copy any of Phoenix's thoughts or spoken words that they do not fully understand. In the second column, they should rewrite them in Standard English. **COLLAB. LEARN.**

Phoenix's Words	Phoenix's Words in Standard English

Additional Resources
📁 *English Language Learners Sourcebook*

Eudora Welty ✌

in some parade, she began to march across. Then she opened her eyes and she was safe on the other side.

"I wasn't as old as I thought," she said.

But she sat down to rest. She spread her skirts on the bank around her and folded her hands over her knees. Up above her was a tree in a pearly cloud of mistletoe. She did not dare to close her eyes, and when a little boy brought her a plate with a slice of marble-cake on it she spoke to him. "That would be acceptable," she said. But when she went to take it there was just her own hand in the air.

So she left that tree, and had to go through a barbed-wire fence. There she had to creep and crawl, spreading her knees and stretching her fingers like a baby trying to climb the steps. But she talked loudly to herself: she could not let her dress be torn now, so late in the day, and she could not pay for having her arm or her leg sawed off if she got caught fast where she was.

At last she was safe through the fence and risen up out in the clearing. Big dead trees, like black men with one arm, were standing in the purple stalks of the withered cotton field. There sat a buzzard.

"Who you watching?"

In the furrow[4] she made her way along.

"Glad this not the season for bulls," she said, looking sideways, "and the good Lord made his snakes to curl up and sleep in the winter. A pleasure I don't see no two-headed snake coming around that tree, where it come once. It took a while to get by him, back in the summer."

She passed through the old cotton and went into a field of dead corn. It whispered and shook and was taller than her head. "Through the maze now," she said, for there was no path.

Then there was something tall, black, and skinny there, moving before her.

___

4. A *furrow* is a long, narrow channel in the ground made by a plow.

At first she took it for a man. It could have been a man dancing in the field. But she stood still and listened, and it did not make a sound. It was as silent as a ghost.

"Ghost," she said sharply, "who be you the ghost of? For I have heard of nary[5] death close by."

But there was no answer—only the ragged dancing in the wind.

She shut her eyes, reached out her hand, and touched a sleeve. She found a coat and inside that an emptiness, cold as ice.

"You scarecrow," she said. Her face lighted. "I ought to be shut up for good," she said with laughter. "My senses is gone. I too old. I the oldest people I ever know. Dance, old scarecrow," she said, "while I dancing with you."

She kicked her foot over the furrow, and with mouth drawn down, shook her head once or twice in a little strutting way. Some husks blew down and whirled in streamers about her skirts.

Then she went on, parting her way from side to side with the cane, through the whispering field. At last she came to the end, to a wagon track where the silver grass blew between the red ruts. The quail were walking around like pullets,[6] seeming all dainty and unseen.

"Walk pretty," she said. "This the easy place. This the easy going."

She followed the track, swaying through the quiet bare fields, through the little strings of trees silver in their dead leaves, past cabins silver from weather, with the doors and windows boarded shut, all like old women under a spell sitting there. "I walking in their sleep," she said, nodding her head vigorously.

In a ravine[7] she went where a spring was silently flowing through a hollow log. Old

___

5. *Nary* means "not one."
6. *Pullets* are young hens.
7. A *ravine* is a deep, narrow valley, especially one eroded by running water.

Vocabulary
vigorously (vig′ ər əs lē) *adv.* with power, energy, and strength

INTERDISCIPLINARY CONNECTION

Geography Explain to students that a fundamental goal of geography is to translate real places into graphic representations, or maps. Maps allow people to view a large area and to see the relationships between places, such as their relative distance, direction, and size. Topographical maps even represent changes in elevation.

Activity Have students reread "A Worn Path," looking for details to use in creating a map of Phoenix's journey. Direct them to be aware of clues and details that reveal the nature of the terrain, distances, and directions. Have them work individually or in pairs to translate these verbal clues into a map. **L2**

INFERRING Ask students why Eudora Welty has Phoenix comment about the spring, and what her comment means.

Model: First, I think the writer introduces the spring because all living things need water, so it's a symbol for life. Phoenix says it was here before she was born, so the spring has been around a long time, and it will probably be around long after she's gone. I think this suggests that life goes on. People live their lives and die, but life itself continues.

H Literary Elements

SYMBOLISM Explain to students that the dog might be a symbol of death. Ask them to explain how this is shown. *(The dog is black, a color associated with death, and acts as a predator. Phoenix fights him off so she can continue her journey to town, just as she is fighting off death in her life's journey. When she is knocked down, the dog waits, as if in anticipation.)*

I Literary Elements

CHARACTER What does the hunter's attitude and speech reveal about his character? *(His amusement at Phoenix's plight indicates that he is not very concerned about her condition. He does, however, help her up and on her way.)*

❋ A Worn Path

Phoenix bent and drank. "Sweet-gum[8] makes the water sweet," she said, and drank more. "Nobody know who made this well, for it was here when I was born."

The track crossed a swampy part where the moss hung as white as lace from every limb. "Sleep on, alligators, and blow your bubbles." Then the track went into the road.

Deep, deep the road went down between the high green-colored banks. Overhead the live-oaks met, and it was as dark as a cave.

A black dog with a lolling tongue came up out of the weeds by the ditch. She was meditating, and not ready, and when he came at her she only hit him a little with her cane. Over she went in the ditch, like a little puff of milkweed.[9]

Down there, her senses drifted away. A dream visited her, and she reached her hand up, but nothing reached down and gave her a pull. So she lay there and presently went to talking. "Old woman," she said to herself, "that black dog come up out of the weeds to stall you off, and now there he sitting on his fine tail, smiling at you."

A white man finally came along and found her—a hunter, a young man, with his dog on a chain.

"Well, Granny!" he laughed. "What are you doing there?"

"Lying on my back like a June-bug waiting to be turned over, mister," she said, reaching up her hand.

He lifted her up, gave her a swing in the air, and set her down. "Anything broken, Granny?"

"No sir, them old dead weeds is springy enough," said Phoenix, when she had got her breath. "I thank you for your trouble."

"Where do you live, Granny?" he asked, while the two dogs were growling at each other.

"Away back yonder, sir, behind the ridge. You can't even see it from here."

"On your way home?"

"No sir, I going to town."

"Why, that's too far! That's as far as I walk when I come out myself, and I get something for my trouble." He patted the stuffed bag he carried, and there hung down a little closed claw. It was one of the bob-whites, with its beak hooked bitterly to show it was dead. "Now you go on home, Granny!"

"I bound to go to town, mister," said Phoenix. "The time come around."

He gave another laugh, filling the whole landscape. "I know you old colored people! Wouldn't miss going to town to see Santa Claus!"

But something held old Phoenix very still. The deep lines in her face went into a fierce and different radiation.[10] Without warning, she had seen with her own eyes a flashing nickel fall out of the man's pocket onto the ground.

"How old are you, Granny?" he was saying.

"There is no telling, mister," she said, "no telling."

Then she gave a little cry and clapped her hands and said, "Git on away from here, dog! Look! Look at that dog!" She laughed as if in admiration. "He ain't scared of nobody. He a big black dog." She whispered, "Sic him!"

"Watch me get rid of that cur," said the man. "Sic him, Pete! Sic him!"

Phoenix heard the dogs fighting, and heard the man running and throwing sticks. She even heard a gunshot. But she was slowly bending forward by that time, further and further forward, the lids stretched down over her eyes, as if she were doing this in her sleep. Her chin was lowered almost to her knees. The yellow palm of her hand came out from the fold of her apron. Her fingers slid down and along the ground under the piece of money with the grace and care they would have in lifting an egg from under a setting hen. Then she slowly straightened up, she stood erect, and the nickel was

---

8. The *sweet-gum* tree discharges a fragrant gum through cracks and crevices in its trunk.
9. The pods of a *milkweed* plant split open and release seeds with puffs of white, silky down.

10. Here, *radiation* means "a pattern of rays or waves."

Teaching Options

REAL-WORLD CONNECTION

Marathon Races In 1998, 32,398 people started the New York City Marathon. Of that number, 31,539 finished the race. Eighty-five wheelchair racers finished the marathon.

Activity Have students research to find interviews with marathon racers to answer the question: Why do you participate in marathons? **L2**

MEETING INDIVIDUAL NEEDS — MULTIPLE LEARNING STYLES

Logical and Mathematical Students who learn best by organizing information into logical patterns may find it useful to organize details of the extended metaphor in "A Worn Path."

Activity Review with students the idea that Phoenix's journey is a metaphor for her life journey and for the life journey of all people. Have them create a chart to identify and organize details of the metaphor. In the first column of the chart, they should identify the places and events in Phoenix's journey to town. In the second and third columns, they should identify the metaphoric meaning of each place or event in Phoenix's life and life in general. **L2**

School Children, Jackson, 1930s. Eudora Welty. Photograph. Mississippi Department of Archives and History, Jackson, MS. Eudora Welty Collection.

Viewing the photograph: Do you think Eudora Welty might have had her story "A Worn Path" in mind when she took this photograph? Why or why not?

in her apron pocket. A bird flew by. Her lips moved. "God watching me the whole time. I come to stealing."

The man came back, and his own dog panted about them. "Well, I scared him off that time," he said, and then he laughed and lifted his gun and pointed it at Phoenix.

She stood straight and faced him.

"Doesn't the gun scare you?" he said, still pointing it.

"No, sir, I seen plenty go off closer by, in my day, and for less than what I done," she said, holding utterly still.

He smiled, and shouldered the gun. "Well, Granny," he said, "you must be a hundred years old, and scared of nothing. I'd give you a dime if I had any money with me. But you take my advice and stay home, and nothing will happen to you."

"I bound to go on my way, mister," said Phoenix. She inclined her head in the red rag.

Then they went in different directions, but she could hear the gun shooting again and again over the hill.

She walked on. The shadows hung from the oak trees to the road like curtains. Then she smelled wood-smoke, and smelled the river, and she saw a steeple and the cabins on their steep steps. Dozens of little black children whirled around her. There ahead was Natchez shining. Bells were ringing. She walked on.

In the paved city it was Christmas time. There were red and green electric lights strung and crisscrossed everywhere, and all turned on in the daytime. Old Phoenix would have been lost if she had not distrusted her eyesight and depended on her feet to know where to take her.

She paused quietly on the sidewalk where people were passing by. A lady came along in the crowd, carrying an armful of red-, green- and silver-wrapped presents; she gave off perfume

INCLUSION STRATEGIES

Learning Disabled Since they often are hampered by short attention spans, students with learning disabilities face a special challenge when reading longer selections like "A Worn Path."

Activity Have students write numbered lists of key events in the story as they read. If they need to take breaks have them review the list each time before they resume reading the story. **L1**

Language Note

Point out the term "grandma" and explain that it is used here as a familiar but respectful term of address.

K **Literary Elements**

CHARACTERIZATION Ask students why Phoenix asks the woman to tie her shoe. What does this reveal about her character? *(Phoenix doesn't want to be seen in the big, magnificent building looking like a country woman with her shoes untied. It indicates that although Phoenix generally seems very humble, she has pride as well.)*

L **Critical Thinking**

COMPARING AND CONTRASTING Have students compare and contrast Phoenix's words and feelings when she finally arrives with the attendant's reaction. *(Phoenix is proud, even triumphant. The unfeeling attendant is only irritated.)*

like the red roses in hot summer, and Phoenix stopped her.

"Please, missy, will you lace up my shoe?" She held up her foot.

"What do you want, Grandma?"

"See my shoe," said Phoenix. "Do all right for out in the country, but wouldn't look right to go in a big building."

"Stand still then, Grandma," said the lady. She put her packages down on the sidewalk beside her and laced and tied both shoes tightly.

"Can't lace 'em with a cane," said Phoenix. "Thank you, missy. I doesn't mind asking a nice lady to tie up my shoe, when I gets out on the street."

Moving slowly and from side to side, she went into the big building, and into a tower of steps, where she walked up and around and around until her feet knew to stop.

She entered a door, and there she saw nailed up on the wall the document that had been

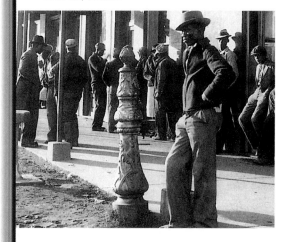

The Store, Madison County, 1930s. Eudora Welty. Photograph. Mississippi Department of Archives and History, Jackson, MS. Eudora Welty Collection.

stamped with the gold seal and framed in the gold frame, which matched the dream that was hung up in her head.

"Here I be," she said. There was a fixed and ceremonial stiffness over her body.

"A charity case, I suppose," said an attendant who sat at the desk before her.

But Phoenix only looked above her head. There was sweat on her face, the wrinkles in her skin shone like a bright net.

"Speak up, Grandma," the woman said. "What's your name? We must have your history, you know. Have you been here before? What seems to be the trouble with you?"

Old Phoenix only gave a twitch to her face as if a fly were bothering her.

"Are you deaf?" cried the attendant.

But then the nurse came in.

"Oh, that's just old Aunt Phoenix," she said. "She doesn't come for herself—she has a little grandson. She makes these trips just as regular as clockwork. She lives away back off the Old Natchez Trace." She bent down. "Well, Aunt Phoenix, why don't you just take a seat? We won't keep you standing after your long trip." She pointed.

The old woman sat down, bolt upright in the chair.

"Now, how is the boy?" asked the nurse.

Old Phoenix did not speak.

"I said, how is the boy?"

But Phoenix only waited and stared straight ahead, her face very solemn and withdrawn into rigidity.

"Is his throat any better?" asked the nurse. "Aunt Phoenix, don't you hear me? Is your grandson's throat any better since the last time you came for the medicine?"

With her hands on her knees, the old woman waited, silent, erect and motionless, just as if she were in armor.

Vocabulary
ceremonial (ser′ ə mō′ nē əl) *adj.* formal
solemn (sol′ əm) *adj.* serious; grave

Grammar and Language *Minilesson*

Incorrect Verb Tense Point out that Eudora Welty has constructed the dialogue to mirror the way her characters would really talk, which often means using incorrect verb tenses. Phoenix makes various kinds of errors with verb tenses. Many of the errors are errors of agreement as when Phoenix says, "I doesn't mind asking a nice lady to tie up my shoe . . ." Other errors include, for example, the failure to

provide an auxiliary verb, as when Phoenix says, "I going to the store . . ."

Activity Ask students to scan the story for dialogue and then analyze the use of verbs. Have them write statements containing usage errors and then rewrite them correctly. Ask students to compare their lists of errors and corrections. **L2**

Additional Resources

✍ *Grammar and Language Transparency 63*

📖 *Grammar and Language Workbook,* pp. 135–143

📕 *Grammar and Composition Handbook,* Lesson 5.6

📗 *Writer's Choice,* Lesson 15.6

"You mustn't take up our time this way, Aunt Phoenix," the nurse said. "Tell us quickly about your grandson, and get it over. He isn't dead, is he?"

At last there came a flicker and then a flame of comprehension across her face, and she spoke.

"My grandson. It was my memory had left me. There I sat and forgot why I made my long trip."

"Forgot?" The nurse frowned. "After you came so far?"

Then Phoenix was like an old woman begging a dignified forgiveness for waking up frightened in the night. "I never did go to school, I was too old at the Surrender,"[11] she said in a soft voice. "I'm an old woman without an education. It was my memory fail me. My little grandson, he is just the same, and I forgot it in the coming."

"Throat never heals, does it?" said the nurse, speaking in a loud, sure voice to old Phoenix. By now she had a card with something written on it, a little list. "Yes. Swallowed lye. When was it?—January—two-three years ago—"

Phoenix spoke unasked now. "No, missy, he not dead, he just the same. Every little while his throat begin to close up again, and he not able to swallow. He not get his breath. He not able to help himself. So the time come around, and I go on another trip for the soothing medicine."

"All right. The doctor said as long as you came to get it, you could have it," said the nurse. "But it's an obstinate case."

"My little grandson, he sit up there in the house all wrapped up, waiting by himself," Phoenix went on. "We is the only two left in the world. He suffer and it don't seem to put him back at all. He got a sweet look. He going to last. He wear a little patch quilt and peep out holding his mouth open like a little bird. I remembers so plain now. I not going to forget him again, no, the whole enduring time. I could tell him from all the others in creation."

"All right." The nurse was trying to hush her now. She brought her a bottle of medicine. "Charity," she said, making a check mark in a book.

Old Phoenix held the bottle close to her eyes, and then carefully put it into her pocket.

"I thank you," she said.

"It's Christmas time, Grandma," said the attendant. "Could I give you a few pennies out of my purse?"

"Five pennies is a nickel," said Phoenix stiffly.

"Here's a nickel," said the attendant.

Phoenix rose carefully and held out her hand. She received the nickel and then fished the other nickel out of her pocket and laid it beside the new one. She stared at her palm closely, with her head on one side.

Then she gave a tap with her cane on the floor.

"This is what come to me to do," she said. "I going to the store and buy my child a little windmill they sells, made out of paper. He going to find it hard to believe there such a thing in the world. I'll march myself back where he waiting, holding it straight up in this hand."

She lifted her free hand, gave a little nod, turned around, and walked out of the doctor's office. Then her slow step began on the stairs, going down.

❧

---

11. The *Surrender* of Robert E. Lee to Ulysses S. Grant in 1865 ended the Civil War.

Vocabulary

comprehension (kom prì hen′ shən) *n.* the act of grasping mentally; understanding

M **Author's Craft**

SETTING How does Eudora Welty imply the time setting of the story? *(If Phoenix were too old to go to school in 1865, and is "very old," probably in her seventies or eighties now, the story must take place in the 1930s.)*

FYI

Lye Lye, a solid, white substance, is an extremely caustic chemical. It causes terrible pain and injury if it contacts a person's eyes or skin. Swallowing lye can be fatal, and would at least cause extensive damage to the tissue of the mouth and throat. Lye, once a staple in rural homes, is used for making homemade soap.

N **Active Reading**

QUESTION Ask students how Phoenix is similar to her grandson. *(Both suffer, yet don't let hardships set them back.)*

Thematic Focus

Personal Discoveries Ask students to identify at least three personal discoveries that Phoenix has made in her life. Then have them identify lessons they can learn from her example.

✔ **ASSESSMENT OPTIONS**

📁 *Quick Checks,* p. 98

Listening and Speaking *Minilesson*

Mini Readers Theater Readers theater is a cross between oral reading and dramatic presentation. Students, assuming the role of characters from the story, read passages in character, as if from a script.

Activity Assign students to work in groups of two or three and to present the interaction between Phoenix and the hunter or Phoenix's encounter at the doctor's office in a mini readers theater. Encourage them to stay in character during the presentation and to read their lines as realistically as possible. **L2**

Personal Response

You may want to have students share their choices with the class and tally them on the board.

ANALYZING LITERATURE

1. She is a small, elderly black woman with her hair tied in a red rag; she carries an old umbrella for a cane and wears a dark striped dress, a sugar-sack apron, and lace-up shoes. Her eyes are blue with age, her hair is black, and her skin is wrinkled with golden undertones.

2. She follows a path through pine woods, up a hill, then down the hill through oaks. At the bottom she crosses a log bridge over a creek. She goes through a barbed wire fence into a cotton field and then into a corn field. She then follows a wagon track past cabins and a spring through a swampy area and under trees until she reaches Natchez.

3. She encounters a hunter who helps her out of a ditch. He is amused by her, chases off a dog that had bothered her, and points his gun at her. He drops a nickel and Phoenix keeps it.

4. Phoenix is headed to a doctor's office to obtain medicine for her grandson. The reader learns this on page 838, near the end of the story.

5. The second nickel is given to her by the attendant in the doctor's office. Phoenix plans to buy a toy windmill for her grandson.

6. She is old and poor.

7. It is a long and difficult path. It may symbolize Phoenix's and perhaps other people's path through life.

8. The most important thing may be that she is strong, clever, brave, and willing to do what is necessary to survive.

9. She is kind, self-sacrificing, and decent.

10. She is generous and loving.

11. Students may or may not feel empathy with Phoenix, but they should feel sympathy for her. They should provide examples to support their responses.

12. Welty might have named her character Phoenix in order to symbolize her resilience and triumph over life's obstacles.

13. Most students will agree that Phoenix is an admirable character who belongs on their lists.

Responding to Literature

Personal Response

What is your favorite incident or image from "A Worn Path"? What is it about the image or incident that especially appeals to you?

ANALYZING LITERATURE

RECALL

1. What does Phoenix Jackson look like?
2. Describe in detail the path Phoenix is taking.
3. Who is the first person Phoenix encounters? What happens?
4. What is Phoenix's destination and purpose? At what point in the story do you learn this?
5. How does Phoenix get her second nickel, and what does she decide to do with this money?

INTERPRET

6. What does Phoenix Jackson's appearance tell you about her?
7. From its description, what can you infer about the path Phoenix is on? What might the path be a **symbol** of? (See Literary Terms Handbook, page R16.) Support your answers with evidence from the selection.
8. What is the most important thing that Phoenix's first encounter reveals about her? Explain.
9. What does the purpose of Phoenix's trip tell you about her character?
10. What does Phoenix's decision about the way to spend her money tell you about her?

EVALUATE AND CONNECT

11. Do you feel empathy toward Phoenix? Why or why not? Relate your answer to events in the story as well as to your own experiences.
12. In Greek mythology, the *phoenix* is a bird that, at the end of its life, burns itself to death; from its ashes, a new phoenix rises. Why might Welty have named her main character Phoenix?
13. Refer to the list that you made for the Focus Activity on page 832. Would you put Phoenix Jackson on your list? Why or why not?
14. Theme Connections   Phoenix's approach to the physical challenges of the path reveals much about her. Think about a physical challenge you have faced. What did you discover about yourself as a result?
15. An author uses **descriptive writing** to create a picture of a person, place, or thing. In your opinion, how effective is Welty's descriptive writing in creating a picture of Phoenix Jackson? of the "worn path"?

Literary ELEMENTS

Characterization

Characterization is the way an author develops the personalities of characters. In **direct characterization**, the writer simply states a character's personality—for example, "The man was without imagination." In **indirect characterization**, the writer reveals a character's personality through the character's thoughts, words, and actions or through the way other characters react to him or her. The reader must then use these clues to infer the character's personality.

1. In developing Phoenix Jackson's personality, does Welty use mostly direct or indirect characterization? Explain briefly.
2. What do the things Phoenix says reveal about her personality?

● See **Literary Terms Handbook**, p. R3.

---

14. Students may relate discoveries of new strengths and abilities.
15. Most students will find the use of description very effective in creating a picture of both Phoenix and the path.

LITERARY ELEMENTS

1. She uses indirect characterization, directly describing her appearance, but revealing her personality through her thoughts, words, and actions.
2. Her words reveal that she is strong, has a sense of humor and proportion, and is appreciative, respectful, and kind.

Additional Resources

 Literary Elements Transparency 81

The Portrait

Tomás Rivera

As soon as the people returned from up north the portrait salesmen began arriving from San Antonio. They would come to rake in. They knew that the workers had money and that was why, as Dad used to say, they would flock in. They carried suitcases packed with samples and always wore white shirts and ties; that way they looked more important and the people believed everything they would tell them and invite them into their homes without giving it much thought. I think that down deep they even longed for their children to one day be like them. In any event, they would arrive and make their way down the dusty streets, going house to house carrying suitcases full of samples.

I remember once I was at the house of one of my father's friends when one of these salesmen arrived. I also remember that that particular one seemed a little frightened and timid. Don Mateo asked him to come in because he wanted to do business.

"Good afternoon, traveler. I would like to tell you about something new that we're offering this year."

"Well, let's see, let's see . . ."

"Well, sir, see, you give us a picture, any picture you may have, and we will not only enlarge it for you but we'll also set it in a wooden frame like this one and we'll shape the image a little, like this—three dimensional, as they say."

"And what for?"

"So that it will look real. That way . . . look, let me show you . . . see? Doesn't he look real, like he's alive?"

"Man, he sure does. Look, vieja.[1] This looks great. Well, you know, we wanted to send some pictures to be enlarged . . . but now, this must cost a lot, right?"

"No, I'll tell you, it costs about the same. Of course, it takes more time."

"Well, tell me, how much?"

"For as little as thirty dollars we'll deliver it to you done with inlays just like this, one this size."

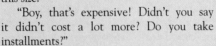

Did You Know?
Inlays are pieces of material, such as wood or ivory, set or embedded into the surface of something else to form a design.

"Boy, that's expensive! Didn't you say it didn't cost a lot more? Do you take installments?"

"Well, I'll tell you, we have a new manager and he wants everything in cash. It's very fine work. We'll make it look like real. Shaped like that, with inlays . . . take a look. What do you think? Some fine work, wouldn't you say? We can have it all finished for you in a month. You just tell us what color you want the clothes to

---

1. Here, the Spanish word *vieja* (vē ā′ hä′) is used as a term of endearment; literally, it means "old" or "old woman."

SUMMARY

The narrator recalls an episode from his youth. One of his father's friends, Don Mateo, is visited by a traveling salesman who promises to enhance and frame a picture of Don Mateo's son, who was killed in the Korean War. The price is high, and the picture is the only one Don Mateo and his wife have of their son, but they pay for the enlargement and entrust the picture to the salesman. Other families do the same. The pictures never come, however, and then the pictures are found; they had been thrown out and are now ruined by the weather. Don Mateo goes to San Antonio, finds the salesman, and forces him to create a picture of his son.

📁 **Spanish Summaries,** p. 91

A Active Reading

PREDICT Point out the narrator's implied opinion of the salesmen. Ask students what they think will happen? *(Students may correctly predict that the salesmen will exploit the poor workers.)*

Additional Resources
📁 *Active Reading Guide,* p. 101
🎧 *Audio Library*
🎧 *Spanish Audio Library*

Teaching Options

Photography Students may want to learn more about portrait photography. Do photographers still visit peoples' homes? Is being a portrait photographer a good career choice? Suggest students search for keywords *portrait photography.*

Historical Note

In the Korean War (1950–1953), the United Nations, led by the United States, supported South Korea in its fight against invading communist North Korea. More than 50,000 Americans died, and twice that number were wounded or missing in action.

B Literary Elements

RISING ACTION Don Mateo repeats that the picture of his son that he is about to surrender to the salesman is the only one that he and his wife have. Ask students why this is significant. *(Giving the picture to the salesman is an act of trust and a significant risk for the parents.)*

C Literary Elements

CLIMAX Point out to students that the revelation of the swindle is the climax of the story. The finding of the pictures will motivate Don Mateo to travel to San Antonio.

D Author's Craft

IRONY Challenge students to explain the irony in the sentence, "Everybody caught on right away." *(The people of the community didn't actually catch on "right away"; they had already been swindled.)*

Teaching Options

FINE ART
TRANSPARENCY 3

You may want to use **Fine Art Transparency 3** to discuss the importance of mementos of loved ones, such as photographs.

---

be and we'll come by with it all finished one day when you least expect, framed and all. Yes, sir, a month at the longest. But like I say, this man, who's the new manager, he wants the full payment in cash. He's very demanding, even with us."

"Yes, but it's much too expensive."

"Well, yes. But the thing is, this is very fine work. You can't say you've ever seen portraits done like this, with wood inlays."

"No, well, that's true. What do you think, *vieja?*"

"Well, I like it a lot. Why don't we order one? And if it turns out good . . . my Chuy . . . may he rest in peace. It's the only picture we have of him. We took it right before he left for Korea. Poor m'ijo,[2] we never saw him again. See . . . this is his picture. Do you think you can make it like that, make it look like he's alive?"

"Sure, we can. You know, we've done a lot of them in soldier's uniforms and shaped it, like you see in this sample, with inlays. Why, it's more than just a portrait. Sure. You just tell me what size you want and whether you want a round or square frame. What do you say? How should I write it down?"

"What do you say, vieja, should we have it done like this one?"

"Well, I've already told you what I think. I would like to have m'ijo's picture fixed up like that and in color."

B "All right, go ahead and write it down. But you take good care of that picture for us because it's the only one we have of our son grown up. He was going to send us one all dressed up in uniform with the American and Mexican flags crossed over his head, but he no sooner got there when a letter arrived telling us that he was lost in action. So you take good care of it."

"Don't you worry. We're responsible people. And we understand the sacrifices that you people make. Don't worry. And you just wait and

---

2. In Spanish, *m'ijo* (mē′ hō) is the colloquial form of mi hijo, meaning "my son."

---

see, when we bring it, you'll see how pretty it's gonna look. What do you say, should we make the uniform navy blue?"

"But he's not wearing a uniform in that picture."

"No, but that's just a matter of fixing it up with some wood fiber overlays. Look at these. This one, he didn't have a uniform on but we put one on him. So what do you say? Should we make it navy blue?"

"All right."

"Don't you worry about the picture."

And that was how they spent the entire day, going house to house, street by street, their suitcases stuffed with pictures. As it turned out, a whole lot of people had ordered enlargements of that kind.

"They should be delivering those portraits soon, don't you think?"

"I think so, it's delicate work and takes more time. That's some fine work those people do. Did you see how real those pictures looked?"

"Yeah, sure. They do some fine work. You can't deny that. But it's already been over a month since they passed by here."

"Yes, but from here they went on through all the towns picking up pictures . . . all the way to San Antonio for sure. So it'll probably take a little longer."

"That's true, that's true."

C And two more weeks had passed by the time they made the discovery. Some very heavy rains had come and some children, who were playing in one of the tunnels leading to the dump, found a sack full of pictures, all worm-eaten and soaking wet. The only reason that they could tell that these were pictures was because there were a lot of them and most of them the same size and with faces that could just barely be made out. Everybody caught on **D** right away. Don Mateo was so angry that he took off to San Antonio to find the so and so who had swindled them.

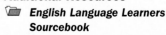
Spanish Words in an English Text
The presence of Spanish words in "The Portrait" provides an opportunity for fluent Spanish speakers to make a unique contribution to class.

Activity Have fluent Spanish speakers identify all of the Spanish words in the selection. For each, they should compare and contrast their own sense of the denotation and connotation of the word with the explanations given in the selection's footnotes.

Additional Resources
📁 *English Language Learners Sourcebook*

The Beautiful Changes

Richard Wilbur

One wading a Fall meadow finds on all sides
The Queen Anne's Lace° lying like lilies
On water; it glides
So from the walker, it turns
5   Dry grass to a lake, as the slightest shade of you
Valleys my mind in fabulous blue Lucernes.°

The beautiful changes as a forest is changed
By a chameleon's tuning his skin to it;
As a mantis, arranged
10   On a green leaf, grows
Into it, makes the leaf leafier, and proves
Any greenness is deeper than anyone knows.

Your hands hold roses always in a way that says
They are not only yours; the beautiful changes
15   In such kind ways,
Wishing ever to sunder°
Things and things' selves for a second finding, to lose
For a moment all that it touches back to wonder.

---

2   *Queen Anne's Lace* is a meadow weed with delicate white flowers.
6   Here, *Lucernes* refers to the Lake of Lucerne, located in central Switzerland.
16   *Sunder* means "to separate" or "to tear apart."

Reading the Selection

A Active Reading

VISUALIZE Have students describe the mental picture the first stanza creates. *(The speaker is walking in a field of fall colors, filled with dry grass topped by Queen Anne's Lace that sways away from the speaker as he wades through the tall grasses.)*

Additional Resources
📁 *Active Reading Guide,* p. 103
🎧 *Audio Library*

B Critical Thinking

COMPARING AND CONTRASTING
Point out that the tone and subject of "The Beautiful Changes" are starkly different from those of "The Death of the Ball Turret Gunner." Ask students to discuss how these two poems are alike and different, and why they fit into a collection of works on the theme of personal discoveries.

✔ ASSESSMENT OPTIONS

📁 *Quick Checks,* p. 103

Teaching Options

MEETING INDIVIDUAL NEEDS — MULTIPLE LEARNING STYLES

Spatial "The Beautiful Changes" presents a number of clear visual images that may appeal to learners with spatial learning abilities.

Activity Ask spatial learners to complete drawings of the vivid images mentioned in the poem—the Queen Anne's Lace, a chameleon, a mantis, hands holding the roses. Display the drawings in the classroom, and have the students discuss the ways in which these particular images are beautiful—both in their execution as drawings and as the actual objects in nature. **L2**

Personal Response

Students may say that they do not usually think of mantises or lizards as beautiful and therefore find those lines memorable. Some may say the "wading" in the meadow grass is memorable.

ANALYZING LITERATURE

1. It turns the meadow into a lake. The Queen Anne's Lace blankets the speaker's mind with images of "blue Lucernes."
2. It changes the forest by blending into it, adding a hidden layer of meaning. A mantis appears to extend a leaf. The beauty comes from these natural changes, the harmony of colors and the levels of beauty that appear as one looks more closely.
3. They hold the roses in a non-possessive manner. It is significant because beauty belongs to all who look, not to one person. The hands might belong to someone the speaker loves.
4. The beautiful changes in "kind ways." This lets people see beauty and then look at it again in new ways to find more beauty.
5. Many students will have identified specific kinds of beautiful things—forests, wild flowers, clouds, oceans, or mountains. Explore with the students the ways in which all of these things change.
6. The title is constructed so that both readings are valid. The adjective-noun combination emphasizes the beauty of the change itself; the noun-verb combination emphasizes the changes in beauty itself.
7. Students should recognize that things, including beauty, change constantly. They may not all agree that beauty always changes in "kind ways," pointing out that sometimes beauty is lost through change.
8. Wilbur may be likening the growth and change of a relationship to growth and change in nature.

Responding to Literature

Personal Response

Which lines from the poem did you find the most memorable or surprising? Take a few minutes to copy these lines into your journal.

——— ANALYZING LITERATURE ———

RECALL AND INTERPRET

1. What does the Queen Anne's lace turn the meadow into? What does the "you" in line 5 do to the speaker's mind?
2. How does a chameleon change a forest? How does a mantis change a leaf? In what ways are these beautiful changes?
3. How do the hands mentioned in stanza 3 hold roses, and why is this significant? To whom might the hands belong?
4. According to stanza 3, in what ways does the beautiful change? What opportunity do the changes offer to people?

EVALUATE AND CONNECT

5. Think about your response to the Focus Activity on page 860. How does your impression of what is beautiful in nature compare with what Wilbur describes in this poem?
6. The word *beautiful* can be a noun or an adjective, and the word *changes* can be a noun or a verb. How do you read the title of this poem: as an adjective and noun combination or as a noun and verb combination? Why? How would your reading of the poem change if you read the title differently?
7. Do you agree with the speaker that the beautiful is always changing and that it changes in "such kind ways"? Explain your response.
8. Why do you think Wilbur writes about changes in nature and a love relationship in the same poem?

Literary ELEMENTS

Sensory Details

Sensory details are those images in a literary work that appeal to one or more of the five senses. Poets use sensory details to help the reader imagine or experience more deeply the content of their poems. "The Beautiful Changes" consists primarily of visual images, which help the reader to picture the splendors of the natural world. In the first stanza, for instance, the reader may visualize how lilies look floating on water.

1. Identify another image in the poem that appeals to your sense of sight. Tell what you see in your mind's eye.
2. What role do you think color plays in this poem? Use details to support your conclusions.

⊙ See **Literary Terms Handbook,** p. R14.

——— EXTENDING YOUR RESPONSE ———

Writing About Literature

Identify the Sound Devices   In this poem, Wilbur enhances our appreciation of beautiful changes in nature by using such sound devices as **assonance,** the repetition of vowel sounds within words, and **alliteration,** the repetition of sounds at the beginnings of words. In a short paper, identify two or more examples of each device in the poem and explain how each example enriches the poem.

Performing

So from the Reader, It Turns   Create a dramatic reading of this poem. Begin by making a copy of the poem that you can write on. Make notes indicating where to speed up or slow down your reading, where to emphasize words, and where to add gestures or movements. Practice the reading several times; then perform it for the class.

📖 **Save your work for your portfolio.**

LITERARY ELEMENTS

1. Images may include the forest, the chameleon, the mantis, the leaf, or the hands holding roses.
2. The colors white and blue and the other implied colors figure prominently in the first stanza; the color green dominates the second stanza; the colors of roses and skin open the third stanza. All of them help form pictures in the reader's mind.

Additional Resources

✍ *Literary Elements Transparency 86*

✔ ASSESSMENT OPTIONS

📁 *Quick Checks,* p. 103
📁 *Selection and Theme Assessment,* p. 154
📁 *Performance Assessment,* p. 87
💾 *Testmaker*

Before You Read

The Rockpile

Meet
James Baldwin

> "I am . . . listening to my own demons and no one else's, and I am going to keep working until they have all said what it is they are trying to tell me—and you. I am not going to stop until the last voice within me has been stilled."
>
> —*Baldwin*

The world would agree that James Baldwin never did stop: he wrote, and wrote, and wrote, producing a body of work that is acclaimed in American literature. Baldwin overcame many handicaps to do so. His own grandparents had been enslaved, and Baldwin himself grew up in Harlem during the economic hard times of the depression.

During high school, Baldwin worked as a youth minister at the Fireside Pentecostal Assembly. After graduating from high school in 1942, Baldwin took a series of jobs to help support his brothers and sisters. He worked as a handyman, dish washer, office worker, and waiter.

The author of plays, short stories, and novels, Baldwin is perhaps most highly regarded as an essayist. Among his most famous essay collections are *Notes of a Native Son*, *Nobody Knows My Name*, and *The Fire Next Time*. In these essays, Baldwin explored, among other things, the forces that shaped American racial identity. In both fiction and nonfiction, Baldwin explored issues of African American identity in twentieth-century America.

Baldwin's first novel, *Go Tell It on the Mountain*, was published in 1953. This novel reflected Baldwin's search for his roots. More and more, however, Baldwin's eloquent voice became one of protest and social outrage against racial inequality. He urged whites to treat African Americans with fairness and justice. With uncompromising realism, he exposed his readers to some basic truths about the society in which they lived.

Besides achieving fame as a writer, Baldwin was in great demand as a speaker during the Civil Rights struggles of the 1950s and 1960s. His insights, his ear for the spoken language, and his early experience as a minister combined to make him a powerful force at the podium. As the years went by, however, Baldwin became disillusioned about the prospect of social change. In 1969 Baldwin moved to Europe, and he lived primarily in France for the rest of his life. In many respects, France proved friendlier to him than his own country. In the United States, Baldwin was for a time put under FBI surveillance, and, despite all his critical and popular success, he never won any major American literary prize during his lifetime. France, on the other hand, honored him with one of its most prestigious awards: Commander of the Legion of Honor.

In death, however, Baldwin returned to Harlem. His funeral was held only a few blocks from the house where he had been born. More than five thousand mourners gathered to pay respects to the man whom the writer E. L. Doctorow credited with the ability "not to make you question but to make you see."

> "Trust life, and it will teach you, in joy and sorrow, all you need to know."
>
> —*Baldwin*

James Baldwin was born in 1924 and died in 1987.

Objectives

- To read and analyze a short story about making choices
- To identify the effect of foil in a short story
- To write an analysis of the internal and external conflicts in a short story

Skills

Reading/Thinking: Previewing; Inferring; Drawing Conclusions; Paraphrasing
Writing: Journal Entry
Vocabulary: Etymology; Analogies
Grammar/Language: Double Negatives
Life Skills: Problem Solving
Collaboration: Literature Groups; Conversational Dialogue

More About James Baldwin

James Baldwin first went to France in 1948. He lived there for eight years. He returned to Europe in 1969, remaining there until his death except for occasional, brief trips to the United States. Remarkably, Baldwin did most of his writing, which is marked by tremendous insight into American life, while abroad. The geographic and cultural distance between the United States and France apparently enhanced, rather than diminished, his ability to decipher life in his home country.

RESOURCE MANAGER

Lesson Planning Resource
The **Unit Six Planning Guide** (pp. 81–88) provides additional lesson notes and reduced versions of all print resources.

📁 **Other Print Resources**
- Active Reading Guide, p. 104
- Vocabulary Practice, p. 50
- Reading Workbook, pp. 79–80
- Grammar and Language Workbook, p. 203

- Grammar and Composition Handbook, Lesson 8.6
- Quick Checks, p. 104
- Selection and Theme Assessment, pp. 155–156
- Performance Assessment, p. 88
- Spanish Summaries, p. 94
- Inclusion Strategies
- English Language Learners Sourcebook

🖎 **Transparencies**
- Selection Focus 94
- Literary Elements 87
- Grammar and Language 64

Technology
🎧 Audio Library
🖥 Glencoe Literature Web Site
💾 Testmaker

Motivating
→OPTIONS

Selection Focus Transparency 94: Have students view the transparency and then answer the question provided.

Focus Activity: Invite students to discuss their experiences. Ask them how they determine the right thing to do when faced with deciding between loyalty and responsibility.

Reading Further

Be sure to review these titles for appropriateness for your class before recommending them to students.

Novel: *Baldwin, James. Go Tell It on the Mountain.* New York: Random House, 1995.

Essays: *Baldwin, James. Notes of a Native Son.* Beacon Press, 1984.

Morrison, Toni (editor). *Collected Essays of James Baldwin.* Library of America, 1998.

Biography: Leeming, David Adams. *James Baldwin: A Biography.* New York: Holt, 1995.

Before You Read

— FOCUS ACTIVITY —

Have you ever known someone who chose to side with a brother, a sister, or a friend even though it meant breaking the rules?

JOURNAL Explain what the person chose to do, and what happened as a result.

SETTING A PURPOSE Read to discover the choices two brothers make and the consequences of their choices.

— BACKGROUND —

The Time and Place

This story is set in the New York neighborhood of Harlem. Although no precise time is given, it appears to be the 1930s—the time of Baldwin's own youth. The story may well be set near the first home Baldwin remembered living in at Park Avenue and 131st Street. The author recalled playing at a garbage dump near the house.

Harlem, 1935.

Autobiographical References

Like John in "The Rockpile," Baldwin was the oldest child in a large family, and his stepfather was a minister. His mother married David Baldwin three years after James's birth. David Baldwin raised James, and James referred to him as Dad. Like the father in the story, David Baldwin was a stern man. He did not want his children playing in the streets. In fact, going outside, except to go to church or to the store, was certain, in his mind, to lead to sin. As John W. Roberts wrote, James Baldwin's "relationship with his stepfather served as a constant source of tension during his formative years." Yet Baldwin knew his father took care of him. He once said, "I would not be here had it not been for him."

— VOCABULARY PREVIEW —

intriguing (in trēg′ ing) *adj.* arousing curiosity or interest; fascinating; captivating; p. 865

grapple (grap′ əl) *v.* to struggle in hand-to-hand combat; to wrestle; p. 866

loiter (loi′ tər) *v.* to stand or linger idly or aimlessly about a place; p. 866

intimidated (in tim′ ə dāt′ əd) *adj.* made timid or fearful; frightened into submission or inaction; p. 866

engrossed (en grōst′) *adj.* fully attentive to; completely engaged in; absorbed; p. 867

clamber (klam′ bər) *v.* to climb hastily or awkwardly, using hands and feet; p. 867

jubilant (jōō′ bə lənt) *adj.* extremely happy; triumphantly joyful; p. 867

864 ❦ UNIT 6

CONNECTING TO OTHER SELECTIONS

The chart at the right shows three ways to connect "The Rockpile" to selections in this book.

For specific teaching strategies, see the *Unit Six Planning Guide*, pp. 84–85.

Connection	Title
Critical Thinking: Synthesizing →	"Sonnet to a Negro in Harlem," p. 749
Thematic: Generations →	"Picture Bride," p. 1083
Literary: Dialect →	"The Celebrated Jumping Frog of Calaveras County," p. 462

The Rockpile

James Baldwin ✥

Across the street from their house, in an empty lot between two houses, stood the rockpile. It was a strange place to find a mass of natural rock jutting out of the ground; and someone, probably Aunt Florence, had once told them that the rock was there and could not be taken away because without it the subway cars underground would fly apart, killing all the people. This, touching on some natural mystery concerning the surface and the center of the earth, was far too <u>intriguing</u> an explanation to be challenged, and it invested the rockpile, moreover, with such mysterious importance that Roy felt it to be his right, not to say his duty, to play there.

Vocabulary
intriguing (in trēg′ ing) *adj.* arousing curiosity or interest; fascinating; captivating

SUMMARY

Two brothers, John and Roy, sit on their apartment's fire escape in Harlem and stare at the rockpile—a natural rock outcropping where the children of the neighborhood play roughly. Their parents forbid the brothers to join in, but Roy, who is younger, sneaks away to the rockpile and is injured by a thrown can. Shortly before the father returns home from work, the reader learns that John is his stepson. The father treats his wife and John harshly, blaming them for Roy's injury. The story is a study in strained family relationships.

📁 *Spanish Summaries,* p. 94

Ⓐ Active Reading

PREDICT Point out that rockpile forms the title of the story and is the subject of the first sentence (dramatically placed at the end), and that the entire first paragraph is devoted to the rockpile. What can students predict about the story from these facts? *(The rockpile will be central to the story, either as an element of the plot or as a symbol—or both.)*

Additional Resources
📁 *Active Reading Guide,* p. 104
🎧 *Audio Library*

Teaching Options

Reading *Minilesson*

Previewing Photographs that accompany "The Rockpile" may depict the story's characters and events, symbolize aspects of the story, and enhance the reading experience. Explain that the photographs are also an effective previewing tool.

Activity Before students read "The Rockpile," challenge them to use the photographs to infer as much as possible about the setting, characters, and other aspects of the story. After they read the story, have them review the story to find examples that support or contradict their inferences. **L2**

Additional Resources
📁 *Reading Workbook,* pp. 79–80

EVALUATE Have students explain how John and Roy are contrasted in this passage. *(Their mother directs her warning at Roy; she knows that he, who gazes longingly at the rockpile, is the one who really wants to go there. John, in contrast, is afraid of it and of the boys who play there.)*

C Critical Thinking

INFERRING Ask students what they can infer about the boys' father and their relationship to him from this sentence.

Model: I can see that this sentence is written from the boys' point of view. The father probably doesn't come home with the idea of "ending their freedom," but the boys look at it this way, suggesting a strained relationship. I can infer from this that the father is a disciplinarian—and it might hint that he is particularly harsh.

Teaching Options

The Rockpile

Other boys were to be seen there each afternoon after school and all day Saturday and Sunday. They fought on the rockpile. Sure-footed, dangerous, and reckless, they rushed each other and grappled on the heights, sometimes disappearing down the other side in a confusion of dust and screams and upended, flying feet. "It's a wonder they don't kill themselves," their mother said, watching sometimes from the fire escape. "You children stay away from there, you hear me?" Though she said "children," she was looking at Roy, where he sat beside John on the fire escape. "The good Lord knows," she continued, "I don't want you to come home bleeding like a hog every day the Lord sends." Roy shifted impatiently, and continued to stare at the street, as though in this gazing he might somehow acquire wings. John said nothing. He had not really been spoken to: he was afraid of the rockpile and of the boys who played there.

Did You Know?
A *fire escape* is a metal stairway attached to the outside of a building, used as an emergency exit in a fire.

Each Saturday morning John and Roy sat on the fire escape and watched the forbidden street below. Sometimes their mother sat in the room behind them, sewing, or dressing their younger sister, or nursing the baby, Paul. The sun fell across them and across the fire escape with a high, benevolent indifference; below them, men and women, and boys and girls, sinners all, loitered; sometimes one of the church-members passed and saw them and waved. Then, for the moment that they waved decorously back, they were intimidated. They watched the saint, man or woman, until he or she had disappeared from sight. The passage of one of the redeemed made them consider, however vacantly, the wickedness of the street, their own latent wickedness in sitting where they sat; and made them think of their father, who came home early on Saturdays and who would soon be turning this corner and entering the dark hall below them.

But until he came to end their freedom, they sat, watching and longing above the street. At the end of the street nearest their house was the bridge which spanned the Harlem River[1] and led to a city called the Bronx;[2] which was where Aunt Florence lived. Nevertheless, when they saw her coming, she did not come from the bridge, but from the opposite end of the street. This, weakly, to their minds, she explained by saying that she had taken the subway, not wishing to walk, and that, besides, she did not live in *that* section of the Bronx. Knowing that the Bronx was across the river, they did not believe this story ever, but, adopting toward her their father's attitude, assumed that she had just left some sinful place which she dared not name, as, for example, a movie palace.

In the summertime boys swam in the river, diving off the wooden dock, or wading in from the garbage-heavy bank. Once a boy, whose name was Richard, drowned in the river. His mother had not known where he was; she had even come to their house, to ask if he was

---

1. The *Harlem River* separates the Bronx and Manhattan, two boroughs of New York City.
2. The *Bronx* is actually one of five boroughs, or divisions, that make up New York City. It is not a separate city.

Vocabulary
grapple (grap′ əl) *v.* to struggle in hand-to-hand combat; to wrestle
loiter (loi′ tər) *v.* to stand or linger idly or aimlessly about a place
intimidated (in tim′ ə dāt′ əd) *adj.* made timid or fearful; frightened into submission or inaction

Dialect The dialect Baldwin uses in "The Rockpile" may pose a challenge to English language learners. Point out that dialect varies among regions and cultural groups. Baldwin uses it to reinforce the setting.

Activity Pair English language learners with fluent English speakers. Have each pair create a chart like the one shown. In the first column, students should write examples of dialect from "The Rockpile." In the second column, they should write the same sentences in Standard English. **COLLAB. LEARN.**

Dialect	Standard English

Additional Resources
📁 *English Language Learners Sourcebook*

there. Then, in the evening, at six o'clock, they had heard from the street a woman screaming and wailing; and they ran to the windows and looked out. Down the street came the woman, Richard's mother, screaming, her face raised to the sky and tears running down her face. A woman walked beside her, trying to make her quiet and trying to hold her up. Behind them walked a man, Richard's father, with Richard's body in his arms. There were two white policemen walking in the gutter, who did not seem to know what should be done. Richard's father and Richard were wet, and Richard's body lay across his father's arms like a cotton baby. The woman's screaming filled all the street; cars slowed down and the people in the cars stared; people opened their windows and looked out and came rushing out of doors to stand in the gutter, watching. Then the small procession disappeared within the house which stood beside the rockpile. Then, *"Lord, Lord, Lord!"* cried Elizabeth, their mother, and slammed the window down.

One Saturday, an hour before his father would be coming home, Roy was wounded on the rockpile and brought screaming upstairs. He and John had been sitting on the fire escape and their mother had gone into the kitchen to sip tea with Sister McCandless. By and by Roy became bored and sat beside John in restless silence; and John began drawing into his schoolbook a newspaper advertisement which featured a new electric locomotive. Some friends of Roy passed beneath the fire escape and called him. Roy began to fidget, yelling down to them through the bars. Then a silence fell. John looked up. Roy stood looking at him.

"I'm going downstairs," he said.

"You better stay where you is, boy. You know Mama don't want you going downstairs."

"I be right *back*. She won't even know I'm gone, less you run and tell her."

"I ain't *got* to tell her. What's going to stop her from coming in here and looking out the window?"

"She's talking," Roy said. He started into the house.

"But Daddy's going to be home soon!"

"I be back before *that*. What you all the time got to be so *scared* for?" He was already in the house and he now turned, leaning on the windowsill, to swear impatiently, "I be back in *five* minutes."

John watched him sourly as he carefully unlocked the door and disappeared. In a moment he saw him on the sidewalk with his friends. He did not dare to go and tell his mother that Roy had left the fire escape because he had practically promised not to. He started to shout, *Remember, you said five minutes!* but one of Roy's friends was looking up at the fire escape. John looked down at his schoolbook: he became <u>engrossed</u> again in the problem of the locomotive.

When he looked up again he did not know how much time had passed, but now there was a gang fight on the rockpile. Dozens of boys fought each other in the harsh sun: <u>clambering</u> up the rocks and battling hand to hand, scuffed shoes sliding on the slippery rock; filling the bright air with curses and <u>jubilant</u> cries. They filled the air, too, with flying weapons: stones, sticks, tin cans, garbage, whatever could be picked up and thrown. John watched in a kind of absent amazement—until he remembered that Roy was still downstairs, and that he was one of the boys on the rockpile. Then he was afraid; he could not see his brother among the figures in the sun; and he stood up, leaning over the fire-escape railing. Then Roy appeared from the other side of the rocks; John

---

Vocabulary
engrossed (en grōst′) *adj.* fully attentive to; completely engaged in; absorbed
clamber (klam′ bər) *v.* to climb hastily or awkwardly, using hands and feet
jubilant (jōō′ bə lənt) *adj.* extremely happy; triumphantly joyful

---

Literary Elements

F

SYMBOLISM Point out that Roy is hurt when he is happy and has just reached the very top of the rockpile. Invite students to suggest the symbolism of this coincidence. *(It might symbolize a life that frustrates hopes, dreams, and triumphs.)*

Literary Elements

G

FORESHADOWING John looks to see if his father will appear; Elizabeth looks "with apprehension" at the clock. Ask students what these actions might foreshadow. *(They may foreshadow the appearance of the father and his angry reaction to Roy's injury.)*

Literary Elements

H

CHARACTERIZATION Ask students what Sister McCandless's statement to John—and his reaction—tells them about the father. *(He is evidently a stern disciplinarian, not a father that children would lie to or test.)*

Teaching Options

saw that his shirt was torn; he was laughing. He moved until he stood at the very top of the rockpile. Then, something, an empty tin can, flew out of the air and hit him on the forehead, just above the eye. Immediately, one side of Roy's face ran with blood, he fell and rolled on his face down the rocks. Then for a moment there was no movement at all, no sound, the sun, arrested, lay on the street and the sidewalk and the arrested boys. Then someone screamed or shouted; boys began to run away, down the street, toward the bridge. The figure on the ground, having caught its breath and felt its own blood, began to shout. John cried, "Mama! Mama!" and ran inside.

"Don't fret, don't fret," panted Sister McCandless as they rushed down the dark, narrow, swaying stairs, "don't fret. Ain't a boy been born don't get his knocks every now and again. *Lord!*" they hurried into the sun. A man had picked Roy up and now walked slowly toward them. One or two boys sat silent on their stoops; at either end of the street there was a group of boys watching. "He ain't hurt bad," the man said, "Wouldn't be making this kind of noise if he was hurt real bad."

Did You Know?
A *stoop* is a structure at the entrance of a building or house, consisting of stairs and a raised platform.

Elizabeth, trembling, reached out to take Roy, but Sister McCandless, bigger, calmer, took him from the man and threw him over her shoulder as she once might have handled a sack of cotton. "God bless you," she said to the man, "God bless you, son." Roy was still screaming. Elizabeth stood behind Sister McCandless to stare at his bloody face.

"It's just a flesh wound," the man kept saying, "just broke the skin, that's all." They were

moving across the sidewalk, toward the house. John, not now afraid of the staring boys, looked toward the corner to see if his father was yet in sight.

Upstairs, they hushed Roy's crying. They bathed the blood away, to find, just above the left eyebrow, the jagged, superficial scar. "Lord, have mercy," murmured Elizabeth, "another inch and it would've been his eye." And she looked with apprehension toward the clock. "Ain't it the truth," said Sister McCandless, busy with bandages and iodine.

"When did he go downstairs?" his mother asked at last.

Sister McCandless now sat fanning herself in the easy chair, at the head of the sofa where Roy lay, bound and silent. She paused for a moment to look sharply at John. John stood near the window, holding the newspaper advertisement and the drawing he had done.

"We was sitting on the fire escape," he said. "Some boys he knew called him."

"When?"

"He said he'd be back in five minutes."

"Why didn't you tell me he was downstairs?"

He looked at his hands, clasping his notebook, and did not answer.

"Boy," said Sister McCandless, "you hear your mother a-talking to you?"

He looked at his mother. He repeated:

"He said he'd be back in five minutes."

"He said he'd be back in five minutes," said Sister McCandless with scorn, "don't look to me like that's no right answer. You's the man of the house, you supposed to look after your baby brothers and sisters—you ain't supposed to let them run off and get half-killed. But I expect," she added, rising from the chair, dropping the cardboard fan, "your Daddy'll make you tell the truth. Your Ma's way too soft with you."

He did not look at her, but at the fan where it lay in the dark red, depressed seat where she had been. The fan advertised a

Less-Proficient Readers There are few characters in "The Rockpile," but identifying them and the relationships among them can prove difficult for less-proficient readers.

Activity Have students create web diagrams to identify the characters and their relationships to John. **L1**

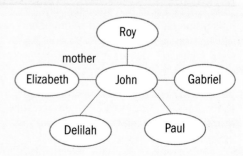

pomade[3] for the hair and showed a brown woman and her baby, both with glistening hair, smiling happily at each other.

"Honey," said Sister McCandless, "I got to be moving along. Maybe I drop in later tonight. I don't reckon you going to be at Tarry Service tonight?"

Tarry Service was the prayer meeting held every Saturday night at church to strengthen believers and prepare the church for the coming of the Holy Ghost on Sunday.

"I don't reckon," said Elizabeth. She stood up; she and Sister McCandless kissed each other on the cheek. "But you be sure to remember me in your prayers."

"I surely will do that." She paused, with her hand on the door knob, and looked down at Roy and laughed. "Poor little man," she said, "reckon he'll be content to sit on the fire escape *now*."

Elizabeth laughed with her. "It sure ought to be a lesson to him. You don't reckon," she asked nervously, still smiling, "he going to keep that scar, do you?"

"Lord, no," said Sister McCandless, "ain't nothing but a scratch. I declare, Sister Grimes, you worse than a child. Another couple of weeks and you won't be able to *see* no scar. No, you go on about your housework, honey, and thank the Lord it weren't no worse." She opened the door; they heard the sound of feet on the stairs. "I expect that's the Reverend," said Sister McCandless, placidly, "I *bet* he going to raise cain."[4]

A scene in Harlem, 1943.

"Maybe it's Florence," Elizabeth said. "Sometimes she get here about this time." They stood in the doorway, staring, while the steps reached the landing below and began again climbing to their floor. "No," said Elizabeth then, "that ain't her walk. That's Gabriel."

"Well, I'll just go on," said Sister McCandless, "and kind of prepare his mind." She pressed Elizabeth's hand as she spoke and started into the hall, leaving the door behind her slightly ajar. Elizabeth turned slowly back into the room. Roy did not open his eyes, or move; but she knew that he was not sleeping; he wished to delay until the last possible moment any contact with his father. John put

---

3. *Pomade* is a perfumed ointment, especially one used as a hair dressing.
4. *To raise cain* is an idiom meaning "to make a great disturbance" or "to lose one's temper."

I **Literary Elements**

SYMBOLISM Ask students what the image on the fan might symbolize. *(The image of the loving mother and baby might symbolize John's relationship with his mother. It stands in sharp contrast to the type of relationship that John longs for but does not have with his father.)*

J **Literary Elements**

CHARACTERIZATION Ask students why Roy pretends to be asleep when it's time for Gabriel to come home. *(The implication is that Elizabeth knows why Roy is feigning sleep. Through her thoughts, the reader learns that Roy, too, is afraid of his father.)*

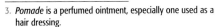

MEETING INDIVIDUAL NEEDS · MULTIPLE LEARNING STYLES

Linguistic Linguistic learners are attuned to the denotations, connotations, and nuances of words. This ability will help them and other students gain greater insight into the characters and relationships explored in the story.

Activity Have students list the main characters and then the main relationships between *pairs* of characters, such as John and Roy, Gabriel and John, and Gabriel and Elizabeth. Ask students to write adjectives and phrases that describe each character and each relationship. Have students share their lists with the class and explain why they selected the adjectives and phrases to describe each character and relationship. **L2**

EVALUATE Have students evaluate the truthfulness of Elizabeth's statement. Does she or John really believe what she is saying?

Model: I don't think either one of them believes what is said because of the way they act. John challenges her with a direct look, but he doesn't say anything, probably because he doesn't need to: there is an unspoken truth between them. I can also see that Elizabeth immediately looks to see if Sister McCandless is making any headway with the father.

L Critical Thinking

DRAWING CONCLUSIONS Ask students what crucial conclusion they draw about the family from the facts in these statements. (*John is Elizabeth's child but not Gabriel's. Therefore, Gabriel is John's stepfather, which explains the tension between them. Moreover, John may remind Gabriel of his wife's "days in sin," which he resents.*)

M Literary Elements

FOIL Ask students how Elizabeth is now acting as a foil for Gabriel. (*Elizabeth's gentleness is used as a contrast to Gabriel's anger, emphasizing his temper.*)

The Rockpile

his newspaper and his notebook on the table and stood, leaning on the table, staring at her.

"It wasn't my fault," he said. "I couldn't stop him from going downstairs."

"No," she said, "you ain't got nothing to worry about. You just tell your Daddy the truth."

He looked directly at her, and she turned to the window, staring into the street. What was Sister McCandless saying? Then from her bedroom she heard Delilah's thin wail and she turned, frowning, looking toward the bedroom and toward the still open door. She knew that John was watching her. Delilah continued to wail, she thought, angrily, *Now that girl's getting too big for that,* but she feared that Delilah would awaken Paul and she hurried into the bedroom. She tried to soothe Delilah back to sleep. Then she heard the front door open and close—too loud, Delilah raised her voice, with an exasperated sigh Elizabeth picked the child up. Her child and Gabriel's, her children and Gabriel's: Roy, Delilah, Paul. Only John was nameless and a stranger, living, unalterable testimony to his mother's days in sin.

"What happened?" Gabriel demanded. He stood, enormous, in the center of the room, his black lunchbox dangling from his hand, staring at the sofa where Roy lay. John stood just before him, it seemed to her astonished vision just below him, beneath his fist, his heavy shoe. The child stared at the man in fascination and terror—when a girl down home she had seen rabbits stand so paralyzed before the barking dog. She hurried past Gabriel to the sofa, feeling the weight of Delilah in her arms like the weight of a shield, and stood over Roy, saying:

"Now, ain't a thing to get upset about, Gabriel. This boy sneaked downstairs while I had my back turned and got hisself hurt a little. He's alright now."

Roy, as though in confirmation, now opened his eyes and looked gravely at his father. Gabriel dropped his lunchbox with a clatter and knelt by the sofa.

"How you feel, son? Tell your Daddy what happened?"

Roy opened his mouth to speak and then, relapsing into panic, began to cry. His father held him by the shoulder

"You don't want to cry. You's Daddy's little man. Tell your Daddy what happened."

"He went downstairs," said Elizabeth, "where he didn't have no business to be, and got to fighting with them bad boys playing on that rockpile. That's what happened and it's a mercy it weren't nothing worse."

He looked up at her. "Can't you let this boy answer me for hisself?"

Ignoring this, she went on, more gently: "He got cut on the forehead, but it ain't nothing to worry about."

"You call a doctor? How you know it ain't nothing to worry about?"

"Is you got money to be throwing away on doctors? No, I ain't called no doctor. Ain't nothing wrong with my eyes that I can't tell whether he's hurt bad or not. He got a fright more'n anything else, and you ought to pray God it teaches him a lesson."

"You got a lot to say *now,*" he said, "but I'll have *me* something to say in a minute. I'll be wanting to know when all this happened, what you was doing with your eyes *then.*" He turned back to Roy, who had lain quietly sobbing eyes wide open and body held rigid: and who now, at his father's touch, remembered the height, the sharp, sliding rock beneath his feet, the sun, the explosion of the sun, his plunge into darkness and his salty blood; and recoiled, beginning to scream, as his father touched his forehead. "Hold still, hold still," crooned his father, shaking, "hold still. Don't cry. Daddy ain't going to hurt you, he just wants to see this bandage, see what they've done to his little man." But Roy continued to scream and would not be still and Gabriel dared not lift the bandage for fear of hurting him more. And he

Grammar and Language *Minilesson*

Double Negatives In this story, the characters' dialect includes the use of double negatives, as when Elizabeth says, "he didn't have no business. . . ." Explain that clauses should not include more than one negative. Common negatives include *none, never, nothing, hardly, scarcely,* and *barely.* Students should also be aware of contractions constructed with negatives and expressions formed with *but,* such

as, "I can't help but go." Emphasize that many of the double negatives in the story are formed with the word *ain't,* which is both nonstandard English and a negative.

Activity Ask students to work in teams to identify and write sentences from the story that contain double negatives. Have the teams rewrite those sentences correctly. Then have teams meet and compare results. **L2** **COLLAB. LEARN.**

Additional Resources

Grammar and Language Transparency 64

Grammar and Language Workbook, p. 203

Grammar and Composition Handbook, Lesson 8.6

Writer's Choice, Lesson 18.6

looked at Elizabeth in fury: "Can't you put that child down and help me with this boy? John, take your baby sister from your mother—don't look like neither of you got good sense."

John took Delilah and sat down with her in the easy chair. His mother bent over Roy, and held him still, while his father, carefully—but still Roy screamed—lifted the bandage and stared at the wound. Roy's sobs began to lessen. Gabriel readjusted the bandage. "You see," said Elizabeth, finally, "he ain't nowhere near dead."

"It sure ain't your fault that he ain't dead." He and Elizabeth considered each other for a moment in silence. "He came mightly close to losing an eye. Course, his eyes ain't as big as your'n, so I reckon you don't think it matters so much." At this her face hardened; he smiled. "Lord, have mercy," he said, "you think you ever going to learn to do right? Where was you when all this happened? Who let him go downstairs?"

"Ain't nobody let him go downstairs, he just went. He got a head just like his father, it got to be broken before it'll bow. I was in the kitchen."

"Where was Johnnie?"

"He was in here?"

"Where?"

"He was on the fire escape."

"Didn't he know Roy was downstairs?"

"I reckon."

"What you mean, you reckon? He ain't got your big eyes for nothing, does he?" He looked over at John. "Boy, you see your brother go downstairs?"

"Gabriel, ain't no sense in trying to blame Johnnie. You know right well if you have trouble making Roy behave, he ain't going to listen to his brother. He don't hardly listen to me."

"How come you didn't tell your mother Roy was downstairs?"

John said nothing, staring at the blanket which covered Delilah.

"Boy, you hear me? You want me to take a strap to you?"

"No, you ain't," she said. "You ain't going to take no strap to this boy, not today you ain't. Ain't a soul to blame for Roy's lying up there now but you—you because you done spoiled him so that he thinks he can do just anything and get away with it. I'm here to tell you that ain't no way to raise no child. You don't pray to the Lord to help you do better than you been doing, you going to live to shed bitter tears that the Lord didn't take his soul today." And she was trembling. She moved, unseeing, toward John and took Delilah from his arms. She looked back at Gabriel, who had risen, who stood near the sofa, staring at her. And she found in his face not fury alone, which would not have surprised her; but hatred so deep as to become insupportable in its lack of personality. His eyes were struck alive, unmoving, blind with malevolence—she felt, like the pull of the earth at her feet, his longing to witness her perdition.[5] Again, as though it might be propitiation,[6] she moved the child in her arms. And at this his eyes changed, he looked at Elizabeth, the mother of his children, the helpmeet given by the Lord. Then her eyes clouded; she moved to leave the room; her foot struck the lunchbox lying on the floor.

"John," she said, "pick up your father's lunchbox like a good boy."

She heard, behind her, his scrambling movement as he left the easy chair, the scrape and jangle of the lunchbox as he picked it up, bending his dark head near the toe of his father's heavy shoe.

---

5. *Perdition* (pər dish′ ən) means "the loss of one's soul and of heavenly salvation" or "eternal damnation."
6. *Propitiation* is a pleasing act intended to soothe, pacify, or win favor.

N Literary Elements

FOIL How is John serving as a foil for Gabriel? *(John's meekness and terror show in contrast to the violence and anger of Gabriel.)*

O Critical Thinking

PARAPHRASING Have students paraphrase what happens at the end of the story and explain its significance. *(Elizabeth stands up to Gabriel, protecting John. His response, despite her status as the mother of his children and his "help-meet given by the Lord," is initially one of absolute hatred. John, at the end, symbolically bows to Gabriel's shoe, trapped under his domination.)*

Thematic Focus

Personal Discoveries Have students identify a personal discovery each of the following characters makes in "The Rockpile": John, Roy, Elizabeth, Gabriel. Are any of the discoveries uplifting or hopeful?

✔ ASSESSMENT OPTIONS

📁 *Quick Checks,* p. 104

REAL-WORLD CONNECTION

1930s Harlem The setting of "The Rockpile" is Harlem, probably in the 1930s, but the events in the story, the emotions of the characters, and the painful family dynamic stretch across time and place.

Activity Have students, working in small groups, list elements of "The Rockpile" that are not unique to the setting but that exist in today's world as well. Discuss with the class how such universality is a fundamental quality of good literature. Invite students to explain why this is true. **L2** COLLAB. LEARN.

Personal Response

Most students will find the ending of the story depressing; they may feel that John's treatment is demeaning and unfair.

ANALYZING LITERATURE

1. The rockpile is "a mass of natural rock jutting out of the ground." Children play and fight on it.
2. The family see themselves as religious and upstanding; the children are not allowed to play with the other children on the rockpile.
3. Roy decides to sneak away and play on the rockpile. John tries to persuade Roy not to go. Roy is hit in the head and cut and must be carried back home by adults.
4. He is Roy's father and John's stepfather.
5. His emotions change from anger to malevolence.
6. It is a place of adventure, excitement, and fun. Perhaps John won't allow himself the temptation because his spirit has been suppressed by Gabriel.
7. The rockpile and the world outside the family are mysterious, unknown, and somewhat dangerous. Therefore both are frightening yet alluring.
8. Most students will not blame John for Roy's actions. John tried to dissuade him from going, and he can't be expected to tattle on his brother.
9. John is his mother's biological child, and she feels sympathetic toward him. John is his father's stepchild and represents his wife's past life, which Gabriel despises.
10. Although the mother stands up to the father, tension remains between them.
11. The author may use this tactic to surprise the reader or to let the reader compare his or her own conclusions about the first part of the story to its actual explanation.
12. The father's return home and his harsh actions are foreshadowed. The effect is to create suspense.
13. It may symbolize a life of freedom outside the stifling home environment and the father's domination.
14. The setting is fundamental to the story, although the characters' emotions and conflicts are universal. The author paints a drab picture of unhappy, discordant families.

Responding to Literature

Personal Response

How did you react to the ending of this story?

——— ANALYZING LITERATURE ———

RECALL

1. What was the rockpile? What usually happened on the rockpile?
2. In what ways does the family in the story see themselves as different from others in the neighborhood?
3. What does Roy decide to do that he should not do? What is John's reaction? What happens to Roy?
4. What important fact is revealed about the father just before he arrives?
5. Describe the father's changing emotions toward his wife.

INTERPRET

6. Why might the rockpile seem to call out to Roy? Why might John not be tempted by the rockpile?
7. How, in your opinion, does the difference between John and Roy's family and others affect the brothers' attitudes toward the rockpile? toward the world outside their family?
8. Do you think John can be blamed for what has happened to Roy?
9. Why, do you think, do John's mother and father disagree over whether John can be blamed for what happens to his brother?
10. Do you think the **conflict** between the father and mother is resolved by the end of the story? Explain. (See Literary Terms Handbook, page R3.)

EVALUATE AND CONNECT

11. The author does not tell the reader an important fact about the father until well into the story. Why do you think the author uses this tactic and what effect did it have on you as a reader?
12. Using **foreshadowing**, a writer provides hints to something that will occur later in the story. In your opinion, what event or events are foreshadowed in this story? What effect does this foreshadowing have on the story? Explain, using details from the selection.
13. What do you think the rockpile symbolizes? Explain.
14. How important is the **setting** (see page R14) to the story? What picture of life does the author create with this setting?
15. Think about your response to the Focus Activity on page 864. How does John's experience compare with the one you described?

Foil

In literature a **foil** is a character who is used as a contrast with a second character. The purpose of a foil is to highlight a particular quality of the second character. Although "The Rockpile" may appear to be about Roy, it actually tells just as much or more about John. The reader gets a clearer understanding of both John and Roy through the many contrasts presented between them, including the differences in their parents' reactions to them.

1. Explain how John and Roy differ in terms of their status within the family.
2. Name two more differences between John and Roy. Explain how these differences help the reader see both characters more clearly.
3. Who else might be a foil in this story? Support your response with evidence from the selection.

● See **Literary Terms Handbook**, p. R6.

15. Like John, students may have been witness to misbehavior that they were powerless or unwilling to prevent.

LITERARY ELEMENTS

1. As a stepson John doesn't benefit from Gabriel's love, support, and encouragement as does Gabriel's biological son, Roy.
2. Roy is adventuresome; John is not. Roy is brash; John is thoughtful. The differences are clear in the boys' actions and words.
3. Gabriel is a foil to Elizabeth, who is kind in contrast to Gabriel's harshness. Similarly, Gabriel is domineering in contrast to John's meekness.

Additional Resources

 Literary Elements Transparency 87

LITERATURE AND WRITING

Writing About Literature

Identify Conflict   The plot of "The Rockpile" includes several **conflicts.** Remember that conflicts can be **external** or **internal.** Conflicts exist when a character struggles with another person, with himself or herself, with nature, with society, or with fate. Write a one-page analysis of the conflicts in this story, describing each conflict and telling how it affects the outcome of the story.

Personal Writing

Your Own "Rockpile"   Was there a "rockpile" in your childhood, or at least something like it? Is it the source of good memories, bad memories, or a mixture of both? In your journal, describe the "rockpile" in your own past. Tell how it helped make you the person you are today.

EXTENDING YOUR RESPONSE

Literature Groups

Defend Yourself   In your group, discuss how each character in the story might explain or defend his or her actions. For example, how might John explain why he did not tell his mother that Roy had gone to the rockpile? How might the father explain his reactions against Roy, John, and Elizabeth? Compile a list of your group's explanations and compare it with lists from other groups.

Internet Connection

Harlem on the Web   Use your research skills to locate four or more Web sites that present a picture of Harlem in the 1930s—what it looked like and what was going on

there. Record each address, visit the site, and write a summary of the information that can be found there.

Performing

Later That Day   With a partner, write a conversation that might have occurred later on the same day between John and Roy. What might they have spoken about? What attitudes might they have had toward each other, toward the "rockpile" event, or toward their parents' reactions? Practice reading the conversation dramatically; then, when you are ready, perform it for the class.

 Save your work for your portfolio.

VOCABULARY • **Analogies**

Analogies are comparisons based on relationships between words and ideas. Some analogies are based on a relationship of *manner,* for example:

whisper : talk :: tap : hit

To *whisper* is to *talk* in a gentle manner; to *tap* is to *hit* in a gentle manner.

To finish an analogy, decide on the relationship represented by the first two words. Then apply that relationship to the second set of words.

● For more on analogies, see **Communications Skills Handbook,** p. R83.

Choose the pair that best completes each analogy.

1. clamber : climb ::
   a. jump : leap
   b. run : jog
   c. creep : cringe
   d. strut : sway
   e. stroll : walk

2. loiter : stand ::
   a. dawdle : rush
   b. wander : travel
   c. wait : linger
   d. visit : depart
   e. search : ramble

Writing About Literature

Students' conflict analyses should
- identify and correctly classify all of the conflicts in the story, such as John's internal conflict about Roy's actions; the external conflict between John and his father; the external conflict between the family's values and those of their community; Elizabeth's internal conflict as she must keep harmony in the family; and the external conflict between Elizabeth and Gabriel.
- accurately describe each conflict and its effect on the story's outcome.

Personal Writing

Students' journal entries should
- describe the "rockpile" of their own childhoods, which may be any "forbidden" place.
- explore the memories they associate with it.

EXTENDING YOUR RESPONSE

Literature Groups   Have students expand on the activity by evaluating the explanations and determining whether the actions are, in fact, justified. **COLLAB. LEARN.**

Internet Connection   Help students create keywords that combine the time and the place about which they are seeking information.

Performing   Remind students that the dialogue and attitudes of the characters should be in keeping with what is presented in the selection. **COLLAB. LEARN.**

VOCABULARY • Analogies

1. e   2. b

Additional Resources
📁 *Vocabulary Practice,* p. 50

✔ **ASSESSMENT OPTIONS**

📁 *Quick Checks,* p. 104

📁 *Selection and Theme Assessment,* pp. 155–156

📁 *Performance Assessment,* p. 88

💾 *Testmaker*

Before Reading

Objectives

- To read a short story about one young man's search for a wife
- To identify and evaluate the effect of dialect on characterization
- To write an essay about a love relationship in a short story

Skills

Reading/Thinking: Interpreting; Comparing and Contrasting; Making Critical Judgments; Inferring; Drawing Conclusions

Writing: Extended Definition; Evaluating Elements; Story

Vocabulary: Word Families; Word Meaning; Latin Roots *ami*, *anim*, and *ama* (*amo*)

Grammar/Language: Subject Complements

Listening/Speaking: Reading Dialogue

Life Skills: Decision Making; Dating Service Brochure

Collaboration: Literature Groups

Before You Read

The Magic Barrel

Meet Bernard Malamud

"People say I write so much about misery, but you write about what you know best."

—*Malamud*

Bernard Malamud was born to Russian Jewish immigrants who worked sixteen hours a day in their small grocery store on New York City's East Side. Reflecting on his childhood, he would recall that there were no books in his home, no records or musical instruments, and no pictures on the walls. He would, however, recall the generosity of his father, who bought him the twenty-volume *Book of Knowledge* when he was a nine-year-old recovering from pneumonia.

Malamud grew to become one of America's foremost writers. Most of the characters in his stories and novels are Jewish, but Malamud thought of Jewishness as a spiritual condition rather than his cultural heritage or a religious creed. To be Jewish, he felt, was to struggle with life's limitations and responsibilities. Malamud said that he wrote about Jews "because they set my imagination going. I know something about their history, the quality of experience and belief, and of their literature, though not as much as I would like."

Malamud's first novel, written when he was in his late thirties, was *The Natural*, the story of the rise and fall of a baseball player. The novel was later made into a popular movie starring Robert Redford. Malamud won highest acclaim, however, as a writer of short stories, and "The Magic Barrel" is considered one of his best.

Bernard Malamud was born in 1914 and died in 1986.

FOCUS ACTIVITY

How would you choose a spouse? Would you make a list of qualities you wanted, or would you simply rely on a gut feeling?

FREEWRITE Write about ways you think would be best to meet a spouse and about ways you've heard of.

SETTING A PURPOSE Read to learn of one young man's search for a wife.

BACKGROUND

The Time and Place

"The Magic Barrel" takes place in New York City, probably during the 1950s. Between 1880 and 1914, about two million Jews from eastern Europe immigrated to the United States. The largest concentration of Jewish immigrants settled on the Lower East Side of Manhattan. They brought with them their culture and traditions, which included the use of matchmakers, people paid to bring young men and women together for the purpose of marriage.

VOCABULARY PREVIEW

meager (mē′ gər) *adj.* deficient in quantity or completeness; p. 875
amiable (ā′ mē ə bəl) *adj.* friendly; p. 876
animated (an′ ə mā′ tid) *adj.* full of life; active; lively; p. 876
enamored (en am′ ərd) *adj.* inspired with love; charmed; captivated; p. 881
abjectly (ab jekt′ lē) *adv.* in a humiliating, mean, or degrading manner; p. 882
affirm (ə furm′) *v.* to declare firmly; to assert; p. 885

Portrait of Abraham Wolkowitz, 1907. Max Weber. Oil on canvas, 25 x 30⅛ in. The Brooklyn Museum, New York.

The Magic Barrel

Bernard Malamud ∿

NOT LONG AGO THERE LIVED IN UPTOWN New York in a small, almost <u>meager</u> room, though crowded with books, Leo Finkle, a rabbinical student in the Yeshivah University.[1] Finkle, after six years of study, was to be ordained in June and had been advised by an acquaintance that he might find it easier to win himself a congregation if he were married.

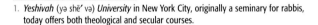

1. *Yeshivah* (yə shē′ və) *University* in New York City, originally a seminary for rabbis, today offers both theological and secular courses.

Vocabulary
meager (mē′ gər) *adj.* deficient in quantity or completeness

SUMMARY

Young Leo Finkle is a rabbinical student who wants to marry to improve his chances of getting a congregation. With no prospects, he asks Pinye Salzman, a marriage broker, for help. Finkle rejects all of Salzman's prospects except one. His date with Lily Hirschorn makes him realize that he has never truly loved anyone but his parents. Later, Finkle finds a girl's photograph in a group left by Salzman and directs his love toward her. Salzman at first refuses to introduce the two because the girl is his daughter. Eventually he consents.

📁 *Spanish Summaries,* p. 95

Ⓐ Active Reading

PREDICT Ask students to discuss the information presented in the opening paragraph that will help them predict the plot. *(The exposition reveals setting, protagonist, and motivation.)* Ask students to write predictions and to check them as they read.

Additional Resources
📁 *Active Reading Guide,* p. 105
🎧 *Audio Library*
🎧 *Spanish Audio Library*

Teaching Options

CONNECTING TO OTHER SELECTIONS

The chart at the right shows three ways to connect "The Magic Barrel" to selections in this book.

For specific teaching strategies, see the *Unit Six Planning Guide,* pp. 92–93.

Connection	Title
Life Skills: Planning and Designing	→ from *My Bondage and My Freedom,* p. 330
Thematic: Self-Discovery	→ "The Bridal Party," p. 652
Literary: Foreshadowing	→ from *His Promised Land,* p. 350

B Literary Elements

CHARACTERIZATION The author paints a striking portrait of Salzman. Ask students what the author also reveals about his personality. *(He is amiable but deeply sad.)*

C Literary Elements

CHARACTERIZATION Salzman detects an "apology" in Finkle's explanation. Ask students if they have the same reaction. What does it reveal about Finkle's character? *(Finkle goes to great lengths to explain and justify his decision. He has thought about it a great deal—earlier, the author speaks of his "two tormenting days of turning it over in his mind"—and so may be embarrassed and self-conscious about his decision.)*

D Critical Thinking

INTERPRETING Challenge students to draw on their prior knowledge to explain the symbolism in this sentence.

Model: The moon has long symbolized love. This makes sense, since Finkle is hoping to gain love for himself. I also think the image of the hen laying an egg, since it is in the same sentence, might also carry a symbolic meaning. The image is one of birth, and it may be that Finkle hopes to have children with the wife he finds. At any rate, if the moon symbolizes love, and it is being laid like an egg, I'm at least sure that the sentence refers to the birth of love.

Teaching Options

Since he had no present prospects of marriage, after two tormented days of turning it over in his mind, he called in Pinye Salzman, a marriage broker whose two-line advertisement he had read in the *Forward*.[2]

The matchmaker appeared one night out of the dark fourth-floor hallway of the graystone rooming house where Finkle lived, grasping a black, strapped portfolio that had been worn thin with use. Salzman, who had been long in the business, was of slight but dignified build, wearing an old hat, and an overcoat too short and tight for him. He smelled frankly of fish, which he loved to eat, and although he was missing a few teeth, his presence was not displeasing, because of an <u>amiable</u> manner curiously contrasted with mournful eyes. His voice, his lips, his wisp of beard, his bony fingers were <u>animated</u>, but give him a moment of repose and his mild blue eyes revealed a depth of sadness, a characteristic that put Leo a little at ease although the situation, for him, was inherently tense.

He at once informed Salzman why he had asked him to come, explaining that his home was in Cleveland, and that but for his parents, who had married comparatively late in life, he was alone in the world. He had for six years devoted himself almost entirely to his studies, as a result of which, understandably, he had found himself without time for a social life and the company of young women. Therefore he thought it the better part of trial and error—of embarrassing fumbling—to call in an experienced person to advise him on these matters. He remarked in passing that the function of the marriage broker was ancient and honorable, highly approved in the Jewish community, because it made practical the necessary without

hindering joy. Moreover, his own parents had been brought together by a matchmaker. They had made, if not a financially profitable marriage—since neither had possessed any worldly goods to speak of—at least a successful one in the sense of their everlasting devotion to each other. Salzman listened in embarrassed surprise, sensing a sort of apology. Later, however, he experienced a glow of pride in his work, an emotion that had left him years ago, and he heartily approved of Finkle.

The two went to their business. Leo had led Salzman to the only clear place in the room, a table near a window that overlooked the lamp-lit city. He seated himself at the matchmaker's side but facing him, attempting by an act of will to suppress the unpleasant tickle in his throat. Salzman eagerly unstrapped his portfolio and removed a loose rubber band from a thin packet of much-handled cards. As he flipped through them, a gesture and sound that physically hurt Leo, the student pretended not to see and gazed steadfastly out the window. Although it was still February, winter was on its last legs, signs of which he had for the first time in years begun to notice. He now observed the round white moon, moving high in the sky through a cloud menagerie,[3] and watched with half-open mouth as it penetrated a huge hen, and dropped out of her like an egg laying itself. Salzman, though pretending through eyeglasses he had just slipped on, to be engaged in scanning the writing on the cards, stole occasional glances at the young man's distinguished face, noting with pleasure the long, severe scholar's nose, brown eyes heavy with learning, sensitive yet ascetic[4] lips, and

---

2. The Yiddish-language newspaper the *Jewish Daily Forward* was published daily in New York.

3. A *menagerie* (mi naj′ ər ē) is a collection of wild or unusual animals.

4. Here, *ascetic* means "severe" or "stern."

Vocabulary
amiable (ā′ mē ə bəl) *adj.* friendly
animated (an′ ə mā′ tid) *adj.* full of life; active; lively

Reading *Minilesson*

Comparing and Contrasting There are two main characters in "The Magic Barrel": Leo Finkle and Pinye Salzman. Explain to students that comparing and contrasting two characters often leads to a better understanding of each as well as to better insight into the theme and plot of a piece of literature.

Activity Have students create a Venn diagram like the one shown to compare and contrast Leo Finkle and Pinye Salzman. They should list character traits unique to each character in areas where the circles do not overlap. Where the circles overlap, students should identify traits the two characters have in common. **L2**

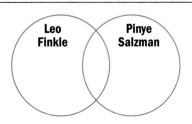

Leo Finkle   Pinye Salzman

Additional Resources
📁 *Reading Workbook,* pp. 79–80

Bernard Malamud :~

a certain, almost hollow quality of the dark cheeks. He gazed around at shelves upon shelves of books and let out a soft, contented sigh.

When Leo's eyes fell upon the cards, he counted six spread out in Salzman's hand.

"So few?" he asked in disappointment.

"You wouldn't believe me how much cards I got in my office," Salzman replied. "The drawers are already filled to the top, so I keep them now in a barrel, but is every girl good for a new rabbi?"

Leo blushed at this, regretting all he had revealed of himself in a curriculum vitae[5] he had sent to Salzman. He had thought it best to acquaint him with his strict standards and specifications, but in having done so, felt he had told the marriage broker more than was absolutely necessary.

He hesitantly inquired, "Do you keep photographs of your clients on file?"

"First comes family, amount of dowry,[6] also what kind promises," Salzman replied, unbuttoning his tight coat and settling himself in the chair. "After comes pictures, rabbi."

"Call me Mr. Finkle. I'm not yet a rabbi."

Salzman said he would, but instead called him doctor, which he changed to rabbi when Leo was not listening too attentively.

Salzman adjusted his horn-rimmed spectacles, gently cleared his throat and read in an eager voice the contents of the top card:

"Sophie P. Twenty-four years. Widow one year. No children. Educated high school and two years college. Father promises eight thousand

Salzman hunched his shoulders in an almost imperceptible gesture of disappointment.

dollars. Has wonderful wholesale business. Also real estate. On the mother's side comes teachers, also one actor. Well known on Second Avenue."

Leo gazed up in surprise. "Did you say a widow?"

"A widow don't mean spoiled, rabbi. She lived with her husband maybe four months. He was a sick boy she made a mistake to marry him."

"Marrying a widow has never entered my mind."

"This is because you have no experience. A widow, especially if she is young and healthy like this girl, is a wonderful person to marry. She will be thankful to you the rest of her life. Believe me, if I was looking now for a bride, I would marry a widow."

Leo reflected, then shook his head.

Salzman hunched his shoulders in an almost imperceptible gesture of disappointment. He placed the card down on the wooden table and began to read another:

"Lily H. High school teacher. Regular. Not a substitute. Has savings and new Dodge car. Lived in Paris one year. Father is successful dentist thirty-five years. Interested in professional man. Well Americanized family. Wonderful opportunity."

"I knew her personally," said Salzman. "I wish you could see this girl. She is a doll. Also very intelligent. All day you could talk to her about books and theyater[7] and what not. She also knows current events."

"I don't believe you mentioned her age?"

"Her age?" Salzman said, raising his brows. "Her age is thirty-two years."

Leo said after a while, "I'm afraid that seems a little too old."

5. A *curriculum vitae* (kə rik′ yə ləm   vē′ tī) is a summary of a person's education and work experience, usually given to a prospective employer. Finkle has provided Salzman with a summary of the "highlights" of his life.
6. A *dowry* is money or property a woman brings to her husband at the time of marriage.

7. *Theyater* is the way Salzman is pronouncing the word "theater."

H Critical Thinking

INFERRING Here and elsewhere Finkle rushes Salzman. Why does he do this? *(He is embarrassed by the situation and is uncomfortable about looking for a spouse in an almost clinical way. He doesn't like the choice offered him and doesn't want to know more.)*

VIEWING THE PAINTING

William Gropper (1897–1977) grew up in New York City in great poverty. He managed to escape this condition when his sidewalk chalk paintings were discovered, which allowed him to go to art school. He later began his professional career as a cartoonist for the *New York Tribune*.

Viewing Response *The men in the painting appear to have a friendly or collegial relationship; there is nothing to indicate the tension of Finkle and Salzman's relationship.*

Salzman let out a laugh. "So how old are you, rabbi?"

"Twenty-seven."

"So what is the difference, tell me, between twenty-seven and thirty-two? My own wife is seven years older than me. So what did I suffer?—Nothing. If Rothschild's[8] a daughter wants to marry you, would you say on account her age, no?"

"Yes," Leo said dryly.

Salzman shook off the no in the yes. "Five years don't mean a thing. I give you my word that when you will live with her for one week you will forget her age. What does it mean five years—that she lived more and knows more than somebody who is younger? On this girl, God bless her, years are not wasted. Each one that it comes makes better the bargain."

---

8. The *Rothschilds* were a prominent, wealthy Jewish family.

Memoir, c. 1960. William Gropper. Watercolor. Marcus Gilden Collection.
Viewing the painting: What do you think the relationship might be between the two men in the painting? Do you think Finkle and Salzman have a similar relationship? Why or why not?

"What subject does she teach in high school?"

"Languages. If you heard the way she speaks French, you will think it is music. I am in the business twenty-five years, and I recommend her with my whole heart. Believe me, I know what I'm talking, rabbi."

"What's on the next card?" Leo said abruptly.

Salzman reluctantly turned up the third card:

"Ruth K. Nineteen years. Honor student. Father offers thirteen thousand cash to the right bridegroom. He is a medical doctor. Stomach specialist with marvelous practice. Brother-in-law owns own garment business. Particular people."

Salzman looked as if he had read his trump card.

"Did you say nineteen?" Leo asked with interest.

"On the dot."

"Is she attractive?" He blushed. "Pretty?"

Salzman kissed his finger tips. "A little doll. On this I give you my word. Let me call the father tonight and you will see what means pretty."

But Leo was troubled. "You're sure she's that young?"

"This I am positive. The father will show you the birth certificate."

"Are you positive there isn't something wrong with her?" Leo insisted.

"Who says there is wrong?"

"I don't understand why an American girl her age should go to a marriage broker."

A smile spread over Salzman's face.

"So for the same reason you went, she comes."

Teaching Options

Grammar and Language *Minilesson*

Subject Complements There are two types of subject complements, predicate nominatives and predicate adjectives. A noun which follows a linking verb and renames the subject of the sentence is called a predicate nominative. It completes the subject by further identifying that subject. *My father is a lawyer.* The word *lawyer* refers to the same person as *father*. Predicate adjectives also follow

linking verbs, and describe the subject. *The horse was beautiful.* The term *beautiful* describes the subject, horse.

Activity Ask students to write five sentences describing one of the characters in the story. Their sentences should use both kinds of subject complements. Students may exchange papers with a partner to check their accuracy. **L2**

Additional Resources

📖 *Grammar and Language Transparency 65*

📘 *Grammar and Language Workbook,* p. 81

📘 *Grammar and Composition Handbook,* Lesson 2.5

📘 *Writer's Choice,* Lesson 11.5

Bernard Malamud ⸻

Leo flushed. "I am pressed for time."

Salzman, realizing he had been tactless, quickly explained. "The father came, not her. He wants she should have the best, so he looks around himself. When we will locate the right boy he will introduce him and encourage. This makes a better marriage than if a young girl without experience takes for herself. I don't have to tell you this."

"But don't you think this young girl believes in love?" Leo spoke uneasily.

Salzman was about to guffaw but caught himself and said soberly, "Love comes with the right person, not before."

Leo parted dry lips but did not speak. Noticing that Salzman had snatched a glance at the next card, he cleverly asked, "How is her health?"

"Perfect," Salzman said, breathing with difficulty. "Of course, she is a little lame on her right foot from an auto accident that it happened to her when she was twelve years, but nobody notices on account she is so brilliant and also beautiful."

Leo got up heavily and went to the window. He felt curiously bitter and upbraided himself for having called in the marriage broker. Finally, he shook his head.

"Why not?" Salzman persisted, the pitch of his voice rising.

"Because I detest stomach specialists."

"So what do you care what is his business? After you marry her do you need him? Who says he must come every Friday night in your house?"

Ashamed of the way the talk was going, Leo dismissed Salzman, who went home with heavy, melancholy eyes.

Though he had felt only relief at the marriage broker's departure, Leo was in low spirits the next day. He explained it as arising from Salzman's failure to produce a suitable bride for him. He did not care for his type of clientele. But when Leo found himself hesitating whether to seek out another matchmaker, one more polished than Pinye, he wondered if it could be—his protestations to the contrary, and although he honored his father and mother—that he did not, in essence, care for the match making institution? This thought he quickly put out of mind yet found himself still upset. All day he ran around in the woods[9]—missed an important appointment, forgot to give out his laundry, walked out of a Broadway cafeteria without paying and had to run back with the ticket in his hand; had even not recognized his landlady in the street when she passed with a friend and courteously called out, "A good evening to you, Doctor Finkle." By nightfall, however, he had regained sufficient calm to sink his nose into a book and there found peace from his thoughts.

Almost at once there came a knock on the door. Before Leo could say enter, Salzman, commercial cupid, was standing in the room. His face was gray and meager, his expression hungry, and he looked as if he would expire on his feet. Yet the marriage broker managed, by some trick of the muscles, to display a broad smile.

"So good evening. I am invited?"

Leo nodded, disturbed to see him again, yet unwilling to ask the man to leave.

Beaming still, Salzman laid his portfolio on the table. "Rabbi, I got for you tonight good news."

"I've asked you not to call me rabbi. I'm still a student."

"Your worries are finished. I have for you a first-class bride."

"Leave me in peace concerning this subject." Leo pretended lack of interest.

"The world will dance at your wedding."

"Please, Mr. Salzman, no more."

"But first must come back my strength," Salzman said weakly. He fumbled with the portfolio straps and took out of the leather case an oily paper bag, from which he extracted a hard, seeded roll and a small, smoked white fish. With a quick motion of his hand he stripped the fish

---

9. *[ran . . . woods]* Here, this phrase means that Finkle "was nervous and distracted."

❶ Critical Thinking

COMPARING AND CONTRASTING Have students compare this description of Salzman with the way he was described during his first appearance at Finkle's home. *(The first description alludes to his age and frailty but emphasizes positive qualities. This description is more negative, though Salzman is still said to be smiling.)*

❶ Literary Elements

DIALECT Point out the inverted syntax typical of a dialect influenced by Yiddish. Have students point out other, similar examples in the story.

MEETING INDIVIDUAL NEEDS — MULTIPLE LEARNING STYLES

Interpersonal Interpersonal learners learn especially well through cooperation and collaboration.

Activity Invite students to explore the characters of Finkle and Salzman by improvising conversations between them. Have students work in groups to discuss the two main characters and identify their attitudes, motivations, and speech patterns. Then have two students take the roles of the characters and have a conversation. The rest of the group should analyze and critique the conversation. Students should then rotate so that everyone has a chance to perform and to critique. What new aspects of Finkle and Salzman have students discovered? **L2 COLLAB. LEARN.**

out of its skin and began ravenously to chew. "All day in a rush," he muttered.

Leo watched him eat.

"A sliced tomato you have maybe?" Salzman hesitantly inquired.

"No."

K The marriage broker shut his eyes and ate. When he had finished he carefully cleaned up the crumbs and rolled up the remains of the fish, in the paper bag. His spectacled eyes roamed the room until he discovered, amid some piles of books, a one-burner gas stove. Lifting his hat he humbly asked, "A glass tea you got, rabbi?"

Conscience-stricken, Leo rose and brewed the tea. He served it with a chunk of lemon and two cubes of lump sugar, delighting Salzman.

After he had drunk his tea, Salzman's strength and good spirits were restored.

"So tell me, rabbi," he said amiably, "you considered some more the three clients I mentioned yesterday?"

"There was no need to consider."

"Why not?"

"None of them suits me."

"What then suits you?"

Leo let it pass because he could give only a confused answer.

Without waiting for a reply, Salzman asked, "You remember this girl I talked to you—the high school teacher?"

"Age thirty-two?"

But, surprisingly, Salzman's face lit in a smile. "Age twenty-nine."

Leo shot him a look. "Reduced from thirty-two?"

"A mistake," Salzman avowed. "I talked today with the dentist. He took me to his safety deposit box and showed me the birth certificate. She was twenty-nine years last August. They made her a party in the mountains where she went for her vacation. When her father spoke to me the first time I forgot to write the age and I told you thirty-two, but now I remember this was a different client, a widow."

"The same one you told me about? I thought she was twenty-four?"

"A different. Am I responsible that the world is filled with widows?"

"No, but I'm not interested in them, nor for that matter, in school teachers."

Salzman pulled his clasped hands to his breast. Looking at the ceiling he devoutly exclaimed, "Yiddishe kinder,[10] what can I say to somebody that he is not interested in high school teachers? So what then you are interested?"

Leo flushed but controlled himself.

"In what else will you be interested," Salzman went on, "if you not interested in this fine girl that she speaks four languages and has personally in the bank ten thousand dollars? Also her father guarantees further twelve thousand. Also she has new car, wonderful clothes, talks on all subjects, and she will give you a first-class home and children. How near do we come in our life to paradise?"

"If she's so wonderful, why wasn't she married ten years ago?"

"Why?" said Salzman with a heavy laugh. "—Why? Because she is *partikiler*.[11] This is why. She wants the *best*."

L Leo went silent, amused at how he had entangled himself. But Salzman had aroused his interest in Lily H., and he began seriously to consider calling on her. When the marriage broker observed how intently Leo's mind was at work on the facts he had supplied, he felt certain they would soon come to an agreement.

M Late Saturday afternoon, conscious of Salzman, Leo Finkle walked with Lily Hirschorn along Riverside Drive.[12] He walked briskly and erectly, wearing with

---

10. *Yiddishe kinder* (yid´ ish ə kint´ ər) means "Jewish children" or "Jewish young people."
11. *Partikiler* is the way Salzman is pronouncing the word "particular."
12. *Riverside Drive,* a major road on the west side of Manhattan, runs beside the Hudson River.

LIFE SKILLS CONNECTION

Decision Making Leo Finkle must make a difficult decision: which, if any, of the women should he meet? Like many important decisions, it is difficult to make. However, both Finkle and Salzman seek to determine what suits Finkle. In other words, they are trying to establish criteria on which to base their decision. Explain that establishing criteria is a valuable tool when faced with tough decisions.

Activity Challenge students to create a list of criteria for Finkle based on what they are told and what they can infer about him, his needs, and his desires. Then have them write a statement defining what suits Finkle, suggesting which, if any, of the women he should meet. Have students share their criteria and conclusions in class discussion. **L2**

distinction the black fedora[13] he had that morning taken with trepidation out of the dusty hat box on his closet shelf, and the heavy black Saturday coat he had thoroughly whisked clean. Leo also owned a walking stick, a present from a distant relative, but quickly put temptation aside and did not use it. Lily, petite and not unpretty, had on something signifying the approach of spring. She was au courant[14] animatedly, with all sorts of subjects, and he weighed her words and found her surprisingly sound—score another for Salzman, who he uneasily sensed to be somewhere around, hiding perhaps high in a tree along the street, flashing the lady signals with a pocket mirror; or perhaps a cloven-hoofed Pan, piping nuptial ditties as he danced his invisible way before them, strewing wild buds on the walk and purple grapes in their path, symbolizing fruit of a union, though there was of course still none.

Did You Know?
In Greek mythology, *Pan* was a god of pastures, flocks, and shepherds who was believed to foster reproduction and growth. He was traditionally depicted as a musician who was part man and part goat.

Lily startled Leo by remarking, "I was thinking of Mr. Salzman, a curious figure, wouldn't you say?"

Not certain what to answer, he nodded.

She bravely went on, blushing, "I for one am grateful for his introducing us. Aren't you?"

He courteously replied, "I am."

---

13. A *fedora* (fĭ dôr′ ə) is a soft felt hat with a curved brim and a lengthwise crease in the crown.
14. The French words *au courant* (ō′ kŏŏ rän′) literally mean "in the current" but are most often used to mean "fully informed" or "up-to-date."

"I mean," she said with a little laugh—and it was all in good taste, or at least gave the effect of being not in bad—"do you mind that we came together so?"

He was not displeased with her honesty, recognizing that she meant to set the relationship aright, and understanding that it took a certain amount of experience in life, and courage, to want to do it quite that way. One had to have some sort of past to make that kind of beginning.

He said that he did not mind. Salzman's function was traditional and honorable—valuable for what it might achieve, which, he pointed out, was frequently nothing.

Lily agreed with a sigh. They walked on for a while and she said after a long silence, again with a nervous laugh, "Would you mind if I asked you something a little bit personal? Frankly, I find the subject fascinating." Although Leo shrugged, she went on half embarrassedly, "How was it that you came to your calling? I mean was it a sudden passionate inspiration?"

Leo, after a time, slowly replied, "I was always interested in the Law."

"You saw revealed in it the presence of the Highest?"

He nodded and changed the subject. "I understand that you spent a little time in Paris, Miss Hirschorn?"

"Oh, did Mr. Salzman tell you, Rabbi Finkle?" Leo winced but she went on, "It was ages ago and almost forgotten. I remember I had to return for my sister's wedding."

And Lily would not be put off. "When," she asked in a trembly voice, "did you become enamored of God?"

He stared at her. Then it came to him that she was talking not about Leo Finkle, but of a total stranger, some mystical figure, perhaps even passionate prophet that Salzman had dreamed up for her—no relation to the living

Vocabulary
enamored (en am′ ərd) *adj.* inspired with love; charmed; captivated

---

N **Critical Thinking**

DRAWING CONCLUSIONS Have volunteers interpret this passage for the class. What does it reveal about Finkle's state of mind? *(Finkle is painfully aware of how he came to meet Lily. His awareness of the active role Salzman played not just in bringing them together but in skewing their response to each other has colored the entire experience for him; it seems artificial and false, and it makes him uncomfortable.)*

O **Active Reading**

RESPOND Have students share their opinions about Lily. Is she a likable character? What adjectives would they use to describe her? Does she seem like a good match for Finkle?

Vo•cab•u•lar•y Skills

Word Families Explain that a word family is a group of words derived from the same root. By identifying its root, students can often decipher the meaning of an unfamiliar word. Point out that the root word for *enamored* is the Latin *ama* or *amo*, meaning "love." Have students brainstorm a list of words with the same root. Then have them check a dictionary to see if the words really belong to the same word family.

INTERDISCIPLINARY CONNECTION

Geography The setting of "The Magic Barrel" is New York City. Explain to students that such settings help make fiction more realistic, and that by locating these settings on a real map, they can bring the story to life for themselves.

Activity Have students make a list of all the specific places mentioned in "The Magic Barrel." They should consult a street map of New York City and/or a guide to the city. They can find these in their library or on the Internet. Have students locate each place on their lists on the map. Then ask them to identify other landmarks located nearby—the buildings, parks, and other places that Finkle and Salzman would have known. **L2**

Teaching Options

Literary Elements

CHARACTERIZATION Ask students what this confession means. What does it reveal about Finkle? *(It may be that Finkle is a man longing for meaning in his life, and he has sought this understanding through religious studies. Or perhaps there was a particular event in his life that caused him not to love God. This revelation suggests that Finkle has never been totally honest with himself and that he has questions, anxieties, or personal issues that he has never confronted.)*

Vo•cab•u•lar•y Skills

Word Meaning *Machinations* are crafty schemes or plots, usually of an evil intent.

Author's Craft

IMAGERY The reference to "winged loaves" is curious. Challenge students to explicate it. *(The image is Finkle's soporific, like counting sheep. That he thinks of it at this point reflects his dashed hopes of a relationship with Lily.)*

or dead. Leo trembled with rage and weakness. The trickster had obviously sold her a bill of goods, just as he had him, who'd expected to become acquainted with a young lady of twenty-nine, only to behold, the moment he laid eyes upon her strained and anxious face, a woman past thirty-five and aging rapidly. Only his self control had kept him this long in her presence.

"I am not," he said gravely, "a talented religious person," and in seeking words to go on, found himself possessed by shame and fear. "I think," he said in a strained manner, "that I came to God not because I loved Him, but because I did not."

This confession he spoke harshly because its unexpectedness shook him.

Lily wilted. Leo saw a profusion of loaves of bread go flying like ducks high over his head, not unlike the winged loaves by which he had counted himself to sleep last night. Mercifully, then, it snowed, which he would not put past Salzman's machinations.

He was infuriated with the marriage broker and swore he would throw him out of the room the minute he reappeared. But Salzman did not come that night, and when Leo's anger had subsided,[15] an unaccountable despair grew in its place. At first he thought this was caused by his disappointment in Lily, but before long it became evident that he had involved himself with Salzman without a true knowledge of his own intent. He gradually realized—with an emptiness that seized him with six hands—that he had called in the broker to find him a bride because he was incapable of doing it himself. This terrifying insight he had derived as a result of his meeting and conversation with Lily Hirschorn. Her probing questions had somehow irritated him into

revealing—to himself more than her—the true nature of his relationship to God, and from that it had come upon him, with shocking force, that apart from his parents, he had never loved anyone. Or perhaps it went the other way, that he did not love God so well as he might, because he had not loved man. It seemed to Leo that his whole life stood starkly revealed and he saw himself for the first time as he truly was—unloved and loveless. This bitter but somehow not fully unexpected revelation brought him to a point of panic, controlled only by extraordinary effort. He covered his face with his hands and cried.

The week that followed was the worst of his life. He did not eat and lost weight. His beard darkened and grew ragged. He stopped attending seminars and almost never opened a book. He seriously considered leaving the Yeshivah, although he was deeply troubled at the thought of the loss of all his years of study—saw them like pages torn from a book, strewn over the city—and at the devastating effect of this decision upon his parents. But he had lived without knowledge of himself, and never in the Five Books and all the Commentaries[16]—mea culpa[17]—had the truth been revealed to him. He did not know where to turn, and in all this desolating loneliness there was no *to whom*, although he often thought of Lily but not once could bring himself to go downstairs and make the call. He became touchy and irritable, especially with his landlady, who asked him all manner of personal questions; on the other hand, sensing his own disagreeableness, he waylaid her on the stairs and apologized abjectly, until

---

15. *Subsided* means "decreased in intensity."

16. The Pentateuch (pen′ ta took′), or first *Five Books* of the Hebrew Bible (Genesis, Exodus, Leviticus, Numbers, and Deuteronomy), are known collectively in Judaism as the Torah, or the Law. *Commentaries* provide explanatory and scholarly information about the biblical texts.

17. *Mea culpa* (mā′ ə ˌ kool′ pə) means "my own fault" in Latin.

Vocabulary
abjectly (ab jekt′ lē) *adv.* in a humiliating, mean, or degrading manner

Writing Minilesson

Extended Definition: Love Point out that although we use the word *love* frequently, its meaning is often imprecise. People may love Mexican food, love someone's new car, love their parents, or love a spouse. Each of these uses seems to mean something different. Are there common elements? Can we write a definition that fits all of these uses, or is the word *love* misused in some of these contexts?

Activity Have students write an extended definition of *love,* making sure it does not include things other than love, nor exclude important kinds of love. Have volunteers share and discuss their definitions in the context of "The Magic Barrel." **L2**

Additional Resources

Writer's Choice, Lessons 3.1, 3.3

Before You Read

The Crucible

Meet Arthur Miller

Arthur Miller saw a play for the first time when he was a boy. From that experience, he "learned that there were two kinds of reality, but that of the stage was far more real." Miller began writing plays of his own while in college, but it was not until 1947, when he was thirty-two, that he scored his first major critical success. That year, his play *All My Sons* was produced, received the New York Drama Critics Circle Award, and was sold for movie rights. Two years later, Miller's play *Death of a Salesman* began a highly successful run and received a Pulitzer Prize.

By his late thirties, Miller's work had won him fame. Fame, however, would involve him in a dark chapter of U.S. history. Fear of communism—the "Red Scare"—had taken hold of Americans. Congress established the House Un-American Activities Committee (HUAC) to investigate an alleged communist conspiracy. Among the main targets of the investigation were people in the entertainment business. These people were called before HUAC and asked not only to "confess" to earlier involvement in socialist or communist organizations but also to name others who had held similar views. People who refused to cooperate were often blacklisted, or denied employment.

The way HUAC questioned people and pressured them to testify against their colleagues reminded Miller of the witch trials in colonial America. In the spring of 1952, Miller visited Salem, Massachusetts. On his way, he stopped to visit his friend Elia Kazan. Kazan told Miller that he had been called to testify by HUAC, and that he had decided to save his career by confessing and naming names. Weighed down with his friend's news, Miller went on to Salem to bury himself in what he called "one of the strangest and most awful chapters in human history."

Miller's research inspired him to write *The Crucible*, which was first staged on Broadway in 1953. Its relevance to the political situation of the times was clear, even in other countries. When a Belgian group invited Miller to see its production of *The Crucible* late in 1953, the U.S. State Department refused to renew Miller's passport, so he could not travel abroad. This was Miller's first run-in with the government.

The second came in 1956 when Miller, too, was called to testify before HUAC. When he refused to name names, he was charged with contempt, fined, and sentenced to jail. His case, however, was reversed on appeal in 1958, and he never served a jail term.

In 1965 Miller became the president of P.E.N., an international literary organization. Through P.E.N. he helped free writers in many countries who had been imprisoned for their political views. Miller's most famous works have remained *Death of a Salesman* and *The Crucible*. In fact, on almost any given day, *The Crucible* is being produced somewhere in the world.

"If only we could stop murdering one another we could be a wonderfully humorous species."

"One of the strongest urges in the writer's heart . . . is to reveal what has been hidden and denied."

—*Miller*

Arthur Miller was born in 1915.

THE CRUCIBLE 911

Objectives

- To read and analyze a play about persecution of individuals for religious and personal reasons
- To identify and understand the uses of dialogue
- To write an analysis of exposition in a drama

Skills

Reading/Thinking: Drawing Conclusions; Identifying Cause and Effect; Building Background Knowledge; Evaluating; Interpreting; Identifying Assumptions; Inferring; Summarizing; Comparing and Contrasting; Analyzing; Problem and Solution

Writing: Choosing a Voice; Expository Paragraphs

Vocabulary: Unlocking Meaning

Grammar/Language: Latin Roots; Exclamation Point

Listening/Speaking: Presenting Puritan Theocracy

Life Skills: Goal Setting

Collaboration: Literature Groups

More About Arthur Miller

In his testimony before HUAC, Miller admitted that, as a young man, he had attended meetings at which communist writers were present. However, he denied having applied for membership in the Communist Party. With respect to his refusal to name others, Miller has stated that his decision was based strictly on conscience. Miller believed that the principle of betrayal violated "the norm of good citizenship."

RESOURCE MANAGER

Lesson Planning Resource
The *Unit Six Planning Guide* (pp. 116–126) provides additional lesson notes and reduced versions of all print resources.

📁 **Other Print Resources**
- Active Reading Guide, pp. 108–111
- Vocabulary Practice, pp. 54–57
- Reading Workbook, pp. 81–82
- Grammar and Language Workbook, pp. 243,

233–237, 281, 293
- Grammar and Composition Handbook, Lessons 11.2, 10.1–10.3, 11.1, 13.4
- Quick Checks, pp. 108–111
- Selection and Theme Assessment, pp. 163–170
- Performance Assessment, pp. 92–95
- Spanish Summaries, p. 98
- Inclusion Strategies
- English Language Learners Sourcebook

📄 **Transparencies**
- Selection Focus 98
- Fine Art 1
- Literary Elements 91–94
- Grammar and Language 68–73

Technology
- 💿 Literature Launchers
- 🎧 Audio Library
- 🎧 Spanish Audio Library
- 💻 Glencoe Literature Web Site
- 💾 Testmaker

Motivating

→OPTIONS

Literature Launchers:
"Witch Hunts in American History"

Videodisc Side B, Segment 19 ‖‖‖‖‖‖‖

Also available in VHS.

Selection Focus Transparency 98: Have students view the transparency and then answer the question provided.

Focus Activity: To extend the Focus Activity, you might have students discuss peer pressure and ways in which people either give in to its influence or resist it.

Reading Further

Be sure to review these titles for appropriateness for your class before recommending them to students.

Moss, Leonard. *Arthur Miller.* Boston: Twayne Publishers, 1980. Part of the Twayne's United States authors series.

Huftel, Sheila. *Arthur Miller: The Burning Glass.* New York: The Citadel Press. Penetrating literary analysis with biographical information.

912

Before You Read

— FOCUS ACTIVITY —

Has your character ever been questioned? Or has someone you know or have heard about–perhaps even a character in a TV show or movie–undergone a test of character?

CHART IT! Create a flow chart like the one below to organize the details of that person's test of character.

| Event that led to test: | → | Response: | → | Reactions of others: | → | Outcome: |

SETTING A PURPOSE Read to learn how certain characters deal with their own tests of character.

— BACKGROUND —

The Time and Place

The Crucible takes place in 1692 in and near Salem, a small town in the Massachusetts Bay Colony that had been founded in the early 1600s by a group of Christians called Puritans. The Puritans had fled England for North America to establish a religious community. However, by the 1660s, English merchants had immigrated to the colony, attracted by business opportunities. Most did not share the religious beliefs of the Puritan founders. Against this backdrop, many Puritans felt they were losing hold of their ideals. Their sense of insecurity, frustration, and loss of control helped create a climate of guilt and blame. This climate pervaded the town of Salem and especially nearby Salem Village, where, in the winter of 1691–1692, several teenage girls began behaving strangely. Many people in the community suspected that the girls were victims of witchcraft. These events and the trials that followed form the basis for Miller's play *The Crucible.*

About the Title

A crucible is a pot or vessel commonly made from porcelain or other highly heat-resistant material. For centuries, people have used crucibles for melting metals, such as gold or silver, to test them for purity. In modern times, chemists use crucibles for heating materials in the process of chemical analysis and in conducting chemical reactions that require extremely high temperatures. Today the term *crucible* has also come to mean "a severe test," or "a place or situation in which concentrated forces interact to cause or influence change or development."

— VOCABULARY PREVIEW —

compromise (kom′ prə mīz′) *v.* to endanger the reputation or interests of; to expose to suspicion; p. 916
contention (kən ten′ shən) *n.* verbal argument or struggle; quarreling; p. 917
subservient (səb sur′ vē ənt) *adj.* useful, in an inferior capacity, to promote an end; submissive; p. 919

naive (nä ēv′) *adj.* lacking knowledge of the ways of the world; unsophisticated; innocent; p. 919
pretense (prē′ tens) *n.* a false show or appearance, especially for the purpose of deceiving; falseness; p. 922
evade (i vād′) *v.* to escape or avoid, as by cleverness; p. 931

912 🐾 UNIT 6: MIDCENTURY VOICES

CONNECTING TO OTHER SELECTIONS

The chart at the right shows three ways to connect *The Crucible* to selections in this book.

For specific teaching strategies, see the **Unit Six Planning Guide,** pp. 122–123.

Connection	Title
Life Skills: Synthesizing →	"Let Us Examine the Facts," p. 519
Thematic: Between Heaven and Hell →	"Sinners in the Hands of an Angry God," p. 101
Literary: Tone →	"Crisis #1," p. 155

PARRIS. No, Goody Putnam, it is—

MRS. PUTNAM. [*Glancing at* BETTY.] How high did she fly, how high?

PARRIS. No, no, she never flew—

MRS. PUTNAM. [*Very pleased with it.*] Why, it's sure she did. Mr. Collins saw her goin' over Ingersoll's barn, and come down light as bird, he says!

PARRIS. Now, look you, Goody Putnam, she never—[*Enter* THOMAS PUTNAM, *a well-to-do, hard-handed landowner, near fifty.*] Oh, good morning, Mr. Putnam.

PUTNAM. It is a providence[13] the thing is out now! It is a providence. [*He goes directly to the bed.*]

PARRIS. What's out, sir, what's—?

[MRS. PUTNAM *goes to the bed.*]

PUTNAM. [*Looking down at* BETTY.] Why, *her* eyes is closed! Look you, Ann.

MRS. PUTNAM. Why, that's strange. [*To* PARRIS.] Ours is open.

PARRIS. [*Shocked.*] Your Ruth is sick?

MRS. PUTNAM. [*With vicious certainty.*] I'd not call it sick; the Devil's touch is heavier than sick. It's death, y'know, it's death drivin' into them, forked and hoofed.

PARRIS. Oh, pray not! Why, how does Ruth ail?

MRS. PUTNAM. She ails as she must—she never waked this morning, but her eyes open and she walks, and hears naught,[14] sees naught, and cannot eat. Her soul is taken, surely.

[PARRIS *is struck.*]

PUTNAM. [*As though for further details.*] They say you've sent for Reverend Hale of Beverly?

PARRIS. [*With dwindling conviction*[15] *now.*] A precaution only. He has much experience in all demonic arts, and I—

MRS. PUTNAM. He has indeed; and found a witch in Beverly last year, and let you remember that.

PARRIS. Now, Goody Ann, they only thought that were a witch, and I am certain there be no element of witchcraft here.

PUTNAM. No witchcraft! Now look you, Mr. Parris—

PARRIS. Thomas, Thomas, I pray you, leap not to witchcraft. I know that you—you least of all, Thomas, would ever wish so disastrous a charge laid upon me. We cannot leap to witchcraft. They will howl me out of Salem for such corruption in my house.

PUTNAM. [*At the moment, he is intent upon getting* PARRIS, *for whom he has only contempt, to move toward the abyss.*] Mr. Parris, I have taken your part in all <u>contention</u> here, and I would continue; but I cannot if you hold back in this. There are hurtful, vengeful spirits layin' hands on these children.

PARRIS. But, Thomas, you cannot—

PUTNAM. Ann! Tell Mr. Parris what you have done.

MRS. PUTNAM. Reverend Parris, I have laid seven babies unbaptized in the earth. Believe me, sir, you never saw more hearty babies born. And yet, each would wither in my arms the very night of their birth. I have spoke nothin', but my heart has clamored intimations.[16] And now, this year, my Ruth, my only—I see her turning strange. A secret child she has become this year, and shrivels like a sucking mouth

---

13. Here, *providence* means "a blessing" or "an act of divine care."
14. *Naught* means "nothing."

15. Here, *conviction* means "certainty."
16. A heart that has *clamored intimations* has nagged its owner with suggestions (of possible witchcraft).

Vocabulary
contention (kən ten´ shən) *n.* verbal argument or struggle; quarreling

Active Reading

REVIEW Have students review the Putnams' reasons for believing that the girls and Tituba are involved in witchcraft. *(Possible answers: Their babies were murdered. Ruth was close to conjuring up their spirits. Some power of darkness struck her dumb. A murdering witch is hiding among the people.)*

Cultural Note

Sneezing can occur when dust or pollen irritates the lining in the nasal passages. Congestion from colds or allergies can also force a person to sneeze. Ruth Putnam may have had a physical illness. However, superstition also held that sneezing might indicate that a possessed person was expelling demons through the nose. This may be the origin of the practice of saying "God bless you" when a person sneezes. It also may be why Mercy suggests that sneezing may restore Ruth's senses.

Active Reading

INFER Remind students that Mrs. Putnam, on first entering, asked how high Betty had flown. Have students infer the meaning of Parris's remark about the window. *(He fears that Betty, if she is possessed by demons, may try to fly out the window.)*

Teaching Options

---

were pullin' on her life too. And so I thought to send her to your Tituba—

PARRIS. To Tituba! What may Tituba—?

MRS. PUTNAM. Tituba knows how to speak to the dead, Mr. Parris.

PARRIS. Goody Ann, it is a formidable sin to conjure up the dead!

MRS. PUTNAM. I take it on my soul, but who else may surely tell us what person murdered my babies?

PARRIS. [*Horrified.*] Woman!

MRS. PUTNAM. They were murdered, Mr. Parris! And mark this proof! Mark it! Last night my Ruth were ever so close to their little spirits; I know it, sir. For how else is she struck dumb now except some power of darkness would stop her mouth? It is a marvelous sign, Mr. Parris!

PUTNAM. Don't you understand it, sir? There is a murdering witch among us, bound to keep herself in the dark. [*PARRIS turns to BETTY, a frantic terror rising in him.*] Let your enemies make of it what they will, you cannot blink it more.

PARRIS. [*To ABIGAIL.*] Then you were conjuring spirits last night.

ABIGAIL. [*Whispering.*] Not I, sir—Tituba and Ruth.

PARRIS. [*Turns now, with new fear, and goes to BETTY, looks down at her, and then, gazing off.*] Oh, Abigail, what proper payment for my charity! Now I am undone.

PUTNAM. You are not undone! Let you take hold here. Wait for no one to charge you—declare it yourself. You have discovered witchcraft—

PARRIS. In my house? In my house, Thomas? They will topple me with this! They will make of it a—

[*Enter MERCY LEWIS, the PUTNAMS' servant, a fat, sly, merciless girl of eighteen.*]

MERCY. Your pardons. I only thought to see how Betty is.

PUTNAM. Why aren't you home? Who's with Ruth?

MERCY. Her grandma come. She's improved a little, I think—she give a powerful sneeze before.

MRS. PUTNAM. Ah, there's a sign of life!

MERCY. I'd fear no more, Goody Putnam. It were a grand sneeze; another like it will shake her wits together, I'm sure. [*She goes to the bed to look.*]

PARRIS. Will you leave me now, Thomas? I would pray a while alone.

ABIGAIL. Uncle, you've prayed since midnight. Why do you not go down and—

PARRIS. No—no. [*To PUTNAM.*] I have no answer for that crowd. I'll wait till Mr. Hale arrives. [*To get MRS. PUTNAM to leave.*] If you will, Goody Ann . . .

PUTNAM. Now look you, sir. Let you strike out against the Devil, and the village will bless you for it! Come down, speak to them—pray with them. They're thirsting for your word, Mister! Surely you'll pray with them.

PARRIS. [*Swayed.*] I'll lead them in a psalm, but let you say nothing of witchcraft yet. I will not discuss it. The cause is yet unknown. I have had enough contention since I came; I want no more.

MRS. PUTNAM. Mercy, you go home to Ruth, d'y'hear?

MERCY. Aye, mum.

[*MRS. PUTNAM goes out.*]

PARRIS. [*To ABIGAIL.*] If she starts for the window, cry for me at once.

ABIGAIL. I will, uncle.

PARRIS. [*To PUTNAM.*] There is a terrible power in her arms today. [*He goes out with PUTNAM.*]

MEETING INDIVIDUAL NEEDS — MULTIPLE LEARNING STYLES

Logical and Mathematical Students with acute logical and mathematical abilities may respond well to activities that involve finding fallacies in reasoning. Point out that Mrs. Putnam's reasoning can be paraphrased this way.

"I know Ruth was close to spirits because she is struck dumb. She had to be close to spirits, or she wouldn't be struck dumb." This is sometimes called circular reasoning.

Activity As they read, encourage students to look for other examples of fallacies in reasoning. You might suggest that they look for the following types: confusing fact and opinion, faulty assumptions, bias, mistaking cause and effect, and guilt by association. **L3**

ABIGAIL. [*With hushed trepidation.*][17] How is Ruth sick?

MERCY. It's weirdish, I know not—she seems to walk like a dead one since last night.

ABIGAIL. [*Turns at once and goes to* BETTY, *and now, with fear in her voice.*] Betty? [BETTY *doesn't move. She shakes her.*] Now stop this! Betty! Sit up now!

[BETTY *doesn't stir.* MERCY *comes over.*]

MERCY. Have you tried beatin' her? I gave Ruth a good one and it waked her for a minute. Here, let me have her.

ABIGAIL. [*Holding* MERCY *back.*] No, he'll be comin' up. Listen, now; if they be questioning us, tell them we danced—I told him as much already.

MERCY. Aye. And what more?

ABIGAIL. He knows Tituba conjured Ruth's sisters to come out of the grave.

MERCY. And what more?

ABIGAIL. He saw you naked.

MERCY. [*Clapping her hands together with a frightened laugh.*] Oh, Jesus!

[*Enter* MARY WARREN, *breathless. She is seventeen, a subservient, naive, lonely girl.*]

MARY WARREN. What'll we do? The village is out! I just come from the farm; the whole country's talkin' witchcraft! They'll be callin' us witches, Abby!

MERCY. [*Pointing and looking at* MARY WARREN.] She means to tell, I know it.

MARY WARREN. Abby, we've got to tell. Witchery's a hangin' error, a hangin' like they done in Boston two year ago! We must tell the truth, Abby! You'll only be whipped for dancin', and the other things!

ABIGAIL. Oh, *we'll* be whipped!

MARY WARREN. I never done none of it, Abby. I only looked!

MERCY. [*Moving menacingly toward* MARY.] Oh, you're a great one for lookin', aren't you, Mary Warren? What a grand peeping courage you have!

[BETTY, *on the bed, whimpers.* ABIGAIL *turns to her at once.*]

ABIGAIL. Betty? [*She goes to* BETTY.] Now, Betty, dear, wake up now. It's Abigail. [*She sits* BETTY *up and furiously shakes her.*] I'll beat you, Betty! [BETTY *whimpers.*] My, you seem improving. I talked to your papa and I told him everything. So there's nothing to—

BETTY. [*Darts off the bed, frightened of* ABIGAIL, *and flattens herself against the wall.*] I want my mama!

ABIGAIL. [*With alarm, as she cautiously approaches* BETTY.] What ails you, Betty? Your mama's dead and buried.

BETTY. I'll fly to Mama. Let me fly! [*She raises her arms as though to fly, and streaks for the window, gets one leg out.*]

ABIGAIL. [*Pulling her away from the window.*] I told him everything; he knows now, he knows everything we—

BETTY. You drank blood, Abby! You didn't tell him that!

ABIGAIL. Betty, you never say that again! You will never—

BETTY. You did, you did! You drank a charm to kill John Proctor's wife! You drank a charm to kill Goody Proctor!

---

17. *Trepidation* means "fear" or "anxiety."

Vocabulary

subservient (səb sur′ vē ənt) *adj.* useful, in an inferior capacity, to promote an end; submissive

naive (nä ēv′) *adj.* lacking knowledge of the ways of the world; unsophisticated; innocent

---

M Critical Thinking

EVALUATE Ask students to describe the change in Abigail's behavior. Do they find it believable? *(Some students may say that she reveals a cruel side to her nature in the way she treats the other girls. Others may say that, with the adults gone, Abigail becomes the dominant personality in the group. Most will probably say that the change is believable because she is revealing her true nature.)*

N Literary Elements

FIGURATIVE LANGUAGE Help students recognize the double meaning in Mercy's use of "peeping" to describe Mary's courage. *(In the literal sense, Mercy uses peeping to refer to the act of looking cautiously or sneakily. In an ironic sense, peeping is also associated with the weak sound of a newborn bird, especially a chicken. So the remark can be interpreted as scorn for Mary's lack of courage.)*

O Active Reading

PREDICT Ask students to predict why Abigail might want John Proctor's wife dead. *(Some students may say that Abigail wants revenge because Elizabeth Proctor dismissed her. Others may say that the earlier reference to a rumor being spread by Mrs. Proctor about Abigail suggests that the girl may have had romantic notions concerning John Proctor.)*

INTERDISCIPLINARY CONNECTION

History Remind students that the residents of Salem were part of the theocracy, or church state, founded when the Pilgrims landed in Massachusetts about 70 years before the events in this play occurred. Suggest that they learn more about the early history of Massachusetts.

Activity Have students form small groups. Have each member research one of the following topics: *Puritan Beliefs, Why the Pilgrims Left England; Puritan Government in Massachusetts; Puritan Treatment of Religious Dissenters.* Afterward, have group members collaborate on a written summary of each topic. Ask groups to share their findings and encourage classmates to ask questions and contribute additional information. **L2**

COLLAB. LEARN.

Teaching Options

P Literary Elements

CHARACTERIZATION Ask student what Abigail's threats toward the other girls reveal about her character. *(She speaks of coming to them in the night with a "pointy reckoning." She has witnessed the brutal murder of her parents and suggests that she is, herself, capable of violence.)*

Q Literary Elements

DIALOGUE Help students recognize how Miller uses names to imply relationship. *(The others say Mr. Proctor; Abigail calls him John. Her uncle always said Abigail; Proctor calls her Abby. This suggests an intimacy borne out in the flirtatious exchange.)*

R Active Reading

EVALUATE Ask students to evaluate the offhand way Abigail describes events to Proctor in light of what we know about her character. *(It illustrates her ability to adapt her manner to suit a situation. With her uncle, she feigns concern and righteous indignation. With the girls, she is domineering and cruel. With Proctor, she is coy and seductive.)*

ABIGAIL. [*Smashes her across the face.*] Shut it! Now shut it!

BETTY. [*Collapsing on the bed.*] Mama, Mama! [*She dissolves into sobs.*]

ABIGAIL. Now look you. All of you. We danced. And Tituba conjured Ruth Putnam's dead sisters. And that is all. And mark this. Let either of you breathe a word, or the edge of a word, about the other things, and I will come to you in the black of some terrible night and I will bring a pointy reckoning that will shudder you. And you know I can do it; I saw Indians smash my dear parents' heads on the pillow next to mine, and I have seen some reddish work[18] done at night, and I can make you wish you had never seen the sun go down! [*She goes to BETTY and roughly sits her up.*] Now, you—sit up and stop this!

[*But BETTY collapses in her hands and lies inert on the bed.*]

MARY WARREN. [*With hysterical fright.*] What's got her? [*ABIGAIL stares in fright at BETTY.*] Abby, she's going to die! It's a sin to conjure, and we—

ABIGAIL. [*Starting for MARY.*] I say shut it, Mary Warren!

[*Enter JOHN PROCTOR. On seeing him, MARY WARREN leaps in fright.*]

MARY WARREN. Oh! I'm just going home, Mr. Proctor.

PROCTOR. Be you foolish, Mary Warren? Be you deaf? I forbid you leave the house, did I not? Why shall I pay you? I am looking for you more often than my cows!

MARY WARREN. I only come to see the great doings in the world.

PROCTOR. I'll show you a great doin' on your arse one of these days. Now get you home; my wife is waitin' with your work! [*Trying to retain a shred of dignity, she goes slowly out.*]

---

18. *Reddish work* means "bloody deeds."

MERCY LEWIS. [*Both afraid of him and strangely titillated.*][19] I'd best be off. I have my Ruth to watch. Good morning, Mr. Proctor.

[*MERCY sidles out. Since PROCTOR's entrance, ABIGAIL has stood as though on tiptoe, absorbing his presence, wide-eyed. He glances at her, then goes to BETTY on the bed.*]

ABIGAIL. Gah! I'd almost forgot how strong you are, John Proctor!

PROCTOR. [*Looking at ABIGAIL now, the faintest suggestion of a knowing smile on his face.*] What's this mischief here?

ABIGAIL. [*With a nervous laugh.*] Oh, she's only gone silly somehow.

PROCTOR. The road past my house is a pilgrimage to Salem all morning. The town's mumbling witchcraft.

ABIGAIL. Oh, posh! [*Winningly she comes a little closer, with a confidential, wicked air.*] We were dancin' in the woods last night, and my uncle leaped in on us. She took fright, is all.

PROCTOR. [*His smile widening.*] Ah, you're wicked yet, aren't y'! [*A trill of expectant laughter escapes her, and she dares come closer, feverishly looking into his eyes.*] You'll be clapped in the stocks[20] before you're twenty.

[*He takes a step to go, and she springs into his path.*]

ABIGAIL. Give me a word, John. A soft word. [*Her concentrated desire destroys his smile.*]

PROCTOR. No, no, Abby. That's done with.

ABIGAIL. [*Tauntingly.*][21] You come five mile to see a silly girl fly? I know you better.

PROCTOR. [*Setting her firmly out of his path.*] I come to see what mischief your uncle's brewin' now. [*With final emphasis.*] Put it out of mind, Abby.

---

19. To be *titillated* is to be pleasantly excited or stimulated.
20. The word *stocks* refers to a heavy wooden frame with holes for confining the ankles and wrists of someone found guilty of a crime.
21. *Tauntingly* means "in a scornful or mocking way."

LIFE SKILLS CONNECTION

Goal Setting Arthur Miller set out to be a playwright early in life. Along the way, he took a number of practical steps to help him reach his goal. As a teenager, he enrolled in the journalism program at the University of Michigan. While in college, he wrote his first plays. After graduation, Miller worked as a radio scriptwriter while he continued to pursue success in the theater.

Activity Have students think about a career goal that they might like to achieve. Tell them to list practical actions that they could take as intermediate steps toward achieving that goal. Remind them that Miller's educational pursuits and early work experience both were related to his ultimate goal. Suggest that they try to think of short-range accomplishments that could prove useful to fulfilling their dreams. **L2**

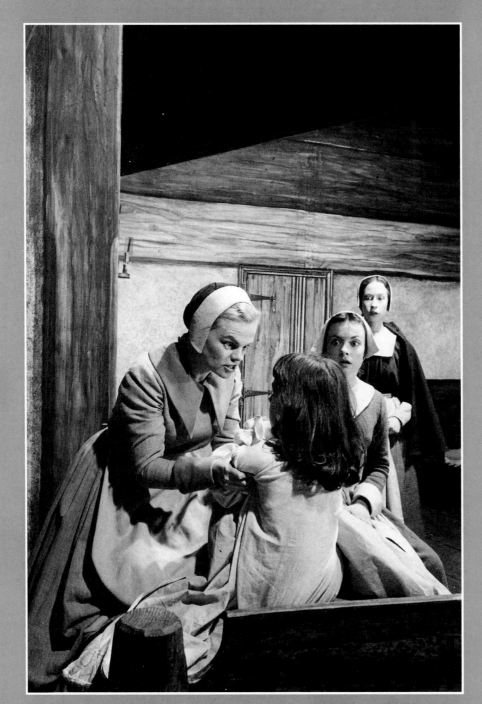

Photographs are from the original 1953 Broadway production of Arthur Miller's *The Crucible.*

interNET CONNECTION

***The Crucible* on Film** Have students use a search engine to locate reviews of the 1996 film version of the play starring Daniel Day-Lewis and Winona Ryder. After reading and analyzing the reviews, interested students may wish to view the film on home video. Have students write a comparison of thier responses with those of the reviewers.

S Literary Elements

PLOT Discuss with students how this passage reveals central conflicts in the plot. *(The conflict between Abigail and Mrs. Proctor: Abigail's motivation is now known. There was a romantic link between her and John, which is why Mrs. Proctor dismissed her. Abigail believes John loves her. Mrs. Proctor's death would clear the way for marriage between them. The conflict between Abigail and John: He denies that he ever gave her reason to believe there was hope for marriage.)*

T Critical Thinking

DRAWING CONCLUSIONS Have students draw conclusions about the conflicting accounts John and Abigail give of their relationship. *(Some may say he is unconvincing. He admits he had come to her in the past. He does not deny having looked up at her window. "Wipe it out of mind" is his way of telling her to pretend nothing ever happened. Others may say he is guilty of flirting with her, but she exaggerates the seriousness of the relationship.)*

U Active Reading

INTERPRET Be certain students understand the relationship between Betty's reaction to the psalm and the plot. *(The words "going up to Jesus" cause her to cover her ears. One tradition was that demons could not bear to hear the name of Jesus, so they tormented possessed persons.)*

Teaching Options

ABIGAIL. [*Grasping his hand before he can release her.*] John—I am waitin' for you every night.

PROCTOR. Abby, I never give you hope to wait for me.

ABIGAIL. [*Now beginning to anger—she can't believe it.*] I have something better than hope, I think!

PROCTOR. Abby, you'll put it out of mind. I'll not be comin' for you more.

ABIGAIL. You're surely sportin' with me.

PROCTOR. You know me better.

ABIGAIL. I know how you clutched my back behind your house and sweated like a stallion whenever I come near! Or did I dream that? It's she put me out, you cannot pretend it were you. I saw your face when she put me out, and you loved me then and you do now!

PROCTOR. Abby, that's a wild thing to say—

ABIGAIL. A wild thing may say wild things. But not so wild, I think. I have seen you since she put me out; I have seen you nights.

PROCTOR. I have hardly stepped off my farm this sevenmonth.

ABIGAIL. I have a sense for heat, John, and yours has drawn me to my window, and I have seen you looking up, burning in your loneliness. Do you tell me you've never looked up at my window?

PROCTOR. I may have looked up.

ABIGAIL. [*Now softening.*] And you must. You are no wintry man. I know you, John. I *know* you. [*She is weeping.*] I cannot sleep for dreamin'; I cannot dream but I wake and walk about the house as though I'd find you comin' through some door. [*She clutches him desperately.*]

PROCTOR. [*Gently pressing her from him, with great sympathy but firmly.*] Child—

ABIGAIL. [*With a flash of anger.*] How do you call me child!

PROCTOR. Abby, I may think of you softly from time to time. But I will cut off my hand before I'll ever reach for you again. Wipe it out of mind. We never touched, Abby.

ABIGAIL. Aye, but we did.

PROCTOR. Aye, but we did not.

ABIGAIL. [*With a bitter anger.*] Oh, I marvel how such a strong man may let such a sickly wife be—

PROCTOR. [*Angered—at himself as well.*] You'll speak nothin' of Elizabeth!

ABIGAIL. She is blackening my name in the village! She is telling lies about me! She is a cold, sniveling woman, and you bend to her! Let her turn you like a—

PROCTOR. [*Shaking her.*] Do you look for whippin'?

[*A psalm is heard being sung below.*]

ABIGAIL. [*In tears.*] I look for John Proctor that took me from my sleep and put knowledge in my heart! I never knew what pretense Salem was, I never knew the lying lessons I was taught by all these Christian women and their covenanted[22] men! And now you bid me tear the light out of my eyes? I will not, I cannot! You loved me, John Proctor, and whatever sin it is, you love me yet! [*He turns abruptly to go out. She rushes to him.*] John, pity me, pity me!

[*The words "going up to Jesus" are heard in the psalm, and* BETTY *claps her ears suddenly and whines loudly.*]

---

22. A covenant is an agreement or promise. Among the Puritans, a *covenanted* person had made a commitment to the church and had signed an agreement testifying to his or her faith.

Vocabulary
pretense (prē′ tens) *n.* a false show or appearance, especially for the purpose of deceiving; falseness

---

MEETING INDIVIDUAL NEEDS   GIFTED AND TALENTED ACTIVITY

Writing an Original Scene Gifted and talented students may respond well to activities that allow them to use creativity and demonstrate insight. Other students may benefit from their abilities as well.

Activity Tell students to imagine that the play begins seven months earlier. Have them write an original scene describing Abigail's dismissal from the Proctor farm. Suggest that they include a private conversation between John and Elizabeth prior to the confrontation between Elizabeth and Abigail. Encourage them to share their work with the class by distributing written copies or directing friends in a performance of the scene. **L3**

PUTNAM. He had no right to sell it. It stands clear in my grandfather's will that all the land between the river and—

PROCTOR. Your grandfather had a habit of willing land that never belonged to him, if I may say it plain.

GILES. That's God's truth; he nearly willed away my north pasture but he knew I'd break his fingers before he'd set his name to it. Let's get your lumber home, John. I feel a sudden will to work coming on.

PUTNAM. You load one oak of mine and you'll fight to drag it home!

GILES. Aye, and we'll win too, Putnam—this fool and I. Come on! [*He turns to PROCTOR and starts out.*]

PUTNAM. I'll have my men on you, Corey! I'll clap a writ[32] on you!

[*Enter REVEREND JOHN HALE of Beverly. He appears loaded down with half a dozen heavy books.*]

HALE. Pray you, someone take these!

PARRIS. [*Delighted.*] Mr. Hale! Oh! it's good to see you again! [*Taking some books.*] My, they're heavy!

HALE. [*Setting down his books.*] They must be; they are weighted with authority.

PARRIS. [*A little scared.*] Well, you do come prepared!

---

32. A *writ* is a judge's order.

Ocean Greyness, 1953. Jackson Pollock. Oil on canvas, 4 ft 9¾ in x 7 ft 6⅛ in. Solomon R. Guggenheim Museum, New York.

Viewing the painting: Look at the interplay of colors in this painting. What characters or events in act 1 might these colors represent? Explain.

THE CRUCIBLE, ACT 1 ✿ 927

EE Critical Thinking

INTERPRET Discuss with students the significance of Proctor's remarks. *(Proctor does not see the question of witchcraft as one that involves him or his family. Therefore, he does not wish to be drawn into the argument. Also, he is not foolish. He will state his opinion as a church member on matters involving policy and as a community member over property disputes. However, he will not risk being called a heretic by disputing accepted theology without good cause.)*

FF Author's Craft

IRONY Discuss with students the irony in Hale's remarks. *(He tells the others that they cannot rely on superstition in matters such as witchcraft. There are scientific ways to determine whether someone is possessed, and they must trust his educated judgment in such matters. To Hale and the Puritans, this may sound reasonable. To a modern audience, his remarks are absurd.)*

GG Active Reading

QUESTION Ask students what is happening here. *(Ann Putnam actually is the one responsible for her daughter's trying to conjure spirits. She has just confessed to the crime of which others will be accused. Rebecca Nurse is appalled, especially by the fact that Ann sent a child to do this.)*

HALE. We shall need hard study if it comes to tracking down the Old Boy.[33] [*Noticing* REBECCA.] You cannot be Rebecca Nurse?

REBECCA. I am, sir. Do you know me?

HALE. It's strange how I knew you, but I suppose you look as such a good soul should. We have all heard of your great charities in Beverly.

PARRIS. Do you know this gentleman? Mr. Thomas Putnam. And his good wife Ann.

HALE. Putnam! I had not expected such distinguished company, sir.

PUTNAM. [*Pleased.*] It does not seem to help us today, Mr. Hale. We look to you to come to our house and save our child.

HALE. Your child ails too?

MRS. PUTNAM. Her soul, her soul seems flown away. She sleeps and yet she walks . . .

PUTNAM. She cannot eat.

HALE. Cannot eat! [*Thinks on it. Then, to* PROCTOR *and* GILES COREY.] Do you men have afflicted children?

PARRIS. No, no, these are farmers. John Proctor—

GILES COREY. He don't believe in witches.

PROCTOR. [*To* HALE.] I never spoke on witches one way or the other. Will you come, Giles?

GILES. No—no, John, I think not. I have some few queer questions of my own to ask this fellow.

PROCTOR. I've heard you to be a sensible man, Mr. Hale. I hope you'll leave some of it in Salem.

[PROCTOR *goes.* HALE *stands embarrassed for an instant.*]

PARRIS. [*Quickly.*] Will you look at my daughter, sir? [*Leads* HALE *to the bed.*] She has tried to leap out the window; we discovered her this

---

33. **Old Boy** is another name for Satan.

---

morning on the highroad, waving her arms as though she'd fly.

HALE. [*Narrowing his eyes.*] Tries to fly.

PUTNAM. She cannot bear to hear the Lord's name, Mr. Hale; that's a sure sign of witchcraft afloat.

HALE. [*Holding up his hands.*] No, no. Now let me instruct you. We cannot look to superstition in this. The Devil is precise; the marks of his presence are definite as stone, and I must tell you all that I shall not proceed unless you are prepared to believe me if I should find no bruise of hell upon her.

PARRIS. It is agreed, sir—it is agreed—we will abide by your judgment.

HALE. Good then. [*He goes to the bed, looks down at* BETTY. *To* PARRIS.] Now, sir, what were your first warning of this strangeness?

PARRIS. Why, sir—I discovered her—[*Indicating* ABIGAIL.]—and my niece and ten or twelve of the other girls, dancing in the forest last night.

HALE. [*Surprised.*] You permit dancing?

PARRIS. No, no, it were secret—

MRS. PUTNAM. [*Unable to wait.*] Mr. Parris's slave has knowledge of conjurin', sir.

PARRIS. [*To* MRS. PUTNAM.] We cannot be sure of that, Goody Ann—

MRS. PUTNAM. [*Frightened, very softly.*] I know it, sir. I sent my child—she should learn from Tituba who murdered her sisters.

REBECCA. [*Horrified.*] Goody Ann! You sent a child to conjure up the dead?

MRS. PUTNAM. Let God blame me, not you, not you, Rebecca! I'll not have you judging me any more! [*To* HALE.] Is it a natural work to lose seven children before they live a day?

PARRIS. Sssh!

[REBECCA, *with great pain, turns her face away. There is a pause.*]

HALE. Seven dead in childbirth.

Teaching Options

Grammar and Language *Minilesson*

Latin Roots Point out that many English words are formed by adding prefixes and/or suffixes to Latin roots. Note that the words *conjure* and *instruct* are formed in this way. The Latin root *jure* means "to swear." *Conjure* literally means "to swear together." The Latin root *struct* means "to build." *Instruct* literally means "to build in [another]."

Activity Knowing the meaning of the following words, formed from the Latin roots *jure* and *struct,* may help students in writing assignments related to this selection.

abjure: to renounce upon oath
perjure: to lie under oath
obstruct: to hinder or block

Have students find the meaning of each word in the dictionary and write original sentences using each word. **L2**

Additional Resources

📠 ***Grammar and Language Transparency 68***

📗 ***Grammar and Language Workbook,*** p. 293

📗 ***Grammar and Composition Handbook,*** Lesson 13.4

📗 ***Writer's Choice,*** Lesson 25.2

MRS. PUTNAM. [*Softly.*] Aye. [*Her voice breaks; she looks up at him. Silence. HALE is impressed. PARRIS looks to him. He goes to his books, opens one, turns pages, then reads. All wait, avidly.*][34]

PARRIS. [*Hushed.*] What book is that?

MRS. PUTNAM. What's there, sir?

HALE. [*With a tasty love of intellectual pursuit.*] Here is all the invisible world, caught, defined, and calculated. In these books the Devil stands stripped of all his brute disguises. Here are all your familiar spirits—your incubi and succubi;[35] your witches that go by land, by air, and by sea; your wizards of the night and of the day. Have no fear now—we shall find him out if he has come among us, and I mean to crush him utterly if he has shown his face! [*He starts for the bed.*]

REBECCA. Will it hurt the child, sir?

HALE. I cannot tell. If she is truly in the Devil's grip we may have to rip and tear to get her free.

REBECCA. I think I'll go, then. I am too old for this. [*She rises.*]

PARRIS. [*Striving for conviction.*] Why, Rebecca, we may open up the boil of all our troubles today!

REBECCA. Let us hope for that. I go to God for you, sir.

PARRIS. [*With trepidation—and resentment.*] I hope you do not mean we go to Satan here! [*Slight pause.*]

REBECCA. I wish I knew. [*She goes out; they feel resentful of her note of moral superiority.*]

PUTNAM. [*Abruptly.*] Come, Mr. Hale, let's get on. Sit you here.

GILES. Mr. Hale, I have always wanted to ask a learned man—what signifies the readin' of strange books?

HALE. What books?

GILES. I cannot tell; she hides them.

HALE. Who does this?

GILES. Martha, my wife. I have waked at night many a time and found her in a corner, readin' of a book. Now what do you make of that?

HALE. Why, that's not necessarily—

GILES. It discomfits[36] me! Last night—mark this—I tried and tried and could not say my prayers. And then she close her book and walks out of the house, and suddenly—mark this—I could pray again!

HALE. Ah! The stoppage of prayer—that is strange. I'll speak further on that with you.

GILES. I'm not sayin' she's touched the Devil, now, but I'd admire to know what books she reads and why she hides them. She'll not answer me, y' see.

HALE. Aye, we'll discuss it. [*To all.*] Now mark me, if the Devil is in her you will witness some frightful wonders in this room, so please to keep your wits about you. Mr. Putnam, stand close in case she flies. Now, Betty, dear, will you sit up? [*PUTNAM comes in closer, ready-handed. HALE sits BETTY up, but she hangs limp in his hands.*] Hmmm. [*He observes her carefully. The others watch breathlessly.*] Can you hear me? I am John Hale, minister of Beverly. I have come to help you, dear. Do you remember my two little girls in Beverly? [*She does not stir in his hands.*]

PARRIS. [*In fright.*] How can it be the Devil? Why would he choose my house to strike? We have all manner of licentious[37] people in the village!

HALE. What victory would the Devil have to win a soul already bad? It is the best the Devil wants, and who is better than the minister?

GILES. That's deep, Mr. Parris, deep, deep!

---

34. *Avidly* means "with intense interest."
35. *Incubi* (ing′ kyə bī′) and *succubi* (suk′ yə bī′) are evil spirits or demons.
36. *Discomfits* means "confuses and frustrates."
37. *Licentious* people disregard commonly accepted standards of right and wrong or good and evil.

COMPARING AND CONTRASTING
Have students compare and contrast Rebecca's character with those of Parris and Hale. (*Her immediate concern is for the welfare of the child. Parris can only think of himself at the moment and ask "Why me?" Hale, though well-intentioned, is egotistical. He has no doubt at all about his actions or his abilities. Rebecca has a healthy skepticism about both.*)

II Active Reading

REVIEW Be certain that students understand what Rebecca is saying here. (*She is going to pray for Parris, who is allowing his daughter to be subjected to this treatment.*)

JJ Author's Craft

IRONY Ask students to explain the irony in this exchange between Parris and Hale. (*Parris asks why the devil would choose his house when there are so many less worthy people in Salem. He does not recognize his own lack of good character. Hale's question assumes that the minister must be the best person in the village, an assumption at odds with the facts.*)

Critical Thinking

ANALYZING Ask students to discuss the significance of the kettle. *(The kettle is a witches' cauldron. Superstition held that witches would boil water in a cauldron, or large, round kettle, when casting spells or conjuring spirits. Often they would throw in small animals or animal parts as part of the mixture they were brewing.)*

Active Reading

PREDICT Before they read, have students predict what Abigail's response will be to the Reverend Hale's question. *(Some students may say that she will place the blame on someone else. Others may say that she will continue to deny the accusation.)*

VIEWING THE PAINTING

The indistinct images in this work suggest something ominous and disconcerting. There is an intense and powerful emotional quality to the use of different shades of orange and the materials of oil and spackle on wood.

Viewing Response *Like the events of the night in the woods, what is actually revealed in this piece of art is at once strongly intense, but difficult to see clearly or to interpret accurately.*

PARRIS. [*With resolution now.*] Betty! Answer Mr. Hale! Betty!

HALE. Does someone afflict you, child? It need not be a woman, mind you, or a man. Perhaps some bird invisible to others comes to you—perhaps a pig, a mouse, or any beast at all. Is there some figure bids you fly? [*The child remains limp in his hands. In silence he lays her back on the pillow. Now, holding out his hands toward her, he intones.*] In nomine Domini Sabaoth sui filiique ite ad infernos.[38] [*She does not stir. He turns to ABIGAIL, his eyes narrowing.*] Abigail, what sort of dancing were you doing with her in the forest?

ABIGAIL. Why—common dancing is all.

---

38. *[In nomine . . . infernos.]* "In the name of the God of the Heavenly Hosts and of His Son, go to hell." Hale is performing an exorcism, a ritual intended to drive out evil spirits.

Omen, 1993. Katherine Bowling. Oil and spackle on wood, 24 x 24 in. The SBC Collection of Twentieth Century American Art. Courtesy SBC Communications.

Viewing the painting: What connections might you make between this painting and the description of the night the girls went to the forest?

PARRIS. I think I ought to say that I—I saw a kettle in the grass where they were dancing.

ABIGAIL. That were only soup.

HALE. What sort of soup were in this kettle, Abigail?

ABIGAIL. Why, it were beans—and lentils, I think, and—

HALE. Mr. Parris, you did not notice, did you, any living thing in the kettle? A mouse, perhaps, a spider, a frog—?

PARRIS. [*Fearfully.*] I—do believe there were some movement—in the soup.

ABIGAIL. That jumped in, we never put it in!

HALE. [*Quickly.*] What jumped in?

ABIGAIL. Why, a very little frog jumped—

PARRIS. A frog, Abby!

HALE. [*Grasping ABIGAIL.*] Abigail, it may be your cousin is dying. Did you call the Devil last night?

ABIGAIL. I never called him! Tituba, Tituba . . .

PARRIS. [*Blanched.*] She called the Devil?

HALE. I should like to speak with Tituba.

PARRIS. Goody Ann, will you bring her up? [*MRS. PUTNAM exits.*]

Teaching Options

MULTIPLE LEARNING STYLES
MEETING INDIVIDUAL NEEDS

Bodily-Kinesthetic Students who have bodily-kinesthetic intelligence may respond well to interpretations of physical actions that accompany thoughts and words.

Activity Organize students into groups of three. Ask each group member to imagine and demonstrate the movements and gestures of one of the characters who is onstage but who plays no active role during Reverend Hale's interrogation of Abigail (pages 930–931). These characters are Ann Putnam, Thomas Putnam, and Giles Corey. Ask students to decide how they would react to each new revelation. You might ask volunteers to read the dialogue as the student performers react. **L2 COLLAB. LEARN.**

HALE. How did she call him?

ABIGAIL. I know not—she spoke Barbados.

HALE. Did you feel any strangeness when she called him? A sudden cold wind, perhaps? A trembling below the ground?

ABIGAIL. I didn't see no Devil! [*Shaking* BETTY.] Betty, wake up. Betty! Betty!

HALE. You cannot evade me, Abigail. Did your cousin drink any of the brew in that kettle?

ABIGAIL. She never drank it!

HALE. Did you drink it?

ABIGAIL. No, sir!

HALE. Did Tituba ask you to drink it?

ABIGAIL. She tried, but I refused.

HALE. Why are you concealing? Have you sold yourself to Lucifer?

ABIGAIL. I never sold myself! I'm a good girl! I'm a proper girl!

[MRS. PUTNAM *enters with* TITUBA, *and instantly* ABIGAIL *points at* TITUBA.]

ABIGAIL. She made me do it! She made Betty do it!

TITUBA. [*Shocked and angry.*] Abby!

ABIGAIL. She makes me drink blood!

PARRIS. Blood!!

MRS. PUTNAM. My baby's blood?

TITUBA. No, no, chicken blood. I give she chicken blood!

HALE. Woman, have you enlisted these children for the Devil?

TITUBA. No, no, sir, I don't truck[39] with no Devil!

HALE. Why can she not wake? Are you silencing this child?

TITUBA. I love me Betty!

HALE. You have sent your spirit out upon this child, have you not? Are you gathering souls for the Devil?

ABIGAIL. She sends her spirit on me in church; she makes me laugh at prayer!

PARRIS. She have often laughed at prayer!

ABIGAIL. She comes to me every night to go and drink blood!

TITUBA. You beg *me* to conjure! She beg *me* make charm—

ABIGAIL. Don't lie! [*To* HALE.] She comes to me while I sleep; she's always making me dream corruptions!

TITUBA. Why you say that, Abby?

ABIGAIL. Sometimes I wake and find myself standing in the open doorway and not a stitch on my body! I always hear her laughing in my sleep. I hear her singing her Barbados songs and tempting me with—

TITUBA. Mister Reverend, I never—

HALE. [*Resolved now.*] Tituba, I want you to wake this child.

TITUBA. I have no power on this child, sir.

HALE. You most certainly do, and you will free her from it now! When did you compact with[40] the Devil?

TITUBA. I don't compact with no Devil!

PARRIS. You will confess yourself or I will take you out and whip you to your death, Tituba!

PUTNAM. This woman must be hanged! She must be taken and hanged!

TITUBA. [*Terrified, falls to her knees.*] No, no, don't hang Tituba! I tell him I don't desire to work for him, sir.

---

39. *Truck* is another way of saying "to have dealings."

40. To *compact with* is to make an agreement or contract with.

Vocabulary
evade (i vād′) *v.* to escape or avoid, as by cleverness

REAL-WORLD CONNECTION

Unfair Attacks? Some critics have characterized negative political ads as a kind of "witch-hunt" against those running for office. Candidates' records are often distorted and false charges may be difficult to defend against.

Activity Have students conduct research on negative campaign advertising to answer such questions as the following: How effective are such ads? How damaging are they to the political process? Are such ads unfair? What parallels are there to the events in Salem?

L2 **COLLAB. LEARN.**

PREDICT Before they read, ask students to predict how Tituba will respond to the accusation of witch-craft. *(Students probably will make the following prediction. Abigail has blamed Tituba to escape punishment. Tituba probably will employ the same tactic and try to shift the blame to someone else.)*

PP Critical Thinking

INFERRING Who is the first person to name specific individuals? What can you infer from this? *(Thomas Putnam is the first. Students might infer from this that Sarah Good and Osburn are people whom the Putnams do not like or against whom the Putnams have grievances.)*

QQ Literary Elements

IRONY Help students understand the irony in Hale's argument. *(He tells Tituba that she is God's instrument doing his work and helping cleanse the village. In reality, he is persuading her to make false accusations of witchcraft against innocent people.)*

RR Critical Thinking

INTERPRET Ask students why Hale speaks in a "kindly" tone. *(Some students may say that he believes he really is helping her and wants to win her soul back to God. Others may say that he realizes that threats will terrify her, but cajoling will gain her confidence and win her cooperation.)*

The Crucible

PARRIS. The Devil?

HALE. Then you saw him! [*TITUBA weeps.*] Now Tituba, I know that when we bind our-selves to Hell it is very hard to break with it. We are going to help you tear yourself free—

TITUBA. [*Frightened by the coming process.*] Mister Reverend, I do believe somebody else be witchin' these children.

HALE. Who?

TITUBA. I don't know, sir, but the Devil got him numerous witches.

HALE. Does he! [*It is a clue.*] Tituba, look into my eyes. Come, look into me. [*She raises her eyes to his fearfully.*] You would be a good Christian woman, would you not, Tituba?

TITUBA. Aye, sir, a good Christian woman.

HALE. And you love these little children?

TITUBA. Oh, yes, sir, I don't desire to hurt lit-tle children.

HALE. And you love God, Tituba?

TITUBA. I love God with all my bein'.

HALE. Now, in God's holy name—

TITUBA. Bless Him. Bless Him. [*She is rocking on her knees, sobbing in terror.*]

HALE. And to His glory—

TITUBA. Eternal glory. Bless Him—bless God . . .

HALE. Open yourself, Tituba—open yourself and let God's holy light shine on you.

TITUBA. Oh, bless the Lord.

HALE. When the Devil comes to you does he ever come—with another person? [*She stares up into his face.*] Perhaps another person in the village? Someone you know.

PARRIS. Who came with him?

PUTNAM. Sarah Good? Did you ever see Sarah Good with him? Or Osburn?

PARRIS. Was it man or woman came with him?

TITUBA. Man or woman. Was—was woman.

PARRIS. What woman? A woman, you said. What woman?

TITUBA. It was black dark, and I—

PARRIS. You could see him, why could you not see her?

TITUBA. Well, they was always talking; they was always runnin' round and carryin' on—

PARRIS. You mean out of Salem? Salem witches?

TITUBA. I believe so, yes, sir.

[*Now HALE takes her hand. She is surprised.*]

HALE. Tituba. You must have no fear to tell us who they are, do you understand? We will pro-tect you. The Devil can never overcome a minister. You know that, do you not?

TITUBA. [*Kisses HALE's hand.*] Aye, sir, I do.

HALE. You have confessed yourself to witch-craft, and that speaks a wish to come to Heaven's side. And we will bless you, Tituba.

TITUBA. [*Deeply relieved.*] Oh, God bless you, Mr. Hale!

HALE. [*With rising exaltation.*][41] You are God's instrument put in our hands to discover the Devil's agents among us. You are selected, Tituba, you are chosen to help us cleanse our village. So speak utterly, Tituba, turn your back on him and face God—face God, Tituba, and God will protect you.

TITUBA. [*Joining with him.*] Oh, God, protect Tituba!

HALE. [*Kindly.*] Who came to you with the Devil? Two? Three? Four? How many?

[*TITUBA pants, and begins rocking back and forth again, staring ahead.*]

TITUBA. There was four. There was four.

PARRIS. [*Pressing in on her.*] Who? Who? Their names, their names!

---

41. Here, *exaltation* means "great enthusiasm" or "joyful ecstasy."

Reading *Minilesson*

Problem and Solution Remind stu-dents that external conflict, or a struggle between a character and his or her envi-ronment, is a central element of plot. Note that the people in Salem face an external conflict. However, different characters may perceive the problem in different terms.

Activity Have partners write a sen-tence defining the problem from the differing perspectives: John Proctor, Abigail Williams, Reverend Parris, Rebecca Nurse. Have them collaborate on a sentence explaining how they think each of these characters would define the solution. **L2** **COLLAB. LEARN.**

Additional Resources
📁 *Reading Workbook,* pp. 81–82

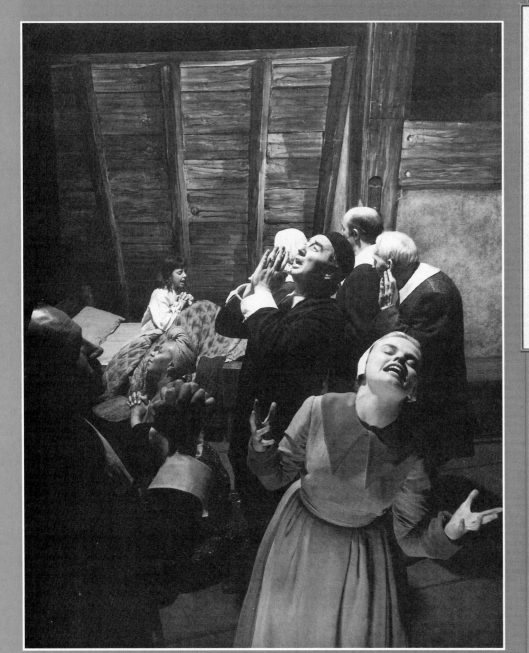

VIEWING THE PHOTOGRAPH

This photograph relates to the dialogue that begins on page 934.

Responding to the Photograph
Discussion questions:
- What are Abigail and Betty doing? *(Students should recognize that they are calling out the names of witches.)*
- Who is the character who is looking heavenward with hands clasped and mouth open? How do you know? *(Parris; the stage direction says that he is shouting a prayer of thanksgiving.)*
- Who is the character holding his hand to his ear? How do you know? *(Giles Corey; he is an old man as stated in the stage directions, and John Proctor has stated that he is hard of hearing.)*

MEETING INDIVIDUAL NEEDS — MULTIPLE LEARNING STYLES

Spatial Students with acute spatial abilities may respond well to activities that involve elements of stage direction.

Activity Explain the concept of actors' "marks" that show where characters stand or move to during a scene. Ask students to visualize the front of the classroom as a stage. At the beginning of each act, have groups read the stage directions and decide where each character might be standing. As you progress through the play, encourage groups to plot the marks on which new characters stand after entering. Challenge them to visualize movements of characters already onstage. Students might also demonstrate their ideas in the front of the class. **L2 COLLAB. LEARN.**

QUESTION Ask students who Tituba has identified as witches. *(She has named Sarah Good and Goody Osburn.)* Why do you think she chose those people? *(Some students may say that Tituba is telling her inquisitors what she thinks they want to hear. Others may say that it is the power of suggestion working on her in her frightened state.)*

TT **Author's Craft**

PLOT Remind students that Miller described act 1 as an overture. Help them see how the plot structure reinforces this concept. *(Act 1 opens with a scene that resembles a religious tableau, or motionless depiction. A minister is kneeling in silent prayer by the bedside of a sick child. The act ends with a crescendo, or the peak of a gradual increase in action and sound. Abigail rises; Betty sits up. Both are shouting accusations. Putnam leaves to get the marshal. Parris is shouting a prayer. The "sound and the fury" are like a storm unleashed on Salem.)*

Thematic Focus

Acting on an Idea Have students discuss the conflicts in the minds of Proctor and Rebecca. Do they think these characters act realistically? Ask for examples to support their opinions.

✔ **ASSESSMENT OPTIONS**

📁 **Quick Checks**, p. 108

Teaching Options

The Crucible

TITUBA. [*Suddenly bursting out.*] Oh, how many times he bid me kill you, Mr. Parris!

PARRIS. Kill me!

TITUBA. [*In a fury.*] He say Mr. Parris must be kill! Mr. Parris no goodly man, Mr. Parris mean man and no gentle man, and he bid me rise out of my bed and cut your throat! [*They gasp.*] But I tell him, "No! I don't hate that man. I don't want kill that man." But he say, "You work for me, Tituba, and I make you free! I give you pretty dress to wear, and put you way high up in the air, and you gone fly back to Barbados!" And I say, "You lie, Devil, you lie!" And then he come one stormy night to me, and he say, "Look! I have *white* people belong to me." And I look—and there was Goody Good.

PARRIS. Sarah Good!

TITUBA. [*Rocking and weeping.*] Aye, sir, and Goody Osburn.

MRS. PUTNAM. I knew it! Goody Osburn were midwife[42] to me three times. I begged you, Thomas, did I not? I begged him not to call Osburn because I feared her. My babies always shriveled in her hands!

HALE. Take courage, you must give us all their names. How can you bear to see this child suffering? Look at her, Tituba. [*He is indicating* BETTY *on the bed.*] Look at her God-given innocence; her soul is so tender; we must protect her, Tituba; the Devil is out and preying on her like a beast upon the flesh of the pure lamb. God will bless you for your help.

[ABIGAIL *rises, staring as though inspired, and cries out.*]

---

42. A *midwife* is a woman who assists other women in childbirth.

ABIGAIL. I want to open myself! [*They turn to her, startled. She is enraptured,[43] as though in a pearly light.*] I want the light of God, I want the sweet love of Jesus! I danced for the Devil; I saw him; I wrote in his book; I go back to Jesus; I kiss His hand. I saw Sarah Good with the Devil! I saw Goody Osburn with the Devil! I saw Bridget Bishop with the Devil!

[*As she is speaking,* BETTY *is rising from the bed, a fever in her eyes, and picks up the chant.*]

BETTY. [*Staring too.*] I saw George Jacobs with the Devil! I saw Goody Howe with the Devil!

PARRIS. She speaks! [*He rushes to embrace* BETTY.] She speaks!

HALE. Glory to God! It is broken, they are free!

BETTY. [*Calling out hysterically and with great relief.*] I saw Martha Bellows with the Devil!

ABIGAIL. I saw Goody Sibber with the Devil! [*It is rising to a great glee.*]

PUTNAM. The marshal, I'll call the marshal!

[PARRIS *is shouting a prayer of thanksgiving.*]

BETTY. I saw Alice Barrow with the Devil!

[*The curtain begins to fall.*]

HALE. [*As* PUTNAM *goes out.*] Let the marshal bring irons!

ABIGAIL. I saw Goody Hawkins with the Devil!

BETTY. I saw Goody Bibber with the Devil!

ABIGAIL. I saw Goody Booth with the Devil!

[*On their ecstatic cries.*]

THE CURTAIN FALLS

---

43. *Enraptured* means "filled with intense joy or delight."

Grammar and Language *Minilesson*

Exclamation Point Remind students that exclamation points are used to show strong feelings and to indicate a forceful command. Write the following sentences on the board to illustrate the rule.

    I saw Sarah Good with the Devil!
    Their names, their names!

The exclamation point is to be reserved for use after true exclamations (expressions of strong feeling) or commands.

    Listen to me!
    Halt!

Activity Have students review what has happened since Reverend Hale began questioning Abigail. Tell them to write five original sentences related to those events that call for the use of exclamation points. Then have them write five original sentences related to the events that should end in periods. **L1**

Additional Resources

📖 ***Grammar and Language Transparency 69***

📓 ***Grammar and Language Workbook***, p. 243

📓 ***Grammar and Composition Handbook***, Lesson 11.2

📓 ***Writer's Choice***, Lesson 21.2

Responding to Literature

Personal Response

What was your response to the end of act 1? Which events or details inspired your response?

ANALYZING ACT 1

RECALL AND INTERPRET

1. What is Reverend Parris praying about at the beginning of act 1? What else might explain why he is praying so desperately?
2. What reasons does Abigail give Parris for her discharge as the Proctors' servant? What might be another reason? What can you infer about Abigail's character from her words?
3. Describe the feelings the characters have toward each other: the Putnams toward John Proctor and Rebecca Nurse, Proctor toward the Putnams and Parris, and Parris toward the congregation. What effect might these feelings have on the future action of the play?
4. How does Tituba first respond to Hale's accusation of witchcraft? How does she change her response? Why might she, as well as Abigail and Betty, make accusations at the end of act 1?

EVALUATE AND CONNECT

5. Which character or characters arouse your sympathy most? Explain.
6. What is the overall **atmosphere,** or prevailing mood, of act 1? How does Miller create this atmosphere?
7. Is Miller's portrayal of the teenage girls and their behavior believable? Why or why not?
8. What similarities do you see between the interactions among the Salemites of 1692 and interactions among people today?

Literary ELEMENTS

Dialogue

Conversation between characters is called **dialogue.** Through dialogue, a playwright reveals the feelings, thoughts, and intentions of characters, sets out conflicts, and moves the plot forward. Much of the dialogue in *The Crucible* centers on series of questions and answers among the characters. In fact, the play opens with Tituba's question "My Betty be hearty soon?"

1. Which characters do the main questioning in act 1? Which characters are the subjects of the questioning?
2. What do the characters hope to determine by asking their questions?
3. Do you think the questions and methods of questioning are fair? Explain.

● See **Literary Terms Handbook,** p. R4.

EXTENDING YOUR RESPONSE

Writing About Literature

Setting the Stage   Miller called act 1 an overture—an introduction. In literary terms, it would be called an **exposition.** Write two or three paragraphs analyzing how Miller has "set the stage" for the rest of the play with the setting, characters, and plot of act 1. What, for you, is the **narrative hook,** or the story element that grabs your attention?

Literature Groups

Put Yourself in the Characters' Shoes   In your group, work together to create character webs that profile each character in act 1. Include the character's age, personality traits, standing in the community, and conflicts with others. Then, as a group, predict the role each character will play in this drama. Share your predictions with the class.

 Save your work for your portfolio.

THE CRUCIBLE 935

LITERARY ELEMENTS

1. Main questioners: Parris and Hale; questionees: Abigail and Tituba.
2. The characters want to know why two children are ill, or whether the girls practiced witchcraft.
3. Those who think the questioning is fair may say Salem is in danger; those being questioned are concealing information; those saying it is unfair may mention threats and intimidation.

Additional Resources

🎵 *Literary Elements Transparency 91*

Before Reading

Objectives

- To read and analyze a play about persecution of individuals for religious and personal reasons
- To identify and understand the uses of stage directions

Skills

Reading/Thinking: Drawing Conclusions; Monitoring Comprehension; Evaluating; Interpreting; Identifying Fallacies in Reasoning; Inferring; Identifying Errors in Logic; Distinguishing Fact and Opinion; Analyzing

Writing: Precise Words

Vocabulary: Dictionary Skills: Definitions

Grammar/Language: Capitalization

Listening/Speaking: Interviewing

Life Skills: Supporting and Contributing

Collaboration: Literature Groups

Skill Minilesson

VOCABULARY • Unlocking Meaning

Often you must use clues outside a word to figure out its meaning. The dictionary and context clues are both useful. However, you will sometimes come across a new word that contains internal clues to its meaning—familiar parts that can provide significant help if you notice them. Every time you learn a new word, you learn something important about a number of other words, ones that share the same base or root or combining form. The more able you are to notice these similarities in words, the easier it is to use what you already know to figure out what you don't yet know.

PRACTICE Use what you know about the vocabulary words in parentheses to complete the sentences.

1. (compromise) If you are in a <u>compromising</u> situation, you appear to be
   a. agreeable.   b. critical.   c. guilty.
2. (naive) An good antonym for <u>naiveté</u> is
   a. rudeness.   b. sophistication.   c. intelligence.
3. (contention) A <u>contentious</u> remark would be
   a. "Make me!"   b. "No, thanks!"   c. "I'm fine."
4. (evade) An <u>evasive</u> response to "When can we get together?" would be
   a. "Tonight."   b. "Soon."   c. "Never!"

 ——Before You Read

The Crucible, Act 2

BACKGROUND

The Puritans and Their Beliefs

The Puritans believed that if one member of the community sinned, misfortune could befall the entire community. Blame, therefore, was a common way to deal with personal misfortune. The Puritans also believed that all aspects of life must be guided by the Christian Bible. In fact, communities built schools so that all could learn to read the Bible. These efforts were intended to counteract the work of Satan, who tried to "keep men from the knowledge of the scriptures."

For most Puritans, witchcraft and black magic were real. Books such as *The Discovery of Witches* (1647) and those used by Reverend Hale described how "bewitched" people behaved.

VOCABULARY PREVIEW

reprimand (rep′ rə mand′) *v.* to reprove or correct sharply; p. 937

base (bās) *adj.* morally low; dishonorable; p. 943

covet (kuv′ it) *v.* to desire, especially to an excessive degree, something belonging to another; p. 947

misgiving (mis giv′ ing) *n.* a feeling of doubt, distrust, or anxiety; p. 947

subtle (sut′ əl) *adj.* not open, direct, or obvious; crafty; sly; p. 949

ineptly (i nept′ lē) *adv.* incompetently; awkwardly; clumsily; p. 951

936 ❧ UNIT 6: MIDCENTURY VOICES

Skill Minilesson

VOCABULARY • Unlocking Meaning

1. c   2. b
3. a   4. b

Additional Resources

📁 *Vocabulary Practice,* p. 55

Act Two

[*The common room of* PROCTOR's *house, eight days later.*

At the right is a door opening on the fields outside. A fireplace is at the left, and behind it a stairway leading upstairs. It is the low, dark, and rather long living room of the time. As the curtain rises, the room is empty. From above, ELIZABETH *is heard softly singing to the children. Presently the door opens and* JOHN PROCTOR *enters, carrying his gun. He glances about the room as he comes toward the fireplace, then halts for an instant as he hears her singing. He continues on to the fireplace, leans the gun against the wall as he swings a pot out of the fire and smells it. Then he lifts out the ladle and tastes. He is not quite pleased. He reaches to a cupboard, takes a pinch of salt, and drops it into the pot. As he is tasting again, her footsteps are heard on the stair. He swings the pot into the fireplace and goes to a basin and washes his hands and face.* ELIZABETH *enters.*]

ELIZABETH. What keeps you so late? It's almost dark.

PROCTOR. I were planting far out to the forest edge.

ELIZABETH. Oh, you're done then.

PROCTOR. Aye, the farm is seeded. The boys asleep?

ELIZABETH. They will be soon. [*And she goes to the fireplace, proceeds to ladle up stew in a dish.*]

PROCTOR. Pray now for a fair summer.

ELIZABETH. Aye.

PROCTOR. Are you well today?

ELIZABETH. I am. [*She brings the plate to the table, and, indicating the food.*] It is a rabbit.

PROCTOR. [*Going to the table.*] Oh, is it! In Jonathan's trap?

ELIZABETH. No, she walked into the house this afternoon; I found her sittin' in the corner like she come to visit.

PROCTOR. Oh, that's a good sign walkin' in.

ELIZABETH. Pray God. It hurt my heart to strip her, poor rabbit. [*She sits and watches him taste it.*]

PROCTOR. It's well seasoned.

ELIZABETH. [*Blushing with pleasure.*] I took great care. She's tender?

PROCTOR. Aye. [*He eats. She watches him.*] I think we'll see green fields soon. It's warm as blood beneath the clods.

ELIZABETH. That's well.

[PROCTOR *eats, then looks up.*]

PROCTOR. If the crop is good I'll buy George Jacob's heifer. How would that please you?

ELIZABETH. Aye, it would.

PROCTOR. [*With a grin.*] I mean to please you, Elizabeth.

ELIZABETH. [*It is hard to say.*] I know it, John.

[*He gets up, goes to her, kisses her. She receives it. With a certain disappointment, he returns to the table.*]

PROCTOR. [*As gently as he can.*] Cider?

ELIZABETH. [*With a sense of reprimanding herself for having forgot.*] Aye! [*She gets up and goes and pours a glass for him. He now arches his back.*]

PROCTOR. This farm's a continent when you go foot by foot droppin' seeds in it.

ELIZABETH. [*Coming with the cider.*] It must be.

PROCTOR. [*Drinks a long draught, then, putting the glass down.*] You ought to bring some flowers in the house.

ELIZABETH. Oh! I forgot! I will tomorrow.

Vocabulary
reprimand (rep′ rə mand′) *v.* to reprove or correct sharply

Reading the Selection

A

B

C

SUMMARY—ACT 2

It is eight days later. A Salem court is convicting people of witchcraft. Relations between the Proctors are strained. John wavers when Elizabeth urges him to expose Abigail. Mary Warren says Abigail has mentioned Elizabeth's name in court. Reverend Hale comes to question the Proctors. Giles Corey and Francis Nurse reveal that their wives have been arrested. Court officials arrest Elizabeth despite John's violent objections. John vows to expose the pretense and bring down the court.

📁 *Spanish Summaries,* p. 98

A Active Reading

QUESTION Ask students how Miller establishes the atmosphere and plot line of act 2. *(John does not want Elizabeth to know he has added salt. It might imply displeasure with her in light of their strained relationship. She begins with a question rather than a greeting. The audience sees the hidden suspicion—Was he with Abigail?)*

Additional Resources
📁 *Active Reading Guide,* p. 109
🎧 *Audio Library*
🎧 *Spanish Audio Library*

Teaching Options

REAL-WORLD CONNECTION

Comparing Reviews Have students attend a performance of *The Crucible* or another play of your choice in your local community. Suggest that they take along a small notebook to jot down their responses to aspects of the performances of the individual actors. Afterwards have each student read and analyze one or more reviews of the play from local newspapers and then write a brief essay comparing his or her own responses with those of the reviewers. **L2**

B Author's Craft

DIALOGUE Review the dialogue and help students recognize how Miller uses it to show the strain between John and Elizabeth. *(Their enthusiasm seems forced—"Oh, is it!" "Oh . . . a good sign . . ." "That's well." "Aye, it would." He makes a point of complimenting the seasoning, but he added salt. They give each other what seem unnecessary assurances—"I took great care." "I mean to please you." He is reluctant to point out that there is no cider on the table. Their talk about the farm has an air of two people trying to avoid an unsettling topic.)*

C Literary Elements

STAGE DIRECTIONS Review the stage directions and help students recognize how Miller uses them. *(Elizabeth watches him eat; it is important to her that he like the food. Her "blushing with pleasure" confirms that. She finds it hard to say she knows he means to please her. She "receives" his kiss, meaning she does not return it. He reminds her of the cider as "gently as he can." She responds as though "reprimanding herself.")*

D Critical Thinking

DRAWING CONCLUSIONS Ask students why they think John knows nothing of Mary or the court. *(Students may say that because of the strained relationship, he and Elizabeth have not been speaking, or that he has been spending as much time as possible in the fields to avoid the situation at home.)*

Teaching Options

The Crucible

PROCTOR. It's winter in here yet. On Sunday let you come with me, and we'll walk the farm together; I never see such a load of flowers on the earth. [*With good feeling he goes and looks up at the sky through the open doorway.*] Lilacs have a purple smell. Lilac is the smell of nightfall, I think. Massachusetts is a beauty in the spring!

ELIZABETH. Aye, it is.

[*There is a pause. She is watching him from the table as he stands there absorbing the night. It is as though she would speak but cannot. Instead, now, she takes up his plate and glass and fork and goes with them to the basin. Her back is turned to him. He turns to her and watches her. A sense of their separation rises.*]

PROCTOR. I think you're sad again. Are you?

ELIZABETH. [*She doesn't want friction, and yet she must.*] You come so late I thought you'd gone to Salem this afternoon.

PROCTOR. Why? I have no business in Salem.

ELIZABETH. You did speak of going, earlier this week.

PROCTOR. [*He knows what she means.*] I thought better of it since.

ELIZABETH. Mary Warren's there today.

PROCTOR. Why'd you let her? You heard me forbid her go to Salem any more!

ELIZABETH. I couldn't stop her.

PROCTOR. [*Holding back a full condemnation of her.*] It is a fault, it is a fault, Elizabeth—you're the mistress here, not Mary Warren.

ELIZABETH. She frightened all my strength away.

PROCTOR. How may that mouse frighten you, Elizabeth? You—

ELIZABETH. It is a mouse no more. I forbid her go, and she raises up her chin like the daughter of a prince and says to me, "I must go to Salem, Goody Proctor; I am an official of the court!"

PROCTOR. Court! What court?

ELIZABETH. Aye, it is a proper court they have now. They've sent four judges out of Boston, she says, weighty magistrates[1] of the General Court, and at the head sits the Deputy Governor of the Province.

PROCTOR. [*Astonished.*] Why, she's mad.

ELIZABETH. I would to God she were. There be fourteen people in the jail now, she says. [PROCTOR *simply looks at her, unable to grasp it.*] And they'll be tried, and the court have power to hang them too, she says.

PROCTOR. [*Scoffing, but without conviction.*] Ah, they'd never hang—

ELIZABETH. The Deputy Governor promise hangin' if they'll not confess, John. The town's gone wild, I think. She speak of Abigail, and I thought she were a saint, to hear her. Abigail brings the other girls into the court, and where she walks the crowd will part like the sea for Israel. And folks are brought before them, and if they scream and howl and fall to the floor—the person's clapped in the jail for bewitchin' them.

PROCTOR. [*Wide-eyed.*] Oh, it is a black mischief.

ELIZABETH. I think you must go to Salem, John. [*He turns to her.*] I think so. You must tell them it is a fraud.

PROCTOR. [*Thinking beyond this.*] Aye, it is, it is surely.

ELIZABETH. Let you go to Ezekiel Cheever—he knows you well. And tell him what she said to you last week in her uncle's house. She said it had naught to do with witchcraft, did she not?

PROCTOR. [*In thought.*] Aye, she did, she did. [*Now, a pause.*]

1. *Weighty* means "important." *Magistrates* are judges.

Painting, 1948. Willem de Kooning. Enamel and oil on canvas, 42⅝ x 56⅛ in. ©2000 Willem de Kooning Revocable Trust/Artists Rights Society (ARS), New York/ The Museum of Modern Art, New York.

Viewing the painting: What emotions does this painting evoke in you? How might it represent the emotions that John Proctor and Elizabeth are expressing at this point in the play?

MEETING INDIVIDUAL NEEDS — ENGLISH LANGUAGE LEARNERS

Understanding Historical Context
English language learners may need to learn more about colonial America. The Massachusetts Bay Colony, founded by the Puritans, at first governed all British settlements in New England. By 1692 politics, religion, and economics had led to the formation of other colonies.

Activity Have small groups conduct research on the founding of New Hampshire, Connecticut, and Rhode Island prior to 1692, and contrast developments in New England with specific historical events from their own cultures. Have the groups prepare oral reports for the class. **COLLAB. LEARN.**

Additional Resources
📁 *English Language Learners Sourcebook*

ELIZABETH. [*Quietly, fearing to anger him by prodding.*] God forbid you keep that from the court, John. I think they must be told.

PROCTOR. [*Quietly, struggling with his thought.*] Aye, they must, they must. It is a wonder they do believe her.

ELIZABETH. I would go to Salem now, John—let you go tonight.

PROCTOR. I'll think on it.

ELIZABETH. [*With her courage now.*] You cannot keep it, John.

PROCTOR. [*Angering.*] I know I cannot keep it. I say I will think on it!

ELIZABETH. [*Hurt, and very coldly.*] Good, then, let you think on it. [*She stands and starts to walk out of the room.*]

PROCTOR. I am only wondering how I may prove what she told me, Elizabeth. If the girl's a saint now, I think it is not easy to prove she's fraud, and the town gone so silly. She told it to me in a room alone—I have no proof for it.

ELIZABETH. You were alone with her?

PROCTOR. [*Stubbornly.*] For a moment alone, aye.

ELIZABETH. Why, then, it is not as you told me.

PROCTOR. [*His anger rising.*] For a moment, I say. The others come in soon after.

ELIZABETH. [*Quietly—she has suddenly lost all faith in him.*] Do as you wish, then. [*She starts to turn.*]

PROCTOR. Woman. [*She turns to him.*] I'll not have your suspicion any more.

E Active Reading

EVALUATE Based on the evidence so far, ask students to form an opinion about the existence of witchcraft in Salem. *(Students might argue that there is no evidence to show that the events in the woods were anything other that adolescent mischief or an attempt by Abigail to get rid of Elizabeth Proctor. They might also say that the unusual behavior of Betty and Ruth proves the girls were under some kind of spell.)*

ⅤIEWING THE PAINTING

Willem de Kooning (1904–1997) was one of America's leading abstract expressionist artists. This work is an excellent example of *action painting*, a technique for expressing what the artist was experiencing in his or her subconscious during the painting process. Action painting emerged among abstract expressionists in the late 1940s.

Viewing Response *Students may answer that the painting evokes a sense of confusion, anxiety, or anger, all of which feelings might be represented in the characters at this point in the play.*

THE CRUCIBLE, ACT 2 ❦ 939

Reading *Minilesson*

Monitoring Comprehension Remind students that playwrights use dialogue to reveal character, define conflict, and advance plot. Identifying and remembering several important bits of dialogue can help the reader understand key ideas in the play.

Activity Before students continue reading act 2, have them scan act 1 for key lines that help them interpret what they have learned thus far. Suggest that they create charts with the headings **Character**, **Conflict**, and **Theme**. Tell them to copy under each heading phrases or sentences they think are crucial to their understanding of the play. Suggest that they add in parentheses the name of the character speaking and the text page on which the dialogue is found. Suggest that students add to their charts as they read the remaining acts. For longer quotes, tell them to copy only key words and to use ellipses to indicate omissions. **L2**

Additional Resources
📁 *Reading Workbook,* pp. 81–82

F Critical Thinking

EVALUATING Ask students their opinions of Proctor's reluctance. Is Elizabeth right? *(Some may say yes because this cautious, indecisive man is not the John Proctor we saw stand up to Reverend Parris and Thomas Putnam. Others may say no because he has a valid point about proof. Also, he knows how seriously the Puritans take witchcraft. Denying the existence of witches is questioning the authority of the Bible. Proctor quickly corrected Corey when Corey said "He don't believe in witches.")*

G Active Reading

INTERPRET Have students explain what Proctor means when he tells Elizabeth "your justice would freeze beer!" *(Beer usually contains between 2 and 6 percent alcohol. The "home brew" of the Puritans may have been stronger. The freezing point of alcohol is significantly below that of water. Proctor equates Elizabeth's justice to extreme cold.)*

H Literary Elements

STAGE DIRECTIONS Ask students how the stage directions help them understand the sudden change in Proctor's behavior. *(Students should recognize that Miller's description of Mary Warren makes it clear that she appears ill and strangely distant, as though coming out of a trance. This helps us understand why her appearance confuses Proctor.)*

Teaching Options

ELIZABETH. [*A little loftily.*] I have no—

PROCTOR. I'll not have it!

ELIZABETH. Then let you not earn it.

PROCTOR. [*With a violent undertone.*] You doubt me yet?

ELIZABETH. [*With a smile, to keep her dignity.*] John, if it were not Abigail that you must go to hurt, would you falter now? I think not.

PROCTOR. Now look you—

ELIZABETH. I see what I see, John.

PROCTOR. [*With solemn warning.*] You will not judge me more, Elizabeth. I have good reason to think before I charge fraud on Abigail, and I will think on it. Let you look to your own improvement before you go to judge your husband any more. I have forgot Abigail, and—

ELIZABETH. And I.

PROCTOR. Spare me! You forget nothin' and forgive nothin'. Learn charity, woman. I have gone tiptoe in this house all seven month since she is gone. I have not moved from there to there without I think to please you, and still an everlasting funeral marches round your heart. I cannot speak but I am doubted, every moment judged for lies, as though I come into a court when I come into this house!

ELIZABETH. John, you are not open with me. You saw her with a crowd, you said. Now you—

PROCTOR. I'll plead my honesty no more, Elizabeth.

ELIZABETH. [*Now she would justify herself.*] John, I am only—

PROCTOR. No more! I should have roared you down when first you told me your suspicion. But I wilted, and, like a Christian, I confessed. Confessed! Some dream I had must have mistaken you for God that day. But you're not, you're not, and let you remember it! Let you look sometimes for the goodness in me, and judge me not.

ELIZABETH. I do not judge you. The magistrate sits in your heart that judges you. I never thought you but a good man, John—[*With a smile.*]—only somewhat bewildered.

PROCTOR. [*Laughing bitterly.*] Oh, Elizabeth, your justice would freeze beer! [*He turns suddenly toward a sound outside. He starts for the door as* MARY WARREN *enters. As soon as he sees her, he goes directly to her and grabs her by her cloak, furious.*] How do you go to Salem when I forbid it? Do you mock me? [*Shaking her.*] I'll whip you if you dare leave this house again!

[*Strangely, she doesn't resist him, but hangs limply by his grip.*]

MARY WARREN. I am sick, I am sick, Mr. Proctor. Pray, pray, hurt me not. [*Her strangeness throws him off, and her evident pallor[2] and weakness. He frees her.*] My insides are all shuddery; I am in the proceedings all day, sir.

PROCTOR. [*With draining anger—his curiosity is draining it.*] And what of these proceedings here? When will you proceed to keep this house, as you are paid nine pound a year to do—and my wife not wholly well?

[*As though to compensate,* MARY WARREN *goes to* ELIZABETH *with a small rag doll.*]

MARY WARREN. I made a gift for you today, Goody Proctor. I had to sit long hours in a chair, and passed the time with sewing.

ELIZABETH. [*Perplexed, looking at the doll.*] Why, thank you, it's a fair poppet.

MARY WARREN. [*With a trembling, decayed voice.*] We must all love each other now, Goody Proctor.

ELIZABETH. [*Amazed at her strangeness.*] Aye, indeed we must.

MARY WARREN. [*Glancing at the room.*] I'll get up early in the morning and clean the house. I must sleep now. [*She turns and starts off.*]

---

2. *Pallor* refers to a pale complexion.

MEETING INDIVIDUAL NEEDS — INCLUSION STRATEGIES

Learning Disabled Elliptical constructions in dialogue may be difficult for learning disabled students. Ask students to explain Elizabeth's elliptical clause: "And I." *(She is saying "And I have forgotten Abigail also.")* Tell students to rely on the case of the personal pronoun to help them complete elliptical clauses. *I* is the nominative case. Therefore, it is the subject. If Elizabeth had meant that John had forgotten her too, she would have said: "And *me*" (the objective case).

Activity Have students make charts listing nominative and objective cases for personal pronouns to help determine meanings of elliptical clauses.

Additional Resources
📁 *Inclusion Strategies*

PROCTOR. Mary. [*She halts.*] Is it true? There be fourteen women arrested?

MARY WARREN. No, sir. There be thirty-nine now—[*She suddenly breaks off and sobs and sits down, exhausted.*]

ELIZABETH. Why, she's weepin'! What ails you, child?

MARY WARREN. Goody Osburn—will hang!

[*There is a shocked pause, while she sobs.*]

PROCTOR. Hang! [*He calls into her face.*] Hang, y'say?

MARY WARREN. [*Through her weeping.*] Aye.

PROCTOR. The Deputy Governor will permit it?

MARY WARREN. He sentenced her. He must. [*To ameliorate[3] it.*] But not Sarah Good. For Sarah Good confessed, y'see.

PROCTOR. Confessed! To what?

MARY WARREN. That she—[*In horror at the memory.*]—she sometimes made a compact with Lucifer, and wrote her name in his black book—with her blood—and bound herself to torment Christians till God's thrown down—and we all must worship Hell forevermore.

[*Pause.*]

PROCTOR. But—surely you know what a jabberer she is. Did you tell them that?

MARY WARREN. Mr. Proctor, in open court she near to choked us all to death.

PROCTOR. How, choked you?

MARY WARREN. She sent her spirit out.

ELIZABETH. Oh, Mary, Mary, surely you—

MARY WARREN. [*With an indignant[4] edge.*] She tried to kill me many times, Goody Proctor!

ELIZABETH. Why, I never heard you mention that before.

---

3. To *ameliorate* is to improve a situation that was unpleasant or unbearable before.
4. *Indignant* means "expressing righteous anger."

MARY WARREN. I never knew it before. I never knew anything before. When she come into the court I say to myself, I must not accuse this woman, for she sleep in ditches, and so very old and poor. But then—then she sit there, denying and denying, and I feel a misty coldness climbin' up my back, and the skin on my skull begin to creep, and I feel a clamp around my neck and I cannot breathe air; and then—[*Entranced.*]—I hear a voice, a screamin' voice, and it were my voice—and all at once I remembered everything she done to me!

PROCTOR. Why? What did she do to you?

MARY WARREN. [*Like one awakened to a marvelous secret insight.*] So many time, Mr. Proctor, she come to this very door, beggin' bread and a cup of cider—and mark this: whenever I turned her away empty, she *mumbled*.

ELIZABETH. Mumbled! She may mumble if she's hungry.

MARY WARREN. But *what* does she mumble? You must remember, Goody Proctor. Last month—a Monday, I think—she walked away, and I thought my guts would burst for two days after. Do you remember it?

ELIZABETH. Why—I do, I think, but—

MARY WARREN. And so I told that to Judge Hathorne, and he asks her so. "Sarah Good," says he, "what curse do you mumble that this girl must fall sick after turning you away?" And then she replies—[*Mimicking an old crone.*][5] — "Why, your excellence, no curse at all. I only say my commandments; I hope I may say my commandments," says she!

ELIZABETH. And that's an upright answer.

MARY WARREN. Aye, but then Judge Hathorne say, "Recite for us your commandments!"—[*Leaning avidly toward them.*]—and of all the ten she could not say a single one. She never knew no commandments, and they had her in a flat lie!

---

5. A *crone* is a withered old woman.

RESPOND Ask students to respond to learning that 39 women have been arrested. *(Students may be shocked that the number imprisoned has almost tripled. This suggests that the witch-hunt is gathering force and speed like an avalanche or a storm.)*

J **Active Reading**

PARAPHRASING Ask students to describe Mary's mental state in their own words. *(Some may say that in court, she is acting like someone hypnotized or in a trance. Others may say that she is acting like someone in the grip of mob psychology, hearing others shouting accusations and then realizing that she is one of those shouting.)*

K **Critical Thinking**

IDENTIFYING FALLACIES IN REASONING Discuss cause and effect with students. Ask them to explain how Mary and the judge are assuming a faulty cause-and-effect relationship. *(There is no reason to believe that Goody Osburn's mumbling was the cause of Mary's sickness. Mary is assuming without any evidence that Goody Osburn placed a curse on her. The judge hears Mary's unproved statement and questions Osburn as though the statement is proven fact.)*

GIFTED AND TALENTED ACTIVITY

"Repressed Memories" Gifted and talented students may respond well to activities that allow them to explore complex or advanced topics.

Activity Call students' attention to Mary Warren's statement: *"and all at once I remembered everything she done to me!"* Point out that this comment suggests what modern psychologists refer to as "repressed memories."

Have students research the definition and theory of repressed memories and circumstances under which they can force their way into the conscious mind. Also, tell them to include concerns that have arisen when people, claiming they have suddenly recalled repressed events, have made accusations that turned out to be false. **L3**

Active Reading

L

QUESTION As they read this passage, ask students what accounts for the reversal in demeanor and attitude that takes place between Proctor and Mary. *(Students should recognize that, as she "wraps herself in the mantle" of the court, Mary becomes a more assertive and dominant figure. Proctor rants at first, but his threats are empty gestures. He gradually loses his power over her, giving in and, in effect, telling her to do whatever she likes.)*

Critical Thinking

M

ANALYZE Ask students to explain the change in Proctor. *(Some may say he realizes that he has no control over her anymore, and it is useless to make idle threats. Others may say Mary's revelation that Elizabeth's name was mentioned frightens him. He is worried about his wife's welfare and beginning to realize how dangerous Abigail is.)*

Active Reading

N

QUESTION Ask students whom Elizabeth is talking about when she says, "She wants me dead." *(She is talking about Abigail.)*

Literary Elements

O

STAGE DIRECTIONS Ask students what they think the stage direction "Without conviction" means. *(Students should recognize that John is trying to reassure Elizabeth that she has nothing to fear. However, he is worried about this turn of events.)*

Teaching Options

PROCTOR. And so condemned her?

MARY WARREN. [*Now a little strained, seeing his stubborn doubt.*] Why, they must when she condemned herself.

PROCTOR. But the proof, the proof!

MARY WARREN. [*With greater impatience with him.*] I told you the proof. It's hard proof, hard as rock, the judges said.

PROCTOR. [*Pauses an instant, then.*] You will not go to court again, Mary Warren.

MARY WARREN. I must tell you, sir, I will be gone every day now. I am amazed you do not see what weighty work we do.

PROCTOR. What work you do! It's strange work for a Christian girl to hang old women!

MARY WARREN. But, Mr. Proctor, they will not hang them if they confess. Sarah Good will only sit in jail some time—[*Recalling.*]—and here's a wonder for you; think on this. Goody Good is pregnant!

ELIZABETH. Pregnant! Are they mad? The woman's near to sixty!

MARY WARREN. They had Doctor Griggs examine her, and she's full to the brim. And smokin' a pipe all these years, and no husband either! But she's safe, thank God, for they'll not hurt the innocent child. But be that not a marvel? You must see it, sir, it's God's work we do. So I'll be gone every day for some time. I'm—I am an official of the court, they say, and I—[*She has been edging toward offstage.*]

PROCTOR. I'll official you! [*He strides to the mantel, takes down the whip hanging there.*]

MARY WARREN. [*Terrified, but coming erect, striving for her authority.*] I'll not stand whipping any more!

ELIZABETH. [*Hurriedly, as PROCTOR approaches.*] Mary, promise now you'll stay at home—

MARY WARREN. [*Backing from him, but keeping her erect posture, striving, striving for her way.*]

The Devil's loose in Salem, Mr. Proctor; we must discover where he's hiding!

PROCTOR. I'll whip the Devil out of you! [*With whip raised he reaches out for her, and she streaks away and yells.*]

MARY WARREN. [*Pointing at ELIZABETH.*] I saved her life today!

[*Silence. His whip comes down.*]

ELIZABETH. [*Softly.*] I am accused?

MARY WARREN. [*Quaking.*] Somewhat mentioned. But I said I never see no sign you ever sent your spirit out to hurt no one, and seeing I do live so closely with you, they dismissed it.

ELIZABETH. Who accused me?

MARY WARREN. I am bound by law, I cannot tell it. [*To PROCTOR.*] I only hope you'll not be so sarcastical no more. Four judges and the King's deputy sat to dinner with us but an hour ago. I—I would have you speak civilly to me, from this out.

PROCTOR. [*In horror, muttering in disgust at her.*] Go to bed.

MARY WARREN. [*With a stamp of her foot.*] I'll not be ordered to bed no more, Mr. Proctor! I am eighteen and a woman, however single!

PROCTOR. Do you wish to sit up? Then sit up.

MARY WARREN. I wish to go to bed!

PROCTOR. [*In anger.*] Good night, then!

MARY WARREN. Good night. [*Dissatisfied, uncertain of herself, she goes out. Wide-eyed, both, PROCTOR and ELIZABETH stand staring.*]

ELIZABETH. [*Quietly.*] Oh, the noose, the noose is up!

PROCTOR. There'll be no noose.

ELIZABETH. She wants me dead. I knew all week it would come to this!

PROCTOR. [*Without conviction.*] They dismissed it. You heard her say—

ELIZABETH. And what of tomorrow? She will cry me out until they take me!

REAL-WORLD CONNECTION

Using Logic Students might not be aware of how often they use the principles of logic in their daily lives. Explain that the *syllogism* is a basic tool of logic, and write this example on the board:

 All people are mortal. (major premise)
 John Proctor is a person. (minor premise)
 Therefore, John Proctor is mortal. (conclusion)

Point out the distinction between *valid* (logically correct) and *true* (factual). The example is valid and true. However, a syllogism may be valid but not true. Write this example on the board:

 All people who do not know the commandments are witches. (major premise)
 Goody Osburn does not know the commandments. (minor premise)
 Therefore, Goody Osburn is a witch. (conclusion)

This syllogism is valid; the conclusion follows logically from the premises. However, it is not true because the major premise is false. Point out that it is important to determine the truth of a premise.

Activity Have students create other syllogisms about *The Crucible* and its theme. Challenge them to create ones that are valid but not true as well as those that are valid and true. **L3**

PROCTOR. Sit you down.

ELIZABETH. She wants me dead, John, you know it!

PROCTOR. I say sit down! [*She sits, trembling. He speaks quietly, trying to keep his wits.*] Now we must be wise, Elizabeth.

ELIZABETH. [*With sarcasm, and a sense of being lost.*] Oh, indeed, indeed!

PROCTOR. Fear nothing. I'll find Ezekiel Cheever. I'll tell him she said it were all sport.

ELIZABETH. John, with so many in the jail, more than Cheever's help is needed now, I think. Would you favor me with this? Go to Abigail.

PROCTOR. [*His soul hardening as he senses . . .*] What have I to say to Abigail?

ELIZABETH. [*Delicately.*] John—grant me this. You have a faulty understanding of young girls. There is a promise made in any bed—

PROCTOR. [*Striving against his anger.*] What promise!

ELIZABETH. Spoke or silent, a promise is surely made. And she may dote on[6] it now—I am sure she does—and thinks to kill me, then to take my place.

[*PROCTOR's anger is rising; he cannot speak.*]

ELIZABETH. It is her dearest hope, John, I know it. There be a thousand names; why does she call mine? There be a certain danger in calling such a name—I am no Goody Good that sleeps in ditches, nor Osburn, drunk and half-witted. She'd dare not call out such a farmer's wife but there be monstrous profit in it. She thinks to take my place, John.

PROCTOR. She cannot think it! [*He knows it is true.*]

---

6. To *dote on* is to show extreme affection for or to pay excessive attention to.

ELIZABETH. [*"Reasonably."*] John, have you ever shown her somewhat of contempt? She cannot pass you in the church but you will blush—

PROCTOR. I may blush for my sin.

ELIZABETH. I think she sees another meaning in that blush.

PROCTOR. And what see you? What see you, Elizabeth?

ELIZABETH. [*"Conceding."*] I think you be somewhat ashamed, for I am there, and she so close.

PROCTOR. When will you know me, woman? Were I stone I would have cracked for shame this seven month!

ELIZABETH. Then go and tell her she's a whore. Whatever promise she may sense—break it, John, break it.

PROCTOR. [*Between his teeth.*] Good, then. I'll go. [*He starts for his rifle.*]

ELIZABETH. [*Trembling, fearfully.*] Oh, how unwillingly!

PROCTOR. [*Turning on her, rifle in hand.*] I will curse her hotter than the oldest cinder in hell. But pray, begrudge me not my anger!

ELIZABETH. Your anger! I only ask you—

PROCTOR. Woman, am I so base? Do you truly think me base?

ELIZABETH. I never called you base.

PROCTOR. Then how do you charge me with such a promise? The promise that a stallion gives a mare I gave that girl!

ELIZABETH. Then why do you anger with me when I bid you break it?

PROCTOR. Because it speaks deceit, and I am honest! But I'll plead no more! I see now your spirit twists around the single error of my life, and I will never tear it free!

Vocabulary
base (bās) *adj.* morally low; dishonorable

P Literary Elements

PLOT Explain that plots can develop a sense of suspense when one character conspires against another. The hatched plan depends for its success on the ignorance or naiveté of the person being conspired against. Ask students whether Abigail's plot will succeed. *(Some may say yes because she has hatched it in private and put it into effect before the Proctors knew what she was up to. Others may say no because Abigail must have realized that Elizabeth saw through her from the beginning and would not be fooled.)*

Q Critical Thinking

INTERPRET Ask students to explain what is being revealed here. *(For the first time, Proctor openly admits that he had an affair with Abigail.)* Ask if they feel more sympathetic toward Abigail at this point. *(Many may say they feel more sympathetic toward her, but the revelation does not justify her actions.)*

R Active Reading

EVALUATE Have students share their opinions of Proctor's character. What do they think of his viewpoint? *(Most will probably say he is unsympathetic. However, some may say that even though he is unsympathetic, Abigail is a schemer and a liar who entrapped him, and she deserves his scorn. Others may say that Elizabeth is right. Proctor is responsible for his actions; he misled her into believing there was a future in their relationship.)*

MEETING INDIVIDUAL NEEDS INCLUSION STRATEGIES

Less-Proficient Readers The physical setting is confined to the Parris house in act 1 and to the Proctor home in act 2, but both acts refer to events that have happened earlier or are taking place elsewhere at the same time.

Activity Have less-proficient readers work in small groups with proficient readers to create time lines of major plot events. For events that are occurring simultaneously, suggest that students enter the event that is occurring onstage above the line and the event that is happening elsewhere below the line. **L1** **COLLAB. LEARN.**

Additional Resources
📁 *Inclusion Strategies*

VIEWING THE PHOTOGRAPH

In the original production, the following actors played the parts of the characters shown in this photograph:

Original Cast Members

Elizabeth Proctor . . Beatrice Straight

John Proctor . . . . . Arthur Kennedy

Reverend Hale . . . E. G. Marshall

Responding to the Photograph

Discussion question:
• Who do you think the three main characters in the photograph are? *(Elizabeth Proctor, John Proctor, Reverend Hale)*

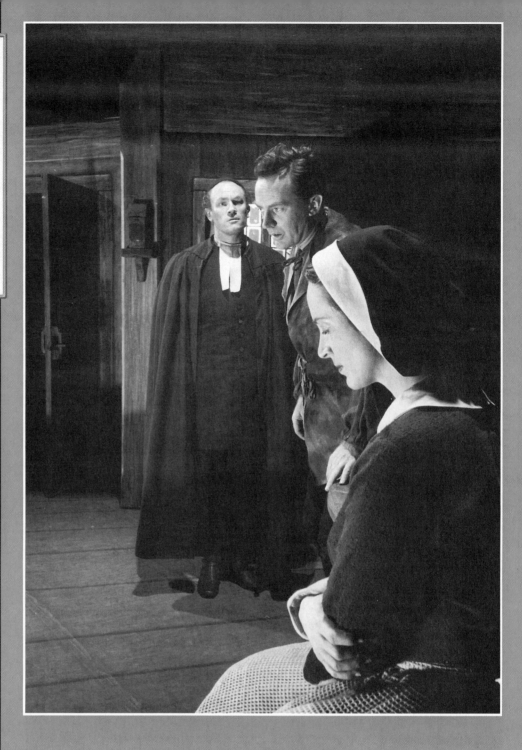

Teaching Options

ELIZABETH. [*Crying out.*] You'll tear it free—when you come to know that I will be your only wife, or no wife at all! She has an arrow in you yet, John Proctor, and you know it well!

[*Quite suddenly, as though from the air, a figure appears in the doorway. They start slightly. It is* MR. HALE. *He is different now—drawn a little, and there is a quality of deference, even of guilt, about his manner now.*]

HALE. Good evening.

PROCTOR. [*Still in his shock.*] Why, Mr. Hale! Good evening to you, sir. Come in, come in.

HALE. [*To* ELIZABETH.] I hope I do not startle you.

ELIZABETH. No, no, it's only that I heard no horse—

HALE. You are Goodwife Proctor.

PROCTOR. Aye; Elizabeth.

HALE. [*Nods, then.*] I hope you're not off to bed yet.

PROCTOR. [*Setting down his gun.*] No, no. [HALE *comes further into the room. And* PROCTOR, *to explain his nervousness.*] We are not used to visitors after dark, but you're welcome here. Will you sit you down, sir?

HALE. I will. [*He sits.*] Let you sit, Goodwife Proctor.

[*She does, never letting him out of her sight. There is a pause as* HALE *looks about the room.*]

PROCTOR. [*To break the silence.*] Will you drink cider, Mr. Hale?

HALE. No, it rebels my stomach; I have some further traveling yet tonight. Sit you down, sir. [PROCTOR *sits.*] I will not keep you long, but I have some business with you.

PROCTOR. Business of the court?

HALE. No—no, I come of my own, without the court's authority. Hear me. [*He wets his lips.*] I know not if you are aware, but your wife's name is—mentioned in the court.

PROCTOR. We know it, sir. Our Mary Warren told us. We are entirely amazed.

HALE. I am a stranger here, as you know. And in my ignorance I find it hard to draw a clear opinion of them that come accused before the court. And so this afternoon, and now tonight, I go from house to house—I come now from Rebecca Nurse's house and—

ELIZABETH. [*Shocked.*] Rebecca's charged!

HALE. God forbid such a one be charged. She is, however—mentioned somewhat.

ELIZABETH. [*With an attempt at a laugh.*] You will never believe, I hope, that Rebecca trafficked with the Devil.

HALE. Woman, it is possible.

PROCTOR. [*Taken aback.*] Surely you cannot think so.

HALE. This is a strange time, Mister. No man may longer doubt the powers of the dark are gathered in monstrous attack upon this village. There is too much evidence now to deny it. You will agree, sir?

PROCTOR. [*Evading.*] I—have no knowledge in that line. But it's hard to think so pious[7] a woman be secretly a Devil's bitch after seventy year of such good prayer.

HALE. Aye. But the Devil is a wily[8] one, you cannot deny it. However, she is far from accused, and I know she will not be. [*Pause.*] I thought, sir, to put some questions as to the Christian character of this house, if you'll permit me.

PROCTOR. [*Coldly, resentful.*] Why, we—have no fear of questions, sir.

HALE. Good, then. [*He makes himself more comfortable.*] In the book of record that Mr. Parris keeps, I note that you are rarely in the church on Sabbath Day.

---

7. **Pious** means "having a sincere reverence for God."
8. **Wily** means "crafty" or "sly and full of tricks."

Dreaming Cathedrals

Proctor is accusing Parris of more than simple avarice and vanity when he says, "the man dreams cathedrals." Puritans wanted to "purify" the Anglican church. Part of this purification included elimination of certain beliefs and practices of the Catholic church. Gold candlesticks and ornate cathedrals, to Proctor, might represent Catholicism and "impure" ideas. In this sense, Proctor is accusing Parris of beliefs and practices that are unacceptable to a good Puritan.

Ⓥ Critical Thinking

ANALYZING Help students recognize how this part of the discussion again introduces the question of authority versus individual conscience. *(In act 1, Parris and Proctor argued over an individual's right to question a minister—"the Lord's man in the parish." Hale is taking the same position Parris took—"That is not for you to decide. . . . the light of God is in him.")*

The Crucible

PROCTOR. No, sir, you are mistaken.

HALE. Twenty-six time in seventeen month, sir. I must call that rare. Will you tell me why you are so absent?

PROCTOR. Mr. Hale, I never knew I must account to that man for I come to church or stay at home. My wife were sick this winter.

HALE. So I am told. But you, Mister, why could you not come alone?

PROCTOR. I surely did come when I could, and when I could not I prayed in this house.

HALE. Mr. Proctor, your house is not a church; your theology[9] must tell you that.

PROCTOR. It does, sir, it does; and it tells me that a minister may pray to God without he have golden candlesticks upon the altar.

HALE. What golden candlesticks?

PROCTOR. Since we built the church there were pewter[10] candlesticks upon the altar; Francis Nurse made them, y'know, and a sweeter hand never touched the metal. But Parris came, and for twenty week he preach nothin' but golden candlesticks until he had them. I labor the earth from dawn of day to blink of night, and I tell you true, when I look to heaven and see my money glaring at his elbows—it hurt my prayer, sir, it hurt my prayer. I think, sometimes, the man dreams cathedrals, not clapboard meetin' houses.

HALE. [*Thinks, then.*] And yet, Mister, a Christian on Sabbath Day must be in church. [*Pause.*] Tell me—you have three children?

PROCTOR. Aye. Boys.

HALE. How comes it that only two are baptized?

---

9. Here, Hale uses the term *theology* to refer to Proctor's own religious beliefs.
10. *Pewter* is an alloy, or a substance composed of two or more metals or of a metal and a nonmetal. Tin is the main metal in pewter, and it is often mixed with lead.

PROCTOR. [*Starts to speak, then stops, then, as though unable to restrain this.*] I like it not that Mr. Parris should lay his hand upon my baby. I see no light of God in that man. I'll not conceal it.

HALE. I must say it, Mr. Proctor; that is not for you to decide. The man's ordained, therefore the light of God is in him.

PROCTOR. [*Flushed with resentment but trying to smile.*] What's your suspicion, Mr. Hale?

HALE. No, no, I have no—

PROCTOR. I nailed the roof upon the church, I hung the door—

HALE. Oh, did you! That's a good sign, then.

PROCTOR. It may be I have been too quick to bring the man to book, but you cannot think we ever desired the destruction of religion. I think that's in your mind, is it not?

HALE. [*Not altogether giving way.*] I—have—there is a softness in your record, sir, a softness.

ELIZABETH. I think, maybe, we have been too hard with Mr. Parris. I think so. But sure we never loved the Devil here.

HALE. [*Nods, deliberating this. Then, with the voice of one administering a secret test.*] Do you know your Commandments, Elizabeth?

ELIZABETH. [*Without hesitation, even eagerly.*] I surely do. There be no mark of blame upon my life, Mr. Hale. I am a covenanted Christian woman.

HALE. And you, Mister?

PROCTOR. [*A trifle unsteadily.*] I—am sure I do, sir.

HALE. [*Glances at her open face, then at JOHN, then.*] Let you repeat them, if you will.

PROCTOR. The Commandments.

HALE. Aye.

PROCTOR. [*Looking off, beginning to sweat.*] Thou shalt not kill.

HALE. Aye.

Teaching Options

Writing *Minilesson*

Precise Words Remind students that they need to use words precisely. Provide this example from the stage directions: "Nods, deliberating this." *Deliberate* and *reflect* are verbs with similar meanings. *Deliberate* suggests careful reasoning before reaching a conclusion. *Reflect* suggests unhurried consideration of something recalled to the mind. Hale is not thinking about something recalled to

mind; he is considering what Elizabeth has said. Therefore, *deliberate* is more precise than *reflect*.

A dictionary or thesaurus may include synonymies that explain subtle differences in word meanings. In a dictionary, synonymies often are found after the entry for one of the related words.

Activity Have students select five pieces of dialogue on this page for which

Miller has not provided stage directions. Tell them to write a stage direction for each, which includes a precise noun, verb, adjective, or adverb to describe the speaker's emotion. Have students use a dictionary, thesaurus, or a synonymy. **L2**

Additional Resources

📓 *Writer's Choice,* Lessons 5.1, 24.1, 24.2

PROCTOR. [*Counting on his fingers.*] Thou shalt not steal. Thou shalt not covet thy neighbor's goods, nor make unto thee any graven image.[11] Thou shalt not take the name of the Lord in vain; thou shalt have no other gods before me. [*With some hesitation.*] Thou shalt remember the Sabbath Day and keep it holy. [*Pause. Then.*] Thou shalt honor thy father and mother. Thou shalt not bear false witness. [*He is stuck. He counts back on his fingers, knowing one is missing.*] Thou shalt not make unto thee any graven image.

HALE. You have said that twice, sir.

PROCTOR. [*Lost.*] Aye. [*He is flailing for it.*]

ELIZABETH. [*Delicately.*] Adultery, John.

PROCTOR. [*As though a secret arrow had pained his heart.*] Aye. [*Trying to grin it away—to* HALE.] You see, sir, between the two of us we do know them all. [HALE *only looks at* PROCTOR, *deep in his attempt to define this man.* PROCTOR *grows more uneasy.*] I think it be a small fault.

HALE. Theology, sir, is a fortress; no crack in a fortress may be accounted small. [*He rises; he seems worried now. He paces a little, in deep thought.*]

PROCTOR. There be no love for Satan in this house, Mister.

HALE. I pray it, I pray it dearly. [*He looks to both of them, an attempt at a smile on his face, but his misgivings are clear.*] Well, then—I'll bid you good night.

ELIZABETH. [*Unable to restrain herself.*] Mr. Hale. [*He turns.*] I do think you are suspecting me somewhat? Are you not?

HALE. [*Obviously disturbed—and evasive.*] Goody Proctor, I do not judge you. My duty is to add what I may to the godly wisdom of the court. I pray you both good health and good fortune. [*To* JOHN.] Good night, sir. [*He starts out.*]

ELIZABETH. [*With a note of desperation.*] I think you must tell him, John.

HALE. What's that?

ELIZABETH. [*Restraining a call.*] Will you tell him?

[*Slight pause.* HALE *looks questioningly at* JOHN.]

PROCTOR. [*With difficulty.*] I—I have no witness and cannot prove it, except my word be taken. But I know the children's sickness had naught to do with witchcraft.

HALE. [*Stopped, struck.*] Naught to do—?

PROCTOR. Mr. Parris discovered them sportin' in the woods. They were startled and took sick.

[*Pause.*]

HALE. Who told you this?

PROCTOR. [*Hesitates, then.*] Abigail Williams.

HALE. Abigail!

PROCTOR. Aye.

HALE. [*His eyes wide.*] Abigail Williams told you it had naught to do with witchcraft!

PROCTOR. She told me the day you came, sir.

HALE. [*Suspiciously.*] Why—why did you keep this?

PROCTOR. I never knew until tonight that the world is gone daft[12] with this nonsense.

HALE. Nonsense! Mister, I have myself examined Tituba, Sarah Good, and numerous others that have confessed to dealing with the Devil. They have *confessed* it.

PROCTOR. And why not, if they must hang for denyin' it? There are them that will swear to

---

11. Here, a *graven image* is an idol.

12. *Daft* means "without sense or reason," "crazy," or "silly."

Vocabulary
covet (kuv′ it) *v.* to desire, especially to an excessive degree, something belonging to another
misgiving (mis giv′ ing) *n.* a feeling of doubt, distrust, or anxiety

W Critical Thinking

INTERPRET Discuss with students the significance of Proctor's failure to remember the one commandment. *(It is the one he is guilty of breaking. Psychologists today might say he has blocked it from his mind because of its painful association, which for him is awareness of his sin.)*

X Author's Craft

DIALOGUE Help students recognize how the organization of Proctor's thoughts reveals how difficult it is for him to make the accusation. *(He typically speaks in a blunt, straightforward manner. Here, he fumbles, and first says he has no proof before he says that Abigail is lying.)*

Y Active Reading

CHARACTERIZATION Point out how Proctor's attitude and demeanor change once the truth begins to come out. He seems to regain his strength of character and forcefulness. He calls the trials "nonsense." He immediately points out the weakness in Hale's argument—". . . why not [confess], if they must hang for denying it?"

LITERATURE & HUMANITIES

🎧 **"Ainsworth Psalm 100,"** from ***American Music***
Volume 1, Track 4

Have students listen to this song Puritan congregations once sang.

MULTIPLE LEARNING STYLES

Musical Students with musical skills may respond well to activities relating song to the selection. Others can benefit from their skills as well. Point out that Elizabeth is "softly singing to the children" as act 2 begins. Miller does not explain what she is singing, but it is quite likely a religious song.

Activity Have students research examples of songs Elizabeth might have sung. Tell them to find examples of songs colonists might have sung and the musical instruments they may have used to accompany their voices. Ask them to share their findings with the class. Encourage students to play recordings or perform the music for the class. **L2**

Ben Shahn

anything before they'll hang; have you never thought of that?

HALE. I have. I—I have indeed. [*It is his own suspicion, but he resists it. He glances at ELIZABETH, then at JOHN.*] And you—would you testify to this in court?

PROCTOR. I—had not reckoned with goin' into court. But if I must I will.

HALE. Do you falter here?

PROCTOR. I falter nothing, but I may wonder if my story will be credited in such a court. I do wonder on it, when such a steady-minded minister as you will suspicion such a woman that never lied, and cannot, and the world knows she cannot! I may falter somewhat, Mister; I am no fool.

HALE. [*Quietly—it has impressed him.*] Proctor, let you open with me now, for I have a rumor that troubles me. It's said you hold no belief that there may even be witches in the world. Is that true, sir?

PROCTOR. [*He knows this is critical, and is striving against his disgust with HALE and with himself for even answering.*] I know not what I have said, I may have said it. I have wondered if there be witches in the world—although I cannot believe they come among us now.

HALE. Then you do not believe—

This photograph shows the scene in which Mary Warren, at John Proctor's urging, testifies that the accusations of witchcraft are false.

Responding to the Art Discussion questions:

• How can you tell that the action shown in the photograph comes before Cheever's comment that Ruth Putnam is not in court? *(Abigail and the other girls are not onstage.)*

• Who do you think is pointing at John Proctor? What do you think he is saying? Why? *(Judge Danforth is pointing. Because he is pointing at Proctor but looking at Mary, he is probably asking, "Has Mr. Proctor threatened you for this deposition?")*

PROCTOR. She has not been a girl these fifteen years, Your Honor.

HATHORNE. But a poppet will keep fifteen years, will it not?

PROCTOR. It will keep if it is kept, but Mary Warren swears she never saw no poppets in my house, nor anyone else.

PARRIS. Why could there not have been poppets hid where no one ever saw them?

 PROCTOR. [*Furious.*] There might also be a dragon with five legs in my house, but no one has ever seen it.

PARRIS. We are here, Your Honor, precisely to discover what no one has ever seen.

PROCTOR. Mr. Danforth, what profit this girl to turn herself about? What may Mary Warren gain but hard questioning and worse?

DANFORTH. You are charging Abigail Williams with a marvelous cool plot to murder, do you understand that?

PROCTOR. I do, sir. I believe she means to murder.

DANFORTH. [*Pointing at* ABIGAIL, *incredulously.*][15] This child would murder your wife? **Y**

PROCTOR. It is not a child. Now hear me, sir. In the sight of the congregation she were twice this year put out of this meetin' house for laughter during prayer.

DANFORTH. [*Shocked, turning to* ABIGAIL.] What's this? Laughter during—!

PARRIS. Excellency, she were under Tituba's power at that time, but she is solemn now.

---

15. *Incredulously* means "in a disbelieving manner."

THE CRUCIBLE, ACT 3 🦋 969

X Literary Elements

COMIC RELIEF Ask students to identify the comic relief on this page. *(Students should recognize that Proctor's line about a five-legged dragon is comic relief.)* Note that the comic relief is for the benefit of the audience, but it does not affect the mood onstage.

Y Literary Elements

RISING ACTION Be certain that students recognize the plot development that brings the rising action nearer to the climax. *(For the first time, Proctor suggests that Abigail has a motive for wanting his wife dead. Revelation of his involvement with Abigail is surfacing.)*

GIFTED AND TALENTED ACTIVITY

Historical Research Point out that Cheever mentions that Ruth Putnam (as well as other children) is not in the court. Her father had been there a short time ago. Have students consider whether Thomas left with his daughter to avoid further questions.

Activity Remind students that from his research, Miller believed that Thomas Putnam, for reasons of vengeance and greed, was one of the principal villains behind the actual Salem witchcraft trials. A number of historians also believe that Thomas Putnam and others used the hysteria to accuse enemies and benefit financially. Have students use library and Internet resources to research this topic. Tell them to evaluate the evidence and draw conclusions in a written report. **L3**

Author's Craft

SUSPENSE Discuss with students how Miller sustains suspense throughout act 3. *(It is clear that Danforth is the dominant force on the court. Throughout the act, each of the two opposing groups tries to win him over. Miller maintains suspense by having the balance constantly swing back and forth. First one side appears to be winning, then the other. At this point, Proctor and his friends seem close to victory. The revelation about dancing has shaken Danforth's faith in Abigail.)*

Active Reading

CONNECT Ask students what they admire most about Mary Warren at this point in the play. *(Some may say that although she is frightened, she refuses to lie. Others may say that she places her concern for the innocent Elizabeth above fears for her own safety.)*

GILES. Aye, now she is solemn and goes to hang people!

DANFORTH. Quiet, man.

HATHORNE. Surely it have no bearing on the question, sir. He charges contemplation of murder.

DANFORTH. Aye. [*He studies* ABIGAIL *for a moment, then.*] Continue, Mr. Proctor.

PROCTOR. Mary. Now tell the Governor how you danced in the woods.

PARRIS. [*Instantly.*] Excellency, since I come to Salem this man is blackening my name. He—

DANFORTH. In a moment, sir. [*To* MARY WARREN, *sternly, and surprised.*] What is this dancing?

MARY WARREN. I—[*She glances at* ABIGAIL, *who is staring down at her remorselessly. Then, appealing to* PROCTOR.] Mr. Proctor—

PROCTOR. [*Taking it right up.*] Abigail leads the girls to the woods, Your Honor, and they have danced there naked—

PARRIS. Your Honor, this—

PROCTOR. [*At once.*] Mr. Parris discovered them himself in the dead of night! There's the "child" she is!

DANFORTH. [*It is growing into a nightmare, and he turns, astonished, to* PARRIS.] Mr. Parris—

PARRIS. I can only say, sir, that I never found any of them naked, and this man is—

DANFORTH. But you discovered them dancing in the woods? [*Eyes on* PARRIS, *he points at* ABIGAIL.] Abigail?

HALE. Excellency, when I first arrived from Beverly, Mr. Parris told me that.

DANFORTH. Do you deny it, Mr. Parris?

PARRIS. I do not, sir, but I never saw any of them naked.

DANFORTH. But she have *danced?*

PARRIS. [*Unwillingly.*] Aye, sir.

[DANFORTH, *as though with new eyes, looks at* ABIGAIL.]

HATHORNE. Excellency, will you permit me? [*He points at* MARY WARREN.]

DANFORTH. [*With great worry.*] Pray, proceed.

HATHORNE. You say you never saw no spirits, Mary, were never threatened or afflicted by any manifest of the Devil or the Devil's agents.

MARY WARREN. [*Very faintly.*] No, sir.

HATHORNE. [*With a gleam of victory.*] And yet, when people accused of witchery confronted you in court, you would faint, saying their spirits came out of their bodies and choked you—

MARY WARREN. That were pretense, sir.

DANFORTH. I cannot hear you.

MARY WARREN. Pretense, sir.

PARRIS. But you did turn cold, did you not? I myself picked you up many times, and your skin were icy. Mr. Danforth, you—

DANFORTH. I saw that many times.

PROCTOR. She only pretended to faint, Your Excellency. They're all marvelous pretenders.

HATHORNE. Then can she pretend to faint now?

PROCTOR. Now?

PARRIS. Why not? Now there are no spirits attacking her, for none in this room is accused of witchcraft. So let her turn herself cold now, let her pretend she is attacked now, let her faint. [*He turns to* MARY WARREN.] Faint!

MARY WARREN. Faint?

PARRIS. Aye, faint. Prove to us how you pretended in the court so many times.

MARY WARREN. [*Looking to* PROCTOR.] I—cannot faint now, sir.

Vocabulary

contemplation (kon′ təm plā′shən) *n.* the act of thinking about something long and seriously

---

Teaching Options

Listening and Speaking *Minilesson*

Dramatic Reading Discuss these guidelines for giving a dramatic reading:
- Listen for cues so that you know when to speak.
- Vary pitch, tone, and speed to express meaning and emotion.
- Use facial expressions and gestures to reinforce vocal interpretations.
- Use stress and pause to build suspense and convey a sense of danger or urgency.

Activity Have groups give dramatic readings of selected passages from the play. To maximize involvement and dramatic effect, select passages with a number of characters. One possibility is the passage that begins with Reverend Hale's interrogation of Abigail on page 930 and ends with the chanting of the accusations that concludes act 1 on page 934. Another is the passage that begins with Danforth's question to Mary on page 967 and ends with Abigail's line "Oh, Heavenly Father, take away this shadow" on page 972. Allow group members to decide which parts each will read. **L2** **COLLAB. LEARN.**

PROCTOR. [*Alarmed, quietly.*] Can you not pretend it?

MARY WARREN. I—[*She looks about as though searching for the passion to faint.*] I—have no *sense* of it now, I—

DANFORTH. Why? What is lacking now?

MARY WARREN. I—cannot tell, sir, I—

DANFORTH. Might it be that here we have no afflicting spirit loose, but in the court there were some?

MARY WARREN. I never saw no spirits.

PARRIS. Then see no spirits now, and prove to us that you can faint by your own will, as you claim.

MARY WARREN. [*Stares, searching for the emotion of it, and then shakes her head.*] I—cannot do it.

PARRIS. Then you will confess, will you not? It were attacking spirits made you faint!

MARY WARREN. No, sir, I—

PARRIS. Your Excellency, this is a trick to blind the court!

MARY WARREN. It's not a trick! [*She stands.*] I—I used to faint because I—I thought I saw spirits.

DANFORTH. *Thought* you saw them!

MARY WARREN. But I did not, Your Honor.

HATHORNE. How could you think you saw them unless you saw them?

MARY WARREN. I—I cannot tell how, but I did. I—I heard the other girls screaming, and you, Your Honor, you seemed to believe them, and I—It were only sport in the beginning, sir, but then the whole world cried spirits, spirits, and I—I promise you, Mr. Danforth, I only thought I saw them but I did not.

[*DANFORTH peers at her.*]

PARRIS. [*Smiling, but nervous because DANFORTH seems to be struck by MARY WARREN's story.*] Surely Your Excellency is not taken by this simple lie.

DANFORTH. [*Turning worriedly to ABIGAIL.*] Abigail. I bid you now search your heart and tell me this—and beware of it, child, to God every soul is precious and His vengeance is terrible on them that take life without cause. Is it possible, child, that the spirits you have seen are illusion only, some deception that may cross your mind when—

ABIGAIL. Why, this—this—is a base question, sir.

DANFORTH. Child, I would have you consider it—

ABIGAIL. I have been hurt, Mr. Danforth; I have seen my blood runnin' out! I have been near to murdered every day because I done my duty pointing out the Devil's people—and this is my reward? To be mistrusted, denied, questioned like a—

DANFORTH. [*Weakening.*] Child, I do not mistrust you—

ABIGAIL. [*In an open threat.*] Let *you* beware, Mr. Danforth. Think you to be so mighty that the power of Hell may not turn *your* wits? Beware of it! There is—[*Suddenly, from an accusatory attitude, her face turns, looking into the air above—it is truly frightened.*]

DANFORTH. [*Apprehensively.*] What is it, child?

ABIGAIL. [*Looking about in the air, clasping her arms about her as though cold.*] I—I know not. A wind, a cold wind, has come. [*Her eyes fall on MARY WARREN.*]

MARY WARREN. [*Terrified, pleading.*] Abby!

MERCY LEWIS. [*Shivering.*] Your Honor, I freeze!

PROCTOR. They're pretending!

HATHORNE. [*Touching ABIGAIL's hand.*] She is cold, Your Honor, touch her!

MERCY LEWIS. [*Through chattering teeth.*] Mary, do you send this shadow on me?

MARY WARREN. Lord, save me!

SUSANNA WALCOTT. I freeze, I freeze!

THE CRUCIBLE, ACT 3 🐚 971

Historical Note

Were the girls of the Salem witch trials suffering from the illness hysteria? Some people believe so. Psychologists have found a relationship between emotional conflict and the illness. Growing up in a repressive Puritan society could have caused emotional conflicts that led to hysteria. Other people doubt the girls were true hysterics, noting, for one thing, that they seemed able to control when they did or did not exhibit symptoms. A true hysteric cannot do this.

BB **Critical Thinking**

Critical Thinking

EVALUATING Ask students if Abigail is a true hysteric or a fake. Guide students in making a judgment about her character based on the information provided.

Model: Miller tells us in the beginning that Abigail has "an endless capacity for dissembling." She seems to be a natural actress. Her hallucinations seem controlled and spring from motive. They come when she feels threatened. When Judge Danforth begins questioning Abigail as though he doubts her, she suddenly begins hallucinating, to deflect attention from herself to Mary. Apparently, Abigail can turn her hallucinations off and on; for example, when Proctor accuses her of sin, her fit ends as suddenly as it began. She says rationally, "Mr. Danforth, he is lying." Clearly, Abigail is faking.

VIEWING THE PHOTOGRAPH

This photograph shows the scene in which Elizabeth, in response to Judge Danforth's question, denies her husband has committed lechery.

Responding to the Art Discussion question:

• Who are the two characters in the foreground? How do you know? *(John Proctor and Abigail Williams. They stand with their backs turned as Judge Danforth instructed.)*

Teaching Options

The Crucible

ABIGAIL. [*Shivering visibly.*] It is a wind, a wind!

MARY WARREN. Abby, don't do that!

DANFORTH. [*Himself engaged and entered by* ABIGAIL.] Mary Warren, do you witch her? I say to you, do you send your spirit out?

[*With a hysterical cry* MARY WARREN *starts to run.* PROCTOR *catches her.*]

MARY WARREN. [*Almost collapsing.*] Let me go, Mr. Proctor, I cannot, I cannot—

ABIGAIL. [*Crying to Heaven.*] Oh, Heavenly Father, take away this shadow!

[*Without warning or hesitation,* PROCTOR *leaps at* ABIGAIL *and, grabbing her by the hair, pulls her to her feet. She screams in pain.* DANFORTH, *astonished, cries,* "What are you about?" *and* HATHORNE *and* PARRIS *call,*

"Take your hands off her!" *and out of it all comes* PROCTOR's *roaring voice.*]

PROCTOR. How do you call Heaven! Whore![16] Whore!

[HERRICK *breaks* PROCTOR *from her.*]

HERRICK. John!

DANFORTH. Man! Man, what do you—

PROCTOR. [*Breathless and in agony.*] It is a whore!

DANFORTH. [*Dumfounded.*][17] You charge—?

ABIGAIL. Mr. Danforth, he is lying!

---

16. Here, *whore* refers to a "loose" woman, not that she has taken money for sexual services.
17. *Dumfounded* means "speechless."

REAL-WORLD CONNECTION

Criminal Law in the United States
Remind students that the accused in the Salem did not enjoy the protections of the Bill of Rights. These 10 amendments protect the rights of individual liberty and of persons accused of crimes. In the last half-century, the Supreme Court has issued numerous rulings involving the rights of criminals. Some of these decisions are controversial.

Activity Have small groups research contemporary controversies related to constitutional rights and criminal law. You might suggest the following topics as guidelines: *the Exclusionary Rule, Due Process, Probable Cause, Search and Seizure.* Tell each group to reach consensus on one of the following positions:

• Supreme Court decisions in these areas generally have provided necessary protections for those accused of crimes.

• Supreme Court decisions in these areas have allowed guilty persons to escape punishment on technical grounds.

Each group should be prepared to defend its conclusions in an informal classroom debate. **L2** **COLLAB. LEARN.**

PROCTOR. Mark her! Now she'll suck a scream to stab me with, but—

DANFORTH. You will prove this! This will not pass!

PROCTOR. [*Trembling, his life collapsing about him.*] I have known her, sir. I have known her.

DANFORTH. You—you are a lecher?

FRANCIS. [*Horrified.*] John, you cannot say such a—

PROCTOR. Oh, Francis, I wish you had some evil in you that you might know me! [*To DANFORTH.*] A man will not cast away his good name. You surely know that.

DANFORTH. [*Dumfounded.*] In—in what time? In what place?

PROCTOR. [*His voice about to break, and his shame great.*] In the proper place—where my beasts are bedded. On the last night of my joy, some eight months past. She used to serve me in my house, sir. [*He has to clamp his jaw to keep from weeping.*] A man may think God sleeps, but God sees everything, I know it now. I beg you, sir, I beg you—see her what she is. My wife, my dear good wife, took this girl soon after, sir, and put her out on the highroad. And being what she is, a lump of vanity, sir—[*He is being overcome.*] Excellency, forgive me, forgive me. [*Angrily against himself, he turns away from the Governor for a moment. Then, as though to cry out is his only means of speech left.*] She thinks to dance with me on my wife's grave! And well she might, for I thought of her softly. God help me, I lusted, and there *is* a promise in such sweat. But it is a whore's vengeance, and you must see it; I set myself entirely in your hands. I know you must see it now.

DANFORTH. [*Blanched,[18] in horror, turning to ABIGAIL.*] You deny every scrap and tittle of this?

ABIGAIL. If I must answer that, I will leave and I will not come back again!

---

18. Here, *blanched* means "drained of color."

[*DANFORTH seems unsteady.*]

PROCTOR. I have made a bell of my honor! I have rung the doom of my good name—you will believe me, Mr. Danforth! My wife is innocent, except she knew a whore when she saw one!

ABIGAIL. [*Stepping up to DANFORTH.*] What look do you give me? [*DANFORTH cannot speak.*] I'll not have such looks! [*She turns and starts for the door.*]

DANFORTH. You will remain where you are! [*HERRICK steps into her path. She comes up short, fire in her eyes.*] Mr. Parris, go into the court and bring Goodwife Proctor out.

PARRIS. [*Objecting.*] Your Honor, this is all a—

DANFORTH. [*Sharply to PARRIS.*] Bring her out! And tell her not one word of what's been spoken here. And let you knock before you enter. [*PARRIS goes out.*] Now we shall touch the bottom of this swamp. [*To PROCTOR.*] Your wife, you say, is an honest woman.

PROCTOR. In her life, sir, she have never lied. There are them that cannot sing, and them that cannot weep—my wife cannot lie. I have paid much to learn it, sir.

DANFORTH. And when she put this girl out of your house, she put her out for a harlot?

PROCTOR. Aye, sir.

DANFORTH. And knew her for a harlot?

PROCTOR. Aye, sir, she knew her for a harlot.

DANFORTH. Good then. [*To ABIGAIL.*] And if she tell me, child, it were for harlotry, may God spread His mercy on you! [*There is a knock. He calls to the door.*] Hold! [*To ABIGAIL.*] Turn your back. Turn your back. [*To PROCTOR.*] Do likewise. [*Both turn their backs—ABIGAIL with indignant slowness.*] Now let neither of you turn to face Goody Proctor. No one in this room is to speak one word, or raise a gesture aye or nay. [*He turns toward the door, calls.*] Enter! [*The door opens. ELIZABETH enters with PARRIS. PARRIS leaves her. She stands alone,*

CLIMAX Ask students to explain how this passage sets up the climax. *(Students should recognize the internal conflict that plagues Proctor. He is torn by guilt over his affair with Abigail. He knows he must expose her as a fraud. However, he has tried every way possible to avoid publicly admitting his shame. By accusing her of sin, he has made a commitment from which he cannot turn back. His charge must be proved. Proving it means he must admit his own sin. The emotional intensity and suspense now approach their peak as the climax and resolution near.)*

DD **Active Reading**

QUESTION Ask students why Proctor refers to the barn as the proper place for his sin to have occurred. *(Puritan preachers often compared sinners to "beasts.")*

EE **Author's Craft**

CHARACTERIZATION Help students recognize how Miller illustrates the significant change that has come about in Proctor as we near the climax. *(Earlier he fought against admitting the extent of his guilt. On page 943, Elizabeth tells him there is a promise made in a relationship between a man and a woman. He angrily denies that, comparing his affair with Abigail to a relationship between animals. Now he admits the reality of that promise. In effect, he is admitting that he shares responsibility for what has happened.)*

INCLUSION STRATEGIES

MEETING INDIVIDUAL NEEDS

Less-Proficient Readers
Paraphrasing may aid students who are experiencing comprehension difficulties.

Activity Have groups of three or four students restate difficult dialogue or longer speeches in their own words in short written summaries. Suggest that they keep the summaries for later use as study guides. You may want to review sample summaries to monitor comprehension. If you find that problems remain, consider reforming groups so that each contains students reading at various levels. **L1** **COLLAB. LEARN.**

Additional Resources
📁 *Inclusion Strategies*

Active Reading

PREDICT Before they read the page, ask students to predict what Elizabeth will say. *(Some students may say that she will tell the truth but ask that John be shown mercy because he is a good man who made one mistake for which he has paid with his own guilty feelings. Others may say that she will lie to protect him because she knows the court is merciless.)*

Active Reading

REVIEW Be certain that students understand what Elizabeth is saying here. *(She is not denying that Abigail made advances toward John. She is saying only that, in her weakened condition, she imagined he gave into the temptation.)*

Critical Thinking

EVALUATE Ask students to explain how they judge Elizabeth's response. *(Most will probably say it is wrong to lie. However, under the circumstances, they might agree with Hale: She lied only to protect her husband. The real villains are Abigail and Danforth. Some may say, however, that her lie shows that she has not regained complete trust in John. Otherwise she would have realized that he had confessed his sin.)*

Teaching Options

The Salem Witch Trials of 1692 Students might enjoy learning more about the Salem witch trials. They can use a search engine to look for information about the accused individuals, their accusers, and the judges. Suggest that they enter keywords such as *Salem Witch Museum* or *Salem Witchcraft Trials of 1692*.

The Crucible

her eyes looking for PROCTOR.] Mr. Cheever, report this testimony in all exactness. Are you ready?

CHEEVER. Ready, sir.

DANFORTH. Come here, woman. [ELIZABETH *comes to him, glancing at* PROCTOR'S *back.*] Look at me only, not at your husband. In my eyes only.

ELIZABETH. [*Faintly.*] Good, sir.

DANFORTH. We are given to understand that at one time you dismissed your servant, Abigail Williams.

ELIZABETH. That is true, sir.

DANFORTH. For what cause did you dismiss her? [*Slight pause. Then* ELIZABETH *tries to glance at* PROCTOR.] You will look in my eyes only and not at your husband. The answer is in your memory and you need no help to give it to me. Why did you dismiss Abigail Williams?

ELIZABETH. [*Not knowing what to say, sensing a situation, wetting her lips to stall for time.*] She—dissatisfied me. [*Pause.*] And my husband.

DANFORTH. In what way dissatisfied you?

ELIZABETH. She were—[*She glances at* PROCTOR *for a cue.*]

DANFORTH. Woman, look at me! [ELIZABETH *does.*] Were she slovenly?[19] Lazy? What disturbance did she cause?

ELIZABETH. Your Honor, I—in that time I were sick. And I—My husband is a good and righteous man. He is never drunk as some are, nor wastin' his time at the shovelboard,[20] but always at his work. But in my sickness—you see, sir, I were a long time sick after my last baby, and I thought I saw my husband somewhat turning from me. And this girl—[*She turns to* ABIGAIL.]

DANFORTH. Look at me.

---

19. To be *slovenly* is to be untidy or careless, especially in appearance.
20. *Shovelboard* is a tabletop version of shuffleboard.

ELIZABETH. Aye, sir. Abigail Williams—[*She breaks off.*]

DANFORTH. What of Abigail Williams?

ELIZABETH. I came to think he fancied her. And so one night I lost my wits, I think, and put her out on the highroad.

DANFORTH. Your husband—did he indeed turn from you?

ELIZABETH. [*In agony.*] My husband—is a goodly man, sir.

DANFORTH. Then he did not turn from you.

ELIZABETH. [*Starting to glance at* PROCTOR.] He—

DANFORTH. [*Reaches out and holds her face, then.*] Look at me! To your own knowledge, has John Proctor ever committed the crime of lechery? [*In a crisis of indecision she cannot speak.*] Answer my question! Is your husband a lecher!

ELIZABETH. [*Faintly.*] No, sir.

DANFORTH. Remove her, Marshal.

PROCTOR. Elizabeth, tell the truth!

DANFORTH. She has spoken. Remove her!

PROCTOR. [*Crying out.*] Elizabeth, I have confessed it!

ELIZABETH. Oh, God! [*The door closes behind her.*]

PROCTOR. She only thought to save my name!

HALE. Excellency, it is a natural lie to tell; I beg you, stop now before another is condemned! I may shut my conscience to it no more—private vengeance is working through this testimony! From the beginning this man has struck me true. By my oath to Heaven, I believe him now, and I pray you call back his wife before we—

DANFORTH. She spoke nothing of lechery, and this man has lied!

HALE. I believe him! [*Pointing at* ABIGAIL.] This girl has always struck me false! She has—

[ABIGAIL, *with a weird, wild, chilling cry, screams up to the ceiling.*]

DANFORTH. Do you sport with me? You will sign your name or it is no confession, Mister! [*His breast heaving with agonized breathing, PROCTOR now lays the paper down and signs his name.*]

PARRIS. Praise be to the Lord!

[*PROCTOR has just finished signing when DANFORTH reaches for the paper. But PROCTOR snatches it up, and now a wild terror is rising in him, and a boundless anger.*]

DANFORTH. [*Perplexed, but politely extending his hand.*] If you please, sir.

PROCTOR. No.

DANFORTH. [*As though PROCTOR did not understand.*] Mr. Proctor, I must have—

PROCTOR. No, no. I have signed it. You have seen me. It is done! You have no need for this.

PARRIS. Proctor, the village must have proof that—

PROCTOR. Damn the village! I confess to God, and God has seen my name on this! It is enough!

DANFORTH. No, sir, it is—

PROCTOR. You came to save my soul, did you not? Here! I have confessed myself; it is enough!

DANFORTH. You have not con—

PROCTOR. I have confessed myself! Is there no good penitence[9] but it be public? God does not need my name nailed upon the church! God sees my name; God knows how black my sins are! It is enough!

DANFORTH. Mr. Proctor—

PROCTOR. You will not use me! I am no Sarah Good or Tituba, I am John Proctor! You will not use me! It is no part of salvation that you should use me!

DANFORTH. I do not wish to—

PROCTOR. I have three children—how may I teach them to walk like men in the world, and I sold my friends?

_____

9. *Penitence* is humble sorrow for one's wrongdoing.

DANFORTH. You have not sold your friends—

PROCTOR. Beguile me not! I blacken all of them when this is nailed to the church the very day they hang for silence!

DANFORTH. Mr. Proctor, I must have good and legal proof that you—

PROCTOR. You are the high court, your word is good enough! Tell them I confessed myself; say Proctor broke his knees and wept like a woman; say what you will, but my name cannot—

DANFORTH. [*With suspicion.*] It is the same, is it not? If I report it or you sign to it?

PROCTOR. [*He knows it is insane.*] No, it is not the same! What others say and what I sign to is not the same!

DANFORTH. Why? Do you mean to deny this confession when you are free?

PROCTOR. I mean to deny nothing!

DANFORTH. Then explain to me, Mr. Proctor, why you will not let—

PROCTOR. [*With a cry of his whole soul.*] Because it is my name! Because I cannot have another in my life! Because I lie and sign myself to lies! Because I am not worth the dust on the feet of them that hang! How may I live without my name? I have given you my soul; leave me my name!

DANFORTH. [*Pointing at the confession in PROCTOR's hand.*] Is that document a lie? If it is a lie I will not accept it! What say you? I will not deal in lies, Mister! [*PROCTOR is motionless.*] You will give me your honest confession in my hand, or I cannot keep you from the rope. [*PROCTOR does not reply.*] Which way do you go, Mister?

[*His breast heaving, his eyes staring, PROCTOR tears the paper and crumples it, and he is weeping in fury, but erect.*]

DANFORTH. Marshal!

PARRIS. [*Hysterically, as though the tearing paper were his life.*] Proctor, Proctor!

HALE. Man, you will hang! You cannot!

U Active Reading

SUMMARIZING Help students recognize how the contradiction Proctor points out summarizes the evil of the court. *(The judges claim that their purpose is to save souls. If that is true, Proctor has confessed and saved his soul. Insisting that his confession be posted publicly reveals the judges' true motive: they want to use Proctor's confession as evidence that Rebecca Nurse and the others are liars. They hope that this will stem the tide of criticism against their authority.)*

V Active Reading

QUESTION Ask students what they think Miller means by the stage direction, "He knows it is insane." *(Some may say that Proctor realizes his insistence on this point will cost him his life. Others may say that he knows he is making a distinction that has meaning only for him. His name represents what and who he is. Posting his name on the church door will be taking that from him and robbing him of his dignity. He cannot let society do that, but Danforth will never understand this.)*

W Author's Craft

AUTHOR'S PURPOSE Help students recognize why Miller portrays Proctor as "weeping . . . but erect." *(Miller is writing a play about moral courage. Portraying Proctor this way during his test of character adds a human dimension to his courage. He is fearful, but he conquers his fears. He knows he is condemning himself to death, but he will not compromise his principles to save his life.)*

Listening and Speaking *Minilesson*

Debate Post these guidelines for conducting a debate:

- Gather sufficient information and support materials for the position taken.
- Organize information and prepare arguments that support the position.
- Anticipate what the opposition will say and be prepared to rebut arguments.
- Develop a forceful, coherent summary as a closing argument.

Activity Form student teams and have them debate the following proposition: Modern societies rob people of dignity by destroying their individuality.

Have participants research to find materials to help them develop arguments, taking notes on authors and publications. **L3 COLLAB. LEARN.**

VIEWING THE PHOTOGRAPH

Have students discuss this final photograph of John Proctor and comment on his facial expression. What feelings can they see?

Active Reading

INTERPRET Have students explain John's comment "you have made your magic now." *(It is ironic that in trying to ban any use of magic or witchcraft in Salem, those prosecuting John have worked a kind of goodness in John that has allowed him to show an integrity he felt he was missing.)*

Teaching Options

PROCTOR. [*His eyes full of tears.*] I can. And there's your first marvel, that I can. You have made your magic now, for now I do think I see some shred of goodness in John Proctor. Not enough to weave a banner with, but white enough to keep it from such dogs. [*ELIZABETH, in a burst of terror, rushes to him and weeps against his hand.*] Give them no tear! Tears pleasure them! Show honor now, show a stony heart and sink them with it! [*He has lifted her, and kisses her now with great passion.*]

REBECCA. Let you fear nothing! Another judgment waits us all!

DANFORTH. Hang them high over the town! Who weeps for these, weeps for corruption!

[*He sweeps out past them. HERRICK starts to lead REBECCA, who almost collapses, but PROCTOR catches her, and she glances up at him apologetically.*]

REBECCA. I've had no breakfast.

HERRICK. Come, man.

[*HERRICK escorts them out, HATHORNE and CHEEVER behind them. ELIZABETH stands staring at the empty doorway.*]

PARRIS. [*In deadly fear, to ELIZABETH.*] Go to him, Goody Proctor! There is yet time!

[*From outside a drumroll strikes the air. PARRIS is startled. ELIZABETH jerks about toward the window.*]

PARRIS. Go to him! [*He rushes out the door, as though to hold back his fate.*] Proctor! Proctor!

[*Again, a short burst of drums.*]

HALE. Woman, plead with him! [*He starts to rush out the door, and then goes back to her.*] Woman! It is pride, it is vanity. [*She avoids his eyes, and moves to the window. He drops to his knees.*] Be his helper!—What profit him to bleed? Shall the dust praise him? Shall the worms declare his truth? Go to him, take his shame away!

ELIZABETH. [*Supporting herself against collapse, grips the bars of the window, and with a cry.*] He have his goodness now. God forbid I take it from him!

[*The final drumroll crashes, then heightens violently. HALE weeps in frantic prayer, and the new sun is pouring in upon her face, and the drums rattle like bones in the morning air.*]

THE CURTAIN FALLS

QUESTION Discuss the meaning of Elizabeth's remark. (*Within the context of her character and the play, she is saying that he finally realizes the goodness that was always within him.*)

Historical Note

In actuality, Rebecca Nurse and John Proctor were not hanged on the same day. She was hanged on July 19, 1692; Proctor on August 19. In October the famed Puritan minister, Increase Mather, visited the Salem prison and interviewed prisoners. Mather concluded that the confessions were not sufficient proof of guilt because they had been obtained under threats and torture. Mather helped persuade Massachusetts Governor, Sir William Phips to overturn the convictions. A reprieve from the governor saved Elizabeth Proctor.

Thematic Focus

Acting on an Idea Have students discuss whether they think John Proctor won a victory by his refusal to compromise his principles. If so, was it a personal victory only, or did it benefit the community?

✓ ASSESSMENT OPTIONS

📁 *Quick Checks,* p. 111

MULTIPLE LEARNING STYLES

Interpersonal Students with acute interpersonal skills may respond well to activities in which they can use ideas expressed by others as the basis for new insights.

Activity Have students imagine that they are with a group of friends who have just seen a live performance of *The Crucible.* They are talking about the play over a post-theater meal. What particular element are they likely to discuss? What character did they admire most? Do they agree with Miller's ideas about modern society and tragedy? Challenge students to add other topics and write notes to develop impromptu conversations. Ask them to present their improvisation to the class.
L2 COLLAB. LEARN.

Personal Response

Responses will reflect individual perceptions and attitudes.

ANALYZING LITERATURE

1. More people have been condemned. There are signs of rebellion, and rumors spread that another town, Andover, has repudiated witchcraft trials. Orphans and abandoned cattle wander about, and crops rot.

2. Abigail and Mercy Lewis have vanished after stealing money from Parris.

3. He recommends that the scheduled hangings be postponed for a time.

4. Hale tries to convince the condemned to confess, even though they are innocent, to save their lives.

5. Proctor is torn between confessing to spare his family hardships and refusing to submit. He needs to preserve his dignity and desires to live. He resolves the conflict by agreeing to sign a confession but refusing to have it posted publicly or to accuse others.

6. The mood is fearful, tense, and resigned. Some may say that fear of losing their authority leads the judges to proceed; others say that the resignation convinces the condemned that there is no point in seeking mercy.

7. He is surprised and worried. He fears that her sudden disappearance may increase doubts.

8. Parris knows that John Proctor and Rebecca Nurse are widely respected. Their executions may strengthen opposition to Parris. The discussion is ironic because "being brought to God" means confessing to witchcraft.

9. Hale's dealings reveal that he has lost faith and values life more than piety.

10. Proctor's choice may mean that he retains his dignity and self-respect. For Salem, it might serve as an inspiration. Elizabeth probably means he realizes that he is good despite his failings.

11. The trials created a climate of fear and suspicion in which innocent people confessed to crimes to avoid punishment and betrayed innocent friends to save themselves. Students should recognize that the Red Scare created the same emotional environment in the United States.

12. Miller presents Hathorne as a flat character because he represents impersonal and dehumanizing forces of modern society. John and Elizabeth Proctor are rounded characters

Responding to Literature

Personal Response

What were your thoughts at the end of the play?

——— ANALYZING ACT 4 ———

RECALL

1. What has happened in Salem during the three months since the end of act 3?
2. What news does Parris give Danforth about Abigail?
3. What recommendation does Parris make about the condemned?
4. What has Hale been trying to do with the condemned?
5. Summarize the **conflict** (see page R3) that John Proctor is experiencing. How does Proctor finally meet the test before him?

INTERPRET

6. Describe the **mood** of Salem at the beginning of act 4. (See Literary Terms Handbook, page R10.) In what ways might this mood be responsible for what finally happens?
7. What is Danforth's reaction to Parris's news about Abigail? Why do you think he reacts this way?
8. What might Parris's motives be for his pleas with the judges and his attempts to get Proctor to confess? What is **ironic** about the officials' discussion of which of the condemned might be "brought to God"?
9. What do Hale's dealings with the condemned reveal about his values and his character?
10. What might Proctor's decision mean for him? for Salem? What might Elizabeth mean when she says that John has "his goodness now"?

EVALUATE AND CONNECT

11. What message do you think Miller was trying to give about the witch trials by his portrayal of Salem at the opening of act 4? How might this message also apply to the emotional environment of the HUAC hearings described on page 911?
12. Which characters in this play are **static**, or unchanging, and which ones are **dynamic characters**, capable of growth? How does Miller use these character types to stress his main points?
13. Besides the events of the 1950s, what other historical events might be similar to those covered in the play?
14. Theme Connections   In what ways are the characters in *The Crucible* acting on an idea? With which ideas do you identify most? Why?
15. What do you think makes this play universally popular?

Literary ELEMENTS

Tragedy and Tragic Hero

A **tragedy** is a drama that ends with the downfall of a main character. This character, or **tragic hero**, generally has many admirable qualities, so the audience responds sympathetically to him or her. However, the tragic hero usually has a single flaw or makes a single mistake, which ultimately brings about his or her downfall.

1. Who is the tragic hero of *The Crucible*? Is there more than one? Explain your response.
2. What was the tragic flaw or mistake of this hero or these heroes?

● See **Literary Terms Handbook**, p. R16.

---

because they face complex decisions and take controversial stands.

13. Responses will reflect individual experience.

14. Identification with one side or the other will reflect personal attitudes and convictions.

15. Conflict between defending principles and being accepted is a universal human experience.

LITERARY ELEMENTS

1. John Proctor. Students who accept traditional views of tragedy may reject Rebecca Nurse because she has no tragic flaw (vice), and Elizabeth because she survives.
2. Possible flaws include Proctor's sin with Abigail because it ultimately causes his destruction or his pride in refusing to admit that mistake until it was too late to prevent the tragedy.

Additional Resources

🖋 *Literary Elements Transparency 94*

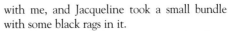
I knew then that she had been with us, for she knew all the answers to the questions I asked.

"I think you do know who I am," she said, staring deeply into the pupils of my eyes. "I know who *you* are. You are Josephine. And your mother knew how to make the Madonna cry."

I let Jacqueline into the house. I offered her a seat in the rocking chair, gave her a piece of hard bread and a cup of cold coffee.

"Sister, I do not want to be the one to tell you," she said, "but your mother is dead. If she is not dead now, then she will be when we get to Port-au-Prince. Her blood calls to me from the ground. Will you go with me to see her? Let us go to see her."

We took a mule for most of the trip. Jacqueline was not strong enough to make the whole journey on foot. I brought the Madonna

with me, and Jacqueline took a small bundle with some black rags in it.

When we got to the city, we went directly to the prison gates. Jacqueline whispered Manman's name to a guard and waited for a response.

"She will be ready for burning this afternoon," the guard said.

My blood froze inside me. I lowered my head as the news sank in.

"Surely, it is not that much a surprise," Jacqueline said, stroking my shoulder. She had become rejuvenated, as though strengthened by the correctness of her prediction.

"We only want to visit her cell," Jacqueline said to the guard. "We hope to take her personal things away."

The guard seemed too tired to argue, or perhaps he saw in Jacqueline's face traces of some long-dead female relative whom he had not done enough to please while she was still alive.

He took us to the cell where my mother had spent the last year. Jacqueline entered first, and then I followed. The room felt damp, the clay breaking into small muddy chunks under our feet.

I inhaled deeply to keep my lungs from aching. Jacqueline said nothing as she carefully walked around the women who sat like statues in different corners of the cell. There were six of them. They kept their arms close to their bodies, like angels hiding their wings. In the middle of the cell was an arrangement of sand and pebbles in the shape of a cross for my mother. Each woman was either wearing or holding something that had belonged to her.

Vocabulary
rejuvenated (ri jōō′ və nā′ təd) *adj.* restored to youthful vigor or appearance; renewed

---

Q Critical Thinking

DRAWING CONCLUSIONS Help students draw conclusions about why the survivors of the massacre use a secret code to communicate. *(They realize they are under constant suspicion and may be accused of witchcraft at any time. Therefore, they want assurance that the other person is a fellow survivor and that they can speak freely before revealing themselves.)*

R Literary Elements

MAGICAL REALISM Discuss with students the reasons for the suspicion and the way it relates to a mixture of magic and realism. *(Other Haitians may believe it was impossible for a normal human to escape the fearful massacre by the river. To explain it, they may have resorted to superstition. One superstitious explanation might be that only witches who could fly on wings of flame escaped. Another explanation might be that no one survived, but the spirits of some who died flew away on wings of flame and now seek to steal the life of infants so they can go on living.)*

S Active Reading

EVALUATE Ask if there is any realistic explanation for Jacqueline's claim that Manman's blood spoke to her from the ground. *(Students should recognize that this is a purely magical element without any rational explanation.)*

Haiti Students may be interested in using the Internet to research and write reports on the troubled history of Haiti. Students should try the keywords *Haiti, Toussaint L'Ouverture,* "Papa Doc" *Duvalier,* "Baby Doc" *Duvalier,* and *Jean Bertrand Aristide.* You might use the reports as the basis for a class discussion.

One of them clutched a pillow as she stared at the Madonna. The woman was wearing my mother's dress, the large white dress that had become like a tent on Manman.

I walked over to her and asked, "What happened?"

"Beaten down in the middle of the yard," she whispered.

"Like a dog," said another woman.

"Her skin, it was too loose," said the woman wearing my mother's dress. "They said prison could not cure her."

The woman reached inside my mother's dress pocket and pulled out a handful of chewed pork and handed it to me. I motioned her hand away.

"No no, I would rather not."

She then gave me the pillow, my mother's pillow. It was open, half filled with my mother's hair. Each time they shaved her head, my mother had kept the hair for her pillow. I hugged the pillow against my chest, feeling some of the hair rising in clouds of dark dust into my nostrils.

Jacqueline took a long piece of black cloth[10] out of her bundle and wrapped it around her belly.

"Sister," she said, "life is never lost, another one always comes up to replace the last. Will you come watch when they burn the body?"

---

10. The tying of a *black cloth* in this manner is a sign of mourning that precedes weeping for the deceased.

"What would be the use?" I said.

"They will make these women watch, and we can keep them company."

When Jacqueline took my hand, her fingers felt balmy and warm against the lifelines in my palm. For a brief second, I saw nothing but black. And then I *saw* the crystal glow of the river as we had seen it every year when my mother dipped my hand in it.

"I would go," I said, "if I knew the truth, whether a woman can fly."

"Why did you not ever ask your mother," Jacqueline said, "if she knew how to fly?"

Then the story came back to me as my mother had often told it. On that day so long ago, in the year nineteen hundred and thirty-seven, in the Massacre River, my mother did fly. Weighted down by my body inside hers, she leaped from Dominican soil into the water, and out again on the Haitian side of the river. She glowed red when she came out, blood clinging to her skin, which at that moment looked as though it were in flames.

In the prison yard, I held the Madonna tightly against my chest, so close that I could smell my mother's scent on the statue. When Jacqueline and I stepped out into the yard to wait for the burning, I raised my head toward the sun thinking, One day I may just see my mother there.

"Let her flight be joyful," I said to Jacqueline. "And mine and yours too."

Vocabulary
balmy (bä′ mē) *adj.* soothing

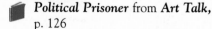

REAL-WORLD CONNECTION

Human Rights Around the World Point out that the arrests and the prison conditions described in the story violate today's human rights standards. Organizations such as Amnesty International try to focus public attention on countries that engage in such violations. On occasion, nations, including the United States, have imposed trade sanctions, or penalties, on countries that repeatedly violate accepted human rights standards.

Activity Form small groups. Have each group use library and Internet resources to research recent issues of human rights standards, violations, and sanctions. Each group should share its findings with the class through an oral presentation. Encourage them to include charts or other graphic aids that support their main ideas. **L2 COLLAB. LEARN.**

Writing Skills in this unit

Writing Skills

The Student Edition of Unit Seven offers strong instructional support for writing skills:

In **Extending Your Response**, which follows each selection:
- Writing About Literature
- Personal/Creative Writing

In **Writing Skills** Lessons:
- Using Quotations (p. 1148)

See also the **Writing Minilessons** throughout the unit in this Teacher's Wraparound Edition.

Writing Workshops

Each of the two themes in Unit Seven concludes with a **Writing Workshop** that guides students through the writing process.
- Persuasive Writing: Speech (pp. 1112–1116)
- Expository Writing: Research Report (pp. 1200–1203)

Writing Resources

Writer's Assistant CD-ROM
Each Writing Workshop is supplemented by an interactive writing guide on the Writer's Assistant CD-ROM. This easy-to-use writing guide provides prompts, templates, and other tools that lead students through the writing process.

Writing and Proofreading Practice
Blackline masters present in-depth instruction and practice on a specific step in the writing process and proofreading. (pp. 81–96)

Writing and Proofreading Transparencies
Transparencies (19–24, 45–48) provide graphic organizers and proofreading exercises for whole class instruction.

Research and Report Writing Guide
This resource provides extensive tips and activities to guide students in their writing projects in the literature classroom as well as in classes across the curriculum.

Style and Documentation Sourcebook for Writers
This sourcebook is a combination reference and work-book, giving students the most up-to-date information and guidance regarding traditional as well as technological research strategies and documentation.

Grammar and Composition Handbook
The Grammar and Composition Handbook provides instruction that supplements activities in the student textbook.

Assessment Resources

Selection Quick Checks
For each selection, a Quick Check of three to five short-answer questions measures students' literal comprehension.

Selection and Theme Assessment
The Selection and Theme Assessment instrument tests students' abilities to recall, interpret, and evaluate what they've read. The tests consist of multiple-choice, short-answer, and essay questions.

Performance Assessment
Alternative assessment instruments and rubrics for Unit Seven are found in the Performance Assessment ancillary.

Writing Assessment and Portfolio Management
These notes and strategies, student models, and assessment tools assist with the task of measuring students' progress as writers and as monitors of their own writing.

Testmaker
Teachers can customize selection, theme, and Unit Seven tests by accessing the Testmaker database.

MindJogger Videoquizzes
Using a popular game show format, MindJogger Videoquizzes enable teachers to evaluate students' understanding of Unit Seven in a quick and fun manner.

Toward the Twenty-First Century

Unit Objectives

- To enjoy reading a variety of literary forms, including poetry, short stories, and memoirs
- To analyze techniques such as imagery and point of view in poetry and fiction
- To apply strategies for reading fiction, nonfiction, and poetry

VIEWING THE PHOTOMOSAIC

Robert Silvers developed his photomosaic techniques as a graduate student at the Massachusetts Institute of Technology Media Lab. Each of his photomosaics is a composite of 1,200 to 3,000 small photographs. His work has been featured on magazine covers and television.

Responding to the Art Discussion questions:

- What message might the artist want to convey by making all these smaller images create one larger image of the Statue of Liberty? What other ways do you see this message conveyed in your everyday life? (*Possible answer: Our nation is made up of a great diversity of people of different races, beliefs, and customs. This diversity arises from and supports ideas of liberty and freedom. Students may provide other examples of this message from their own communities, television, movies, books, or magazines.*)

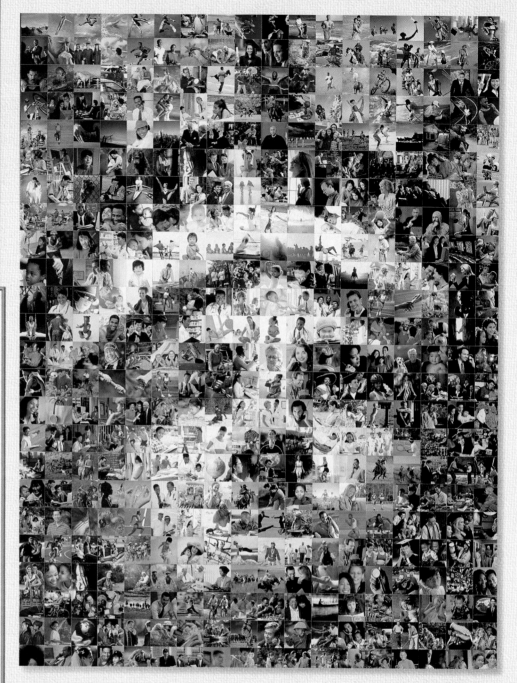

Liberty, 1996. Robert Silvers. Photomosaic™. Photos by The Stock Market.

1018

TEACHER to TEACHER

HUNTINGTON HIGH SCHOOL • HUNTINGTON, WEST VIRGINIA

Like the writers in this unit, my students represent a variety of heritages. Throughout the unit, students delve into their histories and those of their families. They pick one person they find interesting and tell a story based on an incident in his or her life. One student wrote to his grandfather in New York and learned what life was like for him as a boy in Nazi Germany. Students also write an "I Am" poem that celebrates who they are. At the end of the unit, students bring in foods from their family heritage, and we have a Celebration of Diversity Day.

ROSEMARY S. GRANT

UNIT ❧ SEVEN

Toward the Twenty-First Century

1960 to the Present

"Let the word go forth from this time and place, to friend and foe alike, that the torch has been passed to a new generation of Americans, born in this century, tempered by war, disciplined by a hard and bitter peace, proud of our ancient heritage, and unwilling to witness or permit the slow undoing of those human rights to which this nation has always been committed, and to which we are committed today, at home and around the world!"

—John F. Kennedy, *Inaugural Address, 1961*

Theme 11
Generations
pages 1029–1116

Theme 12
Variety Is Richness
pages 1117–1203

Introducing the Unit

Have students read the quotation. Then pose these questions for discussion:

- What lessons from the past do you think guide the work of our country today?
- List some of the differences between your generation and the generations before you, focusing on attitudes toward war and peace, history, human rights, and family relationships. How well do you think your generation is equipped to handle the challenges of the future? Why do you think so?

Theme 11: Generations

The literature in Theme 11 highlights struggles, as members of different generations—whether they are generations in one country or in one family—try to understand each other. The memoirs, short stories, and poems show how much is passed from generation to generation: stories, advice, customs, and attitudes.

Theme 12: Variety Is Richness

The rich diversity of literature in Theme 12 shows that amazement, confusion, and the search for self can be found in many situations.

GLENCOE
TECHNOLOGY
LITERATURE CLASSICS
CD-ROM

Search for other selections by theme, author, or title.

RESOURCE MANAGER

See the *Unit Seven Planning Guide* (p. 1) for additional teaching notes, strategies, and resources for introducing the Toward the Twenty-first Century unit.

Toward the Twenty-First Century

Introducing the Time Period

Ask students to share what they think are the most significant events since 1960. You might write categories on the board, such as technology, human rights, the environment, and politics. Include a few ideas, such as the Vietnam War, the destruction of the rain forests, the boom in personal computing, the end of the cold war, and other events that define the time period.

Setting the Scene

"'Ten, nine, eight, seven, six . . .' At the count of five I put my right hand on the stopwatch button, which I had to push at liftoff to time the flight. I put my left hand on the abort handle, which I would move in a hurry only if something went seriously wrong and I had to activate the escape tower.

"Just after the count of zero, Deke said, 'Liftoff . . . you're on your way . . .'"

Astronaut Alan Shepard Jr. certainly was on his way—rocketing more than 115 miles above the earth. The flight, launched from Cape Canaveral, Florida, on May 5, 1961, traced a neat arc and landed Shepard about 300 miles from the launch site just fifteen minutes later. With this short flight, Shepard became the first American in space, less than a month after Soviet cosmonaut Yuri Gagarin had become the first person to circle the earth. The space age had arrived.

Alan Shepard, 1961, just before his successful flight into space.

U.S.A.					
	1963 Martin Luther King Jr. delivers his "I Have a Dream" speech in Washington, DC	1965 Voting Rights Act becomes law	1967 U.S. population passes 200 million	1972 President Nixon visits China	1976 U.S. celebrates its bicentennial birthday
1960			**1970**	1979	
World	Mali, Senegal, Nigeria, and other African nations gain independence	1968 Soviets invade Czechoslovakia to stop liberal reforms		In Iran, a revolution lead by Shiite Muslims overthrows the Shah; Soviet troops invade Afghanistan	

interNET CONNECTION

NASA Students may want to explore the history of NASA at the National Aeronautics and Space Administration Web site. At the site, they can learn about the non-aerospace applications of technology developed by NASA as well as the rich and detailed history of the space agency.

Extra Credit Projects

• Have students choose one aspect of life, such as technology or the environment, and document the changes that have occurred since 1960. Urge them to find interesting ways to present their findings, such as time lines and charts, news reports, panel discussions, and multimedia presentations. **L2**

• Have students work independently or in teams to trace the course of music from 1960 to the present. Suggest that they link music and its changes to historical or social events. Students may focus on folk music, the surge of Beatlemania and the British Invasion, Woodstock, disco, punk rock, funk and rap, and so on. **L2**

History of the Time

Years of Turbulence

The stormy sixties were launched, appropriately, with a flight into space and an energetic young president—John F. Kennedy. The space program's great accomplishments included astronaut Neil Armstrong stepping onto the surface of the moon in 1969. President Kennedy's term ended in tragedy, however—he was assassinated on November 22, 1963, in Dallas, Texas.

Kennedy's successor, Texan Lyndon Baines Johnson, pushed landmark legislation through Congress, hoping to move the country toward becoming a Great Society without racial discrimination or poverty. Among Johnson's major achievements was the passage of the Civil Rights Act of 1964. With the help of Johnson's Great Society programs, the percentage of families living in poverty declined by one-third between 1964 and 1972.

However, in the words of Martin Luther King Jr., this Great Society was "shot down on the battlefields of Vietnam." The United States sent troops to the civil war in that nation hoping to halt a victory by communist forces. By the late 1960s, there were about 540,000 American troops in Vietnam.

At home, antiwar protests spread through the nation. In 1973 United States troops finally withdrew from Vietnam. The war ended two years later and Vietnam was united under communist rule.

A Change in Direction

In 1968 the assassinations of Martin Luther King Jr. and presidential candidate Robert Kennedy shocked Americans. In 1974 the nation witnessed the resignation of President Richard Nixon over the Watergate scandal. Disenchantment with government solutions to problems helped bring about the election in 1980 of Ronald Reagan, who promised cuts in taxes and social programs and increases in military spending.

In 1992 and again in 1996 Bill Clinton was elected president. Clinton focused on such issues as reducing the budget deficit and fostering free trade with Canada and Mexico.

Facing Challenges

With the breakup of the Soviet Union in 1991 into separate countries, the cold war ended. Other challenges and opportunities remained.

- Hispanics, Native Americans, and others struggled to seek their rightful place in American society.
- Women demanded equal access to good jobs, high salaries, and opportunities of all kinds.
- Immigration to the United States from Latin America, Asia, and the former Soviet Union created an even more diverse population.
- Computers and other technological innovations transformed the way people worked and lived.

Historical Note

The best-known war protest occurred at Kent State University in Ohio following Richard Nixon's announcement that American and South Vietnamese forces had invaded Cambodia on April 30, 1970. Student demonstrations resulted in some damage to businesses, and the governor ordered the National Guard to dispel the demonstrators. During an antiwar rally on May 4, one of the guard members thought that he heard gunfire and opened fire on the students. By the time the ensuing chaos had ended, four students were dead and several others were wounded. The incident fueled the ongoing protest movement, prompting a protest march on Washington.

NOW Advancing the causes of feminism, NOW (the National Organization for Women) was formed in October 1966 by women who were frustrated by the government's inattention to women's issues. NOW has used peaceful methods such as letter-writing campaigns and lobbying to bring about changes in the law and in society's attitudes. The group now has about 250,000 members.

1981
Henry Cisneros of San Antonio, Texas, is elected the first Mexican American mayor of a large U.S. city

1991
The United States attacks Iraq for invading Kuwait and defeats Iraqi forces

1996
Madeline Albright becomes the first female Secretary of State

1998
At age 77, John Glenn becomes the oldest astronaut in space

1980

1986
The overthrow of Jean-Claude Duvalier in Haiti ends a twenty-nine-year family dictatorship

1989
China crushes demonstrators in Tiananmen Square; Berlin Wall is torn down

1990

1991
Soviet Union dissolves into independent republics

1994
Nelson Mandela is elected president of South Africa

1998
India and Pakistan test nuclear weapons

2000

TOWARD THE TWENTY-FIRST CENTURY 🐦 1021

Listening and Speaking *Minilesson*

Political Rhetoric Many recordings of speeches from the 1960s are available. You may want to make these available for students, assigning different groups particular subject areas: the rhetoric of the Civil Rights movement, of women's issues, of the Vietnam debate, or of the presidents.

Activity Have students listen to representative selections from the era, noting style and content. Allow time for students to share with one another, perhaps as a panel presentation, the similiarities and differences among the speakers and their arguments. **L3**

Life of the Time

FYI

The Americans with Disabilities Act The Americans with Disabilities Act, or ADA, became law on July 26, 1990. The ADA ensures rights for people with disabilities by requiring that buildings are handicapped-accessible and by ensuring that people with disabilities have access to government programs offered to the public.

People are talking about

Civil Rights   Inspired by Martin Luther King Jr., activists in the 1960s carry out nonviolent protests—sit-ins, marches, freedom rides—often confronted by tear gas, fire hoses, and dogs. In crowded urban ghettos of the North, frustration over the slow passage of Civil Rights programs erupts into riots each summer from 1964 through 1968. In addition to an impressive string of judicial and legislative victories, the Civil Rights movement creates a growing consciousness against racism. ▶

Martin Luther King Jr.

"High Tech"   Americans in the 1980s and 1990s use more and more amazing new devices. People begin to transmit documents by fax, chat on cell phones, and use personal computers for information, advice, and social interaction. By the late 1990s, the number of Internet users exceeds 30 million.

1960s computer

Laptop computer

The Changing American   As immigration soars in the 1980s and 1990s to levels not seen since the early 1900s, the American population becomes increasingly diverse. By 1995 almost nine percent of Americans are foreign born. Newcomers bring with them new ideas, new words, new foods, new literature, new music.

Firsts

- Dr. Michael DeBakey implants the first successful artificial heart. (1966)
- Margaret A. Brewer becomes the first female Marine Corps general. (1978)
- Chan Ho Park, first Korean major leaguer, pitches for Dodgers. (1994)

U.S.A.

1964
The Beatles appear on television's *Ed Sullivan Show*

1967
The Green Bay Packers win the first Super Bowl

1971
Tennis player Billie Jean King becomes first female athlete to win more than $100,000 in a year

1972
Educational Amendments Act prohibits sex discrimination in school programs

1977
The movie *Star Wars* opens and becomes the largest-selling motion picture to date

1960

World

1962
In Sweden, the Nobel Prize is awarded to three scientists who identified the structure and function of DNA

1967 **1970**
In South Africa, Dr. Christiaan Barnard performs first successful human heart transplant

1974
In China, archaeologists unearth statues of warriors more than 2,000 years old

1022   UNIT 7

MEETING INDIVIDUAL NEEDS   MULTIPLE LEARNING STYLES

Linguistic Linguistic learners may gain a better understanding of the Civil Rights movement by listening to some of the speeches of the time. Students may investigate some of the speeches of Martin Luther King Jr. as well as other leaders of the time.

Activity Have students locate audio clips of Civil Rights movement speeches using the library and Internet sites. Have them select excerpts to play for the class. Then ask: What do you think about these speeches? Are the messages still valid today? **L2**

Food & Fashion

- By the late 1960s, some young people wear "hippie" styles, such as scruffy blue jeans and brightly tie-dyed T-shirts. ▶

- Long hair becomes fashionable among men, and some African Americans demonstrate their pride in their heritage with full-shaped natural Afro hairstyles. ▶

- The growing concern with fitness and the environment begins to affect how Americans think about food. "Natural," "Pesticide-free," "No Preservatives," and "Organic" become increasingly sought-after terms on food labels in the 1970s, 1980s, and 1990s.

Arts & Entertainment

- Almost 90 percent of households own television sets by 1960. In 1981 MTV arrives, and its use of bright colors and quick cuts from scene to scene sets new trends in telecasting.

- Music lovers in the 1960s help the Supremes skyrocket to fame with the "Motown sound." In 1964 the Beatles explode on the U.S. scene. The 1971 musical *Godspell* draws huge crowds. In the 1990s, Garth Brooks wins numerous country music awards.

Amusements

- In the 1990s, the Latin dance style known as salsa grows in popularity, and the jitterbug, tango, and swing are revived.

The Supremes

Garth Brooks

1980

1982
The Vietnam Veterans Memorial in Washington, DC, designed by Maya Lin, is dedicated

1984
Toxic gas from a chemical plant kills thousands in Bhopal, India

1986
Polish composer Witold Lutoslawski's Third Symphony premiers in West Germany

1990

Americans with Disabilities Act protects rights of disabled people

Total world population exceeds 5 billion

1993
The Family and Medical Leave Act requires that large companies allow unpaid leave for family emergencies

1996
Dolly, a cloned sheep, is born in Scotland

1998
Singer Frank Sinatra dies

2000

TOWARD THE TWENTY-FIRST CENTURY 🛰 1023

MEETING INDIVIDUAL NEEDS — MULTIPLE LEARNING STYLES

Musical During the 1960s, artists wrote songs that made strong social and political statements. Have students find out more about these pieces of music and present them to the class.

Activity Have students work alone or with partners to research songs that make statements. Consider playing a few songs to get them started. Try to choose songs that express a variety of opinions and perspectives. Students could perform the pieces live or play recordings, interspersing them with narration that explains the significance and meanings of the songs. **L2 COLLAB. LEARN.**

Literature of the Time

Literature of the Time

PEOPLE ARE READING . . .

About Their Times In the "Me Decade" of the 1970s, self-help books such as Gail Sheehy's *Passages: Predictable Crises of Adult Life* are popular. In the 1980s and 1990s, racial and ethnic concerns, as well as poverty, continue to inspire thoughtful books. They include Richard Rodriguez's *Hunger of Memory* (1981) and *There Are No Children Here* (1991), by Alex Kotlowitz, which describes life in a housing project.

THERE ARE NO CHILDREN HERE

THE STORY OF TWO BOYS GROWING UP IN THE OTHER AMERICA

ALEX KOTLOWITZ

New-Style News In 1982 the new national newspaper *USA Today* zooms to success with its brief articles and bold use of color and graphics. Many Americans read news and feature articles in on-line magazines and news sources on the Internet.

Newcomer Publications The resurgence in immigration revives the foreign-language press. Among the 300 newspapers and magazines written in languages other than English are *La Voz de Houston* in Texas, *Nguoi Viet* in California, and *Korea Times* in New York City.

People Are Writing

Computer Programs As personal computers become more popular, a need arises for technical writers, software developers, and programmers. Some self-taught programmers distribute their creations without charge as "freeware," or for a minimal cost as "shareware."

Timeline

U.S.A.

- Lillian Hellman, *Toys in the Attic*
- 1965 Flannery O'Connor, *Everything That Rises Must Converge*
- 1971 Dee Brown, *Bury My Heart at Wounded Knee*
- 1974 Studs Terkel, *Working*
- 1978 Adrienne Rich, *The Dream of a Common Language*; John Cheever, *The Stories of John Cheever*

1960 — **1970**

World

- Nigeria: Wole Soyinka, *A Dance of the Forests*
- 1967 Japan: Ōe Kenzaburō, *The Silent Cry*
- 1975 Argentina: Jorge Luis Borges, *The Book of Sand*; Ireland: Seamus Heaney, *North*
- 1978 Czechoslovakia: Václav Havel, *Protest*

Literary Trends: Personalizing the Heritage

"The postwar world, the cultural drive toward what has become known as the Postmodern, can be viewed as . . . a root disagreement reducible to the distinction between the adjectives *the* and *a:* . . . can we hope for *the* meaning of a historical event or poem, or must we make do as best we can with *a* meaning?"
—*Richard Ruland and Malcolm Bradbury*

Greater diversity and amazing advances in communications greatly aid the proliferation of ideas, but many of these ideas do not quite fit together in a neat package. Writers of this period experiment with forms and topics, many insisting that no fixed standard exists for contemporary literature. This trend in writing—questioning an ordered view of the world—becomes known as Postmodernism.

In this period of uncertainty, topics such as personal change, generational change, and cultural identity concern such writers as Anne Sexton, John Updike, Simon J. Ortiz, Julia Alvarez, Maxine Hong Kingston, and many others. Writers search for the language and the form that help them make sense of and communicate their own experiences.

FOCUS ON . . .

Diversity

With immigration increasing and opportunities for women expanding, American literature draws upon a wider range of experience than ever before. Americans read stories, poems, and nonfiction by writers of African American heritage, such as Henry Louis Gates Jr. and Rita Dove; of Native American heritage, such as N. Scott Momaday and Louise Erdrich; of Latin American heritage, such as Sandra Cisneros and Victor Hernandez Cruz; and of Asian American heritage, such as Amy Tan and Garrett Hongo. Such writers show that their own cultural traditions have become part of the American cultural experience.

N. Scott Momaday

Rita Dove

1983
Sandra Cisneros, *The House on Mango Street;* Raymond Carver, *Cathedral*

1991
Diana Chang, *Earth, Water, Light: Landscape Poems Celebrating the East End of Long Island*

1988
Bharati Mukherjee, *The Middleman and Other Stories*

1992
Edward O. Wilson, *The Diversity of Life*

1993
Rita Dove is named the first African American poet laureate

1980

1983
Israel: Yehuda Amichai, *Great Tranquility*

1987: Mexico: Octavio Paz, *The Collected Poems of Octavio Paz, 1957–1987*

West Indies: Derek Walcott, *Omeros*

1990

1995: Poland: Wislawa Szymborska, *View with a Grain of Sand*

1997: India: Vikram Chandra, *Love and Longing in Bombay*

2000

MEETING INDIVIDUAL NEEDS — MULTIPLE LEARNING STYLES

Interpersonal Exploring the poetry and prose of the period through dramatic readings can provide students with a fresh way of experiencing the literature.

Activity Have small groups of students choose a single work or several short pieces to present as dramatic readings. For example, they could select literature related to the Vietnam War or poetry written by Hispanic-American authors. As they practice for presentations, students should consider the tone, volume, emphasis, and pacing that will best convey the messages of the works. They should also critique each other's practice sessions in order to refine them for class presentation. **L2**
COLLAB. LEARN.

1025

Introductory Note

Review with students the definition of a novel—an extended prose narrative about fictional events. Then read aloud the titles of the novels shown on the time line or described on these two pages. Ask students to recall and summarize any of these novels they have read. Invite them to add the names of more novels from this period that they have read. Then ask: What common literary elements do all these novels share? Why do you think so many writers have chosen the novel form for presenting their ideas?

.... FYI

The Joy Luck Club

Made into a motion picture, the novel *The Joy Luck Club* has spoken to mothers and daughters across cultures. Regarding the influence Tan has had on the American novel, one critic remarked, "[It is out of the] experience of being caught between countries and cultures that writers such as Maxine Hong Kingston and now Amy Tan have begun to create what is, in effect, a new genre of American fiction."

Novels of the Time

The past and present, families, love, memory, heritage—the themes of late twentieth-century novels are as varied as the authors who write them. Still, many have a common element. They tell a good story, one that is the author's own, not strictly autobiographical, yet revealing and personal.

Breathing Lessons
by Anne Tyler (1988)

The events of Anne Tyler's Pulitzer-Prize novel take place in one day, as Maggie and Ira Moran—an ordinary middle-aged couple—drive to a friend's funeral. Flashbacks and the characters' own musings, however, take the reader deep into their lives. Maggie, a compulsive meddler, decides to reunite her son with his estranged wife and baby. In the process, she and Ira come to certain realizations about reality, hope, and their own relationship. With insight, compassion, and humor, Tyler portrays this family's private struggles.

Anne Tyler

Amy Tan

The Joy Luck Club
by Amy Tan (1989)

This novel by first-generation Chinese American Amy Tan draws upon her own family history. Four immigrant Chinese women meet regularly to play mahjong, eat, talk, raise money, and provide support for one another. Skillfully interweaving the voices of the immigrant mothers and their Chinese American daughters, Tan confronts issues of gender, generation, culture, and family through a powerful and touching narrative.

U.S.A.								
Harper Lee, *To Kill a Mockingbird*	1961 Joseph Heller, *Catch-22*	1962 James Baldwin, *Another Country*	1967 William Styron, *The Confessions of Nat Turner*	1971 Wallace Stegner, *Angle of Repose*	1975 Anne Tyler, *Searching for Caleb*	1976 Ishmael Reed, *Flight to Canada*	1978 Isaac Bashevis Singer, *Shosha*	

1960 ———————————————— **1970** ————————————————

World						
1961 Trinidad and Tobago: V. S. Naipaul, *A House for Mr. Biswas*	1964 Egypt: Naguib Mahfouz, *The Search*	1967 Colombia: Gabriel García Márquez, *One Hundred Years of Solitude*	1976 Canada: Margaret Atwood, *Lady Oracle*	1979 South Africa: Nadine Gordimer, *Burger's Daughter*		

LIFE SKILLS CONNECTION

Problem Solving You may wish to show a clip or read an excerpt from Anne Tyler's novel *Breathing Lessons*. Organize the class into groups, and ask them to take different approaches to solving the problem Tyler's character undertakes—reuniting her son and his wife. Ask students to take into account all facets of the problem by considering it from the perspectives of all persons involved. Students may wish to prepare scripts and perform dialogue between the characters to demonstrate the solutions students developed. **L2 COLLAB. LEARN.**

Critics Corner

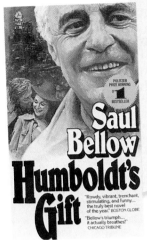

Hurrahs for Humboldt

Humboldt's Gift is an exuberant comedy of success and failure, in which Bellow deals directly for the first time with the writer's life in America, including, implicitly, his own. It is his funniest book and his most openly affectionate, even in its satiric side glances. It speaks most movingly of aging and the felt loss of the sorely missed dead.

—Walter Clemons and Jack Kroll, *Newsweek*, September 1, 1975

Bellow's own great gifts as a storyteller and his talent for vital characterization save what could have been a morose and tedious novel.

—R. Z. Sheppard, *Time*, August 25, 1975

Humboldt's Gift
by Saul Bellow (1975)

Charles Citrine is an aging, award-winning writer, somewhat like Bellow himself. When his old friend and mentor, Von Humboldt Fleisher, dies, Citrine begins reviewing his life and thinking about death. Colorful characters, wild episodes, and Bellow's glorious writing create a thoughtful, at times comic, story. Bellow wins the 1976 Pulitzer Prize for Fiction for *Humboldt's Gift*; he also wins the 1976 Nobel Prize for Literature.

Saul Bellow

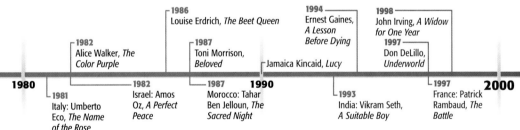

1982 Alice Walker, *The Color Purple*
1986 Louise Erdrich, *The Beet Queen*
1987 Toni Morrison, *Beloved*
Jamaica Kincaid, *Lucy*
1994 Ernest Gaines, *A Lesson Before Dying*
1998 John Irving, *A Widow for One Year*
1997 Don DeLillo, *Underworld*

1980 — **1990** — **2000**

1981 Italy: Umberto Eco, *The Name of the Rose*
1982 Israel: Amos Oz, *A Perfect Peace*
1987 Morocco: Tahar Ben Jelloun, *The Sacred Night*
1993 India: Vikram Seth, *A Suitable Boy*
1997 France: Patrick Rambaud, *The Battle*

GIFTED AND TALENTED ACTIVITY
MEETING INDIVIDUAL NEEDS

Novels in Progress Discuss with students the definition of the twentieth-century novel: "one that is the author's own, not strictly autobiographical, yet revealing and personal."

Activity Invite students to create writer's notebooks to explore ideas for novels they might write. They may jot down random thoughts, note interesting events in their lives, record intriguing quotations, and so on. Then have students choose one idea to develop, keeping in mind that their stories should be revealing and personal, even if those stories are not autobiographical. Students may develop outlines or brief sketches of individual chapters. Have students share and discuss their outlines. **L3 COLLAB. LEARN.**

Language of the Time

How People Speak

Language Equality   The success of the feminist movement changes the way people talk, reflecting an effort to avoid gender stereotyping. For example, "fireman" becomes "firefighter," and "stewardess" becomes "flight attendant." ▶

CB Talk   Long before cellular phones become common, truckers talk to each other via citizens band (CB) radios. In the mid-1970s, automobile drivers discover CBs, and colorful code terms fill the airwaves. Each operator chooses a "handle," or nickname, such as "Lone Coyote," and uses terms such as "10-4 good buddy" for "good-bye."

Machine Messages   Talking to an answering machine makes many Americans feel silly and awkward at first, but they adjust. Some phone owners can't resist recording personal or funny messages, while others get right to the point with "Please leave your message after the beep."

How People Write

Out with the Old   The typewriter, the workhorse of the office for most of the century, gives way rapidly in the 1980s to the computer. The new machines help workers revise their memos with ease, allow companies to generate personalized form letters, and help everyone spell correctly.

In with the New   Speedy and convenient electronic mail, called E-mail, is rapidly replacing the personal letter—even the personal phone call. In 1995, more than one billion E-mail messages are sent. The new technology leads to new forms of expression, as writer John Seabrook noted of his E-mail correspondence with computer mogul Bill Gates:

"There was no beginning or end to Gates's messages—no time wasted on stuff like 'Dear' and 'Yours'. . . . Thoughts seemed to burst from his head *in medias res* [halfway formed] and to end in vapor trails of ellipses. He never signed his mail, but sometimes he put an '&' at the end, which, someone told me, means 'Write back' in E-mail language."

New Words and Expressions

From the Environmental Movement

alternative energy	biodiversity	ozone hole
biohazards	ecocatastrophe	PCBs
biodegradable	greenway	

From Politics

character issue	reinventing government
hot-button issue	shuttle diplomacy
new world order	silent majority

Technology Words As the material on this page suggests, many words come into English because of new processes or new technologies.

Activity Ask English language learners to provide examples of words in their first language that come from technology or new processes. Do they hear these words being used in English as well? Are technology words they hear or read in English difficult to learn, or have they already learned these words in their first language? Invite the entire class to join the discussion and to build a class list of technology words like the new words and expressions listed above.

Additional Resources

 English Language Learners Sourcebook

Although the term *language equality* refers to language that is devoid of gender bias, other debates over language use rage on. California, for example, recently passed a law prohibiting schoolchildren from being taught in Spanish. In other parts of the country, educators have debated whether "African American Vernacular English" is a separate language or dialect and whether it should be taught or acknowledged. These debates involve more than just language; they encompass arguments about race relations, national identity, cultural preservation, and the adequacy of American schools and teachers.

Language Note

Share these definitions with students:

alternative energy—energy, such as wind, solar, and water power, that does not come from fossil fuels

ecocatastrophe—a massive disaster caused by pollutants

greenway—a long, narrow park specifically for pedestrians and bicyclists

ozone hole—a segment of the earth's upper atmosphere in which the ozone layer that prevents high levels of ultraviolet light from reaching Earth has been depleted

biodegradable—able to be decomposed by bacteria or other microbes

PCBs—polychlorinated biphenyl: toxic compounds formed as waste in certain industrial processes

FOCUS ACTIVITY

Does someone you care about hold beliefs or attitudes or behave in ways that you just don't understand?

JOURNAL Think of a few examples of times when the attitudes or customs of a close friend or relative confused or embarrassed you. Describe one of these situations in your journal. Try to determine why you were confused or embarrassed and what the person's words or actions really meant.

SETTING A PURPOSE Read to discover the different attitudes of some close family members.

BACKGROUND

The Time and Place
This story about a family of Chinese immigrants takes place in 1969 in San Francisco, at the time United States forces were involved in the Vietnam War.

Did You Know?
Chinese immigrants first came to California during the gold rush of the late 1800s after hearing the region described as "Gold Mountain." Instead of finding gold and a land of plenty, many of these immigrants ended up with backbreaking jobs as laborers for the railroad that would connect the East and West Coasts.

Many more Chinese came to the United States in the 1930s and 1940s to escape warfare and poverty. After 1949, many left China to escape persecution by the communist government that had taken hold of China. The Communists persecuted many who owned land or were well educated.

Chinese railroad workers of the late 1800s.

VOCABULARY PREVIEW

downy (dou′ nē) *adj.* soft and fluffy, like the feathers of young birds; p. 1038
hover (huv′ ər) *v.* to remain nearby, as if suspended in the air over something; p. 1041
inaudibly (in ô′ də blē) *adv.* in a manner not able to be heard; p. 1041

gravity (grav′ ə tē) *n.* seriousness; importance; p. 1041
oblivious (ə bliv′ ē əs) *adj.* without conscious awareness; unmindful; p. 1041
dusk (dusk) *n.* the time of day just before nightfall; p. 1041

Motivating → OPTIONS

Selection Focus Transparency 101: Have students view the photograph and discuss the question.

Focus Activity: As an extension of the Focus Activity, students can turn their writing into dialogues or skits that show both the surface and deeper meanings of the situations.

Reading Further

Be sure to review these titles for appropriateness for your class before recommending them to students.

Kingston, Maxine Hong. *China Men*. New York: Vintage, 1989. A mixture of fact and fiction, the book explores the lives of early Chinese male immigrants to the United States.

Kingston, Maxine Hong. *Tripmaster Monkey: His Fake Book*. New York: Vintage, 1990. The story of a Chinese American playwright struggling to make a living in Berkeley in the late 1960s.

Kingston, Maxine Hong. *The Woman Warrior: Memoirs of a Girlhood Among Ghosts*. New York: Vintage, 1989.

CONNECTING TO OTHER SELECTIONS

The chart at the right shows three ways to connect this excerpt from *The Woman Warrior* to selections in this book.

For specific teaching strategies, see the **Unit Seven Planning Guide,** pp. 16–17.

Connection	Title
Life Skills: Supporting and Contributing →	from *Of Plymouth Plantation*, p. 69
Thematic: Starting Over →	"Letter to Her Daughter from the New and Unfinished White House," p. 183
Literary: Description →	"Soldiers of the Republic," p. 689

Reading the Selection

It is 1969, and Brave Orchid waits at the airport for her sister, Moon Orchid, to arrive from China. They have not seen each other in 30 years. This selection describes Brave Orchid's thoughts: how she came to America; how she feels about the impending reunion; and what she thinks of her children, who are more American than Chinese. The reunion, although warm, is bittersweet, as both sisters cannot believe how much time has passed since they were last together and how old they have become.

📁 *Spanish Summaries,* p. 101

A Active Reading

QUESTIONING Invite students to preview the selection by looking at the art, reading the captions, and reading the first three paragraphs of the story. After this brief preview, have students write questions about what might happen in the selection. As they read, they should look for answers to their questions.

Additional Resources
📁 *Active Reading Guide,* p. 114
🎧 *Audio Library*
🎧 *Spanish Audio Library*

Teaching Options

---

from The Woman Warrior

Maxine Hong Kingston ∾

When she was about sixty-eight years old, Brave Orchid took a day off to wait at San Francisco International Airport for the plane that was bringing her sister to the United States. She had not seen Moon Orchid for thirty years. She had begun this waiting at home, getting up a half-hour before Moon Orchid's plane took off in Hong Kong.

Brave Orchid would add her will power to the forces that keep an airplane up. Her head hurt with the concentration. The plane had to be light, so no matter how tired she felt, she dared not rest her spirit on a wing but continuously and gently pushed up on the plane's belly. She had already been waiting at the airport for nine hours. She was wakeful.

Next to Brave Orchid sat Moon Orchid's only daughter, who was helping her aunt wait. Brave Orchid had made two of her own children come too because they could drive, but they had been lured away by the magazine racks and the gift shops and coffee shops. Her American children could not sit for very long. They did not understand sitting; they had wandering feet. She hoped they would get back from the pay T.V.'s or the pay toilets or wherever they were spending their money before the plane arrived. If they did not come back soon, she would go look for them. If her son thought he could hide in the men's room, he was wrong.

"Are you all right, Aunt?" asked her niece.

"No, this chair hurts me. Help me pull some chairs together so I can put my feet up."

She unbundled a blanket and spread it out to make a bed for herself. On the floor she had two shopping bags full of canned peaches, real peaches, beans wrapped in taro[1] leaves, cookies, Thermos bottles, enough food for everybody, though only her niece would eat with her. Her bad boy and bad girl were probably sneaking hamburgers, wasting their money. She would scold them.

Many soldiers and sailors sat about, oddly calm, like little boys in cowboy uniforms. (She thought "cowboy" was what you would call a Boy Scout.) They should have been crying hysterically on their way to Vietnam. "If I see one that looks Chinese," she thought, "I'll go over and give him some advice." She sat up suddenly; she had forgotten about her own son, who was even now in Vietnam. Carefully she split her

---

1. *Taro* (tär′ ō) is a tropical Asian plant with broad leaves. It is customary in Chinese cooking to wrap rice, vegetables, or fish in the leaves for steaming.

1036 ❦ UNIT 7

A Sunny Day with Gentle Breeze, 1993. Zifen Qian. Oil on canvas, 56 x 42 in. Private collection.
Viewing the painting: In what way might this painting depict a scene from Brave Orchid's past? Explain.

Chinese-born artist Zifen Qian (1957–) is known for combining traditional and modern techniques in paintings that contain elements of both East and West.

Viewing Response *Students may say that the women in the painting could represent Moon Orchid and Brave Orchid as they looked 30 years ago in China.*

Fleeing to Canada
Thousands of American men fled to Canada during the Vietnam War to avoid serving in the armed forces. According to Canadian immigration figures, about 30,000 American immigrants legally settled in Canada between 1965 and 1972. Some estimate that perhaps another 50,000 slipped into Canada illegally.

Reading *Minilesson*

Connecting The art chosen to accompany this selection conveys messages about generations and about the ideas in the selection. Having students connect the art with the text deepens both their understanding of the story and the art.

Activity Have small groups of students imagine they are editors of this book. After selecting the art that will accompany this story, they should outline the reasons for their choices by citing specific details from the selection. Ask students what additional pieces they might include. They can choose existing art, write descriptions of what they would recommend, or create sketches. Have students explain their choices. **L2** **COLLAB. LEARN.**

Additional Resources
📁 *Reading Workbook,* pp. 83–84

B Literary Elements

EXPOSITION Point out that Kingston periodically uses exposition in telling this story, first at the beginning of the selection and again here. What kind of information does the author give in this paragraph? Why does Kingston use it here? *(The paragraph describes the setting at the customs and immigration station and tells what Brave Orchid does there. Kingston uses exposition here because the scene has shifted from the setting she had established earlier, and she wants her readers to see this new place and how the characters interact with it.)*

C Critical Thinking

DRAWING CONCLUSIONS What kind of relationship does Brave Orchid have with her children? How can you tell? *(Brave Orchid does not seem to understand her children. Their "Americanisms" alternately confuse and anger Brave Orchid. She even feels that her children have "no feelings and no memory.")*

---

attention, beaming half of it to the ocean, into the water to keep him afloat. He was on a ship. He was in Vietnamese waters. She was sure of it. He and the other children were lying to her. They had said he was in Japan, and then they said he was in the Philippines. But when she sent him her help, she could feel that he was on a ship in Da Nang.[2] Also she had seen the children hide the envelopes that his letters came in.

"Do you think my son is in Vietnam?" she asked her niece, who was dutifully eating.

"No. Didn't your children say he was in the Philippines?"

"Have you ever seen any of his letters with Philippine stamps on them?"

"Oh, yes. Your children showed me one."

"I wouldn't put it past them to send the letters to some Filipino they know. He puts Manila[3] postmarks on them to fool me."

"Yes, I can imagine them doing that. But don't worry. Your son can take care of himself. All your children can take care of themselves."

"Not him. He's not like other people. Not normal at all. He sticks erasers in his ears, and the erasers are still attached to the pencil stubs. The captain will say, 'Abandon ship,' or, 'Watch out for bombs,' and he won't hear. He doesn't listen to orders. I told him to flee to Canada, but he wouldn't go."

She closed her eyes. After a short while, plane and ship under control, she looked again at the children in uniforms. Some of the blond ones looked like baby chicks, their crew cuts like the downy yellow on baby chicks. You had to feel sorry for them even though they were Army and Navy Ghosts.[4]

Suddenly her son and daughter came running. "Come, Mother. The plane's landed early. She's here already." They hurried, folding up their mother's encampment. She was glad her children were not useless. They must have known what this trip to San Francisco was about then. "It's a good thing I made you come early," she said.

Brave Orchid pushed to the front of the crowd. She had to be in front. The passengers were separated from the people waiting for them by glass doors and walls. Immigration Ghosts were stamping papers. The travelers crowded along some conveyor belts to have their luggage searched. Brave Orchid did not see her sister anywhere. She stood watching for four hours. Her children left and came back. "Why don't you sit down?" they asked.

"The chairs are too far away," she said.

"Why don't you sit on the floor then?"

No, she would stand, as her sister was probably standing in a line she could not see from here. Her American children had no feelings and no memory.

To while away time, she and her niece talked about the Chinese passengers. These new immigrants had it easy. On Ellis Island[5] the people were thin after forty days at sea and had no fancy luggage.

"That one looks like her," Brave Orchid would say.

"No, that's not her."

Ellis Island had been made out of wood and iron. Here everything was new plastic, a ghost trick to lure immigrants into feeling safe and spilling their secrets. Then the Alien Office could send them right back. Otherwise, why did they lock her out, not letting her help her sister answer questions and spell

---

2. *Da Nang* (dä näng), a port city in South Vietnam, was the site of a major U.S. military base during the Vietnam War.
3. *Manila* (mə nil' ə) is the capital of the Philippines and its largest city.
4. Here, *ghosts* refers to white people.

5. From 1892 to 1943, *Ellis Island,* in upper New York Bay, was the chief U.S. immigration station.

Vocabulary
downy (dou' nē) *adj.* soft and fluffy, like the feathers of young birds

---

Teaching Options

Grammar and Language *Minilesson*

Question Marks and Quotations
Remind students that, when questions appear as parts of direct quotations, the question marks need to appear inside the quotation marks.

Activity Have students find question marks in the selection that follow the rule stated above. *("Do you think my son is in Vietnam?" "Why don't you sit down?"*

"Why don't you sit on the floor?") Then tell students to imagine that they are reuniting with a long-lost friend or relative. What questions would they ask him or her? Have them write a brief dialogue that includes questions they would ask at the reunion. Remind them to punctuate the questions correctly. **L2**

Additional Resources

Grammar and Language Transparency 74

Grammar and Language Workbook, pp. 243, 271

Grammar and Composition Handbook, Lesson 11.10

Writer's Choice, Lesson 21.10

Vo·cab·u·lar·y Skills

Using a Thesaurus

The selection from *The Woman Warrior* begins with a description of the main character, Brave Orchid, as she awaits her sister's flight from China. To ensure her sister's safety, Brave Orchid decides to "add her will power to the forces that keep an airplane up." *Power* and *forces* are **synonyms**, words with similar meanings. Many synonyms, like *force* and *power*, are interchangeable. However, some synonyms have small differences in meaning. Recognizing these differences can help a reader's understanding and improve a person's writing and speaking vocabularies. A **thesaurus** is a specialized dictionary of synonyms and antonyms, words with opposite meanings. There are two types of thesauruses.

Traditional Style

Probably the best-known thesaurus is the traditional *Roget's Thesaurus,* which organizes large categories of words related to a basic concept. To find a synonym for the verb *taste,* for example, browse the index of categories until you find the category *senses,* which includes the subentry *taste.* The index will refer you to the page for the subentry, where you will find a list of synonyms for *taste.*

Dictionary Style

This type of thesaurus presents words in alphabetical order, exactly as a dictionary does. Each word is followed by several synonyms, which are listed by parts of speech. The entry also refers the reader to cross-referenced entries. In this type of thesaurus, you must look for a specific word, such as "taste" or "sweet," to find its synonyms. When you find a synonym, look for it in the alphabetical listing to find additional synonyms.

EXERCISES

1. Using a thesaurus, find three synonyms for each word below. Then look up the definitions of these synonyms in a dictionary to identify the precise meanings for each one.

   a. wait   c. control   e. authorities

   b. scold   d. approval

2. For each word above, try to find one synonym whose meaning has a small but important difference from the original word. Then, for each pair of words, write two sentences—one using the original word and a second using the synonym. Be sure your sentences reflect the slight differences in meaning between the synonyms.

Vo·cab·u·lar·y Skills

Objective

- To use a thesaurus to find synonyms

Teaching Strategies

Write a sentence from one of the selections on the board and ask students to find synonyms for words in the sentence. Rewrite the sentence with various substitutions. Then discuss the degree to which changing the words changes the connotative meaning of the sentence. To extend the lesson, have students select recent pieces of writing from their portfolios and use a thesaurus to find synonyms to replace words like *nice* and *really.*

Exercises

1. *Acceptable responses:*
   a. linger, remain, stay
   b. admonish, criticize, reprimand
   c. mastery, discipline, restraint
   d. consent, endorsement, support
   e. experts, professionals, administrators
2. Students' sentences should correctly use the meanings of the words, showing the nuances of the synonyms.

Additional Resources
 Vocabulary Power: Weekly Lessons and Activities

MEETING INDIVIDUAL NEEDS — ENGLISH LANGUAGE LEARNERS

Synonyms English language learners will find the thesaurus useful for expanding their vocabulary and improving their writing. Emphasize that every word has shades of meaning, so synonyms are not necessarily exact substitutes.

Activity Ask students to select a paragraph from their portfolios and identify a variety of verbs, modifiers, or nouns to replace. Have them use a thesaurus to replace those words with synonyms. Guide students as they work by asking questions, such as: Do you think there is a difference between *caution* and *warn*? What is the difference?

Additional Resources
English Language Learners Sourcebook

MEDIA Connection

Objective

- To understand and apply strategies for reading comic strips

Literature LINK

Son Both Updike and Watterson explore the relationships and differences between sons and their fathers. In "Son" (page 1047), Updike explores those relationships by showing how the father affects the son as the son becomes an adult. Ask students to speculate about Calvin. What will he be like as an adult? As a father? Why do students think so?

Respond

1. Riding a bicycle is a step toward independence.
2. Students may suggest that parents and their children do not always understand each other, and they do not always have similar motives. Calvin, however, is probably a bit more outspoken than many children his age!

Additional Resources
📁 *Media Connections,* p. 20

MEDIA Connection

Comic Strip

Parents and children don't always see things the same way. How different can their perspectives be? *Calvin and Hobbes* cartoonist Bill Watterson finds humor in a misunderstanding between generations.

Respond

1. Why would Calvin's father want to teach his son to ride a bike?
2. In what ways might Calvin represent all sons and daughters? How is he different?

Teaching Options

interNET CONNECTION

Calvin and Hobbes Students can use a search engine to find more *Calvin and Hobbes* comic strips and information about Bill Watterson.

Reading Minilesson

Focusing on a Question Point out the question at the top of the page: "Parents and children don't always see things the same way. How different can their perspectives be?" Explain that this is a framing question to guide students' reading and thinking.

Activity Have small groups meet to discuss how the perspectives of children and parents differ. Then have them read the comic strips aloud and discuss how Watterson portrays these differences. How closely did Watterson's ideas match students' ideas? If students were going to create a similar cartoon strip from their own ideas, what subjects would their cartoons comment on? **L2 COLLAB. LEARN.**

Additional Resources
📁 *Reading Workbook*

Before You Read

Son

Meet John Updike

At an age when some people retire, John Updike stuck his head "into the mouth of the electronic lion"—cyberspace publishing. An on-line book-seller invited the sixty-five-year-old novelist to write the first and last installments of a serial mystery. On-line submissions from more than forty other writers completed the story that unfolded for thousands of readers in cyberspace. The project was a first for Updike, a prolific writer whose novels, short stories, and numerous other works had appeared only on paper. Despite his well-established literary reputation, Updike continues to take chances in his work and to meet new challenges. As he noted himself, "What's a writer for if not to venture out onto the thin ice."

An only child, Updike spent much of his childhood drawing and writing. As a teenager he dreamed of being a cartoonist. After graduating from Harvard University, he studied art at Oxford University in England.

Updike was in his early twenties when he returned to the United States and joined the staff of the *New Yorker*, where he wrote poetry, stories, reviews, and editorials.

When he was just twenty-six years old, Updike's first book, a collection of poetry titled *The Carpentered Hen and Other Tame Creatures*, was published. A year later, in 1959, his first novel, *Poorhouse Fair*, appeared in print. This book won an award, but it was Updike's second novel, *Rabbit, Run*, that

brought him wider recognition the following year. It was the first of four novels about Harry "Rabbit" Angstrom, a suburban husband and father approximately Updike's age. Two books in this series won separate Pulitzer Prizes.

From the 1960s through the 1990s, Updike has continued to write novels and short stories. He has also written essays, poems, and a play. Many of these works focus on the small details of ordinary life: families, chores, and sports. Most are set either in the writer's native Pennsylvania or in New England, where Updike has lived since the 1960s. His fiction is precise and realistic, reflecting Updike's belief that "fiction is a tissue of lies that refreshes and informs our sense of actuality."

❝Writing doesn't require drive. It's like saying a chicken has to have drive to lay an egg.❞

❝I have from the start been wary of the fake, the automatic.❞

—*Updike*

❝Those who admire [Updike's] work consider him one of the keepers of the language; those who don't say he writes beautifully about nothing very much.❞

—*Joseph Kanon*

John Updike was born in 1932.

Objectives

- To read and analyze a short story that shows how father-son relationships affect both sons and fathers as they grow older
- To analyze the use of first person point of view in the story
- To write a paragraph or two analyzing the title of the story

Skills

Reading/Thinking: Drawing Conclusions; Making Critical Judgments
Grammar/Language: Using Commas
Collaboration: Literature Groups

More About John Updike

John Updike was born in Reading, Pennsylvania, and grew up in the small town of Shillington, Pennsylvania, where his father was a junior high school mathematics teacher. While studying in England, Updike met E. B. White, the editor of *The New Yorker*, who offered him a position on the magazine. Updike worked as staff writer and produced articles for "The Talk of the Town." Updike remained at *The New Yorker* less than two years before leaving to devote himself to writing fiction and poetry. "Son," the short story that follows, was selected for *Best American Short Stories 1974*.

RESOURCE MANAGER

Lesson Planning Resource
The *Unit Seven Planning Guide* (pp. 21–26) provides additional lesson notes and reduced versions of all print resources.

📁 **Other Print Resources**
- Active Reading Guide, p. 115
- Vocabulary Practice, p. 61
- Reading Workbook, pp. 83–84
- Grammar and Language Workbook, p. 253

- Grammar and Composition Handbook, Lesson 11.6
- Quick Checks, p. 115
- Selection and Theme Assessment, pp. 175–176
- Performance Assessment, p. 98
- Spanish Summaries, p. 102
- Inclusion Strategies
- English Language Learners Sourcebook

📽 **Transparencies**
- Selection Focus 102
- Literary Elements 98
- Grammar and Language 75

Technology
🎧 Audio Library
🎧 Spanish Audio Library
💻 Glencoe Literature Web Site
💾 Testmaker

1045

Motivating
→OPTIONS

Selection Focus Transparency 102: Read the quote out loud and discuss it with students.

Focus Activity: As an extension of the Focus Activity, have students write lists of tips for parents or children to help them in their roles.

Reading Further

Be sure to review these titles for appropriateness for your class before recommending them to students

Updike, John. *Golf Dreams: Writings on Golf.* Knopf, 1996. Students interested in sports may be interested to read how a literary writer approaches the sport of golf.

Updike, John. *Collected Poems: 1953–1993.* New York: Knopf, 1995.

interNET
CONNECTION

Literature Awards Students may be interested in reading more award-winning short stories. Have them use a search engine to find more short-story award winners using keywords *short stories, American literature*, and *literature awards*.

FOCUS ACTIVITY

Do you think it is more difficult to be a parent or a child?

DISCUSS With a group, discuss this question. Consider all aspects of the roles of both parents and children. Think about the expectations and responsibilities that parents and children have for themselves and for each other.

SETTING A PURPOSE Read this short story to explore the different roles played by fathers and sons.

BACKGROUND

The Time and Place
Updike grew up in a small town in Pennsylvania and developed a keen eye and ear for its physical and emotional landscape. Like most Updike stories, "Son" is set mainly in suburban America; the time is somewhat different, though, in that events occur in 1973, 1949, 1913, and the 1880s.

Literary Influences
"I learned a lot from [J. D.] Salinger's short stories," wrote Updike. Salinger's first novel, *The Catcher in the Rye,* created a literary sensation while Updike was in college, and his shorter fiction appeared frequently in the *New Yorker.* Updike said, "Like most innovative artists, he made new room for shapelessness, for life as it is lived."

VOCABULARY PREVIEW

symmetrical (si met' ri kəl) *adj.* having the same shape or structure on either side of a central line or plane; p. 1047

grotesque (grō tesk') *adj.* bizarre; weird; p. 1047

heedless (hēd' lis) *adj.* careless; thoughtless; reckless; p. 1047

charade (shə rād') *n.* a false show or pretense; p. 1048

incessant (in ses' ənt) *adj.* continuing or following without interruption; p. 1048

submissive (səb mis' iv) *adj.* willing to yield to the power or authority of another; meek; p. 1048

radical (rad' i kəl) *adj.* deviating greatly from the usual or customary; extreme; p. 1049

legible (lej' ə bəl) *adj.* able to be read; p. 1049

valor (val' ər) *n.* courage; bravery; p. 1049

lucid (lōō' sid) *adj.* rational; sane; p. 1050

1046 ❧ UNIT 7

Son

John Updike

Portrait of a Young Man in a White Shirt. Bessie Lowenhaupt (1881–1968). Oil on canvas board, 23¾ x 18⅞ in. Collection of Mr. and Mrs. Charles A. Lowenhaupt.

He is often upstairs, when he has to be home. He prefers to be elsewhere. He is almost sixteen, though beardless still, a man's mind indignantly captive in the frame of a child. I love touching him, but don't often dare. The other day, he had the flu, and a fever, and I gave him a back rub, marvelling at the symmetrical knit of muscle, the organic tension. He is high-strung. Yet his sleep is so solid he sweats like a stone in the wall of a well. He wishes for perfection. He would like to destroy us, for we are, variously, too fat, too jocular,[1] too sloppy, too affectionate, too grotesque and heedless in our ways. His mother smokes too much. His younger brother chews with his mouth open. His older sister leaves unbuttoned the top button of her blouses. His younger sister tussles with the dogs, getting them overexcited, avoiding doing her homework. Everyone in the house talks nonsense. He would be a better father than his father. But time has tricked him, has made him a son. After a quarrel, if he cannot go outside and kick a ball, he retreats to a corner of the house and reclines on the beanbag chair in an attitude of strange—infantile or leonine—torpor.[2] We exhaust him, without meaning to. He takes an interest in the newspaper now, the front page as well as the sports, in this tiring year of 1973.

---

1. *Jocular* (jok′ yə lər) means "tending to joke or jest" or "merry."
2. *Leonine* (lē′ ə nīn′) means "characteristic of, or resembling, a lion." *Torpor* is a state of inactivity.

Vocabulary

symmetrical (si met′ ri kəl) *adj.* having the same shape or structure on either side of a central line or plane
grotesque (grō tesk′) *adj.* bizarre; weird
heedless (hēd′ lis) *adj.* careless; thoughtless; reckless

TOWARD THE TWENTY-FIRST CENTURY 1047

POINT OF VIEW Ask students how the point of view has changed. Who is the "he" in this section? *(The point of view has switched from first person to third person. The "he" referred to in this section is the narrator. In section one, he details his feelings toward his son. This section reveals what his life was like when he was a teenager.)*

C **Literary Elements**

FIGURATIVE LANGUAGE Ask students to give some examples of the figurative language describing the parents and the house. What impression does the figurative language create? *(The parents' voices are like machines, the world is used as a flail, the books are hopeful, and the photographs are docile. The figurative language creates an impression of a hostile place, as though the house falls victim to the unhappy relationship between the parents.)*

He is upstairs, writing a musical comedy. It is a Sunday in 1949. He has volunteered to prepare a high-school assembly program; people will sing. Songs of the time go through his head, as he scribbles new words. *Up in de mornin', down at de school, work like a debil for my grades.* Below him, irksome voices grind on, like machines working their way through tunnels. His parents each want something from the other. "Marion, you don't understand that man like I do; he has a heart of gold." His father's <u>charade</u> is very complex: the world, which he fears, is used as a flail[3] on his wife. But from his cringing attitude he would seem to an outsider the one being flailed. With burning red face, the woman accepts the role of aggressor as penance for the fact, the <u>incessant</u> shameful fact, that *he* has to wrestle with the world while she hides here, in solitude, at home. This is normal, but does not seem to them to be so. Only by convolution[4] have they arrived at the dominant/<u>submissive</u> relationship society has assigned them. For the man is maternally kind and with a smile hugs to himself his jewel, his certainty of being victimized; it is the mother whose tongue is sharp, who sometimes strikes. "Well, he gets you out of the house, and I guess that's gold to you." His answer is "Duty calls," pronounced mincingly.[5] "The social contract is a balance of compromises." This will infuriate her, the son knows; as his heart thickens, the downstairs overflows with her hot voice. "*Don't* wear that smile at me! And *take* your hands off your hips; you look silly!" Their son tries not to listen. When he does, visual details of the downstairs flood his mind: the two antagonists, circling with their coffee cups; the shabby mismatched

furniture; the hopeful books; the docile[6] framed photographs of the dead, docile and still like cowed[7] students. This matrix of pain that bore him—he feels he is floating above it, sprawled on the bed as on a cloud, stealing songs as they come into his head (*Across the hallway from the guidance room / Lives a French instructor called Mrs. Blum*), contemplating the view from the upstairs window (last summer's burdock[8] stalks like the beginnings of an alphabet, an apple tree holding three rotten apples as if pondering why they failed to fall), yearning for Monday, for the ride to school with his father, for the bell that calls him to homeroom, for the excitements of class, for Broadway, for fame, for the cloud that will carry him away, out of this, out.

He returns from his paper-delivery route and finds a few Christmas presents for him on the kitchen table. I must guess at the year. 1913? Without opening them, he knocks them to the floor, puts his head on the table, and falls asleep. He must have been consciously dramatizing his plight: his father was sick, money was scarce, he had to work, to win food for the family when he was still a child. In his dismissal of Christmas, he touched a nerve: his love of anarchy,[9] his distrust of the social contract. He treasured this moment of revolt; else why remember it, hoard a memory so bitter, and confide it to his son many Christmases later? He had a teaching instinct, though he claimed that life miscast him as a schoolteacher. I suffered in his

---

3. A *flail* is a hand tool used to thresh grain by beating.
4. *Convolution* means "a twisting or turning."
5. *Mincingly* means "in an artificially dainty or refined manner."

6. *Docile* means "submissive" or "passive."
7. *Cowed* means "frightened" or "intimidated."
8. The weedy *burdock* plant produces purplish flowers and burs. Its stalks can grow from four to nine feet tall.
9. *Anarchy* (an′ ər kē) is confusion due to the absence of authority or law.

Vocabulary

charade (shə rād′) *n.* a false show or pretense
incessant (in ses′ ant) *adj.* continuing or following without interruption
submissive (səb mis′ iv) *adj.* willing to yield to the power or authority of another; meek

---

Teaching Options

Grammar and Language *Minilesson*

Using Commas Review the rules for using commas, in sentences containing nonessential elements. Remind students that nonessential elements in sentences may be eliminated without changing the basic meaning of the sentence.

Activity Write the following on the board and have students identify the nonessential elements in the sentences. Then have

them place the commas in the correct place.
1. My father, a submissive failure, returned the presents.
2. He was, oh man, so distressed.
3. He was not, surely, going back to work.

Additional Resources

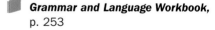 *Grammar and Language Transparency 75*

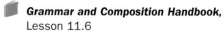 *Grammar and Language Workbook,* p. 253

Grammar and Composition Handbook, Lesson 11.6

Writer's Choice, Lesson 21.6

John Updike ❧

classes, feeling the confusion as a persecution of him, but now wonder if his rebellious heart did not court confusion, not as Communists do, to intrude their own order, but, more <u>radical</u> still, as an end pleasurable in itself, as truth's very body. Yet his handwriting (an old pink permission slip recently fluttered from a book where it had been marking a page for twenty years) was always considerately <u>legible</u>, and he was sitting up doing arithmetic the morning of the day he died.

And letters survive from that yet prior son, written in brown ink, in a tidy tame hand, home to his mother from the Missouri seminary where he was preparing for his vocation. The dates are 1887, 1888, 1889. Nothing much happened: he missed New Jersey, and was teased at a church social for escorting a widow. He wanted to do the right thing, but the little sheets of faded penscript exhale a dispirited calm, as if his heart already knew he would not make a successful minister, or live to be old. His son, my father, when old, drove hundreds of miles out of his way to visit the Missouri town from which those letters had been sent. Strangely, the town had not changed; it looked just as he had imagined, from his father's descriptions: tall wooden houses, rain-soaked, stacked on a bluff. The town was a sepia[10] postcard mailed homesick home and preserved in an attic. My father cursed: his father's old sorrow bore him down into depression, into hatred of life. My mother claims his decline in health began at that moment.

He is wonderful to watch, playing soccer. Smaller than the others, my son leaps, heads, dribbles, feints, passes. When a big boy knocks him down, he tumbles on the mud, in his green-and-black school uniform, in an ecstasy of falling. I am envious. Never for me the jaunty pride of the school uniform, the solemn ritual of the coach's pep talk, the camaraderie of shook hands and slapped backsides, the shadow-striped hush of late afternoon and last quarter, the solemn vaulted universe of official combat, with its cheering mothers and referees exotic as zebras and the bespectacled timekeeper alert with his claxon.[11] When the boy scores a goal, he runs into the arms of his teammates with upraised arms and his face alight as if blinded by triumph. They lift him from the earth in a union of muddy hugs. What spirit! What <u>valor</u>! What skill! His father, watching him from the sidelines, inwardly registers only one complaint: he feels the boy, with his talent, should be more aggressive.

They drove across the Commonwealth of Pennsylvania to hear their son read in Pittsburgh. But when their presence was announced to the audience, they did not stand; the applause groped for them and died. My mother said afterwards she was afraid she might fall into the next row if she tried to stand in the dark. Next morning was sunny, and the three of us searched for the house where once they had lived. They had been happy there; I imagined, indeed, that I had been conceived there, just before the slope of the Depression steepened and fear gripped my family. We found the library where she used to read Turgenev,[12] and the little park where the bums slept close as paving stones in the summer night; but their street kept eluding us, though we circled in the car. On foot,

---

10. *Sepia* (sē′ pē ə) is a brown tone or pigment.

11. *Claxon* (more correctly, Klaxon) is an electronic warning signal or horn. It is also the trademark of such a device.
12. Ivan Sergeyevich *Turgenev* (toor gā′ nyev) (1818–1883) was a Russian novelist, short-story writer, and playwright.

Vocabulary
radical (rad′ i kəl) *adj.* deviating greatly from the usual or customary; extreme
legible (lej′ ə bəl) *adj.* able to be read
valor (val′ ər) *n.* courage; bravery

Language Note
Explain to students that a *seminary* is a religious school or college that trains students to be priests, ministers, or rabbis. A *vocation* is an inner call or summons, especially to the ministry.

D Author's Craft

TONE What tone does the author use? How does he sustain that tone? *(Overall, the tone is bitter and melancholy. Many of the words and images depict people who are unhappy because of the chances in life that have passed them by or who are unhappy because of their situation in life—inadequate parents, the wrong job. The image of the boy pushing away his Christmas presents is especially sober. Even a happy scene, the one in which the boy joyfully plays soccer, is tempered by the father's regret over not having had the same experiences. He even inwardly criticizes his son's play.)*

The Depression
The Depression referred to here is the Great Depression of the 1930s, a period marked by a serious and extensive reduction of business activity with resulting massive unemployment.

INCLUSION STRATEGIES

Less-Proficient Readers If less-proficient readers are having trouble following the story line, encourage them to use a time line or story map to help them keep track of the sections.

Activity Suggest that students read the selection once and then go back to analyze each part. Pair them to discuss how the narrator and the person described in a given section relate to the narrator and subject of the other sections. Students could use time lines or other graphic organizers to map the story. Encourage them to compare their work with that of other pairs. Did they arrive at the same conclusions?
L1 **COLLAB. LEARN.**

Additional Resources
📁 *Inclusion Strategies*

E Critical Thinking

DRAWING CONCLUSIONS Why are the parents and son happy? *(Some students may suggest that the parents and son have reached some sort of understanding—they are functioning as a team. Other students may suggest that they are relieved that the house is gone. All of the bitterness of the past is gone along with the physical house.)*

F Author's Craft

STYLE Here, the author uses bursts of short sentences, clauses, and questions. What is the effect of his style? *(This style feels more personal, as if the writer and reader are having a conversation. While the previous section takes place in the past, using this technique here jolts the reader into the present, creating immediacy, intimacy, and involvement.)*

Thematic Focus

Generations Write the following saying on the board: *The child is father to the man.* How do you think this selection illustrates this quotation? What other statements does "Son" make about the relationships between fathers and sons? Might your parents or grandparents interpret the story differently than you?

✓ ASSESSMENT OPTIONS

📁 *Quick Checks*, p. 115

Teaching Options

---

my mother found the tree. She claimed she recognized it, the sooty linden tree she would gaze into from their apartment windows. The branches, though thicker, had held their pattern. But the house itself, and the entire block, was gone. Stray bricks and rods of iron in the grass suggested that the demolition had been recent. We stood on the empty spot and laughed. They knew it was right, because the railroad tracks were the right distance away. In confirmation, a long freight train pulled itself east around the curve, its great weight gliding as if on a river current; then a silver passenger train came gliding as effortlessly in the other direction. The curve of the tracks tipped the cars slightly toward us. The Golden Triangle, gray and hazed, was off to our left, beyond a forest of bridges. We stood on the grassy rubble that morning, where something once had been, beside the tree still there, and were intensely happy. Why? We knew.

"'No,' Dad said to me, 'the Christian ministry isn't a job you choose, it's a vocation for which you got to receive a call.' I could tell he wanted me to ask him. We never talked much, but we understood each other, we were both scared devils, not like you and the kid. I asked him, Had he ever received the call? He said No. He said No, he never had. Received the call. That was a terrible thing, for him to admit. And I was the one he told. As far as I knew he never admitted it to anybody, but he admitted it to me. He felt like hell about it, I could tell. That was all we ever said about it. That was enough."

He has made his younger brother cry, and justice must be done. A father enforces justice. I corner the rat in our bedroom; he is holding a cardboard mailing tube like a sword. The

challenge flares white-hot; I roll my weight toward him like a rock down a mountain, and knock the weapon from his hand. He smiles. Smiles! Because my facial expression is silly? Because he is glad that he can still be overpowered, and hence is still protected? Why? I do not hit him. We stand a second, father and son, and then as nimbly as on the soccer field he steps around me and out the door. He slams the door. He shouts obscenities in the hall, slams all the doors he can find on the way to his room. Our moment of smilingly shared silence was the moment of compression; now the explosion. The whole house rocks with it. Downstairs, his siblings and mother come to me and offer advice and psychological analysis. I was too aggressive. He is spoiled. What they can never know, my grief alone to treasure, was that lucid many-sided second of his smiling and my relenting, before the world's wrathful pantomime of power resumed.

As we huddle whispering about him, my son takes his revenge. In his room, he plays his guitar. He has greatly improved this winter; his hands getting bigger is the least of it. He has found in the guitar an escape. He plays the Romanza[13] wherein repeated notes, with a sliding like the heart's valves, let themselves fall along the scale:

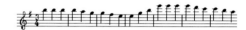

The notes fall, so gently he bombs us, drops feathery notes down upon us, our visitor, our prisoner.

---

13. The *Romanza* (rō män' zə) is a musical composition, written for the guitar, that has sentimental or romantic qualities.

Vocabulary
lucid (lōō' sid) *adj.* rational; sane

Reading *Minilesson*

Making Critical Judgments Making judgments about a piece of writing not only helps students hone their skills in backing up assertions with proof, but also prompts them to delve below the surface of a story. Students should be encouraged to make judgments about the pieces they read.

Activity Pose a statement such as "John Updike accurately portrays relationships between fathers and sons" as the basis for critical judgment. As students form their judgments, they should find evidence in the story and in real life to support their ideas. Have them present their opinions in written critiques or in panel discussions. **L2**

Additional Resources
📁 *Reading Workbook*, pp. 83–84

Responding to Literature

Personal Response

Were you surprised by the final sentence of the story? Why or why not?

Literary ELEMENTS

First-Person Point of View

In a story with **first-person point of view,** the story is told by a character who refers to himself or herself as "I." A first-person narrator can be a participant or an observer. In "Son," the narrator takes both roles. For example, he participates when he says that he gave his son a back rub. He observes in a later passage when he says, "I must guess at the year."

1. In what sections of the story is the narrator a participant? To whom does the pronoun *he* refer in each of those sections?

2. When the narrator is an observer, to whom does the pronoun *he* refer?

3. How might the effect be different if the story were written from third-person point of view?

 See **Literary Terms Handbook,** p. R12.

ANALYZING LITERATURE

RECALL AND INTERPRET

1. Who is the narrator at the beginning and the end of the story? How do you know?
2. Explain the different points of view from which this story is told.
3. Describe the characters in the passages from 1973, 1949, 1913, and the 1880s. What does each passage reveal about the attitudes of the time and the personalities of the characters?
4. How does the narrator of 1973 feel as he watches his son play soccer? Why might he feel this way?
5. What words does the narrator use to describe his son at the end of the story? What might he mean by these words?

EVALUATE AND CONNECT

6. Theme Connections   Find examples of father-son relationships from each time period in the story. What do these scenes suggest about the relationships between fathers and sons during the twentieth century?
7. Compare the relationships in this story with those in your own life. How are your relationships similar to any of those in the story? How are they different?
8. Think about your responses to the Focus Activity on page 1046. How do you think Updike might answer that same question? Explain.

EXTENDING YOUR RESPONSE

Writing About Literature

Analyzing Title   Do you think the title "Son" is a good one for this story? Why or why not? Write your answer in a paragraph or two, and support it with information from your own experience and details from the story. If you disagree with the choice of title, suggest alternative titles.

Literature Groups

Identifying the Theme   A story's **theme** is its underlying message about life or human nature. What do you think is this story's theme? Discuss this question in your group, using details from the story as evidence. Then compare your answer with the answers of other groups.

📖 **Save your work for your portfolio.**

TOWARD THE TWENTY-FIRST CENTURY 🐾 1051

Personal Response

Most students will not find the end of the story surprising. It is consistent with the other passages of the story.

ANALYZING LITERATURE

1. The narrator is the father of the boy who plays soccer and reads the newspaper. He is the son of the teacher. The dates help place the different relationships as generations of a family.
2. The story is told from both the first- and third-person points of view. The narrator describes his own son. When the story reverts to the past, it is told in the third person.
3. 1973: the narrator describes his relationship with his son. 1949: The narrator's life as a teenager is described. He seems to feel many of the same sentiments as his son. 1913: This passage shows the narrator's father as a young boy. He is bitter and depressed as a child and as an adult. 1880s: The passage describes the narrator's grandfather, who is also sorrowful. His bitterness becomes a legacy for the entire family.
4. He seems to feel jealous because he did not have those same opportunities.
5. The narrator describes his son as a visitor (someone who touches other lives, but only for a short time) and a prisoner (someone who is being confined).
6. Fathers and sons have certain expectations of each other, but are often not able to connect with each other beyond the surface level.
7. Students should offer specific examples.
8. Updike would consider both roles difficult. Students should support their answers.

✔ ASSESSMENT OPTIONS

📁 **Quick Checks,** p. 115
📁 **Selection and Theme Assessment,** pp. 175–176
📁 **Performance Assessment,** p. 98
💾 **Testmaker**

LITERARY ELEMENTS

1. The narrator participates in sections 1, 5, and 7. *He* is the narrator's son.
2. The narrator is an observer in the other sections. In sections 2 and 6, the narrator is the son. In section 3, the narrator's father is described. Section 4 describes the narrator's grandfather.
3. The story would not be as personal or credible. Readers would not feel as drawn in to the story.

Additional Resources

 Literary Elements Transparency 98

Objectives

- To read and analyze an excerpt from a memoir that links the author's past with his present identity
- To examine the use of narrative in the selection
- To write an expanded narrative

Skills

Reading/Thinking: Monitoring Comprehension; Drawing Conclusions
Writing: Description with Spatial Order; Travel Brochure
Vocabulary: Etymology
Grammar/Language: Using Semicolons
Listening/Speaking: Interview
Collaboration: Literature Groups

More About N. Scott Momaday

Part of this selection is a retelling of a legend about a boy who becomes a bear. Of this legend, Momaday says, "I identify with that boy. I have for many years. And I have struggled with my bear power through those years. . . . My notion is that the boy and the bear are divisible. That after the end of the story, the bear remains and the boy remains and they come together now and then. The boy becomes a boy again and becomes a bear again, and this goes on and has gone on through the centuries, and probably in every generation there is a reincarnation of the bear— the boy bear. And I feel that I am such a reincarnation, and I am very curious about it. The way I deal with it, finally, is to write about it— to imagine it and to write a story about it. . . ."

Before You Read

from *The Way To Rainy Mountain*

Meet N. Scott Momaday

"I believe that one can work miracles in language. Language itself is a kind of miracle."
—*Momaday*

The Man Made of Words, the title of one of his books, describes N. Scott Momaday (mə mä′ dā) well. He is a distinguished novelist, poet, and teacher who relishes words—their sounds, meanings, and power. "Words are instruments of infinite possibility," he observes, and he uses them to preserve the oral traditions and the culture of Native Americans.

Momaday, of Kiowa descent, was born in Oklahoma and grew up in the Southwest. His mother was a teacher and a writer; his father was an artist, a teacher, and a "great story-teller" who repeatedly told his son Kiowa tales and legends. When Momaday grew up, he realized how fragile these stories were: "They exist only by word of mouth, always just one generation away from extinction." He began retelling these stories on paper, thus starting down a lifelong path as a writer.

Momaday's first novel, *House Made of Dawn,* was groundbreaking for its realistic depiction of modern Native American life. The book won a Pulitzer Prize for Fiction, making Momaday the first Native American writer to win this award. In *The Way To Rainy Mountain,* Momaday blends Kiowa myths, legends, and history, as well as autobiographical details.

Through his writing, Momaday has helped to break down negative stereotypes of Native Americans as well as to share his Kiowa heritage with others.

"When I was growing up on the reservations of the Southwest, I saw people who were deeply involved in their traditional life, in the memories of their blood," he recalls. "They had, as far as I could see, a certain strength and beauty that I find missing in the modern world at large. I like to celebrate that involvement in my writing."

Momaday's talents extend beyond novels and stories, however. He is also an artist and illustrator whose work has been displayed in Europe and appears in several of his books, including *The Gourd Dancer.* In addition, Momaday's trademark voice—described by many as rich, powerful, and booming—can be heard narrating many of the exhibits at the Smithsonian's Museum of the American Indian.

"I believe that the Indian has an understanding of the physical world and of the earth as a spiritual entity that is his, very much his own. The non-Indian can benefit a good deal by having that perception revealed to him."
—*Momaday*

N. Scott Momaday was born in 1934.

Reading Further
If you would like to read more by or about N. Scott Momaday, you might enjoy the following:

Collections: *The Way To Rainy Mountain,* by N. Scott Momaday, is a collection of anecdotes and folktales about the Kiowas, with illustrations by Momaday's father.

Ancestral Voice: Conversations with N. Scott Momaday, by Charles L. Woodard, is a collection of discussions with Momaday about his writing and personal experiences.

Poetry: *The Gourd Dancer* contains poems and illustrations by Momaday.

RESOURCE MANAGER

Lesson Planning Resource
The *Unit Seven Planning Guide* (pp. 27–34) provides additional lesson notes and reduced versions of all print resources.

Other Print Resources
- Active Reading Guide, p. 116
- Vocabulary Practice, p. 62
- Reading Workbook, pp. 83–84
- Grammar and Language Workbook, p. 247

- Grammar and Composition Handbook, Lesson 11.5
- Quick Checks, p. 116
- Selection and Theme Assessment, pp. 177–178
- Performance Assessment, p. 99
- Spanish Summaries, p. 103
- Inclusion Strategies
- English Language Learners Sourcebook

Transparencies
- Selection Focus 103
- Literary Elements 99
- Grammar and Language 76

Technology
- Audio Library
- Spanish Audio Library
- Glencoe Literature Web Site
- Testmaker

——— FOCUS ACTIVITY ———

Where are you from? What places define who you are?

CHART IT! Chart the places that contribute to your identity. These might include your school, your place of birth, your native land, or your favorite place. Write words or phrases that explain how each place contributes to your identity.

Place	How It Defines Me

SETTING A PURPOSE Read to learn how a place influences a person, a family, and a culture.

——— BACKGROUND ———

The Time and Place
The story shifts in time between present-day Oklahoma, the childhood of the narrator's grandmother, and the more distant past.

Literary Influences
Two English-language writers who have influenced Momaday are writer Herman Melville and poet Emily Dickinson. In an interview, Momaday noted that Melville "had a wonderful ear, like the ear of a storyteller." He described Emily Dickinson as "a good teacher." Momaday believes that readers can learn a lot about language from Dickinson: "How it used to be used, how it ought to be used, what risks are involved in the use, and so on." For more about Melville and Dickinson, see pages 381–383 and 423–439.

——— VOCABULARY PREVIEW ———

writhe (rīth) *v.* to twist, as in great pain; p. 1054

preeminently (prē em′ ə nənt lē) *adv.* chiefly; primarily; p. 1054

pillage (pil′ ij) *n.* looting or plundering; p. 1054

luxuriant (lug zhoor′ ē ənt) *adj.* marked by rich or plentiful growth; abundant; p. 1056

profusion (prə fū′ zhen) *n.* a plentiful amount; abundance; p. 1056

engender (en jen′ dər) *v.* to give rise to; to cause; to produce; p. 1056

consummate (kon′ sə māt′) *v.* to bring to completion; to finish; p. 1057

opaque (ō pāk′) *adj.* not letting light through; p. 1058

domain (dō mān′) *n.* a territory over which control is exercised; a realm; p. 1058

enmity (en′ mə tē) *n.* deep-seated hatred; hostility; p. 1059

Motivating
→ OPTIONS

Selection Focus Transparency 103: Have students study the chart. Then pose the question to the class.

Focus Activity: As an extension of the Focus Activity, students can use their charts to write personal character sketches that describe how these important places have contributed to their personality traits.

Reading Further

Be sure to review these titles for appropriateness for your class before recommending them to students.

Momaday, N. Scott. *House Made of Dawn.* New York: Harper, 1968. This story of a young Native American man has been described by one critic as "a creation myth—rife with fabulous imagery . . . suffused with violence and telling a story of culture loss."

Momaday, N. Scott. *The Gourd Dancer.* New York: Harper, 1976. This collection of poems includes illustrations by Momaday.

Momaday, N. Scott. *In the Presence of the Sun: Stories and Poems, 1961–1991.* St. Martin's, 1992. Momaday also illustrated this collection of poetry and prose.

CONNECTING TO OTHER SELECTIONS

The chart at the right shows three ways to connect this excerpt from *The Way to Rainy Mountain* to selections in this book.

For specific teaching strategies, see the *Unit Seven Planning Guide*, pp. 30–31.

Connection	Title
Life Skills: Lifelong Learning →	"The Three Piece Suit," p. 279
Thematic: Heritage →	"The Names of Women," p. 1181
Literary: Narrator →	"The Sky Tree," p. 50

from The Way to

 Active Reading

VISUALIZE Momaday uses figurative language and vivid imagery to create a picture of the landscape surrounding Rainy Mountain. Encourage students to look for language that helps them see, hear, and feel exactly what Rainy Mountain is like.

Additional Resources
📁 **Active Reading Guide,** p. 116
🎧 **Audio Library**
🎧 **Spanish Audio Library**

A single knoll rises out of the plain in Oklahoma, north and west of the Wichita Range. For my people, the Kiowas,[1] it is an old landmark, and they gave it the name Rainy Mountain. The hardest weather in the world is there. Winter brings blizzards, hot tornadic winds arise in the spring, and in summer the prairie is an anvil's edge. The grass turns brittle and brown, and it cracks beneath your feet. There are green belts along the rivers and creeks, linear groves of hickory and pecan, willow and witch hazel. At a distance in July or August the steaming foliage seems almost to writhe in fire. Great green and yellow grasshoppers are everywhere in the tall grass, popping up like corn to sting the flesh, and tortoises crawl about on the red earth, going nowhere in the plenty of time. Loneliness is an aspect of the land. All things in the plain are isolate;[2] there is no confusion of objects in the eye, but *one* hill or *one* tree or *one* man. To look upon that landscape in the early morning, with the sun at your back, is to lose the sense of proportion. Your imagination comes to life, and this, you think, is where Creation was begun.

I returned to Rainy Mountain in July. My grandmother had died in the spring, and I wanted to be at her grave. She had lived to be very old and at last infirm.[3] Her only living daughter was with her when she died, and I was told that in death her face was that of a child.

I like to think of her as a child. When she was born, the Kiowas were living the last great moment of their history. For more than a hundred years they had controlled the open range from the Smoky Hill River to the Red, from the headwaters of the Canadian to the fork of the Arkansas and Cimarron. In alliance with the Comanches, they had ruled the whole of the southern Plains. War was their sacred business, and they were among the finest horsemen the world has ever known. But warfare for the Kiowas was preeminently a matter of disposition rather than of survival, and they never understood the grim, unrelenting advance of the U.S. Cavalry. When at last, divided and ill-provisioned, they were driven onto the Staked Plains in the cold rains of autumn, they fell into panic. In Palo Duro Canyon they abandoned their crucial stores to pillage and had nothing then but their lives. In order to save themselves, they surrendered to the soldiers at

---

1. *Kiowas* (kī′ ə wäz)
2. *Isolate* (ī′ sə lāt) means "solitary."

3. *Infirm* means "physically weak" or "feeble."

Vocabulary
writhe (rīth) *v.* to twist, as in great pain
preeminently (prē em′ ə nənt lē) *adv.* chiefly; primarily
pillage (pil′ ij) *n.* looting or plundering

Teaching Options

Reading Minilesson

Monitoring Comprehension Some students may find Momaday's piece difficult. His writing juxtaposes memories with legends, exposition, and Kiowa history. Students may need different strategies to check their comprehension and to understand confusing passages.

Activity Before students read, have them list strategies they use to monitor

their understanding, such as asking questions, restating the author's ideas, and answering questions posed by the teacher or by the text. Then have students expand the list of strategies they use to include rereading, reading more slowly, using a dictionary or other reference source, or creating a graphic organizer. As students read, encourage them to keep

track of their comprehension and use strategies to help them gain a clearer understanding of the selection. **L2**

Additional Resources
📁 **Reading Workbook,** pp. 83–84

Rainy Mountain

N. Scott Momaday

Fort Sill and were imprisoned in the old stone corral that now stands as a military museum. My grandmother was spared the humiliation of those high gray walls by eight or ten years, but she must have known from birth the affliction of defeat, the dark brooding of old warriors.

Her name was Aho, and she belonged to the last culture to evolve in North America. Her forebears came down from the high country in western Montana nearly three centuries ago. They were a mountain people, a mysterious tribe of hunters whose language has never been positively classified in any major group. In the late seventeenth century they began a long migration to the south and east. It was a journey toward the dawn, and it led to a golden age. Along the way the Kiowas were befriended by the Crows, who gave them the culture and religion of the Plains. They acquired horses, and their ancient nomadic spirit was suddenly free of the ground. They acquired Tai-me,[4] the sacred Sun Dance doll, from that moment the object and symbol of their worship, and so shared in the divinity of the sun. Not least, they acquired the sense of destiny, therefore courage and pride. When they entered upon the southern Plains they had been transformed. No longer were they slaves to the simple necessity of survival; they were a lordly and dangerous society of fighters and thieves, hunters and priests of the sun. According to their origin myth, they entered the world through a hollow log. From one point of view, their migration was the fruit of an old prophecy, for indeed they emerged from a sunless world.

B

---

4. *Tai-me* (tī′ mā), the Sun Dance doll, wears a robe of white feathers.

Rock Tree, 1987. N. Scott Momaday. Graphite and wash, 14 x 11 in. Courtesy of the artist.

1055

B Author's Craft

DICTION What words does Momaday use to describe the Kiowas? What feelings do those words convey?
(Momaday describes them as lordly and dangerous, fighters and thieves, hunters and priests of the sun. He shows the strength of the people through the words he uses. All of these words connote power.)

MEETING INDIVIDUAL NEEDS — GIFTED AND TALENTED ACTIVITY

Native Americans Momaday's memoir may stimulate students to delve deeper into the history and culture of Native Americans.

Activity Have a group of students prepare a series of lessons for younger students on Native American culture. Ask students to use sources other than encyclopedias, such as Internet searches, documentaries, or periodical articles in their research. Tell students to use a variety of methods to present the information: time lines, diagrams, charts, video documentaries, or multimedia presentations, for example. Encourage students to compare their presentations with Momaday's memoir.

L3 COLLAB. LEARN.

C Critical Thinking

DRAWING CONCLUSIONS Momaday says that he has made this journey to visit his grandmother's grave. Ask students if this is his only reason. *(He also seems to be searching for his own past, trying to find peace with his grandmother's death while reconciling his heritage with his present.)*

D Author's Craft

DESCRIPTION Ask students why they think Momaday provides so much description throughout his memoir. *(To Momaday, the descriptions seem to be more important than mere physical descriptions. The harshness of Rainy Mountain helps explain the strength of the Kiowas. The description of the landscape from the Yellowstone to the base of the mountain reflects the journey of the Kiowas through beauty to barrenness.)*

C Although my grandmother lived out her long life in the shadow of Rainy Mountain, the immense landscape of the continental interior lay like memory in her blood. She could tell of the Crows, whom she had never seen, and of the Black Hills, where she had never been. I wanted to see in reality what she had seen more perfectly in the mind's eye, and traveled fifteen hundred miles to begin my pilgrimage.

D Yellowstone, it seemed to me, was the top of the world, a region of deep lakes and dark timber, canyons and waterfalls. But, beautiful as it is, one might have the sense of confinement there. The skyline in all directions is close at hand, the high wall of the woods and deep cleavages of shade. There is a perfect freedom in the mountains, but it belongs to the eagle and the elk, the badger and the bear. The Kiowas reckoned their stature by the distance they could see, and they were bent and blind in the wilderness.

Descending eastward, the highland meadows are a stairway to the plain. In July the inland slope of the Rockies is luxuriant with flax and buckwheat, stonecrop and larkspur.[5] The earth unfolds and the limit of the land recedes. Clusters of trees, and animals grazing far in the distance, cause the vision to reach away and wonder to build upon the mind. The sun follows a longer course in the day, and the sky is immense beyond all comparison. The great billowing clouds that sail upon it are shadows that move upon the grain like water, dividing light. Farther down, in the land of the Crows and

Blackfeet, the plain is yellow. Sweet clover takes hold of the hills and bends upon itself to cover and seal the soil. There the Kiowas paused on their way; they had come to the place where they must change their lives. The sun is at home on the plains. Precisely there does it have the certain character of a god. When the Kiowas came to the land of the Crows, they could see the dark lees[6] of the hills at dawn across the Bighorn River, the profusion of light on the grain shelves, the oldest deity ranging after the solstices.[7] Not yet would they veer southward to the caldron of the land that lay below; they must wean their blood[8] from the northern winter and hold the mountains a while longer in their view. They bore Tai-me in procession to the east.

A dark mist lay over the Black Hills, and the land was like iron. At the top of a ridge I caught sight of Devil's Tower[9] upthrust against the gray sky as if in the birth of time the core of the earth had broken through its crust and the motion of the world was begun. There are things in nature that engender an awful quiet in the heart of man; Devil's Tower is one of them. Two centuries ago, because they could not do otherwise, the Kiowas made a legend at the base of the rock. My grandmother said:

---

5. *Flax* is a flowering plant whose fibers are spun to make cloth. *Buckwheat* is a plant whose seeds are used as a cereal grain. *Stonecrop* is a flowering plant found on rocks and walls. *Larkspur* is known for its showy flower stalks.

6. *Lees* are sheltered places, as the sides of hills that are away from the wind.
7. The *solstices* (sol' sti sez) refers to the longest day of the year (about June 21) and the shortest day (about December 21) in the Northern Hemisphere.
8. *Wean their blood* means "to become acclimated by removing themselves gradually."
9. *Devil's Tower,* an 856-foot-high column of volcanic rock in Wyoming, was the first national monument in the United States.

Vocabulary
luxuriant (lug zhoor' ē ənt) *adj.* marked by rich or plentiful growth; abundant
profusion (prə fū' zhen) *n.* a plentiful amount; abundance
engender (en jen' dər) *v.* to give rise to; to cause; to produce

Teaching Options

Writing Minilesson

Description with Spatial Order
Remind students that one way a writer can describe a scene is in spatial order; that is, the way a viewer would see the same scene. Possibilities include left to right, top to bottom, east to west, and near to far. Ask students to reread this page and determine the spatial order that Momaday uses. *(He begins his description from the farthest point that the Kiowas can see.*

Then he works his way toward the Kiowas' home, the base of Rainy Mountain.)

Activity Ask students to write short descriptive paragraphs that depict scenes important to their cultures or to their families. Have them use spatial order to organize their descriptions. Then have them trade paragraphs with partners who can then identify the pattern of

spatial organization used in each other's paragraphs. **L2**

Additional Resources

📘 *Writer's Choice,* Lesson 3.1

Eight children were there at play, seven sisters and their brother. Suddenly the boy was struck dumb; he trembled and began to run upon his hands and feet. His fingers became claws, and his body was covered with fur. Directly there was a bear where the boy had been. The sisters were terrified; they ran, and the bear after them. They came to the stump of a great tree, and the tree spoke to them. It bade them climb upon it, and as they did so it began to rise into the air. The bear came to kill them, but they were just beyond its reach. It reared against the tree and scored the bark all around with its claws. The seven sisters were borne into the sky, and they became the stars of the Big Dipper.[10]

E

From that moment, and so long as the legend lives, the Kiowas have kinsmen in the night sky. Whatever they were in the mountains, they could be no more. However tenuous their well-being, however much they had suffered and would suffer again, they had found a way out of the wilderness.

My grandmother had a reverence for the sun, a holy regard that now is all but gone out of mankind. There was a wariness in her, and an ancient awe. She was a Christian in her later years, but she had come a long way about, and she never forgot her birthright. As a child she had been to the Sun Dances; she had taken part in those annual rites, and by them she had learned the restoration of her people in the presence of Tai-me. She was about seven when the last Kiowa Sun Dance was held in 1887 on the Washita River above Rainy Mountain Creek. The buffalo were gone. In order to consummate the ancient sacrifice—to impale the head of a buffalo bull upon the medicine tree—a delegation of old men journeyed into Texas, there to beg and barter for an animal from the

Goodnight herd. She was ten when the Kiowas came together for the last time as a living Sun Dance culture. They could find no buffalo; they had to hang an old hide from the sacred tree. Before the dance could begin, a company of soldiers rode out from Fort Sill under orders to disperse the tribe. Forbidden without cause the essential act of their faith, having seen the wild herds slaughtered and left to rot upon the ground, the Kiowas backed away forever from the medicine tree. That was July 20, 1890, at the great bend of the Washita. My grandmother was there. Without bitterness, and for as long as she lived, she bore a vision of deicide.[11]

Now that I can have her only in memory, I see my grandmother in the several postures that were peculiar to her: standing at the wood stove on a winter morning and turning meat in a great iron skillet; sitting at the south window, bent above her beadwork, and afterwards, when her vision failed, looking down for a long time into the fold of her hands; going out upon a cane, very slowly as she did when the weight of age came upon her; praying. I remember her most often at prayer. She made long, rambling prayers out of suffering and hope, having seen many things. I was never sure that I had the right to hear, so exclusive were they of all mere custom and company. The last time I saw her she prayed standing by the side of her bed at night, naked to the waist, the light of a kerosene lamp moving upon her dark skin. Her long, black hair, always drawn and braided in the day, lay upon her shoulders and against her breasts like a shawl. I do not speak Kiowa, and I never understood her prayers, but there was something inherently sad in the sound, some merest hesitation upon the syllables of sorrow. She began in a high and **F**

---

10. The *Big Dipper* is part of a larger constellation called Ursa Major, the Great Bear.

11. *Deicide* (dē´ ə sīd´) is the killing of a god.

Vocabulary
consummate (kon´ sə māt´) *v.* to bring to completion; to finish

E **Literary Elements**

NARRATIVE Remind students that narrative can include many kinds of storytelling. Ask students how the narrative has changed at this point and why Momaday has introduced this different type of narrative. *(He has changed from narrating his own travels and the travels of the Kiowa to telling the legend of Devil's Tower. The legend lends insight to the beliefs and character of the Kiowa and, hence, of his grandmother and of Momaday himself.)*

F **Literary Elements**

CHARACTERIZATION Momaday characterizes his grandmother by describing her actions and traits. What do you learn about her from Momaday's description? *(Her life was difficult, so she was a woman who had both strength and sorrow. She was a woman of prayer and hospitality.)*

MEETING INDIVIDUAL NEEDS

ENGLISH LANGUAGE LEARNERS

Cultural Traditions The Kiowa Sun Dance may be far removed from English language learners' experiences. Discussing traditions from their own cultures may help students understand how important the tradition was to the Kiowas.

Activity Have small groups discuss cultural traditions. Ask: How do you celebrate holidays? What special traditions are associated with marriage? With the birth of babies? Help students see that traditions may have common threads in many cultures. Ask groups to consider how the Sun Dance is similar to some of their cultural traditions. **COLLAB. LEARN.**

Additional Resources
📁 *English Language Learners Sourcebook*

Momaday earned his reputation as a writer first, but he is slowly becoming equally well-known for his art. He sees a close connection between the Native Americans and the land they inhabit, which he tries to express in his art. "They don't live on the land," he has said, "they live *in* it, in a real sense . . . and I like to evoke as best I can that sense of belonging to the earth."

Viewing Response *Many students will say that the sketch portrays strength, determination, courage, and pride—qualities Momaday attributes to Kiowas.*

Faces, 1987. N. Scott Momaday. Graphite and wash, 14 x 11 in. Courtesy of the artist.
Viewing the sketch: Which qualities of the Kiowas—according to Momaday—do you see portrayed in this sketch? Explain your reasoning.

G Literary Elements

FIGURATIVE LANGUAGE: *Simile*
Ask students to explain the simile Momaday uses to describe a house. *(Momaday compares houses to sentinels. He says that they are watchers of the weather, and then describes how houses change under the stress of the weather.)*

H Author's Craft

STYLE Invite students to characterize Momaday's style in this description. What is its effect? *(Momaday uses poetic devices such as consonance, assonance, and repetition. The poetical quality of the writing adds emphasis to his description of the house.)*

little while, wood takes on the appearance of great age. All colors wear soon away in the wind and rain, and then the wood is burned gray and the grain appears and the nails turn red with rust. The windowpanes are black and opaque; you imagine there is nothing within, and indeed there are many ghosts, bones given up to the land. They stand here and there against the sky, and you approach them for a longer time than you expect. They belong in the distance; it is their domain.

   Once there was a lot of sound in my grandmother's house, a lot of coming and going, feasting and talk. The summers there were full of excitement and reunion. The Kiowas are a summer people; they abide the cold and keep to themselves, but when the season turns and the land becomes warm and vital they cannot hold still; an old love of going returns upon them. The aged visitors who came to my grandmother's house when I was a child were made of lean and leather, and they bore themselves upright. They wore great black hats and bright ample shirts that shook in the wind. They rubbed fat upon their hair and wound

descending pitch, exhausting her breath to silence; then again and again—and always the same intensity of effort, of something that is, and is not, like urgency in the human voice. Transported so in the dancing light among the shadows of her room, she seemed beyond the reach of time. But that was illusion; I think I knew then that I should not see her again.

   Houses are like sentinels in the plain, old keepers of the weather watch. There, in a very

Vocabulary
opaque (ō pāk′) *adj.* not letting light through
domain (dō mān′) *n.* a territory over which control is exercised; a realm

Teaching Options

Grammar and Language *Minilesson*

Using Semicolons Remind students that semicolons are used
• to separate main clauses that are not joined by a coordinating conjunction.
• to separate main clauses that are joined by conjunctive adverbs (such as *however*) or by expressions such as *for example* or *that is*.
• to separate items in a series when those items contain commas.

Activity Have students write a description of a house or other building that is meaningful to them, modeling their work on Momaday's description. Ask them to use semicolons in at least five sentences. **L2**

Additional Resources

✎ *Grammar and Language Transparency 76*

📕 *Grammar and Language Workbook,* p. 247

📕 *Grammar and Composition Handbook,* Lesson 11.5

📕 *Writer's Choice,* Lesson 21.5

their braids with strips of colored cloth. Some of them painted their faces and carried the scars of old and cherished enmities. They were an old council of warlords, come to remind and be reminded of who they were. Their wives and daughters served them well. The women might indulge themselves; gossip was at once the mark and compensation of their servitude. They made loud and elaborate talk among themselves, full of jest and gesture, fright and false alarm. They went abroad[12] in fringed and flowered shawls, bright beadwork and German silver.[13] They were at home in the kitchen, and they prepared meals that were banquets.

There were frequent prayer meetings, and great nocturnal feasts. When I was a child I played with my cousins outside, where the lamplight fell upon the ground and the singing of the old people rose up around us and carried away into the darkness. There were a lot of good things to eat, a lot of laughter and surprise. And afterwards, when the quiet returned, I lay down with my grandmother and could hear the frogs away by the river and feel the motion of the air.

Now there is a funeral silence in the rooms, the endless wake of some final word. The walls have closed in upon my grandmother's house. When I returned to it in mourning, I saw for the first time in my life how small it was. It was late at night, and there was a white moon, nearly full. I sat for a long time on the stone steps by the kitchen door. From there I could see out across the land; I could see the long row of trees by the creek, the low light upon the rolling plains, and the stars of the Big Dipper. Once I looked at the moon and caught sight of a strange thing. A cricket had perched upon the handrail, only a few inches away from me. My line of vision was such that the creature filled the moon like a fossil. It had gone there, I thought, to live and die, for there, of all places, was its small definition made whole and eternal. A warm wind rose up and purled[14] like the longing within me.

The next morning I awoke at dawn and went out on the dirt road to Rainy Mountain. It was already hot, and the grasshoppers began to fill the air. Still, it was early in the morning, and the birds sang out of the shadows. The long yellow grass on the mountain shone in the bright light, and a scissortail hied[15] above the land. There, where it ought to be, at the end of a long and legendary way, was my grandmother's grave. Here and there on the dark stones were ancestral names. Looking back once, I saw the mountain and came away.

Did You Know?
A *scissortail,* a type of fly-catcher, is a small gray and pink bird with a forked tail.

---

12. Here, *abroad* means "away from one's home."
13. *German silver* is an alloy that resembles real silver.

14. *Purled* means "rippled with a murmuring sound."
15. *Hied* means "went quickly."

Vocabulary
enmity (en′ mə tē) *n.* deep-seated hatred; hostility

Sidebar

I Critical Thinking

DRAWING CONCLUSIONS What does Momaday mean when he says "gossip was at once the mark and compensation of their servitude"? *(The women served the men, but the gossiping revealed how much the women knew about the goings-on of the community, marked by their hard work and indispensable contributions. It also provided an escape, or compensation, for their work.)*

J Literary Elements

NARRATIVE Ask students how the type of narrative changes in these two paragraphs. *(In the first paragraph, the narrator tells of a memory. In the second, he tells of the present.)* Explain that these narratives draw the past and present together to contribute to the theme of personal identity.

K Literary Elements

SYMBOLISM What does the cricket symbolize for Momaday? *(It represents a beginning and an end. Although Momaday's grandmother is gone, his journey marks a deeper understanding of his own identity.)*

Thematic Focus

Generations What do you think is the most valuable thing that Momaday learned from his grandmother's example? What have you learned from a grandparent?

☑ ASSESSMENT OPTIONS

📁 *Quick Checks,* p. 116

INTERDISCIPLINARY CONNECTION

Social Studies Momaday describes in detail the gathering of the elder members of the community at his grandmother's house. Elderly people are regarded differently in various cultures. What place do elderly people have in Kiowa society? What place do children have? How can you tell?

Activity Ask students to compare and contrast the treatment of elderly people and children in various other cultures with their treatment in Kiowa society. Students may have ideas from their own experiences, but they will probably need to do additional research. Encourage them to focus on specific issues, such as who takes care of the elderly and what attitudes younger people have toward the older members of society. **L2**

Responding to
the Selection

Personal Response

Encourage students to explain what they learned, showing how the selection helped form their thoughts and insights.

ANALYZING LITERATURE

1. Rainy Mountain is a knoll in Oklahoma where Momaday grew up. He returns there to visit his grandmother's grave.

2. She was born into "a sunless world." Her people had been captured and imprisoned without the freedom or even the right to worship tribal deities.

3. The legend links the Kiowas to the sky and gives them a place to escape from the troubles of the world. Traditional beliefs include a reverence for the sun and the ceremony of the Sun Dance.

4. He remembers what they wore and how they looked, their stories and gossip. They came for prayer meetings and feasts.

5. He notices the cricket silhouetted against the moon on his last night. When he sees his grandmother's grave, he looks up and sees the mountain.

6. The landscape is stark and simple, as if at the beginning, before growth clutters things.

7. The Kiowa people are stoic and resilient. They carry on regardless of anything that happens to them.

8. The destruction of the environment mirrors the destruction of the Kiowas and their religious traditions.

9. He knows that his childhood had a great impact on him. His childhood was probably a happy one.

10. The grave symbolizes the "death" of the traditional Kiowa way of life, but also stands as a permanent marker, memorializing the effect the Kiowa had on the area.

11. Most students will suggest that the Kiowas valued nature and tried to preserve ancient teachings and ways of life.

12. Students will probably find that it gives a personal rather than an objective and impersonal view of history.

13. Most students will suggest that the grandmother saw more changes.

14. Tourists would see Rainy Mountain as just another knoll on the landscape, not understanding its significance to the Kiowa.

15. Students should be able to relate the influence of important people in their lives.

Responding to Literature

Personal Response

What new insights did you gain from reading this selection? Share your thoughts with a classmate.

—— ANALYZING LITERATURE ——

RECALL

1. Where and what is Rainy Mountain? Why does Momaday return there?
2. What does Momaday call the era in which his grandmother was born? How did being born at that time affect her life?
3. Of what significance to the Kiowas is the **legend** the grandmother tells? (See Literary Terms Handbook, page R9.) What other elements of Kiowa traditional beliefs were part of the grandmother's life?
4. What memories does Momaday have of his grandmother and her "aged visitors"? What sparked their coming together?
5. What does Momaday notice during his last night and morning on Rainy Mountain? Where does he go, and what does he see?

INTERPRET

6. Why, do you think, does Momaday feel that Rainy Mountain "is where Creation was begun"?
7. What do you learn about the Kiowa people from the way that they respond to the end of their traditional lifestyle?
8. What do you think is the relationship between Momaday's "vision of deicide" and the changes in the environment of the Kiowa people?
9. What might the wealth of details Momaday recalls about his grandmother's life suggest about his childhood?
10. What, do you think, is symbolized in the description of the grandmother's grave?

EVALUATE AND CONNECT

11. In what ways, do you think, does the narrator capture the culture of the Kiowas? Give details from the selection to support your opinion.
12. How is this history like others you have read? How is it different?
13. Theme Connections   In your opinion, which generation witnessed more changes, that of the narrator or his grandmother? Explain your answer.
14. Compare and contrast Momaday's response to Rainy Mountain with the response a tourist today might have to the same place.
15. Momaday's grandmother was an important figure in his life. Who in your life has influenced you? In what ways?

Literary ELEMENTS

Narrative

A **narrative** tells a story. The story may be fiction, a legend, a memoir or an anecdote, a factual account, or even a poem or a song. Many writers use only one kind of story in a work. In *The Way To Rainy Mountain,* Momaday combines fiction, anecdotes, and historical facts. For example, the scene of the grandmother at prayer is an anecdote, and the account of the last Sun Dance and what followed is historical fact.

1. Momaday writes, "the Kiowas have kinsmen in the night sky." What type of narrative does Momaday use to support this idea?
2. What do anecdotes add to a narrative that historical facts cannot? What do historical facts provide that anecdotes or legends may not?

● See **Literary Terms Handbook,** p. R10.

LITERARY ELEMENTS

1. Momaday supports the idea with a legend explaining the origin of Devil's Tower.
2. Memories add personal insights and allow greater connection with someone's personal story. History provides objectivity and facts.

Additional Resources

 Literary Elements Transparency 99

LITERATURE AND WRITING

Writing About Literature

Expanding a Narrative What information about Momaday or his grandmother do you think could add to a reader's appreciation of this narrative? In a few paragraphs, describe the specific parts of the narrative that you would expand, what kinds of information you would include, and how the narrative would benefit from these additions.

Creative Writing

Time Travel Reread the chart you made for the Focus Activity on page 1053. Select one place and think about how you would describe it. Consider Momaday's description of Rainy Mountain as you list details about your special place. Then create a travel brochure for your place. Include details about its landscape and its history.

EXTENDING YOUR RESPONSE

Literature Groups

Examine Ideas Momaday once said, "I don't see any validity in the separation of man and landscape." He called human alienation from nature "one of the great afflictions of our time." In your group, discuss how Momaday's anecdote reflects the idea that people and places are linked and whether or not you agree with this idea. Share your conclusions with the class.

Listening and Speaking

Listen to Oral History Momaday's grandmother witnessed many events in the history of the Kiowas. Whom do you know has been an eyewitness to important historical events? Interview a person about an event or period that the person is familiar with, asking questions to elicit detailed personal recollections about what the person saw and how she or he reacted to it. Share your notes in a brief discussion with the class.

Internet Connection

Other Native American Voices There are many Internet sites that contain works by Native Americans, as well as reviews and discussions of those works. Search the Internet for sites about Native American writers and their writing. With your classmates, assemble a list of Native American authors and titles that you would like to read.

 **Save your work for your portfolio.**

VOCABULARY • *Etymology*

A word's etymology is its history, the story of its origins. This information often gives clues to the meaning and spelling of a word.

The word *wreit*, for example, is an Old English word meaning "to turn." Several modern words can be traced back to *wreit*; for example, *writhe, wreath, wriggle, wrench,* and *wring.* Notice how these words are similar to their ancestor in meaning and spelling.

PRACTICE Use a dictionary and your understanding of word origins to trace the history of the words listed below from their original meanings and languages to their modern definitions.

1. knoll   4. billow
2. range   5. canyon
3. panic   6. cavalry

LITERATURE AND WRITING

Writing About Literature
Students' paragraphs should
- follow a clear pattern of organization.
- include specific ideas for expanding the narrative.
- include ideas that make sense given the rest of the narrative.

Creative Writing
Students' travel brochures should
- describe the area and its history.
- show why the chosen place is so special.

EXTENDING YOUR RESPONSE

Literature Groups Students may want to create illustrations or diagrams that show the links between people and nature.

Listening and Speaking Remind students to prepare questions in advance and to use skills such as paraphrasing answers and establishing direct eye contact.

Internet Connection Encourage students to list their findings in ways that make sense, such as by category or time period. They might include critiques of Web sites in their guides, letting potential users know which sites will be most helpful.

VOCABULARY • *Etymology*
1. *knoll,* from Old English *cnoll,* meaning "lump"; it now means a hillock
2. *range,* from the Old French *ranger,* meaning "to put in a circle or row"; it now means "roam or travel about"
3. *panic,* from the Greek *panikos,* meaning "of Pan"; it now means "to have sudden, great fear"
4. *billow,* from the Old Norse *bylgja,* meaning "sack" or "belly"; it now means "to bulge or swell"
5. *canyon,* from the Latin *canna,* meaning a "reed"; it now means "a narrow valley between cliffs"
6. *cavalry,* from the Italian *cavaliere,* meaning "horse"; it now means "soldiers riding horses or mechanized vehicles"

Additional Resources
📂 *Vocabulary Practice,* p. 62

✔ ASSESSMENT OPTIONS

📂 ***Quick Checks,*** p. 116

📂 ***Selection and Theme Assessment,*** pp. 177–178

📂 ***Performance Assessment,*** p. 99

💾 ***Testmaker***

Motivating
→ OPTIONS

Selection Focus Transparency 104: Give students time to read the information on the time line. Then discuss the question.

Focus Activity: As an extension of the Focus Activity, invite volunteers to share their journal entries. Have the class compare and contrast these experiences.

LITERATURE & HUMANITIES

"Echo of a Scream" from *Art in Focus*, p. 545.

Have students examine what details in the painting express the horrors of war and how these details relate to the story.

Before You Read
Ambush

Meet
Tim O'Brien

"The object of storytelling, like the object of magic, is not to explain or to resolve, but rather to create and to perform miracles of the imagination," says Tim O'Brien. As a foot soldier in Vietnam, O'Brien had to perform miracles of the imagination just to get through each day. He was drafted into the army right after college in 1968. In Vietnam, he became a sergeant and earned a Purple Heart, an award given to U.S. soldiers wounded or killed in battle. His first book, *If I Die in a Combat Zone, Box Me Up and Ship Me Home*, was a memoir of his tour of duty.

O'Brien then wrote a novel called *Going After Cacciato* (kä chä′ tō), about a soldier who decides one day to simply walk away from the war. He won the National Book Award for it in 1979. O'Brien was nominated for a Pulitzer

Prize in 1991 for his short-story collection *The Things They Carried*.

O'Brien's work has been compared to that of Ernest Hemingway and Joseph Heller. Like them, he builds a picture of soldiers' daily lives by compiling masses of sensory details. Unlike them, he intertwines fantasy with reality in his war stories.

Besides writing novels and short stories, O'Brien has worked as a national affairs reporter for the *Washington Post* and as a writing teacher.

"My passion[s] as a human being and as a writer intersect in Vietnam, not in the physical stuff but in the issues of Vietnam—of courage, rectitude, enlightenment, holiness, trying to do the right thing in the world."

—*O'Brien*

Tim O'Brien was born in 1946.

FOCUS ACTIVITY

When have you reacted quickly to a situation and then regretted your actions later?

JOURNAL In your journal, describe a situation in which you reacted without thinking, and what you later felt about your reaction.

SETTING A PURPOSE Read this short story to find out how a single action haunts a man for the rest of his life.

BACKGROUND

The Time and Place
The story takes place in Vietnam, near the village of My Khe (mē   kā), around 1968. From 1965 to 1973, U.S. troops fought alongside the South Vietnamese in their struggle against a communist movement from the North.

The Vietcong, nicknamed *Charley* by U.S. soldiers, were guerrilla soldiers who supported communist North Vietnam. They sometimes disguised themselves as innocent civilians before ambushing South Vietnamese and U.S. troops.

VOCABULARY PREVIEW

grope (grōp) *v.* to feel about uncertainly with the hands; to search blindly; p. 1063
stooped (stōopt) *adj.* bent forward and downward; p. 1063
ponder (pon′ dər) *v.* to think about thoroughly and carefully; p. 1063
gape (gāp) *v.* to stare with the mouth open, as in wonder or surprise; p. 1064
dwell (dwel) *v.* to think about at length; p. 1064

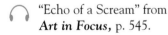

AMBUSH

Tim O'Brien

When she was nine, my daughter Kathleen asked if I had ever killed anyone. She knew about the war; she knew I'd been a soldier. "You keep writing these war stories," she said, "so I guess you must've killed somebody." It was a difficult moment, but I did what seemed right, which was to say, "Of course not," and then to take her onto my lap and hold her for a while. Someday, I hope, she'll ask again. But here I want to pretend she's a grown-up. I want to tell her exactly what happened, or what I remember happening, and then I want to say to her that as a little girl she was absolutely right. This is why I keep writing war stories:

He was a short, slender young man of about twenty. I was afraid of him—afraid of something—and as he passed me on the trail I threw a grenade that exploded at his feet and killed him.

Or to go back:

Shortly after midnight we moved into the ambush site outside My Khe. The whole pla-toon[1] was there, spread out in the dense brush along the trail, and for five hours nothing at all happened. We were working in two-man teams—one man on guard while the other slept, switching off every two hours—and I remember it was still dark when Kiowa shook me awake for the final watch. The night was foggy and hot. For the first few moments I felt lost, not sure about directions, groping for my helmet and weapon. I reached out and found three grenades and lined them up in front of me; the pins had already been straightened for quick throwing. And then for maybe half an hour I kneeled there and waited. Very gradually, in tiny slivers, dawn began to break through the fog, and from my position in the brush I could see ten or fifteen meters up the trail. The mosquitoes were fierce. I remember slapping at them, wondering if I should wake up Kiowa and ask for some repel-lent, then thinking it was a bad idea, then look-ing up and seeing the young man come out of the fog. He wore black clothing and rubber san-dals and a gray ammunition belt. His shoulders were slightly stooped, his head cocked to the side as if listening for something. He seemed at ease. He carried his weapon in one hand, muzzle down, moving without any hurry up the center of the trail. There was no sound at all—none that I can remember. In a way, it seemed, he was part of the morning fog, or my own imagination, but there was also the reality of what was hap-pening in my stomach. I had already pulled the pin on a grenade. I had come up to a crouch. It was entirely automatic. I did not hate the young man; I did not see him as the enemy; I did not ponder issues of morality or politics or military duty. I crouched and kept my head low. I tried to swallow whatever was rising from my stomach, which tasted like lemonade, something fruity and sour. I was terrified. There were no thoughts about killing. The grenade was to make him go away—just evaporate—and I leaned back and felt my mind go empty and then felt it fill up again. I had already thrown the grenade before telling myself to throw it. The brush was thick and I had to lob it high, not aiming, and I remember the grenade seeming to freeze above

---

1. A *platoon* is a military unit, usually commanded by a lieu-tenant, that forms part of a company.

Vocabulary
grope (grōp) *v.* to feel about uncertainly with the hands; to search blindly
stooped (stōopt) *adj.* bent forward and downward
ponder (pon' dər) *v.* to think about thoroughly and carefully

VIEWING THE PAINTING

Before turning to painting images of war, Mort Kunstler worked as an illustrator for *National Geographic* and *Newsweek* magazines. His work has also been featured on A&E's *Time Machine*. Kunstler's paintings create near-photographic images.

Viewing Response *Students may say that the man's face shows anxiety and fear, much as the narrator describes it.*

B Literary Elements

MOOD O'Brien uses carefully chosen words to create the mood of this story. What are some words, phrases, or images that most powerfully create the mood of this story? What is the mood these elements create? *(Students may mention, for example, "the young man coming out of the fog" or "the grenade seeming to freeze above me for an instant" as elements that help create the story's tense, anxious, worried mood.)*

Thematic Focus

Generations Ask students how this story speaks to their generation, even though they were not yet born during the Vietnam War. What modern-day situations might be similar to that of the narrator?

✔ ASSESSMENT OPTIONS

📁 **Quick Checks**, p. 117

Teaching Options

me for an instant, as if a camera had clicked, and I remember ducking down and holding my breath and seeing little wisps of fog rise from the earth. The grenade bounced once and rolled across the trail. I did not hear it, but there must've been a sound, because the young man dropped his weapon and began to run, just two or three quick steps, then he hesitated, swiveling to his right, and he glanced down at the grenade and tried to cover his head but never did. It occurred to me then that he was about to die. I wanted to warn him. The grenade made a popping noise—not soft but not loud either—not what I'd expected—and there was a puff of dust and smoke—a small white puff—and the young man seemed to jerk upward as if pulled by invisible wires. He fell on his back. His rubber sandals had been blown off. There was no wind. He lay at the center of the trail, his right leg bent beneath him, his one eye shut, his other eye a huge star-shaped hole.

It was not a matter of live or die. There was no real peril. Almost certainly the young man would have passed by. And it will always be that way.

Later, I remember, Kiowa tried to tell me that the man would've died anyway. He told me that it was a good kill, that I was a soldier and this was a war, that I should shape up and stop staring and ask myself what the dead man would've done if things were reversed.

None of it mattered. The words seemed far too complicated. All I could do was gape at the fact of the young man's body.

Even now I haven't finished sorting it out. Sometimes I forgive myself, other times I don't. In the ordinary hours of life I try not to dwell on it, but now and then, when I'm reading a newspaper or just sitting alone in a room, I'll look up and see the young man coming out of the morning fog. I'll watch him walk toward me, his shoulders slightly stooped, his head cocked to the side, and he'll pass within a few yards of me and suddenly smile at some secret thought and then continue up the trail to where it bends back into the fog.

Vocabulary
gape (gāp) *v.* to stare with the mouth open, as in wonder or surprise
dwell (dwel) *v.* to think about at length

Reading *Minilesson*

Making Critical Judgments The central question in this story is whether or not the narrator does the right thing by killing the young soldier. The narrator grapples with the question while his companion tells him that, if the situation were reversed, the enemy soldier would have probably done the same thing. Allow time for students to discuss this central question and make judgments about the character's actions.

Activity Assemble students in small groups and present this scenario: You are members of a war crimes commission, and you are deciding if the narrator of the story acted in a way that is justifiable. With your group of commissioners, come to a conclusion. Support your conclusion with evidence from the story as well as your own ideas about what is right and

wrong. Have groups share their findings with the class. **L2 COLLAB. LEARN.**

Additional Resources

📁 **Reading Workbook**, pp. 85–86

She plucked a blade of grass from its roots and twisted it back and forth, watching a streak of feeble, yellow sun play on its linear edges. "I expected it to be a celebration. He'd just finished his first novel, not quite a love story, he says, and he wanted me to read it." She spoke more softly. "When I arrived, he had set tiny blossoms in water dishes throughout the apartment. It smelled wonderful. The food was delicious, everything so lovely, so tranquil I didn't know where to begin. After dinner he led me into the living room.

" 'Rain music,' he said. 'It's for you.' After the last note on the piano had stopped to echo, he turned toward me and kissed me for a long, long time. I didn't know what I was doing. I just couldn't stop. I didn't breathe. When he let me go, I kept thinking of his hands and fingers, seeing them fly over the ivory keys like little Russian men dancing in their black fur hats and noticing how his brown was different from mine. I was raging inside, screaming in my head, 'Why can't his fingers be brown like mine, be my brown? Why is his hair curly, not straight, like mine?' I saw brown pigments run across my eyes, all different colored browns. Those pigments keep us apart. How do I stand there and tell this man who writes me music and whose hands burn my cheeks that I can't be who he wants me to be?"

"But he doesn't want to change you."

"No, I can't be who he thinks I am. He's a damned starving writer. He can't give me anything, just himself. And he doesn't even know that I'm using him. Damn it! He doesn't even know." She choked on her tears, swallowed, and cried quietly, hugging her knees, until exhausted. The leaves rustled softly while I waited.

After a while she grew calm, her eyes gazing steadily at the flashing water of the stream below. "I love Thanh. I would never hurt him for anything. Throughout the four years at UCSF, he has been so patient, so kind, so dedicated to medicine for its own good, not for just its technology, even though he's brilliant and understands these details completely. He's so perfect for me, just perfect. It's like he stepped out of my story and came to life. We speak the same language and share the same past. Everything. And Mom and Dad, they've done so much for us. Now they think they've won the lottery from God for being good all their life."

"But how do you feel about Thanh? How does he make you feel?"

"He will be my lifelong friend. He'll make a wonderful father. That's what a husband should be. Our children will know the culture and customs of our homeland. They'll speak Vietnamese and English, just like us."

"And how does David make you feel?" I tugged at her gently.

She bowed her head for a long while reflecting. Then she softly murmured, "It's just not possible."

"But why? I don't understand."

The picnic basket remained quite full. Neither of us was hungry. It threatened to rain as we packed up to go home. On the drive back, we were silent. I watched the windshield wipers swing back and forth, clearing rain cascading down the front window.

Vocabulary
pigment (pig′ mənt) *n.* a substance that gives color
cascade (kas kād′) *v.* to fall or flow as if in a waterfall or series of waterfalls

VIVID LANGUAGE Point out that Longhang Nguyen uses vivid language, especially in Linh's emotional words conveying her feelings about David. Ask students to characterize the language. What is its effect? *(When Linh describes David, she uses figurative expressions, especially when describing his fingers and his skin, that convey the differences between her and David. The words vividly express her anguish and frustration over having to make a choice.)*

Thematic Focus

Generations Many factors are involved in the decision that Linh faces at the end of the story. Ask students these questions: Do you think that the conflict in this story is a generational conflict? A cultural conflict? Explain. If Linh does marry Thanh, what advice do you think Linh will give her own children about the relationships they might form in the future?

ASSESSMENT OPTIONS

📁 *Quick Checks,* p. 118

ENGLISH LANGUAGE LEARNERS

Dialogue English language learners may be confused by the dialogue on this page. The narrator describes what Linh says, and Linh's dialogue contains a flashback. Students may need help sorting out who says what and when.

Activity Draw students' attention to the first two paragraphs on this page. Have students make a chart with three columns headed *What Linh Says Now,* *What David Said Then, What Linh Thought Then.* As students work with partners to reread these paragraphs, have them summarize the characters' words and thoughts and place their summaries in the correct columns. **COLLAB. LEARN.**

Additional Resources

📁 *English Language Learners Sourcebook*

Responding to the Selection

Personal Response

Students should support their answers with details from the story and their own experiences.

ANALYZING LITERATURE

1. Linh is beautiful, intelligent, and hard-working. Her parents expect her to marry Thanh and become a successful surgeon.
2. She learns about Linh's conflicting feelings for David and Thanh. The narrator feels confused by Linh's situation.
3. She points out that she and David do not share the same pigments; she and Thanh do. The pigment represents culture and race–barriers with David and bonds with Thanh.
4. Linh and David's relationship is playful and friendly, and she seems to love him. She considers Thanh a friend and respects and admires him.
5. Linh struggles with her choice between David and Thanh. She is motivated by loyalty to her culture and her parents.
6. Linh is faced with a difficult decision, an example of internal conflict. She also faces an external conflict between social expectations and her own desires.
7. Many students will say that the story shows more of a clash of generations. David and Linh show that people of different cultures can find common ground.
8. Encourage students to provide specifics to back up their responses.

EXTENDING YOUR RESPONSE

Literature Groups Remind students to rebut arguments that do not reflect story details accurately.

Creative Writing

Students' dialogues should
- reflect an understanding of the two characters.
- accurately create a conversation between David and Linh.

Responding to Literature

Personal Response

Do you think Linh made the right choice? Why or why not?

———— ANALYZING LITERATURE ————

RECALL AND INTERPRET

1. Describe Linh's personality, appearance, and achievements. What expectations do you think Linh's parents have for her?
2. What does the narrator learn on the picnic? How do you think the narrator feels about her sister's predicament? Explain.
3. What does Linh say about the pigment of her skin? What might pigment represent to her? Give reasons for your answer.
4. Describe Linh's relationship with David. How does she feel about him? How does she feel about Thanh? Support your answer with details from the story.
5. What problem does Linh struggle with in this story? What ideas or principles motivate her decision at the end of the story?

EVALUATE AND CONNECT

6. Is the conflict in this story an **internal conflict,** a struggle within a character, or an **external conflict,** a struggle between a character and an outside force? Use details from the story to support your answer.
7. In your opinion, how well does the writer capture the clash of cultures that some immigrants face when they settle in a new country? Explain.
8. What decisions in your life will be as important as the one Linh makes? Review the map you made for the Focus Activity on page 1066. Which factors will be most important to you when you make those decisions?

> ### *Literary* ELEMENTS
>
> **Crisis**
> In many stories a character faces a **crisis,** a moment of high tension that requires a decision. In "Rain Music," the crisis occurs the evening that David and Linh kiss. Instead of just enjoying the moment or being repulsed by it, Linh experiences an emotional storm within herself.
>
> In some stories, like this one, only one crisis occurs. In other stories and in novels, a character may face several crises.
>
> 1. What conflicting feelings does Linh have after the kiss?
> 2. What issues does this scene expose for Linh?
> 3. Why is this moment a crisis for Linh?
> ◉ See **Literary Terms Handbook,** p. R4.

———— EXTENDING YOUR RESPONSE ————

Literature Groups
Predict the Future Do you think Linh will have a happy marriage with Thanh? Hold a debate in your group. Divide into two teams, one to argue in the affirmative and one in the negative. Use story details and personal knowledge to develop support for your team's position. Compare your conclusions with those of other groups.

Creative Writing
Dialogue with David Imagine that Linh and David meet ten years after this story takes place. What kind of life might each have at that point, and what might they say to each other? Imagine both the situation and the conversation. Then write a dialogue that captures it.

📖 **Save your work for your portfolio.**

LITERARY ELEMENTS

1. She seems to love David, but realizes that Thanh shares her culture, a very important part of her life.
2. Linh has to decide what will be best for her. She also must face the fact that she has treated David unfairly and led him on.
3. No matter what decision she makes, Linh will hurt someone. She may hurt herself, her parents, David, or Thanh.

Additional Resources

 Literary Elements Transparency 101

✔ ASSESSMENT OPTIONS

📁 *Quick Checks,* p. 118
📁 *Selection and Theme Assessment,* pp. 181–182
📁 *Performance Assessment,* p. 101
💾 *Testmaker*

Reading & Thinking Skills

Identifying Cause and Effect

If you fail your driver's test, you immediately ask *why.* Did you forget to signal before pulling into traffic? Did you miss a stop sign? Whatever it was, your error **caused** you to fail a test. The **effect** of failing the test may be another few months without a license. These situations have a **cause-and-effect relationship.**

You will find cause-and-effect relationships in your reading as well as in your life. By identifying these relationships, you can better understand what you are reading and the author's purpose for writing. To determine a cause, ask *why.* Identify an effect by looking for a result. Note the following examples.

Heat causes water to evaporate. This is a clear, physical principal with an obvious cause and a predictable effect. The writer's purpose is to inform.

People are social beings. Every culture expects certain kinds of behavior. People of a culture often feel pressure to fulfill the group's expectations. This is a more complex relationship. More than one cause is named, and the effect is not automatic, as indicated by the word "often."

There are several kinds of cause-and-effect relationships:

- one cause, one effect
- several causes, one effect
- one cause, several effects
- a cause-and-effect chain

When reading about causal relationships, be alert for clues—words and phrases that signal the relationship. These clues can also indicate the degree of certainty that is present in the relationship.

As a result, because, if . . . then, and *therefore* are common indicators of cause-and-effect relationships. Words such as *may, perhaps, certainly,* and *possibly* are clues to the certainty of the relationship.

- For more about related comprehension skills, see **Reading Handbook,** pp. R86–R93.

ACTIVITIES

1. Find two examples of cause-and-effect relationships in "Rain Music" and explain each one. One example should be a cause-and-effect chain. In your explanations, point out any clue words that identify each cause and its effect, and the words that indicate the degree of certainty for each relationship.

2. From the reading you have done recently, identify examples of the four kinds of cause-and-effect relationships and explain each one briefly. You may use examples from nonfiction selections in any field you are studying, or from stories and articles.

Reading & Thinking Skills

Objective

- To locate and explain cause-and-effect relationships in text

Teaching Strategies

After students read the first two paragraphs, ask them to give examples of cause-and-effect relationships. When you reach the bulleted list, have students work in pairs to list examples of each type of cause-and-effect relationship. Finally, to help students understand cause-and-effect relationships in their reading, ask them to contribute to a class list of signal words. Start with the examples and encourage students to add more clue words.

Activities

1. *Sample answers:*
   Cause-and-effect relationship:
   David kisses Linh—Linh becomes confused and realizes she must make a decision.
   Cause-and-effect chain:
   Linh does well in school—Linh earns a surgical residency—Linh's parents have high expectations of her in every facet of her life.
2. Accept cause-and-effect relationships in which causes clearly lead to effects.

Additional Resources
📁 *Reading Workbook*

Teaching Options

MEETING INDIVIDUAL NEEDS INCLUSION STRATEGIES

Less-Proficient Readers Some students may need help identifying and remembering cause-and-effect relationships.

Activity Single out an obvious cause and effect in a story the class is reading. Explain that what happened is an *effect.* Write the effect in a box on the board. Why did it happen? Identify the why as the *cause.* Write the cause, draw a box around it, and draw an arrow from the cause to the effect. Encourage students to use the graphic organizer to keep track of other causes and effects.
L1

Additional Resources
📁 *Inclusion Strategies*

Objectives

- To read a selection that shows how shared experiences contribute to one's cultural and family heritage
- To analyze the use of onomatopoeia in the selection

Skills

Reading/Thinking: Evaluating
Life Skills: Create a Menu
Collaboration: Literature Groups

Motivating
→ OPTIONS

Selection Focus Transparency 106: After viewing the painting, ask students if they can name any of the utensils in it. Then discuss the question.

Focus Activity: As an extension of the Focus Activity, students can use their lists as the basis for poems about kitchens. Students' poems should capture definite feelings or moods.

Before You Read

Kitchens

Meet Aurora Levins Morales

"I have a commitment to myself not to take the easy route, to not say things that I don't believe in, to tackle things in a truthful way."

—*Morales*

Aurora Levins Morales (ə rōr′ ä le′ vinz mōr äl′ ās) was thirteen when her family came to the United States from Puerto Rico. It was 1967, and the feminist movement was spreading across the country. Morales read the works of many feminist writers and felt encouraged to write about her own experiences.

Morales joined women's writing groups and developed a love for the works of African American writers Alice Walker and Toni Morrison. She also began writing with her mother, Rosario Morales. Together, they have published their works in anthologies and in their own book, *Getting Home Alive*, a collection of prose and poetry about identity, family, and the experiences of immigrants.

Morales often writes about what it is like to be part Puerto Rican and part Jewish. "As a fiction writer, I feel a responsibility to write material that can be used by my communities in our struggle for survival and identity," she says.

Morales has a Ph.D. in women's studies and history. She teaches writing at the University of Minnesota. She also travels frequently, giving lectures on multicultural histories, especially those of women of Latin American or Jewish descent.

Aurora Levins Morales was born in 1954.

FOCUS ACTIVITY

Which of your senses is the first to respond when you think of the word *kitchen?* What sensory images come to mind?

LIST IT! Make a list of the sensory images the word *kitchen* evokes for you.

SETTING A PURPOSE Read to learn of an awakening that takes place amid the sensory images of a kitchen.

BACKGROUND

Puerto Rican Cuisine
The island of Puerto Rico is home to a number of Caribbean crops: rice, beans, pumpkins, guava, coconuts, and plantains. Puerto Rican meals commonly feature these foods served with fish or meat and seasoned delicately. Puerto Rican desserts include custards, puddings, and cakes, and many meals end with Puerto Rican coffee, served black or with hot milk and sugar.

VOCABULARY PREVIEW

deftly (deft′ lē) *adv.* skillfully; p. 1074
instinct (in′ stingkt) *n.* a natural ability or impulse; p. 1074

murky (mur′ kē) *adj.* characterized by dimness, as from fog or smoke; p. 1074

RESOURCE MANAGER

Lesson Planning Resource
The *Unit Seven Planning Guide* (pp. 46–51) provides additional lesson notes and reduced versions of all print resources.

 Other Print Resources
- Active Reading Guide, p. 119
- Reading Workbook, pp. 85–86
- Quick Checks, p. 119
- Selection and Theme Assessment, p. 183

- Performance Assessment, p. 102
- Spanish Summaries, p. 106
- Inclusion Strategies
- English Language Learners Sourcebook

Transparencies
- Selection Focus 106
- Literary Elements 102

Technology
- Audio Library
- Spanish Audio Library
- Glencoe Literature Web Site
- Testmaker

Vegetable Market (St. Kitts). Frane Lessac (b. 1954). Oil on board, 30 x 25 in. Private collection.

Kitchens

Aurora Levins Morales ∾

A Active Reading

VISUALIZE Morales uses rich imagery to put readers into her kitchens, the current one and the one in which she cooked with her ancestors. As students read, urge them to choose images that evoke strong responses.

Model: When Morales describes the beans, for example, she writes about their speckled surfaces and the clicking sounds they make when being poured into a pot. The description is soothing.

Additional Resources
📁 *Active Reading Guide,* p. 119
🎧 *Audio Library*
🎧 *Spanish Audio Library*

Teaching Options

COMPARING selections

This selection is paired with "Bread" on page 1078. A lesson for teaching a comparison of the two selections appears on page 1081.

ONOMATOPOEIA Onomatopoeia is
the use of words that imitate actual
sounds. Ask students what words
Morales uses to describe the action
of the mortar. What is the effect of
using these words? *(Morales uses
the words* pound, thump, *and* grind *in
succession. These words help readers
more vividly respond to the events
being described.)*

C **Author's Craft**

STRUCTURE Morales includes a
poem in the middle of the selection.
Why do you think she breaks the
flow of the narrative to insert the
poem? What does the poem
describe? *(The rest of the selection
juxtaposes images from the past and
the present, while the poem creates
one sustained image of cooking as
dancing.)*

**Teaching
Options**

Kitchens

I went into the kitchen just now to stir the
black beans and rice, the shiny black beans
floating over the smooth brown grains of rice
and the zucchini turning black, too, in the
ink of the beans. Mine is a California
kitchen, full of fresh vegetables and whole
grains, bottled spring water and yogurt in
plastic pints, but when I lift the lid from that
big black pot, my kitchen fills with the hands
of women who came before me, washing rice,
washing beans, picking through them so <u>deft-
ly</u>, so swiftly, that I could never see what <u>the</u>
defects were in the beans they threw quickly
over one shoulder out the window. Some
<u>instinct</u> of the fingertips after years of sorting
to feel the rottenness of the bean with a worm
in it or a chewed-out side. Standing here, I
see the smooth red and brown and white and
speckled beans sliding through their fingers
into bowls of water, the gentle clicking rush
of them being poured into the pot, hear the
hiss of escaping steam, smell the bean scum
floating on the surface under the lid. I see
grains of rice settling in a basin on the
counter, turning the water milky with rice
polish and the talc they use to make the
grains so smooth; fingers dipping, swimming
through the <u>murky</u> white water, feeling for
the grain with the blackened tip, the brown
stain.

From the corner of my eye, I see the knife
blade flashing, reducing mounds of onions, garlic, cilantro, and green peppers into *sofrito*[1] to be
fried up and stored, and best of all is the pound
and circular grind of the *pilón:*[2] *pound, pound,
thump, grind, pound, pound, thump, grind. Pound,*

B

pound (the garlic
and oregano mashed
together), THUMP!
(the mortar lifted
and slammed down
to loosen the crushed
herbs and spices from
the wooden bowl),
grind (the slow rota-
tion of the pestle
smashing the oozing
mash around and
around, blending the
juices, the green stain

Did You Know?
A *mortar* (môr′ tər) is a bowl
in which grains, spices, or
herbs are pounded into a
powder or paste. A *pestle*
(pes′ əl) is the instrument,
usually club-shaped, used for
pounding.

of cilantro and oregano, the sticky yellowing garlic, the grit of black pepper).

It's the dance of the *cocinera:*[3] to step outside
fetch the bucket of water, turn,
all muscular grace and striving,
pour the water, light dancing in the pot,
and set the pail down on the blackened wood.
The blue flame glitters in its dark corner,
and coffee steams in the small white pan.
Gnarled fingers, *mondando ajo,
picando cebolla, cortando pan,
colando café,*[4]
stirring the rice with a big long spoon
filling ten bellies
out of one soot-black pot.

C

It's a magic, a power, a ritual of love and
work that rises up in my kitchen, thousands of
miles from those women in cotton dresses
who twenty years ago taught the rules of its
observance to me, the apprentice, the novice,
the girl child: "Don't go out without wrapping

---

1. *Cilantro* (sē län′ trō) is an herb that resembles parsley in
   shape but not in taste. *Sofrito* (sō frē′ tō) is a thick sauce used
   as a cooking base in many Puerto Rican dishes.
2. Here, *pilón* (pē lōn′) means "mortar."

3. A *cocinera* (cō sē när′ ä) is a female cook.
4. *Mondando ajo* (mōn dän′ dō   ä′ hō) means "peeling garlic";
   picando cebolla (pē cän′ dō   sä boi′ yä) means "mincing
   onion"; *cortando pan* (côr tän′ dō   pän) means "cutting
   bread"; and *colando café* (cō län′ dō   kä fä′) means
   "preparing coffee by passing it through a strainer."

Vocabulary
deftly (deft′ lē) *adv.* skillfully
instinct (in′ stingkt) *n.* a natural ability or impulse
murky (mur′ kē) *adj.* characterized by dimness, as from fog or smoke

---

MEETING INDIVIDUAL NEEDS **ENGLISH LANGUAGE LEARNERS**

Setting English language learners may
have trouble following the changes in
setting in this story as the narrator
jumps back and forth between the past
and the present.

Activity Ask students to work with
partners and make two-column charts
with the headings *Kitchen Now* and
Kitchen of the Past. As they read
through the selection together, they

should list details about the two
kitchens and about the events of the
present and the past. When students
have completed their charts, ask them
to look for similarities between the two
columns. **COLLAB. LEARN.**

Additional Resources
📁 *English Language Learners
Sourcebook*

your head, child, you've been roasting coffee, *y te va' a pa'mar!*[5] "This much coffee in the *colador*,[6] girl, or you'll be serving brown water." "Dip the basin in the river, so, to leave the mud behind." "Always peel the green bananas under cold water, *mijita*,[7] or you'll cut your fingers and get *mancha*[8] on yourself and the stain never comes out: that black sap stain of *guineo verde* and *plátano*,[9] the stain that marks you forever."

So I peel my bananas under running water from the faucet, but the stain won't come out, and the subtle earthy green smell of that sap follows me, down from the mountains, into the cities, to places where banana groves are like a green dream, unimaginable by daylight: Chicago, New Hampshire, Oakland. So I travel miles on the bus to the immigrant markets of other people, coming home laden with bundles, and even, now and then, on the plastic frilled tables of the supermarket, I find a small curved green bunch to rush home, quick, before it ripens, to peel and boil, bathing in the scent of its cooking, bringing the river to flow through my own kitchen now, the river of my place on earth, the green and musty river of my grandmothers, dripping, trickling, tumbling down from the mountain kitchens of my people.

Produce market in Mayaguez, Puerto Rico.

5. *Y te va' a pa'mar!* (ē   tä   vä   ä   pä mär) is an idiom meaning "you're going to die."
6. A *colador* (cō' lä dôr') is a strainer.
7. *Mijita* (mē hē' tä) means "my daughter" or "my child."
8. A *mancha* (män' chä) is a stain.
9. *Guineo verde* (gi nä' ō   vär' dä) is a green banana. A *plátano* (plä' tä nō), or *plantain*, is a variety of banana that must be cooked. Plaintains are harvested as green vegetables and may be baked, fried, or boiled.

FLASHBACK What does this flashback reveal? How does Morales connect the flashback to the rest of the selection? *(This flashback shows the advice that adults gave to the narrator when she was young. The next paragraph shows the narrator trying to apply that knowledge. Although much of the advice is useless to her now, the narrator finds comfort and a connection when she recalls the advice and follows it.)*

E **Author's Craft**

STYLE Characterize Morales's style. How do you think the style adds to the meaning of the selection? *(Morales uses long sentences that are rich in visual images. Her sentences are almost like thoughts—they don't have distinct beginnings and ends. They reflect Morales's musings about her connection to the past.)*

Thematic Focus

Generations Although Morales mentions specific advice and skills she got from her ancestors, she learned other important lessons in life. Ask students to imagine that Morales has children with whom she is sharing lessons from the past. What do they think she will tell them?

✔ ASSESSMENT OPTIONS

📁 *Quick Checks,* p. 119

Reading *Minilesson*

Evaluating Having students evaluate literature helps them learn about forming solid opinions and reinforces the need to support their opinions with evidence.

Activity Have students write a review of this selection in which they respond to its impact. They should establish their criteria for evaluation, including the use of specific literary elements such as theme, figurative language, flashbacks, and characterization. After they identify their criteria, students should state their opinions, and provide evidence from the story and their own experiences as support. **L2**

Additional Resources

📁 *Reading Workbook,* pp. 85–86

Personal Response

Encourage students to use the text for specific support.

ANALYZING LITERATURE

1. Her current kitchen is more modern. The narrator works alone rather than with family members.
2. She is preparing black beans and rice. Her preparations remind her of her ancestors, the women who prepared the same foods. She feels warmth for these women and their work and proud to carry on the ritual.
3. She believes that cooking, like dancing, is an art, not a science.
4. The narrator learned to keep her head warm when going outside and to peel bananas under running water. The lessons link her to her ancestors and make her proud of her heritage.
5. Students should compare their sensory details with those of Morales. Most will say the sensory details create the atmosphere of a real kitchen.
6. Students should specifically state the source of their traditions.
7. Although people move and may begin to do things differently, traditions bind a family and bring comfort. Students should describe their connections with generations of their family.
8. The Spanish terms connect her to her family. The language is something that she shares with them.

EXTENDING YOUR RESPONSE

Literature Groups Students may do this exercise with their own refrigerators. They can draw diagrams of their refrigerators, reflecting on how the contents convey cultural heritages.

Learning for Life Students may want to actually create meals to reflect their families' heritages. They could also compile recipes into a class cookbook.

Responding to Literature

Personal Response

What kitchen sights and smells did you find most appealing?

——— ANALYZING LITERATURE ———

RECALL AND INTERPRET

1. Describe the narrator's kitchen. How does it compare with the kitchens of her childhood? Explain.
2. What is the narrator preparing in the kitchen, and what do these preparations remind her of? What seems to be her attitude toward these memories? Support your response with details from the selection.
3. Summarize the comparison the narrator makes between cooking and dance. What does this comparison suggest about her view of cooking?
4. What lessons has the narrator learned from her ancestors? What effect have those lessons had on her life as she has grown up and moved away from her childhood home? How do you know?

EVALUATE AND CONNECT

5. How do the sensory details the writer uses compare with those you listed for the Focus Activity on page 1072? In your opinion, does the writer effectively describe the sights and smells of a kitchen? Why or why not?
6. What bonds and traditions influence your behavior? Do they come from family, friends, or other groups? Explain.
7. Theme Connections   What do you think the narrator is saying about the connections between generations? What connections do you have to older generations in your family?
8. In your opinion, does Morales's use of Spanish terms contribute to the effectiveness of this piece? Why or why not?

Literary ELEMENTS

Onomatopoeia
The use of words that imitate the actual sounds associated with those words is known as **onomatopoeia** (on′ ə mat′ ə pē′ ə). *Buzz, roar,* and *tap* are some examples of onomatopoetic words. This technique helps the reader not just to "see" the actions going on but to "hear" them as well. By combining onomatopoeia with repetition, ". . . circular grind of the pilón: *pound, pound, thump, grind, pound, pound, thump, grind,*" Morales brings to life the sound and motion of the mortar and pestle.

1. Find two more examples of onomatopoeia in the selection and explain how they add to the sensory description of the essay.
2. List five other onomatopoetic words that relate to kitchens or cooking. Explain your choices.

● See **Literary Terms Handbook**, p. R11.

——— EXTENDING YOUR RESPONSE ———

Literature Groups
Tales from the Refrigerator   In your group, discuss the following questions: In what ways do the contents of the narrator's refrigerator reflect her upbringing? her personality? the place where she lives? What can you learn about a person from the foods he or she eats? Outline your conclusions and present them to the class.

Learning for Life
Food for Thought   Create a dinner menu—a beverage, an appetizer, a main course with at least one side dish, and a dessert—that reflects your family's heritage. If you can, include recipes. Then share your menu with the class.

■ **Save your work for your portfolio.**

LITERARY ELEMENTS

1. **Onomatopoeia:** Sample answers include "*clicking* rush" and "*hiss* of escaping steam." These words give the piece immediacy and depth.
2. Accept examples of onomatopoeia that have to do with cooking, such as *whisk* and *sizzle.*

Additional Resources

Literary Elements Transparency 102

✔ ASSESSMENT OPTIONS

📁 *Quick Checks,* p. 119
📁 *Selection and Theme Assessment,* p. 183
📁 *Performance Assessment,* p. 102
💾 *Testmaker*

MEDIA
Connection

Newspaper Article

Pictures still have their place in the world of matchmaking, but videos also have a place in today's dating market.

Love and Money
Singles Pay Services a Bundle for a Date—And Maybe a Mate

by Ellen Futterman, staff writer—*St. Louis Post-Dispatch,* June 12, 1994

In the wacky, unpredictable world of dating, mating, and relating, Jennifer Stephens knows exactly what she wants: a single man with whom she can fall in love, marry, and eventually raise a family.

Rather than leave the meeting to chance, Stephens shelled out big bucks to join Great Expectations, one of several pay-for-romance services in the St. Louis area that cater to singles. Between work and social obligations, Stephens says she doesn't have much time, or for that matter the inclination, to go searching for bright, attractive, available men. She'd rather let a dating service do the field work.

"I don't hang out at bars or attend church regularly," says Stephens, 33, who has bright blue eyes and a good-natured energy. "I've never met anyone at the grocery store. And I have my own washer and dryer, so I don't go to Laundromats."

Today, six months after joining, she hasn't fallen in love or, for that matter, in like. In fact, she hasn't even had what she would consider a good date with anyone she's met through Great Expectations' video-screening process.

The whole system felt awkward at first—especially the notion of paying to meet a man and talking into a camera about what she likes to do: watching *Seinfeld* on Thursday nights, going to movies, and reading (yes, she sheepishly admits) trashy Danielle Steel-type novels.

But Stephens, who works in accounting for a food distributor, says she has met nice people through the dating service. And she continues to visit the Great Expectations office in Maryland Heights each week to pore over books containing thumbnail descriptions and pictures of more than 1,500 eligible bachelors.

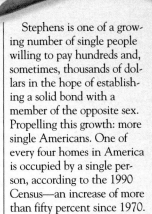

Stephens is one of a growing number of single people willing to pay hundreds and, sometimes, thousands of dollars in the hope of establishing a solid bond with a member of the opposite sex. Propelling this growth: more single Americans. One of every four homes in America is occupied by a single person, according to the 1990 Census—an increase of more than fifty percent since 1970.

Respond

1. In your opinion, what are the advantages and disadvantages of using a dating service?
2. Do you think your generation will rely on such a service? Explain.

Before Reading

Objectives

- To read and analyze a memoir that examines race relations in the 1950s
- To examine the use of sarcasm in the selection
- To write an analysis of the emotional appeals in the memoir

Skills

Reading/Thinking: Drawing Conclusions; Inferring; Analyzing Opinions
Grammar/Language: Quotation Marks
Collaboration: Literature Groups

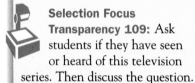

Motivating OPTIONS

Literature Launchers:
"An Integration Story"

Videodisc Side B, Segment 21

Also available in VHS.

Selection Focus Transparency 109: Ask students if they have seen or heard of this television series. Then discuss the question.

Focus Activity: As an extension of the Focus Activity, have students share their lists with a small group. What common elements do students see in their lists?

Before You Read
Prime Time

Meet Henry Louis Gates Jr.

"The society we have made simply won't survive without the values of tolerance. And cultural tolerance comes to nothing without cultural understanding."

—*Gates*

Bridging cultures is a habit for Henry Louis Gates Jr. He grew up in an Appalachian village and became a professor at Harvard. He faced segregation as a child, marched for black power, and spent a year in Tanzania at age twenty. "We were pioneers, people my age, in cross-race relations, able to get to know each other across cultures and classes in a way that was unthinkable in our parents' generation," he says.

After the Civil Rights movement of the 1960s, Gates studied at Yale University, where he was director of student affairs for John D. Rockefeller's campaign for governor. He later worked as a London correspondent for *Time* magazine and earned a Ph.D. in English literature from Cambridge University in England. Gates went on to author several books and has won an American Book Award and a genius grant from the MacArthur Foundation. He also has written dozens of magazine articles, edited numerous anthologies, and created the Public Broadcasting System series, *The Image of the Black in the Western Imagination.*

"I want to be black, to know black, to luxuriate in whatever I might be calling blackness at any particular time—but to do so in order to come out the other side, to experience a humanity that is neither colorless nor reducible to color. Bach *and* James Brown. Sushi *and* fried catfish."

—*Gates*

Henry Louis Gates Jr. was born in 1950.

FOCUS ACTIVITY

When you watch a movie or a television program, do you look for people you can identify with? Explain.

SHARE IDEAS With a partner list movies or TV shows with characters who remind you of yourself or people you know. Then list some movies and programs you don't relate to at all.

SETTING A PURPOSE Read to understand the influence of television on one writer's childhood.

BACKGROUND

The Time and Place
This selection takes place in the late 1950s and 1960s in a small town in West Virginia. During this time, many African Americans began to protest laws that denied them the same access to public places that white people enjoyed.

VOCABULARY PREVIEW

mundane (mun dān') *adj.* ordinary or usual; commonplace; p. 1087
impediment (im ped' ə mənt) *n.* an obstacle; p. 1087
allude (ə lood') *v.* to refer to indirectly; p. 1088
facade (fə säd') *n.* a false or artificial front; p. 1091
ritual (rich' ōō əl) *n.* a regularly followed routine; p. 1092
proverbial (prə vur' bē əl) *adj.* commonly spoken of; well-known; p. 1094
tumult (too' məlt) *n.* uproar; p. 1094

RESOURCE MANAGER

Lesson Planning Resource
The *Unit Seven Planning Guide* (pp. 62–69) provides additional lesson notes and reduced versions of all print resources.

Other Print Resources
- Active Reading Guide, p. 122
- Vocabulary Practice, p. 67
- Reading Workbook, pp. 85–86
- Grammar and Language Workbook, pp. 271, 273

- Grammar and Composition Handbook, Lesson 11.10
- Quick Checks, p. 122
- Selection and Theme Assessment, pp. 185–186
- Performance Assessment, p. 104
- Spanish Summaries, p. 109
- Inclusion Strategies
- English Language Learners Sourcebook

Transparencies
- Selection Focus 109
- Literary Elements 105
- Grammar and Language 77

Technology

- Literature Launchers
- Audio Library
- Spanish Audio Library
- Glencoe Literature Web Site
- Testmaker

Prime Time

Henry Louis Gates Jr.

Family Group, 1955. Charles Alston. Oil on canvas, 48¼ x 35¾ in. Whitney Museum of American Art, New York.

I guess some chafed more than others against the <u>mundane</u> <u>impediments</u> of the color line. "It's no disgrace to be colored," the black entertainer Bert Williams famously observed early in this century, "but it is awfully inconvenient." For most of my childhood, we couldn't eat in restaurants or sleep in hotels, we couldn't use certain bathrooms or try on clothes in stores. Mama insisted that we dress up when we went to shop. She was a fashion plate when she went to clothing stores, and wore white pads called shields under her arms so her dress or blouse would show no sweat. We'd like to try this on, she'd say carefully, articulating[1] her words precisely and properly. We don't buy clothes we can't try on, she'd say when they declined, as we'd walk, in Mama's dignified manner, out of the store. She preferred to shop where we had an account and where everyone knew who she was.

---

1. *Articulating* (är tik′ yə lāt′ ing) means "pronouncing distinctly and carefully."

Vocabulary
mundane (mun dān′) *adj.* ordinary or usual; commonplace
impediment (im ped′ ə mənt) *n.* an obstacle

SUMMARY

In this selection, Henry Louis Gates Jr. describes what it was like to grow up during the 1950s in Piedmont, West Virginia, where he, his family, and other African American residents faced discrimination. As a boy, Gates looked for role models—even for just a familiar face—on television, but found no one to whom he could relate. The Civil Rights movement was a "spectator sport" in his town.

📁 *Spanish Summaries,* p. 109

A Active Reading

CONNECT Point out to students the quotation from Bert Williams (the second sentence in the first paragraph). Ask students to connect it to the information in the selection as they read. Students may want to write the quotation at the top of a sheet of paper. As they read, they can write details from the selection that support the quotation.

Additional Resources
📁 *Active Reading Guide,* p. 122
🎧 *Audio Library*
🎧 *Spanish Audio Library*

Teaching Options

CONNECTING TO OTHER SELECTIONS

The chart at the right shows three ways to connect "Prime Time" to selections in this book.

For specific teaching strategies, see the *Unit Seven Planning Guide,* pp. 65–66.

Connection	Title
Life Skills: Leading and Organizing	→ "Frederick Douglass," p. 1146
Thematic: I Shall Not Be Moved	→ "If We Must Die," p. 734
Literary: Tone	→ "I Will Fight No More Forever," p. 514

As for me, I hated the fact that we couldn't sit down in the Cut-Rate. No one colored was allowed to, with one exception: my father. It was as if there were a permanent TAKE-AWAY ONLY sign for colored people. You were supposed to stand at the counter, get your food to go, and leave. I don't know for certain why Carl Dadisman, the proprietor, wouldn't stop Daddy from sitting down. But I believe it was in part because Daddy was so light-complected, and in part because, during his shift at the phone company, he picked up orders for food and coffee for the operators, and Dadisman relied on that business. At the time, I never wondered if it occurred to Daddy not to sit down at the Cut-Rate when neither his wife nor his two children were allowed to, although now that I am a parent myself, the strangeness of it crosses my mind on occasion.

Even when we were with Daddy, you see, we had to stand at the counter and order take-out, then eat on white paper plates using plastic spoons, sipping our vanilla rickeys[2] from green-and-white paper cups through plastic flexible-end straws. Even after basketball games, when Young Doc Bess would set up the team with free Cokes after one of the team's many victories, the colored players had to stand around and drink out of paper cups while the white players and cheerleaders sat down in the red Naugahyde[3] booths and drank out of glasses. Integrate? I'll shut it down first, Carl Dadisman had vowed. He was an odd-looking man, with a Humpty-Dumpty sort of head and bottom, and weighing four or five hundred pounds. He ran the taxi service, too, and was just as nice as he could be, even to colored people. But he did not want us sitting in his booths, eating off his plates and silverware,

putting our thick greasy lips all over his glasses. He'd retire first, or die.

He had a heart attack one day while sitting in the tiny toilet at his place of business. Daddy and some other men tried to lift him up, while he was screaming and gasping and clutching his chest, but he was stuck in that cramped space. They called the rescue squad at the Fire Department. Lowell Taylor and Pat Amoroso came. Lowell was black and was the star of the soccer team at the high school across the river in Westernport. He looked like Pelé,[4] down to the shape of his head.

They sawed and sawed and sawed, while the ambulance and the rescue squad sat outside on Third Street, blocking the driveway to the town's parking lot. After a while, Carl Dadisman's cries and moans became quieter and quieter. Finally, they wedged in a couple of two-by-fours and dragged out his lifeless body. By then it made little difference to Carl that Lowell was black.

Maybe Carl never understood that the racial dispensation[5] he took for granted was coming to an end. As a child, I must once have assumed that this dispensation could no more be contested than the laws of gravity, or traffic lights. And I'm not sure when I realized otherwise.

I know that I had rich acquaintance early on with the inconveniences to which Bert Williams alluded. But segregation had some advantages, like the picnic lunch Mama would make for the five-hour train ride on the National Limited to Parkersburg,[6] where you had to catch the bus down to the state capital, Charleston, to visit her sister Loretta. So what if we didn't feel comfortable eating in the dining car? Our food was

---

2. *Rickeys* (ri′ kēz) are drinks often made with soda water, sugar, and flavoring.
3. *Naugahyde* (nô′ gə hīd) is a type of artificial leather.

4. *Pelé* (pā lā′) is a world-famous Brazilian soccer player.
5. A *dispensation* (dis′ pən sā′ shen) is a system of ordering things or of regulating human affairs.
6. *Parkersburg* is a city in northwestern West Virginia.

Vocabulary
allude (ə lōōd′) *v.* to refer to indirectly

Historical Note

In 1896 the Supreme Court ruled that laws creating "separate but equal" facilities for African Americans and whites were constitutional. As a result, many states, particularly in the South, segregated public facilities such as schools and public transportation. In 1954 the Supreme Court ruled in *Brown* v. *Board of Education* that racially segregated schools were unconstitutional.

B **Critical Thinking**

DRAWING CONCLUSIONS Why do you think that Gates's father sat down at the Cut-Rate while the rest of his family stood? What does this action reveal about him? *(Students may suggest that Gates's father did it "because he could"—to make a show of being able to sit in the store.)*

C **Literary Elements**

SARCASM Remind students that sarcasm is ironic or satirical language that typically uses humor to criticize a person or an idea. Point out that Gates's tone in this passage is sarcastic. Ask: How does the sarcasm affect you? *(Some will say that the sarcasm helps them become personally involved in the events. Others may say that the sarcasm reveals the speaker's true attitude and shows how ridiculous people like Carl Dadisman really were.)*

ENGLISH LANGUAGE LEARNERS

MEETING INDIVIDUAL NEEDS

Segregation Some English language learners may be unfamiliar with the overall concepts described in this piece—segregation and the hope for integration. Take the time to discuss the general effects of segregation.

Activity Ask students to work independently to research segregation and the Civil Rights movement in the United States. They might search the Internet for first-person accounts, documentary photographs, and other resources. Then have them meet as a group to discuss what they've learned. As a second part of this activity, ask students to share their knowledge of civil rights in their native countries. **COLLAB. LEARN.**

Additional Resources
📁 *English Language Learners Sourcebook*

Jackie Robinson, 1949.

better. Fried chicken, baked beans, and potato salad . . . a book and two decks of cards . . . and I didn't care if the train ever got there. We'd sing or read in our own section, munching that food and feeling sorry for the people who couldn't get any, and play 500 or Tonk or Fish with Mama and Daddy, until we fell asleep.

The simple truth is that the civil rights era came late to Piedmont, even though it came early to our television set. We could watch what was going on Elsewhere on television, but the marches and sit-ins were as remote to us as, in other ways, was the all-colored world of *Amos and Andy*[7]—a world full of black lawyers, black judges, black nurses, black doctors.

7. The television show *Amos and Andy* was a situation comedy based in Harlem. The show, which aired from 1951 to 1953, is now considered by many to be racist.

Politics aside, though, we were starved for images of ourselves and searched TV to find them. Everybody, of course, watched sports, because Piedmont was a big sports town. Making the big leagues was like getting to Heaven, and everybody had hopes that they could, or a relative could. We'd watch the games day and night, and listen on radio to what we couldn't see. Everybody knew the latest scores, batting averages, rbi's, and stolen bases. Everybody knew the standings in the leagues, who could still win the pennant and how. Everybody liked the Dodgers because of Jackie Robinson,[8] the same way everybody still voted Republican because of Abraham Lincoln. Sports on the mind, sports in the mind. The only thing to rival the Valley in fascination was the big-league baseball diamond.

I once heard Mr. James Helms say, "You got to give the white man his due when it comes to technology. One on one, though, and it's even-steven. Joe Louis[9] showed 'em that." We were obsessed with sports in part because it was the only time we could compete with white people even-steven. And the white people, it often seemed, were just as obsessed with this primal confrontation between the races as we were. I think they integrated professional sports, after all those years of segregation, just to capitalize on this

8. *Jackie Robinson* (1919–1972) was the first African American to play major league baseball in the twentieth century. He played for the Brooklyn *Dodgers* (1947–1956).
9. African American *Joe Louis* (1914–1981) was the world heavyweight boxing champion from 1937 to 1949.

TOWARD THE TWENTY-FIRST CENTURY 1089

D Critical Thinking

DRAWING CONCLUSIONS Ask students why the narrator said the world characterized by the Amos and Andy show was remote. *(The African American characters were not true to the narrator's experiences. The all-African American cast suggested that segregation and discrimination were not issues. They were professionals, but in the narrator's town, all professional positions were held by white people.)*

Pop Culture

Integration in Baseball Brooklyn Dodgers general manager Branch Rickey believed segregation was morally wrong. He signed Jackie Robinson to a contract. Two years later, Robinson was named the league's Most Valuable Player. In 1962 Robinson was elected to the Major League Baseball Hall of Fame.

Pop Culture

Television Shows Gates mentions numerous programs and celebrities that students may not know. A few of these are:

Jack Benny—a comedian (1894–1974) who hosted radio (1932) and television shows (1950)

Wyatt Earp—a show about an American frontiersman (1848–1929) famous for being a law enforcer, 1955

The $64,000 Question—a popular quiz show during the 1950s

I Love Lucy—a show adapted from Lucille Ball's radio show that ran from 1951–1957

Gunsmoke—one of the longest-running shows about the settling of the Western frontier that aired from 1955–1975

voyeuristic thrill of the forbidden contact. What interracial sex was to the seventies, interracial sports were to the fifties. Except for sports, we rarely saw a colored person on TV.

Actually, I first got to know white people as "people" through their flickering images on television shows. It was the television set that brought us together at night, and the television set that brought in the world outside the Valley. We were close enough to Washington to receive its twelve channels on cable. Piedmont was transformed from a radio culture to one with the fullest range of television, literally overnight. During my first-grade year, we'd watch *Superman, Lassie,* Jack Benny, Danny Thomas, *Robin Hood, I Love Lucy, December Bride,* Nat King Cole (of course), *Wyatt Earp, Broken Arrow,* Phil Silvers, Red Skelton, *The $64,000 Question, Ozzie and Harriet, The Millionaire, Father Knows Best, The Lone Ranger,* Bob Cummings, *Dragnet, The People's Choice, Rin Tin Tin, Jim Bowie, Gunsmoke, My Friend Flicka, The Life of Riley, Topper,* Dick Powell's *Zane Grey Theater, Circus Boy,* and Loretta Young—all in prime time. My favorites were *The Life of Riley,* in part because he worked in a factory like Daddy did, and *Ozzie and Harriet,* in part because Ozzie never seemed to work at all. A year later, however, *Leave It to Beaver* swept most of the others away.

With a show like *Topper,* I felt as if I was getting a glimpse, at last, of the life that Mrs. Hudson, and Mrs. Thomas, and Mrs. Campbell, must be leading in their big mansions on East Hampshire Street. Smoking jackets and cravats, spats[10] and canes, elegant garden parties and martinis. People who wore suits to eat dinner! This was a world so elegantly distant from ours, it was like a voyage to another galaxy, light-years away.

---

10. A *smoking jacket* is a man's loose-fitting jacket usually worn at home and made of a fine fabric. A *cravat* is a man's scarf. *Spats* are cloth or leather coverings worn over the upper shoe and ankle, usually fastened under the shoe with a strap.

1090 UNIT 7

Leave It to Beaver, on the other hand, was a world much closer, but just out of reach nonetheless. Beaver's street was where we wanted to live, Beaver's house where we wanted to eat and sleep, Beaver's father's firm where we'd have liked Daddy to work. These shows for us were about property, the property that white people could own and that we couldn't. About a level of comfort and ease at which we could only wonder. It was the world that the integrated school was going to prepare us to enter and that, for Mama, would be the prize.

If prime time consisted of images of middle-class white people who looked nothing at all like us, late night was about the radio, listening to *Randy's Record Shop* from Gallatin, Tennessee. My brother, Rocky, kept a transistor radio by his bed, and he'd listen to it all night, for all I knew, long after I'd fallen asleep. In 1956, black music hadn't yet broken down into its many subgenres, except for large divisions such as jazz, blues, gospel, rhythm and blues. On *Randy's,* you were as likely to hear The Platters doing "The Great Pretender" and Clyde McPhatter doing "Treasure of Love" as you were to hear Howlin' Wolf do "Smokestack Lightning" or Joe Turner do "Corrine, Corrine." My own favorite that year was the slow, deliberate sound of Jesse Belvin's "Goodnight, My Love." I used to fall asleep singing it in my mind to my Uncle Earkie's girlfriend, Ula, who was a sweet caffé latté[11] brown, with the blackest, shiniest straight hair and the fullest, most rounded red lips. Not even in your dreams, he had said to me one day, as I watched her red dress slink down our front stairs. It was my first brush with the sublime.

We used to laugh at the way the disc jockey sang "Black Strap Lax-a-teeves" during the commercials. I sometimes would wonder if the kids we'd seen on TV in Little Rock or

---

11. *Caffé latté* (kä′ fā lä′ tā), a type of coffee with steamed milk, is a smooth tan color.

Grammar and Language *Minilesson*

But Kubota would not let it go. In session after session, for months it seemed, he pounded away at his story. He wanted to tell me the names of the FBI agents. He went over their questions and his responses again and again. He'd tell me how one would try to act friendly toward him, offering him cigarettes while the other, who hounded him with accusations and threats, left the interrogation room. Good cop, bad cop, I thought to myself, already superficially streetwise from stories black classmates told of the Watts[11] riots and from my having watched too many episodes of *Dragnet* and *The Mod Squad*.[12] But Kubota was not interested in my experiences. I was not made yet, and he was determined that his stories be part of my making. He spoke quietly at first, mildly, but once into his narrative and after his drink was down, his voice would rise and quaver with resentment and he'd make his accusations. He gave his testimony to me and I held it at first cautiously in my conscience like it was an heirloom too delicate to expose to strangers and anyone outside of the world Kubota made with his words. "I give you story now," he once said, "and you learn speak good, eh?" It was my job, as the disciple of his preaching I had then become, Ananda to his Buddha,[13] to reassure him with a promise. "You learn speak good like the Dillingham," he'd say another time, referring to the wealthy scion of the grower family who had once run, unsuccessfully, for one of Hawaii's first senatorial seats. Or he'd then invoke a magical name, the name of one of his heroes, a man he thought particularly exemplary and righteous. "Learn speak dah good Ing-rish like *Mistah Inouye*," Kubota shouted. "He *lick* dah Dillingham even in debate. I saw on *terre-bision* myself." He was remembering the debates before the first senatorial election just before Hawaii was admitted to the Union as its fiftieth state. "You *tell* story," Kubota would end. And I had my injunction.[14]

Did You Know?
Daniel K. Inouye (in' ō ye') (born 1924), was the first Japanese American to serve in Congress as a U.S. Senator from Hawaii.

The town we settled in after the move from Hawaii is called Gardena, the independently incorporated city south of Los Angeles and north of San Pedro harbor. At its northern limit, it borders on Watts and Compton, black towns. To the southwest are Torrance and Redondo Beach, white towns. To the rest of L.A., Gardena is primarily famous for having legalized five-card draw poker after the war. On Vermont Boulevard, its eastern border, there is a dingy little Vegas-like strip of card clubs with huge parking lots and flickering neon signs that spell out "The Rainbow" and "The Horseshoe" in timed sequences of varicolored lights. The town is only secondarily famous as the largest community of Japanese Americans in the United States outside of Honolulu, Hawaii. When I was in high school there, it seemed to me that every *sansei*[15] kid I knew wanted to be a doctor, an engineer, or a pharmacist. Our fathers were gardeners or electricians or nurserymen or ran small businesses catering to other Japanese

---

11. *Watts,* a section of Los Angeles, was the site of severe racial violence in 1965.
12. *Dragnet* and *The Mod Squad* were popular television police shows.
13. *Buddha* (563?–483? B.C.) was the title given to Siddhartha Gautama (si där' tə gou' tə mə), the founder of Buddhism. *Ananda* (ä nän' dä) was his cousin and "Beloved Disciple."

14. An *injunction* is a command or an order.
15. The *sansei* (sän' sā') are the children of the nisei.

Vocabulary
invoke (in vōk') *v.* to call forth

1105

Author's Craft

TONE Ask students to describe Hongo's tone as he describes his grandfather. What does it reveal about his feelings? *(Hongo's tone seems respectful and also questioning and uncertain. He speaks of how his grandfather "would not let it go." He seems to admire his grandfather's persistence, but he does not at this point seem to understand the urgency and insistence in his grandfather's story.)*

Literary Elements

MEMOIR Point out that *Kubota* is a memoir. Based on students' reading of *Kubota*, what is a memoir? *(Students may speculate that the writer of a memoir recreates a period of personal discovery and/or shows his or her relation to a specific historical event or development.)*

Critical Thinking

DRAWING CONCLUSIONS What story does Kubota want Hongo to tell? Why is Kubota different from the other Japanese Americans? *(Kubota wants Hongo to speak openly about the experiences of Japanese Americans during World War II. Unlike the others who want to bury this part of history as though it were their shame, Kubota seems to think that if the story is told, the mistakes of the past will not be repeated.)*

Writing *Minilesson*

Describing a Character Hongo not only tells readers what his grandfather was like, he paints a picture of Kubota, showing Kubota's character through what he says and how he acts. Ask students to find specific words and phrases that explain Kubota's personality.

Activity Using Hongo's work as a springboard, have each student write a description of someone in his or her family. Before they write, have them list things the person says and does that reveal specific traits. Encourage students to write in the form of an anecdote, as Hongo does in the selection. **L2**

Additional Resources

Writer's Choice, Lesson 3.4

AUTHOR'S PURPOSE Hongo includes long descriptions of the area in which his family lives and of the students at his high school. Why do you think he includes these details? *(Hongo wants to emphasize the desire of the Japanese Americans to assimilate.)*

Historical Note

Robert Kennedy (1925–1968) was appointed U.S. Attorney General by his brother, President John F. Kennedy. Robert Kennedy actively enforced Civil Rights laws during his tenure. In June 1968, while campaigning for the Democratic presidential nomination, he was shot just after declaring victory in the California Primary.

Thematic Focus

Generations Ask students these questions: Why do you think that members of Kubota's generation reacted the way they did? What do Hongo's words say to your generation? What lessons does his story teach?

☑ ASSESSMENT OPTIONS

📁 *Quick Checks*, p. 124

---

from **Kubota**

Americans. Our mothers worked in civil service for the city or as cashiers for Thrifty Drug. What the kids wanted was a good job, good pay, a fine home, and no troubles. No one wanted to mess with the law—from either side—and no one wanted to mess with language or art. They all talked about getting into the right clubs so that they could go to the right schools. There was a certain kind of sameness, an intensely enforced system of conformity. Style was all. Boys wore moccasin-sewn shoes from Flagg Brothers, black A-1 slacks, and Kensington shirts with high collars. Girls wore their hair up in stiff bouffants solidified in hairspray and knew all the latest dances from the slauson to the funky chicken. We did well in chemistry and in math, no one who was Japanese but me spoke in English class or in history unless called upon, and no one talked about World War II. The day after Robert Kennedy was assassinated, after winning the California Democratic primary, we worked on calculus and elected class coordinators for

Did You Know?
A *bouffant* (boo fänt′) is a hairstyle in which the hair is puffed out.

the prom, featuring the 5th Dimension.[16] We avoided grief. We avoided government. We avoided strong feelings and dangers of any kind. Once punished, we tried to maintain a concerted emotional and social discipline and would not willingly seek to fall out of the narrow margin of protective favor again.

But when I was thirteen, in junior high, I'd not understood why it was so difficult for my classmates, those who were themselves Japanese American, to talk about the relocation. They had cringed, too, when I tried to bring it up during our discussions of World War II. I was Hawaiian-born. They were mainland-born. Their parents had been in camp, had been the ones to suffer the complicated experience of having to distance themselves from their own history and all things Japanese in order to make their way back and into the American social and economic mainstream. It was out of this sense of shame and a fear of stigma I was only beginning to understand that the *nisei* had silenced themselves. And, for their children, among whom I grew up, they wanted no heritage, no culture, no contact with a defiled history. I recall the silence very well. The Japanese-American children around me were burdened in a way I was not. Their injunction was silence. Mine was to speak.

---

16. The *5th Dimension* was a popular music group in the late 1960s.

Vocabulary
concerted (kən sur′ tid) *adj.* planned or carried out by mutual agreement

---

Grammar and Language *Minilesson*

Inverted Word Order In English, complete sentences have a subject, a predicate (verb), and perhaps a direct object or subject complement, typically in that order. For variety and emphasis, writers may change that order. For example:

- an interrogative sentence that begins with an auxiliary verb
- a sentence that begins with the word

there or *here* followed by a form of the verb *to be*

Remind students that even with inverted order, the subject and verb should agree in number.

Activity Have students write five sentences about this selection using inverted word order, exchange their work with a

partner, and identify the subject and predicate of each sentence. **L2** **COLLAB. LEARN.**

Additional Resources

🔊 *Grammar and Language Transparency 78*

📙 *Grammar and Language Workbook,* p. 77

📙 *Grammar and Composition Handbook,* Lesson 2.4

📙 *Writer's Choice,* Lesson 16.3

Responding to Literature

Personal Response

What was your reaction to the events described in the memoir?

─────── **ANALYZING LITERATURE** ───────

RECALL AND INTERPRET

1. How does Hongo learn about his family's life at the outbreak of World War II? Why, do you think, does Hongo first disbelieve the stories?
2. What is the difference between the attitude of Kubota toward these events and the attitudes of his contemporaries? What might explain this difference? Use details from the selection to support your answer.
3. Where does Hongo live and go to school at the time he learns of Kubota's experience? How does the **setting** affect his acceptance of Kubota's story? (See Literary Terms Handbook, page R14.)
4. What does Kubota ask his grandson to do with the story he is telling? In your opinion, why does Kubota ask this?

EVALUATE AND CONNECT

5. Hongo begins with a vivid scene from the past and then moves to events that happened later. In your opinion, what does the opening scene contribute to the overall impact of the story?
6. What connection does Hongo make between his life as a writer and his family's past? Why, do you think, does he make this connection?
7. Suppose the author chose to delete the last paragraph from this selection. Would your view of his attitude toward his schoolmates be different? Explain.
8. How do your stories affect the way you view yourself and the world? Compare the impact of the stories you considered for the Focus Activity on page 1100 with the impact Kubota's story had on his grandson.

Literary ELEMENTS

Memoir

In a **memoir**, a writer narrates a portion of his or her past. Unlike an autobiography, a memoir focuses on a specific period or instance in history and deals peripherally with other parts of the writer's life. Many writers of memoirs, like Garrett Hongo, try to re-create an experience of discovery or growth. They may write about a new understanding of a time, a person, or an experience that is important to them. A memoir may include additional information about historical, scientific, or other developments of the time that are relevant to the writer.

1. What in-depth information must Hongo include in this portion of his memoir to make the story clear?
2. In what way does this memoir show a discovery or growth made by the narrator?

⬤ See **Literary Terms Handbook,** p. R9.

─────── **EXTENDING YOUR RESPONSE** ───────

Literature Groups

To Speak, or Not to Speak Is Kubota right to urge his grandson to tell about what happened to Japanese Americans during World War II? Debate this question in your group. Support your position with details from the selection and with historical information. Then share your group's opinions with the class.

Learning for Life

A Pilot Program Imagine that you want to persuade a television station to air a documentary on *Kubota.* Create a storyboard for the program. Develop at least six scenes showing who is in the scene, where it takes place, and the major action of the scene.

 Save your work for your portfolio.

✔ ASSESSMENT OPTIONS

📁 ***Quick Checks,*** p. 124
📁 ***Selection and Theme Assessment,*** pp. 189–190
📁 ***Performance Assessment,*** p. 106
💾 ***Testmaker***

LITERARY ELEMENTS

1. Hongo needs to include historical information to help readers understand his moment of truth. He must explain why this knowledge of his family's history had been hidden from him.
2. The memoir shows Hongo's understanding about his heritage and about his task of preserving the truth.

Additional Resources

 Literary Elements Transparency 107

Personal Response

Students should support their responses with specific passages from the text.

ANALYZING LITERATURE

1. Hongo's grandfather shares the history with him. Hongo finds it unbelievable because he hadn't learned about it from his family or in his history class.
2. His contemporaries want to forget about the events while Kubota wants to discuss them. His contemporaries seem to feel ashamed of the episode and want to forget it and fit in. It might be easier for Kubota to talk about it because he was only detained for four days.
3. He lives in a Japanese American community with students whose parents had been interned in the camps. He wants to accept his grandfather's stories, but the other students and the teacher are reluctant to discuss them.
4. Kubota asks him to tell the story. The injustice of his history angers him, and he doesn't want to let it be forgotten. Perhaps he hopes the story will ensure that the same mistakes do not happen again.
5. The opening scene conveys the incredible disrespect shown to Japanese Americans on the basis of their heritage. It angers readers and makes them want to find out more.
6. Hongo writes about his family's past. He does so, at least in part, because of his grandfather's injunction to speak about it.
7. Many students will suggest that if the last paragraph were deleted, they would have less understanding and empathy for the other Japanese American students who did not want to talk about the story.
8. Students should compare and contrast stories, using specific details.

Objectives

- To read two poems that reflect on family relationships
- To write a poem

Skills

Reading/Thinking: Drawing Conclusions; Making Critical Judgments
Writing: Poem
Listening/Speaking: Storytelling

Motivating
→OPTIONS

Selection Focus Transparency 112: Have students read the quotation and discuss what they have learned from older people in their lives.

Focus Activity: As an extension of the Focus Activity, have students write letters to their family members and friends, thanking them for the lessons they have taught.

Before You Read

Speaking and *apprenticeship 1978*

Meet Simon J. Ortiz

Simon J. Ortiz (ôr tēz′) says that he has been a writer "forever," since his voice comes from the oral tradition of Native American storytelling. Ortiz, a Native American from Acoma Pueblo in New Mexico, has actually been writing for thirty years or more. He has published numerous books, including poetry and short-story collections and essay anthologies. Recently, Ortiz edited a book titled *Speaking for the Generations: Native Writers on Writing*.

Ortiz teaches creative writing and Native American literature at universities and writing workshops throughout the country.

Two of his recent works are *The Good Rainbow Road*, a children's book, and *Before the Lightning*, a poetry collection.

Simon J. Ortiz was born in 1941.

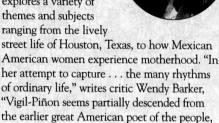

Meet Evangelina Vigil-Piñon

In her poetry, Evangelina Vigil-Piñon (vē hēl pē nyōn′) explores a variety of themes and subjects ranging from the lively street life of Houston, Texas, to how Mexican American women experience motherhood. "In her attempt to capture . . . the many rhythms of ordinary life," writes critic Wendy Barker, "Vigil-Piñon seems partially descended from the earlier great American poet of the people, Walt Whitman."

Vigil-Piñon was born in San Antonio, Texas, and graduated from the University of Houston in 1974. Since then, she has taught literature at various universities. In 1983 Vigil-Piñon won the prestigious American Book Award for her poetry collection *Thirty an' Seen a Lot*.

Evangelina Vigil-Piñon was born in 1949.

FOCUS ACTIVITY

What family member or friend has taught you something that has influenced how you live your life? What exactly did you learn?

FREEWRITE Spend three or four minutes freewriting to explore your response to these questions.

SETTING A PURPOSE Read to find out what one speaker teaches a son and what another learns from a grandmother.

BACKGROUND

Oral tradition—the passing down of stories by word of mouth—is important to both Native American and Chicano cultures. Simon Ortiz believes that the oral tradition brings "a sense of cultural being, continuity, and identity" to Native Americans. Evangelina Vigil-Piñon, in her poem "apprenticeship 1978," celebrates the ways oral tradition keeps the past alive, and she works to reflect that tradition in her own writing. For example, the speaker of "apprenticeship 1978" describes how her grandmother's stories inspire and guide her. By remembering the oral tradition, Vigil-Piñon says, a writer can convey "values to her family members . . . and, as such, she represents a tie to the cultural past."

RESOURCE MANAGER

Lesson Planning Resource
The *Unit Seven Planning Guide* (pp. 83–87) provides additional lesson notes and reduced versions of all print resources.

📁 **Other Print Resources**
- Active Reading Guide, p. 125
- Reading Workbook
- Quick Checks, p. 125
- Selection and Theme Assessment, pp. 191–192

- Performance Assessment, p. 107
- Spanish Summaries, p. 112
- Inclusion Strategies
- English Language Learners Sourcebook

✋ **Transparencies**
- Selection Focus 112

Technology
 Audio Library
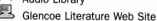 Glencoe Literature Web Site
 Testmaker

Speaking

Simon J. Ortiz

I take him outside
under the trees,
have him stand on the ground.
We listen to the crickets,
5   cicadas,° million years old sound.
Ants come by us.
I tell them,
"This is he, my son.
This boy is looking at you.
10   I am speaking for him."

The crickets, cicadas,
the ants, the millions of years
are watching us,
hearing us.
15   My son murmurs infant words,
speaking, small laughter
bubbles from him.
Tree leaves tremble.
They listen to this boy
20   speaking for me.

---

5 *Cicadas* (si kā′ däz) are large, winged insects.
The males produce a loud, shrill sound.

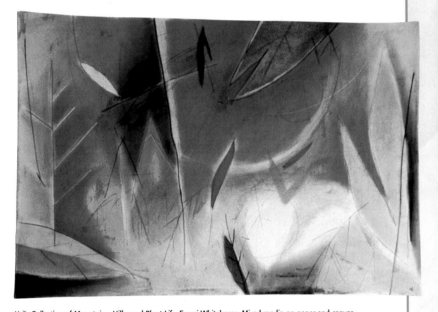

Yei's Collection of Mountains, Hills, and Plant Life. Emmi Whitehorse. Mixed media on paper and canvas, 38 x 48½ in. Telluride Gallery of Fine Art, Telluride, CO.

A **Active Reading**

VISUALIZING As students read this poem, encourage them to visualize the scenes. What details help them clearly picture the scenes? What mood do these details create?

Additional Resources
📁 *Active Reading Guide,* p. 125
🎧 **Audio Library**

B **Literary Elements**

PERSONIFICATION Ask students how Ortiz uses personification in the poem. *(Ortiz personifies nature, showing the insects as listening to the speaker and his son and characterizing the trees as "trembling." The personification exemplifies the link between people and nature.)*

C **Critical Thinking**

DRAWING CONCLUSIONS Why do the tree leaves tremble when the baby speaks? *(Although trembling may denote fear, in this case the tree trembles because of the excitement and connection between nature and humans.)*

Teaching Options

INTERDISCIPLINARY CONNECTION

Science Students who have spent time out of doors in late summer may have wondered how small cicadas produce such loud sounds.

Activity Challenge students to find out more about the cicada. Suggest that students conduct research to answer such questions as the following: Why do cicadas make noise? How loud is their song? How do they produce the sounds?

How long do cicadas live? Do they damage crops? Have students share their findings in a class discussion.

Maria Izquierdo (1902–1955) was born in Jalisco, Mexico. She was the first Mexican woman artist to have an individual show in New York City and said of her work, "I strive to make my work reflect the authentic Mexico."

Viewing Response Discussion questions:

• How does the painting provide a glimpse into the culture of Mexico? (*The woman's dress shows symbols that reflect traditional art forms.*)

• What features are emphasized in the painting? (*The artist emphasizes the lines in the woman's face, probably to show her wisdom and experience.*)

D Literary Elements

EXTENDED METAPHOR Invite students to explain the extended metaphor that Vigil-Piñon uses in the poem. (*Comparing words and memories to masterpieces emphasizes the beauty and timelessness of the grandmother's memories.*)

Thematic Focus

Generations Ask students: In each of these poems, who is learning from whom? What do the lessons being taught and being learned say about the relationship between generations?

☑ ASSESSMENT OPTIONS

🗀 **Quick Checks,** p. 125

Teaching Options

D apprenticeship
1978

Evangelina Vigil-Piñon ∾

I hunt for things
that will color my life
with brilliant memories
because I do believe
5   lo que nos dice
la mano del escritor:°
that life is remembering

when I join my grandmother
for a tasa de café°
10   and I listen to the stories
de su antepasado°
her words paint masterpieces
and these I hang
in the galleries of my mind:

15   I want to be an artist like her.

───────────────────

5–6 *lo que nos dice / la mano del escritor* (lō kā nōs dē′ sā / lä mä′ nō del e skrē′ tôr′) means "what the writer's hand tells us."

9 *tasa de café* (tä′ sä dā kä fā′) means "cup of coffee."

11 *de su antepasado* (dā sōō än′ tä pä sä′ dō) means "of her past."

Retrato de Mujer, 1944. Maria Izquierdo. Watercolor on paper, 20 x 14 in. Private collection.

Reading *Minilesson*

Making Critical Judgments Making critical judgments focuses students' attention on the structure, theme, images, and other elements of a poem.

Activity Have the class brainstorm a list of literary elements to use as a basis for evaluating and judging a poem, such as sound devices, rhyme, rhythm, figures of speech, mood, and imagery. Each student may choose three or four elements to judge either "Speaking" or "apprenticeship 1978." Have students record their judgments briefly. Caution them to provide specific examples from the poem to support their judgments. Then have them meet with others who evaluated the same poem to share critical judgments. **L3**
COLLAB. LEARN.

Additional Resources
🗀 *Reading Workbook*

Responding to Literature

Personal Response

What went through your mind when you finished each poem?

— ANALYZING LITERATURE —

Speaking

RECALL AND INTERPRET

1. Where does the speaker of this poem take his son and what does he have him do? Why might this place be important to the speaker?
2. What sounds does the son make? How would you describe the father's response to these sounds? What does this response suggest about the relationship between the father and son?

EVALUATE AND CONNECT

3. What two words does the poet **rhyme** in lines 3–5? What idea might he be trying to emphasize through this rhyme? (See Literary Terms Handbook, page R13.)
4. The speaker notices the ants, crickets, and cicadas all around him. What aspects of the natural world do you notice in your community? What can you learn from these natural elements? Explain.

apprenticeship
1978

RECALL AND INTERPRET

5. What does the speaker hunt for? How would you characterize the nature of her hunt?
6. What effect do the grandmother's words have on the speaker? What might the speaker mean when she says, "I want to be an artist like her"?

EVALUATE AND CONNECT

7. The poet incorporates Spanish words throughout "apprenticeship 1978." In your opinion, how do these words contribute to the meaning and impact of the poem?
8. In your opinion, is "apprenticeship 1978" a fitting title for this poem? What does it suggest about the speaker's relationship with her grandmother?

— EXTENDING YOUR RESPONSE —

Performing
Tell a Story   In Native American cultures, storytelling is an important activity. Storytellers pass on the myths and legends of the people. Imagine that you are a storyteller who feels that "Speaking" has an important message to preserve. Transform "Speaking" into an oral story and then perform it for a friend.

Creative Writing
Write a Poem   Using your response to the Focus Activity on page 1108 for inspiration, write a poem that conveys what you have learned from someone and how this knowledge has influenced you.

 **Save your work for your portfolio.**

TOWARD THE TWENTY-FIRST CENTURY ❧ 1111

✔ ASSESSMENT OPTIONS

📁 **Quick Checks,** p. 125
📁 **Selection and Theme Assessment,** pp. 191–192
📁 **Performance Assessment,** p. 107
💾 **Testmaker**

Creative Writing
Students' poems should
• convey what students have learned from someone else.
• describe the impact of this knowledge.

Responding to the Selection

Personal Response

Encourage students to link their thoughts to specific details in the poems.

ANALYZING LITERATURE

1. The speaker takes his son outside under trees to stand on the ground and to listen and watch. The place is important because it allows communion with nature.
2. The son murmurs infant words and laughs. The father seems nearly in awe of his son and respectful of the developing relationship.
3. He rhymes ground and sound. He might be trying to emphasize the idea that they are in contact with nature, standing on the earth and listening to nature's sounds.
4. Expect students to tell what they have learned from specific aspects of nature.
5. The speaker hunts for things that will color her life. She is looking for links between the past and the present.
6. The speaker admires her grandmother and cherishes what she says. She wants to carry on as a family storyteller like her grandmother.
7. The words show the link between the speaker and her culture. She is trying to blend the past with the present to hold on to her cultural legacy.
8. Most students will say that the title is appropriate because the speaker learns from her grandmother and, like her, wishes to create masterpieces of memory and tradition.

EXTENDING YOUR RESPONSE

Performing Encourage students to practice storytelling. Stress the importance of using tone and gestures to add drama to their performances.

Objectives

- To write a speech to persuade others that something should or should not be changed
- To plan, draft, revise, rehearse, and present a speech
- To reflect on and assess the speech

GLENCOE
TECHNOLOGY

WRITER'S ASSISTANT CD-ROM

Students can use Glencoe's templates and guidelines software for persuasive writing to aid them in working through the steps in the writing process in this lesson.

Teaching Strategies

PREWRITING

Explore ideas As students generate ideas for their writing, encourage them to meet in small groups to discuss possible topics. They can use the questions in the book to focus their discussions. They can also look through current newspapers and magazines to find topics. During group work, they can refine their ideas and can use other group members as sounding boards to see if their ideas can be effective in a persuasive speech.

Teaching Options

⌁Writing ✎ Workshop⌁

Persuasive Writing: Speech

"A living thing is distinguished from a dead thing by the multiplicity of the changes at any moment taking place in it."

—*Herbert Spencer,* English philosopher

What were you like at thirteen? What songs were popular a year ago? What were schools like when your parents were young? The world is changing all the time.

Sometimes change happens by itself; sometimes people make it happen. Just as frequently, people try to resist change. **In this workshop you will write a speech to persuade others that something should or should not be changed.** What change would you like to promote? What change would you like to prevent?

● As you write your persuasive speech, refer to the **Writing Handbook,** pp. R62–R77.

The Writing Process

PREWRITING

PREWRITING TIP

Keep your topic narrow and specific. You'll be able to target your audience more easily and cover your topic more effectively.

Explore ideas

Persuasive speeches are everyday events: an advertisement encourages you to buy a product, a candidate wants your vote, or a coach charges you up before the big game. When you try to persuade your parents to let you have a party, you become a persuasive speaker. Now you're going to focus your persuasive skills on change. In what ways would you like to go back to the past or move ahead? For ideas, just look around you—at your home, your school, your community, your world. Skim newspapers and magazines. Think about what is on television and radio. Talk to others. Consider the literature you read.

● Look back on the "good old days" an older person has described, as N. Scott Momaday does in *The Way to Rainy Mountain.* What do you think made those days better?

● As Longhang Nguyen does in "Rain Music," consider whether children of immigrant parents should follow traditional ways.

● Think about the lives of immigrants as described by Norma Elia Cantú and Julia Alvarez. How might their lives be made easier?

Focus on an issue that interests you—one about which you have an opinion and some information. Be sure you can justify your reasoning with good examples.

⬭ MEETING INDIVIDUAL NEEDS ⬭ ENGLISH LANGUAGE LEARNERS

Word Connotations In persuasive writing and speaking, a word's connotations may be critically important. English language learners may find this aspect of persuasive writing difficult.

Activity As students write, urge them to consult a dictionary or thesaurus to ensure effective word choices. When students have completed their drafts, pair them with fluent English speakers who can assist them as peer readers to identify the connotations of key words. Paired students should work together throughout the revising and rehearsal stages. **COLLAB. LEARN.**

Additional Resources
📁 *English Language Learners Sourcebook*

Choose an audience

Your topic will probably point you to your audience: a school audience for a school issue, a community audience for a community issue, and so on. Try to target listeners who are in a position to do something—such as pass a law, sign a petition, or write a letter. Talk to your audience in the kind of language they will understand, and give them the kind of information they will need to draw the conclusion you want.

Consider your purpose

Your purpose, as in any persuasive piece, is to persuade an audience to support your view on an issue and perhaps take some action. In this case, however, you will try to accomplish your goal with spoken words rather than written ones.

Build your argument

When you've found a compelling topic, map out your arguments. Include those that support your position and also those that oppose it. Do some research to back up your arguments, recording each fact and its source on one side of a note card. You can be profound and serious, or light and humorous, but in all cases, your arguments have to make sense. You might want to organize your thoughts on a diagram like this one:

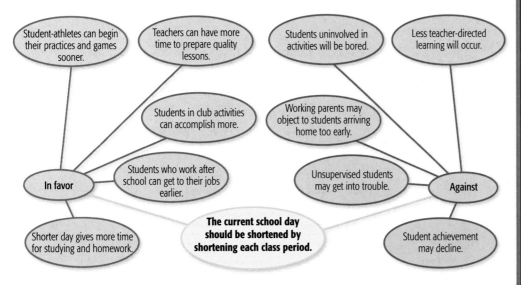

Make a plan

Check on whether you will be able to use visual aids, especially if any of your arguments involve data or diagrams that your audience will need to see. When you have all your information, spread out your note cards and make piles of those that speak to the same point. Then arrange your cards, with your arguments, in a logical order. You may want to prepare an outline from your cards to help you draft your speech.

Choose an audience Suggest that students consider these questions about their audience: What does the audience already know about the issue? What does the audience need to know? What feelings and attitudes might the audience have toward the issue?

Consider your purpose Have students write a position statement that defines the issue, what they think about it, and how they want the audience to respond.

Build your argument Give students permission to use other graphic organizers besides the organizational web to map out their thoughts. Some students may feel more comfortable with outlines or numbered lists.

Make a plan Discuss the different strategies for organizing students' speeches. Order of importance is an obvious organization strategy. Suggest that students also consider comparison and contrast to show the pros and cons of the positions, or examine cause-and-effect organization to show what could happen as a result of taking either position. Most students will decide to use a combination of strategies.

Additional Resources

📁 **Writing and Proofreading Practice,** pp. 1–7, 81–87

✒ **Writing and Proofreading Transparencies 1–6, 19–20, 45–46**

📕 **Writer's Choice,** Lesson 29.2

 MULTIPLE LEARNING STYLES

Interpersonal For students who feel more comfortable working in small groups, you might alter the assignment and ask students to participate in panel discussions.

Activity Organize students into small groups and tell group members to agree on the topic of their presentation and write a thesis statement. Have students plan how to present their materials, with one member serving as discussion leader, another giving the introduction, and a third summarizing the presentation. Other group members should argue one point each. Invite the groups to be creative in choosing ways to make their presentations. **L2** **COLLAB. LEARN.**

1113

Draft your speech Remind students to consider the tone of their speeches. Because they will actually be presenting, they need to think of the overall tone conveyed by their words and their delivery. Listeners may be put off by an angry or argumentative tone, inspired by a rousing and emphatic tone, or become supportive if they hear a sympathetic tone. Students need to be aware of the subtleties of language and how it is presented.

Develop your arguments As students develop their arguments, have them look again at the graphic organizers they created during the planning stage. Urge them to choose the strongest points. Students may want to consult with partners and ask these questions: Which of these arguments would most convince you to agree with my position? Why?

Writing Workshop

DRAFTING

DRAFTING TIP
Find out if there is a time limit for your speech. If not, you may want to set a limit of about twelve minutes. A longer speech can lose its impact, as well as the attention of the audience.

Draft your speech
As you draft your speech, remember that you're writing to be *heard*. Read your draft aloud as you write, and determine if your word choices will *sound* good to an audience. Keep in mind that a persuasive speech is like a persuasive piece of writing. It demands strong arguments, and it is shaped by a good introduction, a cohesive body, and a logical conclusion.

Introduction
- Grab your audience's attention immediately. Try an anecdote, a startling fact, a challenging question, an interesting visual aid, a moving quotation, or a personal connection.
- Tell what the speech will be about.

Body
- Use your notes. Shift things around as you draft if you think of a better arrangement.
- Try building your arguments so that they peak with your most important point.

Conclusion
- Remind your audience of what your position is and why they should agree with it.
- Leave them with something to think about or something to do.

Develop your arguments
Don't just list your arguments, elaborate on them with facts, stories, examples, and visual aids. On the other hand, don't throw too much information at your listeners. They have to understand your argument from hearing it just once. Remember, listeners cannot turn back the pages for another look. Choose words that clarify, rather than confuse, your argument.

STUDENT MODEL

> We never seem to have enough time in our busy lives. Students are no different from adults in this regard, having to balance school and homework with sports, extracurricular activities, and sometimes even an after-school job. Since there's not that much time in a day, one way to accomplish all we need to do is to modify the school day by shortening each class period. Cutting even five minutes from each class period would improve our lives in a number of significant ways. There would be more time to study and do homework. Those of us who participate in athletics or after-school clubs could begin practices and activities earlier, leaving more time later in the day for our studies. For those students who have after-school jobs, an earlier start might mean more money for college or more time for homework. Lastly, shortened class periods would mean more teacher preparation time and better lessons.

Teaching Options

Writing *Minilesson*

Avoiding Faulty Reasoning Work with students to find and correct faulty reasoning in their work. Discuss these types of faulty reasoning with students:

Loaded Language—The unfair use of highly emotional language.

Circular Reasoning—An argument that takes you back to where it started.

Name Calling—Attacking an individual rather than dealing with the issue.

Faulty Either-Or Reasoning—An argument based on the false assumption that there are only two sides to an issue.

Faulty Cause-and-Effect Reasoning—Arguing that one event causes another just because it happens first.

Bandwagon—Telling listeners to do or believe something because everyone else does.

Activity As students draft and revise their speeches, have them test each argument or reason they use against the list of faulty reasons. As a final check, have them trade speeches with partners to look for faulty reasoning. **L2** **COLLAB. LEARN.**

Additional Resources
Writer's Choice, Lesson 6.5

~ **Writing Workshop** ~

REVISING

Review your work

First read over your speech. Look for weak or incomplete arguments, words that need sharpening, or ideas that need linking. Then be your own audience. Practice your speech by yourself, thinking about how it sounds and how persuasive the arguments are. Mark places that strike you as awkward, unconvincing, unclear, or tedious.

Rehearse for others

Using your draft, your outline, or notes on cards, give your speech to family members, friends, classmates—anyone who is willing to listen and to make helpful comments. Ask your listeners to concentrate on how you look and sound as well as on what you say. The way a speech is delivered can significantly affect its message. Suggest that they use the **Questions for Revising** as a guide. Consider the comments you receive carefully, and incorporate those you find useful.

TECHNOLOGY TIP
With a computer, you can save and print out different versions of your speech. Test them all by reading them aloud—to yourself and to others. Use the one that seems most comfortable and convincing.

QUESTIONS FOR REVISING

☑ How might the opening be strengthened?

☑ Do the arguments flow smoothly? Where should the order be changed? Where do I need better transitions?

☑ Where can I eliminate weak arguments? Which points need more elaboration?

☑ Which parts are boring or hard to follow?

☑ Which parts have an inappropriately casual tone?

☑ How can I make the closing encourage action? Does it strongly support my opinion?

STUDENT MODEL

> *If your life is as hectic as mine, I think you'll agree that*
> ~~To summarize, everybody's life is nuts.~~ Shortening the school day
> *by five minutes*
> is a good idea. Shortening each class period is one good solution.
> ~~Five minutes isn't that much.~~ Athletes, students ~~in various clubs~~
> *students* *club members,*
> ~~and activities,~~ ~~kids~~ with jobs ~~and stuff~~—all of us could benefit
> from having extra time. ~~Then we'd be home for dinner early and~~
> *Certainly our parents would be pleased*
> *about that.*
> ~~our moms would be overjoyed.~~ Finally, our teachers would have
> *to prepare lessons*
> extra planning time ~~and that would be good for us too.~~

TOWARD THE TWENTY-FIRST CENTURY ✖ 1115

REVISING

Review your work As students review their work, you might play for them an audiotape or videotape of an especially effective speech. Ask students these questions: What makes this speech effective? The words? The tone of voice? The strength of the arguments? The organizational pattern? What else? Have students list their ideas and consider them as they review.

Rehearse for others If students are shy about rehearsing for others, suggest that they read their speeches aloud alone in front of mirrors before trying them out on actual audiences. Before they ask friends or family members to listen to their speeches, students might write the questions for revising on a separate sheet of paper so that listeners can answer the questions as they listen to the speech.

MEETING INDIVIDUAL NEEDS — MULTIPLE LEARNING STYLES

Spatial Strong spatial learners may want to enhance their presentations by using visual aids. Some information that is hard to articulate may be easy to represent visually.

Activity Work with students to list visual aids and discuss the ways that such aids can enhance presentations. Visuals might include charts, diagrams, tables, graphs, photographs, posters, illustrations, or artifacts. Ask students to brainstorm a list of tips, such as making sure that visuals are uncluttered and using bright, bold colors and large letters. Leave students' lists on the board for reference throughout the writing process. Invite students to work in pairs to suggest and create suitable visual aids. **L2 COLLAB. LEARN.**

Have students use the Proofreading Checklist on the inside back cover of their textbooks. Emphasize that editing speeches is different from editing written work. Students must listen to their speeches as well as read them; listeners can't go back and reread if something is unclear. Students may want to consider shortening sentences and inserting more transitional words.

Additional Resources

 Grammar and Composition Handbook, Lesson 14

PUBLISHING/PRESENTING

Point out that it is normal to be nervous when delivering a speech. Encourage students to take a deep breath before beginning and to avoid rushing when speaking. If they make a mistake, they should calmly correct themselves and continue the speech.

Reflecting

Portfolio Encourage students to ask these questions.

In writing this speech did I
- avoid using faulty reasoning?
- present my ideas clearly and concisely?
- find ways to improve my persuasive writing in the future?

If students answer "yes" to two or more questions have them consider including their speeches in their portfolios.

Teaching Options

~: *Writing* \ *Workshop* :~

EDITING/PROOFREADING

PROOFREADING TIP
Make sure that all changes from previous versions have been made correctly.

When you are satisfied with your speech, go over it for errors in grammar, usage, mechanics, and spelling, using the **Proofreading Checklist** on the inside back cover of this book. Even if no one but you will see the written version, you still want to be sure it is correct.

Grammar Hint

An irregular past participle cannot stand alone as a verb. Use the past participle with a form of *have,* or use the past tense form of the verb instead.

I have known many students who had after-school jobs.

● For information on related usage problems, see **Language Handbook,** pp. R27–R28.

STUDENT MODEL

Since september, I *have* gone to work at the grocery store every day after school.

PUBLISHING/PRESENTING

PRESENTING TIP
The audience will be looking as well as listening. Don't wear or hold anything that will distract them from your speech.

Prepare any visual aids or props in advance. Also decide whether you prefer to read your speech, memorize it, or speak from brief notes. Reading guarantees you will say what you intend, but you may not connect as well with your audience. Memorizing carries the danger of forgetting things and may increase your nervousness. Speaking from notes also involves such dangers, but the notes do provide cues.

No matter how you deliver the speech, remember to speak slowly and loudly, make frequent eye contact with your audience, and vary your pace, volume, and tone to keep listeners awake. Stand straight, keep both feet on the floor, and avoid nervous movements.

Reflecting

What was most challenging about preparing a persuasive speech? What was most fun? Set goals for your next piece of writing. Will you do something differently? If so, what?

 **Save your work for your portfolio.**

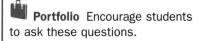

✔ ASSESSMENT OPTIONS

📁 **Writing Assessment and Portfolio Management**
- Writing Assessment, pp. 1–13, 44–46
- Portfolio Management, pp. 51–58

Our Life on His Back, 1993. Julie Lankford Olds. Oil on canvas, 12 x 16 in. Minnetrista Cultural Center & Oakhurst Gardens, Muncie, IN.

Prayer to the Pacific

Leslie Marmon Silko

A Active Reading

PREDICT Have students predict the content of the poem by looking at the title, the poem's structure, and the accompanying illustration. What first impressions do they have of the poem?

Additional Resources
Active Reading Guide, p. 126
Audio Library

VIEWING THE PAINTING

Born in Oklahoma in 1962, Julie Lankford Olds is a member of the Native American group known as the Miami. In this painting as in others, Olds attempts to communicate important Native American beliefs such as the close tie between humanity and nature.

Viewing Response What do you think the turtle represents in this painting? What do you think the man represents? (*The turtle may represent the islands or Earth, while the man represents the birth of the human race.*)

Teaching Options

Listening and Speaking *Minilesson*

Dramatic Reading The poem's structure, with its many pauses; the poem's tone, with its simple language and images; and the fact that this poem reads like a story all invite dramatic reading.

Activity Have students work with partner "critics" to prepare readings of the poem. Encourage students to read the poem as if it were a dramatic story. Ask students: How can you use your tone of

voice, volume, and dramatic pauses to make the poem seem like a story—a story that has deep significance? As students consider their answers, they can work their ideas into their readings. Partners can guide each other, offering suggestions to make the reading reflect the form, content, and intent of the work.
L2 COLLAB. LEARN.

FIGURATIVE LANGUAGE: *Personification*
Ask students how Silko personifies the ocean. What is the effect of the personification? *(The speaker mentions the ocean's birth and speaks to the ocean. The ocean becomes a living being; people can interact with it.)*

C **Literary Elements**

POETIC LICENSE Explain that lines 15 and 16 are an example of poetic license: the poet has deliberately disregarded the rules of grammar to create the effect. Invite students to paraphrase the lines, using a complete sentence and proper grammar. *(In my pocket, I carry back four round stones from the ocean so that I can suck on them and taste the ocean.)* How does the poet's version create a more evocative image?

Thematic Focus

Variety Is Richness Silko draws upon the stories and myths of Native Americans. Ask students to imagine that they are going to write using their cultural backgrounds as a basis for their work. What stories, events, and images would they want to include? In what ways would sharing their cultures enrich the lives of those who read their work?

☑ **ASSESSMENT OPTIONS**

📁 *Quick Checks,* p. 126

Teaching Options

Prayer to the Pacific

I traveled to the ocean
      distant
             from my southwest land of sandrock
             to the moving blue water
5   Big as the myth of origin.

Pale
pale water in the yellow-white light of
        sun   floating west
           to China
10   where ocean herself was born.
Clouds that blow across the sand are wet.

Squat in the wet sand and speak to the Ocean:
     I return to you   turquoise   the red coral you sent us,
        sister spirit of Earth.
15 Four round stones in my pocket   I carry back the ocean
         to suck and to taste.

Thirty thousand years ago
       Indians came riding across the ocean
       carried by giant sea turtles.
20 Waves were high that day
       great sea turtles waded   slowly out
             from the gray sundown sea.
Grandfather Turtle rolled in the sand   four times
       and disappeared
25   swimming into the sun.

And so   from that time
      immemorial,°
         as the old people say,
rain clouds drift from the west
30   gift from the ocean.

Green leaves in the wind
Wet earth on my feet
      swallowing raindrops
        clear from China.

---

27 *Immemorial* means "extending back beyond memory or record."

Reading *Minilesson*

Responding This poem may be different from many more traditional poems. You might simply allow students to respond to the poem. Their responses can be as simple as telling whether or not they liked the poem. Encourage students to think about the work as a whole. Ask students: How does the poem "speak" to you? What do you think of the ideas the poem presents?

Activity Have students form individual responses to the poem through free-writing. Use the questions provided or formulate questions of your own. Then encourage them to share their responses with others, questioning and discussing to clarify their ideas. **L2**

Additional Resources
📁 *Reading Workbook,* pp. 89–90

Responding to Literature

Personal Response

Which images appealed to you most? Note them in your journal.

——— ANALYZING LITERATURE ———

RECALL AND INTERPRET

1. Where did the speaker begin and end her journey? Why, in your opinion, did the speaker make this journey?
2. According to the speaker, where was the ocean born, and in what direction is it floating? Why might the speaker believe the ocean is floating in this direction?
3. What does the speaker say to the ocean? How would you characterize the speaker's relationship to the ocean? Why, in your opinion, is the ocean so important to her?
4. Summarize the story that the speaker tells. What natural phenomenon does the story explain? Why might this phenomenon be important to the Pueblo people?

EVALUATE AND CONNECT

5. Silko describes the Pacific Ocean as "Big as the myth of origin." Why is this comparison particularly fitting for this poem?
6. Review the word web that you created for the Focus Activity on page 1118. How is your view of the ocean different from or similar to the view expressed in this poem?
7. In what ways does the **form** of this poem connect to its subject?
8. Based on this poem, what can you infer about the Pueblos' relationship to nature? Do you think that other groups in American society have a similar relationship to nature? Explain.

Literary ELEMENTS

Poetic License

Poetic license is the freedom allowed poets to ignore the standard rules of grammar or proper diction in order to create a desired artistic effect. Although the term most frequently refers to liberties taken with language, it can also refer to liberties taken with facts. Silko uses poetic license throughout this poem. For example, in the line "Squat in the wet sand and speak to the Ocean," she does not include a subject in the clause.

1. What word in line 3 cannot be found in any dictionary? Why might Silko have coined this word?
2. What example of poetic license does line 25 include? How might this example contribute to the meaning of the poem?

● See **Literary Terms Handbook**, p. R12.

——— EXTENDING YOUR RESPONSE ———

Interdisciplinary Activity

History: Research Myths   According to this poem, "Indians came riding across the ocean / carried by giant sea turtles." Locate one or more collections of Pueblo myths in the library or on the Internet and look for myths that either describe the migration of the Pueblo people to North America or that include turtles. Then tell the class what you have learned about Pueblo origin myths and the significance of turtles in Pueblo culture.

Personal Writing

Picture Postcard   Create a postcard message about the Pacific Ocean to send to your family or a friend. If you have actually seen an ocean or another large body of water, describe your own response. If not, you might base your message on the impressions you get from the poem.

✊ **Save your work for your portfolio.**

TOWARD THE TWENTY-FIRST CENTURY ❧ 1121

Responding to the Selection

Personal Response

Expect students to single out images and to explain why those images appeal to them.

ANALYZING LITERATURE

1. The speaker begins her journey from her home in the "southwest land of sandrock" and ends at the Pacific Ocean. She wishes to fulfill a quest to find out more about herself and where she comes from.
2. She says that the ocean was born in China and floats west toward the United States. The speaker may feel this way because her people originally came from the East to the West.
3. The speaker tells the ocean that she is returning a turquoise to the sea. She feels kinship and respect for the ocean. The ocean is part of the origin of her people who migrated to North America from a land across the ocean.
4. Thirty thousand years ago, Indians crossed the ocean on sea turtles. After arriving, Grandfather turtle rolled on his back and then returned to his home. Since then, rain comes from the west, a gift from the ocean. The story tells of the origin of rain, which is important to a desert people.
5. The comparison is fitting because the entire poem shows the ocean's importance to the survival of the speaker's people.
6. Students should be able to point to specific similarities and differences.
7. The shape of the poem mirrors the shape of ocean waves and suggests movement.
8. The Pueblo are dependent upon nature, but they also have respect for the forces of nature and feel kinship with them. Be sure that students support their opinions about the relationship to nature of other groups.

Objective

• To learn about the geography of the Pacific Ocean

Teaching Strategies

Consider having students create outlines or another type of graphic organizer to keep track of what they learn about the Pacific Ocean. Ask students to describe the organization of this article. Students should note that topics are organized by paragraph, and some paragraphs have bold headings to identify topics.

The Magnificent Pacific

Silko's "Prayer to the Pacific" describes the Pacific as an ocean of legend and myth, and indeed, the facts about the Pacific can be as fascinating as any legend or myth. The largest, deepest, and most life-sustaining ocean on Earth, this magnificent body of water stretches from Asia and Australia to the Americas.

Millions of Miles of Water The total surface area of the Pacific is about 63,800,000 square miles—an area greater than that of the entire land surface of the earth. In other words, the Pacific is so large that all of the continents could fit inside of it.

The widest part of the ocean from east to west lies between Colombia, South America, and the Malay Peninsula in Asia, a distance of about 12,000 miles. The longest part of the ocean from north to south stretches about 9,600 miles from the Bering Strait between Alaska and Asia to Antarctica.

Not Really So Pacific? Historians believe that the first people to sail the Pacific may have been seafaring Southeast Asians, about 3,000 years ago. It was Portuguese explorer Ferdinand Magellan (c. 1480–1521), however, who named the ocean *Pacífico*, which means "peaceful," after having sailed its calm waters for several weeks. The name is misleading, however. Underground volcanoes and earthquakes have caused powerful and deadly tidal waves called *tsunamis*, and typhoons have destroyed fleets of ships.

How Deep Is the Ocean? Although the Pacific Ocean bottom is extremely uneven, its average depth is about 14,000 feet. Its deepest spot—in fact, the deepest spot of any ocean—lies near Guam in the Mariana Trench. Here, the ocean bottom is about 36,200 feet below the surface.

Ocean Life The Pacific has the most varied mix of life forms of all the oceans. They range from tiny plankton, to species of seaweed that stretch 100 feet in length, to giant clams and whales. The western Pacific is also known for its spectacular coral reefs, ridges formed by the stacked skeletons of small sea creatures.

1122   UNIT 7

Teaching Options

Grammar and Language *Minilesson*

Using Hyphens Point out the term *mineral-rich* in the article. *Mineral-rich* is a compound adjective formed with a hyphen. Point out the following methods of forming compound adjectives with hyphens:

1. noun plus present participle (*thirst-quenching*)
2. adjective plus past participle (*fine-grained*)
3. adjective plus noun (*small-scale*)

4. number plus unit of measurement (*two-foot*)

Activity Have students list or create compound adjectives that describe the Pacific Ocean or some aspect of it. They can work independently or in pairs to create compound adjectives using each of the formulas above. **L2**

Additional Resources

Grammar and Language Transparency 79

Grammar and Language Workbook, p. 279

Grammar and Composition Handbook, Lesson 11.13

Writer's Choice, Lesson 21.14

A Wealth of Resources For centuries, traders have used the Pacific for transporting goods between continents. The ocean itself provides a wealth of products, including over half of the world's fish and shellfish catch. Northern Pacific fishers catch salmon, hake, and Alaska pollack. In addition, more than half of the world's tuna catch comes from the Pacific. Other products of the Pacific include pearls, seaweed, tropical fish for aquariums, and minerals, such as salt, sand, and magnesium. Major deposits of oil and natural gas from under the seafloor provide these important fuels for many countries.

Hot Vents In the eastern Pacific, structures called hot vents occur where water, heated by underlying molten rock, rises to create mineral-rich hot water springs. Near these hot vents live large communities of unusual marine life, including giant clams, mussels, and tube worms.

Coral reef

Activity

Think of two or three questions you have about the Pacific Ocean and do research to find the answers. Then report your findings to the class.

Teaching Strategies

As students begin to formulate their questions for investigation, suggest that they think about questions that begin with *who, what, when, where, why,* and *how.* Encourage them to focus on extending and developing information in this lesson. Remind students to keep track of the sources they use and to avoid plagiarism by carefully paraphrasing or summarizing their research rather than lifting entire phrases or sentences.

Activity

Students' reports should include in-depth information on some aspect of the Pacific Ocean. Expect reports to be clearly organized around a main idea and to include ample supporting details. Students' reports should not simply mirror the information in this article.

MEETING INDIVIDUAL NEEDS — MULTIPLE LEARNING STYLES

Spatial Some students may find it difficult to picture the information given about the Pacific Ocean because most of the information is given in numbers. Working with maps will help these students form a clearer picture of the immensity of the Pacific Ocean.

Activity Provide students with maps on which they can write. Have them locate the continents and countries that have Pacific coasts. Then ask students to transpose the numbers from the article onto the map. They could, for example, find the widest part of the ocean and record the distance on the map. You might also provide a globe so that students can compare the sizes of the other oceans to the Pacific and verify that all of the earth's land could fit into the Pacific Ocean. **L2**

Objectives

- To read and analyze a poem about self-discovery
- To analyze the emotional effect of surrealistic images in a poem
- To use evocative images in a descriptive poem

Skills

Reading/Thinking: Drawing Conclusions
Collaboration: Literature Groups

Motivating

→OPTIONS

Selection Focus Transparency 114: Have students view the transparency and then answer the question provided.

Focus Activity: As an extension of the Focus Activity, students can write a series of journal entries that detail moments of self-discovery. Ask students what they explored. To what self-discoveries did these explorations lead?

FINE ART
TRANSPARENCY 29

You may want to use *Fine Art Transparency 29* to discuss sensations related to height and motion.

Before You Read

Riding the Elevator into the Sky

Meet Anne Sexton

"**Sexton was uneven and excessive, but that was because she dared to be a fool and dared to explore the dark side of the unconscious.**"

—*Erica Jong*

Anne Sexton once said that poetry "should almost hurt." In describing her personal nightmares with brutal honesty, Sexton's poems sometimes illuminate those of her readers as well and may, in fact, "hurt." After encountering many of her poems, readers may also find themselves feeling frustrated, as many critics have, by Sexton's exclusive focus on her own inner turmoil.

To outward appearances, Sexton led a fairly conventional life. She was born into a wealthy family in Newton, Massachusetts, and, like other young women of her background, attended a finishing school for girls.

At nineteen she dropped out of junior college to marry Alfred Muller Sexton, settling in a Boston suburb where she soon gave birth to the first of two daughters. For the next ten years, she focused on being a housewife and mother, roles that left her feeling restless and bored.

Sexton began writing poetry at the age of twenty-nine as a form of therapy for her ongoing struggles with depression. Through vivid imagery and bold metaphors, she explored motherhood, the breakdown of relationships, and the dramatic highs and tragic lows of mental illness. These poems catapulted Sexton into literary stardom and earned her a Guggenheim Fellowship and the Pulitzer Prize for Poetry in 1967. Despite her literary success, Sexton remained deeply troubled and ultimately took her own life.

Anne Sexton was born in 1928 and died in 1974.

FOCUS ACTIVITY

Think about a time in your life when you explored something unknown to you.

LIST IT! Make a list of images that describe the experience you had and the effects it had on your life.

SETTING A PURPOSE Read to learn about one speaker's experience exploring the unknown.

BACKGROUND

Literary Influences

In her poetry and in her emotionally charged life, Anne Sexton was greatly influenced by her fellow poets. Shortly after she began writing poetry, she attended the Antioch Writers' Conference, where she studied with the "confessional" poet W. D. Snodgrass. His very personal poems, she once said, "gave her permission" to explore her own emotional troubles. Later that year, Sexton participated in a writing seminar led by poet Robert Lowell at Boston University, where she forged lasting friendships with such poets as Sylvia Plath, Maxine Kumin, and Randall Jarrell.

RESOURCE MANAGER

Lesson Planning Resource
The *Unit Seven Planning Guide* (pp. 99–103) provides additional lesson notes and reduced versions of all print resources.

📁 **Other Print Resources**
- Active Reading Guide, p. 127
- Quick Checks, p. 127
- Selection and Theme Assessment, p. 194
- Performance Assessment, p. 109

- Spanish Summaries, p. 114
- Inclusion Strategies

📖 **Transparencies**
- Selection Focus 114
- Fine Art 29
- Literary Elements 109

Technology
🎧 Audio Library
💻 Glencoe Literature Web Site
💾 Testmaker

administration from the University of Wisconsin (although we are not in Wisconsin, we are in Utah, Montana or Idaho). When we went down it was in either Utah, Montana or Idaho, I don't remember. We have been here for one hundred thirty-three days owing to an oversight. The pale green reinforced concrete walls sweat and the air conditioning zips on and off erratically[7] and Shotwell reads *Introduction to Marketing* by Lassiter and Munk, making notes with a blue ballpoint pen. Shotwell is not himself, but I do not know it, he presents a calm aspect and reads *Introduction to Marketing* and makes his exemplary notes with a blue ballpoin pen, meanwhile controlling the .38 in my attaché case with one-third of his attention. I am not well.

We have been here one hundred thirty-three days owing to an oversight. Although now we are not sure what is oversight, what is plan. Perhaps the plan is for us to stay here permanently, or if not permanently at least for a year, for three hundred sixty-five days. Or if not for a year for some number of days known to them and not known to us, such as two hundred days. Or perhaps they are observing our behavior in some way, sensors of some kind, perhaps our behavior determines the number of days. It may be that they are pleased with us, with our behavior, not in every detail but in sum. Perhaps the whole thing is very successful, perhaps the whole thing is an experiment and the experiment is very successful. I do not know. But I suspect that the only way they can persuade sun-loving creatures into their pale green sweating reinforced concrete rooms under the ground is to say that the system is twelve hours on, twelve hours off. And then lock us below for some number of days

known to them and not known to us. We eat well although the frozen enchiladas are damp when defrosted and the frozen devil's food cake is sour and untasty. We sleep uneasily and acrimoniously.[8] I hear Shotwell shouting in his sleep, objecting, denouncing, cursing sometimes, weeping sometimes, in his sleep. When Shotwell sleeps I try to pick the lock on his attaché case, so as to get at the jacks. Thus far I have been unsuccessful. Nor has Shotwell been successful in picking the locks on my attaché case so as to get at the .38. I have seen the marks on the shiny surface. I laughed, in the latrine, pale green walls sweating and the air conditioning whispering, in the latrine.

I write descriptions of natural forms on the walls, scratching them on the tile surface with a diamond. The diamond is a two and one-half carat solitaire I had in my attaché case when we went down. It was for Lucy. The south wall of the room containing the console is already covered. I have described a shell, a leaf, a stone, animals, a baseball bat. I am aware that the baseball bat is not a natural form. Yet I described it. "The baseball bat," I said, "is typically made of wood. It is typically one meter in length or a little longer, fat at one end, tapering to afford a comfortable grip at the other. The end with the handhold typically offers a slight rim, or lip, at the nether[9] extremity, to prevent slippage." My description of the baseball bat ran to 4500 words, all scratched with a diamond on the south wall. Does Shotwell read what I have written? I do not know. I am aware that Shotwell regards my writing-behavior as a little strange. Yet it is no stranger than his jacks-behavior, or the day he appeared in black bathing trunks

---

7. Here, *erratically* (ə rat′ ik lē′) means "irregularly," or "unpredictably."

8. *Acrimoniously* (ak′ rə mō′ nē əs lē) means "with bitterness and resentment."
9. *Nether* means "lower."

Vocabulary
exemplary (ig zem′ plə rē) *adj.* worthy of imitation; commendable
denounce (di nouns′) *v.* to condemn; to criticize

INFERRING Ask students what Shotwell wants the narrator to do. *(Possible answer: Cooperate with him in firing the missile.)* What does the narrator's insistence about getting the jacks reveal about him? Ask students to explain how they know. *(He has lost control and can no longer reason effectively, which is clear because he no longer knows the difference between fair play in getting the jacks and firing a missile that may kill millions of people.)*

Thematic Focus

Variety Is Richness The quotation at the beginning of Donald Barthelme's biography describes the author as both a comedian and a thinker. Ask students if they see anything comedic about the situation in the story. What thoughts does the story provoke? How might this story enrich students' understandings of human relationships and of the frailty of people and their governments?

✓ ASSESSMENT OPTIONS

📁 *Quick Checks,* p. 128

GAME

with the .25 caliber Beretta strapped to his right calf and stood over the console, trying to span with his two arms outstretched the distance between the locks. He could not do it, I had already tried, standing over the console with my two arms outstretched, the distance is too great. I was moved to comment but did not comment, comment would have <u>provoked</u> countercomment, comment would have led God knows where. They had in their infinite patience, in their infinite foresight, in their infinite wisdom already imagined a man standing over the console with his two arms outstretched, trying to span with his two arms outstretched the distance between the locks.

Shotwell is not himself. He has made certain overtures.[10] The burden of his message is not clear. It has something to do with the keys, with the locks. Shotwell is a strange person. He appears to be less affected by our situation than I. He goes about his business <u>stolidly</u>, watching the console, studying *Introduction to Marketing,* bouncing his rubber ball on the floor in a steady, rhythmical, conscientious manner. He appears to be less affected by our situation than I am. He is stolid. He says nothing. But he has made certain overtures, certain overtures have been made. I am not sure that I understand them. They have something to do with the keys, with the locks. Shotwell has something in mind. Stolidly he shucks the shiny silver paper from the frozen enchiladas, stolidly he stuffs them into the electric oven. But he has something in mind. But there must be a

quid pro quo.[11] I insist on a quid pro quo. I have something in mind.

I am not well. I do not know our target. They do not tell us for which city the bird is targeted. I do not know. That is planning. That is not my responsibility. My responsibility is to watch the console and when certain events take place upon the console, turn my key in the lock. Shotwell bounces the rubber ball on the floor in a steady, stolid, rhythmical manner. I am aching to get my hands on the ball, on the jacks. We have been here one hundred thirty-three days owing to an oversight. I write on the walls. Shotwell chants "onesies, twosies, threesies, foursies" in a precise, well-modulated voice. Now he cups the jacks and the rubber ball in his hands and rattles them suggestively. I do not know for which city the bird is targeted. Shotwell is not himself.

G

Sometimes I cannot sleep. Sometimes Shotwell cannot sleep. Sometimes when Shotwell cradles me in his arms and rocks me to sleep, singing Brahms' "Guten abend, gute Nacht,"[12] or I cradle Shotwell in my arms and rock him to sleep, singing, I understand what it is Shotwell wishes me to do. At such moments we are very close. But only if he will give me the jacks. That is fair. There is something he wants me to do with my key, while he does something with his key. But only if he will give me my turn. That is fair. I am not well.

---

10. *Overtures* are actions or proposals that indicate a willingness to begin a new course of action or a new relationship.

11. The Latin expression *"quid pro quo"* (kwid′ prō kwō′) (literally, "what for what") means "an equal exchange."

12. The German words *"Guten abend, gute Nacht"* (gōō′ tən ä′ bənt, gōō′ tə näкнt) mean "good evening, good night." This is the opening phrase in the musical piece commonly known as "Brahms' Lullaby" by German composer Johannes Brahms (1833–1897).

Vocabulary
provoke (prə vōk′) *v.* to bring about; to incite
stolidly (stol′ id lē) *adv.* with little or no emotion; impassively

Teaching Options

Grammar and Language *Minilesson*

Using Italics Point out to students that the title of the book *Introduction to Marketing* is italicized in the story. Remind students to italicize the following:

- Titles of books, long poems and musical compositions, plays, films, television shows, paintings and sculptures, court cases, newspapers, and magazines
- Names of ships, trains, airplanes, and spacecraft

- Foreign words and expressions
- Words, letters, and numerals used to represent themselves

Activity Ask students to rewrite these phrases correctly using italics:

1. the opera Vanessa
2. Louise Erdrich's novel Love Medicine
3. the spacecraft Apollo 11
4. the French phrase mangez bien **L2**

Additional Resources

🔖 *Grammar and Language Transparency 80*

📓 *Grammar and Language Workbook,* p. 275

📓 *Grammar and Composition Handbook,* Lesson 11.11

📓 *Writer's Choice,* Lesson 21.12

Responding to Literature

Personal Response

Were you surprised by the way this poem ended? Explain.

──── ANALYZING LITERATURE ────

RECALL AND INTERPRET

1. What is the identity of the speaker in the first stanza? What qualities does the speaker possess? What does the **metaphor** (see page R9) in the first stanza suggest about the speaker?
2. How does the speaker view the wall in lines 7–8? How would you characterize the speaker's relationship to the wall?
3. How has the speaker changed in the second stanza? What does the woman want from the speaker? What might "those liars, the candle or the moon" offer the woman that the speaker can't?
4. In your opinion, why is the speaker important to the woman? What can you infer about the woman's attitude toward aging from lines 17–18?

EVALUATE AND CONNECT

5. Why might Plath have chosen the speaker of this poem to be an inanimate object instead of a human being? In what ways might the poem have been different if told from the perspective of the woman?
6. In this poem, the mirror claims that it is not cruel but truthful. Do you agree, or do you think this mirror distorts what it reflects? Explain.
7. Read over your response to the Focus Activity on page 1139. Are mirrors as important to you as they are to the woman in the poem? Explain.
8. The elderly are often valued because of their wisdom and experience. How might an elderly person react to this poem? Why?

Literary ELEMENTS

Internal Rhyme
One of the sound devices that poets use is **rhyme,** or the repetition of sounds in the final accented syllables of words. When the rhyme occurs within a single line of poetry, it is called **internal rhyme.** Poets use internal rhyme, like **end rhyme,** to convey meaning, to evoke a mood, or simply to create a musical effect. In "Mirror," Plath incorporates internal rhyme as well as **alliteration** (<u>l</u>ooked, <u>l</u>ong) and **assonance** (<u>rea</u>ches, <u>rea</u>lly).

1. What two words rhyme in line 8? What is the effect of linking these two words?
2. What syllables rhyme in line 16? What image does this rhyme reinforce? What does this contribute to the meaning of the poem?

◉ See **Literary Terms Handbook,** p. R13.

──── EXTENDING YOUR RESPONSE ────

Performing

Mirror, Mirror on the Wall   Imagine that you are asked to read "Mirror" on the radio. How would you present it? Would you add sound effects, such as footsteps or a voice crying? How and where would you vary the volume and pitch of your voice? Plan a dramatic reading of the poem. As you plan, write down why you are making these choices about your performance. Then practice your reading and present it to the class.

Creative Writing

New View   Write a poem from the perspective of a mirror that describes what the mirror reflects in the course of an hour or a day. In your poem, try using the sound devices mentioned in the Literary Elements box above.

🖐 **Save your work for your portfolio.**

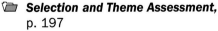
✔ ASSESSMENT OPTIONS

📁 ***Quick Checks,*** p. 130
📁 ***Selection and Theme Assessment,*** p. 197
📁 ***Performance Assessment,*** p. 111
💾 ***Testmaker***

LITERARY ELEMENTS

1. In line 8, *part* and *heart* rhyme, creating a musical effect.
2. In line 16, *face* and *replaces* are near-rhymes. The rhyme reinforces the image of the face emerging from the darkness, and contributes to the idea that the changes happen gradually—age slowly comes into view, and youth slowly disappears.

Additional Resources

 Literary Elements Transparency 112

Responding to the Selection

Personal Response

Many students will be surprised. Until the end of the poem, the images are not particularly shocking. The end of the poem takes a menacing turn.

ANALYZING LITERATURE

1. The speaker is a mirror. It reflects truthfully, without judgment or bias. The speaker is important and all-knowing. It can speak the truth.
2. The mirror believes that the wall is part of its heart. The wall is all that is constant for the mirror. They are separated, however, by "faces and darkness."
3. The speaker describes itself as a lake in which the woman looks at herself. While the candles and the moon can soften the effects of aging, the mirror does not flinch—it shows the truth.
4. The woman wants desperately to see herself staying young. Each morning the woman looks at the mirror to see if she has changed. She has kept her watch for many years, and the young girl is gone, replaced by the aging woman she has become. The woman is upset to see herself age.
5. An inanimate object does not have emotions or feelings. It can be truthful about the subject. If told from the woman's point of view, the poem might be more emotional and less detached.
6. Some students will say that the mirror is truthful, while others will say that its choice of words ("like a terrible fish") shows its cruelty.
7. Some students will feel that mirrors are important because they help create an individual's sense of personal identity.
8. An elderly person would probably react negatively, thinking that comparing an older person to a "terrible fish" is inappropriate—elderly people are much more valuable than that. They might also respond that looks and youth are not all that important.

Before You Read

Traveling Through the Dark

Motivating
→OPTIONS

Selection Focus Transparency 118: Have students view the transparency and then answer the question provided.

Focus Activity: As an extension of the Focus Activity, have students write personal letters describing both the circumstances of the decision and the effects that making the decision had on their lives.

Meet William Stafford

"If I am to keep on writing, I cannot bother to insist on high standards. I must get into action and not let anything stop me, or even slow me much."

—*Stafford*

Writing, William Stafford once wrote, is like fishing. The writer must wait patiently for an idea or an impression to appear and then must seize upon it. "If I put something down," he adds, "that thing will help the next thing come, . . . a process that leads so wildly and originally into new territory." Stafford's method of writing certainly served him well. During his lifetime, he created an immense and compelling body of work that is recognized among the finest of the twentieth century.

Stafford was born in Kansas to parents who were avid readers. From his father he received a deep and abiding love of the natural world and from his mother, a particular view of events and people. "The voice I hear in my poems," he once said, "is my mother's voice." As a young man, Stafford worked on farms and oil refineries, and later he taught at various universities in the Midwest and West.

Stafford, wrote critic Stephen Stepanchev, is a "Western Robert Frost, forever amazed by the spaces of America, inner and outer." Like Frost, Stafford deftly captured American speech patterns in his poetry and discovered universal truths in the particulars of the natural world. Also like Frost, he was interested in exploring the ties that bind people to the earth and to each other.

William Stafford was born in 1914 and died in 1993.

FOCUS ACTIVITY

Think about a time in your life when you were forced to make a difficult decision.

SHARE IDEAS Share your experience with a partner. Describe the circumstances surrounding the decision and what happened as a result.

SETTING A PURPOSE Read to find out how one speaker responds when faced with a difficult decision.

BACKGROUND

The Time and Place

Many of Stafford's poem are set in rural areas of the Midwest and West in this century. The Kansas of his youth was primarily agricultural—what one critic called "rural, austere, inhabited by companionable neighbors and dominated by family." It was a beautiful, peaceful place that affected the poet deeply. "The earth was my home," he said. "I would never feel lost while it held me."

Kansas farmland, 1920s.

RESOURCE MANAGER

Lesson Planning Resource
The *Unit Seven Planning Guide* (pp. 122–126) provides additional lesson notes and reduced versions of all print resources.

📁 **Other Print Resources**
- Active Reading Guide, p. 131
- Reading Workbook
- Quick Checks, p. 131
- Selection and Theme Assessment, p. 198

- Performance Assessment, p. 112
- Spanish Summaries, p. 118
- Inclusion Strategies

 **Transparencies**
- Selection Focus 118
- Literary Elements 113

Technology
- 🎧 Audio Library
- 🎧 Spanish Audio Library
- 💻 Glencoe Literature Web Site
- 💾 Testmaker

Traveling Through the Dark

William Stafford :~

Moonlit, 1991. Benny Alba. Oil on paper, 25 x 18 in. Collection of the artist.

Traveling through the dark I found a deer
dead on the edge of the Wilson River road.
It is usually best to roll them into the canyon:
that road is narrow; to swerve might make more dead.

5 By glow of the tail-light I stumbled back of the car
and stood by the heap, a doe, a recent killing;
she had stiffened already, almost cold.
I dragged her off; she was large in the belly.

My fingers touching her side brought me the reason—
10 her side was warm; her fawn lay there waiting,
alive, still, never to be born.
Beside that mountain road I hesitated.

The car aimed ahead its lowered parking lights;
under the hood purred the steady engine.
15 I stood in the glare of the warm exhaust turning red;
around our group I could hear the wilderness listen.

I thought hard for us all—my only swerving—
then pushed her over the edge into the river.

Reading the Selection

A Active Reading

EVALUATE As students read, have them evaluate how the tone and form enhance the poem's message. *(The arrangement of the poem in stanzas and its tone are matter-of-fact, even though the speaker is faced with an emotionally charged decision. The tone and the form may suggest that unfortunate events in nature are commonplace.)*

Additional Resources
- 📁 **Active Reading Guide,** p. 131
- 🎧 **Audio Library**
- 🎧 **Spanish Audio Library**

B Literary Elements

CAESURA Point out the use of a caesura, or pause, after the word group. Ask students to explain what effect the caesura has. *(The caesura causes the reader to pause, which gives more emphasis to the words that immediately follow. The effect is almost like placing the words that follow on a separate line.)*

✔ **ASSESSMENT OPTIONS**

📁 **Quick Checks,** p. 131

Teaching Options

LIFE SKILLS CONNECTION

Decision Making The speaker in the poem is faced with a very difficult decision. Many factors influence what he decides to do. Ask students what the speaker must decide. *(whether or not to rescue the unborn fawn)* What factors influence his final decision?

Activity Have students participate in a decision-making exercise. Ask them to consider difficult decisions they have had to make, or supply a dilemma. Have students work in groups to make decisions. They should make lists of pros and cons to show the reasoning behind their decisions. **L2** **COLLAB. LEARN.**

Responding to the Selection

Personal Response

Some students may think he is cruel and uncaring; others will suggest that it would have been even crueler to bring a motherless fawn into the world; still others will say he is caring but recognizes his powerlessness to change events.

ANALYZING LITERATURE

1. The best thing to do is to roll a dead deer into the canyon. If it is left in the road, a car may hit it, causing harm or death to the passengers. The speaker seems to be practical. He isn't emotional about the deer.
2. The speaker notices that the deer is pregnant. He hesitates, wondering what to do about the unborn fawn.
3. The engine continues to hum, a reminder of the speaker's own world that continues to roll steadily on. The car, a man-made machine, is juxtaposed to nature.
4. The speaker hears the wilderness listening. He implies that people are outsiders—the wilderness is waiting to see what he will do.
5. The speaker rolls the deer into the canyon. Some students may suggest that he realizes that there is nothing he can do except bring the tragedy to its inevitable conclusion. Moving the deer out of the road may also prevent traffic accidents.
6. Some students will say that the speaker is right not to interfere with nature, while others will say that people caused the deer's death, and the narrator should take responsibility. Others will say that little could be done except what he did. He probably couldn't deliver the fawn and it almost certainly would not have survived anyway.
7. The first *swerve* describes a car—swerving to avoid the deer could cause an accident. The second *swerve* describes the speaker's thinking process. His swerving is his moment of hesitation.
8. Students should support their answers with evidence from the poem and from their own experiences.

Responding to Literature

Personal Response

What did you think of the speaker in this poem? Explain.

—— ANALYZING LITERATURE ——

RECALL AND INTERPRET

1. According to the speaker, what should one do with a dead deer? Why? Based on the first stanza, what can you infer about the personality of the speaker and his attitude toward deer?
2. What does the speaker notice about the deer? Why might he hesitate after touching the deer?
3. What is the speaker's car doing in the fourth stanza? In your opinion, what is the significance of the car in the poem?
4. What does the speaker hear in line 16? What does this line suggest about the relationship between human beings and the natural world?
5. What does the speaker finally decide to do with the deer? Why, in your opinion, does he make this decision?

EVALUATE AND CONNECT

6. In your opinion, did the speaker make the right decision about the deer? Explain your answer.
7. What connection can you make between the words *swerve* in the first stanza and *swerving* in the last stanza? What idea might Stafford have been trying to emphasize through this **repetition** (see page R13)?
8. Compare your response to the Focus Activity on page 1142 with the decision faced by the speaker. Who had the more difficult decision?

Caesura

Poets control the sound of a poem in many ways: they arrange stressed and unstressed syllables into patterns, and they place pauses in strategic locations. A pause that falls within a line of poetry is called a **caesura**. Generally, a caesura falls within the middle of a line and follows a punctuation mark. Sometimes, however, a pause occurs in the absence of punctuation. In the following line, the caesura is marked by double slanted lines: "I dragged her off;// she was large in the belly."

1. Find an example of a caesura in lines 1–2. What idea might it serve to emphasize?
2. What is the caesura in line 4? How does it affect how you read that line?

● See **Literary Terms Handbook,** p. R2.

—— EXTENDING YOUR RESPONSE ——

Literature Groups

Where Do You Stand? Stafford, writes critic Greg Orfalea, "is, at core, a moralist." In your group, debate whether or not "Traveling Through the Dark" includes a moral judgment. In other words, how might Stafford want the reader to view the speaker's decision? How do you know? Have each side give its opinion, using evidence from the poem as support. Then share your conclusions with the class.

Interdisciplinary Activity

Drivers Education: Heads Up As deer populations in the United States increase, so does the likelihood of automobiles hitting deer on highways and back roads. Use the Internet or library resources to research this problem. Then write a guide for drivers showing how they might decrease the likelihood of hitting a deer on the road.

🖐 **Save your work for your portfolio.**

LITERARY ELEMENTS

1. In line 1, the pause after the word *dark* emphasizes what follows, calling attention to the speaker's being alone and experiencing the discovery of the deer by himself.
2. The caesura follows *narrow*. The pause forces the reader to think about the line: this situation is serious and calls for action to prevent further deaths.

Additional Resources

🖎 *Literary Elements Transparency 113*

✔ ASSESSMENT OPTIONS

📁 *Quick Checks,* p. 131
📁 *Selection and Theme Assessment,* p. 198
📁 *Performance Assessment,* p. 112
💾 *Testmaker*

Before You Read

Frederick Douglass

Meet Robert Hayden

"Hayden is ceaselessly trying to achieve . . . transcendence, which must not be an escape from the horror of history, . . . but an ascent that somehow transforms the horror and creates a blessed permanence."

—*Gary Zebrun*

Although Robert Hayden often wrote about African American heroes and history, he wanted to be known as a poet, not a black poet. Such labeling, Hayden believed, placed African American writers "in a kind of literary ghetto, where the standards of other writers" were not applied to them. It also, he felt, "restricted them to racial themes." During the Civil Rights movement, his beliefs provoked the ire of African American authors intent on writing political poetry. Hayden, however, continued to follow his own course.

Hayden's interest in African American history originated from research he did for the Federal Writers' Project in his native Detroit. He learned about the history of his people from the time of slavery to the present. Later, he used this material to write formal, graceful poems about the Underground Railroad, the Civil War, the experiences of enslaved people, and such historical figures as Frederick Douglass, Harriet Tubman, Nat Turner, and Malcolm X.

Although he taught for many years, Hayden saw himself as "a poet who teaches in order to earn a living." His first book of poetry, *Heart-Shape in the Dust,* was published in 1940. He received little critical attention, however, until the publication of *Selected Poems* in 1966. Ten years later, he became the first African American poet to become Poetry Consultant to the Library of Congress.

Robert Hayden was born in 1913 and died in 1980.

FOCUS ACTIVITY

Who has changed the world for you in ways that matter?

CHART IT! Use a simple chart like the one on this page to record the names of, and a few details about, people who have greatly influenced your life.

SETTING A PURPOSE Read to learn about one man and his influence on people's lives.

Person	Influence	Details

BACKGROUND

A Closer Look at Frederick Douglass

Frederick Douglass (c. 1818–1895) escaped from slavery and became an important figure in the Abolitionist movement. He was known both for his rousing speeches denouncing slavery and for his autobiography, *Life and Times of Frederick Douglass,* which poignantly described his experiences under slavery. Following the Civil War (1861–1865), Douglass fought for civil rights for newly emancipated African Americans and championed the women's rights movement. To learn more about Frederick Douglass, see pages 328–335.

Before Reading

Objectives

- To read a poem about an important African American leader
- To analyze diction in a poem
- To write a poem, song, or essay about an admirable person

Skills

Writing: Personal Tribute
Collaboration: Literature Groups

Motivating →OPTIONS

Selection Focus Transparency 119: Have students view the transparency and then answer the question provided.

Focus Activity: As an extension to the Focus Activity, students might choose one person from their charts to nominate as most influential in their lives, and then write a paragraph describing how this person has influenced them.

RESOURCE MANAGER

Lesson Planning Resource
The *Unit Seven Planning Guide* (pp. 127–131) provides additional lesson notes and reduced versions of all print resources.

📁 **Other Print Resources**
- Active Reading Guide, p. 132
- Reading Workbook
- Quick Checks, p. 132
- Selection and Theme Assessment, p. 199

- Performance Assessment, p. 113
- Spanish Summaries, p. 119
- Inclusion Strategies
- English Language Learners Sourcebook

🔊 **Transparencies**
- Selection Focus 119
- Literary Elements 114

Technology
🎧 Audio Library
💻 Glencoe Literature Web Site
💾 Testmaker

A Active Reading

CONNECT Before students read, invite them to tell what they already know about Frederick Douglass. Record their responses on the board. As students read, encourage them to connect to their prior knowledge of Douglass.

Additional Resources
📁 **Active Reading Guide,** p. 132
🎧 **Audio Library**

Teaching Options

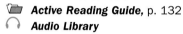

A FREDERICK DOUGLASS

Robert Hayden ⌇

When it is finally ours, this freedom, this liberty, this beautiful
and terrible thing, needful to man as air,
usable as earth; when it belongs at last to all,
when it is truly instinct, brain matter, diastole,° systole,°
5   reflex action; when it is finally won; when it is more
than the gaudy mumbo jumbo of politicians:
this man, this Douglass, this former slave, this Negro
beaten to his knees, exiled, visioning a world
where none is lonely, none hunted, alien,
10 this man, superb in love and logic, this man
shall be remembered. Oh, not with statues' rhetoric,
not with legends and poems and wreaths of bronze alone,
but with the lives grown out of his life, the lives
fleshing his dream of the beautiful, needful thing.

---

4 *Diastole* (dī as′ tə lē′) is the period of normal relaxation of the heart between beats. The period of normal contraction between diastoles is called *systole* (sis′ tə lē).

The Contribution of the Negro to Democracy in America, 1943. Charles White. Egg tempera, 141 x 207 in. Hampton University Museum, Hampton, VA. Choose two people in this painting whom you think exemplify what Hayden describes as "fleshing [Douglass's] dream of the beautiful, needful thing." Explain your choices.

MEETING INDIVIDUAL NEEDS — INCLUSION STRATEGIES

Less-Proficient Readers This poem's complex sentence structure and sophisticated vocabulary will challenge less-proficient readers. Help them cull the most important ideas from the poem—that freedom is essential for life and freedom fighters feel honored to see people live out their visions.

Activity Read the poem aloud as students listen. Then write these sentence openers on the board:
• To the speaker, freedom means . . .
• To the speaker, Douglass represents . . .
• Douglass will be remembered by . . .

Students can reread the poem with partners and complete the sentences. **L1**
COLLAB. LEARN.

Responding to Literature

Personal Response

What is your impression of Frederick Douglass after reading this poem?

ANALYZING LITERATURE

RECALL AND INTERPRET

1. In what ways is freedom described in lines 1–5? What does the poet convey by using these particular details? Explain.
2. How does the speaker describe the talk of politicians? From this description, what can you infer about his attitude toward politicians?
3. In your own words, describe Frederick Douglass and the world he envisioned as portrayed in lines 7–10. What does this portrayal suggest to you about Hayden's opinion of Douglass? Explain.
4. According to lines 11–14, in what ways will Douglass be remembered? What does this tell you about the impact of Douglass's life?

EVALUATE AND CONNECT

5. Do you agree with the statement that freedom is both a "beautiful and terrible thing"? Why or why not?
6. In this poem, Hayden uses **parallelism**–the repeated use of phrases that are the same or similar in structure. In your opinion, how does the use of this device reinforce the message of the poem?
7. Do you think the tribute described in lines 13–14 is a fitting memorial to Douglass? Why or why not?
8. Many poets, including Langston Hughes and Paul Laurence Dunbar, have written about Frederick Douglass. Who from recent times might poets choose to honor? Explain.

> ### *Literary* ELEMENTS
>
> **Diction**
> Poets choose words carefully, paying close attention to both their sounds and their meanings. Sometimes poets use specialized vocabulary, which can give a piece of writing more authority, enhance its sense of realism, create a certain musical effect, or provide contrast with other vocabulary. In this poem, Hayden's **diction**, or word choices, incorporates words commonly used by doctors and biologists, such as *diastole* and *systole*.
>
> 1. Why might Hayden have chosen to use specialized vocabulary in this poem?
> 2. How do the words *diastole* and *systole* contribute to the musical quality of the poem?
>
> ● See **Literary Terms Handbook,** p. R5.

EXTENDING YOUR RESPONSE

Literature Groups
Timely or Not?   In your group, discuss the following question: Is this poem still relevant to the lives of African Americans and other groups in this country, or is it interesting mainly as a historical piece? Use evidence from the poem to support your answer. Then summarize your opinions and share them with the class.

Personal Writing
Personal Tribute   Review your responses to the Focus Activity on page 1145. Then, using "Frederick Douglass" for inspiration, write a poem, song, or essay that celebrates the life of a person whom you admire. In your tribute, express the special qualities and accomplishments of this person and the impact he or she has had on the world.

 Save your work for your portfolio.

✔ ASSESSMENT OPTIONS

📁 ***Quick Checks,*** p. 132
📁 ***Selection and Theme Assessment,*** p. 199
📁 ***Performance Assessment,*** p. 113
💾 ***Testmaker***

LITERARY ELEMENTS

1. Hayden chose medical and biological words to express his ideas because he wanted to portray freedom as the "life blood" of people. These words make freedom seem as important as oxygen in sustaining human life.
2. Although these are technical words, they sound more poetic than "blood pressure."

Additional Resources
📑 ***Literary Elements Transparency 114***

Personal Response

Responses will vary, but most students will suggest that they view Douglass as brave and inspirational.

ANALYZING LITERATURE
---

1. The poet conveys freedom as "beautiful and terrible," instinctive, and both physical and intellectual. Hayden shows that freedom is as much a part of a person as the heart and lungs—freedom is life-sustaining.
2. He calls their talk "gaudy mumbo jumbo." Students can infer that the speaker's attitude is that politicians are more adept with words than with actions; they talk about freedom but do little to make it a reality.
3. He envisioned a world in which all belong, all are loved, and none are isolated. Hayden views Douglass as loving and logical. He could reach people in many different ways.
4. Rather than being remembered with memorials or statues, Douglass left a living legacy: people are living his dreams.
5. Students will probably agree. Although freedom is beautiful, it is also terrible in that it comes with tremendous responsibility.
6. The parallelism gives this poem a lyrical quality, like that of an eloquent speech, which reinforces the idea that people living in freedom are living Douglass's dream.
7. Students will probably say that the lines are a fitting tribute. Although this is not a tangible tribute, Douglass would have wanted people to live his vision rather than erect a statue or other tribute.
8. Students might suggest humanitarians, activists, political figures, or anyone who has had an important impact on society. They should support their answers with concrete reasons.

Writing Skills

Writing Skills

Objective

- To format quotations and cite sources correctly

Teaching Strategies

Ask students to find quotations in this textbook to use for each type of quotation formatting. Then provide students with quotations and have them apply the correct formatting:

At the announcement of the Emancipation Proclamation, Douglass wrote

"We were waiting and listening as for a bolt from the sky . . . longing for the answer to the agonizing prayers of centuries."

Exercise

Students' writing should
- include quotations that directly relate to the research topic.
- include at least one block quotation.
- show source citations in the text and include a works-cited list.
- follow the rules for formatting quotations.

Additional Resources

Writer's Choice, Lessons 7.4, 21.11

Teaching Options

Using Quotations

Hayden's poem "Frederick Douglass" is just one of many tributes to this American hero. If you were to write a research paper about Douglass, you would need quotations by and about Douglass to support and elaborate on your main points.

Citing Sources

When you use quotations in a research paper, you need to document the source of each quote by using a **citation**—the author's last name and the page number on which you found the material. *(McFeely 312)*

You will also need to include a **works-cited list,** which presents information about each source you refer to in your paper. The reader can then use the information in the citation to find the title of the book in the works-cited list.

Formatting Quotations

● When quoting an entire sentence, introduce it with your own words. Set off the quotation with quotation marks. Use a comma or colon before the quote:

> *No historian can state Frederick Douglass's date of birth, because this important fact was unknown to Douglass himself: "I have no accurate knowledge of my age, never having seen any authentic record containing it." (Douglass 15).*

● When quoting part of a sentence within your own sentence, set off the quotation with quotation marks:

> *After the end of the Civil War, Douglass was not surprised that "all across the South black people were demonstrating a fierce interest in politics" (McFeely 240).*

● When quoting only part of a sentence, use ellipses (three periods separated by spaces) to indicate omitted words:

> *Douglass "did not wait . . . for a formal summons from the White House." (McFeely 261).*

● When you use a quotation that runs more than four typed lines, create a **block quotation:**

1. Set the quotation off from the rest of the text by beginning a new line.
2. Indent the entire quotation one inch, or ten spaces, from the left margin.
3. Type the quotation double-spaced, without quotation marks.

EXERCISE

Generate one or two questions about a topic that interests you. Then research the answers in more than one source. Write three paragraphs with four or five examples of quotations. Use at least one block quote. Be sure to document your sources and to include a works-cited list.

Grammar and Language *Minilesson*

Quotation Marks with Other Punctuation Marks Remind students that commas and periods always go inside closing quotation marks; semi-colons and colons go outside closing quotation marks.

Activity Have students work individually to create sentences illustrating each of these rules. **L2**

Additional Resources

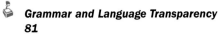

- **Grammar and Language Transparency 81**
- **Grammar and Language Workbook,** p. 273
- **Grammar and Composition Handbook,** Lesson 11.10
- **Writer's Choice,** Lesson 21.11

A Weaver

Sandra María Esteves

Awe Series, 1990.
Susan Stewart.
Monotype,
40⅛ x 28½ in.
Collection of the artist.

For Phil George

Weave us a song of many threads

Weave us a red of fire and blood
that tastes of sweet plum
fishing around the memories of the dead
5   following a scent wounded
our spines bleeding with pain

1153

A Active Reading

QUESTION Before students begin reading, ask them what a poet and a weaver might have in common. How does each communicate a message through his or her work? How can a poem and a weaving communicate similar messages? Have students pose other questions like these, and encourage them to look for the answers as they read.

Additional Resources
📁 *Active Reading Guide,* p. 134
🎧 *Audio Library*

B Literary Elements

IMAGERY Have students identify the images Esteves uses in these opening lines. What is the overall effect of her imagery? *(Esteves uses images of sight through her reference to color, weaving, and fishing. She uses images of taste [sweet plum], smell [scent], and touch [spines bleeding with pain]. These images produce sensory responses that add power to Esteves's ideas.)*

Teaching Options

MEETING INDIVIDUAL NEEDS — INCLUSION STRATEGIES

Less-Proficient Readers Read this poem aloud, and ask students to describe its organization. Guide students to understand that the speaker structures the poem around colors: each color is a thread for weaving, and each color has specific associations.

Activity Ask students to pair up to reread the poem. Before they read, help students construct two-column charts.

One column should be labeled *Colors,* and the other column should be labeled *Associations.* As partners read, they can record the colors as well as what the speaker associates with each color. Ask students to think about what these colors represent. What will happen when these colors are combined?

L1 COLLAB. LEARN.

REPETITION Read these lines aloud and discuss how the musical quality is created by the repetition of sounds. Point out the repetition of the *w* sound in *weave*, *wings*, and *wild growth*; and the repetition of the *s* sound in *passion*, *beats*, *smoky*, and *song*. Explain that musicality is also enhanced by repeating vowel sounds, such as *o* in *blows*, *so*, *cold*.

D Author's Craft

POETIC LICENSE Ask students to identify Esteves's use of poetic license in this poem. What is the effect? *(Sample responses: wild-growth (line 12), sweatseeds (line 15), venom stalking (line 28), moon breezes (line 32). Esteves uses poetic license to create evocative, powerful images.)*

Thematic Focus

Variety Is Richness Esteves says she and other minority writers "shared a common condition." How would students characterize this "common condition"? In what way does Esteves address this condition in her writing? How does her writing speak to all readers?

☑ ASSESSMENT OPTIONS

🗀 **Quick Checks,** p. 134

Teaching Options

Weave us a red of passion
that beats wings against a smoky cloud
and forces motion into our lungs
10 Weave us a song
C of yellow and gold and life itself
a wildgrowth
into the great magnetic center
topaz canyons
15 floral sweatseeds
in continuous universal suspension

Weave us a song of red and yellow and brown
that holds the sea and sky in its skin
the bird and mountain in its voice
20 that builds upon our graves a home
with fortifications
strength, unity and direction

And weave us a white song to hold us
D when the wind blows so cold to make our children wail
25 submerged in furious ice
a song pure and raw
that burns paper
and attacks the colorless venom stalking hidden
in the petal softness of the black night

30 Weave us a rich round black that lives
in the eyes of our warrior child
and feeds our mouths with moon breezes
with rivers interflowing
through ALL spaces of existence

35 Weave us a song for our bodies to sing
a song of many threads
that will dance with the colors of our people
and cover us with the warmth of peace.

Reading *Minilesson*

Analyzing Structure Although this poem does not follow a traditional structure, the poem does have a definite pattern of organization.

Activity Ask pairs of students to analyze the structure of the poem. Guide students to see that after the introductory sentence, each stanza links a color to a quality. Invite students to find ways to map the organizational pattern. They could, for example, make outlines or graphic organizers such as diagrams or flowcharts. Have students speculate on why Esteves may have used this structure and then share their ideas with the class. **L2 COLLAB. LEARN.**

Additional Resources
🗀 *Reading Workbook*

Responding to Literature

Personal Response

Which lines from the poem did you find most powerful? Why?

--- ANALYZING LITERATURE ---

RECALL AND INTERPRET

1. What does the speaker say in line 1? In your opinion, what does this mean and who is the speaker addressing? Explain.
2. In lines 2–22, what colors does the speaker note? What does the speaker associate with the colors and what might they add to the "song"?
3. What colors does the speaker ask for in lines 23–34? Why might she include these colors? Support your response with details from the poem.
4. What does the speaker think people could accomplish if they united? Review your response to the Focus Activity on page 1152. Do you agree with the speaker? Why or why not?

EVALUATE AND CONNECT

5. What contrasting images does Esteves use in lines 23–29? In your opinion, how does the contrast help get Esteves's main idea across? Support your response with evidence from the poem.
6. Which words and phrases are repeated throughout the poem? How does this **repetition** affect your reading of the poem? Explain.
7. What is the **tone** (see page R16) of this poem? Does the tone change at any point? How does the poem's tone help express the poet's main idea?
8. Theme Connections   Based on the ideas expressed in this poem, what do you think Esteves would say about the phrase, "variety is richness"? Explain, using details from the poem to support your response.

Literary ELEMENTS

Assonance and Consonance

Poets commonly use sound devices to contribute to the tone or the musical quality of a poem. The repetition of similar vowel sounds is called **assonance,** and the repetition of consonant sounds within or at the ends of words is called **consonance.** For example, in the line "in continuous universal suspension," the repetition of the long *u* sound in "contin*uous*" and "*u*niversal" is assonance. The repetition of the *s* sound in "continuou*s* universal *s*uspension" is consonance.

1. What effect does the consonance in lines 11–12 have on your reading of the poem?
2. Find two more examples of consonance and assonance in the poem and explain the effects they have.

 See **Literary Terms Handbook,** pp. R2 and R4.

--- EXTENDING YOUR RESPONSE ---

Literature Groups

Lasting Peace?   In your group, discuss Esteves's message about breaking barriers. Does she seem to think people are capable of uniting? If they did unite, does she think peace would last? Support your ideas with details from the poem. Then sum up the poet's message in a sentence. Compare your statement with those of other groups.

Interdisciplinary Activity

Art: Weave a "Song of Many Threads"   Use the poem as inspiration to create your own weaving out of string, yarn, paper, or another material. Try to reflect the imagery and symbolism of the poem in your weaving. Then display your weaving in the classroom.

Save your work for your portfolio.

TOWARD THE TWENTY-FIRST CENTURY 🕊 1155

Personal Response

Students will probably identify powerful images such as those found in line 6 and lines 28 and 29.

ANALYZING LITERATURE

1. The speaker asks a weaver to weave "a song of many threads." The speaker could be making a plea for people of many diverse backgrounds to weave together to form a whole.
2. The colors chosen are red, yellow, gold, and brown. These colors may be meaningful in the speaker's culture; she may be referring to common skin tones; or the colors may be symbolic of pain, wealth, and so on. The colors make the song universal; they are colors common to humanity.
3. The speaker asks for white and black. These colors may represent skin tones or light and darkness. Students should support their answers with details from the poem.
4. If people united, they would live in warmth and peace. Students will probably agree with the speaker, and they may offer more concrete suggestions.
5. Esteves uses the contrasting images of ice and fire and of black and white. She is trying to convey the idea that the world is full of contrast and sharply contradictory views, yet there is hope of uniting these opposite forces.
6. The words "weave us" and "song" are repeated throughout the poem. The repetition helps the reader appreciate the speaker's intense desire for this song to become a reality.
7. With the exception of the last stanza, the tone is vehement and urgent. In the last stanza, the tone softens as the speaker contemplates unity.
8. Most students will reply that Esteves thinks that a blending of the colors makes the whole stronger than its parts—a collective group of people, united in spite of their differences, is stronger than the individuals it comprises.

✔ ASSESSMENT OPTIONS

📁 *Quick Checks,* p. 134
📁 *Selection and Theme Assessment,* pp. 201–202
📁 *Performance Assessment,* p. 115
💾 *Testmaker*

LITERARY ELEMENTS

1. The consonance creates a feeling of perpetual movement and binds the words together, echoing the poem's theme of weaving people together.
2. The repetition of the *t* in line 13 and the *w* in line 24 is consonance. In line 30, the *i* in *rich* and *lives* and in line 32, the *e* in *feeds* and *breezes* are assonance. These devices create rhythm and musicality.

Additional Resources

✍ *Literary Elements Transparency 115*

Objectives

- To read and analyze two poems about the relationship between people and nature
- To write paragraphs describing two poems' messages about nature's effect on people

Skills

Reading/Thinking: Making Critical Judgments

Motivating

→OPTIONS

Literature Launchers: "Pat Mora and Southwestern Images"

Videodisc Side B, Segment 24

Also available in VHS.

Selection Focus Transparency 122: Have students view the transparency and then answer the question provided.

 Focus Activity: As an extension of the Focus Activity, students can use ideas generated during their freewriting as the basis for a postcard. The postcard could show a scene and describe in a line or two the effect that the scene had on the writer.

Before You Read

For Georgia O'Keeffe and Most Satisfied by Snow

Meet Pat Mora

"The desert persists in me," writes Pat Mora, "both inspiring and compelling me to sing about her and her people."
Mora grew up in the Chihuahua desert in Texas and often writes about the Native Americans and Mexican Americans who live there, their rich cultural traditions, and their relationship to the land. "I write," she says, "because I believe Mexican Americans need to take their rightful place in U.S. literature. We need to be published . . . so that the stories and ideas of our people won't quietly disappear." Mora's books include a collection entitled *Borders and Chants* and *Nepantla: Essays from the Land in the Middle.*

Pat Mora was born in 1942.

Meet Diana Chang

"I guess it's in my temperament to seek variety and change." Diana Chang told an interviewer. "I not only write," she says, "but I also paint." Both Chang's life and work reflect her love of change. She was born in New York City, but spent her early years in China. After World War II, her family returned to New York, where Chang attended high school and Barnard College, graduating in 1955. Chang then worked as a book editor and creative writing instructor. In addition to writing poetry, Chang has produced six novels, which explore issues of identity through a vast array of characters.

Diana Chang was born in 1934.

FOCUS ACTIVITY

How might something in nature have an impact on one's life? Have you ever been changed by an experience related to nature? How?

FREEWRITE Spend a few minutes freewriting to explore your ideas about how nature can affect one's life.

SETTING A PURPOSE Read to discover how two speakers grow from their experiences related to nature.

BACKGROUND

Georgia O'Keeffe

The title of Pat Mora's poem refers to Georgia O'Keeffe, a painter who is linked with the southwestern United States. While in her thirties, O'Keeffe began painting magnified views of flowers. Then, following a visit to New Mexico in 1929, where she eventually settled, she turned her attention to the desert's spare beauty. She painted canvases that capture its colors and dramatic forms, including the bleached bones she found there. One series of studies from this period, the *Pelvis Series,* focuses exclusively on bones.

Georgia O'Keeffe, 1937.

1156 UNIT 7

RESOURCE MANAGER

Lesson Planning Resource
The *Unit Seven Planning Guide* (pp. 142–146) provides additional lesson notes and reduced versions of all print resources.

 Other Print Resources
- Active Reading Guide, p. 135
- Reading Workbook
- Quick Checks, p. 135
- Selection and Theme Assessment, pp. 203–204

- Performance Assessment, p. 116
- Spanish Summaries, p. 122
- Inclusion Strategies
- English Language Learners Sourcebook

 Transparencies
- Selection Focus 122

Technology
 Literature Launchers
Audio Library
Glencoe Literature Web Site
Testmaker

— FOCUS ACTIVITY —

Think of a time when you have been baffled by homework, a difficult task, or a problem with a relationship and then suddenly understood what to do.

JOURNAL In your journal, describe how you felt when you understood something that had been a mystery.

SETTING A PURPOSE Read to find out how suddenly understanding the answer to a difficult problem makes one speaker feel.

— BACKGROUND —

Geometry: From Ancient Days to Modern Times

In mathematics, a theorem is a statement that can be proved based on certain other assumptions and definitions.

The word *geometry* literally means "earth measuring." The study of geometry began in ancient Egypt and Mesopotamia as people surveyed and farmed land. Knowledge about points, lines, planes, and solid objects was based on practical experience with landmarks, footpaths, farmers' fields, and blocks of granite. Around 300 B.C., the mathematician Euclid took hundreds of geometrical theorems that had accumulated over the centuries and developed ten postulates (fundamental rules or principles) that could explain them all. More than two thousand years later, in the 1820s, several mathematicians proved that Euclidian geometry is only one of many possible kinds of geometry.

Proving Theorems

Although geometry homework may be a chore for some students to hurry through, certain mathematicians devote much of their time—even years—to proving theorems. And some theorems go unproved for centuries. For example, a note left in a book by seventeenth-century mathematician Pierre Fermat stated that he had proved a proposition relating to an equation written in the sixth century. However, this proof—for Fermat's Last Theorem—was never found, and mathematicians tried unsuccessfully for years to prove the theorem.

Mathematician Andrew Wiles has been fascinated with the problem since he was just ten years old. Years of on-and-off work on the problem paid off when, in 1995, Wiles finally did prove Fermat's theorem. But is his proof the same as the one Fermat claimed to have developed? Impossible, according to Wiles, who says that his is a twentieth-century proof. In fact, he doubts that Fermat really had a proof but leaves the door open for future mathematical sleuths: ". . . What has made this problem special for amateurs is that there's a tiny possibility that there does exist an elegant seventeenth-century proof."

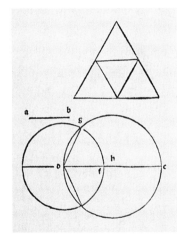

From Euclid's *Elementa geometria*.

A Active Reading

VISUALIZE Point out that Rita Dove uses an extended metaphor to show her feelings when she finally understands geometry. What does Dove's metaphor reveal about her feelings? *(Dove compares her sudden understanding to the breaking apart of a concrete object; Dove feels she has broken free of her confusion.)*

Additional Resources
- *Active Reading Guide,* p. 136
- *Audio Library*

VIEWING THE ART

Elizabeth B. Heuer, a contemporary American artist, studied at universities in the United States and in Italy. Her work *Blue* is a collage—made up of various materials (such as paper or cloth) glued on a surface.

Viewing Response *Students may say that the colors of the collage reflect the speaker's happiness as she unlocks a mystery. The piece's distinct curves, lines, and angles suggest geometry.*

✓ ASSESSMENT OPTIONS

- *Quick Checks,* p. 136

Teaching Options

Blue, 1994. Elizabeth B. Heuer. Collage. Collection of the artist. Look closely at the lines and shapes in this painting. How might they reflect the mood of "Geometry"?

Geometry

Rita Dove ∿

I prove a theorem and the house expands:
the windows jerk free to hover near the ceiling,
the ceiling floats away with a sigh.

As the walls clear themselves of everything
but transparency, the scent of carnations
leaves with them. I am out in the open

and above the windows have hinged into butterflies,
sunlight glinting where they've intersected.
They are going to some point true and unproven.

Reading *Minilesson*

Evaluating Evaluating different aspects of the poem can improve students' comprehension.

Activity Ask small groups of students to evaluate "Geometry." Groups should first establish evaluation criteria. These might include appropriateness of tone, vivid images, effective sound devices, useful figures of speech, and strong symbols. Have each group discuss and evaluate the poem and identify examples to support their judgments. Students might use a chart like the one shown to organize their evaluations. **L2 COLLAB. LEARN.**

Criteria	Examples	Rating	Images

Additional Resources
- *Reading Workbook*

LISTENING, SPEAKING, and VIEWING

Discussing Literature

After reading a thought-provoking poem like "The House," readers often enjoy expressing their opinions. A group discussion is a useful way for people to exchange opinions and enhance their understanding of a piece of writing. People use discussions to solve problems, plan group actions, explore ideas, and exchange information. Here are some guidelines for planning and joining a group discussion about literature.

● Assign roles to people in your group, such as *group leader-facilitator, group participants,* and *note-taker.* This chart will help you understand these roles:

Role	Duties
Leader-facilitator	• introduces the discussion topic • invites each participant to speak • keeps the discussion focused and interactive • keeps track of the time • helps participants arrive at a consensus • summarizes major points at the end of the discussion
Group Participants	• form ideas and questions about the literature before the discussion • contribute throughout the discussion • support any opinions with facts • avoid repeating what has been said earlier • listen carefully to other group members • evaluate opinions of others • respect the opinions of others
Note-taker	• keeps track of the most important points • helps the group leader form conclusions based on the discussion • helps the group leader summarize the discussion

● If the topic for discussion has not been assigned, develop a topic and define a goal for the discussion. Choose a topic that interests the group. Try to state the topic as a question that will inspire an interesting discussion.
● After your discussion, take some time to evaluate how well you worked as a group.

ACTIVITY

Hold a twenty-minute discussion about "The House" or another piece of literature. Follow the guidelines above. Then together, write a brief evaluation of the discussion.

LISTENING, SPEAKING, and VIEWING

Objective

• To learn and apply strategies for discussing literature in groups

Teaching Strategies

After briefly discussing the process and the roles of the various group members, you might want to model this process for the class. With a small group, develop and discuss a topic for a selection read previously in this theme. Then lead an evaluation and analysis of the presentation. Discuss the following questions: What can the group leader, note-taker, and participants do to make the group run more smoothly? How can members resolve differences? Who is responsible for keeping the discussion going if interest wanes?

Activity

Encourage students to develop rubrics or some other method to assess how well group members performed their roles. Students can assess the group as a whole, while individuals can reflect on their own contributions to their groups. Students can decide how their groups could function better and make a list of tips for future discussions.

Teaching Options

MEETING INDIVIDUAL NEEDS — ENGLISH LANGUAGE LEARNERS

Group Discussions English language learners may feel awkward during group discussions if their level of English comprehension prevents their full participation. Help students develop strategies for following a group discussion.

Activity Have students work in small pre-discussion groups to prepare for the group discussion. For example, students could write down their ideas about a piece of literature. They might devise roles for those who feel more comfortable listening than speaking. One student might be responsible for looking up dictionary meanings of words in the literature that the group does not understand.

Additional Resources
📁 *English Language Learners Sourcebook*

Before You Read

Salvador Late or Early

Objectives

- To read and analyze a short prose piece that describes living in poverty
- To examine the emotional effect of imagery
- To write a paragraph analyzing sound devices

Skills

Reading/Thinking: Drawing Conclusions

More About Sandra Cisneros

The House of Mango Street, Sandra Cisneros's first book, earned her a Before Columbus American Book Award in 1985, but in 1997 another house, this one on Guenther Street in San Antonio, Texas, again put Cisneros in the spotlight.

Cisneros painted her Victorian cottage in shades of amethyst, lilac, and violet. The colors put her at odds with the San Antonio Historic and Design Review Committee, a group of 15 architects, historians and other experts who say her choice of colors violates the guidelines for homes in historic districts because the shades of purple are unapproved.

Cisneros says she has tried to consider other shades in a "Tejano palette." Speaking to June Naylor Rodrigues of the *San Antonio Express News,* Cisneros commented, "I believe in divine providence, which took me this route. . . . The issue isn't about my house; it's about (Hispanic) heritage. Otherwise why would it have gotten such a community response?"

Meet Sandra Cisneros

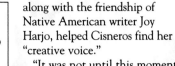

When Sandra Cisneros (sis nā′ rōs) was a child, one of her favorite books was *The Little House,* by Virginia Lee Burton, the story of a stable family that lives permanently in one house even as the neighborhood around it changes. Perhaps she was drawn to the story because her own family moved constantly from one ghetto neighborhood to another. They also moved back and forth between Mexico and the United States, because her father was often homesick and was devoted to his mother in Mexico.

Cisneros was born in Chicago, Illinois, to a Mexican American mother and a Mexican father. As the only girl in a family of seven children, she often felt like she had "seven fathers," she says, because her six brothers, as well as her father, tried to control her. She felt shy and lost in the shuffle and retreated into books. Despite her love of reading, she did not do well in elementary school because her family moved so often and because she was too shy to participate.

In high school, with the encouragement of one particular teacher, Cisneros improved her grades and worked on the school literary magazine. Her father encouraged her to go to college because he thought it would be a good way for her to find a husband. Cisneros did attend college, but instead of searching for a husband, she found a teacher who helped her enroll in the prestigious graduate writing program at the University of Iowa. At the university's Writers' Workshop, however, she felt isolated—a Mexican American from a poor neighborhood among students from wealthy families and the best colleges. The feeling of being so different,

along with the friendship of Native American writer Joy Harjo, helped Cisneros find her "creative voice."

"It was not until this moment when I separated myself, when I considered myself truly distinct, that my writing acquired a voice. I knew I was a Mexican woman, but I didn't think it had anything to do with why I felt so much imbalance in my life, whereas it had everything to do with it! My race, my gender, my class! That's when I decided I would write about something my classmates couldn't write about."

Cisneros published her first prose work, *The House on Mango Street,* when she was twenty-nine. In a series of interlocking stories, the book tells about a young Chicana girl growing up in a Chicago barrio, much like the neighborhoods in which Cisneros lived as a child. The book was awarded the Before Columbus American Book Award in 1985 and has been used in classes from high school through graduate school level in many types of courses. Since then, Cisneros has published several books of poetry, a children's book, and a short-story collection. Many of her works, including "Salvador Late or Early," have appeared in literary journals.

"**I'm trying to write the stories that haven't been written. I feel like a cartographer. I'm determined to fill a literary void.**"

"**To me, the definition of a story is something that someone wants to listen to. If someone doesn't want to listen to you, then it's not a story.**"

—*Cisneros*

RESOURCE MANAGER

Lesson Planning Resource
The ***Unit Seven Planning Guide*** (pp. 162–166) provides additional lesson notes and reduced versions of all print resources.

📁 **Other Print Resources**
- Active Reading Guide, p. 139
- Reading Workbook
- Quick Checks, p. 139
- Selection and Theme Assessment, p. 208

- Performance Assessment, p. 120
- Spanish Summaries, p. 126
- Inclusion Strategies
- English Language Learners Sourcebook

📊 **Transparencies**
- Selection Focus 126
- Literary Elements 119

Technology
🎧 Audio Library
💻 Glencoe Literature Web Site
💾 Testmaker

FOCUS ACTIVITY

What does it mean to be poor? In your opinion, how might poverty affect a person's personality and outlook on life?

MAP IT! Create a word web with the word *poverty* at the center. Around that word, write the words and images you associate with poverty. Then think about the reactions these words and images bring out in you.

Poverty

SETTING A PURPOSE Read to discover one boy's experience of poverty.

BACKGROUND

Literary Influences

When Sandra Cisneros looks back on her years in high school and college, she admits she did not know that she was a Chicana, or Mexican American, writer. Although she had an identity that was Mexican, when it came to literature, she simply thought of herself as American because she read mainstream literature and wrote in English. Though she spoke Spanish at home, Cisneros did not know any Mexican American writers, so she did not think of them as belonging to a separate category. She admired the "big male voices" of poets such as James Wright, Richard Hugo, and Theodore Roethke. Those voices, however, "were all wrong for me," Cisneros now says. Not until graduate school in Iowa did she realize how different her experience was from that of most of her classmates.

Yet even as Cisneros was shaping her own Chicana identity, much of the inspiration for *The House on Mango Street* came from the memoirs of Russian American writer Vladimir Nabokov.

Cisneros admires Latin American writers such as Manuel Puig, for his compassion for the underdog, and Juan Rulfo, "for his rhythms and what he's doing with voices." She is also interested in the writing of American working-class women who publish with small presses, which Cisneros says can be "more fearless about things that they take" than large publishing companies. The writers who touch her "passion buttons" she says, are those who, like Rulfo and Puig, are "doing something new."

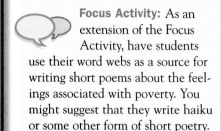

Motivating
→ OPTIONS

Selection Focus Transparency 126: Have students view the transparency and then answer the question provided.

Focus Activity: As an extension of the Focus Activity, have students use their word webs as a source for writing short poems about the feelings associated with poverty. You might suggest that they write haiku or some other form of short poetry.

Reading Further

Be sure to review these titles for appropriateness for your class before recommending them to students.

Novels: Cisneros, Sandra. *The House on Mango Street.* New York: Random House, 1994. This highly acclaimed novel tells the story of a girl growing up in a Hispanic part of Chicago.

Cisneros, Sandra. *Woman Hollering Creek.* New York: Random House, 1991.

Sandra Cisneros Have students use a search engine to find out more about Sandra Cisneros. Suggest they enter *Sandra Cisneros* as a keyword.

Salvador
Late or Early

Sandra Cisneros ✍

Salvador with eyes the color of caterpillar, Salvador of the crooked hair and crooked teeth, Salvador whose name the teacher cannot remember, is a boy who is no one's friend, runs along somewhere in that vague direction where homes are the color of bad weather, lives behind a raw wood doorway, shakes the sleepy brothers awake, ties their shoes, combs their hair with water, feeds them milk and corn flakes from a tin cup in the dim dark of the morning.

Salvador, late or early, sooner or later arrives with the string of younger brothers ready. Helps his mama, who is busy with the business of the baby. Tugs the arms of Cecilio, Arturito, makes them hurry, because today, like yesterday, Arturito has dropped the cigar box of crayons, has let go the hundred little fingers of red, green, yellow, blue, and nub of black sticks that tumble and spill over and beyond the asphalt puddles until the crossing-guard lady holds back the blur of traffic for Salvador to collect them again.

Salvador inside that wrinkled shirt, inside the throat that must clear itself and apologize each time it speaks, inside that forty-pound body of boy with its geography of scars, its history of hurt, limbs stuffed with feathers and rags, in what part of the eyes, in what part of the heart, in that cage of the chest where something throbs with both fists and knows only what Salvador knows, inside that body too small to contain the hundred balloons of happiness, the single guitar of grief, is a boy like any other disappearing out the door, beside the schoolyard gate, where he has told his brothers they must wait. Collects the hands of Cecilio and Arturito, scuttles off dodging the many schoolyard colors, the elbows and wrists criss-crossing, the several shoes running. Grows small and smaller to the eye, dissolves into the bright horizon, flutters in the air before disappearing like a memory of kites.

El Patio de la Casa del Artista, 1884. Martin Tovar y Tovar. Oil on canvas, 18¼ x 21⅝ in. Private collection. Do you think Salvador might have liked to live in a house like this? Why or why not?

1174

Responding to Literature

Personal Response

What would you want to say to Salvador if you were to meet him?

ANALYZING LITERATURE

RECALL AND INTERPRET

1. List the colors the narrator mentions in the first sentence of "Salvador Late or Early." What do these colors suggest about Salvador's life?
2. Describe Salvador's role in his household. What does his role reveal about how Salvador is viewed in his family?
3. What does the narrator reveal about Salvador's appearance in the third paragraph of the selection? about how Salvador speaks and feels? What do these details indicate about Salvador's history?
4. What images describe Salvador in the third paragraph? What do these images tell you about Salvador's character? about what he thinks of himself? about the narrator's attitude toward him?

EVALUATE AND CONNECT

5. Theme Connections   How might Cisneros's writing style reflect the idea that "variety is richness"? Support your answer with examples.
6. A major part of Cisneros's **style** (see page R15) in "Salvador Late or Early" is her use of unusually long sentences. In your opinion, do these long sentences add to or detract from the effectiveness of Cisneros's writing? Explain, using examples.
7. Think of someone you know who reminds you of Salvador. How is this person like Salvador? How is this person different?
8. Are the ideas about poverty you mapped out for the Focus Activity on page 1173 similar to those conveyed in "Salvador Late or Early"? Does Cisneros's story make you think differently about poverty? Explain.

Literary ELEMENTS

Imagery

Imagery is the word pictures a writer creates to evoke an emotional response. For example, Cisneros writes that Salvador "arrives with the string of younger brothers ready." These words create an image of a line of boys following behind Salvador. This image also conveys the idea that Salvador is always attached to his brothers.

1. What image do the words "Salvador inside that wrinkled shirt" create for you? How does this image make you feel about Salvador?
2. Which image in Cisneros's story do you find most striking? Why?

● See **Literary Terms Handbook,** p. R8.

EXTENDING YOUR RESPONSE

Writing About Literature

Poetic Prose   In "Salvador Late or Early," Cisneros uses many sound devices—**alliteration, assonance, rhyme,** and **rhythm**—that are more commonly associated with poetry than with prose. (See pages R1, R2, and R13.) Using specific examples from the story as evidence, write a paragraph explaining the effect these devices have on your reading of the story.

Internet Connection

Leading the Way   Sandra Cisneros is one of the leading figures in Hispanic American literature today. Search the Internet for information about other Hispanic Americans who are leaders in their fields. You may choose any area you like, such as art, science, sports, or politics. Present your findings to the class.

 Save your work for your portfolio.

LITERARY ELEMENTS

1. Salvador appears both disheveled and small. These words evoke a feeling of sympathy for Salvador.
2. Students should provide an example of an image and explain why it is especially striking to them.

Additional Resources

Literary Elements Transparency 119

Responding to the Selection

Personal Response

Students will probably say that they would offer words of encouragement and reassurance that his life can and will improve.

ANALYZING LITERATURE

1. Cisneros mentions "the color of caterpillar," "the color of bad weather," and "dim dark." The colors are bleak and desolate, much like Salvador's life.
2. Salvador takes care of his little brothers. He has a father role in the family even though he is a young boy.
3. Salvador always wears a wrinkled shirt and is covered with scars. His appearance is nondescript and his voice is apologetic. These details could indicate that Salvador has suffered from abuse.
4. Students should list the series of images presented in the paragraph. They reveal that Salvador is responsible, unassuming, and fearful. He probably feels small, hopeless, and sad. The narrator is sympathetic; she seems to view him as having the potential to be like any other boy, except that he can't be because of the abuse and poverty he's experienced.
5. Cisneros's style is unique. She writes prose using poetic techniques like sound devices and images. Her sentences are unconventional; they are long with few breaks.
6. Most students will say that the long sentences give a feel of breathlessness to the writing. They mirror the way Salvador feels, running to care for his brothers, running to school, running home.
7. Students should offer specific points of comparison and contrast.
8. Students' own ideas about poverty will reflect those expressed in the story in varying degrees. Many students will say that reading about Salvador puts a face on poverty. It makes the problems of poverty more real.

Objectives

- To read and analyze two poems that examine relationships between parents and children
- To compose an E-mail message in response to a warning that forgetting one's heritage is a dangerous thing

Skills

Reading/Thinking: Connecting
Life Skills: Planning and Designing

Motivating
→OPTIONS

Selection Focus Transparency 127: Have students view the transparency and then answer the question provided.

Focus Activity: As an extension of the Focus Activity, have students meet in groups to discuss and compare their quickwrites.

 # Before You Read

Embroidering: A Response to "Somnad" by Carl Larrson and
El Olvido (Según las Madres)

Meet Rita Magdaleno

The daughter of a Mexican American father and a German mother, Rita Magdaleno (mäg' dä lä' nō) writes to reconcile the two landscapes of her life. Born in Germany, she says that the sounds and landscapes of Germany shaped her, just as those of Phoenix, Arizona, did when she was growing up there.

Magdaleno remembers keeping a journal during her first visit to Germany, when she was ten years old. She traveled on a boat for seven days and kept a record of all that she observed.

She didn't consider writing professionally until her early thirties, when she entered a creative writing program. Since that time, she has published fiction and poetry in numerous anthologies. In addition, she has worked with high school students as a poet in the schools and has taught photo narrative writing, a type of writing that creates a story from a single photograph.

Rita Magdaleno was born in 1947.

Meet Judith Ortiz Cofer

Culture clash is a familiar theme in the work of Judith Ortiz Cofer (ôr tēz' kō' fer). Many of her poems, novels, and autobiographical essays touch on the conflicts between the old values of her Puerto Rican ancestors and those of the United States.

Cofer was born in Puerto Rico, but she moved with her family to New Jersey as a young girl. Her father worked for the U.S. Navy, and whenever he went to sea, the family visited relatives in Puerto Rico.

Cofer praises "Nuyoricans"—Americans of Puerto Rican descent—who use both Spanish and English in their writing. Although some criticize this practice, Cofer says, "My view is that these young people mixing English and Spanish are energizing the language. Writers do what teenagers do, taking on and changing the language."

A professor of literature and creative writing, Cofer continues to write.

Judith Ortiz Cofer was born in 1952.

FOCUS ACTIVITY

How does where you live affect the way you look at the world?

QUICKWRITE Jot down ways that the place, or places you've lived have affected your views.

SETTING A PURPOSE Read to discover how geography and culture affect two speakers.

BACKGROUND

Did You Know?
Rita Magdaleno wrote "Embroidering" after the death of her mother. A friend sent her a condolence card showing a sketch by artist Carl Larrson, of two women doing needlework. The sketch, "Somnad" (meaning "sewing"), inspired Magdaleno to reflect on her relationship with her mother.

RESOURCE MANAGER

Lesson Planning Resource
The *Unit Seven Planning Guide* (pp. 167–171) provides additional lesson notes and reduced versions of all print resources.

 **Other Print Resources**
- Active Reading Guide, p. 140
- Reading Workbook
- Quick Checks, p. 140

- Selection and Theme Assessment, pp. 209–210
- Performance Assessment, p. 121
- Spanish Summaries, p. 127
- Inclusion Strategies
- English Language Learners Sourcebook

 Transparencies
- Selection Focus 127

Technology
- 🎧 Audio Library
- 💻 Glencoe Literature Web Site
- 💾 Testmaker

Embroidering:
A Response to "Somnad" by Carl Larsson

Rita Magdaleno ∿

A vase of hydrangeas on the table, this room
blue and clear, everything solid
and in its place. Here, two women
sit together, their knees
5 touching, stroking the beautiful
threads. One is pale green
like a single blade of weed
at the edge of a small pond. Another
strand is the color of deep wood
10 roses, wild and very sweet.
Also, threads like filaments°
of fish tails, gold
and a blue string curled
like a child's ball, color
15 of sky on early desert mornings.
This afternoon, pale
and warm, the daughter listens
to her mother's breath, soft

   and steady like a small animal
20 full of milk, nearly asleep,
this rhythm of breathing and needles
sliding slowly through the cloth.
They have planned this thing,
a tablecloth to spread out
25 for guests who will come
to this room, who will sit
and bow their heads to the white
plates of food. And this will become
a cloth to be passed through
30 generations, needle of the mother,
needle of the daughter crossing
through the cloth over
and over. A choreography°
of hands and needles,
35 and the daughter wonders
how this cloth will sing.

---

11 Here, *filaments* probably refers to thin rods or rays that support the web of skin in fish fins.

33 *Choreography* (kôr′ ē og′ rə fē) is the composition and arrangement of dances.

Sömnad, 1916. Carl Larsson. Watercolor. Private collection.

Reading the Selection

A Active Reading

EVALUATE In addition to sight, Magdaleno appeals to several other senses. What kinds of sensory responses do the poet's images evoke? What overall mood is created by the images? *(In addition to sight images, such as colors, the speaker appeals to the sense of touch [warm] and the sense of sound [the soft, steady sound of the mother's breathing]. The images contribute to feelings of comfort and warmth.)*

Additional Resources
- *Active Reading Guide,* p. 140
- *Audio Library*

B Literary Elements

FIGURATIVE LANGUAGE: Symbol Ask students what is symbolized by the tablecloth and by the act of embroidering. *(The tablecloth is a symbol of the unification of generations in a family. The act of embroidering might symbolize knowledge or traditions passing from one family member to another.)*

Teaching Options

MEETING INDIVIDUAL NEEDS ENGLISH LANGUAGE LEARNERS

Figurative Language Although the figurative language adds a rich, lyrical quality to the poem's images, English language learners may have difficulty with the similes.

Activity Have small groups of students skim through the poem for similes, such as "One is pale green/ like a single blade of weed" and "threads like filaments/of fish tails,"

and work together to find the meanings of the expressions. Encourage them to reread the poem aloud, inserting their translations. Do their interpretations capture the writer's intent? **COLLAB. LEARN.**

Additional Resources
- *English Language Learners Sourcebook*

Ancestral Dream I, 1996. Maria Eugenia Terrazas. Watercolor, 70 x 60 cm. Private collection.

El Olvido
(Según las Madres)

Judith Ortiz Cofer

It is a dangerous thing
to forget the climate of
your birthplace; to choke out
the voices of the dead relatives when
5   in dreams they call you by
your secret name; dangerous
to spurn° the clothes you were
born to wear for the sake of fashion;
to use weapons and sharp instruments you
10 are not familiar with; dangerous
to disdain° the plaster saints before
which your mother kneels praying for you with
embarassing fervor that you survive in
the place you have chosen to live; a costly,
15 bare and elegant room with no pictures
on the walls: a forgetting place where
she fears you might die of exposure.
Jesús, María y José.
El olvido is a dangerous thing.

El Olvido (el   ōl vē′ dō) is Spanish for "the forgotten." *Según las Madres* (sə gōōn′   läs   mä′drəs) means "according to mothers."

7 *Spurn* means "to reject with contempt" or "to scorn."
11 *Disdain* means "to look down on" or "to despise."

Responding to Literature

Personal Response

Which poem was more meaningful for you? Why?

——— ANALYZING LITERATURE ———

Embroidering:
A Response to "Somnad"
by Carl Larsson

RECALL AND INTERPRET

1. What are the mother and daughter in the poem doing? What feature of the threads does the speaker describe? What might the threads **symbolize**, or stand for, in the poem? Explain your response.
2. What do you think the tablecloth represents? Support your ideas with specific details from the poem.

EVALUATE AND CONNECT

3. How does the poet engage your senses in this poem? List several examples.
4. When have you made something with another person or for another person? How was it different from making something by yourself or for yourself?

El Olvido
(Según las Madres)

RECALL AND INTERPRET

5. According to lines 1–12, what kinds of things are dangerous? Why, do you think, does the speaker call them dangerous?
6. What fear does the mother have? Why might she have this fear? What seems to be the relationship between the speaker, the mother, and the person called "you"? What can you infer about their values?

EVALUATE AND CONNECT

7. Are you convinced that forgetting one's roots "is a dangerous thing"? Why or why not?
8. Consider one of the places you wrote about for the Focus Activity on page 1176. What aspects of this place or of a place your ancestors came from do you think are most important to remember? Why?

——— EXTENDING YOUR RESPONSE ———

Personal Writing

Your Point of View "El Olvido" contains a Spanish subtitle that means "According to Mothers." Imagine that you are a young person living in a "costly, bare, and elegant room with no pictures on the walls." Compose an E-mail message that responds to the mother who has told you that forgetting is a dangerous thing.

Learning for Life

Letter of Request Using Magdaleno's poem for inspiration, write a letter to a relative, asking him or her to help you create a visual-arts project celebrating an aspect of your family's culture or history. In your letter, describe what you want to make, the materials you will use, and how this person could help you carry out your project.

 **Save your work for your portfolio.**

Personal Response

Students should give specific reasons for their choices.

ANALYZING LITERATURE

1. The mother and daughter are embroidering a tablecloth. The speaker describes the color and texture of the threads. The threads might symbolize the shared experiences of the mother and daughter.

2. The tablecloth might represent the history of the family and the common elements that hold a family together.

3. The poet engages the senses of sight, sound, and touch. Sight images include descriptions of color; sound images include the mother's breath; and touch images include the knees touching and the needles sliding through cloth.

4. Students may suggest that working on a project with someone else results not just in a finished product, but also in a shared experience.

5. It is dangerous to forget your past and to scorn family traditions because these things are necessary to retain a sense of self and to remain spiritually and psychologically healthy.

6. The mother fears that the child will not survive without her family traditions and sense of where she comes from. The speaker and mother seem to have a very close relationship; they care about each other deeply. The "you" may be a close friend of the speaker, or it may be the reader. "You" is a confidant(e), someone the speaker feels compelled to talk to.

7. Some students may believe that forgetting one's roots is dangerous because roots are important to one's identity. Others may think that roots are less important than what one makes of oneself.

8. Students should identify the most important aspects of the place they chose in the Focus Activity and give reasons for their choices.

✔ ASSESSMENT OPTIONS

🗀 **Quick Checks,** p. 140

🗀 **Selection and Theme Assessment,** pp. 209–210

🗀 **Performance Assessment,** p. 121

💾 **Testmaker**

EXTENDING YOUR RESPONSE

Personal Writing

Students' E-mail messages should
- respond to the mother's concern about forgetting their roots.
- defend or explain their reasons for living as they do.

Learning for Life As part of their letters, students can include diagrams or schematics that help the reader visualize what their completed projects will look like.

Before Reading

Objectives

- To read and analyze a prose piece about the significance of names
- To recognize and examine the use of a catalog in writing
- To write an analysis of the use of factual information in a selection

Skills

Reading/Thinking: Inferring; Distinguishing Between Fact and Opinion; Using Text Structure
Writing: Descriptive Names
Vocabulary: Antonyms
Grammar/Language: Using Apostrophes
Listening/Speaking: Readers Theater
Collaboration: Literature Groups

Motivating

→OPTIONS

Selection Focus Transparency 128: Have students view the transparency and then answer the question provided.

Focus Activity: As an extension of the Focus Activity, ask students to meet in small groups and respond to this question: What name would you give yourself if you could choose your own name? Explain why.

—Before You Read—

The Names of Women

Meet Louise Erdrich

❝People in [Native American] families make everything into a story. . . . People just sit and the stories start coming, one after another.❞

—*Erdrich*

The daughter of a German American father and an Ojibwa (ō jib′wā′) mother, Louise Erdrich grew up in Wahpeton, North Dakota, the oldest of seven children. Erdrich's parents, who both worked in a Bureau of Indian Affairs boarding school, encouraged their daughter to write. "My father used to give me a nickel for every story I wrote, and my mother wove strips of construction paper together and stapled them into book covers. So at an early age I felt myself to be a published author earning substantial royalties."

Erdrich entered Dartmouth College in 1972, the first year of the college's new Native American studies department. From Dartmouth, Erdrich went to the Johns Hopkins University, where she wrote poems and stories and earned a master's degree. She then returned to Dartmouth as a writer in residence.

Before she turned thirty, Erdrich published her first novel, *Love Medicine*. The book was well received by readers and critics, earning the National Book Award in 1984. Erdrich has continued her successful writing career, publishing novels, nonfiction, and children's books.

Louise Erdrich was born in 1954.

FOCUS ACTIVITY

What's in a name? Does your name tell people anything about you?

JOURNAL Write about your own name or the names of some of your relatives or ancestors. What can people learn about you and your family from your names?

SETTING A PURPOSE Read to learn what one writer thinks about the names in her family.

BACKGROUND

Erdrich's People

The *Anishinabe* (a nish′ i nä′ bā)—also known as the Ojibwa, Ojibway, or Chippewa—are one of the largest groups of Native Americans in North America. After the mid-1600s, they migrated west from the Great Lakes region to areas such as Wisconsin, North Dakota, and Montana.

VOCABULARY PREVIEW

decimated (des′ ə māt′ əd) *adj.* destroyed or killed in large numbers; p. 1182

presumptuous (pri zump′ chōō əs) *adj.* going beyond what is proper; excessively bold; p. 1182

ecclesiastical (i klē′ zē as′ ti kəl) *adj.* of or relating to the church; p. 1182

undeviating (un dē′ vē āt′ ing) *adj.* not turning away from; p. 1183

intricately (in′ tri kit lē) *adv.* in a complicated manner; elaborately; p. 1183

novel (nov′ əl) *adj.* new and unusual; p. 1183

wane (wān) *v.* to decrease gradually; to decline; p. 1184

RESOURCE MANAGER

Lesson Planning Resource
The *Unit Seven Planning Guide* (pp. 172–179) provides additional lesson notes and reduced versions of all print resources.

📁 **Other Print Resources**
- Active Reading Guide, p. 141
- Vocabulary Practice, p. 71
- Reading Workbook, pp. 91–92
- Grammar and Language Workbook, p. 277

- Grammar and Composition Handbook, Lesson 11.12
- Quick Checks, p. 141
- Selection and Theme Assessment, p. 211
- Performance Assessment, p. 122
- Spanish Summaries, p. 128
- Spanish Translations
- Inclusion Strategies
- English Language Learners Sourcebook

 Transparencies
- Selection Focus 128
- Literary Elements 120
- Grammar and Language 82

Technology
🎧 Audio Library
🎧 Spanish Audio Library
💻 Glencoe Literature Web Site
💾 Testmaker

and torn calendars, in the nest of a sagging bed, I listen to mice rustle and the scratch of an owl's claws as it paces the shingles.

Elise Eliza's daughter-in-law, my grandmother Mary LeFavor, kept that house of hand-hewed and stacked beams, mudded between. She managed to shore it up and keep it standing by stuffing every new crack with disposable diapers. Having used and reused cloth to diaper her own children, my grandmother washed and hung to dry the paper and plastic diapers that her granddaughters bought for her great-grandchildren. When their plastic-paper shredded, she gathered them carefully together and one day, on a summer visit, I woke early to find her tamping[13] the rolled stuff carefully into the cracked walls of that old house.

I t is autumn in the Plains, and in the little sloughs ducks land, and mudhens, whose flesh always tastes greasy and charred. Snow is coming soon, and after its first fall there will be a short, false warmth that brings out the sweet-sour odor of highbush cranberries. As a descendant of the women who skinned buffalo and tanned and smoked the hides, of women who pounded berries with the dried meat to make winter food, who made tea from willow bark and rosehips, who gathered snakeroot, I am affected by the change of seasons. Here is a time when plants consolidate[14] their tonic and drop seed, when animals store energy and grow thick fur. As for me, I start keeping longer hours, writing more, working harder, though I am obviously not a creature of a traditional Anishinabe culture. I was not raised speaking the old language, or adhering to the cycle of religious ceremonies that govern the Anishinabe spiritual relationship to the land and the moral order within human configurations. As the wedding of many backgrounds, I am free to do what simply feels right.

> As the wedding of many backgrounds, I am free to do what simply feels right.

My mother knits, sews, cans, dries food and preserves it. She knows how to gather tea, berries, snare rabbits, milk cows and churn butter. She can grow squash and melons from seeds she gathered the fall before. She is, as were the women who came before me, a repository[15] of all of the homely virtues, and I am the first in a long line who has not saved the autumn's harvest in birch bark *makuks*[16] and skin bags and in a cellar dry and cold with dust. I am the first who scratches the ground for pleasure, not survival, and grows flowers instead of potatoes. I record rather than practise the arts that filled the hands and days of my mother and her mother, and all the mothers going back into the shadows, when women wore names that told us who they were.

---

13. *Tamping* means "forcing or packing in with a series of light taps."

14. To *consolidate* (kən sol′ ə dāt′) means "to combine."
15. Here, a *repository* (ri poz′ ə tôr′ ē) is a person who stores something.
16. *makuks* (mä′ kuks)

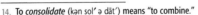

Personal Response

Students should give reasons for their reactions.

ANALYZING LITERATURE

1. She reveals that her heritage is partly a mystery. Because of factors such as the mixing of cultures, wars, and destruction caused by illness, the culture was radically altered.

2. Sample names include *Standing Strong*, *Fish Bones*, *Different Thunder*, *Lightning Proof*, and *Steps Over Truth*.

3. She describes Elise Eliza McCloud as "elevated in her pride." Virginia Grandbois is "fearsome and fascinating."

4. Like her great-grandmother, Erdrich feels she has energy and purpose.

5. Her mother practices home arts like sewing, canning, and drying food. Erdrich writes about these arts, finding a connection to her past not by participating directly in the activities, but by examining them.

6. Erdrich seems fascinated by her past and by the strengths that the women possessed. She also seems saddened by the fact that she does not possess those same strengths in the same ways.

7. The names reveal their personalities and their strengths, make the women seem more real, and reveal the truth—the people who possess those names cannot hide anything about their traits.

8. Erdrich seems in awe of their strengths and abilities and impressed by their sense of purpose.

9. Erdrich is saying that she, too, is determined to get home by exploring and preserving her family history. She hopes she has the same determination and strength of will her great-grandmother had in walking straight toward her home regardless of obstacles.

10. Erdrich seems to feel almost apologetic that she does not need to perform the same tasks as her ancestors. While her mother worked hard, Erdrich does the same tasks for pleasure rather than for work.

11. The search for identity should include a careful examination of the past. The strength of our ancestors can fortify us and give us a sense of purpose.

12. Smell: "sweet-sour odor of high-bush cranberries." Sight: "a patchwork

---

Responding to Literature

Personal Response

Discuss your initial impression of this selection with a partner.

ANALYZING LITERATURE

RECALL

1. What does Erdrich reveal in the first paragraph about her ethnic heritage and about the history of her ancestors?
2. List five names that, according to Erdrich, appeared on the rolls of the Turtle Mountain Reservation in 1892.
3. What words does Erdrich use to describe her great-grandmothers?
4. What do Virginia Grandbois and Erdrich have in common?
5. Compare the things her mother does with the things Erdrich does.

INTERPRET

6. In your opinion, what is Erdrich's attitude about her ancestors' history?
7. What sense of the Anishinabe women do you get based on the listing of their names? Explain.
8. How do you think Erdrich feels about her great-grandmothers? Use specific details from the selection to explain your answer.
9. What do you think Erdrich is saying about herself when she explains what she has in common with her great-grandmother Virginia Grandbois? Use details from the selection to support your response.
10. What conclusions can you make about the kind of person Erdrich is, based on the last paragraph? How do you think she feels about being the kind of person she is? Explain.

EVALUATE AND CONNECT

11. In your opinion, what is the **theme**, or message, of this selection? Support your response with evidence from the selection.
12. Find three examples of **sensory details** (see page R14) in "The Names of Women," and describe how they affect your appreciation of the selection. Use a chart like the one on this page to help you.
13. Theme Connections   How does the fact that Erdrich's ancestors are both Anishinabe and French relate to the theme "Variety Is Richness"?
14. How do the names you wrote about for the Focus Activity on page 1180 compare with the ones in this selection for telling about the people they name? Which names do you prefer? Explain.
15. Do you think that writing about what people have done in the past is important? Why or why not?

Literary ELEMENTS

Catalog

A **catalog** is a list of people, things, or attributes. Many forms of literature include catalogs. For example, ancient epic poems listed the names of heroes or ships. The poets Walt Whitman and Carl Sandburg often included catalogs in their poems as Erdrich does in "The Names of Women."

1. Describe two catalogs that appear in this selection.
2. Why might Erdrich present this information in the form of catalogs?

● See **Literary Terms Handbook**, p. R3.

Sensory detail	Effect
1.	
2.	
3.	

---

of shirts, pants, other worn-out scraps, bordered with small rinsed and pressed Bull Durham sacks." Sound: "the scratch of an owl's claws as it paces the shingles." The details bring the setting and characters to life, making readers feel more involved.

13. Erdrich's mixed ancestry gives her a varied and rich ethnic identity. This ancestry accounts for her determination to discover who she is.

14. Students should give specific reasons for their responses.

15. Most students will suggest that understanding the past is essential to interpreting the present.

LITERARY ELEMENTS

1. Erdrich catalogs the names of her ancestors, the items her ancestors peddled on their carts, and the tasks her mother performs.
2. The catalogs provide a detailed historical record; they also draw the reader's attention to the content of each list, giving it emphasis.

Additional Resources

Literary Elements Transparency 120

LITERATURE AND WRITING

Writing About Literature
Analyzing the Author's Use of Factual Information
Reread "The Names of Women" and find three facts that strike you as particularly interesting or surprising. Analyze each fact and explain how Erdrich uses it, what makes it so interesting, and how it adds to your understanding of the world she describes.

Creative Writing
Name Your Friends   Make a list of ten friends or relatives. What distinctive characteristics or events in their lives might best be used to illustrate their personalities? Make up names for these people, using the kind of descriptive names listed in the first part of "The Names of Women."

EXTENDING YOUR RESPONSE

Interdisciplinary Activity
History: Family Tree   Using the information in the selection, create a family tree for Louise Erdrich. Leave empty spaces where no information is provided, but show the relationships among the ancestors of Erdrich who are named in the selection.

Listening and Speaking
Readers Theater   Read parts of this selection aloud, dramatizing, through sound or pantomime, the names or activities described. You might use this technique for the opening paragraphs or for the final paragraphs.

Literature Groups
Will She Make It?   In this selection, Erdrich describes herself as someone with the "urge to get home, even if I must walk straight across the world." What does she mean? Will she make it? As a group, agree on a statement of Erdrich's goal and discuss why you think she will succeed or fail in reaching it. Use passages from the selection to support your view. Have one group member take notes on the explanations people offer. Outline your group's ideas and supporting details, and then share your conclusion with the class.

 Save your work for your portfolio.

Antonyms are words that have opposite meanings from each other. Some antonyms are "true," with meanings that are exactly opposite; for example, *hot* and *cold* or *night* and *day*. Often, a word will have several antonyms, each with a slightly different meaning. For example, *courageous* and *valiant* are antonyms for *cowardly*.

While most words have at least one synonym, or word that has the same or nearly the same meaning, not all words have an antonym; for example, *run* and *dog* have no antonyms.

PRACTICE   Choose an antonym for each of the vocabulary words listed below.

1. decimate
   a. build   b. destroy   c. create
2. intricately
   a. simply   b. elaborately   c. curiously
3. novel
   a. innovative   b. dated   c. literary
4. wane
   a. increase   b. slacken   c. subside

LITERATURE AND WRITING

Writing About Literature
Students' writing should
- discuss three specific facts.
- explain why those facts are striking.
- explain how Erdrich uses those facts to help readers understand her heritage.

Creative Writing
Students' names should
- accurately reflect the personalities, characteristics, and important events in the lives of those who will receive the names.
- be descriptive and evocative.

EXTENDING YOUR RESPONSE

Interdisciplinary Activity   Have students meet in groups to compare the family trees. Allow students to modify the trees as they discuss each other's work. **COLLAB. LEARN.**

Listening and Speaking
Encourage students to practice with partners to get feedback on the tone, rhythm, pauses, and gestures that best convey the meaning of the piece. **COLLAB. LEARN.**

Literature Groups   Have students respond to the questions individually before meeting in groups. Groups should select a leader-facilitator whose responsibilities will include providing opportunities for each student to share ideas. **COLLAB. LEARN.**

1. c   2. a
3. b   4. a

Additional Resources
📁 *Vocabulary Practice,* p. 71

✔ ASSESSMENT OPTIONS

📁 *Quick Checks,* p. 141
📁 *Selection and Theme Assessment,* p. 211
📁 *Performance Assessment,* p. 122
💾 *Testmaker*

MEDIA
Connection

Objective

- To understand and apply strategies for reading a newspaper article

Literature
LINK

The Names of Women Both this article and Erdrich's "The Names of Women" (p. 1181) deal with how people get names. Erdrich seems to prefer the descriptive names originally given to her ancestors rather than the more ordinary names of later generations, such as Marie, Jeanne, and Catherine. This article discusses how some parents have tried to give their children fresh and different names to set them apart, only to find that the names they chose were equally appealing to thousands of other parents that same year.

Respond

1. Encourage students to give reasons for their responses.
2. People use different criteria or traditions to name their children, but they are always looking for new ideas and ways to give their children special distinction.

Additional Resources
📁 *Media Connections,* p. 23

Teaching Options

inter**NET**
CONNECTION

Names Have students search for additional information about names. Suggest that they enter the keywords *baby* and *names*.

MEDIA
Connection

Newspaper Article
Names certainly come in a great variety. What is the origin of your name? In this article, you'll learn about recent trends in names for babies.

The Name Reign:
New Parents Balance the Trendy and Unique

by Janet Simons—Rocky Mountain News, January 18, 1998

Fashions in names seem as arbitrary as fashions in carpet. One day everyone wants orange shag, then suddenly it's green berber.

What else explains Mary, the top name for girls in 1930, 1940 and 1960? (It was temporarily displaced in 1950 by Linda.) At one point, one of every six females in the United States was named Mary. Now the name ranks 72nd. Or Heather, so popular in 1989 that the movie *Heathers* featured three popular girls all named Heather. At No. 100, Heather barely clings to the 1997 list.

On the flip side, countless parents thought Austin or Hannah sounded fresh when their children were born, then wound up inviting two kids with the same name to the third birthday party.

Duncan Drechsel is willing to predict which names will be popular in 1998. Drechsel is marketing director for the BabyCenter, a San Francisco–based Web site for expectant and new parents. The BabyCenter recently released a list of the 100 most popular baby names based on a sample of new Social Security registrations from the first eight months of 1997. "Diana. I see a lot of Dianas in the future,"

he says. "And Mabel. I'd put money on Mabel moving up."

Diana, which ranked only 92 for the first eight months of 1997, before the princess died, seems obvious. But Mabel? It's not even on the current list of 100. Drechsel says Mabel meets several criteria for a name on the rise. It's an "antique" name, like Sarah and Emily, numbers 1 and 2 on the list. It has a long A sound, like Kaitlyn, Taylor and Megan, ranked 3,

7 and 8, respectively. Most important, it's the name of the baby in the television sitcom *Mad About You,* so it . . . is fresh in the minds of expectant parents.

"Parents today are looking for something different," Drechsel says. "That's why we're seeing so much more variation in the names on the list."

The nation's most popular names for 1997:

1.	Michael	Sarah
2.	Matthew	Emily
3.	Nicholas	Kaitlyn
4.	Jacob	Brianna
5.	Christopher	Ashley
6.	Austin	Jessica
7.	Joshua	Taylor
8.	Zachary	Megan
9.	Andrew	Hannah
10.	Brandon	Samantha

Respond

1. Which names in the article and on the list are your favorites? Which do you like least? Explain.

2. From this article, what do you learn about the theme "Variety Is Richness"? Explain.

Reading *Minilesson*

Scanning Point out that this article contains many dates, facts, and figures. Discuss with students what reading strategy they would use to find the year that the name *Diana* was popular. Explain that scanning is looking quickly over the text to find certain numbers or words.

Activity Help students sharpen their scanning skills by posing questions about the article and challenging students to

find the answers as quickly as they can. You might ask the following questions:
- What was the most popular name for girls in 1950?
- What is Duncan Drechsel's occupation?
- Why might Mabel become a more popular name? **L2**

Additional Resources
📁 *Reading Workbook*

Reading on Your Own

If you have enjoyed the literature in this unit, you might also be interested in the following books.

. . . And the Earth Did Not Devour Him

By Tomás Rivera This classic of Chicano literature tells the unique story of a young boy trying to recall the events of a "lost year," a year that has clearly been a difficult one for him.

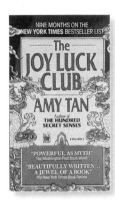

The Joy Luck Club

by Amy Tan Spanning four decades, this novel traces the tragedies and joys of four Chinese women who immigrate to the United States and the complex lives of their American-born daughters.

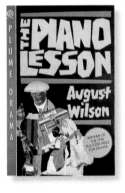

The Piano Lesson
by August Wilson
Written by a Pulitzer Prize–winning author, this two-act play takes place in 1936, in the house of an African American family. Wilson tells the story of a brother and sister and their conflict over whether or not to sell a piano that has been in the family for three generations and is reminiscent of the family's painful history.

Eyes On the Prize: America's Civil Rights Years, 1954–1965

by Juan Williams This important and inspiring book about personal activism records eleven years that changed America's history. It includes the story of the Montgomery bus boycott and numerous other Civil Rights struggles.

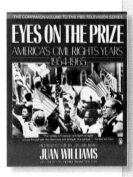

Reading on Your Own

Glencoe Literature Library

. . . And the Earth Did Not Devour Him by Tomás Rivera is available in the *Glencoe Literature Library*. For a complete listing, see p. T48 in this book.

The *Study Guides for Glencoe Literature* provide instructional support and student activities for works in the *Glencoe Literature Library*.

MEETING INDIVIDUAL NEEDS — INCLUSION STRATEGIES

You may wish to recommend *Eyes on the Prize* by Juan Williams to your less-proficient readers. The accessible writing style, vivid photographs, interviews, short biographies, and brief notes make this book particularly appropriate for less-proficient readers. **L1**

The books listed at the right are rated for average readers (**L2**) or for students who need more challenging reading material (**L3**):

- *. . . And the Earth Did Not Devour Him* by Tomás Rivera **L2**
- *The Joy Luck Club* by Amy Tan **L3**
- *The Piano Lesson* by August Wilson **L2**

Additional Resources
 Inclusion Strategies

Standardized Test Practice

 TEST-TAKING TIP

On essay revision questions, students do not need to worry about the content of passage. In addition, they may not even be asked to pick out every error in the passage.

Answers and Analyses

1. **D** Students should read sentences (1) and (2) then consider the answer that best connects the two. Answer D connects the general statement about the automobile's place in life with the specific example of the compact car.

2. **B** Again, students need to read sentence 3 in the context of the paragraph. Answer B makes clear that the sedan has a different function than do compact cars.

Standardized Test Practice

> Directions: The following passage is an early draft of an essay. Some parts of the passage need to be rewritten.
>
> Read the passage and answer the questions that follow. Some questions are about particular sentences or parts of sentences and ask you to improve sentence structure and word choice. Other questions refer to parts of the essay or the entire essay and ask you to consider organization and development. In making your decisions, follow the conventions of standard written English. Select the letter of the correct answer and write it on your paper.

(1) *In the last twenty years, automobiles in many forms have been increasingly necessary for modern life.* (2) *For example, today the compact car is regarded as indispensable for basic transportation for business people and homemakers.* (3) *The sedan, is something most executives, chauffeurs, and taxi drivers could not do without.* (4) *Moreover, many families use the mini-van to transport baseball teams to games, to travel on a vacation, and to help move their children to college.*

(5) *Despite our obvious reliance on cars, some people do not want to buy new cars with advanced technology in them.* (6) *They fear that because the new automobiles have computers that they will take control over people and the road.* (7) *Because of this fear, cars that have computers that diagnose problems and control safety devices are not selling.*

(8) *This is unfortunate.* (9) *The technology that is being developed for automobiles performs many important functions, and could do even more.* (10) *What would have happened if people had been afraid to buy the very first car, and it had been taken off the market?* (11) *Not only would the cost of transportation be greater, and many trips would require more time than before to make.* (12) *Further, major industries would never have been able to grow without trucks and other larger versions of the automobile.* (13) *Cars have become an essential part of almost everyone's lives.* (14) *To those of you who are afraid, we should remember that our new, high-tech cars are simply advanced model Ts!*

1. Which of the following would be the most suitable sentence to insert immediately after sentence 1?
   (A) The race is on to produce the "ultimate" car.
   (B) I have found the new automobiles somewhat difficult to learn to operate.
   (C) Many people are understandably intimidated by new technology.
   (D) They are now so common that they have a wide-ranging effect on daily life.
   (E) Motorcycles belong to the family of automobiles.

2. To best connect sentence 3 to the rest of the first paragraph, which is the best word or phrase to insert after "*The sedan,*" in sentence 3 (shown below)?

   The sedan, is something most executives, chauffeurs, and taxi drivers could not do without.

   (A) surely,
   (B) however,
   (C) another form of automobile,
   (D) you see,
   (E) in contrast,

TEST-TAKING TIP

Suggest to students that if they don't know the definition of a word, they can usually work through the question by thinking about how they've heard the word used before. If they find the word *abominable* on the test, they can think of the phrase or situation in which they've heard it, as in *abominable snowman*. They can then think about how that context limits what the word might mean.

3. In context, sentence 8 could be made more precise by adding which of the following words after *"This"*?
   - (A) technology
   - (B) control
   - (C) example
   - (D) automobile
   - (E) situation

4. The function of sentence 10 is to
   - (A) set up a hypothetical condition
   - (B) raise doubt in the reader's mind about the usefulness of automobiles
   - (C) allow the writer to show modesty
   - (D) contest a common claim about automobiles
   - (E) show the writer's astonishment about the new automobiles

5. Which of the following is the best revision of the underlined portion of sentence 11 (reproduced below)?

   Not only would the cost of transportation be great, and many trips would require more time than before to make.

   - (A) but so would the many trips require more time to make
   - (B) and also many trips require more time to make
   - (C) but they would require more time to make the trip
   - (D) as well as to require more time for many trips to be made
   - (E) but many trips would require more time to make, as well.

6. Which of the following versions of the underlined portion of sentence 14 (reproduced below) best suits the context?

   To those of you who are afraid, we should remember that our new, high-tech cars are simply advanced model Ts!

   - (A) (As it is now)
   - (B) You who are fearing it should remember that our new, high-tech cars
   - (C) But remember, you may be afraid that our new, high-tech cars
   - (D) Those who are fearful should remember that our new, high-tech cars
   - (E) What we fear about the new, high-tech cars is that we see that they

STOP

THE PRINCETON REVIEW **TEST-TAKING TIP**

Explain to students that on the SAT there are questions that do not count towards student scores. Students will not be able to tell which ones they are. This is done to try out new questions for the first time, for use on future exams. Some experimental questions will be poor questions—they will be discarded before ever going on a test as a real question. They may be harder than they should be, so students should be prepared. Students should answer each question as if it counted, but if they hit a tough question or section, they should just do their best and when they're done, assume it was experimental.

THE PRINCETON REVIEW **TEST-TAKING TIP**

There are many places where students may hear and see unfamiliar words every day—in newspapers, schoolbooks, novels, conversations, and even on television. Suggest to students that when they come across a word they can't define, they write it down on an index card. This way they can look it up in a dictionary later, writing down the definition and any helpful word parts on the reverse side. This is an excellent way for students to improve their vocabulary as well as their SAT scores.

---

3. **E** Ask students, "to what does the word 'this' refer?" The answer in the lack of popularity of cars containing advanced technology. Answer E, situation, is the closest choice.

4. **A** Sentence 10 attempts to encourage the reader to consider what would have happened in the past if people reacted negatively to the first car. He then answers his own question.

5. **E** The words *not only* at the beginning of the sentence should let students know that the second clause will add another point to the first. This requires a conjunction other than *and*. Answer E uses the conjunction *but* and is the only answer free of additional errors.

6. **D** Answer D is the only choice that retains the meaning of the original, while making it clearer and eliminating the confusion of pronouns involved in "those of you who are afraid" and "we."

MORE PRACTICE

For additional practice with the SAT II: Writing Test, assign pp. 28–33 from the *College Entrance Exams Preparation and Practice Workbook*.

Reference Section

Literary Terms Handbook

A

Abstract language   Language that expresses an idea or intangible reality, as opposed to a specific object or occurrence or a concrete reality. The Declaration of Independence uses such abstract language as *safety, happiness, prudence,* and *laws of nature.*

> See also CONCRETE LANGUAGE.

Act   A major unit of a **drama,** or play. Many modern dramas have two or three acts. A short drama may have only one act. Acts may comprise one or more scenes.

> See page 908.
> See also DRAMA, SCENE.

Allegory   A narrative work of fiction or drama in which the elements—characters, settings, and plot— work together to teach a moral lesson. Frequently, this involves using things, persons, and settings as symbols. Nathaniel Hawthorne sometimes used allegorical techniques—for example, in "The Minister's Black Veil."

> See also SYMBOL.

Alliteration   The repetition of similar sounds, most often consonant sounds, at the beginnings of words. For example, James Weldon Johnson uses alliteration in the following line from "My City":

But, ah! Manhattan's sights and sounds, her
   smells

> See pages 383, 399, and 845.
> See also SOUND DEVICES.

Allusion   A reference in a work of literature to a character, a place, or a situation from history or from music, art, or another work of literature. For example, in "A Narrative of the Captivity and Restoration of Mrs. Mary Rowlandson," Rowlandson makes a number of allusions to the Bible.

> See page 609.

Ambiguity   The expression in a single term or passage of more than one meaning. The richness of literary language lies in its ability to evoke multiple layers of meaning. The title of Richard Wilbur's poem "The Beautiful Changes" is intentionally ambiguous.

Analogy   A comparison to show similarities between two things that are otherwise dissimilar. Writers often use an analogy to explain something unfamiliar by comparing it to something familiar.

> See page 91.
> See also METAPHOR, SIMILE.

Anecdote   A brief account of an interesting event. An anecdote may be used to raise or illustrate a point, to explain an idea, or to describe a personality.

> See page 901.

Antagonist   A person or a force that opposes the protagonist, or central character, in a story or drama. The reader is generally meant not to sympathize with the antagonist. For example, in "The Open Boat," by Stephen Crane, the sea is the antagonist.

> See pages 472 and 1099.
> See also CONFLICT, PROTAGONIST.

Aphorism   A short, pointed statement that expresses a wise or clever observation about human experience. Américo Paredes's "Dichos" is composed largely of aphorisms.

> See page 136.
> See also EPIGRAM.

Apostrophe   A figure of speech in which a speaker addresses an inanimate object, an idea, or an absent person. Ezra Pound's poem "A Pact," in which he addresses the long-dead Walt Whitman, is an example of apostrophe.

> See pages 390 and 673.
> See also PERSONIFICATION.

Argument   Writing in which reason is used to influence ideas or actions. An argument is a form of persuasion. While some persuasive writing depends on emotion, an argument uses logic, reasons, and evidence.

>See pages 262 and 521.
>See also PERSUASION.

Aside   In a play, a comment made by a character that is heard by the audience or another character but is not heard by other characters on stage. The speaker turns to one side, or "aside," away from the main action on stage. Asides, which are rare in modern drama, reveal what a character is thinking or feeling.

Assonance   The repetition of similar vowel sounds, especially in a line of poetry. For example, the *o* sound is repeated in this line from an Emily Dickinson poem:

The Soul selects her own Society . . .

>See pages 399 and 1155.
>See also SOUND DEVICES.

Atmosphere   The dominant mood or feeling conveyed by a piece of writing.

>See also MOOD.

Author's note   A note accompanying a piece of writing and containing explanatory information. Author's notes usually include helpful but nonessential information. Randall Jarrell provides an author's note along with his poem "The Death of the Ball Turret Gunner."

>See page 858.

Author's purpose   An author's intent in writing a piece of literature. Authors typically write to accomplish one or more of the following purposes: to persuade, to inform, to explain, to entertain, or to describe.

>See pages 150 and 611.
>See also DICTION, STYLE, THEME.

Autobiography   The story of a person's life written by that person. An example of this genre is *The Autobiography of Benjamin Franklin.*

>See page 335.
>See also BIOGRAPHY, MEMOIR, NONFICTION.

B

Ballad   A narrative song or poem. **Folk ballads,** which usually recount an exciting or dramatic episode, were passed down by word of mouth for generations before being written down. **Literary ballads** are written in imitation of folk ballads.

>See also FOLKLORE, NARRATIVE POETRY, ORAL TRADITION.

Bias   The author's personal inclination toward a certain opinion or position on a topic.

>See page 67.
>See also NONFICTION.

Biography   The account of a person's life written by someone other than the subject.

>See pages 26–27.
>See also AUTOBIOGRAPHY, MEMOIR, NONFICTION.

Blank verse   Poetry written in unrhymed **iambic pentameter.** Each line has five pairs of syllables, with each pair made up of an unstressed syllable followed by a stressed syllable. Because it may attempt to imitate spoken English, every line need not be perfectly regular. Robert Frost wrote "Birches" in blank verse:

Whĕn Í sĕe bírchĕs bénd tŏ léft ănd ríght

>See page 218.
>See also IAMBIC PENTAMETER, SCANSION.

C

Caesura   A pause within a line of poetry. A caesura is used to produce variations in rhythm and to draw attention to certain words. The following lines from "The Tide Rises, the Tide Falls," by Henry Wadsworth Longfellow, have caesuras after the words *rises* and *darkens.*

The tide rises, the tide falls,

The twilight darkens, the curlew calls.

>See page 1144.
>See also RHYTHM.

Catalog   The listing of images, details, people, or events in a piece of writing. In *Song of Myself,* for example, Walt Whitman catalogs different kinds of workers from all over the United States.

> See page 1186.

Character   An individual in a literary work. A **main character** is central to the story and is typically characterized fully. A **minor character** displays few personality traits and is used to help develop the story. Characters who show varied and sometimes contradictory traits, such as Michael Curly in F. Scott Fitzgerald's "The Bridal Party," are called **round.** Characters who reveal only one personality trait are called **flat.** A **stereotype,** or stock character of a familiar type, is typically flat. A **dynamic character** grows and changes during the story, as does the captain in Stephen Crane's "The Open Boat." A **static character** remains basically the same throughout the story.

> See pages 472 and 485.
> See also CHARACTERIZATION, STEREOTYPE.

Characterization   The methods a writer uses to reveal the personality of a character. In **direct characterization** the writer makes explicit statements about a character. In **indirect characterization** the writer reveals a character through the character's words and actions and through what other characters think and say about that character.

> See pages 666, 840, and 1033.
> See also CHARACTER.

Classicism   A style that reflects the principles and concerns of the art and literature of ancient Greece and Rome. Typically, a classical style displays simple, harmonious purity of form.

Climax   The point of greatest emotional intensity, interest, or suspense in a narrative. Usually the climax comes at the turning point in a story or drama, the point just before the resolution of the conflict, as in Ernest Hemingway's "In Another Country," when the bereft major loses his temper with the narrator.

> See pages 473, 492, and 979.
> See also CONFLICT, DÉNOUEMENT, PLOT, RESOLUTION.

Colloquial language   Informal speech that people use in everyday conversation.

> See page 469.
> See also DIALECT, VERNACULAR.

Comedy   A type of drama that often has a happy ending and is humorous. A **heroic comedy** focuses on the exploits of a larger-than-life hero.

> See also DRAMA, FARCE, HUMOR, PARODY, SATIRE, WIT.

Comic relief   A humorous episode inserted into a serious drama, customarily used to break the tension yet highlight the seriousness of the story.

Conceit   An elaborate extended metaphor that dominates a passage or an entire poem. The conceit makes an analogy between some object from nature or everyday life and the subject or theme of the poem.

> See page 1166.
> See also EXTENDED METAPHOR, IMAGERY.

Concrete language   Clear language about actual things or occurrences. Words like *dog* and *sky* are concrete, while words like *truth* and *evil* are not concrete but abstract.

> See also ABSTRACT LANGUAGE.

Confessional poetry   A movement in poetry begun in the 1950s in which the poet writes about his or her own personal experiences. These writers described their problems with mental illness, alcohol abuse, and troubled relationships in an open and direct style. Poets such as Robert Lowell, Anne Sexton, and Sylvia Plath became known as members of the **Confessional school** of poets.

> See page 818.

Conflict   The central struggle between two opposing forces in a story or drama. An **external conflict** exists when a character struggles against some outside force, such as another person, nature, society, or fate. An **internal conflict** is a struggle between two opposing thoughts or desires within the mind of a character.

> See pages 473 and 788.
> See also ANTAGONIST, PLOT, PROTAGONIST.

Connotation   The suggested or implied meanings associated with a word beyond its dictionary definition, or **denotation**. A word can have a positive, negative, or neutral connotation.

> See pages 83 and 173.
> See also AMBIGUITY, DENOTATION, FIGURATIVE
>   LANGUAGE.

Consonance   The repetition of similar consonant sounds typically within or at the ends of words, as in the succession of echoing *d* sounds in this line from "Naming Myself," by Barbara Kingsolver:

I could shed my name in the middle of life,

> See pages 399 and 1155.
> See also SOUND DEVICES.

Couplet   Two consecutive, paired lines of poetry, usually rhymed, and usually forming a stanza. For example, the following lines from "Recuerdo," by Edna St. Vincent Millay, make up a couplet:

We were very tired, we were very merry—
We had gone back and forth all night on the ferry.

> See page 180.
> See also HEROIC COUPLET, RHYME, SONNET,
>   STANZA.

Crisis   In a narrative, a moment of high tension that requires a decision. In Bret Harte's "The Outcasts of Poker Flat," the crisis comes when the "outcasts" are stranded in a cabin during a blizzard and begin to run out of food.

> See page 1070.
> See also CLIMAX, RISING ACTION.

D

Denotation   The literal, or dictionary, meaning of a word. In his "Author's Note" to "The Death of the Ball Turret Gunner," Randall Jarrell uses many words that are intended simply to signify their literal, or exact, meanings.

"A ball turret was a plexiglass sphere set into the belly of a B-17 or B-24 . . ."

See also CONNOTATION, LITERAL LANGUAGE.

Dénouement   The outcome, or resolution, of the plot.

> See page 473.
> See also CLIMAX, CONFLICT, FALLING ACTION,
>   PLOT, RESOLUTION.

Description   A detailed portrayal of a person, a place, an object, or an event. Description appeals to the senses, helping the reader see, hear, smell, taste, or feel what the writer is describing. The following passage from Eudora Welty's "A Worn Path" is an example of deft description:

Her eyes were blue with age. Her skin had a pattern all its own of numberless branching wrinkles and as though a whole little tree stood in the middle of her forehead. . . .

> See pages 18 and 186.
> See also FIGURATIVE LANGUAGE, SENSORY
>   DETAILS.

Dialect   A variation of a language spoken by a particular group, often within a particular region and time. Dialects may differ from the standard form of a language in vocabulary, pronunciation, or grammatical form. Mark Twain's story "The Celebrated Jumping Frog of Calaveras County" contains the following example of dialect:

Well, thish-yer Smiley had a yaller one-eyed cow that didn't have no tail, only jest a short stump like a bannanner . . .

> See page 888.
> See also COLLOQUIAL LANGUAGE, LOCAL
>   COLOR, REGIONALISM, VERNACULAR.

Dialogue   Conversation between characters in a literary work. These lines from "Rain Music," by Longhang Nguyen, provide an example of dialogue:

"Will your daughter become a surgeon?" our relatives ask.
"It's possible," my father says, beaming.

> See pages 909 and 935.
> See also MONOLOGUE.

Diary   An individual's personal, daily record of impressions, events, or thoughts, written for the individual's personal use rather than for publication.

> See also JOURNAL.

Diction   A writer's choice of words; an important element in the writer's "voice" or style. Skilled writers choose their words carefully to convey a particular tone and meaning. Ernest Hemingway, for example, was known for his spare, simple, sturdy diction, as exemplified in these lines from "In Another Country":

In the fall the war was always there, but we did not go to it any more. It was cold in the fall in Milan and the dark came very early.

> See pages 73, 365, and 1147.
> See also AUTHOR'S PURPOSE, STYLE, VOICE.

Drama   A story intended to be performed before an audience by actors on a stage. The script of a dramatic work may include **stage directions** that explain how characters should look, speak, move, and behave. The script might also specify details of the setting and scenery, such as lighting, **props,** and sound effects. A drama may be divided into **acts,** which may also be broken up into **scenes,** indicating changes in location or the passage of time.

> See pages 908–909.
> See also COMEDY, TRAGEDY.

Dramatic monologue   A form of dramatic poetry in which one speaker addresses a silent listener. Edgar Allan Poe's poem "To Helen," in which the speaker passionately addresses his beloved, is an example of a dramatic monologue.

> See page 550.
> See also DRAMATIC POETRY, MONOLOGUE.

Dramatic poetry   Poetry in which characters are revealed through dialogue and monologue, as well as through description. Robert Frost's "The Death of the Hired Man" is an example of dramatic poetry.

> See page 709.
> See also DIALOGUE, DRAMATIC MONOLOGUE.

E

Elegy   A poem mourning a death or other great loss. Walt Whitman's "Sight in Camp in the Daybreak Gray and Dim" is an elegy to soldiers killed in the Civil War.

Enjambment   In poetry, the continuation of a sentence across a line break without a punctuated pause between lines. For example, the following lines from Robert Frost's "Stopping by Woods on a Snowy Evening" are enjambed:

My little horse must think it queer
To stop without a farmhouse near

> See page 649.
> See also RHYTHM.

Epic   A long narrative poem that traces the adventures of a hero. Epics intertwine myths, legends, and history, reflecting the values of the societies in which they originate. Homer's *Iliad* and *Odyssey* are two famous epics.

> See also LEGEND, MYTH, ORAL TRADITION.

Epigram   A short, witty poem; a saying. For example, much of Benjamin Franklin's *Poor Richard's Almanack* is made up of epigrams.

> See also APHORISM.

Epiphany   The sudden intuitive recognition of the meaning or essence of something. At the end of "The Second Tree from the Corner," by E. B. White, the main character has an epiphany when he finally realizes what he wants from life.

Epithet   An apt phrase, nickname, or adjective; in oral or written epics, a formalized nickname or adjective phrase used to identify or describe a recurring character, place, event, or object. For example, in his poem "Fiddler Jones," Edgar Lee Masters uses an epithet when he refers to "Red-headed Sammy."

Essay   A short piece of nonfiction writing on any topic. The purpose of the essay is to communicate an idea or opinion. The **formal essay** is serious and impersonal. The **informal essay** entertains while it informs, usually in light, conversational style. A **personal essay** is an informal essay that makes personal references. Ralph Waldo Emerson's "Nature" is an example of a formal essay. Ralph Ellison's "February" is a personal essay.

> See pages 34, 152–153, and 848.
> See also NONFICTION.

Exaggeration. See HYPERBOLE.

Exemplum   A brief story that illustrates a moral point by serving as an example.

> See also ANECDOTE, FABLE, PARABLE.

Exposition   At the beginning of a story, novel, or other narrative, the part of the plot line that sets the scene by introducing the characters, setting, and situation. Exposition also refers to expository writing, a type of prose that informs and explains.

> See pages 143, 473, and 1042.
> See also PLOT.

Extended metaphor   A metaphor that compares two unlike things in various ways throughout a paragraph, a stanza, or an entire piece of writing. For example, in *Song of Myself,* Walt Whitman answers the question "What is the grass?" with this extended metaphor:

I guess it must be the flag of my disposition, out
   of a hopeful green stuff woven.

Or I guess it is the handkerchief of the Lord,
A scented gift and remembrancer designedly dropt,
Bearing the owner's name someway in the
   corners, that we may see and remark, and say
   Whose?

> See page 81.
> See also METAPHOR.

F

Fable   A short, usually simple tale that teaches a moral and sometimes uses animal characters. Themes are usually stated explicitly.

> See also LEGEND, PARABLE, THEME.

Falling action   In a narrative, the action that follows the **climax.**

> See page 473.
> See also CLIMAX, DÉNOUEMENT, PLOT, RESOLUTION.

Farce   A type of comedy with ridiculous situations, characters, or events.

> See COMEDY, HUMOR, PARODY, SATIRE.

Fiction   A narrative in which situations and characters are invented by the writer. Some aspects of a fictional work may be based on fact or experience. Fictional works include short stories, novels, and dramas.

> See pages 4–5.
> See also DRAMA, NONFICTION, NOVEL, SHORT STORY.

Figurative language   Language used for descriptive effect, in order to convey ideas or emotions. Figurative expressions are not literally true but express some truth beyond the literal level. Figurative language is especially prominent in poetry. A **figure of speech** is a specific device or kind of figurative language such as metaphor, personification, simile, or symbol.

> See pages 248 and 399.
> See also CONNOTATION, IMAGERY, METAPHOR, PERSONIFICATION, SIMILE, SYMBOL.

Flashback   An interruption in the chronological order of a narrative to show an event that happened earlier. A flashback gives readers information that may help explain the main events of the story. For example, in "An Occurrence at Owl Creek Bridge," Ambrose Bierce presents a flashback in the middle of the story.

> See pages 380 and 813.
> See also FLASH-FORWARD.

Flash-forward   An interruption in the chronological sequence of a narrative to leap forward in time. Richard Wright uses this device in his autobiography, *Black Boy,* when he describes a visit to his father that occurs many years after the time of the story.

> See page 828.
> See also FLASHBACK.

Foil   A minor character whose contrast with a main character highlights particular traits of the main character. The dog in Jack London's "To Build a Fire," for example, exhibits a caution and respect for the cold of the Yukon that the man obviously lacks.

> See page 872.
> See also ANTAGONIST, CHARACTER, CHARAC-TERIZATION, PROTAGONIST.

Folklore   The traditional beliefs, customs, stories, songs, and dances of a culture. Folklore is passed down through oral tradition and is based in the concerns of ordinary people.

> See also BALLAD, EPIC, FOLKTALE, LEGEND, MYTH, ORAL TRADITION, TALL TALE.

Folktale   An anonymous traditional story passed down orally long before being written down. Folktales include animal stories, trickster stories, fairy tales, myths, legends, and tall tales.

> See also EPIC, FOLKLORE, LEGEND, MYTH, ORAL TRADITION, TALL TALE.

Foot   The basic unit in the measurement of a line of metrical poetry. A foot usually contains one stressed syllable (ˊ) and one or more unstressed syllables (˘). The basic metric feet are the **anapest** (˘˘ˊ), the **dactyl** (ˊ˘˘), the **iamb** (˘ˊ), the **spondee** (ˊˊ), and the **trochee** (ˊ˘).

> See also METER, RHYTHM, SCANSION, STANZA.

Foreshadowing   The use of clues by the author to prepare readers for events that will happen later in a story. In "The Portrait," by Thomas Rivera, the salesman's demand for full cash payment foreshadows the fact that the transaction is a swindle.

> See page 353.
> See also PLOT, RISING ACTION, SUSPENSE.

Form   The structure of a poem. Many contemporary writers use loosely structured poetic forms instead of following traditional or formal patterns. These poets vary the lengths of lines and stanzas, relying on emphasis, rhythm, pattern, or the placement of words and phrases to convey meaning.

> See page 1170.
> See also RHYTHM, STANZA, STRUCTURE.

Frame story   A plot structure that includes the telling of one story within another story. The frame is the **outer** story, which usually precedes and follows the **inner,** more important story. For example, Mark Twain uses a frame in "The Celebrated Jumping Frog of Calaveras County."

Free verse   Poetry that has no fixed pattern of meter, rhyme, line length, or stanza arrangement. "Prayer to the Pacific," by Leslie Marmon Silko, is an example of free verse.

> See pages 416 and 1149.
> See also RHYTHM.

G–H

Genre   A category or type of literature. Examples of genres are poetry, drama, fiction, and nonfiction.

Haiku   A traditional Japanese form of poetry that has three lines and seventeen syllables. The first and third lines have five syllables each; the middle line has seven syllables. Usually about nature, a haiku presents striking imagery to evoke in the reader a variety of feelings and associations.

Hero   The chief character in a literary work, typically one whose admirable qualities or noble deeds arouse the admiration of the reader. Although the word *hero* is applied only to males in traditional usage–*heroine* being the term used for females–contemporary usage applies the term to either gender.

> See also EPIC, LEGEND, MYTH, PROTAGONIST, TALL TALE, TRAGEDY.

Heroic couplet   A pair of rhymed lines in iambic pentameter. For example, Anne Bradstreet uses the heroic couplet in "To My Dear and Loving Husband":

Ĭ príze / thy̆ lóve / mŏre thán / whŏle mínes / ŏf góld

Ŏr áll / thĕ rích/ĕs thát / thĕ Eást / dŏth hóld

> See page 180.
> See also IAMBIC PENTAMETER, METER, RHYTHM.

Historical fiction   A story that sets fictional characters against a backdrop of history and contains many details about the period in which it is set.

> See pages 110–113.
> See also FICTION.

Historical narrative   A work of nonfiction that tells the story of important historical events or developments. In *La Relación,* Cabeza de Vaca provides a historical narrative of the experiences of a group of Spanish explorers.

See page 166.

Humor   The quality of a literary work that makes the characters and their situations seem funny, amusing, or ludicrous. Mark Twain's story "The Celebrated Jumping Frog of Calaveras County" is told with humor.

See also COMEDY, FARCE, PARODY, SATIRE, WIT.

Hyperbole   A figure of speech that uses exaggeration to express strong emotion, to make a point, or to evoke humor. For example, the expression "I'm so hungry I could eat a horse" is hyperbole.

See page 158.
See also FIGURATIVE LANGUAGE, UNDERSTATEMENT.

I

Iambic pentameter   A specific poetic meter in which each line is composed of five feet (**pentameter**), most of which are iambs.

See page 218.
See also BLANK VERSE, FOOT, HEROIC COUPLET, METER, RHYTHM, SCANSION.

Idiom   A saying or group of words that takes on special meaning, different from the usual meaning of the words that make it up. For example, "I'm leading a hand-to-mouth existence" really means "I don't have much money." Idioms add realism to the dialogue in a story and can expand characterization.

See page 854.
See also DIALECT.

Imagery   The "word pictures" that writers create to evoke an emotional response. In creating effective images, writers use **sensory details,** or descriptions that appeal to one or more of the five senses: sight, hearing, touch, taste, and smell. For example, in the following lines from "Snow," Julia Alvarez uses visual imagery to make a scene vivid to the reader.

All my life I had heard about the white crystals that fell out of American skies in the winter. From my desk I watched the fine powder dust the sidewalk and parked cars below.

See pages 105, 399, and 1175.
See also FIGURATIVE LANGUAGE, SENSORY DETAILS.

Imagist poetry   The works of a group of early twentieth-century poets who believed that the image was the essence of poetry, conveying a poem's meaning and emotion. The language of poetry, they believed, should be brief, clear, and concrete, and it should also be similar to spoken language. A classic Imagist poem is "In a Station of the Metro," by Ezra Pound.

See pages 598 and 612.
See also MODERNISM.

Internal rhyme   Rhyme that occurs within a single line of poetry. Poets use internal rhyme to convey meaning, to evoke mood, or simply to create a musical effect. For example, Edgar Allan Poe uses internal rhyme in the poem "The Raven":

Once upon a midnight <u>dreary</u>, while I pondered, weak and <u>weary</u>

See page 1141.
See also RHYME.

Inversion   Reversal of the usual word order in a prose sentence or line of poetry, for emphasis or variety. Writers use inversion to maintain rhyme scheme or meter, or to emphasize certain words.

See page 76.

Irony   A contrast or discrepancy between appearance and reality. **Situational irony** exists when the actual outcome of a situation is the opposite of someone's expectations, as at the end of Kate Chopin's "The Story of an Hour," when the narrator's husband, thought to be dead, arrives at the front door. In **verbal irony,** a person says one thing and means another, as when someone says of a mean person, "Nice guy!" **Dramatic irony** occurs when the audience has important information that the characters do not know.

See pages 228 and 1133.

J–L

Journal. A daily record of events kept by a participant in those events or a witness to them.

> See page 361.

Juxtaposition The placing of two or more distinct things side by side in order to contrast or compare them. It is commonly used to evoke an emotional response in the reader. For example, in her poem "Richness," Gabriela Mistral juxtaposes the images of a rose and a thorn.

I have a faithful joy
And a joy that is lost.
One is like a rose,
The other, a thorn.

> See page 601.

Legend A traditional story handed down from the past, based on actual people and events, and tending to become more exaggerated and fantastical over time. For example, "The Sky Tree," as retold by Joseph Bruchac, is a legend about how the earth came to be.

> See also FABLE, FOLKLORE, FOLKTALE, HERO,
> MYTH, ORAL TRADITION, TALL TALE.

Literal language Language that is simple, straightforward, and free of embellishment. It is the opposite of figurative language, which conveys ideas indirectly.

> See page 677.
> See also DENOTATION.

Local color The evocative portrayal of a region's distinctive ways of talking and behaving. Bret Harte's story "The Outcasts of Poker Flats" is classic for its use of local color.

> See pages 455, 475, and 730.
> See also DIALECT, REGIONALISM,
> VERNACULAR.

Lyric poetry Poetry that expresses a speaker's personal thoughts and feelings. Lyric poems are usually short and musical. Emily Dickinson's "This is my letter to the World" is an example of a lyric poem.

> See page 746.
> See also POETRY.

M

Magical realism A literary style in which the writer combines realistic events, settings, characters, dialogue, and other details with elements that are magical, supernatural, fantastic, or bizarre. For example, in "Nineteen Thirty-Seven," the narrator's suggestion that certain women could fly with "wings of flames" implies a magical or supernatural quality about these women.

> See page 1007.

Memoir An account of an event or period emphasizing the narrator's own experience of it. "Prime Time," by Henry Louis Gates Jr., is an example of a memoir.

> See page 1107.
> See also AUTOBIOGRAPHY, BIOGRAPHY.

Metaphor A figure of speech that compares or equates two seemingly unlike things. In contrast to a simile, a metaphor implies the comparison instead of stating it directly; hence there is no use of connectives such as *like* or *as.* For example, in her story "Rain Music," Longhang Nguyen writes of her sister and herself:

She is the rose of the family and I am the green thorn.

> See pages 399 and 794.
> See also EXTENDED METAPHOR, FIGURATIVE
> LANGUAGE.

Meter A regular pattern of stressed (´) and unstressed (˘) syllables that gives a line of poetry a more or less predictable rhythm. The basic unit of meter is the **foot.** The length of a metrical line can be expressed in terms of the number of feet it contains: a **dimeter** has two feet, a **trimeter** three, a **tetrameter** four, a **pentameter** five, a **hexameter** six, and a **heptameter** seven. The following lines from "Old Ironsides," by Oliver Wendell Holmes, show one line of iambic tetrameter and one line of iambic trimeter:

Aˇy, teár heˇr táttěred eńsǐgn dówn!

Lońg haˇs ǐt waˊveˇd oˇn hiǵh

> See page 1163.
> See also FOOT, IAMBIC PENTAMETER, METER,
> SCANSION.

Metonymy   The use of one word to stand for a related term. When Emerson writes that the "sun shines into a child's heart," he uses *heart* to stand for soul, or deep emotions.

> See page 241.
> See also FIGURATIVE LANGUAGE.

Modernism   A term applied to a variety of twentieth-century artistic movements that shared a desire to break with the past. The poetry of T. S. Eliot and Ezra Pound, with its novel subject matter, diction, and metrical patterns, came to define Modernism. One example is Eliot's "The Love Song of J. Alfred Prufrock."

> See page 593.
> See also IMAGIST POETRY, STREAM OF
> CONSCIOUSNESS, SYMBOLIST POETRY.

Monologue   A long speech by a character in a literary work.

> See also DRAMATIC MONOLOGUE, SOLILOQUY.

Mood   The emotional quality or atmosphere of a literary work. A writer's choice of language, subject matter, setting, and tone, as well as such sound devices as rhyme and rhythm, contribute to creating mood.

> See page 1065.
> See also ATMOSPHERE, SETTING, TONE.

Moral   A practical lesson about right and wrong conduct.

Motif   A significant phrase, image, description, idea, or other element repeated throughout a literary work and related to the theme.

> See page 1137.

Motivation   The stated or implied reason or cause for a character's actions.

> See also PSYCHOLOGICAL REALISM.

Myth   A traditional story that deals with goddesses, gods, heroes, and supernatural forces. A myth may explain a belief, a custom, or a force of nature. "How the World Was Made" is an origin myth.

> See pages 46, 1118, and 1196.
> See also EPIC, FOLKLORE, FOLKTALE, LEGEND,
> ORAL TRADITION.

N

Narrative   Writing or speech that tells a story. Narrative writing is used in novels, short stories, and poetry, and it may also be an important element in biographies, autobiographies, memoirs, and essays.

> See page 1060.
> See also NARRATIVE POETRY.

Narrative poetry   Verse that tells a story. Narrative poetry includes narrative ballads and epics as well as shorter forms that are usually more selective and concentrated than are prose stories. "The Raven," by Edgar Allan Poe, for example, is a narrative poem.

> See also BALLAD, EPIC, NARRATIVE.

Narrator   The person who tells a story. The narrator may be a character in the story, as in Ali Deb's "The Three-Piece Suit." At other times the narrator stands outside the story, as in F. Scott Fitzgerald's "The Bridal Party."

> See page 66.
> See also NARRATIVE, POINT OF VIEW.

Naturalism   The literary movement characterized by a belief that people have little control over their own lives. Naturalist writers such as Frank Norris and Stephen Crane focus on the powerful economic, social, and environmental forces that shape the lives of individuals. In Crane's "The Open Boat," for example, four men face the power of the relentless sea.

> See pages 455 and 576.
> See also PSYCHOLOGICAL REALISM.

Nonfiction   Factual prose writing about real people, places, and events. Written from either the first- or third-person point of view, works of **narrative nonfiction** tell a story and commonly have characteristics of fiction, such as setting, characters, theme, and plot. Biographies, autobiographies, memoirs, and narrative essays are types of narrative nonfiction. Works of **informative nonfiction** include essays, speeches, and articles that explain a topic or promote an opinion.

> See pages 26–27.
> See also AUTOBIOGRAPHY, BIOGRAPHY, ESSAY,
> FICTION.

Novel   A book-length fictional prose narrative. The novel has more scope than a short story in its presentation of plot, character, setting, and theme.

>   See also FICTION, SHORT STORY.

O

Octave.   The first eight lines of a **Petrarchan,** or **Italian, sonnet.**

>   See page 721.
>   See also SONNET.

Ode   An elaborate **lyric poem** expressed in a dignified and sincere way. An ode may be imaginative as well as intellectual.

>   See page 791.
>   See also LYRIC POETRY.

Onomatopoeia   The use of a word or phrase that actually imitates or suggests the sound of what it describes. The word *murmur,* used in "Speaking," by Simon J. Ortiz, is an example of onomatopoeia.

>   See pages 399 and 1076.
>   See also SOUND DEVICES.

Oral tradition   Literature that passes by word of mouth from one generation to the next.

>   See page 46.
>   See also BALLAD, EPIC, FOLKLORE, FOLKTALE,
>   LEGEND, MYTH, TALL TALE.

Oxymoron   A figure of speech in which opposite ideas are combined. Examples are "bright darkness," "wise fool," and "hateful love."

>   See also FIGURATIVE LANGUAGE, PARADOX.

P–Q

Parable   A simple story pointing to a moral or religious lesson. Nathaniel Hawthorne's short story "The Minister's Black Veil" is a parable.

>   See page 265.
>   See also FABLE.

Paradox   A situation or statement that seems to be impossible or contradictory but is nevertheless true, literally or figuratively. For example, in "The Useless," Chuang Tzu concludes with a paradox.

This shows
The absolute necessity
Of what has "no use."

>   See also OXYMORON.

Parallelism   The use of a series of words, phrases, or sentences that have similar grammatical form. Parallelism emphasizes the items that are arranged in similar structures. For example, Walt Whitman uses parallelism in *Song of Myself*:

What do you think has become of the young and
   old men?
And what do you think has become of the
   women and children?

>   See page 386.
>   See also REPETITION.

Parody   A humorous imitation of another literary work. A parody imitates another work's plot, characters, or style, usually through exaggeration. See the parodies of Emily Dickinson's poetry on page 439.

>   See also COMEDY, FARCE, HUMOR, SATIRE.

Personification   A figure of speech in which an animal, an object, a force of nature, or an idea is given human characteristics. The following lines from Emily Dickinson's "Because I could not stop for Death" exemplify personification:

Because I could not stop for Death—
He kindly stopped for me—

>   See pages 399 and 1192.
>   See also APOSTROPHE, FIGURATIVE
>   LANGUAGE.

Persuasion   Writing, usually nonfiction, that attempts to influence the reader to think or act in a particular way. Writers of persuasive works use appeals to logic or emotion, entreaty, salesmanship, and other techniques to sway their readers. Thomas Paine's "The Crisis" is an excellent example of persuasive writing.

>   See pages 347, 348, and 392–396.
>   See also ARGUMENT.

Petrarchan sonnet. See SONNET.

Plain style A style of writing common among the Puritan settlers that focused on communicating ideas as clearly as possible. This marked a change from ornate style, the complicated and decorative style used by writers in Europe at that time. Colonial writers such as William Bradford thought of writing as a practical tool for spiritual self-examination and religious instruction, not as an opportunity to demonstrate cleverness.

> See page 43.

Plot The sequence of events in a drama or a narrative work of fiction. The plot begins with **exposition,** which introduces the story's characters, setting, and situation. The plot catches the reader's attention with a **narrative hook.** The **rising action** adds complications to the **conflicts,** or problems, leading to the **climax,** or the point of highest emotional pitch. The **falling action** is the logical result of the climax, and the **resolution,** or **dénouement,** presents the final outcome.

> See pages 276, 473, 528, and 909.
> See also CLIMAX, CONFLICT, DÉNOUEMENT,
> EXPOSITION, FALLING ACTION,
> RESOLUTION, RISING ACTION.

Poetic license The freedom given to poets to ignore standard rules of grammar or proper diction in order to create a desired artistic effect.

> See page 1121.

Poetry A form of literary expression that differs from prose in emphasizing the line, rather than the sentence, as the unit of composition. Many other traditional characteristics of poetry apply to some poems but not to others. Some of these characteristics are emotional, imaginative language; use of **metaphor, simile,** and other **figures of speech;** division into **stanzas;** and the use of **rhyme** and regular patterns of **meter.**

> See pages 20–21, 398–399, 440–443, and
> 762–765.

Point of view The relationship of the narrator, or storyteller, to the story. In a story with **first-person point of view,** the story is told by one of the characters, referred to as "I." The reader sees everything through that character's eyes. In a story with a **third-person limited point of view,** the narrator reveals the thoughts, feelings, and observations of only one character, but refers to that character as "he" or "she." In a story with an **omniscient,** or **all-knowing point of view,** the narrator knows everything about the characters and events and may reveal details that the characters themselves could not reveal.

> See pages 377, 472, 540, and 1051.
> See also NARRATOR, SPEAKER.

Props Theater term (a shortened form of *properties*) for objects and elements of the scenery of a stage play or movie set. For example in act 1 of *The Crucible,* Arthur Miller writes:

[*There is a narrow window at the left. Through its leaded panes the morning sunlight streams. A candle still burns near the bed, which is at the right.*]

> See also DRAMA.

Prose Written language that is not versified. Novels, short stories, and essays are usually written in prose.

Protagonist The central character in a literary work, around whom the main conflict revolves. Generally, the audience is meant to sympathize with the protagonist.

> See pages 472 and 1099.
> See also ANTAGONIST, CONFLICT, HERO.

Psychological realism An attempt to portray characters in an objective, plausible manner. Above all else, psychological realism insists that characters be clearly motivated; they should not act without apparent reason.

> See also MOTIVATION, NATURALISM, REALISM.

Quatrain A four-line poem or stanza.

> See also COUPLET, OCTAVE, SESTET, STANZA.

R

Rationalism A philosophy that values reason over feeling or imagination.

> See also ROMANTICISM.

Realism   A literary manner that seeks to portray life as it really is lived. More specifically, Realism was a nineteenth-century literary movement that usually focused on everyday middle- or working-class conditions and characters, often with reformist intent.

> See page 323.
> See also NATURALISM, PSYCHOLOGICAL
>   REALISM.

Refrain   A line or lines repeated regularly, usually in a poem or song. For example, the line "If you follow the drinking gourd" is a refrain in the song "Follow the Drinking Gourd."

> See page 341.
> See also REPETITION.

Regionalism   An emphasis on themes, characters, and settings from a particular geographical region. For example, much of the work of Mark Twain deals with life in Missouri and along the Mississippi River, where he passed his boyhood and youth.

> See also DIALECT, LOCAL COLOR, VERNACULAR.

Repetition   The recurrence of sounds, words, phrases, lines, or stanzas in a speech or piece of writing. Repetition increases the sense of unity in a work and can call attention to particular ideas.

> See pages 58 and 743.
> See also PARALLELISM, REFRAIN.

Resolution   The part of a plot that concludes the falling action by revealing or suggesting the outcome of the central conflict.

> See pages 473 and 492.
> See also CLIMAX, CONFLICT, DÉNOUEMENT,
>   FALLING ACTION, PLOT.

Rhetorical question   A question to which no answer is expected. A rhetorical question is used to emphasize the obvious answer to what is asked. In his biography, Olaudah Equiano uses rhetorical questions to argue against slavery:

Why are parents to lose their children, brothers their sisters, or husbands their wives?

> See page 97.

Rhyme   The repetition of the same stressed vowel sounds and any succeeding sounds in two or more words. For example, *notation* rhymes with *vacation.* **End rhyme** occurs at the ends of lines of poetry. **Internal rhyme** occurs within a single line. **Slant rhyme** occurs when words include sounds that are similar but not identical. Slant rhyme typically involves some variation of **consonance** (the repetition of similar consonant sounds) or **assonance** (the repetition of similar vowel sounds).

> See pages 398, 438, and 1141.
> See also ASSONANCE, CONSONANCE, INTERNAL
>   RHYME, RHYME SCHEME, SOUND
>   DEVICES.

Rhyme scheme   The pattern that end rhymes form in a stanza or a poem. The rhyme scheme is designated by the assignment of a different letter of the alphabet to each new rhyme. For example, the rhyme scheme in Edgar Allan Poe's "To Helen" is:

Helen, thy beauty is to me	*a*
Like those Nicéan barks of yore,	*b*
That gently, o'er a perfumed sea,	*a*
The weary, way-worn wanderer bore	*b*
To his own native shore.	*b*

> See pages 398 and 702.
> See also RHYME.

Rhythm   The pattern of beats created by the arrangement of stressed and unstressed syllables, especially in poetry. Rhythm gives poetry a musical quality, can add emphasis to certain words, and may help convey the poem's meaning. Rhythm can be regular, with a predictable pattern or meter, or irregular. Notice how the rhythm of the first two lines of E. E. Cummings's "anyone lived in a pretty how town" gives a lilting quality to the poem.

Anyone lived in a pretty how town

(with up so floating many bells down)

> See pages 237, 398, and 644.
> See also IAMBIC PENTAMETER, METER.

Rising action   The part of a plot in which actions, complications, and plot twists lead up to the **climax** of a story.

> See pages 282 and 473.
> See also CLIMAX, CONFLICT, PLOT.

Romanticism   An artistic movement that valued imagination and feeling over intellect and reason. Ralph Waldo Emerson, Henry David Thoreau, and Walt Whitman were heavily influenced by Romanticism.

> See pages 125, 218, and 323.
> See also RATIONALISM, TRANSCENDENTALISM.

Round character.   **See CHARACTER.**

S

Sarcasm   Satire or irony that often uses bitter and caustic language to point out shortcomings or flaws.

> See page 1095.
> See also IRONY, SATIRE.

Satire   Literature that exposes to ridicule the vices or follies of people or societies. Donald Barthelme's story "Game" is an example of satire.

> See also COMEDY, FARCE, HUMOR, PARODY,
>   SARCASM, WIT.

Scansion   The analysis of the meter of a line of verse. To scan a line of poetry means to note the stressed and unstressed syllables and to divide the line into its feet, or rhythmical units. Stressed syllables are marked (´) and unstressed syllables (˘). Note the scansion of these lines from Claude McKay's "The Tropics in New York":

Bă·nán / ăs rípe / ănd gréen, / ănd gín / gĕr-roót,

   Cócŏa / ĭn póds / ănd áll / ĭgát / ŏr peárs,

> See page 750.
> See also FOOT, METER, RHYTHM.

Scene   A subdivision of an act in a play. Typically, each scene takes place in a specific setting and time. A scene is shorter than or as long as an act.

> See page 909.
> See also ACT, DRAMA.

Science fiction   Fiction that deals with the impact of science and technology—real or imagined—on society and on individuals. Sometimes occurring in the future, science fiction commonly portrays space travel, exploration of other planets, and possible future societies.

Screenplay   The script of a film, which, in addition to dialogue and stage directions, usually contains detailed instructions about camera shots and angles.

> See also STAGE DIRECTIONS.

Sensory details   Evocative words or phrases that appeal to one or more of the five senses. "The Beautiful Changes," by Richard Wilbur, uses sensory details that appeal to the sense of sight.

> See page 862.
> See also IMAGERY.

Sestet   A six-line poem or stanza.

> See page 721.
> See also SONNET.

Setting   The time and place in which the events of a literary work occur. Setting includes not only the physical surroundings, but also the ideas, customs, values, and beliefs of a particular time and place. The setting often helps create an atmosphere, or mood.

> See pages 472, 510, and 908.
> See also ATMOSPHERE, MOOD.

Shakespearean sonnet.   **See SONNET.**

Short story   A brief fictional narrative in prose that generally includes the following major elements: setting, characters, plot, point of view, and theme.

> See pages 276 and 472–473.
> See also CHARACTER, PLOT, POINT OF VIEW,
>   SETTING, THEME.

Simile   A figure of speech using a word or phrase such as *like* or *as* to compare seemingly unlike things. For example, this famous simile appears at the opening of T. S. Eliot's "The Love Song of J. Alfred Prufrock":

Let us go then, you and I,
When the evening is spread out against the sky
Like a patient etherised upon a table. . . .

> See pages 25, 399, and 637.
> See also ANALOGY, FIGURATIVE LANGUAGE,
>   METAPHOR.

Slave narrative   An autobiographical account of the life of a former enslaved person. These documents helped expose the cruelty and inhumanity of slavery.

> See page 195.
> See also AUTOBIOGRAPHY, MEMOIR.

Soliloquy In a drama, a long speech by a character who is alone on stage. A soliloquy reveals the private thoughts and emotions of that character.

> See also DRAMATIC MONOLOGUE, MONOLOGUE.

Sonnet A lyric poem of fourteen lines, typically written in iambic pentameter and usually following strict patterns of stanza divisions and rhymes.

The **Shakespearean,** or **English, sonnet** consists of three **quatrains,** or four-line stanzas, followed by a **couplet,** or pair of rhyming lines. The rhyme scheme is typically *abab, cdcd, efef, gg.* The rhyming couplet often presents a conclusion to the issues or questions presented in the three quatrains.

In the **Petrarchan,** or **Italian, sonnet,** fourteen lines are divided into two stanzas, the eight-line **octave** and the six-line **sestet.** The sestet usually responds to a question or situation posed by the octave. The rhyme scheme for the octave is typically *abbaabba;* for the sestet the rhyme scheme is typically *cdecde.*

> See page 545.
> See also COUPLET, RHYME SCHEME, STANZA.

Sound devices Techniques used, especially in poetry, to appeal to the ear. Writers use sound devices to enhance the sense of rhythm, to emphasize particular sounds, or to add to the musical quality of their writing. Examples of sound devices include alliteration, assonance, consonance, onomatopoeia, and rhyme.

> See page 399.
> See also ALLITERATION, ASSONANCE, CONSONANCE, ONOMATOPOEIA, RHYME.

Speaker The voice of a poem, similar to a narrator in a work of prose. Sometimes the speaker's voice is that of the poet, sometimes that of a fictional person or even a thing. The speaker's words communicate a particular **tone,** or attitude, toward the subject of the poem. For example, in Anne Bradstreet's "To My Dear and Loving Husband," the speaker addresses her husband in a tone of passionate devotion.

> See pages 398 and 633.
> See also TONE.

Stage directions Instructions written by the dramatist to describe the appearance and actions of characters, as well as the sets, costumes, and lighting. Arthur Miller's play *The Crucible* contains numerous stage directions.

> See page 956.
> See also DRAMA, SCREENPLAY.

Stanza A group of lines forming a unit in a poem. A stanza in a poem is similar to a paragraph in prose. Typically, stanzas in a poem are separated by a line of space.

> See page 761.
> See also COUPLET, OCTAVE, QUATRAIN, SESTET, SONNET, TRIPLET.

Stereotype A character who is not developed as an individual, but instead represents a collection of traits and mannerisms supposedly shared by all members of a group.

> See also CHARACTER.

Stream of consciousness The literary representation of a character's free-flowing thoughts, feelings, and memories. Much stream-of-consciousness writing does not employ conventional sentence structure or other rules of grammar and usage. Parts of T. S. Eliot's poem "The Love Song of J. Alfred Prufrock" exemplify stream of consciousness.

> See pages 603 and 629.
> See also SURREALIST POETRY.

Structure The particular order or pattern a writer uses to present ideas. Narratives commonly follow a chronological order, while the structure of persuasive or expository writing may vary. Listing detailed information, using cause and effect, or describing a problem and then offering a solution are some other ways a writer can present a topic.

> See page 895.

Style The expressive qualities that distinguish an author's work, including word choice and the length and arrangement of sentences, as well as the use of figurative language and imagery. Style can reveal an author's attitude and purpose in writing.

> See page 684.
> See also AUTHOR'S PURPOSE, FIGURATIVE LANGUAGE, IMAGERY, TONE.

Surrealist poetry   Poetry that expresses the workings of the unconscious mind and how these workings interact with outer reality. This poetry is characterized by the use of images from dreams and stream-of-consciousness associations. Anne Sexton's poem "Riding the Elevator into the Sky" has elements of surrealism.

> See page 1126.
> See also STREAM OF CONSCIOUSNESS.

Suspense   A feeling of curiosity, uncertainty, or even dread about what is going to happen next. Writers increase the level of suspense in a story by creating a threat to the central character, or **protagonist,** and giving readers clues to what might happen.

> See page 305.
> See also PROTAGONIST.

Symbol   Any object, person, place, or experience that exists on a literal level but also represents something else, usually something abstract. For example, in "The Bridal Party," F. Scott Fitzgerald writes:

> . . . the Graf Zeppelin, shining and glorious, symbol of escape and destruction—of escape, if necessary, through destruction—glided in the Paris sky.

> See pages 399 and 618.
> See also ALLEGORY, FIGURATIVE LANGUAGE.

Symbolist poetry   A kind of poetry that emphasizes suggestion and inward experience instead of explicit description. The symbolist poets influenced twentieth-century writers such as T. S. Eliot and Ezra Pound.

> See also IMAGIST POETRY, MODERNISM.

T

Tall tale   A type of folklore associated with the American frontier. Tall tales are humorous stories that contain wild exaggerations and invention. Typically, their heroes are bold but sometimes foolish characters who may have superhuman abilities or who may act as if they do. Tall tales are not intended to be believable; their exaggerations are used for comic effect, as in Mark Twain's "The Celebrated Jumping Frog of Calaveras County," when Simon Wheeler describes the frog:

> "[Y]ou'd see that frog whirling in the air like a doughnut—see him turn one summerset, or maybe a couple, if he got a good start, and come down flat-footed and all right, like a cat."

> See page 214.
> See also FOLKLORE, FOLKTALE.

Technical vocabulary   Words that are unique to a particular art, science, profession, or trade. Technical vocabulary may provide authority or enhance the sense of realism. In her poem "Geometry," Rita Dove uses the terms *theorem* and *intersect* from the technical vocabulary of geometry.

> See also DICTION.

Theme   The central message of a work of literature that readers can apply to life. Some works have a **stated theme,** which is expressed directly. More works have an **implied theme,** which is revealed gradually through events, dialogue, or description. A literary work may have more than one theme.

> See pages 233, 276, 473, and 801.
> See also AUTHOR'S PURPOSE, FABLE, MORAL.

Thesis   The main idea of a work of nonfiction. The thesis may be stated directly or implied.

> See also NONFICTION.

Third-person point of view. See POINT OF VIEW.

Tone   A reflection of a writer's or a speaker's attitude toward the subject matter, as conveyed through elements such as word choice, punctuation, sentence structure, and figures of speech. A writer's tone might convey a variety of attitudes such as sympathy, objectivity, or humor.

> See pages 109 and 515.
> See also AUTHOR'S PURPOSE, DICTION, FIGURATIVE LANGUAGE, STYLE, VOICE.

Tragedy   A play in which a main character suffers a downfall. That character, the **tragic hero,** is typically a person of dignified or heroic stature. The downfall may

Lack of Clear Pronoun Reference

Problem: A pronoun reference that is weak or vague.

The cast performed well, (which) was the result of hard work. *ref*

There were no prices on the merchandise, and (that) bothered me. *ref*

The book says to sand (it) before painting it. *ref*

Solution A: Rewrite the sentence, adding a clear antecedent for the pronoun.

The cast gave a wonderful performance, which was the result of hard work.

Solution B: Rewrite the sentence, substituting a noun for the pronoun.

There were no prices on the merchandise, and the lack of information bothered me.

The book says to sand the wood before painting it.

Problem: A pronoun that could refer to more than one antecedent

When Marta and Helen picked up the magazines, (they) were dirty. *ref*

Midori told her mother that (she) should look for a new job. *ref*

Solution A: Rewrite the sentence, substituting a noun for the pronoun.

When Marta and Helen picked up the magazines, the covers were dirty.

Solution B: Rewrite the sentence, making the antecedent of the pronoun clear.

Midori told her mother to look for a new job.

Problem: The indefinite use of *you* or *they*

Is there still a law that (you) cannot drive faster than 55 miles per hour? *ref*

In Australia, (they) have winter when it is summer here. *ref*

Solution A: Rewrite the sentence, substituting a noun for the pronoun.

Is there still a law that motorists cannot drive faster than 55 miles per hour?

Solution B: Rewrite the sentence, eliminating the pronoun entirely.

In Australia, the winter season arrives when it is summer here.

Shift in Pronoun

Problem: An incorrect shift in person between two pronouns

I always study in the library because (you) can concentrate there. *pro*

One should feel lucky when (you) have good health. *pro*

They looked for a new television at the mall, where (you) can find bargains. *pro*

Solution A: Replace the incorrect pronoun with a pronoun that agrees with its antecedent.

I always study in the library because I can concentrate there.

One should feel lucky when one has good health.

They looked for a new television at the mall, where they can find bargains.

Solution B: Replace the pronoun with an appropriate noun.

I always study in the library because students can concentrate there.

They looked for a new television at the mall, where shoppers can find bargains.

Shift in Verb Tense

Problem: An unnecessary shift in tense

Since the clinic was so busy, the doctor (sees) ten patients in an hour. *shift t*

I rented a video while Maria (is making) popcorn for all of us. *shift t*

Solution: When two or more events occur at the same time, be sure to use the same verb tense to describe each event.

Since the clinic was so busy, the doctor saw ten patients in an hour.

I rented a video while Maria made popcorn for all of us.

Problem: A lack of correct shift in tenses to show that one event precedes or follows another

By the time I finished my homework, my sister (came) home from work. *shift t*

Solution: When two events have occurred at different times in the past, shift from the past tense to the past perfect tense to indicate that one action began and ended before another past action began.

By the time I finished my homework, my sister had come home from work.

> **Rule of Thumb:** When you need to use several verb tenses in your writing, it may help to first jot down the sequence of events you're writing about. Be clear in your mind what happened first, next, and last.

Incorrect Verb Tense or Form

Problem: An incorrect or missing verb ending

Krista (heat) the frying pan before she added the eggs. *tense*

The guard had (question) the visitor at the bank. *tense*

Solution: Add *-ed* to a regular verb to form the past tense and the past participle.

Krista heated the frying pan before she added the eggs.

The guard had questioned the visitor at the bank.

Problem: An improperly formed irregular verb

The pitcher (throwed) the ball to second base. *tense*

The runner on third had already (stealed) home. *tense*

Solution: Irregular verbs form their past and past participles in some way other than by adding *-ed.* Memorize irregular verb forms, or look them up.

The pitcher threw the ball to second base.

The runner on third had already stolen home.

Problem: Confusion between the past form and the past participle

Teka's new shoes (have tore) her pantyhose. *tense*

The poet (has wove) a theme of sorrow throughout her new poem. *tense*

Solution: Use the past participle form of an irregular verb, not the past form, when you use any form of the auxiliary verb *have*.

Teka's new shoes have torn her pantyhose.

The poet has woven a theme of sorrow throughout her new poem.

Problem: Improper use of the past participle

Jon (seen) the squirrel carry nuts from the tree. *tense*

The officers (given) medals to the war veterans. *tense*

Solution A: The past participle of an irregular verb cannot stand alone as a verb. Add a form of the auxiliary verb *have* to the past participle to form a complete verb.

Jon has seen the squirrel carry nuts from the tree.

The officers have given medals to the war veterans.

Solution B: Replace the past participle with the past form of the verb.

Jon saw the squirrel carry nuts from the tree.

The officers gave medals to the war veterans.

Misplaced or Dangling Modifier

Problem: A misplaced modifier

Emily borrowed a sweater from her cousin (that was too small.) *mod*

(With no horn or brakes,) the twins bought the old car. *mod*

Solution: Modifiers that modify the wrong word or that seem to modify more than one idea in a sentence are called misplaced modifiers. Move the misplaced phrase as close as possible to the word or words it modifies.

Emily borrowed a sweater that was too small from her cousin.

The twins bought the old car with no horn or brakes.

Problem: Incorrect placement of the adverb *only*

We (only) have study hall twice a week. *mod*

Solution: Place the adverb *only* immediately before the word or group of words it modifies.

Only we have study hall twice a week.

We have only study hall twice a week.

We have study hall only twice a week.

> **Rule of Thumb:** Note that each time *only* is moved, the meaning of the sentence changes. Check to be sure your sentence says what you mean.

Problem: A dangling modifier

(Knowing little Spanish,) the textbook was difficult to understand. *mod*

(Coming home late last night,) the front door was locked and bolted. *mod*

(Driving through the tunnel,) the tollbooth was blocked by traffic. *mod*

Solution: Dangling modifiers do not logically seem to modify any word in the sentence. Rewrite the sentence, adding a noun to which the dangling phrase clearly refers. Often you will have to add other words, too.

Knowing little Spanish, Jenny found that the textbook was difficult to understand.

Coming home late last night, I realized that the front door was locked and bolted.

Driving through the tunnel, my father reached the tollbooth, which was blocked by traffic.

Missing or Misplaced Possessive Apostrophe

Problem: Singular nouns

My (aunts) dog is a beagle. *poss*

(Jess) story was fascinating. *poss*

Solution: Use an apostrophe and *-s* to form the possessive of a singular noun or a proper name, even if the noun ends in *s*.

My aunt's dog is a beagle.

Jess's story was fascinating.

Problem: Plural nouns ending in -s

The (birds) songs sounded sweet, even so early in the morning. *poss*

Solution: Use an apostrophe alone to form the possessive of a plural noun that ends in -s.

The birds' songs sounded sweet, even so early in the morning.

Problem: Plural nouns not ending in -s

The (childrens) grandparents baked them chocolate chip cookies. *poss*

Solution: Use an apostrophe and -s to form the possessive of a plural noun that does not end in -s.

The children's grandparents baked them chocolate chip cookies.

Problem: Pronouns

(Someones) package is at the lost and found desk. *poss*

Is it (your's?) *poss*

Solution A: Use an apostrophe and -s to form the possessive of a singular indefinite pronoun.

Someone's package is at the lost and found desk.

Solution B: Do not use an apostrophe with any of the possessive personal pronouns.

Is it yours?

Problem: Confusion between *its* and *it's*

As the dragon roared, (it's) fiery breath consumed everything around it. *poss*

The detective said, ("Its) true that the butler committed the crime." *cont*

Solution A: Do not use an apostrophe to form the possessive of *it*.

As the dragon roared, its fiery breath consumed everything around it.

Solution B: Use an apostrophe to form the contraction of *it is*.

The detective said, "It's true that the butler committed the crime."

Missing Commas with Nonessential Elements

Problem: Missing commas with nonessential participles, infinitives, and their phrases

Lynda delighted with the message immediately called Rick with the news. *com*

The professor browsing through some old books found a rare first edition. *com*

To be honest a gardener does not need a green thumb. *com*

Solution: Determine whether the participle, infinitive, or phrase is essential to the meaning of the sentence or not. If it is not essential, set off the phrase with commas.

Lynda, delighted with the message, immediately called Rick with the news.

The professor, browsing through some old books, found a rare first edition.

To be honest, a gardener does not need a green thumb.

Problem: Missing commas with nonessential adjective clauses

My running shoes which have reflective patches were falling apart. *com*

Solution: Determine whether the clause is essential to the meaning of the sentence or not. If it is not essential, set off the clause with commas.

My running shoes, which have reflective patches, were falling apart.

Problem: Missing commas with nonessential appositives

The librarian a creative woman held a story hour for beginning readers. *com*

Solution: Determine whether the appositive is essential to the meaning of the sentence or not. If it is not essential, set off the appositive with commas.

The librarian, a creative woman, held a story hour for beginning readers.

> **Rule of Thumb:** To determine whether a word, phrase, or clause is essential, try reading the sentence without it.

Problem: Missing commas with interjections and parenthetical expressions

Oops I dropped the glass on the floor! *com*

The junior class party I think will be held in the gym. *com*

Solution: Set off the interjection or parenthetical expression with commas.

Oops, I dropped the glass on the floor!

The junior class party, I think, will be held in the gym.

Missing Comma in a Series

Problem: Missing commas in a series of words, phrases, or clauses

Meg bought new pillows sheets and curtains. *com*

I walked into the attic through the closet and behind the bed to find the trunk with the costumes. *com*

Victor saved his money so he could fly to Chicago stay in a hotel and go sightseeing. *com*

The clowns performed tricks the lions roared the elephants paraded and the ringmaster cracked his whip. *com*

Solution: When there are three or more elements in a series, use a comma after each element that precedes the conjunction.

Meg bought new pillows, sheets, and curtains.

I walked into the attic, through the closet, and behind the bed to find the trunk with the costumes.

Victor saved his money so he could fly to Chicago, stay in a hotel, and go sightseeing.

The clowns performed tricks, the lions roared, the elephants paraded, and the ringmaster cracked his whip.

> **Rule of Thumb:** When you're having difficulty with a rule of usage, try rewriting the rule in your own words. Then check with your teacher to be sure you have grasped the concept.

Troublesome Words

This section will help you choose between words that are often confused. It also alerts you to avoid certain words and expressions in school or business writing.

a, an

Use *a* when the word that follows begins with a consonant sound, including a sounded *h,* or with the "yew" sound. Use the article *an* when the word that follows begins with a vowel sound.

> **A** little puppy might become **a** huge dog.
>
> The ballplayer wore **a** uniform and carried **an** umbrella and **an** overcoat.

a lot, alot

The expression *a lot* means "a large amount" or "a great deal" (as in "I like him a lot") and should always be written as two words. Some authorities discourage its use in formal English.

> Informal: There have been **a lot** of tourists in town this summer.
>
> Formal: There have been **many** tourists in town this summer.

a while, awhile

An article and a noun form the expression *a while.* Often the preposition *in* or *for* precedes *a while,* forming a prepositional phrase. The single word *awhile* is an adverb.

> Once in **a while,** I like to walk to the lake.
>
> For **a while,** I walked to the lake each day.
>
> I waited **awhile** before I walked to the lake.

ability, capacity

Ability and *capacity* both mean "the power to do something." *Ability* also means "skill or talent." *Capacity* also means "the maximum amount that can be contained."

> Not all birds have the **ability** to fly. For example, the ostrich does not have the **capacity** to fly.
>
> My guitar teacher says I have a great deal of musical **ability.**
>
> The tank has a **capacity** of twenty gallons.

accept, except

Accept is a verb meaning "to receive" or "to agree to." *Except* may be a preposition or a verb. As a preposition, it means "but." As a verb, it means "to leave out."

> I **accept** the nomination for president of the student council. **Except** for Ari, the other candidates are not good campaigners.
>
> If we **except** him, I don't have any strong opponents.

adapt, adopt

Adapt means "to change something so that it can be used for another purpose" or "to adjust." *Adopt* means "to take something for one's own."

The writer will **adapt** his novel for a film.

Dogs often **adapt** to the cold weather by growing a thick undercoat of fur.

The city council agreed to **adopt** the new ordinance.

advice, advise

Advice (əd vīs′), a noun, means "helpful opinion." *Advise* (əd vīz′), a verb, means "to give advice or offer counsel."

To **advise** Ramona to exercise more and to eat less was good; unfortunately, she hasn't taken the **advice.**

affect, effect

Affect, a verb, means "to cause a change in" or "to influence." As a noun, *effect* means "result." *Effect* as a verb means "to bring about or accomplish."

Will the heavy traffic **affect** our travel time?

The **effect** of the heavy traffic was to make us late.

We should **effect** a right turn, away from the heavy traffic.

ain't

Ain't is never used in formal speaking or writing unless you are quoting the exact words of a character or real person. Instead of using *ain't,* say or write, *am not; is not;* and so on.

They **aren't** playing by the rules.

all ready, already

All ready means "completely ready." *Already,* an adverb, means "before" or "by this time."

By the time Danielle was **all ready** to go hiking, everyone else was **already** on the trail.

all right, alright

This expression should always be written as two words.

Everything seemed **all right** after the storm.

all together, altogether

All together means "in a group." *Altogether* is an adverb meaning "completely" or "on the whole."

Nana was **altogether** delighted when the family went **all together** to the reunion.

allusion, illusion

Allusion means "an indirect reference." *Illusion* refers to "a false idea or appearance."

Mr. Kim made an **allusion** to the designer's ability to create an **illusion** of elegance using commonplace objects.

anxious, eager

Anxious means "uneasy or worried about some event or situation." *Eager* means "having a keen interest, feeling impatient for something expected."

Anxious for the skiers' safety, the ski patrol closed the mountain. The skiers were **eager** to get back on the slopes.

anywheres, everywheres

Write these words and others like them without a final *s: anywhere, everywhere, somewhere.*

The family searched **everywhere** for their lost pet.

assure, ensure, insure

Assure means "to guarantee something to someone." *Ensure* means "to make a situation safe." *Insure* means "to assure the payment of a sum of money in certain circumstances."

At the garage sale, Cassie **assured** everyone that the stereo worked perfectly.

To **ensure** the financial security of the condominium, the board of directors voted to **insure** the building against fires.

bad, badly

Use *bad* as an adjective (to modify nouns and pronouns). *Bad* often follows a linking verb. Use *badly* as an adverb (to modify verbs, adjectives, or other adverbs). *Badly* almost always follows an action verb.

I felt **bad** after I snapped at my little sister.

The shortstop played so **badly** that the coach took him out of the game.

being as, being that

Although these expressions sometimes replace *because* or *since* in informal conversation, you should always avoid them in formal speaking and writing.

Because of my cold, I could not taste my food.

Since that galaxy is far away, the light we see in the telescope is thousands of years old.

beside, besides

Beside means "next to." *Besides* means "moreover" or "in addition to."

David insisted on sitting **beside** Sara at the restaurant. **Besides** eating three tacos, he finished the salad and the guacamole.

between, among

Between and *among* are prepositions that are used to state a relationship. Use *between* to refer to two persons or things or to compare one person or thing with another person or thing or with an entire group. Use *between* to refer to more than two persons or things considered equals in a close relationship or viewed individually in relation to one another.

Rosalia could not decide **between** the pink sweater and the beige blouse.

We had to choose **between** one large lilac bush and three small rose bushes.

The agreement was worked out **between** the president, the Senate, and the House of Representatives.

Use *among* to show a relationship in which more than two persons or things are considered as a group.

The teacher divided the toys **among** the children.

The eagles flew **among** the clouds.

bring, take

Bring means "to carry from a distant place to a closer one." *Take* means "to carry from a nearby place to a more distant one."

Tasha will **bring** her video camera when she comes.

"**Take** all of these groceries to Mrs. Hall's car," said the manager to the clerk.

can, may

Can implies the ability to do something. *May* implies permission to do something or the possibility of doing it.

I **can** run to the top of the hill without stopping.

May I have some fruit instead of ice cream?

> **Rule of Thumb:** Although *can* is sometimes used in place of *may* in informal speech, a distinction should be made when speaking and writing formally.

can't hardly, can't scarcely

Can't hardly and *can't scarcely* are considered double negatives, since *hardly* and *scarcely* by themselves have a negative meaning. Do not use *hardly* and *scarcely* with *not* or *-n't*.

I **can hardly** believe that the holiday is next week.

The cafeteria food is so bad I **can scarcely** eat it.

capital, capitol

Use *capital* to refer to the city that is the center of government of a state or nation, to money or other assets, or to an uppercase letter. Use *capitol* to refer to the building in which a state or national legislature meets.

She needed a loan, because she did not have enough **capital** to open a shop.

We saw members of Congress on our visit to the **Capitol**, in Washington D.C., the nation's **capital.**

Rule	Example
Use a **hyphen** a. after any prefix joined to a proper noun or proper adjective.	all-American pre-Columbian
b. after the prefixes *all-*, *ex-*, and *self-* joined to any noun or adjective, after the prefix *anti-* when it joins a word beginning with *i*, after the prefix *vice-* (except in *vice president*), and to avoid confusion between words that begin with *re-* and look like another word.	ex-president self-important anti-inflammatory vice-principal re-creation of the event recreation time re-pair the socks repair the computer

> **Rule of Thumb:** Remember that the prefix *anti-* requires a hyphen when followed by a word that begins with *i* in order to prevent spelling words with two successive *i*'s. Otherwise, *anti* does not require a hyphen except before a capitalized word.

Rule	Example
c. in a compound adjective that precedes a noun.	a bitter-tasting liquid
d. in any spelled-out cardinal or ordinal numbers up to *ninety-nine* or *ninety-ninth*, with a fraction used as an adjective, or to separate two numbers in a span.	twenty-three eighty-fifth one-half cup 1914-1918
e. to divide a word at the end of a line between syllables.	air-port scis-sors fill-ing fin-est

Abbreviations

Abbreviations are shortened forms of words.

Rule	Example
Use only one period if an abbreviation occurs at the end of a sentence. If the sentence ends with a question mark or exclamation point, use the period and the second mark of punctuation.	We didn't get home until 3:30 A.M. Did you get home before 4:00 A.M.? I can't believe you didn't get home until 3:30 A.M.!
Capitalize abbreviations of proper nouns and abbreviations related to historical dates.	John Kennedy Jr. P.O. Box 333 800 B.C. A.D. 456 C.E. 1066
Use all capital letters and no periods for most abbreviations of organizations and government agencies.	CBS CIA PIN CPA IBM NFL MADD GE FBI

Rule	Example
Use abbreviations for some personal titles.	Ms. Kasuga; Dr. Platt; Sandra Held, D.D.S.
Abbreviate units of measure used with numerals in technical or scientific writing, but not in ordinary prose.	ft. (foot) in. (inch) oz. (ounce) g (gram) l (liter) m (meter) km (kilometer)

Numbers and Numerals

This section will help you understand when to use numerals and when to spell out numbers.

Rule	Example
In general, spell out cardinal and ordinal numbers that can be written in one or two words.	We just celebrated my brother's twenty-third birthday.
Spell out any number that occurs at the beginning of a sentence.	One hundred forty people bought tickets for the concert.
In general, use numerals (numbers expressed in figures) to express numbers that would be written in more than two words. Extremely high numbers are often expressed as a numeral followed by the word *million* or *billion*.	There are 513 students in our school. The Suarez family donated $1.2 million to the new children's hospital.
If related numbers appear in the same sentence, use all numerals.	Our grammar school had 150 students, but my cousin's had more than 2,000.
Use numerals to express amounts of money, decimals, and percentages.	$45.99 4.59 20.5%
Use numerals to express the day and year in a date and to express the precise time with the abbreviations *A.M.* and *P.M.*	He was supposed to be at the airport on August 31, 1997, at 3:30 P.M.
To express a century when the word century is used, or a decade when the century is clear from the context, spell out the number. When a century and a decade are expressed as a single unit, use numerals followed by -s.	The nineteenth century was a time of turmoil in the United States, especially during the sixties. Do you remember the 1980s?
Use numerals for streets and avenues numbered above ten and for all house, apartment, and room numbers.	Ramona lived at the corner of Fourth and Elm streets. Todd worked in Suite 412, at 1723 West 18th Avenue.

Spelling

The following basic rules, examples, and exceptions will help you master the spellings of many words.

Forming plurals

English words form plurals in many ways. Most nouns simply add -*s*. The following chart shows other ways of forming plural nouns and some common exceptions to the pattern.

GENERAL RULES FOR FORMING PLURALS		
If a word ends in	**Rule**	**Example**
ch, s, sh, x, z	add -*es*	glass, glasses
a consonant + *y*	change *y* to *i* and add -*es*	caddy, caddies
a vowel + *y* or *o*	add only -*s*	cameo, cameos monkey, monkeys
a consonant + *o* common exceptions	generally add -*es* but sometimes add only -*s*	potato, potatoes cello, cellos
f or *ff* common exceptions	add -*s* change *f* to *v* and add -*es*	cliff, cliffs hoof, hooves
lf	change *f* to *v* and add -*es*	half, halves

A few plurals are exceptions to the rules in the previous chart, but they are easy to remember. The following chart lists these plurals and some examples.

SPECIAL RULES FOR FORMING PLURALS	
Rule	**Example**
To form the plural of proper names and one-word compound nouns, follow the general rules for plurals.	Cruz, Cruzes Mancuso, Mancusos crossroad, crossroads
To form the plural of hyphenated compound nouns or compound nouns of more than one word, make the most important word plural.	passer-by, passers-by ghost writer, ghost writers
Some nouns have unusual plural forms.	goose, geese child, children
Some nouns have the same singular and plural forms.	moose scissors pants

Adding prefixes

When adding a prefix to a word, keep the original spelling of the word. Use a hyphen only when the original word is capitalized or with the prefixes *all-*, *ex-*, and *self-* joined to a noun or adjective.

co + operative = cooperative   inter + change = interchange

pro + African = pro-African   ex + partner = ex-partner

Suffixes and the silent *e*

Many English words end in a silent letter *e*. Sometimes the *e* is dropped when a suffix is added. When adding a suffix that begins with a consonant to a word that ends in silent *e*, keep the *e*.

like + ness = likeness   sure + ly = surely

COMMON EXCEPTIONS awe + ful = awful; judge + ment = judgment

When adding a suffix that begins with a vowel to a word that ends in silent *e*, usually drop the *e*.

believe + able = believable   expense + ive = expensive

COMMON EXCEPTION mile + age = mileage

When adding a suffix that begins with *a* or *o* to a word that ends in *ce* or *ge*, keep the *e* so the word will retain the soft *c* or *g* sound.

notice + able = noticeable   courage + ous = courageous

When adding a suffix that begins with a vowel to a word that ends in *ee* or *oe*, keep the final *e*.

see + ing = seeing   toe + ing = toeing

Drop the final silent *e* after the letters *u* or *w*.

argue + ment = argument   owe + ing = owing

Keep the final silent *e* before the suffix *-ing* when necessary to avoid ambiguity.

singe + ing = singeing

Suffixes and the final *y*

When adding a suffix to a word that ends in a consonant + *y*, change the *y* to *i* unless the suffix begins with *i*. Keep the *y* in a word that ends in a vowel + *y*.

try + ed = tried   fry + ed = fried

stay + ing = staying   display + ed = displayed

copy + ing = copying   joy + ous = joyous

Descriptive Writing

Description recreates an experience primarily through the use of sensory details. However, good descriptive writing is more than just a collection of sensory details. A writer should always strive to create a single impression that all the details support. To do so requires careful planning as well as choices about order of information, topic sentences, and figurative language.

Use the checklist at the right as you revise your descriptive writing.

☑ Did I create interest in my introduction?

☑ Are my perspective and my subject clearly stated in my topic sentence?

☑ Did I organize details carefully and consistently?

☑ Did I vary my sentences, including gerund, participial, and infinitive structures where appropriate?

☑ Did I order information effectively?

☑ Have I chosen precise, vivid words?

☑ Do transitions clearly and logically connect the ideas?

☑ Have I used fresh, lively figures of speech and sensory details?

☑ Have I created a strong, unified impression?

Narrative Writing

Narrative writing, whether factual or fictional, tells a story and has these elements: characters, plot, point of view, theme, and setting. The plot usually involves a conflict between a character and an opposing character or force.

Use this checklist as you revise your narrative writing.

☑ Did I introduce characters and a setting?

☑ Did I develop a plot that begins with an interesting problem or conflict?

☑ Did I build suspense, lead the reader to a climax, and end with a resolution?

☑ Did I use dialogue to move the story along?

☑ Did I present a clear and consistent point of view?

☑ Is my writing vivid and expressive?

Persuasive Writing

Persuasive writing expresses a writer's opinion. The goal of persuasion is to make an audience change its opinion and, perhaps, take action. Effective persuasive writing uses strong, relative evidence to support its claims. This kind of writing often requires careful research, organization, and attention to language.

Use this checklist for persuasive writing.

☑ Did I keep my audience's knowledge and attitudes in mind from start to finish?

☑ Did I state my position in a clear thesis statement?

☑ Have I included ample supporting evidence, and is it convincing?

☑ Have I addressed opposing viewpoints?

☑ Have I avoided errors in logic?

☑ Have I used strong, specific words to support my argument?

Research Paper Writing

More than any other type of paper, research papers are the product of a search—a search for data, for facts, for informed opinions, for insights, and for new information.

Kinds of Research Papers

Three common approaches to writing a research paper are listed below. Sometimes writers combine approaches. For example, they might evaluate the research of others and then conduct original research.

- A **summary paper** explores a topic by summing up the opinions of other writers. The author of the paper does not express an opinion about the subject.
- An **evaluative paper** states an opinion and backs it up with evidence found in primary and secondary sources.
- An **original paper** is based on the writer's own original research—for example, observation, experimentation, interviews. It leads to new insights or information about the topic.

Guidelines for Writing a Research Paper

A research paper is almost always a long-term assignment. Set a schedule. If you have six weeks to complete the assignment, your schedule might look like this.

Week 1	Week 2	Week 3	Week 4	Week 5	Week 6
Prewriting Researching and Outlining			**Drafting**	**Revising**	**Editing and Presenting**

Selecting a topic

- If a specific topic is not assigned, choose a topic. Begin with the assigned subject or a subject that interests you. Read general sources of information about that subject and narrow your focus to some aspect of it that interests you. Good places to start are encyclopedia articles and the tables of contents of books on the subject. A computerized library catalog will also display many subheads related to general topics. Find out if sufficient information about your topic is available.
- As you read about the topic, develop your paper's central idea, which is the purpose of your research. Even though this idea might change as you do more research, it can begin to guide your efforts. For example, if you were assigned the subject of the Civil War, you might find that you're interested

- Also credit original ideas that are expressed graphically in tables, charts, and diagrams, as well as the sources of any visual aids you may include, such as photographs.
- You need not cite the source of any information that is common knowledge, such as "John F. Kennedy was assassinated in 1963 in Dallas, Texas."

In-text citations The Modern Language Association (MLA) recommends citations in the text that refer readers to a list of works cited. This style of documentation is parenthetical and consists of two main elements: the author's name and the page number or numbers on which the information is found. Put the documentation at the end of a clause or sentence. The parentheses that enclose it should come before commas and periods, but after quotation marks.

Type of Source	Style of Citation	Example
The author is named in text.	Put page number only in parentheses.	McDonald claims . . . (178)
The author is not named in the text.	Put author's last name and page number in parentheses.	(Goodrich 70–71)
The text has more than one author.	Put authors' last names in parentheses if all are not named in the text.	(McKnight and Williams 145)
No author is listed (usually in magazine articles).	Give title of article, or abbreviation of it, and page number in parentheses.	("Realism" 993)
More than one work by the same author is in the paper.	Include words from the title in the reference.	(Pratt, *Modern Art* 99–102)
You use a quotation that appears in a work written by another author.	Place the abbreviation "qtd. in" before author and page.	(qtd. in Dennis 47)
You refer to a novel, play, or poem.	Include: page and chapter in a novel; part (if there is more than one part) and line number in a poem; act and scene for a play, plus line number for a verse play	(Cather 72, ch. 3) (*Iliad* 9.19) (Jackson 2.2.15–18)
You cite more than one volume of a multivolume work.	Include the volume number and page number.	(Hawaii Volcano Observatory 2:140)
A work in an anthology.	Cite the name of the author not the anthology editor.	(Jeffers 16)

Compiling a list of works cited

At the end of your text, provide an alphabetized list of published works or other sources cited.

- Include complete publishing information for each source.
- For magazine and newspaper articles, include the page numbers. If an article is continued on a different page, use + after the first page number.
- For on-line sources, include the date accessed.
- Cite only those sources from which you actually use information.
- Arrange entries in alphabetical order according to the author's last name. Write the last name first. If no author is given, alphabetize by title.
- For long entries, indent five spaces every line after the first.

Some sample citations follow. Notice how each entry is punctuated and indented.

How to cite sources

Books	
One author	Settle, Mary Lee. <u>All the Brave Promises</u>. Charlotte: University of South Carolina Press, 1995.
Two or more authors	Haynesworth, Leslie, and David Toomey. <u>Amelia Earhart's Daughters</u>. New York: Morrow, 1998.
More than one work by an author	Levinson, Jay Conrad, and Seth Godin. <u>Get What You Deserve!</u> New York: Avon Books, 1997. ——. <u>The Guerilla Marketing Handbook</u>. New York: Houghton Mifflin, 1995.
One editor	Baker, Russell, ed. <u>The Norton Book of Light Verse</u>. New York: W.W. Norton, 1986.
Selections within books	
One selection from a book of one author's works	Bradstreet, Anne. "Of the Four Ages of Man." <u>The Works of Anne Bradstreet</u>. Ed. Jeannine Hensley. Cambridge: Harvard University Press, 1967. 51–64.
One selection from a book of several authors' works	Kingston, Maxine Hong. "The Grandfather of the Sierra Nevada Mountains." <u>American Mosaic</u>. Ed. Barbara Roche Rico and Sandra Mano. Boston: Houghton Mifflin, 1995. 122–141.
One selection from a collection of longer works	Shakespeare, William. <u>Cymbeline</u>. <u>The Riverside Shakespeare</u>. Ed. G. Blakemore Evans. Boston: Houghton Mifflin, 1974.

Articles from magazines, newspapers, and journals	
Weekly magazine article	Darr, A. "The Long Flight Home." <u>U. S. News and World Report</u> 17 Nov. 1997: 66–68.
Monthly magazine article	Chelminski, R. "The Maginot Line." <u>Smithsonian</u> June 1997: 90–96+.
Newspaper article with byline	Wells, Ken. "View from a Canoe." <u>The Wall Street Journal</u> 4 Aug. 1998: 1+.
Newspaper or magazine article, no byline	"Accounts of Blast at Odds." <u>Saint Paul Pioneer Press</u> 9 Aug. 1998: 1+.
Scholarly journal article	Rubinstein, William, and Richard Levy. "No Substitute for Victory." <u>The Wilson Quarterly</u> 21 (1997): 119–120.

Electronic sources: Sources accessed by computer, either on CD-ROM or on-line	
CD-ROM	"Time Warner, Inc.: Sales Summary, 1988–1992." <u>Disclosure/Worldscope. W/D Partners</u>. Oct. 1993.
Article in reference database	"Fresco." <u>Britannica Online</u>. Vers 97.1.1. Mar. 1997. Encyclopaedia Britannica. 18 Dec. 1998 <http://www.eb.com.180>.
Article in electronic journal	Machlis, Sharon. "Bookseller Beefs Up Products, Searches." <u>Computerworld</u> 2 Nov. 1998. 17 Dec. 1998 <http://www.elibrary.com/search.cgi?id=119940369x0y6229w3>.
Article at a professional site	<u>The Botany Libraries</u>. Harvard University. 17 Dec. 1998 <http://www.herbaria.harvard.edu/libraries/libraries.html>.

Other sources	
Radio/television interview	Berry, Wendell. Interview with Noah Adams. <u>All Things Considered</u>. Natl. Public Radio. WBEZ, Chicago. 24 Dec. 1998.
Television or radio program	"The cost of winning at all costs." <u>Dateline NBC</u>. NBC. WMAQ, Chicago. 31 July 1998.

Preparing a manuscript

Follow the guidelines of the Modern Language Association when you prepare the final copy of your research paper.

- **Heading** On separate lines in the upper left-hand corner of the first page, include your name, your teacher's name, the course name, and the date.
- **Title** Center the title on the line below the heading.
- **Numbering** Number the pages one-half inch from the top of the page in the right-hand corner. Write your last name before each page number after the first page.
- **Spacing** Use double spacing throughout.
- **Margins** Leave one-inch margins on all sides of every page.

Business and Technical Writing

Business writing and technical writing are specialized forms of expository writing.

Business Writing

Business writing might include documents such as letters, memorandums, reports, briefs, proposals, and articles for business publications. Business writing must be clear, concise, accurate, and correct in style and usage.

Business letters

Three common types of business letters are inquiry or order letters, complaint letters, and opinion letters. Whenever possible, address your letter to a specific person. Business letters are usually written in one of two forms: the modified block form (illustrated below) or the full block form.

> 66 Glenwood Drive
> Teller, NJ 07324
> June 8, 1999
>
> Ms. Barbara Neill
> Personnel Manager
> Riverside Press
> 35 Clinton Road
> Rutledge, NJ 07321
>
> Dear Ms. Neill:
>
> I am writing to express my interest in the summer word processing position, which you advertised in the *Rutledge Herald* of June 6.
>
> I have a great deal of word processing experience. This past semester, I typed and formatted every edition of our monthly school newspaper, *The Teller High News.* Mr. John Greene, faculty adviser to the newspaper, praised my neatness, attention to detail, and ability to work quickly under tight deadlines.
>
> I would be available to work full-time from the end of June until the beginning of September. I will be available for an interview at your convenience.
>
> Yours truly,
>
> Michael Costello

Memos

A memorandum (memo) conveys precise information to another person or a group of people. A memo begins with a heading block. It is followed by the text of the message. A memo does not have a formal closing.

- Make a monthly assignment calendar. By writing down due dates, test dates, and notes about upcoming assignments, you can see at glance what work you need to do and when. It will also bring to your attention the times when you will be especially busy, allowing you to plan ahead.
- At the beginning of your study period, when your attention and energy are at their highest levels, work on the assignments you find hardest.
- Take a short break after completing each task. Stay alert by stretching, walking, or having a light snack.
- Review material before stopping. Even a short review will greatly increase the amount of material you are able to remember.

Preparing for Classroom Tests

This section will help you learn how to prepare for classroom tests.

Thinking ahead

- Write down information about an upcoming test–when it will be given, what it will cover, and so on–so you can plan your study time effectively.
- Review your textbook, quizzes, homework assignments, class notes, and handouts. End-of-chapter review questions often highlight key points from your textbook.
- Develop your own questions about main ideas and important details, and practice answering them. Writing your own practice tests is an excellent way to get ready for a real test.
- Make studying into an active process. Rather than simply rereading your notes or a chapter in your textbook, try to create a summary of the material. This can be an outline, a list of characters, or a time line. Try to include details from both your lecture notes and your textbook reading so you will be able to see connections between the two.
- Form study groups. Explaining information to a peer is one of the best ways to learn the material.
- Sleep well the night before a test. Spreading your study time over several days should have given you enough confidence to go to bed at your regular time the night before a test.
- Remember that eating well helps you remain alert. Students who eat a regular meal on the morning of a test generally score higher than those who do not.

Taking objective tests

Many of the tests you take in your high school classes will be objective tests, meaning that they ask questions that have specific, correct answers. Time is often limited for these tests, so be sure to use your time efficiently.

- First, read the directions carefully. If anything is unclear, ask questions.
- Try to respond to each item on the test, starting with the easier ones.
- Skip difficult questions rather than dwelling on them. You can always come back to them at the end of the test.
- Try to include some time to review your test before turning it in.

Below are tips for answering specific kinds of objective test items:

Kind of item	Tips
Multiple-choice	Read all the answer choices provided before choosing one; even if the first one seems nearly correct, a later choice may be a better answer. Be cautious when choosing responses that contain absolute words such as *always, never, all,* or *none.* Since most generalizations have exceptions, absolute statements are often incorrect.
True/False	If *any* part of the item is false, the correct answer must be "false."
Short-answer	Use complete sentences to help you write a clear response.
Fill-in	Restate fill-ins as regular questions if you are not sure what is being asked.
Matching	Note in the directions whether some responses can be used more than once, or not used at all.

Taking subjective (essay) tests

You will also take subjective tests during high school. Typically, these tests ask questions that require you to write an essay. Your grade is based more on how well you are able to make your point than on whether you choose a correct answer.

- When you receive the test, first read it through. If there are several questions, determine how much time to spend on each question.
- Begin your answer by jotting down ideas on scratch paper for several minutes. Read the test question again to make sure you are answering it. Then create a rough outline from which you can create your essay.
- Start your essay with a thesis statement in the first paragraph, and follow with paragraphs that provide supporting evidence. Give as much information as possible, including examples and illustrations where appropriate.
- Finish your essay with a conclusion, highlighting the evidence you have provided and restating your thesis.
- You will probably not have time to revise and recopy your essay. After you are finished writing, spend any remaining time proofreading your answer and neatly making any necessary corrections.

Preparing for Standardized Tests

Standardized tests are designed to be administered to very large groups of students, not just those in a particular class. Three of the most widely known standardized tests, all part of the college application process, are the ACT (American College Testing), the PSAT (Preliminary Scholastic Assessment Test), and the SAT (Scholastic Assessment Test). The strategies in this handbook refer specifically to the PSAT and SAT tests, but they also can apply to preparing for the ACT and other standardized tests.

The PSAT is generally administered to students in the 11th grade, though some schools offer it to students in the 10th grade as well. This test is designed to predict how well you will do on the SAT. For most students, the PSAT is simply a practice test. Those who perform exceptionally well on the 11th grade PSAT, however, will qualify for National Merit Scholarship competition.

The Scholastic Assessment Tests consist of the SAT-I: Reasoning Test and a variety of SAT-II: Subject Tests. The SAT-I is a three-hour test that evaluates your general verbal and mathematics skills. The SAT-II: Subject Tests are hour-long tests given in specific subjects and are designed to show specifically how much you have learned in a particular subject area.

Tips for taking standardized tests

Standardized tests are often administered outside of regular class time and require registration. Ask your teacher or guidance counselor how you can register early to ensure that you can take the test at a time and location most convenient for you. In addition, follow these tips:

- Skip difficult questions at first. Standardized tests are usually timed, so first answer items you know. You can return later to those you skipped.
- Mark only your answers on the answer sheet. Most standardized tests are scored by a computer, so stray marks can be read as incorrect answers.
- Frequently compare the question numbers on your test with those on your answer sheet to avoid putting answers in the wrong spaces.
- If time permits, check your answers. If you are not penalized for guessing, fill in answers for any items you might have skipped.

Preparing for the PSAT and the SAT-I

The verbal sections of the PSAT and SAT-I contain analogies, sentence completion items, and reading comprehension questions.

Analogies

Nearly half of the items on the verbal sections of the PSAT and SAT-I are designed to test your vocabulary. Therefore, the more words you know, the higher your score will be. Refer to pages R86–R87 of the **Reading Handbook** for information on how to build your vocabulary.

COMMUNICATIONS SKILLS HANDBOOK R83

One type of vocabulary-based question is the analogy, which tests your ability to grasp the relationships between concepts. The best way to pinpoint the relationship is to connect the words in a simple sentence that defines one of the words. Some of the most common relationships seen on the PSAT and the SAT-I are shown below.

Relationship	Example
Cause and effect	heat : perspiration :: sadness : tears
A person to the normal action of that person	comedian : amuse :: journalist : write
An object to its normal function	telescope : magnify :: aircraft : fly
User to tool	teacher : book :: carpenter : hammer
Degree	terrified : frightened :: destitute : poor
Object to characteristic	water : wet :: brick : hard
Class to subclass (or subclass to class)	grain : rye :: music : rap

Answering analogy items will be easier if you know some facts about them.

- Each group of analogy items is roughly arranged from easiest to hardest.
- Many analogy items use only nouns. The rest involve a noun and an adjective, a noun and a verb, or a verb and an adjective.
- All the answer choices will have the same parts of speech, in the same order, as the words in the initial analogy.
- If you can eliminate even one answer choice, take a guess at the correct answer.

Sentence completion

Sentence completion items provide a sentence with one or two blanks and ask you to select the word or pair of words that best fits in the blank(s). Here is some general information to help you with these questions on the PSAT and SAT-I.

- Start by reading the sentence and filling in your own word to replace the blank. Look for words that show how the word in the blank is related to the rest of the sentence–*and, but, since, therefore, although.*
- Do not read the sentence with the words from each answer choice inserted. This may leave you with several choices that "sound good."
- Once you have chosen your own word to fill in the blank, pick the word from the answer choices that is closest in meaning to your word.
- If you have trouble coming up with a specific word to fill in the blank, try to determine whether the word should be positive or negative. Even this bit of information can help you eliminate some answer choices. If you can eliminate even one answer choice, take a guess at the correct answer.

chart to see how you might show the chronological sequence of a story. Use a flow chart to make a **change frame,** recording causes and effects in sequence to illustrate how something changed.

A **web** can be used for a variety of purposes as you read a selection.

- To **map out the main idea and details** of a selection, put the main idea in the middle circle, and, as you read, add supporting details around the main thought.
- To **analyze a character in a story,** put the character's name in the middle, and add that character's actions, thoughts, reputation, plot involvement, and personal development in the surrounding circles.
- To **define a concept,** put a word or idea in the middle circle, and then add a more general category, descriptions, examples, and non-examples in the surrounding circles.

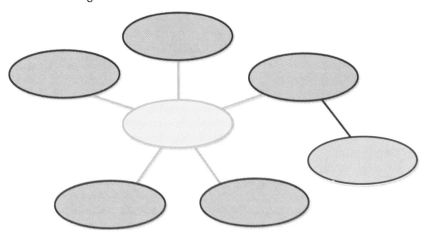

Analyzing text structures

To follow the logic and message of a selection and to remember it, analyze the **text structure,** or organization of ideas, within a writer's work. In narrative as well as in informational text, writers may embed one structure within another, but it is usually possible to identify one main pattern of organization. Recognizing the pattern of organization can help you discover the writer's purpose and will focus your attention on the important ideas in the selection. **Look for signal words** to point you to the structure.

- **Chronological order** often uses words like *first, then, after, later,* and *finally.*
- **Cause-and-effect order** can include words like *therefore, because, subsequently,* or *as a result of.*
- **Comparison-contrast order** may use words like *similarly, in contrast, likewise,* or *on the other hand.*

Interpreting graphic aids

Graphic aids provide an opportunity to see and analyze information at a glance. Charts, tables, maps, and diagrams allow you to analyze and compare information. Maps include a compass rose and legend to help you interpret direction, symbols, and scale. Charts and graphs compare information in categories running horizontally and vertically.

Tips for Reading Graphic Aids

- Examine the title, labels, and other explanatory features.
- Apply the labels to the graphic aid.
- Interpret the information.

Look carefully at the models below.

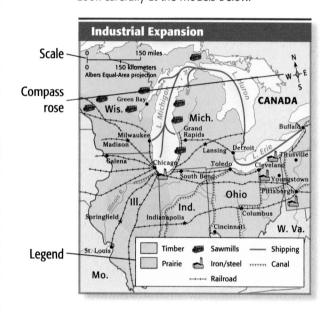

Scale

Compass rose

Legend

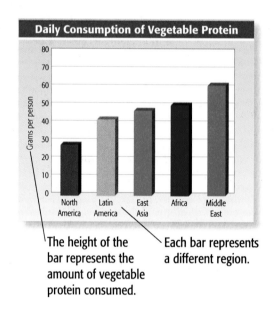

The height of the bar represents the amount of vegetable protein consumed.

Each bar represents a different region.

Sequencing

The order in which thoughts are arranged is called a **sequence.** A good sequence is one that is logical, given the ideas in a selection. **Chronological order, spatial order,** and **order of importance** are common forms of sequencing. Think about the order of a writer's thoughts as you read, and pay particular attention to sequence when **following complex written directions.**

Summarizing

A summary is a short restatement of the main ideas and important details of a selection. Summarizing what you have read is an excellent tool for understanding and remembering a passage.

Tips for Summarizing

- Identify the **main ideas** or most important thoughts within a selection.
- Determine the essential **supporting details.**
- Relate all the main ideas and the essential details in a **logical sequence.**
- **Paraphrase,** that is, use your own words.
- Answer **who, what, why, where,** and **when** questions when you summarize.

The best summaries can easily be understood by someone who has not read the selection. If you're not sure whether an idea is a main idea or a detail, try taking it out of your summary. Does your summary still sound complete?

Drawing inferences and supporting them

An **inference** involves using your reason and experience to come up with an idea based on what a writer implies or suggests, but does not directly state. The following strategic reading behaviors are examples of inference:

- **Making a prediction** is taking an educated guess about what a text will be about based on initial clues a writer provides.
- **Drawing a conclusion** is making a general statement you can explain with reason or with supporting details from a text.
- **Making a generalization** is generating a statement that can apply to more than one item or group.

What is most important when inferring is to be sure that you have accurately based your thoughts on supporting details from the text as well as on your own knowledge.

Reading silently for sustained periods

When you read for long periods of time, your task is to avoid distractions. Check your comprehension regularly by summarizing what you've read so far. Using study guides or graphic organizers can help get you through difficult passages. Take regular breaks when you need them, and vary your reading rate with the demands of the task.

Synthesizing information

You will often need to read across texts; that is, in different sources, combining or **synthesizing** what you've learned from varied sources to suit your purposes. Follow these suggestions:

- Understand the information you've read in each source.
- Interpret the information.
- Identify similarities and differences in ideas or logic.
- Combine like thoughts in a logical sequence.
- Add to the information or change the form to suit your purposes.

Literary Response

Whenever you share your thoughts and feelings about something you've read, you are responding to text. While the way you respond may vary with the type of text you read and with your individual learning style, as a strategic reader you will always need to adequately support your responses with proofs from the text.

Responding to informational and aesthetic elements

When you respond both intellectually *and* emotionally, you connect yourself with a writer and with other people. To respond in an intellectual way, ask yourself if the ideas you have read are logical and well supported. To respond emotionally, ask yourself how you feel about those ideas and events. Choose a way to respond that fits your learning style. Class discussions, journal entries, oral interpretations, enactments, and graphic displays are some of the many ways to share your thoughts and emotions about a writer's work.

Comparing responses with authoritative views

Critics' reviews may encourage you to read a book, see a movie, or attend an event. They may also warn you that whatever is reviewed is not acceptable entertainment or is not valued by the reviewer. Deciding whether or not to value a review depends on the credibility of the reviewer and also on your own personal views and feelings. Ask yourself the following questions:

- What is the reviewer's background?
- What qualifies the reviewer to write this evaluation?
- Is the review balanced? Does it include both positive and negative responses?
- Are arguments presented logically?
- Are opinions supported with facts?
- What bias does this reviewer show?
- Do I agree? Why or why not?

Analysis and Evaluation

Good readers want to do more than recall information or interpret thoughts and ideas. When you read, read critically, forming opinions about characters and ideas, and making judgments using your own prior knowledge and information from the text.

Analyzing characteristics of texts

To be a critical reader and thinker, start by analyzing the characteristics of the text. Think about what specific characteristics make a particular selection clear, concise, and complete. Ask yourself these questions:

- What **pattern of organization** has this writer used to present his or her thoughts? Cause/effect? Comparison/contrast? Problem/solution? Does this organization make the main ideas clear or vague? Why?

dissembling (di sem′ bling) *n.* the act of concealing one's true character, feelings, or intentions; p. 690

dissipate (dis′ ə pāt′) *v.* to cause to scatter and gradually vanish; to break up and drive off; p. 798

distinctive (dis ting′ tiv) *adj.* different in quality or kind; separate; p. 139

doctrine (dok′ trin) *n.* a principle that is taught and advocated; a tenet; p. 520

doggedly (dô′ gid lē) *adv.* in a stubbornly persistent manner; obstinately; p. 535

doleful (dōl′ fəl) *adj.* full of grief or sorrow; sad; p. 85

domain (dō mān′) *n.* a territory over which control is exercised; a realm; p. 1058

downy (dou′ nē) *adj.* soft and fluffy, like the feathers of young birds; p. 1038

dupe (do͞op) *v.* to fool; to trick; p. 1079

dusk (dusk) *n.* the time of day just before nightfall; p. 1041

dutiful (do͞o′ ti fəl) *adj.* careful to fulfill obligations; p. 622

dwell (dwel) *v.* to think about at length; p. 1064

dwindle (dwin′ dəl) *v.* to become gradually smaller; p. 628

E

ecclesiastical (i klē′ zē as′ ti kəl) *adj.* of or relating to the church; p. 1182

efface (i fās′) *v.* to destroy; to erase; p. 373

elusive (i lo͞o′ siv) *adj.* difficult to explain or grasp; p. 526

embark (em bärk′) *v.* to set out on a venture; p. 64

embody (em bod′ ē) *v.* to give concrete or material form to; p. 900

emphatic (em fa′ tik) *adj.* forceful; p. 562

enamored (en am′ ərd) *adj.* inspired with love; charmed; captivated; p. 881

endeavor (en dev′ ər) *v.* to make an effort to; to try; p. 171

engender (en jen′ dər) *v.* to give rise to; to cause; to produce; p. 1056

engrossed (en grōst′) *adj.* fully attentive to; completely engaged in; absorbed; p. 867

enlighten (en līt′ ən) *v.* to give knowledge or wisdom to; p. 31

enmity (en′ mə tē) *n.* deep-seated hatred; hostility; p. 1059

enormity (i nôr′ mə tē) *n.* outrageousness; the state of being monstrous; p. 93

ensure (en shoor′) *v.* to make certain; to guarantee; p. 96

enterprising (en′ tər prī′ zing) *adj.* showing energy and initiative, especially in beginning new projects; p. 468

enunciate (i nun′ sē āt′) *v.* to pronounce distinctly; p. 1032

ephemeral (i fem′ ər əl) *adj.* lasting for a very brief time; short-lived; p. 900

equanimity (ek′ wə nim′ ə tē) *n.* evenness of temper; calmness; p. 479

espionage (es′ pē ə näzh′) *n.* spying; p. 1102

esteem (es tēm′) *v.* to regard favorably; to value highly; p. 108

evade (i vād′) *v.* to escape or avoid, as by cleverness; p. 931

exalt (ig zôlt′) *v.* to lift up; to put in high spirits; p. 726

exalted (ig zôl′ təd) *adj.* elevated; p. 527

exclusively (iks′ klo͞o′ siv lē) *adv.* without the inclusion or involvement of others; p. 30

exemplary (ig zem′ plə rē) *adj.* worthy of imitation; commendable; p. 1131

exhilarated (ig zil′ ə rā təd) *adj.* cheerful, lively, or excited; filled with vigor; p. 656

exhilaration (ig zil′ ə rā′ shən) *n.* a feeling of strength and energy, joy, or excitement; p. 847

exorbitant (ig zôr′ bə tənt) *adj.* exceeding what is reasonable; excessive; p. 519

expatriated (eks pā′ trē āt′ əd) *adj.* banished; exiled; p. 477

expedient (iks pē′ dē ənt) *n.* something employed to bring about a desired result; a means to an end; p. 258

exploit (eks′ ploit) *n.* a notable, heroic deed; a feat; p. 156

exploit (iks ploit′) *v.* to use or develop for profit, often in a selfish, unjust, or unfair way; p. 657

extricate (eks′ trə kāt′) *v.* to set free from; to remove; p. 183

F

facade (fə säd′) *n.* a false or artificial front; p. 1091

feigned (fānd) *adj.* fictitious; not genuine; p. 72

feint (fānt) *n.* a deceptive movement intended to draw an opponent's attention from the real attack; a deception; p. 162

futile (fū′ til) *adj.* useless; worthless; pointless; p. 823

G

gape (gāp) *v.* to stare with the mouth open, as in wonder or surprise; p. 1064

garrulous (gar′ ə ləs) *adj.* talkative; p. 462

gaunt (gônt) *adj.* thin, bony, and hollow-eyed, as from hunger or illness; p. 8

grapple (grap′ əl) *v.* to struggle in hand-to-hand combat; to wrestle; p. 866

gratify (grat′ ə fī′) *v.* to satisfy or indulge; p. 193

grave (grāv) *adj.* dignified and gloomy; somber; p. 833

gravity (grav′ ə tē) *n.* seriousness; importance; p. 1041

grievously (grē′ vəs lē) *adv.* very seriously; gravely; p. 490

grimace (grim′ is) *v.* to contort the face, especially to express pain or displeasure; p. 1001

grope (grōp) *v.* to feel about uncertainly with the hands; to search blindly; p. 1063

grotesque (grō tesk′) *adj.* bizarre; weird; p. 1047

guile (gīl) *n.* cunning; deceit; slyness; p. 968

H

hallow (hal′ ō) *v.* to make or select as holy; to regard or honor as sacred; p. 385

hallucination (hə lōo′ sə nā′ shən) *n.* a false sensory perception of something that is not really there; p. 1079

haughty (hô′ tē) *adj.* conceited; arrogant; p. 808

heedless (hēd′ lis) *adj.* careless; thoughtless; reckless; p. 1047

hemorrhage (hem′ ər ij) *n.* a severe discharge of blood; p. 785

holocaust (hol′ ə kôst′) *n.* great or complete destruction, especially by fire; p. 1032

hostile (host′ əl) *adj.* feeling or showing hatred; antagonistic; p. 823

hover (huv′ ər) *v.* to remain nearby, as if suspended in the air over something; p. 1041

hypocrisy (hi pok′ rə sē) *n.* an expression of feelings or beliefs not actually possessed or held; p. 156

hypothesis (hī poth′ ə sis) *n.* an unproved explanation or assumption; p. 480

I

idiom (id′ ē əm) *n.* an expression peculiar to a people or to a specific region; p. 1103

illumination (i lōo′ mə nā′ shən) *n.* intellectual enlightenment; p. 527

immaculate (i mak′ yə lit) *adj.* unblemished; flawless; pure; p. 966

imminent (im′ ə nənt) *adj.* about to take place; p. 652

immortality (im′ ôr tal′ ə tē) *n.* the condition of having eternal life; p. 499

impede (im pēd′) *v.* to slow or block progress or action; to obstruct; p. 295

impediment (im ped′ ə mənt) *n.* an obstacle; p. 1087

imperative (im per′ ə tiv) *n.* something absolutely necessary; an essential; p. 894

imperious (im pēr′ ē əs) *adj.* imperative; urgent; p. 371

imperviousness (im pur′ vē əs nəs) *n.* the state of being unaffected or undisturbed; p. 808

impetuously (im pech′ ōo əs lē) *adv.* impulsively; suddenly; rashly; p. 658

impious (im′ pē əs) *adj.* lacking in reverence; disrespectful; p. 568

impose (im pōz′) *v.* to inflict, as by authority; to dictate; p. 527

impregnable (im preg′ nə bəl) *adj.* incapable of being taken by force; able to resist attack; p. 205

impropriety (im′ prə prī′ ə tē) *n.* the quality of being improper; improper behavior; p. 477

impudently (im′ pyə dənt lē) *adv.* in an offensively bold manner; arrogantly; p. 565

inaudibly (in ô′ də blē) *adv.* in a manner not able to be heard; p. 1041

incensed (in senst′) *adj.* made very angry; p. 102

incessant (in ses′ənt) *adj.* continuing or following without interruption; p. 1048

indentured (in den′ chərd) *adj.* bound by contract to serve another person for a period of time; p. 131

indictment (in dīt′ mənt) *n.* a formal legal accusation, charging the commission or omission of an act, which is punishable by law; p. 989

indifferent (in dif′ ər ənt) *adj.* lacking feeling or concern; p. 729

indignation (in′ dig nā′ shən) *n.* restrained, dignified anger in response to meanness, injustice, or ingratitude; p. 161

induce (in dōōs′) *v.* to lead by persuasion or influence; p. 330

ineptly (i nept′ lē) *adv.* incompetently; awkwardly; clumsily; p. 951

inert (i nurt′) *adj.* inactive; sluggish; p. 536

inevitable (i nev′ ə tə bəl) *adj.* incapable of being avoided or evaded; p. 96

infidel (in′ fə del′) *n.* an unbeliever; p. 131

ingenious (in jēn′ yəs) *adj.* exhibiting creative ability; inventive; p. 131

ingenuously (in jen′ ū əs lē) *adv.* honestly; frankly; candidly; p. 564

inherent (in hēr′ ənt) *adj.* existing as a basic quality; belonging to by nature; p. 258

iniquity (in ik′ wə tē) *n.* sin; wickedness; p. 268

initially (i nish′ ə lē) *adv.* at the beginning; first; p. 1102

inquisitor (in kwiz′ ə tər) *n.* one who asks questions; p. 786

insidious (in sid′ ē əs) *adj.* slyly treacherous and deceitful; deceptive; p. 148

instinct (in′ stingkt) *n.* a natural ability or impulse; p. 1074

intangible (in tan′ jə bəl) *adj.* not easily defined or evaluated by the mind; p. 498

integrate (in′ tə grāt) *v.* to bring all parts together into a whole; p. 242

integrity (in teg′ rə tē) *n.* moral uprightness; honesty; p. 247

interminable (in tur′ mi nə bəl) *adj.* seemingly endless; p. 463

intervene (in′ tər vēn′) *v.* to come or lie between; p. 502

intimation (in′ tə mā′ shən) *n.* a hint; a suggestion; p. 787

intimidated (in tim′ ə dāt′ əd) *adj.* made timid or fearful; frightened into submission or inaction; p. 866

intricately (in′ tri kit lē) *adv.* in a complex or complicated manner; elaborately; p. 1183

intrigue (in′ trēg) *n.* the use of devious schemes to achieve a goal; secret plotting; p. 823

intriguing (in trēg′ ing) *adj.* arousing curiosity or interest; fascinating; captivating; p. 865

invigorated (in vig′ ə rā′ tid) *adj.* filled with strength and energy; p. 787

invoke (in vōk′) *v.* to call forth; p. 1105

irk (urk) *v.* to annoy; to bother; p. 822

irreproachable (ir′ i prō′ chə bəl) *adj.* free from blame; faultless; p. 274

irrevocable (i rev′ ə kə bəl) *adj.* not possible to undo; p. 96

J

jilt (jilt) *v.* to drop or reject as a sweetheart; p. 625

jocular (jok′ yə lər) *adj.* humorous; p. 480

jostle (jos′ əl) *v.* to bump, push, or shove while moving, as in a crowd; p. 681

jubilant (jōō′ bə lənt) *adj.* extremely happy; triumphantly joyful; p. 867

K

kindle (kind′ əl) *v.* to stir up; to excite; p. 533

L

lament (lə ment′) *v.* to express deep sorrow or grief; p. 89

latent (lā′ tənt) *adj.* present but not evident; hidden; p. 245

legacy (leg′ ə sē) *n.* an inheritance; p. 533

legible (lej′ ə bəl) *adj.* able to be read; p. 1049

lethargy (leth′ ər jē) *n.* sluggish inactivity or drowsiness; p. 298

limber (lim′ bər) *adj.* able to bend or move easily; nimble; p. 834

list (list) *v.* to tilt or lean to one side; p. 8

loiter (loi′ tər) *v.* to stand or linger idly or aimlessly about a place; p. 866

lucid (lōō′ sid) *adj.* rational; sane; p. 1050

lurch (lurch) *v.* to move suddenly and unevenly; p. 680

luxuriant (lug zhoor′ ē ənt) *adj.* marked by rich or plentiful growth; abundant; p. 1056

M

malevolence (mə lev′ ə ləns) *n.* a disposition to wish harm to others; ill will; p. 478

manifest (man′ ə fest′) *adj.* apparent to the eye or the mind; evident; obvious; p. 246

meager (mē′ gər) *adj.* deficient in quantity or completeness; p. 875

meandering (mē an′ dər ing) *adj.* following a winding course; p. 33

melancholy (mel′ ən kol′ ē) *adj.* depressing; dismal; gloomy; p. 205

mentor (men′ tər) *n.* a wise and trusted adviser; p. 57

mimic (mim′ ik) *v.* to copy; to reproduce; to imitate; p. 1067

minutely (mī nōōt′ lē) *adv.* in a very small degree; p. 1068

misgiving (mis giv′ ing) *n.* a feeling of doubt, distrust, or anxiety; p. 947

mishap (mis′ hap′) *n.* an unfortunate accident or mistake; a misfortune; p. 520

morose (mə rōs′) *adj.* bad-tempered, gloomy, and withdrawn; p. 14

mortification (môr′ tə fi kā′ shən) *n.* a feeling of shame, humiliation, or embarrassment; p. 132

mundane (mun dān′) *adj.* ordinary; usual; commonplace; p. 1087

murky (mur′ kē) *adj.* characterized by dimness, as from fog or smoke; p. 1074

myriad (mir′ ē əd) *adj.* countless; innumerable; p. 255

N

naive (nä ēv′) *adj.* lacking knowledge of the ways of the world; unsophisticated; innocent; p. 919

novel (nov′ əl) *adj.* new and unusual; p. 1183

O

obesity (ō bē′ sə tē) *n.* the condition of being extremely fat; p. 806

obliquely (ə blēk′ lē) *adv.* in a slanting or sloping direction; p. 537

obliterate (ə blit′ ə rāt) *v.* to remove all traces of; to erase; p. 207

oblivious (ə bliv′ ē əs) *adj.* without conscious awareness; unmindful; p. 1041

occult (ə kult′) *adj.* beyond human understanding; mysterious; p. 243

ominous (om′ ə nəs) *adj.* like an evil omen; threatening; p. 1032

onslaught (on′ slôt′) *n.* a vigorous or destructive attack; p. 163

opaque (ō pāk′) *adj.* not letting light through; p. 1058

oppressed (ə prest′) *adj.* controlled or governed by a cruel and unjust use of force or authority; p. 892

ordeal (ôr dēl′) *n.* a circumstance or experience that is painful or difficult; a trial; p. 892

P

pall (pôl) *n.* that which covers with an atmosphere of darkness and gloom; p. 498

paradigm (par′ ə dīm′) *n.* an example that acts as a model; a pattern; p. 33

parsimony (pär′ sə mō nē) *n.* excessive frugality; stinginess; p. 211

perception (pər sep′ shən) *n.* an awareness; an insight; p. 527

perennial (pə ren′ ē əl) *adj.* continuing year after year; enduring; p. 243

perish (per′ish) *v.* to pass from existence; to disappear; p. 385

perpetual (pər pech′ ōō əl) *adj.* lasting forever; eternal; p. 242

perplexed (pər plekst′) *adj.* puzzled; confused; p. 1098

persistence (pər sis′ təns) *n.* stubborn or determined continuance; p. 527

perturbation (pur′ tər bā′ shən) *n.* agitation; anxiety; uneasiness; p. 268

perusal (pə rōō′ zəl) *n.* the process of examining carefully; p. 363

pervade (pər vād′) *v.* to spread through every part; p. 360

petrified (pet′ rə fīd) *adj.* paralyzed with fear; stiff or like stone, p. 156

piety (pī′ ə tē) *n.* religious devoutness; goodness; p. 627

pigment (pig′ mənt) *n.* a substance that gives color; p. 1069

pillage (pil′ ij) *n.* looting or plundering; p. 1054

plague (plāg) *v.* to annoy; to pester; p. 623

plumage (plōō′ mij) *n.* the feathers of a bird; p. 847

poignant (poin′ yənt) *adj.* sharp; severe; causing emotional or physical anguish; p. 372

poised (poizd) *adj.* having a calm, controlled, and dignified manner; composed; p. 827

ponder (pon′ dər) *v.* to think about thoroughly and carefully; p. 1063

posterity (pos ter′ ə tē) *n.* generations of the future; all of one's descendants; p. 56

preeminently (prē em′ ə nənt lē) *adv.* chiefly; primarily; p. 1054

preposterous (pri pos′ tər əs) *adj.* absurd; ridiculous; p. 566

presumptuous (pri zump′ chōō əs) *adj.* going beyond what is proper; excessively bold; p. 1182

pretense (prē′ tens) *n.* a false show or appearance, especially for the purpose of deceiving; falseness; p. 922

pretension (pri ten′ shən) *n.* a claim; an assertion; p. 519

prevail (pri vāl′) *v.* to use persuasion successfully; p. 539

prevalent (prev′ ə lent) *adj.* widespread; p. 204

procure (prə kyōōr′) *v.* to obtain by care or effort; p. 72

profound (prə found′) *adj.* coming from the depth of one's being; intensely felt; p. 560

profusion (prə fū′ zhen) *n.* a plentiful amount; abundance; p. 1056

progenitor (prō jen′ ə tər) *n.* a direct ancestor; an originator of an ancestral line; p. 57

proposal (prə pō′ zəl) *n.* something put forward for consideration as a plan of action; p. 108

propriety (prə prī′ ə tē) *n.* the quality of being proper; appropriateness; p. 520

prosperity (pros per′ ə tē) *n.* success; wealth; good fortune; p. 364

prostrate (pros′ strāt) *adj.* bowing or kneeling down in humility, adoration, or submission; p. 359

protrude (prō trōōd′) *v.* to stick out; to project; p. 369

proverbial (prə vur′ bē əl) *adj.* commonly spoken of; well-known; p. 1094

providence (prov′ ə dəns) *n.* divine care or guidance; foresight; p. 70

provoke (prə vōk′) *v.* to bring about; to incite; p. 1132

proximity (prok sim′ ə tē) *n.* closeness in space, time, sequence, or degree; nearness; p. 302

prudence (prōōd′ əns) *n.* exercise of good and cautious judgment; p. 102

Q

querulous (kwer′ ə ləs) *adj.* complaining; whining; p. 483

quivering (kwiv′ ər ing) *n.* a shaking with a slight, rapid vibration; a trembling; p. 834

R

radical (rad′ i kəl) *adj.* deviating greatly from the usual or customary; extreme; p. 1049

random (ran′ dəm) *adj.* lacking a definite pattern; haphazard; p. 1032

ration (rash′ ən) *n.* a fixed portion or share; p. 62

ravage (rav′ ij) *n.* a destructive or ruinous action or its result; p. 156

ravenous (rav′ ə nəs) *adj.* extremely hungry; p. 11

reciprocate (ri sip′ rə kāt′) *v.* to give, feel, or show in return; p. 652

recourse (rē′ kôrs′) *n.* a resorting to a person or thing for help; p. 185

rectitude (rek′ tə tōōd′) *n.* uprightness of moral character; honesty; p. 172

redress (rē′ dres′) *n.* compensation, as for wrong done; p. 364

refugee (ref′ū jē′) *n.* a person who flees to safety, especially one who leaves home or a homeland because of persecution, war, or danger; p. 352

rejuvenated (ri jōō′ və nā′ təd) *adj.* restored to youthful vigor or appearance; renewed; p. 1005

relinquish (ri ling′ kwish) *v.* to give up control of; to surrender; p. 156

reminiscence (rem′ ə nis′ əns) *n.* an account of a past experience or event; p. 462

remonstrate (ri mon′ strāt) *v.* to object; to protest; p. 148

remorselessly (ri môrs′ lis lē) *adv.* in a way that shows no pity or compassion; mercilessly; p. 165

render (ren′ dər) *v.* to cause to be; to make; p. 184

repertoire (rep′ ər twär′) *n.* the stock of skills that a person or group has and is prepared to demonstrate or perform; p. 280

repression (ri presh′ ən) *n.* the state of being held back or kept under control; p. 526

reprieve (ri prēv′) *n.* official postponement of the carrying out of a sentence; p. 985

reprimand (rep′ rə mand′) *v.* to reprove or correct sharply; p. 937

reproach (ri prōch′) *n.* an expression of disapproval; a reprimand; p. 533

repudiate (ri pū′ dē āt′) *v.* to refuse to accept as valid; to reject; to renounce; p. 894

resign (ri zīn′) *v.* to make oneself accept; p. 683

resignation (rez′ ig nā′ shən) *n.* unresisting acceptance; submission; p. 253

resolution (rez′ ə lōō′ shən) *n.* firmness of purpose; p. 156

resolve (ri zolv′) *v.* to decide; to determine; p. 70

resonant (rez′ ə nənt) *adj.* having a full, rich sound; p. 1068

retaliation (ri tal′ ē ā′ shən) *n.* the act of repaying an injury or wrong by committing the same, or a similar, act; p. 985

retractable (ri trak′ tə bəl) *adj.* capable of being drawn back or in; p. 784

revive (ri vīv′) *v.* to give new strength and vitality; to bring back to consciousness; p. 62

rigorously (rig′ ər əs lē) *adv.* precisely; strictly; p. 1130

ritual (rich′ ōō əl) *n.* a regularly followed routine; p. 1092

rouse (rouz) *v.* to awaken from sleep; p. 62

rudiment (rōō′ də mənt) *n.* an imperfect or undeveloped part; p. 254

rue (rōō) *v.* to regret; to be sorry for; p. 16

S

sagacious (sə gā′ shəs) *adj.* having or showing wisdom and keen perception; p. 269

sage (sāj) *n.* a person of profound wisdom and judgment; p. 245

sanction (sangk′ shən) *n.* approval or support; p. 261

savory (sā′ vər ē) *adj.* agreeable to the taste or smell; appetizing; p. 89

scavenger (skav′ in jər) *n.* one who searches through discarded materials for something useful; p. 1078

score (skôr) *n.* a group of twenty items; p. 385

scruple (skrōō′ pəl) *n.* moral principle that restrains action; p. 194

scrupulously (skrōō′ pyə ləs lē) *adv.* with extreme care and attention to detail; painstakingly; p. 1130

scuffle (skuf′ əl) *v.* to move with a quick, shuffling gait; p. 798

seclusion (si klōō′ zhən) *n.* separation from others; isolation; p. 481

sibling (sib′ ling) *adj.* relating to a brother or a sister; p. 1067

signal (sig′ nəl) *adj.* remarkable; striking; notable; p. 165

simultaneously (sī′ məl tā′ nē əs lē) *adv.* at the same time; p. 1129

sluggard (slug′ ərd) *n.* one who is usually or always lazy or idle; a loafer; p. 141

sluggishly (slug′ ish lē) *adv.* slowly; without strength or energy; p. 805

snicker (sni′ kər) *n.* a snide, partly suppressed laugh, often expressing disrespect; p. 727

solemn (sol′ əm) *adj.* serious; grave; p. 838

speculate (spek′ yə lāt′) *v.* to engage in risky business ventures, hoping to make quick profits; p. 210

obliterate/arrasar *v.* borrar; destruir por completo; p. 207

oblivious/abstraído *adj.* distraído; ensimismado; p. 1041

occult/sobrenatural *adj.* más allá de la comprensión humana; misterioso; p. 243

ominous/ominoso *adj.* que da mal presagio; siniestro; p. 1032

onslaught/embestida *s.* ataque vigoroso o destructivo; p. 163

opaque/opaco *adj.* que no deja pasar la luz; p. 1058

oppressed/oprimido *adj.* controlado o gobernado mediante el uso cruel e injusto de la fuerza o autoridad; p. 892

ordeal/tribulación *s.* circunstancia o experiencia dolorosa o difícil; p. 892

P

pall/palio *s.* manto que obscurece o cubre y da una atmósfera sombría; p. 498

paradigm/paradigma *s.* ejemplo que sirve como modelo; p. 33

parsimony/parquedad *s.* excesiva moderación o economía; tacañería; p. 211

perception/percepción *s.* conocimiento; idea; p. 527

perennial/perenne *adj.* que continúa año tras año; duradero; p. 243

perish/perecer *v.* dejar de existir; desaparecer; p. 385

perpetual/perpetuo *adj.* que dura por siempre; eterno; p. 242

perplexed/perplejo *adj.* asombrado; confundido; p. 1098

persistence/persistencia *s.* perseverancia; continuación; p. 527

perturbation/perturbación *s.* agitación; ansiedad; inquietud; p. 268

perusal/escudriñamiento *s.* proceso de examinar cuidadosamente; p. 363

pervade/penetrar *v.* saturar; llenar por todos lados; p. 360

petrified/petrificado *adj.* paralizado de miedo; inmóvil como una piedra; p 156

piety/piedad *s.* devoción religiosa; bondad; p. 627

pigment/pigmento *s.* substancia que da color; p. 1069

pillage/pillaje *s.* robo o saqueo; p. 1054

plague/fastidiar *v.* molestar; importunar; p. 623

plumage/plumaje *s.* conjunto de plumas de un ave; p. 847

poignant/punzante *adj.* agudo; lacerante; que causa angustia emocional o física; p. 372

poised/sereno *adj.* que tiene un modo de ser calmado y equilibrado; p. 826

ponder/ponderar *v.* pensar algo detenida y cuidadosamente; p. 1063

posterity/posteridad *s.* generaciones del futuro; todos los descendientes; p. 56

preeminently/preeminentemente *adv.* de modo principal; predominantemente; p. 1054

preposterous/disparatado *adj.* absurdo; ridículo; p. 566

presumptuous/insolente *adj.* que va más allá de lo apropiado; atrevido; p. 1182

pretense/simulación *s.* falsa apariencia, especialmente con el propósito de engañar; falsedad; p. 922

pretension/pretensión *s.* reclamo; aspiración; p. 519

prevail/prevalecer *v.* persuadir; convencer; p. 539

prevalent/prevaleciente *adj.* frecuente; generalizado; p. 204

procure/procurarse *v.* obtener mediante esfuerzos; p. 72

profound/profundo *adj.* que viene del fondo; que se siente intensamente; p. 560

profusion/profusión *s.* gran cantidad; abundancia; p. 1056

progenitor/progenitor *s.* ancestro directo; ascendiente; padre o abuelo; p. 57

proposal/propuesta *s.* algo que se presenta a consideración como plan de acción; p. 108

propriety/corrección *s.* cualidad de ser correcto o apropiado; p. 520

prosperity/prosperidad *s.* éxito, riqueza o fortuna; p. 364

prostrate/postrado *adj.* agachado o arrodillado en señal de humillación, adoración o sumisión; p. 359

protrude/sobresalir *v.* resaltar; proyectarse; p. 369

proverbial/proverbial *adj.* conocido y notable; p. 1094

providence/providencia *s.* cuidado o guía divina; disposición; p. 70

provoke/provocar *v.* inducir; incitar; p. 1132

proximity/proximidad *s.* cercanía en espacio, tiempo, secuencia o grado; p. 302

prudence/prudencia *s.* ejercicio del buen juicio y la cordura; cautela; p. 102

Q

querulous/quejumbroso *adj.* que se queja mucho; lastimero; p. 483

quivering/estremecimiento *s.* temblor repentino; sacudida; sobresalto; p. 834

R

radical/radical *adj.* que se desvía de lo usual o común; extremo; p. 1049

random/causal *adj.* que no sigue un patrón definido; fortuito; p. 1032

ration/ración *s.* porción definida; p. 62

ravage/asolamiento *s.* acción destructiva o resultado de una acción destructiva; p. 156

ravenous/voraz *adj.* extremadamente hambriento; p. 11

reciprocate/corresponder *v.* dar, sentir o mostrar a cambio; p. 652

recourse/recurso *s.* ayuda; medio que, en caso de necesidad, sirve para conseguir lo que se pretende; p. 185

rectitude/rectitud *s.* buena condición moral; honestidad; p. 172

redress/desagravio *s.* compensación por un error o mala actitud; p. 364

refugee/refugiado *s.* persona que huye por razones de seguridad, especialmente quien abandona su hogar o país debido a persecución, guerra o peligro; p. 352

rejuvenated/rejuvenecido *adj.* que ha recuperado el vigor o la apariencia joven; renovado; p. 1005

relinquish/rendir *v.* ceder el control; doblegarse; p. 156

reminiscence/reminiscencia *s.* relato de una experiencia o suceso pasado; p. 462

remonstrate/rezongar *v.* objetar; protestar; p. 148

remorselessly/despiadadamente *adv.* de un modo que no muestra piedad ni compasión; sin misericordia; p. 165

render/producir *v.* causar; generar; p. 184

repertoire/repertorio *s.* conjunto de destrezas que una persona o grupo tiene y está preparado para demostrar en una actuación; p. 280

repression/represión *s.* situación en la que se frena o mantiene bajo control; p. 526

reprieve/aplazamiento *s.* demora oficial de una sentencia; p. 985

reprimand/reprender *v.* regañar o corregir severamente; p. 937

reproach/reproche *s.* expresión de desacuerdo; censura; p. 533

repudiate/repudiar *v.* negarse a aceptar como válido; rechazar; renunciar; p. 894

resign/resignarse *v.* obligarse a aceptar; conformarse; p. 683

resignation/resignación *s.* aceptación; conformismo; sumisión; p. 253

resolution/resolución *s.* acción de decidir con firmeza; p. 156

resolve/resolver *v.* decidir; determinar; p. 70

resonant/resonante *adj.* que tiene un sonido fuerte y vibrante; p. 1068

retaliation/represalia *s.* acto de vengarse o devolver un mal acto cometiendo un acto similar o igual; p. 985

retractable/retráctil *adj.* capaz de encogerse; p. 784

revive/revivir *v.* dar nueva fuerza y vitalidad; hacer que recupere el conocimiento; p. 62

rigorously/rigurosamente *adv.* precisamente; estrictamente; p. 1130

ritual/ritual *s.* rutina que se sigue regularmente; ceremonial; p. 1092

rouse/despertar *v.* dejar de dormir; p. 62

rudiment/rudimento *s.* parte imperfecta o sin desarrollar; p. 254

rue/deplorar *v.* lamentar; sentir; p. 16

S

sagacious/sagaz *adj.* que tiene o demuestra astucia y agudeza mental; p. 269

sage/sabio *s.* persona con profundo conocimiento y buen juicio; p. 245

sanction/ratificación *s.* aprobación o respaldo; p. 261

savory/apetitoso *adj.* agradable al paladar o al olfato; sabroso; p. 89

scavenger/trapero *s.* el que busca y recoge cosas útiles de la basura; p. 1078

score/veintena *s.* grupo de veinte objetos; p. 385

scruple/escrúpulo *s.* principio moral que limita una acción; p. 194

scrupulously/escrupulosamente *adv.* con extremo cuidado y atención; esmeradamente; p. 1130

scuffle/arrastrar los pies *v.* moverse con pasos rápidos y torpes; p. 798

seclusion/reclusión *s.* separación de otros; aislamiento; p. 481

sibling/fraterno *adj.* relativo a un hermano o hermana; p. 1067

signal/insigne *adj.* admirable; asombroso; notable; p. 165

simultaneously/simultáneamente *adv.* al mismo tiempo; p. 1129

sluggard/haragán *s.* alguien que por lo general es perezoso o vago; ocioso; p. 141

sluggishly/perezosamente *adv.* lentamente; sin energía ni entusiasmo; p. 805

snicker/risita burlona *s.* risa solapada que puede demostrar burla o falta de respeto; p. 727

solemn/solemne *adj.* serio; grave; p. 838

speculate/especular *v.* participar en negocios arriesgados con el deseo de obtener ganancias rápidas; p. 210

spurn/desdeñar *v.* rechazar con menosprecio o desdén; p. 149

stately/majestuoso *adj.* noble; imponente; espléndido; p. 12

stature/estatura *s.* nivel alcanzado; posición; p. 894

stoically/estoicamente *adv.* de modo calmado y sin emoción, especialmente en momentos de dolor o sufrimiento; p. 691

stolidly/impasiblemente *adv.* con poca o ninguna emoción; sin perturbarse; p. 1132

stooped/encorvado *adj.* doblado hacia adelante y hacia abajo; p. 1063

subjugation/subyugación *s.* acto de someter o poner bajo control; dominación; p. 148

sublime/sublime *adj.* de gran valor espiritual o intelectual; noble; p. 253

submissive/sumiso *adj.* dispuesto a ceder el poder o autoridad a otro; dócil; p. 1048

subservient/subordinado *adj.* útil, en una capacidad inferior, para conseguir un fin; sumiso; p. 919

subtle/sutil *adj.* que no es obvio ni directo; p. 949

subversive/subversivo *adj.* que busca destruir o debilitar; p. 1079

succor/socorro *s.* ayuda en momentos de necesidad; auxilio; p. 71

succumb/sucumbir *v.* rendirse; ceder; p. 893

sumptuous/suntuoso *adj.* que implica un gran gasto; extravagante; espléndido; p. 1068

supplication/súplica *s.* solicitud humilde de ayuda; ruego; p. 280

surmise/suponer *v.* conjeturar con poca o ninguna evidencia; presumir; p. 207

sustenance/sustento *s.* que conserva la vida, especialmente alimento; p. 520

symmetrical/simétrico *adj.* que tiene la misma forma o estructura a ambos lados de una línea o plano central; p. 1047

synthesis/síntesis *s.* combinación de partes o elementos separados para formar un todo; p. 893

T

tactful/discreto *adj.* capaz de hablar o actuar sin ofender a otros; p. 622

temper/atemperar *v.* modificar o moderar; suavizar; p. 57

tentative/tentativo *adj.* que no se ha definido por completo; p. 658

tenure/tenencia *s.* condiciones o términos bajo los cuales se posee algo; p. 171

thicket/espesura *s.* área de vegetación densa con muchos arbustos; p. 834

torpor/entumecimiento *s.* incapacidad de moverse o sentir; p. 274

treacherous/traicionero *adj.* que tiende a engañar; desleal; p. 1079

trek/travesía *s.* viaje, especialmente si es lento o difícil; p. 1098

trepidation/perturbación *s.* anticipación nerviosa; ansiedad; p. 536

tumult/tumulto *s.* alboroto; conmoción; p. 1094

tumultuously/tumultuosamente *adv.* de modo agitado; violentamente; p. 526

turmoil/disturbio *s.* estado de agitación; conmoción; p. 537

tyranny/tiranía *s.* uso cruel de la autoridad; poder opresivo; p. 155

U

uncanny/espectral *adj.* inquietante y extraño; misterioso; p. 562

undeviating/recto *adj.* que no se desvía o extravía; p. 1183

unorthodox/no ortodoxo *adj.* que no es usual ni tradicional; p. 33

unperturbed/inalterado *adj.* que no se molesta o altera; calmado; p. 975

upbraiding/reprochador *adj.* que da una crítica o recriminación severa; p. 333

usurpation/usurpación *s.* acto de tomar el poder sin derecho o autoridad legal; p. 169

V

vagabond/vagabundo *s.* alguien que vaga de un lugar a otro, sin tener medios aparentes de ganarse la vida; p. 468

valedictorian/orador *s.* estudiante de más alto rango que pronuncia el discurso de despedida; p. 1098

valor/valor *s.* coraje; valentía; p. 1049

vanity/vanidad *s.* orgullo excesivo, particularmente por la apariencia física; p. 625

vanquish/subyugar *v.* derrotar; conquistar p. 333

vault/bóveda *s.* estructura arqueada que forma un techo o cielo raso; p. 48

vehemently/vehementemente *adv.* de modo fuerte, intenso o apasionado; p. 690

venerable/venerable *adj.* que merece respeto debido a la edad, carácter o posición; p. 268

venture/empresa *s.* negocio o acto aventurado; p. 351

vigilance/vigilancia *s.* condición de estar alerta o vigilante; p. 520

vigorously/vigorosamente *adv.* con poder, energía y fuerza; p. 835

vile/vil *adj.* malvado; bajo; repulsivo; degradante; p. 960

vindicate/vindicar *v.* justificar; demostrar que es correcto ante nuevas circunstancias; p. 807

vindictive/vengativo *adj.* que desea venganza; p. 823

virtuous/virtuoso *adj.* recto; bueno; p. 363

virulent/virulento *adj.* extremadamente nocivo o dañino; p. 810

vital/vital *adj.* de enorme importancia; esencial; p. 826

vivid/vívido *adj.* auténtico; realista; distintivo; p. 826

W

wane/declinar *v.* menguar o disminuir gradualmente; p. 1184

warily/cautelosamente *adv.* de modo cuidadoso o alerta; p. 1032

warranted/justificado *adj.* que se explica en vista de las circunstancias; p. 1102

whimsically/caprichosamente *adv.* de modo extravagante; p. 691

wistful/nostálgico *adj.* lleno de melancolía o añoranza; p. 1067

withered/marchito *adj.* seco; arrugado; p. 680

wrath/ira *s.* furia extrema; castigo vengativo; p. 102

writhe/retorcerse *s.* flexionar, como cuando se siente gran dolor; p. 1054

Z

zealous/fervoroso *adj.* lleno de entusiasmo y devoción; apasionado; p. 274

Index of Skills

Index of Authors and Titles

Index of Art and Artists

Acknowledgments

(Continued from page ii)

Literature

Active Reading Models

"The Life You Save May Be Your Own" from *A Good Man Is Hard to Find and Other Stories,* copyright © 1953 by Flannery O'Connor and renewed 1981 by Reginia O'Connor, reprinted by permission of Harcourt Brace & Company.

"The Fish" from *The Complete Poems 1927–1979* by Elizabeth Bishop. Copyright © 1979, 1983 by Alice Helen Methfessel. Reprinted by permission of Farrar, Straus & Giroux, Inc.

"Thoughts on the African-American Novel" by Toni Morrison, from *Black Women Writers (1950–1980)* by Mari Evans. Copyright © 1983 by Mari Evans. Used by permission of Doubleday, a division of Bantam Doubleday Dell Publishing Group, Inc.

Unit 1

"The Sky Tree" retold by Joseph Bruchac, from *Keepers of Life,* by Michael Caduto and Joseph Bruchac. Copyright © 1994, Fulcrum Publishing, 350 Indiana St., Suite 350, Golden, CO 80401. (800) 992–2908.

"Shipwreck Survivors Recall Ordeal" by Patrick McDonnell. Copyright © 1997, Los Angeles Times. Reprinted by permission.

Excerpt from *The Account: Alvar Nunez Cabeza de Vaca's Relacion,* edited and translated by José Fernandez and Martin Favata is reprinted with permission from the publisher (Houston: Arte Publico Press—University of Houston, 1993).

"In Your Eyes" by Peter Gabriel. Copyright © 1986 Real World Music, Ltd. Reprinted with permission of Lipservices.

From Lang, Amy Schrager, ed. "A True History of the Captivity and Restoration of Mary Rowlandson," in Andrews, William L., Sargent Bush Jr., Annette Kolodny, Amy Schrager Lang and Daniel B. Shea, eds. *Journeys in New Worlds: Early American Women's Narratives.* Copyright 1990. Reprinted by permission of The University of Wisconsin Press.

Reprinted with the permission of The Free Press, a Division of Simon & Schuster from *Stay Alive, My Son* by Pin Yathay. Copyright © 1987 by Pin Yathay. Excerpt from *Stay Alive, My Son,* copyright © 1987 by Pin Yathay. Reprinted by permission of the author.

Unit 2

"Dichos" by Americo Paredes from *Mexican-American Authors.* Copyright © 1976, 1972 by Houghton Mifflin Company. All rights reserved. Reprinted by permission of McDougal Littell Inc.

"Give Me Rhetoric!" by Wen Smith, from the *Saturday Evening Post,* September/October 1996. Reprinted by permission of the author.

"Thermopylae" from *The Histories* by Herodotus, translated by Aubrey de Selincourt, revised by A. R. Burn (Penguin Classics 1954, Revised edition 1972) copyright © the Estate of Aubrey de Selincourt, 1954 copyright © A. R. Burn, 1972. Reprinted by permission of Penguin Books Ltd.

"To His Excellency, George Washington" from *The Poems of Phillis Wheatley,* edited by Julian D. Mason. Copyright © 1989 by the University of North Carolina Press. Used by permission of the publisher.

"Amistad America" reprinted by permission of the Amistad Project, Mystic Seaport, Connecticut.

From "Bart Sells his Soul," *The Simpsons*™ and © 1996 Twentieth Century Fox Film Corporation. All rights reserved. Reprinted by permission.

"Dead Singer Buckley's Voice Haunts Poe Disc" by Steve James © Reuters Limited 1998. Used by permission.

Unit 3

"Swing Low, Sweet Chariot" and "Go Down, Moses" from *Religious Folk-Songs of the Negro,* edited by R. Nathaniel Dett. Reprinted courtesy of AMS Press, Inc.

"Follow the Drinking Gourd," adapted by John L. Haag, from *All American Folk, Vol. #1.* Copyright © 1982 and 1986 Creative Concepts Publishing Corp. Used by permission.

"Mars Robot 'Sojourner' Named by Black Girl to Honor Abolitionist Sojourner Truth," *Jet* magazine, July 29, 1997. Reprinted by permission.

From *His Promised Land: The Autobiography of John P. Parker* by Stuart Selly Sprague, editor. Copyright © 1996 by The John P. Parker Historical Society. Reprinted by permission of W. W. Norton & Company, Inc.

Excerpt from *Mary Chestnut's Civil War,* edited by C. Vann Woodward. Copyright © 1986 by C. Vann Woodward, Sally Bland Metts, Barbara G. Carpenter, Sally Bland Johnson, and Katherine W. Herbert. Reprinted by permission of Yale University Press.

"An Occurrence at Owl Creek Bridge" from *The Twilight Zone Companion* by Marc Scott Zicree. Copyright © 1982 by Marc Scott Zicree. Reprinted by permission of the author.

"The Gift in Wartime" by Tran Mong Tu. Reprinted by permission of the author.

"Stolen Whitman Papers Surface After 50 Years" by David Streitfeld and Elizabeth Kastor. Copyright © 1995, The Washington Post. Reprinted with permission.

"The Useless" by Thomas Merton from *The Way of Chuang Tzu.* Copyright © 1965 by The Abbey of Gethsemane. Reprinted by permission of New Directions Publishing Corp.

"Butterfly Dream" from *The Book of Chuang Tzu,* translated by Martin Palmer, with Elizabeth Breuilly, Chang Wai Ming, and Jay Ramsey (Arkana, 1996) copyright © ICOREC 1996. Reproduced by permission of Penguin Books Ltd.

Poems #511, #303, #67, #435, #1624, #1732, #465, #1078, #712, #258, #441 reprinted by permission of the publishers and the Trustees of Amherst College from *The Poems of Emily Dickinson,* Thomas H. Johnson, ed., Cambridge, Mass: The Belknap Press of Harvard University Press, copyright © 1951, 1955, 1979, 1983 by the President and Fellows of Harvard College.

Emily Dickinson parody ("The Apple falls—its own Society—") by Christopher C. Lund. Reprinted by permission of the author.

Unit 4

Excerpt from *Frogs,* text © David Badger, photo © John Netherton, reprinted with permission of the publisher, Voyageur Press, Inc., Stillwater, MN 55082. 1-800-888-9653.

"Chief Sekoto Holds Court" from *Tales of Tenderness and Power,* published by Heinemann International in their African Writers Series, 1990. Copyright © 1989 The Estate of Bessie Head.

Unit 5

"In a Station of the Metro" and "A Pact" by Ezra Pound, from *Personae.* Copyright © 1926 by Ezra Pound. Reprinted by permission of New Directions Publishing Corp.

"The Red Wheelbarrow," and "This Is Just to Say" by William Carlos Williams, from *Collected Poems: 1909–1939, Volume I.* Copyright © 1938 by New Directions Publishing Corp. Reprinted by permission of New Directions Publishing Corp.

"Anecdote of the Jar" from *Collected Poems* by Wallace Stevens. Copyright © 1923 and renewed 1951 by Wallace Stevens. Reprinted by permission of Alfred A. Knopf, Inc.

From "Let's Call the Whole Thing Off" by Leila Cobo-Hanlon. Reprinted with the permission of the *St. Louis Post-Dispatch,* copyright © 1995.

"The Jilting of Granny Weatherall" from *Flowering Judas and Other Stories,* copyright © 1930 and renewed 1958 by Katherine Anne Porter, reprinted by permission of Harcourt Brace & Company.

"Richness" by Gabriela Mistral, translated by Doris Dana. Reprinted by arrangement with Doris Dana, c/o Joan Daves Agency as agent for the proprietor. Copyright © 1971 by Doris Dana.

"Ars Poetica" from *Collected Poems 1917–1982* by Archibald MacLeish. Copyright © 1985 by The Estate of Archibald MacLeish. Reprinted by permission of Houghton Mifflin Company. All rights reserved.

"Dirge Without Music" by Edna St. Vincent Millay. From *Collected Poems,* HarperCollins. Copyright © 1928, 1955 by Edna St. Vincent Millay and Norma Millay Ellis. All rights reserved. Used by permission of Elizabeth Barnett, literary executor.

"Recuerdo" by Edna St. Vincent Millay. From *Collected Poems,* HarperCollins. Copyright © 1922, 1950 by Edna St. Vincent Millay. All rights reserved. Used by permission of Elizabeth Barnett, literary executor.

"anyone lived in a pretty how town," copyright 1940, © renewed 1968, 1991 by the Trustees for the E. E. Cummings Trust, from *Complete Poems: 1904–1962* by E. E. Cummings. Edited by George J. Firmage. Reprinted by permission of Liveright Publishing Corporation.

"Poetry," reprinted with the permission of Simon & Schuster from *Collected Poems* by Marianne Moore. Copyright © 1935 by Marianne Moore; copyright renewed © 1963 by Marianne Moore and T. S. Eliot.

"The Bridal Party," reprinted with the permission of Scribner, a division of Simon & Schuster, from *The Short Stories of F. Scott Fitzgerald,* edited by Matthew J. Bruccoli. Copyright © 1930 by Curtis Publishing. Copyright renewed © 1958 by Frances Scott Fitzgerald Lanahan.

Excerpts from *Songs of Gold Mountain: Rhymes from San Francisco Chinatown* by Marion K. Hom. Copyright © 1987 The Regents of the University of California. Reprinted by permission of the University of California Press.

"In Another Country," reprinted by permission of Scribner, a division of Simon & Schuster, from *Men Without Women* by Ernest Hemingway. Copyright © 1927 by Charles Scribner's Sons. Copyright renewed 1955 by Ernest Hemingway.

"Soldiers of the Republic" by Dorothy Parker, and "Penelope" by Dorothy Parker, from *The Portable Dorothy Parker* by Dorothy Parker, Introduction by Brendan Gill. Copyright 1928, renewed © 1956 by Dorothy Parker. Used by permission of Viking Penguin, a division of Penguin Books USA, Inc.

"Stopping by Woods on a Snowy Evening," "Mending Wall," "Birches," and "The Death of the Hired Man" from *The Poetry of Robert Frost,* edited by Edward Connery Lathem. Copyright 1944, 1951, © 1956, 1958 by Robert Frost, © 1967 by Lesley Frost Ballantine, copyright 1916, 1923, 1928, 1930, 1939 © 1969 by Henry Holt & Co., Inc. Reprinted by permission of Henry Holt & Co., Inc.

"My City," copyright 1935 by James Weldon Johnson, © renewed 1963 by Grace Nail Johnson, from *Saint Peter Relates an Incident* by James Weldon Johnson. Used by permission of Viking Penguin, a division of Penguin Books USA Inc.

"A Place to Be Free" by Constance Johnson. Copyright © March 2, 1992, *U.S. News & World Report.* Reprinted by permission.

Excerpt from *Dust Tracks on a Road* by Zora Neale Hurston. Copyright © 1942 by Zora Neale Hurston. Copyright renewed 1970 by John C. Hurston. Reprinted by permission of HarperCollins Publishers, Inc.

"Artist Jacob Lawrence" © Copyright NPR® 1998. The news report by NPR's William Drummond was originally broadcast on National Public Radio's "Morning Edition®" on June 9, 1998, and is used with the permission of National Public Radio, Inc. Any unauthorized duplication is strictly prohibited.

"I, Too" from *Collected Poems* by Langston Hughes. Copyright © 1996 by the Estate of Langston Hughes. Reprinted by permission of Alfred A. Knopf, Inc.

"The Negro Speaks of Rivers" from *Selected Poems* by Langston Hughes. Copyright © 1926 by Alfred A. Knopf and renewed 1954 by Langston Hughes. Reprinted by permission of the publisher.

"And We Shall Be Steeped" from *Nocturnes* by L. S. Senghor. Copyright © Editions du Seuil, 1964. Reprinted by permission of Editions du Seuil.

"Storm Ending" from *The Collected Poems of Jean Toomer,* edited by Robert B. Jones and Margery Toomer Latimer. Copyright © 1988 by the University of North Carolina Press. Used by permission of the publisher.

"November Cotton Flower" from *Cane* by Jean Toomer. Copyright 1923 by Boni & Liveright, renewed 1951 by Jean Toomer. Reprinted by permission of Liveright Publishing Corporation.

"A Black Man Talks of Reaping" from *Personals* by Arna Bontemps. Reprinted by permission of Harold Ober Associates Incorporated. Copyright © 1963 by Arna Bontemps.

"Any Human to Another" from *On These I Stand* by Countee Cullen. Copyrights held by the Amistad Research Center, administered by Thompson and Thompson, New York, NY.

From *A Brief History Of Time* by Stephen W. Hawking. Copyright © 1988 by Stephen W. Hawking. Used by permission of Bantam Books, a division of Random House, Inc.

Unit 6

"The Second Tree from the Corner" from *The Second Tree from the Corner* by E. B. White. Copyright © 1947 by E. B. White. Copyright renewed. Reprinted by permission of HarperCollins Publishers, Inc.

Excerpt from "The Mystery of Happiness" an ABC Special Report, September 4, 1997. Special thanks to ABC News.

"Ode to My Socks" from *Neruda and Vallejo: Selected Poems,* translated by Robert Bly and James Wright, Boston, Beacon Press 1976. © 1972 by Robert Bly. Reprinted with the translator's permission.

"Breakfast" from *The Long Valley* by John Steinbeck. Copyright 1938, renewed © 1966 by John Steinbeck. Used by permission of Viking Penguin, a division of Penguin Putnam Inc.

"A Rose for Emily" from *Collected Stories of William Faulkner* by William Faulkner. Copyright © 1930 and renewed 1958 by William Faulkner. Reprinted by permission of Random House, Inc.

"Upon Receiving the Nobel Prize for Literature" from *Essays, Speeches & Public Letters by William Faulkner* by William Faulkner, edited by James B. Meriwether. Copyright © 1950 by William Faulkner. Reprinted by permission of Random House, Inc.

"Father's Bedroom" from *Selected Poems* by Robert Lowell. Copyright © 1976 by the Estate of Robert Lowell. Reprinted by permission of Farrar, Straus & Giroux, Inc.

Excerpt from *Black Boy* by Richard Wright. Copyright © 1937, 1942, 1944, 1945 by Richard Wright. Copyright renewed 1973 by Ellen Wright. Reprinted by permission of HarperCollins Publishers, Inc.

"100-Mile Run to Agony and Ecstasy" by Sonia Nazario. Copyright © 1996, Los Angeles Times. Reprinted by permission.

"A Worn Path" from *A Curtain of Green and Other Stories,* copyright 1941 and renewed 1969 by Eudora Welty, reprinted by permission of Harcourt Brace & Company.

"The Explorer" by Gwendolyn Brooks, from *Blacks,* published by Third World Press, Chicago. © 1991. Reprinted by permission of the author.

"February" from *The Collected Essays of Ralph Ellison* by Ralph Ellison. Copyright © 1995 by Random House, Inc. Reprinted by permission of Random House, Inc.

"The Portrait" by Tomás Rivera, translated by Evangelina Vigil-Piñon, is reprinted with permission from the publisher of . . . *And the Earth Did Not Devour Him* (Houston: Arte Publico Press-University of Houston, 1987).

"The Death of the Ball Turret Gunner" from *The Complete Poems* by Randall Jarrell. Copyright © 1969 by Mrs. Randall Jarrell. Reprinted by permission of Farrar, Straus & Giroux, Inc.

"The Beautiful Changes" from *The Beautiful Changes and Other Poems,* copyright © 1947 and renewed 1975 by Richard Wilbur, reprinted by permission of Harcourt Brace & Company.

"The Rockpile" is collected in *Going to Meet the Man* © 1965 by James Baldwin. Copyright renewed. Published by Vintage Books.

Reprinted by arrangement with the James Baldwin Estate.

"The Magic Barrel" from *The Magic Barrel* by Bernard Malamud. Copyright © 1950, 1958 and copyright renewed © 1977, 1986 by Bernard Malamud.

Excerpt from *Stride Toward Freedom* reprinted by arrangement of The Heirs to the Estate of Martin Luther King Jr., c/o Writers House, Inc. as agent for the proprietor. Copyright 1963 by Martin Luther King Jr., copyright renewed 1991 by Coretta Scott King.

"Choice, A Tribute to Dr. Martin Luther King, Jr." from *In Search of Our Mothers' Gardens, Womanist Prose,* copyright © 1983 by Alice Walker, reprinted by permission of Harcourt Brace & Company.

"Blacklisted Women Vindicated by Federal Court Ruling" © Copyright NPR® 1996. The news report by NPR's Daniel Zwerdling was originally broadcast on National Public Radio's "Morning Edition®" on March 16, 1996, and is used with the permission of National Public Radio, Inc. Any unauthorized duplication is strictly prohibited.

The Crucible by Arthur Miller. Copyright 1952, 1953, 1954, renewed © 1980, 1981, 1982 by Arthur Miller. Used by permission of Viking Penguin, a division of Penguin Books USA Inc.

"Nineteen Thirty-Seven" from *Krik? Krak!* by Edwidge Danticat. Copyright © 1991, 1992, 1993, 1994, 1995 by Edwidge Danticat. Reprinted by permission of Soho Press.

Unit 7

"Snow" from *How the Garcia Girls Lost Their Accents.* Copyright © 1991 by Julia Alvarez. Published by Plume, an imprint of Dutton Signet, a division of Penguin USA, Inc., and originally in hardcover by Algonquin Books of Chapel Hill. Reprinted by permission of Susan Bergholz Literary Services, New York. All rights reserved.

Excerpt from *The Woman Warrior* by Maxine Hong Kingston. Copyright © 1975, 1976 by Maxine Hong Kingston. Reprinted by permission of Random House.

"Son" from *Problems and Other Stories* by John Updike. Copyright © 1973 by John Updike. Reprinted by permission of Alfred A. Knopf, Inc.

Excerpt from *The Way to Rainy Mountain* by N. Scott Momaday. Copyright © 1969 by the University of New Mexico Press. Reprinted by permission of the author.

"Ambush" from *The Things They Carried.* Copyright © 1990 by Tim O'Brien. Reprinted by permission of Houghton Mifflin Co./Seymour Lawrence. All rights reserved.

"Kitchens" by Aurora Levins Morales from *Getting Home Alive* by Aurora Levins Morales and Rosario Morales. Copyright © 1986 by Aurora Levins Morales and Rosario Morales. Reprinted by permission of Firebrand Books.

"Bread" from *Good Bones and Simple Murders* by Margaret Atwood. Copyright © 1983, 1992, 1994 by O. W. Toad Ltd. A Nan A. Talese Book. Used by permission of Doubleday, a division of Bantam Doubleday Dell Publishing Group, Inc.

"Bread" from *Murder in the Dark* by Margaret Atwood. Used by permission, McClelland & Stewart, Inc., *The Canadian Publishers.*

"Picture Bride" from *Picture Bride* by Cathy Song. Copyright © 1983 by Cathy Song. Reprinted by permission of Yale University Press.

"Love and Money" by Ellen Futterman. Reprinted with permission of the *St. Louis Post-Dispatch.* Copyright © 1994.

"Prime Time" from *Colored People* by Henry Louis Gates Jr. Copyright © 1994 by Henry Louis Gates Jr. Reprinted by permission of Alfred A. Knopf, Inc.

Excerpt from "Kubota" from *Volcano* by Garrett Hongo. Copyright © 1995 by Garrett Hongo. Reprinted by permission of Alfred A. Knopf, Inc.

"Speaking" from *Woven Stone* by Simon J. Ortiz. Copyright © 1992 by Simon J. Ortiz. Reprinted by permission of the author.

"apprenticeship" reprinted by permission of the author, Evangelina Vigil-Piñon.

"Prayer to the Pacific," copyright © 1981 by Leslie Marmon Silko. Reprinted from *Storyteller* by Leslie Marmon Silko, published by Seaver Books, New York, New York.

"Riding the Elevator Into the Sky" from *The Awful Rowing Toward God* by Anne Sexton. First published in the *New Yorker.* Copyright © 1975 by Loring Conant Jr., executor of the Estate of Anne Sexton. Reprinted by permission of Houghton Mifflin Company. All rights reserved.

Excerpt from "Need a Lift?" by Randy Brown, from *Buildings,* December 1996. Copyright © 1996 Stamats Communications. Reprinted by permission.

"Game" by Donald Barthelme. Copyright © 1982 by Donald Barthelme, as printed in *60 Stories.* Reprinted with the permission of The Wylie Agency.

"Waiting for the Barbarians" from Keeley, Edmund, and Sherrard, Philip (translators); *C. P. Cavafy: Selected Poems.* Copyright © 1972 by Edmund Keeley and Philip Sherrard. Reprinted by permission of Princeton University Press.

"Mirror" from *Crossing the Water* by Sylvia Plath. Copyright © 1963 by Ted Hughes. Originally appeared in the *New Yorker.* Reprinted by permission of HarperCollins Publishers, Inc.

"Traveling Through the Dark," copyright © 1962, 1998 by the Estate of William Stafford. Reprinted from *The Way It Is: New & Selected Poems* by William Stafford with the permission of Graywolf Press, Saint Paul, Minnesota.

"Frederick Douglass," copyright © 1966 by Robert Hayden, from *Collected Poems of Robert Hayden* by Frederick Glaysher, editor. Reprinted by permission of Liveright Publishing Corporation.

"#2 Memory" and "Poem" from *Mainland* by Victor Hernandez Cruz. Copyright © 1973 by Victor Hernandez Cruz. Reprinted by permission of Random House, Inc.

"Weaver" copyright © 1974 Sandra María Esteves, reprinted with permission from the author.

"For Georgia O'Keeffe," by Pat Mora, is reprinted with permission from the publisher of *Chants* (Houston: Arte Publico Press— University of Houston, 1985).

"Most Satisfied By Snow" first appeared in *The Virginia Quarterly Review,* Autumn, 1973. Copyrighted by Diana Chang and reprinted by permission of the author.

"Geometry" from *Rita Dove, Selected Poems,* © 1980, 1993 by Rita Dove. Used by permission of the author.

"The Welder" from *This Bridge Called My Back: Writings by Radical Women of Color.* Copyright © 1983 by Cherrie Moraga and Gloria Anzaldua. NY: Kitchen Table Press, 1983.

"The House" and "La Casa" by Maria Herrera-Sobek, from *Chasqui,* published in *Infinite Divisions,* by Tey Diana Rebolledo (University of Arizona Press, 1993).

"Salvador Late or Early" from *Woman Hollering Creek.* Copyright © 1991 by Sandra Cisneros. Published by Vintage Books, a division of Random House, Inc., and originally in hardcover by Random House, Inc. Reprinted by permission of Susan Bergholz Literary Services, New York. All rights reserved.

"Embroidering: A Response to 'Somnad' by Carl Larsson" by Rita Magdaleno, from *New Chicano/Chicana Writing 2,* University of Arizona Press, 1992. Reprinted by permission of the author.

"El Olvido" by Judith Ortiz Cofer is reprinted with permission from the publisher of *Terms of Survival* (Houston: Arte Publico Press - University of Houston, 1987).

"The Names of Women," copyright © 1992 by Louise Erdrich (from *Granta* 41, Autumn 1992). This story first appeared in Granta and was later adapted and made part of Ms. Erdrich's novel *Tales of Burning Love* (HarperCollins 1996). Reprinted by permission of the author.

"The name reign: new parents balance the trendy and the unique" by Janet Simons. Reprinted by permission from the Rocky Mountain News.

"Naming Myself" and "Poniendome un Nombre" by Barbara Kingsolver. Copyright © 1994 by Barbara Kingsolver. Reprinted from *Another America,* by Barbara Kingsolver, and published by Seal Press.

"A Poet's Job" by Alma Villanueva, from *Bloodroot,* Place of Herons Press, 1982. Reprinted by permission of the author.

Maps

Ortelius Design, Inc.

Photography

Abbreviation key: **AH** = Aaron Haupt Photography; **AP** = Archive Photos; **AR** = Art Resource, New York; **BAL** = Bridgeman Art Library, London/New York; **CB** = Corbis/Bettmann; **CI** = Christie's Images; **FMWPC** = Frank & Marie-Therese Wood Print Collections, Alexandria VA; **LPBC/AH** = book provided by Little Professor Book Company. Photo by Aaron Haupt; **LOC** = Library of Congress; **NWPA** = North Wind Picture Archives; **SIS** = Stock Illustration Source; **SS** = SuperStock; **TSI** = Tony Stone Images.

Cover (coin)Aaron Haupt, (painting)The Patrick Henry National Memorial, Brookneal VA; **vii** (t–b)NWPA, Chateau de Versailles, France/E.T. Archive, London/SS, Gene Ahren/Bruce Coleman Inc., Culver Pictures, private collection. Courtesy Terry Dintenfass Gallery, NY, CB, Wayne Miller/Magnum Photos; **viii** Ashmolean Museum, Oxford, UK/BAL; **ix** Robert Llewellyn/Uniphoto; **x** (t)Collection of the New York Public Library. Astor, Lenox and Tilden Foundations (b)Independence National Park; **xi** CI; **xii** (t)private collection, photo courtesy Robert M. Hicklin Jr., Inc., Spartanburg SC, (b)High Impact Photography/Time Life Books; **xiv** National Gallery of Art, Washington DC. Gift of the W.L. and May T. Mellon Foundation; **xv** The Museum of Modern Art, New York. Philip L. Goodwin Collection; **xvi** (t)National Gallery of Art, Washington DC. Collection of Mr. and Mrs. Paul Mellon, (b)CB; **xvii** Wide World Photos; **xviii** (t)CI, (b)Tom Till/DRK Photo; **xix** (l)First Image, (r)SAFECO Insurance Company, Seattle WA. Courtesy the artist and the

Francine Seders Gallery, Seattle WA; **xxi** The Stock Market; **xxii** Hampton University Museum, Hampton VA; **xxvii** Cambodian Artists Assistance Program; **xxviii** (t)Ron Watts/Corbis Los Angeles, (b)Art Wolfe/TSI; **xxix** LOC/CB; **4** AH; **6** Flannery O'Connor Collection, Ina Dillard Russell Library, GA College & State University; **7** Courtesy Hubert Shuptrine; **9** O.K. Harris Works of Art, New York; **10** Kactus Foto, Santiago, Chile/SS; **15** O.K. Harris Works of Art, New York; **17** Reprinted with permission of Mrs. Emil J. Kosa Jr.; **20, 21** AH; **22** UPI/CB; **24** BAL; **26, 27** AH; **28** Erin Elder/SABA; **29** Ackland Art Museum, University of NC at Chapel Hill. Ackland Fund; **31** Collection, High Museum at Georgia-Pacific Center, Atlanta GA; **32** Wadsworth Atheneum, Hartford CT. The Ella Galup Sumner and Mary Catlin Sumner Collection; **36** Ashmolean Museum, Oxford, UK/BAL; **38** SS; **39** Hand-colored engraving, NWPA; **40** (tl)AP, (tr)FMWPC, (b)CI; **41** (t)Robert Llewellyn/Uniphoto, (bl)from *Historic Samplers* by Patricia Ryan and Allen D. Bragdon, Bulfinch Press. Collection of The Bennington Museum, Bennington VT, (br)Peabody Essex Museum; **42** (l)American Bible Society, New York/SS, (r)CB; **43** Wadsworth Atheneum, Hartford CT; **44** (t)Culver Pictures/SS; (b)The Newberry Library/Stock Montage; **45** Philbrook Art Center, Tulsa OK; **46** Ron Watts/Corbis Los Angeles; **47** Jose Galvez/PhotoEdit; **50** Rochester Museum & Science Center, Rochester NY; **51** Stock Montage; **53** Arthur Rothstein/CI; **54** Drawing by Seth Eastman; **55** NY State Museum; **60** Flip Nicklin/Minden Pictures; **61** Amanita Pictures; **63** Frederic Remington Art Museum, Ogdensburg NY; **68** CB; **69** Museum of the City of New York/CB; **70** CB; **76** E.T. Archive; **77** Tom Stewart/The Stock Market; **79** The CT Historical Society, Hartford CT; **82** (t)John Henley/The Stock Market, (b)Peter Cade/TSI; **83** NWPA; **84** Trustees of the Boston Library; **85, 87** NWPA; **92** Sophie Bassouls/Sygma; **93** Gamma Liaison; **94** (t)Cambodian Artists Assistance Program, (b)Gamma Liaison; **95, 96** Gamma Liaison; **98** Cambodian Artists Assistance Program; **99** Larry Moore/SIS; **100** Yale University Art Gallery, New Haven CT; **101** Loaned by the Dept. of Parks and Recreation, City of Boston. Courtesy Museum of Fine Arts, Boston; **103** National Portrait Gallery, London; **108** Publishers Depot; **115** LPBC/AH; **118** Collection of the New York Public Library. Astor, Lenox and Tilden Foundations; **120** Private collection/BAL; **121** Bowdoin College of Art Museum; **122** (t)CB, (b)H. Armstrong Roberts; **123** (tl)The Newark Museum/AR, (tr)FMWPC, (b)Museum of Fine Arts, Boston. Gift of Joseph W. Revere, William B. Revere, and Edward H.R. Revere; **124** (l)Brown Brothers, hand coloring by Lorene Ward, (r)LOC/Corbis; **125** (tl)Peabody Essex Museum, Salem MA, (tr)H. Armstrong Roberts, (b)NWPA; **126** (t)Stock Montage/SS, (b)CB; **127** (c)CI, (others) NWPA; **128** (t)National Portrait Gallery, Washington DC/AR, (b)CB; **129** (t)file photo, (b)CB; **130, 132** Collection of The NY Historical Society; **135** AH; **138** Courtesy Arte Publico Press; **139** Reproducción autorizada por el Instituto Nacional De Belles Artes Y Literatura. © 2000 Reproducción autorizada por el Banco de México/Museu de Arte, Sao Paulo, Brazil; **144** Giraudon/AR; **145** Larry Moore/SIS; **146** National Portrait Gallery, Smithsonian Institution/AR; **147** VA Historical Society; **151** Photodisc; **154** AP; **155** Jim Barber; **156** Stock Montage; **160** Scala/AR; **161** Smithsonian Institution; **163** Ronald Sheridan/Ancient Art & Architecture; **164** The Trustees of the National Museums of Scotland; **168** H. Armstrong Roberts; **170** Yale University Art Gallery, New Haven CT; **176** Engraving published by Archibald Bell in 1773, LOC; **177** AH; **182** NY State Historical Association, (b)Smithsonian Institution; **183, 184** The White House Collection, ©White House Historical Association; **187** Courtesy Mystic Seaport; **188** The Royal Albert Memorial Musem, Exeter/BAL; **189** National Maritime Museum, London/BAL; **191** FMWPC; **192** Courtesy Tom Feelings. From *The Middle Passage, White Ships/Black Cargo*, ©1995 Dial Books;

193 The Newberry Library/Stock Montage; **201** Courtesy Robin Holder; **202** CB; **203** Cleveland Museum of Art. Mr. & Mrs. William H. Marlatt Fund, 1967.18; **204** Breck P. Kent/Earth Scenes; **205** (l) Photo Researchers, (r)John Gerlach/Animals Animals; **208** The Ogden Museum of Southern Art, University of New Orleans; **212** The Fine Arts Museums of San Francisco. Gift of Mr. & Mrs. John D. Rockefeller III. 1979.7.84; **216** The Simpsons™ and ©Twentieth Century Fox Film Corporation. All rights reserved; **218** National Academy, New York; **219** National Gallery of Art. Gift of Mrs. Walter B. James; **221** The Metropolitan Museum of Art, New York. Gift of J. Pierpont Morgan; **224** AP; **225** The PA Academy of the Fine Arts, Philadelphia. Gift of Caroline Gison Taitt; **226** Private collection/SS; **229** David M. Dennis; **230** FPG; **232** CI; **235** CB; **236** Dallas Museum of Art; **238** AP; **239** By permission of the Houghton Library, Harvard University. Shelf mark MS Am 1280H, vol. 918, pp. 68, 69; **240** SS; **246** National Portrait Gallery, London/SS; **247** Bruce Satterthwaite; **250** CB; **251** LOC; **254** CI; **257, 262** Charles Philip/Corbis Los Angeles; **264** H. Armstrong Roberts; **267** National Museum of American Art, Washington DC/AR; **268** NWPA; **273** The *Hartford Times*; **278** (t)Middle East News Agency, (b)CI; **279** Sotheby's; **281** Amanita Pictures; **283** NWPA; **285** CB; **286** David David Gallery, Philadelphia/SS; **287** CI; **293** Courtesy William Morrow & Company and R. Michelson Galleries; **295** Courtesy Christa Naher, photo by Lothar Schnepf; **299** Eric van den Brulle/Photonica; **300** Bowes Museum, Co. Durham, UK/BAL; **307** Steve Eichner/Retna Ltd; **313** LPBC/AH; **316, 317** Private collection, photo courtesy Robert M. Hicklin Jr., Inc., Spartanburg SC; **318** The Museum of the Confederacy, Richmond VA, photo by Katherine Wetzel; **320** (t)Mark Burnett; (inset)LOC/Corbis, (bl)National Portrait Gallery, Smithsonian Institution, Washington DC/AR, (br)CB; **321** (t)Mary Evans Picture Library, (bl)National Gallery of Art, Washington DC, (br)file photo; **322** (tl)from the collection of Edith Hariton/Antique Textile Resource, Bethesda, MD, (tr)file photo, (c)LOC, (b)National Portrait Gallery, Smithsonian Institution/AR; **323** CB; **324** (t)E.T. Archive, (b)NWPA; **325** (t)AP, (b)CB, hand coloring by Lorene Ward; **326** (t)Mark Twain Memorial, Hartford CT, (b)LOC/Corbis; **327** The Seventh Regiment Fund, Inc., photograph courtesy The Metropolitan Museum of Art, New York; **328** Corbis; **331** Hampton University Museum, Hampton VA; **336** Collection of the Blue Ridge Institute & Museums/Ferrum College; **337** National Museum of American Art, Washington DC/AR; **338, 339** Hampton University Museum, Hampton VA; **342** (t)Frank Driggs/AP, (b)David Redfern/Retna; **343** NASA; **344** AP; **345** Hampton University Museum, Hampton VA/©Elizabeth Catlett/Licensed by VAGA, New York, NY; **348** Larry Moore/SIS; **350** CB; **355** Doug Martin; **356** National Portrait Gallery, Smithsonian Institution/AR; **357** Corbis, hand coloring by Lorene Ward; **359** CB; **360** Museum of the Confederacy, Richmond VA; **362** West Point Museum Collections, U.S. Military Academy; **363** Cook Collection, Valentine Museum, Richmond VA; **364** High Impact Photography/Time Life Books; **367** CB; **368** The Metropolitan Museum of Art, New York. Gift of Mr. and Mrs. John A. Rutherford, 1914. (14.141); **369** (l)Time Life, (r)SS; **370** CB; **372** Courtesy Rodrigue Studios; **376** The Detroit Institute of Arts. Founders Society Purchase, Merrill Fund; **379** British Film Institute; **381** From a painting by Asa W. Twitchell/CB; **382** Gene Ahren/Bruce Colemman Inc.; **384** CB; **385** David Muench/Corbis; **388** Courtesy Tran Mong Tu; **389** Francis Bailly/Gamma Liaison; **391** David Muench/Corbis; **397** NWPA; **400** Assoc. Press Photo/Eric Miller; **401** Collection of Walt Whitman House, NJ State Historic Site, Camden NJ; **402** Museum of the Confederacy; Larry Sherer/Time Life Books, High Impact Photography; **403** The St. Louis Art Museum; **404** Peter Sickles/SS; **406** Archival Research International/

National Archives; **407** The Brooklyn Museum of Art, New York. Dick S. Ramsay Fund 59.9; **409** The Metropolitan Museum of Art, New York. Gift of Thomas Kensett; **411** The Columbus Museum of Art, Columbus OH. Museum Purchase, Howald Fund; **414** Brooklyn Museum, New York/SS; **419** Private collection/CI; **421** CI; **423** CB; **424** Trustees of Amherst College; **425** Private collection/CI; **426** Shiko Nakano/Photonica; **428** Fine Arts Museums of San Francisco. Gift of Mr. and Mrs. John D. Rockefeller III. 1993.35.20; **429** Collection of the Birmingham Museum of Art, Birmingham AL. Gift of John Meyer; **431** Jane Vollers/Photonica; **432** Tony Craddock/TSI; **435** Heath Robbins/Photonica; **436** CI; **445** LPBC/AH; **448–449** National Gallery of Art, Washington DC. Gift of the W.L. and May T. Mellon Foundation; **450** (l)CA State Railroad Museum, Sacramento/SS, (r)file photo; **451** Culver Pictures; **452** CB; **453** (l) Culver Pictures, (others)file photo; **454** (t)CB, (b)CI; **455** (t)NWPA, (b)The Metropolitan Museum of Art, New York/SS; **456** (tl)Culver Pictures, (tr)CI, (bl)CB, (br)Amanita Pictures; **457** (t)Culver Pictures, hand coloring by Lorene Ward, (b)painting by Isaac Radu, 1903. Photo: Archivio G.B.B./G. Neri/Woodfin Camp & Assoc.; **458** (l)CB, (r)LOC, hand coloring by Lorene Ward; **459** The Fine Arts Museums of San Francisco. Gift of the Charles E. Merrill Trust with matching funds from The de Young Museum Society; **460** AP; **461** North Wind Pictures; **462** Mark Burnett; **463** (t)Mark Burnett, (b)Hirshhorn Museum and Sculpture Garden, Smithsonian Institution. Gift of Joseph H. Hirshhorn; **464** LOC; **465** Museum of the City of New York/BAL; **466** SS; **471** John Netherton; **474** UPI/CB; **475** FMWPC; **476** SS; **478** Roy Bishop/Stock Boston; **481** file photo; **483** The Columbus Museum of Art, Columbus OH. Bequest of Frederick W. Schumacher; **487** J. Goldblatt/Globe Photos; **488** (l)courtesy Thames & Hudson Inc., (r)private collection/BAL; **490, 491** Courtesy Thames & Hudson Inc.; **494** Larry Moore/SIS; **496** AP; **497** CB; **498** Cavalry Club/E.T. Archive/SS; **500** Biophoto Assoc./Photo Researchers; **503** Tom Stock/TSI; **505** Photodisc; **507** Berhard Otto/FPG; **508** Giraudon/AR; **513** National Portrait Gallery, Washington DC/AR; **514** ©1979 Howard Terpning, courtesy The Greenwich Workshop Inc., Shelton CT. For information on limited edition fine art prints by Howard Terpning call 1-800-577-0666; **517** (t)MN Historical Society/Corbis, (b)LOC/Corbis; **519** The Philbrook Museum of Art, Tulsa OK; **523** MO Historical Society; **524** file photo; **525** The Butler Institute of American Art; **530** LOC/Corbis; **531** Ira Nowinski/Corbis; **532** The Hayden Collection, courtesy Museum of Fine Arts, Boston; **532–533** AH; **534** David David Gallery, Philadelphia/SS; **535** NWPA; **537** file photo; **538** Museum of Fine Arts, Boston. Charles Henry Hayden Fund; **542** AP; **543** University of Rochester, photo by Joe Gawlowicz; **544** National Museum of American Art, Washington DC/AR; **546** CB; **547** The Museum of Modern Art, New York. Philip L. Goodwin Collection; **548** The Museums at Stony Brook, NY; **552** (t)FPG, (b)ME Historic Preservation Commission; **553** Portland Museum of Art, Portland ME; **557** AP; **558** The *New York Journal;* **559** Private collection/CI; **563** Collection Mr. & Mrs. Robert A. Kopp Jr., courtesy Mrs. Carol McAdoo; **566** National Museum of American Art, Washington DC/AR; **572** Fischbach Gallery, NY; **583** LPBC/AH; **586–587** National Gallery of Art, Washington DC. Collection of Mr. and Mrs. Paul Mellon; **588** CB; **589** FPG; **590** (l)Underwood & Underwood/ CB, (r)UPI/CB; **591** (l)courtesy AZ Historical Society, Tucson. AHS# 69493–Luisa Ronstadt Espinel, c. 1921, (r)PNI; **592** (t)James Westwater, (c)FMWPC, (b)UPI/CB; **593** (tl)by permission of the Houghton Library, Harvard University, (tr)The Metropolitan Museum of Art, New York. Bequest of Gertrude Stein, 1947, (b)Schomburg Center for Research in Black Culture; **594** (tl)CI, (tr)AP, (b)FPG; **595** (t)Wide World Photos, (bl)AP, (br)Photofest/Jagarts;

596 (l)FPG, (r)CI; **597** Museum of Modern Art, New York. Abby Aldrich Rockefeller Fund; **598, 599** CB; **602** Hulton Getty/TSI; **603** LOC; **605** San Diego Museum of Art. Gift of Anne R. and Amy Putnam; **610** Collection of the Newark Museum. Anonymous gift, 1929. (cat. No. 55); **612** UPI/CB; **613** Courtesy Frank Jensen, photo by Marlin Carter; **614** Kenneth Gabrielson Photography/ Gamma Liaison; **616** (t)CB, (b)Carr Clifton/Minden Pictures; **617** LOC/Corbis; **619** Peter Gridley/FPG; **620** CB; **621** Collection, Hirschl & Adler Galleries; **623** E.T. Archive, London/SS; **626** CI; **627** Photodisc; **631** LOC/Corbis; **635** UPI/CB; **638** CB; **639** Private collection; **640** Collection of The Newark Museum. Purchase, 1939. Felix Fuld Bequest Fund. (cat. No. 22); **642** Culver/PNI; **643** CI; **645** Wide World Photos; **646** UPI/CB; **647** The Metropolitan Museum of Art, New York. Gift of Georgia O'Keeffe through the generosity of The Georgia O'Keeffe Foundation and Jennifer and Joseph Duke, 1997; **650** PhotoAssist/AP; **651** Hulton-Deutsch Collection/Corbis; **654** CB; **659** CI; **662** Private collection/BAL, London/SS; **669** Yousuf Karsh/Woodfin Camp & Assoc.; **670** LOC/Corbis; **671, 672** UPI/CB; **674** LOC/Corbis; **675, 676** Philip Gould/Corbis; **678** Karsh/Woodfin Camp & Assoc.; **679** file photo/The *Kansas City Star.* Reprinted by permission; **683** Scala/ AR; **688** AP; **692** National Gallery, London/SS; **694** CB; **695** Walter Bibikow/FPG; **697** Yale University Art Gallery, New Haven CT. Gift of Walter Bareiss, B.A. 1940; **698** Geir Jordahl/Graphistock; **701** Museum of Fine Arts, Boston. Abraham Shuman Fund (1970.47); **703** Collection of Harrison Young, Beijing, China. Reproduced in *Spirit of Place* by John Arthur; **710** A. Corton/Visuals Unlimited; **711** Larry Moore/SIS; **717** The Schomburg Center for Research in Black Culture, The New York Public Library. Photo: Manu Sassoonian; **718** FPG; **719** LOC/Corbis; **720** Private collection. Courtesy Terry Dintenfass Gallery, New York; **723** National Portrait Gallery, Smithsonian Institution/AR; **724** Photograph owned by Louise Franklin. Courtesy The Association to Preserve the Eatonville; **725** Philadelphia Museum of Art: The Louis E. Stern Collection; **727** Anne Heimann/The Stock Market; **728** Geoff Butler; **733** National Portrait Gallery, Smithsonian Institution/AR; **734** Collection of Martin & Sondra Sperber, New York. Courtesy Heritage Gallery, Los Angeles; **735** Private collection/SS; **738** National Portrait Gallery, Smithsonian Institution/AR; **739** Penguin/CB; **740** Collection of Harry Belafonte. Courtesy Heritage Gallery, Los Angeles; **741** Tom Till/DRK Photo; **744** Peter Jordan/Network/SABA; **745** CI; **749** Museum of Art, Rhode Island School of Design. Gift of Miss Eleanor B. Green; **751** (t)The Beinecke Rare Book and Manuscript Library, Yale University, (b)National Museum of American Art, Smithsonian Institution, Washington DC/AR; **752** (t)UPI/CB, (b)George Lepp/Corbis; **753** Sheldon Ross Gallery, Birmingham MI; **754** The Harmon and Harriet Foundation for the Arts, San Antonio TX; **756** (l)Wide World Photos, (r)The Amistad Research Center, Tulane University, New Orleans; **757** Frank & Marie-Therese Wood Print Collections, Alexandria VA; **758** San Diego Museum of Art, San Diego CA. Museum purchase with funds provided by Mrs. Leon D. Bonnet; **759** National Museum of American Art, Washington DC/AR; **767** LPBC/AH; **770** SAFECO Insurance Company, Seattle WA. Courtesy the artist and the Francine Seders Gallery, Seattle WA; **772** (l)CB, (r)FPG; **773** Hulton Getty Collection/Liaison Agency; **774** (t)Camerique/AP, (c)FPG, (b)Wide World Photos; **775** (t)CB, (c)UPI/CB, (b)Everett Collection; **776** (tl)AH, (tr)Jon Hammer/AP, (b)Walter Sanders/Life Magazine ©Time, Inc.; **777** (t)Willinger/FPG, (bl)Wide World Photos, (br)Geoff Butler; **778** (tl)Hulton Getty Collection/Liaison Agency, (tr)CI, (bl)Geoff Butler, (br)UPI/CB; **779** (t)B. Gotfryd/Woodfin Camp & Assoc., (b)AH; **780** (t)AP, (b)Hulton Getty Collection/Liaison Agency; **781** The Lucy Drake

Marlow Collection Trust; **782** National Portrait Gallery, Smithsonian Institution. Gift of Irving Penn. Courtesy *Vogue*. ©1948 (renewed 1976) by The Conde Nast Publications Inc./AR; **783** David Findlay Jr. Fine Art, New York/BAL; **784** (t)Clay Perry/Corbis, (b)NWPA; **787** Jeff Greenberg/Photo Researchers; **790** The Stock Market; **791** Sovfoto/Eastfoto; **792** Kactus Foto, Santiago, Chile/SS; **796** CB; **797** Everett Collection; **798, 799** UPI/CB; **802** Cofield Collection, Center for the Study of Southern Culture, University of MS; **803** Ted Spiegel/Corbis; **804** First Image; **805** The Art Institute of Chicago. Frank Russell Wadsworth Memorial; **808** SS; **809** Columbus Museum of Art, Columbus OH; **811** First Image; **816** Hulton Getty/Gamma Liaison; **817** Private collection. Courtesy Tibor de Nagy Gallery, New York; **820, 821** AP; **823** Schomburg Center for Research in Black Culture, The New York Public Library; **827** Loïs Mailou Jones Pierre-Noel Trust; **830** Bob Gomel/The Stock Market; **831, 833, 834, 837, 838** Department of Archives and History; **842** The Contemporary Forum. Photo by Bill Tague; **843** National Portrait Gallery/AR; **844** Courtesy Raymond McGuire; **846** B. Gotfryd/Woodfin Camp & Assoc.; **847** Private collection/CI/ SS; **850** Courtesy Arte Publico Press; **851** Scala/AR, (bkgd)courtesy Robert C Buitrón; **853** Courtesy Robert C. Buitrón; **855** Geoff Butler; **856** (t)Wide World Photos, (b)Hulton-Deutsch Collection/ Corbis; **857** Baldwin H. Ward/CB; **860** Nancy Crampton; **863** Richard Kalvar/Magnum Photos; **864** UPI/CB; **865** Gwen Akin/Graphistock; **866** Jonathan Taylor Photography/Uniphoto; **868** E.C. Stangler/Uniphoto; **869** LOC/Corbis; **874** David Lee/Corbis; **875** The Brooklyn Museum, New York; **878** Marcus Gilden Collection; **881** NWPA; **883** Hirshhorn Museum and Sculpture Garden, Smithsonian Institution. Gift of Joseph H. Hirshhorn, May 14, 1981. Photo by Lee Stalsworth; **885** PNI; **890** Flip Schulke/Corbis; **891** Danny Lyon/Magnum Photos. From the book *Memories of the Southern Civil Rights Movement;* **892** Courtesy Reginald Gammon; **893** Culver Pictures; **896** F. Capri/Saga/AP; **897** Aristock, Inc.; **898** Collection of the artist; **907** Museum of the City of New York, Theatre Collection; **910** FPG; **911** UPI/CB; **912** Thomas Lindley/FPG; **913** Daniel Root/ Photonica, (inset)Gjon Mili/Life Magazine ©Time, Inc.; **914** Daniel Root/Photonica; **921** Gjon Mili/Time Life Syndicate; **924** Sande Webster Gallery, Philadelphia, PA; **927** Solomon R. Guggenheim Museum, New York. 54.1408; **930** Courtesy SBC Communications; **933** Gjon Mili/Life Magazine ©Time, Inc.; **937** Daniel Root/ Photonica; **939** The Museum of Modern Art, New York. Purchase/ ©2000 Willem de Kooning Revocable Trust/Artists Rights Society (ARS), New York; **944** Gjon Mili/Life Magazine ©Time, Inc.; **948** The Lane Collection, courtesy Museum of Fine Arts, Boston; **952** Albright-Knox Art Gallery, Buffalo, NY. Gift of Seymour H. Knox, 1957; **954** Courtesy The Robert Miller Gallery, NY/©2000 Pollock-Krasner Foundation/Artists Rights Society (ARS), New York; **958** Daniel Root/Photonica; **963** Sande Webster Gallery, Philadelphia PA; **969, 972** Gjon Mili/Life Magazine ©Time, Inc.; **977** Estate of Elaine DeKooning; **981** Daniel Root/Photonica; **982** Gayle Ray/SS; **989** The Lane Collection, courtesy Museum of Fine Arts, Boston; **992, 994** Gjon Mili/Life Magazine ©Time, Inc.; **998** Nancy Crampton; **999** Collection of Jonathan Demme; **1000** Amanita Pictures; **1001** Collection of Astrid and Halvor Jaeger, Neu-Ulm, West Germany; **1005** Yale University Art Gallery, New Haven CT. Gift of Seldon Rodman; **1008** Gjon Mili/Life Magazine ©Time, Inc.; **1009** Larry Moore/SIS; **1015** LPBC/AH; **1018** The Stock Market; **1020** NASA; **1021** Wayne Miller/Magnum Photos; **1022** (t)Hulton Getty/Gamma Liaison, (c)AP, (bl)H. Armstrong Roberts, (br)John Coletti/Stock Boston; **1023** (t)Gerald Israel/AP, (bl)UPI/CB, (br)Paul Natkin/Outline; **1024** (tl)AH, (tr)Amanita Pictures, (b)Dan Lamont/Corbis; **1025** (t)Cynthia Farah, (b)Tim Wright/Corbis; **1026** (tl)Diana Walker/Gamma Liaison, (tr bl)AH; (br)James D. Wilson/Gamma Liaison; **1027** (t)AH, (b)J. Lowenthal/Woodfin Camp & Assoc.; **1027** (tl)AH, (tr)Bob Peterson/FPG, (c)Geoff Butler, (b)Ian Lloyd/Corbis Los Angeles; **1030** Daniel Cima; **1031** UPI/CB; **1034** Miriam Berkley; **1035** CB; **1037** SS; **1039** Phil Schermeister/Corbis; **1041** NWPA; **1044** Calvin & Hobbes ©1995 Watterson. Reprinted with permission of UNIVERSAL PRESS SYNDICATE. All rights reserved; **1045** Levine/Gamma Liaison; **1046** Jerry Cooke/Corbis; **1047** The St. Louis Art Museum; **1052** Nancy Crampton. **1055, 1058** Courtesy N. Scott Momaday; **1059** Animals Animals/Bates Littlehales; **1062** Miriam Berkley; **1064** Collection National Guard Bureau, Pentagon, Washington DC. From the original painting by Mort Kunstler. ©1984 Mort Kunstler, Inc.; **1066** Jonathan Nourok/PhotoEdit; **1067** Color Box/FPG; **1072** Barry Kleider; **1074** Photodisc; **1075** Tony Arruza/Corbis; **1077** Sophie Bassouls/Sygma; **1079** The Cummer Museum of Art and Gardens, Jacksonville, FL/SS; **1082** (t)John Eddy, (b)Hawaiian Legacy Archive/Pacific Stock; **1083** CI; **1085** Photodisc; **1086** James M. Kelly/Globe Photos; **1087** Whitney Museum of American Art, New York; **1089** UPI/CB; **1093** Francis Miller/Life Magazine ©Time, Inc.; **1096** J. Michael Short; **1097** The Cleveland Museum of Art. Gift of Mrs. Malcolm L. McBride; **1100** Courtesy Alfred A. Knopf Inc. Photo by Shuzo Uemoto; **1101** Collection of Michael D. Brown; **1103** Richard Hutchings/PhotoEdit; **1104** Collection of Yo Kasai; **1105** Terry Ashe/Gamma Liaison; **1106** Corry/AP; **1108** (l)Nancy Crampton, (r)Arte Publico Press. Photo by George McInnis; **1109** Telluride Gallery of Fine Art; **1110** CI; **1117** SS; **1118** Nancy Crampton; **1119** Minnetrista Cultural Center & Oakhurst Gardens, Muncie IN; **1122** Vince Cavataio/Pacific Stock; **1122, 1123** Art Wolfe/TSI; **1123** Kelvin Aitken/Peter Arnold, Inc.; **1124** Wide World Photos; **1125** Minneapolis Institute of Arts. Gift of the Regis Corporation, W. John Driscoll, and the Beim Foundation; the Larsen Fund; and by Public Subscription. ©1999 The Georgia O'Keeffe Foundation; **1127** Walt Disney Company/Gamma Liaison; **1128** Nancy Crampton; **1129** Michael Barson Collection/Past Perfect; **1134** Margot Granitsas Archives/The Image Works; **1135** SS; **1138** Michael Barson Collection/Past Perfect; **1139** UPI/CB; **1140** Margo Weinstein/Swanstock; **1142** (t)Wide World Photos, (b)Culver Pictures; **1143** Courtesy Benny Alba; **1145** CB; **1146** Hampton University Museum, Hampton VA; **1149** Courtesy Coffee House Press, photo by William Lewis; **1150** Private collection of Sylvia Asturias; **1152** Courtesy Arte Publico Press; **1153** Courtesy Susan Stewart, photo by Pascale Productions; **1156** (tl)Cynthia Farah, (tr)Gordon Robotham, courtesy of Diana Chang, (b)Ansel Adams Publishing Rights Trust/Corbis; **1157** Philadelphia Museum of Art, The Alfred Stieglitz Collection; **1158** David David Gallery/SS; **1160** Robert Severi/Gamma Liaison; **1161** CB; **1162** Collection of the Artist/Elizabeth Heuer/SS; **1164** (t)Patrick "Pato" Hebert, (b)Kevin Laubacher/FPG; **1165** Steve Kahn/FPG; **1167** Courtesy Maria Herrera-Sobek; **1169** Gallery Contemporanea, Jacksonville, FL/SS; **1171** Larry Moore/SIS; **1172** Cynthia Farah; **1173** AH; **1174** CI; **1176** (l)courtesy Rita Magdaleno, (r)Miriam Berkley; **1177** Courtesy Nordén Auktioner AB, photo by Hans Winter; **1178** Kactus Foto/SS; **1180** Christopher Little/Outline; **1181** Courtesy Louise Erdrich, c/o Rembar and Curtis, (bkgd) William Self/Photonica; **1183** (t)Peter Harholdt/SS, (b)Richard B. Spencer/SS; **1188** Cydney Conger/Corbis Los Angeles; **1189** (t)Miriam Berkley, (b)LOC/Corbis; **1190** ©1976 Helen Hardin, photo ©2000 Cradoc Bagshaw; **1196** (l)courtesy Alma Luz Villanueva, (r)Bettina Larrude, courtesy Children's Press; **1197** Telegraph Colour Library/FPG; **1198** Danny Lehman/Corbis; **1205** LPBC/AH.